P. J. DE LOUTHERBOURG
self-portrait

A
BIOGRAPHICAL
DICTIONARY

OF

Actors, Actresses, Musicians, Dancers,
Managers & Other Stage Personnel
in London, 1660–1800

Volume 4: Corye *to* Dynion

by

PHILIP H. HIGHFILL, JR., KALMAN A. BURNIM
and
EDWARD A. LANGHANS

SOUTHERN ILLINOIS UNIVERSITY PRESS

CARBONDALE AND EDWARDSVILLE

Library of Congress Cataloging in Publication Data (Revised)

Highfill, Philip H., Jr
    A biographical dictionary of actors, actresses, musicians, dancers, managers & other stage personnel in London, 1660–1800.

    Includes bibliographical references.
    CONTENTS: v. 1. Abaco to Belfille.—v. 2. Belfort to Byzand. —v. 3. Cabanel to Cory.—v. 4. Corye to Dynion.
    1. Performing arts—London—Biography. I. Burnim, Kalman A., joint author. II. Langhans, Edward A., joint author. III. Title.
PN2597.H5   790.2′092′2   [B]   71–157068
ISBN 0–8093–0693–X (v. 4)

List of Illustrations

THEATRE PLANS AND SITES

Volume 4

Corye *to* Dynion

Corye. *See* COREY *and* CORY.

Cosby. *See also* CROSBY.

Cosby, Thomas   [*fl.* *1663–1670*],
ropedancer, booth operator.

On 22 February 1663 Thomas Cosby,
along with Jacob Hall and William Fuller,
was sworn one of Charles II's "Valters &
Dancers on ye Rope and other agillity of
Body." Sometime during 1663–64 he was
granted a license to ropedance, along with
his wife and servants, and on 24 October
1667 he was given permission to erect a
booth in Little Lincoln's Inn Fields for
ropedancing. He must have forgotten to get
a license in 1670, for on 29 August that
year a warrant was issued for his apprehension for putting on dumb shows and ropedancing.

Possibly an entry in the St Margaret,
Westminster, parish registers concerned the
ropedancer: on 27 October 1672 Thomas
and Ann Cosbey baptized a daughter Ann.

Cosby, Mrs Thomas   [*fl.* *1663–1664*],
ropedancer. See COSBY, THOMAS.

Cosh. *See* COYSH.

Cosmopolite. *See* COSTETOMEPOLI-
TAN.

Cossa, Signor   [*fl.* *1785*], *tumbler.*
The bill at Astley's Amphitheatre for 7
April 1785 lists a Signor Cossa as one of
10 tumblers.

Cossins, W.   [*fl.* *1734–1735*], *boxkeeper.*
A Mr W. Cossins was listed as boxkeeper at the Haymarket Theatre in the
winter and spring of 1734–35, when the
house was occupied by a succession of
transient companies. He shared a benefit
on 25 April.

Costa, Gioacchino   [*fl.* *1790*], *singer.*
Gioacchino Costa was a *mezzo carattere*

in comic opera. His first London notice was
in the bill for John Gallini's opera company at the Haymarket Theatre on 7 January 1790, when he sang the part of
Putifare in the Cimarosa-Giardini comic
opera *Ninetta.* He was Valerio in *Li due
castellani burlati* on 2 February, Paolino in
La villanella rapita on 27 February, Ma-
tusio in *L'usurpatore innocente* on 6 April,
Alessandro in *La generosità d'Alessandro*
on 29 April, a principal character unspecified in *Gli schiava per amore* on 27 May,
and Oreste in *Andromaca* on 28 May. (Performances after 15 June were at Covent
Garden.) This tenor was not heard in London after the summer of 1790.

Costain, Mr   [*fl.* *1764–1795*], *dresser,
caller, concessionaire?*
Mr Costain was a men's dresser at Drury
Lane Theatre from at least 1764–65
through 1794–95, at a salary of nine shillings per week. On 27 January 1767 the
theatre paid him £6 6s. "on his note of
hand" and 16s. for stoppages overpaid on
his last note. On 7 December 1771 he was
given £4 4s. "on note" and another £2 2s.
on 19 March 1774. Costain seems to have
served the theatre as caller and in some
other capacity as well, perhaps as a concessionaire. On 18 January 1773 the theatre
paid £6 6s. for "Mr Costain's Rent & c."
and on 10 January 1781 a sum of £1 16s.
for "Mr Costain's bill for calling performers." On 24 October 1795 he received £1
17s. 6d. for 15 days, although he was not
on the regular pay list that season. He may
have been related to Costin, who was a
boxkeeper at Drury Lane between 1746
and 1772.

Costantini. *See also* CONSTANTINI.

Costantini, Signora   [*fl.* *1726*],
singer.
Signora Costantini sang Armira in
Scipione at the King's Theatre on 12
March 1726. Burney said that she was a

contralto with "no abilities." Deutsch in his *Handel* classifies her as a mezzo-soprano, and *The London Stage* turns her into a man and calls her "Constantini."

Costantini, Costantino *b. c. 1634, actor, musician.*

The patriarch of a considerable family of *commedia dell'arte* players, Costantino Costantini (or "Constantini") was born about 1634 in Verona, the son of a merchant. He followed his father's trade for a while, setting up a factory and finding new ways of dying cloth. He married, and, apparently by his first wife, he had two sons, Angelo (who became a famous *Mezzettino*) and Giovanni Battista (who was an *amoroso* who was called Cintio in Italy and Octave in France). Costantino fell in love with a strolling actress named Domenica, a native of Verona, and in time had a natural son, presumably by her, named Antonio who eventually became a popular harlequin. Giving up his business and (so the story goes) forcing his wife and sons to travel along with him, Costantino Costantini became an actor, specializing in the character of Gradellino.

On 11 November 1678 an Italian troupe which included Costantini was given permission to import their belongings custom-free into England, and between then and February 1679 they performed six times, styled as the Duke of Modena's company. Costantini went back to Italy after that, playing in Padua and Vicenza, and in 1687 he made his first appearance in Paris as one of the King's Italian players. A good musician, Costantini oversaw the musical portions of productions there, and it is said that he was banished from the Parisian stage for singing a song in public against the French. He was back in Italy in 1688 but returned to Paris. He died after 1696.

Costantini, Domenica [*fl.* 1674–1686], *actress.*

Domenica Costantini was born in Verona, became a strolling player, attracted the eye of the merchant Costantino Costantini, and lured him, his wife, and his two sons into a life in the theatre. Domenica specialized in servant roles and became known as "Corallina" in the Duke of Modena's company. In time she took Costantini's name and had by him a son, Antonio. She was in Naples in 1674, came to London and played six times between November 1678 and February 1679, was in Padua in 1681, Verona in 1684, and Vicenza in 1686.

Costantini, Giovanni Battista *d. 1720, actor, musician.*

Giovanni Battista Costantini was the son of Costantino Costantini and, presumably, of his first wife. He was born in Verona and with his brother Angelo and his father was lured into the theatre by a strolling actress. He became a member of the Duke of Modena's company, specializing in young lovers, and in time he came to be known in Italy as Cintio and in France as Octave. Before the end of the 1670s he had married Teresa Corona Sabolini, an actress whose chief character was Diana. Together they came to England in November 1678 with Costantino and Domenica Costantini to play six times between then and February 1679. Sometime during 1679 a daughter, Anna Elisabetta, was born to Giovanni Battista and Teresa; she died in Paris on 21 October 1754 after a career as an actress.

Costantini made his Paris debut on 2 November 1688, was in Verona in 1697, was again in Paris in 1708, managed productions at the fairs of St Germain and St Laurent in 1712, and was the leader of a strolling troupe in 1716. Giovanni Battista Costantini was an accomplished dancer and instrumentalist as well as an actor and manager. He died at La Rochelle on 16 May 1720 (or, according to Riccoboni, 1721). His wife Teresa died ten years later.

Costantini, Signora Giovanni Battista, Teresa, née Corona Sabolini *d. 1730, actress.*

Teresa Corona Sabolini was apparently an actress before she married Giovanni Battista Costantini. As a member of the Duke of Modena's company, she played Diana to her husband's Cintio. From November 1678 to February 1679 the pair acted in London, giving six performances; in the troupe were also Costantino and Domenica Costantini, the father of Giovanni Battista and his mistress—or possibly by then, his wife. Teresa was in Padua in 1681, after which she acted in Paris. She and her husband had a daughter, Anna Elisabetta, born in 1679, who, after a career as an actress, died in Paris on 21 October 1754. Teresa Costantini died in Palermo in 1730.

Costanza, Signora [fl. 1742–1743], dancer.

On 21 September 1742, Signora Costanza performed a *Peasant Dance* at Drury Lane with Boromeo. They were announced as making their first appearance on that stage, thus suggesting the possibility that they had danced elsewhere in London previously. On the same night, they offered a *Tyrolean Dance*. On 9 October Signora Costanza appeared in comic dances called *La Mascarada* and *Les Matelotes*, the latter being repeated on 25 October, when a *Turkish Seraglio* dance was also introduced. Signora Costanza continued in similar programs throughout the season. She shared a benefit with Maclelan and Boromeo on 16 May 1743. Her last performance at Drury Lane was in the *Tyrolean Dance* on 20 May 1743.

Costello. See also CASTELLE, CASTELLO, COSTELLOW, and COSTOLLO.

Costello, Miss [fl. 1780], actress.

A Miss Costello acted an unspecified role in a single special performance of *A School for Ladies* at the Haymarket on 5 April 1780. Perhaps she was the Miss Costello who played minor roles at Bristol in 1775.

Costello, Mary Anne. See CANNING, MRS GEORGE.

Costelloro. See COSTELLOW, THOMAS.

Costellow. See also CASTELLE, CASTELLO, COSTELLO, and COSTOLLO.

Costellow, Thomas [fl. 1775–1815?], composer, singer, teacher.

Thomas Costellow was active in many areas of late eighteenth-century musical life in London but evidently earned little distinction in any. In 1787–88 he was paid £4 10s. for singing tenor in the concerts of the Academy of Ancient Music. An overture and recitative of his composition was played at a performance of *The What Is It?* at Hughes's Royal Circus on 12 May 1789. In 1792 he was organist at the Apollo Gardens. Costellow was listed by Doane's *Musical Directory* in 1794 as a singer in the Handelian performances at Westminster Abbey and as living at No 15, Bridge Street, Lambeth.

Upon the death of Stephen Storace in 1796, Costellow became the harpsichordist at Drury Lane Theatre, a position he held at a salary of £2 10s. per week at least through 1803–4. He also may have been the Mr Castello who played double bass in the band at the Haymarket Theatre in 1815 at a salary of £1 16s. per week.

For many years Thomas Costellow was the organist at the Bedford Row Chapel, Bedford Square. One of his apprentices, the musician William E. Heather, was introduced by him as a singer at Drury Lane at the end of the eighteenth century. Payments to Thomas Costellow were made regularly by the theatre treasury for Heather's appearances, as on 12 March 1799, when he received £6 for the young boy's performances in *Feudal Times*.

Published compositions by Costellow include *A Favourite Lesson for the Harpsichord* (1775?); the song *Love and Music* (1775?); the song *Dorilas and Daphne*

(1780?); *Bridal Day, a favorite song sung
by Miss Wingfield at the Apollo Gardens*
(1792); *A Selection of Psalms and Hymns
. . . for Bedford Chapel* (1791); *You
lov'd and I was blest, a song sung by Mr
Mathews at the Royalty Theatre* (1790);
*A Sonata for the Piano-Forte, to which is
added—Arranged as a Rondo—the Favorite
Air in the Ballet of the True Lover's Knot
as performed by Mr O'Farrol . . . and Mr
Weippert at Drury Lane Theatre* (1795?);
some sonatinas and accompaniments for
the harpsichord; *The Fair Huntress, a song
sung at Vauxhall by Miss Daniels*
(1800?), and *An Irish air performed in
the pantomime Harlequin Amulet, adapted
for the pianoforte or harp* (1800).

Costetomepolitan, Mr [*fl.* 1772–
1782], *acrobat, slack-rope walker,
clown, equestrian.*

A versatile Greek performer was nearly
constantly at Astley's Amphitheatre in the
years between 1772 and 1782 under a
number of variant spellings of his name. In
April of 1772 he gave an undescribed performance (as "Cosmethopila"). A bill of
1773 advertised "Several new manly Feats
of Horsemanship and Activity by Mr. Astley, Mr. Griffin, a young Lady (Sister to
Mr. Astley), Mr. Costetomepolitan, &c. on
one, two, three and four Horses in a Manner beyond Conception." In August of
1775 "Costmepolitan" performed numbers
of "vaultings and tumblings." "Costmethopila" was a trick rider in 1775 and
1780. The tortured appellation seems to
have occurred in the bills for the last time
in the summer of 1782, when "Cosmopolite" was said to be "clown to the slack-
rope."

Costin, Mr [*fl.* 1746–1772], *boxkeeper.*

Mr Costin was a boxkeeper at Drury
Lane at least from 1746–47 through 1771–
72. He regularly shared benefit tickets
with other house servants. Perhaps he was

related to Costain, the dresser at the same
theatre between 1764 and 1795.

Costmepolitan or **Costmethopila.**
See **COSTETOMEPOLITAN.**

Costo. *See* **COUSTOS.**

Costollo. *See also* **CASTELLE, CAS-
TELLO, COSTELLO,** and **COSTELLOW.**

Costollo, Patrick *d. 1766, actor.*

Patrick Costollo began his twenty-one-
year career on the London stage as a performer in the fair booths and minor theatres, making his first appearance as
Teague, an Irishman, in *The Committee* at
Shepherd's Market, Mayfair, on 28 February 1745. For his own benefit on 27 October 1746 he again acted Teague and sang
"The Irish Trot" at Southwark. At Goodman's Fields Theatre in 1746–47 he acted
Humphrey in *The Conscious Lovers* on 23
February, Sable in *The Funeral* on 9
March, Lennox in *Macbeth* on 16 March,
and performed in *The Rehearsal* and *Miss
in her Teens* on 23 March, when he shared
benefit tickets. Costollo then joined Foote's
company at the Haymarket to play in *The
Diversions of A Morning* on 22 April 1747
and throughout the summer (when he was
billed by the name of Castalio).

During the next two seasons as an occasional performer under similar circumstances he acted Bullock in *The Recruiting
Officer* at New Wells, Clerkenwell, on 4
April 1748, Thomas, the Idle 'Prentice, in
the droll *The Consequences of Industry and
Idleness* at Bartholomew Fair on 24–27
August 1748, and Obadiah in *The Committee* for the benefit of Lewis Hallam at
the New Wells, Lemon Street, on 27 February 1749. With Foote, again at the Haymarket, he acted Tim in *The Knights* 20
times between 3 April and 1 June 1749
and then went to play during the summer
at Richmond and Twickenham. He was
back at Bartholomew Fair on 23 August

1749 to perform Blunderbuss in the droll of *The Adventures of Sir Lubberly Lackbrain and his Man Blunderbuss.*

By now becoming established as a low comic, Costollo was engaged at Drury Lane for 1749–50 by Garrick, who perhaps took to heart Foote's wish in the preface to the published text of *The Knights* that "the Managers of the Theatres would employ Costello, whose peculiar naiveté and strict propriety would greatly become many characters on our stage." Costollo made his first appearance at Drury Lane as Bully in *The Little French Lawyer* on 7 October 1749 but played a light load of roles for the remainder of the season: Foigard in *The Stratagem*, Tom Errand in *The Constant Couple*, a part in *The Rehearsal*, Lockit in *The Beggar's Opera*, and Swagger in *The Funeral*. Re-engaged for 1750–51, he acted Nym in *The Merry Wives of Windsor*, the Keeper in *The Pilgrim*, a role in *Queen Mab*, and his roles in *The Funeral* and *The Constant Couple*. For his benefit on 1 May 1751, when he lived at Mr Waiter's, chemist, at the Golden Cross in Russell Street, he acted Squire Richard in *The Provok'd Wife*. That night he shared gross receipts of £90 (less about £50 house charges) with Miss Minors.

In his third season at Drury Lane, 1751–52, he acted Blister in *The Virgin Unmask'd*, Charon in *Lethe*, Formal in *Everyman in his Humour*, Caleb in the first performance of Foote's entertainment *Taste* on 11 January 1752, Tubal in *The Merchant of Venice*, Sexton in *Much Ado About Nothing*, and a role in *Harlequin Ranger*. For his benefit on 21 April 1752, when he shared gross receipts of £160 with Scrase and Wilder, he acted William in *As You Like It* and Sancho in *Don Quixote in England*, in the latter role speaking an epilogue "riding on his Ass."

Costollo then left Drury Lane to play at Dublin in 1752–53. He made his first appearance at the Smock Alley Theatre on 8 November 1752 as Moneytrap in *The City Wives Confederacy*. He played Cimberton in *The Conscious Lovers* on 30 November, Tubal in *The Merchant of Venice* on 13 December, Sir Paul Pliant in *The Double Dealer* on 14 December, Snap in *Love's Last Shift* on 8 January 1753, Sir Hugh Evans in *The Merry Wives of Windsor* on 3 February, Don Felix in *The Mistake* on 10 February, Petulant in *The Way of the World* on 2 March, the Counsel in *The Humorous Trial of Ananias Overdone* on 25 April, and Antonio in *Much Ado About Nothing* on 4 May. On 24 May 1753 he shared in benefit tickets. He returned to London by mid-winter to make two appearances as Tim in *The Knights*, one at Drury Lane on 9 February 1754 and the other at Covent Garden (his first appearance there) on 28 March. In the following season he engaged full time at Covent Garden, where he was to remain for twenty years as a journeyman actor of low comedy characters in both comic and serious plays. In 1761–62 his salary was £2 per week.

In addition to many of the parts cited roles in his repertoire at Covent Garden included the Shoemaker in *The Relapse*, Subtle in *The Englishman in Paris*, plebeians in *Coriolanus* and *Julius Caesar*, the Welch Collier in *The Recruiting Officer*, the King of Brentford in *The Rehearsal*, Caleb in *Alzira*, Flash in *Miss in her Teens*, a Carrier in *1 Henry IV*, Sir Joseph in *The Old Bachelor*, Gripe in *The Cheats of Scapin*, Diego in *She Wou'd and She Wou'd Not*, Sneak in *The Country Lasses*, Simple and Shallow in *The Merry Wives of Windsor*, Whisper in *The Busy Body*, Roger in *Wit Without Money*, Menippeus in *The Humourous Lieutenant*, Nym in *Henry V*, Simon Pure in *A Bold Stroke for a Wife*, Sir Frances in *The Provok'd Husband*, a Witch in *Macbeth*, a Gravedigger in *Hamlet*, Sancho in *Love Makes a Man*, Silence in *2 Henry IV*, Grumio in *Catherine and Petruchio*, Sir William Wealthy in *The Minor*, Dapper in *The Citizen*, Argus in

The Contrivances, Stave in *The What D'Ye Call It*, Peter in *The Summer's Tale*, and Butler in *The Drummer*.

Costollo also acted at Plymouth in 1759 and at the Haymarket for Foote again in the summer of 1765, when his roles included Isaac Fungus in *The Commissary*, Honeycombe in *Polly Honeycombe*, Sir Jealous in *The Busy Body*, a part in *The Patron*, Dapper in *The Citizen*, and the physician in *The Rehearsal*.

His last appearance on the stage was as first Gravedigger in *Hamlet* at Covent Garden on 12 May 1766. He died on 9 August 1766 (a widower) and was buried at St Paul, Covent Garden—entered in the burial register as "Patrick Costollow from St Martin in the Fields"—on 13 August. Administration of his estate was granted on 16 January 1767 to his sister and next of kin, Judith Brady, wife of Owen Brady of Dublin.

Costos. *See* **Coustos.**

Cotes, Mr ₁*fl. 1767*₁, *singer.*

A Mr Cotes performed an unspecified vocal part in a single performance of a new afterpiece, *Lycidas* (after Milton), at Covent Garden Theatre on 4 November 1767.

Cotshal, Mr ₁*fl. 1758*₁, *actor.*

Mr Cotshal acted Soto in *She Wou'd and She Wou'd Not* on 16 January and Theodore in *Venice Preserv'd* on 18 and 23 January 1758, out of season, at the Haymarket Theatre.

Cotsona. *See* **Cuzzoni.**

Cott——l——. *See* **Cautherley.**

Cotter, Mrs *See* **Wheeler, Eliza.**

Cotter, Patrick. *See* **O'Brien, Patrick.**

Cottereau, Symon ₁*fl. 1670*₁, *musician.*

Symon Cottereau was appointed an "Italian" musician in ordinary in Charles II's private music on 9 July 1670. He may have been the Simon Cotterell, Gentleman, of Gray's Inn Lane, whose wife Margret gave birth to a son Simon on 27 March 1656; the boy was baptized at St Andrew, Holborn, on the following 3 April.

Cotterel, Miss ₁*fl. 1750*₁, *singer.*

Miss Cotterel sang the role of Mlle Sans Corps in *L'Opéra du gueux*, a French translation of *The Beggar's Opera*, performed by an "Anti-Gallic" company of English singers at the Haymarket Theatre on 16 February and 8 March 1750.

Cottin, Mr ₁*fl. 1700–1706*₁, *dancer.*

Mr Cottin was a dancer in Christopher Rich's company at Drury Lane Theatre at the beginning of the eighteenth century. He danced an entry in *The Pilgrim* on 6 July 1700 and possibly some earlier dates in April and May, and the bills for 1702–3 through 1705–6 occasionally mention Cottin as providing entr'acte dances. His last notice at Drury Lane was on 17 December 1705. Some of his dances were included in *A Collection of the most celebrated Jigs, etc.* in 1705.

Cotton, Mr ₁*fl. 1782*₁, *actor.*

A Mr Cotton acted the role of Vizard in a single specially licensed performance of *The Constant Couple* at the Haymarket Theatre on 14 January 1782.

Cotton, Mrs ₁*fl. 1708*₁, *dresser.*

Mrs Cotton was one of the women dressers at the Queen's Theatre in the Haymarket, a task for which she was being paid 5s. daily, according to a document in the Coke papers at Harvard dated 8 March 1708.

Cotton, John ₁*fl. 1794–1800*₁, *violinist.*

On 1 December 1799 John Cotton was proposed by Thomas Leffler for membership in the Royal Society of Musicians but was rejected on 2 March 1800 by a vote of 12 nays to six yeas. Probably he was the "Cotton, Junr" listed in 1794 in Doane's *Musical Directory* as a violinist who lived in Bride's Passage, Fleet Street, with his father, a flute maker. A William Cotton, a flute maker of Bridewell Lane, no doubt was related.

Couch. *See also* CROUCH.

Couch, Mr [*fl.* 1710–1721?], *impresario, dancing master?, violinist?*

A concert was given at Couch's Drawing Room, Walbrook, on 24 February 1710. Perhaps Couch was John Crouch, the court and theatre violinist of the late Restoration and early eighteenth century, and/or the Crouch or Couch lauded by John Weaver in 1712 and again in 1721 as one of London's dancing masters.

Coulon, Anne Jacqueline, later Mme Pierre Gabriel Gardel the first [*fl.* 1787–1792], *dancer.*

Mlle Anne Jacqueline Coulon had danced in Paris before making her first appearance at the King's Theatre, London, on 8 December 1787 with Vestris, Signora Bedini, and the two Misses Simonet—all former members of Noverre's company at the Paris Opéra—in a new ballet by Noverre, *Les Offrandes à l'amour*, and a new divertissement. The bill was repeated throughout that season. On 12 January 1788 she appeared in another new ballet, *The Military Dance*, and on 15 January performed with Didelot in a *pas de deux* composed by Noverre. Other ballets in which she danced that season were *L'Amour et Psiché*, *Les Fêtes de tempe*, *Euthryme et Eucharis*, a new untitled "serious ballet" (3 April), *Adela de Ponthieu*, *The Deserter*, and *La Bonté du seigneur*. She also danced specialty numbers fre-

quently, as on 21 February, when she gave a *Pas de Bernois* with Didelot and a *pas seul*. At the time of her benefit on 3 April 1788 she was living at No 8, Great Suffolk Street, Charing Cross. Probably she was the person advertised as Madame Cologne who danced in the new burletta *The Boarding School* at Hughes's Royal Circus in 1787.

Dancing in the King's Theatre company at the time was a Monsieur Coulon, perhaps her husband, but more likely her father or brother, for by this time she was probably already married to the ballet master Pierre Gabriel Gardel (1758–1840), by whom she had two children. Under the pseudonym "Peter Lindar," in his *Ode upon Ode* (1787), John Wolcot hinted at a liaison between Mlle Coulon and Lord Brudenwell:

> So much by dancing is his Lordship won,
> Behind the Op'ra scenes he constant goes,
> To kiss the little finger of COULON,
> To mark her knees, and many-twinkling toes.

After this single season, Mlle Coulon seems not to have danced again at London. She was back in Paris in 1792, when *Le Petit almanach des grands spectacles de Paris* observed that since her return from England she had become a negligent and mediocre dancer. She died before December 1795, for in that month her husband Pierre Gabriel Gardel married the French dancer Marie Elizabeth Millard (1770–1823), sometimes known as "Miller," who also performed in London.

Coulon, [Eugene?] [*fl.* 1787–1830?], *dancer.*

Monsieur Coulon was a member of the French company of dancers who performed at the King's Theatre in 1787–88. He made his first appearance with Vestris, the two Simonet girls, and Signora Bedini in a new ballet by Noverre, *Les Offrandes à l'amour*, and a new *divertissement*, on 8

December 1787. On the same bill was Mademoiselle Coulon, perhaps his wife, but probably his daughter or sister.

On 12 January 1788 Coulon participated in *The Military Dance*, on 29 January was Mercury in *L'Amour et Psiché*, on 21 February danced a *pas de trois* with the Simonet sisters, on 28 February was Bellone in *Les Fêtes de tempe*, and on 15 March took Didelot's place in *Pas de Bernois*.

He was perhaps Eugene Coulon, dancing master, still active at Paris in 1830, whose portrait was engraved by C. Baugniet, published at London by Julien. A caricature by T. Sinclair, published by Lee and Walker, Philadelphia, depicts a Mr Coulon, with the dancer Cellarius and the musicians Laborde and Coralli.

Coulton, Mr (*fl.* 1789–1790), *house servant?*

A Mr Coulton was paid 9s. per week at Drury Lane in 1789–90, probably as a house servant.

Count. *See* LA COUNT.

"Count." *See* HAINES, JOSEPH.

Counts, Mr (*fl.* 1794), *clarinetist, violoncellist.*

A Mr Counts, alias Kauntz, was listed in 1794 by Doane's *Musical Directory* as a clarinetist and violoncellist, in the band of the Second Regiment of Guards, a player at Apollo Gardens, and living at No 34, Charles Street, Westminster.

Cour. *See* DE LA COUR.

Courco. *See* CURCO.

Court. *See* LA COURT.

Courtenay. *See also* COURTNEY.

Courtenay, Miss, stage name of Miss Crawley (*fl.* 1777), *actress, singer.*

A Miss Courtenay from Bath acted an unspecified part and sang a song (which was published "as sung by" her) in *Love Finds the Way* at Covent Garden on 18 November 1777. She was identified in the bill only as "A Young Lady." Her real name seems to have been Crawley. She did not appear again in London.

Courtenay, Denis 1760–1794, *piper.*

Denis Courtenay (or Courtnay, Courtney) was born in 1760. He was an itinerant Irish musician of great fame in the British provinces who came to Covent Garden Theatre in the spring of 1791 to perform occasional specialty numbers. His instrument was the so-called "Union Pipes." (The term was a corruption of the Gaelic *piob uilleann* f. *piob* 'pipe' + *uilleann, gen.* singular of *uille* 'elbow.' "A form of bag pipes in which the wind-bag is inflated by bellows worked by the elbow; Irish bagpipes," according to the *New English Dictionary*.)

On 20 May 1791 "Between the Acts of the afterpiece the favourite air of *Moggy Lauder*" was played on the Union Pipes by "the celebrated Courtney." He returned on 24 October 1791 to play, assisted by C. Meyer on the harp, in the afterpiece *Oscar and Malvina*. He repeated that performance 13 times down to 19 December. On 29 March 1792 he and John Michael Weippert the harpist were at the Lyceum in the Strand, on the same program with John Collins and his "Evening Brush." Courtney was in the bill for 31 May 1792 but did not appear, and Weippert filled in for him.

On 25 October 1792 Courtenay resumed his performance in *Oscar and Malvina* at Covent Garden, again assisted by Weippert on the harp. They repeated on 1, 20, and 26 November and 6 December 1792. They returned to the theatre toward the middle of the next season, on 6 February 1794, repeating their offering six times that month, but were not seen again until 11

Harvard Theatre Collection

DENIS COURTENAY, in *Oscar and Malvina*
engraving by Barlow, after Cruikshank

The funeral procession was exceedingly numerous, and extended from the Hampshire Hog, in Broad-Street, St Giles's, a considerable way into Tottenham-Courtroad. The number of those in mourning could not be less than 80 or 90 couples, who were preceded by two Irish pipers, one of whom played on the union pipes used formerly with such wonderful effect by the deceased. The body was *waked* at the Hampshire Hog, and all the expenses of the burial and [wake] were defrayed by Capt Leeson; whose motive for ordering the wake to be held there was his great success in recruiting by means of the deceased, who had, some time since, enlisted in his corps, and had, by that gentleman, been appointed a serjeant. Courtenay was a wet soul, and everything about the body, to its interment, was entirely correspondent. During the continuance of the wake, the greatest profusion of liquors was distributed. At the church-yard the same liberality in the distribution of liquors to every one who chose to drink was observed; and the company happily parted without fighting.

Cruikshank drew and Barlow engraved a portrait of him, in Scottish dress and playing the bagpipes in the pantomime *Oscar and Malvina*. It was published by J. Roach in 1792.

June, when they played "several favorite pieces of music" at the end of the main-piece. These were Courtenay's last recorded performances in London.

The Secret History of the Green Room (1792) was reminded, when Miss Broadhurst sang, "of Courtnay, on the Union Pipes, who certainly commands great power, and produces the most bewitching and various sounds on that Instrument which possibly can be conceived. His ingenuity seems to have made a new discovery in Instrumental Music."

Courtenay's legal residence was No 1, York Street, St James's, when he died in the Middlesex Hospital on 2 September 1794. He was buried in Pancras Church-yard three days later. The *Gentleman's Magazine* attributed his demise to "a dropsy, which he is supposed to have contracted by hard-drinking." The magazine's description of the obsequies is diverting:

Courteville, Raphael *d. 1675, singer.*

Raphael Courteville was a Gentleman of the Chapel Royal under Charles I and was reappointed under Charles II. The Lord Chamberlain's accounts mentioned him infrequently, but we know that he participated in the coronation ceremonies on 23 April 1661, was among those exempted from subsidies on 10 December 1663, and accompanied the King to Windsor in May, June, and July 1671 at an extra fee of 8*s.* daily. After Courteville died on 28 December 1675, his son and grandson carried on his name and profession.

Courteville, Raphael *d. c. 1735, organist, composer, singer.*

The second Raphael Courteville—or, as

he frequently seemed to be styled, Ralph— was brought up as a chorister in the Chapel Royal under his father. In 1683 he was the recipient of a bequest in the will of his fellow musician John Hingeston. Hingeston left Courteville a number of music books and an organ with two "setts of keys." On 7 September 1691 Courteville was appointed the first organist of St James, Westminster (now Piccadilly), at £20 annually.

His chief contribution to music, however, was as a composer. His works included six sonatas for two flutes (c. 1690), a popular hymn tune entitled *St James's*, and a good number of light songs, many of which are listed in the British Museum *Catalogue of Printed Music*. Among his songs were several for plays: "Virtumnus, Flora, you that bless" in *3 Don Quixote*, "To Convent streams" in *A Duke and No Duke*, "A Lass there lives upon the green" in *Oroonoko*, "The Charms of bright Beauty" in *Aureng-Zebe*, and "The Prerogatives of Love" in *The Female Vertuosos*. Other songs by him were printed in collections dated 1685, 1696, and 1699. Courteville also wrote songs used as entr'acte entertainments at the playhouses, such as "To touch your Heart," which Mr Hughes sang at Drury Lane about 1700, and songs featured at York Buildings concerts, such as "Phillis would her charms improve," which Mrs Roberts sang about 1700. Courteville died about 1735, leaving a son Raphael to carry on the family musical tradition.

Courteville, Raphael *d. 1772, organist.*

The third Raphael Courteville was the son of the popular songwriter and organist of the same name and succeeded him as organist at St James, Westminster (now Piccadilly). He was referred to as "Courteville Junior" to distinguish him from his father on 1 April 1720 when he shared a benefit concert at York Buildings. At some point Courteville married Elizabeth Abbot, who was buried at St James's in May 1735;

by the following September he had remarried. His second wife was Lucy Green, a lady of considerable wealth. On 28 August 1739 he became one of the original members of the Royal Society of Musicians.

Though Courteville kept his post as organist at St James's until his death, he turned his attention in the late 1730s to politics and produced, in 1738, one of his earliest works, *Memoirs of the Life and Administration of William Cecil, Baron Burleigh*. He went on to publish a number of pamphlets and to gain sufficient fame to be ridiculed as "Court-Evil" and described as an "Organ-blower, Essayist, and Historiographer." The wardens of his church took umbrage at his neglect of his duties and warned him in both 1753 and 1754 to curtail his outside activities. He was just as negligent in paying his assistant at St James's his salary, for in 1771 the assistant complained he was supposed to be receiving half of what Courteville was paid (since he was doing at least half of the organist's work), but that Raphael had paid him only a quarter. Courteville was buried on 10 June 1772.

Courtney. *See also* COURTENAY and HENDERSON, JOHN.

Courtney, Mr   [*fl.   1749–1762*], *singer.*

For over a dozen years a Mr Courtney, a tenor singer, hung about the fringes of London musical and theatrical activity, now appearing at a public garden, now among specially hired singers for an extravaganza, sometimes assisting in a solemn performance of a Handelian oratorio, but rarely on the regular pay list of a patent house, and then only to swell choruses. Like many such singers, he certainly worked more frequently in London than he was named in the bills, and when he was not in London he was doubtless on the road. His kind of person was indispensable to the theatres of the eighteenth century.

Courtney was first noticed on 4 May 1749 at Covent Garden Theatre singing in a "representation of the Coronation of Anne Bullen" at a performance of *Henry VIII* commanded by the Prince of Wales. The "Coronation" was repeated on 16 April 1751. He was one of four Cyclopses in the pantomime *Perseus and Andromeda* on 10 October 1752.

He was listed in the report of the Treasurer of the Foundling Hospital as receiving 10s. 6d. for his part in the great performance of *Messiah* given at the Hospital's chapel on 15 May 1754, and the same sum was paid him at another performance of the work there on 27 April 1758. He must have seen considerable service at Covent Garden Theatre in the season of 1759–60, for he was allowed tickets to sell for the benefit performance of 6 May. But he was in the bills only twice: on 10 December, when he was one of a number of "Recruits" in the pantomime *The Fair*, and on 18 January, when he was one-ninth of a chorus in *Comus*.

By 28 April 1761 Courtney had left Covent Garden, for he was named in the Drury Lane bill as a choral assistant in the music-filled *Macbeth* which was then popular. Drury Lane allowed him a benefit shared with Scrase and Miss Reed on 29 May. He was still obscurely at that theatre when he shared another benefit (with Stevens and Western) on 17 May 1762.

Courtney, Mr ₁*fl. 1773–75₁*, *actor, singer.*

A Mr Courtney played at the Haymarket on 24 May 1773 the role of Thomas in the afterpiece *The Virgin Unmask'd*, Leander in *The Mock Doctor* on 31 May, and from then until the middle of September the following: unspecified parts in *The Bankrupt, She Stoops to Conquer, A Trip to Portsmouth,* and *The Rehearsal,* the First Spouter in *The Apprentice,* Bridoun in *The Commissary,* Jasper in *Miss in Her Teens,* Frankly in *The Register Office,* Knowlife

in *The Tobacconist*, and Old Kecksy in *The Irish Widow*.

Courtney was at Drury Lane as a regular by 9 October 1773, when he was paid for "3 days not on list 7s. 6d.," and he achieved notice in the bills on 2 November as one of several Soldiers in the afterpiece *The Deserter*. His other parts at Drury Lane that season were: one of the singing participants in a procession in *The Genii*, an unspecified part in *The Christmas Tale*, a Sailor in *The Brothers*, and a Beggar in *The Ladies' Frolick*.

By 16 May 1774 Courtney had rejoined Foote at the Haymarket, where he played a round of his parts already named and added a few others: ones unspecified in *The Nabob* and *The Cozeners*, Francis in *Cross Purposes*, Lint in *The Mayor of Garratt*, Cook in *The Devil to Pay*, and the Music Master in *Catherine and Petruchio*.

Though he did not show up in the bills, Courtney served Drury Lane for one more season, 1774–75, for in the summary list of expenses in the Treasurer's Book, dated 29 May 1775, occurs "Mr Courtney Chorus 27 nights at 5s. per night in full £6 15s."

Courts, Mr ₁*fl. 1760–1761₁*, *singer.*

A Mr Courts was briefly and sporadically a chorus singer at Covent Garden Theatre. The first time he was noticed in the bills was on 18 January 1760, when he sang in the background to the alteration of Milton's masque *Comus*, repeated several times. He was not named again until 11 December 1760, when he sang again in *Comus*, with a few more scattered performances during that season. He sang once again in that piece on 26 September 1761 and on 13 October in the chorus of *The Fair* (being paid 5s. as an extra that night and for 22 subsequent nights, according to the account book).

Courtup. *See* COUSTUP.

Courtvill. *See* COURTEVILLE.

Cousins, Mr [*fl. 1748*], *fair booth proprietor.*

A Mr Cousins was in partnership with a Mr Reynolds at Bartholomew Fair, in the "Great Tiled Booth over against Cow Lane," presenting the *"True and Ancient History of King Henry IV or The Blind Beggar of Bethnal Green*, with several diverting Scenes between Squire Punch and his Man Gudgeon," during the time of Bartholomew Fair in August 1748 (according to Morley in *The Memoirs of Bartholomew Fair*; the performance is not listed in *The London Stage*). Cousins also maintained at the booth a waxwork representation of the Court of the Queen of Hungary. Italian sword dancers rounded off the program, for which pit spectators paid 1s., those in the first gallery gave up 6d., and those in the upper gallery 3d.

Coustos, Mr [*fl. 1747–1750*], *singer.*

At Drury Lane Theatre on 16 May 1747, Mr Coustos sang a song "at the particular desire of the grand master of the Fraternity of the Antient and Honourable Society of Free and Accepted Masons." The *Daily Advertiser* of that day reported that Coustos had been "long confin'd in the Inquisition in Portugal, upon the account of Free Masonry; and with the greatest resolution [had undergone] torture Nine Times without either renouncing his Religion, or having the secret of Free Masonry extorted from him."

Two years later Coustos sang the role of Captain Dubutin in *L'Opéra du gueux*, a French translation of *The Beggar's Opera*, which was performed at the Haymarket by an "Anti-Gallic" group of English players nine times between 27 April and 31 May 1749, with the last performance being for Coustos's benefit. The same company again played at the Haymarket in the following season when they gave *L'Officer en recrue*, translated from *The Recruiting Officer*, with Coustos as La Ramee, on 8, 12, and 13 February 1750. *L'Opéra du gueux* was

repeated on 16 February and 8 March 1750. Coustos acted Le Commissaire in performances of *L'Avare* on 26 February and 1, 7, and 13 March 1750. On the last date he also played Dumelange in the pantomime afterpiece *Arlequin fourbe Anglois*.

Coustup, George [*fl. 1785–1799*], *musician.*

George Coustup (or Courtup) was a member of the Court of Assistants of the Royal Society of Musicians in 1785 and attended meetings in January, March, and May. On 3 February 1799 he informed the Governors of the Society of the death of one Elizabeth Jackson and was granted the usual funeral allowance of £5. Mrs Jackson was doubtless the widow of the organist George Jackson, one of the Society's earlier members.

Coutchee Noyai [*fl. 1795–1796*], *performer.*

A Catawba Indian called Coutchee Noyai, or Green Bird, performed with his compatriot Kaiew Neika, or White Man, on 18, 19, 20 and later dates in June 1795 at Sadler's Wells. Coutchee Noyai's name derived from his shrill voice and agility in the woods, according to the press descriptions. The Indians performed feats of archery, illustrated the management of the tomahawk, and gave examples of war songs and dances. Toward the end of their engagement they presented "an Indian Interlude of connected action, called The Ambuscade," which featured an attack on a hunting party. Ten London players in makeup helped them with this. One of the Indians was about 32 and the other about 20, but which was which the bills did not make clear. Both were called "well-looking." The Catawba Indians who performed at Astley's Amphitheatre in April and May 1796 must have been the same pair.

Couteux. *See* LE COUTEUX.

Coutreau. *See* COTTEREAU.

Coutts, Miss ₍fl. 1779₎, *actress.*

A Miss Coutts appeared for the first time in London on 11 January 1779 playing the part of Jenny in *The Gentle Shepherd* at a specially licensed performance at the Haymarket Theatre for the benefit of actors named Stewart and M'Donald. The bill for that all-Scots evening included *The Students; or, The Humours of St Andrews*, in which Miss Coutts played Mrs Macdowell, and was studded with names like Campbell, Henderson, and Sinclair. It assured the auditors of hearing "proper Scotch Music between the Acts." Miss Coutts was herself probably from North Britain. When on 8 March, for the benefit of Riddle, *The Gentle Shepherd* was again presented at the Haymarket, Jenny was played by "A Gentlewoman, who appeared in it lately with applause." It seems reasonable to suppose that she was Miss Coutts, though why she then chose to conceal her name is unfathomable.

Coutts, Mrs Thomas. *See* MELLON, HARRIET.

Coval. *See* COVILL.

Covey. *See* COREY.

Covill, Mr ₍fl. 1786–1794₎, *singer, dancer?*

A Mr Covill performed a character in an unnamed pantomime at Hughes's Royal Circus in October 1786 and Pluto in the pantomime *What You Please* at the same arena on 23 August 1788. No doubt he was the Mr Coval listed in 1794 in Doane's *Musical Directory* as a tenor at the Circus and living in Gunpowder Alley, Shot Lane.

Cowcher, Mr ₍fl. 1781₎, *actor.*

A Mr Cowcher played the Officer in *Love and a Bottle* at the Haymarket Theatre on 26 March 1781.

Cowdy. *See* COREY and CORY.

Cowley, Francis Laurence ₍fl. 1739₎, *musician.*

Francis Laurence Cowley was listed as one of the original subscribers ("being musicians") to the Royal Society of Musicians of Great Britain in the "Declaration of Trust" dated 28 August 1739 establishing the Society.

Cowper, Mr ₍fl. 1785–1794₎, *singer.*

Mr Cowper, a lay vicar of Lincoln Cathedral and "alto" (countertenor) singer, is listed in Doane's *Musical Directory* (1794) as having been concerned in the "grand performances" commemorating Handel in Westminster Abbey. The likelihood is that he was in one or more of the later celebrations (1785, 1786, 1787 or 1791), inasmuch as he is not on Charles Burney's list of the performers who were in the first one in 1784.

Cowper, Miss ₍fl. 1771–1780?₎, *singer.*

A soprano singer named Miss Cowper seems on the evidence of published songs to have sung occasionally at Vauxhall Gardens from about 1775 through about 1780. A "Rondeau, sung by Miss Cowper in Vauxhall-Gardens, and set by Mr. [Johann Christian] Bach" is in the Enthoven Collection, hand-dated 1771. The British Museum's *Catalogue of Printed Music* contains the following (with the Museum's dating): *In vain I seek to calm to rest* (1775?), J. C. Bach, *A Third Collection of Favourite Songs sung at Vaux Hall by Miss Cowper* (1775?), *In a secret wish'd for bow'r*, [from] *The Relenting Shepherdess Sung by Miss Cowper at Vauxhall*. J[ohn] R[utherford]: London, (1780?).

Cowper, Mrs ₍fl. 1748–1760₎, *actress.*

Mrs Cowper's name was on the playbill

of Covent Garden Theatre for 11 April 1749, when she played the small comic part of Sylvia in *The Double Gallant*. She probably had already come on the stage ("a Young Gentlewoman, who never appeared on that stage before") as Angelina in *Love Makes a Man* on 22 December 1748, for she was named in the part on 12 April 1749. On 25 April she played a similar secondary ingenue role, Isabinda in *The Busy Body*, for her own benefit shared with Mrs Bambridge, Miss Ferguson, and Mr Collins. In the summer she played briefly at Richmond and Twickenham and then moved to Bath, where she acted until she appeared at the Haymarket Theatre on 10 July 1753 as Lady Betty Modish in *The Careless Husband*. She was again at Richmond that summer.

On 9 October 1753 she made her debut at Drury Lane Theatre as a more famous Sylvia, in *The Recruiting Officer*. The prompter Cross wrote in his journal: "(she came from Bath, Richmond, &c.) — Toll [erable]." The next night she was Charlotte Weldon in *Oroonoko*, and on 24 October still another Sylvia, in *The Old Bachelor*. She returned to her first Sylvia, in *The Double Gallant*, on 14 November and then shifted her line startlingly, becoming Regan in *King Lear* on the following night, but on 16 November she went back to her specialty, as Lucinda in *The Conscious Lovers*. She played Emilia in *The Man of Mode* for the first time on 26 November. On 7 January 1754 she was featured as Viola in *Twelfth Night*, on 25 March returned to tragedy as Selima in *Zara*, played the title part in Whitehead's new tragedy *Creusa, Queen of Athens* on 20 April, and on 4 May assumed Lucinda once more, for her benefit, shared with the actor Phillips. At that time she lodged at Mr Fryer's, a hosier at the corner of James Street, Long Acre.

Mrs Cowper went to tour in Ireland in 1754–55, with what success is not now known. She returned to Drury Lane on 10 October 1755 to play Lady Macduff in

Macbeth. She played often that season in her established characters and added several new ones. There were some gaps in her engagements, and she may have been ill. She was Nottingham in *The Earl of Essex* on 24 October, a night when Mrs Cibber played Rutland. Her other new parts were Mrs Conquest in *The Lady's Last Stake* (for her benefit on 30 April), Hillaria in *Love's Last Shift*, Mistress Page in *The Merry Wives of Windsor*, and Mariana in *The Miser*.

Mrs Cowper was similarly engaged in 1756–57, principally in light comedy roles, with a judicious admixture of the tragedy secondary parts she did best. The only new role she added was that of Oriana in *The Inconstant*.

She was probably acting in the English provinces or in Ireland or Scotland during the next two years. She was certainly at Edinburgh in the winter of 1758–59 and was still there in the summer of 1759 when *A View of the Edinburgh Theatre During the Summer Season, 1759* (almost certainly a collaboration of James Boswell and the actor-critic Francis Gentleman) praised the "charming" lady as "a valuable Acquisition to our Theatre; as she had the finest Person, the most agreeable Face, and the politest Carriage of any Actress we remember to have seen on this Stage, which makes her deservedly fill the capital characters in genteel Comedy." This puff sounds suspiciously like Boswell pursuing his usual purposes where young actresses were concerned; and so it was. Boswell's enthusiasm waxed hotter with the summer. Her Mrs Sullen in *The Beaux' Stratagem* "outdid her usual excellence," and as Lady Townly in *The Provok'd Husband* "our favourite Actress was entirely the Woman of Quality." Her "strength" lay "principally in Comedy," wherefore the critic was "agreeably surprised at her succeeding so well [in acting Juliet], in which the Softness of her voice inspired us with the most tender Feelings, while the Sweetness and Sensibility of Virtue sat on her Face." The critic added:

It is more than probable, that the envy-posioned Tongue of *a certain blustering Zoilus* may wickedly endeavor to falsify, or turn into Ridicule, our Commendations of this amiable Lady; but, let him know, that we have it from undoubted Authority, that the celebrated Mr QUIN, after seeing Mrs *Cowper* play this character at *Bath*, exclaimed with an Air of the highest Satisfaction, *She is indeed a Juliet!*

Again and again the critic singled Mrs Cowper out for special praise. For example, on 11 July, of her Sylvia in *The Recruiting Officer* he said:

The common Proverb, slow and sure, is justly exemplified in this Lady; who, as she is not very quick at Study, has this very superior Advantage, that she may boast of being the perfectest Actress upon any Stage in the three Kingdoms; by which Means, she not only plays her Parts, but plays with them. To use the *Green-Room* Phrase, she *lays* Clap-traps, with the finest Taste and Judgment, and is peculiarly happy in her Transitions from one Passion to another. Her arch Attention to the Captain's Embarrassment about his *little Boy*, plainly evinced her Depth in theatric Knowledge. . . . There is a Particularity about this Lady, which ever attracts our respectful Notice; and that is the unaffected, modest Blush, which reddens her Face, at hearing an indecent Word: And the delicacy with which she glides over any Expressions that border the least on Licentiousness, prevents their poisonous Effects, and almost renders them Innocent.

In Boswell's letters she was called "Sylvia." In his "Epistle to Temple" she was styled "Lavinia." In January 1760 William Temple wrote to Boswell disdainfully: "By marrying [Cowper] her musick-master she [had] given but a bad specimen of her taste and judgment." By the time she became Boswell's mistress, however, she was the music-master's widow.

Mrs Cowper was a good many years older than Boswell, but, in an outline for the sketch of his life which he prepared for Rousseau, Boswell wrote that he had been "madly in love" with her and "wanted to marry her." Frederick A. Pottle, in *James Boswell, the Earlier Years, 1740–1769*, cites Boswell's verse "Epistle to Temple," (in manuscript in the Bodleian Library) in which she is styled "Lavinia," and credited with a daughter. Mrs Cowper was a Roman Catholic, and Pottle conjectures that it was she who interested Boswell in Catholicism.

Cowslade, Miss ₍fl. 1755₎, actress.

A Miss Cowslade was a member of a company of new performers managed by Theophilus Cibber at the Haymarket Theatre in the summer of 1755. Her name appeared in the bills for Rose in *The Recruiting Officer* on 9 September and for Amarillis in *The Rehearsal* on 11 and 15 September 1755.

Cox, Mr ₍fl. 1729–1730₎, house servant.

A house servant named Cox shared a benefit with another named Wingate at Goodman's Fields Theatre on 29 June 1730. Their functions are not known.

Cox, Mr ₍fl. 1732–1736₎, dancer.

A Mr Cox first appeared on the London stage when he danced a Pierrot Man opposite Miss Mann as a Pierrot Woman in *Harlequin Restored* at Drury Lane Theatre on 14 December 1732. The bill of the evening was a command performance before the Prince of Wales. Cox was one of four "Mandarin Gormogons" in the afterpiece *Cephalus and Procris* on 26 December. These pieces were repeated, and he probably danced also on occasions when he was not represented in the printed bill, but his name did not reappear until 14 May 1735 when, again at Drury Lane, he was a "Mandarin Gormogon."

It is highly probable that this rather unsuccessful dancer had been apprenticed originally to a City trade, to which he returned between appearances, for a Cox "a Pewterer of the City of London, who [the bill claimed had] never appeared on any stage before," danced at Lincoln's Inn Fields Theatre for Pritchard's benefit on 31 March 1736. He represented "a Harlequin and a Scaramouch" in a specialty turn.

Cox, Mr *(fl. 1741)*, actor.

At the little old disused tennis-court theatre in James Street on 30 November 1741, a group of "Persons for their Diversion" staged *Oroonoko* for the benefit of one Cox who played the title part in his "first time on any stage." Evidently it was also his last, unless he took his talents to some dark corner of the provinces.

Cox, Mr *(fl. 1761)*, actor.

On 13 October 1761 the company at Covent Garden Theatre presented as an afterpiece *The Fair, A Grotesque Pantomime Entertainment* in which various activities, performers, and spectators of a typical day at one of the popular fairs— equilibrists, pantomimes, gingerbread sellers, recruiting officers, puppet shows—were shown. Various actors and dancers were named in the bills. A Mr Cox, who was not thus cited, was nevertheless present, in an unusual role, as the Covent Garden manuscript account book at the Folger Library shows. On 13 October the entry, under the rubric "Sundry persons us'd in the Fair," included "The Ox−Cox−2 [s.] 6 [d.]." He performed this odd deception for 23 nights.

Cox, Mr *(fl. 1781–1789)*, house servant.

At the end of every season from 1781–82 through 1788–89, with the exception of 1784–85, a male named Cox delivered benefit tickets at Covent Garden Theatre. His duties in the house were never indicated by the bills, but he was a house servant, not a performer.

Cox, Mr *(fl. 1788–1792)*, actor, singer.

Mr Cox bore a "Vocal Part" in the solemn dirge sung by the mourners in Juliet's funeral procession at Drury Lane Theatre on 17 November 1788. He was one of the "Spouters" in *The Apprentice* on 6 December and had an unspecified part in the extravagant pantomime *Robinson Crusoe; or, Harlequin Friday* on 22 December. He continued throughout the season, with occasional repetitions of these or similar chores, not often named in the bills, but pretty certainly often in background choruses and pantomimes. The account book entry of 29 May 1788 shows him to have been already at the theatre for 17 days at that time though not on the regular pay list. He was paid 3s. 4d. per day then and the same amount when he was dropped from the list on 6 November 1789. But an entry of 1 July 1790 seems to indicate that he came back to the Drury Lane company for one week in the spring of that year.

This performer may have been the Cox who contributed his services on 15 October 1792 to a specially licensed benefit performance by minor professionals for the actor Sims at the Haymarket. He played William, a bumpkin in *The Country Girl*. At another such benefit, for Silvester, on 26 November, he was Simon in *The Apprentice*. After that he disappeared from the record.

Cox, Mrs *(fl. 1760)*, singer.

The single appearance of Mrs Cox a singer, so far as the bills show, was at Drury Lane Theatre on the occasion of a benefit for Mrs Yates on 14 April 1760. She sang some unspecified part in the "Burlesque Opera of two acts" called *Galligantus*.

Cox, Mrs *(fl. 1781–1782)*, singer, actress.

Mrs Cox (or Coxe) made her first London appearance at a benefit for Walker, specially licensed, on 12 November 1781 at the Haymarket Theatre, usually dark at that season. She played Priscilla Tomboy in *The Romp* and sang. She emerged again from obscurity a year later, on 25 November 1782, at another specially licensed Haymarket performance, evidently for the benefit of the pick-up company which gave it. On this occasion she was Lucy "(with a *song*)" in *Wit Without Money*. Mrs Cox evidently failed to find employment in one of the regular companies.

Cox, Mrs (*fl. 1783–1785*), *dresser.*
A Mrs Cox was dresser for opera singers at the King's Theatre in the Haymarket from 1783 through 1785 and probably earlier and later.

Cox, Mrs (*fl. 1798*), *dancer?*
A Mrs Cox labored obscurely as one of the (dancing?) Female Domesticks in the popular afterpiece *Oscar and Malvina* at Covent Garden on 19 March 1798 and several nights thereafter that season. Mrs Cox may have been the *Miss* Cox of 1795–1804.

Cox, Miss (*fl. 1795–1804*), *actress, dancer, singer?*
A Miss Cox was first named in the bills as one of a number of "English Amazonians" performing some duty—probably dancing and possibly singing—in a two-act afterpiece spectacle called *Lord Mayor's Day* at Covent Garden Theatre on 16 November 1795. She repeated the performance on 23 November. Though she was not given billing in anything else that season, she was probably in the company, toiling anonymously through an apprenticeship.

She may have been retained in the next few seasons, but she did not appear again by name until 29 January 1799 when she was one of several Haymakers in an extravagant pantomime, requiring dozens of singers and dancers, called *The Magic Oak*. She was a Female Domestick in *Oscar and*

Malvina on 2 March and also a Domestic in *Raymond and Agnes; or, The Castle of Lindenbergh* on 13 April. She was a "Principal Character" in the afterpiece *The Jew and the Doctor* on 12 June. All of these afterpieces were repeated, and there is no doubt that she, like other minor folk, was concealed under many an "*&c.*" at the end of lists of chorus members.

Miss Cox was given £1 per week salary for the 1799–1800 season, continuing in precisely the same line of assistance to her betters but now rising occasionally to a named part in a mainpiece (e.g., the Milliner in *The Suspicious Husband* on 20 September and Serina in *The Orphan* on 9 October). She continued at Covent Garden until at least the season of 1803–4, at the same salary. She was also at the Haymarket during the summer of 1801.

Cox, Elizabeth (*c. 1639?–1688?*), *actress.*
On 30 November 1661 a marriage license was granted to a John Bateman of St Paul, Covent Garden, whose age was about 27, and an Elizabeth Cox, spinster, whose age was about 22. There is no certainty that she was the actress of a decade later, but if Elizabeth Cox kept her maiden name on stage, perhaps she was. John Bateman may have been the Mr Bateman who was in the King's Company in 1667.

The first known role for Betty Cox, as she came to be called, was Lydia in *Love in a Wood*, performed by the King's Company at the Bridges Street Theatre in March 1671. With that troupe at Lincoln's Inn Fields Theatre (probably) she acted Palmyra in *Marriage à la Mode,* Violetta in *The Assignation,* and Constantia in *The Amorous Old Woman.* Her first certain role at the new Drury Lane playhouse was Octavia in *Nero* on 16 May 1674. On 25 January 1675 she took over the role of Desdemona in *Othello*; on 23 April she acted Panthea in *A King and no King*; and on 30 April either she or Mrs Coysh played the title role in *Sophonisba*. Subsequently she acted Claudia in *Lucina's Rape*, Indamora in *Aureng-Zebe*, and Artemira in *The Heir of Morocco*, and she spoke the epilogue to *Sophonisba* both in London and at Oxford.

She was off the stage between 1676 and 1681 and upon her return spoke the epilogue to *Mithridates* in mid-October 1681:

> *What shall I say? I have been hence so long*
> *I've e'ne forgot my Mother Tongue . . .*

(She had presumably been on the Continent.) Then she asked the audience:

> *Will you be pleas'd to take me as I am.*
> *Quite out of Countenance, with a down cast look,*
> *Just like a Truant that returns to Book:*
> *Yet I'me not old, but if I were this place*
> *Ne're wanted Art to peice a ruin'd Face.*
> . . . .
> *These young Beginners may grow up in time,*
> *And the Devil's in't if I'me past my Prime.*

If Betty was the Elizabeth Cox who married in 1661, she would now have been about 42, an age appropriate to these remarks.

And, indeed, she was not past her prime. About this time she was apparently the actor Cardell Goodman's mistress, as a scandalmongering versifier noted:

> *Lett Lumley Coax his Mrs Fox,*
> *And help his younger Brother;*
> *Let Goodman Pox faire Mrs Cox,*
> *And all Six flux together.*

The last theatrical mention of Elizabeth Cox was on 7 April 1683 when Charles Killigrew, the United Company co-manager, was told by the Lord Chamberlain to answer a petition of some sort which Mrs Cox had submitted. Since this was not long after the union of the King's and Duke's troupes, perhaps Betty had been dropped from the roster and was asking to be readmitted. She is not known to have done any performing after the union. The *Satire to Julian* in 1683 indicated that she was still Goodman's mistress, but *The Session of the Ladies* in 1688 suggests that she switched her affections: she was spoken of therein as "Lord Lumley's cast player the fam'd Mrs Cox."

Cox, Gabriel *1747–1792, master carpenter, machinist.*

During the seasons of 1789–90, 1790–91, and 1791–92 Gabriel Cox was master carpenter at Covent Garden Theatre in charge of directing and paying a large squad of under-carpenters. He worked in close conjunction with Richards and the other scene-designers and probably was deviser of at least some of the machinery. He was no doubt the Cox, machinist, who had received a benefit at Richmond, Surrey, on 8 August 1781.

Gabriel Cox was almost certainly the individual who was proprietor of Cox's Museum, Spring Garden. This enterprise, on the evidence of a printed song in the British Museum's collection, included organ music and vocalizing (*The Celebrated Music which is on the Organ at Mr. Cox's Museum Spring Garden. Properly adapted for the Harpsichord* [1770?], by Theodore Smith.) Its character is further suggested—and so is Cox's work at Covent Garden—by Mrs Hester Thrale's entry in her *Diary* on 7 December 1784:

> When I saw Cox the Mechanist in the midst of his fine Show-Room at Spring Gardens about 12 Years ago; where Gold & Silver, and Diamonds and Pearls were exhibited in a surprizing Quantity (he made a Lottery for them some Time after)—I was shocked at the sight of his only Son sneaking about the Room in a Coloured Coat when it was a Year of publick Mourning—but his Father thought him an *Incumbrance* I believe, & saved all he could from his Family to make more Elephants twist their Trunks,

and more Rhinoceroses roll their Eyes, as they did by great Mechanical Powers, very ingeniously managed, and very splendidly adorned.

Gabriel Cox's career was cut short by death at the age of 45, on 5 June 1792. He was buried at St Paul, Covent Garden, on 13 June. The inscription on his tomb praised him as "a tender Husband, a good Father, and a sincere Friend." On 24 July administration of unspecified property was granted to his widow Margaret.

Cox, Hugh *1731–1763, singer, harpsichordist.*

Hugh Cox was a Gentleman of the Chapel Royal, a member of the Choir of Westminster Abbey, a harpsichordist, and a teacher. At the time of his death, aged 32, on 16 December 1763 he lived in Bridge Street, Westminster, in the parish of St Margaret's. He was buried on 20 December in the North Cloister of the Abbey. On 29 December following, his relict Dorothy was granted administration of his property. He had one son, Hugh.

Cox, [John?] [fl. *1751–1764?],* *singer, publisher, instrument maker.*

Winton Dean, in *Handel's Dramatic Oratorios and Masques*, conjecturally identified as the music seller and publisher John Cox the Cox who was a regular member of G. F. Handel's chorus and a bass, who sang Habdonah in *Esther* in 1751, and who sang in the Foundling Hospital *Messiah* performances of 1754, 1758, and 1759. He was paid 10s. 6d. for each of these efforts. The publisher had in 1751 married the widow of John Simpson and had taken over Simpson's music business in Sweeting's Alley, opposite the east door of the Royal Exchange. *Mortimer's London Directory* of 1764 furnished the additional information that the John Cox of that address was also a musical-instrument maker.

On 25 March 1757 a Cox was advertised as among singers of the Hasse-Giardini oratorio *I pellegrini* in a charity performance at Drury Lane Theatre. On 12 February 1762 a Cox sang Polypheme in *Acis and Galatea* for Miss Robinson's benefit at Hickford's Room in Brewer Street.

Cox, John George *d. 1758, oboist, dancing master.*

John George Cox is identified as a dancing master and musician by a clipping from an unidentified newspaper in the Burney Collection in the British Museum, which also gives the date of his death as 20 March 1758 and the place of his death as Hackney.

He was, no doubt, the John George Cox who was elected a member of the Sublime Society of Beefsteaks on 3 December 1736, who was mentioned in the club's minutes of 9 January 1741, and who (as "J. G. Cox") witnessed the actor Dennis Delane's will in 1750. He was also very probably the George Cox who was mentioned as a member of the King's Band of Music in the Lord Chamberlain's Records of 1752. The identification is rendered certain by a second entry in these records dated 20 February 1759 which attests the swearing of John Hebden and John Perkins into the places of Talbot Young and George Cox, "deceased." The other three musicians named were oboists of the King's Musick, and hence it seems Cox was also.

Cox, Susannah [fl. *1702–1715],* *actress.*

Susannah Cox may have been related to the Restoration actress Elizabeth Cox, but the evidence is inconclusive. *The London Stage* first lists Susannah as a member of the company at Lincoln's Inn Fields Theatre in 1702–3, though no parts are known for her, the season being one which is very incompletely documented. She transferred to Drury Lane Theatre where she is known to have played Betty in *Vice Reclaimed* on 23 June 1703, Betty in *The Lying Lover* the following 2 December, and Duchess Semorin in *Love the Leveller* on 26 January

1704. She shared a benefit with Mrs Allison on 1 July. No roles are recorded for her during the regular 1704–5 season, but she appeared in June and July 1705 as Jaculine in *The Royal Merchant* and Petesca in *The Loyal Subject*.

She was not mentioned again in the London bills until 1707–8 when she acted Lucy in *The Recruiting Officer*, Jenny Trapes in *Tunbridge Walks*, Honoria in *Love Makes a Man*, Ardelia in *The Persian Princess*, and Ariadne in *The Sea Voyage*. She continued playing at Drury Lane through 1714–15, adding such new parts as Mrs Overdo in *Bartholomew Fair*, Trusty in *The Silent Woman*, Leonora in *The Mourning Bride*, the "Widow" in *The Alchemist*, Cleone in *The Distrest Mother*, Mrs Foresight in *Love for Love*, and, at her last appearance on 1 July 1715, Violante in *Greenwich Park*. Her favorite role would appear to have been Theodosia in *The Lancashire Witches*, which she first acted on 4 September 1708, used for a number of her shared benefits, and excelled in to the end of her career.

Coyle, Mr [fl. 1784], *organist, violinist*.

A "Mr Coyle (Jr)" organist of Ludlow, Shropshire, was listed by Charles Burney as among the first violins assisting at the Handel Commemoration performances at Westminster Abbey and the Pantheon in May and June of 1784. He was probably the son of Miles Coyle (1714–1796?).

Coyle, Miles 1714–1796?, *singer, violinist, violist*.

A letter of attorney from Miles Coyle, "late Child of his Majesty's Chapel to Mas Kaye of Russel Street Covent Garden London Musician" dated 16 December 1768, empowered Kaye to demand and receive £10 due Coyle from the Exchequer.

The Miles Coyle of the document was probably the Mr Coyle who was listed by Charles Burney as among the first violins who assisted at the Handel Commemora-

tion performances at Westminster Abbey and the Pantheon in May and June of 1784. Miles Coyle was named as a "Tenor Voice" in the accounts of money paid to musicians employed from time to time in concerts sponsored by the Academy of Ancient Music in the season of 1787–88.

A Mr Coyle played either the violin or the viola for the Ashleys in the Covent Garden oratorios in the spring of 1797 and again in the spring of 1798. Miles Coyle was by these dates very old and infirm. The Royal Society of Musicians, to which he belonged, had received on 6 November 1791 a petition stating that he was 77 years of age, deprived of the sight on one of his eyes, had "very little winter business," and was requesting the Society's aid until the opening of Sadler's Wells (where he was employed in the band). He was allowed four guineas per month until further notice. On 6 May he wrote advising that his engagement had commenced at the Wells. This seasonal charity continued through 3 April 1796, with Coyle humbly requesting aid and being awarded four guineas a month when Sadler's Wells was closed and scrupulously advising the Society of the remission of his need when he resumed work. No further entries survive, and he perhaps died sometime in 1796. He published *Six Lessons for the Harpsichord or Pianoforte* (c. 1785). The younger Coyle, organist and violinist (fl. 1784), was doubtless his son.

Coyners. *See* CONYERS.

[Coysh, Miss?] [fl. 1682], *actress*.

"Mrs Coysh's Girl," dressed as Cupid, delivered the epilogue to *The Heir of Morocco* on 11 March 1682 at Drury Lane. *The London Stage* indexes the young lady as "Mrs Coysh Junior," though she may have been a servant to the actress Mrs Coysh rather than her daughter.

Coysh, John [fl. 1667–c. 1697], *actor, manager*.

John Coysh was a strolling player who spent some time acting in London. He may have started his career early in 1667 at the Hatton Garden "Nursery" for young actors, operated by Edward Bedford for the patent companies. Before March 1668 he had had a troupe at Cambridge and had persuaded the comedian Joe Haines to join him. The company played at several towns, one of their offerings possibly being *The Comedy of Errors*, in which at some point Coysh acted Dromio of Ephesus and his wife played Adriana. Perhaps the John Coysh mentioned in the parish registers of St Margaret, Westminster, was the actor: on 8 July 1669 John and Dorothy Coysh christened a daughter, Theodorah. From other sources we know that the actor John Coysh and his wife probably had a daughter.

About 1670 Coysh rejoined (or possibly joined for the first time) Bedford's Hatton Garden troupe of young players. In 1672 "strowling Coish," as he was called in "A Satyr upon the Players" (1683), probably managed a group styled The Duke of Monmouth's Company. The personnel was largely drawn from the Nursery in London, and promptbooks which have survived may pertain to Nursery or touring performances, or both. One of the books is for *The Wise Woman of Hogsdon*, in which Coysh acted Spencer and in which his wife played Gratiana. On 6 August 1672 Coysh was given permission to act for a week at Norwich. A week later his stay was extended when he donated 40s. to the "hamper" for the poor of the town. Probably after this engagement and possibly in Edinburgh, Coysh played Sir Arthur Addell in *Sir Salomon*. Perhaps it was during this strolling period that Theophilus Keene came under Coysh's tutelage.

Mr and Mrs Coysh apparently joined the King's Company in London playing at Lincoln's Inn Fields Theatre in 1672–73. Coysh's first known role there was Mingo in *The Spanish Rogue* in March 1673. The next season he acted Muly Labas and spoke the prologue to *The Empress of Morocco*, and he followed this with Riccamare in *The Amorous Old Woman* and Plautus in *Nero*. He was a member of the King's Company again in 1674–75 at their new Drury Lane Theatre, but by the end of the season he had set off for the provinces again.

Sometime between May 1673 and the end of September 1675 – the summer of 1675 seems most likely – Coysh and Martin Powell apparently played in a private performance of *The Indian Emperor*, possibly in London or perhaps at Newmarket; Coysh appeared as Cortez, and the troupe was called the Duchess of Portsmouth's Servants. During the summer of 1675 *Sir Salomon* was also in the company's repertory.

Coysh was back in London by 27 August, playing Jeffrey in *Psyche Debauch'd* at Drury Lane, and though reputedly he stayed with the King's Company in 1675–76, no other parts are known for him. On 16 March, however, a suit was brought against Coysh and Powell for a debt of £5 – possibly in connection with their touring activity the previous summer. At Drury Lane in 1676–77 Coysh played Sir Robert Malory in *The Country Innocence*, Aristander in *The Rival Queens*, and Dick Slywit in *Wits Led by the Nose*. In 1677–78 he was Myris (one of the Priests) in *All for Love*, Bramble in *The Rambling Justice*, Pricknote in *The Man of Newmarket*, and one of the physicians in *Trick for Trick*. He may have stayed with the King's players in 1678–79, but no parts are recorded for him. He was in London, however, for on 11 January 1679 a warrant was issued by the Lord Chamberlain concerning a suit for debt brought against Coysh by one Alexander Hatchett.

By the spring of 1679 Coysh was in Edinburgh, playing in the Duke of Monmouth's Company. In 1681–82 he was again with the King's troupe at Drury Lane where, in late October 1681, he is known to have acted Swift in *Sir Barnaby Whigg*. By November 1682, according to the *State Papers Domestic*, the playwright Elkanah Settle "designed to carry down one Coish and others to act some plays or drolls in York"—but whether or not the trip materialized is not known. On 12 March 1683 Coysh and his strolling players were acting at the Red Lion in Norwich. They were granted five extensions and apparently acted into June. Coysh was spoken of as the assignee of the strolling patent that had belonged to the late George Jolly. Coysh returned to Norwich in late February to act for a week, and on 16 October 1686 he was granted permission to play there during the Duke of Norfolk's visit.

Coysh's name disappeared from the records in the ten years which followed, but by 23 September 1696 he was leading the Duke of Norfolk's company and had hired a fellow stroller, Anthony Aston. They acted at Norwich for a month around Christmas, but by October 1697 the leadership of the company had passed into the hands of Thomas Doggett, and John Coysh was heard of no more.

Coysh, Mrs John, ⌊Dorothy?⌋ ⌊*fl.* 1668–1679⌋, *actress*.

Mrs Coysh was doubtless the wife of the strolling actor John Coysh, and it may be that they were the John and Dorothy Coysh who baptized a daughter Theodorah at St Margaret, Westminster, on 8 July 1669. Mrs Coysh acted Adriana in *The Comedy of Errors*—probably about 1668 though possibly later—in her husband's touring production. She was Gratiana in *The Wise Woman of Hogsdon* in 1672, possibly on tour or at the Hatton Garden "Nursery" for young players in London—or both. She and her husband acted with the King's Company in London for a time, though we know of only one role she may have played: on 30 April 1675 either she or Mrs Cox acted Sophonisba. The 1676 edition lists her, but the 1681 edition names Mrs

Cox; both doubtless played the role at some time. Mrs Coysh was presumably touring with her husband in the spring of 1679 and possibly appeared at Edinburgh in the Duke of Monmouth's Company, which John Coysh led.

Crace, Mr ⌊*fl.* 1789–1803⌋, *scene painter*.

The Covent Garden Theatre accounts contain several references to the scene painter Crace. In the 1789–90 season he was paid £200. In 1790–91 he received £34 5*s*. On 23 June 1801 he received £146 18*s*. for the season, but in 1802–3 he worked only intermittently and the books specify no payments to him.

Cradock, William ⌊*fl.* 1669⌋, *musician*.

William Cradock and several others were ordered arrested on 18 June 1669 "for keeping playhouses and sounding trumpets, drums and fifes at dumb shows and modells without paying the fee due to his Majesty's serjeant trumpeter . . ."

Craford. *See* CRAWFORD.

Craggs. *See also* CRAIG.

Craggs, Mr ⌊*fl.* 1744⌋, *actor*.

Mr Craggs was a member of a company headed by Charles Macklin which acted occasionally at the Haymarket Theatre in the spring of 1744. Craggs's name was on the bills for Sir Tunbelly in *The Relapse* on 6 and 9 April and Clerimont in *The Miser* on 10 May 1744.

Craig, Master ⌊*fl.* 1792⌋, *singer*.

A Master Craig sang a minor chorus role in performances of *Orpheus and Eurydice* at Covent Garden Theatre on 28 February and 6 and 13 March 1792.

Craig, ⌊Adam? *d.* 1741⌋, *violinist*.

The Mr Craigg (or "Craggs") who played at the Queen's Theatre in the Haymarket in the early eighteenth century was possibly the violinist Adam Craig. Craig had been born in Edinburgh. From 1695 he had played principal second violin at the Edinburgh concerts. On 24 December 1709 an instrumentalist, "Craigg," identified in the Coke papers at Harvard as a second violinist, was listed as a member of the band at the Queen's Theatre. Craigg was paid 10s. daily for his service, which ranked him among the lower half of the musicians at the opera. A document dated 1711 but referring to "Last Year" shows that Igl replaced Craig among the second violins in 1710.

Adam Craig compiled *A Collection of the Choisest Scots Tunes* which was published in 1730 but which had apparently been issued earlier as well. He died in Edinburgh in October 1741.

Crail. *See* CERAIL.

Cramer, Charles *d. 1799, violinist.*

Charles Cramer was the eldest of four children of the eminent violinist and composer Wilhelm Cramer (1745–1799) by that musician's second wife, the singer Miss Maria Maddan of Dublin. Charles was acclaimed at a benefit concert held in London for his father in 1792 and he was, in the season of 1791–92, carried on the roster of the band at the King's Theatre. He may have played there in later years also, but evidently he died before finishing his musical education and apprenticeship. He died in December 1799.

Cramer, Franz *1772–1848, violinist, impresario.*

Franz Cramer was born on 12 June 1772 at Schwetzingen, near Mannheim, the second son of the violinist Wilhelm Cramer by his first wife. He is variously denominated Franz, François, Francis, and Frank in English printed and manuscript records. In 1771 Wilhelm came to London, leaving

Franz behind in Mannheim with his grandfather. But Franz was certainly the child "5 or 6 years of age" whom his father mentions as being with him in London in 1777.

Franz was a delicate child, and his early musical education, undertaken by his father, was interrupted when the eminent physician Sir Richard Jebb advised that he should discontinue practicing. At 15 he resumed study at the most elementary level. But he schooled himself through incessant work on Corelli's solos, then through those of Geminiani and Tartini, and on to the *capuccios* of Benda and Stamitz, until finally he commanded his instrument with professional skill. His father placed him, at 17, in the band of the Opera House to accustom him to various styles of music and to the necessity for instant sight-reading. In the 1790–91 season Franz was also in the band at the Pantheon where his father was leader. Fétis called him a mediocre violinist,

Harvard Theatre Collection

FRANZ CRAMER

engraving by Moitte, after Minasi

but though he certainly was assisted professionally by his father's ubiquity in the musical affairs of the day, he can hardly have been less than an adequate executant, and he inherited Wilhelm's leadership ability.

When Franz was 22 William Dance proposed him for membership in the Royal Society of Musicians on 6 July 1794. He was unanimously elected on 5 October. At the time of his nomination he was said to be single, a performer "on the Violin and Tenor [i.e. viola]." He was at that time "engaged as principal Second [violin] at the King's Theatre," and played in the Concerts of Ancient Music. "Francis" was active in the Royal Society, as its Minute Books show, being named a Governor in 1797 when he was only 25. He was listed as a violinist among the musicians detailed by the Society to play the annual charity concert for the clergy of St Paul's Cathedral in 1797, 1799, 1800, 1802, 1804, 1806, and 1811. In 1800 he was one of the Court of Assistants, as he was in 1813, 1814, 1828, 1830, 1832, 1838, and 1840.

From 1799 to 1814, inclusive, he was the director of music for the Ancient Concerts and from 1834 through 1838 was Master of the King's Band. He employed his string quartet in the Vocal Concerts at Willis's Rooms and was either leader or player at virtually every provincial musical festival during his maturity. By the express command of William IV he was leader of the band at that monarch's coronation. He was a power in the Philharmonic Society, co-founded by his brother Johann. In 1793, 1827, and 1831 (and probably in other years as well) he played and led the band at the Oxford Music Room.

On 2 October 1813 a son, William, was born to "François and Anne Cramer." He was baptized at St John, Hampstead, on 13 October. These facts are taken from the files of the Royal Society of Musicians, to which William was admitted on 3 August 1834. His instrument was the violin.

By permission of the Trustees of the British Museum

FRANZ CRAMER

engraving by Gibbon, after Watts

On 9 November 1826, at the "actors' church," at St Paul, Covent Garden, were baptized "Charles Edward Son of François and Ann Cramer: Red Lyon Square: Professor of Music: Born 11th Septr 1824" and "Frederick Moralt Cramer . . . Born 11th Septr 1824." It is not known whether or not these twins survived.

Franz Cramer died on 1 August 1848. Unlike his brother Johann, Franz evidently was not much interested in composing. Only a single violin *capriccio* survives.

A portrait of Cramer by William Watts was engraved by Benjamin Gibbon and published by J. Wyatt at Oxford in 1826. A vignette portrait by J. Slater was published by the engraver I. W. Slater in 1832. Another vignette by Minasi, engraved by C. Moitte, was published by Galignani at Paris.

Cramer, Johann Baptist *1771–1858, pianist, violinist, composer, publisher.*

Johann Baptist Cramer was the eldest child of the violinist Wilhelm Cramer and his first wife. Johann was born in Mannheim on 24 February 1771, while his father was on a tour of France, Germany, and Italy. In 1772 Wilhelm was invited to London by J. C. Bach and in 1774 was joined by his wife and his elder son, leaving behind for the time being a younger son, Franz.

Johann very early received training on the violin from his father. Sainsbury declared that "he was discovered, when about six years old, to take every opportunity of practising privately on an old pianoforte [so] that his friends perceived the true bias of his mind, shortly after which his father apprenticed him for three years to a Ger-

Harvard Theatre Collection

JOHANN B. CRAMER

engraving by Scriven, after Pocock

man professor named Benser." The ambiguous statement probably means that Johann was sent at about age six to study piano in Germany. This would be approximately consonant to Wilhelm's deposition made to the Royal Society of Musicians in 1777 that he had two children, one of whom was in Germany and "about 7 or 8 years of age." Johann Cramer's next teacher was Johann Samuel Schröeter, and his fourth and most important was Muzio Clementi, with whom he studied for two years. In 1785 Cramer also took a course of lessons in thorough-bass from Karl Friedrich Abel.

Cramer's early professional activities in London are submerged in and to some extent obscured by those of his famous father. In 1781 Johann played for pay for the first time in public at his father's annual benefit concert. The elder Cramer's eminence, as leader of the band at the opera, in the Drury Lane oratorios, at the Pantheon, and at musical festivals and celebrations, seems to have procured concert work in London for the young pianist, even while his musical education continued. In 1783 he played at Trinity College Hall, Oxford, for the benefit of the violinist Antony Manini. In 1784 he played at one concert in a two-piano duet with Jane Mary Guest, and at another with Muzio Clementi.

In 1788, when he was 17 years old, Johann left England and began his famous tours to the Continent in which he established his enormous reputation as teacher and keyboard executant. In Vienna he made Haydn's acquaintance, and in Paris he heard for the first time the works of J. S. Bach. He returned to England in 1791 but in 1798 was back on the Continent. This time he met Beethoven. Between tours he lived in London (in Titchfield Street, according to Doane's *Musical Directory* of 1794).

Curiously, not until 3 May 1802, when he was nearing 30, was Cramer admitted (by unanimous vote) to the Royal Society of Musicians. At this time he was certified

Harvard Theatre Collection

JOHANN B. CRAMER

engraving by Thomson, after Wivell

as a performer on both piano and violin. Though no other accounts seem aware of it, he must have kept up practice on the violin, for he was named by the Governors of the Society in 1803, 1804, 1806, and 1812 (and perhaps in other years) as a violinist in the select company of musicians appointed annually to play the annual benefit concert for the clergy of St Paul's Cathedral. It is more than likely that he had assisted his father in many of the bands in which the older man had been "leader."

On 17 January 1813 Cramer, Philip Anthony Corri, and William Dance issued a circular proposing that several musicians meet them on 24 January to plan the establishment of a Philharmonic Society. The plan was carried into effect with thirty members, and on 8 March the society began a program of concerts in Argyll Rooms, Regent Street. In 1912 the organization became known as the Royal Philharmonic Society.

By 1805 the versatile Cramer had become a partner in the music publishing company of Cramer and Keys and in 1812 had become a partner of Samuel Chappell in the same business. In 1815 he lived at No 29, Sloane Street, Knightsbridge. In 1824 he established the firm of J. B. Cramer and Company. From 1816 to 1818 he traveled again in Germany. From 1835 to 1845 he lived principally abroad, at first at Munich, then at Paris. Returning to London, he lived retired until his death on 16 April 1858. He was buried at Brompton on 22 April.

Cramer was highly esteemed by his pupils, among them Thomas Welsh, Joseph B. Hart, and John Beale. He was a kindly, gregarious man with a wide acquaintanceship among musicians all over Europe. He was a close friend of Haydn and Clementi, and Beethoven ranked him first among all contemporary pianists (even though Cramer did not much care for Beethoven). Domenico Dragonetti left him "2 bonds old Portuguese funds value £10 annual interest."

Edward Dannreuther, writing in *Grove's Dictionary*, has provided a highly sensitive brief technical appreciation of Cramer's keyboard technique.

Cramer's many compositions are nowadays much neglected, despite their solid virtues. He wrote 105 sonatas, as well as lessons, rondos, fantasies, and concertos. The only attempt to list his compositions was by Sainsbury's *Dictionary* (1824), and that list was very incomplete. A few publications which do not appear in the Sainsbury list may be found in the British Museum's *Catalogue of Printed Music*.

Following is a list of portraits of J. B. Cramer:

1. An oil, "Trial Scene in *Henry VIII*," by G. H. Harlow, in which Mrs Sarah Siddons is the central figure, also shows J. B.

Cramer, among others. A copy of the painting is in the Garrick Club.

2. Portrait engraving by J. Thomson after David Barber, published by T. Boosey, 1826.

3. Portrait engraving by E. Scriven after J. Pocock, published by G. Clementi, 1819.

4. Portrait drawn and engraved by W. Sharp.

5. Engraving by B. Holl after A. Wivell, 1831.

6. Engraving by Thomson after A. Wivell, published by W. Pinnock, 1823.

7. Anaglyptograph of medal struck in Cramer's honor, engraved by A. B. Freebairn after the medal by Wyon.

8. Lithograph by Alfred Le Moine, Paris.

Cramer, Wilhelm *1745–1799, violinist, composer, impresario.*

Wilhelm Cramer was born in Mannheim, Germany, in 1745, the second son of Jacob Cramer (1705–1770), a violinist and flutist in the service of the Elector Palatine. Wilhelm studied with Johann Stamitz and Christian Cannabich, both friends and associates of his father who had entered the band at Mannheim three years before Wilhelm was born and who had influenced him from his earliest years. Stamitz was the founder of the important Mannheim "school" of violin playing, and Cramer brought the school's manner to England.

Stories of Cramer's startling precocity are too pervasive for his early facility to be doubted, though the assertion of Gerber in the *Lexikon der Tonkünstler* that Wilhelm was already playing regularly and professionally in the band at Mannheim by 1750 cannot be true if the birthdate of 1745 is acceptable. It seems probable, however, that the boy was playing occasionally in concert by the age of six or seven. The chronology of his early triumphs is highly uncertain, but apparently by age 12 at latest he had joined the Mannheim band,

and by age 16 he had toured successfully in the Netherlands.

The date of Wilhelm's first marriage is not known, nor is the maiden name of his bride, but the marriage occurred in 1770 and his first child, Johann Baptist, was born at Mannheim on 24 February 1771. Wilhelm seems to have obtained in 1770 leave from the Elector and a grant of £200 a year during his absence, to travel through Germany, Italy, and France. In the fall of 1772, on the invitation of Johann Christian Bach (who had just brought out his *Temistocle* at Mannheim) he came to London. Cramer lived for a while with Bach, first in Queen Street, Golden Square, and then in Newman Street. Bach counseled him on his compositions, introduced him to Bach's fellow impresario Karl Friedrich Abel, and helped him arrange a benefit concert at Hickford's Rooms on 22 March 1773. At the little Theatre in the Haymarket on 19 April 1773 he appeared, along with Abel, Crosdill, Eichner, Fischer, Pinto, and Spandau, on the bill of a "Concert of Vocal and Instrumental Music" for the benefit of Pinto and Eichner. He played a violin concerto at another benefit, this time "For the Support and Increase of a Fund established for the Support of decay'd Musicians, or their Families" at the King's opera house on 10 February 1774. By that time he was, very likely, in the regular band at the Opera, as he surely was in the 1774–75 season. Beginning with the charity concert for the Musicians' Fund on 26 January, he was featured in the bills 10 times through 7 April, almost always in new *concerti* composed by his friend J. C. Bach.

Sometime in 1774 Cramer was joined by his wife and his first son, Johann. They seem, however, to have been with him for a short time only. Cramer was proposed for membership in the Royal Society of Musicians on 3 August and admitted on 7 December 1777. According to the deposition furnished by his sponsor, the violinist

Thomas Shaw, he was "in great business." His wife was said then to be dead, and he was reported to have two children, one in Germany "about 7 or 8 years of age" (no doubt this was Johann Baptist, sent home for musical training) and one in London, "about 5 or 6 years of age" (doubtless Franz). (Michael Kelly in his *Reminiscences* asserted that "Mrs Cramer, first wife of the celebrated leader, and mother of John Cramer and F. Cramer . . . a beautiful woman, a charming singer, and a distinguished professional favourite of Tenducci, Leoni, and Rauzzini" had sung in Ireland in Kelly's youth. But he must have been thinking of the second wife.) Wilhelm's father Jacob died in 1770.

In 1779 Cramer was distinguished in a preseason advertisement of the opera house as first violinist and leader of the band, in which position he was perennial until 1796–97 when he was succeeded by Giovanni Battista Viotti (though Cramer continued playing in the violin section that season). It was publicly charged at the time that his demotion from his £300-a-year job was caused by the machinations of Viotti and Brigitta Banti.

Cramer earned £5 5s. each spring from 1779 through 1781 performing and assisting at the Drury Lane oratorios. In 1780 he succeeded Hay as leader of the concerts which were given several times a year by the Society of Ancient Music at Tottenham Court, and he continued in this position through 1789, frequently heard and commended by royalty. He was not, however, the leader of the King's Band (as is sometimes stated), though he may have been a member. Around 1780 he found additional lucrative employment as a member of the Duke of Cumberland's fine private band, organized by Karl Friedrich Baumgarten.

In 1783 Cramer became leader of the band at the Professional Concerts and in this capacity wrote Haydn an urgent invitation to come to England. He was leader also at the second Chester Musical Festival,

Harvard Theatre Collection

WILHELM CRAMER
by T. Hardy

held 16 through 19 September 1783. In 1784 and 1787 he was leader of the strings under Joah Bates at the Handel Commemorations at Westminster Abbey and the Pantheon. In 1791–92 he was leader of the band for 48 nights of opera and ballet at the Pantheon. He belonged to the Anacreontic Society until its dissolution in 1794, walking frequently to its meetings at the Crown and Anchor Tavern in Fleet Street from his home at No 7, Newman Street, off Oxford Street, in the parish of St Marylebone.

Cramer performed but seldom away from London once he took up residence in the British capital, though he was at Dublin with his wife at some date not determined. He played at the Music Room in Oxford, first on 26 April 1773, again in a series of concerts from 20 May 1776 (when, upon the sudden illness of the violinist La Motte, Cramer was "sent by express" to take his place), and on numbers of other occasions up to 19 November 1796. Farmer's *History of Music in Scotland* speaks of his having been *maestro di capella* at the concerts of the Musical Society of Edinburgh at some unspecified date. His last public appearance was at the Three Choirs Festival meeting at Gloucester in September 1799.

This energetic musician also busied himself with teaching, and among his many prominent pupils were George Baker, James Bartleman, John Beale, George Griesbach, and Henry Smart. He composed sonatas, solos, string trios, and a concerto for the harpsichord. Despite all his activity, however, he was frequently in financial difficulties and near the end of his life had to be extricated from financial disaster by a process of bankruptcy.

Wilhelm Cramer died at his house in Charles Street, Marylebone, on 5 October 1799 and was buried in a vault near the entrance to the old Marylebone burying ground.

Cramer had taken a second wife not long after the death of his first. She was a Miss Maria Maddan of Dublin, and apparently she was the beautiful singer of Kelly's recollection. By her Cramer had a second family, four children. The eldest, Charles, was an infant prodigy who played the violin with success at a benefit concert for his father in 1792. In 1791–92 this boy was carried on the roster of the band at the King's Theatre and perhaps played there in subsequent seasons. He died in 1799 before his education in music was finished. The marriage produced two daughters, Julia Augusta and Jane (one of whom married Captain John D'Esterre), and a son, Henry, who was either feeble-minded or a chronic invalid. Jane is said to have been early "distinguished by her extraordinary talents for elocution." A Folger Library manuscript notes that on 22 June 1810 "Miss Jane Cramer made her first appearance on this [the Haymarket] stage, and received great applause in Collins' Ode on the Passions."

Maria Cramer, Wilhelm's widow, married with perhaps scandalous haste after his death. The story unfolds through several entries in the Minute Books of the Governors of the Royal Society of Musicians: On 6 October 1799, Maria was granted £8 for Wilhelm's funeral expenses and £2 12*s.* 6*d.* per month for herself and £3 per month for her four children. On 3 November she applied for an allowance for mourning and for an apothecary's bill incurred by Wilhelm's illness. The plea was rejected. On 5 October 1800, it being reported that Mrs Cramer was remarried, her allowance was suspended until the truth could be ascertained. On 2 November the Minute Book recorded with indignation that the register of St Mary, Islington, had revealed the marriage of Maria Cramer to Edward Martin on 13 March 1800. The Governors then wrote to the lady that, inasmuch as she had for six months fraudulently continued to receive the Society's allowance for widows, her name was to be stricken from the records and that no claim from her would ever be allowed, "on any account whatever." She was told, further, that by removing her children from the Kingdom (of England) she had also made their allowances invalid. In fact her malefaction was such a *cause célèbre* that an extraordinary meeting of the Society was called for 14 December 1800 to amend the bylaws relative to relicts so as to "prevent frauds in future."

The Governors' outrage does not, however, seem to have prejudiced the membership rights of the sons of Wilhelm's first marriage, and the Society eventually relented in the matter of support for the younger children also. On 7 November 1800 a motion was made by one of the Ashleys, and carried, that the usual allowance to orphans should commence for the support of *three* children of "the late Mr Cramer." Franz Cramer had already informed the Governors on 5 January 1800 that he was going to support his half-brother Henry.

Cramer's violin playing was celebrated

for its deep and pure tone and accurate execution. His sight-reading capability was legendary. His teaching was not confined to his instrument; he was evidently competent in voice, other instruments, and theory. He wrote much music, but none survives. Of the stream of German musicians who settled in England from the time of Handel onward, Wilhelm Cramer was one of the most influential.

J. Roberts drew a pencil vignette of Cramer in 1778, but its present location is not known. A portrait of him by T. Hardy was published by Bland in 1794. This was copied by J. F. Schröter at Leipzig. A portrait of him by T. Bragg, after G. Place, was published in 1803. About 1805 Luigi Scotti included him and his son J. B. Cramer in a huge canvas depicting Apollo in a nimbus of light presiding over 31 of the great violinists of the eighteenth century.

Cramerer, Mlle [fl. 1779–1780], dancer.

A note among the Burney manuscripts in the British Museum lists a "Madlle. Cramerer" as one of the "1st serious dancers" at the Opera House during the season of 1779–80.

Cranfeldt. See CRANFIELD.

Cranfield, Mr [fl. 1780–1800?], dancer, actor.

A Mr Cranfield danced professionally in London for the first known time on 17 May 1780 when he was Pierrot in *The Norwood Gypsies* at Covent Garden Theatre, but he may have been performing for some time without being noticed in the bills. He was, according to *The London Stage*, carried on the roster as an actor at £1 5s. per week. His name does not occur on any document in 1780–81 but he was back, this time as a dancer, at Covent Garden in the spring of 1782, when he was named along with many other dancers in the quadrilles and

cotillions at the end of the mainpieces. Again, it is impossible to guess how long or how much he performed that season, though his presence on the pay list at £1 10s. per week seems to indicate that he was a company regular for at least some part of the season. The same observation applies to his activities in 1782–83, when he was named only as Mars in *The Royal Chace; or, Harlequin Skeleton.*

Not until toward the end of the season of 1787–88 did Cranfield's name appear again in London theatrical records, though he had danced at Richmond in July 1785. He was, according to the account book, still earning £1 10s. per week when on 12 and 16 May 1788 he reappeared in *The Royal Chace,* but this time dancing as Hercules. The following season, 1788–89, he was carried in the company list as an actor, though at the same salary. He rose somewhat in the manager's trust, achieving the title role in the new adaptation from the French called *The Death of Captain Cook,* an elaborate series of scenes from the explorer's voyages, presented as an afterpiece which ran for many nights. He was also Don Juan in *Don Juan, or, The Libertine Destroyed,* which was popular for several seasons, and Pierrot in *Poluscenicon.* He danced again at Richmond in the summer of 1789.

In 1789–90 Cranfield worked for the same salary and played the same roles but danced also in such new devices as *Nootka Sound; or, Britain Prepar'd.* In 1790–91 he was joined at Covent Garden by his wife, also a dancer, who earned £1 5s. His own salary was unchanged. They were together on 20 December in Charles Bonnor and Robert Merry's new pantomime *Picture of Paris,* he as a Pioneer and she as a Dancing Nymph. His salary was raised to £2 per week in 1791–92, and she disappeared from the roster, so far as the record shows, until 11 March 1793. Cranfield was there for the entire season of 1792–93, from 25 October through 10 June. He was Draco in *Oscar and Malvina,* General Sanguinaire in

The Shipwreck, a Butler in *The Invasion*, she only a Creolian Woman in several performances of *The Governor; or, The Creolian Insurrection*. Their salaries were level at £2 and £1 5*s.* through 1795–96 and probably through 1797–98, the last season Mrs Cranfield can be followed in London. Their parts remained in the same lines: for her always as one of shoals of servants, shepherdesses, "native women," and the like in pantomimes, for him the occasional specialty dance and the tertiary comedy characters in the harlequinades. They were both absent from Covent Garden in 1796–97. He was at Jones's Royal Circus on 20 August 1796.

A Mr T. Cranfield was at Covent Garden that year but he was not the Cranfield we have been following, for he was present along with the subject of this entry in 1795–96 and in subsequent years also. In 1797–98 not only were Cranfield, Mrs Cranfield, and T. Cranfield dancing at Covent Garden, often in the same performances, but a Miss Cranfield, subsequently identified as Louisa and later to become the second Mrs. John Watts, began to appear. It may be guessed that she was the daughter of the Cranfields of this entry and that T. Cranfield was her uncle.

T. Cranfield was named, with the other Cranfield, as one of the crowd of "Persians and Arabs" dancing in *Harlequin's Treasure* on 15 March 1796. That was the only named appearance for him that season. He performed some function in *Harlequin and Oberon* on 26 May 1797 and subsequently until 12 June. His name was in the bills again several times between 19 and 26 March 1798 as a Male Domestic in *Oscar and Malvina*, and he was back for the next (1798–99) season from 11 December through 16 May in a "procession and dance of Swabian Peasants" in *Albert and Adelaide*, and similar menial appearances. He was also present from 23 December through 5 June 1799–1800, always in unspecified "Pantomimic Characters."

It is not possible to say which of the Cranfield brothers was referred to by the Royal Circus bill of 28 November 1803: "A Hornpipe by Miss Cuerton (Pupil to Mr. Cranfield, late of the Covent Garden Theatre)" or which was at the Circus as Mattes in the pantomime *Abellino; or, the Bravo's Bride* in the summer of 1805, advertised as from the Theatre Royal, Covent Garden, making his first appearance there. If the latter assertion was true, it was T. Cranfield. He was carried in the bill as "Mr Cranfeldt." A Miss P. Cranfield was on the Drury Lane Company lists in 1801–2, and a George Cranfield was earning £1 5*s.* per week at Drury Lane in 1807–8.

Cranfield, Mrs [*fl.* 1790–1798], *dancer.* See **CRANFIELD, MR** [*fl.* 1780–1800?].

Cranfield, Louisa. See **WATTS, MRS JOHN THE SECOND.**

Cranfield, T. [*fl.* 1796–1805?], *dancer.* See **CRANFIELD, MR** [*fl.* 1780–1800?].

Cranford, Miss [*fl.* 1784–1794], *singer, actress.*
Miss Cranford was first noticed in a London playbill on 7 January 1784 at Drury Lane Theatre, when she filled the minor role of a Spirit in the afterpiece *Harlequin Junior; or, the Magic Castle*, which was repeated some 15 times thereafter that season. The role probably required rudimentary dancing and chorus singing and she may have given similar background services to other offerings, but her name did not occur again in the bills that season.

She resumed the same tiny part in *Harlequin Junior* next season, on 23 September 1784. She sang in the chorus of *Arthur and Emmeline* on 22 November and following and performed the same obscure function in *The Caldron; or, Pantomimical Olio* on 20 January and several subsequent dates.

Miss Cranford returned to Drury Lane company each season through 1788–89, playing an occasional minor role and singing specialty songs once in a great while. After her initial appearance at the Haymarket Theatre on 16 June 1786, singing a song at the end of the mainpiece, she was also a summer regular there. She was never given any character more ambitious than Sabrina in *Comus* (her most recurrent one), Jenny in *The Gentle Shepherd*, Colette in *Richard Coeur de Lion*, Jenny Diver in *The Beggar's Opera*, or Dorcas in Garrick's alteration of *The Winter's Tale*.

The *Oracle* of 15 October 1789 stated that the younger Colman had discharged her from the Haymarket, along with a dozen other players, when he assumed the management. She was acting in the summer theatre at Richmond, Surrey, in 1792. On 20 November 1792 and 16 January 1793 she was at Londonderry in Ireland and was at Belfast on 17 April and 15 May. She acted briefly in 1794 at the Theatre Royal, Windsor, and also sang in concerts at Windsor Town Hall. The *Theatrical Journal* found that she possessed "a charming pipe."

Crathorn, Mr ₁fl. 1776–1794₁, *violoncellist, composer.*

Mr Crathorn, of Liverpool, a violoncellist, was listed in Doane's *Musical Directory* in 1794 as a player in the Handelian performances at Westminster Abbey. He probably was the Mr Crathorn who had played in the band and composed music at the Theatre Royal, Liverpool, between 1776 and 1778. The account books of that theatre during those years list payments to Mr Crathorn for wages at 11s. 3d. per week and for writing a score to *Cymon* (21 December 1776). Occasionally he was paid for wages to "his Nephew" at 13s. 6d. per week. No doubt the uncle and his nephew were related to the William Crathorn who was elected to membership in the Royal Society of Musicians on 1 January 1826, who served that society as a Governor in 1827 and 1828 and who was alive in 1830.

Crauford, Mrs ₁fl. 1765₁, *dancer.*

A pay list for Drury Lane Theatre dated 9 February 1765 belonged to the Shakespeare editor H. H. Furness and had been given him by Fanny Kemble as from her father's files. The document purportedly is in Garrick's hand. It contains the names of several minor performers not to be found in other sources. Included is one Mrs Crauford, a dancer, who earned £1 per week.

Craven, Mr ₁fl. 1749₁, *actor, singer.*

A Mr Craven acted the role of Story in a performance of *The Committee* given at the New Wells, Lemon Street, for the benefit of a Hallam on 27 February 1749. He also sang Jaques in the *L'Opéra du gueux*, a French translation of *The Beggar's Opera*, which was performed six times by an "Anti-Gallic" company of English players at the Haymarket between 29 April and 29 May 1749. On 26 May he shared in benefit tickets. Perhaps he was the Mr Graven who played Jemmy Twitcher in a regular version of *The Beggar's Opera* at Twickenham on 26 September 1749.

Craven, Miss ₁fl. 1771–1773₁, *actress.*

Miss Craven was a member of Foote's summer company in 1773 at the Haymarket, where she acted Mrs Trippet in *The Lying Valet* on 17 May, Biddy in *Miss in Her Teens* on 19 May, a role in *She Stoops to Conquer* on 14 June, a role in *The Rehearsal* on 18 June, Margery in *The Register Office* on 28 July, Miss Flint in *A Trip to Portsmouth* on 11 and 27 August, and Lissni in *The Pantheonites* on 3 September. For the performance of *A Trip* to *Portsmouth* on 17 September 1773 she was replaced by Mrs Jewell. Probably she was the Miss Craven who had acted earlier at Norwich (in 1771–72). If so, the Mr Craven who was also a member of the Norwich Company was her father.

Craven, Katharine. *See* STEVENS, KATHARINE.

Craven, William ₁*fl.* 1770–1774₁, *proprietor.*

In 1770 William Craven subleased premises at Ducking Pond in Spa Fields from Rosoman of Sadler's Wells, where at a cost of £6000 he laid out a garden and built a great teahouse on the site of the old inn. The establishment was called the Pantheon and, later, the Little Pantheon, to distinguish it from the larger building which was opened in Oxford Street in January 1772. Craven went bankrupt in 1774 and was required to sell his Little Pantheon.

Crawford, Mrs ₁*fl.* 1760–1761₁, *dancer.*

A "Mrs Craford," a dancer, was on the list of performers at Covent Garden Theatre in the season of 1760–61 at a salary of 3*s.* 8*d.* per day. "Mrs Crawford" was among 11 dancers in *Comus* on 11 December 1760. She no doubt performed many times during the year but was named only in the playbill on 9 March as one of 23 dancers in "A Grand Comic Ballet call'd *The Hungarian Gambols, or a Provincial Rendezvous*" and on 11 and 24 April, when she shared a benefit and danced hornpipes. The account book shows that her annual salary of £35 was (like those of the rest of the company) reduced by a little more than 10 percent—in her case £3 14*s.* 3*d.*—because of the loss attending the closing of the theatres for 19 nights following the death of George III. She disappeared from the Covent Garden roster and from the London playbills after the season of 1760–61.

Crawford, Miss ₁*fl.* 1770–1771₁, *actress.*

A Miss Crawford played Lavinia, a secondary part in *The Fair Penitent*, with an irregular company at the Haymarket Theatre on 28 January 1771.

Crawford, Miss ₁*fl.* 1785?–1794?₁, *singer.*

A Miss Crawford who was located by Doane's *Musical Directory* (1794) at the Bath Theatre had sung in some of the Handel Commemoration performances at Westminster Abbey. Inasmuch as Burney does not list her in those of the first year (1784), she probably sang in one or more of the later ones (1785, 1786, 1787, 1791).

Crawford, Peter *d. 1793, treasurer, manager.*

Peter Crawford was treasurer of the opera at the King's Theatre in the Haymarket from about 1749. But he seems to have had some share in the administration of the theatre from about 1740. On 20 May 1749 Dr Croza signed a letter in the *General Advertiser* identifying a "Mr C——d" in the office of treasurer. On 20 August 1757, Crawford wrote a letter to the *Public Advertiser* signing himself as treasurer. That paper's edition of 13 September 1775 again called him treasurer. On 27 December 1779 he succeeded Le Texier as acting manager and thereafter he discharged both functions until near the end of the season 1783–84.

His employment at the opera house came as a consequence, perhaps, of his connection, through his mother's second marriage, to Benjamin May. May was manager of the theatre, according to James Winston, "for many years" before his death on 1 January 1759. May's will, signed on 28 June 1753, which appointed his wife Theresia May sole executrix, stated "I desire my said executrix to pay into the hands of Peter Crawford her son of the parish of St.

James, Westminster . . . Jeweller, and Henry Kipling of St George Bloomsbury . . . the full sum of one thousand pounds sterling" to be laid out for securities to be purchased for Mrs May's benefit. Crawford himself was left £500.

It was announced by a newspaper clipping dated 31 May 1763, that

As Signora Mattei will leave England after the Operas are over; and as Mr Crawford will have no further concern with the Management of Operas, all the Cloaths used in the Burlettas and Dances, with many other articles, being his own Property and that of Signora Mattei's will be sold. The particulars of which may be had of Mr Crawford at the finishing of the season.

Crawford was caught in the dispute between the Taylor and Gallini factions at the King's Theatre in 1783. According to a circumstantial account, *The Case of the Opera-House Disputes* (1784), at one point—apparently 1763—he had lost his job, though "as principal and conductor of the theatre for so long a period as forty-three years, [he] had acquired that veteran experience necessary to afford general satisfaction." At some other point in the quarrel "P. Crawford, Jun" published a letter asserting (according to Burney's undated transcription in the British Museum) "that there is no other Manager."

The interruption to Crawford's career was slight, however, for 1784–85 saw him back in charge as manager and treasurer. He retired from the theatre in 1786. He was said to be a particular favorite of the nobility during his tenure at the house. Crawford died at Salisbury in 1793.

Crawford, Thomas   1750–1794, *actor, musician, manager.*

Thomas Crawford (called "Billy") was born in 1750 to an upper-middle-class family and bred as an attorney. He became infatuated with the stage and then with Ann

Street Dancer Barry, a renowned and talented actress and at that time most recently the widow of the theatrical luminary Spranger Barry. She was 16 years Crawford's senior, but he became her third husband in mid-July of 1778. She was apparently his second wife. On 13 July, in preparation for the marriage, Ann had secured "to herself by law the Crow-street Theatre properties left to her by her late husband Spranger Barry," according to a manuscript in the Dublin Office of the Registry of Deeds. Clark, in *The Irish Stage in the County Towns*, says that Crawford acted in Dublin that summer of 1778, but his roles are not known.

Mrs Crawford proceeded to Bristol for a brief engagement on her way to London in the early fall of 1778, and Crawford accompanied her. Hannah More saw them at Bristol and wrote to Garrick on 22 September:

Her new husband is handsome, volatile, noisy, a dozen years younger than herself, and by his own account not worth a penny, but in debt. He is most desperately in love with his new wife, and in mourning for his old one . . . Poor man! I believe he thinks her an angel;—pity those fine delusions cannot last.

The couple arrived at London a few days later and took an apartment at No 3, Adam Street, the Adelphi.

Mrs Crawford was then the leading tragedienne at Covent Garden and through her influence (and after her tutelage) Billy Crawford was thrust onstage as Pierre in *Venice Preserv'd* on 22 March 1779, on the occasion of his wife's benefit. The "young adventurer," remarked a newspaper critic the next day, "was so awed on this occasion, as to be able to do little more than rehearse his part." He was given encouragement, however, for he had "a fine person and a good voice." After receiving more polishing Crawford made another try, as Posthumus in *Cymbeline*, for Richard Daly's benefit on 20 April, a performance about which criticism was silent.

On 17 July 1779 a Dublin newspaper announced that "Mr Crawford and his wife intend to take command of Crow-street Theatre the ensuing winter." Ann was doubtless in effective control as an owner, but Thomas Ryder was the manager, and Crawford "for the sake of his wife," as Gilliland bluntly put it, was hired to act. Possibly for the sake of his ego his small worth was concealed under their joint salary of £25 per night for 40 nights. The Crawfords journeyed from London accompanied by the Irish actor Richard Daly, whom they had befriended after he failed to find an opening in London. They opened at Crow Street in May, Ann rejecting the more suitable role of the Countess for that of the virginal Adelaide in *The Count of Narbonne* in order that she might play the love scenes with her young husband as Theodore.

The Crawfords were employed at the summer theatre in the Haymarket from 2 June through 16 August 1780. On 24 July, again for Ann's benefit, Crawford played Othello for the first time. His wife was Desdemona. Tickets were to be had at their house "in Salisbury-street, Strand." The performance was repeated on 4 August. Crawford played no more in London that summer.

The Crawfords signed articles with the Drury Lane company for 1780–81. She earned £14 per night; his salary is not known. She played her usual round of capital roles in tragedy, including her famous Desdemona on 29 November, on which night he essayed Othello again for his debut at Drury Lane. Not until 19 March 1781 was Crawford allowed to act again. Then he played Jaffeir in *Venice Preserv'd* for the first time, once again because of Mrs Crawford's influence, and also for her benefit. His first appearance in comedy (in London, anyway) was on 18 April 1781, as Captain Plume in *The Recruiting Officer*. No assess-

ments of his effectiveness in the part are known.

Notwithstanding his small value to the theatre, his wife's professional weight was enough to give him an unshared benefit night on 19 May. On this occasion, the last time of his acting in London, he showed versatility of not great skill. He played the title role in Home's tragedy *Douglas* and starred as Petruchio opposite his wife in the farce altered from Shakespeare called *Catherine and Petruchio*. The bill also stated: "End of mainpiece a favorite *trio* performed on a guittar (composed by Giardini) for a violin, guittar, and violoncello, by Crawford." Crawford spoke the prologue for the opening of the Dublin summer season of 1781, and he and his wife both played at Crow Street in June and July.

A disagreement with the Drury Lane management caused Mrs Crawford to break off her engagement to that house at the beginning of the season of 1781–82. The tragedy of *Zara* had been advertised for 11 October but *The Lord of the Manor* was substituted: "Mrs Crawford, refusing to fulfill her Engagement at this Theatre, *Zara* cannot be performed." Ann had returned to Ireland to join her husband.

The details of Thomas Crawford's partnership in management (if that is what it was) with Thomas Ryder in 1781–82 are not well understood. They are not much elucidated by the amusing anecdotes which James Gilliland related in his *Dramatic Mirror* of 1808. Crawford, Gilliland says, was forced out of his contract after his first Dublin season because of "a piece of economy he practiced on his benefit night, that provoked the indignation of both the performers and the audience." The highly colored account continues:

The farce was High Life below Stairs, and instead of a supper, he provided wooden fowls, and other mock dishes. Mr. G. Dawson, who played one of the servants, finding the fowl so very tough that he could not possibly carve it, showed it to the audience, who immediately expressed their contempt. Notwithstanding Mr. Ryder, on this occasion, was very satirical on Mr. Crawford, yet soon after the latter not only returned to his theatre, but became a partner in the management of it. Such was, however, its distracted state, that Mr. Ryder left it all to himself, and went over to Mr. Daly, while Mr. Crawford supported it as long as he could. His wife, however, would never appear on the stage till she was paid; and her husband was frequently obliged to collect the money from the door-keepers, and send her the sum she demanded. The band likewise mutinied, and the poor manager, one night that he was to perform Othello, there being no musicians in the orchestra, offered to play on the violin himself between the acts, which proposal being cheerfully accepted by the audience, he played that night the double part of Moor and Fiddler, and his performance in the orchestra was more applauded than that on the stage. . . . This gentleman had a most unfortunate Newcastle *burr* in his throat, but was totally unconscious of it himself; otherwise his address to Banquo's ghost would have cured him of his passion for Macbeth. He was encored in "Approach thou like the rugged Russian bear," &c. which he took for applause, and very obligingly repeated it to a quizzing Dublin audience.

Whatever the authenticity of several such stories about him, Billy Crawford was even worse as a manager than as an actor, and by December 1782 the receipts had fallen so low that, almost certainly at frugal Ann's insistence, her husband had relinquished direction of the enterprise and she had rented the house to William Dawson, Robert Owenson, and others of the company for three months for £150. She continued to extract £17 1s. 3d. from the management for each night she acted. The theatre fared no better, however, nor did she, her husband now being entirely at liberty to dissipate. In 1783 the theatre at Crow Street closed its doors and it did not reopen them until 1787. Mrs Crawford,

thoroughly disenchanted, gave Billy £100 a year and cast him loose. She went back to London to compete frustratedly with Mrs Siddons.

Crawford kept trying to make a success of acting, but his fading career can be glimpsed after 1785 only in the scattered playbills of the Irish provinces. He was at Kilkenny in February and June of 1792 and at Wexford in July and December and again in January 1793. But he returned to England. The *European Magazine* of June 1794 reported his death "aged 44" at Hampstead "lately." A manuscript note by J. P. Kemble gives the place of his death as Hackney.

Crawford, Mrs Thomas. *See* **BARRY, MRS SPRANGER.**

Crawley. *See also* **COURTENAY, MISS.**

Crawley, Mr [*fl.* 1695–*c.* 1727], *puppeteer.*

In September 1695 at Southwark Fair Mr Crawley (or Crowley) the puppeteer presented a show at the Golden Lion, near St George's Church, dealing with the creation of the world and the deluge. About 1727 he, or one of his progeny, was still at it, as a surviving bill from the time attests:

At Crawley's Booth,
Over against the Crown Tavern, in Smithfield,
during the time of
Bartholomew Fair
will be presented a little opera called
THE OLD CREATION OF THE WORLD
yet newly revived with the addition of
NOAH'S FLOOD

Also several fountains playing water during the time of the play. The last scene does represent Noah and his family coming out of the ark with all the beasts, two by two, and all the fowls of the air are seen in a prospect sitting upon trees; likewise over the ark is seen the sun rising in a most glorious manner: moreover a multitude of angels will be seen in a double rank which presents a double prospect, one for the sun the other for a palace; when will be seen 6 Angels *ringing of bells*. Likewise machines descend from above, double and treble, with Dives rising out of hell, and Lazarus is seen in Abraham's bosom, beside several *figures* dancing *jiggs, sarabonds,* and country dances to the admiration of the spectators, with the merry conceits of Punch.

Crawley, Mr ₁fl. 1784₁, *singer.*

A Mr Crawley, bass, was listed by Charles Burney among the vocal performers at the Handel Memorial Concerts in Westminster Abbey and the Pantheon in May and June of 1784.

Creed, Mr ₁fl. 1794–1795₁, *singer.*

A Mr Creed was first noticed in a London theatrical bill when he was one of a Chorus of Guards singing in George Colman and Dr Samuel Arnold's musical spectacle called *The Mountaineers* at Drury Lane Theatre on 31 October 1794. This offering was repeated several times. Creed was mentioned again on 12 February 1795 as one of the several Satraps attendant on Alexander and Statira in a song-and-dance afterpiece, by the choreographer James Harvey D'Egville, called *Alexander the Great; or, The Conquest of Persia*, a piece much admired and long played. Creed was mentioned for the last time in the bill of Drury Lane on 28 February 1795, in this vocal and trivial part.

Creek, Thomas ₁fl. 1668–1670?₁, *actor?*

Montague Summers in *The Playhouse of Pepys* identified Thomas Creek as one of the members of the Duke's Company about 1668 or 1670. Creek is otherwise unknown, and *The London Stage* does not list him.

Creitch. *See* KYTCH *and* CRAIG.

Cremonini, Clementina ₁fl. 1763–1766₁, *singer.*

Clementina Cremonini was first noticed in the opera bills in London when she sang the small part of Nice in the first performance in England of Johann Christian Bach's opera *Orione, ossia Diana vendicata* at the King's Theatre in the Haymarket on 19 February 1763. The opera was repeated several times during the season. She was almost certainly also in *La calamita de' cuori* on 21 February, *Il tutore e la pupilla* on 14 March, *La serva padrona* (Pergolesi) on 24 March, and J. C. Bach's "new serious" opera *Zanaida* on 7 May, though no casts were advertised for either the first or repeated performances. She sang two arias in a "Concert of Vocal and Instrumental Music" held for the benefit of the "Fund for Decay'd Musicians" on 25 April. Two nights later she assisted in another benefit concert, at Drury Lane, "for the Colleges of Philadelphia and New York." (She was then called "Signora Clementina.") She, with other opera performers, generously lent her voice to a benefit concert "for Capitani, now in the King's Bench, for 20 years past," held at the Haymarket on 9 June.

Her name did not occur in the opera bills for the 1763–64 season (there is no conclusive proof, however, that she was not there). At Drury Lane on 24 February 1764 she bore the only foreign name among the singers in Rush's "New English Opera," *The Royal Shepherd*. Hopkins noted in his prompter's diary:

Signora Cremonini, Clementini, made her first appearance on this Stage in the Character of Eliza. Sings very well, very Graceful Deportm.ᵗ & is a great Support to the Opera. Many of the Songs were Encor'd. Some few Hisses, but on the Whole, was pretty well receiv'd.

It is not clear whether or not she sang at Drury Lane in any other work or capacity. The bills did not reflect another performance, yet she shared a benefit night with the Drury Lane managers on 5 April, the occasion of the third performance of *The Royal Shepherd*. Her profit was £63 12*s*.

On 5 June 1764, Signora Cremonini was one of two vocalists (Signor Quilici being the other) on the historic occasion when the seven-year-old Wolfgang Amadeus Mozart and his eleven-year-old sister Marianne made their first public appearance in England, billed truly as "Prodigies of Nature," at the Great Room, Spring Garden, St James's Park.

Signora Cremonini must have figured in the two performances of *Enea e Lavinia*, one (12 June) at the King's Theatre and one (16 June) at the Haymarket in the summer of 1764, for when she went to Smock Alley, Dublin, later that summer, she was billed as from the Little Theatre in the Haymarket. By (at latest) 2 November she was back at Drury Lane, singing Aspatia in a "Serious English Opera never performed before," *Almena* by Richard Rolt, the music by Michael Arne and Jonathan Battishill. She performed the part five times through 23 November 1764 and was Onori in *Ezio* a "new serious opera" at the King's Theatre on 24 and 27 November. But on 30 November the scheduled performance of *Almena* was "oblig'd to be deferr'd until Siga Cremonini's place [could] be supplied."

It is extremely likely that the "Sig." Cremonini in the *Daily Advertiser*'s announcement of the Mozarts' benefit concert at Hickford's Room on 13 May 1765 should really be "Siga.," inasmuch as the only male of that name ever in London was the *castrato* Domenico Cremonini, who was there from 1784 to 1787.

Clementina Cremonini went back again to Dublin, singing there with Tenducci and Peretti in July of 1765. She is traceable to two performances—1 September and 15 October 1766—and there the record terminates.

Cremonini, Domenico ₁*fl.* 1784–1787₎, *singer.*

The *castrato* Domenico Cremonini probably came to England from Genoa. He made his English debut in the role of Aurelio at the first presentation in London of Anfossi's comic opera *Il curioso indiscreto*, at the King's Theatre on 18 December 1784. On 25 January 1785 he was Serpione in *Il pittor parigino*, on 26 February Bubaste in *Nitteti*, on 2 April an unspecified character in *La finta principessa*, and on 15 April an unspecified character in *Artaserse*. These operas were several times repeated. He received £100 for the season.

The next season he was in the cast on the Opera's opening night, 23 December 1786, as Mitrane in *Alceste*. On 9 January 1787 he was Masino in *Giannina e Bernardone* and on 17 April an unspecified character in *Virginia*, a serious opera. He continued in the grave strain on 16 June when he replaced Mengozzi as Tolomeo in *Giulio Cesare in Egitto*. After the end of the season he was heard no more in opera in England. (The announcement in the *Daily Advertiser* of the young Mozarts' benefit at Hickford's Room on 13 May 1765 cites "Sig." Cremonini as singing. The citation is very probably a mistake for Signora Clementina Cremonini.)

Crescentini, Girolamo 1762–1846, *singer.*

Girolamo Crescentini was born in Urbania near Urbino on 2 February 1762. He began his study of music at the age of 10 and was later the student of Gibelli at Bologna. He made his debut in Rome in 1783, somewhat later in life than was usual with the *castrati*, as Angus Heriot observes, and he then went on tour in Italy, obtaining an engagement as *primo uomo* at Leghorn, where he appeared in Cherubini's *Artaserse*.

Crescentini came to London in 1784 and was engaged in opera at the King's Theatre, appearing first on 8 January 1785 as Alceste in the *premier* performance of Metastasio's *Demetrio*. He was then said to

be from the Opera at Lucca. According to
the theatre's account book, he was paid
£850 but, wrote Lord Mount-Edgcumbe, he
"was thought so moderate a performer and
so little liked that before the season was
half over, he was succeded by [the elderly]
Tenducci." Charles Burney thought his
voice "feeble and uncertain." Though he
sang Alceste a few times, he had only two
more parts at London: Sammete in Anfossi's *Nitteti* on 26 February and Arbace in
the *pasticcio Artaserse* on 16 April. But, as
Mount-Edgcumbe charitably remarked "It
is but justice to add that, when he was here,
Crescentini was very young, and had not
attained that excellence which has since
gained him the reputation of a first-rate
singer. He never returned to this country."

But Crescentini's powers were great; he
had a beautiful and agile mezzo-soprano
voice, and he rapidly become one of the
foremost singers on the Continent. He had
profound successes at Padua, Venice, and
Turin in 1785, at Milan in 1787, and at the
San Carlo in Naples in 1788–89. In 1791
he sang at the Argentina in Rome and in
1794 at Venice and Milan. He was at Venice again in 1796, and Cimarosa composed
for him the "Gli orazi ed i Curiazi." He
went over to Vienna, returned for the Carnival of 1797 at Milan, and then departed
for Lisbon. He sang there for the next four
years, becoming a director of the Opera. He
reappeared at Milan in 1803, sang at the
opening of the new theatre at Piacenza, and
then took up an appointment as professor
of singing to the Imperial family at Vienna,
where he was first heard by Napoleon, who
occupied the city in 1805. The French con-
queror was enchanted with the voice which
the youthful Schopenhauer described that
year as being "supernaturally beautiful."

When he sang the air "Ombra adorata"
in *Romeo and Juliet*, standing in Juliet's
garden, two doves descended from the
clouds and brought him a crown of laurels,
while garlands were thrown at him from
the wings. After seeing three performances

Harvard Theatre Collection

GIROLAMO CRESCENTINI
engraving by Grobert

of this opera, Napoleon made Crescentini
a Knight of the Iron Cross of Lombardy
and invited him to the Parisian court,
where he arrived in 1806. He remained six
years in Paris, singing frequently at the
Tuileries. Fétis says that he "reduced the
prince, the courtiers, and all the assembly
to tears when he sang the role of Romeo."
Alfred de Vigny in his "La canne de jonc"
describes an occasion when the Emperor,
the Kings and Queens of Spain, West-
phalia, Württemberg, Saxony, and Naples,
the princes of the Confederation of the
Rhine, and crowds of dukes and ambassadors listened raptly to Crescentini singing in
Cimarosa's *Les Horaces* "with a Seraph's
voice that came from an emaciated and
wrinkled face."

In 1812, his voice showing the strain of
long overuse, and imagining the climate of
France inimical to his health, Crescentini

obtained the reluctant permission of Napoleon to withdraw to Italy. He retired to Rome, abandoning public performance until 1816, and then went to Naples where he began teaching singing at the Royal College of San Pietro a Majella. He died at Naples on 24 April 1846.

Crescentini composed some music and published a number of airs in Vienna in 1797. He also wrote and published, at Paris, a treatise on vocalization.

A portrait of Crescentini by Stainhaüser von Treuberg hangs in the National Library, Vienna. His likeness was drawn and engraved at Milan by Rados in 1821, by Della Rocca at Milan c. 1822, by Giovanni Bernardoni in 1830, and by Grobert at some date undetermined. He was one of a large group of musicians engraved in 1801 after a picture by Antonio Fedi.

Crespi, Signora *[fl. 1773–1786],* *dancer.*

Signora Crespi (sometimes "Crispi") first danced in London at Drury Lane on 30 September 1773 when she appeared with Signor Como in "A New Comic Dance call'd the *Mountaineers.*" She was a regular member of the ballet corps and performed fairly often in solo or duo dances for the next seven seasons, attaining after about two years the status of a principal dancer and dancing dramatic and descriptive ballets with intriguing titles like *The Grand Garland Dance, The Triumph of Love, The Savage Hunters, The Dockyard, The Sportsman Deceived,* and *Rural Sights,* as well as the usual quota of hornpipes, chaconnes, and "peasant dances."

In addition, in 1779–1780 she doubled her duties for part of the year as a principal dancer in the *corps de ballet* of the opera at the King's Theatre. At Drury Lane in 1774–75 and also in 1777–78 she was earning £3 13*s.* 6*d.* per week. From at latest 22 April 1777 through 17 May 1779, she lived at No 26, Poland Street, Oxford Street, "opposite the Back door to the Pantheon." In 1782–83 and 1785–86 she confined her activities entirely to the opera where she was "second dancer."

In the summer of 1776 Signora Crespi danced at the Liverpool Theatre from 15 July through 16 September and was paid £1 per week. She returned there on 2 June 1777 and performed through 29 September at a salary of £2 per week.

On 8 May 1775 Drury Lane granted a benefit "for Sign^r and Sign^a Crespi," at which she danced three dances with Como after the play. Signor Crespi did not dance then or (apparently) ever in London.

Crespion, Stephen *c. 1649–1711,* *singer.*

Stephen Crespion was born about 1649 to Germain and Cornelia Nau Crespion, both apparently French immigrants. Stephen matriculated at Christ Church, Oxford, on 13 July 1666 at the age of 17, received his A.B. degree on 17 May 1670, and was granted his A.M. on 22 March 1673. The following 13 May he was sworn a Gentleman of the Chapel Royal in London, and on 1 November 1675 he was made Confessor to the royal household. As one of the choristers, he accompanied the King to Windsor in the summers of 1675 and 1678, and on 13 August of the latter year he was made Prebendary of Bristol. He became Sacrist of Westminster Abbey on 25 July 1683 and Chanter on 16 January 1684. He died on 25 November 1711 and was buried at the Abbey on 2 December.

Crespion married twice. By his first wife, Margaret, he had a daughter Elizabeth, who was born on 4 April 1675 and christened at Westminster Abbey the next day; the child expired on 21 May and was buried the following day. They had a son Stephen, who was christened on 1 August 1676 and buried on 22 August. Their daughter Margaret was christened on 8 July 1677 and buried on 11 October 1679. Following this sad history of infant death, Mrs Crespion

died and was buried at the Abbey on 22
March 1688.

Crespion's second wife was named Mary.
Their daughter Mary was born on 16 Janu-
ary 1694, christened on 23 January, and
buried on 22 September 1715. The second
Mrs Crespion was buried at the Abbey on 1
January 1759.

Cressea, Mrs *[fl. 1698],* *impresaria.*
The *Post Boy* of 28–31 May 1698 advertised that "At the Request of several
Persons of Quality, Mrs Cressea's Entertainments of Vocal and Instrumental Musick
will be performed in York Buildings, on
Wednesday next, the first of June." "Cressea" could be a misspelling, and she might
have been related to the John Cressett who
is said to have been a concert organizer
during the Restoration.

Cressett, John *[fl. Restoration],* *impresario.*
John Cressett is said to have been a concert organizer during the Restoration period. It is possible that the Mrs Cressea who
sponsored a concert in 1698 was related to
him, and perhaps "Cressea" is a misspelling.

Cresswell, Mr *[fl. 1780–1809?],* *actor.*
A Mr Cresswell acted the part of Var-
land in a performance of *The West Indian*
at the Crown Inn, Islington, on 29 February 1780 in a company made up of novices,
most of whom did not then or subsequently
amount to much on the London stage. Certainly Mr Cresswell did not, for that would
seem to have been his only recorded appearance in London.

It is a temptation to identify him with
the Cresswell who turned up at Hull (as
from Exeter) on 18 November 1783 and
who was at York (as "Tresswell") in
1784–85. One of that name played at Liverpool under Dickens's management in
January and June 1797, along with his

wife. The Cresswells were in Edinburgh in
the winter of 1797–98. Cresswell was de-
rided by "Timothy Plain," the local satirical
critic, when he played Lord Randolph in
Douglas: "in the lover and the warrior [he]
was awkwardness personified." He pleased
Plain even less as Bridgemore in *The Fashionable Lover,* which "was very poorly represented by Mr Creswell."

By the way, I can neither see the necessity
nor propriety in representing every citizen of
London with a pillow under his waistcoat;
nay, of doing so at the hazard of being
ridiculous, which must be the case, when the
man's lantern jaws proclaim the deception.
. . . But, perhaps, Mr Creswell did this to
fill up the *stock* waistcoat.

On 16 November 1798 the Cresswells
made their Dublin debut at the Crow Street
Theatre, having come there from Manchester. On 31 August 1799 Mrs Cresswell
was acting at Cork.

An anonymous manuscript criticism in
the Royal Irish Academy shows Mr Cresswell, at least, to have been at Crow Street
in *Romeo and Juliet* in 1801: "Mrs. Norman and Mr. Cresswell, two of the most
stupid, execrable performers, that ever trod
a stage, were selected for the Capulets. The
principal scenes were, of course, spoiled."
Probably the Mrs Cresswell who was appointed to assist in the Handel Commemo-
rative concert given by the Irish Musical
Fund on 9 March 1803 was the lady we
have been following. She sang again in this
annual affair in 1810. A Cresswell was on
the company list of the theatre at Brighton
in the summer of 1809.

Cresswell, John *[fl. 1796–1814],* *carpenter, scene painter, machinist, chorus
singer?*
John Cresswell was evidently hired as
painter (or perhaps elevated from the car-
pentry crew) during the temporary absence
of Lupino from Covent Garden Theatre,

first appearing in the company's payment ledgers on 13 February 1796, at a salary of £3 3s. per week.

He was first credited with a design in a production when he appeared on the bill of 5 November 1796 on the occasion of the premier performance of John O'Keeffe's elaborate afterpiece burlesque *Olympus in an Uproar*: "The Dragon, the Car and Machinery designed and executed by Cresswell." The *Morning Herald* of 7 November thought: "The beauty of the scenery is only to be equalled by the ingenuity of the machinery. The descents and ascents of the Deities were managed with astonishing regularity and adroitness; and the Flying Cupids hovered in the air in very pleasing attitudes."

Cresswell very quickly consolidated his position as machinist by his contribution to the new pantomime *Harlequin and Oberon* on 19 December: "Machinery, Trick, and Changes of Scenery invented and executed by Cresswell and Sloper [the Master Carpenter]." The *Oracle* of 20 December explained the "tricks":

Among the changes are a trunk into a gingerbread nut-man's wheel-barrow—a poor man's hut into an old oak, with a group of Gypsies boiling their kettle under it—one of the clowns into a thick candle, and the candle afterwards into a green-house tub, with a large shrub in it.

For the fifteen changes of elaborate scenery in the new afterpiece *Raymond and Agnes; or, the Castle of Lindenbergh*, a preposterous but colorful piece taken from an incident in Matthew Lewis's *The Monk*, Cresswell and Sloper devised even more complicated effects. It opened on 16 March 1797. On 17 April Cresswell was paid £12 for "tricks" in the revival of Leonard Macnally's *Robin Hood*.

In the season of 1797–98 Cresswell received a raise in salary to £4 4s. per week. On 26 December 1797 he was credited,

along with Goosetree and Sloper, with the machinery for *Harlequin and Quixotte*, involving East India Company warehouses being instantly changed to Chinese dwellings, "Magic Arms" appearing in flames, and various transformations. Similar subtleties and spectacularities were achieved by him alone or—more usually—with Goosetree or Sloper, in connection with *Harlequin Woodcutter* on 29 January 1799; *The Volcano* on 23 December 1799 ("The representation of the Volcano, and the fight in the air between Floridel and Cratero, may with justice claim the epithet of grand and magnificent," said Dutton in *The Dramatic Censor*); *Harlequin, Tom, Perouse,* and *The Blind Girl* in 1800–1801; *Harlequin's Almanack* in 1801–2; *Harlequin's Habeas* in 1802–3; and *Pizarro* (for which he furnished decorations) and *Valentine and Orson* (machinery) in 1803–4.

In 1799–1800 he had been raised to £5 5s. per week, but no further salary raises are recorded. John Cresswell was paid £134 for the season of 1805–6 at Covent Garden, and a Cresswell, machinist, was still on the Covent Garden roster as late as 1813–14. In 1803–4 a Cresswell was on the Covent Garden List as "Extraordinary Chorus." This may, however, have been the Miss Cresswell who was on the Covent Garden roster as an actress from 1804–5 through at least 1805–6.

Cresswell, Thomas [*fl.* 1660–1679], trumpeter.

Thomas Cresswell was probably the son of the trumpeter of the same name who was in the King's Musick under Charles I but who was placed on pension after 1660. The elder Cresswell apparently died before 1666. Thomas the younger became a member of the King's Musick in 1660, but an entry in the Lord Chamberlain's accounts indicates that he was sworn to come in on the next "avoidance"; this expression probably meant that he served without fee until a salaried post became vacant. By 12 November 1664—the next mention of him in the records—he was at least receiving a £19 17s. 8d. payment for livery due him for the previous year, but a warrant dated 8 April 1665 shows that he was still serving without an annual salary. To keep body and soul together he accepted other opportunities; from 29 March 1672 to 6 January 1673, for instance, he was with the Duke of Richmond in Denmark, the sort of task that brought daily fees plus special livery.

Cresswell's patience was finally rewarded on 16 June 1674 when he was appointed a trumpeter in ordinary "in the place and upon the surrender of John Jones." The post was well worth waiting for: trumpeters were paid £60 annually, much more than most of the other court musicians. The last mention of Thomas Cresswell in the records is in a payroll list dated 13 December 1679. At some time after that date he must have retired or died.

Creswick, Mr [W.?] d. 1792, actor, monologist.

Mr Creswick (or Cresswick) made his first appearance "on any stage" as Beau in the afterpiece *The Toyshop* ("with alterations by himself") billed only as "A Gentleman," at Drury Lane on 22 April 1758, for Holland's benefit. (The identification was made 50 years later by James Winston, early nineteenth-century stage manager at the theatre, but it seems probable.) It was late in the season and the novice learned no new part and found no professional home at Drury Lane. But he signed articles at Covent Garden for the following season and on 29 September was permitted to play the engaging farcical part of the Fine Gentleman in the afterpiece of *Lethe*. Doubtless he was serviceable in unconsidered trifles during the rest of the season, but he played characters important enough to be mentioned in the bills on only four additional occasions: Osric in *Hamlet* on 27 February and 30 April, Drunken Man in *Lethe* on 5 May, and, for his joint benefit

with Desse and Lucas on 21 May, Jack Meggot in *The Suspicious Husband* (with a new epilogue spoken by him).

Creswick was absent from the Covent Garden bills during the first half of the 1759–60 season, and he appeared on only four bills during the second half, adding only one new character, Don Manuel in *Love Makes a Man*. At his benefit he spoke an "Epilogue in Imitation of Shakespeare's Stages of Human Life," which was delivered well enough to be repeated on several other nights. Creswick's share of the benefit came to £27 14s.

Creswick's salary of 3s. 4d. per day in 1760–61 was one of the lowest in the company, and he was obscurely or infrequently employed. At the end of November he was fined 5s. for "not waiting in [*The Earl of*] *Essex* 27th October." Not until 19 December was he named in the bills. He played then Mordecai in *Love à-la-Mode* before the King and other members of the Royal family. He added Witling in *The Refusal* to his repertoire on 28 February and played both Brazen in *The Recruiting Officer* and Fribble in *Miss in Her Teens* for the first time on 8 May, when he shared a benefit.

He was given a place in the bills only twice in the season of 1761–62 (10 October as Osric; 6 November as Don Manuel), earned only £42, and had to suffer the insolence of the anonymous author of *The Rosciad of C——v——nt G——rd——n* (1762):

> . . . CR——SW——CK, who vainly tries,
> With action not his own, to cheat our eyes;
> With cadence forc'd, and imitation mean,
> He apes OBR{IE}N in each mangled scene.
> . . . .
> When, as a Fop, in lace, superbly dress'd,
> What thousand joys are in his eyes express'd!
> Form'd, in his own opinion, quite to please;

Striving at humour, and affecting ease;
He thinks no actor can with him com-
    pare,
For graceful manner, and engaging air.
. . . .
His voice refusing nature to obey,
With misplac'd accents murders ev'ry
    play;
And whilst he violates her sterling laws,
Stares at the wond'ring gall'ries for ap-
    plause.
. . . .
His hoarse rough voice removes our first
    delight,
And all the Coxcomb *stands before our*
    sight.

Creswick faded disconsolately out of the London picture after that season and presumably took to touring in the country towns. He turned up at Edinburgh in the winter seasons of 1763 and 1764 and settled down to secondary parts at York from the season beginning January 1766 through the one beginning in January 1773. He was at Hull for a brief stay beginning on 30 September 1765. On 16 September 1773, in London at the Haymarket, he played an unspecified part in *The Macaroni* and on 18 September an unspecified part in *The Modish Wife*, as well as Sir Patrick in *The Irish Widow.* On both occasions he was advertised as "from York."

The next time Creswick appeared in a London bill was on 2 May 1776 when he played Lord Trinket in *The Jealous Wife* at a specially licensed benefit performance at the Haymarket. He was again absent from London's theatres until 23 March 1778 when he repeated Lord Trinket at the Haymarket in a "Benefit for a Lady in Distress." Once again Creswick sank back into obscurity. On 28 October 1779 *The Morning Chronicle* gave a clear clue to his whereabouts between the occasional engagements when it carried the following advertisement:

At the Old Theatre, No 5, in Portugal Street, Lincoln's-inn-fields, this Day, the 28th instant, at Seven in the Evening, Mr Cresswick's Third Lecture on Elocution will be exemplified in reciting part of

    Dr. Young's Night Thoughts;
    An Affecting Story from the Fool of
        Quality
    Thompson's Palaemon and Lavinia
    Several Passages from Shakespeare;
    A few extracts from the Lecture on
        Hearts;
    Some Observations on Scandal and Def-
        amation;

And Mr. George Stevens' remarks on the origin of Lectures, and practice of snuff-taking.
    tickets for two people for *6d.*

Creswick was said to be gratified at the response to two former lectures. There was yet another of the Haymarket's specially licensed performances on 20 December 1779, this "By Desire of the Most Noble Order of Bucks." Creswick was then Dumont in *Jane Shore* and Sancho in *The Wrangling Lovers.* So far as the record reveals, this was his last public performance in London.

Creswick played occasional small parts with Mrs Siddons, Brunton, Keasberry, Didier, and others in Dimond's company at Bath and Bristol in the spring and summer of 1782. For Haughton's benefit on 22 May at Bath, he delivered a "Lecture upon Hearts" at the end of the mainpiece.

Creswick, who lodged at a Mr Carter's house in the Strand, had, according to the *Thespian Dictionary* (1805), "latterly occupied himself in teaching elocution and lectures." He died suddenly at Kensington on 18 January 1792, having just finished "teaching the young gentlemen at the Prince of Wales's academy," according to the *Gentleman's Magazine* (which called him "Cheswick").

Tate Wilkinson, who suffered him patiently, has left his impressions of Creswick:

. . . a simpering, ogling, inoffensive character; a great admirer of *himself*. We did not long agree, he left me as a discarded actor in 1773, and from that period, by dint of industry, without talents, he, to my astonishment, got an existence by his assiduity and perseverance in giving stupid lectures to the entertainment of no one but himself, and that person was gratified in the highest degree; . . . he did not want a tolerable education, but was a bad speaker. He would read *wold* for *world*; for *superfluous, supufluous,* &c. . . . he acted Beau Mordecai and some trifling characters at Covent Garden, but not with estimation, either in town or country; he had also a very bad memory, and to make that worse, was always frightened out of his small wits. . . . He was utterly deprived of pronouncing the letter *r*.

Wilkinson thought, nonetheless, that when Creswick died, he was "regretted as an honest man, by the few that were acquainted with him." Some rather cruel lines on Creswick from Robertson's *Rosciad*-like poem *The Fragment* (1764) are quoted by Wilkinson:

> *On* Dulness' *form, begot by* Impudence,
> *Of both his parents the true quintescence*
>   [sic],
> *Creswick approaches; but alas, so dull,*
> *So* empty, *though of self so very full;*
> *So flatly pert, he tires our patience quite*
> *We yawn, and wish the creature out of*
>   *sight;*
> *Of vile Monotonists the very worst,*
> *On Lethe's bank with foggy opiates*
>   *nurst:*
> *The boxes ogling with a saucy leer,*
> *He seems to say, with self-applauding*
>   *sneer,*
> *"Ladies your most— What think ye?*
>   *Did ye ever*
> *See any thing so handsome, smart, or*
>   *clever?"*
> *And yet in archness should some female*
>   *own*
> *"She loves," he stops, retreats, and pug is*
>   *gone.*
> *The reputation's all, give that, and then—*

> Daffodil *leaves the* something else *to*
>   men.
> *Others may raise our laughter or disdain,*
> *But Creswick's nauseous impudence*
>   *gives pain.*

Creta, Joachim Frederic [*fl.* 1729], *horn player.*

On 16 January 1729 at the Lincoln's Inn Fields Theatre Joachim Frederic Creta blew "the First and Second Treble on Two French Horns, in the same Manner as if Two Persons: Being the first Time of his appearing in Publick, since his Arrival in Great-Britain."

Crewe, Mr [*fl.* 1792], *actor.*

A Mr Crewe played Richmond in *Richard III* in a company of irregulars performing by special permission of the Lord Chamberlain for the benefit of the Literary Fund at the Haymarket on 16 April 1792. He evidently did not play well enough to attract the attention of the patent houses, for his name does not appear again in the London bills.

Crewes, Jeremiah [*fl.* 1630–1665?], *drummer.*

Jeremiah (or Jeremy) Crewes was sworn a drummer in ordinary in the King's Musick on 14 January 1630, a position in which he was re-established on 21 June 1660. Robert Mawgridge replaced him on 24 August 1665, and an order in the Lord Chamberlain's accounts dated 15 December 1669 indicates that by that time he had died.

Cridland, Mr [*fl.* 1761–1773], *box-keeper.*

A Mr Cridland (once called "Gridland") was a boxkeeper at Drury Lane Theatre every season from 1761–62 through 1772–73. A surviving pay list of 9 February 1765 gives him a salary of 12s. per week during that season.

Crieve, Mrs [*d.* 1787?], *sweeper.*

Nothing is known of Mrs Crieve, a sweeper at Drury Lane, except the notice in the theatre's manuscript account book for 10 January 1787: "Given to the funeral of Mrs Crieve, sweeper 1 / 1 / –."

Crig. *See* LA CRIG.

Crippen, Mr ₍fl. 1784₎, *singer.*

A Mr Crippen was listed by Charles Burney among the vocal performers at the Handel Memorial Concerts at Westminster Abbey on 26 and 29 May and 3 and 5 June and at the Pantheon on 27 May 1784. His was a bass voice.

Crisp, Mrs ₍fl. 1787₎, *actress.*

A Mrs Crisp played the role of Lady Rusport in *The West Indian* in a specially licensed performance by a group of irregulars at the Haymarket on 12 March 1787. She may have been related to the Crisps who acted at York in the 1760s and at Exeter and York in the 1790s, or to Charles, John, and George Crisp, or to both groups.

Crisp, Miss ₍fl. 1799₎, *actress. See* CRISP, JOHN.

Crisp, Charles ₍fl. 1799–1821?₎, *actor, manager.*

Charles Crisp was perhaps related to the Mrs Crisp who acted once at the Haymarket and the Crisps who acted principally at Exeter and York. He had at least two brothers—John, who was older, and George, who was younger—and a sister whose name is not known.

Charles is known certainly to have been concerned in only one London performance, though he probably was in others. He appeared playing a "Boy" in the afterpiece *The Poor Soldier* at the Old Crown Inn, Highgate, on 15 May 1799.

Charles was at first joint manager, with his brother John, of the Hereford circuit (after Watson's death in 1813) and at

some later date succeeded him as sole manager. That was probably in 1821, when he was said by a country newspaper to have succeeded his brother as manager on the Cheltenham circuit, where he had supervised rehearsals since 1819.

"Alpha," writing in *Notes and Queries* in 1868, remembered Charles Crisp as an excellent Richard III, Macbeth, Shylock, and Ghost in *Hamlet*. He had married "a niece of the late Sir Astley Cooper, Bart., M.D., and [had] had two daughters, both accomplished actresses, but the youngest (Miss Cecilia Crisp) left the profession soon, and married a medical practitioner at Cheltenham."

Crisp, John ₍fl. 1799–1819?₎, *actor, manager.*

John Crisp may have been closely related to the Mrs Crisp who acted at the Haymarket on one occasion and to the Crisps who performed at Exeter and York. He had at least two brothers, Charles and George, and a sister whose name is not known. John is known certainly to have been concerned in only one performance in the London area, though he probably was in others. He appeared (as "Master Crisp") playing a servant in Home's tragedy *Douglas* at the Old Crown Inn, Highgate, on 15 May 1799, in a pickup company evidently managed by one Frimbley. Douglas in the mainpiece and Patrick, the lead in the farce *The Poor Soldier*, were played by an unidentified "Person of Highgate." John's younger brother Charles and his sister were also on the bill. Charles played "Boy" and Miss Crisp Norah in the afterpiece.

John was probably the Crisp who was acting at Worcester in 1807. He certainly succeeded the elder John Boles Watson (d. 1813) as manager at Hereford. *Authentic Memoirs of the Green Room* (1814) cite John and his brother Charles as joint managers of a circuit which included Hereford, Worcester, Chester, Wolverhampton, Kidderminster, Ludlow, and Shrewsbury. A newspaper of May 1819 carried an announcement by John Crisp of the "General improvement of the [Cheltenham] Theatre which is now lighted with Gas upon an enlarged scale, after the most improved plan of the London Theatres. The Rehearsals and Stage Management will fall under the superintendence of his brother, Mr. Charles Crisp. . . ." A Crisp (possibly John) joined the company of the Haymarket Theatre in the summer of 1816 at a salary of £3 per week. He was not re-engaged in 1817.

Crisp, Samuel   1707–1768, actor.

Samuel Crisp (or Crispe) was born in 1707. He apparently served a provincial theatrical apprenticeship and was acting at Norwich in 1734–35. He joined the company of Henry Giffard, which was then evading the Licensing Act at Goodman's Fields Theatre, on 10 February 1741 and played the title role in *Richard III*. He was Old Wilmot in *The Fatal Curiosity* on 14 February, Osmond in *King Arthur* on 19 February, Jupiter in the pantomime *Harlequin Student* on 3 March, and the King of France in *All's Well That Ends Well* on 7 March. On 7 April he shared a benefit with William Giffard, a relative, according to Tate Wilkinson. Crisp did not act again in London.

For 23 years "Sammy," as Wilkinson called him, either went into some line of work outside the theatre or dropped into such country obscurity that his name was not carried in theatrical bills. A few years before his death he and his wife "Henny" turned up at the York Theatre and acted there together from 1764 until near the time of Sammy's death, which occurred on 4 April 1768. He was buried in St Olave's Churchyard, York. His wife continued to act at York through the season which began in January 1772. It is probable that the Samuel Crisps were the parents of Charles, George, and John Crisp, theatrical people of the next generation.

Tate Wilkinson remembered the Crisps in *The Wandering Patentee*. Samuel had been Wilkinson's unsuccessful rival for the managership at York. Though "well made in person" and allowed to play "most of the principal characters," Crisp was "very awkward in deportment, entirely possessed of the old strut and bounce, and was ever at the top of his voice." Wilkinson quoted the theatrical satirist Robertson on Sammy's acting:

> *Lo! Nature's direst foe, King* Crisp *appears,*
> *And with discordance vile torments our ears;*
> *The signal cue when giv'n, the* machine *moves,*
> *It strikes the same whether it chides or loves;*
> *An octave higher always than the rest;*
> *Sweet harmony ne'er touched that callous breast,*
> *A wooden poor Automaton at best:*
> *With toes turn'd in, thumbs cock'd, and bellman's cant,*
> *It scolds, nay whispers always in a rant:*
> *Ended in the speech, fix'd to the spot it stands,*
> *Till cue-struck, once again it lifts its hands:*
> *Deaf to the anguish of a wounded heart,*
> *Automaton can but repeat its part:*
> *Ye gods! that such a lump should e'er engage,*
> *To quit the plough, and vilify the stage;*
> *Hence with th' unfeeling, bawling, stupid block,*
> *He's only fit to cry — past twelve o'clock.*
> *In one tone he can mouth, growl, rant, and roar,*
> *And make flat nonsense what was sense before.*

Crisp, Mrs Samuel, Henrietta Maria, née Tollett   1709–1780, actress, dancer, singer.

Henrietta Maria Tollett was born sometime in 1709, evidently into a family with theatrical connections. The "Mrs" Tollett to whom *The London Stage* gives the character of the Page in *The Orphan* on the occasion of a special benefit for the actor Huddy at the Haymarket on 24 February 1726 was doubtless Henrietta Maria (the Latreille manuscript at the British Museum cites "Miss"). It is a juvenile part.

Miss Tollett appeared as Nell in *The Devil to Pay* at the Lee and Harper booth at Bartholomew Fair in August and September 1731, moved on to Fielding's booth at Southwark Fair by 28 September to attempt Mrs Lovely in *A Bold Stroke for a Wife*, and on 25 October 1731 was advertised as appearing for the first time on the stage of the Goodman's Fields Theatre, in the character of Betty in the afterpiece *Flora*. Thereafter that season she danced occasionally and played Flora in *Love's Opera*, Rose in *The Recruiting Officer*, Jenny in *The Fair Quaker*, Prue in *Love For Love*, Serina in *The Orphan*, Jenny in *The Tender Husband*, Lucetta in *The Rover*, Cleone in *The Distress'd Mother*, Leonora in *The Mourning Bride*, Lucy in *Oroonoko*, Tippet in *Phoebe*, Myrtilla in *The Provok'd Husband*, Molly in *The Footman*, Gipsey in *The Stratagem*, and an Attendant on Columbine in *Harlequin's Contrivance*. A Mrs Tollett was active at Goodman's Fields that season, often playing or dancing on the same program with Miss Tollett. Occasionally, the printer confused the two women, who were probably mother and daughter.

Henrietta Maria Tollett continued to act at Goodman's Fields through 1735–36. She added the following new parts: Mrs Vixen in *The Beggar's Opera*, Situp in *The Double Gallant*, Lamorce in *The Inconstant*, Teresa in *The Spanish Fryar*, Mrs Chat in *The Committee*, Donna Rodriguez in *Don Quixote*, Scentwell in *The Busy Body*, the Ghost in *The Indian Emperor*, Honoria in *Love Makes a Man*, an Attendant on Britannia in *Britannia*, Wishwell in *The Double Gallant*, Isabella in *The Stage Coach*, Inis in *The Wonder*, Parly in *The Constant Couple*, Jenny in *The Tender Husband*, Clara in *The Lover's Opera*, Florella in *The Orphan*, Betty in *The Fond Husband*, Necessary in *Woman is a Riddle*, Lucy in *George Barnwell*, Busy in *The Man of Mode*, Wheedle in *The Miser*, Finesse in *A Tutor for the Beaus*, Lady Graveairs in *The Careless Husband*, Mrs Starch in *Sir Cockle at Court*, and Juliet in *Measure for Measure*. In addition, at the Ryan-Laguerre-Chapman-Hall booth at Bartholomew Fair on 24 August 1734, she was one of Don John's Wives in *Don John; or, The Libertine Destroy'd*. Also, at Lincoln's Inn Fields on 27 December 1736 she was Surda in *Ignoramus* and played her minor part in *Britannia* on 28 and 29 December.

The date of Henrietta Maria Tollett's marriage to Samuel Crisp is unknown. Samuel, usually a provincial actor, had acted briefly early in 1741 at Goodman's Fields for his kinsman Giffard. He had then disappeared from London and for 23 years is not recorded as playing anywhere else. Henrietta was absent from the record for 28 years. They were both at the York Theatre from 1764 until Samuel died in April 1768, and "Henny," as she was called, acted there until the spring of 1772 or perhaps even later.

Like her husband, Henny was pilloried by the theatrical satirist Robertson. Wilkinson, in *The Wandering Patentee*, quotes:

[Crisp's] *royal spouse, that wither'd,*
    antique dame,
Murders the youthful parts; oh, shame!
    shame! shame!
Patches and paints in vain their aid
    supply,
The old crack'd wall, tho' varnish'd o'er,
    we spy;
To age, tho' rev'rence and respect is due,
An old coquette we nauseate when we
    view:
In vain she twines, writhes, jerks, the hag
    still glares,
And thro' the flimsey veil old Abigail
    appears

But Wilkinson himself was far kinder: "Mrs CRISP [was] neat in dress to a degree, and a genteel made woman, but quavered her tragedy in imitation, as I was told, of Mrs Porter. . . . She was a pattern for actresses as to neatness and propriety of behaviour." She died in 1780.

Wilkinson testified that the Crisps "lived in great credit and were much esteemed by several worthy persons at York, Hull, and Newcastle."

Crispi. *See* CRESPI.

Crispin. *See* CRESPION.

"Croaker, Alley" *(fl. 1759), singer.*
A singer operating under the topical pseudonym "Alley Croaker," punning on the Indian rebel's name, rendered with a Signora Ciperini a duet, "The Humours of Bartholomew Fair," at Shuter's New Booth at that same fair on 3 September 1759.

Croce. *See* VIVIANI.

Croft. *See also* CROFTS.

Croft, Henry *(fl. 1771–1772), actor.*
Henry Croft (or Crofts) was the very type of the stagestruck gentleman who has made life miserable for managers in all eras. According to the *Town and Country Magazine* (1771) he was "the son of a clergyman, and served his time to a stationer in the Temple." Charmed by the superficial glamor of the theatre, with no real appreciation of its requirements of either talent or hard work, Croft badgered David Garrick for six months until he extracted a promise for an audition, which was held at the Drury Lane manager's house at Hampton. In a letter of 6 August 1771 Garrick made a desperate effort to avert—both for Croft and himself—the sure consequences of the amateur's persistence, telling him bluntly "You have not talents for the stage," and "You will fail." But Croft was

not to be deterred. He wrote Garrick on 13 August a three-page letter insisting that the manager had promised him a chance. Croft had "calmly consider'd the Event" and was determined. On 18 August Garrick was writing resignedly "I have a character in mind for you."

Garrick contrived to delay and excuse, but finally, on 4 December 1771, the novice was allowed to come out in the important part of Alcibiades in *Timon of Athens* (as altered by Cumberland). The result was as Garrick had foretold. The *Town and Country Magazine* found his action and walk "aukward and improper," saying, "He is not a bad figure, but is too little for his part; his voice is strong and powerful, but a glaring deficiency of judgment and method is apparent in his delivery." The *Theatrical Review* roasted Croft at some length:

his deportment is aukward and void of grace to an extreme; and he labors under the disadvantage of having a face destitute of expression. His gestures are extremely ungraceful, and the whole of his execution is glaringly untutored, and misconceived. His person is very ill formed, and therefore it makes greatly against him, especially as he is the representative of Alcibiades, who was the handsomest man in all Athens, and we never remember any one's attempting to set out as a capital performer with so few requisites . . . as this gentleman appears to have.

The prompter Hopkins was more succinct in his diary: "bad figure bad voice & Play'd bad."

The atrocious notices notwithstanding, Croft was given a second role, this time Chamont in *The Orphan* on 21 February 1772. This time the *Theatrical Review* was outraged:

If necessity has obliged Mr. Croft, to tread the Actor's walk, he is truly an object of pity, but this will not justify Mr. *Garrick's* neglect of that duty he owes to the Public. If he means to serve Mr. Croft, let him be employed in a cast of Characters to which his abilities are adequate. . . . to place him in capital Characters . . . is an affront to common sense, and consequently an insult offered to the Public.

Yet the Public seems to have regarded the novice with kindness personally if not professionally. He was given a benefit on 7 May and played Posthumus in *Cymbeline*. After paying house charges of £49 10s. 6d. he still had the remarkably large sum of £179 5s. 6d. left for himself. Nevertheless, he had prudence enough to withdraw quietly—or Garrick had firmness enough to refuse him a place in the company.

Croft, William 1678–1727, *organist, composer.*

William Croft (sometimes Crofts) was christened at Nether Ettington, Warwickshire, on 30 December 1678. At an early

National Portrait Gallery

WILLIAM CROFT, c. 1690

artist unknown

age he was placed under John Blow as one of the Children of the Chapel Royal in London. Unlike many of the boys who left the Chapel never to return, Croft was sworn a Gentleman of the Chapel Royal on 7 July 1700. At first he served without fee, no position being vacant. He and Jeremiah Clarke were to succeed as organists "according to merit" when a place became available. While waiting, Croft accepted a post as organist of St Anne, Westminster (now St Anne, Soho), in 1700.

Though only 22, Croft was already an established composer. Three of his sonatas for violin and bass were announced in the *Post Boy* of 30 September–3 October 1699; in early 1700 some of his works appeared in *A Choice Collection of Ayres for the Harpsichord or Spinnet*; he was represented in *The Harpsichord Master* in 1700 and 1701; and the *Post Boy* of 5 December 1700 announced the publication of *A Set of New Ayres* which Croft had composed for *Courtship à la Mode* at Drury Lane on 9 July. Other plays for which Croft provided overtures and act tunes were *The Funeral* in 1701, *The Twin Rivals* in 1702, *The Lying Lover* in 1703, *The Northern Lass* in 1704, and *The Modern Prophets* in 1709. The Bodleian and Christ Church collections include other music composed by Croft for unidentified plays.

In later years Croft turned out a great number of religious and secular works, as the British Museum's *Catalogue of Printed Music* testifies. He published in 1724 a two-volume folio, *Musica Sacra*, which included his most famous work, a burial service still used in Anglican ritual. His lighter works were popular in London concert halls, and Croft in his early years helped organize such events. The *Diverting Post* of 20 January 1705, for instance, noted that Croft and Jeremiah Clarke were preparing a concert "on the late successful campaign."

Croft and Clarke had to wait from 1700 to 24 May 1704 before they received permanent positions in the Chapel Royal. They were sworn jointly to the organist's post made vacant by the death of Francis Piggott. Now secure, Croft married Mary George on 7 February 1705. His colleague Clarke committed suicide on 1 November 1707, and four days later Croft succeeded to the full position of organist to the Chapel Royal. At the death of John Blow on 1 October 1708 he was appointed organist of Westminster Abbey and made Composer and Master of the Children. He was given a special allowance of £80 to cover his extra duties in connection with teaching the boys writing, musical composition, arithmetic, and organ. Though still only 30, he had established himself as one of the foremost musicians in England and the logical successor to Henry Purcell. Gould made the assumption in his *Works* in 1709:

Only, inchanting Crofts! 'tis only Thee,
Whose Soul has Seeds of equal Har-
*   mony:*
On Thee (if Poets Wishes may befriend)
A double Portion of his Skill descend:
You follow fastest the bright Path he
*   trod;*
Keep, Lovely Youth, in the Harmonious
*   Road.*

In January 1712 Croft gave up his position at St Anne's, probably to provide himself more time for composing and teaching. Among his students at Court was the organist Charles Stroud, but he also taught outside the Court, one of his private pupils being the singer Anastasia Robinson. On 9 July 1713 he received the Doctor of Music degree from Oxford, composing two odes for delivery at his graduation exercise on 13 July.

In 1724 *The Session of Musicians* poked fun at most of the prominent musical artists in England by having them appear before Apollo to see who would be judged the finest (Handel, of course, won):

Gr[ee]n, C[ro]fts, and some of the
*   Cathedral Taste,*
Their Compliments in Form to Phoebus
*   past;*
Whilst the whole Choir sung Anthems in
*   their Praise,*
Thinking to chant the God out of the
*   Bays;*
Who, far from being pleas'd, stamp'd,
*   fum'd, and swore,*
Such Musick he had never heard before;
Vowing he'd leave the Laurel in the
*   lurch,*
Rather than place it in an English
*   Church.*

This deprecation was all in sport, however. In 1725, when the Academy of Vocal Music was founded, Croft became one of its honored members.

When Croft died at Bath on 14 August 1727, the newspapers described him as "the eminent Dr. Crofts, Organist and composer to his Majesty, Master of the Chil-

Courtesy of Faculty of Music, Oxford

WILLIAM CROFT
by T. Murray

dren of the Chapel Royal, and Instrument Keeper and Organist of St. Peter's Westminster." He was buried at Westminster Abbey on 23 August. Mary Croft survived her husband, but only by a few years. Administration of both their estates was granted to her father, Robert George, on 28 July 1733.

William Croft was the subject of a painting by an anonymous artist, showing him as one of the Children of the Chapel Royal about 1690; the painting is now at the National Portrait Gallery. A second painting, done by Thomas Murray about 1720, is at Oxford; engravings of it were made by Vertue in 1724 and by J. Caldwell. A Kneller portrait, perhaps of Croft, is at the Trinity College of Music; a reproduction of it is in the National Portrait Gallery archives.

Crofts. *See also* **CROFT.**

Crofts, Mr ₁*fl. 1740–1757?*₁, *actor, dancer?*

Mr Crofts was first seen in London at Goodman's Fields Theatre on 21 October 1740 in the part of Vainlove in *The Old Bachelor.* The next evening he played Scale in *The Recruiting Officer* and two nights later was Freeman in *A Bold Stroke for a Wife.* He was steadily employed in good secondary parts for the rest of the season, adding: Zaura in *Tamerlane,* Blunt in *George Barnwell,* Thomas in *The Virgin Unmask'd,* Suffolk in *Lady Jane Gray,* Sir John Friendly in *The Relapse,* Seward in *Macbeth,* the Turnkey in *The Imprisonment . . . of Harlequin,* the First Lord in *The Winter's Tale,* an Old Woman in *The Stratagem,* Montano in *Othello,* Valentine in *The Wife's Relief,* Ratcliff in *Richard III,* Aurelius in *King Arthur,* the Second Watchman in *Harlequin Student,* the Lawyer in *The Miser,* Thomas in *Lethe,* and Frederick in *The Wonder.*

On 22 August 1741 he was at Turbutt and Yates's Great Theatrical Booth, opposite the King's Head and Greyhound Inn, West Smithfield, at the time of Bartholomew Fair, playing the lead in *Thomas Kouli Kan, The Persian Hero.*

Crofts opened his season at Goodman's Fields on 16 September 1741, playing Buckram in *Love for Love.* He added to his repertoire Pedro in *The Spanish Fryar* on 18 September, Manuel in *Love Makes a Man* on 28 October, Tanais in *Tamerlane* on 7 November, the original Robin in *Pamela* (James Dance's adaptation of Richardson's novel) on 9 November, and Sancho in *Rule a Wife and Have a Wife* on 16 December 1741.

After the season of 1740–41 Crofts dropped from the records in London. He may have been the Crofts who acted at York around 1748 or the one who acted and danced at Edinburgh for a short period in 1749 (or both). He may even have been the Croft who played at Norwich in 1755–56 and 1756–57.

Crofts, Mrs ₁*fl. 1680–1687*₁, *actress.*

Mrs Crofts is known to have acted Teresa in *The Spanish Fryar* on 1 November 1680 and Aurelia in *2 Rover* in January 1681 at the Duke's Company's theatre in Dorset Garden. She seems to have been a member of the United Company in the 1685–86 and 1686–87 seasons, but no roles are known for her.

Crofts, Mrs *d. 1778. See* **SHERRIFFE, MRS JOHN.**

Crofts, Miss ₁*fl. 1786–1790*₁, *equestrienne, dancer, actress, singer.*

Miss Crofts (sometimes Croft) first came to public attention acting and dancing at Hughes's Royal Circus in St George's Fields. On 28 October 1786 she was an unspecified character in the burletta *The Peckham Gardener.* On 31 October the Royal Circus bill announced, amongst other pleasures, "N.B. Hughes's Famous horse Chiliby, will be rode every Evening this

Week by Miss Croft, which horse no riding master or groom dare approach before Mr Hughes made him obedient." In April 1787 Miss Crofts was last on a list of 20 "principal Dancers" presenting "A New Burletta, called The FROLICKSOME WIFE. And a New OPERA, called BOTANY BAY."

Miss Crofts accompanied the troupe of Hughes to Stourbridge Fair, near Cambridge, in 1788, a year in which a defector from Hughes's company, one Benjamin Handy, brought a rival company to the Fair. There were many "challenges" thrown between Hughes and Handy to perform difficult equestrian feats, with large sums riding on the outcomes. Among them was a challenge by Hughes to Handy to bring forth an equestrienne to equal Miss Crofts, riding either one or two horses, for £20.

The versatile Miss Crofts could also sing, and so she did on 22 July 1790, the night of her benefit shared with Mr Peile, a night signalized by "A grand display of Horsemanship, By the whole of Hughes's Troop" and exhibitions of athleticism by "Signor FORTISSIMO (commonly called AT-LAS)," and "The Whole to conclude with the Siege and Demolition of the BAS-TILE." It was also the last recorded performance by Miss Crofts.

Crofts, Mary ₁fl. 1740–1741₁, *lamp woman.*
Mary Crofts served the Covent Garden Theatre as a lamp woman at 10s. per week during the 1740–41 season. She was perhaps related to the actor named Crofts who was at Goodman's Fields Theatre that season.

Croix. *See* DE LA CROIX.

Crome, Robert ₁fl. c. 1745–c. 1765₁, *violinist, composer.*
Robert Crome was a violinist at Covent Garden Theatre in the middle of the eighteenth century, according to van der Straeten. He wrote a "tutor," *The Fiddle New Model'd . . . ,* published by Thompson about 1750, and *The Complete Tutor, for Violoncello . . . To which is added a favourite Collection of Airs, Marches, Minuets, Song-tunes & Duetts,* published by Thompson about 1765. Songs, mostly patriotic, composed by him are listed in *The Catalogue of Printed Music in the British Museum.*

Cromer. *See* COMER.

Crook, Miss ₁fl. 1747–1748₁, *actress.*
A Miss Crook played Sukey Tawdrey in *The Beggar's Opera* at Drury Lane on 13 May 1747 and Angelica in *The Anatomist* at the same theatre on 29 October 1748.

Croome, Mr ₁fl. 1667₁, *booth operator.*
In 1667 at Bartholomew Fair a Mr Croome advertised his show:

At Mr Croome's, at the Sign of the Shoe and Slap, near the Hospital Gate in West Smithfield, is to be seen, THE WONDER OF NATURE, A Girl, above Sixteen Years of Age, born in Cheshire, and not above Eighteen Inches long, having shed the Teeth seven several Times, and not a perfect Bone in any part of her, only the Head; yet she hath all her senses to Admiration, and Discourses, Reads very well, Sings, Whistles, and all very pleasant to hear. Sept. 4, 1667. GOD SAVE THE KING.

Cropponi, Mr ₁fl. 1733–1734₁, *dancer, actor.*
Mr Cropponi was an actor-dancer in Theophilus Cibber's company of Drury Lane deserters playing at the Haymarket Theatre in 1733–34. He appeared as Merlin on 29 October 1733 and as Grizzle on 28 January 1734 in *The Opera of Operas.*

Crosa. *See* CROZA.

Crosara. *See* CROSSARO.

Crosbie. *See* CROSBY.

Crosby. *See also* COSBY.

Crosby, Mr [*fl.* 1786], *house servant.*

A Mr Crosby shared benefit tickets with minor house servants at Covent Garden on 1 June 1786. A notation in the account book of that theatre indicates that on 2 December 1786 Crosby was replaced by Atkins, a known house servant.

Crosby, Miss [*fl.* 1800], *singer.*

A Miss Crosby sang in the oratorios at Covent Garden in the spring of 1800. She made her first appearance singing "Jehovah crowned" in a concert of Handel's sacred music on 28 February; on 5 March she sang "Light a bright cherub," from *Gideon*, with Miss Capper and Miss Tennant. She also sang roles in the *Messiah* on 7 and 26 March, in *Alexander's Feast* on 14 March, and in *Acis and Galatea* on 21 March, and rendered "Return, O God," from *Samson*, on 19 March. On 28 March 1800 she sang in the first London performance of Haydn's *The Creation*.

Crosby, John *d. 1724, actor.*

The earliest mention of John Crosby in contemporary documents seems to have been in the manuscript of *Ignoramus* (now at Harvard), where he was noted as having played Banacar—presumably at court with the Duke's Company on 1 November 1662. His name did not occur in public theatrical records, however, until the 1669–70 season; the prompter John Downes recorded Crosby as first being "entertain'd in the Duke's House" about 1670. On 20 September 1670 Crosby acted Cleontius in *The Forc'd Marriage*, and during the rest of the 1670–71 season he played Andrages in *The Women's Conquest*, Otanes in *Cambyses*, Featlin in *The Six Days' Adventure*, and Alexey in *Juliana*.

Between that season and his retirement in 1679, he acted mostly "young lover" roles but occasionally had heavier parts: Pheroras in *Herod and Mariamne*, Lewis in *Charles VIII*, Mr Cleverwit in *The Citizen Turn'd Gentleman*, Don Sebastian in *The Fatal Jealousy*, Rash in *The Morning Ramble*, Leandro in *The Reformation*, Abdelcador in *The Empress of Morocco*, Lewis in *Love and Revenge*, Claudius in *Hamlet*, Patroclus in *Alcibiades*, the Marquis of Posa in *Don Carlos*, Alonzo in *Abdelazer*, Courtly in *Tom Essence*, Arsaces in *Titus and Berenice*, Sylvio in *Pastor Fido*, Thyreus in the Sedley version of *Antony and Cleopatra*, Frederick in *The Rover*, Claudio in *The French Conjuror*, Noble in *The Counterfeit Bridegroom*, Ptolemy in *The Siege of Babylon*, Leander Fancy in *Sir Patient Fancy*, Lovell in *Squire Oldsapp*, Haemon in *Oedipus*, Paris in *The Destruction of Troy*, and Julio in *The Feign'd Curtizans*. (He spoke the epilogue to *The Counterfeit Bridegroom*, though *The London Stage*, in error, gives his name as *Mrs* Crosby.) Diomedes in Dryden's *Troilus and Cressida* in April 1679 at the Dorset Garden Theatre was Crosby's last recorded role, after which he left the stage.

The *True Protestant Mercury* of 29 July–2 August 1682 reported an altercation involving John Crosby after he retired from acting:

Sunday Evening [presumably 30 July] some Gentlemen sitting in Peter's Coffee-House in Covent Garden among them Mr Tho. Merry, one Crosby late a Player at the Dukes Theatre coming therein, began with very foul language to give Mr Merry, and stepped back to draw his sword, they began to tilt, but the Gentlemen taking away their swords from each, they began to scufle with blows, but being parted, the said Crosby fell upon his friend and beat him severly, thinking it had been Mr Merry, but being also taken off, and he sitting at the table, he proceeded to abuse the other gentlemen, whereupon Sir Thomas Amestrond [Armstrong] with his sword blade, began to chastise him but the company enterposing one of them struck Sir Thomas-ses sword out of his hand, who stooping to pick up the same this Crosby took the advantage and made a thrust and gave Sir Thomas a prick in the breast for which Cowardly action the Gentlemen turned him down stairs, and the footman as he passed gave him the farwel, and so the fray ended which has caused much discourse.

The *Loyal Protestant* of 3 August, less breathlessly, dated the event 31 July and described Merry as the one who had started the argument by calling Crosby a "Papist, Rascal, &c."

In time, however, John Crosby became a respectable citizen, serving as one of the justices of the peace for Middlesex and one of the governors and benefactors of the hospitals of Christ Church, Bethlehem, and Bridewell. He died on 8 April 1724 at his home in Charter House Yard "in a very advanced Age." He was buried the night of 16 April at St Sepulchre with much pomp, still remembered in the papers as an actor from the time of Charles II.

Possibly the following marriage was the player's: on 20 October 1668 a John Crosbie of St Clement Danes (a parish in which several actors in the Duke's Company lived), a gentleman and bachelor aged about 25, married Mrs Susan Smeeton of St Andrew, Holborn, a widow aged about 21. An actor named Smeaton (or Smeton) who played in Dublin in the 1670s and early 1680s and acted in London in the 1690s may have been related to the bride.

Crosdill, John   *1751?–1825, violoncellist, violist.*

The violoncellist John Crosdill was born at London probably about 1751 as stated by Grove; the alternative date of 1755 given by *The Dictionary of National Biography* would appear incorrect in view of the fact that Crosdill became a member of the Royal Society of Musicians on 4 December 1768. To be accepted by this society at the age of 17 was extraordinary enough,

but election at the age of 13 would have been most unlikely. Indeed, it may well be that many of the activities previously ascribed to the earlier years of John Crosdill's career were actually those of his father, Richard Crosdill (1698–1790), also a violoncellist.

John Crosdill is said to have been educated at Westminster School, but the registers of that school, which begin in 1763, do not list his name. He was, however, a member of the Westminster Abbey choir under the direction of John Robinson and Benjamin Cooke. He then took up the violoncello with the French musician Jean Pierre Duport (1741–1818), perhaps in Paris in the early 1760s or in 1769 when Duport came to London. Some confusion exists over Fétis's account in his *Biographie des Musiciens* as to when Crosdill went to Paris. Fétis gives the date as 1772, and indicates that Crosdill remained there until 1780 studying with the elder Janson and playing in an amateur orchestra directed by the Chevalier de Saint-Georges. But Crosdill is known to have been at London during these years. Indeed, either Crosdill or his father apparently played in the Concert Spirituel at Paris in 1768 with Jean Louis Duport (1749–1819), younger brother of Jean Pierre Duport. (*The Dictionary of National Biography* seems confused, however, in stating that in 1768 Crosdill "played in a duet at a concert given by Siprutini.")

In 1769, Crosdill was a principal cellist at the concerts of the Three Choirs in Gloucester, a position he held annually until his retirement, except for the year 1778 when it was filled by the younger Cervetto. A "Mr Crusdile," either John or his father Richard, played a solo on the violoncello in the oratorio of *The Resurrection* at Covent Garden on 30 March 1770. At the King's Theatre on 5 February 1773, one of the Crosdills played for the benefit of the Musicians' Fund, and again at the same theatre on 12 April 1773 for the

Courtesy of Mr Paul Mellon and the National Portrait Gallery

JOHN CROSDILL

engraving by Daniell, after Dance

benefit of the younger Thomas Linley. On 26 March 1773, a Crosdill played a cello solo during a performance of the *Messiah* at the Haymarket, and on 19 April 1773, at the same theatre, he performed with Cramer and Abel for the benefit of Pinto and Eichner. On 9 May 1774, Crosdill was cellist in a concert given at Hickford's Room in Brewer Street. In the spring of 1775 he played at the King's Theatre in the oratorios sponsored by J. C. Bach. He also played for the oratorios at Covent Garden in 1777 and at Drury Lane in 1779, 1782, and 1784.

Upon the establishment of the Concerts of Ancient Music in 1776 Crosdill became the principal cellist. On 10 March 1778 he succeeded Nares as violist in the Chapel Royal, a position he held until his death.

At about the same time he became a member of the King's band of music. Appointed chamber musician to the Royal Household in 1782, he taught violoncello to the Prince of Wales, later to become George IV. On 11 May 1782 he played at the dedication of the building for the Incorporated Society of Artists. In 1783 Crosdill was appointed composer of state music in Ireland and performed solos at the Second Chester Music Festival held between 16 and 19 September. He was a principal violoncellist in the Handel Memorial Concerts given at Westminster Abbey and the Pantheon in May and June of 1784, and soon after became associated with the band at the Concert Rooms in Hanover Square. He also played a great number of times at the Oxford Music Room from about 1768.

On 6 November 1790, his father Richard Crosdill – "the celebrated performer on the violoncello, who retained his faculties to the last moment," according to his obituary in the *Gentleman's Magazine* (November 1790) – died in his son's arms ("without a groan") at the age of 92 in his house in Nottinghill Street, Marylebone. According to *The Dictionary of National Biography*, "about this time, John Crosdill married a lady of fortune" and retired from his profession to live as a Yorkshire squire for the rest of his days (although he later played at the coronation of George IV in 1821). Perhaps he was, then, the John Crosdill, bachelor, who married Elizabeth Colebrooke, widow, at St Marylebone on 31 May 1785. That marriage was witnessed by the actor Wright Bowden.

According to Doane's *Musical Directory* (1794), Crosdill lived for a time at No 14, Upper Harley Street. For several years he lived in Titchfield Street, where Lord Fitzwilliam was his frequent houseguest, and later in Grosvenor Square, where he shared lodgings with Beilby Thompson of Escrick, M. P. for Hedon. After Thompson's death, Crosdill moved to a house in Berners Street, Marylebone. He died in early

October 1825, by most reports at the home of a nephew of Thompson in Escrick, Yorkshire, but the *Harmonicon* (III, 235) states that his death occurred at his house in Berners Street. By his will, signed at Berners Street on 30 August 1825 and proved at London on 25 October 1825, Crosdill left a substantial fortune to his "son or reputed Son Lieutenant Colonel John Crosdill of the military in service of the honorable the united Company of Merchants of England trading in the East Indies." He left bequests of 19 guineas each, for remembrance rings, to numerous friends, including the musicians Benjamin Blake and William Shield. According to his father's wishes Lieutenant-Colonel Crosdill gave a sum of £1000 to the Royal Society of Musicians.

A portrait of John Crosdill by Thomas Gainsborough was exhibited at the Royal Academy in 1780. A portrait of him by Dance was engraved by Daniell.

Crosdill, Richard *1698–1790, violoncellist. See* **CROSDILL, JOHN.**

Crose, Mr ⟨*fl.* 1794⟩, *double-bass player.*
A Mr Crose was listed in 1794 by Doane's *Musical Directory* as a "double bass," who lived at No 3, Upper James Street, Golden Square.

Crosman. *See also* **CROSSMAN.**

Crosman, Mr ⟨*fl.* 1762⟩, *viola d'amore player.*
Mr Leeming, the landlord and entrepreneur of Lord Cobham's Head, a tavern in Cold Bath Fields, on 19 August 1762 took occasion to warn his customers that "the Season of the Year being far advanc'd; . . . the Musical Entertainment in the Gardens will be continued till Tomorrow Night, and no longer." He had made "an extraordinary Addition for these two nights

to the Band of Musick, with several celebrated Performers" particularly "Mr Crosman on the Violdemore, he being the only Performer on that Instrument in England." Leeming's exaggeration was perhaps not detected by his guests. This is the only notice of Mr Crosman's performance that we have.

Cross, Mr ⟨*fl. c.* 1745?⟩, *animal tamer.*
Hester Lynch Thrale, in her diary in June 1777, reminisced about going as a child to see "A shew of Wild Beasts" made tame by a Mr Cross.

Cross, Mr ⟨*fl.* 1772–1791?⟩, *actor.*
A Mr Cross played Glaud in *The Gentle Shepherd* as one of an irregular company in a specially licensed performance at the Haymarket Theatre on 21 December 1772. There is no way to confirm our suspicion that he was the same Cross who, ten years later, played Abrahamides in the afterpiece *The Taylors* in another special performance at the Haymarket on 25 November 1782. In a third such performance, on 15 December 1783, that Cross was Tressel in *Richard III*, and in another, on 23 February 1784, he had parts unspecified in both *The Patriot* and *The Reprisal*. In yet another, on 8 March 1784, he played Lovely in *The Man's Bewitch'd*.

During the next regular theatrical season of 1784–85 (a time when the Haymarket, a summer house, was usually dark) Cross was one of a small nucleus of professional actors—hardly a company—who appeared together several times at the Haymarket, while tyros and out-of-towners tried their hands. On 16 November he was Orson in *The Romance of an Hour*; on 13 January 1785 he was Kecksy in *The Irish Widow*; on 31 January he delivered a recitation of "Bucks Have at Ye All"; on 15 March he was Harry Stukely in *All the World's a Stage*; on 25 April he was both Lazarillo in *'Tis Well It's No Worse* and Carmine in

The Diversions of a Morning; and on 26 April he played Bellamy in *The Suspicious Husband*.

The Cross of the Haymarket may have been the Cross who was playing for Joseph Fox the Brighton lessee in the summers of 1785, 1788, 1789, 1790, and 1791. In 1789 and 1790 a Mrs Cross was also in that company.

Cross, Miss *[fl. 1740–1741]*, *actress?*

The Covent Garden accounts contain an entry in 1740–41 for a Miss Cross, possibly an actress and perhaps the daughter of Mr and Mrs Richard Cross, who were in the company this season. The daily pay for Miss Cross was 6s. 8d.; an identical sum is noted in the books for Mr Cross, so possibly the "Miss" is an error for "Mr."

Cross, George *d. 1800? violinist?*

A George Cross was cited on a manuscript endorsed by David Garrick: "List of our [Drury Lane] Band for the present year 1775" and dated 20 August 1775. The musician was perhaps the Mr Cross named by Charles Burney among the second violins at the Handel Memorial Concerts at Westminster Abbey and the Pantheon in May and June 1784. He may also have been the George Cross who married Mary Brand, spinster, of Eton, at St Marylebone on 7 April 1790, though the name was so common that this identification is highly uncertain.

George Cross was evidently a member of the Royal Society of Musicians, though his entrance papers are no longer to be found. On 7 July 1799 the Minute Books of the Governors of the Musicians' Fund noted the receipt of thanks from Cross for a benefaction of £5 5s. He was probably in ill health then and he may have been dead by 6 July 1800 when a Mrs Cross (his widow?) returned thanks to the Society for a gift of money sent to her on recommendation of the general meeting of the Society.

Cross, John Cartwright *d. 1809, actor, dramatist, manager.*

John Cartwright Cross came to the attention of the audience at Covent Garden Theatre on 4 October 1790 when he secured a part, unspecified in the playbill but doubtless small, in *The Provocation*. Thereafter that season he played Donalbain in *Macbeth*, a Printer's Devil in *Love in a Village*, a Sportsman in *Harlequin Chaplet*, a Carrier in *1 Henry IV*, a Waiter in *Two Strings to Your Bow*, Kingston in *High Life Below Stairs*, a Sheriff's Officer in *Wild Oats*, Clodpole in *Barnaby Brittle*, and an unspecified role in *The Fugitive*. He also participated in four premieres: as Stephen in James Marshall's comedy *The German Hotel*, as Jacobine in Charles Bonner and Robert Merry's pantomime *The Picture of Paris*, as a Bailiff in Thomas Holcroft's comedy *The School for Arrogance*, and as Filbert in Henry Bate's new comic opera *The Woodman*.

In the 1791–92 season Cross added to his repertoire of small characters: Corin in *As You Like It*, a Waiter in *Blue Beard*, Wittrain in *The Deaf Lover*, a Shepherd in *A Peep Behind the Curtain*, Mr Frost in *The Irishman in London*, and unspecified parts in *The Mermaid* and *The Road to Ruin*. In his third season at Covent Garden, that of 1792–93, he added Napkin in *Modern Antiques*, Jeffrey in *Animal Magnetism*, and a part unassigned by the bill in *Just in Time*. In 1793–94 he added only Bob in *The Woodman* and Peter in *A Day in Turkey* at Covent Garden but was able greatly to expand his repertoire, at least numerically, at the Haymarket in the summer of 1794: a Waiter in *Suicide*, a Crier in *The Surrender of Calais*, a Goatherd in *The Mountaineers*, Rustic in *Auld Robin Gray*, and Farmer Stubble in *The Agreeable Surprise*. He was also the original Joe in his fellow actor Robert Benson's musical farce *Britain's Glory*.

At Covent Garden in 1794–95 Cross augmented his list of characters by Ranger's

Servant in *The Suspicious Husband*, the original Holdfast in Hannah Cowley's comedy *The Town Before You*, and a Tradesman in the first performance of John O'Keeffe's *Life's Vagaries*. In the summer he was again at the Haymarket and there he played, in addition to a selection of his old characters, the Corporal in *The Battle of Hexham*, the Old Man in *Who Pays the Reckoning?* and the original Pinch in Prince Hoare's *Three and the Deuce*. In the 1795–96 winter season at Covent Garden, Cross added Trap in *Wild Oats*, the Servant in *The Rage*, a tradesman in *The Road to Ruin*, Bernardo in *Hamlet*, Robin of Bagshot in *The Beggar's Opera*, Ned in *The Flitch of Bacon*, and a Bailiff in the first performance of Thomas Morton's *The Way to Get Married*. Cross's constant weekly pay during those six seasons at Covent Garden was £1 5s.

But Cross was not so much interested in acting, or even in what he could earn from acting, as in devising entertainments for the stage. On 23 November 1793 his musical interlude *A Divertissement*, with music by Charles Dibdin, was presented at Covent Garden. It achieved 22 performances before the end of that season and was popular through the end of the century. It was followed by his musical interludes *British Fortitude and Hibernian Friendship* on 29 April 1794, *Naples Bay* on the following 2 May and *The New Divertissement* on 26 May, all at Covent Garden. On 8 February he had also produced for Colman (who was operating during that winter season at the Haymarket on a rented patent) *The Purse; or, The Benevolent Tar*. On 3 September at the Haymarket appeared his "Musical Dramatic Romance" *The Apparition*. All except the last-named were played several or many times during the seasons in which they emerged, though they were not always revived in later seasons.

Cross seems to have come to an agreement in the spring of 1796 with the equestrian performer George Jones, suc-

cessor to Hughes as proprietor of the Royal Circus in St George's Fields, Southwark, to bring his talents to that amphitheatre, and from the summer season of 1796 until his death Cross was associated in the extravagant spectacles, hippodramas, and overblown pantomimes purveyed there. By 1797 the *Monthly Mirror* was calling him "deputy manager" of the Circus.

J. C. Cross had two wives. The first, very likely, was the singer Mrs Cross who first appeared at Covent Garden on 6 October 1790 and who left that house in the spring of 1793. At any rate Cross's first spouse was dead by 23 August 1798 when, according to the marriage register of St Paul, Covent Garden, "John Cartwright Cross of this Parish, a Widower" married "Sarah Sophia Jones of St George's Southwark." She was the youngest daughter of James Jones, who with George his brother was coproprietor of the New Royal Circus and Philharmonic Academy (not to be confused with Astley's Royal Circus or Royal Grove). Apparently she was never a performer. Also in 1798 Jones retired from active management and Cross "was admitted as a propietor to the extent of one-fourth of the concern," according to E. W. Brayley in his *Historical and Descriptive Accounts of the Theatres* (1826).

When Cross was elevated to the coproprietorship at the New Royal Circus, he left his commitment as pantomime maker at Covent Garden (where he was succeeded by Thomas Dibdin) and began to devote his energies entirely to the business of the Circus, where he wrote, directed, and at first occasionally acted.

Charles Dibdin had hoped when he opened his Royal Circus in 1782 "That the business of the stage and ring might be united," and that, professional horsemanship being "very much admired" by the English public, he could "divest it of its blackguardism," in order to make it "an object of public consequence." But after Dibdin's confinement for debt in the King's

Bench in 1784 and the quarrels and litigation between him, Charles Hughes, and the property's proprietors, the enterprise had steadily lost patronage. Cross revitalized the company and won back much of the lost audience with his spirited pantomimes employing ingenious new scenes and machines.

Cross continued as principal manager of the Royal Circus until near the time of his death, though he seems at various periods to have been assisted by undermanagers. In 1804, according to Winston in the *Theatric Tourist*, he was said to be part of a quadripartite managerial arrangement along with the clown Follett, the actor Thomas Haymes, and Rees the imitator. In the summer of 1809 the bills began to carry the heading "under the direction of Mr. Elliston.—Stage Manager Mr Cross" and the admonition "every Department has been under the Direction and Inspection of Mr Elliston."

On "Mr CROSS'S NIGHT Stage Manager and Author of the principal Pieces produced during the present Season," 25 September 1809, the "ingenious caterer," as the *Monthly Mirror* had called him, took his last bows. He died on either 1 or 14 December 1809, at either Manchester or Liverpool, but apparently while he was on tour with Elliston. His recent permanent London addresses had been: in September 1800, No 13, Temple Place and, from at latest 20 September 1802 until his death, No 4, Lambeth Road.

The popular spectacle theatre was incessant in its demands for novelty. Many of Cross's productions were quickly devised and no one knows the extent of his work. The following list, assembled principally from Nicoll's "Hand List of Plays" in *A History of English Drama 1660–1900* (where the author is called "James C. Cross") and from *The London Stage, 1660–1800*, supplies for each title the year of production: *The Apparition* (1794); *British Fortitude, and Hibernian Friendship; or, An Escape from France* (1794);

The Charity Boy (1796); *The Cloud King; or, Magic Rose* (1806); *Cora; or, The Virgin of the Sun* (1799); *The Corsican Pirate; or, the Grand Master of Malta* (1803); *Cybele; or, Harlequin's Hour* (1808); *The Eclipse; or, Harlequin in China* (1801); *The Enchanted Harp; or, Harlequin for Ireland* (1802); *An Escape into Prison* (1797); *The False Friend; or, Assassin of the Rocks* (1806); *The Fatal Prediction; or, Midnight Assassin* (1802); *The Fire King; or, Albert and Rosalie* (1801); *The Genoese Pirate; or, Black Beard* (1798); *The Golden Farmer; or, Harlequin Ploughboy* (1802); *Gonsalvo de Cordova; or, The Conquest of Granada* (1802); *Halloween; or, Castles of Athlin and Dunbaine* (1799); *Harlequin and Quixotte; or, the Magic Arm* (1797); *Harlequin's Return* (1798); *In Love, in Debt, and in Liquor; or, Our Way in Wales* (1797); *Joan of Arc; or, the Maid of Orleans* (1798); *Joanna of Surinam* (1804); *John Bull and Buonoparte; or, A Meeting at Dover* (1803); *The Jubilee of 1802; or, The Preston Guild* (1802); *King Caesar; or, The Negro Slaves* (1801); *Lethe* (at Bath, 1812); *Louisa of Lombardy; or, The Secret Nuptials* (1812); *The Magic Flute; or, Harlequin Champion* (1800); *The Mine; or, the Black Forest of Istria* (1800); *Niobe; or, Harlequin's Ordeal* (1797); *The Nymph of the Fountain* (1797); *Number Nip; or, the Elfin King of the Giant Mountains* (songs only, 1803); *Our Native Land, and Gallant Protectors* (1803); *Pedler's Acre; or, Harlequin Mendicant* (1804); *The Purse; or, The Benevolent Tar* (1794); *The Raft; or, Both Sides of the Water* (1798); *Rinaldo Rinaldini; or, the Secret Avengers* (1809); *The Rival Statues; or, Harlequin Humourist* (1803); *Sir Francis Drake and the Iron Arm* (1800); and *The Village Doctor; or, Killing No Cure* (1796). (For classifications and all publication dates and for theatres and exact dates of first performances *after* 1800, see Nicoll; for date of first performance *before* 1800, see *The London Stage*.) Collections of Cross's works were published: *Parnassian Bagatelles: being a Miscellaneous Collection of Poetical Attempts*, 1796 and *Circusiana, or A Collection of the most favourite Ballets, Spectacles, Melodramas, &c. performed at the Royal Circus, St. George's Fields*, 2 vols., 1809 (reprinted as *The Dramatic Works of J. C. Cross*, 1812).

Cross, Mrs [John Cartwright?], [stage name of Mrs Gilbert Hamilton?] [fl. 1790–1793], singer, actress.

A Mrs Cross came on the London Stage for the first time at Covent Garden on 6 October 1790 singing in the chorus supporting *Macbeth*. On 15 October she sang the part of Mrs Casey in O'Keeffe's comic opera *Fontainebleau*. Her performance was criticized by the *European Magazine*: "This lady is possessed of one requisite for the part she performed, that of confidence in a very high degree. She has also no bad figure for the stage. Her singing is but indifferent." Her only other named part that season was Bridget in Henry Bate's new comic opera *The Woodman*, which came out on 26 March, with music by Shield, and enjoyed a long run. She earned her £1 6s. weekly salary for the most part by singing in choruses.

In 1791–92 she was given substantially the same kind of duties for the same stipend but she appeared oftener. She was Nan in *Modern Antiques*, Nancy in *He Wou'd Be a Soldier*, one of the Female Prisoners in *The Crusade*, Bridget in *The Woodman* again, Mrs Hoplove in *Blue Beard*, a Country Girl in *The Cottage Maid*, one of the Furies in *Orpheus and Eurydice*, and Bett Bouncer in *Tony Lumpkin's Ramble to Town*. In addition, she sang in the "Solemn Dirge" during Juliet's funeral procession in *Romeo and Juliet*, in the "Grand Triumphal Entry of Alexander into Babylon" in *Alexander the Great*, and in many other choruses. In the summer of

1792 she was at Brighthelmstone, playing, among other roles, Patty in *Inkle and Yarico*.

In 1792–93 Mrs Cross added nothing to her list of parts except the breeches role of Curtis in *Catherine and Petruchio*, some unspecified role in *Just in Time*, and a Fishwoman in *Harlequin's Museum*, though she repeated several of her old parts and again assisted in choruses.

Mrs Cross disappeared from the London scene after the end of the 1792–93 season. James Winston, in a Folger manuscript, identified her as the Mrs Cross who was playing in Scotland in the summer of 1793. If she was that person, then she was the subject of a curious anecdote in the *London Chronicle*, the truth of which cannot now be verified. The gist of the tale was that when Mrs Cross played at Glasgow, Gilbert Hamilton, the Provost of the city, recognized her from the audience as his wife "from whom he had been separated near 20 years" and whom he had supposed dead. He halted the play, went backstage and confirmed the fact, and took her home with him. Whatever the authenticity of this odd story, Mrs Cross did seem to fade from public notice in the summer of 1793.

Another question arises in connection with John Cartwright Cross the actor and dramatist, who was at Covent Garden during her years at that theatre and for some years afterward. Was the subject of this entry related to him, and if so, how? Hogan in the index to his *Shakespeare on the London Stage* identified the Mrs Cross who appeared as the male servant Curtis in *Catherine and Petruchio* on 10 May 1793 as the first Mrs John Cartwright Cross and guessed at a death date (c. 1797) for her based apparently on the fact that J. C. Cross married for the second time in 1798. In the indexes to his volumes of *The London Stage, 1660–1800*, however, Hogan withdrew the identification in favor of "Cross, Mrs [stage name of Mrs Gilbert Hamilton]." The first identification seems, all things considered, far more likely, though it is by no means impossible that her association with Cross was either bigamous or irregular and that she was both Mrs Cross and Mrs Hamilton, simultaneously or consecutively.

Cross, Letitia c. 1677–1737, actress, singer, dancer.

Born about 1677—not, as some authorities state, about 1683—Letitia Cross was probably the "Girl" who sang a Purcell song which was introduced into 2 *Conquest of Granada* about 1694 at Dorset Garden or Drury Lane. In 1694–95 "A New Song in the *Tempest* [was] sung by Miss Cross to her Lover, who is supposed dead. Set by Mr. *Henry Purcell*." The role would have been Dorinda, a part she was still playing years later. A British Museum manuscript (c. 1695) of the music in *The Indian Queen* includes Miss Cross's name; the fact suggests her participation in a performance in mid-April 1695 at Dorset Garden. Some of the music which she sang was published by a Thomas Cross, who may have been her father (and who is not to be confused with Thomas Cross the theatre treasurer of earlier years).

During the 1695–96 season Miss Cross was busy in a number of productions presented by Christopher Rich at either Drury Lane or Dorset Garden (he then operated both theatres). She sang in *A Wife for Any Man*; spoke the prologue and sang in *The Mock Marriage* (billed as "The Girl"); sang and supposedly played the title role in *Bonduca*; played Alphanta and sang in *The Rival Sisters*; spoke the prologue, sang, and acted Altisidora in *3 Don Quixote*; was possibly the "Girl" who sang in *Oroonoko*; sang Cupid and spoke the epilogue to *Love's Last Shift*; acted Amadine in *Neglected Virtue*; spoke the epilogue to *The Lost Lover*; sang and presented the prologue to *Ibrahim*; and sang in *The Cornish Comedy* and *The Spanish Wives*.

During the season she was indifferently

Harvard Theatre Collection

LETITIA CROSS

engraving by J. Smith, after Hill

referred to as "Miss" and as "Mrs" which at that period usually indicated a young woman close to her majority, and if she played such roles as Dorinda and Bonduca it is doubtful that she would still have been a child. But in late May 1696 in the prologue to *Ibrahim* she was made to say "Look to't, ye Beaus, my Fifteen is coming." This led some authorities to place her birth about 1683, but they were surely taking the information too literally. In the prologue to *3 Don Quixote* in November 1695 the actor Hildebrand Horden was made to remark to Miss Cross, "Your interest with the Sparks is wondrous strong. / Child, th'art three years too young"—that is, three years short of her majority and her "Prime to come." Most of the evidence would suggest that she was born about 1677.

In *The Female Wits* in September 1696

LETITIA CROSS, as St Catherine

engraving by J. Smith, after Kneller

Miss Cross sang, danced, acted a Player (herself), and took the role of Isabella. In the play, Marsilia (a caricature of Mrs Manley the playwright) calls Miss Cross a "Little Cherubim" and, later, "A little inconsiderable Creature." Since the play satirized the very players taking part in it, perhaps these qualities were fairly descriptive of Letitia Cross. During the rest of the 1696–97 season she sang in *Brutus of Alba, The World in the Moon,* and *Aesop*; spoke the first prologue and acted Hoyden in *The Relapse*; spoke the epilogue to *Women's Wit*; and played Isidora in *The Triumphs of Virtue.* Hoydenish roles seem to have been her specialty, and Vanbrugh may have tailored her role in *The Relapse* to her special talents. In 1697–98 she sang in *The Imposture Defeated*, played Eromena in *The Fatal Discovery*, acted Salome in *Caligula*, spoke the

prologue to *Phaeton*, and gave the epilogue and apparently played Zaraida in *Victorious Love*. After two seasons of being referred to alternately as "Miss" and "Mrs," she was now called "Mrs Cross" all season.

Letitia eloped to France after the spring of 1698, causing a lamentation in the epilogue written and spoken by Joe Haines (in mourning) to *Love and a Bottle*. He blamed her flight on Jeremy Collier, the opponent of immorality in drama and theatre:

> O Collier! Collier! Thou's frighted away
>   Miss Cross.
> She, to return our Foreigners Complaisance,
> At Cupid's Call, has made a Trip to
>   France.
> Love's Fire-Arms here are since not
>   worth a Souse;
> We've lost the only Touch-hole of our
>   House.
> Losing that Jewel, gave Us a fatal
>   Blow . . .

It was reported by Anne Oldfield's biographer Egerton that Miss Cross was whisked away by a baronet, thus opening the role of Candiope in *Secret Love* to Mrs Oldfield.

Either Letitia Cross did not marry or, if she did, kept her maiden name for stage use, for she was billed Mrs Cross throughout the rest of her career. It has been suggested that her husband was Richard Cross the elder, who was active in the theatre in the early eighteenth century, but there seems to be no evidence to prove this, and the coincidence of their surnames might mean Letitia and Richard were brother and sister rather than man and wife.

After her sojourn in France, Letitia Cross went to Dublin, where she was active from 1698 to 1704 at the Smock Alley Theatre. Her Dublin career has not yet been fully documented, but she is said to have played there the Orange Woman in *The Man of Mode* in 1698–99.

On 16 December 1704 she was again at Drury Lane, singing a dialogue with the basso Richard Leveridge and billed as "Famous for Singing and Acting in the last Reign." On 2 January 1705 she was belatedly advertised as making her first appearance in London in five years, and on 16 January she appeared as Dorisbe in *Arsinoe*. For her benefit on 8 February she displayed all her talents: she acted Florimel in *Secret Love*, offered an entertainment of dancing, and sang Purcell's "Tell me why, my charming fair" with Leveridge.

In the five years which followed, Mrs Cross played at Drury Lane and (beginning in the fall of 1707) the new Queen's Theatre in the Haymarket. Some of her new parts were Gatty in *She Wou'd If She Cou'd*, Mrs Clerimont in *The Tender Husband*, Jacinta in *An Evening's Love*, the title roles in *The Young Coquet* and *The Northern Lass*, Mrs Sago in *The Basset Table*, Lady Sadlife in *The Double Gallant*, Melantha in *Marriage à la Mode*, Miss Notable in *The Lady's Last Stake*, Meriel in *The Jovial Crew*, Jiltall in *Love for Money*, Mrs Foresight in *Love for Love*, Miranda in *The Busy Body*, Ophelia in *Hamlet*, Laura in *The Man's Bewitched,* Eliza in *Almahide*, Harriet in *The Man of Mode*, and Belinda in *The Old Bachelor*. Summers, in his edition of Shadwell's *Works*, stated that Mrs Cross also played the mistress of Peter the Great when he visited London in 1708. At the theatre during these years she was earning £80 annually, a figure that in time rose to £100. By way of comparison, the prima donna at the Queen's Theatre, Mrs Tofts, was making £500 a year.

In 1710–11 Mrs Cross ran into difficulties with her managers—Wilks, Cibber, Doggett, and Swiney. They had apparently refused to let her act but had put it about that the refusal had come from her. To her rescue on 15 March 1711 came 73 anonymous gentleman admirers of the lady who swore to the managers that they would riot against anyone who presumed to play Mrs Cross's roles. "[W]e are very well assured," the gentlemen stated in their letter to the managers, "that she has constantly attended, and that you have several times forbad her entrance even behind the scenes. . . . Think upon this before Munday night otherwise you may depend upon it that Mr Doggets Benefit will not be very well treated." Her supporters were convinced that the managers wanted to "deprive her of her livelyhood and performance on the stage where she has been bred up from a child." Letitia, on 22 March, wrote to the Lord Chamberlain admitting that she had, indeed, told some of her friends about the wrongs done her but that she had "suffered silently" and was not responsible for the letter sent to the managers. She enclosed "a case of the hardships they have put upon me" (the document is now lost) and begged the Lord Chamberlain's protection. Her plea must have fallen on deaf ears, for she was not seen again on the London stage for four years.

On 4 January 1715 she played Belinda in *The Old Bachelor* at the Lincoln's Inn Fields Theatre under John Rich's management. She acted through 21 March 1717, playing such important new parts as Arabella in *The Fair Quaker of Deal*, Cidaria in *The Indian Emperor*, Sylvia in *The Recruiting Officer*, Marcella in *2 Don Quixote*, Olivia in *The Plain Dealer*, Lady Fanciful in *The Provok'd Wife*, Elvira in *The Spanish Fryar*, Victoria in *The Fatal Marriage*, Miranda in *Woman is a Riddle*, and Morayma in *Don Sebastian*. As in earlier years, she also sang and danced and frequently delivered epilogues. Her attraction for the public was still strong, for on 28 April 1715 her benefit brought in £98 16s. 6d. and on 22 March 1716 the income was £128 8s. 6d.

Once again Letitia Cross disappeared from the London stage, but she was back on 4 October 1720 at Lincoln's Inn Fields, playing Marcella in *2 Don Quixote* and offering in it the popular song, "I burn, I burn." She revived several more of her old roles in 1720–21, such as Elvira, Sylvia, Lady Fanciful, and Miranda, and she tried (apparently for the first time) Mrs Ford in *The Merry Wives of Windsor*, Colombine in both *The Jealous Doctor* and *Amadis*, Corinna in *A Woman's Revenge*, an unnamed role in *Much Ado About Nothing*, and Alinda in *The Pilgrim*. She danced frequently and often sang songs within plays. Her 23 March 1721 benefit brought in £109 9s., but a second benefit (shared with Hulett and Newhouse) on 9 May made only £85 7s.

Mrs Cross remained at Lincoln's Inn Fields through 1724–25 and added to her repertoire such roles as Narcissa and Hillaria in *Love's Last Shift*, the Wanton Wife in *The Amorous Widow*, Domitilla in *Domitian* (*The Roman Actor*), Araminta in *The Old Bachelor*, the Pierrot Woman in *The Necromancer*, and Lady Froth in *The Double Dealer*. Her last season with Rich, 1724–25, saw her featured only infrequently: she was cited in the bills for only one role (in *The Necromancer*) and she shared with Mrs Vincent on 22 April 1725 a benefit which made £131 4s.

Though on the Drury Lane roster in 1726–27, Mrs Cross seems not to have played any role large enough to warrant mention in the bills. She disappeared until 8 May 1732, when she turned up at the Haymarket Theatre as Monimia in *The Orphan* (for her benefit), billed as not having appeared on stage for several years. This desperation benefit seems to have been her last performance.

On 4 April 1737 Letitia Cross died at her lodgings in Leicester Fields. She made a codicil to her undated will the day she died, leaving a number of mourning rings to friends. The bulk of her estate, which may not have been large, she bequeathed to a Mrs Elizabeth Barker. She left a shilling to her sister Mrs Mary Sibourg of Bagshot, Surrey, and a shilling to a Mrs Audrey Cardinell of the same address. Mrs Cross specified that her "share as Renter of Lincoln's Inn Playhouse" should go to Mrs Barker, her residuary legatee.

Pretty Letitia Cross was painted as St Catherine by Kneller. An engraving of the portrait was made by John Smith. Smith also engraved a mezzotint of her done by T. Hill.

Cross, Philip. *See* CADEMAN, PHILIP.

Cross, Richard [*fl. c. 1695?–1725*], *actor.*

The Mr Cross who was active at the Smock Alley Theatre in Dublin about 1695 may have been Richard Cross, the London actor of the early eighteenth century. The earliest of three performers of that name was probably related to the actress-singer-dancer Letitia Cross—a brother, perhaps and, if so, possibly the son of the music publisher Thomas Cross. It is also probable that the later theatrical figures named Richard Cross were descendants of the earliest one.

A Cross was first mentioned in London records on 9 December 1700 when he acted Charino in *Love Makes a Man*. Since the records in the early years of the century are incomplete, perhaps this Cross acted other roles, but he was not mentioned again in any document now extant until 11 March 1703 when he played Major Bombard in *The Old Mode and the New* at Drury Lane. On 8 November 1704 he may have played Vexhem in *The Northern Lass*, for he was so cast in the 1706 edition. In 1705 he was noted thrice at Drury Lane: as Salathiel in *Farewell Folly* on 18 January, as Caudle in *The Quacks* on 29 March, and as a Boor in *The Royal Merchant* on 12 June.

From 4 January 1707 onward more is known of him. On that date he was at the Queen's Theatre in the Haymarket acting Roger in *Wit Without Money*, and he remained at the Queen's through 1 January 1708 playing such parts as Bulfinch in *The Northern Lass*, a Plebeian in *Julius Caesar*, a Citizen in *Caius Marius*, Polonius in *Hamlet*, Thomas in *The Lancashire Witches*, Sir Timothy Treatall in *The City Heiress*, the Constable in *The Old Troop*, Ursula Pigwife in *Bartholomew Fair*, Sir Harry Atall in *The Double Gallant*, and Hearty in *The Jovial Crew*.

He was at Drury Lane from February through December 1708 and acted the servants Anthony and Peter in *The Chances*, alternately with Norris, Roger in *Aesop*, the Gravedigger in *The Funeral,* the Orangewoman in *The Man of Mode*, Sir Lionel in *The Taming of a Shrew*, the Landlord in *Feign'd Innocence*, Boldsprite in *The Sea Voyage*, Pedro in *The Successful Strangers*, Sycorax in *The Tempest*, a Witch in *Macbeth*, Sosia in *Amphitryon*, Sampson in *The Fatal Marriage*, Lolpoop in *The Squire of Alsatia*, and Toby in *Epsom Wells*.

The summer of 1710 found Cross in the company at Pinkethman's playhouse in Greenwich, but he was listed as one of the players drawn from outside London, so it is probable that in 1709 he was off in the provinces or in Ireland. He returned to the Queen's Theatre as early as 20 April 1710 when, according to a Folger promptbook, he acted the part of the Cardinal in *The Force of Friendship*. He was at the Queen's Theatre in October and November 1710 and then moved back to Drury Lane on 18 December to play the Physician in *The Rehearsal*.

Cross remained at Drury Lane through 1724–25, a utility actor who seldom graduated beyond secondary parts. He kept playing Charino, Polonius, Sosia, Bulfinch, and a few other old roles, to which he added over the years such parts as Bloody Bones in *The Soldier's Fortune*, Blunt in *The Volunteers*, Sir Thomas Gaymood in *Love's a Jest*, Doctor Paunchy in *City Politics*, Thrassilius in *Timon of Athens*, the title role in *The Spanish Fryar*, Carbuncle in *The Country Lasses*, Sir Humphrey in *The What D'Ye Call It*, and Leucippe in *The*

Humorous Lieutenant. Most of these parts he added before 1720, and in his last season, 1724–25, he played nothing important enough to warrant mention in the bills.

Cross, Richard *d. 1760, prompter, actor, dancer.*

The astoundingly versatile Richard Cross —the second of that name and probably the son of his namesake earlier in the eighteenth century—may have begun his theatrical career as early as 1729. The edition of *Love and Revenge* published that year lists a Mr Cross as the third Felon; the work was produced on 12 November 1729 at the Haymarket Theatre. During the 1730–31 season at the same house a Mr Cross, presumably the same person and probably Richard, acted Nobody in *The Author's Farce* on 21 October, Dismal in *The Battle of the Poets* on 30 November, a Forester in *The Amorous Adventure* on 28 December, Snip in *The Jealous Taylor* on 18 January 1731, and Nevill in *The Fall of Mortimer* on 12 May. At Yeates's booth at Tottenham Court on 9 August Cross played Damon in *Damon and Phillida*; at the Hall-Hippisley-Fielding booth at Bartholomew Fair on 24 August he was Eugenio in *The Emperor of China*; and on 8 September at Southwark Fair he acted a Demon in *Merlin*.

In 1731–32 Cross was affiliated with the Haymarket Theatre but also served occasionally as an extra at Drury Lane. He was Mars in *Perseus and Andromeda* at Drury Lane on 25 November 1731 and on a number of subsequent dates; at the Haymarket he appeared as Gripe in *The Cheats of Scapin* on 16 February 1732, as Poverty in *The Blazing Comet* on 2 March, and as the Abbé Cadière in *The Wanton Jesuit* on 17 March; he played Mars and one of Pierrot's servants in *Perseus and Andromeda* at Drury Lane on 21 March; and, again at the Haymarket, he acted Periwinkle in *A Bold Stroke for a Wife* on 23

March, a Recruit in *The Recruiting Officer* on 27 April, Damon in *Damon and Phillida* on 8 May, and a role in *The Coquet's Surrender* on 15 May. Drury Lane, in recompense for his services, allowed his benefit tickets from that house to be taken at the Haymarket on 6 May. Cross played Damon again on 27 May at the Great Booth on Windmill Hill and then appeared at Drury Lane in August as Jemmy in *The Beggar's Opera* and Mago in *The Devil of a Duke*. Still not exhausted, the peripatetic Cross then polished off his season at Bartholomew Fair on 23 August as Rochford in *Henry VIII*.

Cross may have worked outside London the following season, for he was next mentioned in London bills on 23 August 1733 when he acted Axalla in *Tamerlane* at the Cibber-Griffin-Bullock-Hallam Bartholomew Fair booth. For the same group he played King Henry in *Sir John Falstaff* on 4 September.

In 1733–34 Cross was at Drury Lane but followed Theophilus Cibber's rebel troupe to the Haymarket and back in the middle of the season. He appeared as Ramilie in *The Miser*, Aldiborontiphoscophornio in *Chrononhotonthologos*, Erastus in *The Country House*, Mons Quadrille in *Cupid and Psyche*, Cabinet in *The Funeral*, Vernon in *1 Henry IV*, Gloster in *2 Henry IV*, Cromwell in *Henry VIII*, and Marcus in *Cato*. His benefit tickets were accepted at Drury Lane on 24 May, after which he joined Cibber at the Haymarket again. On 27 June he was at Richmond playing Worcester in *1 Henry IV*, and on 12 September he shared a benefit there with Bardin.

Cross's 1734–35 season, mostly at Drury Lane, was particularly stunning for the sheer number and variety of new roles he attempted: Selim in *The Mourning Bride*, Plumb in *Cupid and Psyche*, Valentine in *Love for Love*, Pedro in *The Spanish Fryar*, Young Fashion in *The Relapse*, a Justice in *The Harlot's Progress*, Alonzo and Juan in

Rule a Wife and Have a Wife, Tressel in *Richard III*, Neptune in *Cephalus and Procris*, Antony's servant in *Julius Caesar*, Vizard in *The Constant Couple*, Frederick in *The Miser*, Richard and Townly in *The Provok'd Husband*, Francisco in *Wit Without Money*, Young Loveless in *The Scornful Lady*, Gainlove in *A Cure for a Scold*, Lewis in *The Man of Taste*, Rosencrantz in *Hamlet*, Antonio in *The Rover*, Sir Charles in *The Stratagem*, Wormwood in *An Old Man Taught Wisdom*, Sir Charles in *The Careless Husband*, Trueman and Thorowgood in *The London Merchant*, Young Woudbe in *The Twin Rivals*, Martin in *The Anatomist*, and the Player in *The Beggar's Opera*. In between, of course, he played some of his earlier roles. Several times during the season he acted at one or another of the other theatres when Drury Lane was dark, as on 7 October 1734 when he played Valentine in *Love for Love* at the Haymarket Theatre, or in June when he acted briefly at Lincoln's Inn Fields.

Cross somehow found time during the season for some courting, for between 25 January and 4 February 1735 Miss Frances Shireburn, the Drury Lane actress, became Mrs Richard Cross in the playbills. There was no time (perhaps no inclination) to make the union official, however, for not until 16 years later, on 29 May 1751 at St George's Chapel, Hyde Park Corner, did the couple stand before a priest.

Through the 1738–39 season Cross remained at Drury Lane, playing each season a great variety of old and new roles. A fair selection of his new parts might include Malcolm in *Macbeth*, Whisper in *The Busy Body*, Pistol in *The Merry Wives of Windsor*, both Frisure and Subtleman in *The Twin Rivals*, the title role in *The Fall of Phaeton*, a Beggar in *Phebe*, Clerimont in *The Miser*, Bagshot in *The Beggar's Opera*, Jaques in *Love Makes a Man*, Sancho in *Rule a Wife and Have a Wife*, Dorilant in *The Country Wife*, the Duke and Renault in *Venice Preserv'd*, Brisk in *The Double*

Folger Shakespeare Library

Opening from "Prompter's Diary" of RICHARD CROSS, Drury Lane Theatre, September 1749

Dealer, Dick in *The Confederacy*, Poins in *2 Henry IV*, Tattle in *Love for Love*, Haly in *Tamerlane*, Syphax in *Cato*, Curio in *The Pilgrim*, Petit in *The Inconstant*, and Jeffery in *The Amorous Widow*. The full list would be twice as long. Yet during these years the Drury Lane managers did not give Cross much encouragement, for only occasionally was he granted benefit tickets to sell.

Perhaps this caused him to move with Mrs Cross to Covent Garden for the 1739–40 and 1740–41 seasons. He acted only once during his first season there—on 8 December 1729 when he played Witwoud in *The Way of the World*—and it may be that he was already assuming the duties of prompter, the announced task for him the next season. On 23 August 1740 Cross returned to play at Bartholomew Fair for the first time in several years. His situation at Covent Garden seems not to have been

much better financially than what he had known before. His salary was only 6s. 8d. daily, and though he received a benefit on 4 May 1741, he had to share it with three other people.

It was apparently during the 1740–41 season that Cross began keeping his prompter's diary (one part now at the Folger Library and the other at the Rylands). In it he noted some of his own activities, audience reactions to performances, rough estimates of receipts, and other information that has since proved of great value to historians. On 18 December 1740, for instance, when *The Rehearsal* was performed, Cross noted laconically: "Cibber sick, i did Bayes." How often before this Cross may have substituted for other players we have no way of knowing, but it is likely that he had done so frequently.

After the Covent Garden season of 1740–41 Cross returned to Drury Lane in

June, acted at Tottenham Court and Bartholomew Fair in August, and became a permanent member of the Drury Lane company in the fall. There he stayed until his death in 1760, though, as before, he made occasional excursions to other houses, probably to substitute for ailing players. At Drury Lane he continued his new prompting career, wrote out parts, stood in for other actors, kept his diary, and performed in his own right. His benefits, normally shared with Mrs Cross, usually identified him only as the prompter, and the managers apparently paid him accordingly, despite the fact that Cross often undertook leading roles also.

Only a handful of the new parts he played from 1741 to 1760 can be listed here: the Elder and Younger Brothers in *Comus*, Jaques in *As You Like It*, Constant in *The Provok'd Wife*, Sir Fopling in *The Man of Mode*, Horatio in *Hamlet*, Lorenzo and Salanio in *The Merchant of Venice*, Polydore and the Chaplain in *The Orphan*, Smith and Johnson in *The Rehearsal*, Surly and Face in *The Alchemist*, Richmond in *Richard III*, Brazen in *The Recruiting Officer*, Jeremy in *Love for Love*, Manuel in *Love Makes a Man*, Albany in *King Lear*, Young Seward and Duncan in *Macbeth*, Frederick in *The Fatal Marriage*, the Governor in *Oroonoko*, Young Rakish in *The School Boy*, Morelove in *The Careless Husband*, Careless in *The Double Gallant*, and Well Bred in *Every Man in His Humour*.

He occupied most of his summers from 1746 through 1753 playing in Chapman's troupe at Richmond and Twickenham, some of his parts there being: the title role in *Sir Courtly Nice*, Cheatly in *The Squire of Alsatia*, Iago in *Othello*, Lothario in *The Fair Penitent*, the title role in *Philaster*, Buckingham in *Richard III*, the title role in *A Duke and No Duke*, Claudius in *Hamlet*, Freeman and Sir Philip Modelove in *A Bold Stroke for a Wife*, Gibbet in *The Stratagem*, Belvil Junior and Tom in *The Conscious Lovers*, Plume in *The Recruiting*

Officer, Altamont in *The Fair Penitent*, Fainall and Mirabel in *The Way of the World*, Bellmour and Dumont in *Jane Shore*, Don Pedro in *Much Ado About Nothing*, Montague in *Romeo and Juliet*, Archer and Aimwell in *The Beaux' Stratagem*, Kitely in *Every Man in His Humour*, Manly in *The Provok'd Husband*, Truewit in *The Silent Woman*, Count Cogdie in *The Gamester*, Lord Foppington in *The Careless Husband*, Macduff in *Macbeth*, and Southampton in *The Earl of Essex*. He was not mentioned as prompter at Richmond and Twickenham (the number of his appearances would almost have ruled out the possibility). If he was acting the above roles at his own choice rather than as an understudy, perhaps they give a true picture of his talents. Still, it is almost impossible to discern a "line" for Cross; apparently he could play anything.

But acting with Chapman's group up the river did not consume all the summer vacation, so Cross appeared off and on at the fairs. At Southwark Fair on 16 October 1746, for instance, he played Sullen in *The Stratagem*; on 24 August 1748 he ran a booth at Bartholomew Fair with Bridges, Burton, and Vaughan (and also acted); from 23 to 28 August 1749 he and Bridges operated a Bartholomew Fair booth (and Cross again acted); and on 26 July 1750 Cross turned up at the Haymarket Theatre to play Volatil in *The Wife's Relief*.

In his spare time he did some writing. On 10 May 1739 he advertised *The Adventures of John Le Brun* for publication, and on 1 May 1749 his play *The Henpecked Captain* was advertised—but apparently not printed. His play was performed at his benefit on 29 April at Drury Lane, and Cross noted honestly in his diary: "A farce of my own, damn'd before half over." Cross also published, in 1747, *A Collection of Poems on Several Occasions*, an anthology of works by Rochester, Dryden, Prior, and others.

The Drury Lane accounts seldom mentioned Cross over the years, though in 1749–50 he was several times cited as being paid money for writing out parts (4s. on one occasion, 12s. on another), for pens and paper (1s. 6d. once, 7s. another time), and for playing Young Worthy on 3 February 1750 (£1 1s.—presumably he was paid over and above his salary whenever he acted for someone else).

Of Cross's family not much is known. On 4 June 1749 Charles, the son of Richard Cross from St Martin-in-the-Fields, was buried at St Paul, Covent Garden; on 11 December 1749 at the same church a daughter Frances was buried. Cross noted sadly in his diary at the theatre on 9 December 1749: "Aged 4ʸ 2ᵐ my dear Fann dy'd poor Girl." Could it have been these calamities that caused Richard and Frances Cross to solemnize their marriage on 29 May 1751? The couple had another son, Richard, who has not yet been located in a parish register. By 1752 Richard was sharing benefits with his parents; he performed in London from 1748 to 1757. As of 1748 the Crosses were living "over against" the Rose Tavern in Russell Street, Covent Garden, but by 1752 (after their marriage) they had moved to Crown Court, Little Russell Street, where they lived until Cross's death.

During the last few years of his life Cross did little acting, but he served as the Drury Lane prompter to the last. The final entry in his hand in the diary he kept was dated 23 January 1760. On the following 20 February Richard Cross died. He was buried four days later at St Paul, Covent Garden. *The Present State of the Stage* had praised him in 1753 for supplying

in proper Time the Defects of treacherous Memory: No Man understands better the Business of the Stage, and from a long Acquaintance with all the Pieces that have been play'd for some Years past, he is perfect in a Number of Characters, and can, at an Hour's Warning, fill up a Chasm caused by the sudden Sickness, or any other unexpected Accident befalling a Performer.

The *Public Advertiser* waited until after Richard Cross was dead to say what doubtless would have pleased him most; on the afternoon of his death the paper said Cross's "abilities in his station were equal to any in the theatre, and [his] integrity would have done credit to any profession."

Cross, Richard [*fl. 1748–1760*], actor, dancer, violinist.

Richard Cross, the third of that name, was the son of the Drury Lane prompter-actor and his wife Frances. The younger Cross was first noticed in the bills on 19 March 1748 when, billed as Master Cross, he played Fleance in *Macbeth* at Drury Lane. Since Frances Shireburn becames Mrs Cross (without benefit of clergy) in 1735, perhaps Richard was born that year or the next. On 8 July 1748 at Twickenham and on 16 July at Richmond Master Cross shared benefits with Master Shawford; the bills there that summer rarely listed casts, so Cross's activity is not known. At Bartholomew Fair on the following 24 August he danced at a booth operated by his father and others.

In 1748–49 the younger Cross appeared again at Drury Lane, repeating Fleance and also playing Tom in *The London Cuckolds* and the Page in *Romeo and Juliet*. At Bartholomew Fair on 23 August 1749 he acted Master Clack in *Modern Madness* at the booth run by Bridges and the elder Cross. Back at Drury Lane again in 1749–50, Master Cross was paid £7 12s. 6d. for performing 61 nights at 2s. nightly—much more activity than his few billings suggest. During the season he was again Fleance and played the Page in *Friendship in Fashion* and Fribble in *Miss in Her Teens*. He also danced in *The Tempest*, for which he received an extra 5s. for each performance.

Richard added no new parts to his limited repertoire at Drury Lane in 1750–51, but he tried to expand his opportunities by acting at the James Street Theatre. The elder Cross noted in his diary on 15 November 1750: "My son Dick taken up for playing Timoleon at ye Tennis Court & Disch^d by Jus: Fielding." In the summer of 1751 at Richmond and Twickenham young Cross had a chance to add at least three roles to his list legally: Daniel in *The Conscious Lovers*, John in *The Recruiting Officer*, and Balthazar in *Romeo and Juliet*. In 1751–52 at Drury Lane he played pages in *The Relapse* and *Eastward Ho* and the Boy in *Taste*.

The summer of 1752 at Richmond and Twickenham brought him Simon Pure in *A Bold Stroke for a Wife*, Master Stephen in *Every Man in His Humour*, Squire Richard in *The Provok'd Husband*, Amble in *A New Way to Pay Old Debts*, John in *Don Quixote in England*, Selim in *The Mourning Bride*, Douglas in *Henry IV*, and Burgundy in *King Lear*. At Drury Lane in 1752–53 he added Donalbain in *Macbeth* and the second Spirit in *Comus*, and the summer of 1753 at Richmond saw him in Master Tosty in *The Fine Lady's Airs*, Jack Ranger in *The Suspicious Husband*, Scrub in *The Beaux' Stratagem*, and Taylor in *Lethe*. The bills listed him only in Poins in *The Humourists* at Drury Lane in 1753–54, though doubtless he appeared regularly in unmentioned parts.

Billed as "Cross Junior" instead of "Master Cross" on 15 December 1755, Richard "had his Oratorio at ye Haymarket," according to the diary of the elder Cross. This was a benefit performance of *Acis and Galatea* which Richard shared with Miss Thomas, but it is not clear in what capacity he served. Perhaps he fiddled, for on 28 April 1757 at Drury Lane, Cross Junior played a concerto on the violin at his mother and father's benefit. On 27 May the Mr Cross who acted Young Rakish in *The School Boy* at Covent Garden was probably the younger Cross, not the elder (who at this date seldom performed). After that, he apparently gave up his career. In August 1760, identified as the son of the late prompter, Richard Cross married the widow of Samuel Chitty, born Elizabeth Norris.

Cross, Mrs Richard, Elizabeth. *See* **Norris, Elizabeth.**

Cross, Mrs Richard, Frances, née Shireburn *1707–1781, actress, singer.*

Born in 1707, Frances Shireburn (or Sherburn) first came to public notice about 1725 when the song *Would you live a stale Virgin for ever?* was published, naming her as the singer. On 18 April 1727 at Drury Lane she played Mrs Chat in *The Committee*, following this on 3 May with Mrs Buskin in *The Strollers*. She appeared as Flora in *Jane Shore* on 21 August at the Miller-Hall-Milward booth at Bartholomew Fair. During the 1727–28 Drury Lane season she added to her repertoire Foible in *The Way of the World*, a Country Maid in *Acis and Galatea*, and the Aunt in *The What D'Ye Call It*, and shared a benefit with Mrs Burton on 14 May. On 24 August she was at Bartholomew Fair again, playing Ursula in *Bateman* at the Hall-Miller booth.

At Drury Lane in 1728–29 Miss Shireburn played for the first time some of the roles which were to be her stock in trade for many years, notably Mlle D'Epingle in *The Funeral*, Mademoiselle in *The Provok'd Wife*, and Regan in *King Lear*. She also tried for the first time Leonora in *The Mourning Bride*, Juno and Cassiopea in *Perseus and Andromeda*, Dame Pliant in *The Alchemist*, Doll Tearsheet in *2 Henry IV*, Lucy in *The Country Wife*, and Betty in *The Contrivances*—among others. In August 1729 she again played at Bartholomew Fair.

During the rest of her long career she acted a great many parts, but for the following 50 years she concentrated on a small group of roles which she considered her property. In addition to Mlle D'Epingle, Mademoiselle, and Regan, the roles most closely associated with her over the years (with the dates when she first essayed them) were: Mrs Motherly in *The Provok'd Husband* on 1 November 1731, Lady Bountiful in *The Stratagem* on 20 November, the Aunt in *Sir Courtly Nice* on 9 December, Mrs Sealand in *The Conscious Lovers* on 4 April 1733, Mrs Day in *The Committee* on 3 October, the Nurse in *The Relapse* on 6 October, Mrs Quickly in *1* and *2 Henry IV* on 6 and 10 October, Lady Darling in *The Constant Couple* on 28 March 1734, Mrs Peachum in *The Beggar's Opera* on 3 June, Mrs Wisely in *The Miser* on 8 October, Mrs Clearaccount in *The Twin Rivals* on 3 January 1736, Doll Common in *The Alchemist* on 10 December 1740, and Patch in *The Busy Body* on 12 December 1741. She was still acting virtually all of these parts in the 1770s when she was in her sixties. Her last recorded role was Mrs Motherly in *The Provok'd Husband* on 5 November 1776, a part she had first played 45 years before.

There were many other characters of importance which she played during her career, among them Mrs Overdo in *Bartholomew Fair*, Mrs Tipkin in *The Tender Husband*, Lady Laycock in *The Amorous Widow*, Lady Woodville and Pert in *The Man of Mode*, Wishwell in *The Double Gallant*, Araminta in *The Old Bachelor*, Widow Lackit in *Oroonoko*, Lavinia in *The Fair Penitent*, Dorinda in *The Stratagem*, Lady Grace in *The Provok'd Husband*, Teresa in *The Spanish Fryar*, Altea in *Rule a Wife and Have a Wife*, the Duchess of York in *Richard III*, the Player Queen in *Hamlet*, Lady Haughty and Mrs Otter in *The Silent Woman*, Mrs Anne in *Love's Last Shift*, Ruth in *The Squire of Alsatia*, Sisygambis in *The Rival Queens*, Mrs Marwood and Lady Wishfort in *The Way of the World*, Lady Falconbridge in *King*

John, Mrs Foresight and Mrs Frail in *Love for Love*, Amanda in *The Relapse*, Melinda in *The Recruiting Officer*, and Alithea in *The Country Wife*. Despite the attention she gave to her stock roles, only in the 1760s did she reduce the number of new parts she tried each year.

Most of her career was spent at Drury Lane, but she followed Theophilus Cibber and his seceders to the Haymarket Theatre in the fall of 1733 for a short stay; in 1739–40 and 1740–41 she played at Covent Garden; she made occasional appearances at the fairs; and she acted at Richmond during the summers from 1765 to 1777. For the most part, however, she was content to stay at Drury Lane, year in and year out, rarely getting leading roles but seldom being assigned tiny ones. Judging by her occasional appearances for a night or two in roles normally assigned others, she probably stood in for ailing actresses when needed.

Frances was one of the workhorses of the company, and her wages were hardly commensurate with her heavy schedule. At Covent Garden in 1740–41, for instance, we know that she was paid only 8s. daily, and in 1765 at Drury Lane she received only 5s. daily or £1 10s. per week. She received twice as much as the lowest performers on the scale, but only a twelfth of that which such luminaries as Mrs Cibber or Mrs Pritchard could demand. Her benefits, normally shared with from one to three others, sometimes brought her only £25. Her biggest boon came not from the theatre at all: when the painter James Worsdale died in 1767, he left her £100.

Miss Shireburn became (actually though not canonically) Mrs Richard Cross between 25 January and 4 February 1735, the change in her name on the bills being our only evidence of the couple's cohabitation at that time. They were not actually married until 29 May 1751 at St George's Chapel, Hyde Park Corner. The Crosses had at least three children: Richard, who may have been the cause of Miss Shireburn's taking Cross's name in 1735; Charles, who was buried at St Paul, Covent Garden, on 4 June 1749; and Frances, who was buried at the same church on 11 December 1749.

Frances Shireburn Cross, widowed after 1760, died in Hart Street, Bloomsbury, on 29 June 1781 at the age of 74, still remembered as an actress who had entertained Londoners for nearly 50 years.

Cross, Thomas   *b. c. 1630, treasurer.*

Thomas Cross was born about 1630, the son of Thomas and Anne Cross. The elder Thomas was an apothecary who died early in the Civil Wars, leaving his widow with young Thomas and at least two other boys, Paul and John. Anne married a second time, to Sir Thomas Cademan, and by him (if not by her first husband) she had another son, Philip, who was later called Philip Cademan, alias Cross. Sir Thomas died in 1651, about the time that young Thomas Cross gave up a secretarial position he had held under Sir William Davenant and voyaged out to Barbados to be clerk to Lord Willoughby of Parham. When Thomas returned to England some time after October 1652, he found that his mother had married a third time to none other than his old employer Davenant.

Cross and his brothers lived in Davenant's newly acquired house in Tothill Street. Sir William, plagued by creditors, put the house and furnishings in Thomas Cross's name to save them from attachment and entered into a weird bond concerning £800 of the elder Thomas Cross's money which Dame Anne had loaned Davenant. The bond was drawn up in February 1654. By it Davenant agreed to pay the four boys £100 within a year and provide them with maintenance; if he failed to carry out his agreement the £800 bond was to be forfeited. But Davenant included a clause to the effect that if he continued supporting the boys until £100 was paid to

each of them—even if this took more than a year—the penalty would not be exacted. According to Thomas Cross's later testimony, Davenant managed to get out of all these obligations, but Thomas, in the 1650s, was too naive to see that his stepfather was cheating him out of his inheritance.

Thomas dutifully spent his time running errands for Sir William, copying papers, and performing sundry duties, for which he received no reimbursement beyond board, room, and clothing. Even after his mother died in March 1655, he remained faithful to Davenant and, in lieu of his promised £100, accepted employment in Sir William's theatrical ventures. His earliest such work seems to have been secretarial and financial in connection with Davenant's productions at Rutland House and elsewhere from 1656 to 1660. When Davenant married Henrietta Maria du Tremblay and began a new family at Rutland House, Thomas still (it appears) stayed with his stepfather.

At the Restoration, Cross was made one of the treasurers of the Duke's Company, a position he held until 1675. Later, when Lady Davenant accused Cross of embezzlement, he described in considerable detail his duties:

. . . delivering out Tickets to his fellow Treasurers (who had an equal power with this Defendant both in Receipts of money, payment of charges, and making up the Charge of the Theatre), and then to receive the Tickets in again from all the Doorkeepers of the Pit, Galleries, and Boxkeepers' moneys, as also making up the whole Receipts and expenses of the day, comparing the number of Tickets with the money brought in, wherein the Company had always a check upon this Defendant, and they might and did almost daily view and examine this Defendant's Accounts, which one or other of them did or might have done when they pleased; And also this Defendant had the sole trouble of paying the whole charge of the House weekly, that is to say, the Salaries of all hireling Players both men and Women, Music Masters, Dancing Masters, Scene men, Barbers, Wardrobekeepers, Doorkeepers, and Soldiers, besides Bills of all kinds, as for Scenes, Habits, Properties, Candles, Oil, and other things, and in making and paying (if called for) all the Dividends of the Sharers, dividing each man his particular share according to his proportion, and often in the crowd of this Defendant's [business], and all this done by this Defendant without having any Receipts from any of the Company, or any of the Hirelings or any others belonging to the Company for any one Sum paid them by this Defendant. And also this Defendant had the paying the sharers of the Ten Shares (being the Assignees of the said Sir William Davenant) who came or sent for their moneys when they pleased, having free access by themselves, servants, or Agents, to the Books of Accounts of all the Receipts and disbursements of the foregoing week with the several Dividends, this Defendant being ever ready when required to Satisfy them in every particular, and to deliver them their shares at every week's end. . . . [For this work] he did receive, for such weeks only as they acted, after the rate of Twenty Five Shillings *per* week; and some time after [Davenant's] decease was by the said Company advanced to Thirty shillings, in consideration (as he conceives) of his great pains and care, and no more.

Davenant died in 1668, and his chief creditor, John Alway, was granted administration of his estate. This was apparently prearranged, and in time the estate came back into the hands of Davenant's widow, Dame Mary. Despite his growing suspicions about the way Alway and Lady Davenant handled the estate, Cross continued to serve the Duke's Company. On 12 August 1670, for example, the lease on the plot of ground on which the Dorset Garden Theatre was being built was assigned to Cross and Nicholas Davenant (then a child) in trust for Dame Mary. As a representative for the troupe, Cross occasionally received payments for plays the company performed at the Middle Temple. By 18 July 1674 he

had purchased or come into a half share in the company—not much, but the largest shareholder, Dame Mary, had only 3.3 shares of the total of 20. On the surface, at least, it would seem that Thomas Cross was building a creditable career in the troupe and had long since forgotten about that £100.

On 30 November 1675 Alexander Davenant replaced Cross as treasurer. It is not clear what happened to Cross in the ten years that followed, but his later statement that he became aware in 1677–78 of how the Davenants were handling the company accounts would suggest that he was still employed in the theatre office but in a lesser capacity than before. Alexander Davenant had schemes of his own afoot and had his own reasons for wanting Cross out of the treasurer's post, but Cross may, nevertheless, have been fired for cause. Dame Mary later testified that Cross had "imbecelled misimployed or detayned great sums of money of the sayd sharers" and was "forced to abscond himselfe for fear of being sued by the said sharers for a great parte of their respective monyes by him recd and with him deposited and misimployed or detayned as aforesaid . . ."

In 1684–85 Cross bethought himself of that £100 of long before and in behalf of himself and his brothers sued Dame Mary. The case brought out, in addition to many of the above particulars, Dame Mary's fear that Cross was conspiring to defraud her of the Davenant estate and Cross's complaint that he had been bilked of his inheritance. The outcome of the case is not known, but since both sides seem to have behaved rather shabbily, some kind of compromise settlement was probably reached. In fact, when on 19 November 1686 Dame Mary Davenant drew up her will, Thomas Cross served as one of the witnesses.

Perhaps the following entry in the registers of St Olave, Hart Street, concerns our subject: on 14 December 1676 Thomas Crosse and Elizabeth Burton, both of the parish of Whitechapel, were married at St Olave's.

Cross, Thomas *d. 1737, numberer.*

On 17 May 1717 at Lincoln's Inn Fields the numberer Thomas Cross shared a benefit, the earliest mention of him in the bills. Thereafter, through 29 April 1726, he received annual benefits, once by himself but usually shared with one or two others. The theatre accounts show salary payments to him through 9 June 1727 and indicate that his daily pay in the mid-1720s was 6s. 8d.

If the following will was the numberer's, he had activities that lay outside the theatre and may have spent his last years enjoying them: Cross the numberer died on 19 December 1737; a will made by a Thomas Cross on 9 October 1735, attested on 3 January 1738 (since he had drawn it up himself), and proved on 31 January reveals a man who was possibly a tavern keeper. This Thomas Cross identified himself as from Hammersmith. He left his estate to be divided equally between his mother Margaret and his three sisters—Ann Cross, Katherine Harmon, and Mary Rogers. He also left a number of legacies to various friends and tradesmen, some of whom he identified as distillers, but one a poulterer, and one a vintner. The will was originally drafted on 12 March 1733, but Cross kept making additions—such as noting in 1734 that his wife had been dead for almost six years—through 9 October 1735. Since many theatre people, especially the house servants, had secondary occupations, it is not at all unlikely that the will was that of Thomas Cross the numberer.

Crossaro, Signor [*fl. 1787–1789*], *dancer.*

Announced as a dancer from Venice, Signor Crossaro performed in a new dance called *Nobody, or Two Faces are Better than One*, at the Royal Circus in 1789. He was no doubt the "Mr Crosara" who had

been added to the Drury Lane list on 13 October 1787 at 3s. 4d. per day, probably as a chorus dancer inasmuch as his name appeared in no bills.

Crossby. *See* CROSBY.

Crossdill. *See* CROSDILL.

Crossfield, Mr [*fl. 1698–1699*], *singer.*

Mr Crossfield, otherwise unknown, sang in *The Island Princess* at Drury Lane in November 1698 and at subsequent performances through April 1699.

Crossman, Master [*fl. 1785–1793*], *equestrian.*

Master Crossman was performing feats of horsemanship at Astley's Amphitheatre, Westminster Bridge, as early as 1785. Probably he was the son of the famous equestrian John Crossman, but there is some slight possibility that "Master" and "Mr" were actually the same person. Curiously, no extant bill or advertisement from Astley's that we have seen lists both of them as performing on the same night. Mr Crossman appeared as early as September 1787; in 1791 the bills listed variously a Master and a Mr Crossman, so that we assume them to be different people.

A characteristic performance by Master Crossman was the one on 6 May 1791 when he was listed for horsemanship and to perform exercises typical of the Light Dragoons. Called "Young" Crossman by 1793, he was performing at the Royal Circus where, on 7 August of that year, he challenged all the horsemen of Europe in "Fricasee Dancing, Vaulting, Tight-Rope Dancing, Pyramids, Ground and Lofty Tumbling" and presented an "unparalleled Peasant Hornpipe, and Hag Dance, not to be equalled by any Horseman in this Kingdom." His other feats included vaulting "over the Horse backwards and forwards, with his Legs Tied," and "leaping from a single Horse over Two Garters, 12 feet high," and alighting again on the saddle, all the while playing the violin in various attitudes. See also the entry for John Crossman.

Crossman, John [*fl.* 1787–1817], *equestrian, dancer.*

John Crossman, whom the younger Charles Dibdin coupled with George Smith, calling them "the two greatest Equestrian Performers of their time," was exhibiting feats of horsemanship at Astley's Amphitheatre, Westminster Bridge, as early as September 1787 when he appeared in *The Siege of Quebec.* There is a possibility that he was also billed as "Master Crossman," although we assume that person to have been his son (see Master Crossman, fl. 1785–1793). Extant advertisements for Astley's list him also as a dancer in *The Animated Statue* in July and September 1791. The bill for 30 August 1791 contained the curious statement that one Crossman was performing horsemanship for "the first time in England," suggesting that there was yet another equestrian of this name.

About 1793 Crossman left Astley to join the competition at the Royal Circus, St George's Fields, where he remained until 1799. In that latter year he became partner with William Parker, William Davis, Robert Handy, George Smith, and Richard Johannot in a venture to play in temporary circuses throughout Britain and Ireland. With these partners (except Johannot), in 1804 Crossman took over a half-interest in the rebuilt Astley's Amphitheatre (it had burned in September 1803). He was still active as a performer at the Amphitheatre in 1811, but by 1817 he had retired. He was dead by the time the younger Charles Dibdin wrote his *Memoirs* in 1830. The Mrs Crossman who acted at Drury Lane in 1797 was very likely his wife.

Crossman, Mrs [John?] [*fl.* 1797], *actress.*

A Mrs Crossman, probably the wife of the accomplished equestrian John Crossman (fl. 1787–1817), acted the maid in *The Suspicious Husband* at Drury Lane on 7 February 1797 and possibly on 14 June. On 6 March 1797 she played Helen in *Cymbeline.*

Crotch, William *1775–1847, musician, composer, teacher.*

William Crotch, who at the age of two was celebrated as an infant musical prodigy and in his mature years became an eminent composer and Doctor of Music, was born in Green's Lane, St George Colgate, Norwich, on 5 July 1775. He was the youngest son of Isabella and Michael Crotch (d. 1813), a master carpenter of that city. About Christmas 1776, not yet two years of age, William showed an unusual curiosity for a small organ which his father, an amateur of

By permission of the Trustees of the British Museum

WILLIAM CROTCH, as a child
by Mrs Harrington

music, had built for his own pleasure. By
next midsummer, the child was able to pick
out the keynote of his favorite tunes, which
his father had regularly played for him, and
soon afterward he could manage the first
two or three notes of these tunes.

According to Charles Burney's report to
the Royal Society which was printed as an
"Account of an Infant Musician" in the
Philosophical Transactions (1779), by the
time William was but two years and three
weeks old, he had taught himself to play
first the air and then the bass part of "God
save the King." Burney relates several anecdotes about William's persistence at practice. Soon crowds of visitors flocked to the
house to see and hear the precocious lad,
till "at length, the child's parents were
forced to limit his exhibition to certain days
and hours, in order to lessen his fatigue,
and exempt themselves from the inconven-
ience of constant attendance on the curious
multitude." Daines Barrington, an amateur
musician, also provided an account of the
lad's feats, much of which was reprinted by
Sainsbury in his *Dictionary of Music*:

The accuracy of the child's ear is such,
that he not only pronounces immediately
what note is struck, but in what key the music
is composed. I was witness of an extraordinary
instance of his being able to name the note
touched, at Dr. Burney's, who has a pianoforte, with several keys, both in the bass and
treble, beyond the scale in the common instruments of the same sort.

Upon any of these, very high or very low
notes being struck, he distinguished them as
readily as the intermediate notes of the instrument. Now it is well known that the
harpsichord tuners do not easily manage the
extreme, as their ears are not used to such
tones, and more particularly the lowest notes.

Soon William taught himself to play on
the violin, which he held as a violoncello,
and touched with only two fingers. His
young acquaintance, one of the Rev Mr

National Portrait Gallery

WILLIAM CROTCH
by Linnell

Wesley's sons, who was also a musical
prodigy but not at so tender an age, used to
anger William by mistuning the violin. So
exquisite was young Crotch's ear that he
could distinguish the quarter tones of the
violin. Later in life, Crotch wrote his own
musical memoirs—"Extracted by himself,
for himself, from old letters"—in which he
recollected the precocity of his musical talents, perhaps having been prompted by the
available published stories about him.

In November 1778, his mother took him
to Cambridge, where, according to the *London Magazine* (April 1779), "he played on
all the College and Church organs to the
astonishment of the gentlemen of the University." On 2 December 1778 he was
taken to London and introduced to J. C.
Bach and Lady Dartmouth; and then on 1
January 1779 he was summoned with his
mother to Buckingham House to perform
on the organ in an evening concert before

the Royal Family in which he played ten tunes including, of course, the national anthem. On Sunday, 31 January, after divine service, Crotch, now three-and-a-half years old, again performed before their Majesties. Still in London on 5 June 1779, he played in St James's Palace for the princesses. In the following month he was in Oxford where his mother advertised in the *Oxford Journal* of 3 July that her child, not yet four, would "play upon the ORGAN at the Musick Room this day at Twelve o'Clock," by permission of the vice-chancellor and the stewards of the Musical Society.

Mother and son made a second visit to London in the fall beginning on 4 October 1779. On 18 October an advertisement announced that "Mrs Crotch is arrived in town with her son, the Musical Child, who will perform on the organ every day as usual, from one o'clock to three, at Mrs. Hart's, milliner, Piccadilly," two doors west of St James's Street. Presumably these were concerts for which admission was charged, thereby constituting Crotch's only known professional appearances in London before 1801 and thus qualifying him for inclusion in these volumes.

In 1781 the "Infant Musician" played before large audiences at the Bridgegate Hall and the Saracen's Head Hall in Glasgow. Crotch gave concerts in Oxford in 1785 and went to Cambridge in 1786, remaining for two years to assist and study with Dr Randall, Professor of Music and organist of Trinity and King's Colleges. He had a benefit concert at King's College Hall on 19 May 1786, and on 4 June 1789, when he was 14, his oratorio *The Captivity of Judah* was sung at Trinity Hall. In this latter year he also gave concerts at Oxford. About this time he moved to Oxford with the intention of entering the Church, under the patronage of the Rev. A. C. Schomberg, tutor at Magdalen. When Schomberg began to experience ill health, Crotch found it necessary to give up his studies and resume his professional music

work. In September 1790 Crotch succeeded the late Thomas Norris as organist of Christ Church, a post he continued to hold until about 1808. He took his Bachelor of Music degree at Oxford on 5 June 1794, and his degree exercise, dated 28 May 1794, is in the Music School collection. He succeeded Dr Philip Hayes as organist of St John's and Professor of Music in March 1797. The latter appointment he held until 1806. He was also at this time organist to St Mary's, Oxford. Crotch received his Doctor of Music degree on 21 Nov 1799, composing for the occasion a setting for Warton's "Ode to Fancy."

Dr Crotch devoted the rest of his life, almost five decades in the nineteenth century, to teaching and composing, and to drawing and sketching; the graphic talents he had also developed as a mere child. His appointments included the first principalship of the Royal Academy of Music upon its establishment in 1822. Details of his later career are found in Grove and *The Dictionary of National Biography*. Lists of his compositions are given in Sainsbury's *Dictionary of Music* and by John S. Bumpus in *Musical News*, 17 and 24 April 1897.

On 10 June 1834, Crotch produced a new oratorio entitled *The Captivity of Judah* (entirely different from his earlier composition of the same title) for the installation of the Duke of Wellington as Chancellor of Oxford. Several weeks later on 28 June 1834 he played the organ at Westminster Abbey for the Handel festival, an event which proved to be his last public appearance.

During his later years Crotch resided at Kensington Gravel Pits and finally moved to Taunton to live with his son, the Rev William Robert Crotch, who was master of the grammar school in that city. He died at the age of 72, on 29 December 1847, while seated at dinner, and was buried in the churchyard at Bishop Hull, near Taunton. In his will, drawn in 1844, he left his manuscripts and musical copyrights to his son, and most of his estate, about £18,000, to his wife.

Crotch's achievement was distinguished in his own time, although he never, in the manner of Mozart, rose to the extraordinary genius that his childhood prowess promised. But he became an accomplished and learned musician and a teacher who enjoyed high public esteem.

Portraits of Crotch include:

1. An oil painting of him as a boy, sometimes attributed to George Romney but probably by William Beechey. In the Royal Academy of Music. A copy of this painting, inscribed "From the original by Sir William Beechey in the Royal Academy of Music—London" is with the Faculty of Music, Oxford, to whom it was presented before 1776 by a Mr Whytley.

2. As a mature man, by W. Derby, engraved by J. Thomson, and published in the *European Magazine*, 1822.

3. An engraving by W. T. Fry, published 1 September 1822.

4. A drawing "taken from life" at age three years and seven months, playing the organ, by Mrs Harrington of No 62, South Moulton Street, Oxford Road, who held a royal patent "for her improved and expeditious method of obtaining the most perfect likeness in one minute." An engraving was published 2 April 1779. A variant was printed in the *London Magazine* in April 1779, and another was engraved by James Titler and published by Mrs Crotch on 12 May 1779. Mrs Harrington also published a silhouette profile of the head in 1779, and an anonymous version of the same under the title of "The Musical Phenomenon" also appeared.

5. A watercolor of him as an old man, by John Linnell. In the National Portrait Gallery.

6. An oil painting by J. Sanders. Exhibited at the Royal Academy in 1785.

7. A drawing of Crotch in his academic gown, by F. W. Wilkins. In the possession of D. C. Bell in the late nineteenth century.

Crouch. *See also* COUCH and CRUDGE.

Crouch, Mr [*fl. 1743*], *actor.*

A Mr Crouch acted the title role in a performance of *Oroonoko* at the James Street Theatre on 2 February 1743, by "particular desire" and for the benefit of "a Family under misfortunes and in great Distress."

Crouch, John [*fl. 1679–1710?*], *violinist, dancing master?*

John Crouch's initial appointment to the King's Musick on 22 December 1679 was among the wind instruments, replacing the deceased Humphrey Madge. On 5 July 1682, however, he was described as a violinist and given a post previously held by Thomas Greeting; the first appointment may have been a temporary administrative arrangement to provide Crouch with a place in the royal musical establishment. A warrant in the Lord Chamberlain's accounts dated 26 January 1685 ordered Crouch and others to go to His Majesty's Theatre (at court, presumably) to practice for a ball. Crouch attended both Charles II and James II at Windsor during his time in the royal service. His salary by 5 July 1687 was £50 annually, but it dropped under William III to £30 on 25 March 1689. Crouch was not mentioned again in the accounts until 1 December 1707 when he and other court musicians were given leave to play for the operas at the Queen's Theatre in the Haymarket.

Crouch may have been the "Mr Couch" who had a concert room in 1710 and / or the Mr Couch or Crouch who was a dancing master in the decade following.

Crouch, John *1762–1793, instrumentalist.*

When John Crouch was recommended by John Bassett for membership in the Royal Society of Musicians on 1 April 1784, it was certified that he was then an unmarried man, 22 years of age, had studied music for seven years, was a player on the violin, viola, and harpsichord and was a member of the Drury Lane orchestra. Admitted on 6 June 1784, subsequently he played at the Society's annual concerts at St Paul's for benefit of the clergy in 1785, 1789, and 1790; in 1793 he served the Society as a governor.

In 1789–90, John Crouch's name was on the Drury Lane salary list for 2s. per day. On 6 April 1793 his name was removed from the list as "dead."

William Crouch (1749–1833), also a musician, was evidently his elder brother.

Crouch, Mrs Rawlings Edward, Anna Maria, née Phillips, *1763–1805, actress, singer.*

ANNA MARIA CROUCH
by Romney

The principal details of Anna Maria Crouch's parentage and early life, with a running account of her career, were furnished by her friend Maria Julia Young in two volumes of *Memoirs* published in 1806, a few months after the death of her subject. Miss Young's account must be supplemented and corrected from many other sources.

Anna Maria Phillips was born in Gray's Inn Lane, London, on 20 April 1763, one of six children of Peregrine Phillips, a lawyer and official of the Wine License Office and of his wife, who had been Miss Gascoyne, daughter of a substantial Worcestershire farmer. Phillips was descended on his paternal side from an old Welsh family with noble connections and, through his French mother, a Mlle Corday, was said to be connected with Charlotte Corday, the assassin of Marat. He was sent to America in his boyhood and was patronized by Benjamin Franklin, who imbued him with republican principles. These "radical" ideas surfaced later in his writings, such as the series of letters signed "An Old English Merchant," at one time attributed to Franklin himself. Phillips published also occasional poems and satirical pamphlets and a description of Brighthelmstone called *The Diary* (1778); and in 1785 he edited a selection of the works of Richard Crashaw. For his political activities he was dismissed from his government post, but he continued the practice of law until disabled by illness.

Anna Maria's childhood was saddened by the death of her mother at 42 and of a brother, Edward Erasmus, in his infancy, but otherwise she seems to have experienced an early life of tranquil happiness in the cultivated household with her father, her sisters—Mary Anne, Sophia, and Henrietta—and an older brother, Peregrine. Her striking beauty and her exceptional voice brought her to the attention of the organist of Berwick Street Chapel, a teacher of music named Wafer, who undertook her instruction in voice and harpsichord. About

Harvard Theatre Collection

ANNA MARIA CROUCH, with MRS BLAND, in *The Prisoner*

engraving by Barlow, after Charles

this time, probably before she was 14 years old, she went to live in Princes Street, Cavendish Square, with a widowed sister of her father's, Mrs Le Clerc, a silk trimming maker.

Soon after her seventeenth birthday Anna Maria was apprenticed for three years to Thomas Linley, music master and joint patentee of Drury Lane Theatre. At the same time, says Miss Young, she was "engaged as first singer at the said theatre for six seasons, at a rising salary from six pounds to twelve per week, out of which [for those first three years] Mr Linley was to have a stipulated share" (which Boaden later said was actually half).

Miss Phillips made her first professional appearance at Drury Lane on 11 November 1780 under the conventionally modest de-

Harvard Theatre Collection

ANNA MARIA CROUCH

engraving by Barlow, after Cruikshank

scription "A Young Lady who never appeared on any stage," as Mandane in a revival of Arne's opera *Artaxerxes.* Her success was threatened by an attack of beginner's nerves, but she quelled her fears and was applauded. She assisted in the half-dozen repetitions of the piece but did not get a new part until her appearance as Clarissa in *A School for Fathers* for her own unshared benefit on 21 April 1781. (Ticket seekers were sent to her at No 56, Drury Lane.) The then-incumbent Lord Mayor of London, Sir Watkin Lewes, and his lady, early friends of her father and to her talent, brought a large party. The receipts were £201 12*s.* and no house charges were levied, a circumstance attributable, no doubt, to the fact that Linley, a proprietor, was to receive that "stipulated share" of her net receipts—perhaps half her benefit pro-

ceeds as well as of her salary. Yet, even though the determination of financial matters was partly in her mentor's control, the fact that the other managers agreed to give a young girl of her limited experience her own unshared and uncharged benefit indicated their confidence in her future. Before the end of the season Anna Maria added to her slim repertoire Emily in *The Runaway* on 5 May and Narcissa in *The Rival Candidates* on 7 May. Linley wisely held his valuable property under tight control this first season and did not overwork her fine young voice, which critics were already applauding as an uncommonly good instrument for speaking the parts of comedy as well as for singing.

At the end of the Drury Lane season of 1780–81 Anna Maria set out from London for Liverpool with her father and Mrs Le Clerc. George Mattocks, the manager at Liverpool, had engaged her for the summer, and she sang Polly in *The Beggar's Opera* for her first appearance at Liverpool's Theatre Royal on 11 June. A letter from her father to a London friend, dated 18 July 1781 subjoined a list of parts she had played up to that point in the summer. They included: Sabrina in *Comus,* Narcissa in *The Rival Candidates,* Patty in *The Maid of the Mill,* Clarissa in *Lionel and Clarissa,* Gillian in *The Quaker,* Clara in *The Duenna,* and Rosetta in *Love in a Village.* She sang specialty songs in several other performances. In Drury Lane's winter season of 1781–82, Anna Maria was much admired as Venus in the masque *King Arthur* and was praised therein by an anonymous poet:

Methinks I see you in your iv'ry car,
Sparkling in gems, like the bright morn-
ing-star;
In purple cloth'd, your head with roses
crown'd,
And your moist hair with golden fillets
bound
Drawn by your doves, as thro' the air
you fly

*The winds, enamour'd, breathe a gentle
        sigh,
E'en Boreas faintly dims the glassy sky;
As to the bless'd abodes, you floating
        move,
All heaven, all earth, harmonious, sing
        their love.*

This was neither the worst nor the lengthiest effusion addressed to Anna Maria in the public prints during that season, one other such "poem" running to 92 lines and to such expressions as: "She looks, she moves, and I adore her, / Without the courage to implore her."

But her popularity survived even such celebration, and that season she added to her roles Emily in *The Runaway*, Miranda in *The Tempest*, and the original Emily in Richard Tickell's *The Carnival of Venice*, singing several exquisite songs probably written expressly for her by Sheridan. She was the original London representative of Angelica in Frederick Pilon's *The Fair American* and Laura in *The Chaplet*. In the summer she returned to Liverpool to act. Late in October she came back to open her new season as Patty in *The Maid of the Mill*, her first attempt in London with the character, which soon became almost her finest.

Anna Maria had made a close study of the acting style of the great comic actress Frances Abington, whom she idolized, but Mrs Abington left Drury Lane for Covent Garden after the 1782–83 season, and her influence over Miss Phillips gradually diminished. Anna Maria then quickly developed an irresistible comic style of her own which kept her in public favor for exactly 20 years. She was always at Drury Lane in the winter seasons from 1780–81 through 1800–1801.

In the summer of 1781 Anna Maria engaged at Smock Alley Theatre in Dublin and also sang with great éclat and acclaim at the Rotunda concerts there. In July and August she played at Cork and in August

also at Limerick. She and her father had come to the Irish capital armed with letters of introduction to various influential persons, one of the letters being, indeed, to William Windham from Samuel Johnson. The professional and social reception of father and daughter was so favorable that they returned hopefully to Dublin in June of 1783.

Anna Maria went once again to Cork in the summer of 1783 (but not, as Professor Clark has asserted, billed as Mrs Crouch). On the way from London to Ireland she was thrust into one of those adventures to which she seems to have been all too liable. In the Burney manuscripts in the British Museum is the "Extract of a Letter from Portsmouth" dated June 1783: "Miss Phillips from the T[heatre] R[oyal] D[rury] L[ane], was engaged to perform here six nights; but the conduct of some sea officers has deprived us of that excellent singer." They had "offered her liberties which modesty could not permit" and "Mr Phillips, for shewing an honest resentment to the insult offered his daughter, had nearly lost his life."

According to her biographer, Anna Maria also had a narrow escape that summer in Dublin from assassination at the hands of a maniacal disappointed suitor who was apprehended after threatening to shoot her on the stage. Shortly afterward she was said to have eloped (with the help of her brother) with a young scion of wealth and Irish aristocracy; but they were both under age and they were parted after being apprehended in their flight to Scotland by both fathers.

When the Phillips family returned to London in the fall of 1784 Anna Maria was sequestered in the house of one of her older sisters in Charles Street, St James's Square, and later that winter her father took the upper floors of a house in Charles Street, Covent Garden, near the theatre, for his and Anna Maria's residence.

On 9 January 1785 at Twickenham

Anna Maria married a young lieutenant in the Navy named Rawlings (or Rollings) Edward Crouch. She continued, however, to act and sing under her maiden name through the end of the season of 1784–85, both in London and in provincial places like the Oxford Music Room, where she sang in April and May 1785, and Liverpool, where she was in June and July. Later that summer she and her husband shared a seaside cottage at Broad Stairs, near Margate. The marriage was revealed only after the premature birth of a child, who lived for only two days. Anna Maria's father moved in with the young couple at No 3, Adam Street, Adelphi, and Anna Maria found herself supporting to a considerable extent a gout-ridden parent, a mad aunt, an orphaned niece, a spendthrift brother, and an indolent husband, and paying for the education of one of her sisters.

Anna Maria's marriage lasted formally for some seven years, but long before it broke up she had taken up residence with the dashing tenor singer Michael Kelly. She had met him on his return from Italy in March 1787, and in his Drury Lane debut had played Clarissa to his Lionel. He had soon moved to lodgings in Rathbone Place, near her house. He coached her in singing and they shortly became inseparable off the stage and virtually so onstage. On 12 May 1787 she reappeared at the Oxford Music Room. In June, accompanied by both her husband and Kelly, she returned to Ireland to play at Dublin, Cork, and Limerick. Later that summer the trio traveled to York, Leeds, Chester, Manchester, and Worcester. In the summer of 1788 the Crouch-Kelly duet sang at Liverpool, Chester, Manchester, and Birmingham.

In the summer of 1789 Anna Maria and her lover had returned to the Irish circuit with great success when, according to *The Secret History of the Green Room* (1795), Mrs Crouch had "so charmed the people of Limerick, that on her Benefit Night she was presented with a large Gold Medal by the Ladies and Gentlemen of the Town; with a tribute inscribed to her great abilities on one side, and on the other, the Arms of the City most beautifully engraved." They were also at Cork and Waterford before going on to Liverpool. In October they sang at "a grand musical festival" at Norwich. They had been with Joseph Fox when he opened his Duke Street Theatre in Brighton on 13 July 1790. In August 1790 Mr and Mrs Crouch and Kelly had taken a trip to France.

In 1791 Anna Maria sent Crouch packing with a sizable allowance after a legal separation occasioned, according to rumor, by an intimacy which had sprung up between Mrs Crouch and the Prince of Wales. The charge was vigorously denied by both Anna Maria and her public partisans in the newspapers. It certainly did not disturb relations between her and Kelly—indeed the Prince was one of the favored and frequent guests at the brilliant routs they sponsored over the next few years. She and her husband (and possibly Kelly) had lived at No 6, Leicester Street, Leicester Fields, at the time of her benefit in April 1787. They had removed by April 1789 to No 56, Titchfield Street, Oxford Street, and by October 1789 to No 26, Bridges Street. Early in 1792 she and Kelly moved into a large house at No 4, Pall Mall, and then into a larger one in Suffolk Street, Haymarket. They saw much of the Storaces, Madame Mara, Sheridan, and other professional friends, but their familiar acquaintance extended to all ranks and kinds. During these years she was the toast of every assembly. The author of *The Final Farewell* (1787) thought that her only "fault originates in an extreme but amiable diffidence," and he hymned her charms:

> And Crouch, endued with every gentle grace,
> A voice celestial, and an angel face:
> Sweet Harmonist! whose silver tones impart

*The soothing melody that charms the
heart.*

Anna Maria and Kelly had sung together
in the *Messiah* and *Sampson* at the elaborate Fourth Chester Musical Festival in
1791 and had appeared with great acclaim
in York that same summer. They were to
be found together in subsequent summers
at many of the leading theatres of the British Isles—for instance, at Manchester's
Theatre Royal (for a music festival) in
1792, at Liverpool and in Ireland in 1793,
at Chester and Edinburgh in 1794, at
Wakefield and Scarborough in 1795, 1796,
and 1797, and nearly always and everywhere to crowded houses. At Drury Lane
for a number of seasons they were paid
jointly, like man and wife, especially for
the oratorios. Before the end of the 1796–
97 season they had moved to No 9, Lisle
Street, Leicester Square, to a house they
shared until Mrs Crouch's death.

During her last ten years on the stage
Anna Maria suffered several accidents and
some periods of illness. On 13 November
1787 she was on her way to the theatre in
a hackney coach when it was overturned
and her face was so badly cut that the scars
were visible always afterward. She was on
that occasion away from the theatre for
some weeks. On a summer professional ex-
cursion with Kelly in 1793 her own carriage overturned and a heavy dressing case
fell across her throat, so that for some time
she was unable to sing. Her voice was ever
afterward much weaker both for speaking
and singing, though "she herself thought
that she found the greatest benefit from
being bled in the throat with leeches, an
operation to which she frequently submitted."

A volume of notes left by John Philip
Kemble contains many notations which reflect Mrs Crouch's worsening health (e.g.,
that for 10 November 1790: "Mrs Crouch
acted in the play tonight for the first time
since the eleventh of October," and for 4

May 1795: "Mrs Crouch acted for the first
time these ten weeks," the playbill of 10
April having noted that "The new Opera
of Jack of Newbury is obliged to be postponed on account of Mrs Crouch's illness"). F. G. Waldron, in his *Candid and
Impartial Strictures on the Performers*
(1795) called her

A most delightful singer, but considerably
decreased of late in power, by what means
we know not. There is a plaintive, heart-felt
tone in this lady's voice, that we never heard
from any other singer since the late Mrs.
Sheridan. Her face is, or rather has been
beautiful, for of late it is puffed up with
bloated flesh, and her person possesses the
same appearance of unsound encrease.

"Anthony Pasquin," in his *Pin Basket to
the Children of Thespis* (1796), con-
curred: "Mrs Crouch, the once beautiful
and admired Crouch, is now hastily losing
all her attraction. . . . she is at the present
moment learning from Monsieur —— to
sing a note lower."

Mrs Crouch's weekly salary at Drury
Lane seems to have remained level from
1791–92, when it rose from £12 to £14
for five days' service, until the end of her
career. But she and Kelly earned other substantial sums: for the spring oratorios, for
concertizing, and for summers at the Haymarket or in the provinces—and their benefit receipts were often huge: for example,
total receipts for her on 15 April 1799
were £673 6s. 6d., with a charge for use
of the house of £250. In addition, the pair
were successful teachers of singing (and
she of acting). Among their many pupils
sent to theatres and the opera house were
Clara Dixon, Miss Davies, Jane Jackson
(later Mrs Mathews), the Misses E. and R.
Jacobs, Miss Dufour, Bella and Mary
Menage, and Miss Tyrer, as well as Anna
Maria's two neices, Miss Scadgall and Miss
Horrebow.

At the peak of her powers Anna Maria
Crouch combined extraordinary beauty and

grace of person very effectively with a good stage presence and a fine singing voice to seize the affections of a large public. She was not a powerful actress, but most of the parts she sustained required no great power. She was a sweet-natured and charitable woman, amiable and democratic in manner, and her influential acquaintances were legion.

She was the original representative of the following characters: Nancy in John Dent's comic afterpiece *Too Civil by Half* (singing Thomas Hooke's music), Julia in William Jackson's comic opera *The Metamorphosis*, Emily in Harriet Horncastle Hook's operatic farce *The Double Disguise*, Anna in James Cobb's farce *The Doctor and the Apothecary*, Ormellina in Cobb's comic opera *Love in the East*, Catherine in the James Cobb–Stephen Storace *Siege of Belgrade*, Lady Elinor in the Cobb-Storace opera *The Haunted Tower*, Donna Aurora in the Cobb-Storace opera *The Pirates*, Zilipha in their spectacle *The Cherokee*, Clara in Attwood's *The Prisoner*, Dame Eleanor in James Hook's comic opera *Jack of Newbury*, the Countess in Prince Hoare's comic opera *A Friend in Need*, Claribel in George Colman and Michael Kelly's melodrama *Feudal Times*, Helena Caustic in Samuel Jackson Pratt's comedy *The School for Vanity*, and Harriet in *The Adventures of a Night*, a comedy by William Hodson. In Sheridan's lavishly produced tragedy *Pizarro* she headed the list of "Vocal Parts" as Priestess of the Sun.

Some of her other characters were: Patty in *The Maid of the Mill*, Rachel in *The Ladies Frolick*, Narcissa in *The Rival Candidates*, Louisa in *The Deserter*, Phoebe in *Belphegor*, Dorinda in an alteration of *The Tempest*, Gillian in *The Country Girl*, Chloris in *Acis and Galatea*, Clarissa in *A School for Fathers*, Louisa Dudley in *The West Indian*, Emily in *The Runaway*, Laura in *The Chaplet*, Sophia in *The Lord of the Manor*, Polly in *The Beggar's Opera*, Olivia in *Twelfth Night* ("with songs"),

Urganda and Sylvia in *Cymon*, Sylvia in *The Recruiting Officer*, Matilda in *Richard Coeur de Lion*, Rosetta in *Love in a Village*, and Miss Neville in *Know Your Own Mind*—some joyful maidens, some tuneful, but all of them young. She played them until the very end of her career.

Numbers of the songs she sang, both within the actions of operas and plays and as specialty offering entr'acte and after the curtain, were published "as sung by" her (the conjectural dates are from the British Museum's *Catalogue of Printed Music*): Thomas Linley's *Still the lark finds repose*, from *The Spanish Rivals* (1784); the duet (with Miss Romanzini) *Swei mädchen*, by von Dittersdorf (1788); Kelly's *To see thee so gentle* and *What new delights* (for which Mr Crouch did the instrumental parts) (1789?); *In thee each joy*, a duet with Kelly (1790?); *What makes this new pain in my breast*, from *Twelfth Night* (1790?); I. J. Pleyel's song from *The Haunted Tower*, "Pity I cannot deny" and G. Sarti's song "Hush, such counsel do not give" (published together in the March 1790 issue of *Walker's Hibernian Magazine*, Dublin); *On Love's best altar* and *The summer heats bestowing* by Stephen Storace, from *The Doctor and the Apothecary* (Dublin, 1790?); Hayes's *The New Soger Laddie* (1790?); *On that lone bank where Lubin died*, duet with Dignum (1794?); *Adieu my Floreski*, from *Lodoiska* (1794); and *Fair Rosalie* (1795?).

In 1795 Anna Maria Crouch installed Mr Phillips, her father, in a little house in Battersea (which she used as a summer retreat) until she built an elaborate cottage for him off the King's Road, Chelsea, in 1798. There "the Gothic hall" would "contain a dinner party of fifteen, if not twenty persons, commodiously," Miss Young remembered. Anna Maria spent much time at Chelsea with her young nephews Peter and Henry Horrebow. At some time after her retirement—her last appearance was for Kelly's benefit on 14 May 1801—she and

Kelly removed their town abode from Lisle Street to the Saloon, Pall Mall. There they continued to entertain, but on a diminishing scale as her health declined.

Anna Maria began to suffer her last illness in the spring of 1805. In August she went to Brighton in hope that the sea air would revive her. But by September she had worsened and had sent for her attorney William Fisher to reaffirm her will. She gave calm direction to be buried according to old custom in a woollen shroud "neither flounced nor trimmed" and that her coffin be black and her obsequies simple. She died at Brighton on 2 October 1805 of what Termier and Bankhead, the physicians who attended her, decided was "an internal mortification." (The details of her decline make it seem probable that her malady was cancer.) She was buried in Brighton churchyard, and a monument to her memory was soon erected there by Michael Kelly.

Her will left her "moiety or half part" of the house in Pall Mall and other property unvalued and unitemized in trust to her executors William Sewell, Esq of the Haymarket and Thomas Shaw, Esq of the Inner Temple (despite his address, perhaps the leader of the band at Drury Lane). In effect, Kelly, who (obviously) owned the other part of the leasehold messuage in Pall Mall, was to have her half for the term of his life "upon condition the said Michael Kelly do and shall pay . . . to my sister Mrs Diana Horrebow one Annuity or clear yearly sum of fifty pounds for . . . the term of her natural life . . . exclusive of what [he] now . . . allows the said Sophia Diana Horrebow." Residuary legatees were Peter Rawlings Horrebow, her nephew, and two nieces, Sophia Horrebow and Sophia Scadgall.

Mrs Crouch was a favorite subject for portraiture. The following pictures of her were executed:

1. Portrait, oil on canvas, by George Romney. In the Iveagh Bequest at Kenwood.

2. Oil on canvas, by Romney. In the McFadden Collection at the Pennsylvania Museum.

3. Pen drawing, with sepia and indigo wash, by J. H. Ramberg. In the British Museum. It was engraved for *Bell's British Theatre* in 1785.

4. Pencil drawing, tinted, by a "Revd. Mr. Thomas." Now at the Garrick Club.

5. Portrait in oils, full length, by Samuel De Wilde. Mrs Crouch as Polly in *The Beggar's Opera*. Now in the Garrick Club.

6. Portrait engraving, Bartolozzi after Romney, published by Boydell in 1788. Same portrait engraved by Greatbach (1789?).

7. In a seated pose, playing harp, engraved by Barlow after Cruikshank, 1789.

8. Oval portrait drawn and engraved by T. Lawrence as plate to the *General Magazine and Impartial Review*, 1792.

9. Engraved portrait by J. Condé as a plate to *The Thespian Magazine* (1792).

10. Engraved portrait by C. Blackberd after Schuder, published by T. Bellamy, 1795.

11. Engraved portrait by J. Hutchinson as a plate to the *Monthly Mirror*, 1801, and by A. Pope and W. Ridley as a plate to the *European Magazine*, 1805, and published by J. Asperne.

12. Anonymous woodcut depicting Mrs Crouch, standing with a man in front of a cottage, over three verses and chorus of a song, *Little Bess the Ballad Singer*, published by Howard and Evans, 1800.

13. Anonymous engraving of Mrs Crouch, hands manacled, headdress with feathers.

14. Engraved portrait by E. Harding after J. Barry.

15. When Miss Phillips, in the character of Emily in *The Double Disguise*. Engraved by Cook for *Bell's British Library*, 1784.

16. As Princess Lodoiska in *Lodoiska* by J. Rogers after Stevens, published by Simkin and Marshall, 1824.

17. When Miss Phillips, as Mandane

in *Artaxerxes*, published by Harrison and Company, 1781.

18. As Miranda in *The Tempest*, engraved by Sherwin and Grignion after H. Ramberg, for *Bell's British Library*, 1785.

19. As Peggy in *Patie and Peggy*, with Michael Kelly as Patie, engraved by Barlow, published by J. Roach, 1789.

20. "As Rosetta," engraved by E. Phillips, published by E. Hedges, 1785.

21. As Rosina in *Rosina*, by J. Rogers after J. Kennerley, as a plate to Oxberry's *New English Drama*, 1824.

22. As Selima in *Selima and Azor*, by J. R. Smith after J. Barry.

23. With Mrs Bland, in *The Prisoner*, by Barlow after Charles.

Crouch, William *1749–1833, instrumentalist.*

When William Crouch, the organist of St Luke's, Old Street, was recommended by John Bassett for membership in the Royal Society of Musicians on 4 April 1784, it was certified that he was a player on the violin and viola, had many music students, and was engaged at Drury Lane Theatre as a harpsichordist. At that time he was 35 years old, married, with two children, ages four and five. Crouch was elected to the Society on 6 June 1784, the same day that his younger brother, John Crouch (1762–1793), was elected. William played the violin at the Society's annual concerts at St Paul's Cathedral for the benefit of its clergy in 1789, 1790, 1792, and 1794. In the latter year, Doane's *Musical Directory* listed him as a player in the grand performances at Westminster Abbey. Probably he was the Crouch who played at Covent Garden Theatre in 1812–13.

By 1820 his first wife was dead (perhaps she was the Ann Crouch who was buried at St Paul, Covent Garden, on 8 September 1818, age 59), for on 4 April 1820, described as a widower, he married Mary Williams, a spinster, at St Nicholas, Deptford, Kent. William Crouch died in 1833,

having paid his subscription to the Fund of the Royal Society of Musicians through Christmas of that year. In a petition by ten members of the Society in support of Mary Crouch's application for widow's relief, it was stated that she was 57 years old "and has no means of support but that of letting apartments, furnished, in the house she occupies, No 8, Sidmouth Place, Gray's Inn Road, which are at present and have been for some time wholly unoccupied." The Governors of the Society, however, delayed action, not convinced that the property left her by Crouch would realize an income of less than £30 per year. In 1836, Mary Crouch attested that after her death the house left to her by her husband, with the furniture, was to be sold and the money was to be paid to his daughter Mrs Bonner. Finally on 3 January 1836 the Governors granted her the £2 12s. 6d. monthly widow's allowance. On 4 August 1839 she wrote to advise the Governors that she had just become the wife of John Elliott (probably the musician), and she was granted the usual widow's dowry.

Frederick William Crouch (c. 1780–1844), William Crouch's son by his first wife, became an eminent cellist in the nineteenth century and was a member of the orchestra at the King's Theatre in 1817 and 1818. In 1823 he lived at Clapham Rise. His son was Frederick William Nicholls Crouch (1808–1896), who married Lydia Pearson at St Paul, Covent Garden, on 15 October 1832, and whose daughter Ciantha was born on 19 August 1833 and baptized at the same church on 14 November 1833. Frederick William Nicholls Crouch performed at the Royal Coburg and Drury Lane Theatres in the nineteenth century. In 1849 he went to the United States, where he was engaged at the Astor Place Opera House and at Boston, Philadelphia, Richmond, and Portland, Maine. He died at Portland on 18 August 1896.

Compositions published by William

Crouch include *Six Sonatas or Lessons for the Harpsichord or Piano Forte* (1775? and 1790?), instrumental music to *The Tempest* (1789), *To see thee so gentle* (1789?), and *What new delights invade my bosom* (1789?), the latter two being instrumental accompaniments for Michael Kelly's songs.

Crowder, John   *d. 1674, trumpeter.*

On 23 May 1663 John Crowder (or Crowther) was appointed a trumpeter extraordinary (without fee) in the King's Musick, and on 16 May 1664 a permanent and salaried position became available to him at the death of Edward Simpson. He served under Prince Rupert in the fall of 1664, but the Lord Chamberlain's accounts show that he was so little satisfied that he deserted and had to be apprehended. Nevertheless, in the summer of 1666 he was serving Prince Rupert again, this time also working under the Duke of Albemarle at sea. A year later Crowder attended the ambassadors to the United Netherlands; in the summer of 1669 he was paid £20 extra for accompanying Lord Henry Howard, the ambassador to Morocco, to his post; and in 1672–73 he made an official trip to Denmark. The trumpeter may have died abroad, for the next mention of him is dated 24 June 1674 when he was reported as recently deceased. His position was given to James Castle.

Crowe, [Eleanor?]   [*fl.* 1796–1801], *actress.*

A Miss Crowe acted the role of Miss Tittup in *Bon Ton* at the Haymarket (usually dark at that season) on 22 February 1796. She acted at Crow Street, Dublin, in 1796–97. Perhaps she was the Miss Eleanor Crowe who was a member of Winston's company at Richmond, Surrey, in 1799 and 1801. In 1799 Eleanor Crowe signed her full name to the articles of agreement between the company and Winston which are now in the Richmond Library.

Crowe, William   [*fl.* 1792–1796], *dancer. See* CROWE, MRS WILLIAM, JANE.

Crowe, Mrs William, Jane, née Rowson   [*fl.* 1791–1799], *dancer.*

Miss Jane Rowson, later Mrs William Crowe, was the daughter of the actors William Rowson (d. 1842) and Susanna Rowson (d. 1862), who were acting at London in the early 1790s and who then, in 1793, went to America to perform. Her sister Elizabeth Rowson danced at Covent Garden in the 1780s and died young on 19 October 1790.

Jane Rowson first performed at London in the season of 1791–92 when she was engaged at Covent Garden (where her parents were also employed) at a salary of £1 5s. per week. Her name appeared in the bills for dancing in the chorus of *Blue Beard* on 32 nights between 22 December 1791 and 18 February 1792, but probably she worked in other pieces at different times during the season. Still billed as "Miss Rowson" she began the next season by dancing again in *Blue Beard* on 8, 15, and 22 October 1792. On 11 November she married the dancer William Crowe at St Martin-in-the-Fields, with her mother and father signing the register as witnesses. Now billed as "Mrs Crowe" she continued the season at Covent Garden, dancing in the chorus for 48 performances of *Harlequin's Museum* (first time 26 December 1792) and as a black woman in seven performances of the ballet pantomime, *The Governor* (first time, 11 March 1793). Re-engaged at a salary of £1 5s. per week in 1793–94, she danced in 52 performances of *Harlequin and Faustus*, beginning on 19 December 1793. In the following two seasons she still earned £1 5s. per week for chorus dancing in such pieces as *The Lord Mayor's Day* and the first performance of O'Keeffe's comic opera *The Lad of the Hills* (9 April 1796).

Mrs Crowe's name did not appear on the

Covent Garden bills or pay list for 1796–97. She was back, however, in 1797–98 and 1798–99, appearing in *Oscar and Malvina* on 19 March 1798 (and eight other times) and in the first performance of T. J. Dibdin's *The Magic Oak* on 29 January 1799 (and 31 other times that season). Her husband, William Crowe, seems to have appeared only once at London in the eighteenth century; he danced the pantomime character of a Jew in a single performance of *Harlequin's Treasure* at the Haymarket, out of season, on 15 March 1796.

Crowley. *See* CRAWLEY.

Crowther. *See also* CROWDER.

Crowther, Mr ₁*fl.* 1782₁, *actor.*
A Mr Crowther played an unspecified character in a single performance of the burlesque *The Taylors* at the Haymarket on 25 November 1782.

Croza, John Francis ₁*fl.* 1748–1750₁, *manager.*
An Italian company under the direction of Dr John Francis Croza arrived at London on 21 September 1748 "to entertain the Town the approaching Season, at the King's Theatre in the Haymarket, with Operas of a new kind, call'd Burlettas," reported the *General Advertiser* (23 September 1748). They gave their first performance of this Neapolitan form of comic opera on 8 November 1748, a piece called *La commedia in commedia*, the libretto by Francesco Vanneschi, with music by Rinaldo da Capua, "Being the first of this Species of Musical Drama ever exhibited in England."

The company consisted of Francesco Bianci, Gaetano Guadagni, Filippo Laschi, Pietro Pertici, and Signoras Amoretti, Frasi, Galli, Laschi, Mellini, Pertici, and Saiz. Dancers were the young Charles and Jenny Poitier, with the senior Poitier as choreog-

rapher. Ciampi was the maestro and the composer of some of the burlettas. It was a good company, by Burney's account, with Pertici and Laschi being two of the best *buffo* actors he ever saw. Walpole, on the other hand, reported their slow start in a letter to Mann on 2 December: "The burlettas are begun; I think, not decisively liked or condemned as yet, their success is certainly not rapid."

Croza's company did survive 43 performances of seven different comic operas and a "Serenade," all given largely by subscription and many by royal commands. Croza himself received a benefit on 28 March 1749. He was beginning to have difficulties by then with the other promoters at the King's Theatre, and in a statement to the *General Advertiser* on 16 May 1749 he explained:

Dr. CROZA, to prevent any Discredit he may suffer, by the many Actions brought against him, and others with which he is threatened, is under a Necessity of informing the Publick, that, in fact, he is not the Undertaker of the Operas; but came hither in consequence of Articles, which he entered into with an English Gentleman of Distinction, who employ'd Mr. V——i as a Director, and Mr. C——d as Treasurer, the former of whom engaged the Dancers, and others who receiv'd Salaries, as the Sequel will evince; wherefore the said Doctor is not a little surprized, that he, V——i, should also pretend to make any Demand upon him as a Poet, since it will appear under his own Hand, that the said Doctor was under his Directions as to the Operas, and that the said V——i retain'd every Night Three per cent out of the Treasury, as a Gratuity for his Trouble.

Croza was taking exception to Vanneschi's claiming payments for his work as librettist of *La commedia in commedia* in addition to taking profits as one of the promoters. The quarrel resulted in Croza removing his players from the King's Theatre for several months in the next season and attempting to perform at the Haymarket. On 8–10 November 1749 the *Penny London Post* announced that Croza had lost three of his best performers, apparently because of the director's "tyrannical treatment," but evidently they were all reconciled, for they opened on 21 November at the Haymarket with Ciampi's *Il negligente*. The printed libretto by Goldoni was dedicated by Croza "to the British Ladies."

Paragraphs antagonistic to Croza appeared in the press, including a burlesque "Prologue for the Italian Strollers, at their Opening in the Little Theatre in the Haymarket; Spoke by Don John Francisco Charlatano, the Raree-show Doctor." Exception was also taken to Croza's having announced the performance for the King's Theatre but having played at the Haymarket. As pointed out by Sybil Rosenfeld in her account of the opera events of this season (*Foreign Theatrical Companies in Britain*), Croza was "catering for the wealthy," with the especially high prices of eight shillings for pit and boxes and four shillings for the gallery. He had a poor house on the first night, a circumstance which persuaded Colley Cibber to write to Benjamin Victor that the burletta company "like a sickly Plant, will die, before it takes any great Root among us."

Il negligente was performed eight times before the Haymarket closed in December, and then Croza took his group back to the King's Theatre on 13 January 1750 with a production of Latilla's *Madama Ciana*. After four performances of the piece were unenthusiastically received, it was withdrawn, to be replaced by *Don Colascione* on 10 February. Croza tried a serious opera, *Adriano in Siria* on 20 February, but when it too played to thin houses for six performances, he returned to burletta. He offered *La serva padrona* for the first time in England on 27 March and *Il trionfo di Camilla* on 31 March and again on 7 April, this time for his own benefit.

When the season ended on 28 April 1750 with *Don Colascione*, Croza made a hasty departure in order to evade his creditors. They sought, apparently unsuccessfully, to apprehend him. The *General Advertiser* of 8 May 1750 bore the following bailiff's notice:

Whereas Doctor John Francis Croza, late Master of the Company of Comedians at the Opera House in the Haymarket, escaped from me on Tuesday Evening last: whoever will secure or cause him to be secured, so that I may re-take him, shall have a reward of thirty pounds immediately, paid by me HENRY GIBBS, one of the Tipstaffs attending the court of Common Pleas, Southampton St., Covent Garden, Tea Merchant. N. B. The said John Francis Croza is a thin man, about Five feet five inches high of a swarthy Complexion, with dark brown eyebrows, pitted with the small pox, stoops a little in the Shoulders, is about 50 years of age, and takes a remarkable deal of Snuff talks Italian and French, but speakes very little English.

Crozier, Miss   [*fl.* 1742], *dancer, singer.*

A Miss Crozier gave entertainments of singing and dancing with Madam Debon and Master Fremble at Woodhouse's booth on the Bowling Green, Southwark, on 16 September 1742, at the time of the fair.

Crudge. *See also* CROUCH.

Crudge, Alexander   *d. 1759, doorkeeper, housekeeper.*

Alexander Crudge became a housekeeper and stage doorkeeper at Covent Garden in 1752–53, situations he retained until his death in 1759. He regularly shared annual benefits with other house servants. Crudge died a widower on 16 January 1759 at his apartments in the theatre and was buried at St Paul, Covent Garden, on 21 January. Administration of his estate was granted on 20 June 1759 to Willoughby Crudge, spinster, his daughter. Crudge was a man (by testimony of the *Public Advertiser* of 19 January 1759) "whose Behaviour gained him esteem and makes his loss lamented by his Acquaintance." He had been a witness to the will of the actor Dennis Delane, proved on 3 April 1750. He had also been elected a member of the Sublime Society of Beefsteaks on 15 December 1744, a circumstance which suggests that he was employed by Covent Garden Theatre by that date.

Cruisdile or Crusdile. *See* CROSDILL.

Cruys, Francis *(fl. 1673–1700)*, *violinist.*

On 16 September 1673 Francis Cruys was appointed to John Smyth's place as a violinist in the private music of Charles II at £40 annually plus the usual livery allowance of £16 2s. 6d.

The Lord Chamberlain's accounts seldom cite Cruys (once spelled Cryme) except in connection with arrears in livery payments (on 22 January 1677 he still had not been paid for the previous four years, for example). We know, though, that on 7 May 1679 he was paid 5s. daily for attending the King at Newmarket and that in January 1691 he went with William III to the Hague. A warrant of 1697 listed him as still receiving a base pay of £40 but, unlike the other musicians, his stipend was "for life." This suggests that perhaps by that time he had been pensioned. He was still connected with the royal service at the end of the century.

Cryme. *see* CRUYS.

Cubit, Mr *(fl. 1794–1807)*, *violoncellist, violist.*

A Mr Cubit was listed in 1794 by Doane's *Musical Directory* as a violoncellist and principal tenor at Covent Garden Theatre and as then living at No 12, Royal Row, Lambeth. No doubt he was the same

Mr Cubit who, with his son, played in the band for a performance of the *Messiah* given at the Haymarket on 15 January 1798 for the benefit of the Choral Fund. A Cubit was also in the Haymarket band in the summer of 1807. (On 5 August 1824, a G. Cubitt was elected to the Royal Society of Musicians; he was still alive in 1839.)

Cubitt, William *(fl. 1775–1830?)*, *actor, singer, violinist, dancer?*

William Cubitt, a singer in the earlier part of his career, is known to have been a member of the summer company at Richmond, Surrey, in 1775. He made his first appearance at Drury Lane on 5 October 1775 (when the *Public Advertiser* misspelled his name as "Cupid") in the role of Mungo in Bickerstaffe's comic opera *The Padlock.* He played a role in *Harlequin's Jacket* on 11 October, Scaramouche in *The Elopement* on 17 October, and Harlequin in *The Theatrical Candidates* on 24 October, performances which suggest he was also a dancer. During the rest of the 1775–76 season he performed a variety of small supporting and chorus roles, which included a Country Lad in *May Day,* the Doctor in *Cymbeline,* Spendall in *Old City Manners,* a Servant in *The Blackamoor Wash'd White* and *The Runaway,* a Soldier in *The Deserter,* and unspecified singing parts in *Queen Mab, The Maid of the Oaks, Macbeth, The Genii, A Peep Behind the Curtain, The Spanish Fryar,* and *Romeo and Juliet.* He had a small role in *The Rehearsal* on 11 May 1776, for his benefit shared with La Mash, Griffith, and Blurton, which brought no profit, but rather a deficit of about £3 10s. He subscribed 10s. 6d. to the Drury Lane Theatrical Fund in that season, at the conclusion of which, according to Winston's notation in the Folger Library copy of the Fundbook, Cubitt was "discharged" from the theatre.

Unable to obtain a situation in London, Cubitt toured the provinces for some years, playing at Bristol in 1776, 1778, and 1779 and at Plymouth, where on 19 July 1780 he performed Don Antonio in *The Duenna*. He had a short and temporary engagement at Covent Garden between 28 April and 14 May 1781, at £2 per week, during which he played Vinegar in *The Son-in-Law* and sang "O what a charming thing's a battle" in performances of *Phusimimesis*. On 3 May 1781 he shared benefit tickets with many other lowly personnel.

In 1782, Cubitt became a principal singer at Vauxhall Gardens. In that year he also performed at the Capel Street Theatre, Dublin. On 6 September 1783 he acted at Cork and was at the Smock Alley Theatre, Dublin, in 1783–84, where on 3 January 1784 he signed his full name to a paper listing the actors of that theatre. In Ireland he "was received with a slight degree of favour," according to *The Secret History of the Green Room* (1792), and had some success playing "Ruffians, Jailers, Highwaymen, &c." He also took to playing the violin in the theatre band, according to the testimony of *The Thespian Dictionary* (1805).

When Cubitt finally secured a permanent engagement at Covent Garden in 1784–85, determined to do "all in his power to make himself useful," he gave up singing, for the most part, and turned to straight acting, playing a large number of minor roles in that season, which included Rosencrantz in *Hamlet*, Lodovico in *Othello*, Douglas in *1 Henry IV*, Tibalt in *Romeo and Juliet*, Noodle in *Tom Thumb*, Fenton in *The Merry Wives of Windsor*, Trueman in *Retaliation*, Leander in *The Mock Doctor*, Stanmore in *Oroonoko*, Spinosa in *Venice Preserv'd*, Conrade in *Much Ado About Nothing*, Woodley in *Three Weeks after Marriage*, Rapino in *The Castle of Andalusia*, Simpkin in *The Deserter*, Manuel in *Love Makes a Man*, Strutter in *Lawyer's Panic*, Sergius in *The Siege of Damascus*, and parts in *The Musical Lady*, *The Critic*, and *The Arab*. He

acted Bowman in *Robin Hood* on 12 October 1784, but when Mrs Kennedy became ill after the first act, "Davies came forward," reported the *London Chronicle* the next day, informed the audience of the sudden misfortune, "and hoped that Cubitt might be permitted to read the remainder of her part [Allen a Dale]; a request that was immediately complied with." A similar emergency was met by Cubitt at the beginning of the next season, when, on 19 September 1785, Johnstone was to have played Ferdinand in *The Duenna* but became suddenly ill, and Cubitt, reported the *Town and Country Magazine* (September 1785), "did all in his power to supply his place."

He remained at Covent Garden through 1793–94, at a salary of £5 per week by 1789–90, £3 10*s*. in 1791–92, and £6 10*s*. in 1793–94. He also played at Plymouth in the summer of 1788. The roles he performed in his final season at Covent Garden were typical of the dozens of journeyman tasks by which he served the theatre: Gammon in *Wild Oats*, Cacafogo in *Rule a Thumb*, Don John in *Much Ado About Nothing*, the Duke in *Othello*, Hecate in *Macbeth*, Rapine in *Netley Abbey*, Anthony in *The Chances*, Cassander in *Alexander the Great*, Moody in *The Speechless Wife*, a part in *The World in a Village*, and Gibbet in *The Beaux' Stratagem*—the last being a character which the author of *The Secret History of the Green Room* believed "he personates with most excellence . . . which he *looks* so completely, that it is impossible to mistake him for anything but a Highwayman."

After leaving Covent Garden, Cubitt played for a while at the Royal Circus in April and October 1795, one of his roles there being the "serjeant" in the burletta *The Recruiting Serjeant* on 17 April 1795. He was a member of the company at Birmingham in the summer of 1796. On 15 May 1798, he made a final appearance at Covent Garden, when, Fawcett being ill,

Cubitt undertook the part of Bobadil in *Every Man in His Humour*. The critic of the *Monthly Mirror* (June 1798) reported that "though we admire the promptitude with which he came forward on the present emergency," his performance had not reached the level of merit which he had attained some years before in Gibbet.

In addition to the roles mentioned above, a selected list of Cubitt's typical parts while at Covent Garden might include the Lieutenant in *Richard III*, Croudy in *The Highland Reel*, Colonel Epaulette in *Fontainebleau*, the Doctor in *The Little Hunchback*, a Corporal in *Love and War*, Gregory in *Rose and Colin*, the Marquis of Montague in *The Battle of Hexham*, the Earl of Mersia in *Peeping Tom*, Roundfee in *Ways and Means*, Bounce in *The Suicide*, Bruin in *The Mayor of Garratt*, Lucianus in (an altered version of) *Hamlet*, and Farmer in *Oscar and Malvina*.

Nothing is known of Cubitt's first wife. On 17 September 1789, described in the register as a widower, he married Anne Milbourne, spinster, of the parish, at St Paul, Covent Garden. Their daughter, Maria Caroline Cubitt, who was born in Lambeth on 6 April 1800, sang at the age of seven before the Prince Regent in the Nobility's Concerts at the Argyle Rooms and made her debut at Drury Lane on 10 June 1817 as Margaretta in *No Song No Supper*. On 26 September 1818, Peake, the treasurer of Drury Lane, advanced £150 to Cubitt "to release his Daughter from her Apprenticeship to Mr Nathan to be repay'd out of Miss Cubitt's Salary as Pr. Agreement." Miss Cubitt enjoyed a successful career but took to drink after being jilted by an actor. She died prematurely on 20 July 1830, and was buried at St Paul, Covent Garden, on 26 July. Maria died a spinster, notwithstanding Oxberry's rumor that she had been secretly married to the son of a rich East India director, whose parents had disapproved of the match. According to a Winston manuscript at the

Folger Library, she had a brother, who may have been the Cubitt who played in the Haymarket band in 1807; but William Cubitt had played the violin in theatre bands in his early days, and this Haymarket musician may have been the father himself.

In 1819, "The Manager's Notebook" declared that William Cubitt "for many years has been an annuitant" on the Covent Garden Fund. The date of his death is not known to us, but remarks in the Winston manuscripts suggest that he may have been alive still at the time of his daughter's death in 1830.

Cuckow. *See* CURCO.

Cudmore, Richard *1787–1840, instrumentalist, composer.*

The musician Richard Cudmore was born at Chichester in 1787, according to an autobiographical account in his own hand which he provided to Sainsbury in 1823. The manuscript, which formed the basis of the entry on Cudmore in Sainsbury's *Dictionary of Musicians* (1824), is presently in the Library of Glasgow University. Under the tutelage of his first master James Forgett, an organist at Chichester, the young Cudmore proved to be musically precocious. At the age of nine he played the violin in public at Chichester, was taught by Reinagle (who was residing in Oxford) in the following year, and at the age of 11 played a concerto of his own composing in his native city. He was then introduced by the Reverend Mr Marwood to Salomon, under whose instruction at London he remained, intermittently, for about two years.

By his own account, Cudmore led the band at the theatre in Chichester when he was but 12 years of age and he also played a concerto there for the benefit of the comic actor Richard Suett. He claimed that in the same year (presumably 1799) he also "play'd among the *Primo Violins* at the

Italian Opera in London," but no record exists of such an engagement.

Cudmore returned soon to Chichester where he lived for nine years, during which period he played two violin concertos at Oxford when Morelli and Mrs Mountain were also engaged. About 1808 he went again to London where he studied pianoforte under Woelfi and soon became a regular performer in concert circles, playing the violin and pianoforte for Salomon, Madame Catalani, and others. Cudmore was also a member of the Philharmonic Concerts. On 7 May 1815 he was proposed by Potter for membership in the Royal Society of Musicians and was elected (13 ayes, 2 nays) on 6 August 1815. On one occasion, according to Cudmore's story, he was summoned to fill in for Salomon, who had rehearsed with Dr Crotch and Jacobs for a particular concert at the Rowland Hill's Chapel but had been suddenly subpoenaed to court. Cudmore performed the music at sight before an audience of two or three thousand persons. Another time he performed at sight a very difficult concerto brought by "a professional Man" to a party given by Mr C. Nicholson. In his brief autobiography Cudmore boasted of regularly executing three solos in a given night at concerts in Manchester and of performing at Liverpool on a single evening a concerto on the violin by Rode, one on the violoncello by Cervetto, and a third on the piano by Kalkbrenner.

Cudmore remained the leader of the Gentlemen's Concerts at Manchester for some years and was occasionally leader at Liverpool. In 1823 he was living at No 26, Brazen-nose St, in Manchester. He died in his lodgings in Wilton Street, Oxford Road, Manchester, on 29 December 1840, leaving a widow named Mary and a family which included a child who had been baptized at St Giles in the Fields, London, in 1814.

His best musical composition was the oratorio "The Martyr of Antioch," based on Milman's poem, selections from which were performed at Birmingham, Liverpool, and Manchester, and which was published by subscription. Six songs from his opera *Jeanie Graham, or the Year Forty-Five* (evidently never performed) were published about 1830. He also composed some concertos for his various instruments.

Cudworth, Mr [fl. c. 1675–1691], actor.

Mr Cudworth acted at the Smock Alley Theatre in Dublin from about 1675 to 1680, one of his parts being the title role in *Julius Caesar*. While in Dublin he also participated in a production of *Belphagor*, but his role is not known. By 20 November 1689 he was with the United Company at Drury Lane, acting Fearless in *The Widow Ranter*. In December 1690 he played Dingboy in *The Scowrers*, and sometime during the 1690–91 season he acted Captain Tilbury in *Madam Fickle*.

Cudworth, Mr [fl. 1794], violinist.

A Mr Cudworth was listed in 1794 in Doane's *Musical Directory* as a violinist, a member of the New Musical Fund, and as then living in Margaret Street, Cavendish Square.

Cue. See **KEW.**

Cuerton, Mr [fl. 1800–1804], dancer, whistler.

A Mr Cuerton made a single appearance at the end of the eighteenth century on 23 May 1800 at Covent Garden when he danced a hornpipe. No doubt he was the "sibilist," or whistler, who performed at Sadler's Wells in 1803 and at the Royal Circus on 28 November 1803, on the latter date whistling "several airs in an astonishing manner, particularly the grand Overture to Oscar and Malvina." On the same bill a Miss Cuerton, presumably his daughter, and a pupil to the dancer Cranfield, offered a hornpipe. At the Royal Circus again in October 1804, Cuerton, "in a variety of new and melodious cadences," whistled the favorite air of "Lullaby."

Cuiler. *See* CUYLER.

Culcup, the Misses [*fl. 1797*], *actresses.*
Two sisters named Culcup were actresses in the Richmond company in the summer of 1797. The nature and extent of their activity are unknown.

Culkin. *See* CALKIN.

Culver, Mr [*fl. 1772–1794*], *singer.*
A Mr Culver sang at Marylebone Gardens in the summer of 1772; he received a benefit there on 1 September and also sang an ode by Arnold in honor of the birthday of the Prince of Wales. Probably he was the same Mr Culver who was a bass (vocal) performer in the Handel Memorial Concerts at Westminster Abbey and the Pantheon in May and June 1784. In 1794 this Mr Culver, according to Doane's *Musical Directory*, lived in Aldersgate Street.

Cummerford. *See* COMERFORD.

Cundell. *See* CONDELL.

Cunisbo. *See* CONINGSBY.

Cunningham, [Thomas?] [*fl. 1795–1817?*], *actor.*
A Mr Cunningham was in the Richmond, Surrey, company during the summer of 1795. His roles are not furnished by the bills, nor is his first name, but it is conceivable that he was Thomas Cunningham the actor who was at Ennis in Ireland in 1790 and 1792, Kilkenny in 1791, Cork in 1792, and Galway and Crow Street, Dublin, in 1793. That Cunningham made his debut at Manchester (as from Dublin) on 25 May 1795 and his debut at Bath (again as from Dublin) on 7 May 1796. He was probably the "young actor, of the

name of Cunningham," who was "a very excellent addition to the old Company at Exeter," according to the *Monthly Mirror* of December 1795.

Was he the Cunningham who was settled down at Bristol during every season from 1796–97 through 1816–17 and who on 28 January 1798 married Miss Loder? She was perhaps Harriet, a daughter of John Loder, leader of the band at the Bristol Theatre. She was a singer and served in the Bristol company from before 1799 through 1816–17 (except for the 1804–5, 1806–7, 1810–11, and 1811–12 seasons). Those Bristol Cunninghams had five children, all of whom were on the Bath stage in the second decade of the nineteenth century: Miss Cunningham, Miss E. Cunningham, Miss F., Miss J., and a boy whose first name is also unknown.

Cunningham, W. [*fl. 1733–1754?*], *dancer, singer, actor.*
The first appearance in the bills of the name of "Young Cunningham" was opposite the character Fame in the masquelike afterpiece *The Judgment of Paris* at Drury Lane Theatre on 12 February 1733. He doubtless assisted at other performances, perhaps before as well as after this date, but the next time he was featured was on 31 March when he again represented Fame. On 7 May following he was Cupid in *Damon and Daphne*, and he was again Cupid in *Venus, Cupid, and Hymen* on 21 May.

Young Cunningham sang between the acts of *Sophonisba* at the new Covent Garden Theatre on 10 August and perhaps at other performances of that play during the short summer season at that house. He ended his introductory year with an appearance at Bartholomew Fair on 23 August when once again he was Cupid in *The Garden of Venus; or, The Triumphs of Love.*

Our subject was doubtless "Cunningham, from Drury Lane" who sang the part of

Kalib in *The Indian Emperor* at Goodman's Fields on 14 January 1734. He is shown in the Goodman's Fields bill for 4 November 1734 as one of the lowly Spirits in *The Necromancer*. His name did not occur again in the bills until the advertisement for the Goodman's Fields performance on 6 March 1735 when he played Mercury in the pantomime *Jupiter and Io*. At that point the Cunningham we have been following disappeared from London notice.

Nine years later, on 2 March 1744, at the seldom-used James Street Theatre in London "At the desire of the Hon. Bell Ara Moleck, and the worshipful Fraternity of Free-Masons," Cunningham "from Edinburgh" took a benefit. He sang the lead part of Macheath in *The Beggar's Opera*. At May Fair on 7 June 1744 he joined Charlotte Charke's little company and performed entr'acte turns of singing and dancing. He performed one of the masque characters which seemed to be his humble specialty, Neptune in the Dryden-Davenant version of *The Tempest* at Goodman's Fields on 15 April 1745. At the same house nearly a year later on 20 March 1746, he sang again between the acts, on the last night of the season. He sang between the acts of the play at the New Theatre, Bowling Green, Southwark, on 7 October 1746, was Mordecai in *The Harlot's Progress* there on 16 October, and sang there again on 20 and 27 October.

What shift he made to live between these meager commissions is not known. He may have been performing in the country; more likely he was in trade in London. No doubt many of his performances are unknown to us because of lost or uninformative bills. Yet it is clear that Cunningham was on the starveling fringes of the profession, and there he stayed despite his renewed efforts to stimulate interest in his talents by means of a self-induced benefit at the Haymarket on 27 November 1746. The benefit had been scheduled for the theatre in South-wark but had been shifted away because of a hue and cry in the newspapers and the Court Leets for the Borough of Southwark against "a pack of Strolling-Players, who by the Laws now in force are liable to be punished by His Majesty's Justices of the Peace as vagrants and vagabonds" and who had "lately infested the villages of Clapham, Stockwell and Borough of Southwark and other places in the County of Surrey . . ." They had "made several riots and . . . contracted several debts with His Majesty's liege subjects and [had] given out printed handbills and Tickets for several of their benefits."

Cunningham staged another benefit for himself at James Street on 1 April 1747, when *Patie and Roger; or, The Gentle Shepherd* was played. He sang "Select Songs." In September 1747 he was at Southwark Fair, dancing in the booth of Yeates Junior and Mrs Warner. On 24 August 1748 he was singing and dancing between the acts of the drolls at Bartholomew Fair at "Hussey's Great Theatrical Booth facing the Hospital Gate." On 7 September he was with the Yeateses and Warner at Southwark Fair as Sir John Lovewell in *The Fair Maid of the West*. These are the last notices we have of Cunningham unless he was the performer of that name who was in the Smock Alley company at Dublin in 1752–53 and 1753–54. In the latter season a Mrs Cunningham also acted there.

"Cuochetina, La." *See* **GABRIELLI, CATERINA.**

Cuper. *See also* **COOPER.**

Cuper, Boyder ⟨*fl. c. 1691*⟩, *proprietor.*

About 1691 or earlier Boyder Cuper rented a narrow strip of land surrounded by water courses in Lambeth near where Waterloo Station stands today. He laid out walks, arbors, and bowling greens and decorated his pleasure gardens with statuary that had previously stood at Arundel House before its destruction. A waterside tavern called The Feathers was connected with Cuper's grounds, and the trumpeter Matthias Shore's floating palace of entertainment, called by the wits "Shore's Folly," later docked near Cuper's (or, waggishly, "Cupid's") stairs.

By 1717 John Cuper, probably Boyder's son, was the proprietor of the gardens, and in that year he sold the statuary for £75. Except for the entertainment offered on Shore's barge, Cuper's Gardens during the late seventeenth and early eighteenth centuries may not have included performances by musicians, though these were common to pleasure gardens later.

The control of the gardens passed on to others in time, notably Ephraim Evans and his wife, but the pleasure spot was still called Cuper's Gardens in the 1750s.

Cuper, John [fl. 1717], *proprietor.* *See* **CUPER, BOYDER.**

Cupid. *See* **CUBITT, WILLIAM.**

"Cupid." *See* **HALLET, BENJAMIN.**

Curco, Mr [fl. 1687–1700], *singer.* References in contemporary documents to Courco, Cuckow, and Curkaw are probably all to the singer Mr Curco. As of 5 July 1687 he was one of the Gregorians at the Chapel Royal earning £50 yearly, and in the summers of 1687 and 1688 he attended at the Court at Windsor. He sang in a performance of *Macbeth* at either Drury Lane or Dorset Garden late in 1694 (at the earliest), and as part of Betterton's company at Lincoln's Inn Fields he sang in *Lover's Luck* in December 1695. About 1700 was printed a song by John Eccles, *The Pow'r of Wine*, which, according to the British Museum *Catalogue of Printed Music*, was sung by Messrs Gouge, Courco, and

Spalding in *The Morose Reformer*—a play otherwise unknown.

Curioni, Rosa [fl. 1754–1762], *singer.*
The Italian singer Signora Rosa Curioni made her debut at London, as *seconda donna* in the Opera, singing the role of Plisthenes in *L'Ipermestra* at the King's Theatre on 9 November 1754. The offering was repeated a number of times during the season, including the night of Curioni's benefit on 10 April 1755.

Signora Curioni's name appeared in the bills for the role of Lysander in the first performance of Garrick's *The Fairies*, taken from *A Midsummer Night's Dream*, at Drury Lane on 3 February 1755, but the manuscript diary of the prompter Cross and the first edition of the text place Guadagni in the role. *The Fairies* was performed at Drury Lane a number of times in that and the subsequent season. Signora Curioni played the male role of Ferdinand in a musical version of *The Tempest* when it was produced as "a New English Opera" at Drury Lane on 11 February 1756 and five other times that season. According to Dean (*Handel's Dramatic Oratorios and Masques*), she probably sang in *Judas Maccabaeus* in 1755 or 1756 and in *Jeptha* in 1756.

Signora Curioni had returned to Venice by 1757. She was back at London for the opera season of 1761–62 when at the King's Theatre she sang Gandartes in *Alessandro nell' Indie*, the Conte della Roca in *Il mercato di Malmantile*, and the song "Sperai vicino al lido," in a concert for the benefit of the Fund for Decay'd Musicians on 11 May 1762.

Curkaw. *See* **CURCO.**

Curona. *See* **CUZZONI.**

Currer, Elizabeth [fl. 1673–1743?], *actress.*

The wayward orthography of Restoration times turned Elizabeth Currer's surname into Carrier, Corar, Corer, Correr, Corror, Coror, Currar, Currier, and Curryer. She was apparently from Ireland and she became a member of the Duke's Company at the Dorset Garden Theatre in London as early as 1673–74. Her first recorded role was the small part of Alcinda in *The Conquest of China* on 28 May 1675. Between then and the union of the two patent companies in 1682 Mrs Currer played Betty Frisque in *The Country Wit*, Asteria in *Ibrahim*, Clarinda in *The Virtuoso*, Mrs Hadland in *The Counterfeit Bridegroom*, Lady Fancy in *Sir Patient Fancy*, Madame Tricklove in *Squire Oldsapp*, Marcella in *The Feign'd Curtizans*, Jenny Wheedle in *The Virtuous Wife*, the Queen in *The Loyal General*, Lady Eleanor Butler in *The Misery of Civil War*, Ariadne in *2 The Rover*, Isabella in *The False Count*, Eugenia in *The London Cuckolds*, Lady Medler in *Mr Turbulent*, Aquilina in *Venice Preserv'd*, Diana in *The City Heiress*, possibly Lady Desbro in *The Roundheads*, and a part in *Like Father, Like Son*. Over the years she became one of the company's most popular speakers of prologues and epilogues and a specialist in playing breeches parts and bawds.

During these years few references were made to Elizabeth Currer beyond the parts she played, but on 25 May 1676 she was for some reason ordered arrested by the Lord Chamberlain, and in March 1679 she spoke the prologue to *The Feign'd Curtizans* which Aphra Behn wrote for her:

Who says this Age a Reformation wants,
When Betty Currer's Lovers all turn
*   Saints?*
In vain, alas, I flatter, swear, and vow,
You'll scarce do any thing for Charity
*   now:*
Yet I am handsom still, still young and
*   mad,*
Can wheedle, lye, dissemble, jilt—egad,
As well and artfully as e'er I did;

Yet not one Conquest can I gain or
*   hope . . .*

Mrs Behn then caused her to say, "Who wou'd have thought such hellish Times to have seen, / When I shou'd be neglected at Eighteen?"—that is, because of new legal and church regulations. It is not likely that Betty Currer was anywhere near 18 when she spoke this, so the age reference should not be taken literally. By 1679 she was probably in her mid-twenties.

Mrs Currer joined the United Company in 1682, but between early 1685 and the fall of 1689 no roles are known for her in London. Possibly she followed the advice in the *Satyr on the Players* (c. 1684):

Currer 'tis time thou wert to Ireland gone
Thy utmost Rate is here but half a
*   Crown*
Ask Turner if thou art not fulsom
*   grown—*

During the seasons in which she did act with the United Company, she played Mrs Featly in *Dame Dobson*, Sylvia in *The Atheist*, Isabella in *A Duke and No Duke*, the title role in *The Widow Ranter*, and (the last known role for her, in 1690–91) the title part in *Madam Fickle*. The last specifically dated reference to her in the Restoration period was on 8 March 1690 when she was to attend a hearing because of a "difference between Mr Killigrew & Mrs Currer."

There is a slim chance that the Mrs Carrier who played the Queen of Hungary in Charlotte Charke's unpublished "Tit for Tat" on 1 February 1743 at Punch's Theatre in James Street was Elizabeth Currer, for she was described as "the celebrated Actress tho' now almost out of date . . ." Mrs Currer would have been out of date indeed by 1743—probably in her nineties—but it would have been just like crazy Charlotte to dig up such a relic from the past.

Currier. *See* CURRER *and* CURRYER.

Curry, Mr (*fl.* *1708–1716*), box-keeper.

Mr Curry was one of the front box-keepers at the Queen's Theatre in the Haymarket, his salary as of 8 March 1708 being 4*s.* daily. On 15 December 1716 at a performance of *Cleartes* he was recorded as having taken in £2 8*s.*

Curryer. *See also* **CURRER.**

Curryer, Mr (*fl.* *1744–1747*), office keeper.

A Mr Curryer was a pit office keeper at Drury Lane from 1744–45 through 1746–47; in each of his three seasons he shared benefits with other house servants.

Curtal or **Curtat.** *See* **CURTET.**

Curteen, Mr (*fl.* *1772–1795*), box-keeper.

Mr Curteen was a boxkeeper at Covent Garden Theatre at least from 1772–73 through 1794–95, at a salary of 12*s.* per week.

Curten, Miss (*fl.* *1791–1795*), house servant? performer?

In 1791–92 a Miss Curten, sometimes Kerton or Curtin, was on the Drury Lane list at £1 10*s.* per week. In 1793–94 and 1794–95, a woman by the name of Kerton, variously Miss or Mrs, was at Covent Garden at £1 5*s.* per week as a house servant or possibly as a performer, although her name appeared on no bills. It may be that all the spellings refer to one person, that her name was, after all, properly spelled "Curteen," and that she was related to the Covent Garden boxkeeper of that name.

Curtet, Pierre (*fl.* *1762–1774*), dancer.

Pierre Curtet made his first advertised appearance on the London stage dancing as one of the Bride's Men in *The Witches* at Drury Lane on 23 November 1762. Pre-sumably he worked the rest of that season at the same theatre as a member of the dancing ensemble. In 1763–64 he went off to Covent Garden where he remained for at least ten years through 1773–74 as a minor dancer. His name occasionally occurred in the bills for specific pieces, as an Infernal in *Perseus and Andromeda* (14 January 1764), a minuet with Miss Barrowby (22 May 1765), Pan in *The Royal Chace* (28 October 1765), dancing in *Harlequin Doctor Faustus* (18 November 1766), and the new ballet *The Wapping Landlady* (27 April 1767).

Curtet's salary in 1767–68 was five shillings per day. For a minor figure he did well at his shared benefits, taking for himself £22 10*s.* 6*d.* on 9 May 1767, £26 3*s.* on 25 May 1768, £36 6*s.* on 17 May 1769, £11 12*s.* on 25 May 1770, £44 11*s.* on 16 May 1772, £42 13*s.* 6*d.* on 26 May 1773, and £56 6*s.* for his final benefit on 18 May 1774. His name sometimes appeared as "Curtat" or "Curtal," but in a letter sent to Colman by a group of Covent Garden performers on 5 November 1768, he signed as "Pierre Curtet."

Curties, Mr (*fl.* *1794–1801*), actor, singer.

A Master Curties appeared in that favorite introductory role for young actors, Prince Edward in *Richard III*, at Covent Garden on 15 October 1794. He was given 12*s.* per week but performed no other named parts during the rest of the season. He was raised to 15*s.* per week in 1795–96, playing Fleance in *Macbeth* on opening night, 14 September 1795, and thereafter and helping to fill up crowds in such musical spectacles as O'Keeffe's new comic opera *The Lad of the Hills.*

After September 1796 he appeared as Mr Curties. His salary was raised to £1 per week in 1796–97, a season in which he was confined to nameless servants, waiters, and Irish peasants. He opened 1798–99 singing, with numerous others, Shield's "Dirge" in

Act V of *Hamlet* and continued for the rest of the season to earn his salary of £1 anonymously in choruses and crowds. His salary was once again raised (to £1 10*s*.) in 1799–1800 but his professional condition did not much improve, though he was given his old part of Fleance on 30 September and twice more during the season. Curties was carried again on the company books during 1800–1801, but after that the record is mute.

Curtin. *See* **CURTEEN.**

Curtis. *See* **CORTES.**

Curtz, Mlle [*fl.* 1769–1776], *dancer.* Mademoiselle Curtz (sometime Curz) was a dancer at the King's Theatre in 1769–70 and 1771–72 and possibly in 1770–71. Her name is found, however, only twice on the bills: for dancing in the opera *Il disertore* on 19 May 1770 and in a new ballet, *La Clauchette*, with Signora Crespi and others, on 11 June 1772. In a letter to Mr Greville on 8 December 1775, the great ballet master Noverre wrote that "La Curtz who is a pretty woman and by consequence inconsistent, has just let herself win the cavaliers of Turin, they have engaged her for the carnival of '76."

Cusanino. *See* **CAPELLETTI.**

Cushing, John 1719–1790, *actor.* Although his career on the London stage spanned some 41 years, almost all that is known about John Cushing consists of the list of numerous parts of every variety which he performed at the theatres and fairs. He was probably the actor of the name who was a strolling player in Wales in the earlier part of 1741. Cushing's first appearance in London was on 4 August 1741 when he played a witch in a production of the pantomime *Harlequin Sorcerer* at Lee and Woodward's booth, near the Turnpike, during the Tottenham Court Fair. At that time his name appeared in the advertisements as "Cushion." In the following season he was a member of a transient company which gave occasional performances at the James Street Theatre; billed now as "Mr Cushing," he was advertised on 7 April 1742 for the title role in *The Lying Valet*, a part which was to remain his specialty for many years.

Cushing appeared occasionally at the various London fairs over the next several years. On 9 May 1743 he acted Harlequin in *Trick Upon Trick* in Yeates, Warner, and Rosomon's booth in the upper end of Little Brookfield, at the Mile End Fair. In this performance his wife was first noticed in London, playing Colombine. For some years their theatrical careers were to be intertwined, with their names appearing together in the casts of innumerable pieces, especially under the management of the Hallams in the 1740s. On 1 May 1743, in a booth which he operated in partnership with Middleton at the May Fair, Cushing produced *The Wandering Prince of Troy* and *Le Marriage de Pesant*, pieces in which, no doubt, he and his wife performed. At the Southwark Fair on 8 September 1743 Cushing performed Momford to Mrs Cushing's Arabella in *The Blind Beggar of Bethnal Green.*

In 1744–45 the Cushings joined the Hallam company at the theatre in Goodman's Fields. He made his first appearance there as Sir George in *The Busy Body* on 4 December 1744, the day after Mrs. Cushing had first appeared as Polly in *The Beggar's Opera.* For several years they both performed a series of capital roles of young heroes and heroines suitable to their ages. (Cushing at this time was 25, and his wife presumably was about the same age.) In his first season Cushing acted Colonel Fainwell in *A Bold Stroke for a Wife* on 10 December 1741, the title role in *George Barnwell* (with Mrs Cushing as Millwood) on 11 December, Sharp in *The Lying Valet* on 12 December, Plume in *The Recruiting*

Officer (with Mrs Cushing as Melinda) and Harlequin in *The Amorous Sportsman* on 26 December, Ventoso in *The Tempest* (with Mrs Cushing as Dorinda) on 14 February 1745, Clerimont in *The Miser* (with Mrs Cushing as Wheedle) on 7 March, and the title role in *Richard III* for his benefit on 18 March.

In the following season, 1745–46, at Goodman's Fields, Cushing acted no fewer than 34 roles, suggesting an extensive schooling in the provinces. Most of them, if they had been performed at one of the patent houses, would have established him as a major actor. They included Charles IX in *The Massacre of Paris*, the title role in *The Mock Doctor*, Young Wou'dbe in *The Twin Rivals*, Sharp in *The Lying Valet*, Archer in *The Stratagem*, Fainwell in *A Bold Stroke for a Wife*, Sir George in *The Busy Body*, Silvio in *The Humours of Purgatory*, Belmour in *The Old Bachelor*, Butler in *The Drummer*, Macheath in *The Beggar's Opera*, George Barnwell in *The London Apprentice*, Torrismond in *The Spanish Fryar,* Horatio in *Hamlet*, Blandford in *Oroonoko*, Prince Hal in *1 Henry IV*, Ventoso in *The Tempest*, Hastings in *Jane Shore*, Juba in *Cato*, Juan in *Rule a Wife and Have a Wife*, the title role in *The Earl of Essex*, Richmond in *Richard III*, James IV in *Perkin Warbeck*, Clerimont in *The Miser*, the title role in *The Royal Merchant*, Plume in *The Recruiting Officer*, Castalio in *The Orphan*, Octavio in *She Wou'd and She Wou'd Not*, Rovewell in *The Fair Quaker*, Reynard in *Tunbridge Walks*, Courtwell in *A Woman is a Riddle*, Campley in *The Funeral*, and Valentine in *Love for Love*. For his benefit on 10 May 1746 (when he and his wife lived at No 3, Lambeth Street), he acted Tom in *The Conscious Lovers* and she acted Phyllis. At Bartholomew Fair on 25 August 1746 they played Harlequin and Colombine in *Harlequin Incendiary*. (For the rest of his wife's career, see her entry.)

With similar fortitude and flexibility,

Cushing was again at Goodman's Fields in 1746–47 and was still living at No 3, Lambeth Street. Before the season he also acted Lopez in *The Fate of Villainy* in Warner's booth at Southwark Fair on 8 September 1746, Castalio at the New Wells, May Fair, on 6 October, and the Miser, Archer, and Prince Hal at Southwark on 7, 16, and 20 October, respectively. In the following summer, Cushing was a member of the Haymarket company, which performed Foote's *The Diversions of a Morning*, first on 22 April 1747 and on numerous occasions thereafter.

Cushing's association with Foote continued into the fall of 1747 when he acted Wagtail in *Foote's Tea*, the bill for which at Covent Garden on 11 November marked the beginning of his long stay at this patent house. In that season, however, he acted only a few other roles there: Fribble in *Miss in Her Teens* on 14 January 1748, Maiden in *Tunbridge Walks* on 8 March, a character in *The Muses' Looking-Glass* on 14 March, and Dr Orator in *The Author's Farce* on 28 March. On 30 March he played Archer and Fribble at the Haymarket and on 4 April Plume at the New Wells, Clerkenwell, the latter again with the Hallam company.

After engagements at Richmond and at the Jacob's Wells Theatre at Bristol in the summer of 1748, Cushing took up a full-time situation at Covent Garden in September 1748. His first role of the season, however, was a portent of the significantly lower position he was to hold in this metropolitan house. Whereas previously he had been seen in the leading role of Plume when he appeared in *The Recruiting Officer* at Covent Garden on 23 September 1748, he now played one of the recruits, having given way to Ryan in the main part. That night Cushing also acted his familiar role of the valet in *The Lying Valet*. Several days later, on 26 September, instead of Macheath he played Filch in *The Beggar's Opera*. So it continued throughout the season: the Gentleman Usher in *King Lear*, Pistol in *The Merry Wives of Windsor*, Sir Joseph in *The Old Bachelor*, Lucio in *Measure for Measure*, Varole in *The Relapse*, the First Carrier in *1 Henry IV*, Abel in *The Committee*, Poins in *2 Henry IV*, Young Clincher and Dicky in *The Constant Couple*, Smirk in *The Man of Mode*, and Guilford in *Henry VIII*. He did perform the featured role in *The Busy Body* on 27 October, Harlequin in *The Emperor of the Moon* on 26 December, and Fribble in *Miss in her Teens* for his benefit, shared with Anderson and Delagarde on 19 April 1749. In the following summer Cushing operated his own booth at Bartholomew Fair, "facing the King's Head, Smithfield," where on 23–26 and 28 August he produced *King John*, interspersed with a comic piece called *The Adventures of Sir Lubberly Lackbrains, and his Man Blunderbuss,* playing Sir Lubberly in the latter. For his own benefit at Southwark Fair on 22 September 1749, Cushing acted the Earl of Essex and Fribble.

Returning to Covent Garden in 1749–50, Cushing played Osric in *Hamlet* on 27 September. He was paid 10s. on 29 September for two days, and on 6 October his salary was raised 10s. per week, presumably providing him with wages of £2 for a six-day week. His wife, now engaged for the first time at Covent Garden, was receiving 15s. per week. In that season he augmented his repertory of minor roles with Tressel in *Richard III*, Roderigo in *Othello*, Brisk in *The Double Dealer*, Meggot in *The Suspicious Husband*, Roger in *The London Cuckolds*, Finder in *The Double Gallant*, Sancho in *Love Makes a Man*, Gardener in *The Drummer*, Balthazar in *Romeo and Juliet*, and Archer in *A Cure for a Scold*. His share of benefit tickets on 17 April 1750 amounted to £20 17s.

In the circumstances of a very serviceable journeyman actor, Cushing remained at Covent Garden for another 31 years, at a constant salary of 6s. 8d. per day, or £2 per

week. In his last season, 1781–82, his repertoire still consisted of some of the familiar roles he had played throughout much of his career: Verges in *Much Ado About Nothing*, Pistol in *The Merry Wives of Windsor*, a character in *The Rehearsal*, Mother's Ghost in *The What D'Ye Call It*, and (for his last performance on 28 May 1782) Whisper in *The Busy Body*.

According to a notice in the *European Magazine* (November 1790), John Cushing died at Liverpool in October 1790, at the age of 71. His wife, who did not act at Covent Garden after 1751–52, presumably had died before him.

In addition to the roles mentioned above, an incomplete list of Cushing's numerous roles at Covent Garden would include: Petulant in *The Way of the World*, Nettle in *The What D'Ye Call It*, Petit in *The Inconstant*, a witch in *Macbeth*, Tibalt in *Romeo and Juliet*, Lory in *The Relapse*, Titus in *Coriolanus*, Alcander in *Oedipus*, a servant in *Julius Caesar*, Heli in *The Mourning Bride*, Fabian in *The Fatal Marriage*, Amorous in *The Counterfeit Heiress*, Dapper in *The Citizen*, Simon in *The Apprentice*, a waiter in *The Oxonian in Town*, Blunt in *George Barnwell*, an unspecified part in the first performance of Goldsmith's *The Good Natur'd Man* on 29 January 1768, William in *The Way to Keep Him*, Lucianus in *Hamlet*, Thrift in *The Cheats of Scapin*, Biondello in *Catharine and Petruchio*, Charino in *Love Makes a Man*, Francis in *1 Henry IV*, Lory in *A Man of Quality*, and Trapland in *Love for Love*. Despite his 41 years on the stage, no portrait or engraving of him is known to exist.

Cushing, Mrs John [*fl.* 1743–1751], *actress, singer.*

As in the case of her husband, about all that is known of the career of Mrs John Cushing on the London stage is a list of her many roles. Her first noted appearance was as Colombine, with her husband as Harlequin, in a performance of *Trick Upon Trick* at the Yeates, Warner, and Rosomon booth in the upper end of Little Brookfield, at the Mile End Fair on 9 May 1743. On 8 September of that year she acted Arabella to her husband's Momford in *The Blind Beggar of Bethnal Green* at the Southwark Fair.

With her husband, Mrs Cushing joined the Hallam company at the theatre in Goodman's Fields in 1744–45, acting in that season Polly in *The Beggar's Opera* on 3 December, Millwood in *George Barnwell* on 11 December, Melinda in *The Recruiting Officer* on 26 December, Dorinda in *The Tempest* on 14 February, and Wheedle in *The Miser* on 7 March. At Goodman's Fields in 1745–46 she added Lady Grace in *The Provok'd Husband*, Melissa in *The Lying Valet*, Gipsey in *The Stratagem*, Constantia in *The Humours of Purgatory*, Beatrice in *The Debauchees*, Laetitia in *The Old Bachelor*, Teresa in *The Spanish Fryar*, the Player Queen in *Hamlet*, Lucia in *Cato*, the Countess of Nottingham in *The Earl of Essex*, Jaqueline in *The Royal Merchant*, Florella in *The Orphan*, Flora in *She Wou'd and She Wou'd Not*, Arabella in *The Fair Quaker*, Belinda in *Tunbridge Walks*, Clarinda in *A Woman is a Riddle*, Harriet in *The Funeral*, Mrs Frail in *Love for Love*, and for her benefit on 10 March 1746, Phyllis in *The Conscious Lovers*. At Bartholomew Fair that summer she played Colombine in *Harlequin Incendiary* on 25 August 1746 in Warner and Fawkes's booth, and at Southwark Fair on 8 September she again played Colombine in *The Imprisonment of Harlequin*. At the New Wells, May Fair, she acted Monimia in *The Orphan* on 6 October, and at the new theatre in Southwark she played Mrs Sullen in *The Stratagem* on 16 October 1746.

Mrs Cushing's new roles at Goodman's Fields in 1746–47 were: Mrs Clearaccount in *The Twin Rivals*, Mariana in *The Miser*, Elvira in *Love Makes a Man*, Ophelia in *Hamlet*, Imoinda in *Oroonoko*, Lady Fanciful in *The Provok'd Wife*, Berintha in *The Relapse*, Mistress Ford in *The Merry Wives of Windsor*, Amphitrite in *The Tempest*, Regan in *King Lear*, a part in *The Battle of Poictiers*, Flora in *The Wonder*, and Tag in *Miss in her Teens*. On 17 December 1746 she also played the boy's role of Edward V in *Richard III*, a part which suggests tender age and slight body.

In the summer of 1748 she acted with her husband at Richmond and at the Jacob's Wells Theatre, Bristol. She was not to be found with him as a member of the Covent Garden company in 1748–49, but she acted occasionally that season at the fairs and minor theatres. At the New Wells, Lemon Street, she played Arabella in *The Committee* on 27 February 1749, for the benefit of Lewis Hallam. On 29 April and 29 May she sang Lucie in *L'Opéra du gueux,* a French translation of *The Beggar's Opera* which was performed at the Haymarket by a company of "Anti-Gallic" players. Her other performances included Constance in *King John* on 23 August at a booth operated by her husband during Bartholomew Fair and Rutland in *The Unhappy Favourite* at Southwark Fair on 22 September.

In 1749–50 Mrs Cushing was engaged at Covent Garden at a salary of 15s. per week; she made her first appearance at that theatre on 29 September as Mrs Motherly in *The Provok'd Husband*. This was the only role for which her name appeared in the bills that season, but no doubt she acted other supernumerary parts. In the following season her name was on the bills only for the First Lady in *Rule a Wife* on 6 February 1751. She played Dolly Trull in *The Beggar's Opera* at the beginning of the next season on 27 and 30 September 1751 and on the latter date also appeared as one of the Amazons in the afterpiece *Perseus and Andromeda*. When both pieces were repeated on 2 October her name was still on the bills, but it was omitted from both casts when they were given again on 12 October 1751. Presumably she gave up the stage at this point or perhaps died. See also the entry for her husband, John Cushing (1719–1790).

Cushion. *See* CUSHING.

Cussans, Mrs, later Mrs Higginson and Mrs Egerson [*fl.* 1797–1800], *actress.*

An actress who had performed previously in the provinces under the name of Mrs Cussans made her first appearance at Covent Garden, billed as "A Young Lady," in the role of Julia in *The Mysteries of the Castle* on 11 November 1799. No doubt she was the Mrs Cussans who had an affair with the Duke of Bedford in 1797, according to the *Monthly Mirror* (September 1797). The *European Magazine* identified her as a Mrs Higginson, who had acted at Richmond, Cheltenham, and Birmingham under the name of Cussans. Several days earlier *The Oracle*, 7 November 1799, had announced "Mrs Cussans, so well known in the World of Gallantry, and who is shortly to appear at Covent Garden, has changed her name to Higginson." Still billed as "A Young Lady," however, she acted Juliet for her second appearance on 18 November 1799. The *Monthly Mirror* (November 1799), which called her "Mrs Cussans, or Mrs Higginson, or Mrs —— any body, her name is Legion, for they are many," complained that she had been "permitted to lisp out" the important character of Juliet, and commented further on her talent and person:

As far as a pretty face and a pleasing figure are concerned in the business of acting, we have seen few ladies so agreeably gifted as Mrs Cussans; nor does she appear to be materially deficient of sense; but, to the higher excellencies of the art—voice, dignity, feeling, and spirit, her pretensions are feeble in the extreme.

In the earlier part of *Juliet* . . . the *masquerade*, and the garden scenes, there was not the slightest room for censure—the text

was accurately given, the emphasis rightly placed, and the purpose of the poet completely answered: but, when she should have awakened the sensibilities of the audience, by piercing exclamations of distress, or animated bursts of tender affection, on being told of her husband's *banishment*—or when the situation required vehemence of gesture or rapidity of utterance, it was still simply correct, and uniformly torpid—cold, impotent, flat, tedious, wearisome, and heavy.

After another performance in *The Mysteries of the Castle* on 3 February 1800, she played but once more, Julia in *The Rivals*, for her own benefit on 20 May 1800, curiously enough now appearing under the name of Mrs Egerson. There was an overflow crowd which brought her receipts of £263 5s., and tickets could be had of her at No 79, Lower Gower Street, Bedford Square. (The ratepayer at her address was a person named Egerson.) "To whatever cause it might be owing," reported *The Dramatic Censor* (1800), "probably to her excessive modesty, she spoke in so low a key, that it was almost impossible to understand her part of the dialogue." She seems not to have performed again at London under any of her known names. Perhaps she was related to the eccentric singer and actor, John P. Cussans.

Cussans, John P., sometimes William [*fl.* 1797–1803], *actor, singer.*

Mr Cussans acted the role of Jeremy Sneak ("with an old new song") in a single performance of *The Mayor of Garratt* at the Haymarket on 26 March 1798. About this time the song "When I was a lad" was published as sung by him at the Royal Circus and Sadler's Wells. He was no doubt the colorful eccentric noticed in *The Thespian Dictionary* of 1805:

CUSSANS, (Mr.) has been an occasional actor in characters of low humour, but seems never to have had a permanent engagement at a theatre; his flighty disposition being ill calculated for study and regularity. He was a member of the law, and possessed of a considerable fortune, which he spent—at present he has a decent income, which was left him by a relation, and which is regularly paid to him, according to the directions of the will, at half a guinea per day. His whimsical adventures are so truly romantic and ridiculous that they exceed credibility.

His "whimsical adventures" included disguising himself as a street ballader, serving for three months as a servant in a public house to win a wager, riding an ass many miles a day "for his diversion," and falling into silences for long periods of time and deigning to answer questions with nods and

other signs. Notwithstanding such eccentricities and the fact that he was often referred to as "Mad Cussans," it was reported that Cussans was "by no means deficient in understanding, for, when he pleases he can evince much rationality and learning."

In his *Memoirs of Robert William Elliston* (1844), George Raymond stated that an account of "The insane exploits of Cussans would occupy a volume," and he described Cussans' presiding over antic improvisations called "Fortune's Wheel" at a club called the "Court of Comus" in Wych Street. Such clubs, open to anyone who would pay sixpence, were frequented "chiefly by a class of persons who had but one plan in life, which was, to give over work the first moment they had earned enough to get drunk for the remainder of the week."

According to Raymond, who was writing some 50 years after the times, Cussans was "a considerable actor," who played frequently at Sadler's Wells in the 1790s, usually in the role of Jeremy Sneak in *The Mayor of Garratt*. Cussans was "much celebrated" for his characteristic song of "Oh, Poor Robinson Crusoe," which was often called back for encores three or four times in an evening. The song was written by Cussans himself, and the words and music were published in 1797 by E. Bates, Blackfriar's Road. The words were also later printed in *The Universal Songster* in 1825.

Confusion exists over this eccentric's pedigree and Christian names. He was described variously as a native of Barbados, the son of an opulent West Indian, and the reputed natural son of Lord Scarborough. Raymond claimed that Cussans was educated at Marylebone School. His Christian name was given as William by J. T. Smith, the editor of *Nollekens and His Times* (1828) and by John Green in *Evan's Music and Supper Rooms, Covent Garden* (1866). A satirical colored engraving in the British Museum, drawn "from Life by R. Newton," is entitled "The Celebrated M^r

TL CELEBRATED Mr J^{no} CUSSANS.

By permission of the Trustees of the British Museum

JOHN CUSSANS
by Newton

J^{no} Cussans," and depicts him as a waiter.

In 1802 Cussans brought his singularities to Jamaica in the West Indies, where advertisements for 4 March (which also provided his initials) announced his programs of songs and passages from approved authors as to be presented at the Kingston Theatre. He offered similar entertainments in Jamaica regularly throughout 1803. Lady Nugent, in her *Journal* of 25 February 1803 recorded going with her family in the evening to Spanish Town to see "Mr Cussan's exhibition":

It was a performance something in the style of Dibdin. We could not help laughing at the nonsense; but, at the same time, it made me melancholy to think, that the folly and extravagance of a person who had been brought up as a gentleman, and who is really of a respectable family, should compel him to expose himself in that way to the public. The audience were of all colours and descriptions; blacks, browns, Jews, and whites.

Accounts of Cussans's death are also contradictory. According to Raymond, "brandy was his death, and water his grave, for he died on his voyage to a softer climate, and was buried in the deep." In *Nollekens and his Times*, it was reported that Cussans had remained in "Barbadoes"—presumably an inclusive term for the West Indies—for about three years, "after which, on his return to England, he died," but the syntax does not make clear whether he died during the return voyage or in England.

The Mrs Cussans who acted at Richmond, Surrey, and then at Covent Garden Theatre in 1799–1800 under the names of both Mrs Higginson and Mrs Egerson was perhaps at one time his wife or was otherwise related.

Cussans, William. *See* CUSSANS, JOHN P.

Custonelli, Signora [*fl. 1752*], *singer.*
Signora Custonelli, "just arrived from Italy," sang some serious pieces in *The Old Woman's Oratory* performed by "Mrs Midnight" (Christopher Smart) and company at the Haymarket on 9 May 1752 and probably again on 13 May. "Custonelli" may have been a pseudonym.

Custos. *See* COUSTOS.

Cuthbert, Mr [*fl. 1743–1755*], *actor.*
Mr and Mrs Cuthbert acted at the Yeates-Warner-Rosoman booth at Tottenham Court on 4 August 1743, the fare being a droll, taken from *Richard III*, "Into which will be introduc'd an exact Representation of the Battle of Dettingen, intermix'd with a Comedy call'd *The Wanton Trick; or, All Alive and Merry*." On 23 August they were with the same managers at Bartholomew Fair in the cast of *The Cruel Uncle*.

Mrs Cuthbert, apparently without her husband, played Lady Betty in *The Careless Husband* at the playhouse in James Street on 10 December 1744, and Mr Cuthbert, apparently without his wife, played Lord Worthy in *The Fair Maid of the West* on 7 September 1748 at the Lee-Yeates-Warner Southwark Fair booth. The Cuthberts were together again on 2 October 1755 at Widow Yeates's "Large Theatrical BARN" in Croydon, playing in *A Bold Stroke for a Wife*, he acting Obadiah Prim and she Betty.

Cuthbert, Mrs [*fl. 1708–1726*], *dresser.*
Mrs Cuthbert was one of the women dressers at the Queen's Theatre in the Haymarket as of 8 March 1708 when she was earning 5s. daily. She was doubtless the same Mrs Cuthbert who was paid £5 19s. 4d. on 2 March 1726 by John Rich at Lincoln's Inn Fields for making clothes for Mrs Younger in "Proserpine"—possibly an error for *Apollo and Daphne* (which had opened on 14 January with Mrs Younger as Colombine), since *The Rape of Proserpine* was not performed until a year later.

Cuthbert, Mrs _(fl. 1743–1755)_, actress. See CUTHBERT, MR.

Cuthbert, Thomas _d. 1737, violinist, copyist._

On 5 March 1703 Thomas Cuthbert and Mr Latour performed on the violin and lute respectively at a concert in the Great Dancing Room, Mincing Lane, Fenchurch Street. In April and May 1711 Cuthbert had benefit concerts at Stationers' Hall, and on 21 July that year he and Teno undertook a concert at Richmond Wells. On 14 May 1712 he shared a benefit concert at Stationers' Hall with Smith. Cuthbert became attached to the Drury Lane company at some point, perhaps as a violinist in the band, but certainly as a music copyist, for several bills have survived which show payments to him for copying out music for _Oroonoko, The Comical Lovers,_ and _Macbeth._ For this work he was paid £2 3s., probably about 1714 or 1715. Two of Cuthbert's dated bills for writing out the music for dances were drawn up on 24 October 1715 and 11 April 1716.

On 23 August 1737 Thomas Cuthbert died at Kentish Town, described as "an eminent Performer on the Violin" and one of the senior musicians in ordinary in the King's Musick.

Cutler, James _(fl. 1678–1683)_, singer.

James Cutler was a boy singer under John Blow in the mid-1670s, but by 3 July 1678 his voice had broken and he was granted clothes as a former Chapel boy. Blow was still providing for him on 28 July 1683, the last mention of Cutler in the Lord Chamberlain's accounts.

Cutting, Master _b. 1718, singer._

On 28 November 1732 "Master Cuttin, a Youth of 14 Years of Age, who never appear'd on any Stage before," sang at the Goodman's Fields Theatre. He made several appearances during the 1732–33 season, being noted as a student of Eversman on the bill for 30 November 1732. His name was not mentioned in 1733–34, but he reappeared as "Young Mr Cutting" and sang in Italian at Goodman's Fields on 6 May 1735.

Cuyler, Margaret, later Mrs Dominic Rice _1758–1814, actress._

Most of the details of the early life of Mrs Margaret Cuyler (b. 1758) a professional beauty and adventuress who turned actress in 1777, are furnished by the 1790 and 1792 editions of _The Secret History of the Green Room._ Some of these data are as suspect as they are vivid. At least some of the principal incidents recounted seem, nevertheless, to have occurred, though they are almost hidden under fictive embellishment.

According to that account, Mrs Cuyler was the daughter of a gentleman (whose name was not furnished) of great inherited wealth. She was born while her father was a captain in the 55th Regiment of Foot. His last commission was as Lieutenant-Colonel of the 18th, or Royal Irish, Regiment, from which he had been for some time retired when he died about 1790, leaving his considerable estate to the mistress he had kept for 20 years.

Mrs Cuyler was brought up and adopted by the "late Deputy Governess to the Royal Children"; she received her education and passed her childhood at St James's Palace and was the playmate of "the present princesses." When she was not quite 14 years of age, she was somehow lured, "by the machinations of the Park-Gate-Keeper's Daughter at Buckingham-Gate," into the house of the notorious procuress Mother Kelly (then Mrs Nelson), where she was starved for several days but where she "resisted every overture." Indeed, "several titled Miscreants were introduced to reap the treasure, but none of them were hardy enough" to force her to yield. She was said to be a large, though beautifully-proportioned, girl, and she bloodied the nose of

Harvard Theatre Collection

MARGARET CUYLER, as Cressida

engraving by Thornthwaite, after E. F. Burney

one of the insistent lordlings. Captain Cuyler, of the 46th Regiment of Foot, "rescued" her from this perilous situation and made her his common-law wife. But he had only his army pay and when, after two years of their blissful association, Cuyler was ordered to America, she was left destitute in England. She had borne one child but it had died in its first month.

Mrs Cuyler, still only 16, was said to have been literally starving when she met the wealthy Major Metcalf, with whom she lived for three years. He wished to marry her, but she refused to accompany him when he left for India on some business scheme. Metcalf left her well provided for but she foolishly lent £1000 to a Captain Maundel, who was lost in the *Ville de Paris* returning from the West Indies. (In the 1790 version, corrected by the 1792 account above, it was Cuyler who had the wealth. He it was, also, who perfected her

education. He "provided her a chariot and they lived together in Paris, London, and Dublin, in the most splendid stile." It was Metcalf, in this version, who was drowned in returning from the West Indies.)

Margaret had long been solicited by a young Lord who finally succeeded in persuading her into "keeping" and gave her a sum of money to set up house in London. But this connection was swiftly broken by the Earl his father. According to the *Secret History*, Margaret was then kept, successively, by an auctioneer named Sands, by R. B. Sheridan (who introduced her to the stage), and by Thomas Harris, the Covent Garden Theatre manager.

Only at about this point in the hapless lady's adventures—the point at which she came onto the London stage—are verifiable facts at hand. Since even the *Secret History* concedes that "it would be tedious to enumerate all her admirers," we will record only the claim by R. B. Peake (in his *Memoirs of the Colman Family*, 1841) that she married Dominic Rice of Gray's Inn on 21 February 1778 and move onto the higher, firmer ground of her theatrical career.

Margaret Cuyler's "first appearance on any stage" occurred at Drury Lane on 4 January 1777 when, billed only as "A Young Lady," she played Miranda in *The Tempest*. She played no other part all season, so far as the bills show, but *The Tempest* was often repeated through 30 May. The reviewer for the *London Magazine* in January had not been encouraging:

The lady, Mrs Scuyler [*sic*], who appeared for the first time, in Miranda, had been handsome, or rather approaching to the beautiful. She is at present a mere piece of still life. She wants almost every requisite for her new vocation but face and figure, and seems while on the stage to be in a state of incurable stupidity or inattention, or which is much more inexcusable, to affect a species of insolent indifference, of which, if the sacredness of her sex did not forbid, she deserved long since to be warmly and loudly reminded.

Her voice is not disagreeable, nor does her countenance want expression when she happens to *betray* any feeling.

Nevertheless, when the new season opened with *The Tempest* on 20 September 1777, Mrs Cuyler was serenely in her place as Miranda, and she retained the part through half a dozen performances during the season. Maybe, as the *Secret History* suggests, she was kept there by the managerial influence of Sheridan, who was then riding high on the phenomenal success of his new comedy *The School for Scandal*. But not even Sheridan was powerful enough to obtain a line of first-rate parts for the statuesque beauty. She did not dance, she could not sing, and her acting ability, such as it ever became, developed slowly. On 17 October she was allowed to appear among a distinguished cast in a revival after seven years of *1 Henry IV*. She was Lady Percy that night and a dozen times more during the season. But in a theatre then dominated by Jane Pope and Mrs Abington, Mrs and the Misses Hopkins, Mrs Yates, and Sophia Baddeley, she could not compete even with Miss Sherry, Mrs Wrighten, Miss Collett, and Mrs Colles.

Lady Percy and Miranda she continued to be as often as they were required at Drury Lane, but for several years, so far as the bills show, Sheridan made little further use of her at the theatre. On 31 May 1779, however, she came under the summer management of the elder George Colman at the Haymarket and was immediately allowed four more characters for her sparse repertoire: Second Daughter in Colman's alteration of Beaumont and Fletcher's *Bonduca*, Dorinda in *The Stratagem*, Anne Bullen in *Henry VIII*, and Mrs Revel in *Separate Maintenance*.

A brief attack on Mrs Cuyler's abilities signed "Heigh-Ho" in the *Morning Post* for 3 August 1779 brought forth in the issue of 5 August a spirited defense of her from "An Advocate for the Fair Sex":

It is extremely hard on this lady to be the subject of newspaper ridicule: she is a most elegant woman, and conducts herself with great propriety and decency. If she is possessed of theatrical abilities, they have never been called forth, though one of the finest figures on the stage. She has been equally neglected by the winter and summer managers.

Margaret Cuyler returned to Drury Lane in the winters of 1779–80 and 1780–81 and was at the Haymarket in the summers of 1780 and 1781. But rumors of her enforced departure from the winter house began to circulate early in 1781, and the *Morning Herald* of 21 September reported her discharge, adding that "it has surprised all her acquaintance that a woman of her spirit and independent circumstance should have continued so long in a situation so mortifying as hers must have been in that theatre." She was absent from Drury Lane after the spring of 1781 until the beginning of the 1785–86 season (though she played at the Haymarket both in the summers and occasionally in specially licensed performances in the winter). But she was never far away from the *haut monde*. For example, the *Morning Herald* of 24 May 1783 reported a masquerade held to give the visiting Duchesse de Chartres et Fitz-James some idea of England's fashionable amusements. The Prince of Wales was present, and "The lovely Mrs C——r appeared in the circle with peculiar éclat . . . the beautiful simplicity of her dress proved the delicacy of her taste in that important article, and exhibited her gracefully *elegant form* to the utmost advantage."

In 1784 she was resident in lavish quarters at No 7, St Albans Street. She returned to Drury Lane Theatre in 1785–86 and remained there in the winters through 1788–89, playing also some part of each summer at the Haymarket. In 1789–90 she was on the pay book at Drury Lane at a salary of £1 10*s.* per week but appeared in the bills only for the performance of 18 February

1790, as Elmira in the afterpiece *The Sultan*, one of her oft-repeated roles. In 1790 she played at Drury Lane on 30 September only (again as Elmira) and then disappeared from town until the summer season of 1791 when she played fitfully at the Haymarket. She had probably been in Ireland meanwhile.

She was at Drury Lane from 1791–92 through 1792–93 but was absent from London again in the winter of 1793–94. She returned to the Haymarket in the summer of 1794. Back at both houses in 1794–95 and 1795–96, she was absent from Drury Lane again until 1 February 1797. In 1797–98 she appeared once only – on 1 June – at Drury Lane, though she was that summer again at the Haymarket. From 1799–1800 (when for the first time she made as much as £2 per week) until the close of her career in the season of 1808-9, she was pretty steadily at Drury Lane in the winters and the Haymarket in the summers.

Gradually after her very tentative start Margaret Cuyler had assembled a fairly respectable list of roles in farce to complement her slender repertoire in comedy. She acquired most of her new parts in the summertime at the Haymarket. There she demonstrated by the frequency of her change of parts that she was by no means the slow study that she would appear to have been if one judged only by her winter appearances, so perhaps there was truth in the charge that she did not receive justice at Drury Lane.

Among the parts she accumulated over the years were Lady Gorget in the first presentation of Sheridan's *The Camp*, "Actress" in *The Manager in Distress*, Almadine in *Nature Will Prevail*, Mrs Revel in *The Separate*, Ismene in *Phaedra and Hippolitus*, Miss Mortimer in *The Chapter of Accidents*, Lady Dorville in *The Female Captain*, Arabella in *The Author*, Sophy in *The Nabob*, Sheba in *A Mogul Tale*, Kitty in *Seeing is Believing,* the original Donna Clara in Hannah Cowley's *School*

for Greybeards, Elmira in *The Sultan*, Bloom in *I'll Tell You What!*, Lucy in *The Guardian*, the original Circassian in *The Test of Love*, the original Kitty in *The New Peerage*, French Lady in *Harlequin Junior*, a Lady in *The London Hermit*, and Lady Godiva in *Peeping Tom*.

Margaret Cuyler's "wit, which is poignant and ready," avowed the *Secret History* in 1792, "has long been the terror of the Green-Room," and perhaps this was accurate, for the *European Magazine* reported in 1813 that she was preparing to publish a novel. But the enduring image of Mrs Cuyler is physical rather than intellectual, and Amazonian at that. Peake called her "a full-grown Irish Venus, without the Graces." Boaden, in his *Memoirs of Mrs Siddons* (1827), harked back over 40 years to the 1785 revival of Garrick's *Jubilee* procession of Shakespeare's characters and sundry abstract figures. Mrs Siddons (who had already been apotheosized by Sir Joshua Reynolds's famous picture) appeared as the Tragic Muse. Boaden thought Thalia's representative should have been Dora Jordan; instead, it was "a tall lifeless woman whose name was Cuyler, exceedingly pallid, and whose features were ridiculously small for her size . . ."

Margaret Cuyler was subjected to her quota, and more, of newspaper gossip. There was, for instance, a long series of squibs, full of witty allusion and innuendo, in the *World* and the *Morning Post* from 2 August 1790 to about the middle of August 1791. They concern the intrusion into her dressing room of a Dr Patence, a dental surgeon and amateur playwright, who had his ardour cooled by a basin of water she threw over him. A false apology purporting to be from Mrs Cuyler to Patence brought a reply from him and a sequence of furious denials, counterdenials, and threats of legal action.

Mrs Cuyler had subscribed £1 1s. to the Drury Lane actors' Fund in 1777, had neglected payment in 1782, when she had left the theatre, and had been readmitted in 1788. On 23 March 1811 she was made an annuitant of the Fund. In her latter years she lived at Lambeth. She died on 14 March 1814 at Walworth and was buried on 22 March in St Paul, Covent Garden, churchyard.

E. F. Burney drew Mrs Cuyler's likeness as Cressida in *Troilus and Cressida*, and Thornthwaite engraved the picture for John Bell in 1785.

Cuzzoni, Francesca, later Signora Pietro Giuseppe Sandoni and / or Signora San-Antonio Ferre *c. 1700– 1770, singer.*

Born about 1700 in Parma, Francesca Cuzzoni studied voice under Lanzi before making her debut in the fall of 1718 in Venice singing Dalinda in *Ariodante*. Her splendid soprano enthralled audiences at most of the major Italian theatres and won her an invitation from Heidegger and Handel to come to England for the 1722–23 season. The emissary who delivered the offer and brought her to England was supposedly Pietro Giuseppe Sandoni, the harpsichord master and composer. He and Signora Cuzzoni were said to have married secretly, apparently before her arrival in London. Heidegger advanced the singer £250 and guaranteed her £2000 for the season, a salary equal to that of the famous *castrato* Senesino.

Cuzzoni's first appearance in London was on 12 January 1723 at the King's Theatre in the Haymarket as Teofane in Handel's *Ottone*. The *Daily Journal* said she performed "to the surprize and admiration of the Audience, which was very numerous." The *London Journal* reported that she had "already jump'd into a handsome Chariot, and an Equipage accordingly. The Gentry seems to have so high a Taste of her fine Parts, that she is likely to be a great Gainer by them." And indeed she was: when *Ottone* was presented again on 15 January the ticket prices had jumped from half a guinea to four guineas, and for her benefit on 26 March "some of the Nobility gave her 50 Guineas a Ticket," helping to bring her income at that performance to over £700.

In *Ottone* she sang exquisitely the aria "Falsa immagine," which, in rehearsal, she had refused even to try, simply because she did not like it. Handel, the story goes, raised the window, seized the singer by the waist, and threatened to throw her out if she remained obstinate. She sensibly consented, and the aria established her reputation with the audience as the greatest soprano England had ever heard.

From the beginning, however, Signora Cuzzoni had her critics. The *London Journal* on 30 March 1723 reminded everyone that

there are several who believe that Mrs. Tofts was equal to her in every Respect; but she was born in Italy. Why Musick should be confined only to that Country is what we cannot perceive; since no person that ever came out of it equal'd the Harmony of our famous Purcell. As we delight so much in Italian Songs, we are likely to have enough of them, for as soon as Cuzzoni's Time is out, we are to have another over; for we are well assured *Faustina*, the fine Songstress at Venice, is invited, whose Voice, they say, exceeds that we have already here . . .

Faustina did not come to England for another three years, but her reputation already matched that of Cuzzoni, and the rivalry that eventually developed led, as will be seen, to a battle royal. In the meantime, however, London had to be satisfied with Cuzzoni, even if it was her great misfortune to have been born in another country.

On 23 March 1723, after *Ottone* finished its run, Signora Cuzzoni sang Volumnia in *Coriolano*; on 30 March she was Ennone in *Erminia*; and on 14 May she sang Emilia in *Flavio*. After repetitions of *Ottone* on 4 and 8 June she probably went to Paris with four of the other leading singers who had

FRANCESCA CUZZONI
by Mercier

been offered 25,000 *livres* to perform 12 times.

She was back at the King's Theatre for the 1723–24 season and sang Tomiri in *Farnace*, Arricidi in *Vespasiano*, Cleopatra in *Giulio Cesare*, the title role in *Calfurnia*, and Emilia in *Aquilio Consolo*. So popular had she become that Signora Durastanti and Anastasia Robinson, both previous favorites, had left the field. Yet it was reported that Signora Cuzzoni would leave

England on 25 May 1724, and the broken-hearted Ambrose Phillips even went so far as to write a farewell poem to her. There must have been a mistake, however, for she was still at the King's Theatre in 1724–25, triumphant as ever, singing Asteria in *Tamerlano*, Aspasia in *Artaserse*, the title role in *Rodelinda*, Statira in *Dario*, and the title role in *Elpidia*—in addition to repeating her Cleopatra. Up to this point her greatest part had been Rodelinda. When she sang it in the spring of 1725 she and Handel both triumphed. Her brown silk dress trimmed with silver started a new fashion amongst the ladies of quality, since they could not imitate her singing of the finest aria in the work, "Ho perduto il caro sposo."

Meanwhile, the soprano was leading a rather mysterious personal life. The *Daily Journal* on 11 January 1725 reported that "ToMorrow Signiora Cuzzoni the famous Chauntress, is to be married to San-Antonio Ferre, a very rich Italian, at the Chapel of Count Staremberg, the Imperial Ambassador." Had the singer divorced Sandoni—or had she never married him in the first place? She still used his name offstage. Indeed, on 22 August 1725 Mrs Pendarves wrote to her sister that

Mrs. Sandoni (who was Cuzzoni) is brought to bed of a daughter: it is a mighty mortifi-

cation it was not a son. Sons and heirs ought to be out of fashion when such scrubs shall pretend to be dissatisfied at having a daughter: 'tis pity indeed, that the noble name and family of the Sandoni's should be extinct. The minute she was brought to bed, she sang "La Speranza", a song in Otho [*Ottone*].

No further notice seems to have been taken of Signora Cuzzoni's husband or husbands for some time.

The 1725–26 season—actually just the period January through May 1726, for the opera season was shorter than the theatrical one—brought Signora Cuzzoni the title role in *Elisa*, Berenice in *Scipione*, and Lisaura in *Alessandro*. *Alessandro* opened on 5 May, and Cuzzoni faced on stage the other great prima donna of the era, the mezzo-soprano Signora Faustina. The advantage that Faustina had over her rival was probably slight vocally, but she was a far more

Harvard Theatre Collection

FRANCESCA CUZZONI, with FARINELLI and SENESINO
by Hogarth ?

attractive woman, and single to boot. Handel hired her at £2000 a season, carefully matching Cuzzoni's salary to avoid a squabble, and in *Alessandro* he wrote parts for the two singers which exploited, contrasted, and flattered their individual talents. All this, instead of helping to keep the peace, only led in time to a contest which had ruinous effects on Italian opera in London.

The 1726–27 season opened on 7 January 1727 with Signora Cuzzoni singing Lucilla in *Lucio Vero*, after which she appeared as Antigona in *Admeto* and Andromaca in *Astianatte*. Sides were chosen by opera patrons, some supporting Cuzzoni, others cheering on Faustina (and almost forgotten by the enthusiasts on both sides was the fact that Handel had brought together one of the most remarkable associations in the history of opera: Cuzzoni, Faustina, Senesino, and Handel himself). Mary, Countess of Pembroke, was the leader of the Cuzzoni partisans; opposing her were the Countess of Burlington, Lady Delawar, and their factions. At one performance, possibly of *Astianatte* in May, Princess Amelia was present when the audience disrupted the performance. Lady Pembroke wrote to Mrs Charlotte Clayton (Lady of the Bedchamber to the Princess of Wales) that

every one who wishes well to Cuzzoni is in the utmost concern for what happened last Tuesday at the Opera, in the Princess Amelia's presence; but to show their innocence of the disrespect which was shown to her Highness, I beg you will do them the justice to say, that Cuzzoni had been publicly told, to complete her disgrace, she was to be hissed off the stage on Tuesday; she was in such concern at this, that she had a great mind not to sing, but I, without knowing anything that the Princess Amelia would honour the Opera with her presence, positively ordered her not to quit the stage, but let them do what they would: though not heard, to sing on, and not to go off till it was proper; and she owns now that if she had not that order she would have

quitted the stage when they cat-called her to such a degree in one song, that she was not heard one note, which provoked the people that like her so much, that they were not able to get the better of their resentment, but would not suffer Faustina to speak afterwards.

When Princess Caroline attended the King's Theatre on 6 June—apparently after the perturbations described above—the rival factions in the audience showed their respect for royalty and for music by "hissing, catcalls, and other disturbances."

Given such an audience, it is a wonder that the performers were willing to waste their talent on them, but the singers were also jealous of one another and ultimately engaged in hair-pulling bouts on stage. The satirists were quick to make capital of all this unseemly behavior. One piece that came out in 1727 was *The Contretemps; or, Rival Queans*, published in Colley Cibber's *Dramatic Works* but probably not written by him. The scene is the Temple of Discord, with ranks of aristocratic patrons on each side of the stage and the thinly disguised opera personnel arguing their differences in the middle. "F——s——na" blasts "C——z——ni" for her excessive girth, among other things, to which Cuzzoni replies:

My Person touch'd!—your Malice I despise;
I'll spoil your Singing and tare out your Eyes;
Each Limb, each Motion mar, each graceful Air,
Those Ornaments you practice with such Care . . .

Soon the pair are pulling at one another's headdresses, while their rooters on each side cheer them on:

The Queen and Princess again engage: Both Factions play all their Warlike Instruments; Cat-calls, Serpents and Cuckoos make a dreadful Din. F——s——na lays flat C——z——ni's Nose with a Sceptre;—

Thou tunefull Scarecrow, & thou warbling Bird,
No shelter for your Notes, these lands afford
This Town protects no more thi Sing-Song Strain
Whilst Balls & Masquerades Triumphant Reign
Sooner than midnight revels ere shoud fail
And ore Ridotto's Harmony prevail.
That Cap (a refuge once) my Head Shall Grace
And Save from ruin this Harmonious face

Drawn by Dorothy Countess of Burlington.

Harvard Theatre Collection

FRANCESCA CUZZONI, with FARINELLI and HEIDEGGER
engraving by Goupy, after Ricci

C——z——ni *breaks her Head with a gilt Leather Crown:* H[ande]l *desirous to see an End of the Battle, animates them with a Kettle-Drum; a Globe thrown at Random hits the High-Priest* [Heidegger] *on the Temples, he staggers off the Stage:* S[an]d[o]ni *and* M[un]ro [in charge of the claques] *quit their Posts and take Shelter behind the Scenes— The Queen loses her Head of Hair, and the Princess her Nose in the Skirmish: At last the Goddess Discord inspires* C——z——ni *with more than mortal Bravery, she plys her Antagonist so warmly, the Queen is obliged to fly—*

the Princess follows; S[ene]s[i]no *creeps from under the Altar where he lay hid, and moralizes in the following Simile.*

The character of Senesino ends his "Simile" with:

> *So much the Shew of Greatness is their Care,*
> *They'll lose the Substance for a Puff of Air.*

The disgraceful behavior of the two prima donnas and their adherents brought the downfall of the Royal Academy of Music and its opera venture within a year.

In 1727–28 Cuzzoni and Faustina continued singing, but after the bloodletting of the previous spring the furor over their respective talents quieted. Signora Cuzzoni sang at the St Cecilia's Day concert at the Crown and Anchor on 22 November 1727, but the rest of her activity was confined to the King's Theatre. There she sang Zelinda in *Teuzzone*, Costanza in *Riccardo I*, Laodice in *Siroe*, and Seleuce in *Tolomeo*. At the end of the season the Academy held a general court to consider the accumulated debts. One decision made was to offer Cuzzoni one guinea less than Faustina in the future, knowing that the former had sworn never to sing for less than her rival. But this was all pointless, for the Academy could not continue its operas in any case, and the season just ended was its last. Cuzzoni, Faustina, and Senesino returned to the Continent.

Cuzzoni's departure pleased those chauvinists who disliked imported performers generally. One poem, not printed until 1731 but probably composed before Cuzzoni left England, was appended to a satirical print by George Bickham showing a young lady (not Cuzzoni) reclining on a couch:

THE SYREN OF THE STAGE

A Satire on Madame Cuzzoni

Little Syren of the Stage,
Charmer of an idle Age,
Empty Warbler, breathing Lyre,
Wanton gale of fond desire,
Bane of ev'ry manly Art,
Soft enfeebler of the Heart,
O too pleasing is the strain.
Hence to Southern Climes again
Tuneful mischief. Vocal spell
To this Island bid fare-well
Leave us as we ought to be
Leave us Britons rough and free!

Signora Cuzzoni accepted the invitation of Count Kinsky to sing at the court in Vienna, but her salary demands were too high for the theatre there. In 1729 she and Faustina were both in Venice, singing at different theatres. That year Cuzzoni sang in *Onorio*, and the following year found her in *Idaspe*, *Artaserse*, and *Mitridate*. In 1732 she sang in *Euristeo*.

By June 1733 the new Opera of the Nobility in London was forming, and it engaged Senesino and Cuzzoni for the forthcoming season. Cuzzoni arrived in the spring of 1734 to sing the title role in *Arianna in Naxo* on 20 April at the Lincoln's Inn Fields Theatre; this was Porpora's opera, running in opposition to Handel's *Arianna in Creta*. The following 11 May Cuzzoni sang Lavinia in *Enea nel Lazio*. In 1734–35 she was with Porpora's company at the King's Theatre (Handel used Covent Garden), singing Mandane in *Artaserse*, Galatea in *Polifemo*, and the title roles in *Issipile* and *Ifigenia in Aulide*. During the season she and Farinelli also sang at concerts at the Crown and Anchor and the Crown taverns. In 1735–36 she was Eminera in *Adriano*, Semandra in *Mitridate*, and Termanzio in *Onorio*. She also sang in *Orfeo* that season, but her role was not named in the bills.

After the 1735–36 season Signora Cuzzoni returned once more to the Continent. The newspapers in September 1736 reported that she was under sentence of death in Italy for having poisoned her husband (not cited by name, unfortunately). Apparently this was only gossip. She was not beheaded, as she was rumored to have been, and perhaps she came to England again in 1748, as Hawkins reported in his *General History*, to sing in *Mitridate*—though the opera is not otherwise reported to have been performed that year. She did return to England in 1750, however, for a benefit concert at Hickford's Room on 18 May. Burney said that by that time Cuzzoni had been "almost deprived of her voice, by age and infirmities" and drew only small audiences. Horace Walpole wrote to Horace Mann on 2 August that "Another celebrated Polly has been arrested for thirty pounds [debt], even old Cuzzoni. The Prince of Wales baled her—who will do as much for him?"

She sang in concerts on 16 April 1751 at the King's Theatre, on 27 April at the Haymarket, and on 23 May at Hickford's. The last concert was for her benefit which, she advertised, "shall be the last I will ever trouble [the public] with." She claimed to be "Unhappily Involved in a few Debts" and anxious to pay them before leaving England. To prove her honesty, she arranged that Hickford should receive the money taken in and pay the debts for her. She apparently then went to Holland, but there she was thrown into debtors' prison. She sang her way out by giving occasional performances with the permission of the prison governor. Finally she returned to Bologna, where she was seen by Baretti, selling greens at a stall. Another report has it that she was reduced to making buttons for a living. Perhaps the poor lady did both. She died in poverty at Bologna in 1770.

Dr Burney was extravagant in his praise for Signora Cuzzoni:

A native warble enabled her to execute divisions with such facility as to conceal every appearance of difficulty; and so grateful and touching was the natural tone of her voice, that she rendered pathetic whatever she sung, in which she had leisure to unfold its whole volume. The art of conducting, sustaining, increasing, and diminishing her tones by minute degrees, acquired her among professors, the title of complete mistress of her art. In a cantabile air, though the notes she added were few, she never lost a favourable opportunity of enriching the cantilena with all the refinements and embellishments of the time. Her shake was perfect, she had a creative fancy, and the power of occasionally accelerating and retarding the measure in the most artificial and able manner, by what the Italians call *tempo rubato*.

Tosi in his *Observations* in 1743 spoke of Signora Cuzzoni's "delightful, soothing Cantabile . . . joined with the Sweetness of a fine Voice, a perfect Intonation, and Strictness of Time . . ." Her voice, reported the *London Magazine* in 1777, frequently melted audiences into tears. "D—— her!" shouted one gallery admirer, according to the *Theatrical Jester* about 1795, "she has a nest of nightingales in her belly!" From all reports it would seem that Cuzzoni had a perfect shake and full control over *tempo rubato*, immaculate high notes, and perfect pitch.

E. Seeman painted a portrait of her which Van der Gucht and James Caldwall engraved. The British Museum has an original drawing of her by Philippe Mercier. She was also shown in several satirical prints. In Hogarth's "Masquerades and Operas," for instance, she was pictured receiving £8000 from the Earl of Peterborough. Mario Ricci sketched her about 1728–29 with Farinelli and Heidegger, showing her as dumpy as most verbal descriptions make her out to have been; Joseph Goupy engraved Ricci's drawing. Hogarth may have been the artist who drew another caricature of Cuzzoni about 1723: she, Berenstadt, and Senesino are shown on the stage of the King's Theatre in a variation of a section of the "Masquerades and Operas" drawing. An anonymous artist about 1730 pictured little Cuzzoni with tall Senesino in a print called "On loosing their Toast and Butter."

(*The London Stage*, in the roster for the 1732–33 season at the King's Theatre, lists a "Signora Gismondi (Cuzzoni)"; this appears to be a confusion of Celeste Hempson, who was Signora Gismondi, and Cuzzoni. Under the date of 30 April 1728 *The London Stage* cites the 1728 edition of *Ptolemy* as containing the names "Signora Cuzzoni Bardoni" and "Signora Faustina Bardoni"—the first being clearly a mistake.)

Cymber, Miss *fl. 1747*, *actress.*
A Miss Cymber and her backers rented

the disused Haymarket Theatre on 24 March 1747 to allow her to play the title role in *Jane Shore* for her benefit. The meaningless formula "At the Desire of several Ladies of Quality" was used in the bill. Criticism is silent about the performance of Miss Cymber in her taxing role, as well as of a Mrs Clarke who played Alicia and of the anonymous "Young Gentleman" who played Hastings. *Miss in her Teens* was offered as the afterpiece, but the bill yields no cast.

Miss Cymber displayed her talents once more, on 20 April, as Monimia in *The Orphan*. Castalio was presented by the shy

"Young Gentleman that played Hastings, and rest by [the] company that played *Jane Shore*." A notice in the *Daily Advertiser* admonished that "Several of Miss Cymber's Friends mistaking the House for the Theatre in James St., are desir'd to observe this is facing the Opera House in the Haymarket." Since Miss Cymber failed in these attempts to catch the eye of management, it seems especially pitiful that her friends could not find the theatre.

Cypriani. *See* **CIPRIANI.**

Cyri. *See* **CIRRI.**

= D =

D Jr, Mr (fl. 1766–1767), *property man.*

A "D Jr" was on the Drury Lane pay list for 24 January 1767 as a property man at a salary of 1s. 9d. per day, or 10s. 6d. per week.

Dabell, Mr (fl. 1772), *actor.*

A Mr Dabell played the role of the Taylor in seven performances of *The Cooper* given by Foote's summer company at the Haymarket between 12 June and 31 August 1772.

Dabney. *See* DOBNEY.

Dace, Mr (fl. 1735), *dancer.*

A Mr Dace was a member of the chorus which danced a grand ballet in performances of *Harlequin Orpheus* at Drury Lane on 3 March 1735 and many other times during the season.

Dacres, Mr (fl. 1661), *actor.*

As a member of the Duke's Company at Lincoln's Inn Fields, Mr Dacres is known to have played the second Gravedigger in *Hamlet* on 24 August 1661 and Parson Soaker in *Cutter of Coleman Street* on the following 16 December.

Dacres, Andrew d. 1669, *painter.*

Andrew Dacres, a painter-stainer from the parish of St Giles, Cripplegate, had apparently been in the civil wars, for he was styled "Captain." He helped paint the pageants for the Lord Mayor's shows in 1659 and 1660, and he worked, probably on the figure subjects, on the triumphal arches for the coronation procession of Charles II on 22 April 1661. Dacres died in 1669.

Dacrow. *See* DUCROW.

"Dagger." *See* MARR, HENRY.

Daggs. *See* DANKS.

Daglish, Master (fl. 1790), *actor.*

Master Daglish was billed as the Child in *Isabella* at Drury Lane Theatre on 7 December 1790, a part he repeated on 21 December. He was not seen in London again.

Daglish, Thomas (fl. 1776–1794), *music copyist, house servant.*

Thomas Daglish's principal responsibility during the more than 16 years in which he regularly appeared on the Drury Lane Theatre's pay list was as music copyist. But he turned his hand to other chores for the management. He was occasionally disburser of funds to dancers, instrumental musicians, and the chorus, and to certain tradesmen; he was caller for the practice sessions of the band; and he was also purchasing agent, as a few excerpts from the account books will demonstrate: November 1776: "Daglish and Music Bills 4/6/—"; June 1779: "Daglish . . . to pay Mr Lolli for practice of Dancers for the season 10/10/0"; 23 December 1779: "Mr Daglish for calling Music Band —/13/6"; June 1780: "Daglish . . . Bill for Cleaning Harpsichords 1/17/6"; December 1780: "Daglish . . . for Chorus in full to 1st inst. 12/5/0 . . . for K:[ettle] Drum to 24th Nov.

2/15/0"; March 1784: "Mr Daglish to pay Mr Markordt's funeral P^r: order of Mr Linley 5/15/8"; November 1784: "Daglish's bill for Sundries —/9/4". His salary ranged from £1 per week in 1776 upward to £2 in 1793–94, but he received extra payments for copying music.

On 11 September 1792 Thomas Daglish married a Miss Jones at St Martin-in-the-Fields. She may have been his second wife, inasmuch as a "Master Daglish" appeared as a performer at Drury Lane twice in 1790. Daglish belonged to the New Musical Fund, and Doane's *Musical Directory* (1794) gave his home address as No 15, Little Drury Lane.

Dagnall, Mr [fl. 1661], *singer.*

A member of the Chapel Royal, Mr Dagnall was given a partial payment of 4s. on 30 March 1661 for having performed at the funeral of Princess Mary, the King's eldest sister. He was due 8d. more.

Dagueville or **Dagville.** *See* **D'EG-VILLE.**

Dahl. *See* **DALL.**

Dahmen, Hermanus *1755–1830, horn player.*

The horn player Hermanus Dahmen was born at Sneek, Holland, on 26 September 1755, the son of the musician Wilhelm Dahmen (1731–1780). He played in the band of the Municipal Theatre at Amsterdam and in 1787, according to Grove, went to Dublin and then to London, where he played with various musical groups until 1790. We find no record of any performances by him at London. He went to Steinfurt in 1790 to play with the grand-ducal orchestra. He died at Rotterdam in 1830.

Dahmen, Johan Arnold *b. c. 1760, violinist, violoncellist, composer.*

Johan Arnold Dahmen was born at the Hague about 1760. Probably he was the son of Wilhelm Dahmen (1731–1780), the patriarch of a very large family of musicians. Known as an excellent instrumentalist, Johan Dahmen lived for many years in England, according to Sainsbury's *Dictionary of Musicians.* Grove gives his year of death at London as 1794, but he was undoubtedly the Dahmen who played the violin and violoncello in the opera band at the King's Theatre in 1795–96 and 1796–97. He composed *Trois Quatuors pour 2 violons, alto et bass* and *Trois Trios pour violons et basse,* published at Paris, and sonatas and duets for the violoncello. Hermanus Dahmen (1755–1830), who evidently performed at London as a horn player, was his brother. (See Grove for brief notices of the continental careers of this numerous family.)

Dahmen, Wilhelm *b. 1769, horn player.*

Wilhelm Dahmen was born in Harlingen in Holland in 1769, the fifth son of the elder Wilhelm Dahmen (1731–1780), a performer and teacher of music. He played the horn. *Grove's Dictionary* says of him only that he "had considerable success in Amsterdam, Rotterdam, and London, in which latter city he joined the army against Napoleon." He died in Spain at some time during the campaigns against the French (1808–13).

Dahuron, [Francis?] [fl. 1719–1728], *flutist, singer.*

The Mr Dahuron who performed at concerts in London in 1719 was probably Francis Dahuron, whose name appears twice in the St Paul, Covent Garden, parish registers. On 6 July 1727 he and his wife Mary baptized a daughter Frances, and on 20 July 1728 they baptized a son Anthony.

Dahuron played the German flute at a concert for his benefit at Hickford's Music Room on 13 February 1719, and on the following 7 May he sang at another Hickford's concert. No other public appearances are known for him, but he must have been a well-known musician—perhaps a teacher—for on 3 February 1741, after his death, his name was still remembered. On that date Christopher Smith held a benefit concert for himself at the Haymarket Theatre and noted that he had, at his own expense, provided for and brought up the children of the late Mr Dahuron.

Daigueville or **Daigville.** *See* **D'EG-VILLE.**

Daily. *See* **DALY.**

Dakers. *See* **DACRES.**

Dalagarde. *See* **DELAGARDE.**

Dalby, Mr ₍*fl. 1785–1790*₎, *house servant.*

A Mr Dalby, a house servant, shared annual benefit tickets with other servants at Covent Garden Theatre between 1785–86 and 1789–90.

Dale, Mr ₍*fl. 1784*₎, *singer.*

A Mr Dale was listed by Burney as one of the tenor singers in the Handel Memorial Concerts given at Westminster Abbey and the Pantheon in May and June 1784.

Dale, Mr ₍*fl. 1794*₎, *violinist.*

A Mr Dale, violinist, was listed in 1794 by Doane's *Musical Directory* as a performer at Covent Garden Theatre. His address was No 26, Stanhope Street, Clare Market, the same as that of William Dale, who was a boxeeper at Drury Lane for many years.

Dale, Joseph *1750–1821, instrumentalist, music seller.*

Joseph Dale was born in 1750. He established himself as a music seller as early as 1783. His first business address was No 19, Chancery Lane—a private house. In Janu-

ary 1786 he moved to No 132, Oxford Street and took over the circulating music library of Samuel Babb. By 1791 Dale also had quarters at No 19, Cornhill, and about 1802 he established a third office at No 151, New Bond Street. In 1805 he went into partnership with his son William, but in 1809 the younger Dale went into business on his own and Joseph managed his affairs alone until his death in 1821.

Doane's *Musical Directory* of 1794 listed a J. Dale—doubtless Joseph—as a violist, organist, composer, and participant in the concerts presented by the Academy of Ancient Music. In 1805 Dale was organist of St Anthony and St John Baptist, Watling Street. He composed sonatas, arranged vocal airs, and invented improvements for the tambourine, an instrument for which J. Dale Jr—presumably Joseph's son—composed.

One may see in the *Catalogue of Printed Music* of the British Museum an indication of the extent and variety of Joseph Dale's music publishing activities. The business he founded flourished well into the nineteenth century.

Dale, Thomas ₍*fl. c. 1699*₎, *booth operator.*

Morley's *Memoirs of Bartholomew Fair* quoted an advertisement dating about 1699 for Thomas Dale's booth:

THOMAS DALE, Drawer at the Crown Tavern at Algate, keepeth the TURK'S HEAD *Musick Booth,* in Smithfield Rounds, over against the *Greyhound*-Inn during the Time of *Bartholomew Fair,* Where is a Glass of good Wine, Mum, Syder, Beer, Ale, and all other Sorts of Liquors, to be Sold; and where you will likewise be entertained with good Musick, Singing, and Dancing. You will see a Scaramouch Dance, the Italian Punch's Dance, the Quarter Staff, the Antick, the Countryman and Countrywoman's Dance, and the Merry Cuckolds of Hogsden.

Also, a Young-Man that dances an Entry, Salabrand, and Jigg, and a Woman that dances with Six Naked Rapiers, that we Challenge the whole Fair to do the like. There is likewise a Young-Woman that Dances with Fourteen Glasses on the Backs and Palms of her Hands, and turns round with them above an Hundred Times, as fast as a Windmill turns; and another Young Man that Dances a Jigg incomparably well, to the Admiration of all Spectators.

Dale, William   ₁fl. 1774–1805?₁, boxkeeper.

William Dale was a house servant at Drury Lane as early as 1774–75. In 1775–76 he was the box bookkeeper, and in 1776–77 he was paid 15s. per week as a lobby keeper. Dale continued at Drury Lane until 1804–5, by which year his salary was about £1 16s. per week. Throughout the years, as a supervisor of other house functionaries, he was paid regular sums of money to be distributed as salaries to the sweepers, dressers, doorkeepers, and other servants. By 1792, Dale was living at No 26, Stanhope Street, Clare Market. For some years around the turn of the century, he was in charge of the box office at the Theatre Royal in Margate during summers.

His son, William, commonly carried in the accounts as "Dale Junior," was a boxkeeper at Drury Lane from 1788–89 until his death in 1807. By 1805 he had replaced his father at Margate. Another Mr Dale, a violinist, who performed at Covent Garden in the 1790s and also lived at No 26, Stanhope Street, was undoubtedly another son. Also probably related were William Dale, the organist at Whitehall and assistant organist at the King's Chapel in 1784, and Joseph Dale, composer, organist, member of the Academy of Ancient Music, and in 1794 an operator of music shop and circulating library at No 132, Oxford Street, and Cornhill.

William Dale the elder died sometime between 1805 and 1807. His son William, who died in the latter year, left his modest estate to his mother, Frances Dale, widow of the elder William.

Dale, William   d. 1807, boxkeeper.

William Dale, the son of the Drury Lane Theatre's boxkeeper of the same name, by his wife Frances, was also a boxkeeper at Drury Lane by the season of 1788–89. On 10 June 1789, as "Dale junior," he shared benefit tickets with many other house servants. His salary in that year was 12s. per week. It was still that in 1803–4.

By 1805 (perhaps as early as 1801) the younger Dale had replaced his father as summer box office keeper at the Theatre Royal in Margate. His father died sometime between 1805 and 1807. The younger William Dale died a bachelor, at Stanhope Street, on 4 April 1807, according to the *Annual Register*. Administration of his estate, valued at £40, was granted on 23 October 1807 to his father's widow, Frances Dale, "mother and next of kin of deceased."

Daley. *See* DALY.

Dall, Miss   ₁fl. 1776–1794₁,   singer, actress, composer.

Miss Dall was the daughter of Nicholas Thomas Dall, the artist and Covent Garden scene painter, by his wife Mary. She was born before 1776, the year of her father's death; on 3 May 1777 her widowed mother was given a benefit at Covent Garden. Miss Dall was educated in singing by Joseph Mazzinghi, and under the direction of Harrison and Ashley she sang in the oratorios at Covent Garden in 1790, making her debut in the *Messiah* on 19 February. In concerts of sacred music on 24 and 26 February and 17 March, she sang "Praise the Lord" (from *Esther*), "Come ever smiling Liberty" (*Judas Maccabaeus*), and "Hark—'tis the Linnet" (*Joshua*), and also performed in *Judas Maccabaeus* on 5 March 1790. According to *The Secret History of the Green Room* (1792), "she met with that liberal reception which modest merit is ever certain of." In the spring of 1790, Miss Dall appeared as the fourth principal soprano in the Fifth Grand Musical Festival at Westminster Abbey, and in September she sang with Storace at the Colchester Musical Festival.

At Covent Garden on 10 March 1791, Miss Dall took over the role of Emily in *The Woodman* after only one rehearsal, when the regular incumbent, Madame Pieltain, was too intoxicated to play, and, according to the *European Magazine,* performed the character "with much diffidence and modesty, and no inconsiderable share of effect." She presented a good voice and person and was encouraged with the prediction that "when she had achieved carriage and ease of manner, she will represent the character in a manner to deserve applause." Miss Dall played Emily another 17 times before the end of the season. On 14 May she played Eliza in *The Flitch of Bacon,* and on 20 May Rosetta in *Love in a Village.* For her performances that season she was paid £52 10*s.*

In August of 1791 she went to play at the theatre in York and to sing in the Subscription Concerts. When Mrs Billington found herself too busy to prepare the role of Augusta in the new comic opera *Just in Time,* by Thomas Hurlstone, which was scheduled to open at Covent Garden on 10 May 1792, Miss Dall, again seizing opportunity, volunteered to go on in the role without pay. This was her only appearance in that season, but in the fall of 1792 she returned to Covent Garden to play Emily in *The Woodman* on 19 October and Augusta again eight times between 27 October and 23 November. The song "A linnet, just fledg'd," with words by Hurlstone, was published in 1792 as composed and sung by her. She also sang in the oratorios at Covent Garden in 1793.

In the following summer Miss Dall joined Colman's company at the Haymarket at a salary of £6 per week. She made her first appearance there as a villager in *The Battle of Hexham* on 12 June 1793; this was followed by regular appearances in

various musical pieces—Narcissa in *Inkle and Yarico* on 13 June, Amelia in *Summer Amusements* on 15 July, a role in *The Mountaineers* on 3 August, Louisa in *No Song No Supper* on 6 August, a role in *The London Hermit* on 12 August, Laura in *The Agreeable Surprise* on 27 August, and Euphrosyne in *Comus* on 2 September. We find no further notice of Miss Dall at London, although in 1794 she was listed in Doane's *Musical Directory* as a soprano, a member of the Academy of Ancient Music, and at Covent Garden Theatre.

In assessing her talents, *The Secret History of the Green Room* (1792) found that her voice "though not the most powerful, possesses much sweetness, and she runs the most difficult passages with singular ease, neatness, and rapidity, her shake, which is a natural one, is remarkably fine." In person she was short but "perfectly well-formed," and her manners were "genteel and interesting." Her conduct in private life, we are told, was "unblemished."

Dall, Nicholas Thomas   *d. 1776, scene painter, landscape painter.*

A native of Denmark and at one time a scene painter at the King's Opera House in Copenhagen, Nicholas Thomas Dall arrived in London in the early 1750s. There he settled, working as a landscape painter and also finding steady employment as a scene painter at Covent Garden Theatre. By his own testimony in the course of litigation between Colman and other managers of Covent Garden in 1769, Dall claimed to have been working at that theatre "16 ys or thereabouts," thus establishing the date of his initial employment at around 1753. His name first appeared in the theatre's account books on 16 September 1757 when he was put down for a salary of £1 10*s.* per week. On 31 December of that year he was paid for extra work provided for *Alexander.*

Dall continued at Covent Garden for some 19 years, painting first with Lambert and his assistant Austin and then with Richards. In 1759–60 and 1760–61 he was paid £100 for each season at the rate of 12s. per day. He earned £2 per week in 1761–62. By 1766 he was being paid £120 for the season; in 1767–68, £150; 1768–69, £180; 1769–70, £200; 1771–72, £200; 1772–73, £193 10s., and 1773–74, £250. In 1763 he was living in Castle Street, opposite Cranbourn Alley.

Dall painted a new scene of Imogen's chamber, possibly for the revival of *Cymbeline* on 28 December 1767. With Richards, he painted two new scenes for the afterpiece *Harlequin Dr Faustus* on 15 March 1768. In October 1769, he and Richards were paid a total of £14 14s. for expenses of a trip to Stratford in connection with the great jubilee and apparently for studying on location for the preparation of appropriate scenes (including "Drop Cloth Transp Rainbow & Clouds") for *Harlequin's Jubilee*, a new pantomime by Woodward which opened at Covent Garden on 27 January 1770 and for Colman's new comedy *Man and Wife; or, the Shakespeare Jubilee* on 7 October 1769. On 7 December 1771 Dall was paid £6 17s. 11d. for expenses of a similar journey to Windsor in connection with scenes for Colman's *The Fairy Prince, with Installation of Knights of the Garter*, a masque which opened on 12 November 1771. His remaining work at Covent Garden included scenes for Fisher's new pantomime *The Sylphs* on 3 January 1774, Fisher's masque *The Druids* on 19 November 1774, the new pantomime entertainment of *Prometheus* (first and last scenes, of a convent and a landscape) on 26 December 1775, and Thompson's new masque *The Sirens* on 26 February 1776. He also contributed scenes to the productions of *The Rape of Proserpine* and *The Brothers*. "Dall's Hall" and "Dall's Town" are found as notations for stock pieces in a promptbook of *Measure for Measure* (New York Public Library) and "Dall's Hall" is called for in a promptbook of *All's Well*

(Folger Library). In 1773 he painted a scene of Venice, with the Rialto, for William Hanbury's private theatre at Kelmarsh, and in October of that year he provided a "New Curtain Scene" in *Harlequin Sorcerer* for Tate Wilkinson at Hull.

Dall also kept himself busy as a landscape artist. Between 1761 and 1770 he exhibited about 40 pictures at the Society of Artists (of which he was a member), mostly in oils and tempera, with some drawings, all of landscapes, castles, and waterfalls. In 1768 he was awarded the first premium given by the Society of Artists for landscape painting. In 1771 he was elected an associate of the Royal Academy. Works he exhibited at the academy included Yorkshire landscapes he had done while in the employ of the Duke of Bolton and Lord Harewood. A landscape which he painted of Sir John Coghill's estate, Coghill Hall, near Halifax, became widely circulated in an engraving by W. Angus. Dall also did a number of paintings for Shugborough, Great Haywood, Staffordshire (the seat of the Earls of Lichfield) which are still in that house.

In the middle of the season of 1776–77, while still in the employ of Covent Garden, Dall died in Great Newport Street. The date of 10 December 1776 given by the *London Magazine* would appear to be correct; a manuscript notation by Reed in the British Museum cites 7 January 1777. Administration of his possessions was granted to his widow, Ann Dall, of the parish of St Ann, Westminster, on 21 January 1777. She was accorded benefit tickets at Covent Garden on 3 May 1777, from which she took £91 6s.

Ann Dall was a linen draper who supplied Covent Garden and the King's Theatre. She was the daughter of Edward Ayrton (1698–1774), a "barber chirurgian" of Ripon who later became mayor, and the sister of the distinguished musician Edmund Ayrton (1734–1808). By his will, at his death in 1808, the latter left "all the pictures paintings Drawings and Copies of Drawings painted and drawn by my late Brother in Law Nicholas Thomas Dall" to his son William Ayrton. No mention of Ann Dall was made in her brother's will, so presumably she was dead by that time.

It was reported that at his death Nicholas Thomas Dall left a young family. A daughter sang on the London stage as Miss Dall between 1790 and 1793, but nothing is known of her subsequent life. A Robert Nicholas Dall, whose name is found in the registers of St Paul, Covent Garden, in the 1810s, was probably his son. Robert Nicholas Dall's children, by his wife Jane Mary Dall, were: Jane, born 1 December 1805 and baptized 2 February 1806; William Vincent, born 13 September 1807 and baptized 8 February 1808; and Elizabeth Margaret, baptized 15 April 1810.

Scene pieces painted by Dall persisted as stock pieces at Covent Garden long after his death. Some of his scenes were used for *Harlequin's Chaplet* in 1789–90 and for *Harlequin's Treasure* in 1796–97.

There was no evident relationship between Dall and Michael Dahl (1656–1743), the portrait painter.

Dall' Abaco, Giuseppe Marie Clément 1710–1805, *violoncellist, composer.*

Giuseppe Marie Clément Dall' Abaco was born in the Netherlands but was of Italian descent. Baptized at Ste Gudule in Brussels on 27 March 1710, he was the son of the violinist and composer Evaristo Dall' Abaco and his wife Clemence Bultinck Dall' Abaco. Young Giuseppe was taught music by his father and then sent to Bonn. He was there enrolled on 29 March 1729 as a violoncellist in the chapel of the Elector of Cologne. His earliest appearance in London was on 15 April 1736 when he held a benefit concert at Hickford's Music Room. He must then have been only visiting, however, for on 26 August 1738, at Bonn, he was appointed director of the chamber music and councillor at a salary of 1000 florins.

Burney said that Dall' Abaco was in England in 1740, but this may have been an error for his 1736 visit. The violoncellist played in concerts in Vienna, returned to Bonn, but left there in 1753 and settled with his wife Thérèse, née Cosman, near Verona. On 22 September 1766 he was made a Baron by Prince Maximilian of Bavaria. He composed during his lifetime at least 30 cello sonatas, 17 sonatas for cello and continuo, and a cantata. Manuscripts of his music are at the British Museum and at Vienna and Berlin. Dall' Abaco died at Arbizzano di Valpolicello, near Verona, on 31 August 1805 after a remarkably long life.

Dallas, John 1fl. 1780–1787₁, *scene painter.*

The first notice of the scene painter John Dallas was a payment of £8 14s., "in full," entered in the Drury Lane account book on 21 November 1780. On 11 December 1781 "Mr Dalla painter" was paid £3 12s. 11d. "in full to 10th Oct." Numerous payments to him in varying amounts continued during 1781–82. He also painted scenery at Drury Lane in 1782–83.

Dallas was working for Covent Garden in 1785–86 and received £10 on 19 December 1785 for work to that date. Covent Garden also paid him £32 11s. on 7 February 1786 and £17 3s. on 9 January 1787. In 1782 he was a subscriber to George Parker's *Humourous Sketches.*

Dallon. *See* DALTON.

Dalrymple, Mrs 1fl. 1782–1783₁, *house servant?*

A Mrs Dalrymple shared benefit tickets with a group of house servants and minor performers at Covent Garden on 10 May 1782 and 28 May 1783.

Dalton, Mr 1fl. 1759–1763₁, *ticket taker.*

On 22 December 1759 a Mr "Dallon" was paid by the treasurer of Covent Garden Theatre "on account of salary omitted 15th inst. £1 10s. and salary of 22 inst. £1 10s." On 15 April 1760 he received another £1 10s. for his weekly salary. His function at the theatre is not known to us. Very likely he was the Mr Dalton, a "receiver," or ticket taker, at Drury Lane Theatre for three seasons, 1760–63, who shared annual benefits with other house servants.

Dalton, Miss [*fl. 1791*], *actress.*

A Miss Dalton acted the leading female role of Rosamond in a single performance of *King Henry II* at the Haymarket, in a specially licensed performance, on 26 December 1791.

Dalton, Amy [*fl. 1664–1667*], *actress.*

An actress whose roles were apparently too small to warrant inclusion on cast lists, Amy Dalton was first mentioned as a member of the King's Company in a Lord Chamberlain's warrant dated 13 September 1664. Her name was cancelled on a livery warrant dated 8 February 1668.

Daly, Mr [*fl. 1732*], *actor.*

Mr Daly played Lockit in *The Beggar's Opera* when it was performed at the Haymarket Theatre on 4 September 1732 for Signora Violante's benefit.

Daly, Mr [*fl. 1779*], *actor.*

A Mr Daly played Freeman in *A Bold Stroke for a Wife* in a specially licensed performance for the benefit of the actor Massey at the Haymarket Theatre on 13 October 1779. This Mr Daly seems not to have been Richard Daly, who had performed a few times at Covent Garden during the previous spring but who by May had left for Ireland.

Daly, Mrs [*fl. 1756?–1763*], *actress.*

A Mrs Daly made her first appearance at Drury Lane in the title role of *The Old Maid* on 24 March 1763 on the occasion of Yates's benefit. She had joined Foote's summer theatre at the Haymarket by 20 June 1763, at which time the playbill showed "Mrs Daily" playing Mrs Sneak in *The Mayor of Garratt*. This afterpiece had a run of 24 consecutive performances, and 36 before the end of the summer. In addition Mrs Daly played several times as Parthenope and Moon in *The Rehearsal*, Louisa in *Love Makes a Man*, and (for a benefit shared with Weston) both Mrs Sullen in *The Beaux' Stratagem* and an unspecified part in *The Contented Cuckold*. On that date, 5 September 1763, she was living at Mr Allen's in Great Suffolk Street, near the Haymarket.

There is no record of her playing again before or after those dates, either in or out of London, unless she was the Mrs Daly who had played at Tralee in Ireland in September and October of 1756.

Daly, Richard *1758–1813,* *actor, manager.*

Richard Daly was born in County Galway, Ireland, the second son of a prosperous farmer. The *Alumni Dubliniensis* indicates that he was 15 years of age when he enrolled at Trinity College, Dublin, in the fall of 1773. He is not, however, recorded in *A Catalogue of Graduates Who Have Proceeded to Degrees . . .* (1869), and it is probable that he did not remain in college long enough to take a degree.

Whatever the length of Daly's residence at Trinity, it seems to have been little more than an excuse for roistering with a set of young ruffians, fellow students nearly as dissolute as himself. One of them, Jonah Barrington, was responsible for the incredible assertion, later repeated by James Boaden (and still later, by the historian of duelling Lorenzo Sabine) that Daly "in two years, fought three duels with sword, and thirteen with pistol, yet received no material harm." (Barrington swore that he had fought a duel with Daly in which his adversary was saved from death only because the ball from Barrington's pistol struck and broke a diamond brooch over Daly's breastbone.) Barrington often drew the longbow in his memoirs, but whether or not the astonishing total of duels which he gave is correct, there is sufficient testimony to Daly's irresponsible challenges and to his brutal behavior as a young man-about-Dublin. Twenty years after his matriculation *An Answer to the Memoires of Mrs Billington . . .* (1792) suggested that, as an undergraduate, he had had a hand in the murder of two watchmen by a group of young hoodlums, and that, in a fit of anger over a decision in a billiard game at Mara's tables in Cope Street, Daly had hurled a ball at the marker, hitting him in the eye and fatally injuring him. Shortly after that incident, his patrimony exhausted, and (very likely) sought by the

RICHARD DALY

artist unknown

Irish authorities, Daly turned up in London, where for a time he lived nearly in destitution.

Tall and elegantly made and (though with a squint) very handsome, Daly as a young man had considerable charm when he was not being deliberately offensive. When it was suggested to him that he might follow the lead of innumerable other Irishmen and take to the London stage he submitted himself briefly to the tutelage of his aged and famous fellow-countryman Charles Macklin. He made his stage debut, as Othello, at Covent Garden on 4 March 1779 billed as "A Young Gentleman," the cloak of anonymity usually employed for initial appearances in leading roles. The notorious difficulties posed by the character of Othello were no doubt exacerbated for Daly by the contrast with the experienced Iago of Robert Bensley and the Desdemona of Mrs Ann Crawford, Spranger Barry's widow. At any rate, his debut in tragedy was a failure and he was next groomed for high comedy in the part of Lord Townly in *The Provok'd Husband*, again opposite Mrs Crawford, she as Lady Townly. He appeared in the role, again anonymously, on 8 April. Daly was given a benefit on 20 April and chose to play Iachimo in *Cymbeline*; he was assisted by Thomas Crawford as Posthumus, and solicited patronage from his residence at No 8, George Street, York Buildings.

Daly had been befriended by the Crawfords and when they left London for a Dublin engagement in May of 1799 he accompanied them, playing young Norval and other parts at Cork on the way. Daly could have had few better patrons in Ireland than Ann Dancer Barry Crawford. A wise and experienced actress and an owner of theatrical property (shares in Crow Street Theatre, Dublin, inherited from Spranger Barry), she wielded much influence and she evidently exerted it in Daly's behalf with Thomas Ryder, the Dublin lessee and manager. Daly soon played Lord Townly to the Lady Townly of Jane Barsanti Lyster, a beautiful and respected London actress and singer then well established in the Crow Street company and but recently (in January 1779) widowed. She owned a well-earned reputation as a woman of rigid principles and strict morality, yet she very quickly capitulated to Daly's charming manner, and before the middle of September 1779 they had married and she had settled on him an income of £20 per week.

Thomas Ryder, Daly's Crow Street manager, also held a lease of the empty Smock Alley house. Without revealing his identity to Ryder, Daly obtained the lease from the owner, Dr. Thomas Wilson, who acted as go-between in offering Ryder remission of a debt of between £12,000 and £15,000. Daly signed the celebrated John Philip Kemble to a short-term contract, quickly refurbished the house, and in November 1780 opened it with an expensive gala. So far as the public knew, at first he was a successful manager, rotating through his excellent resident repertory company a succession of London stars: the Kembles, his old tutor Macklin, Mrs Jordan, Mrs Billington, and dozens of prominent but lesser lights. But it was charged that he neglected his business for debauchery, and squandered receipts at gambling and in elaborate suppers for his intimates on stage after performances. He seldom went to England to engage actors himself, but sent a succession of henchmen ("absolute theatrical kidnappers," according to the author of *An Answer to the Memoirs of Mrs Billington*) who promised actors large returns which were never realized because of Daly's parsimony and dishonesty and his habit of reducing performers' salaries by unreasonable fines and forfeits. Such success as Daly had, moreover, was in large measure due to the loyal exertions of his wife Jane, who had to witness the constant pursuits (and frequent captures) of the young actresses Daly lured to his company and then black-mailed into submission by threats of cancelled contracts and humiliating roles. Among his young victims was Dorothy Phillips, later the celebrated actress Dorothy Jordan, by whom he had a daughter, who became (as Mrs Alsop) an actress on the British and American stages.

Despite his deficiencies of character and ability Daly prospered for several seasons, withstanding stiff competition. His old patrons Ann and Thomas Crawford had reopened Crow Street in the fall of 1781, and they were succeeded there by Dawson, Owenson, Robert Glenville (a dissident from Daly's company), and Sparks. But by the spring of 1783 Crow Street was boarded up again. In 1782 the little Capel Street Theatre reopened and in 1783 Giordani and Leoni began giving operas and light musical pieces there, but by the spring of 1784 this venture also had failed. Finally, Owenson challenged Daly by opening up the Fishamble Street Music Hall as a theatre. But Daly was spared whatever threat that enterprise posed by the intervention of Parliament which, on 25 November 1786, granted him an exclusive patent for fourteen years for the performance of drama in Dublin and gave him also the title of Deputy Master of the Revels. Daly's company continued to play at Smock Alley through the 1786–87 season and then removed to Crow Street, where a completely redecorated and partly rebuilt theatre reopened on 18 January 1788.

But in 1789 Daly came under attack by various factions led by John Magee, editor of the Dublin *Post*, who charged Daly with having wrongfully obtained large sums from the government lottery offices in Dublin by having certain information sent from London by carrier pigeon before its official reception by packet boat. Magee was subsequently convicted of libel, but not before he had stirred up riots and disturbances which reduced patronage at the house. In 1792 he and his brother Cuthbert were jailed briefly for fighting in the theatre. In

1793 Frederick Edward Jones and several young aristocrats opened the private theatre in Fishamble Street; Jane Barsanti Daly died in 1795; and on 12 August 1797, Daly, exhausted with struggle, sold to Jones both his theatre and the remainder of his patent, for an annuity of £400.

For fifteen seasons after 1781 Daly was also manager at the George's Street Theatre in Cork, and he had complicated managerial interests at various times also at Limerick, Newly, and Waterford. (See William Smith Clark, *The Irish Stage in the County Towns*, 1965.) In 1798 the Crown granted a pension of £100 to Daly. On 1 December 1800 he transferred his ownership of Crow Street Theatre to Frederick Jones. He died at Dublin in September 1813.

A profile portrait of Daly, crudely made by an unknown engraver, was published in the *Town and Country Magazine*, 1787.

Daly, Mrs Richard. *See* **BARSANTI, JANE.**

Damascene, Alexander *d. 1719, singer, composer.*

Born in France, probably of Italian parents, Alexander Damascene came to England because of his Protestantism and the imminence of the revocation of the Edict of Nantes, and was made an Englishman by domicile on 22 July 1682. On 18 July 1689 he was appointed to the vocal music at court and made the composer for the King's private music. Not until 6 December 1690 was he sworn a Gentleman of the Chapel Royal extraordinary (without fee). On 10 December 1695, upon the death of Henry Purcell, he was appointed to a full place with salary.

In 1691, while waiting for his ordinary appointment, he had accompanied William III to the Hague, and on 30 April 1693 and 1694 had sung at the Court in London to celebrate the Queen's birthday.

Damascene composed a large number of secular songs which appeared in such collections as *Choice Ayres and Songs* (1676–84), *The Theatre of Musick* (1685–87), *Vinculum societatis* (1687–91), *Comes amoris* (1687–94), *The Banquet of Musick* (1688–92), *The Gentleman's Journal* (1692–94), and *Wit and Mirth* (1719).

He died in London on 14 July 1719, having drawn up a will on 16 May 1715 leaving his estate to his daughter Sara Powell. He described himself as of the parish of St Anne, Westminster (now St Anne, Soho). Sara Powell proved the will on 27 July 1719.

Dame, Mr *[fl. 1783], musician.*

According to a manuscript "List of Persons" now in the Public Record Office, a Mr. Dame was a musician at the King's Theatre in 1783. Perhaps he was related to the William Dame of Manchester Street who received 19 guineas for a ring of remembrance in the will of the musician John Crosdill, dated 30 August 1825.

Damen. *See* **DAHMEN.**

Damiani, Vitale *[fl. 1799–1800], singer.*

Vitale Damiani, a singer of some reputation in Italy, had been engaged by W. Taylor, the manager of the Opera, for the latter half of the 1798–99 season, but did not arrive in London until about 9 July 1799, too late to perform at all. Although he also had been articled at £1200 to perform the whole of the next season, Damiani fell out with the management over the details of his contract and again did not perform at the Opera. (The disagreement was laid out in a memorandum by Taylor which he published on behalf of the King's Theatre in August 1799.) An ambiguous notice in the *Monthly Mirror* for March 1800 suggests the likelihood that Damiani did perform in at least one concert room: "Raimondi's Concert—Willis's Room. With the principal aid of the first vocal performer in this country, we mean Madame Mara, aided by the novel attractions of Damiani, these concerts have been, and are likely to continue to be, extremely productive."

Damiani was pictured in a large and idealized composite group of singers by Fedi, engraved by Bettelini and published at Milan early in the nineteenth century.

D'Amicis. *See* **DE AMICIS.**

Danby, Master   ₍*fl.* *1792–1814?*₎, *singer.*

The "Danby, Jun." alto (i.e., counter-tenor singer) whose address in 1794 was in Tottenham Street, according to Doane's *Musical Directory*, was probably the son of Charles Danby the bass singer and actor. He may be identified as the "Master Danby" who sang in the chorus supporting *The Enchanted Wood* at the Haymarket Theatre on 25 August 1792 and several times thereafter. From the spring of 1799 through perhaps the season of 1814 he served Drury Lane intermittently as a chorus singer.

Danby, Charles   ₍*fl.* *1776–1814?*₎, *actor, singer.*

Charles Danby, the actor and bass singer, was probably the younger brother of the better-known bass singer and composer, John Danby (1757–1798).

Charles was singing in the chorus at Drury Lane by September 1776 or earlier at 5*s.* a performance. On 26 December 1776 the account book distinguishes a "Danby" and a "C. Danby." The former was probably John Danby. From this point on until John's death in 1798 it is often impossible to say which Danby is being mentioned in the accounts, though it seems obvious, from certain indications, that John was more constant in the chorus and for a long while disbursed money to its members. Charles was doubtless the "Danby, Jr." cited by Burney as among the basses in the

Handel Commemoration concerts at Westminster Abbey and the Pantheon in May and June, 1784.

The *London Chronicle* of 20 October 1781 identified Charles Danby as a bass singer and he was listed in the part of Æolus in the dramatic opera *King Arthur* on 19 October 1781. He sang in the piece repeatedly until the end of the following January, but the bills do not show him in anything else that season.

Charles was not named in the Drury Lane bills again until 29 April 1785 when he played the Daemon of Revenge in *Cymon*. He sang several times during May in the afterpiece entertainment *The Convivial Coterie* or *Sons of Anacreon*. By the season of 1789–90 he was earning £1 10*s.* per week. He was fairly often employed in tiny singing parts and choruses of plays and in comic opera and melodrama until perhaps 1813–14. The record is again complicated, however, after the debut of a "Master Danby" at the Haymarket in the summer of 1792 and especially after the appearance, around the fall of 1802, of "Danby, Jr" (at £1 10*s.* per week) and "Danby, Sr" (at £1 5*s.*) in the Drury Lane pay list.

Charles Danby's address in 1794 was No 24, Tottenham Street, according to Doane's *Musical Directory* (1794). The records of the Royal Society of Musicians contain no mention of him.

Danby, Humphrey   ₍*fl.* *1709–1739*₎, *flutist.*

The Mr Denby who played on the "flute a-la-main" (a German flute?) at Hampstead Wells on 3 September 1709 may have been Humphrey Danby (or Denby), who was later a member of the Prince of Denmark's Musick. A warrant in the *Calendar of Treasury Books* concerns a sum for pensions for nine of the Prince's musicians from 15 December 1715 to 20 December 1716 and it names Danby. A Humphrey Danby became one of the original subscribers to the Royal Society of Musicians on 28 August 1739.

Danby, John *1757–1798, singer, composer.*

John Danby the bass singer was born in 1757, according to the inscription on his tombstone, but nothing is known of his parentage. He may have come from a musical family, however, and the singer and actor Charles Danby was probably his brother.

John studied singing under Samuel Webbe and by (at latest) 1776 he was finding frequent professional employments, including occasional five-shilling engagements helping to fill up the chorus at Drury Lane. From this period until after John Danby's death it is difficult to determine whether payments in the manuscript account books refer to John or to Charles. A notation of 26 December 1776 distinguished a C. Danby and a Danby (doubtless John) and this would seem to imply John's seniority; a notation of 20 December 1784 reads "Mr Charles Danby 3 weeks before put on list 4/10/0." Long before the latter date one Danby had risen to some position of direction in the chorus and was disbursing money to it, and thus it seems that functionary must have been John. He evidently held the position until the end of the 1788–89 season.

On 2 January 1785 S[amuel] Webbe signed the following statement of nomination to the Governors of the Royal Society of Musicians:

Gentlemen, I beg leave to recommend Mr John Danby Musician, as a proper person to be a Member of this Society, he has no Family, being unmarried—Served a Regular Apprenticeship to me, has practised music for a livelihood for more than 7 years, is 28 years of age. . . . His present engagements are Drury Lane Theatre—Concert of Antient Music, Oratorios, Academy of Antient Music, at all which he sings in Chorus, has several scholars and a variety of other engagements.

John Danby was unanimously elected to the Society on February 1785, and on 6 March he attended, signed the books of admission, and paid his subscription. One or both of the Danbys resided in Wardour Street, Soho, in 1786.

Danby had, indeed, the "variety of other engagements" spoken of by his sponsor. He was singing at Ranelagh and Vauxhall (often with his old master Samuel Webbe) and composing glees and songs in great profusion. Between 1781 and 1794 he won ten prizes from the Catch Club for eight glees and ten canons. Burney lists him among the bass singers in the Handel Memorial Concerts at Westminster Abbey and the Pantheon in May and June 1784. He wrote music for two plays and composed masses and motets for the service of the Spanish Chapel near Manchester Square, where he, a Catholic, had been made organist. Probably to be nearer Vauxhall he moved to No 7, Gilbert's Buildings "near the Asylum," in the late eighties, and later lived at No 26, Henrietta Street, Covent Garden.

Danby became virtually paralyzed with arthritis from having slept in a damp bed at an inn and in the final years of his life was forced to abandon his profession. He died at 11:30 on the evening of 16 May 1798 at a house in Upper John Street, Fitzroy Square, even as a concert held for his benefit at Willis's Rooms was concluding. He was buried in Old St Pancras Churchyard.

One of John Danby's daughters, Caroline Melissa (1797–1857), married the well-known organist and composer, Henry George Nixon (1796–1849), and this couple had 13 children, among whom were the excellent organist and composer Henry Cotter Nixon (1842–1907), and the violinist James Cassana Nixon (1823–1842).

The fortunes of John Danby's widow and children can be followed for many years in the Minute Books of the Governors of the Musicians Fund in the Royal

Society of Musicians: on 1 July 1798 Sarah Danby, the widow, prayed for relief and was granted £4 17s. 6d. per month, which was increased by 15s. on 6 January 1799 when the Governors were informed that Mrs Danby had been delivered of a daughter (Teresa). Various payments for children's schooling followed. On 1 December 1805 Mrs Danby informed the Society that on 27 January 1806 her daughter Louisa Mary would be 14; and on 2 February the Society took steps to place the girl for seven years with Mrs Potter, the Headmistress of Wimbledon School, probably as an apprentice teacher. A similar report was made of Marcella Danby who was 14 on 14 April 1810 but she developed scrofula and was not fit for service. Caroline (born 20 July 1797) and Teresa (born in January 1799) were apprenticed to another schoolmistress, a Madame Bernard who kept "the school in the New Road near Lisson Green" and who, on 6 February 1814, was said to have "left her school and deserted her apprentice[s]." Mrs Danby sent the Society thanks for a Christmas donation on 4 February 1838. In April and again in July 1840 she was given £1 for medical relief. At that point the entries ceased.

John Danby's compositions were numerous. He published three collections, and a fourth was issued after his death. An extensive list of his works can be found in the *Catalogue of Printed Music in the British Museum.*

Dance, James. *See* LOVE, JAMES.

Dance, Mrs James. *See* LOVE, MRS JAMES.

Dance, William   *1755–1840, pianist, violinist, composer.*

William Dance was born on 20 December 1755, entering a numerous family of practitioners of several arts. He was the great-great-grandson of James and Elizabeth Dance of Winchester. His great-grandfather was Giles Dance (1670–1751), stonemason of London, and his great-grandmother, Giles's wife, was Sarah Brett of Carshalton. William's paternal grandfather was the elder George Dance (1695–1768), Clerk of the City Works and the architect of the Mansion House and several important churches, and his grandmother was Elizabeth Gould. William's father was George's eldest son, the Oxford-educated actor, manager, and playwright James Dance (1722–1774), who had assumed the name Love, and his mother was James's wife the actress Elizabeth, daughter of James Hooper.

One of William's uncles was Sir Nathaniel Dance-Holland, R. A. (1735–1811), the painter, and another was George Dance the younger (1741–1825), architect of Newgate and other famous London buildings, who was also an amateur musician. William's brother Nathaniel (1748–1827) was an adventurous captain of an East Indiaman who had been knighted for routing a French naval squadron which he had accidentally encountered while returning from the East with a group of British merchant ships. William's cousin Charles Dance (1794–1863) was a prolific popular dramatist.

William turned early to music, probably because of his father's theatrical connections. He studied piano early with Theodore Aylward and then took up the violin, first under the direction of C. F. Baumgarten and later with Giardini. Some early authorities reported that William played in a theatrical band in 1767, when he would have been only 12 years old. James Boswell, an old acquaintance of his father's, visited the Loves at their theatre in Richmond, Surrey, on 18 September 1769 and remarked in his *Journal* that "Billy was grown a surprising musician. He played to me on the pianoforte." Billy was certainly carried on the roster of the Drury Lane band from 1771–72 through 1774–75, for the account books show payments to him all during this period. In 1775 he joined the opera band at the King's Theatre where he remained for 18 years as a second violinist. In 1785 he was paid £5 5*s.* per week. Burney numbered Dance among the first violins at the Handel Memorial Concerts at Westminster Abbey and the Pantheon in May and June 1784. He led the band at that festival in 1790, in the absence of J. B. Cramer. He was leader of the band at the summer theatre in the Haymarket from 1784 through 1790.

From sometime before 1794, in which year Doane's *Musical Directory* reported his address, Dance resided at No 17, Manchester Street, Manchester Square. It was from this house on 17 January 1813 that Dance issued the circular signed by himself, Cramer, and Domenico Corri which led to the establishment of the Philharmonic Society, of which Dance was afterward a director and the treasurer. His son Henry was secretary for the first year.

Dance was active in the Professional

By permission of the Royal Society of Musicians of Great Britain

WILLIAM DANCE
by George Dance

Concerts and played in the King's Band. He had been proposed by John Parke the great oboist for membership in the Royal Society of Musicians on 4 January 1778, and he took a very active part in its affairs. The Minute Books of the Society show him to have been a member of its Court of Assistants in 1785, continuously from 1793 through 1800, again from 1802 through 1816, in 1818, and 1837. On 2 March 1800 "Mr Dance gave in the name of Capt Dance as honorary member" according to an entry of the above date in the Minute Book. An entry of 1 June 1800 proposed George Dance as an honorary member. Doubtless the former was the mariner and the latter William's Uncle George, the amateur musician. William "gave the name of Mr Henry Dance as a subscriber for life and paid £10.10" according to an entry of 4 April 1802; and there is a similar tenguinea entry for Edward Dance on 5 December 1802. These were probably sons of William.

Dance's chief celebrity came from his performance on the violin, but he was also an accomplished performer on the piano, and he gave lessons on both instruments for perhaps sixty years. Among his innumerable successful pupils were Benjamin Blake on the piano and W. T. Parke on the tenor violin. The latter, indeed, testified in his memoirs that he had become a proficient player after only three months of intensive instruction by Dance.

The great age to which he eventually attained, his family and professional connections, and his gregarious temperament, gave Dance an almost unparalleled breadth of acquaintance, especially in artistic, theatrical, and musical circles. He was an intimate of the Parkes, Ignace Pleyel, Domenico Corri, and J. B. Cramer. He introduced Haydn to Mr and Mrs Joah Bates at their house in John Road, Bedford Row, on the evening when Mrs Bates charmed Haydn by singing his songs. He entertained Mendelssohn, who wrote for his daughter

Sophia Louisa No 4 of the *"Lieder ohne Worte."*

William Dance died at Brompton on 5 June 1840. His widow Jane was granted a pension of £2 12s. 6d. per month by the Royal Society of Musicians.

Dance left behind him a quantity of miscellaneous musical composition, and some of it was published during his lifetime. In notes written in 1824 for Sainsbury's 1827 *Dictionary* Dance testified that he had "published various Piano Forte works of merit consisting of Sonatas, Fantasias, Variations, Preludes, &c." and then listed "Six Sonatas for the Piano Forte, Op. 1; Six [Sonatas] for [Piano Forte], Op. 2; Three Sonatas and eight Preludes for [Piano Forte], Op. 3; A Sonata in which is introduced the National Air of Hearts of Oak, Op. 4; God Save the King with New Variations (in Sainsbury's published *Dictionary* he notes that these "have been extremely admired, and the sale has been such as to require four sets of plates." They were published by L. Lavenu in 1800); Preludes in Various Keys; Fantasia for the Piano Forte; with several Song[s] & Airs arranged as Rondos for the Piano Forte."

In addition the British Museum holds three songs published by Dance: *Tell me thou Soul of her I love. A Ballad. The Words from Thomson's Odes* . . . L. Lavenu [1798]; *Address to Contentment, from Lady Manners' Poems* . . . L. Lavenu . . . [1798]; and *The Waterman, a Favorite Air* [from Charles Dibdin's opera *The Waterman*] *arranged as a Rondo for the Piano Forte, by W. Dance.* Dale, for the Author . . . [1796?].

A pencil drawing of William Dance by his brother George is at the Royal Society of Musicians.

Dancer, Mrs (fl. 1766), *house servant?*

Mrs Dancer was the subject of one of James Winston's entries in the Drury Lane fund book which is difficult to interpret:

"Mrs. Dancer died before Estab 1–1." She was apparently a member of the company, possibly a house servant, and she presumably deposited £1 1s. in the fund but died before the fund was sufficient in size for it to help her beneficiaries. Winston's entry was dated simply 1766.

Dancer, Miss (fl. 1782–1788), *actress.*

A Miss Dancer, more than likely the daughter of the York actors Mr and Mrs John Wimperis Dancer, was listed in Wilkinson's company on the York circuit in 1782. On 17 September 1783 a Miss Dancer was given unspecified parts in the anonymous new comedy *Cheapside* and W. C. Oulton's new farce *A New Way to Keep a Wife at Home* in a specially licensed performance at the Haymarket. She was absent from the London bills until 30 September 1788 when she (or some other Miss Dancer) turned up in another Haymarket performance specially licensed by the Lord Chamberlain, playing Corinna in *The Citizen.* She may nevertheless have found some work in London during the interim between 1783 and 1788, for a Miss Dancer was among 17 known minor performers allowed to share in a Drury Lane benefit on 1 June 1787.

Dancer, John Wimperis d. 1790, *actor, singer.*

Though his first name was not given by the bill, it is almost certain that the actor who appeared in the part of Ratcliff in *Richard III* at the Haymarket Theatre on 19 September 1769 was John Wimperis Dancer. Dancer was making his first London appearance on this last night of the summer season.

Where Dancer spent the following winter is not known; it was not in a London patent theatre. But evidently the Haymarket manager, Samuel Foote, had approved him in his debut, for the young actor was on hand when the Haymarket season opened the following May, performing at least 18 times with 15 parts during the summer of 1770: Young Loveit and Gruel in *The Commissary*, Guildenstern in *Hamlet*, Sir Roger Dowlas in *The Patron*, Spinosa in *Venice Preserv'd*, a Scholar in *The Padlock*, Cornwall in *King Lear*, Quaver in *The Virgin Unmask'd*, a Footman in *The Lame Lover*, Carlos in *The Wrangling Lovers*, Mars in *Midas*, Pembroke in *King John*, the Chaplain in *The Orphan*, the Governor in *Oroonoko*, and Raleigh in *The Earl of Essex*—a very thorough apprenticeship in a very short time.

Dancer was certainly in London during the fall of 1770, but he attracted no attention from the patent houses in the three performances he participated in at the Haymarket by special license of the Lord Chamberlain—Sir Charles Freeman in *The Beaux' Stratagem* on 27 September, Cassio in *Othello* on 1 October, and Whisper in *The Busy Body* on 5 October. Probably he did not try very hard to obtain a London berth, for his manager Foote had taken a lease of the Edinburgh Theatre for the winter season of 1770–71, and Dancer accompanied him thither.

By 15 May 1771 Dancer had returned to London, with the rest of Foote's company. He played Loveit in *Miss in Her Teens* and subsequently until 20 September several of his old parts and these new ones: Cash in *Every Man in His Humour*, Jollop in *The Mayor of Garratt*, Charles in *The Busy Body*, Classic in *The Englishman in Paris*, Old Catgut in *The Commissary*, Beaufort in *The Citizen*, Francis in *The Brothers*, Gargle in *The Apprentice*, Puff in *Miss in Her Teens*, Harry in *The Mock Doctor*, Sol Smack in *The Vintner Trick'd*, Stukely in *The West Indian*, Eustace in *Love in a Village*, Count Bassett in *The Provok'd Husband*, and Lorenzo in *The Merchant of Venice*.

J. W. Dancer's movements during the 1771–72 winter season are not known. He was again at the Haymarket on 20 May 1772 and that season he added to his list of parts: the Poet in *The Author*, La Fleur in *The Commissary*, James in *The Mock Doctor*, Argus in *The Contrivances*, Martin in *The Anatomist*, Clerimont in *The Miser*, Setter in *The Old Bachelor*, an unspecified part in *The Rehearsal*, Tressel in *Richard III*, and, on the last night of the season, for his benefit (shared with Mrs Fearon and Van Rymsdyck), Eustace in *Love in a Village*.

The Committee Books of the Norwich Theatre contain the following entry for 26 May 1773: "Ord'd that Mr. Dancer's Salary be advanced to £1. 11. 6," thus indicating the actor's presence in that theatre for at least some part of the previous season. C. B. Hogan furnishes evidence, from a manuscript compilation by A. S. Brown of Norwich, a company member, that a Mr Dancer began to be active in Norwich in the fall of 1772. Certainly this Dancer—who continued at Norwich off and on until 1782—cannot have been William Dancer, as suggested by the editor of the *Committee Books*, William having died in 1759. There is hardly any doubt that the Norwich man was John Wimperis Dancer.

Dancer "held the palm of great preeminence in that city," according to Tate Wilkinson, playing a wide spectrum of roles, from Sileno in *Midas* to Sir George Hastings in *A Word to the Wise*. He spent part of the summer of 1776 in the ill-fated little China Hall Theatre at Rotherhithe. The Norwich Committee Books reveal that in 1775–76 his salary was fixed at £1 1s. per week, that by at latest 30 May 1777 he was married and his wife was also acting, and that he sometimes borrowed heavily against his salary. Hannah More saw him on 16 June that year when the company was at Bungay and thought the portrayal of his character "pretty well conceived . . . though inadequately acted." On 11 May 1781 it was "Ordered That Mr Dancer (who left the Company on Acct of Illness and now having recovered his Health & Applied to the Manager to be readmitted) be informed . . . that this Committee will receive him at a Sallary of 1.11.6 p week & that he may Join the Company on the 4th June at Bungay."

It may have been either the refusal of a loan or the Committee's denial of a place in the company to Mrs Dancer for the next season (reflected in May 1781 entries in the *Committee Book*) or it may have been some other reason which made the Dancers leave the excellent little theatre at Norwich for York the next year. He (and perhaps she) acted in the York company from August 1782. Things went well for over a year, and then, in the words of his York manager, Wilkinson, Dancer, "who had gone on with every imaginable good reception and reward from the public, and who seemed remarkably attentive to his theatrical labours was (without any cause whatever that could be ascribed) on Sunday, July 20 [1783] seized with a violent madness, which continued so alarming and increasing a degree, that the York Asylum was the only possibility of relief, where he was carried to from Leeds . . ." Under the sympathetic care of a Dr Hunter, Dancer recovered his wits sufficiently to act in the winter season beginning in January 1784. But by the spring his condition had once more become pitiable.

In an announcement for the Dancers' benefit on 15 May 1784 Dancer feared that "after so many favours" this benefit would seem "an intrusion on generosity," but since Mr Dancer's state of health made a temporary retirement from the stage necessary the manager (Tate Wilkinson) was providing a second benefit night so that Mrs Dancer might "fix herself in a shop to support herself" and her family. Dancer died at York on 23 May 1790, according to the Leeds *Mercury* of 31 May.

Mrs Dancer does not seem to have acted in London, but a Miss Dancer, probably a daughter, who first came on the stage at

York in 1782, performed in a few pick-up companies at the Haymarket.

Dancer, William *d. 1759, actor.*

The first notice of the actor William Dancer was as a member of the company at Richmond, Surrey, in the summer–fall season of 1747. He is known to have acted Trueman in *Diversions of the Morning* and Horatio in *Hamlet* on 13 October. He was in Foote's company at the Haymarket Theatre in the spring of the following year and he shared a benefit with Poynter on 19 May 1749. In the summer of that year he acted at the Butler Market Theatre in Canterbury. For a brief time in April of 1750, Dancer, with Matthews and Yeates, managed the New Wells at Clerkenwell.

In 1751, Dancer acted at Bath, first at the Orchard Street Theatre, then at Simpson's Theatre. He was in 1752 at York where on 28 February he played King Lear. Playing Cordelia was Ann Street, Dancer's future wife. As a member of the summer company at Richmond in 1753, he played Shrimp in *The Fine Lady's Airs*, Ranger in *The Suspicious Husband*, Morelove in *The Careless Husband*, Archer in *The Beaux' Stratagem*, Macbeth, Myrtle in *The Conscious Lovers*, Hotspur in *1 Henry IV* and Marplot in *The Busy Body*. For his benefit at Richmond on 22 September he offered Ranger and presented a "Dish of Foote's Tea" and some "Choice Spirits from the Old Woman's Oratory." The latter pastiche was also his specialty when he was at York. Dancer returned to Bath to perform at Orchard Street in 1753–54 and at Simpson's in 1754–55.

In a private ceremony at Bath in 1754 Dancer married the young actress Ann Street, who earlier had been acting sometimes under her maiden name and sometimes as Mrs Dancer. The marriage took place against her relatives' wishes, and the couple felt it necessary to place a notice in the *Bath Journal* absolving friends of encouraging them:

Whereas it has been wickedly and maliciously reported, that Mr Richard Stephens and wife were privy and accessory to our late private wedding: In justice therefore, we think it our indispensible duty to certify their innocence, they being in no way concern'd or acquainted with it.

The Dancers continued to act together at York in 1755 and 1756 and at Newcastle in 1756 and 1757. At York he played Gratiano and she played Jessica in *The Jew of Venice*, Granville's adaptation of Shakespeare's play. In the season 1758–59 they engaged with Spranger Barry at his new Crow Street Theatre in Dublin.

At Crow Street, Ann Dancer began an affair with Barry, who was instructing her in acting; it was said that she "sucked in the poison of love by the vehicle of tuition." Stories circulated of the Dancers' domestic discord and of William's jealousy of his wife's professional success. Dancer became the subject of numerous puns and epigrams. He died, of unspecified causes, on 27 December 1759, leaving the way clear for Mrs Dancer to take up openly with Barry, whom she later married. As Mrs Barry, and then Mrs Crawford, Ann became one of the most celebrated actresses of the London stage.

Some 18 years after William Dancer's death, the *Town and Country Magazine* (January 1777) described him as "one of the most disagreeable men, as to person, that ever existed." He should not be confused with the Mr Dancer who acted at Norwich in the 1770s and at York in the 1780s. That actor was John W. Dancer.

Dancer, Mrs William. *See* BARRY, MRS SPRANGER.

Dancey, Mr *fl. 1734*, dancer?

Mr Dancey was one of the Justices (probably a dancing role) in *The Harlot's Progress* at Drury Lane on 21 October 1734.

Dancey, Mrs *fl. 1732–1739*, actress, dancer.

On 16 February 1732 at the Haymarket Theatre a benefit was held for Mrs Dancey, "the famous Dutch Woman," probably the mother of the Miss Dancey active at this time and wife of the Mr Dancey who appeared at Drury Lane in 1734. At her benefit Mrs Dancey may have rope danced. She appeared as Mrs Overdone in *Sir John Falstaff* on 4 September 1733 at Bartholomew Fair and, with Miss Dancey, was a member of the Drury Lane troupe in 1734–35 and 1735–36. At Drury Lane she was cast as a Lady of Pleasure in *The Harlot's Progress* on 21 October 1734 (her first notice) and also played, during her stay there, Mrs Snip in *The Merry Cobler* and a Milkmaid in *Harlequin Restored*.

On 23 August 1736 she was in *The Cheats of Scapin* at Bartholomew Fair, and a year later she danced at Hallam's Bartholomew Fair booth and at the Lee-Hallam Southwark Fair booth. In 1737–38 and 1738–39 she was at Covent Garden playing small parts such as Dainty Fidget in *The Country Wife*, Lucinda in *Love and a Bottle*, and Lucy in *Wit Without Money*. The bills seem sometimes to have confused Miss and Mrs Dancey, and it is difficult to tell which one acted Valeria in *The Rover* on 11 April 1737 and 18 April 1738.

Possibly the following entry in the parish registers of St Paul, Covent Garden, relate to the performing Danceys: on 24 March 1736 George and Elizabeth Dancey christened a daughter Louisa-Sophia Farnanda.

Dancey, Miss *fl. 1731–1740*, actress, dancer.

Miss Dancey (or Dancy) was first mentioned in the bills on 26 August 1731 when she played Betty in *Flora* at Bullock's booth at Bartholomew Fair. At the Haymarket Theatre on 16 February 1732 for the benefit of Mrs Dancey "the famous Dutch Woman" (probably her mother) Miss Dancey appeared as Clara in *The*

Cheats of Scapin. She went on that season and the next to play the Poor Beggarwoman in *The Blazing Comet*, L'Amande in *The Wanton Jesuit*, Lucy in *The Recruiting Officer*, a Shepherdess in *The Festival*, a Peasant Woman in *The Burgomaster Trick'd*, and a Lady in *Chrononhotonthologos*—all at the Haymarket. On 24 August 1734 she was at Bartholomew Fair again, acting one of Don John's wives in *Don John* and Hippolita in *The Barren Island.*

In 1734–35 and 1735–36 she was in the Drury Lane company, except for an appearance as Clara in *Rule a Wife and Have a Wife* at Lincoln's Inn Fields on 12 June 1735. At Drury Lane she was cast as Scentwell in *The Busy Body*, Doll Tearsheet in *2 Henry IV*, and Colombine's Maid in *The Fall of Phaeton*. From 1736–37 through 1739–40 she worked at Covent Garden playing small parts in pantomimes and occasional roles in comedies, some of her parts being a Woman Peasant in *Apollo and Daphne*, an Amazon in *Perseus and Andromeda*, Betty in *The Contrivances*, Wishwell in *The Double Gallant*, Lucy in *Tunbridge Walks*, Betty in *The Gamester*, a Country Lass and a Nymph in *The Royal Chace*, Arbella in *The Honest Yorkshireman*, and Ricotta in *Don Quixote*. The bills may have confused her sometimes with Mrs Dancey, as on 18 April 1738 when *The London Stage* listed her as Valeria in *The Rover*, a part Mrs Dancey was listed to perform on 11 April 1737; which woman actually played it is unclear.

During her years at Covent Garden Miss Dancey appeared only once elsewhere: on 23 August 1737 she and Mrs Dancey danced at Hallam's Bartholomew Fair booth.

Dancy. *See* DANCEY.

Daney, Mr ₁*fl.* 1766₁, *house servant?*
Benefit tickets for Mr Daney, possibly a house servant, were accepted on 19 May 1766 at Drury Lane.

D'Anfoy, Mr ₁*fl.* 1730₁, *dancer.*
Mr D'Anfoy, billed as making his first appearance at Goodman's Fields, performed a new *Dance of Fawns* with Burney on 10 March 1730.

Dangerfield, Mr ₁*fl.* 1791–1804₁, *boxkeeper.*
Mr Dangerfield was a boxkeeper at Drury Lane at least from 1791–92 through 1803–4. By the latter season his salary was 12s. per week. On 13 June 1796 he shared benefit profits of about £292 with 12 other house servants; but on 16 June 1797 he shared an apparent deficit in benefit receipts with 12 others. His wife, Mrs Dangerfield, served the house in an unknown capacity in 1801–2.

Dangeville, Mons ₁*fl.* 1720₁, *dancer.*
Monsieur Dangeville danced with De Grimbergue's troupe at the King's Theatre in the Haymarket and at Lincoln's Inn Fields in the spring of 1720. The troupe began performing on 5 March, but Dangeville's name was not mentioned in the bills until 24 March, when he offered a dance with the performance of *Harlequin a Sham Astrologer.* He was billed as dancing at almost every performance thereafter that spring and apparently was a favorite with the audiences. The manager had to publish an apology in the 2 May *Daily Courant* for Dangeville's failure to appear on 29 April: "he refused to Dance, being puft up by the Applause he had the good Fortune to meet with; fancying he hath a Right to do so whenever he pleases."

The troupe was attacked by Steele and others for lack of decency in some of the performances, but it is not known if Dangeville contributed anything offensive. Mary, Countess Cowper, wrote of the program presented on 31 May 1720: "A most dismal Performance. No Wonder People are

Slaves who can entertain themselves with such Stuff." The play had been *Les Deux arlequins*, and Dangeville had danced.

Dangeville was certainly related to the performing family of that name in France in the first half of the eighteenth century, but which Dangeville he was is not clear. The most famous, Charles Botot (or Claude-Charles Batot) Dangeville (1664–1743), was chiefly an actor; the other likely candidate, Antoine-François Botot (or Batot) Dangeville (1701–1748), was a dancer.

Dangle, Steven ₁*fl. 1794*₁, *violinist.*
Steven Dangle, of No 33, George Street, Manchester Square, was listed in 1794 in Doane's *Musical Directory* as a violinist at Salomon's concerts and in the performances in Westminster Abbey. Perhaps he was related to the musician named Bent Dangle, who according to William Dunlap's *Diary* had been a victim of the Inquisition, had escaped and had arrived, by way of Ireland, in New York by 1798 to play in the orchestra of the Park Theatre.

Daniel. *See also* **DANIELS.**

"Daniel, Dapper." *See* **"DAPPER DANIEL."**

Daniel, Mr ₁*fl. 1782–1789*₁, *actor.*
A Mr Daniel acted the role of Ratcliff in a performance of *Richard III* given at the Haymarket Theatre on 4 March 1782 for the benefit of Mrs Lefevre. Perhaps he was the Mr Daniel who acted Sir William Meadows in *Love in a Village* at the same theatre on 8 January 1787 for the benefit of Mr Harwood, the retired prompter of Drury Lane. A Mr Daniel acted at Brighton in the summers of 1785 and 1789.

Daniel, Mark ₁*fl. 1794–1802?*₁, *singer.*
Mark Daniel, living in Little College Street, Westminster, was listed in Doane's *Musical Directory* in 1794 as a singer in St Peter's choir and in the oratorios at Covent Garden. Perhaps he was the Mark Daniel who witnessed the will of the musician Edmund Ayrton on 6 October 1802.

Daniel, William *d. 1755, actor.*
Prior to his first known appearance in London as a member of a company which performed in 1736 at the old playhouse at the bottom of Mermaid Court during the time of Southwark Fair, William Daniel was no doubt an itinerant actor in the provinces. He had acted Trapland in *Love for Love* in the performance which inaugurated the new theatre in Rainsford Street, Dublin, on 3 February 1733. Daniel was again in London on 16 March 1742 playing an unspecified role in *The Honest Yorkshireman* at the James Street Theatre, for the benefit of the eccentric Charlotte Charke. His wife, Mary Daniel, was a member of the James Street company at this time. Together they managed a booth, with Malone and James, near the Swan, in Tottenham Court Road, in August 1743. On 16 March 1744, the Daniels were again at the James Street Theatre in performances of *The Country Lasses* and *The Fond Husband*. In 1744–45 they joined the Hallam company at Goodman's Fields Theatre, where Daniel acted a recruit in *The Recruiting Officer* on 26 December 1744, Charon in *The Tempest* on 14 February 1745, and the title role in *The Miller of Mansfield* for a benefit he shared with Mrs Bainbridge on 30 March 1745.

Although his wife was engaged at Covent Garden in the spring of 1746 and for the following two seasons, William Daniel was unable to obtain an engagement at a winter patent house. He acted at Warner's booth during the Southwark Fair in September 1747 (when Mrs Garrick was a member of the company) and also Scrub in *The Stratagem* at Southwark on 21 October 1747. During 1748–49, he worked at various London places: at Southwark on 31 October and 13 February (with a benefit on the latter date), at James Street on 20 December when he acted Grise in *The Busy Body,* and on 27 March when again he had a benefit, and at New Wells, Clerkenwell, in December. On 14 November of that season he and his wife had a benefit at the Haymarket, she playing Belvidera in *Venice Preserv'd.* The Daniels were then living at No 17, Stewart Rents, the bottom of Great Wild Street. At the Haymarket on 29 April 1749 he acted Matthieu de la Prison in *L'Opéra du gueux,* a French-language version of *The Beggar's Opera* performed by English actors. According to *The London Stage* he played the same role at the Haymarket about ten months later on 16 February 1750 and again on 8 March, but by these dates, apparently, he had already settled in Jamaica, having gone there with Moody's troupe. For according to the Jamaican Assembly *Journals* of 1749 he that year became the first printer to be authorized by the House of Assembly in Spanish Town to report its votes. His fee was £100 per year.

Daniel also printed the first almanac to be published in Jamaica, *The Merchant's Pocket Companion or an Almanac for the year of our Lord, 1751,* printed in King Street, near the Court House, in Kingston. By 1753 he was named "printer to the Assembly," a position he held until his death several years later. The "Register of Burials, Kingston" (in the Public Record Office, Spanish Town), indicates that William Daniel, printer, was buried in the churchyard on 26 August 1755. In 1756 his widow, through her late husband's executor, Charles Somerset Woodham, presented a claim to the Assembly for printing done by Daniel. On 13 November 1755, Mary Daniel had married Woodham, who had then succeeded Daniel as printer to the Assembly.

Daniel, Mrs William, Mary, later Mrs Charles Somerset Woodham [*fl.* 1742–1756], *actress, dancer.*

Although Mary Daniel probably was performing in itinerant companies with her husband William Daniel during the 1730s, her first recorded stage appearance was as Harriet in *The Miser* at Drury Lane on 27 December 1742. Apparently, however, she was not a regular member of the Drury Lane company at the time. She performed Lady Lurewell in *The Constant Couple,* for her own benefit, at the James Street Theatre on 22 February 1743. Her husband was also in that company. On 5 August 1743 she acted Jenny in *The Glorious Queen of Hungary* at the Tottenham Court Fair in a booth operated by her husband, Malone, and James. Again with her husband she acted in *The Country Lasses* and *The Fond Husband* at the James Street Theatre on 16 March 1744 and then appeared as Sylvia in *The Recruiting Officer* at the Haymarket on 23 April 1744.

In 1744–45 the Daniels joined the company at the Goodman's Fields Theatre where Mrs Daniel acted Miranda in *The Busy Body* on 4 December, Ann Lovely in *A Bold Stroke for a Wife* on 10 December, Sylvia in *The Recruiting Officer* on 26 December, Miranda in *The Tempest* on 14 February, the breeches role of Sir Harry in *The Constant Couple* for her benefit on 26 February, and Lady Townley in *The Provok'd Husband* on 30 March. During this season the Daniels were living at Mrs Cliff's in Buckle Street, near the Lead House, Goodman's Fields.

Late in the season of 1745–46 she took up an engagement at Covent Garden Theatre, where her responsibilities were modest. After her first appearance there on 22 April 1746 as Aura in *The Country Lasses,* she acted the Duchess of York in *Richard III* on 16 June and Lady Bountiful in *The Stratagem* on 23 June 1746. In the following season, when her salary was 7s. 6d. per week, her only known role was Mrs Chat in *The Committee.* She was again at Covent Garden in 1746–47, but on 25 April 1747 her name was taken off the list for the rest of the season. In 1747–48 at Covent Garden she played Mrs Chat and danced in the chorus in such pieces as *The Mouse Trap*. On 30 April 1748 she played Desdemona to Scudamore's Othello at the Haymarket, and at the same theatre several days later, on 2 May, she played the title role in *Jane Shore* for a benefit she shared with the dancer Nicholson.

In the summer of 1748 she performed in Lee and Yeates's booth at Bartholomew Fair, one of her parts being the Fair Maid of the West in the droll *The Unnatural Parents*. With her husband in 1748–49 she acted at various London minor theatres. She essayed the major role of Belvidera in *Venice Preserv'd* at the Haymarket for their benefit on 14 November. They then lived at No 17, Stewart Rents, at the bottom of Great Wild Street. At the James Street Theatre she acted Miranda in *The Busy Body* on 20 December, and on 26 December she managed to perform both the role of Jane Shore at James Street and that of Mrs Prim in *A Bold Stroke for a Wife* at the New Wells, London Spa, Clerkenwell. She acted Lucy in *The Beggar's Opera* at Southwark on 2 January 1749 and the role of Susanne Pimpante in a French-language version of the same play, entitled *L'Opéra du gueux*, at the Haymarket on 29 April 1749. In the following summer at Cross and Bridges' booth at Bartholomew Fair she performed Mrs Clack in *Modern Madness* and Mary in the interlude *The Jovial Jack Tars*.

Early in the fall of 1749 the Daniels left London and sailed to Jamaica to act with Moody's troupe. William, who established himself as a printer to the Assembly at Kingston, died in August 1755. On 13 November 1755, at Kingston, Mrs Daniel married Charles Somerset Woodman, who had been the executor of her husband's estate and was the successor to his printing business.

Daniels. *See also* **DANIEL.**

Daniels, Alicia, later Mrs George Frederick Cooke the second, and **Mrs Windsor** *d. 1826, singer, actress.*

Although she probably performed in the provinces or in London earlier, the first recorded stage appearance of Alicia Daniels was as Leonora in *The Padlock* at Drury Lane on 26 May 1791. On that evening, in Act IV of the mainpiece, *The Belle's Stratagem*, she sang an "Italian Air," and she also shared in benefit tickets. The bills announced that this was her "first appearance" in the character of Leonora, a comment which suggests previous appearances in other roles.

Her name had been entered on the theatre pay list on 22 January 1791 at 3s. 4d. per day, so she must have appeared in chorus roles before playing Leonora. She had probably been one of the priestesses in Prince Hoare's comic opera *The Cave of Trophonius* when it had been performed for the first time several weeks earlier, on 3 May 1791, but the bills for this date had listed only the main performers. When that piece was repeated in the fall of the next season, on 15 October 1791, while the Drury Lane company was playing at the King's Theatre, her name was listed in the bills only as a Priestess. She also played an Italian girl in *The Critic* on 3 October. After a repeat in *The Cave of Trophonius* on 22 October 1791 no other appearances with the company that season are shown; a notation in a manuscript (now at the British Museum) by J. P. Kemble informs us that "Miss Daniels was discharged for nonattendance." Her name was removed from the pay list on 2 December 1791, but by then she was already with the company managed by Banks and Ward at Manchester, where the leading actor was George Frederick Cooke, her future husband.

Miss Daniels remained with the Manchester company for several seasons and no doubt acted in the various towns of the northern circuit when the company went on tour. In 1792–93 her roles in Manchester

Harvard Theatre Collection
ALICIA DANIELS
engraving by Maguire

In voice, look, and action, be ever ex-
press'd

. . . .

Never assume the appearance of an-
guish . . .

She was still in the Manchester company in April 1794, but she seems at this point also to have begun engagements for the summer at Sadler's Wells in London. In his *Musical Directory* (1794) Doane listed a "Miss Daniel" as a soprano at Sadler's Wells Theatre, then living in Fletcher Row, Cold Bath Fields.

Returning to Manchester in 1794–95, she acted Ophelia on 25 May 1795. Hamlet was Mr Cunningham of Dublin. Again at Sadler's Wells in the summer of 1796, she is noted in a Folger Library manuscript as having played a Lass in *England's Glory* on 31 August. The songs *Absence* and *The Gallant Forty Second*, "as sung by Miss Daniels at Vauxhall," were printed about this time. She returned to Manchester once more for 1795–96, when she played Ophelia again, this time to Cooke's Hamlet. During this season, curiously, a "Master Daniels, junior," played the title role in the comic opera *The Adopted Child*.

In his *Reminiscences* (1827), Thomas Dibdin recalled the time when he had served as prompter and actor in the Banks-Ward company and had known Miss Daniels before she married Cooke. At the time, he said, she "had a completely foreign accent," but he did not offer elaboration as to how she came to possess it. During an engagement at Chester, about 1795, Miss Daniels and her mother lodged in the same house where the father of the great French actor Talma lived with his English wife and practised dentistry. Her mother, deeply involved in Miss Daniels's career, used to stand in the wings while the daughter sang, and from nervousness constantly tugged out the pins from her dress—"thus if Miss Daniels happened (as was frequently the case) to be *encored* in a tolerably long song," re-

included Clarissa in *Lionel and Clarissa* and Ariel in *The Tempest*; in the latter piece Cooke played Prospero. The author of *The Thespian Mirror . . . of the Theatres Royal, Manchester, Liverpool, and Chester* characterized her in 1793:

Of some execution and science possess'd
Behold little Daniels a singer profess'd,
Her vanity often mistaking the cause,
Interprets encouragement into applause,
The portion of favor she's thought to in-
herit,
Is more the effect of her youth than her
merit

. . . .

Her efforts are weaken'd by over exer-
tion;
Her artless appearance and infantine
[sic] face,
Forbids the idea of masculine grace:
Her notes when essay'd to be sonorous
and full,
Are tedious, unpleasant, insipid, and dull:
Let the delicate coyness that dwells in
your breast,

ported Dibdin, "mama was very nearly undressed before her daughter arrived at the end of it."

Alicia Daniels married George Frederick Cooke at St Peter's Church in Chester on 20 December 1796. (She was probably his second wife and not his first as commonly believed; a Mrs Cooke had acted with him at Chester in 1785.) Several weeks later they were back in Manchester for the opening of the winter season on 2 January 1796 when he acted Hastings in *Jane Shore* and she was Eliza in the musical piece *The Poor Sailor*. She went with Cooke to play in Dublin in 1797–98, first at Fishamble Street and then in the new Crow Street Theatre. While in Ireland, Cooke's drinking became radically worse so she left him. Several years later on 4 July 1801 she had her marriage to Cooke nullified before Sir William Scott in Doctors' Commons at London.

After leaving Ireland, she played at Bath in January 1799. She remained with the Bath and Bristol company for about five years, appearing under her maiden name of Daniels. At Bristol in September 1801 she advertised she was available for singing lessons. During this period she again sang at Vauxhall Gardens; songs published as sung by her there between 1800 and 1802 included Brooks's *Pastoral Dialogue* and *Ere my dear Laddie gade to Sea*, Costellow's *The Fair Huntress*, Hook's *Hey Derry Down*, Reeve's *Love sounds the Trumpet*, as well as *Happy Art of Pleasing* and *O'er Highlands and Lowlands*. On 16 May 1804 she returned to London, billed as Miss Daniels from the Theatre Royal, Bath, to make her first appearance at the Haymarket Theatre as Rosina in *The Spanish Barber*. At the Haymarket she also played Mrs Flaw in *The Gay Deceivers* on 22 August and Nancy in *The Miller's Maid* on 25 August. Soon she returned to the Bath Theatre, now to play under the name of Mrs Windsor. Perhaps she had become the wife of the musician Windsor, a member of the Bath

Harmonic Society and an accomplished pianist. She died at Bath on 30 April 1826. A portrait of her when she was Mrs Cooke was engraved by P. Maguire.

Daniels, Mary Ann. *See* RYALL, MRS JOHN.

Danjeville. *See* DANGEVILLE.

Danks, John [*fl. 1723–1724*], *violinist.*

The parish registers for St Giles, Cripplegate, twice cite John Danks (or Daggs), describing him as a "fidler." On 10 January 1723 John and Mary Danks had a child, christened Anne on 18 January. Their son James was born on 7 June and baptized on 21 June 1724.

Dannell, Mr [*fl. 1784*], *actor.*

Mr Dannell played Wolf in *The School for Wives* at the Haymarket Theatre when it was given one performance on 16 November 1784.

Danny. *See* DENNY.

Danoyer. *See* DENOYER.

Danser. *See* DANCER.

Dansey. *See* DANCEY.

Danzi, Francesca. *See* LEBRUN, MME LUDWIG AUGUST.

Da Ponte, Lorenzo, earlier Emanuele Conegliano *1749–1838, poet, librettist, impresario, teacher.*

Lorenzo Da Ponte, best known in the history of music as Mozart's librettist, was born on 10 March 1749 in the town of Ceneda, near Venice, the first son of Italian Jews, Geremia and Rachele Conegliano. The Conegliano family, which probably originated in a town of that name not far from Ceneda, enjoyed some prestige in the area, having contributed a number of scholars in the past. One of the most notable had been Dr Israel Conegliano, a physician and statesman who in reward for his diplomatic services to Turkish-Venetian relationships at the end of the seventeenth century had been exempted from the anti-Semitic regulations of the Venetian state.

In 1754, when Emanuele was five, his mother died, leaving the boy and his two younger brothers Baruch and Anania to a poor education under their father's care. When Emanuele was 14, his father married a young girl named Orsola Pasqua Paietta, a Catholic. Geremia Conegliano and his three sons were baptized into the Christian faith on 29 August 1763 in the cathedral at Ceneda in a ceremony performed by Monsignor Lorenzo Da Ponte, the Bishop, from whom they took their new family name. The father became Gaspare Da Ponte, Baruch and Anania became Girolamo and Luigi Da Ponte respectively, and Emanuele, taking the full name of his sponsor, was henceforth known as Lorenzo Da Ponte. Eventually Lorenzo was to gain three more brothers and seven sisters as the result of his father's second marriage.

Lorenzo entered the seminary at Portogruaro near Ceneda, where he remained for five years, learning Latin, studying the great Italian poets under the tutelage of the notable teacher, the Abbé Cagliari, and beginning to write poetry himself. At the age of 21 he became a teacher of Italian at the seminary. He was ordained into the priesthood in March 1773, but his ordination did not prevent him from conducting a bizarre love affair in Venice with a young aristocrat, Angiola Tiepolo, nor would it discourage later amorous adventures. Soon after this episode he entered the seminary at Treviso as Professor of Rhetoric and began to write poems which the audience of the *Accademia* found to be seditious and radical but which Da Ponte himself considered as "mere poetic caprice." He was tried by the Venetian Senate, and, being found guilty,

Harvard Theatre Collection

LORENZO DA PONTE
engraving by Skenino, after Rogers

he was discharged from his post in December 1776, and publicly admonished.

Da Ponte remained in Venice after his trial. He was befriended by Bernardo Memmo, a nobleman, served as secretary to Pietro Antonio Zaguri, another Venetian patrician, and developed friendships with Gozzi and Casanova. He acquired a reputation for writing good improvisatory verse and for conducting his life in a libertine manner worthy of his friend Casanova. His employer Zaguri characterized Da Ponte as "A strange man; known for a scoundrel of mediocre calibre, but gifted with great talents for literature, and with physical attractions which win love for him!" His escapades included eloping with Angioletta Bellaudi, the hot-blooded wife of his landlord, Carlo Bellaudi. Three offspring of their relationship were put in foundling hospitals. Eventually his notorious behavior scandalized authority and on 5 January 1780 Da Ponte was sentenced to 15 years of banishment. But he had already left Venice and Angioletta, and had gone to Austria. He lived for a short time in Gorizia, where, according to his *Memoirs*, his inexpressible attraction for women continued to assert itself. Then he found his way to Dresden, where he assisted the poet Mazzolà at the court opera. Soon, faced with an ultimatum from the mother of two young women named Rosina and Camilletta to choose which one he would marry, Da Ponte decided to leave Dresden.

Fortified with a letter of recommendation from Mazzolà to the composer Salieri, Da Ponte arrived in Vienna in November 1780. He was introduced to the famous Imperial librettist, Pietro Metastasio, who had written for the greatest composers of the day, including Handel, Hasse, and Gluck, and who praised Da Ponte's poetry. After Metastasio's death in 1783, it was decided to establish a company of Italian singers in Vienna to replace the French actors, who had offended the Emperor. Through the influence of Salieri, Da Ponte was appointed to provide comedies and libretti for the Italians at a salary of 1200 florins a year and was named Poet to the Imperial Theatres. His appointment to this important artistic post was indeed irregular, for up to that date, as Da Ponte freely admitted to Emperor Joseph at his first interview with the monarch, he had never written a play. "Good, good!" the Emperor was reported to have replied. "Then we shall have a virgin muse." The two men became good friends.

After some delay, Da Ponte's first work at Vienna, *Il ricco di un giorno*, with music by Salieri, was performed on 6 December 1784, and was a complete failure, caused in part by a cabal against Da Ponte by supporters of a rival librettist, Giovanni Battista Casti. His next piece, *Il burbero di buon cuore*, adapted from Goldoni with music by Vincenzo Martin y Soler, produced on 4 January 1786, was a success. Encouraged, on 20 February 1786 Da Ponte produced his second failure, *Il finto cieco*, an adaptation of a French comedy, with music by Giuseppe Gazzaniga.

At this point in his career Da Ponte began his famous collaboration with Mozart, whom he had met about 1783. Although they were opposites in character and taste, Da Ponte was able to offer the composer what he had been seeking, an "able poet" who, in the assessment of April Fitzlyon (*The Libertine Librettist,* 1955), supplied

. . . good craftsmanship, willing subordination to the music, verse expressed in the contemporary idiom, and the whole work carried out in the closest collaboration with the composer. He supplied him with more — with wit, sound plot construction, good characterisation, and elegant verse. Yet all these qualities . . . do not explain why da Ponte, the licentious, unscrupulous adventurer, the facile, mediocre poet, the very inexperienced dramatist, should be the man, who, above all others, succeeded in providing Mozart with the perfect framework for his music, and in collaborating with him to produce three of the very few operas in existence in which the words blend so perfectly with the music as to produce a truly homogeneous work of art.

Le nozze di Figaro, based on Beaumarchais's controversial play, was a modest success at its opening on 1 May 1786. The cast included two singers well known upon the English stage, but then resident in Vienna — Nancy Storace, who sang Susanna, and Michael Kelly, who played the smaller roles of Don Basilio and Don Curzio. The opera was performed nine times in 1786, but was then replaced in November by Martin's *Una cosa rara*, the libretto for which was also written by Da Ponte. When *Le nozze di Figaro* was performed in Prague in December 1786 its success was enormous, and the city became "Figaro-mad." Da Ponte did not attend the rehearsals or performances at Prague; rather he remained in Vienna to enjoy the enthusiastic reception given to *Una cosa rara*, which proved to be a most outstanding success and long remained in its own day a favorite of the repertory.

After failures with the libretti for *Il Demogorgone* of Righini and the *Bertoldo* of Piticchio, Da Ponte found himself in the difficult position of needing to provide three libretti for three different composers at the same time, which feat he managed to perform by working shut up in a room day and night—with distractions only from the beautiful sixteen-year-old girl who brought him food and comfort regularly—for two months. The results were *Tarare* (actually a translation of Salieri's work), *L'arbore di Diana* for Martin, and *Don Giovanni* for Mozart. *Don Giovanni*, which had its first performance at Prague on 29 October 1787, has, of course, become an acknowledged masterpiece, despite initial criticisms of its libertinism and immorality. His next work for Mozart, *Cosi fan tutte*, a controversial piece in its own day, had its first performance at Vienna on 26 January 1790.

When the Emperor Joseph died in February 1790, Da Ponte's fortune in Vienna changed, largely because of a cabal against him, but partly as the result of his indiscreet verses critical of the new Emperor Leopold. It is not clear whether or not he resigned his post of Poet to the Imperial Theatres or was discharged, but he soon found himself at Trieste in desperate financial straits. Plans to go to St Petersburg fell through when a promised vacancy there was filled by someone else. At the age of 42, Da Ponte had become, as Fitzlyon has put it, the remnant of an epoch which had passed away with the deaths of Joseph II and Mozart. "Fate decreed that he was to live for another forty-six years, that more than half his life was to be spent in that new age with which he had nothing in common, and in which there was no place for him. From henceforward he was to be a spiritual refugee."

While at Trieste, Da Ponte met Ann Celestine Grahl—or Nancy as she was called—the daughter of a Dresden merchant John Grahl, who was probably of Jewish origin. Grahl had lived in England for a number of years, and Nancy claimed that country as her birthplace. In his autobiography Da Ponte states that on 12 August 1792, Nancy was given to him by her parents "after the usual social ceremonies and formalities," but there is found no evidence that an actual marriage ever took place. It was rumored that they had been joined in a Jewish ceremony, but given the climate at Trieste it seems unlikely that any rabbi would have performed such a ceremony between a Jewess and a known Catholic priest. The "marriage," in any event, was a surprising success, broken only by the death of Nancy forty years later.

With his new mate, Da Ponte set off for Paris, passing through Ljubljana, Prague, Dux (where they visited with Casanova), Dresden, and Spires. News of the imprisonment of Marie-Antoinette discouraged their going on to Paris, so they turned toward Holland, and thence to London, where Casanova had advised him to go "If you want to make your fortune." But Casanova had also written, "On arriving in England, a foreigner needs to be fortified with resignation . . ."

Toward the end of 1792, the Da Pontes arrived in London and took lodgings at No 16, Sherard Street, Golden Square. Things went badly, news of some of his more sensational activities having preceded him, and his schemes for teaching Italian, publishing a periodical, and writing poetry, and especially his hopes for an appointment as librettist to the opera having come to naught. In May 1793 he left England for Belgium and Holland, but there for awhile his situation grew even worse. Finally, however, he received a letter notifying him that he was now wanted as Poet to the King's Theatre in London, an appointment which he took up in the fall of 1794 at a salary of £250 per season and which he held for some ten years, through 1804–5.

Da Ponte's first work at the King's Theatre was an alteration and adaptation of Bertati's libretto for *Il Don Giovanni*, a musical *pasticcio*, which was first performed on 1 March 1794. His *Il burbero di buon cuore*, which had been first performed at Vienna in 1786, with music by Martin (who was now a resident composer at the King's) was given on 17 May 1794, with a new duet. In honor of the "Glorious First of June" his cantata *La Vittoria*, with music by Pasiello, was performed on 23 June 1794. His first completely new work to be written for London, and in English, was *La Scola de' maritati*, again with music by Martin, on 27 January 1795. His last collaboration with Martin was *L'isola del piacere*, for the King's Theatre on 26 May 1795. It was their least successful joint effort and had been created during a period when their friendship was strained; the composer had impregnated a servant girl in the Da Ponte household and then had spread the word that the librettist was the father.

In 1796 Da Ponte wrote *Antigona*, music by Bianchi, which was first performed on 24 May; *Il tesoro*, with music by Mazzinghi, first performed on 14 June; and *Zemira e Azore*, a translation of Marmontel's French libretto with music by Grétry, first performed on 23 July. His other writings for the King's Theatre during his tenure as Poet included (with dates of first performances): *Il consiglio imprudente* on 26 December 1796; *Evelina, or The Triumph of the English over the Romans*, on 10 January 1797, and published by Da Ponte in that year from No 134, Pall Mall; *Le nozze del Tamigi e Bellona*, "An Entertainment of Singing and Dancing," originally written as a cantata for the marriage of the Prince of Wales with Caroline of Brunswick and then performed in honor of the victory of Cape St Vincent, on 11 March 1797; *Merope* (from Voltaire) on 10 June 1797; *Armida* on 1 June 1802; *La grotta di Calipso* on 31 May 1803; *Il trionfo dell'amor fraterno*

on 22 March 1804; and *Il ratto di Proserpina* on 31 May 1804.

In 1795, in order to augment his income, Da Ponte leased the theatre café from Taylor, the King's Theatre manager, and his wife operated it for 18 months both for the operas and the masquerades. In the autumn of 1798, Taylor sent him to Italy to engage performers, his first visit to his homeland in 20 years. He returned to England in March 1799, never again to travel on the Continent.

In 1800, Da Ponte was arrested some 30 times in connection with Taylor's debts at the Opera because he had neglected Casanova's warning never to sign any document in England. Foolishly he had backed the manager's debts and actually had often served as his general factotum in the theatre's administration. In order to get out from under heavy financial burdens, Da Ponte bought out a bookshop at No 5, Pall Mall for 30 guineas and, specializing in new books from Italy and France, he quickly built up his inventory to over 8000 volumes. His financial position now vastly improved by a good trade, he ventured into publishing. But he expanded into a disastrous partnership with Corri and Dussek for music publishing which ended with Corri's going to Newgate, Dussek's fleeing abroad, and Da Ponte's being left with the obligations. He then became involved with Dulau and Nardini, printers and publishers, an association which went well at first but which also ended unhappily.

It was time for another change of venue for Da Ponte. In August 1804 he sent his wife and four children off to Philadelphia, where Nancy joined her parents, who had emigrated some years before. Nine months later, leaving his publishing business in the hands of his brother Paola, Da Ponte followed his family, sailing on the *Columbia* on 7 April 1805 and arriving at Philadelphia on 4 June. There he discovered that the family had moved to New York. He made his way there but the intellectual climate in his new country did not favor opportunities for an Italian poet or librettist and Da Ponte opened grocery stores, first in New York and then in Elizabethtown, New Jersey. He gave up that trade in 1807, returned to New York, and through the help of a bookseller named Riley recruited pupils for tuition in modern languages and the classics. His gifts for teaching now evident, he established the Manhattan Academy for Young Gentlemen. This school was praised by Arthur Livingston, the American editor of his *Memoirs*, as "an important moment for the American mind," for "Da Ponte made Europe, poetry, painting, music, the artistic spirit, classical lore, a creative education, live for many important Americans as no one, I venture, had done before." Several of his pupils, including Nathaniel F. Moore and John M. MacVickar, became professors at Columbia University.

In 1811 he became an American citizen, and also, tempted by the possibility of an idyllic life in the countryside, moved to Sunbury, Pennsylvania, where he again traded in groceries and gave language lessons, founded an Academy for Young Ladies and Gentlemen at nearby Northumberland, and ventured into publishing, millinery, and even into distilling. He moved to Philadelphia in 1818, and then back to New York in April 1819. In 1823 Da Ponte began publishing his *Memoirs*, and in September 1825, at the age of 76, he was appointed to the first Professorship of Italian Literature at Columbia College.

On 23 May 1826 his *Don Giovanni* was performed for the first time in the United States, at the Park Theatre in New York. Da Ponte devoted the latest years of his life to advancing the cause of Italian opera in America. In 1830 he persuaded his half-brother Agostino Da Ponte to come to New York with Agostino's daughter Giulia, who was a singer of some talent. The latter made her debut on 31 March 1830 at a "Grand Concert of Vocal and Instrumental

Music," and a month later she sang in Da Ponte's *pasticcio, L'ape musicale*. On 10 May 1830 she sang at a concert for the Musical Fund Society before a large audience at the City Hall, but she was really a mediocre singer—"not made for the stage, nor the stage for her," according to her uncle's judgment. In 1832, Da Ponte raised a subscription and promoted the visit of Jacques Montrésor, a singer and impresario from Bologna, and his company for a season at the Richmond Hill Theatre in New York and later in Philadelphia. Much money was lost on that season, but Da Ponte persisted in his ambitions. He was largely responsible for raising funds for the erection of New York's first Opera House, which opened on 18 November 1833 for a season which lasted until 21 July 1834, with Da Ponte as impresario. A large deficit resulted, and in 1836 the Opera House was converted to a playhouse called the National Theatre. Soon afterward, it burned down.

In 1835 Da Ponte lamented that he had never received proper recognition in America. His teaching diminished, and he complained that he had not had a student in 18 months. "I, the creator of the Italian language in America," he wrote, "the teacher of more than two thousand persons whose progress astounded Italy! I, the poet of Joseph II, the author of thirty-six dramas, the inspiration of Salieri, of Weigl, of Martin, of Winter, and Mozart! After twenty-seven years of hard labour, I have no longer a pupil! Nearly ninety years old, I have no more bread in America!"

His wife Nancy died in December 1831. In the following year, in her memory, he published his *Sonetti per la morte di Anna Celestina Ernestina da Ponte*. Lorenzo Da Ponte himself died of old age on 17 August 1838, after being given the last rites of his church. His funeral, attended by a distinguished assembly of persons from the academic and social circles of New York, was held on 20 August at the Catholic Cathedral, and he was buried in the Roman Catholic Cemetery in that city.

Lorenzo Da Ponte's five children by his wife Nancy included Louisa (1792–1823), who married Miles Franklin Clossey in 1809; Frances (b. 1798), who married Henry James Anderson, Professor of Mathematics and Astrology at Columbia; Joseph (b. 1799), who died of consumption at Philadelphia in 1821; Lorenzo (b. 1803), who became a Professor of Italian at the University of Maryland but died young in 1840; and Charles (b. 1806), about whom little is known.

Additional details of Da Ponte's life and lists of his works may be found in the *Enciclopedia dello spettacolo* and in April Fitzlyon's biography *The Libertine Librettist* (1955). Da Ponte's autobiography was published in New York by the author, in four volumes, between 1823 and 1827, under the title *Memorie di Lorenzo da Ponte da Ceneda scritte da esso.*

Portraits of Da Ponte include an engraving by M. P. Skenino after N. Rogers, and a painting by an unknown artist, showing him in old age.

"Dapper Daniel" [fl. 1699], fencer.

The *Post Boy* for 30 March–1 April 1699 ran the following notice:

This day [1 April] at the New Red Theatre in Winchester Street, Southwark, next Door to the Pair of Tongues and Keys, will be perform'd a curious Trial of Skill at Back-sword, Single-Rapier, Quarter-Staff, &c, between Archibald Macdonald, late of Dublin; and Dapper Daniel of Abington, for Fifty Guinea's: As likewise a Wrestling Match, between the famous Welch Will, of Kidwelly (who had the Honour last Year to divert the Elector of Bavaria) and Hugh Lammerton, Tinman, near Lestiehill, for Twenty Pounds. The Sport will begin at Two in the Afternoon precisely, and will conclude with a Consort of Tartarian Musick, never before heard in England; and six new Entries after the Sclavonian manner. Perform'd by 4 Transilvanian Co-

medians, and the same number of Moldavian Women in long Rustian Vests, and Turkish Head-dresses. The Highest places will go at Ten Shillings; the Lowest at Half a Crown.

Darastanti. *See* DURASTANTI.

Darby. *See also* DERBY and RYDER.

Darby, Mr [fl. 1760], house servant?

On 19 May 1760 Mr Darby's benefit tickets were accepted at Covent Garden. His income was £38 12s., the second highest in the sizeable group given benefits that evening, but he received only half value: £19 6s. His function at the theatre is not known, but many of the other employees named that night were servants working in the front of the house.

Darby, Aaron [fl. 1688–1689], actor.

Aaron Darby was sworn a comedian in the United Company on 23 May 1688, and his name was cited again on a warrant dated 23 August 1689. He doubtless played small roles, for his name was never noted in cast lists.

Darby, Mary. *See* ROBINSON, MRS THOMAS.

D'Arcy, Mr, stage name of Mr Caird [fl. 1797–1802?], singer, actor.

A Mr D'Arcy made what purported to be his first appearance on the London stage at the Haymarket on 23 June 1798 in the character of Captain Greville in the comic opera *The Flitch of Bacon*. He had played at Margate in the summer of 1797. The *Monthly Mirror*, in criticizing the Haymarket performance, reported that

he is a pupil of Mr [Michael] Kelly, and his real name is Caird; but D'Arcy has, no doubt, a much prettier appearance in a play-bill. This gentleman has a remarkably pleasant voice, and no small portion of that taste which so eminently distinguishes his master . . . his deportment requires improvement, and he must learn to articulate *words* as well as sounds; we wish also he would endeavor to sing more like a man, and less like an Italian, for the affectation of shrugging up the shoulders, and heaving the breast, is abominable in an Englishman . . .

The *Authentic Memoirs of the Green Room*, monitoring his second performance, as Cheerly in *Lock and Key* on 10 July 1798, thought that this operetta's songs did not much suit his voice, but "He is, upon the whole, much better than his predecessor, Mr. Phillips." It was, however, thought strange that he would adopt a foreign name when he had a good British one like Caird.

D'Arcy was steadily employed for the rest of the season, as Frederick in *No Song No Supper* on 13 July, in a chorus of peasants for James Boaden's new *Cambro-Britons* on 21 July, as Nicolo in the first performance of George Moultrie's *False and True* on 11 August, as Balthazar (his first Shakespeare character in *Much Ado About Nothing* on 21 August, and as Selwyn in *The Shipwreck* on 23 August (with several repetitions of the new pieces). He helped to ring down the curtain on the season by singing "A Pasticchio, consisting of: *From Shades of Night*, composed by Storace for MAHMOUD."

Despite these evidences of fair success, D'Arcy was not seen in London again but went instead to Salisbury (where his wife also sang) and then to the Bath-Bristol company in August 1799. In 1800 the D'Arcys were briefly at Shrewsbury and in 1800, 1801, and 1802 in Huddart's company at Manchester.

The subject of this entry should not be confused with the "Mr Darcy" who was at Hull in 1787 and at York in 1788 and 1789, acting a young heroic and comic line. That actor's real name was Darcy Lever (1760?–1837).

D'Arcy, Miss ₁*fl. 1770–1771*₁, actress.

Miss D'Arcy made her first appearance on the stage playing the brilliant leading comedy part of Lady Townly in *The Provok'd Husband* at Covent Garden on 7 December 1770. She was billed simply as "A Young Lady," a widespread practice for novitiates at that time, but her identity was revealed by the *Town and Country Magazine* for December 1770, by the *Public Advertiser* of 28 January 1771, and by the *Gentleman's Magazine* for January 1771, and is corroborated by the prompter Hopkins's manuscript notations. The *Town and Country Magazine* reported that Miss D'Arcy

was received with uncommon applause. Her figure and deportment are happily suited to the sprightly, elegant woman of quality. Her countenance is very expressive; her voice is distinct and sweet; and, upon the whole, we think this lady will be an acquisition to the stage in the polite walk of comedy.

This apparent success was followed, on 29 January 1771, by her assumption of Mrs Lessingham's usual role of Mrs Sullen in *The Stratagem.* She repeated Lady Townly on 11 February, chose Imogen in *Cymbeline* for her benefit performance on 15 April, and then dropped out of the bills for that season.

Miss D'Arcy appeared only twice in the London season of 1771–72—on 27 September as Mrs Sullen and on 4 October as Lady Townly. Those six performances and those three parts cited above constitute Miss D'Arcy's entire career and repertoire, so far as can be determined.

Darcy, Stafford ₁*fl. 1660–1662*₁, *singer.*

On 9 August 1660 Stafford Darcy was appointed a tenor in the private vocal music of Charles II, a post which he still held in · 1662.

Darimate, Mlle. *See* DURANCY, MME.

Darion. *See* DORION.

Darkin, Joseph ₁*fl. 1794*₁, *singer.*

Doane's *Musical Directory* of 1794 listed Joseph Darkin, of No 3, Hind Court, Foster Lane, Cheapside, as a singer who participated in concerts by the Choral Fund and the Cecilian Society and sang in the oratorios at Covent Garden and the Handelian concerts at Westminster Abbey.

Darley, William ₁John?₁ *c. 1756–1809, singer, actor.*

William Darley was born, probably about 1756, in Birmingham and, according to both *The Secret History of the Green Room* (1790) and the 1804 edition of the *Authentic Memoirs of the Green Room*, he was "bred a buckle-maker." John Bernard managed him in the United States, and in a note to his *Retrospections of America* he called Darley a "bucket-maker." Bernard also contributed to a massive confusion over Darley's identity, first name, and parentage:

John Darley, Sr., was the son of Matthew Darley, a somewhat eccentric but talented painter of the school of Hogarth, and particularly celebrated as a caricaturist. . . . No mention is anywhere made of the artistic abilities of either his son or his grandson, but several sons of the younger John Darley have been artists, the most distinguished of them being the Felix O. C. Darley of to-day—a marked instance of the transmission of genius.

There appears to be no confirmation of the derivation from the painter Matthew Darley, which in any case sorts poorly with the idea of either buckle- or bucket-making. The first name "John" is hard to dismiss, particularly inasmuch as Bernard also applied it to the elder performer elsewhere in his writings. Yet an authentic pay sheet of Covent Garden surviving at the Huntington Library records the payment of £95 for 190 nights at 10s. each to *William* Darley, and legal documents relative to his death

(see below) call him William. William is the name accepted by C. B. Hogan, in both *Shakespeare in the Theatre* and *The London Stage*. It is possible that he bore both names.

Darley gained his first experience in public performance as a bass singer at the Birmingham Vauxhall, singing popular songs "with a most clear, strong, and various voice," and later obtained an engagement singing at the Birmingham theatre. He was heard there by some London performers who obtained an audition for him at Richmond, where he appeared for the first time on 5 June 1779, according to Isaac Reed's "Notitia Dramatica." From there he went to Covent Garden to sing in the chorus, possibly as early as the season of 1779–80, though his name does not figure in surviving theatrical records until the playbill for 8 May 1782, on which he was mentioned as one of eight performers and others connected with Covent Garden delivering out benefit tickets. He was similarly privileged in the springs of 1783, 1784, and 1786. His salary in 1781–82 and 1782–83 was £2 per week; he was raised to £3 in 1783–84, and his salary stuck at that point through 1789–90. That season he invited seekers of benefit tickets to apply at his lodgings at No 27, Bow Street. He toiled most of this time as a journeyman chorus singer, little favored or even noticed until, as the *Secret History* has it,

occasional accidents brought him forward, particularly one evening, when "Sweet Poll of Plymouth" was loudly called for during the performance of the Positive Man, and in Mrs Kennedy's absence he came forward, and sung it with such eclat, as recommended him to the encouragement of the Managers and favour of the Public.

What this "favour" amounted to was the gain of a few small concessions, such as being permitted to sing Glazier in the first productions (25 November 1782 and after) of John O'Keeffe's successful pantomime *Lord Mayor's Day* and being named in the bills for his participation in the "Solemn Dirge" in Juliet's funeral procession and the background chorus to a musicalized *Macbeth*.

During all this apprenticeship Darley had labored under the disadvantage of an unprepossessing appearance—corpulent and awkward, looking more like "a Jolly Publican or Butcher, than Actor"— which is even said to have caused his discharge from the Birmingham Vauxhall company. As Anthony Pasquin put it:

When he bellows in HAWTHORN, or STERNHOLD, or GILES,
Sweet Poetry shudders, and Irony smiles.
. . . .
Behold! 'mid the harmonic congress he stands,
Distress'd by the weight of two ox-knuckle hands;
. . . .
But tho' Fate to his savage exterior's unkind,
He has blanch'd ev'ry ill by the worth of his mind.

After Charles Bannister went back to Drury Lane in the fall of 1784, Darley, as the only bass singer of any competence in the Covent Garden chorus, gradually inherited a few of Bannister's parts and expanded his meagre repertoire generally by the acquisition of: Harry Puddington and Matt o' the Mint in *The Beggar's Opera*, the original Friar Bungy in O'Keeffe's *Harlequin Rambler*, The Daemon of Revenge in *Cymon*, the original Bowman (and later an Outlaw) in Leonard Macnally's opera *Robin Hood*, Roger in *Hob in the Well*, Charles the wrestler in *As You Like It* (which part his squat, corpulent physique no doubt gained for him), Hecate in *Macbeth*, Jupiter in *Midas*, the Ghost in *Tom Thumb*, the first robin in *Fontainebleau*, a Bacchanal in *Comus*, Sanguino in *The*

Castle of Andalusia, Russet in *The Deserter*, a Counsellor in *The Lawyer's Panic*, the original London represener of Rifle in Jephson's new Irish import *The Campaign*, the Serjeant in *Poor Vulcan*, Otoo in *Omai*, the Mate in *Inkle and Yarico*, and, more importantly for him, the widely acclaimed singing Farmer Blackberry in *The Farmer*.

To the end of his career at Covent Garden Darley was doomed to these and similar small endeavors, his unfortunate appearance trapping him in a range of eccentrics and grotesques, supernaturals, and comic rustics and servants. His melodious bass singing voice, which, if he had been handsomer, might have gained for him more leading roles, did, indeed, make him a favorite with audiences, and he was increasingly employed in entr'acte songs.

Darley was listed by Charles Burney as among the basses at the first Handel Memorial Concerts at Westminster Abbey and the Pantheon in May and June 1784. He sang for the Anacreontic Society's concerts for several years and appeared often in the summers at Astley's and Vauxhall, where he was very popular. The 1792 edition of *The Secret History of the Green Rooms* reported

Whether it was that he had not such principal characters given to him as he thought by his talents he was intitled to, or that he disagreed with the Managers, for refusing him permission to sing at Vauxhall, during the summer of 1791, he deserted Covent Garden; but as his powers are of great use . . . the mutual interest of both parties reinstated him.

The Secret History was off by a year, for an advertisement of 18 May 1790 regretted that "Mr Darley being prevented by his engagement from attending at Vauxhall during the early part of the season, his parts in the concert will be performed by Mr Page." So Darley dropped from the Covent Garden roster in 1790–91. He helped Joseph Fox open the Duke Street

Theatre in Brighton on 13 July 1790, and after summer performances were through there he moved along to the Plymouth Theatre for the following season.

In 1791–92 Darley patched up his difficulties with Harris, the Covent Garden proprietor, and returned to that patent house with a handsome raise to £5 per week. He sang his excellent Farmer Blackberry in the afterpiece *The Farmer* on the season's opening night, 12 September, erroneously advertised "first appearance these two years," and was regularly employed in his familiar repertoire throughout that season and the next.

Thomas Wignell came to England in December 1791 to recruit performers for the Chestnut Street Theatre in Philadelphia,

Harvard Theatre Collection

WILLIAM DARLEY
engraving by Barlow

then in process of construction. Slowly and carefully he chose the company which returned to America in the summer of 1793 in the ship *George Barclay*. Darley and his wife, also a singer, were minor members of that group. (The sole notice we have of her performance in England is a mention in a clipping describing a Vauxhall vocal concert on 30 May 1793.) They remained in America for the next eight years, performing at theatres and singing in concerts in Annapolis, Charleston, Philadelphia, and New York. They introduced their more famous son, John (1775–1853), to the American stage. After a final season, 1800–1801, at the Chestnut Street Theatre, the elder Darleys sailed for England. On 11 October 1802 Darley resumed his situation at Covent Garden Theatre, acting one of his old popular parts, Hecate in *Macbeth*.

Darley died on 30 June 1809 "after a long and painful illness," according to an unidentified clipping. He evidently died intestate and was possessed of property worth only £20, for one William Darley with property of such valuation was entered on the Administration Book of Somerset House on 28 July 1809, when administration of his estate was granted to his widow Anne. She was possibly the Ann Darley of Brompton Place, "Aged 80" at her death, who was buried at the actors' church, St Paul, Covent Garden, on 31 May 1838.

Numbers of popular editions were published of songs "as sung by" Darley, alone or in choral groups. A great many were by James Hook and virtually all were sung at Vauxhall. Examples are: Hook's *Britons be Valiant, Content and a Cot, Cruel Peggy, My Heart is Devoted, Wine and Kisses, The Prince of the People, The Sea-Worn Tar, The Lovers' Quarrel* (all published in 1790), *The Veil* and *Look Ere you Leap* (1792), and *Then Say My Sweet Girl* (1795?), and Upton's *Chelsea Quarters* (1790), Reeves's *The Loyal Tars* (1789), Shields's *'Ere around the huge Oak* (1788), Mould's *The Forecastle Sailor* (1789), and the anonymous *The Day is Departed* (1790).

Darley is shown performing in the band at Vauxhall in an engraving by Barlow which was published by W. Locke in 1792.

Darley, Mrs William [John?], Anne
1758?–1838? singer, actress.

The only notice we have of a London performance by Mrs William [John?] Darley is a clipping describing a Vauxhall vocal concert on 30 May 1793 at which she sang. In the summer of 1793 she accompanied her husband to America in a company recruited by Thomas Wignell for the Chestnut Street Theatre in Philadelphia. She acted and sang for the next eight years in theatres and concert halls in Annapolis, Charleston, Philadelphia, and New York, and in 1801 sailed back to England.

William [John?] Darley died in 1809 and administration of his meagre property was granted to his widow Anne. She was possibly the Ann Darley of Broughton Place, "Aged 80" at her death, who was buried at St Paul, Covent Garden on 31 May 1838.

Darling, Mr [fl. 1785], actor.

Mr Darling made his first and last appearance on the London stage as Guzman in *'Tis Well It's No Worse* at the Haymarket Theatre on 25 April 1785.

Darling, William [fl. 1794], singer.

William Darling, a basso living in Bolsover Street, Marylebone, was a member of the Portland Chapel Society, according to Doane's *Musical Directory* of 1794.

Darly. See DARLEY.

Darney. See DORNEY.

Darrant, Symon [fl. 1672], violinist.

The Lord Chamberlain's accounts on 19 April 1672 show that Symon Darrant was to substitute for anyone in the King's private music who became ill. He must have been a violinist, since the private music was made up only of fiddlers.

Darrell, Mr [fl. 1708], house servant.

Mr Darrell was listed on 8 March 1708 as one of the employees at the Queen's Theatre in the Haymarket earning 5s. daily, but his duties were not specified.

Darvile, Mr [fl. 1784], singer.

Mr Darvile and Mr Darvile Junior, both tenors, sang in the Handel Memorial Concerts at Westminster Abbey and the Pantheon on 26, 27, 29 May and 3, 5 June 1784.

Darvile Junior, Mr [fl. 1784], singer.
See DARVILE, MR.

Dashwood, [John?] [fl. 1799–1813], doorkeeper.

Mr Dashwood was a doorkeeper at Drury Lane from at least as early as the 1799–1800 season. His name appears in the account books through 1803–4 at a salary of 9s. daily. He was at the Lyceum Theatre in 1811–12 and 1812–13, again as a house servant, though his precise function there is not known. Perhaps the following entry in the St Paul, Covent Garden, parish registers concerned him: John and Sarah Dashwood baptized their daughter Pamelia on 31 October 1803.

D'Auberval, Jean, stage name of Jean Bercher *1742–1806, dancer, ballet master, choreographer.*

The dancer Jean Bercher *dit* D'Auberval was born in Montpellier on 19 August 1742, a son of the well-known actor at the Comédie-Française, Etienne-Dominique Bercher D'Auberval, according to Campardon. Etienne-Dominique, who retired in 1780 with a pension of 1,000 livres from the royal treasury, evidently was dead by the end of the century. The careers of father and son overlapped, and there is thus some danger of confusing their activities.

Jean D'Auberval made his debut at the Académie Royal de Musique on 12 June 1761 in *Zais*, an heroical ballet. Deryck Lynham (in *The Chevalier Noverre*) placed D'Auberval as *premier danseur sérieux* in Jean Georges Noverre's company at Stuttgart in the fall of 1762. Lynham cited (and translated) an entry of 1 November 1762 in the Wurtenburg *Landschreiberrechnungen und Rentkammerprotokollen*: "The dancer Jean Dauberval, as *premier danseur*, at 2,500 florins yearly and 130 florins shoe money to Easter 1764 and 25 golden louis for his journey there [to Stuttgart?] and the same for his return."

D'Auberval remained with the Stuttgart company continuously until Easter 1764,

according to Lynham. *The London Stage*, however, shows that on 13 December 1763 "A *New Dance* for Mr Duberval" was one of the features of the bill at the King's Theatre in London. "Duberval" repeated the dance on 14 January 1764 and danced again on 24 January. He appeared with Miss Auretti on 7 and 14 February in unnamed turns and on 21 February they were featured in a figure called *Le Mariage du village*. On 20 March "Duberval" teamed with Berardi and Miss Tetley in a dance called *The Turkish Coffee House*, after Act II of *Alessandro nell' Indie*. He and Miss Auretti were partners again on 29 and 30 March and 14 April 1764. If "Duberval" was D'Auberval, he had evidently returned to the Continent before the opening of the next London season.

D'Auberval's execution of the *pas des*

Harvard Theatre Collection

JEAN D'AUBERVAL, with Mme Allard in *Sylvie*
engraving by Tilliard, after L. C. de Carmontelie

deux with Mlle Allard in the pastoral *Sylvie* at the Opéra in 1766 placed him in the first rank of French dancers, according to Campardon. He began receiving the best parts and his popularity and salary soared. But so did his extravagance. In 1770, already head over heels in debt, he seized upon the expedient of opening his opulent house in the rue de Cléry for subscription balls. But the enterprise apparently did not suffice, for in 1774 he was obliged to hide from his creditors. Madame du Barry, a close friend, used her influence at Court to obtain for him 50,000 livres to settle his affairs.

In 1773 he had been named, jointly with Philippe Gardel, ballet master of the Opéra, succeeding the elder Vestris. In 1776 began his long involvement in the feuds and cabals against Noverre, which led on 15 February 1779 to his expulsion from the Académie Royal de Musique by the Provost of Merchants Caumartin, speaking for the King. By 1781, however, Noverre had retreated and Gardel and D'Auberval were back in control of the *corps de ballet* at the Opéra. They too soon quarrelled, and in 1783 D'Auberval resigned from the Opéra and retired with a pension of 3,500 livres, which a little later was sweetened by the King to the extent of 2,000 livres a year in gratitude for D'Auberval's services to the Court.

D'Auberval had carried on successive affaires with Mlle Dubois of the Comédie-Française (who asserted that he had fathered her child) and with the celebrated tragedienne Mlle Roncourt. But sometime before 1783, and despite the exhortations of his protectress Madame Du Barry, he married the dancer Mlle Théodore.

Whether or not the London dancer of 1763–64 was Jean D'Auberval (and it is possible that he was) certainly Jean was brought to London in the fall or winter of 1783–84 by Gallini and Harris to become ballet master and choreographer for the opera at the King's Theatre in the Hay-

Harvard Theatre Collection, George Chaffee Collection

JEAN D'AUBERVAL
engraving by Legnies, after Le Fevre

market. D'Auberval's first substantial contributions came on 6 December 1783: for Vestris, Jr the "Allegorical Ballet" in *The Pastimes of Terpsycore* and, for Lepicq and others, *Friendship Leads to Love*, both drawing ecstatic notices in the newspapers. On 3 February 1784 he presented *Le Réveil du bonheur*, on 26 February *Le Cocq du Village; ou, La Lotterie ingénieuse*, on 6 March *Orpheo*, and on 11 March *Le Magnifique*. For his benefit on 18 March three ballets composed by him were danced between the acts of the Opera. The ballets constituted "An entirely new Species of Entertainment, after the French style. The Music entirely new composed by Rauzzini." Novosielski painted new scenery, and Lupino devised new dresses. D'Auberval himself danced Old Age in his specialty dance *Four Ages of Man*, partnered by Mme Simonet and "to the celebrated Musette of Handel." Tickets were to be had of the beneficiary, at half a guinea each, at his house, No 5, Great Pultney Street, Golden Square.

On 25 March 1784 D'Auberval presented for the singer Mme Rossi's benefit at the King's a new ballet "*Pygmalion*, taken from the Mono-drama of that name by Jean-Jacques Rousseau, with the original music composed by that very celebrated writer."

D'Auberval danced but seldom in the season of 1783–84, judging by the bills. On 13 May 1784 he took the place of the absent Slingsby in *Le Réveil du bonheur* for the benefit of his wife "Mme Théodore," now a King's Theatre ballerina. He also that night danced Skirmish in his new "Tragi-Comic Dancing Pantomime, *Le Déserteur; ou, la clémence royale*." The *Public Advertiser* thought his "drunkenness was well managed." D'Auberval himself danced again, according to the bills, on 25 May, 10 and 12 June, and 3 July, when some of his ballets were repeated. He was kept sufficiently busy devising the brilliantly spectacular full ballets and the innumerable occasional dances and rehearsing his brilliant corps to the polish which the *Public Advertiser* described: "As to the Dancers, such exquisite perfection was never seen in England before, because there certainly never was before seen such a band of transcendent Dancers simultaneously subsisting on the same Stage . . ."

Mons and Mme D'Auberval were absent from London for the next six seasons and were probably at Bordeaux. They returned in the spring of 1791 to assist in the 55 nights of operas and ballets performed at the Pantheon under the new patent granted Robert O'Reilly. D'Auberval was ballet master and a principal dancer. The entr'acte entertainments for the opera *Armida*, which opened the season on 17 February, were by him: "End of Act I *Divertissement*; End of Act II an entire new Pantomime Ballet, in I act, composed by D'Auberval, *Amphion et Thalie; ou, L'Elève des Muses*." The Muse de la Comédie was danced by "Mme Théodore D'Auberval," as she was now usually billed. For the performance of 24 March, D'Au-

berval "augmented" his *The Deserter* and danced his old part of Skirmish. He had also been responsible for *Telemachus in the Island of Calypso*, performed on 22 March and on several other nights. On 3 May his new divertissement *Le Triomphe de la folie* came out; on 9 May he presented his new pantomime ballet in three acts, *Le Siège de Cythère*; and he is to be credited, no doubt, with several other, slighter, productions that season. But the most notable achievement was the two-act *La Fille mal gardée*, which he had composed in Bordeaux and which he introduced at the Kings on 30 April 1791. (This ballet, in its broad outlines, has survived through the twentieth century.) The couple lived at the time of their benefit on 24 March 1791 at No 52, Poland Street.

The final London season for Mons and Mme D'Auberval was that of 1791–92, when he was again ballet master and she a principal *danseuse*, with the company at the Pantheon from 17 December through 7 January (the Pantheon burned on 14 January) and at the Haymarket from 14 February through 9 June.

Once again D'Auberval assisted in opening the season, this time on 17 December 1791 with an elaborate "new Ballet Demi-Caractère . . . *La Fontaine d'Amour*" at the end of Act I of the opera *La pastorella nobile*, and, at the end of Act II, "a new Pantomimic, Anacreontic Ballet . . . *L'Amant déguisé*." His other contributions in this season, in which the bills do not show him dancing at all, were the revived and revised *La Fête villageoise* (which Haydn saw on 31 December and which he did not approve, even though De La Chapelle was making his first appearance and Mme Hilligsberg also danced), *Le Volage fixé, Le Menuet du volage*, and *La Foire de Smirne; ou, Les Amans réunis*.

The London *Telegraph* of 30 September 1796 reported that the ballet at the King's Theatre was to be augmented by the addition of D'Auberval, Vestris, and L'Aborie,

Harvard Theatre Collection, George Chaffee Collection
JEAN D'AUBERVAL, with Mme Allard and Mme Pelin
artist unknown

but none of these dancers appeared in the company that season. On 26 March 1799 D'Auberval's ballet *Télémaque*, as produced by him at Bordeaux, was brought to the King's Theatre, but there is no evidence that D'Auberval was present in London at the time.

According to Deryck Lynham (citing Bachaumont), D'Auberval, like the elder Vestris, lived from time to time with dancer Marie Allard, the mother of the younger Vestris: "Watching [young Vestris] a few days ago from the wings, [D'Auberval] remarked with as much chagrin as admiration: 'What talent! He is the son of Vestris and not mine! Alas! I missed him but by a quarter of an hour.'"

Jean Bercher *dit* D'Auberval died in

1806. The twentieth-century critic Moore (*Images of the Dance*) declares:

Dauberval had imagination, wit and intelligence. In his choreography he knew how to blend dancing and acting imperceptibly, so that the story flowed naturally through the movement. A performer of enormous vitality and versatility, he relished comedy roles as the classic *pas.*

Jean D'Auberval's portrait was engraved by Legnis after LeFevre. He was pictured with Mme Pelin and Marie Allard in a print of 1779, with Mme Allard in *Sylvie* in an engraving by J. B. Tilliard after a painting by L. C. de Carmontelie, and in a *pas de trois* with Marie Allard and

Marie Madeleine Guimard, in an anonymous engraving dated 1779.

D'Auberval, Mme Jean, née Crépé called Mme Théodore *d. 1798, dancer.*

When the dancing master Lany's young pupil Mlle Crépé was admitted as supernumerary to the *corps de ballet* of the Paris Opéra in 1775–76 she exchanged her patronymic, according to custom, for a stage name, "Mlle Théodore." She made her debut as a dancer of the Académie Royal de Musique in the pastoral *Mirtil et Lycoris* on 26 December 1777.

By the time of Jean Georges Noverre's defection from the Opéra to London's King's Theatre in the fall of 1781, Mlle Théodore had danced her way into some prominence in the *corps.* Deryck Lynham in *The Chevalier Noverre* relates that she found out that in London she might double her Parisian salary of 6,000 livres a year. She therefore wrote to the minister who was responsible for the administration of the Opéra, demanding eight months' leave each year. When her request was refused she appealed directly to the Queen of France, who saw to it that her contract was annulled and that she was free to go where she chose.

Mlle Théodore then joined Noverre and her other French colleagues (who were ignoring the fact that England and France were in a state of war) in London. The group included Mons, Mme, and the Mlles Simonet, and Le Picq, Nivelon, Gardel, Leger, and Bournonville.

Mlle Théodore danced at the opening of the season on 17 November 1781 and at its close on 29 June 1782. She danced frequently and inspired some good reviews, though she seldom danced alone. She paired with the prominent male dancer Nivelon on 29 January 1782 in Noverre's composition *The Emperor's Cossac* and did so again on the occasion of her benefit on 19 March when, in the masquerade scene in

Harvard Theatre Collection

MME THÉODORE D'AUBERVAL

by Henard

La contadina in corte, they danced a minuet. She furnished benefit tickets to her public from her residence at No 39, Tichfield Street, Portland Chapel.

Lynham says that, when Mlle Théodore returned to France at the end of the London season, the autocratic director of the Opéra had her jailed on the pretext that she had in her letters censured the theatre's management. She was confined for eight days as a lesson to other possible defectors. But her determination to return to London only hardened. Furthermore, she persuaded D'Auberval to go there too.

More than a year elapsed, however, before D'Auberval followed her to London, for he did not appear in the King's company roster of 1782–83, when the dancers occupied the expensively renovated opera house. Mlle Théodore was there, however, and once again danced on both the opening and closing nights, 2 November and 28 June, in a season which, despite the dancers' efforts, was financially ruinous for the proprietor William Taylor. She was several times featured in dances partnered by the ballet master Lepicq or the celebrated Slingsby. At the time of her benefit on 8 May 1783 she was living at No 46, Rupert Street, Haymarket.

Sometime in September 1783 Mlle Théodore was married to the dancer Jean Bercher *dit* D'Auberval. It is fairly certain though that he was not in London between 1764 and the winter of 1783–84; and he may not have been there before the appearance of his name in the bill of 18 March 1784. He was probably, however, ballet master at the King's Theatre from the beginning of that season in late November.

Billed now sometimes as "Mme Théodore" and sometimes as "Mme Théodore D'Auberval" the dancer accompanied her husband to London for the seventy-night 1783–84 season at the King's. She danced first on 6 December 1783 in her husband's new ballets *The Pastimes of Terpsycore*, and *Friendship Leads to Love*. During the season she was featured several times with the brilliant Lepicq, with the athletic Slingsby, and with the new sensation among the imported male dancers, Vestris, Jr.

For the next six seasons, the D'Aubervals were absent from the London stage. "They both," writes Lynham, "applied for reinstatement at the Opéra, she as *premier sujet*, he as joint *Maître de Ballet*." But, he says, their application failed, and Jean accepted the post of ballet master and his wife that of principal dancer at Bordeaux, where Jean brought forth some of his best choreography, including *La Fille mal gardée*. The chronology here is uncertain, and it is not clear why Jean should have had to apply for reinstatement at Paris. For the opera season beginning at the Pantheon on 17 February and running through 19 July

1791 D'Auberval was hired as ballet master and Mme D'Auberval as a principal dancer. The couple returned in the same capacities for the full season of 1791–92 at the Pantheon and then were heard of no more in London.

Mme Théodore D'Auberval died in 1798. According to Lynham, "she had been described as a 'free thinker in short skirts' and 'a philosopher in pink satin slippers' because she was said to be more interested in the writings of J. J. Rousseau than in dancing."

Mme D'Auberval was drawn and engraved in peasant costume by C. Henard. She was also the subject of a portrait engraving by J. Palliere after Desmarsoeuvre.

D'Aubigney or **D'Aubney.** *See* **DOBNEY.**

Dause, Mrs [*fl. 1760*], *dancer.*
On 22 September 1760 Mrs Dause was on the Covent Garden payroll as a dancer at 3*s.* 4*d.* daily.

D'Auvigne, Mons [*fl. 1773*], *ballet master.*
On 2 February 1773 a "Grand Ballet" entitled *L'Isle desert* by the ballet master D'Auvigne was presented at the King's Theatre in the Haymarket.

Davain. *See* **DAVANT.**

Davant, Henrick [*fl. 1685–1716*], *trumpeter.*
The Henrick Davant who was a trumpeter in the King's Music in the late Restoration period was probably the trumpeter "Davain" (or Devan, Davin, Devon) who played in theatre bands in the early eighteenth century. Davant was a participant in the coronation ceremonies for James II on 23 April 1685 and was officially appointed a trumpeter in the King's Musick on 23 May. He continued as a court

musician under William III at a salary of
£91 5s. yearly. By about 1708 he was playing trumpet in the band at the Queen's
Theatre in the Haymarket for 8s. daily, a
fee that grew to 10s. by about 1710. He
moved to Drury Lane afterward, but on 2
June 1716 the managers wrote the treasurer
"to let Mr. Devan, Mr. Latour, the Hoboy
and Mr. Pots know that after Saturday, the
9th instant, the company have no further
occasion for their performance in the music-
room."

Davenant, Alexander   b. c. 1658, treasurer, proprietor.

The black sheep of the Davenant family
was Alexander, born about 1658, the
fourth son of Sir William and Dame Henrietta Maria. Curiously, Lady Davenant's
will in later years spoke of Alexander as
her third son, but the Davenant genealogy
in the College of Arms lists, in sequence,
Charles, Edmund, William, Alexander,
Augustin (Ralph?), Thomas, Nicholas,
George, and Richard. Edmund probably
died young, which may account for Dame
Mary's forgetting him.

On 30 November 1675, when he was
about 17 and surely too inexperienced for
the job, Alexander supplanted his stepbrother Thomas Cross as the Duke's Company's treasurer. His appointment may have
been part of an effort by Lady Davenant
and her eldest son, Charles, to keep control
of the troupe within the family and discourage Cross's growing curiosity about the
company's books. Alexander may have
served in a titular capacity at first, for the
records indicate little more than that he
was a member of the troupe in 1675–76.

He quickly showed his colors, however.
One of the Bulstrode papers dated 26 De-
cember 1675 reported that "The earle of
Pembroke had another rencounter yesterday
at a play house at which he wounded one
Davenant, Sir William's son, and got a
hurt himself." There is no proof that the
Earl's opponent was Alexander, but the

young man's later escapades would suggest
that it was he, rather than the steadier
Charles, the only other son who could be
referred to at this time. Pembroke was
known as "a madman when he was sober
and a homocidal maniac when he was
drunk," but even if he started the quarrel,
it is significant that Davenant drew, too.

Alexander's name began appearing in
connection with the Duke's Company's
finances the next year. On 13 November
1676, as treasurer, he was paid by the
Middle Temple for a play presented there,
and on 9 November 1677 and 13 February
1678 he received similar fees in behalf of
the troupe. In May 1683 he married an
heiress, Allett Brome, daughter of Henry,
who brought him a tidy £3000. Either before or just after his marriage he turned
over his treasurer's post in the (now)
United Company to his younger and even
less experienced brother Ralph and set up
as a coal and wood merchant on a wharf
next to the Dorset Garden playhouse. At
some later point affluent Alex purchased a
brewery on Saffron Hill.

He did not, however, drop his interest
in the theatre. In 1686 he established the
system of taking after-money—reduced fees
from latecomers who had always before
then entered free. And in 1687 he bought
control of the shares and patent which his
brother Charles had held. He made the
proposal to Charles in May 1687, offering
£2400, and Charles accepted the money on
30 August. To make this purchase Alexander had cleverly used only £400 of his
own funds, for in secret he had induced the
slippery lawyer Christopher Rich and his
friend Sir Thomas Skipwith to put up the
rest of the money. This trio, then, received
from Charles Davenant all his acting or
venturer's shares; his interest in the costumes, scenery, and properties; his right to
the old Davenant patent; the 19-year lease
(beginning on 9 November 1682) on
Drury Lane; and a number of plays belonging to the old Duke's Company. On 12

Public Record Office

Petition of the Players, concerning ALEXANDER and CHARLES DAVENANT

September 1687 Skipwith made over his ⅝ interest in all this property to Alexander for seven years, in return for which Alexander proposed to pay him £312 a year in weekly sums of £6 by farming out the shares to advantage. Davenant sold his own ⅙ interest to Rich for £400, again making an agreement to farm out the shares and pay Rich £1 4s. weekly.

As the active proprietor, Davenant next eased out Thomas Betterton and William Smith as managers of acting and put still another Davenant, Thomas, the least experienced of all, in their place. He hoodwinked the actress Elizabeth Barry into lending him some £600 to £800; he even milked Skipwith and Rich for over £1300; he stopped share payments to the retired actor Henry Harris, and when the player protested he was put off "with many vaine and trifleing pretences and excuses." He also conned some of the actors into giving him shares in the costumes and scenery in return for £100 should they be disabled or cease acting, but William Smith (who duly remembered Alex in his will) was the only one so paid. Somewhere along the line, according to later complaints by the rather untrustworthy Skipwith and Rich, he committed forgeries. It is doubtful that he needed to do any of this: he had married well and had made money in business, and when Lady Davenant died in 1691 she made him her executor and left him the "overplus" of the estate, which may have been considerable, for her bequests to her other sons came to over £1000.

He must simply have liked money and manipulations; and, chiefly by selling the same property twice and borrowing on property that was not his, he must have made a small fortune. By the time most of his swindling was discovered in 1694, Alexander was out of reach of punishment. By 23 October 1693 he had fled to the Canary Islands, never to be heard from again.

Davenant, Charles 1656–1714, proprietor.

The first of Sir William Davenant's sons by his third wife, Dame Henrietta Maria, Charles Davenant was born in 1656, about the time the poet laureate was attempting his first productions at Rutland House. He went to the grammar school at Cheame, Surrey, and then on to Balliol College in 1671. Though he did not complete his work there, he was later granted "by favour and money" an LL. D. by some university—Cambridge or Dublin, said Wood, but the registers do not list him as resident at either. Charles's mother relinquished to him

control of the Duke's Company about June 1673, and from this time until he sold his interest to his brother Alexander in 1687, Charles was proprietor of the Duke's troupe and, after 1682, of the United Company.

Even before he succeeded his mother, Charles may have been privy to arrangements made by his father before his death to keep control of the company in the family. His stepbrother Thomas Cross later accused Charles of conniving with Lady Davenant and one John Alway in the settlement of Sir William Davenant's estate in 1668, but Charles was only 12 at the time and not sufficiently precocious for conspiracy. He was, however, a bright boy and is said to have written the spectacle play, *Circe*, at the age of 19. It was published in 1677 and produced at the Dorset Garden Theatre in May of that year.

Except for writing *Circe*, Charles Davenant's activities in the Duke's Company between 1673 and 1681 are unrecorded. He did not come into his inheritance of 4.5 shares in the troupe until 1677, and possibly until then he was learning the business and was proprietor in name only. But by 1681 he was more active, and it is clear that he played an important part in the union of the Duke's with the King's Company. The initial agreement was signed on 14 October 1681. There is uncertainty as to whether Davenant took the first step or whether his counterpart in the rival troupe, Charles Killigrew, initiated the proposal, but certainly Davenant's actions were no credit to him. He, Thomas Betterton, and William Smith tried to get two of the leading players from the King's Company, Charles Hart and Edward Kynaston, to desert their failing troupe and sign over their shares in it to the Duke's players. In return Davenant and his colleagues agreed to pay the two actors for every day they did not act for Killigrew. Hart and Kynaston were also to help promote a union of the two companies, even to the extent of going to law against Killigrew.

On 4 May 1682 an agreement was reached on the union, and Davenant clearly had the upper hand. He agreed to pay Killigrew £3 for each day the new company played at either theatre as soon as Killigrew turned over Drury Lane. Killigrew, whose actions in this affair were equally underhanded, had negotiated the union without consulting the King's Company sharers, and he himself had hardly any equity in the troupe. On 9 November 1682 a new agreement was drawn up, leasing Drury Lane to Charles Davenant for 19 years, and the union was thus completed.

Davenant and Killigrew ostensibly shared control of the new United Company, but entries in the Lord Chamberlain's accounts suggest that Davenant held the reins. Payments coming in for plays performed before members of the royal family were made to Davenant, Betterton, and Smith, or to some combination of this trio, while Killigrew was mentioned chiefly in connection with complaints made against the company. It was Davenant who looked over new plays: Aphra Behn in her preface to *The Lucky Chance* said that Charles, "out of Respect to the Commands he had from Court, to take great Care that no Indecency should be in Plays, sent for [my play] and nicely look't it over, putting out anything he but imagin'd the Criticks would play with." This was a foreshadowing of Davenant's later role as Master of the Revels and inspector of plays.

But Charles had higher aims than a lifetime of theatre management, and in May 1687 he accepted his brother Alexander's proposal to sell him Charles's interest in the United Company for £2400. The money passed hands on 30 August 1687, and Charles relinquished virtually all his control in an enterprise which his father had so painfully developed years before. Had young Alexander been something better than a swindler, it might not have mattered, but Sir William would have wept to see the power pass to the scapegrace Alexander,

from whom it would quickly slip into the hands of the rapacious lawyer Christopher Rich.

Freed of his theatrical obligations, Charles Davenant built a different career. In 1678 he had used some of his inheritance to purchase a lucrative place as a commissioner of the excise, a post he held until 1689. Now he sat for St Ives, Cornwall, in James II's first parliament and was made Master of the Revels, with the power to censor and license plays; this post, too, he held until 1689. Luttrell reported on 8 May 1694 that Davenant had been made surveyor general of all the salt pits in England, and on 2 July 1696 that he was appointed surveyor general of the excise. Under William III he sat for Great Bedwin in 1698 (and again in 1700), and on 29 November 1698 Luttrell reported that Davenant had been appointed the old East India Company's chief agent for negotiating with "the great mogull" in India. Charles Sedley, writing to Sir Richard Newgate on 12 January 1699, commented that "Doctor Daveñat hath obligd the world with an other booke but I fear disobligd some of our great men, hee is going agent to Fort St George, for the Old East India company: for 3 yeares . . ." Most of Davenant's tracts on political economy were written and published from these years forward. At the accession of Queen Anne, Davenant was made secretary of the commission to negotiate for a union with Scotland, and Defoe noted in his letters that in May 1707 Charles was inspector general of imports and exports, a post he had been given in 1705.

Though involved in government affairs, Davenant did not lose all interest in theatre. He is said to have encouraged the rebellion of Betterton from the United Company in 1694, and since his wife held half a share in the Drury Lane troupe, Charles maintained a degree of interest in the difficulties Christopher Rich was having in 1709 when the Drury Lane company was silenced. At some time Charles concerned himself with the Davenant heritage and erected a tablet at St Martin's Church, Oxford, commemorating his father's relatives who were buried there.

Charles Davenant died, according to a genealogy drawn up by one of his sons, on 7 November 1714 (*The Dictionary of National Biography* gives 6 November) and was buried at St Bride, Fleet Street, in the vault with his mother.

Of Davenant's own family quite a bit is known, though there is confusion about his wife's identity. On or near Michaelmas 1678 he married. His bride is reported to have been Frances Walden, daughter and heiress of Sir Leoline Walden, but the Davenant genealogy in the College of Arms cites her as Frances Molins, daughter of James Molins, MD., of the parish of St Bride's. The genealogy must be correct, for the Molins name was given to the son who drew up the family tree, yet Charles may have married twice, each time to a girl named Frances. In any case, by using the genealogy prepared in 1727 by Henry Molins Davenant and information from the St Bride's registers, a fairly complete reconstruction of the Davenant offspring can be attempted.

A first son, name unknown, must have died in infancy about 1679. The second son, so described in the genealogy, was Charles, born about 1680 and still alive in 1725. Then came Henrietta, baptized on 26 March 1681 and buried on the following 11 April; a second Henrietta, still alive in 1725, was born sometime after this, perhaps before the next child. Next came Elizabeth, baptized on 8 February 1684 and buried on 29 June 1693. Then there were Charlotte, baptized on 8 February 1685, and Frances, baptized on 29 August 1687—both of whom lived beyond 1725. Henry Molins was the next child. His birth year is not known; he lived beyond 1727. After him were born Philadelphia and then Catherine and Anne, apparently twins, all of whom were alive in 1725.

A character book written about 1705 or 1706, a copy of which is in the Folger Shakespeare Library, contains some caustic comments on Charles Davenant and his namesake. It notes that Davenant had, in the reign of William III, made several advances to the ministry (of Excise, apparently) but "to no purpose, their neglect & his Poverty [had] sowr'd him" and had led to some of the critical comments in his writings. He never made much headway in the House of Commons; "his Talent lay more in writing, then in speaking." "He was very poor at the Revolution & had no business to import him at the Reign of K W^m yet made a good figure, he is a very Cloudy lookt man, fatt of midle Stature, & fifty years Old." His son Charles, who was then an agent at Frankfort, is described as "a very Giddy headed young fellow, with some Witt, about twenty five Years Old."

Davenant, Henrietta Maria du Tremblay *d. 1691, proprietress.*

Sir William Davenant met Henrietta Maria du Tremblay of St Germaine Beaupré during his stay in France, probably about 1646. He may have been married at that point, but the facts concerning his first wife are very dim; it is probable that Henrietta Maria was also then married, though facts of her life at this time are equally scarce. At any rate, the pair may well have had an affair, as Davenant's *Gondibert* implies. About a decade and one wife later, Sir William came back to France, wooed and won the lady (then, apparently, a widow), and brought her back to England in 1655. The couple moved into Rutland House, in which Sir William planned to present his "operas."

Though Dame Henrietta Maria, or, as she came to be called, Dame Mary, may have participated in some way in the theatrical ventures at Rutland House, the Cockpit in Drury Lane, the Salisbury Court Theatre, and finally the Lincoln's Inn Fields Theatre, the only references to her before her husband's death in 1668 have to do with her home and family. Indeed, between 1656 and 1668 Dame Mary bore at least nine sons to her knight, quite enough to keep her occupied at home. In addition, she looked after at least some of the offspring from Davenant's earlier marriages, four of his young actresses, and a young girl that he and she adopted. Her sons were Charles (born in 1656), Edmund (1657?), William (1657), Alexander (1658?), Augustin (Ralph? c. 1659), Thomas (1664), Nicholas (c. 1665), George (c. 1666), and Richard (1668). Her stepsons were Thomas Cross (c. 1632), Paul Cross (c. 1636), John Cross (c. 1641), and Philip Cademan, alias Cross (c. 1643) – but of these, John and Paul had left the household by 1656 and Thomas was in residence with the Davenants only periodically. Dame Mary's stepdaughter was Mary, Sir William's daughter by his first wife, born about 1638 or possibly 1642 and probably living with the Davenants until she married, about 1660.

The actresses, after 1660, were Mary Davis, Mary Saunderson, Miss Davenport, and Miss Long; these must have been supplanted by a different foursome as the girls married or were otherwise provided for. The adopted girl was Elizabeth Barry, who joined the household, at less than ten years of age, sometime before Sir William's death in 1668. The Davenants educated her, and she became Dame Mary's companion before going on to a brilliant and scandalous career as an actress. When Lisle's tennis court in Lincoln's Inn Fields was turned into a theatre by Davenant in 1661, the household moved to quarters in a wing of the building, and there the great brood lived for many years.

Before his death Sir William apparently connived with his wife and one John Alway to stave off creditors and keep control of Davenant's theatrical enterprise in the family. Purposely, it seems, Davenant made no will, and administration of his estate was granted to Alway, Dame Mary renouncing (as planned, apparently) on 6 May 1668.

Not long thereafter Alway resold a deed of his rights to the estate to Dame Mary, and she thus retrieved the 3.3 controlling shares in the Duke's Company. These she held in trust for her son Charles until about June 1673. One of the chief opponents of this private arrangement, though not until 1684, when he had been ousted from the treasurership of the United Company, was Davenant's stepson, Thomas Cross, to whom the knight had legally owed money since 1652. When Cross finally brought his case to court, he styled Alway "an absurd person of no residence" and claimed that Dame Mary and her eldest son, Charles, had so transacted matters after Sir William Davenant's death that Cross could not tell until 1677–78 how much of the estate was actually in Dame Mary's hands. And it was only in the 1680s that Cross had been able to determine which of the shares in the Duke's Company were assets and which were inheritance.

As proprietress, then, from 1668 to 1673, Dame Mary Davenant inherited the virtually dictatorial powers that her husband had held. Most of her activity during these years suggests that she was a shrewd and sensible businesswoman. She put the artistic supervision of the troupe in the hands of the company's best actors, Thomas Betterton and Henry Harris; she started a new Nursery for young actors in the Barbican in 1672; she delegated much of the authority to others when the intricate problems of planning and building the new Dorset Garden Theatre came up – but she saw to it that the lease, though in other names, was in trust for her; she guided her husband's collected *Works* into print and thus stimulated new interest in those of his plays which were in the Duke's Company's repertory; and she took a particular interest in the company accounts, seeing to it that most if not all the payments for plays done before royalty were routed through her.

In connection with her Nursery project, Dame Mary became involved in a quarrel with the actor-manager John Perin and won handily. Perin in 1671 was the leader of a Nursery operating in Finsbury Fields, called Bunhill; it was rather conveniently dissolved and the booth theatre torn down just before Dame Mary pushed forward her plans for the Barbican Nursery. The details of the tiff between Perin and Lady Mary Davenant are missing, but warrants in the Lord Chamberlain's accounts hint at what must have happened. On 21 September 1671 Perin was ordered to be apprehended for abusing Dame Mary—and for other, unnamed, misdemeanors; on 18 December permission was granted for Dame Mary to go to law against Perin. Finally, on 27 December 1671 an order was issued to arrest some group, possibly Perin's, who acted plays without a license from Dame Mary Davenant and Killigrew. In 1672 Dame Mary started her Nursery in the Barbican with no competition. Sir William would have been proud of her.

After Charles, and later Alexander, Davenant took over control of the acting troupe, Dame Mary was less active but still interested. She clung to her 3.3 shares, and in October 1678 her son Charles deeded her a half share more. She also owned, until 30 May 1687, the rights to income from the fruit concession at the Dorset Garden playhouse, and even after the two London companies united in 1682 and Dorset Garden was little used, she contrived to have herself paid her usual 5*s.* every day a play was done at Drury Lane but *not* at Dorset Garden.

Having passed on most of the affairs of the company, Dame Mary by 1676 claimed she was in poverty. This probably was not strictly true, yet Sir William had left a tangle of debts, and supporting a large family with pretensions to wealth and position must have been costly. Her son William could not be maintained in the manner befitting an Oxford student, so she petitioned everyone she knew from the King down to the Earl of St Albans (Henry Jermyn, Sir William's old friend) to support her son's

hope for a fellowship at All Souls. She apparently failed in her attempt, but William stayed at Oxford anyway (at Magdalen) and in time received his A.M. and took orders.

Whether she really had it to give or not, when she made her will on 19 November 1686 Dame Mary left to her sons Nicholas £200, Thomas £400, George £200, and Richard £200. To her eldest, Dr Charles Davenant and his lady, she bequeathed £5 each for rings, and to her "sister" Mrs Elizabeth Cookson (exact relationship unknown) £5 for a ring. All else she left to the scapegrace of the family—though she must not have considered him so—Alexander Davenant. Dame Mary was buried on 24 February 1691 in the vault of St Bride, Fleet Street. A second hand in the registers noted that she died of a fever. Alexander Davenant proved her will on 15 May 1691, two years before his nefarious practices at the theatre forced him to flee the country.

Davenant, Nicholas *b. c. 1665, lessee.*

Though not nearly as involved with theatre affairs as other members of the family, Nicholas Davenant nevertheless served as an important link in maintaining the family's control of the Duke's Company after his father, Sir William Davenant, died in 1668. Nicholas was born about 1665, and when he was only five he was named one of the official lessees of the Dorset Garden Theatre, then under construction. He could not have come into any form of control until he was 16, but his name on the lease was designed to protect the numerous elders who were involved in negotiations for the playhouse.

The arrangements were typically complex. On 12 August 1670 the Duke's Company agreed that Henry Harris and John Roffey (the first an actor-sharer, the second a sharer) would reassign the lease that they had obtained on the site for the new playhouse to Nicholas Davenant and Thomas

Cross, Sir William Davenant's stepson and company treasurer, in trust for Dame Mary Davenant. On 21 July 1674, after the theatre was in operation and debts had piled up, the lease was again reassigned, this time to two trustees, John Baker and Thomas Franklin. The next day Baker and Franklin re-leased the theatre and ground for 35 years to Nicholas Davenant, then only about nine years of age, and John Atkinson. If these elaborate machinations were designed to befuddle any creditors, they certainly must have succeeded.

There is nothing to indicate what happened after this to Nicholas and his paper involvement in the theatre. He may have grown up to serve as something more than a lessee, but the only other notice of him was in his mother's will, dated 19 November 1686 and proved on 15 May 1691. Dame Mary left him £200. Nethercot, in his *Sir William D'Avenant*, suggests that perhaps Nicholas was the "ingenious, sober man" who was one of the English factors in Bengal in the 1680s.

Davenant, Ralph *c. 1659–1698, treasurer.*

Ralph Davenant does not appear in the Davenant genealogy at the College of Arms, but an otherwise unknown son, Augustin, does. It may be that the two names belonged to one person: Augustin Ralph Davenant, perhaps, who preferred to be called Ralph. Ralph Davenant was, if this identification is correct, the fifth of at least nine sons born to Sir William and Dame Henrietta Maria Davenant. It is probable that he was born about 1659—certainly not much earlier if calendar space is to be provided his older brothers Charles, Edmund, William, and Alexander, and certainly no later than about March 1663, since the next son in the family, Thomas, was born in January 1664. After Thomas came Nicholas, George, and Richard.

About 1683 Ralph Davenant succeeded his brother Alexander as treasurer of the United Company when Alexander married and went into the wood business. But the company accounts suggest that Ralph took no active role in the finances until about April 1684. From time to time contemporary documents mentioned Ralph as receiving payments for plays done at the Inner Temple, or being charged as a company representative with not paying exactors their shares, or as being with the actor William Mountfort the night he was killed. But for the most part, Ralph Davenant kept out of the limelight during the 1680s and early 1690s, and there is little indication that he inherited much knack for business affairs from his father.

A John Powell was ordered arrested on 1 May 1698 for having attacked a Davenant (Ralph?) in a coffeehouse, and two days later he was imprisoned, presumably for this affront. This scuffle may have had a connection with the next one: Luttrell recorded in his diary that "about 12 last night [18 May 1698] Mr. D'avent, treasurer of the playhouse, was murthered by 3 soldiers, as he was goeing into his own lodgings in Grayes Inn Lane, who designed to have robbed the house." Ralph lived just long enough to make an abbreviated will. It was dated 18 May 1698, the day of the attack, and described the dying man as from the parish of St Andrew, Holborn. Ralph named his brother William his executor. No bequests were made; there probably was no time, and Ralph would have known that his pious clergyman brother would take care of things properly. Ralph Davenant was buried near his mother in the vault at St Bride, Fleet Street, on 22 May 1698. William Davenant proved the will the following 2 December.

Davenant, Thomas *b. 1664, manager.*

Thomas, one of at least nine sons of Sir William and Dame Henrietta Maria Davenant, was born on 14 January and baptized at St Giles, Cripplegate, on 31 January 1664. In 1687 Alexander Davenant bought his brother Charles's interest in the United Company and began a series of maneuvers that were to end in 1693 with his fleeing to the Canary Islands. One of the first things he did was to depose the veteran actors Thomas Betterton and William Smith as managers of acting and appoint his brother Thomas. Thomas was paid 40*s.* weekly starting on 5 November 1687 for doing (or supposedly doing) a job for which he was, so far as is known, completely untrained. But Alexander was not concerned with such matters; he merely wanted to get control of the troupe into the family; so Thomas may have served in name only and may have let someone more competent manage the acting.

By May 1688 Thomas seems, in fact, to have shifted himself into company work that had more to do with finances than with acting. In that month, according to the Lord Chamberlain's accounts, he and Charles Killigrew were ordered to pay out of the actor Freeman's salary a debt he owed to one Alexander Blayer. Similarly, later the same month, a letter was addressed to Davenant and Betterton concerning the widow Lacy's share in the troupe's income. And in December 1689 Davenant and Killigrew received, or were supposed to receive, payment for plays done before royalty. Such references to Thomas occur through 1695, at which time the United Company split, and he apparently ceased active participation in theatre affairs.

Thomas seems not to have endeared himself to people with whom he associated. On 19 January 1692, for example, the playwright Thomas Shadwell, working in behalf of fellow author Nicholas Brady's play, *The Innocent Impostors*, complained that "Tho Davenant has with great slight turnd mee of[f] and says he will trouble himself noe more about yᵉ play. . . ." When Betterton and his followers complained about the management of Christopher Rich and Sir Thomas Skipwith and pleaded for the formation of a separate company, Thomas

Davenant was mentioned in conjunction with his counterpart from the Killigrew family, Charles. This pair, the complaints stated, had bilked the actor Williams of £1 a week in salary.

On the other hand, in March 1693, according to Thomas Southerne's manuscript memoir of Congreve at the British Museum, Southerne persuaded Thomas Davenant "who then governd the Playhouse, that Mr Congreve should have the privilege of the Playhouse half a year before his play was playd, wh. I never knew allowd any one before." And though Christopher Rich failed to fulfill the agreement, Davenant and Killigrew had ordered £20 to be given from company money for an organ for St Bride, Fleet Street. Perhaps, surrounded as he was by such schemers as Rich, Skipwith, and his brother Alexander, Thomas Davenant could not have become an effectual member of the company even if he had wanted to. One piece of information in the case Betterton versus Rich and Skipwith points to just that: Thomas Davenant was appointed (but to what position and when was not stated) by word of mouth only.

When the United Company split in 1695, Thomas held .084 shares—the smallest of the lot. But he had apparently been paid well for his theatrical work through the years, and his mother left him £400 when she died in 1691. He kept his interest in Rich's company until at least 1704, but after that there is no trace of him.

Davenant, William 1606–1668, *manager, playwright, poet.*

William Davenant—or D'avenant, as he styled himself on title pages, was baptized on 3 March 1606 at St Martin's Church in Oxford, the second son in the family of John Davenant, vintner and owner of the Crown Tavern, and his fetching wife Jane, née Shepherd. William Shakespeare was, according to tradition, godfather to the boy, and John Aubrey, writing after Davenant's death in 1668, was one of the earliest biographers to give credence to the rumor that Davenant was Shakespeare's son:

Mr. William Shakespeare was wont to goe into Warwickshire once a yeare, and did commonly in his journey lye at this house in Oxon, where he was exceedingly respected. . . . Now Sir William would sometimes, when he was pleasant over a glasse of wine with his most intimate friends—e.g. Sam Butler, author of *Hudibras*, etc., say, that it seemed to him that he writt with the very spirit that did Shakespeare, and seemed contented enough to be thought his Son. He would tell them the story as above, in which way his mother had a very light report, whereby she was called a Whore.

That Shakespeare may have been Davenant's godfather could be true, but there is no proof of this, and that he was the boy's father may also be a myth, though a reference to the achievements of bastards in a poetic tribute of Carew to Davenant supports the story. All that is certain is that in later years Davenant became a frequent adaptor and producer of the Bard's plays and a source for much Shakespeare apocrypha, some of it patently untrue.

John and Jane Davenant's family consisted of, in chronological order of birth, Jane (1602), Robert (1603), Alice (1604), William (1606), John (1607), Elizabeth (sometime between 1607 and 1611), and Nicholas (1611). Young William was educated at Edward Sylvester's private school in Oxford but, as Aubrey said, he was "drawne from schoole before he was ripe enough" and placed under Reverend Daniel Hough at Lincoln College about 1620 or 1621.

William's mother died in early April 1622, and on 23 April his father was buried. By John Davenant's will, William was given £150, a seventh of the accrued profits of the wine business, and was to be put "to prentice to some good merchant of London or other tradesman." William went to London but had higher hopes than trade, and by the end of 1623 he had spent his money on fineries and had been arrested for a debt to his tailor. He managed to satisfy his debt by 20 July 1624, but this unpleasant scrape with the law was the beginning of a lifetime of legal problems and confinements in debtor's prisons. The apprenticeship abandoned, the young man became a page to the first Duchess of Richmond, but he was unlucky in this, too, for when the Duke died on 11 February 1624, William's sinecure disappeared.

About this time—perhaps before Richmond's death and when Davenant's post seemed secure—he married. Information about his bride is almost nonexistent, and parish register entries citing William Davenant can be misleading, for they frequently refer to another man of the same name active about the same time. A William and Mary Davenant baptized a son William at

Courtesy of Lincoln College, Oxford

WILLIAM DAVENANT
by Lely

St James, Clerkenwell, on 27 October 1624; this reference was probably to our man, but the following one may not be: a William Davesnett buried a daughter Elizabeth at St Benet and St Peter, Paul's Wharf, on 9 October 1631.

After the loss of his position with the Duchess of Richmond, Davenant found a new one serving Fulke Greville, Baron Brooke, and he lived at Brooke House off and on until the Baron's death in September 1628. Brooke let him go off to serve in "forrain countries" – he was probably at the siege of St Martin's on the Isle of Rhe in 1627 – and on 8 April 1628 the Bishop of Salisbury, Davenant's cousin, wrote the Secretary to the Admiralty in behalf of another request of William's to serve his country:

M^r. Nicholas, this young gentleman, M^r. William Davenant, has heertofore been imployed in ye Warrs abroad in forrain countries. Hee is my neer kinsman, & one whome I wish well; in regard wherof I should bee very gladd, yf it lay in mee to doe him any good. As hee tells mee, hee hath ye place of an Ancient, or Lieftenant already; and is in some hope when any new Regiments shall bee raised, of further advancement. I assure my selfe that you may have opportunity to doe him y^t favour in such busines, wch I have not.

Through his association with Brooke, his experiences in the service, and the acquaintance of new-found friends at the Inns of Court, Davenant was encouraged during the 1620s to try his hand at playwriting.

The Cruell Brother was licensed on 12 January 1627 and later acted (about 1629?) at the Blackfriars Theatre, though it was not published until 1630. *The Tragedy of Albovine*, printed in 1629 but not acted, may have been composed first. If not, it was at least his first effort to be published. A play called "The Colonel," which was never printed under that title, was written about this time; it may have been an early version of *The Siege* or of *Love and Honour*. *The Siege* and *The Just Italian* were licensed and acted in 1629; the former was not printed until 1673 but the latter was published in 1630.

When Baron Brooke died in 1628 he left Davenant a year's wages plus food and clothing allowances for four months. The request for preferment which the good Bishop had supported apparently bore no fruit, so Davenant moved to the Middle Temple. There he cultivated friendships with Bulstrode Whitelock, master of that society's revels, and Edward Hyde, future Earl of Clarendon and nephew of the Lord Chief Justice of England. Davenant also made friends with James Shirley, John Suckling, and other young men with literary aspirations and good connections. His own creative endeavors he dedicated, with the usual flattering epistles, to important men: poems and a play to the Earl of

Harvard Theatre Collection

WILLIAM DAVENANT

engraving by Worthington, after Thurston

Dorset, a play to the Earl of Somerset, and odes to the King. To two young men who became his special patrons, Henry Jermyn and Endymion Porter, he also wrote complimentary lines. By 1630, then, Davenant had established himself in print, on stage, with court and literary circles, and, unfortunately, with some "Black handsome wench" who gave him "a terrible clap . . . which cost him his nose," reported Aubrey. The disease was not "a clap," but syphilis. The cure for venereal disease then not being very far advanced, Davenant suffered not only from the disease but also from the mercury treatment, which ate away the cartilage of his nose.

His disfigurement made much sport for the wits, but Davenant seems to have weathered the cruel jibes and, being a good theatre man, perhaps he felt that even bad publicity was better than none. His friend Suckling's barbs in *A Session of the Poets* were typical of the cruel jibes Davenant endured:

> *Will. Davenant, ashamed of a foolish*
> * mischance,*
> *That he had got lately travelling in*
> * France,*
> *Modestly hoped the handsomeness of's*
> * muse*
> *Might any deformity about him excuse.*

> *And*
> *Surely the company would have been*
> * content,*
> *If they could have found any precedent;*
> *But in all their records either in verse or*
> * prose,*
> *There was not one laureate without a*
> * nose.*

His cure was finally managed by no less than the Queen's own physician, Thomas Cademan, whose widow Davenant would one day marry.

The resulting medical bills drove Davenant into debt, and he was still carrying on a running battle with his tailor, who was hounding him again. Why the tailor, John Urswick, continued dealing with Davenant is a mystery; in 1632 he sued the writer in Chancery and received in return a countersuit for usury. More curious still is the fact that Urswick had been providing Davenant's wife with food and lodging.

In 1633 Davenant was working in London on a new play, *The Witts*. The Master of the Revels, Sir Henry Herbert, who would cross swords with Davenant again later in his life, refused to license the play. The dramatist appealed to the King, Charles considered the manuscript, revisions were made, and Herbert reluctantly licensed it for printing on 19 January 1634. The work was performed at the Blackfriars Theatre on 22 January and presented before the King at court six days later, but it did not appear in print until 1636. The initial reception was mixed: Herbert noted that the "kinge commended the language, but dislikt the plott and characters" and that the work had "a various fate on the stage, and at court." Davenant's friends, (Porter being the chief among them) praised it, and Davenant's enemies of course damned it.

Court masques now captured Davenant's attention. He may have had a hand in Carew's *Coelum Britannicum* in 1634 (it was published in Davenant's *Works* years later, possibly in error for his own *Britannia Triumphans*, which was left out). For Queen Henrietta Maria, Davenant wrote *The Temple of Love*, first performed on 10 February 1635 with scenes and machines by Inigo Jones. The Queen, who performed in it, liked it well enough to have it presented at least three times in succession, but Sir Thomas Roe thought it was done "with much trouble and Wearisomeness." It was published within six weeks, with the playwright styled "her Majesties Servant."

Meanwhile, Davenant's public theatre work went on apace. On 20 November 1634 his *Love and Honour* was licensed, and by 12 December it had been played at the Blackfriars Theatre. It became one of the author's most popular and influential works, however tedious it may now seem. On 1 August 1635 his next play, *News from Plymouth*, was licensed; it was written for and produced at the Globe, then no longer a fashionable playhouse. Davenant's next play was again for the Blackfriars: *The Platonic Lovers*, licensed on 16 November 1635 and probably performed the following year. For the two sons of the Queen of Bohemia the Middle Temple presented Davenant's *The Triumphs of the Prince D'Amour* on 23 February 1636.

The year 1638 was a remarkable one for Davenant. His *Madagascar* and other poems were published; his masque *Britannia Triumphans* was given in a specially built but temporary banqueting hall at court on 7 January; *Luminalia*, written for the Queen, was performed on 6 February; *The Unfortunate Lovers* was played at the Blackfriars on 23 April; *The Fair Favourite* was presented before the King and Queen at the Cockpit on 20 November; and on 13 December the King named Davenant to succeed Ben Jonson as poet laureate. The dramatist's appointment was made retroactive to 25 March 1638 and carried an annual allowance of £100. Oddly, there is no evidence of an investiture ceremony taking place, nor did the King's order for the stipend actually mention the laureateship.

Davenant's next efforts, after all this furious literary activity, concerned plans for a new playhouse. The King granted him letters patent on 26 March 1639 to erect a theatre on a site measuring 120′ square near the Three Kings Ordinary in Fleet Street. Though the project was suspended by the King on 2 October after objections were raised by the manager of the nearby Salisbury Court Theatre, Richard Heton, Davenant was to find the patent useful in later years.

Details of the playwright's personal life during these years are very scarce. One supposes that his wife Mary was still alive and

with him in London, though his infidelity is an established fact and she seems not to have been mentioned by any of his contemporaries save the tailor Urswick back in 1632. The registers of St Giles in the Fields record the burial on 10 September 1639 of a stillborn child of a William Davenett, but there is no certainty that this was the laureate. A Mary Davenant, daughter of William and Mary, was baptized on 11 January 1642 at St Martin-in-the-Fields; this may have been the daughter Mary, thought to have been born about 1638, who later lived with the dramatist and his third wife, but, again, proof is lacking.

Davenant's next play, *The Distresses*, which was probably the same play as "The Spanish Lovers," licensed on 30 November 1639, may have been written with the playwright's projected playhouse in mind. In 1641 it was listed as the property of the old King's Company at the Blackfriars Theatre, and traces of prompt copy in the text printed after the Restoration suggest a possible production before 1642. But it was the court masque *Salmacida Spolia* that crowned Davenant's prewar career. On 21 January 1640 the lavish work was performed at Whitehall with scenes and machines by Inigo Jones and his assistant, John Webb. It was the last of the great court masques of the Caroline period, and only once again, in the 1670s, would the English court put on such a spectacle. How deeply Davenant was involved in this and other productions of his works is not clear, but he must have been gaining theatrical as well as literary experience during these early years. When William Beeston, the master of the company at the Cockpit in Drury Lane, was imprisoned on 4 May 1640 and his troupe silenced, Davenant was appointed to replace him on 27 June—an indication, at least, of budding abilities as a manager. Though the wars were shortly to end the laureate's duties at the Cockpit, this was the beginning of a career in management which was ultimately to be Davenant's greatest contribution to the theatre.

One would suppose that Davenant had quite enough to keep him busy in London in 1639 and 1640, but the Bishop's Wars in May 1639 and 1640–41 found him in the ordnance and transport service. This was not another William Davenant, for Suckling's letters tell of Davenant's using his carrier pigeons in Henrietta Maria's service, and Viscount Conway wrote from Newcastle on 17 July 1640 that "There are 400 Draught horses come hither, 800 more will be here within four days; no order is taken for their payment, and no man knows what to do with them. There is only one man sent down, a deputy to Mr. Davenant; if another man should do so he would put it into a play."

Davenant's involvement in the civil strife deepened, and in early May 1641 he, Henry Jermyn, Sir John Suckling, Henry Percy, and Captain Billingsley were ordered arrested for promoting "designs of great danger to the state, and mischievous ways to prevent the happy success and conclusion of this Parliament"—which was another way of saying they had disturbed the Long Parliament by trying to bring up an army to defend the King. The laureate's cohorts fled across the Channel, but Davenant was arrested at Faversham, Kent, and detained while Parliament decided what to do with him. Under examination he admitted that "Confession is the neerest way to forgivenesse," whereupon he accused himself of using some "mis-becoming words" and "loose Arguments, disputed at Table perhaps" but said he never meant to commit any errors "irreverently or maliciously against Parliamentary government." His part in the conspiracy was minimal, he pleaded, for the others had not taken him into their council. The Earl de la Warr called Davenant's defense "Roguery," but most members of Parliament inclined toward leniency and the dramatist was kept dangling through June 1641. On 8 July the Commons decided to admit Davenant

to £4000 bail, but after this the case was pursued no further. The bail was apparently forfeited, for Davenant quietly slipped off to the Hague where he found protection with some of his friends and Queen Henrietta Maria.

The Queen employed the playwright as a messenger and had him made a lieutenant-general of the ordnance under the Earl of Newcastle. In the Queen's service Davenant piled up in time debts of at least £10,000, a considerable price to pay for the knighthood Charles I bestowed upon him shortly before 5 September 1643. The laureate was roundly jeered by lampooners: "How could *Will* for fighting be a Knight, / And none alive that ever saw *Will* fight," ran one verse. But, encouraged by this new glory, Davenant became more daring. By November 1643 he was at Rotterdam gathering arms and ammunition for the royalist cause, and he finally bought a small frigate and directed it to work the Channel as a privateer. It came back from one voyage with £6000 worth of loot—which the Dutch immediately confiscated—and Davenant was as a consequence accused by Parliament of high treason. One report, on 25 July 1644, implied that the laureate had given his life for the King on the field of battle, but Davenant was very much alive and had probably heard no shots fired in anger at Marston Moor or elsewhere. He was now the "great pirott," helping to break up enemy shipping, keeping various segments of the royalist forces in touch, transporting arms, and sometimes offering debatable advice to his superiors.

In August 1646 two of his children, possibly little Mary and another, were brought suddenly to France. Davenant wrote on 14 August to Sir Richard Browne in Paris saying, "I understand I have 2 children newly arrived at Paris, which a servant of my wives hath stolne from an obscure Country education in which they have continud during this Parliament nere London." Would Browne, he asked, look to the children and furnish them "cheap and handsomely" for him? With equal nonchalance Davenant about this time made the acquaintance of Henrietta Maria du Tremblay, apparently had an affair with her, and then set her aside (since she was probably married at this point) for future reference. She would in time become Lady Davenant.

His religious affections also may have changed in 1646. When the Queen sent him in October to persuade her husband to renounce the Church of England for the Church of Scotland, Davenant may have converted to Catholicism to make his arguments more convincing. If he did so it was of little avail, for the King had "scruples of conscience" and the laureate returned unsuccessful. Since the royalist cause was falling apart, Davenant settled for a while at the Louvre in Paris with Henry, now Lord Jermyn, and his entourage, which included Abraham Cowley. Having altered some of his other affections, Davenant now turned away from thoughts of war and piracy and took up his pen to work on his heroic poem, *Gondibert*, a project which held his attention for several years.

By the end of 1649, with the royalist cause lost and his King beheaded, Davenant tried unsuccessfully to get reimbursed for his wartime expenditures. Young Charles II had no money to give, so he granted Sir William a commission to act as treasurer in Virginia instead. Unable to complete *Gondibert*, Davenant wrote a *Preface* to it which he published in Paris in 1650, meanwhile preparing for his departure to the Colonies with a motley group of ex-convicts who were to serve as craftsmen in the New World. Charles changed his mind at the last moment and reassigned Davenant to Maryland, where he was to be lieutenant governor and help curb the antiroyalist Lord Baltimore. The laureate's departure on a ship loaded with money, stores, and slaves was an open secret, and when he set out from Jersey on 3 May 1650 he was pounced upon by a frigate captained by

John Green, who sailed triumphantly away with his valuable catch.

Held prisoner in Cowes Castle on the Isle of Wight while Parliament considered his fate, Davenant whiled away his time writing more of *Gondibert*. By October he finished the sixth canto and then wrote a postscript to the reader explaining (a little sensationally and prematurely) that he had been interrupted "by so great an experiment as Dying." In this incomplete form the work was published late in 1650, about the time the poet was brought to London. He was confined to the Tower for a while, but his own plea for clemency and, probably, some help from John Milton brought him freedom to move about London.

Davenant's most immediate need was money, and since (apparently) by this time his first wife had died, he searched about for a woman with a compassionate heart and a full purse. In the widow Anne Cademan he found what he was looking for. Her late husband, Sir Thomas Cademan, had been a royalist friend of Davenant's, to say nothing of his having cured the poet of his 1630 affliction. Cademan had died in 1651, and to Davenant Dame Anne brought a fair fortune and four sons: Thomas, Paul, John, and Philip—the first three by her first husband, Thomas Cross, and the fourth (called Philip Cademan "alias Cross") possibly by her second spouse. With money left her by Cross she had bailed Sir Thomas Cademan out of his ruined state, and now she befriended Davenant to the extent of £800 in cash plus another £600 raised by selling her jewelry. In return, Davenant married her in October 1652 and set her up in a house in Tothill Street; there her sons, aged 22, 16, 11, and 9 respectively, lived along with Davenant's only surviving child by his first marriage, Mary, aged somewhere between 10 and 14. Soon this ménage was augmented by the birth of a son to Sir William and Dame Anne. The child's name has been lost, and he died young.

Though Lady Davenant's funds had helped, Sir William was still in financial straits (getting out of the Tower must alone have cost a pretty penny). He therefore did several curious and clever things to protect himself from creditors, one of which was to put the Tothill Street house and furnishings in the name of young Thomas Cross and thus avoid attachment. Then, in February 1654 he entered into a strange bond concerned with the £800 his wife had given him. Since it was money left by the elder Thomas Cross and rightfully belonged to the boys, Davenant agreed to pay each of them £100 within a year and provide them with maintenance, or forfeit the £800. But he contrived the agreement so that if he should not be able to pay them their £100 each at the appointed time, he might continue supporting them, in lieu of forfeiting the bond. In the long run, Davenant managed to get out of all these agreements, and the boys were still trying to get their money years after the laureate died.

Having thus arranged to pay his debts without actually having to pay them, Davenant turned to the problem of gaining a full discharge from the Tower, for he was still only at privileged liberty. On 22 March 1654 he appealed directly to Cromwell, and on the following 4 August he was a free man. Dame Anne died in March 1655. After laying her to rest at St Andrew, Holborn, on 5 March, Davenant turned his thoughts again to France and was granted permission to cross the Channel in August. Perhaps he planned to renew his royalist contacts or work for reimbursement of his war expenditures, but the only visible result of his visit was a third marriage, to Henrietta Maria du Tremblay, now a wealthy widow.

Upon his return to London Davenant moved with his new wife and old family to Charterhouse Yard and leased Rutland House. Theatrical activity had been officially forbidden since 1642, though there had been a fair amount of surreptitious performing. Now, with fresh funds available because of his successful marriage, Davenant laid plans to set up a theatrical company. On 16 February 1656 he signed a contract to establish a troupe capitalized at £4400. This amount was split into 16 shares of £275 each. Davenant interested William Cutler in the venture and they, probably without using any of their own funds, managed to raise between £2000 and £3000. Sir William was to serve as the house poet and Cutler, apparently, as the general administrator. Work was actually started on a building near Charterhouse Yard, and Davenant gathered a troupe of performers and rehearsed wherever he could find space available. That he probably gave performances by April 1656 is evidenced by a ballad, "How Daphne pays his Debts," published shortly before this. It implies that Davenant had several houses for private theatricals: Apothecaries' Hall, the old Cockpit in Drury Lane, Gibbons's tennis court in Vere Street, and "s. Jones's" —possibly the house in St John's which was once the office of the Revels or possibly Rutland House. The poem also suggests that the Clerk of Parliament under Cromwell had promised Davenant the Mastership of the Revels.

By April 1656, in fact, the Council paid Davenant the tribute of being concerned about this budding theatrical activity, but their investigating committee returned a favorable report, possibly because what the playwright was up to was private, not public, or perhaps because his venture was about to collapse anyway. Davenant had to face his irate sharers in court, but this did not deter him from an experiment of his own. He set up benches for an audience and a tiny stage for performers in a small hall in Rutland House, and there on 23 May 1656, or perhaps as early as 20 May, he offered *The First Days Entertainment at Rutland House, by Declamations and Musick: after the Manner of the Ancients,* published in 1657. A government spy was sent to view the performance and submitted an unwittingly amusing report of what he clearly took to be an innocuous presentation:

Vpon friday the 23 of May 1656 These foresaid Declarations [sic] began att the Charterhouse and 5ˢ a head for the entrance. The expectation was of 400 persons, but there appeared not aboue 150 auditors. The roome was narrow, at the end of which was a stage and on ether side two places railed in, Purpled and Guilt, The Curtayne also that drew before them was of cloth of gold and Purple.

After the Prologue (wᶜʰ told them this was but the Narrow passage to the Elizium theire Opera) Vp cam Diogenes and Aristophanes, the first against the Opera, the other for it. Then came up a Citizen of Paris speaking broken English—and a Citizen of London and reproached one another wᵗʰ the Defects of each Citty in theire Buildings, Manners, Customes, Diet &c: And in fine the Londoner had the better of itt, who concluded that hee had seene two crocheteurs in Paris both wᵗʰ heavy burdens on theire backs stand complementing for yᵉ way wᵗʰ, ceste a vous Monsʳ: Monsʳ: uous uous Mocquies de Moy &c: which lasted till they both fell down under their burden.

The Musick was aboue in a loouer hole railed about and couered wᵗʰ Sarcenetts to conceale them, before each speech was consort Musick. At the end were songs relating to the Victor [the Protector] The last song ended wᵗʰ Paris and the french, and concluded.

And though a shipp her scutchen bee
yet Paris hath noe shipp at sea.

The first song was made by Hen: Lawes, yᵉ other by Dʳ Coleman who were the Composers. The Singers were Capᵗ Cooke, Ned Coleman and his wife, a nother wooman and other inconsiderable voyces. It lasted an howre and a haulfe and is to continue for 10 dayes by wᶜʰ time other Declamations wilbee ready.

It may not have been much of a show, and the theatre was makeshift, but Davenant had succeeded in his first step to bring opera to England and reestablish the public theatre.

His next step was more ambitious. *The Siege of Rhodes* was entered in the Stationers' Registers on 27 August 1656 and probably performed at Rutland House in September. This time Davenant introduced scenery by John Webb consisting of three pairs of permanent side wings and changeable shutters to form the prospect. On the cramped stage he set forth in dialogue and music the story of Solyman the Magnificent. Henry Cooke, Matthew Locke, and Henry Lawes provided the music, and orchestral interludes were written by Charles Coleman and George Hudson. The singers were Cooke, Coleman, Mrs Coleman, Gregory Thorndell, Locke, John Harding, and the elder Henry Purcell, understudied by Dubartus Hunt, Roger Hill, Peter Ryman, Alphonso Marsh, and Thomas Blagrave— most of whom, like the instrumentalists, were, in time, to be prominent members of the King's Musick and the Chapel Royal. The band was made up of William Webbe, Christopher Gibbons, Humphrey Madge, Thomas Bates, John Banister, and Thomas Balser.

By avoiding the use of actors and performing in his own house, albeit for a fee, Davenant managed to get around the law. To further his efforts he wrote to Secretary Thurloe in January 1657 arguing the value of public entertainments. They would, he said, divert the minds of citizens from melancholy thoughts that might breed sedition, they would keep wealthy folk in London by providing a diversion for them, and they would serve as useful propaganda for the government by dealing with historical subjects. Perfectly willing to switch his political affections if this would aid his venture, Davenant also wrote a poem in praise of the Protector's daughter Mary when she was wed in November 1657. Finally, on 7 December of this year Davenant's publisher, Henry Herringman, announced

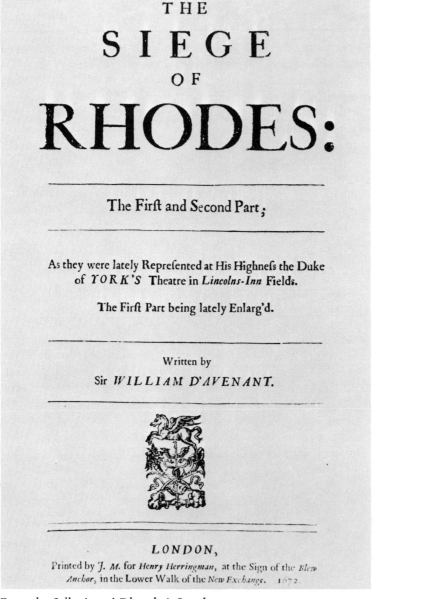

THE
SIEGE
OF
RHODES:

The First and Second Part;

As they were lately Reprefented at His Highnefs the Duke
of *YORK'S* Theatre in *Lincolns-Inn* Fields.

The First Part being lately Enlarg'd.

Written by
Sir *WILLIAM D'AVENANT.*

LONDON,
Printed by *J. M.* for *Henry Herringman*, at the Sign of the *Blew
Anchor*, in the Lower Walk of the *New Exchange.* 1672.

From the Collection of Edward A. Langhans

Title page of WILLIAM DAVENANT's *The Siege of Rhodes*

several works by the laureate to be printed, including "An Essay for the New Theater, Representing the Preparacõn of the Athenians for the Reception of Phocion after hee had gained a victory." (Other Davenant titles, "Satyrical Declamations" in 1658 and "Satyricall Declamations at the Opera" in 1660 may have been references to new editions of *The First Days Entertainment.*)

Davenant's next theatrical production was *The Cruelty of the Spaniards in Peru*, published in 1658 and presented about July of that year at the Cockpit in Drury Lane, refurbished and fitted with scenery. The plotless musical work was dedicated to Cromwell and left undisturbed by the authorities. But the Protector died on 3 September 1658, and his son Richard assumed the leadership of the country. He was less willing to let Davenant's activity go unnoticed, and on 23 December he and his Council ordered an investigation of "the *Opera* shewed at the *Cockpit* in *Drury-lane*" to discover "by what authority the same is exposed to publick view . . ." Fortunately Sir William had by this time cultivated enough friends among the upper orders to prevent his operation being silenced, though the Cockpit was fined several times in 1659 and other groups attempting to stage legitimate drama were stopped. The winter of 1658–59 saw Davenant's next work staged. This was *The History of Sir Francis Drake*, which was also published in 1659. The new piece was still in the manner of an opera, but instead of monologues and declamations, this one had a sound plot and dramatic action. Evelyn saw it (or possibly *The Siege of Rhodes*) on 6 May 1659 and called it "a new opera, after the Italian way, in recitative music and scenes, much inferior to the Italian composure and magnificence; but it was prodigious that in a time of such public consternation such a vanity should be kept up, or permitted."

Meanwhile, on the home front, Dame Henrietta Maria (or Mary, as she came to be called) was producing children faster than her husband was producing operas. To augment the household that had been depleted by the placement of John and Paul Cross in positions with other families, Dame Mary gave birth in 1656 to Charles, about 1657 to Edmund (who apparently died young), in 1657 to William, about 1658 to Alexander, and about 1659 to

"Augustin"—probably the son known as Ralph. Trying valiantly to match this fecundity, Sir William registered in May 1659, and probably soon thereafter staged, *The Second Part of the Siege of Rhodes*, which was published in 1663 along with an enlargement of the first part.

The restoration of the monarchy was close at hand. London was being flooded with returning royalists, and for a brief period in August 1659 Davenant was arrested, probably for participation in a royalist rally held on 5 August. On 3 February 1660 General Monck marched down from Scotland and entered London, and Davenant, always interested in the main chance, penned a "Panegyrick" to Monck and had it in print by March. With remarkable speed old actors and managers came out of hiding and started forming troupes for the public presentation of plays, so that by February or March 1660 three companies were active. One group, headed by John Rhodes and made up largely of younger players, established themselves at the Cockpit in Drury Lane; another, under Michael Mohun and consisting mostly of older actors, set up shop at the old Red Bull playhouse; and a third, led by William Beeston, moved into the Salisbury Court Theatre. (The complex history of the formation of the patent companies has been examined in detail by John Freehafer in *Theatre Notebook*, XX, and only Davenant's own activities can concern us here.)

On 1 May 1660 Parliament declared the restoration of Charles II. Faced for the first time in many years with real theatrical competition, Davenant moved to stake his claim. By the end of March he had leased Lisle's tennis court in Lincoln's Inn Fields, which he intended to convert into a playhouse, and he had requested and received a pass to go to France. Whether or not he crossed the Channel is uncertain, but his motive in seeking to do so must have been to get back in the good graces of those who would now be ruling England. The King returned to London on 29 May, and the laureate, for some reason, blundered by not celebrating the occasion in verse as quickly as he had done for Monck; his "Poem, upon His Sacred Majesties Most Happy Return to His Dominions" was not out until August. Davenant might have secured a favored position with the higher powers sooner had his muse worked faster.

The laureate's chief rival for control of London's theatrical activity was neither Rhodes nor Beeston nor Mohun, but Thomas Killigrew, a groom of the bedchamber and one of the King's favorites. Killigrew and Davenant together had still a more formidable rival in Sir Henry Herbert, who quickly re-established himself as Master of the Revels with the power to license playhouses and approve plays and players—all for a fee, of course. Killigrew wasted no time: on 9 July 1660 he obtained a warrant to form an acting company, and he made certain the order should contain an authorization to suppress all other troupes. This could not touch Davenant, however, for he had held for many years a patent issued by Charles I. A double monopoly was thus set up by the King, and Davenant, willing to settle for this, wrote his own order, which was protested by Sir Henry Herbert on 4 August but approved by Charles II on 21 August. What Herbert resented was Davenant's having slipped into his order a delegation of power to himself and Killigrew for the censorship of plays. Players not under either Killigrew or Davenant kept giving unlicensed performances, however, and on 6 October a temporary group was formed of members from all three companies, to act at the Cockpit under Killigrew but with Davenant sharing in the income. By November two official companies had been established by royal patents, the Duke's under Davenant and the King's under Killigrew.

Davenant's patent, based on his old one of 1639, was not finally issued until 15 January 1663, but it was understood to be operative from November 1660, and he received an exemplification of it on 16 May 1661. Its terms provide us with some idea of the kind of comprehensive control Davenant had over his troupe as well as the responsibilities he accepted in connection with it. In windy and convoluted legal language the patent granted, first of all, permission to build a new theatre near the Three Kings in Fleet Street (which was his 1639 plan) "or in any ground in or about that place; or in the whole street aforesaid . . . or in any other place that was or thereafter should be assigned or allotted out to the said Sir W. Davenant . . ." He was allowed to gather a group of performers and to perform plays, music, scenes, dancing "or other the like" at that theatre or any other and to charge admission for such entertainments. He was given full power to pay his company members "as he or they shall think fit," and "the said company shall be under the sole government and authority of the said Sir W. Davenant, his heirs, etc.; and all scandalous and mutinous persons shall from time to time be ejected, and disabled from playing in the said theatre." The King then declared that he disliked the "divers companies of players [that] have taken upon them to act plays publicly in our cities of London and Westminster, or the suburbs thereof" without authority and that henceforth only the troupes led by Davenant and Killigrew (and their heirs or assigns) would be permitted to perform. No player would be allowed to desert one company for another without the manager's permission; women's parts could now be played by women as long as the plays were "not only harmless delights, but useful and instructive representations of human life"; and the power to rid plays of offensive matter was placed in the hands of the manager. "And we do by these presents declare," stated the patent, "all other company and companies saving the companies before mentioned, to be silenced and suppressed." Killigrew's patent, granted finally on 25

April 1663, repeated essentially the same conditions.

With this as his authority, by 5 November 1660 Davenant had a troupe under contract. The members were chiefly the younger players who had served briefly under Rhodes: Thomas Betterton, Edward Kynaston, James and Robert Nokes, Cave Underhill, Henry Harris, Edward Angel, and others. With the Duke of York as their patron, they set up temporarily at the Salisbury Court playhouse, but from the beginning Davenant, unlike Killigrew apparently, planned for a theatre complete with scenes and machines in Lisle's tennis court, which Davenant had already leased. The sharing arrangements in the Duke's Company were marvelously complicated, for they concerned both playhouses. In connection with the Salisbury Court Theatre, Davenant was the party of the first part; the actors Betterton, Sheppey, both Nokeses, Lovell, Mosely, Underhill, Turner, and Lilleston formed the party of the second part; and Henry Harris (described not as an actor but as a painter) was the party of the third part. They all agreed to play at Salisbury Court until their new theatre was ready. A total of 14 shares was issued, with Davenant's four to be held by Betterton, James Nokes, and Sheppey as deputies and company accountants.

Once the playhouse in Lincoln's Inn Fields was ready, a new sharing arrangement was to be set up totalling 15 shares, two of which were to go to Davenant to cover rent, building, and scenery frames, one more to him to cover costumes, properties, and scenes, and seven to him for managing the company and maintaining the actresses. The remaining five shares were to go to the actors, with Harris getting as great a share as any. It was agreed that Davenant would be responsible for appointing treasurers, doorkeepers, a barber, a wardrobekeeper, and other hirelings, and providing the players with hats, gloves, feathers, and the like. Each actor posted a

£500 bond to keep the covenant, and this, of course, provided the troupe with the necessary £5000 operating capital. The women in the troupe were not among the sharers, and the proviso concerning their maintenance seems to have concerned only four at a time. At the start, Davenant took into his home Mary Davis, Mary Saunderson (later Mrs Betterton), Miss Davenport, and Miss Long—four of his eight actresses, all of whom he had to train. His stepson Thomas Cross he installed as one of the treasurers, and Philip Cademan, another stepson, he brought into the troupe as a minor actor. By June 1661 the company moved into the converted tennis court in Lincoln's Inn Fields, and into a wing of the building Davenant moved his family and actresses.

The Duke's Company did very well: they had a fine stock of old plays, including most of Shakespeare's best works; their scenes and machines at Lincoln's Inn Fields caught the public fancy; and Davenant was a good manager who ran his enterprise wisely and trained his players well. They were, Betterton reported in later years, "obliged to make their Study their Business," and this meant good business at the box-office. By 1662 holders of shares had probably realized a 10 to 15 percent return on their investment.

Though, as will be seen, Davenant spent much of his time in the early 1660s tangling with various adversaries, once his company was in operation he turned again to plays. In possession of the rights to a large number of old plays, including all but one of his own (The Unfortunate Lovers, but he got that one back from Killigrew eventually), the manager went to work revising, editing, compiling, trimming, patching, and sometimes writing anew. For his opening production at his new playhouse he revived both parts of The Siege of Rhodes, with the first part enlarged. The two works ran on alternate days for almost two weeks with considerable success. Pepys reported that the scenery was "very fine and magnificent," and the prompter Downes noted that all the parts (except his) were "Justly and Excellently Perform'd . . ." (Pepys grew more enamoured of *The Siege of Rhodes* the more he saw it, and he finally bought a copy, read it, and pronounced with his usual absolute certainty that it was "the best poem that ever was wrote.") Other works of his own which Davenant revived were *The Witts* and *Love and Honour*. And he took *The History of Sir Francis Drake* and *The Cruelty of the Spaniards in Peru*, added some new material, and produced a variety show on 16 December 1661 called *The Play-House to be Let*, published posthumously in 1673. In this he may have had the help of Henry Howard.

His chief efforts as reviver and reviser, however, were expended on the plays of Shakespeare. He offered *Hamlet* as the third production at Lincoln's Inn Fields in August 1661, with Betterton playing the title role and setting a standard that would not be matched for almost a century. The text as altered by Davenant is probably as we find it in Restoration editions of the play: considerably cut and tidied up, but swift-moving and a good vehicle for Betterton. According to Downes, Davenant handed on to Betterton instructions for playing the role that derived from the Bard himself. *Twelfth Night* Davenant also revived, apparently with all the romance deleted (no Restoration version was ever printed). *Romeo and Juliet* he revised and produced, but again there survives no edition to tell us what he may have done to the text. *King Lear* may have come through the manager's hands unscathed, for Downes was careful to note that it was played "exactly as Mr. Shakespear Wrote it" until Tate eventually tampered with it. *Julius Caesar* was, according to the 1719 edition, altered by Davenant and Dryden, but the play was the property of the King's Company and was not acted by Davenant's

troupe. *Measure for Measure* and *Much Ado About Nothing* appeared, thrown together and disguised as Davenant's *The Law Against Lovers*, first printed in 1673. The laureate produced the mutilation in 1662 with only fair success, and an anonymous scribbler wrote

Then came the Knight agen with his
    Lawe
Against Lovers the worst that ever you
    sawe
In dressing of which he playnely did
    shew it
Hee was a far better Cooke than a Poet
And only he the Art of it had
Of two good Playes to make one bad.

Macbeth came replete with songs, dances, fancy machines, and flying witches, in 1663, and so did *Henry VIII*, which was not so much altered as turned into a sumptuous pageant "all new Cloath'd in proper Habits" to excite London's attention. Another Davenant tampering under a new title was *The Rivals,* published in 1668 but produced in 1664; this was a revision of *The Two Noble Kinsmen* of Shakespeare and Fletcher with a bit of Jonson's *The Sad Shepherd* thrown in for good (or bad) measure. With Dryden Davenant made his last invasion of Shakespeare's canon. On 7 November 1667 they produced their version of *The Tempest*, complete with new characters: a young man named Hippolito who had never seen a woman, a mate for Ariel called Milcha, a sister for Miranda named Dorinda, and sundry other new faces.

Along with revivals and revisions of his own works and his adaptations of earlier plays by others, Davenant, to give him credit, did not neglect the "modern" drama. It was he who first produced a work by Etherege and furthered the cause of Restoration comedy of manners, and by his production of Boyle's *Henry V* Davenant encouraged heroic tragedy. He had a good eye for what was stageworthy, spent much time helping new playwrights correct and alter their works, and probably well deserved the praise given him by Dryden when *The Tempest* was published in 1670. Sir William, wrote Dryden, "was a Man of quick and piercing imagination" and "I must likewise do him that justice to acknowledge, that my writing received daily his amendments, and that is the reason why it is not so faulty, as the rest which I have done without the help or correction of so judicious a friend." Moreover, insisted Dryden:

In the time I writ with him, I had the opportunity to observe somewhat more neerly of him, than I had formerly done, when I had only a bare acquaintance with him: I found him then of so quick a fancy, that nothing was propos'd to him, on which he could not suddenly produce a thought extremely pleasant and surprizing: and those first thoughts of his, contrary to the old Latine Proverb, were not always the least happy. And as his fancy was quick, so likewise were the products of it remote and new. He borrowed not of any other; and his imaginations were such as could not easily enter into any other man. His corrections were sober and judicious: and he corrected his own writings much more severely than those of another man; bestowing twice the time and labour in polishing which he us'd in invention. It had perhaps been easie enough for me to have arrogated more to my self than was my due in the writing of this Play, and to have pass'd by his name with silence in the publication of it, with the same ingratitude which others have us'd to him, whose Writings he hath not only corrected, as he has done this, but has had a greater inspection over them, and sometimes added whole Scenes together, which may as easily be distinguish'd from the rest, as true Gold from counterfeit by the weight.

During the 1660s, then, Sir William was tirelessly managing, producing, directing, and correcting, and one would suppose that for a man now in his fifties that would have been quite enough to fill his waking hours. Not so. Davenant had never been an idler, and he certainly did not slow down after the Restoration. He had his fingers in so many other matters that only a few can be mentioned here to suggest the bustle of his last years.

No sooner had Davenant formed his troupe and started acting in November 1660 than he cast his eye beyond London. On 26 November he somehow contrived to get himself appointed Master of the Revels in Ireland. He planned to "provide a theatre in Dublin," much to the surprise and anger of the old Master, John Ogilby, who protested to the King and had himself reinstated on 8 May 1661.

Then there was Davenant's running battle with Sir Henry Herbert over the powers of censorship. Herbert was more concerned with losing the fees than with losing the opportunity to read the numberless and often tedious scripts, but he seems to have been sincere in his concern for keeping offensive material out of plays. Killigrew was more willing to give Herbert back his powers, but both he and Davenant spent much of 1660 and 1661 countering Herbert's charges. Finally, on 4 June 1662 Killigrew came to terms with Herbert, and later in the year Davenant capitulated. When Sir William wasn't battling in court with Herbert, he was involved with other plaintiffs. In 1661 his old colleagues in the ill-fated Charterhouse venture sued him for fraud, and his negotiations concerning the Lincoln's Inn Fields theatre and improvements to it led to suits against him in 1662 and 1663. Typically, the court cases dragged on, sometimes for years, after the initial hearings.

Money problems also plagued Davenant. The cost of forming a troupe and converting a tennis court into a theatre, despite success at the boxoffice for the company as a whole, burdened Sir William with new debts. Of the ten shares (of the total 15) which he began with, he had to part with 7.7 during the first year or two of the troupe's operations. By the time he died he had retrieved some of what he had been forced to sell, but he still had only 3.3 shares—a controlling interest but not enough to bring him a steady income. And from the start he received no salary, since the shares were supposed to be his pay for services rendered.

Unhappiness came to Davenant and Killigrew from George Jolly, too. A strolling manager for years, Jolly kept trying to establish himself in London. On 30 December 1662, in order to cut him out of competition, the patent house managers made a £2000 bond with Jolly, agreeing to pay him £4 weekly for not acting in London. Jolly went touring on 1 January 1663, supposing that Davenant and Killigrew in London would use his patent to start a third company there, the profits from which would pay Jolly his fee. As soon as the stroller had left town, however, the managers pretended to the King that they owned Jolly's patent outright and with it would set up a Nursery for young actors. Charles revoked Jolly's old patent and, on 30 March 1664, gave Davenant and Killigrew a new license, made out in the name of William Legge, a groom of the chamber who would be a sleeping partner. When Jolly returned to London, the managers refused to pay him his due and then tried to have him arrested for illegal acting. In time they placated the irate Jolly by making him deputy manager of the Nursery they established in Hatton Garden in the spring of 1667.

Meanwhile, Davenant and Dame Mary brought four more boys into the world. Thomas was born on 14 January 1664 and baptized at St Giles, Cripplegate, on 31 January; Nicholas was born about 1665 and George about 1667; and Richard was born just before Davenant died in April 1668. Of the earlier offspring, Charles, the eldest surviving son, was studying at Cam-

Harvard Theatre Collection

WILLIAM DAVENANT
engraving by Faithorne, after Greenhill

bridge by the mid-1660s; young William was then under the tutelage of John Milton; and Mary had married a parson in 1660. Davenant's literary immortality had not yet been completely arranged for, and probably by 1667 he had begun preparing a collection of his works, several of which had not been published. This project he did not live to complete, and as a result we may have lost some of his plays. A work called "The Secrets," for example, was mentioned in *Poems on Affairs of State* in 1703 as having been written by Davenant; a manuscript alteration of Massinger's *The Fatal Dowry* called "The Guiltless Adventuress," said to have been in the laureate's hand, has never been found; and "Greene's Tu Quoque" by Cooke was altered by Davenant and performed at Lincoln's Inn Fields on 12 September 1667, but it was never published. For posterity, too, Davenant dreamed of a theatre more elegant than his converted tennis court, and before his death he must have been involved in some of the initial planning of the Dorset Garden Theatre. He did finish one last play, *The Man's the Master*, based on Scarron's *Jodelet*, performed on 26 March 1668 and printed in 1669. It was only a moderate success at first, but it held the stage for a century.

On 7 April 1668 Sir William Davenant died at the age of 62. The cause of his death is not known, and there is no record of his having been ill. One punster, inevitably, attributed his death to his early bout with venereal disease:

His Exit *then this Record shall have,*
A Clap *did usher* Davenant *to his Grave.*

Whatever the cause of his demise, Davenant had his wits about him to the end. It seems that he purposely drew no will, but arranged with a John Alway to be his principal creditor; administration was granted Alway on 6 May, Dame Mary renouncing, and in time Alway sold back to Lady Davenant a deed of his rights to the estate. So the Duke's Company, and all that it meant to Davenant, stayed in the family's control.

On 9 April 1668, with the members of the acting company forming a procession, Davenant's body was carried from the humble tennis court theatre in Lincoln's Inn Fields to the splendor of Westminster Abbey for burial. Observers noted that the laurel wreath was missing from the walnut coffin, but most concluded that this was an error and not an indication that Davenant had actually never been made poet laureate in the first place. This dignity was one of the few things Davenant left behind which did not remain in the family. It went to his friend, a far greater poet, John Dryden.

In 1673 Dame Mary saw through the press a fine folio of Davenant's *Works*. The frontispiece was an engraving of Davenant by Faithorne, made from J. Greenhill's picture; W. H. Worthington also engraved the portrait, as he did another picture by J. Thurston. Beckett reports a portrait of Davenant by Lely at Lincoln College, Oxford. Not until the 1930s did Davenant receive the biographical treatment he deserved, and then it came double: Alfred Harbage in 1936 and Arthur Nethercot in 1938 published full and valuable treatments of Davenant, the former providing a helpful bibliography of Davenant's works and the second a genealogy and extensive quotations from primary sources. Leslie Hotson's *The Commonwealth and Restoration Stage* also contains so much material, especially on Davenant's finances, that it, too, deserves recommendation.

But perhaps Davenant's contemporaries should have the last word. In 1668 Richard Flecknoe published Sr *William D'avenant's Voyage to the Other World*, which contains both a rollicking satire on what in Davenant was vain and ridiculous and a simple eulogy that recognized his accomplishments. Flecknoe pictured Sir William's journey to the "Poet's Elyzium:" he is overcharged for his passage by Charon because of his wealth, coolly received by the poets whom he had "disoblig'd by his discommendations," and finally given the post of jester. Shakespeare is offended at him for "so spoiling and mangling of his Plays," and Momus gives Davenant his full comeuppance, saying that the laureate had "mar'd more good Plays, than ever he had made, That all his Wit lay in Hyperboles and Comparisons," that his muse was "onely a Mungril, or By-blow of Parnassus," and that his high sounding words were "like empty Hogsheads, the higher they sounded, the emptier still they were."

But Flecknoe also quoted a flattering, if second-rate, poem that summed up Davenant's contribution to the theatre:

Now Davenant's dead, the Stage will mourn,
And all to Barbarism turn:

Since He it was this later Age,
Who chiefly civiliz'd the Stage.

Great was his Wit, his Fancy great,
As e're was any Poets yet:
And more Advantage none e'er made
O' th' Wit and Fancy which he had.

Not onely Dedalus Arts he knew,
But even Promethius's too:
And living Machins made of Men,
As well as dead ones, for the Scene.

And if the Stage or Theatre be
A little World, 'twas chiefly he,
That Atlas-like supported it,
By force of Industry and Wit.

All this, and more, he did beside,
Which having perfected, he dy'd:
If he may properly be said
To dy, whose Fame will ne'er be dead.

Davencourt, Mons   *[fl.* 1705],
dancer.

Monsieur Davencourt (or Serancourt)
danced at the Queen's Theatre in the Haymarket on 12, 14, and 17 December 1705
in a *Grand Dance.*

Davenett, Harriett. *See* PITT, HAR-
RIETT.

Davenport, Mr   *[fl.* 1729–1758?],
dancer, actor, dancing master.

A Mr Davenport acted (and probably
danced and sang) the part of the Miller's
Man in *The Humours of Harlequin* in
Reynolds's little company at Bartholomew
Fair on 25 August 1729, a day on which
the bill boasted that "his Royal Highness
the Duke and their Royal Highnesses the
Princesses Mary and Louisa intend to
honour Mr Reynolds with their Presence
at his Great Theatrical Booth."

Though so auspiciously begun, Davenport's career developed but slowly. He was
seen at the Haymarket on 27 and 29 December 1729 doing a *Pierrot's Dance* with
Nott after performances of *Hurlothrumbo.*
He certainly danced oftener than he was

cited in the bills, but named roles eluded
him, except for that of Sir Farcical Comick
in Henry Fielding's *The Author's Farce*
on 30 March 1730.

Davenport went back to the fair booths
in the summer of 1730, being traceable
in those scattered bills to the Pinkethman
enterprise at Southwark Fair on 9 September, where he danced Harlequin in *Harlequin's Contrivance,* and with "the Company
of Comedians from the Hay-Market at the
Great Theatrical Booth in Bird-Cage Alley," where he performed the same part.

Davenport opened his 1730–31 season
at the Haymarket on 21 October, with Sir
Farcical Comick. He was incessantly employed in dancing during the season and he
added to his repertoire the following characters: a Forester in *The Amorous Adventure,* Mons de Foppery in *The Jealous
Taylor,* Robe in *The Spendthrift,* Sneaksby
in *The Letter Writers,* Master Owen in *The
Welch Opera,* and Sly in *The Fall of
Mortimer.*

In the winter season of 1731–32, the
Haymarket was occupied by several successive companies, and there is no record of
what Davenport was doing before his reappearance at that house on 8 March 1732
when with Miss Jones he performed "A
new *Scots Dance* to Ballad Tunes." He
danced again at the Haymarket on 12 May,
and on 23 August he was back at Bartholomew Fair in the Miller-Mills-Oates booth
diverting the crowds with his dancing between shows.

In 1732–33 Davenport was for the first
time on the regular pay list of a patent
house. He began in September to dance at
Drury Lane. In a full season of dancing he
added: Peasant in *Country Revels,* a Triton
in *Cephalus and Procris,* a Shepherd in *The
Judgment of Paris,* and a Companion of
Paris in *The Harlot's Progress.* He had for
some time supplemented his theatrical income by teaching dancing, and, in the manner of all dancing masters who were
themselves active on the stage, on 14 May

1733 for his joint benefit with Mrs Shireburn he brought pupils to the stage. The *Irish Trot* was danced "by a Youth of ten, scholar to Davenport." Davenport himself danced both *Dutchman and His Wife* and *Long Whitson Holiday* with Miss Price, probably another pupil. He danced once in the following summer, on 14 August 1733. On 23 August he rejoined the Mills-Miller-Oates enterprise at Bartholomew Fair. At this time he lived in Brownlow Street.

Davenport remained with John Highmore and the "Loyal" company at Drury Lane in 1733–34 when Theophilus Cibber drew away the defectors to the New Haymarket in September and he was still with the company when the seceders rejoined in March. He had married during the summer or early autumn and a "Mrs Davenport," dancer, began to appear in the bills on 12 October. (She was probably dancing in the company before her marriage, but the membership of the dance corps was so transient that speculation is idle as to which of the maidens whose names disappeared from the company after 1732–33 became Mrs Davenport.) From this point the careers of husband and wife were inseparable. They frequently performed dance numbers together.

In 1733–34 Davenport was named in the Drury Lane bills some thirty times, and Mrs Davenport at least that many. Besides specialty dances and "grand ballets," Davenport added the following new characters; Pierrot in *Harlequin Doctor Faustus*, a Waterman in *The Tempest*, Dancing Master in *Twin in Love*, and a "Sylvan" in *Cupid and Psyche*. His wife was Jenny in *The Harlot's Progress*, a Syren in *Cephalus and Procris*, Lady of Pleasure in *The Tempest*, Scentwell in *The Busy Body* (her first acting part), a Milkmaid in *The Country Revels*, a Nymph in *Cupid and Psyche*. On 14 May "a Youth of Ten, scholar to Davenport," danced. Both the Davenports went over to Lincoln's Inn Fields three times in the spring to dance for friends'

benefits. Davenport was at the Haymarket all summer and also appeared at the Miller-Mills-Oates booth at Bartholomew Fair time.

The Davenports continued to prosper at Drury Lane during the winter seasons of 1734–35 and 1735–36. Davenport danced on the first night of the season and played or danced at least 38 other nights in 1734–35. His wife was named in the bills 18 times that season but doubtless swelled many a chorus or procession anonymously. Each added a number of characters which were essentially the same as ones named above: peasants, soldiers, swains, nymphs, shepherds, gardeners, satyrs, country maidens, and (not very often) a named part in a pantomime or farce. They played and danced similar roles at the Haymarket in the summers through 1736.

In 1735–36 both the number and importance of their appearances at Drury Lane declined, and they did not appear at the Haymarket at all. Only two performances by Mr Davenport, both at Covent Garden, survive in the record of the 1736–37 season—as an "Infernal" in *Perseus and Andromeda* on 26 November 1736 and as Hercules in *The Royal Chace; or, Merlin's Cave* on 14 February 1737. Mrs Davenport was in the bills only once that season, on 7 September 1736 at Drury Lane, once again as Jenny in *The Harlot's Progress*.

Yet Davenport must have hung on in some capacity of assistance to the Covent Garden house in 1737–38, though he was not featured on a single night, for the bill of 5 May 1738 noted "Tickets for Davenport and Mrs Gould taken." And though he is not recorded as having danced in 1738–39, on 21 May 1739 under the specialty dancing in the Covent Garden bill was noted "*Harlequin* by Master Mathews, Scholar to Davenport." Probably Davenport had been devoting more and more of his time to teaching—perhaps paid by the theatre also as a staff teacher and (in effect) ballet master.

The Davenports danced a few times at Drury Lane in 1739–40 and were also in the notices at Sadler's Wells in September 1740. They were in the company at Goodman's Fields in 1740–41, though she does not appear to have danced after the middle of December. He alone saw occasional service dancing at Covent Garden in 1741–42 and was also on the bill of 19 June 1742 at Sadler's Wells. He was noticed at Drury Lane on 3 May 1744 and on 24 January 1747.

According to Mark Lansdale, a late-eighteenth-century manager of Sadler's Wells, Davenport was one of the figures in a painting done by Francis Hayman in 1754 of the Sadler's Wells Club. This was a name given to a group of his cronies by Thomas Rosoman, proprietor of the Wells. The painting, which for a long time hung in the Sir Hugh Myddleton's Head Tavern, has been lost. The figures included Rosoman, the scene painters Greenwood and Holtham, Maddox the wiredancer, Peter Yarman the ropedancer, the tumbler Billy Williams, and others. The inference should be that Davenport worked more extensively at the Wells than surviving bills show.

A Mr and Mrs Davenport were in the Edinburgh company in the winters from 1748 to 1751. There is no present way of telling whether or not the performer Davenport who was in the Smock Alley company at Dublin in 1757–58 was our man.

Davenport, Mr [*fl.* 1776?–1779], actor.

A specially licensed performance of *Venice Preserv'd* was given "By Authority. For this Night only" on 29 October 1779 at the Haymarket, usually dark at that season. The players were out-of-work London performers and ambitious provincials. An actor named Davenport, not known to have appeared elsewhere in London, played Spinosa. He may have been the Davenport who had played Vizard in *The Constant Couple* at Carmarthen on 20 September 1776, and probably he was in other towns in Wales with Roger Kemble's company.

Davenport, Mrs [*fl.* 1733–1741], dancer, actress. See **DAVENPORT, MR** [*fl.* 1729–1758?].

Davenport, Elizabeth [*fl.* 1664?–1675?], actress.

Elizabeth Davenport may have been the sister of Frances and Jane Davenport, both of whom were also members of the King's Company in the 1660s. Perhaps it was Elizabeth who was cited by Thomas Killigrew in his notes to *Thomaso* as his choice for the role of the servant Kecka in that play when it was done about November 1664, but all he wrote for an identification in his manuscript was "Bette"—which could also refer to Betty Hall.

Elizabeth Davenport played Sabina in *Secret Love* at the Bridges Street Theatre in late February 1667 and a Lady in *The Black Prince* on 19 October of the same year. Her name appeared on livery warrants dated 22 July 1667 and 8 February 1668, and it was probably Elizabeth who was the Mrs Davenport listed on a warrant dated 2 October 1669. A Mrs Davenport, again possibly Elizabeth, played Rosalinda in *Sophonisba* on 30 April 1675, but she relinquished this role to Mrs Bowtell before 1681.

Davenport, Frances [*fl.* 1664–1668], actress.

The "Franki" noted by Thomas Killigrew in his manuscript of *Thomaso* as his choice for the role of Calis in that play, performed about November 1664, was probably Frances Davenport. She was possibly the sister of Elizabeth and Jane Davenport, most modern commentators citing her as the eldest of the three. A Lord Chamberlain's warrant dated 27 June 1666 cites her as a member of the King's

Company, as do livery warrants dated 30 June 1666, 22 July 1667, and 8 February 1668. She acted Flavia in *Secret Love* in late February 1667 and Valeria (a breeches part) in *The Black Prince* on 19 October 1667. On 7 April 1668 Pepys heard from his actress friend Mrs Knepp that the "eldest Davenport is, it seems, gone from this house to be kept by somebody; which I am glad of, she being a very bad actor." J. H. Wilson in *All the King's Ladies* and *A Rake and His Times* suggests that Frances may well have been the "Fr. Damport" (who had a mother similarly named) who was involved in intrigues with the Duke of Buckingham and others in the summer of 1667.

Davenport, George Gosling *c. 1758–1814, actor, manager.*

George Gosling Davenport was first noticed playing in a respectable small company at Exeter with the Hunns, Diddear, the five Jeffersons, and others in 1784–85. He may have remained on that circuit for some years. At his first appearance at Crow Street, Dublin, in 1792, in the part of Fulmer in *The West Indian*, he was billed as "from Exeter." In 1786 he had married Mary Ann Harvey, a young actress whom he had met in Exeter.

In the fall of 1794 George and Mary Ann came to Covent Garden at the insistence of Munden, who had seen them in the provinces. Evidently Mary Ann was intended as a replacement for Mrs Webb, who had died in 1793. The Davenports signed articles at £2 per week each. George appeared first as Boniface in *The Beaux' Stratagem* on 19 September and secured some applause. Mary Ann made her bow on 24 September, deceitfully billed by the management as making her first appearance on any stage, as Mrs Hardcastle in *She Stoops to Conquer*, and she secured good critical notices.

George Davenport settled into a broad variety of eccentric foreigners and dialect provincials when he was lucky and minor old men and anonymous lords when he was not. He played one of the Lords in *Cymbeline*, Captain Vansluisens in *The World in a Village*, Montague in *Romeo and Juliet*, Ready in *The Rage*, Seville in *The Child of Nature*, the Landlord in *Arrived at Portsmouth*, Sulky in *The Road to Ruin*, Father Frank in *The Prisoner at Large*, a tradesman in *Life's Vagaries*, Alonzo in *Barataria*, and Egbert in *The Battle of Hexham*.

Both Davenports pleased Harris and Lewis the managers, and they were advanced to £3 per week apiece for the 1795–96 season. George played Meanwell in the new comedy by Miles Peter Andrews called *Speculation*, the Adjutant in *Love in a Camp*, Thomas in *The Agreeable Surprise*, Major Benbow in *The Flitch of Bacon*, Captain Driver in *Oroonoko*, Mr Hale in *The Banknote*, Don Juan in *The Castle of Andalusia*, Freehold in *The Farmhouse*, Porter in *Jane Shore*, Camillo in Garrick's alteration of *The Winter's Tale*, Barleycorn in *The London Hermit*, Redwald in *The Days of Yore*, the Landlord in *The Way to Get Married*, Furnace in *A New Way to Pay Old Debts*, Father Frank in *The Prisoner at Large*, and the Duke in *The Merchant of Venice*.

An analysis of the parts in these two seasons shows that once George Davenport got a foothold in good secondary and tertiary parts—representations of jolly hosts, sturdy grandfathers, upright yeomen on the land, blustery military men—he seldom slipped down to second lords and minor servants, but he seldom played a primary character either.

In 1796–97 George and his wife each made £3 per week; in 1797–98 each was paid £4. In 1800–1801 they were raised to £4 10s. each. The Davenports had several times made summer engagements at Windsor and she had acted at Richmond, Surrey, in the summer of 1796. The *Authentic Memoirs of the Green Room* approved Mr Davenport in characters "of a dry and caustic nature, clowns and rustics." The writer added that George was "perfect" in his part, however, only when greatness was thrust upon him, when he played Duke, Doge, Lord, or King.

About 1807 George Davenport had been appointed Secretary to the Covent Garden Theatrical Fund. Early in 1812, plagued by ill health, he quit the stage. He died on 13 March 1814, aged 56, and was buried at St Paul, Covent Garden, on 18 March.

Davenport had done a solid service for the theatre and had won many friends, though his performances had tended toward a sameness. He was easy-going and of an almost Johnsonian slovenliness of person. Gilliland reports his constant impatient saying, "What would people have?! always clean! always perfect! —shirt washed to-day, and wig combed not an hour ago!" The usually scornful John Williams, in *A Pin Basket to the Children of Thespis* (1797), treated Davenport with indulgent justice:

He seems hot and red

. . . .
He looks fierce and perturbed in all that he saith

. . . .
His purple-clad visage seems reeking with rage

. . . .
Yet all this to his Locket *and* Sulky *give force*

. . . .
He is not a churl, though his habits are such;
He would do a kind deed and not think he'd done much:
Notwithstanding his frame's so coarse hewn and terrific,
Every nerve in his bosom's 'gainst ill a specific!

George Gosling Davenport was survived by his wife, who did not die until 1843, and by at least three children.

Davenport, Mrs George Gosling, Mary Ann, née Harvey *1759–1843, actress, singer.*

Mary Ann Harvey was born at Launceston in 1759. She made her theatrical debut at Bath on 21 December 1784 as Lappet in *The Miser.* In May 1785 she appeared in Bristol. Acting at Exeter in 1785 she met George Gosling Davenport, a year her senior. They were married in 1786.

Mary Ann and her husband apparently failed to find permanent berths in any good country company and may have been itinerant strollers for a time. She went alone to London at one point but failed to find work. She followed her husband to the stage of the Crow Street Theatre, Dublin, on 4 June 1792, playing Rosalind in *As You Like It* and billed as "from Liverpool." She had sustained young comic characters up to that point in her career, but when she filled in for an absent colleague to play an elderly eccentric and made an astonishing success of the part (the story goes) her Irish audiences would not let her return to younger roles. Certainly from about her thirty-fifth year she confined herself to mature roles in comedy.

In the fall of 1794 the Davenports were hired at Covent Garden, she to replace Mrs Webb, who had died in 1793. Each was signed at £2 per week, but Mary Ann soon began to evince her professional superiority to George. He appeared first as Boniface in *The Beaux' Stratagem* on 19 September and she, deceitfully billed as making her first appearance on any stage, played Mrs Hardcastle in *She Stoops to Conquer* on 24 September. She was immediately adopted as a favorite by the London audience. Yet, for some reason her roles were few that first season. She was billed as the Nurse in *Romeo and Juliet*, the Duenna in *The Duenna* (a singing part), Miss Crotchet in *Crotchet Lodge*, Miss Ann Battledore in *The Poor Sailor*, and Lady Supple in *The Bank Note.*

The Davenports were more than satis-

Harvard Theatre Collection

MARY ANN DAVENPORT, as Miss Von Frump

by Cruikshank

factory to the Covent Garden management, and earned a one-pound advance in salary at the end of their first season. Mary Ann helped open the new season, 1795–96, by singing one of the unnamed "Vocal Parts" in *Macbeth*, in which George played Seward. Thereafter she sang Fidget in *Rose and Colin*, was Dorcas in *Cymon*, sang Deborah in *Love in a Village*, was Cecily in *The Midnight Hour*, Mrs Enfield in *The Deserted Daughter*, Lady Wronghead in *The Provok'd Husband*, Mrs Malaprop in *The Rivals*, Lady Project in *Speculation* (she was the first representer), Mrs Cheshire in *The Agreeable Surprise*, the Hostess in *1 Henry IV*, Mrs Drugget in

Three Weeks After Marriage, Mrs Maggs in *The London Hermit*, Lady Acid in *Notoriety*, Katty Kavanaugh in *The Lie of a Day*, Lady Bull in *Fontainebleau*, Miss Di Clacket in *The Woodman*, Hazlenut in *The Witch of the Woods*, Lady Tacet in *The Positive Man*, and Lady Sorrel in *The Way to Get Married*.

Mary Ann Davenport's roles never declined to the third rank; and although her steady assumption, despite her relative youth, of more and still more elderly women "typed" her, her mastery of the mannerisms of loquacious underlings, affected social climbers, tedious granddams, and a whole group of the elderly odd fish beloved by English audiences kept her securely a favorite. In some roles she was scarcely surpassed down to the end of the century: Mrs Malaprop, Dame Quickly, Juliet's Nurse, Lady Duberly in *The Heir at Law*, Lady Dunder in *Ways and Means*, Mrs Heidelberg in *The Clandestine Marriage*, Mrs Peachum in *The Beggar's Opera*, Widow Warren in *The Road to Ruin*, Mrs Pickle in *The Spoil'd Child*, Mrs Price in *Catch Him Who Can*, and Mrs Dangle in *The Critic*. She was praised when she introduced the new characters Deborah Dowlas in Colman's *Heir at Law*, Dame Ashfield in Morton's *Speed the Plough*, and Monica in Dimond's *The Foundling of the Forest*. Though year by year she added roles to her repertoire, she remained essentially a specialist, going from Hebe Wintertop in *The Dead Alive* to Scout in *The Village Lawyer*.

The Covent Garden management diplomatically paid husband and wife at the same rate: £3 per week in 1796–97, £4 the next year. In 1800–1801 they were raised to £4 10s. each. After her husband's death, in 1814, salary figures are not available, except for 1821–22, when she was earning £10 per week, and 1824–25, when she was earning £12.

George Davenport retired from the stage for reasons of health in 1812. He died on

13 March 1814. After her husband's death Mary Ann withdrew with one of her daughters into almost total social seclusion but she continued to appear on the stage, with very little decline in her powers, through her last performance (at Covent Garden, for her benefit) on 25 May 1830, when she played the Nurse in *Romeo and Juliet*. She died at her house, No 17, St Michael's Place, Brompton, on 8 May 1843, aged 84, and was buried seven days later at St Paul, Covent Garden.

In a will dated 5 November 1840 from No 22, St Michael's Place, Mary Ann left her property in trust to be administered by William Underwood of Vere Street, Oxford Street, woolen draper; William Moore, formerly of Old Bond Street, but now of Cheyne Walk, Chelsea; and Mrs Mary Arnold of No 22, St Michael's Place. Each was to receive 5 guineas. Mrs Ann Smith of Chiswick was to receive immediately Mary Ann's clothes, and £100. The residue of the estate (worth not stated) was to be split between Ann Smith and Mrs Abigail Worthington of Mecklenburg Street, Mecklenburg Square.

Mary Ann's obituary in the *Gentleman's Magazine* stated that at the time of her death she lived alone: "She had a son and daughter; the former died in India, the latter some years since in England." The infant Mary Ann Davenport who was buried at St Paul, Covent Garden, on 25 November 1801 "Aged 1 year" is certain to have been her daughter also. It would seem that the Maria Gosling Davenport of Hammersmith, who was buried at St Paul, Covent Garden, on 1 February 1838 "Aged 47," must have been the daughter of Ann and George Davenport.

The will of the comedian John Quick introduced a puzzle into the genealogy of the Davenport family when it left a bequest to his "daughter" one "Mary Ann Davenport of Great Knight River Street Doctors Commons" and made his "son-in-law John Davenport" joint executor with

Harvard Theatre Collection

MARY ANN DAVENPORT, as Dame Ashfield
(incorrectly titled as Mrs Grundy)
engraving by Ridley, after De Wilde

his son William Quick. A "Mary Ann Frances Davenport, Little Bedford Street, St Martin's" parish, who was buried at St Paul, Covent Garden on 8 April 1835 "Aged 43" may have been Quick's daughter.

Mary Ann Davenport was the subject of the following portraits:

1. An oil painting by George Romney, present location unknown.

2. As Lady Denny in *Henry VIII*. Watercolor by Benjamin Burrell; now at the Garrick Club.

3. As Fiametta in *The Tale of Mystery*. Watercolor by Samuel De Wilde; at the Garrick Club.

4. As Mrs Peachum in *The Beggar's Opera*, with Blanchard as Peachum and Miss Tree as Polly. Oil by G. Clint, engraved by Conrad Cook.

5. Engraved portrait; stipple. Anonymous and undated.

6. As Winifred Evans in *The School for Rakes*. Engraving by W. Leney after J. Roberts; plate to *Bell's British Theatre*, 1795.

7. As "Mrs Grundy" (actually Dame Ashfield) in *Speed the Plough*; by Ridley, after De Wilde. Plate to the *Monthly Mirror*, 1805.

8. As the Nurse in *Romeo and Juliet*. Anonymous; plate to the *Dramatic Magazine*.

9. As the Nurse, with Fanny Kemble as Juliet. By J. S. Templeton after J. Hayter.

10. As Mrs Quickly in *Henry IV*, by J. Rogers after J. Kennerley; plate to Oxberry's *Dramatic Biography*, 1825.

11. As Miss Von Frump in *The Slave*, drawn and engraved by Cruikshank; plate to the *British Stage*, 1817. There is an anonymous reversed copy of this engraving.

Davenport, Hester, later called the Countess of Oxford, later Mrs Peter Hoet *1641?–1717, actress.*

Hester Davenport of the Duke's Company, in Evelyn's description "that faire & famous Comoedian call'd Roxalana," was born either on 2 or 23 March 1641 or on 23 March 1642 (J. H. Wilson in *Theatre Notebook* XII, and in *All the King's Ladies* presents the choice.) She was apparently not related to the three Davenport girls who acted for the King's Company in the 1660s. Hester was one of the four leading actresses housed by Sir William and Dame Mary Davenant when the Duke's Company formed in late 1660. Her first role may have been Cleora in *The Bondman* on 1 March 1661 at Salisbury Court and later dates at Lincoln's Inn Fields. Certainly her most famous role was Roxalana in both parts of *The Siege of Rhodes*, produced at Lincoln's Inn Fields on 28 and 29 June 1661 and subsequent dates. For Davenant, Hester also played Ample in *The Witts*, Gertrude in *Hamlet*, and Evandra in *Love and Honour*—all before the end of 1661. But soon after that promising beginning,

Hester Davenport was "erept the stage" by the Earl of Oxford. By 18 February 1662 Pepys was lamenting the loss of "Roxalana."

The Memoirs of Grammont give the romanticized version of the story:

The Earl of Oxford fell in love with an actress in the Duke of York's company, a charming, graceful creature and one that acted to perfection. Her rendering of the part of Roxalana, in a new play, had brought her into prominence, and the name stuck to her. This young person, full of virtue, prudence, or, if you like it better, obstinacy, proudly refused all the offers of service and the presents that Lord Oxford made her. This resistance irritated his passion; he had recourses to insults and, even, to spells. It was all in vain. Lord Oxford ceased to eat anything—which in him meant very little; but his passion presently became so violent that he ceased to gamble and smoke as well. At this extremity, Love invoked the aid of Hymen. The Earl of Oxford, premier peer of the kingdom, is a handsome person, as you can see for yourself; he belongs to the order of the Garter, which sets off a naturally noble air. In short, to look at him, you would say that he was somebody; but, when you hear him talk, you realize that he is nobody. This ardent lover presented his flame with a fair promise of marriage, authentically signed by his hand—a bait she was not disposed to swallow; however, seeing him arrive next day, accompanied by a minister and a witness, she thought that she would be risking nothing. Another actress, one of her friends, witnessed the contract on her behalf; and thus the marriage was sealed and solemnized. You think, maybe, that the new Countess had nothing else to do but get herself presented at Court, take her rightful place there and assume the arms of Oxford? By no means. When the time came, it was discovered that she had never been married at all; it was discovered, that is to say, that the supposed minister was really a trumpeter of His Lordship's, and the witness his kettle-drummer. After the ceremony, clergyman and witness disappeared, and to the other witness it was explained that the Sultana had apparently thought she was being married while she was acting in some stage play. Poor creature, she might well point to Law and Religion violated, like herself, by this stratagem; well might she go fling herself at the King's feet and beg that he would give her justice. She must needs get up again, only too lucky in having been awarded, as dowry, a pension of a thousand crowns a year and obliged to re-assume the name of Roxalana, instead of that of Oxford. You will tell me that she was but an actress, that all men are not the same, and that there can be no harm in listening to them, when they do no more than pay just tribute to a person of your deserts. Do not trust them . . .

This story, which is apparently fairly close to the truth, was presented in the *Memoirs* as if told by Miss Hobart, one of the Maids of Honor to the Duchess of York who had, incidentally, more interest in women than in men.

The prompter Downes suggests that Hester returned to the stage in 1663 to play Camilla in *The Adventures of Five Hours* and in 1665 to act Roxalana in *Mustapha*. Possibly she did, but it seems unlikely, for most evidence points to her having settled down with the Earl of Oxford as his "wife." On 17 April 1664 she bore Oxford a son, baptized Aubrey (Vere) at St Paul, Covent Garden, on 15 May. Oxford contracted a regular marriage with Diana Kirke on 12 April 1673. He died on 12 March 1703 and his son by Hester was buried on 4 June 1708.

Hester was indeed married on 25 July 1703 at St Paul, Covent Garden, to Peter Hoet of Gray's Inn. She stubbornly described herself on that occasion as "Dame Hester, Countess Dowager of Oxford." Her husband was buried at St Dionis Backchurch on 8 May 1717. On the following 16 November "Dame Hester Countess of Oxford late widow of Peter Hoett Esq. deceased" made her will, leaving virtually all her estate to her friends John Hardy and Dorcas Magenis; she left a shilling to a sister, Anne Walker. Hester died, probably

at her lodgings in Compton Street, Soho, within a day or two after signing her will; she was buried at St Anne, Westminster (now Soho), on 20 November 1717.

In 1723 George Vertue mentioned a portrait of Hester Davenport: "Roxilana the actress (copied after Cooper) who was married to the Lord Oxford."

Davenport, Jane   [*fl. 1667–1668*], *actress*.

No roles are known for Jane Davenport, but she was named in livery warrants for the King's Company on 22 July 1667 and 8 February 1668. She was possibly the sister of Frances and Elizabeth Davenport, most modern authorities assuming her to be the youngest of the trio, all of whom were members of the King's troupe.

Davenport, John   [*fl. 1689*], *musician*.

John Davenport was appointed to the King's private music on 19 July 1689, but there is no further record of his activity.

Davey. *See* **Davy.**

David, Mr   [*fl. 1791*],   *basset-horn player, clarinetist*.

Mr David was a Czech who accompanied his countrymen Dworshak and Springer to London in 1791. All three were engaged as basset-horn players and clarinetists in the band at Vauxhall Gardens. How long they remained there is not known.

Davide, Giacomo   1750–1820, *singer*.

Giacomo Davide, known as *"David le père,"* was born at Presezzo near Bergamo in 1750. He studied composition under Sala.

Evidently he entered into negotiations to sing in the Italian operas at the King's Theatre in London, either for Sheridan and Harris in 1778–79 or for Sheridan and Taylor in 1779–80. A clipping of a newspaper advertisement, dated only 1779, among the Burney materials in the British Museum reads: "Mr David having departed from his proposals, which were signed and agreed to by the Proprietors, either Signor Poggi, or Signor Moriggi will be Buffo caricato." Davide sang instead at Naples that season.

In 1785 Davide was in Paris, where he sang at the Concert Spirituel and was greatly praised in Pergolesi's "Stabat Mater." Returning to Italy, he sang two seasons at Milan in the Teatro alla Scala. In 1790 he returned to Naples.

In the spring of 1791 William Taylor at the newly erected King's Theatre in the Haymarket was confronted with the competition of Robert O'Reilly's superior opera company at the Pantheon. O'Reilly had secured a patent from the Lord Chamberlain, and Taylor had only a precarious license. Davide was brought to London by Taylor expressly to bolster his feeble company, and evidently Davide's reputation attracted other musicians of note. Haydn, who had recently arrived in England, was also at the theatre after the season finally began on 26 March, and he wrote several new pieces for the theatre, including a concert aria for Davide. The season turned out rather successfully after all, largely because of the exertions of Haydn and Davide.

The season opened with "Entertainments of Music and Dancing" in which Davide sang both "Comic Music" and "Serious Music" from various operas. The "Entertainments," which Walpole called "a sort of opera in *déshabille*" with "the singers in their own clothes, the dancers dressed, and no recitative," were given through 9 July. No operas were performed in public, though on 23 February Taylor gave a semi-private rehearsal of *Pirro* at the King's Theatre.

Davide was also prominent at the fifth and last annual Handel Commemoration in Westminster Abbey, and he sang in the concert series offered by Haydn and Salo-

Harvard Theatre Collection

GIACOMO DAVIDE, in *Zelmira*
engraving by Beyer

mon. He lived at No 10, Pall Mall. Francesco Bianchi's duet "Ah qual orrida scena . . . sung by Sig⟨r⟩ Marchetti & Sig⟨r⟩ David" was published at London in 1791.

In 1802 Davide was at Florence. He sang at La Scala in Naples in 1808. By 1812 he was singing at the church of Santa Maria Maggiore in Bergamo. He sang at Lodi in 1820, the year of his death. The famous tenor Giovanni Davide was his son.

Engravings were made of portraits of Giacomo Davide at Venice in 1792 and at Milan (by Sasso) in 1821. There is an undated engraving by L. Beyer of Davide in character in the opera *Zelmira* and another one by Marta. Davide was also included in a painting of a large group of singers done by A. Fedi between 1801 and 1807. "High Committee, or, Operatical Contest," a satirical engraving by Dent (1791), shows Davide among other figures. His portrait was drawn and engraved by Domenico Piggio in 1790, and there is an undated engraving by T. Altini.

Davidge, Mr _[fl. 1792]_, _puppeteer._

A Mr Davidge gave a puppet show at Bartholomew Fair in 1792.

Davids, Joseph _[fl. 1783]_, _house servant?_

A Joseph Davids identified himself as "servant to Mr Gallini" in a published letter of 10 September 1783 (publication not identified). He was probably a "servant" to the Opera House (of which "Sir" John Gallini was then principal manager) rather than a domestic. His purpose in writing was to absolve the other managers, especially Peter Crawford, acting manager and treasurer, of a charge of inhumanity toward playhouse personnel, contained in a previously published attack. Davids testified that the manager had given him money to discharge his obligations after he was threatened with imprisonment for debt.

Davies. _See also_ **DAVIS.**

Davies, Mr _[fl. 1716–1717]_, _music copyist._

Mr Davies was hired by the King's Theatre in the Haymarket for the 1716–17 season of operas as a music copyist, a post he held with Mr Linike. They were paid £8 12s. for copying _Tito Manlio_ and £6 9s. for _Venceslao_, both new works. One entry in the account book for this season at the Hampshire Record Office cites Davies for a £1 5s. payment, which was possibly his weekly salary.

Davies, Mr _[fl. 1783–1817]_, _constable._

A Mr Davies was a constable at the King's Theatre as early as 1783–84. Perhaps he was the same Mr Davies who was a constable at Drury Lane from at least

1812–13 through 1816–17, at a salary of 15s. per week.

Davies, Mr _[fl. 1796–1799]_, _dancer._

A Mr Davies (sometimes Davis) was a chorus dancer at Covent Garden from at least 1796–97 through 1798–99. During his first season he appeared in 60 performances of _Harlequin and Oberon_, during his second in 30 performances of _Harlequin and Quixotte_, and during his third in 32 performances of _The Magic Oak_.

Davies, Master _[fl. 1779]_, _dancer._

A Master Davies, announced as a scholar to Hurst, made his first appearance in public dancing a hornpipe at the end of Act IV of _The Comedy of Errors_ at Covent Garden on 4 May 1779. No other performances by him were noted in the bills.

Davies, Miss _[fl. 1794–1795]_, _singer._

A Miss Davies sang in the chorus for 20 performances of _Lodoiska_ at Drury Lane between 9 June and 4 July 1794. On 31 May she was paid £4 16s. 8d. for 29 days' back pay and was put on the list for 3s. 4d. per day. In the following season she sang in 34 performances of _Lodoiska_ and 16 performances of _The Cherokee_ between 27 September 1794 and 16 January 1795.

Davies, Anna, later Mrs Emanuel Samuel _[fl. 1786–1836]_, _actress._

The actress Anna Davies who performed at the Haymarket and Drury Lane between 1786 and 1789 was the daughter of Thomas Davies, a carver and gilder at Birmingham, and his wife (1732–1827), who acted at Birmingham, Bath, York, and Gloucester in the 1770s, but evidently never at London. Anna Davies was the younger sister of Mary Davies, who acted at London as Mrs Wells and later became Mrs Sumbel. For an account of Anna Davies's parents and early life, see the entry of Mrs Ezra Wells (1762–1829).

Billed only as "A Young Lady," Anna

Davies made her first appearance on any stage in the role of Amelia in *The English Merchant* at the Haymarket on 28 July 1786, for the benefit of her sister Mary Wells. For this debut, an "Introductory Address," written by William Upton, was delivered by John Bannister before the mainpiece. She was identified as Miss Davies by the *European Magazine* (July 1786), which observed "no marks of genius, whatsoever." Her second appearance did not come until 5 June 1788, this time at Drury Lane, when she acted both Louisa Dudley in *The West Indian* and Miss Kitty Sprightly in *All the World's a Stage*. In the latter role, she exhibited "some degree of spirit," according to the *European Magazine* (June 1788), "and met with encouragement enough to warrant her perseverance in her present pursuit."

In the following season at Drury Lane, Anna performed Lucy in *The Devil to Pay* 15 times from 17 December 1788 through 29 May 1789. No doubt she sang chorus roles in other productions, for on 1 November 1788 her name was added to the pay list at ten shillings per day and she was given back pay of £11 10*s*. for 23 days "not on list." On 9 June 1789 she shared benefit tickets with 11 other minor performers and house servants.

On 24 June 1789, Anna Davies married Emanuel Samuel, a widower, at St Clement Danes, in a ceremony witnessed by Mary Wells and Edward Topham. Samuel reputedly was "an apostate Jew," who had written for the *Morning Post* at a guinea per week. Soon after the marriage, according to Mrs Wells's memoirs, Samuel was thrown into Fleet Prison. His release was secured when his sister-in-law, Mrs Wells, paid his debts, amounting to £60. Afterwards she supposedly arranged an appointment for him in the West Indies and provided him with money for the journey. For some years, as Mary Wells told it, Anna had to resort to all sorts of devious stratagems to avoid prison herself on account of

Samuel's debts, and indeed she was arrested several times.

Mrs Samuel did not return to Drury Lane in 1789–90. On 17 September 1789, "Mrs Samuels" was taken off the pay list, lightening it by ten shillings per day, and on 1 July 1790, she was obliged to return a sum of £1 10*s*. for one week's wages already in hand when she was removed from the payroll. Sometime later, she had accompanied her husband to the West Indies. About 1799 the Samuels returned to England and took up residence at Hammersmith, where Mrs Wells lived with them for about a year and a half. Samuel agreed to settle a guinea a week upon Mrs Wells to alleviate her distressed situation, but after several years of "irregular payments" he withdrew the allowance in 1805. Little else is known of the Samuels, except that Mrs Samuel was still living in London, in indigent circumstances, in 1836.

Davies, Cecilia *1753?–1836, singer.*

The soprano Cecilia Davies was the daughter of the musician Richard Davies (d. 1773) and the younger sister of Marianne Davies (1774–1816?), player on the glass armonica. Some confusion prevails over the year of Cecilia's birth. Dr Rimbault (in Lysons, *History of the Three Choirs*) claimed she was 92 years of age in 1832, putting her year of birth at 1740, before that of her presumed elder sister. In 1836 a writer in the *Musical World* claimed she was above 80 and gave her birth year as 1757, a year which also seems improbable in view of the likelihood that she was the Miss Davies who played a fairy in *Queen Mab*, her first appearance on the stage, at Drury Lane on 7 December 1759. In his *First London Notebook*, Haydn said that she sang at Naples at the age of 13; Cecilia went to the Continent in 1767 and sang in Italy soon after. By this calculation her birth year would be about 1753 or 1754, perhaps a more reasonable conjecture.

Earlier editions of Grove stated that Cecilia had made her first appearance in public at a concert in the Great Room in Dean Street, Soho, on 28 April 1756, but her name is not found in the list of vocal performers on that occasion. As stated above, however, she was probably the Miss Davies who played a fairy in performances of *Queen Mab* at Drury Lane in 1759–60. The notice in the *Public Advertiser* of a concert at Spring Gardens on 17 February 1762 fails to corroborate Pohl's (*Mozart in London*) statement that on that date, when Marianne performed on her armonica, Cecilia sang. Perhaps she was involved in the various concerts given by her father and sister in the several music rooms in 1762–64. She did sing at Smock Alley, Dublin, in November 1763 and in 1764, when she accompanied her family to Ireland.

By 1765 she was back at London to sing in a performance of *Solomon* at Marylebone Gardens on 6 August, for a benefit she shared with Legg and Collett. She again sang at Marylebone Gardens in the summer of 1766, under the management of Lowe. In May 1766 the *Jester's Magazine* published "A New Musical Address to the Town, as it is Sung at Marylebone Gardens" by Miss Davies, Lowe, Taylor, Mrs Vincent, and Master Raworth. With these same performers she sang in *Acis and Galatea* there on 26 September 1766. Cecilia returned to Marylebone Gardens in the summer of 1767; on 7 August she participated in a performance of songs, catches, and glees, and on 18 September she sang again in *Solomon*. On 10 August of that summer, perhaps also at Marylebone, her sister gave a concert in which Cecilia sang favorite songs from *Artaxerxes* and *Caractacus*.

After another summer at Marylebone, when her salary was three guineas per week, Cecilia and her family departed in the fall of 1768 for the Continent. They traveled through France and Italy and settled for some time at Vienna. There the sisters became favorite performers at the

court of Maria Theresa, whose daughters (one of whom was Marie Antoinette) they, reportedly, taught to sing and act. At Vienna the Davies family lived in the same house as Hasse, with whom Cecilia studied voice. She sang an ode composed by Hasse, with Metastasio's words, and accompanied by her sister on the armonica, on the occasion of the marriage of the Archduchess Amelia to Duke Ferdinand of Parma on 27 June 1769. In a letter several years after, dated 16 January 1772, Metastasio commented on the virtuosity by which Cecilia had assimilated her voice to the lovely tone of the armonica. At Milan in 1771 she sang in the Hasse-Metastasio opera of *Ruggiero* and became the first English woman to sing as a prima donna on the Italian stage. She also sang at Florence and Venice. Dubbing her "L'Inglesina," the Italians judged her to be a singer second only to Gabrielli.

Cecilia returned to England in 1773 to take up an engagement in the Italian Opera at the King's Theatre, where she appeared in Sacchini's *Lucio Vero* on 20 November. The company gave a poor performance but Cecilia was, according to the *Middlesex Journal*, the salvation of the opera. *Lucio Vero* was repeated several times until 18 December 1773, when it was deferred on account of the death of Miss Davies's father. The other operas in which she sang that season included *Perseo* (29 January 1774), *Antigono* (8 March), *Nitteti* (19 April), *Artaserse* (17 May), and *L'Olimpiade* (3 June). She also sang in benefit concerts of the *Messiah* and *Ruth* at the Chapel of the Foundling Hospital on 26 and 30 March 1774. In a letter on 1 May 1774, Horace Walpole wrote, "Miss Davis, the Inglesina, is more admired than anything I remember of late years in operas." Burney's excellent analysis of Cecilia Davies's singing at this time in her career bears repetition:

Her powers of execution were allowed at this time to be unrivalled by those of any other singer that had been heard in England. . . . Her voice, though not of a great volume, or perhaps sufficiently powerful for a great theatre, yet was clear and perfectly in tune. Her shake excellent, open, distinct, and neither sluggish like French *cadence,* nor so quick as to become a flutter. The flexibility of her throat rendered her execution of the most rapid divisions fair and articulate, even beyond those of instruments in the hands of the greatest performers. The critics, however, though unanimous in this particular, did not so readily allow her excellence to be equal in the cantabile style. She took her notes judiciously, they readily granted; sung them perfectly in tune; but was said by some to want that colouring, passion, and variety of expression, which render *adagios* truly touching. And I own that I felt myself more tranquil when she sung slow songs than quick. In rapid airs of bravura, if I had had as many hands as Briarius, they would have been all employed in her applause; but in cantabile movements, though there was nothing to blame, and much to commend, the transport of pleasure and satisfaction was less violent. Indeed, if both styles had been equal, she would have been two distinct singers.

In the autumn of 1775, Cecilia sang in the *Messiah* and *Judas Maccabaeus* at the Three Choirs Festival, Hereford, but did not engage for the season at the Opera because of a dispute over a clause in her articles which evidently would have prevented her from singing elsewhere. Fanny Burney met her at a party in 1775, but she "would not be prevailed upon to sing . . . [and] said that she *dared* not; for, that a law-suit was not yet decided, and her articles with the Opera-managers tied her down to never singing to any company." She invited the Burney family to her home, however, supposing that there "she might be allowed to *practice,*" for their amusement. The litigation was resolved on 31 May 1775 in the Court of Common Pleas, in a trial which lasted from ten in the morning till six in the evening. Judgment was found in favor of the plaintiff, Miss

Davies; and Richard Bates, the opera manager, was obliged to pay her £1500 plus costs and £500 for her lost benefit.

On 18 November 1775, Miss Davies sang as a soloist at the Oxford Music Room, and a week later on 23 November she sang in the *Messiah* at the Chapel of the Foundling Hospital. She returned to the Opera in the following season, making her reappearance at the King's Theatre on 21 January 1777 as Rosomonda in *Germondo.* She also sang Berenice in *Antigono* (1 March), Amarilli in *Le ali d'amore* (13 March), a role in *Telemaco* (15 March), and Candiope in *Orione* (24 May). For her benefit on 20 March 1777, when tickets were available at her house, No 1, St Albans Street, Pall Mall, she introduced into Act III of *Le ali d'amore* the song " 'Sventurata in van mi lagno," from *Antigono,* with a flute accompaniment.

Soon after, she left England with her sister to live at Florence, where she was discovered in 1784–85 by Lord Mount Edgcumbe in financial straits. The English colony there arranged a benefit for the two sisters, making it possible for them soon to return to England. Cecilia sang in the Professional Concert on 3 February 1787. In March 1791 she appeared for the first time in the oratorios at Drury Lane. On 11 March she sang "Let the bright Seraphim" (*Samson*) and "O Liberty!" (*Judas Maccabaeus*) and then appeared in the *Messiah* (16 March), *Judas Maccabaeus* (17 March), *Redemption* (23 March), *Acis and Galatea* (1 April), and *Israel in Egypt* (13 April). At this time Haydn wrote in his *First London Notebook* that "she is rather old now, but has a good technique."

After the oratorio season of 1791 she did not sing again in public, but she lived on for many years, poor and neglected, especially after the death of her sister Marianne Davies about 1816. She published a collection of six songs by Hasse, Galuppi, and Jommelli about 1817. Bedridden during most of the last years of her life, she subsisted on a pension of £25 per year from the National Benevolent Fund and occasional donations from the Royal Society of Music. On 1 July 1832 she wrote to thank the Governors of that society for a £10 gift. In his *Conversations with Hazlitt*, Northcott wrote of Cecilia Davies's frequent visits (about 1830) to the shop of Mr Rowe, the bookseller; Northcott once asked Hazlitt if he had ever heard of her. "No, never!" replied Hazlitt, and Northcott mused, "She must be very old now. Fifty years ago, in the time of Garrick . . . all England rang with her name." Thus forgotten, she died at No 58, Great Portland Street, on 3 July 1836; the newspapers took no notice of her passing and her funeral was attended only by a faithful servant and her nurse.

Fanny Burney had admired Cecilia Davies's good breeding and her "Modesty and unassuming carriage." In 1773 Cecilia's figure was described as short but pleasing. No portrait of her is known. Songs published as sung by her at Vauxhall and Marylebone included *Young Phillis one morning* (1763), *In all mankind's promiscuous race* (1764), *Where shall Celia fly for shelter* (1764), *Something New* (1765), *The Casuist* (1765), *I like the Man whose soaring Soul* (1765?), *Summer* (1770?), and *My Daddy's a cross old man* (1770?).

Davies, Elizabeth, later Mrs Jonathan Battishill and Mrs Anthony Webster *d. 1777, actress, singer.*

In his "Notitia Dramatica" Isaac Reed identified "the Young Gentlewoman" who made her first appearance on any stage at Drury Lane playing Lucy in *The Virgin Unmask'd* on 26 May 1762 as Elizabeth Davies. She made her second appearance, and her first at Covent Garden, when she acted Nell in *The Devil to Pay* at that theatre on 22 September 1762.

Inasmuch as there was another Miss Davies (Davis) performing at Covent Garden in the season of 1762–63, it is dif-

ficult to ascertain which roles belonged to each, but probably Elizabeth Davies was the person who played Rose in *The Recruiting Officer* on 21 October, Corinna in *The Citizen* on 15 November, and Miss Jenny in *The Provok'd Wife* on 16 November. On 8 December 1762 she created the role of Margery in the first performance of Bickerstaffe's *Love in a Village*, a pastiche which received a total of 40 performances before the end of the season. She also played Charlotte in *The Apprentice* on 14 February 1763 and Miss Hoyden in *The Relapse* and Nell in *The Devil to Pay* again on 7 May. Of her performance as Nell, the critic of the *Theatrical Review* (1763) wrote: "Her person is agreeable; her voice and manner of singing, pleasing; her powers, though at present too weak, we think capable of being heightened and improved. In regard to her speaking, there was discoverable a dawn of merit, which portended she might some day or other hold a no very indifferent rank in the theatrical state."

Returning to Covent Garden in 1763–64, Miss Davies again played her roles of Nell, Rose, Corinna, Miss Jenny, and Margery. On 3 October 1763 she sang a hymn in *The Royal Convent*, on 8 October she played Dorcas in *Thomas and Sally*, and on 22 November she appeared for the first time as Lucy in *The Beggar's Opera*. Miss Davies's name did not appear on any London bills in 1764–65.

On 19 December 1765 she married the musician Jonathan Battishill, then a harpsichordist at Covent Garden, by license at St George's, Bloomsbury. At the time, Miss Davies was described as of the parish of St Paul, Covent Garden. Now retired from the stage, she continued as Battishill's wife for some 10 years, until she met Anthony Webster, a law student turned actor, who made his debut at Covent Garden on 15 January 1776. According to the recollections of the composer Richard John Samuel Stevens, Mrs Battishill lived in open adultery with Webster. "If I ever meet that Rascal," Battishill was supposed to have told his friends, "I'll stick a knife in his heart." She went off with Webster to Ireland in 1776. Billed as Mrs Webster, she acted at Crow Street, Dublin, and at Cork in 1776 and 1777. Her time with Webster, according to the *Thespian Dictionary* (1805), was made unhappy by his vanity and his pursuit of other women, causing her to die "of a broken heart" at Cork in late October 1777.

Davies, George. *See* HARLEY, GEORGE DAVIES.

Davies, Hugh [*fl.* 1742–1743?], actor.

The person who acted Acasto in *The Orphan* at Goodman's Fields Theatre on 19 January 1742 was Hugh Davies, an old man and a former secretary to Bishop Sherlock. For the performance he was paid 10*s.* 6*d.*, according to the testimony of the actor and bookseller Thomas Davies (d. 1785), who provided the information to Isaac Reed ("Notitia Dramatica" in the British Museum). Hugh Davies was possibly the Davis who acted Castalio in *The Orphan* (6 October) and Moneses in *Tamerlane* (5 November) at Drury Lane in the fall of 1743.

Davies, "Kiddy." *See* DAVIES, WILLIAM.

Davies, Marianne 1744–1816?, singer, instrumentalist.

Marianne Davies was born in 1744, a daughter of the flutist and composer Richard Davies (d. 1773) and elder sister of the better known singer Cecilia Davies ("la Inglesina"). By 1751 her family lived "opposite the Golden Leg" in Longacre. On 30 April 1751, at the age of seven, Marianne played a concerto by Handel on the harpsichord during her own benefit concert at

Hickford's Great Room in Brewer Street. She also sang some songs and played a concerto of her own composition on the German flute. Other performers in the concert included Pinto on the violin, Bombardin on the bassoon, and the singers Beard, Master Arne, and Signora Frasi.

Again for her benefit, on 19 March 1753, this time at the Great Room in Dean Street, Soho, Miss Davies–announced as "A Child of Nine Years Old"–played a Handelian concerto on the harpsichord, accompanied by such musicians as the violinist Chabran and the singers Signor Galli, Signor Guadagni, and Miss Bennett. About this time were published at London two pieces by Richard Davies entitled *Ye Sacred Muses now attend. A New Song. The Words by a Gentleman on hearing a little Miss perform on the Harpsichord and German Flute* and *Musick can charm the Human heart. An Extempore Thought, on hearing the Performances of Miss Davies, a Child of Eight Years of Age, in the Great Room in Dean Street. Set . . . for the German Flute.*

The musical prodigy continued to be heard in various concerts about London. At her benefit in Dean Street on 28 February 1757 she and her father played German flutes together, and she performed on the harpsichord. By then, the Davies family had taken a house in Lichfield Street, facing Newport Market. Several months later, on 22 April 1757, Marianne, announced as making her second appearance on any stage, played the German flute in accompaniment to singing by Mrs Lampe. In 1762 she came into possession of a glass armonica, a musical instrument consisting "of a series of glasses fixed on an axle, which was moved by a treadle, and played and tuned something like ordinary glasses." It had been invented by Benjamin Franklin, who was said to have been her uncle. The Franklin family pedigree, however, shows no such relationship. Miss Davies became an accomplished player on the armonica, which she introduced to the public on 18 February 1762 at the Great Room in Spring Gardens, when she also sang and played the German flute. These performances lasted through 27 March, and on 16 April she took another benefit at Dean Street. In May she gaves a series of concerts at the Gold Lamp in King's Square Court, Soho, where her family now lived. Throughout the next several years she and her father gave numerous concerts in the town including one at Spring Gardens on 31 July 1762 before "the Cherokee kings and the two chiefs." There were other concerts periodically at the Pillar and Gold Lamp in the Haymarket in August 1762 and from 10 February until 13 August 1763 and at the Swan and Hoop, Cornhill, from 15 August to 7 October 1763. By 1763 her younger sister, Cecilia Davies, perhaps was singing with the family.

After a trip to Ireland with her family in the winter of 1763–64, Marianne resumed her performances at Spring Gardens and Cornhill in the summer of 1764. The Davieses then traveled to Paris and again were several months in Ireland. They returned to London by June 1767, when they lived at Coventry Court, Haymarket, and gave concerts throughout the summer at various music rooms. In the fall of 1768, the family again went to the Continent, this time remaining for five years, principally in Italy and at Vienna, where they met the Mozart family. At Vienna the Davies sisters became favorites of society and often gave performances at the Imperial court. Her sister Cecilia having proved herself the superior vocalist, Marianne limited herself for the most part to the armonica.

Soon after the family's return to London in 1773, Richard Davies died. Her sister's professional life was on the rise, but Marianne, "whose nerves had been shattered by playing so much on an instrument of so peculiar a nature," performed but infrequently, and apparently not at all after 1784. By that year she had returned to Italy

with her sister. Lord Mount Edgcumbe came upon them in Florence living without employment and in a financial distress which was relieved somewhat when the English resident in that city sponsored a benefit concert for them. Marianne soon returned to England with her sister. Some disagreement exists over the date of her death: Pohl, *Haydn in London*, gives 1792; early editions of Grove give 1793; and in an obituary notice for her sister Cecilia in 1836, a correspondent to the *Muscial World* wrote that Marianne had died "almost twenty years ago."

Davies, Mary Stephens. *See* WELLS, MRS EZRA.

Davies, Richard *d. 1773, flutist, composer.*

The musician Richard Davies was the father of Cecilia and Marianne Davies, in whose entries information on his professional life may be found. He died at London in December 1773; on the eighteenth of that month a performance of *Lucio Vero* at the King's Theatre was deferred because Cecilia Davies could not play, her father having died. In addition to the compositions mentioned in the entry of Marianne Davies, he wrote some songs, set for the German flute, which are listed in the *Catalogue of Printed Music in the British Museum*.

Davies, Thomas *c. 1712–1785, actor, bookseller, printer, proprietor.*

Thomas Davies attended the University of Edinburgh in 1728 and 1729, dates which suggest he was born about 1712. He had acquired, by Johnson's testimony, "learning enough to give credit to a clergyman," but eventually found himself in London as an aspiring actor. In the spring of 1736 he was with Fielding's "Great Mogul's Company of Comedians" at the Haymarket Theatre where on 27 May he acted Young Wilmot in Lillo's *Guilt Its*

Harvard Theatre Collection

THOMAS DAVIES

engraving by Schiavonetti, after Hickey

Own Punishment; or, Fatal Curiosity. The cast was not listed in the announcements but his name, given as "Davis," was printed for the character in the 1737 edition of the play. During the following spring, again with Fielding at the Haymarket, he repeated Young Wilmot, and played Crimcrowsky in *A Rehearsal of Kings*, Pistol in *The Historical Register*, and Honestus in *Eurydice Hiss'd*. Possibly he was the "Davis" who acted Brabantio in a special performance of *Othello* which was given by a group of actors, many from Covent Garden, before the Ambassador Extraordinary from the Emperor of Morocco at the Lincoln's Inn Fields Theatre on 7 September 1737.

When Fielding's theatrical satires were closed by the imposition of the Licensing Act, Davies embarked upon his first venture in bookselling, an occupation he worked at for some eight years before re-

turning to the stage. He may have been the "Davis" who was billed for acting Castalio in *The Orphan* (6 October) and Moneses in *Tamerlane* (5 November) in the fall of 1743 at Drury Lane, but that person was more likely Hugh Davies. At Covent Garden on 24 January 1746 the bill for *Venice Preserv'd* announced that the major role of Pierre was to be "attempted"—for his own benefit—by Mr Davies, a bookseller, from whom tickets could be had in Old Round Court in the Strand. He was also, probably, the "Davis" whose name appeared in the bills to act King Henry in *Richard III* at Drury Lane on 29 April 1746, when he had benefit tickets out.

Davies joined Covent Garden Theatre for the season of 1746–47 at a salary of 15*s.* per week, making his first appearance as a regular member of the company on 20 October 1746 as Stanley in *Richard III*. During that season he also acted Marcus in *Cato*, Henry again to Garrick's Richard III (31 October 1746), Mortimer in *1 Henry IV*, Sylvius in *As You Like It*, and Norfolk in *Henry VIII*. On 11 May 1747, he acted Fainall in *The Way of the World* and took about £24 as his part of a benefit shared with Dunstall. Tickets could be had of Davies at his lodgings with Mrs Cox at the Indian Queen in Cranbourn Street, Leicester Fields.

Evidently Davies enjoyed little success in his brief career at Covent Garden, for he was not re-engaged by Rich and was obliged to move into the provinces. In August of 1750 he joined with Henry Thomson as a manager and proprietor of the New Concert Hall in Edinburgh; on 22 August 1750 he entered into an agreement to engage Elizabeth Storer and Isabella Lampe for six months beginning 29 October 1750 at a total combined salary of £300. He played in *Comus* with Mrs Lampe on 14 January 1751. Also in the production was the woman whom Davies had married in December of 1749, Susannah Davies (1723–1801), a most beautiful woman and the daughter of the York actor Joseph Yarrow. At Edinburgh Davies was accused of retaining all the most popular roles for himself. The two Davieses joined Thomas Sheridan's company at Smock Alley, Dublin, for the season of 1751–52. Davies made his first appearance at Smock Alley on 21 October 1751 in the role of Sciolto in *The Fair Penitent*, in which his wife acted Lavinia. During the season he also played Cimberton in *The Conscious Lovers*, the title role in *King John*, Henry in *Richard III*, Fainall, Cominius in *Coriolanus*, Tribulation in *The Alchemist*, Strictland in *The Suspicious Husband*, and Hotspur in *1 Henry IV*. Announced as from Dublin, the Davieses played in the 1752 summer company at Richmond and Twickenham where Davies acted Bevil Junior in *The Conscious Lovers*, Downright in *Every Man in his Humour*, Fainall, Cutbeard in *The Silent Woman*, Wellborn in *A New Way to Pay Old Debts*, Osmyn in *The Mourning Bride*, Hotspur, Edgar in *King Lear*, and Hastings in *Jane Shore*—the last role he offered at his benefit in Richmond on 27 September 1752, when his wife played the title role.

In the fall of 1752 Davies and his wife began an engagement at Drury Lane which ultimately would last over a decade for each. Mrs Davies made her debut there on 23 September 1752 in the role of Lady Easy in *The Careless Husband*. Davies's first appearance was on 16 October 1752 as Ross in *Macbeth*. Next he acted Cutbeard in *The Silent Woman* on 26 October; during that season he also played Alvarez in *Don Sebastian*, Manly in *The Provok'd Husband*, Bassanio in *The Merchant of Venice*, Fainall in *The Way of the World*, Polydore in *The Orphan*, Sciolto in *The Fair Penitent*, and Stukely in *The Gamester*. The author of *The Present State of the Stage* (1753) noted that, as Stukely, Davies was especially good in his scenes with Garrick in the third act, but added, "notwithstanding that he understands well

what he is to do, he seems always to have a Fear about him upon the Stage, which generally accompanies Merit, and is one of the worst enemies a performer can have." For his benefit with his wife on 26 April 1753 receipts of £140 were taken. They performed *The Fair Penitent*; he acted his usual role of Sciolto and she acted Calista for the first time. Tickets could be had at their lodgings at Mr Evans's in Tavistock Row, Covent Garden.

Davies's wife made an excellent career at Drury Lane, taking on early a number of capital roles. On the other hand, while some first-line roles came to Davies himself, he was assigned mostly to a variety of supporting parts. In his second season he acted Ross again, the Lord Chamberlain in *Henry VIII*, a character in *The Englishman in Paris*, Trinobanitans in *Boadicia*, Granger in *The Refusal*, Gloster in *Jane Shore*, Don John in *Much Ado About Nothing*, King Philip in *King John*, and a role in *Virginia*. Of his performance of Claudius in *Hamlet* (16 October 1753), Samuel Derrick (under the pseudonym Thomas Wilkes) wrote in *A General View of the Stage* (1759) that Davies "manifests great judgment." Ticket receipts for the benefit he shared with his wife on 24 April 1754 were £192, for a revival of *Zara* ("Acted but once these seventeen Years") in which Davies acted Nerestan, his wife Selima, and Garrick Lusignan. The Davieses were still living with Evans in Tavistock Row on this date but by April of 1755 they had lodgings at Mr Marshall's in the same street. By April 1757 they lived at No 16, New Crown Court, Covent Garden, where they were still to be found in the spring of 1759.

Davies remained at Drury Lane through the season of 1761–62, and it seems that he almost never ventured away from London or vicinity to act in the provinces during the summer. On 19 June 1760 he acted in *The Provok'd Husband* at Drury Lane in a performance billed as being given by the

Harvard Theatre Collection

House of THOMAS DAVIES, in Russell Street

by Storer

Richmond company of players. Probably he was the Davies whose name appeared in the bills as acting World in *The Rehearsal* for Theophilus Cibber's short-lived company at the Haymarket on 11 and 15 September 1755. In 1761, Charles Churchill's lines about him in *The Rosciad* evidently disturbed Davies seriously enough to make him think of retiring from the stage:

With him came mighty Davies. On my life,
That Davies hath a very pretty wife:—
Statesman all over!—in plots famous grown!—
He mouths a sentence as curs mouth a bone.

By the spring of 1760 Davies had opened a bookshop opposite Tom's Coffee House at No 8, Russell Street, Covent Garden, but he did continue to act for several more seasons. On 19 April 1763 he took his last benefit with his wife; she played Harriet in *The Jealous Wife* but his name was not on the bills for a role. He gave his last performance on 11 May 1763, as Glenalvon in *Douglas*, a role he had first played on 11 January 1760.

In addition to the ones cited above, Davies regularly played numerous roles in the Drury Lane repertory, a selection of which (with date of first performance) include: Fantome in *The Drummer* (25 October 1754), Claudio in *Measure for Measure* (22 February 1755), Sadi in *Barbarossa* (23 December 1755), Camillo in *The Winter's Tale* (21 January 1756), Siward in *Athelstan* (27 February 1756), Sullen in *The Stratagem* (23 April 1756), Touchwood in *The Double Dealer* (18 October 1757), Carlos in *The Fatal Marriage* (3 December 1757), Euxus in *Agis* (21 February 1758, the first performance), Eumenes in *The Siege of Damascus* (18 November 1758), Eros in *Antony and Cleopatra* (3 January 1759), Mirvan in *The Orphan of China* (21 April 1759, the first performance), Varus in *The Siege of Aquileia,* Cymbeline (28 April 1762), and the King in *1 Henry IV* (30 April 1762).

It was Churchill's verse, according to Dr Samuel Johnson, which eventually drove the ridiculed Davies from the stage. In the summer after Davies's last season at Drury Lane there occurred a heated exchange of correspondence between him and his late manager. Garrick teased Davies about the lines in his letter on 10 August 1763: "it has indeed been said, that the Stage became disagreeable to you from ye first publication of ye Rosciad, & that you were resolv'd to quit it, as you were always *confus'd & unhappy* when you saw Mr Churchill before you." Davies replied on 13 August: "I remember that during the run of Cimbeline I had ye misfortune to disconcert you in one scene of that play, for wch I did immediately beg y^r pardon & did attribute it to my accidentally seeing Mr Churchill in ye Pitt with great truth; & that was ye only time I can recollect of my being confused or unmindful of my business when that Gentleman was before me." Although Davies had put it out to his friends that his reason for leaving the stage was his being unable to attend his shop and his stage business together, he had complained to Dr Johnson that it had been Garrick's temper at rehearsals which had finally prompted him—and many other actors before him—to quit. Garrick, however, retorted that Davies's lack of careful preparation had led to the manager's *"warmth of temper."* Garrick continued, "for I must confess I have been often too much agitated by y^r want of that care and readiness in your parts which I thought I had a right to resent, & which made your leaving us of such little Consequence."

Garrick also berated Davies for having falsely reported to Garrick's brother George that he had refused to give Davies £50 for the deposit on the purchase of his house and bookshop at No 8, Russell Street—"I told You I *would* lend it to you, tho I could not conveniently at ye time you ask'd it"—when indeed he had given him the money, on Davies's bond, over a year earlier. Garrick, in fact, was now prepared to agree to Davies's suggestion ("tho from your Behaviour You have no claim to it") that a twelve-volume set of *Museum florentinum* (1731–1766) be accepted as partial repayment.

Davies kept at his bookselling up to his death. He is best remembered in literary history for having been the person who introduced Boswell to Johnson in his bookshop in 1763 and as the biographer of Garrick. Davies, himself, spent much of his time on the periphery of the Johnsonians, and was mentioned frequently by Boswell, who reported that Beauclerk had once remembered that he could not conceive a more humiliating position than to be patted on the back by Davies. Johnson derisively suggested, "as a superlative expression of contempt," that Swift's *Conduct of the Allies* might well have come from the pen of Tom Davies. In 1773 Davies appropriated without authority many of Johnson's writings which he included in his publication of *Miscellaneous and Fugitive Pieces.* Johnson responded to the piracy with good nature, telling Mrs Thrale that while he would "storm and bluster a little," he was nevertheless somewhat charmed by Davies's good nature: "I believe," Johnson said, "the dog loves me dearly," and suggested that he must "do something for Tom Davies."

Davies enjoyed an agreeable social life and was a member of the booksellers' club which convened first at the Devil Tavern, Temple Bar, and later at the Grecian Coffee House. The diarist Sylas Neville reported that he had dined at Davies's country house in China Walk (now Cheyne Walk), Chelsea, on 29 September 1761 with the Italian Baretti, and that at other times there he had met numerous socially prominent persons.

In 1778 Davies's trade turned bad and he declared himself bankrupt. Johnson wrote to Mrs Montague on 5 March 1778 that "Poor Davies, the bankrupt bookseller, is soliciting his friends to collect a small sum for the repurchase of part of his household stuff. Several of them gave him five guineas; It would be an honour to him to owe part of his relief to Mrs Montague." At Drury Lane on 27 May 1778 a benefit was given for "Davies, bookseller, and Mrs Davies, who formerly belonged to this Theatre," at which they took £134 5s. 6d. after house charges. For the event, Davies acted Fainall in *The Way of the World,* his first appearance on the stage in 16 years. In 1779, when Davies published *The Dramatic Works of Philip Massinger* (4 vols, edited by John Monck Mason), he dedicated the first volume, which contains "The Life of Philip Massinger" written by Davies himself, to Dr Johnson. It was Johnson who later suggested that Davies write a life of Garrick, and he offered information on the great actor's early years. Davies's two-volume work, *Memoirs of the life of David Garrick, Esq. interspersed with characters and anecdotes of his theatrical contemporaries*, appeared in 1780, the year after Garrick's death, and went into a fourth edition by 1784. A copy of this work at the Johnson Birthplace Museum at Lichfield contains in the fly-leaf of volume 1: "To His Honour'd Friend and Patron Dr. Samuel Johnson, from the Author."

Davies then wrote *Dramatic Miscellanies, consisting of critical observations on several plays of Shakespeare, with a review of his principal characters and those of various eminent writers, as represented by Mr. Garrick and other celebrated comedians* in three volumes, which he published in 1785. A second edition came out in the same year. Both works are pleasant, lively, and important sources of information about the English theatre in the eighteenth century. In 1777 he published the first edition of *A genuine narrative of the life and theatrical transactions of Mr John Henderson, commonly called the Bath Roscius*; it had a third edition in 1778. Davies's authorship of the volumes was established in J. Ireland's *Henderson* (1786). Other works written and printed by Davies included *The Works of William Browne, with the Life of the Author* (3 vols., 1772), *A Catalogue of the Library of the late William Oldys* (1762), and *Some Account of the Life of George Lillo* (1775). After his death was published *Roscius Anglicanus, or, an historical review of the stage . . . from 1660, to 1706 by John Downes . . . with additions by the late Mr Thomas Davies, author of the Life of Garrick* (1789). In her *Memoirs*, Letitia Hawkins advised that her father's *History of Music* had first been contracted by Davies, though it eventually went to Payne on "Davies' defalcation." According to her, Davies was a very proud and difficult man to deal with:

"Davies had never lost the strut of the stage; — he practised it in his shop, and . . . when Steevens, the editor of Shakespeare, enquired of him for a Homer without notes . . . he replied — 'I have but one copy, and that I keep for my own reading'."

As an actor, Davies played his many characters "if not with great excellence," by the testimony of the *European Magazine*, "at least with propriety and decency." The *Public Advertiser* on 22 December 1784 recalled that Davies was inclined to employ "his intervals of silence with glances at the side-boxes."

Thomas Davies died on 5 May 1785 and was buried at St Paul, Covent Garden, on 12 May in the vault under the school. In his will, written on 6 July 1784 and proved at London on 19 August 1785, he left all his goods, chattels, and effects to his wife Susannah, whom he also named as executrix. She lived on in London, suffering severe financial hardship in her later years, until her death on 9 February 1801.

A portrait of Davies, engraved by L. Schiavonetti, after T. Hickey, was published by Harding in 1794. An illustration of his house in Russell Street was drawn and engraved by Storer for Cole's *Residence of Actors*.

Davies, Mrs Thomas, Susannah, née Yarrow *1723–1801, actress.*

The beautiful wife of the actor and bookseller Thomas Davies (1712?–1785) was born Susannah Yarrow in 1723. Her father Joseph Yarrow was a performer at York who wrote at least three stage pieces which were performed in that city. The Yarrows were living in London, at least intermittently, in the late 1730s. Yarrow's name appeared in the bills for Young Mirabel in *The Inconstant* at the Haymarket Theatre on 19 February 1736. Susannah's mother was likely the Mary Yarrow, "widow," who was buried at St Paul, Covent Garden, on 9 December 1764, but she may have been the Susannah Yarrow,

"Widow the Relict of John [*sic*] Yarrow late of the parish of St George Hanover Square," who was granted administration of her husband's estate on 9 September 1754. In the latter instance, however, the John Yarrow, deceased, may have been Joseph's brother.

By 1738 Susannah was helping her mother keep an establishment called Dick's Coffee House, located between the Temple Gates; a comedy by James Miller entitled *The Coffee House* which was produced at Drury Lane on 26 January 1738 had two characters designed after them, according to the *Biographia Dramatica* (1812).

In December 1749 Susannah married Thomas Davies, who had interrupted his career as bookseller to take up acting again in the 1740s. Davies entered into a partnership with Henry Thomson in the summer of 1750 at the New Concert Hall in Edinburgh, where Susannah acted the Lady in *Comus* on 14 January 1751. In the fall she and her husband engaged with Thomas Sheridan at the Smock Alley Theatre, Dublin. She made her first appearance there on 18 October 1751 as Indiana in *The Conscious Lovers*. There is no evidence that Susannah had been on the stage prior to her marriage, but during this season at Smock Alley she acted at least 21 roles, many of them in the first line, a repertoire which clearly points to extensive prior experience in the provinces: Lavinia in *The Fair Penitent* (21 October 1751), Rutland in *The Earl of Essex* (15 November), Lady Woodvil in *The Non Juror* (20 November), Dorinda in *The Stratagem* (6 December), Emilia in *The Man of Mode* (19 December), Polly in *The Beggar's Opera* (20 December), Miranda in *The Tempest* (30 December), Amanda in *The Relapse* (8 January 1752), Cynthia in *The Double Dealer* (25 January), Doll Mavis in *The Silent Woman* (7 February), Volumnia in *Coriolanus* (29 February), the Queen in *The Spanish Fryar* (13 March), Araminta in *The City Wives' Confederacy* (16

March), Anne Page in *The Merry Wives of Windsor* (18 March), Jacintha in *The Suspicious Husband* (in boy's clothes, 13 April), Ismene in *Phaedra and Hippolitus* (20 April), Florinda in *The Rover* (8 May), Anna Bullen in *Henry VIII* (13 May), and Julia in *The Fatal Marriage* (30 May).

The Davieses went to play at Richmond and Twickenham in the summer of 1752. There she acted Jane Shore, Millamant in *The Way of the World*, Indiana, the title role in *The Mourning Bride*, the Fine Lady in *Lethe* (for her benefit at Richmond on 16 September), and Belinda in *The Provok'd Wife*. In the same company was a Miss Davis (fl. 1739–1762), no evident relation.

Engaged with her husband by Garrick, she made her debut at Drury Lane on 23 September 1752 as Lady Easy in *The Careless Husband*, at which time the prompter Cross wrote in his diary: "Mrs Davies from Ireland play'd Lady Easy, a pretty Figure—Toll:[erable]." Her second appearance was as Lady Anne to Mossop's Richard III on 30 September; then followed a variety of leading parts which included many she was known to have played before coming to London but also some evidently new, such as Hero in *Much Ado About Nothing*, Selima in *Tamerlane*, Mrs Kitely in *Every Man in His Humour*, Moryama in *Don Sebastian*, Harriet in *The Miser*, Imoinda in *Oroonoko*, and Oriana in *The Inconstant*. As the Lady in *Comus* on 28 November 1752 she was "Excellence itself," according to the author of *The Present State of the Stage* (1753), possessed of a figure which "inspires with infinite pleasure," and a beauty comparable to Milton's description of Eve. There was also "extreme justice in her enunciation." In his *Collection of Original Poems* (1755), Samuel Derrick also waxed enthusiastic about her appearance in *Comus*: "And Milton's self, if living, had admir'd, / To find himself by *thee* still more *in-*

spir'd." Others sang in raptures of her beauty, like the author of *The Battle of the Players* (1762) who wrote "The beautiful Daviesia . . . fairer than *Venus*, and more intrepid than Minerva." And, of course, by his famous cut at Thomas Davies in *The Rosciad* (1761) Charles Churchill assured that posterity would know that "On my life, / That Davies hath a pretty wife."

Mrs Davies remained at Drury Lane for 11 years, continuing there for two years after her husband had retired from the stage to take up bookselling and writing. During her career there she acted dozens of roles, generally in the line of beautiful heroines. In addition to the ones already mentioned, among others her parts included Margaret in *A New Way to Pay Old Debts*, Desdemona, Ophelia, Harriet in *The Jealous Wife*, Araminta in *The Old Bachelor*, Maria in *George Barnwell*, Selima in *Zara*, Viola in *Twelfth Night*, Cordelia, Isabella in *The Wonder*, Lucia in *Cato*, Teresa in *The Squire of Alsatia*, and Mrs Fainall in *The Way of the World*. At her last benefit on 25 April 1764, when she took a profit of £102 6s., she played Imoinda in *Oroonoko*. She gave her last performance on 14 May 1764, as Jane Shore, and then apparently she retired from the stage for good, at a time when her husband's trade was sufficient to allow her to live comfortably at their home and shop at No 8, Russell St, Covent Garden, and at their country house on Cheyne Walk, Chelsea.

When her husband died on 5 May 1785 he left all his goods, chattels, and effects, of unspecified value, to Susannah who, as executrix, was granted administration of his will on 19 August 1785. No children were mentioned in the will or in any other documents or accounts concerning the Davieses. Soon she fell on hard times and was sustained in her last years by the philanthropy of Alderman Thomas Cadell, a bookseller, and a wealthy friend of her late husband. Documents now in the Harvard Theatre

Collection reflect her decreasing fortunes. Cadell had arranged a small annuity for her from the Royal Academy. On 7 December 1787 her niece Mary Yarrow signed a receipt for "Ten Pound for half a Years Annuity due to my Aunt Mrs Davies for the Royal Academy—receivd for Mrs Susannah Davies." Susannah signed her own name to a receipt for £5 "for half a years annuity" on 25 November 1788. She signed similar receipts for £10 on 7 January 1790 and 7 January 1794. In January 1800 Cadell proposed a subscription for the relief of Mrs Davies and solicited the support of his friend George Nicol. A manuscript, probably in Cadell's hand, now at Harvard, provides the text of their proposed announcement:

A Subscription for the Support of M[rs] Davies, Widow of the late M[r] Thomas Davies, of Drury Lane Theatre, and afterwards a Bookseller in Russell Street Covent Garden. She has been enabled to exist, for some years, upon a *very small* annuity, procured to her by her Friends—But Time has swept away many of those kind Hearts, who were acquainted with her Merits, and who knew upon how small a pittance her rigid oeconomy could subsist.—This has unfortunately happened, when the decay of Nature has, by confining her to her Bed, deprived her of the honour of practicing that industry & oeconomy, which she had heretofore exerted, with so much propriety.—She now alas! can no longer assist herself.

It is on these grounds that this Subscription is set on foot, by M[r] Alderman Cadell No. 4 Bloomsbury place, and M[r] George Nicol No. 58 Pallmall.

The amount of the income from the subscription (if it ever actually was circulated) is not known. A year later Susannah Davies died on 9 February 1801 and was buried on 15 February at St Paul, Covent Garden, whose burial register records on that date, "Susanna Davies (From S[t] George Hanover Square) 78 years." Unfortunately no portrait or print of this woman, so widely celebrated for her beauty, is known to exist.

Davies, William *1751–1809, actor, singer.*

William Davies, sometimes called "Kiddy" Davies, was born at London in 1751, according to *The Secret History of the Green Room* (1790), and was apprenticed to a stonemason. His mother was still alive in 1798, serving as a domestic to Lord Thurlow, the Lord Chancellor, a circumstance that Davies often boasted about in company. He began his theatrical career as a singer in the provinces, performing at Portsmouth and Norwich. He and his wife Elizabeth Davies were members of the Norwich company by 1767–68; by 1768–69 their salaries were £1 11s. 6d. and 13s. 6d. per week, respectively. On 22 May 1769 their articles were renewed at that salary for the following season. On 10 April 1770 the manager at Norwich was empowered by the committee of proprietors "to allow Mr and Mrs Davies an Increase of Five Shillings p week to their Joint Salaries." The Davieses, however, did not accept the offer, and after playing the summer at Richmond, they came into London.

Announced as a "Young Gentleman," Davies made his first appearance at Drury Lane on 25 September 1770 as Lord Aimworth in Bickerstaffe's comic opera *The Maid of the Mill*. In his diary the prompter William Hopkins identified and described him: "Mr Davies from the Norwich Company, a tolerable figure, a bad voice & speaks tolerable may be useful pretty well receiv'd." The *Town and Country Magazine* (September 1770) described Davies as having "a very agreeable and expressive countenance, and a happy figure upwards," with a good stage voice when singing was not required of him. "Upon the whole, he went through the part tolerably well," it was thought; but he was advised by the critic that he would appear to greater advantage in polite comedy,

"where no musical exertions are required."

Several nights later, on 29 September 1770, Davies reappeared as Lord Aimworth, and Mrs Davies made her first appearance on the Drury Lane stage in the afterpiece, *Harlequin's Invasion*, playing Sukey Chitterlin. During the rest of the season Davies acted a variety of roles, typical of the diversity he would offer throughout his London career over the next 29 years. His versatility led the *Authentic Memoirs of the Green Room* to write of him in 1799 (rather equivocally) "tragedy, comedy, opera, pantomime—all is the same to him . . . a very useful man." On 25 October 1770 he acted Vincent in *The Ladies' Frolick*. This was followed by a vocal part in *Romeo and Juliet*, Hilliard in *The Ladies' Frolick*, Don Pedro in *'Tis Well It's no Worse*, Amintor in *Daphne and Amintor*, Frankly in *The Register Officer*, Gayless in *The Lying Valet*, Altamont in *The Fair Penitent*, Palaemon in *The Chaplet*, Heartly in *The Reprisal*, Father in *The Ephesian Matron*, and Ford in *The Merry Wives of Windsor*. For his benefit on 14 May 1771, which he shared with Hartry, Davies played Young Meadows in *Love in a Village*, for the first time.

In the following season he repeated many of these roles and added Worthy in *The Recruiting Officer*, Painter in *Timon of Athens*, Antonio in *Twelfth Night*, Frederick in *Amelia*, Rosencrantz in *Hamlet*, a soldier in *The Grecian Daughter* (in its first performance on 26 February 1772), Weldon in *The Absent Man*, Orthagoras in *Timoleon*, Don Lopez in *Marplot in Lisbon*, the captain in *Macbeth*, Rakeit in *The Humours of the Turf*, and Eustace in *Love in a Village*. For his benefit on 20 May 1772, Davies shared a profit of £95 11s. 6d. with Inchbald. Of Davies's performance of the Squire in *Thomas and Sally* on 6 December 1771, Thomas Potter wrote in the *Theatrical Review* that he "discovered no inconsiderable degree of merit."

Davies continued in a similar capacity under Garrick's management through 1775–76 and, after Garrick's retirement, with Sheridan at the same theatre through 1779–80. He also played at Bristol in the summers of 1775 and 1778. He seemed often in financial difficulty, perhaps because of his devotion to the bottle. On 14 January 1772 Garrick advanced him £50 on his note, and at about this time Davies wrote to the manager about his troubles, in an undated letter sent from his lodgings at No 6, Russell Street. Davies protested that he tried to live frugally and was honored by his engagement at Drury Lane, but that his salary was so small and his benefits so disappointing (£50 in the year he was writing) that he now found it impossible to pay most of his bills. He requested an advance of £30 and hoped that Garrick would be patient for the sum already owed him by the previous advance. He asked the manager to deduct an additional 10 shillings per week from his salary to accelerate the repayment. In this letter Davies requested articles to be drawn covering the next six seasons, beginning at £5 per week for the next and following seasons and increasing to £6 for the third and fourth, and £7 for the fifth and sixth. He did not get what he asked for. In 1774–75, his salary was only £3 per week.

In 1775, Davies subscribed £1 1s. to the Drury Lane Theatrical Fund, which with a committee of other actors he had been instrumental in having established. He was one of the signers of a citation presented to Garrick by the Fund. Among the roles which he played for the first time under Garrick's management, in addition to the many mentioned above, were Don Diego in *The Padlock* (22 December 1774); Henry in *The Deserter* (27 November 1775); Sir John in *The Devil to Pay* (5 December 1775); Leander in *The Padlock* (7 December 1775); Clerimont in Garrick's controversial revival on 13 January 1776 of *Epicoene*, when Mrs Siddons played Epicoene. The *Westminster Magazine*

(January 1776) complained that Palmer, Brereton, and Davies had "a bloated vulgarity about them, which should ever deter the manager from assigning them the parts of cavaliers or men of fashion." He was Sebastian in *Twelfth Night* (10 April 1776).

On 8 June 1776, during the last round of Garrick's performances, Davies played the part of Sir John in the afterpiece of *The Devil to Pay* in place of Vernon, who was hoarse. When the audience called for the song of "The Early Horn," traditional in the part of Sir John for over 30 years, Davies came forward—reported Hopkins in his diary—and "told them he did not know of doing the part till after two therefore he was not prepared, they call'd out & bid him go on his own way."

In the summer of 1776 Davies acted at Richmond and then returned to Drury Lane, now under Sheridan's management, at his salary of £3 per week. He remained there for four seasons. For his benefit in March 1778 he took receipts of £80. In 1779–80, his last season at Drury Lane, he crossed over to Covent Garden for a single performance of Amiens in *As You Like It* on 17 December and in the next season engaged full time with Covent Garden at a salary of £4 per week, making his first appearance of the season on 3 October 1780 as Doodle in *Tom Thumb*. Among his other roles in that year, when he lived still in Russell Street, were Cromwell in *Henry VIII*, a bacchanal in *Comus*, and Artaxias in *The Siege of Sinope*. He returned to Drury Lane for a single performance on 8 April 1781 to play Henry in *The Deserter* for the benefit of Mrs Cargill.

Davies remained at Covent Garden for 14 years, at a constant salary of £4 per week until 1783–84, when he was raised to £5, continuing in his familiar and varied repertoire. Frederick Reynolds spoke of him in his *Life and Times* (1826) as the person with the "low bow and melancholy countenance" who was the "usual messenger of woe" when it became necessary to announce illness or refractoriness of an actor before a performance at Covent Garden. One such occasion was on 7 December 1786 when Lewis, having received "a blast in the eye," was rendered unable to go on as Captain Crevelt in *He Wou'd be a Soldier*, and Davies read the part. Sometimes, however, the audience was less indulgent and hooted him off as they called for the manager.

Probably he was the Mr Davies who had a benefit at Richmond on 9 October 1781 —a night he did not play at Covent Garden—and perhaps he was the actor of that name who performed on occasion at Edinburgh in 1782 and 1783, although the latter person was more likely Thomas Dibble Davis, with whom he has often been confused. Thomas Dibble Davis acted at Covent Garden for many years while William Davies was at Drury Lane, but T. D. Davis had left Covent Garden before William transferred to that theatre. With the possible exception of 1783, William seems never to have been acting during summers at the Haymarket at the same time T. D. Davis was also in the company.

William Davies acted Hawthorn in *Love in a Village* at the Haymarket on 16 and 19 September 1782. While at Covent Garden in the regular seasons, he performed during summers at the Haymarket from 1783 through 1795, and after his final season at the winter theatre in 1794–95, he continued at the summer Haymarket through 1799. By 1796, according to the magazine *How Do You Do?* (27 August 1796), "Davies, so long the *walking gentleman* of Dramatists," had changed his line of acting, "and means to take the Old Men." (He was 46 years old at the time.) The writer congratulated him on the transition and looked forward to seeing him again in Old Wilding, "which he played wonderfully" (in *The Lyar*, at the Haymarket, 11 June 1796).

Davies's other roles in the following summer were typical: Harold in *Peeping Tom*, Lord Edmund in *The Prisoner at Large*, Mr Goodwill in *Bannian Day*, Campley in *Inkle and Yarico*, the Governor in *Love Makes a Man*, Edward in *The Dead Alive*, and a robber in *The Iron Chest*. During his years at the Haymarket, Davies also acted, among many other roles, Willford in *Next Door Neighbours* (for the first time on 30 August 1791), Belville in *Rosina* (first time on 10 August 1786), Edward in *The Purse* (18 August 1795), Lord Alford in *The Children in the Wood* (3 July 1795), Lord Glenmore in *The Chapter of Accidents* (3 August 1796), Meanwell in *Tit for Tat* (6 July 1796), Capulet in *Romeo and Juliet* (7 September 1796), and Flood in *Family Distress* (15 June 1799). Davies's last performances at London were at the Haymarket on 16 September 1799: he played Harold in *Peeping Tom*, a robber in *The Iron Chest*, and with others sang "Rule Britannia!" in *Tars at Torbay*. In the summer of 1800, announced as from the Theatres Royal, Covent Garden and the Haymarket, he played at Birmingham.

William Davies died on 25 September 1809, according to his obituary in the *Gentleman's Magazine* (September 1809), which identified him as "Kiddy" Davis, formerly of Drury Lane and Covent Garden. He was buried at St Paul, Covent Garden—entered in the register as "William Davies. From St Mary le Bone. Aged 58 years"—on 1 October 1809. His wife Elizabeth had been buried at the same church 27 years earlier on 31 July 1782. No issue are known, but the Master William Davies who acted at Portsmouth in 1791 may have been their son.

In *Candid and Impartial Strictures on the Performers . . .* (1795), F. G. Waldron termed Davies "a kind of theatrical packhorse" upon whom all sorts of roles could be heaped—"he will never complain, but bear all patiently." No member of any theatre, claimed *The Secret History of the Green Room* (1790), "supports a more variegated list of characters, or more frequently appears before the Public." Davies had a genteel person and face but was reported to be stiff and inanimate in action. He was "a tolerable singer, and a very articulate speaker," but his chief merit was his "extraordinary industry." During the years he was at the Haymarket he drank heavily and his life was said to be "a continual scene of dissipations of the town."

Davies, Mrs William, Elizabeth
d. 1782, actress.

Elizabeth Davies was acting at Norwich by 1767–68 with her husband William Davies (1751–1809). In 1768–69 her salary there was 13s. 6d. per week, at which figure her articles were renewed on 22 May 1769 for the following season. Although she and her husband were offered a total increase of five shillings on their salaries at Norwich for 1770–71, they left to join the Covent Garden Theatre. There she made her first appearance, billed as "A Young Gentlewoman," in the role of Sukey Chitterlin in *Harlequin's Invasion* on 29 September 1770. The prompter Hopkins identified her as Mrs Davies from Norwich —"Smart little figure, some spirit, was well receiv'd." *The Public Advertiser* listed her for Phoebe in *As You Like It* on 9 October 1770, but the posted bills named Miss Platt for the role on that night. Mrs Davies acted Lucille in *The Fair Penitent* on 27 October and on 22 November was named in the bills for Phoebe. On 6 April 1771 she played a role in *The Rehearsal*. In the following season she played Sukey, Phoebe, the chambermaid in *The Clandestine Marriage*, Miss Jenny in *The Provok'd Husband*, the milliner in *The Suspicious Husband*, Miss Frolick in *The Absent Man*, Harriet in *The Upholsterer*, a shepherdess in *Cymon*, and Jenny, a breeches part, in *The Humours of the Turf*.

Specializing mainly in a line of chambermaids and young women, Elizabeth Davies continued at Drury Lane through 1779–80. Among her roles were Wishwell in *The*

Double Gallant (18 February 1773), Melissa in *The Lying Valet* (10 January 1774), Lucy in *The Recruiting Officer* (21 April 1775), and Robinette in *A Christmas Tale* (19 April 1775). In 1775–76 she acted Bridget in *Every Man in his Humour*, Foible in *The Way of the World*, Gypsy in *The Stratagem*, Viletta in *She Wou'd and She Wou'd Not*, Chloe in *The Lottery*, Lucy in *The London Merchant*, Nerissa in *The Merchant of Venice*, Centaur in *Epicoene*, Mlle Florival in *The Deuce is in Him*, a maid in *Zara*, Necessary in *A Woman is a Riddle*, Lady Charlotte in *High Life Below Stairs*, Kitty Pry in *The Lying Valet*, and Miss Fuz in *A Peep Behind the Curtain*. When she acted Miss Tittup in *Bon Ton* on 9 October 1776, Hopkins entered in his diary—"Mrs Davies Miss Tittup—La! La!" She performed Lucy in *The Rivals* for the first time on 9 April 1777. Her salary at Drury Lane in 1774–75 was £2 per week.

She acted soubrettes and maids at Bristol in 1775 and 1778 and at Richmond in the summer of 1776. Probably she was the Mrs Davies who acted Lucy in *The Beggar's Opera* at the Haymarket on 20 September 1776 and Patience (with a song in character) in a performance of *Henry VIII* at China Hall, Rotherhithe, on 25 September 1776.

Mrs Davies died prematurely, probably at the age of 30 or younger, in July 1782. The register of St Paul, Covent Garden, where she was buried on 31 July 1782, listed her as "Elizabeth, wife of William Davies." That this Elizabeth Davies was, indeed, the actress is confirmed by John Moody's notes in the "Drury Lane Fund Book," at the Garrick Club. Her husband continued to act at London until 1799; he died in September 1809 and was buried at St Paul, Covent Garden, on 1 October.

Davin. *See* DAVANT.

Davis. *See also* DAVIES.

Davis, Mr ₍fl. 1696₎, *actor.*

A Mr Davis played a Councellor in *The City Bride* at Lincoln's Inn Fields in March 1696.

Davis, Mr ₍fl. 1722–1723₎, *actor.*

Mr Davis (often "Davies") played Coupee in *The Compromise* at Lincoln's Inn Fields on 15 December 1722 and, for his shared benefit with Huddy on 10 May 1723, Pyramon in *Oedipus*. The two players split £107 7s. 6d.

Davis, Mr ₍fl. 1733–1735₎, *singer, actor.*

A Mr Davis performed Merlin in *The Opera of Operas* at the Haymarket on 4 June 1733. In the following season at the same theatre he performed the bailiff in the same piece on 29 October 1733 and the King of the Fiddlers in *Chrononhotonthologos* on 22 February 1734.

Probably this Davis was the person of that name who had a benefit at the Haymarket on 21 March 1735, when the *London Post* urged a large turnout for him, and, praising him for "probity join'd with uncommon Industry," reported that Davis had been "brought up under the late ingenious Mr Nicolo Haym, and has himself more than once endeavoured to divert the Town, in a Poetical as well as Musical way." The pieces performed at the benefit, for which no casts are known, were *Arlequin Sauvage* and *Les Deux arlequins*. A Widow Davis, who received a benefit "at the particular Desire of several Persons of Quality" on 2 May 1734 at Goodman's Fields Theatre, may have been his wife.

Davis, Mr ₍fl. 1736–1752₎, *dancer.*

A person or persons named Davis (sometimes Davies) danced in various London houses between 1736 and 1752. This male dancer performed in the chorus of *Cupid and Bacchus* at Lincoln's Inn Fields Theatre as early as 10 December 1736. In 1739–40 a Mr Davies danced a

villager in *Orpheus and Eurydice* at Covent Garden, a role for which his name later appeared regularly at that theatre in 1740–41, 1741–42, 1749–50, 1750–51, and 1751–52. No doubt he made other appearances in the Covent Garden dancing ensemble.

On 22 August 1741, Mr Davis played a servant in a performance of *The Modern Pimp* in Hallam's booth at Bartholomew Fair. At that fair on 25 August 1742, either two persons named Davis performed or the same person worked two booths: at Phillips and Yeates's booth opposite the hospital gate a Mr Davis played Puff in *The Indian Merchant*, and at Hippisley and Chapman's booth in the George Inn Yard a Mr Davis performed a *Fingalian Dance* with Mrs Vallois. In the summer of 1743 Davis danced with Bencraft in Hippisley and Chapman's booth at Bartholomew Fair, and on 27 December 1742 he danced the *Dutch Skipper* dance at the New Wells, London Spa, Clerkenwell.

Davis, Mr ₍fl. 1754–1761₎, *violinist.*

A Mr Davis was paid 10s. for playing in performances of the *Messiah* at the Foundling Hospital in May 1754. Perhaps he was the same Mr Davis who was paid 2s. 6d. per night as "Fidler" for 23 performances of *The Fair* at Covent Garden between 13 October and 9 November 1761.

Davis, Mr ₍fl. 1780₎, *actor.*

A Mr Davis acted Catesby in a single performance of *Richard III* at the Crown Inn, Islington, on 6 March 1780. Possibly this person was the actor John Davis (fl. 1771–1813?) or the Mr Davis, the Manchester actor, who died at that city on 12 September 1795.

Davis, Mr ₍fl. 1787–1795?₎, *singer, dancer.*

A Mr Davis was a principal dancer at Hughes's Royal Circus, St George's Fields, in the summer of 1787. Probably he was the Davis who played a principal character in a new burletta *The Boarding School* in April 1787. A Mr Davis sang in a musical piece *The What Is It?* and was the clown in the pantomime *I Don't Know What!* on 12 May 1789. A person by this name, and his wife, both announced as from the Theatre Royal, Dublin, played principal characters in the spectacle of *Veluti in Speculum* at the Royal Circus on 17 April 1795. This latter Mr Davis may have been the actor John Davis (fl. 1771–1813?).

Davis, Mr ₁fl. 1787–1803₁, *costume designer*.

A Mr Davis was a theatrical costumer in London from at least 1787 through 1802. On 6 November 1787 the *Public Advertiser* commented on the beautiful dress worn by Mrs Wells on Saturday evening, 3 November (when she played Stella in *Robin Hood* and Julia in *The Midnight Hour*): "there was a something so simply fascinating in it . . . as entitles it to much praise; it is said to owe its birth to the fancy of Mr Davis, to whom Mrs Siddons, Mrs Wells, Mrs Pope, Miss Farren, &c. are frequently indebted for their elegant & graceful stage habiliments."

Davis was working as a costume designer at the Royal Circus by 1799, and on 25 March of that year provided dresses, with Williams, Miss Williams, Nash, and Liddell, for the oriental spectacle *Almoran and Hamet, or, the Fair Circassian.* At the Royal Circus he also contributed costume designs for *The Fire King* (1801), *Halloween* (1801), *The Golden Farmer* (1802), *The Conquest of Granada* (1802), and *The Jubilee of 1802, or, Preston Guild.* In 1803 he married the Miss Williams, a costumer, who continued as Mrs Davis (fl. 1799–1803) to work with him on the costumes at the Royal Circus.

Davis, Mr ₁fl. 1794₁, *singer*.

A Mr Davis, of Worcester, was listed in 1794 in Doane's *Musical Directory* as an alto and a participant in the Handelian performances at Westminster Abbey.

Davis, Mrs, née Clegg ₁fl. 1726–1745₁, *singer*.

Mrs Davis may have been the sister of the violinist John Clegg; she certainly was the mother of the harpsichord prodigy Miss Davis who performed with her in the 1740s. Mrs Davis was a student of Bononcini and made her first stage appearance at the Lincoln's Inn Fields Theatre on 6 May 1726 singing in Italian and English at a performance of *The Squire of Alsatia.* She held a benefit for herself at York Buildings on 26 April 1727 when she sang songs by Pepusch.

At the King's Theatre in the Haymarket she sang with Handel's company in 1732, taking the part of the First Israelite in *Esther* on 2 May and Eurilla in *Acis and Galatea* on 10 June. On 17 December 1733 she sang at a concert in Dublin, after which the records of her activities are slim until the 1740s. In early December 1742 at Mr Johnson's Hall in Crow Street, Dublin, she sang with her sister Miss Clegg a number of Handel arias. Her daughter, then aged six, accompanied Mrs Davis on the harpsichord in one song. By 10 May 1745 Mrs Davis was back in London with her daughter, billed as lately arrived from Ireland. They performed at Hickford's Music Room for Miss Davis's benefit, with Mrs Davis offering a number of songs.

Davis, Mrs ₁fl. 1741₁, *actress*.

A Mrs Davis acted Celia in a single performance of *The Whim, or the Merry Cheat,* a new musical farce, at Covent Garden on 17 April 1741. Her name was on the Covent Garden pay list that season for 1s. 8d. daily. Probably she was the same Mrs Davis who performed the role of Statira in *The Rival Queens* on 4 August 1741 in Middleton's booth at the Tottenham Court Fair.

Davis, [**Mrs?**] [*fl. 1793–1814*], *dresser.*

A woman named Davis was a women's dresser at Drury Lane Theatre from as early as 1793–94 until 1813–14 or after. Her salary from the season of 1801–2 to the last known year of her employment was 9s. per week.

Davis, Mrs [*fl. 1795*], *singer?, dancer?*

A Mrs Davis and her husband, announced as from the Theatre Royal, Dublin, played principal characters in the spectacle of *Veluti in Speculum* at the Royal Circus on 17 April 1795. She may have been the wife of the actor John Davis (fl. 1771–1813?).

Davis, Mrs [*fl. 1799?–1803*], *singer, actress.*

A Mrs Davis performed at Sadler's Wells regularly during the summer of 1800. She was re-engaged there in 1801 by Charles Dibdin who in his *Memoirs* calls her "a very clever actress and singer of low comedy." She was still at Sadler's Wells in 1803. Probably she was the Mrs Davis who sang the song, *The Way to get married* (published in 1799?), at the Royal Circus.

Davis, Mrs, née Williams [*fl. 1799–1803*], *costume designer.*

A Miss Williams was a costume designer at the Royal Circus, St George's Fields, from as early as 1799 to at least 1803. By the latter date she had married Mr Davis (fl. 1787–1803), who was also a costume designer at that theatre. Miss Williams's mother and father were also involved as set designers, costumers, and performers at the Royal Circus (later the Surrey) between 1790 and 1810. In a newspaper advertisement for *Almoran and Hamet; or, the Fair Circassian* on 25 March 1799, Miss Williams was listed as one of the costume designers. Other productions at the Royal Circus for which she received similar credit were *The Fire King* (1801), *Halloween* (1801), *The Golden Farmer* (1802), and *The Conquest of Granada* (1802). Advertisements of *The Rival Sisters* for 11 April 1803 and *Louisa of Lombardy* on 25 April 1803 announced that the dresses were executed under the direction of Mrs Davis, late Miss Williams.

Davis, Master [*fl. 1792*], *dancer.*

A Master Davis performed in the ensemble of "Shepherds, Furies, and Shades of departed Heroes" in the opera *Orpheus and Eurydice* at Covent Garden on 28 February, 6 and 13 March 1792.

Davis, Miss *b. c. 1736, harpsichordist.*

Born about 1736 to the singer Mrs Davis (née Clegg), Miss Davis was first noticed in *Faulkner's Dublin Journal* on 13 November 1742.

In the Beginning of December next, at Mr Johnson's Hall in Crow-street, will be performed a Concert of Vocal and Instrumental Musick, for the Benefit of Miss Davis, a Child of 6 years old, who will perform a Concerto and some other Pieces upon the Harpsichord; particularly she will accompany her Mother to a Song of Mr Handel's, composed entirely to shew the Harpsichord.

On 10 May 1745, now billed as eight years old and lately arrived from Ireland, Miss Davis had a benefit at Hickford's Music Room. She again accompanied her mother, and the bill noted that "Miss Davis is to perform on a Harpsichord of Mr. Rutgerus Plenius's making, Inventor of the new deserv'd famous Lyrichord."

Davis, Miss [*fl. 1739–1762?*], *actress, dancer, singer?*

During the quarter of a century between 1739 and 1762 a number of young female roles of some variety but mostly of the same general type—ingenues in sentimental comedy, pert serving maids and the like in farce and comic opera, columbines and other characters in pantomime—were filled in London and elsewhere by a Miss Davis who for one reason or another cannot have been identical with any one of the other Misses Davis who performed during this period. The likelihood that an actress would not only remain unmarried but would retain parts of this youthful cast for so long was not great, but neither was such a retention, of name or of roles, unknown. The (by no means confident) assumption of the following account is that only one Miss Davis, an actress, dancer, and singer of satisfactory middling talents, is concerned in all of the roles cited.

A Miss Davis was a chorus singer at Covent Garden from 1739–40 through 1742–43, her name appearing for vocal parts in *Cupid and Bacchus* on 10 December 1739, in *Orpheus and Eurydice* on 12 February and 10 October 1739, 5 January, 24 February and 28 December 1741, and in *Macbeth* on 9 October 1743. She was probably the young woman who performed Betty in *The School Boy* on 7 May and 1 November 1740, a Nymph in *The Royal Chace* on 21 January 1741, an Amazon in *Perseus and Andromeda* on 28 February 1741, and Rose in *The Recruiting Officer* on 11 May 1741. A Miss Davis was Situp in *The Double Gallant* on 14 May 1742; and on 22 August, at Hallam's booth at Bartholomew Fair, A Miss Davis played Cleora in *The True and Ancient History of Rosamond*. An actress of that name acted Mrs Trippet in *The Lying Valet* at the new theatre in Southwark on 18 February 1743.

More than likely this singing actress was the Miss Davis who was at Aungier Street and Smock Alley theatres in Dublin from 1743–44 through 1745–46; she sang Lucy in *The Beggar's Opera* at Smock Alley on 25 April 1746. A Miss Davis sang the role of Manon Delateur in *L'Opéra du gueux*, a French translation of *The Beggar's Opera* performed by an "Anti-Gallic" company of English players at the Haymarket several

times between April 1749 and February 1750. On 9 February 1750 she played Rose in a French version of *The Recruiting Officer* given by the same group. A Miss Davis played at Richmond and Twickenham in the summer of 1751; she was one of two persons by this name—one from the "Theatre Royal, Dublin"—at those theatres in the summer of 1752. One of these persons was at those theatres in 1753.

Between 1750–51 and 1761–62, a Miss Davis was a regular minor performer at Covent Garden. The roles for which her name appeared in the bills (with date of each first performance) were: an Amazon in *Perseus and Andromeda* (19 November 1750); Diana in *Merlin's Cave* (27 December 1750), a vocal part in *Henry VIII* (16 April 1751), Polly in *The Beggar's Opera* (for her benefit on 14 May 1751), Dolly Trull in *The Beggar's Opera* (12 October 1751), a Lady in *Rule a Wife and Have a Wife* (6 November 1751), a vocal part in *Comus* (18 January 1760), Flavia in *The Frenchify'd Lady in Paris* (27 March 1762), a shepherdess in *Harlequin Sorcerer* (14 October 1762), and a role in *The Loves of Pluto and Columbine* (1 November 1762). Her salary in 1760–61 was 3s. 4d. per day. Her share of benefit tickets on 12 April 1760 was £5 11s., and on 11 April 1761, £7 15s. She may have been the Miss Davies who acted at the Haymarket in the summer of 1755, in the roles of Melissa in *The Lying Valet* (1 September), Arabella in *Home at Yorkshire* (3 September), Betty in *The Devil to Pay* (9 September), and Moon in *The Rehearsal* and Mercury in *Lethe* (11 September).

Davis, Miss [fl. 1789–1791], *equestrienne*. See **DAVIS, WILLIAM** [fl. 1789–1824].

Davis, Miss [fl. 1794], *singer*.
A Miss Davis was listed in Doane's *Musical Directory*, 1794, as a singer in the

oratorios at Drury Lane and as living at Lower Lambeth Marsh. Perhaps she was the Miss Davies (fl. 1794–1795) who also was a regular member of the Drury Lane chorus at this time.

Davis, Miss [fl. 1799], actress.

A Miss Davis, according to James Winston in *The Theatric Tourist*, was one of the performers who had acted in a private theatre in Tottenham Court Road —"a place at that time of great consequence in dramatic estimation"—and were then brought by Neville, as an experiment, to play professionally at Richmond, Surrey, in 1799.

Davis, David [fl. 1799–1815?], musician, instrument maker.

David Davis, musician and musical instrument maker, of No 26, Cheapside, became a freeman of the Worshipful Company of Musicians on 22 January 1799. Perhaps he was the Mr Davis of the firm of instrument makers, music sellers, and publishers known in 1815 as Clementi, Banger, Collard, Davis, & Collard.

Davis, Dibble. *See* DAVIS, THOMAS DIBBLE.

Davis, Elizabeth. *See* CHAMBERS, MRS WILLIAM.

Davis, F. [fl. 1768], actor.

On 5 November 1768 the *Theatrical Monitor* printed a letter to George Colman signed by Covent Garden performers, among whom was listed an F. Davis. Thomas Dibble Davis was acting at Covent Garden at the time, so perhaps the "F" was a misprint for "T." No F. Davies is otherwise known.

Davis, Henry [fl. 1756], doorkeeper.

Henry Davis, doorkeeper, received a benefit at Sadler's Wells in 1756.

Davis, "Jew" [fl. 1795?–1819], singer, actor.

Announced as making "his First Appearance on this Stage," the Mr Davis of this notice performed at Sadler's Wells in Thomas John Dibdin's musical interlude *First Come First Served* on 17 April 1797. Perhaps it was in that piece that he introduced *The Snug [or Tight] Little Island*, a song by Dibdin which was published in that year and became enormously popular. Despite the fact that this was said to be his first appearance at Sadler's Wells, perhaps he was the Mr Davis who had earlier performed the role of the hunter in *Chevy Chase, or Douglas and Percy* at that theatre on 4 August 1795. *Arrah who can stand still* and *The Land of Gold*, both songs from *Harlequin Mariner, or the Witch of the Oaks*, were published in 1796 as sung by a Mr Davis at the Royal Circus.

Davis was engaged regularly at Sadler's Wells at least through 1806. During this period he acquired the name of "Jew" Davis by his success at playing stage Jews. He also acted for John Philip Kemble at Drury Lane about 1801 and appeared on occasion at the Royal Circus. At the latter place, on 2 January 1804, Davis sang a comic song "The Rushlight, or the Humours of the Wry-mouthed Family" in a new burletta, *The Village Doctor*.

He was a close friend of the great clown Grimaldi, in whose *Memoirs* (by Charles Dickens) there are several anecdotes about Davis's prankish nature, including a story about Kemble's playing Hamlet in the provinces and being incensed by Davis's buffoonery as the gravedigger, all to the delight of the audience. T. J. Dibdin relates how Davis took revenge on him in 1801 when as manager Dibdin was obliged to turn down some unreasonable request by Davis. The actor had dislocated his shoulder, and although it was "perfectly cured" by the night on which he was to play a Moorish king in Dibdin's *The Ethiop, or the Siege of Granada*, Davis faked a fall and then protested that his shoulder had been injured again. As a last resort Dibdin was forced to go on in Davis's place—"and upon it founded, (as some years subsequent he acknowledged to me)" wrote Dibdin, "the hope of his revenge, and my mortification." Although he had written the piece, Dibdin could not "recollect one incident in the part" and had to be led about the stage by Dubois and Grimaldi.

In later years Dibdin paid tribute to Davis as "a performer of great merit in every department of stage performance, dancing excepted," who, had he "cultivated the graces as much as he did *la grosierté,* . . . might have been an ornament to the Stage." A stage-door keeper at Sadler's Wells named Wheeler described Davis as a perpetrator of nasty practical jokes on the foreign ropedancers and as "unprincipalled in manners and [in] language brutal." Davis was such a favorite with the gallery that when his pranks became too much for the managers to bear and he was dismissed, "it was said they never would be able to get on without him; but they did."

When Dibdin was confined for debt in the King's Bench Prison in 1819, "Jew" Davis came to visit him with tears in his eyes for his former manager's misfortune and offered the loan of half his weekly salary from the Cobourg Theatre until Dibdin's debts should be satisfied.

Davis, John [*fl.* 1700–1705], *singer.*
The earliest mention of the singer John Davis was about 1700 when Philip Hart's song *When Lovely Berenice I view* was published, with John Davis noted as the singer who had presented it at the Lincoln's Inn Fields Theatre. Davis appeared in the bills at this playhouse through 25 January 1705, when he sang Eccles's "Trumpet Song." He is also recorded as having sung at a concert at Hampstead on 21 August 1703, but the bulk of his work was at the theatre. He seems to have been quite popu-

lar, for several theatre songs sung by him were included in the 1704 *Monthly Masks.*

Davis, John [*fl.* 1771–1813?], *actor.*
The actor John Davis was known to be at York in 1782 when his full name was printed as a subscriber to George Parker's *Humourous Sketches.* He was probably the Mr Davis who, with his wife, had performed at York as early as 1771–72. He acted Tom in *The Jealous Wife* when the Norwich company visited Colchester on 12 August 1782 and a role in *The Fair American* at Norwich on 12 February 1783. An entry in the Committee Book of the Norwich Theatre on 30 May 1783 ordered that "Mr Davis be immediately discharged and that Mr Starkey [pay] him One Guinea over and above his Salary."

John Davis was acting at Edinburgh in 1784–85 and 1789. He made his debut at Crow Street, Dublin, on 15 November 1794 and was again at Edinburgh in 1795–96. He may have been the Mr Davis who, with his wife, both announced as from Dublin, had performed in *Veluti in Speculum* at Hughes's Royal Circus, St George's Fields, London, on 17 April 1795.

Engaged at a salary of £1 per week at Covent Garden in 1797–98, Davis made his first appearance at that theatre as a Scotchman in *The Apprentice* on 4 November 1797. He played O'Thunder in *A Trip to the Nore* on 9 November and Abhorson in *Measure for Measure* on 17 November. Davis created the roles of Muley in Monk Lewis's music drama *The Castle Spectre,* which opened on 14 December 1797 and played 47 nights that season, and Aladdin in *Blue-Beard,* which opened on 16 January 1798 and played for 64 nights. Davis acted at Cork and Belfast in 1800 and was probably the Davis who rejoined the Manchester company on 1 December 1804, after an absence. He may have been the Davis who was acting at Edinburgh between 1805 and 1813.

Courtesy of Guildhall Art Gallery

JOHN DAVIS
by Souler

Davis, John *d. 1793, proprietor.*

According to Warwick Wroth in *The London Pleasure Gardens*, a John Davis succeeded Hughes as proprietor of Sadler's Wells about 1775 and continued as lessee until his death on 28 August 1793. In 1792, Davis also became proprietor of Bagnigge Wells.

The will of a Mr John Davis, carpenter, of St Mary, Islington, which was made on 20 July 1793 and proved on 3 September 1793, may have been that of the proprietor. That John Davis left bequests of substantial funds and properties, although no mention was made of interest in either pleasure resort. Included in the bequests were £250 per year in bank annuities to his wife and executrix Jane Davis, £50 to her sister Miss Mary Bignell of Islington, £500 to the Orphan Working School in the City Road, Middlesex, £2000 for the building of almshouses in Islington, £300 to the Quaker School near St John Street Road, and his leases of estates in Gloucester Place, Isling-

ton, and Hampton, Middlesex, to his wife.

An oil painting of Davis by J. Souler is in the Guildhall Art Gallery. An engraving of it was published by Scott.

Davis, John Francis *[fl. c. 1730?–1753], composer, flutist?*

John Francis Davis was listed as one of the original subscribers, "being musicians," in the Declaration of Trust which established the Royal Society of Musicians on 28 August 1739. Possibly he was the Mr Davis, a scholar of Nicola Haym, who sang at the Haymarket between 1733 and 1735. Works composed by him are listed in the *Catalogue of Printed Music in the British Museum* and include *The Musical Companion, being a New Collection of Songs, Minuets, Rigadoons & Country Dances* transposed for the flute (c. 1730) and the dance tune *Locking's Whim, or the Conjurer* (1753).

Davis, Mrs K. *[fl. 1789–1792], dancer.*

Mrs K. Davis was in the Drury Lane company list as a dancer at 15s. per week in 1789–90, although her name appeared in no bills. In the following season she danced in the chorus of *Don Juan* on 16 nights between 26 October and 1 December 1790 and no doubt appeared in other pieces. Her name continued on the company list for 1791–92.

Davis, Katherine *[fl. 1681–1691], actress.*

Katherine Davis played Julia, a young woman of great beauty, in *The False Count* in November 1681 at the Dorset Garden Theatre. Though she remained with the Duke's Company until the union in 1682, her other roles are not known. Similarly, as a member of the United Company from 1682 to 1691 she is known to have acted only two parts: Silvia in *Madam Fickle* in 1690–91 and Miss Molly in *Love for Money* in January 1691 – both at Drury

Lane. She doubtless played other roles, but the records are woefully incomplete for the period during which she was active.

Davis, "Kiddy." *See* DAVIES, WILLIAM.

Davis, Mary, later Mrs James Paisible [*fl. 1660–1698*], *actress, dancer, singer.*

Mary Davis, better known in her time as "Moll," is said by some sources to have been the illegitimate daughter of Colonel Charles Howard, son of Thomas, Earl of Berkshire, but by others to have been the daughter of a blacksmith from Charlton, near the seat of the Howard family in Wiltshire. The prompter Downes claimed that Miss Davis was one of the four "Principal Actresses" housed by Sir William and Dame Mary Davenant when the Duke's Company began playing late in 1660, but though Davenant may have provided Mary with home and hearth, it is most unlikely that she was a principal actress at this early date: Pepys was still referring to her as a little girl as late as 1663.

The first time the diarist saw her perform was on 18 February 1662 at the Lincoln's Inn Fields playhouse when she played Viola in *The Law Against Lovers*. He saw her dance in boy's clothes in *The Slighted Maid* on 23 February 1663 and noted that "the play hath little good in it, being most pleased to see the little girl dance in boy's apparel, she having very fine legs, only bends in the hams, as I perceive all women do," but she "is come to act very prettily, and spoke the epilogue most admirably." Perhaps the legs he was so critical about belonged to some other young actress, but it has been assumed that the little girl he admired was Mary Davis at the beginning of her career.

Miss Davis acted Violinda in *The Step-Mother* in mid-October 1663, Aurelia in *The Comical Revenge* in March 1664, an unnamed role (and the epilogue) in *Heraclius* on 8 March 1664, Princess Anne in Boyle's *Henry V* on 13 August 1664, and the Queen of Hungary in *Mustapha* on 3 April 1665. After the plague and fire Pepys learned, on 17 April 1666, that "the pretty girle, that sang and danced so well at the Duke's house, is dead." Miss Davis was still alive and kicking, however, for when Pepys went to see *The English Princess* on 7 March 1667 he noted that

little Mis Davis did dance a jig after the end of the play, and there telling the next day's play; so that it come in by force only to please the company to see her dance in boy's clothes; and, the truth is, there is no comparison between Nell's [Nell Gwyn's] dancing the other day at the King's house in boy's clothes and this, this being infinitely beyond the other.

This was high praise, for the connoisseur had praised Nell sky-high. Again on 5 August 1667 when Pepys saw *Love Tricks* it was Miss Davis who saved the day: "a silly play, only Mis's dancing in a shepherd's clothes did please us mightily."

On 15 August 1667 Mary Davis played Mrs Millisent in *Feign'd Innocence*; on 7 November she was Ariel in *The Tempest*; on 19 November she acted Celania in *The Rivals*; and on 6 February 1668 she played Gatty in *She Wou'd If She Cou'd*. Many performances by the Duke's Company in which she participated were presented at court or seen by Charles II at Lincoln's Inn Fields, and Miss Davis's talents did not go unobserved by the monarch. What seems to have affected him most was her rendering of the song "My Lodging It Is on the Cold Ground" in *The Rivals*; Downes claimed that soon after the King heard her sing this ditty he took her off the ground and put her in his bed. By 11 January 1668 Pepys had learned of the King's interest in Mary. On this date he reported on a discussion of an amateur performance at court —some of the performers having been

MARY DAVIS

by Kneller
painting at Audley End House

members of the Duke's Company. He had heard that

among the rest [there was] Mis Davis, who is the most impertinent slut . . . in the world; and the more, now the King do show her countenance; and is reckoned his mistress, even to the scorne of the whole world; the King gazing on her, and my Lady Castlemayne being melancholy and out of humour, all the play, not smiling once. The King, it seems, hath given [Miss Davis] a ring of £7000, which she shews to every body, and owns that the King did give it her; and he hath furnished a house for her in Suffolke Street most richly, which is a most infinite shame. It seems she is a bastard of Colonell Howard, my Lord Berkshire, and that he do pimp for her for the King, and hath got her for him; but Pierce says that she is a most homely jade as ever she saw, though she dances beyond any thing in the world.

Poor Pepys, caught between jealousy and outrage, saw Mary Davis's probable last performance when she was in *She Wou'd If She Cou'd* at court on 29 May 1668. He reported that "Mrs Davis was there; and when she was to come to dance her jigg, the Queene would not stay to see it, which people do think it was out of displeasure at her being the King's whore, that she could not bear it." The diarist, on the other hand, apparently stayed for the whole performance. On 31 May he heard "that Mrs Davis is quite gone from the Duke of York's [play]house, and Gosnell comes in her

Harvard Theatre Collection

MARY DAVIS

engraving by Tompson, after Lely

room, which I am glad of." On 15 February 1669 Pepys wrote: "Here in Suffolk Street lives Moll Davis; and we did see her coach come for her to her door, a mighty pretty fine coach."

So ended, for a time, the stage career of Mary Davis. Notorious though she had become, audiences did not forget her talent. In 1669 in *Epigrams of all Sorts* Richard Flecknoe wrote:

To Mis: Davies, on her excellent dancing.

Dear Mis: delight of all the nobler sort,
Pride of the Stage and darling of the Court,
Who wou'd not think to see thee dance so light,
Thou wer't all air? or else all soul and spirit?
Or who'd not say to see thee only tread,
Thy feet were feathers! others feet but lead?
Athlanta well cou'd run, and Hermes flee,
But none e'er mov'd more gracefully than thee;
And Circe charm'd with wand and magick lore,
But none, like thee, e'er charm'd with Feet before.
Thou Miracle! whom all men must admire
To see thee move like air, and mount like fire.
Whoe'er would follow thee or come but nigh
To thy perfection, must not dance but fly.

After her withdrawal from the stage Mary Davis did not disappear from the public eye. On 21 December 1668 Pepys went to the theatre and wrote afterward, "it vexed me to see Moll Davis, in the box over the King's and my Lady Castlemayne's head, look down upon the King, and he up to her; and so did my Lady Castlemayne once, to see who it was; but when she saw her, she looked like fire; which troubled me."

On 16 October 1673 Mary gave birth to the King's daughter, Lady Mary Tudor, who later married Edward, Viscount Radcliffe, who became second Earl of Derwentwater. Lady Mary led almost as scandalous a life as had her mother. She married three times and died in Paris on 5 November 1726. Mary Davis returned to the stage to sing Thames in the court masque *Calisto* on 15 February 1675, a production that involved both court and professional participants. Perhaps it was she who was the "Mrs Davys" who acted Venus in *Venus and Adonis* at court in 1681–82. But her day at court ended with the death of Charles II, if not before.

On 4 December 1686 Mary Davis and the musician James Paisible were granted a license to marry. He was about 30 and she, according to her deposition, about 25 – she must have been past 30. On hearing of this, Sir George Etherege wrote from Ratisbon to Charles Boyle on 12/22 May 1687, "Mrs. Davies has given a proof of the great passion she always had for music, and Monsieur Peasible has another bass to thrum than that he played so well upon." In "A Choyce Collection" at Ohio State is a "Satyr on Bent–g &c. 1688/9" which John Harold Wilson quotes in *All the King's Ladies*:

> *Davis was looking out too for a Hero,*
> *Weary already for her Pypeing Lero.*
> *O Peaceable! thy own sad Farewell set,*
> *And make words to it of thy want of wit:*
> *A Fidlers Name alone is Vile We know,*
> *Must thou then be a Pimp, & Cuckold*
>   *too?*

But if the marriage was beset by infidelities on Mary's part, there seems to be no other notice of it. The Paisibles made some trips to France, one occasion being in 1688 when they followed James II into exile. On 31 January 1698 they were granted permission to make England once again their home.

The date of Mary Davis Paisible's death is not known. Certainly 1687, the date sometimes suggested, is incorrect. James Paisible made a will on 17 January 1721 in which he left £50 to "James Paisible now in London" – possibly a son of James and Mary. He did not mention his wife, so perhaps before that time she had died.

Portraits of Mary Davis include:

1. Painting by Lely, c. 1674. In the Earl of Bradford's collection at Weston. Engraved by G. Valck in 1678 and captioned "Madam Davits;" by Schiavonetti as a plate to the *Memoirs of Count Grammont*, published by E. and S. Harding in 1792; by E. Scriven for the same work, published by Miller and Carpenter in 1810; and by R. Earlom, published by Woodburn in 1815; and by R. Tompson, A. De Blois, and two anonymous engravers.

2. Painting by Lely. In Baptist May's collection in 1677.

3. Painting by Lely, called Mary Davis, c. 1657. In the collection of Lord Brocket at Bramshill. Engraved anonymously.

4. Painting by Lely, said to be of Mary Davis, c. 1674. In the collection of Sir E. Davis in 1939.

5. Painting attributed to Lely, its subject erroneously called Nell Gwyn. At Hatfield House.

6. Painting after Lely, titled Mary Davis as St Mary Magdalen. At the National Portrait Gallery.

7. Another version of the above, in which the subject is called Elizabeth Wriothesley. At Syon House.

8. Another version of the same, formerly at Rushbrooke Hall.

9. A miniature of the same. At the Victoria and Albert Museum.

10. A copy of the same. In Lord Falmouth's collection about 1800, when it was engraved by Van der Berghe as a likeness of Arabella Churchill. An engraving of it by Valck was called a picture of Hortense Mancini.

11. Painting by Kneller. At Audley End House, Saffron Walden, Essex. Engraved by W. N. Gardiner and by an anonymous engraver.

12. An engraving after J. Hoskins. Published in Williamson's *Catalogue of the Pierpont Morgan Collection*, 1906.

13. Anonymous engraving. Published in Volume III of *The Walpole Society* series in 1920.

14. An engraving by E. Bocquet.

Davis, Richard *1697–1785, box office keeper.*

Originally trained as a seal engraver, "in which art he made a considerable proficiency" (by report of the *Gentleman's Magazine*, October 1785), Richard Davis became a box office keeper at Covent Garden Theatre at least by 1735–36. In that season he received a salary of 2*s*. per day. By 1760–61 his salary was 2*s*. 6*d*. per day. For nearly 50 years at Covent Garden "he acquitted himself with civility, industry, and integrity" until his death on 22 October 1785 at the age of 88.

Davis, Solomon *[fl. 1785], musician.*

Solomon Davis was proposed by Napier for membership in the Royal Society of Musicians on 1 May 1785, at the same time that the flutist Teobaldo Monzani was proposed. By ballots on 5 June 1785 both were denied admission (for Davis, three yeas, 22 nays). Monzani at the time was a musician at the Pantheon and the Haymarket, so Solomon Davis perhaps was one of his colleagues.

Davis, Thomas *[fl. 1702], stroller.*

On 8 September 1702 the *Post Man* advertised that Thomas Davis and other strolling players were required to pay 2*s*. daily to town constables. The men named were also called mountebanks, and since the notice appeared in a London paper, they had probably appeared in the city.

Davis, Thomas *[fl. 1739–c. 1778], composer, instrumentalist?*

Thomas Davis was listed as one of the original subscribers, "being musicians," in the Declaration of Trust which established the Royal Society of Musicians on 28 August 1739. About the middle of the century he worked for the publisher Henry Waylett in Exeter Change. A number of songs composed by him, including several which were sung by Hemskirk at Sadler's Wells, were published between 1740 and 1760 and are listed in the *Catalogue of Printed Music in the British Museum*. Davis also published two sets of six solos for the German flute or violin, with a thorough bass for the harpsichord, about 1750 and about 1778.

Davis, Thomas *[fl. c. 1760–1768], watchman, dresser.*

In litigation concerning the Covent Garden managers in 1768, a Thomas Davis deposed that he had been employed at that theatre as "Watchman & Dresser for 8 ys or upwards."

Davis, Thomas Dibble *d. 1795, actor, manager.*

Thomas Dibble, who adopted the stage name of Davis, had a career of some 30 years on the London stage, mostly playing minor supporting roles in slight farces, comedies, and musical offerings. There is probably little truth in the statement by the author of *Theatrical Biography* (1785) that Davis once worked as a servant for Samuel Foote. It was a tale told about others as well.

Davis made his first appearance at Covent Garden as Cabinet in *The Funeral* on 20 October 1758. He next played Montano in *Othello* on 23 October, Fenton in *The Merry Wives of Windsor* on 31 October, and Brutus in *Coriolanus* on 2 November. During the remainder of the season he performed Hali in *Tamerlane*, Perdiccas in *The Rival Queens*, Philippo in *The Rover*, Le Beau in *As You Like It*, the Persian Ambassador in *The Prophetess*, Don Lewis in *She Wou'd and She Wou'd Not*, Selim in *The Mourning Bride*, the

Dauphin in *Henry V*, Belcour in *Wit Without Money*, Slango in *The Honest Yorkshireman*, a part in *The She Gallant*, Ratcliff in *Jane Shore*, Sofarino in *The Merchant of Venice*, Don Manuel in *Love Makes a Man*, Jack Stanmore in *Oroonoko*, Catesby in *Richard III*, and Jenkins in *The Knight*. For a benefit which he shared with Stoppelaer and Wignell on 17 May 1759, Davis acted Flash in *Miss in her Teens*. Davis appeared regularly in most of these roles throughout his years at Covent Garden.

In 1759–60, Davis added to his repertoire such roles as Arenthes in *Theodosius* and Don Duart in *Love Makes a Man*, the latter for his benefit with Wignell on 12 May 1760, when his share of profits amounted to £51 10s. In the following summer Davis joined Foote's company at the Haymarket. He made his first appearance there as Loader in the first performance of Foote's comedy *The Minor*, which opened on 28 June 1760 and continued for a total of 35 times. In the following season at Covent Garden, when his salary was 5s. a day, he played his role in *The Minor* numerous nights and also acted Chatillon in *King John* on 9 December 1760, Gayless in *The Lying Valet* on 8 January 1761, Townly in *The Married Libertine* on 28 January, Horatio in *The Wife's Relief*, Captain Briton in *The English Tars in America* on 30 March, and Friendly in *The School Boy* on 11 May. At his shared benefit on 5 May 1761 Davis took £75 2s. in ticket receipts. In that year *The Anti-Rosciad* wrote:

Davis the Critic views with scornful
    eyes,
And sneering, teaches others to despise;
Yet he in acting never gives offense,
But always rightly hits the poets' sense.

Davis was engaged at Covent Garden for every season through 1777–78, except during 1770–71 when he was in the north.

His salary in 1767–68 was 8s. 4d. per day. In the summer of 1765 he acted in the old theatre at Richmond (a new one was operating that summer as well) where he took a benefit on 17 August. Between 1763 and 1769 Davis acted regularly with Foote's summer company at the Haymarket, making his first appearance there as Bruin in *The Mayor of Garratt* on 20 June 1763. In that summer he also acted roles in *The Lyar* and *The Diversion of a Morning*, Young Wilding in *The Citizen*, Aimwell in *The Beaux' Stratagem*, and Carlos in *Love Makes a Man*. For Foote he played more substantial roles than were his lot during the regular seasons at Covent Garden, thus moving some poetaster to write in *Momus* (1767):

See D——e D——s better half the year
A Mere poltroon—a hero now appear!
Unnotic'd and obscure he struts un-
    known,
An utter stranger to the injur'd town,
Till F——te, his patron, impotent and
    wise,
At once convinces each beholder's eyes,
That merit oft beneath oppression dwells,
For see how D——s now himself ex-
    cells,
Aimwell, Cassio, nay, and many more,
Such parts were never acted so before,
And that my Muse may shew her mean-
    ing plain,
Hopes ne'er to see 'em murder'd so
    again.

In September 1770, Davis joined with Thomas Weston in the management of a theatre in Tooley Street, Southwark. The author of *Theatrical Biography* (1785) claimed that a performance they gave of *Richard III* was stopped in the middle by constables. During that fall Davis also acted several capital roles at the Haymarket (Aimwell on 27 September, Othello on 1 October for his benefit, Loader in *The Minor* on 15 October, and Pierre in *Venice Preserv'd* on 29 October), not for Foote, with whom he quarreled about this time, but apparently under his own temporary license. Instead of returning as usual to Covent Garden for the season of 1770–71, Davis went to play with Wilkinson's company at York. In the spring of 1771 he joined with Thomas Weston at Leeds, where the two "entered into a scheme of taragiging" (as Weston termed it in his *Memoirs*, 1776) which was an entertainment consisting of prologues, epilogues, and some detached scenes from plays and interludes, whereby they "got a few pounds." With the summer coming on and with the antagonism toward Foote now subsided, Davis returned to the Haymarket on 15 May 1771 to play Flash in *Miss in Her Teens* and to take on many of his usual summer roles. In the fall he returned to Covent Garden, where he stayed for another seven years at a pittance of £1 per week and also played at the Haymarket regularly in summer through 1782.

Francis Gentleman somewhat unkindly, but perhaps accurately, in *The Theatre* (1772) described Davis as a "sing-song man of little worth," who was too "feeble" for criticism and "a human ape." The last characterization was harsh, for except for a blemish in an eye, Davis was at this time in his life (perhaps about the age of 35) a handsome man, according to Tate Wilkinson. He did, however, have a disfiguring accident at the Haymarket later, about 1777; the *Morning Post* of 3 August 1781 stated that "It was not Captain Smith who perforated the Nose of Mr Davis a few years since at the Haymarket Theatre, but Mr Dubellamy." It was also in 1777 that Samuel Foote made a burlesque will, leaving among other things "his grace and elegant deportment to Mr Dibble Davis."

In 1779, without an engagement at a winter house, Davis occasionally took over the Haymarket, by permission of the Lord Chamberlain, for benefit performances and to provide a showcase for young talents who came forth after his instruction in act-ing. On 18 October 1779 he presented *The Busy Body*, in which he acted Sir George Airy for his own benefit. Several weeks later, on 13 November, he advertised in the *Gazeteer*:

Mr. Davis being employed to get up two Plays, avails himself of this method of offering any Lady or Gentleman (ambitious of displaying their talents in Comedy) an excellent opportunity of appearing before an audience, whose judgment will stamp a sanction on merit, that may probably be productive of extraordinary future advantages to the possessor. N.B. The first Comedy will be put in rehearsal the week after next—Falstaff's Wedding, written in imitation of Shakespeare, by the late ingenious Dr. Kenrick. Also a Tragi-Comi-Operatic-Pastoral Farce, called The Rival Milliners. A Gentleman, whose figure & deportment will suit the character of Falstaff & a Lady & Gentleman in the vocal way, are particularly wanted. . . . Apply to Mr Davis, at a Chymist's, No. 34, the corner of white-horse-yard, Stanhopestreet, near Clare-market, from twelve to eight.

Falstaff's Wedding was indeed performed on 27 December 1779, with Falstaff played by an unidentified "Gentleman, well known in the literary world, who has been prevailed upon by his Friends to make his [first] attempt on the stage." *The Rival Milliners* was the afterpiece, with Miss Evison making her first appearance in the role of Sukey Ogle and Miss Morris, who had sung the previous season at Ranelagh, as Mrs Cambrick. On 5 April 1780 Davis headed a cast of *A School for Ladies* which included two unidentified young ladies in their first appearances. In the following fall, Davis advertised in *The Morning Chronicle* (8 September 1781):

Since the loss of a Garrick, a Barry, a Mossop, or a Powell, there never was a theatrical period so unpromising as the present. This circumstance induces a veteran of the theatres Royal to offer his assistance to ladies & Gentleman, whose genius & inclination are ripe for an attempt in the Sock or Buskin. N.B.

Apply any day to MR. Thomas Davis, No. 24 (at a Chymist's) in Stanhope-street, near Clare-market, from Twelve at Noon, to Five in the Evening.

Wanted immediately, Six Ladies & Eight Gentlemen, to make their first appearance in a new Piece, to be represented shortly at a Theatre Royal. Likewise two young Ladies in the singing Line.

Instructions (as usual) on moderate terms.

Again in the *Morning Chronicle* on 22 September 1781 Davis urged "Ladies and Gentlemen . . . to be speedy in their application," inasmuch as he was preparing two new pieces. These, *The Spendthrift* and *The Romp*, were produced at the Haymarket on 12 November 1781, with a prologue spoken by Davis. In the *Memoirs of the Countess of Derby* (by "Scriptor Veritatis") published in 1797, the story is told of Davis's practice of allowing young ladies to play any character of their choice provided they would take up tickets for the performance at a goodly sum. One such young lady, the favorite of a colonel, took £50 in tickets for the liberty of playing for one night and then again paid £40 by a note for another night; but when her connection with the colonel was dissolved and the tickets could not be disposed of, Davis had her arrested—"which put a final check to her theatrical mania."

After his final summer engagement at the Haymarket in 1783, Davis made only two other appearances at that theatre: on 8 March 1784 as Heeltap in *The Mayor of Garratt* and on 30 September 1788 as Captain Loveit in *Miss in her Teens*. He then went into the provinces. He was at York in 1783–84. Probably he was the Mr "Davies" who acted at Birmingham in the summers of 1790 and 1791 and at Margate in 1792. Perhaps he was the Davis who performed in Lord Barrymore's private theatricals at Wargrave in 1791–92. By 1790, his fifth wife was a member of the Manchester company, but Davis himself seems not to have performed there, al-though another Mr Davis did. The *Manchester Mercury* for 2 November 1790 reported that "Mrs Davis, who performs the principal comic characters at our theatre, is not, as is generally supposed, the *Cara Sposa* of the gentleman who bears the same name with this our favourtie Thalia, but the wife of a celebrated comedian, who performed under the banners of Garrick, Foote, Barry, & the heroes of old."

In his later years Davis took to drink and whoring. Wilkinson lamented in 1795, after commenting on his younger and handsomer years, "but . . . o! ye gods! how fallen! how changed!" On Monday 22 September 1795 the *Manchester Mercury* reported "Sat. se'nnight [12 September 1795], died Mr Davis, husband of Mrs Davis, late of our theatre." He was, by the estimate of Wilkinson, about 60 years of age in that year and had been subsisting on the Covent Garden Theatrical Fund.

Thomas Dibble Davis had at least five wives. The first was the Elizabeth Dibble, listed as the mother of twin daughters, Elizabeth and Charlotte, by Thomas Dibble, who were baptized at St Paul, Covent Garden, on 25 May 1758, in the spring before Dibble began to act in London under the name of Davis. Was Elizabeth the Mrs Davis who acted Miss Biddy in *Miss in her Teens* at the Haymarket on 8, 13, 22 June and 4 July 1768 to Mr Davis's familiar role of Flash? She seems never to have acted again in London. The second wife acted in London as Miss Ann Ogilvie from 1767 to 1775. Davis married Susanna Sawyer, born Harrison, at St Clement Danes on 10 January 1773. She seems not to have acted. According to the Burney papers at the British Museum, Davis married yet another woman, unidentified, on 5 April 1778. She died on 13 January 1784. His fifth wife, as noted above, acted at Manchester from 1790 to 1792 and was at Covent Garden in 1792–93. For possible connections to people named Dibble, see Robert Dibble.

Among the many roles which Davis acted at Covent Garden, in addition to those mentioned above, were: an Officer and Bardolph in *1 Henry IV*, Prince John in *2 Henry IV*, Laertes in *Hamlet*, Seberto in *The Pilgrim*, Benvolio in *Romeo and Juliet*, Harlow in *The Old Maid*, Lord Rake in *The Provok'd Wife*, Rodolpho in *The Frenchify'd Lady Never in Paris*, Wormwood in *The Virgin Unmask'd*, Trueman in *Every Man in his Humour*, Rovewell in *The Upholsterer*, Richmond in *Richard III*, Albany in *King Lear*, Sanchio in *Rule a Wife and Have a Wife*, Cheatly in *The Squire of Alsatia*, Portius in *Cato*, Conrade in *Much Ado About Nothing*, Essex in *Prince John*, Hortensio in *Catherine and Petruchio*, Alberto in *A Duke and No Duke*, and the Governor in *The Author*. At the Haymarket he acted Prince Volscius in *The Rehearsal*, Young Loveit in *The Commissary*, Dick Rever in *The Patron*, Myrtle in *The Conscious Lovers*, Bernardo in *The Taylors*, Philip in *The Maid of Bath*, Dick in *The Apprentice*, Clerimont in *The Miser*, and parts in *The Nabob, The Orators, Madrigal and Truletta*, and *A Devil Upon Two Sticks*.

Davis, Mrs [Thomas Dibble the first? Elizabeth] [fl. *1758?–1768*], actress.

A Mrs Davis acted Miss Biddy in performances of *Miss in Her Teens* at the Haymarket Theatre on 8, 13, 22 June and 4 July 1768. Playing Flash in the same production was Thomas Dibble Davis (d. 1795). Probably this Mrs Davis was his first wife, the Elizabeth Davis named as the mother, by Thomas Dibble, of twin daughters Elizabeth and Charlotte who were baptized at St Paul, Covent Garden, on 25 May 1758. No other performances by her are known.

Davis, Mrs Thomas Dibble the second, Ann. *See* OGILVIE, ANN.

Davis, Mrs Thomas Dibble the fifth [fl. *1785–1813?*], actress.

Having become the fifth wife of Thomas Dibble Davis sometime after the death of his fourth wife in January 1784, Mrs Davis began her career on the stages at Reading, Margate, Liverpool, and Birmingham in the late 1780s. By 1790 she was playing principal comic characters in the Manchester company; on 2 November 1790 the *Manchester Mercury* identified her as "the wife of a celebrated comedian, who performed under the banners of Garrick, Foote, Barry, & the heroes of old." In the provinces she was "much approved," wrote Wilkinson, but she was "seduced from a good engagement" at Manchester to sign on at Covent Garden where she made her first appearance in the character of Priscilla Tomboy in *The Romp* on 10 March 1792. Identifying her as "the wife of a performer known by the name of Dibble Davis," the *European Magazine* (March 1792) stated that she "displayed talents which promise hereafter to afford considerable entertainment to the public. She was received with a great share of applause and had her second air encored." *Woodfall's Register* (12 March 1792) reported her debut at some length:

Mrs Davis, the Jordan of the Liverpool & Manchester Theatres . . . has happily continued to copy without servility of imitation, & to preserve the spirit unalloyed by the dross of vulgarity. She is a good figure for the Hoyden cast of character, has a clear youthful voice, a lively countenance, & a good deal of easy girlish action & deportment. . . . Mrs Davis kept up the spirit & vivacity of the scene ably, & in one or two incidental circumstances introduced some originality that told well. In her "Oh, how I long to be married!" her byplay with the supposed Baby was laughable, & her boxing Watty Cockney [Blanchard] round the stage and knocking him down, though rather a bold effort at novelty, was highly successful. She certainly is not equal to stand in competition with Mrs Jordan, but Mrs Davis may nevertheless fairly be pronounced a promising performer in the same cast of comic characters.

After this successful debut, Mrs Davis acted Miss Fuz in *A Peep Behind the Curtain* on 31 March and Sophia in *A Cure for a Coxcomb* on 15 May. She was probably the Mrs Davies who acted with her husband at Margate in the summer of 1792. She was re-engaged at Covent Garden for the next season. She acted Louisa in *The Irishman in London* on 1 October 1792 and sang in the choruses of *Macbeth* on 29 October and *Harlequin's Museum* on 31 December. On 2 January 1793 she acted Miss Neville in *She Stoops to Conquer* and on 25 January was Madge in *Love in a Village*. The *Thespian Magazine* (March 1793) wrote that she gave Margery all the innocent simplicity of the character without "o'erstepping the modesty of nature." She acted Melissa in *The Lying Valet* on 15 April. Several days later on 18 April, when Mrs Esten was too indisposed to play her character of Rosa in the first performance of Frederick Reynolds's comedy *How to Grow Rich*, Mrs Davis went on in the role after an apology was made to the audience. Although the house at first raised considerable objection, "Mrs Davis was well received in the part," said the *Thespian Magazine* (June 1793). Her last performance at Covent Garden was as Nancy in *The Pad* on 27 May 1793.

Her husband died in September 1795. In January 1796 the *Monthly Mirror* announced that Mrs Davis, "who performed two or three seasons back very prettily at Covent Garden," was a member of Stephen Kemble's company at Edinburgh. Possibly she was the Mrs Davis who acted at Richmond in the summers of 1796 and 1799. In the latter year, that Mrs Davis's address was given on a manuscript list of the Richmond company (now in the Richmond Reference Library) as No 7, Crown Court, Windmill Street. A Mrs Davis was acting at Edinburgh as late as 1812–13.

Davis, William *fl. 1685*, *singer.*

All that is known of William Davis is that on 23 May 1685 he was sworn a Gentleman of the Chapel Royal extraordinary—without fee until a position became vacant. Since no further mention was made of him in the Lord Chamberlain's accounts, he probably left the group soon after his appointment.

Davis, William *fl. 1789–1824*, *equestrian, manager.*

William Davis, who in the nineteenth century became a well-known circus and hippodrama entrepreneur, was performing feats of horsemanship at Astley's Amphitheatre, Westminster Bridge, as early as 1789. On 16 May of that year he exhibited "extraordinary exercises on two horses," with a child of seven. The exhibition was repeated throughout the summer. Davis offered similar exhibitions at Astley's regularly, sometimes with Taylor, Crossman, and Miss Smith, throughout the last decade of the eighteenth century. By 1797 he and Robert Handy had taken over Astley's Amphitheatre Royal in Dublin, but in December of that year Davis suffered a most severe loss. His wife Sarah and his infant daughter drowned with other members of the company and 20 horses when the packet *Viceroy*, out of Liverpool, went down in the Irish Sea on the way to Dublin.

Soon after, Davis returned to London to take over the management of the horse department at the Royal Circus. In an advertisement for a performance on 23 April 1798 he solicited the patronage of the public, for in addition to losing his wife and child, and his "whole troop and Horses, in which he was concerned, to the amount of £2000," he still had the burden of "a large Family, depending solely on his Industry." He pledged to provide "entirely *New Equestrian Performances* as cannot fail giving universal Satisfaction." In 1799 Davis joined with Handy, William Parker,

Harvard Theatre Collection

WILLIAM DAVIS, as the Georgian Chief
engraving by Scott, after Cooper

George Smith, John Crossman, and Richard Johannot in a partnership to perform in temporary circuses throughout the three kingdoms. The younger Charles Dibdin, in their employ at the time, related in his *Memoirs* the travels of the company and their performances at a temporary circus erected in Union Place, Liverpool.

Davis was back at London in 1800 directing the horsemanship at the New Royal Circus. For performances in that season of *The Magic Flute, or Harlequin Champion*, Davis had "taught the noble 'Horse Turk' to rear up, seize hold of, and tear down a streaming banner from the ramparts, during the representation of a grand tournament in the opening scene."

When Astley's Amphitheatre, which had burned down in September 1803, was rebuilt and opened again in 1804, Davis and his partners of 1797 (except Johannot) took over half interest in it, with the other half remaining in the hands of John Astley. Although Davis sometimes was found else-where, such as at the Royal Circus, St George's Fields, in 1809, or at the Cirque Olympique in Paris in 1817, he spent most of his remaining career as master of the horses at Astley's.

In the summer of 1821, Davis performed the role of the King's Champion in Elliston's coronation spectacle at Drury Lane. In a maneuver which the *Times* (2 August) proclaimed as "one of the most superb *scenes* ever exhibited in a theatre," the King's retinue appeared on horseback during the representation of the traditional banquet at Westminster Hall. The horses were "admirably managed," reported the *Morning Herald* (19 July), "especially the Champion's, which backed out down the narrow platform across the pit as rapidly and dexterously as though he had been going head foremost."

When all of his partners were gone or retired in 1817 Davis became joint partner with John Astley. On 19 October 1821 Astley died, and Davis was faced with the problem of helping the widow, Hannah Astley, meet debts amounting to some £8000. He changed the name of the establishment to Davis's Royal Amphitheatre, and as sole proprietor of the horses managed the enterprise until 1824 when his lease expired. Litigation against Mrs Astley earlier in 1822 had given him two years of grace with his licence, but, unable to remove the widow from an interest in the licence, he left the establishment and was succeeded as master of the equestrian performances there by Andrew Ducrow.

During his time at Astley's, William Davis had introduced such innovations as real fox chasing, horse racing, and large-scale military operations in numerous pieces such as *Tom and Jerry, The High Mettled Racer, Alexander the Great and Thalestris the Amazon,* and *The Battle of Waterloo.* (For an account of these and other equestrian spectaculars, see Arthur H. Saxon, *Enter Foot and Horse* [New Haven, 1968].)

William Davis's wife, Sarah, who drowned in 1797, had been an actress at Drury Lane. The female child of seven who performed with Davis in 1789 may have been theirs. The child who was baptized at St Paul, Covent Garden, on 4 July 1787, as Jane, daughter of William and Sarah Davies (*sic*), was probably also their daughter. Presumably one of these daughters was the Miss Davis who was a colombine at Astley's in the nineteenth century and married the musician and music publisher, Montague Corri (1784–1849), about 1817.

A colored print of Davis as the Georgian Chief in *Timour the Tartar*, drawn by Cooper and engraved by Scott, was published on 1 August 1822.

Davis, Mrs William, Sarah *d. 1797, actress, singer.*

Sarah Davis, the wife of the equestrian William Davis (fl. 1789–1824), was engaged at Drury Lane for three seasons,

1789–92, at a salary of £1 10s. per week. Her first billed appearance was as Dolly Trull in *The Beggar's Opera* on 24 September 1789. On 13 November 1789 she had a choral role in the ballad opera *The Island of St Marguerite,* which was performed a total of 28 times that season, and on 26 December 1789 she sang a similar role in *Harlequin's Frolicks,* which was performed 22 times. In 1790–91 she again sang in *The Island of St Marguerite,* and in 1791–92 she played a priestess in *The Cave of Trophonius* on 15 October and sang a part in *Dido, Queen of Carthage* on 23 May 1792. In 1792 she subscribed 10s. 6d. to the Drury Lane fund; in a postscript to the fundbook Winston identified her as the Mrs Sarah Davis who "drowned." She was at Liverpool in 1793 and at Astley's with her husband in 1795; on 22 August of the latter year she played a haymaker in a performance of *Harlequin Invincible* at Astley's. On 11 November 1795 she signed her full name to a paper subscribed by performers at Astley's.

Sarah Davis and her infant daughter drowned when the packet *Viceroy,* on the way to Dublin from Liverpool, went down in the Irish Sea in December 1797. For information on her children, see her husband's entry.

Davis, William ₍fl. 1794₎, *singer.*

A William Davis, of Green Church Yard, St Catharine's, was listed in 1794 in Doane's *Musical Directory* as a bass singer and a participant in the Handelian performances in Westminster Abbey.

Davison, Mr ₍fl. 1788₎, *actor.*

A Mr Davison performed Pierrot in Delpini's new pantomime *What You Please* at Hughes's Royal Circus on 23 August 1788.

Davison, Mary ₍fl. 1718?–1725₎, *actress.*

Fitzgerald in his *New History* cited a

notice from the Drury Lane managers to John Rich at Lincoln's Inn Fields which said that they had hired Mrs Mary Davison in January 1718 (possibly an error for 1719). They presumably would not have felt such a note necessary unless Mrs (or Miss?) Davison had been working for Rich up until then. She was probably the "Mrs Davidson" who played several parts at Drury Lane in the summer of 1723, according to first editions of several of the works concerned: Cleora in *Sir Thomas Overbury*, Lady Elizabeth in *Henry VI*, Dogood in *A Wife to be Let*, and Beatrice in *The Impertinent Lovers*. A Miss Davison shared a benefit at Drury Lane on 20 May 1724, and she too, was probably Mary. A Mrs Davison acted the Distressed Woman in *A Duke and No Duke* on 4 July 1724 at Richmond, and a Miss Davison shared a benefit at Drury Lane on 17 May 1725. Probably all the references given here are to the same woman, Mary Davison.

Davits, Mary. *See* DAVIS, MARY.

Davy, Master [*fl.* 1741], *dancer.*

A Master Davy, announced as one who had never appeared on any stage before, danced at Goodman's Fields Theatre on 9 April 1741 for the benefit of his dancing master, Lanyon.

Davy, John 1763–1824, *composer, instrumentalist.*

The composer John Davy was born at Creedy Bridge in the parish of Upton Helion, eight miles from Exeter, on 23 December 1763 and was baptized on Christmas Day. The illegitimate son of Sarah Davie or Davy, he was cared for by his mother's brother, a village blacksmith who also played violoncello. At a very early age Davy revealed a remarkable precocity in music. At the age of three, according to his obituary in the *Gentleman's Magazine*

(March 1824), Davy was able to produce tunes on the violoncello.

By the age of five, having been attracted to the fifes played by soldiers quartered at Crediton, a nearby town, Davy soon taught himself several tunes on that instrument, "which he played very decently." The story is told that when he was about six he took 20 to 30 horseshoes from a neighboring smith, and when he was apprehended by the smith it was discovered that the boy had selected eight horseshoes to form an octave, "had suspended each of them by a single cord clear from the wall, and, with a small iron rod, was amusing himself by imitating the Crediton chimes which he did with great exactness."

Soon Davy's musical gift attracted the attention of James Carrington, rector of Upton Helion, who introduced him to the harpsichord. Through Carrington the lad was taken into the patronage of the Rev Mr Richard Eastcott (d. 1828), of Exeter, amateur composer and music historian who later recounted many of Davy's remarkable early accomplishments in his *Sketches of the Origin, Progress, and Effects of Music* (Bath 1793). Upon the recommendation of Eastcott, in 1765, at the age of 12, Davy was articled as apprentice to Dr William Jackson, organist of Exeter Cathedral.

Under Jackson's tutelage the lad made excellent progress in the study of composition and also became an "admirable performer" on the organ, violin, viola, and violoncello. Upon completion of his studies, Davy continued to reside for some years at Exeter, teaching and composing. He also took up amateur acting and played Zanga in *The Revenge*. Playing Alonzo was William Dowton (1764–1851), then an apprentice to an architect in Exeter, but later to become a leading actor in London and America.

Another Exeter friend was Charles Incledon (1763–1826), who was in the cathedral choir under Dr Jackson, and who became one of the chief singing stars of

Harvard Theatre Collection

JOHN DAVY
artist unknown

Covent Garden Theatre in the 1790s. Davy moved to London to take up a position as violinist which Incledon had obtained for him in the Covent Garden orchestra in the season of 1790–91. In London he also attracted a considerable number of music students. Later in the decade, however, he seems to have given up both activities of teaching and playing when his engagements to supply the theatres with musical compositions became more frequent and more lucrative. He composed music for some 22 burlettas, pantomimes, and ballets between 1796 and 1821. His earliest stage work was for *A Pennyworth of Wit, or The Wife and the Mistress*, a burletta by T. J. Dibdin which was performed on 18 April 1796 at Sadler's Wells. At the same house several years later, on 4 June 1798, Davy provided the music for *Alfred the Great*, a "grand historical ballet of action." At Covent Garden on 5 June 1800 his song "The Fox, Stag, and Hare," with

lyrics by T. J. Dibdin, was sung by Incledon at the end of Act II of *Lovers' Vows*. He wrote the overture and all the music for *What a Blunder!*, a three-act comic opera by J. G. Holman which was first performed at the Haymarket on 14 August 1800. A list of his music for nineteenth-century productions may be found in Grove.

Davy's *Six Quartets for Voices* and *Twelve Favourite Songs* were published between 1790 and 1795. His *Charming Kitty*, sung by Incledon at Vauxhall, was printed about 1790. Other published songs include *Crazy Jane*, sung by Mrs Mountain (1799?), and *The Fight is o'er, the Battle won: An Occasional Glee and Chorus on Admiral Nelson's Victory* (1799). He also wrote an "Ode for the Anniversary of Nelson's Victory and Death" which was performed at Covent Garden on 21 November 1806. Manuscripts of his music are in the British Museum.

His last work for the theatre consisted of incidental music, composed with others, for Frederic Reynolds's version of *The Tempest* at Covent Garden in 1821. In his later years Davy fell into drink and debt, became infirm, and died in penury at miserable lodgings in May's Buildings, St Martin's Lane, on 22 February 1824. His burial in St Martin's churchyard on 28 February was paid for by two London tradesmen, one of whom, a Mr Thomas, was a native of Crediton.

A portrait of John Davy by an anonymous engraver was published by T. Williams.

Daw, Miss [*fl.* 1760–1768], *dancer.*

A Miss Daw (sometimes Dawes) was a member of the dancing corps at Covent Garden from 1760–61, when her salary was £1 per week, through at least 1767–68, when her salary was £1 6s. per week. Her first billed appearance was for dancing in *Comus* on 11 December 1760. In that season she also performed as a follower of

Ceres in *The Rape of Proserpine* and in a new comic ballet, *The Hungarian Gambols*, pieces she continued to appear in throughout her stay at Covent Garden. She received £6 16s. in shared benefit tickets on 17 April 1761. For her shared benefit on 17 April 1762 she danced a hornpipe for the first time. Other pieces for which her name appeared on the bills included *Apollo and Daphne* (first time on 28 January 1762), *Thomas and Sally* (first on 12 October 1763), *The Beggar's Opera* (first on 3 November 1764), and *Harlequin Doctor Faustus* (first on 18 November 1766).

Dawe, William (fl. 1792–1795), carpenter, sceneman.
William Dawe received regular payments of £1 4s. per week as an extra carpenter or sceneman at Drury Lane between 11 October 1792 and 17 October 1795. He also seems to have been in charge of the scenemen. Perhaps the Mrs Dawes who was a canvas worker at the same theatre in 1799 was his wife.

Dawes. *See also* **DAW.**

Dawes, Mr (fl. 1791–1792), singer.
A Mr Dawes sang in the chorus at Covent Garden in 1791–92. His name appeared in the bills for Gluck's *Orpheus and Eurydice* on 28 February and 6 and 13 March 1792.

Dawes, Mrs (fl. 1777–1779), actress.
At China Hall, Rotherhithe, in the summer of 1777, a Mrs Dawes acted Calista in *The Fair Penitent* on 18 June and the title role in *Jane Shore* on 25 June. In the following spring at the Haymarket she acted Aura (with the original epilogue) in *The Country Lasses* and a role in *All the World's a Stage* on 29 April 1778 and Fanny in *The Clandestine Marriage* on the following day. No doubt she was the person who, billed as "A Young Lady," acted

Juliet at Covent Garden on 19 April 1779, although this was said to be her first appearance on the stage. She was identified as Mrs Dawes—"who performed the part of Juliet last season at Covent Garden"—by the *Kentish Gazette* on 19 June and 3 July 1779 when she acted Lady Teazle in *The School for Scandal* at Canterbury.

Dawes, Mrs (fl. 1799), canvas worker.
According to Cecil Price in *The Letters of Richard Brinsley Sheridan*, a Mrs Dawes was a canvas worker at Drury Lane in 1799. Perhaps she was the wife of William Dawe, a carpenter and sceneman at the same theater in the 1790s.

Dawson, Mr d. 1748, actor.
Mr Dawson played Worcester in *1 Henry IV* on 25 September 1733 at Goodman's Fields and then switched to Covent Garden to act Duncan in *Macbeth* on 11 October, Nestor in *Troilus and Cressida* on 20 December, and Cleon in *Timon of Athens* on 28 March 1734. He acted Pedro's Ghost in *Don John* on 24 August at Bartholomew Fair. He may have stayed active in the London theatres in the years that followed, but his name did not appear in any bills. On 13 April 1748, the prompter Richard Cross recorded the following in his diary: "Dawson & —— fought in Long Field ye first kill'd on ye spot."

Dawson, Mr (fl. 1767), billsticker. *See* **DAWSON, RICHARD.**

Dawson, Mr (fl. 1776–1782), tumbler, ropedancer.
A Mr Dawson was with Astley's company at the Birmingham Theatre on 27 and 30 December 1776 performing "Several curious and uncommon feats of activity on the slack rope." He was to be found at Astley's Amphitheatre in London several times in 1777 and in a tumbling act, part

of an exhibition called the "Theatre of Florence," on at least eight dates in July, September, and October 1780. The scattered bills for Astley's company show him to have performed several times again in the summer and fall (the latest date being 2 November) in 1782, both as tumbler and "stiff rope dancer."

Dawson, Mr ₍fl. 1789–1797₎, *actor.*
The Mr Dawson who played Davy in *Bon Ton* at a specially licensed winter performance of the Haymarket (usually dark at that season) on 23 February 1789 may have been the Dawson who was Puff in *Miss in Her Teens* at a similar performance at the same theatre on 6 February 1792. He may also have been the Dawson who was Lucius in *Cato* and Sir Jasper Wilding in *The Citizen* on 4 December 1797, also at the Haymarket.

A Mr Dawson, conceivably the subject of this entry, was playing at Limerick on 22 November 1790 and 18 March 1791 and at Cork on 26 April and 28 May 1791.

Dawson, Miss ₍fl. 1779–1782₎, *actress, singer.*
On 5 April 1779 a Miss Dawson sang at Sadler's Wells. She was most likely the same Miss Dawson who appeared as Lucy in *An Adventure in St James's Park* on 21 January 1782 at the Haymarket Theatre.

Dawson, Nancy c. 1730?–1767, *dancer.*
According to the contemporary *Authentic Memoirs of the Celebrated Miss Nancy D——ws——n* [1761?] and the entry on her in *The Dictionary of National Biography,* Nancy Dawson was born about 1730, "within a musket shot of Claremarket." She was reported to be the daughter of one Emmanuel Dawson, who "exercised the compound occupation of pimp and porter," and his wife, who "amused herself with selling greens, &c." The mother died, according to the legend,

Harvard Theatre Collection

NANCY DAWSON

engraving by Watson, after Spooner

when Nancy was a child, and her father ran off somewhere. The *Authentic Memoirs,* however, are sketchy at best, imaginative in many instances, deficient in fact, and ultimately must be regarded as a volume concocted to take advantage of colorful Nancy's popularity. Her will, which was proved at London on 6 June 1767, and is presumably a more reliable document, identifies her father as William Newton, staymaker, then of Martlett Court in the parish of St Paul, Covent Garden, and her mother as Eleanor Newton. She gave her own name as Ann Dawson, "of King Street in the Parish of Saint George the Martyr . . . but now of Averstock Hill in the Parish of Hampstead." Her mother and father, then, were alive at Nancy's death, and her bequests to them in her will indicate the family was not estranged.

The story that Nancy found herself cast

out on her own resources at the age of 16 probably is another fabrication. In his *Book for a Rainy Day*, J. T. Smith wrote he had been informed "that Nancy, when a girl, set up skittles at a tavern in High Street, Marylebone." According to the author of the *Authentic Memoirs*, by the age of 16 she worked her way into the company of a Mr Griffin, the master of a puppet show, who taught her to dance. She was befriended by a figure dancer at Sadler's Wells Theatre who, smitten by her, solicited an invitation for her to join the Sadler's Wells company, where the novelty of her dancing soon made her a favorite of the town. In her second summer season there she was promoted to the role of Columbine. According to *The Dictionary of National Biography* and *The Dramatic History of Master Edward, Miss Ann, and Others*, in the following winter (1757–58) she made her first appearance at Covent Garden, under the auspices of Ned Shuter. Such a chronology of events, if she was 16 when she joined Griffin, would place her birth year at about 1739. The *Authentic Memoirs*, however, claim that after her second season at Sadler's Wells, she appeared as a figure dancer at Drury Lane, "where she remained about three or four seasons, . . . little known, or taken notice of, beyond the neighbouring bawdy-houses, taverns, and whores lodgings; but during the summer she as usual, plied at Sadler's Wells." Then, according to the *Authentic Memoirs*, she made her appearance at Covent Garden. Such a chronology would first place her with Sadler's Wells about 1752 and with Griffin about 1751; if she was 16 when she joined the latter, her birth year would have been about 1735. Unavailability of early bills for Sadler's Wells prevents any resolution on her tenure at that theatre, but the Drury Lane bills do not reveal her name at any time before her first engagement at Covent Garden.

What can be verified, however, is the first notice of her name in the Covent Garden bills on 1 February 1758, when she was one of numerous dancers in the revival of Betterton's dramatic opera *The Prophetess*, a piece she continued to dance in many times throughout the remainder of the season. On 22 May 1758 she was billed for dancing a hornpipe, and from a benefit which she shared with nine other performers she received £20 16s. With other dancers she performed a comic ballet on 22 April.

During the following season at Covent Garden Nancy remained an obscure chorus dancer in productions of *The Prophetess* and other pieces. On 16 May 1759 when she shared a benefit with Mrs Jansolien and Miss Dulies she danced a hornpipe at the end of *The Spanish Fryar*. Early in the next season Mr Miles, who danced the hornpipe in the thieves' dance of *The Beggar's Opera*, fell ill and presented Nancy with the opportunity all young performers dream about. Her name replaced Miles's in the bill for 12 October 1759 – "by Desire, a Hornpipe by Miss Dawson" – and from that moment her professional reputation was assured. Within days she became "vastly celebrated, imitated, and followed by everyone," and appeared regularly throughout the season in her specialty act. Although Nancy's dancing has usually been credited for the long and crowded run of *The Beggar's Opera* that season at Covent Garden, more likely the performance of Charlotte Brent (later Mrs Pinto) in the role of Polly was the real drawing card. But the combination of Nancy and Miss Brent hurt the rival theatre and supposedly made Garrick turn serious thoughts to the idea of a continental vacation. Nancy made her first speaking appearance as the Princess in the droll *The English Sailors in America* on 20 March 1760, for the benefit of the author of the piece, Ned Shuter, with whom she had formed a happy domestic alliance. For her own benefit, which she shared with Collins on 29

April 1760 (taking about £114 as her moiety), she played Colombine in *Harlequin Statue* and, of course, offered her hornpipe.

The tune of the hornpipe by means of which Nancy Dawson danced into fame and upon which she traded for the remainder of her career became a popular household tune of the day. Goldsmith gave it a degree of immortality by mentioning it in the epilogue to *She Stoops to Conquer* and another dramatist, Alexander Dow, spread its fame as far off as India. On 3 December 1769, Dow wrote to Garrick from Bombay, where he was in the service of the East India Company, that "Instead of invoking the Tragic Muse . . . I am employed in teaching puppets to dance, (sad falling off!) *to the tune of Nancy Dawson.*" The tune has taken its place in the repertory of English folk music and still is sung in the nursery as "Here we go round the Mulberry Bush." As with most popular ballads many different versions of the

Folger Shakespeare Library

NANCY DAWSON's hornpipe

words were in circulation. These were rarely printed, but several have survived. An eight-stanza version was printed in her *Authentic Memoirs* and some years later in *The Vocal Magazine, or Compleat British Songster* (1781) (number II, p. 67):

Of all the girls in our town,
The black, the fair, the red, the brown,
That dance and prance it up and
   down,
 There's none like Nancy Dawson!

Her easy mien, her shape so neat,
She foots, she trips, she looks so sweet,
Her ev'ry motion's so complete
 I die for Nancy Dawson!

See how she comes to give surprise,
With joy and pleasure in her eyes;
To give delight she always tries,
 So means my Nancy Dawson.

Was there no task t'obstruct the way,
No Shuter droll, nor house so gay,
A bet of fifty pounds I'll lay,
 That I gain'd Nancy Dawson.

See how the Op'ra takes a run,
Exceeding Hamlet, Lear, or Lun,
Though in it there would be no fun
 Was't not for Nancy Dawson.

The Beard and Brent charm ev'ry
   night,
And female Peachum's justly right,
And Filch and Lockit please the sight,
 'Tis crown'd by Nancy Dawson.

See Little Davy strut and puff —
'P—— on the Op'ra and such stuff,
My house is never full enough,
 A curse on Nancy Dawson!'

Though Garrick he has had his day,
And forc'd the town his laws t'obey,
Now Johnny Rich is come in play,
 With help of Nancy Dawson.

Another four-stanza version was printed at the bottom of a pirated copy of the picture of Nancy Dawson which had been engraved and published by M. Jackson:

Come all ye bucks and bloods so grim,
Who love the rowling hornpipe trim,
Behold how Nancy moves each limb —
 The charming Nancy Dawson.

How easily she trips the stage!
Her heaving breasts all eyes engage,
Love's fire she can best assuage —
 O charming Nancy Dawson!

Yet vainly she each breast alarms
With all love's hoard of heavenly
   charms;
She's only for N—d S——r's arms —
 The smiling Nancy Dawson.

Tho' Poitier treads the passive air
And Baker's always debonair,
Yet none with Nancy can compare —
 The charming Nancy Dawson.

Credit for the composition of *The Ballad of Nancy Dawson* has commonly been given to that whimsical and eccentric character, George Alexander Stevens, the author and actor who is best remembered for his "Lecture on Heads." The facts that Stevens was the author of many of the popular tunes and lyrics of the day and that he was also responsible for *The Dramatic History of Master Edward Shuter, Miss Ann, and Others* make the attribution reasonable. Probably Stevens did prepare some of the better-known lyrics, although none will be found in his published works. The music, however, seems to have been written by the eminent theatrical composer, Dr Thomas Augustine Arne. The Harvard Theatre Collection holds an invoice in the holograph of Arne to Jonathan Tyers, the proprietor of Vauxhall Gardens, "for Compositions this Summer." This invoice lists a charge of £3 3s. for a catch "Call'd Nancy Dawson in 3 vocal parts, besides Instruments." The document is dated "Augst-ye-28th" — but lacks the year. There is no record that Nancy herself performed at Vauxhall, but perhaps she did. If not, Arne probably wrote the music to capitalize on her growing reputation and then she took it over as a professional trademark. Or he may simply have put down an arrangement of the tune whch was already in the public domain. As Nancy's reputation increased various sets of lyrics were applied, but there is no evidence that Nancy herself ever sang as she danced. Other performers at the theatres and pleasure gardens may have offered the lyrics in parody. The attribution of the composition to Arne was firmly established, it would seem, when the tune found its way into *Love in a Village*, which was first performed on 8 December 1762 at Covent Garden, with a musical pastiche of the compositions of at least twelve composers, including many by Arne. In the music, published after the performance, may be found, in a portion of a medley which was credited on the printed page to Arne, the familiar tune of "Here we go round the Mulberry Bush," in a somewhat more sophisticated rendering than the simple ditty to which it has been reduced. The role of the housemaid who sang the medley in *Love in a Village* was not created by Nancy Dawson, who was now at the rival house, but by Miss Davies. In the latter part of this 1762–63 season, however, Nancy accompanied Shuter to Ireland for an engagement at the Crow Street Theatre, where she danced a double hornpipe with Slingsby in a production of *Love in a Village*, certainly to Arne's tune with her name. (For a more extensive discussion of *The Ballad of Nancy Dawson* and its possible connection to the Shakespeare Jubilee of 1769, see K. A. Burnim, "Here We Go Round the Mulberry Bush," *Restoration and 18th Century Theatre Research*, November 1965.)

After a three-year engagement at Covent Garden, Nancy was induced, in a typical flanking action by Garrick against his com-

Permission of the Provost and Fellows of Worcester College, Oxford

NANCY DAWSON
artist unknown

petition, to defect to Drury Lane by the offer of a higher salary. She made her first appearance there with her hornpipe in Act III of *The Beggar's Opera* on 23 September 1760. Her hornpipe was billed regularly at Drury Lane in 1760–61, and she also performed in the dances incident to *The Enchanter*, a new musical entertainment by Garrick which was first given on 13 December 1760. For her benefit on 16 April 1761 in the presence of the Tripoline ambassador she gave her hornpipe and a new comic dance called *The May Day Morning, or Fingalian Lass*. In the summer of 1761 she joined Shuter and Grimaldi in Lee's company at Winchester. Nancy danced at Drury Lane for three more seasons. In 1761–62 she offered a new hornpipe in *Harlequin's Invasion* on 5 September, played a character in *Fortunatus* on 3 November, and danced in the masque in Act II of *Cymbeline* on 28 November. For her benefit on 1 May 1762 she performed the country girl in a new comic dance called *The May Day Frolic*. In 1762–63 she appeared regularly in *Fortunatus* and the comic dance *The Flemish Feast*. On 4 May 1763 she and Walker performed a double hornpipe for the first time. In the season of 1763–64 she danced in the new pantomime of *The Rites of Hecate* on 26 December 1763. After one more time, on 27 December, her name was dropped from the company of dancers in subsequent performances of the piece, never to reappear.

What led to this premature retirement from the stage is not known. There is the possibility she was already suffering from whatever caused her death some four years later. She re-drew a will, made at some prior date, on 24 May 1767. The dates of 26 or 27 May 1767 often given by biographers for her death are incorrect and are based on a premature obituary notice in the *Gentleman's Magazine* for May 1767. Actually, she died on 9 June 1767 at Haverstock Hill; the date is confirmed by Reed's "Notitia Dramatica" in the British Museum and the burial register of St George the Martyr, Bloomsbury. She was buried on 12 June 1767 in the grounds belonging to that church behind the Foundling Hospital, and a notice to that effect appeared in the *Public Advertiser* on 16 June. According to several nineteenth-century sources, the inscription on her headstone supposedly consisted of eight lines of a disreputable ditty commencing "Nancy Dawson was a Whore," and a rector had the stone turned down flat, with the inscription underneath, so as not to offend those who used the grounds for pleasant walks. A visit to the burial ground (now

known as St George's Gardens), however, will dispel the legend. The stone, a very large pylon, still stands. In 1932 the simple inscription "NANCY DAWSON" could still be made out, but all traces of it have completely worn away since. The size of the monument and its prominence in the burial ground evoke interesting queries about Nancy's later years and alliances.

In her will, proved at London on 26 June 1767, she identified herself as Ann Dawson of King Street in the parish of St George the Martyr "but now of Averstock Hill in the Parish of Hampstead." To her father, named as William Newton, staymaker, of Martlett Court, Covent Garden, she left a suit of mourning or £20 in lieu thereof and a mourning ring. To her mother Eleanor Newton she bequeathed her clothes. To her brother William Newton she gave £50, a pair of stone buckles, and a mourning ring, and to his wife Bridgett Newton she left £5 or a suit of mourning. Her niece Elizabeth Newton—if she behaved herself "in a prudent decent and sober manner" and married a good character—was to receive some clothing, "all my ornamental China belonging to the Glasses in both my parlours only together with one Blue Bed," some furniture, a clothes press, and three small chairs from Nancy's house in King Street. (The fact that Nancy had a furnished house in King Street but spent her last days at Haverstock Hill suggests that she may have died in a hospital.) Should the niece not live up to her aunt's expectations, the money from the sale of the aforesaid goods would be given to Nancy's nephew William Newton.

Other bequests included a mourning ring to John Walker, a diamond ring to Mrs Walker, a mourning ring and suit to her friend Mrs Lee of Martlett Court, and some clothes and a ring to her servant Hannah Sidebottom. William Ireland, a japanner, and Robert Allen, a merchant, were named as executors. The will informs that her niece Elizabeth Newton had been regularly bound to her for seven years as an apprentice and Nancy requested that she be turned over to a good master for the remainder of the apprenticeship. This information and the fact that her executors were in trade suggest that Nancy may also have spent her years since leaving the stage in some mercantile activity. Nancy also left a mourning ring to Edward Shuter, whose mistress she had been. Finally, she asked to be buried at St George the Martyr in a grey coffin with white nails and plumes. No mention was made in her will of any husband or children of her own which could support Sir William Musgrave's statement in his "Adversaria," in the British Museum, that "Nancy Dawson was the wife of a publican near Kelso, on the borders of Scotland."

In her day Nancy had a reputation for a shrewish temper and was said to be "heartless and mercenary, and of notoriously immoral life." In his *The Meretriciad* (1761), Edward Thompson included her among the notorious women of the Town and wrote unflattering verses about her and Shuter. She was a person of beauty and grace—"extremely agreeable in her figure"—as her portraits testify. A painting by an unknown artist of "Nancy Dawson, dancing her celebrated Hornpipe" was part of the *Mathews Gallery* (1833) and is presumably the oil now at the Garrick Club which depicts her in straw hat, with one hand on hip and the other raised. A mezzotint similar to this painting was done by M. Jackson, another version was published by R. Sayer, and a third version, with two small figures in the background, by an anonymous engraver, was printed for George Pulley at Rembrandt's Head, Fleet Street, with the verses beginning "Come all ye bucks" which are cited above. A portrait in oils by an unknown artist which depicts a dancer standing full-length and holding a scarf across her skirt is in the Library of Worcester College, Oxford, and is probably

of Nancy. A portrait painted and engraved by C. Spooner showing her leaning on a balustrade was published by R. Sayer; a copy of the Spooner picture was engraved by Watson and was published by J. Bowles. According to J. S. Udal (*Notes and Queries*, 3 July 1915), a colored portrait of Nancy Dawson used to hang in the orderly room of the old Inns of Court Rifle Volunteers in New Square in the 1870s and the regimental air bore her name—"and an excellent one it was to march to, I remember, though I cannot say it reminded me of the tune of the old children's game of 'Here we go round the mulberry bush'." The words of the Nancy Dawson song *Of all the girls in our town* were printed in 1760. A volume entitled *Nancy Dawson's Jests: To Which is Added the Merry Hornpipe; Being a Collection of Songs written for the Delight and Amusement of all her Admirers* was printed for J. Seymour in 1761. A handsome issue of *Dance Perspectives* (volume 26, Summer 1966) is devoted to Nancy Dawson; it includes a printing of the *Authentic Memoirs*.

Dawson, Nancy [*fl.* 1785], *dancer.*
Surviving bills for three performances (on 6 June, in late July, and on 1 August 1785) at Astley's Amphitheatre mention dancing by a Nancy Dawson—twice in a minuet with two horses.

Dawson, Richard [*fl.* 1739–1766], *house servant.*
A number of references to a Mr Dawson in the middle of the eighteenth century probably pertain to Richard Dawson the house servant. The will of musician Henry Symonds, dated 6 March 1739, was witnessed by Richard Dawson, and in 1748 he was an executor of musician William Corbett's will. He may have been the Mr Dawson who received shared benefits at Drury Lane on 4 May 1752 and 17 May 1753. Dawson handled tickets for the King's Theatre benefits for decayed musicians on

30 April 1753 and 6 April 1758. For these concerts, tickets could be had "of Richard Dawson at his house near Henry VII's Chapel, Westminster, who is empowr'd by the [Royal] Society [of Musicians] to deliver them and to receive the subscriptions." A British Museum manuscript names a Mr Dawson as the first gallery officekeeper at Covent Garden in 1766. Arthur Murphy's list of Covent Garden employees on 14 September 1767 has one Dawson, a billsticker, down for 2s. daily salary; this would seem quite a falling off for Richard Dawson. Perhaps that person was Richard's son.

Day, Mr (fl. 1742), *dancer.*

Mr Day danced the *Drunken Man* at the playhouse in James Street on 31 May 1742.

Day, Mr (fl. 1759–1761), *pyrotechnist.*

On 11 April 1761 Mr Day was paid £8 8s. for fireworks which he handled for 56 performances of *The Rape* between 1 March 1759 and 4 April 1761. His fee was 3s. per night.

Day, Mrs 1737–1793. *See* **WEBB, MRS RICHARD.**

Day, Mrs (fl. 1744), *singer.*

Mrs Day made her first (and only?) appearance on any stage singing at the New Wells in May Fair on 16 February 1744.

Day, Charles (fl. 1767), *house servant?*

Throughout the fall and early winter of 1767 Mrs Jane Lessingham, the mistress of Thomas Harris, one of the patentees of Covent Garden Theatre, struggled with her rival Mrs Mary Ann Yates over the possession of a certain dressing room. According to a contemporary manuscript in the British Museum, describing a climactic scene in the dispute, on or about 31 December 1767 "about 40 people," adherents of the Lessingham party, overcame the Yates faction and in the process "took Charles Day out of Mrs. Lessingham's dressing room feet foremost." Day seems to have been of the theatre but his function is not known.

Day, [George?] (fl. 1762?–1799?), *actor.*

The "gentleman" who had "never appeared on any stage" before he took the part of Pierre in *Venice Preserv'd* at Covent Garden Theatre on 4 December 1762 is not identified by *The London Stage.* But he was a Mr Day, according to the *Theatrical Review* of January 1763. The critic was severe:

This gentleman, like too many of our spouting Icarus's, disdaining the inferior rank of characters, and aspiring to the superior, had, we would hope, utterly dissipated all his air-built expectations of future theatrical eminence. In a word, as Mr. Day is no doubt qualified for many other professions, it is with the utmost friendship, that we would advise him to think no more of one, which he has already experienced to be so very arduous and uncertain.

Faulkner's Dublin Journal of 8 December 1770 cited the Irish debut of a Mr Day "from Covent Garden" at Smock Alley on that date. *The London Stage* gives no Mr Day at Covent Garden in the period 1762–70. W. J. Lawrence, quoting from the *Theatrical Review's* strictures in his annotated scrapbooks (now in the National Library of Ireland), "wonders" if that Mr Day was not the one who was in Parker's company at Belfast in the season of 1771–72, and whose benefit bill of 18 December 1771 placed his residence at "Mr Mitchell's, back of the Green."

W. S. Clark, in *The Irish Stage in the County Towns,* identifies the Mr Day who was at Smock Alley in 1770 with one who was at Limerick on 22 October and Belfast on 30 October and 18 December 1771; at Belfast on 17 January 1772; at Kilkenny on 16 February 1773; at Belfast again on 28 and 30 December 1778 and 12 February 1779; and also at Derry on 23 October 1782 and Cork on 20 August 1794. Clark gives him a first name: George. A note in one of Lawrence's scrapbooks asserts that, when Day was advertised to appear under Myrton Hamilton's management in the new Ann Street Theatre at Belfast in 1778, he was said to be appearing "from Dublin, after seven years' absence from Belfast." It is at this date impossible to affirm that all these Irish Days were the same (and named George) or were from Covent Garden. The surname Day appears also in the Norwich company in 1765, the Brighton company in the summer of 1788, at Birmingham in the summer of 1799, and at Sheffield in the following October.

Neither the Irish nor the English provincial Day can be the first husband of the celebrated comedy queen (née Child) who appeared first in Edinburgh in 1772 as Mrs Day, for by late November of 1773 (and always afterward) she was billed as Mrs Webb. That Miss Child was divorced from Mr Day and then married to Mr Webb is of course a possibility—though a remote one. An irregular assumption of either the one name or the other would be a more likely answer. But Professor Clark lists a Mrs George Day who appeared at Smock Alley "from Covent Garden" in 1770 and whose Irish career roughly thereafter closely parallels George Day's engagements for more than a quarter of a century past the date of the first appearance on Edinburgh's bills of "Mrs Webb." Clark lists Mrs George Day in Belfast on 30 October and 18 December 1771 and 24 January 1772; at Kilkenny on 16 February 1773; at Belfast again on 27 March 1780; at Derry on 25 June 1782; at Limerick on 1 October 1798; and at Cork on 4 March 1800. There seems to be a likelihood that it was Mrs George Day who was the Mrs

Day playing Lady Freelove in *The Jealous Wife* at a specially licensed performance at the Haymarket Theatre in London on 29 April 1788. A Mrs Day was reported by the Reading *Mercury* of 12 May 1788 as then coming to Reading from Dublin. A Mrs Day was in specially licensed performances with irregular companies at the Haymarket on 22 December 1788, as Miss Doiley in *Who's the Dupe?* and on 7 March 1791 as Isabinda in *The Busy Body*.

Day, Mrs [George?] [*fl. 1770?–1800?*], *actress.* See **Day, [George?]**.

Day, William [*fl. 1673*], *musician.*
On 17 July 1673 the Lord Chamberlain issued a warrant to apprehend William Day and others for playing music without a permit.

Dayes, Mary. *See* **Morton, Mary.**

Days. *See* **Desse.**

D'Bainville, [Mons] [*fl. 1733*], *dancer.*
At the Goodman's Fields Theatre on 20 April 1733 one D'Bainville (or D'Blainville) danced in a new piece called *La Payzane mantaignez*.

D'Cleve. *See* **De Cleve.**

Deame. *See* **Deane.**

De Amicis, Domenico [*fl. 1759–1763*], *singer.* See **De Amicis, Signora Domenico.**

De Amicis, Signora Domenico, Anna Lucia [*fl. c. 1755–1789*], *singer, dancer.*
Anna Lucia De Amicis, born at Naples, was a singer in comic opera in Italy from about 1755. With her husband, Domenico De Amicis, she managed a traveling opera company which performed at Antwerp and

Brussels in 1759. Sometime in the early part of 1761 the De Amicis family was at London, but there is no record of any performances by them there at that time. While at London, however, they were engaged by Minelli for Smock Alley, Dublin, for a stipend of £1000, with £367 10*s*. of that amount to be paid prior to their leaving London. A disagreement over the engagement erupted after the De Amicis couple arrived at Dublin, and Signor De Amicis published a single-sheet broadside, entitled *The Case of Mr Dominick De Amicis*, in which he set out the contract terms for the engagement to be concluded prior to 15 June 1761. The family had given their stipulated 12 performances, but Minelli had not made his payments by the schedule agreed upon:

And as Mr. *De Amicis* left *London* (where he might have been much more advantageously engaged) on the Faith of Mr. *Minelli*, and the Expectation of such undeniable Security, and was detained there at a vast Expence above two Months, in order on his Part, fully to keep up his Promise and Agreement, which he has punctually adhered to; and as on the Part of Mr. *Minelli*, not one single Point of his Contract has been fulfilled, he thinks himself sufficiently warranted from having quitted any further Obligation or Connection with him.

Anna and Dominick returned to London in the fall of 1762, where, by the testimony of Burney, they were engaged by Signora Mattei, the manager of the Opera, for burlettas at the King's Theatre. Signora De Amicis made her debut on 13 November 1762 in the burletta of *Il tutore e la pupilla*. Although the piece itself received little applause, Signora De Amicis captivated the public sufficiently for the work to receive seven more performances by the end of December and several more thereafter. "Her figure and gestures," reported Burney, "were in the highest degree elegant and graceful; her countenance, though not perfectly beautiful, was extremely high bred and interesting; and her voice and manner of singing, exquisitely polished and sweet." She next sang in a new comic *pasticcio, La cascina*, brought out on 8 January 1763. Despite the opinion of the Italian violinist, Signor Bimolle, who wrote from London to Signora Aquilante at Naples that the piece was "the most perfect *Burletta* that ever was composed, acted by the most accomplished *Buffa* that Italy ever produced," *La cascina* was received with indifference by the audience and achieved only one more performance, that of 10 January.

On 3 February Signora De Amicis appeared in Galuppi's comic opera, *La calamita de' cuori*, which gained applause and several performances though it never managed to fill the house. This was a difficult season for the Opera, and although the talented Signora De Amicis was the chief support of the burlettas, "the rest of the singing was so despicable," wrote Burney, "that only her songs have been printed."

The expectations of the audience were heightened by the engagement of J. C. Bach for the composition of serious operas. Bach, who had arrived in London in 1762, had been successful with dramatic productions in Italy. At the suggestion of Bach, who heard her sing several serious songs in private, Signora De Amicis was given the "first woman's" parts in the serious operas. On 19 February 1763 she sang Andriope in Bach's *Orione, ossia Diana vendicata*, which was "extremely applauded by a very numerous audience," including their Majesties. She appeared in Bach's second serious composition, *Zanaida*, on 7 May. For her benefit on 24 March she sang in *La serva padrona*. On 25 April she participated in a concert at the King's Theatre for the benefit of the musicians' fund, and on 9 June she sang at the Haymarket Theatre in a benefit concert for Signor Capitani, a singer at the Opera who was then imprisoned for debt in the King's Bench. She gave her final performance at the King's Theatre on 11 June 1763 in *Zanaida*.

The testimony of Signor Bimolle was that in the serious opera, Signora De Amicis "had no body of voice, and could not be heard beyond the middle of the pit." On the other hand, Burney recorded that "De Amicis was not only the first who introduced *staccato divisions* in singing on our stage, but the first singer that I had ever heard go up to E flat in altissimo, with true, clear, and powerful *real* voice." After leaving London, she became one of the foremost female singers in serious opera at Naples, where she was active until 1789.

It is not clear that her husband Domenico De Amicis or anyone else in the family ever performed in London during the 1762–63 season. Burney's statement that the family was engaged for the Opera season is ambiguous, for he then wrote, "Indeed, she acted and sung for the whole family; for by her merits and good works, she covered the multitude of their sins, which would otherwise have had no remission." According to *The London Stage*, Signora De Amicis danced—"by Desire" —with Gallini after the burletta *La serva padrona* on 20 April 1763. Perhaps her husband's name was really intended for the bill.

Anna Lucia De Amicis and her husband Domenico were included in a large group of singers which was painted by Antonio Fedi; an engraving of this group by Bettelini was published in Italy between 1801 and 1807.

Dean, Mr [fl. 1761], *trumpeter.*

Mr Dean was hired as an extra trumpeter in the elaborate coronation ceremony staged at Covent Garden as part of *Henry VIII* beginning on 30 September 1761. The account books show a payment of 5s. to Dean on 13 November, presumably for a night's work.

Dean, Mr [fl. 1799], *lamplighter.*

Mr Dean was a lamplighter on the staff of the Richmond Theatre in 1799.

Dean, Henry [fl. 1794], *harpsichordist, horn player.*

Doane's *Musical Directory* of 1794 listed Henry Dean, of No 35, Cockspur Street, Charing Cross, as a harpsichordist and horn player at concerts presented by the New Musical Fund.

Dean, Thomas [fl. 1701–1731], *instrumentalist, composer.*

On 26 March 1701 a Mr Dean, presumably Thomas, shared a benefit with Manshipp at York Buildings, and on 11 May, 1 June, and 27 July 1702 he played the violin at concerts at Hampstead. For the next several years he appeared in concerts at York Buildings, Hampstead, the Lincoln's Inn Fields Theatre, Chestnut House in Herefordshire, Hampstead Wells, Godwin's Dancing School, and Stationers' Hall, and he was for the period 1707–12 one of the treble violinists in the band at the Queen's Theatre in the Haymarket at a salary of £30 yearly.

In 1707–8 Thomas Dean Junior appeared at several concerts with his father, the earliest apparently being on 28 April 1707 at York Buildings. One of the features of their numerous York Buildings concerts at this time was the younger Dean's performances on the arch-lute. At a concert on 21 January 1708 father and son played a work composed by Thomas Junior for the arch-lute and violin, and 4 February the younger Dean sang a song to his own lute accompaniment.

References to a Thomas Dean after this time are probably to the father, for no records after 1708 hint at the son's continuing his career. The senior Dean, then, was presumably the one who played in the Queen's Theatre band, who was frequently noted as playing violin at concerts in

1709–10, and who was still active at the theatre in 1711–12.

Thomas Dean was also a composer. He wrote the incidental music to *The Governor of Cyprus* in 1703, some church music, and a number of violin pieces, which were published in *The Division Violin*. Dean was organist at Warwick and Coventry, is said to have been the first to perform a Corelli sonata in England (in 1709, though the existing bills do not seem to pinpoint this), and was granted a D. Mus. at Oxford on 9 July 1731.

Dean, Thomas *[fl. 1707–1708], instrumentalist, singer, composer. See* **Dean, Thomas** *[fl. 1701–1731].*

Deane, Richard *[fl. 1661–1673?], trumpeter.*
The earliest mention of Richard Deane in the Lord Chamberlain's accounts was on 22 September 1661 when his yearly salary as a trumpeter was noted as £60. He attended Charles II at Bath from 20 August to 1 October 1663 for an extra 5s. daily, and on 17 December 1669, the date of the last mention of him, he was to receive a new silver trumpet as soon as he turned in his old one.

Perhaps the following entries in the registers of St Margaret, Westminster, concern the trumpeter: Richard and Jane Dean baptized a son John on 24 April 1670, a daughter Jane on 17 December 1671, and a son Richard on 21 November 1673.

"Dear Jenny." *See* **Fourmantel, Kitty.**

Dearl, Mrs *[fl. 1765], singer.*
A Drury Lane pay list for 9 February 1765 listed Mrs Dearl as a singer receiving 3s. 4d. daily or £1 weekly, the lowest salary among the singers. She was presumably the wife of the popular singer Mr Dearle.

Dearle, Mr *[fl. c. 1755–c. 1780], singer.*

Judging by the approximate publication dates of songs performed by him, Mr Dearle was a popular entertainer at London's pleasure gardens from about 1755 to about 1780. He sang at Ranelagh Gardens as early as 1755 and continued to appear there through 1764; from 1765 to 1780 he was a featured singer at Finch's Grotto Gardens. Many of the songs he made popular were by composers whose names are lost to us, but at Finch's he frequently sang works by Richard Bride, including "Phillis" and "The Span." It is probable that Dearle was the husband of the Mrs "Dearl" who sang in the Drury Lane chorus in 1765.

Dease, Mr *[fl. 1732], actor.*
A Mr Dease played Mat in *The Beggar's Opera* at the Haymarket Theatre on 4 September 1732 for Signora Violante's benefit.

"Death." *See* **Oliver, Stephen.**

Death, Thomas *1739–1802, actor, lecturer.*
Many of the particulars of Thomas Death's early life and family background are furnished by a convincing account in the *General Magazine* for 1788, printed when he was alive and in a position to challenge any inaccuracy. He was said to have been born in 1739, the son of John Death, an eminent surgeon and apothecary of Greek Street, Soho, a benevolent and highly esteemed local celebrity who left a "numerous family" ill provided for.

Young Thomas became enthralled by the idea of acting when he was 12 and memorized a number of roles from popular plays. When he was 15 his elder brother Michael obtained, through the influence of a Captain Woolsey, R. N., a commission for Thomas as midshipman on board Woolsey's sloop, the *Fennit*. He sailed on one voyage and then applied for and received a discharge despite the Captain's reported reluctance to lose such a terrifying name from his roster.

An acquaintance with William Hogarth introduced Death to the notice of David Garrick who admired the youth's abilities but did nothing for him. One surviving playbill of 14 July 1762 of the Birmingham Theatre contains the name Death, and that was very likely Thomas.

The *General Magazine* account relates that "At eighteen he was introduced, and had the good fortune to be engaged by Mr Foote, whose instructors laid the groundwork of his future excellence." Death may indeed have met Foote when he was 18, but the extant bills do not show him to have been engaged at the Haymarket until 20 June 1763, when he would have been 24 years of age, if the inscription on his tombstone (giving his age at death as 63) is correct.

That playbill of 20 June 1763 lists him only for an unspecified "principal part" in the afterpiece, *The Mayor of Garratt*, but *The Minor* was the mainpiece that night and it is likely that, as the magazine account attests, he "made his first appearance as Sir George Wealthy in The Minor." The double bill was repeated a dozen times during the summer, and the afterpiece ran with other mainpieces also. In addition, Death was cited in an unspecified part in *The Diversions of the Morning*, as Beaufort in *The Citizen*, Prettyman in *The Rehearsal*, and Lord John in *The Englishman Return'd from Paris*.

The *General Magazine* account asserts that he had "succeeded so well" in *The Minor* "that Mr Foote was induced to study the young actor's genius so far as to write the part of Dick Bever in the Patron, in order, as the wit said, that 'his friend Death might bring it to *life*.' " Ignoring the feeble jest (which in one form or another of course pursued poor Death even to his epitaph) we may believe the assertion, for Foote delighted to write parts "from the life," and certainly the first offering of the

Haymarket in the summer of 1764 was *The Patron*, with Death playing Dick Bever. It was a fine success, repeated 15 times that summer. Death also added to his repertoire unspecified parts in *The Orators* and *Tragedy à la Mode*, the President in *The Apprentice*, and Wellbred in *Every Man in His Humour*. He also figured in the parts he had learned the previous summer.

Despite all this apparent success, Death could not secure a place in the winter patent theatres, and he evidently retreated (again?) to the provinces, leaving behind one Maria Churchill, with whom he is said to have contracted an informal alliance.

Harvard Theatre Collection

THOMAS DEATH

engraving by Corner, after Sherratt

Evidently Death went directly from London to the Norwich theatre in the fall of 1764. About 20 March 1765 he married the young comedienne Margaret Sparks, the comedian Luke Sparks's daughter, who was performing under the designation of Miss (or Mrs) Vernon. (She had had her debut with the Norwich company at Yarmouth on 31 December 1764.)

Mr and Mrs Death performed at Norwich—with what regularity is not known—until 1769. A notation in a Committee Book of the Norwich theatre dated 2 March 1769 reads: "This Committee consents that In Consideration of the present Ill State of Health of Mrs Death a Play may be acted on Thursday next for the Benefit of her & Mr Death, on the usual Terms of Benefits." Margaret died on 10 April, at the age of 26, and Death's friend the monologuist George Alexander Stevens contributed the execrable quatrain engraved on her memorial in St Stephen's Church, Norwich:

Her form once lovely now can please no
 more,
And all her melody on earth is o'er;
A wife and mother, tender and sincere,
These she hath been, now, alas, she's here

She had apparently never performed in London. On 22 May 1769 Death signed articles for the following season "at a Salary of 1.11.6 p week," but the Committee Book under the date of 6 March 1770 reported it as "Ord'd That Mr Death be received for the Remainder of this Season & that he be discharged at the Expiration thereof."

Death went back to London and applied to Garrick, who secured him an engagement with John Palmer's company at Bath. There he "entered upon the genteel comic walk, and was well received," according to a contemporary account. But a quarrel with Lee, the deputy manager, contributed to his decision to leave Bath for Dublin on the invitation of his father-in-law Luke Sparks and of Thomas Ryder the Smock Alley manager. Death passed an agreeable winter of excellent success with the Dublin audiences. Tottenham Heaphy offered him a place with the Cork summer company, but he declined and went instead to George Mattocks's management at Portsmouth.

In the fall of 1770 Death again sought a London engagement. On 27 September he and Mrs Gardner shared a specially licensed benefit night at the Haymarket, when she went into breeches as Scrub in *The Beaux' Stratagem* and he was Archer (advertised as "from the theatre in Norwich"). But no London manager took the bait, and Death returned once again to the provinces.

By 1773 at the latest he had accepted an offer from West Digges to come to Edinburgh to portray a line of "walking gentlemen" and young "genteel" parts like Belcour, varied by his "smart" fops like Prattle in *The Deuce is in Him* and his successful old Lord Ogleby. He left Edinburgh after 1774 for a brief engagement at Hull and Liverpool and then a tour on Tate Wilkinson's York circuit in 1775, when he opened with sensational success as Marplot in *The Busy Body*, a success which was sustained for two years and which came soon to the ears of metropolitan managers.

In the season of 1777–78 Death finally achieved the long-sought-for place in a London patent company. He signed for £2 a week with Harris at Covent Garden, appearing first on 8 October (as "from the York Theatre," but identified only as "a Young Gentleman") playing the impudent comic servant Tom in *The Conscious Lovers*. Thereafter that season he is recorded playing the Gentleman Usher in *King Lear* on 8 October, Lint in *The Mayor of Garratt* on 15 January 1778, an unspecified role in *The Rehearsal* on 20 January, and Sancho in *Love Makes a Man* on 25 February. He was announced to play Mellefont in *The Little French Law-yer* on the occasion of Quick's benefit, 27 April, but, said the *London Chronicle* for 28 April, he "was not to be found . . . Hull begged for permission for Lee Lewes to read Death's part in his own undress, which [was] granted." The motive for Death's taking this holiday is not known, but the defection cost him dearly. He was not among the Covent Garden players signing articles for the next season, and he had evidently forfeited his chance for steady London employment. A vagrant manuscript pay sheet at Harvard credits him with 151 days at 6*s.* 8*d.* per day, for a total salary of £50 6*s.* 8*d.* that season. With these small gains he returned yet once more to provincial service.

After his three years' absence, Thomas Death was received again into the York company for the season beginning in January 1780. Then, according to the account in the *General Magazine*, he "quitted the stage for some years; and when he played again it was at Cambridge, with Mr John Palmer . . ." Certainly Death was among a number of experienced actors Palmer assembled to perform at Stourbridge Fair near Cambridge, in 1786, to oppose a monopoly held there by the Norwich company. Palmer is also said to have brought him to London for the ill-starred venture at the Royalty Theatre in 1787, but inasmuch as there is no record of Death's ever having sung or danced, it is unlikely that he remained there through 1788–89, when only entertainments requiring those talents were permitted at the Royalty. He was one of a miscellaneous group of actors performing at the Haymarket in a specially licensed performance for their own benefit on 30 September 1788. He played Young Philpot in *The Citizen* and also spoke a monologue.

The *General Magazine* brought his career up through 1788 with the assertion that "He has . . . lectured in different parts of the country with varied success; and in London at the Freemason's Tavern."

The London managers were censored by that author for not bringing again "to the boards of our winter theatres," this "mild, friendly, and convivial" man who "in person much resembles David Garrick."

Death returned to Norwich, and there are records of his performances in that theatre in 1793. He married one Ann Bowlan at Norwich sometime in 1792, and he died in that city on 16 August 1802. His second wife died on 5 September 1824, "aged 73," according to the memorial to Thomas and his two wives erected over their graves in the east end of St Stephen's Church, Norwich.

Richard Ryan, in his *Dramatic Table Talk* (1825–1830), observed:

This gentleman's name, as might be conjectured, supplied the *minor wits* and "full grown" punsters of his day with witticisms innumerable, which were smuggled into each journal's columns devoted to theatrical criticism: if he performed *well*, they remarked, that "last night, *Death* was quite *alive*;" and if he acted *ill,* they did not fail to add, that "*Death* . . . was devoid of all animation."

When his great namesake, *Death*, claimed a closer acquaintanceship with him, they did not "let him shuffle off this mortal coil" without a few flying shots, in the form of epigrams and epitaphs. . . . The following is selected from the quantity which were so generously administered to the public.

Epitaph on Mr Death.
DEATH *levels all, both high and low,*
Without regard to stations;
Yet, why complain,
If we *are slain?*
For here lies one, at least, to shew
He kills his own relations.

An engraving of Thomas Death by J. Corner, after E. Sherratt, was published as a plate to the *General Magazine and Impartial Review,* 1788.

De Barques. *See* **DESBARQUES.**

De Basson. *See* **BASSANO.**

De Baudin, Baptiste ⟨*fl. c. 1787*⟩, *dancer.*

About 1787 "Monsieur Babdist de Baudin" from Lyons danced at the Royal Circus.

De Beaumont. *See* D'ÉON.

De Blois, Mons ⟨*fl. 1732*⟩, *dancer.*

At Tottenham Court on 4 August 1732 Monsieur De Blois, billed as just arrived from Paris, played the first Infernal in *The Metamorphosis of Harlequin.*

Debon, Mme ⟨*fl. 1742*⟩, *performer.*

At Woodhouse's booth at Southwark Fair on 16 September 1742 Madame Debon and two others offered singing and dancing.

Debourg. *See* DUBOURG.

De Breame, Maxent ⟨*fl. 1675–1678*⟩, *oboist.*

Maxent De Breame (or de Bresmes) played the oboe in the court masque *Calisto* on 15 February 1675, and on 8 June 1678 he and two other Frenchmen were appointed musicians in the Chapel Royal.

De Brécourt, Sieur ⟨**Guillaume Marcoureau**⟩ ⟨*fl. 1674*⟩, *manager.*

A troupe of French comedians played at the English Court from 1 June to 19 August 1674, and it is possible that this was the company of Guillaume Marcoureau, Sieur de Brécourt, the probable author of the *Ballet de musique pour le divertissement du roy de la Grand Bretagne,* published in London in 1674.

Debroc, Mons ⟨*fl. 1720–1743*⟩, *acrobat, dancer.*

Monsieur Debroc (or Debroke, Du Brocq) was a member of De Grimbergue's French troupe, which performed at the King's Theatre in the Haymarket and at Lincoln's Inn Fields from 5 March to 21 June 1720. On 26 April he was noted in the bill for "the Extraordinary Tumbling, call'd Le Saut de la Planche, to be performed by Mr Debroc, who with Links in his Hands will run up to the Top of a Board 16 Foot high, and with a most surprising Activity will tumble from thence." Though the performer was not named on 13 June, Debroc was probably the "Scaramouch" who did a similar feat, throwing himself backward on the stage after running up the board.

Debroc appeared in London again in 1734, apparently after having performed from time to time in the 1720s in Holland. On 24 August 1734 at Bartholomew Fair he joined Vanderhoff, "de Voltore," and Janno in a tumbling act. From 18 December 1735 to 28 February 1736 he appeared with the King of France's Company of Italian Rope-Dancers at the Lincoln's Inn Fields playhouse, billed as the "celebrated equilibrist." On 9 February 1736 he pitted himself against his colleague Corneille in a "match in tumbling." Not until 23 August 1743 at Bartholomew Fair was Debroc mentioned again in London bills; cited then as the "Ballance Master, just arriv'd from Paris," Monsieur "de Broke" played Harlequin in *Harlequin Dissected* at Turbutt and Dove's booth at the end of Hosier Lane in West Smithfield.

De Bryn. *See* DEBUIN.

Debuin, Henry ⟨*fl. 1794*⟩, *singer.*

Doane's *Musical Directory* of 1794 contains two entries which must surely be for the same person: Henry Debuin of No 29, Little Castle Street, Cavendish Square, a tenor, and Henry De Bryn of No 29, Little Castle Street, Oxford Market, an alto. Debuin or De Bryn participated in Handelian Society concerts.

De Camargo. *See* CAMARGO.

De Camp, Mons *(fl. 1727)*, *dancer.*

Monsieur De Camp was a leading dancer at the opera in Brussels before appearing on 23 March 1727 at the King's Theatre in the Haymarket. On that date he and Mlle Mimi l'Post were billed as just arrived and offered both serious and grotesque dancing. The company with which they were associated at the King's Theatre was an Italian *commedia dell'arte* troupe that had been in London since the previous 21 September.

De Camp, Adelaide *(fl. 1776–1791).* *See* SIMONET, MRS LOUIS.

De Camp, Adelaide *1780–1834,* *actress, dancer.*

Adelaide De Camp was born in France in December 1780, the second daughter and third child of the French musician George Louis De Camp and his wife Jeanne, née Dufour. She followed her older sister Maria Theresa and her brother Vincent onto the stage. At 12 she was dancing at Drury Lane under the management of John Philip Kemble, but her name appears in the bills there only a few times between 27 December 1792 and 14 January 1793. Her niece, the great nineteenth-century tragedienne Frances Anne Kemble, recalled that "She . . . found employment in her profession under the kindly protection of Mr Stephen Kemble, my father's brother," manager of Durham and a circuit which embraced Newcastle, Sunderland, and various other towns. But the exact time of this country experience is indeterminable. It was probably after the brief trial at Drury Lane and before her Covent Garden debut on 7 May 1799 as Sophia in *The Road to Ruin.* She was then advertised (with a deception often employed in introducing young provincial performers) as making her first appearance "on any stage." She did not play again at Covent Garden. She was at Brighton in 1799 and when on 3 November 1800 she turned up at the

theatre at Hull she was said to have come from Richmond. She toured Birmingham, Liverpool, Edinburgh, Glasgow, and other cities in 1801 and was at Nottingham and Hull in 1802.

Fanny Kemble knew her as devoted "Aunt Dall," and in the memoir *Records of a Girlhood* spoke with moving affection of her services to the family of Charles Kemble, with whom she lived after leaving Stephen Kemble's shelter following a disappointment in love. She never married:

Obliged, as all the rest of the family were, to earn her own bread, and naturally adopting the means of doing so that they did, she [had gone] upon the stage; but I can not conceive that her nature can ever have had any affinity with her occupation. She had a robust and rather prosaic common-sense, opposed to any thing exaggerated or sentimental, which gave her an excellent judgment of character and conduct, a strong genial vein of humor which very often made her repartees witty as well as wise, and a sunny sweetness of temper and soundness of moral nature that made her as good as she was easy and delightful to live with. Whenever any thing went wrong . . . she used to sing; it was the only indication by which we ever knew that she was what is termed "out of sorts."

Aunt Dall accompanied Fanny on her tour of America in 1832. During a summer outing to Niagara Falls in 1833 their carriage overturned and Adelaide received a spinal injury which left her helpless. She died in Fanny's arms in April 1834. One of the last entries in Fanny's *Records of a Girlhood* reads:

We have buried dear Dall in a lonely, lovely place in Mount Orban's [Auburn] Cemetery, where [Pierce Butler?] and I used to go and sit together last spring, in the early time of our intimacy. I wished her to lie there, for life and love and youth and death have their trysting place at the grave.

De Camp, George Louis *1752–1787,* *flutist.*

The musician Louis De Camp "fils de Jean De Camp, Luneville en Lorraine," married "Jeanne Adrienne fille de Jean Louis Dufour de Nancy" on 7 April 1774, according to their marriage certificate on file at the Royal Society of Musicians. (The 1814 edition of *Authentic Memoirs of the Green Room* calls him George Louis.) The match produced a notable family of theatrical performers.

De Camp played the flute in the band assembled at Covent Garden Theatre for the oratorio season of 1777 and also played for the six oratorios given in March 1779 at the Haymarket. In 1783 his name was on the roster, as musician, at the King's Theatre and he was listed by Charles Burney as among the flutes at the Handel Memorial Concert at Westminster Abbey in May and June 1784.

When William Napier proposed him for membership in the Royal Society of Musicians on 4 December 1784, he was said to be "engaged at the Hanover Square & Pantheon Concerts," to be "about 30 years old," and to have four children. Their names were given as: Theresa, "Venanzio," Adelaide, and "Victore." Louis was "balloted for, and unanimously Elected" on 2 January 1785 and signed the book of admission and paid his subscription on 6 February.

De Camp was playing woodwind in the band at Ranelagh Gardens under Napier in 1784 and 1786, but sometime in 1786 he became ill. A petition to the Royal Society dated 7 October 1787 deposed that De Camp "thirty-five years of age, has a wife and Six Children" and "By a violent disorder (in his Lungs) is totally unable to perform on any instrument." He died later in October, probably in Germany, and in November a petition of his widow "Jane" De Camp to the fund of the Royal Society spoke of six children "the eldest of which only is provided for": Teresa (Maria Theresa), born January 1775, Vincent, born January 1779, Adelaide, born December 1780, Victoire, born December 1782, Sophy (Sophia), born June 1785, and Mary, born August 1787.

The widow was awarded an allowance of unspecified amount. On 7 November 1791 she informed the Society of the death of her youngest child (Mary) and the allowance was reduced to £5 12*s*. 6*d*. per month. On 6 June 1795 Mrs De Camp informed the Governors that her daughter Adelaide had been apprenticed to one Mr Percy (presumably John Percy, the violinist and Vauxhall composer). On 14 December 1800 notification was made that Sophia De Camp, the fifth child of George Louis and Jeanne, had been apprenticed to (the music teacher) Giuseppe Lanza, and on 1 February 1801 the Society paid Lanza a £20 premium for his services.

On 3 March 1816 application was made by the De Camp family to the Society for funeral expenses — amount unspecified — for Mrs De Camp.

Adelaide, Sophia, Maria Theresa (later Mrs Charles Kemble), and Vincent De Camp, children of George Louis and Jeanne, and George Louis's sisters, Sophia and Adelaide (Mrs Louis Simonet), were all performers and are separately noticed. George Louis's wife evidently did not perform in England. She was, no doubt, the "Jane De Camp, King Street" who died at age 60 in 1816 and was buried on 21 February at St Paul, Covent Garden.

The statement in the entry for Maria Theresa (De Camp) Kemble in *The Dictionary of National Biography* that her father had changed his name from De Fleury appears dubious. The assertion was probably taken from a romantic account in the entry for his son Vincent in the 1814 edition of the *Authentic Memoirs of the Green Room*:

His real name . . . was De Fleury, and he was descended from a younger branch of that family in France. Allured by the prospect of riches and fame, which had been promised him by several English noblemen, then resident abroad, he quitted Germany, for England; where, although his great merits were acknowledged, yet his modesty and unassuming diffidence . . . were an unfortunate bar to his success.

De Camp, Maria Theresa, *actress.*
See **KEMBLE, MRS CHARLES.**

De Camp, Sophia   *ifl. 1776–1777*, *dancer.*

The dancer Sophia De Camp evidently accompanied her brother George Louis De Camp, the musician, and his family and her sister Adelaide (later Mrs Louis Simonet), the dancer, from France to England about 1776. Sophia's "first appearance in England" (according to the bill) was at the King's Theatre on 12 April 1777 when she danced an *Entrée*. She was several times employed in ballets composed by the ballet master, her brother-in-law Simonet, to the end of the season.

Strangely, there is no certain record of this Sophia De Camp's dancing again in London (though she is liable to be confused with her niece Sophia), and she may have gone back to France. The dancer Miss S. De Camp, at Drury Lane briefly in the spring of 1797 and receiving Miss Maria Theresa's salary in 1804, is almost certainly the younger woman.

De Camp, Sophia, later Mrs Frederick Brown.   *b. 1785, dancer.*

Sophia De Camp was born in 1785 to the musician George Louis De Camp and his wife Jeanne, née Dufour. She was the fourth daughter and fifth child in a family of at least six children, most of whom were performers.

Sophia (or Sophy, as she seems to have been called) is liable to some confusion with her aunt, the dancer of the same name. But apparently it was the younger woman who danced the part of Lauretta in Giacomo Gentili's ballet *The Labyrinth; or*

The Country Madcap at the end of *Cymbeline* at Drury Lane on 6 March 1797. The dance was twice repeated, and after that "Miss S. De Camp" disappeared from the playbills. A Sophia De Camp signed all salary receipts for Theresa De Camp in 1803–4.

The *Theatrical Inquisitor and Monthly Mirror* for July 1814 carried the following item: "Married on Saturday the 28th of May, at Sunderland, Mr Frederick Brown to Miss Sophia De Camp, youngest sister of Mrs C. Kemble, and late of the Theatre Royal, York."

De Camp, Vincent   *1779–1839, actor, singer.*

Vincent De Camp was the second child and only son of the flutist George Louis De Camp and his wife Jeanne, née Dufour. He was born (probably in London) in January 1779, according to a deposition given by his mother to the Royal Society of Musicians. At least three of his five sisters were on the stage.

Vincent came on the boards playing the traditional juvenile debut role of the Prince of Wales in *Richard III* for the displaced Drury Lane company at the King's Theatre, on 5 November 1792, with John Philip Kemble playing Richard. His sister Maria Theresa was already in the company and danced that night in the afterpiece. His name did not occur again in a public notice until the bill for 26 December, when he was allowed to play Donalbain in *Macbeth.* His third attempt was Arthur in *King John* on 12 February. He repeated Donalbain on 7 May, and, so far as the bills show, that was his season. For Mrs Kemble's benefit at the Haymarket the following 6 August he repeated the Prince of Wales.

Master De Camp signed on again at Drury Lane in the abbreviated season beginning 21 April 1794 for £1 per week. He played Donalbain 10 times, but he was seen in nothing else there. He had, how-

Harvard Theatre Collection

VINCENT DE CAMP, as Duretete

engraving by Thomson, after Wageman

Master De Camp had spoken a prologue after the boys of "Mr Audinet's Academy, Great Russel-Street" had presented *The Village Lawyer* "in French and English." It is probable that he was attending the school at the time.

Vincent became 16 midway through the 1794–95 season. He was still employed in juvenile roles, though very infrequently. He was heard that season for the first time singing in choruses. In the summer of 1795 he accompanied his older sister to the Haymarket again but was named in the bills only on 10 August, when he was Juba in the afterpiece *The Prize*. In the season of 1796–97 Vincent De Camp evidently withdrew to Stephen Kemble's company at Edinburgh where he acted through the season of 1797–98. On 13 November 1799 he reappeared at Drury Lane as Vapour in *My Grandmother*. The *Monthly Mirror* gave him a brief puff for going "through the part with much credit." He had, the *Mirror* said,

been improving himself, in Mr. Stephen Kemble's company, and at Margate—and he has now, we understand, a regular engagement at [Drury Lane]; . . . His figure is remarkably genteel, and his countenance handsome and expressive—his voice is good, but rather defective in articulation.

During the season of 1799–1800, when he earned £2 per week, De Camp played several times Lovel in *High Life Below Stairs*, Count Valentia in *The Child of Nature*, and Careless in *The School for Scandal* and perhaps did some walk-ons and sang in choruses but was not noticed again in the bills.

One of John Philip Kemble's manuscript notes in the British Museum informs us that, on 7 September 1801, "Mr De Camp engaged for three years at 3 Pounds a Week the first year—and 4 Pounds a week the two last years"; and De Camp remained on the Drury Lane roster playing

ever, been able to secure employment with George Colman, who had opened the Haymarket from 19 September through 8 April employing the patent rented from Thomas Harris, and there Vincent acted the Boy in *Henry V*, and, once again, the Prince of Wales in *Richard III*.

Master De Camp and his sister Maria Theresa both accepted the employment at the Haymarket proferred by Colman to members of the disbanded Drury Lane company in the early part of the 1793–94 season. When the magnificent new Drury Lane playhouse opened on 21 April they rejoined that enterprise. During the season young Vincent played Donalbain more than a dozen times and repeated his Prince of Wales in *Richard III*. The *Thespian Magazine* reported early in 1794 that

VINCENT DE CAMP, in "The Three Singles," in *Three and the Deuce*
engraving by R. Jackson

the same round of characters through 1813–14. He was also a regular at the summer theatre in the Haymarket until he resigned in consequence of some dispute with James Winston, Colman's factotum there. He was one of the actors signing an unsuccessful petition to the King, delivered in 1810, asking the monarch to grant a third London theatrical patent. On 9 September 1812 De Camp and R. W. Elliston fought a bloodless duel on Dulwich Common after an altercation at the Surrey Theatre.

The critics were fickle to De Camp, and so was the public. He admitted in a letter to Thomas Dibdin that the part of Laertes in *Hamlet* had been taken away from him as a result of "disapprobations shewn by the audience." Implicated in the melancholy failure of "Monk" Lewis's *Adelgitha* in 1810, De Camp addressed the audience from the stage to inform them that he had not played his role from choice but that it had been thrust upon him. Crabb Robinson's *Diary* contains several strictures on his acting. Robinson thought him "a most

unworthy Prince of Wales." The *Authentic Memoirs of the Green Room* (1814 edition) thought that his representation of "fops, walking gentlemen, &c." brought him "some fame in the comic line . . . but by attempting too much, and particularly by appearing in tragedy [he] . . . has done himself considerable injury."

A Folger manuscript casting book of the early nineteenth century (probably c. 1814–15) gives the following list of parts which De Camp played: Colonel Epaulette in *Fontainebleau*, James in *Blue Devils*, Lovel in *High Life Below Stairs*, Brass in *The Confederacy*, Lovel in *The Clandestine Marriage*, Edward in *The Irishman in London*, Colonel Montfort in *Ella Rosenberg*, Placid in *Every One Has His Fault*, Tom Surfeit in *False Alarms*, Captain Thalwick in *How to Die for Love*, Rolando and Lopez in *The Honeymoon*, Cypher in *Hit or Miss*, Zekiel Homespun in *The Heir at Law*, Duretete in *The Inconstant*, Villeroy in *Isabella*, Lord Trinket in *The Jealous Wife*, Tom Shuffleton in *John Bull*, Mildmay in *The School for Prejudice*, Jessamay in *Lionel and Clarissa*, Jeremy in *Love for Love*, Captain Vain in *Lock and Key*, Claudio in *Much Ado About Nothing*, Marquis in *The Midnight Hour*, Pistol in *The Merry Wives of Windsor*, Vapour in *My Grandmother*, Frank in *Modern Antiques*, Roderigo in *Othello*, Don Carlos in *The Pannel*, Squire Richard in *The Provok'd Husband*, Isidore in *Remorse*, Sarcough in *The Russian*, Young Heartwell in *Riches*, Fitz Edward in *Sons of Erin*, Frankly in *The Suspicious Husband*, Trip in *The School for Scandal*, Kera Khan in *Lodoiska*, Captain Savage in *The School for Wives*, Daggerwood in *Sylvester Daggerwood*, Captain Nightshade in *Seeing's Believing*, Bob Handy in *Speed the Plough*, Wormwood in *The School for Authors*, Young Marlow in *She Stoops to Conquer*, Humphry in *Three and the Deuce*, Granger in *Who's the Dupe?*, Young Random in *Ways and Means*, Dick Dashall in *The Way to Get Married*, Osric in *Hamlet*, Varnish in *Intrigue*, Baron Teraldi in *Devil's Bridge*, Vincentio in *A Bold Stroke for a Husband*, Echo and Loiter in *The World*, Young Pranks in *The London Hermit*, Whiskerandos in *The Critic*, and Sadi in *The Mountaineers*.

After 1814 De Camp seems to have confined his activities pretty much to country theatres for a while. In 1815 he was manager at Canterbury for William Dowton. After many years campaigning in the British provinces, De Camp gravitated to America, where his activities are impossible to follow very far. Mathews said that he managed at Montreal in 1833. At Philadelphia late in 1833 he evidently began an engagement of six nights, 27, 30, and 31 December and 1, 2, and 8 January, at the Chestnut Street Theatre. He then dropped back into obscurity. An obituary notice in the *Columbian Century* of 26 August 1839 reported that Vincent De Camp "of the Mobile Theatre, d. at Houston, Texas, about the middle of July." The *Gentleman's Magazine* said 27 July 1839. But

VINCENT DE CAMP, as Coupée
by De Wilde

T. Allston Brown's *History* gives his death date as 1848.

Gilliland had reported in 1808: "He lately married a very amiable and pretty woman, with a handsome property, which enables him to live in a very comfortable style," but we do not know his wife's name.

Portraits of Vincent De Camp include:

1. As Figaro in *The Follies of a Day*. An oil painting by George Clint now in the Garrick Club, engraved by Cooke for Oxberry's *New English Drama* (1822).

2. As Master Heartwell in *Riches*. An oil by Samuel De Wilde painted in 1810 according to De Wilde's diary. Now in the Garrick Club.

3. Watercolor drawing by William Foster. In the Garrick Club.

4. As Coupée in *The Virgin Unmask'd*, watercolor by De Wilde. In the British Museum.

5. Watercolor portrait by De Wilde. In the Harvard Theatre Collection.

6. As Duretete in *The Inconstant*, engraved in 1820 by Thomson after Wageman.

7. As Hengo in *Bonduca*, engraved by P. Audinet after J. Roberts.

8. "Mr De Camp in the Three Singles," from Hoare's farce *Three and the Deuce* (De Camp is represented by all three figures). Engraved by R. Jackson.

9. "As Raymond," a "tuppence coloured" print engraved in 1823 by Hodgson.

De'Caro. *See* **DEL CARO.**

De Castro, Frances [*fl.* 1795], equestrienne?

A Frances De Castro was one of a group of performers in Astley's company signing a letter to the *Hibernian Journal* of 11 November 1795. She had, presumably, performed with Astley's equestrian company in London.

De Castro, James *b. 1758, actor, monologist, mimic, singer.*

James De Castro in 1824 published a rambling account of his 39 years as a comedian which furnishes most of the facts about his life and is also crammed with brief anecdotes about other performers.

He was born, according to a facsimile of an affidavit from his father, D. De Castro, "on or about the 14th Jan. 1758," in Houndsditch, Bishopsgate Street, London.

In his early days he was intended for a priest [rabbi], and passed the different schools, under the patronage of the Portuguese Jews' Synagogue. His uncle, a very respectable man, was guardian to the principal families of the Portuguese Jews, and his father was 'Rabbi' at the time, and had ninety boys under his care, to teach them the Hebrew Language . . .

De Castro says that he and other boys of the school raised a fund to draw upon whenever Garrick should play and that he quickly became enamoured of the stage and so at age 15 was "organizing plays and farces in commemoration of the *puerim.*"

He bore a strong facial resemblance to the great comedian Tom Weston and owned a good talent for mimicry. At a dinner party at the house of Moses Fernandez, when the actor and monologist Lee Lewes was present, he so astonished the company in imitating Weston that he was invited to perform Tom in *The Irish Widow* at Lewes's benefit at Covent Garden. He says that he did so and that he made his second appearance at Mrs Hunter's benefit later that season. He guessed "1778 or 1779," but the year was actually 1776: 27 April *"The Irish Widow.* Thomas [to be imitated after the manner of Weston]—A Young Gentleman, first appearance on any stage. . . . Benefit for Lee Lewes," and 8 May, "Benefit for Mrs Hunter," the same.

Following these successes he was introduced by Joseph Dalmieda to Thomas Harris, the Covent Garden manager, who gave him a note to Samuel Foote. Foote heard him and said that

he would introduce him to the notice of the King in the "Robin Hood" debating Society scene in the "Orators," and he that night . . . gave his imitations, vocal and rhetorical, of several eminent performers . . . and his Majesty did him the honour to send privately round a message for an *"encore"* of the song "Had I a heart for falsehood framed" . . .

That occasion is again undated in the *Memoirs* but was doubtless the command performance of *The Orators* at the Haymarket on 10 July 1776, though De Castro is not named in that bill. He was for the first time publicly noted when the bill of 18 September showed at the end of Act IV of *Midas*: "*Imitations*—Decastro."

Foote "Gave him a cast of parts, such as Jerry Sneak, Doctor Last, &c. &c." but the sudden retirement of Foote, the sale of his theatre, and his death (on 21 October 1777) were a collective "disappointment so great that for a time [De Castro] gave up all ideas of theatrical life, but still kept up his connexions with the principal comedians of both theatres and now and then played for their benefits at the Haymarket theatre." One certain occasion was on 9 October 1777: "End of mainpiece *Imitations*, Vocal and Rhetorical, by Decastro; several new ones, and those which Foote introduced him in before their Majesties." Other occasions were on 18 October 1779 when he played an unspecified part in *The Touchstone of Invention*; on 20 December 1779 in "a Variety of new *Imitations*"; on 13 December 1784 when he played Thomas in *The Irish Widow*; on 12 February 1785 when he played Taylor in *The Miser*, was Solomon in *The Quaker*, and "took off" the singers; on 6 March 1786 when he was Jerry Sneak in *The Mayor of Garratt* and did "*Imitations*, Vocal and Rhetorical"; and on 6 January 1787 when he tried Dr Last in *The Devil Upon Two Sticks*.

The nature of De Castro's employment during the wide gaps between his services in winter benefits at the Haymarket is suggested by a look at the scattered remaining playbills of the hippodrama at Astley's Amphitheatre. De Castro began his thirty-eight-year service to the remarkable Philip Astley in 1785. The first Astley's notice we find in which De Castro figures is that of 7 April 1785 in which "Our Adventurer," as he liked to call himself in his *Memoirs*, played Sam Strap in the musical farce *The Air Balloon; or, All the World in the Clouds*. In late July he was Beau Dimity in *The Termagant Mistress or Prussian Dragoon*, on 27 September sang the lead in

Harvard Theatre Collection

JAMES DE CASTRO
by Stanfield

Cupid Pilgrim, and on 5 October, in an unnamed burletta, introduced "a new comic song to the air of 'Fal de ral Tit.'" In bills we have read dated from 1785 through 1795 he was reported in all manner of singing parts: the Knave of Hearts in *The Marriage of the Knave of Hearts*, a Servant in *The Two Nannys*, Courier in *The King and the Cobbler*, Mercury in *Jupiter's Vengeance*, Allworth in *The Blunt Tars; or, True Love Rewarded*, a Drummer in *Bagshot-Heath Camp*, and Tom in *The Reasonable Wife; or, a New Way to Cure Tipsy*. These were the overblown harlequinades and quickly concocted musical sketches which supplemented the trick riding and spectacle at Astley's Amphitheatre. De Castro's few movements outside London remain largely undocumented. We do know that he went to Dublin in the winter of 1803–4 to assist John Astley in the Astleys' large establishment there, and very likely he had been there in 1795, for in that year *Walker's Hibernian Magazine* had printed "Miss Jenny don't think that I care for you," as sung by (Richard) Johannot and Mrs De Castro. (De Castro had been married to that lady sometime before July 1791, when she first began to appear in Astley's London bills.) *The Quarrelling Duet.* "Sung . . . by Mr Johannot and Mr. Decastro, in the Pantomime of Harlequin Invincible . . . at Mr Astley's Theatre of Arts" was published at London in 1795.

In 1823, James De Castro was living at No 17, Granby Place, according to a manuscript in the Garrick Club, and the same source declares that he died shortly after the publication of his memoirs in 1824.

A portrait of De Castro was engraved by Stanfield and published as a plate to the performer's *Memoirs*, 1824.

De Castro, Mrs James *(fl. 1791–1795), singer, actress.*

Mrs De Castro married James De Castro, singer and actor, at some time before July 1791. In that month (the bill is no more closely dated) she was at Astley's Amphitheatre as Louisa in a musical offering called *The Tythe Sheaf, or Village Plot*, "being her first appearance." From that date until August 1792 she played only Baucis in *The Good and Bad; or, Jupiter's Vengeance* and Grace in *Bagshot-Heath Camp*, so far as the scarce surviving bills show. She was not recorded as playing again until 22 August 1795 when she sang as Sally in *The Reasonable Wife*. In 1795 *Walker's Hibernian Magazine* printed "Miss Jenny don't think that I care for you" as sung by (Richard) Johannot and Mrs De Castro.

De Celotti. *See* CELOTTI.

De Chaliez. *See* DESCHALLIEZ.

De Champville. *See* CHAMPVILLE.

De Chanlue. *See* DESHALN.

De Chanville. *See* CHAMPVILLE.

De Cleve, Vincent *d. 1827, treasurer.*

According to William Pinks in *The History of Clerkenwell* (1881), Vincent de Cleve was treasurer of Sadler's Wells for many years before he died on 30 July 1827 at the age of 67. Perhaps his tenure began in the eighteenth century. Nicknamed "Polly" for his inquisitiveness, he occupied rooms on the second floor of a building called "Goose Farm," next to the Angel Inn, St John Street Road, Clerkenwell. De Cleve was buried in the churchyard of St Mary, Lambeth.

Dedeschina. *See* DESDECHINA.

Dedier. *See* DIDIER.

Deeble, Mr *(fl. 1767–1794), singer.*

As of 9 May 1767 Mr Deeble was earning 5s. nightly as a member of the singing chorus at Drury Lane. He was apparently still singing there in 1774–75, and he was probably the tenor who participated in the Handel Memorial concerts at Westminster Abbey and the Pantheon on 26, 27, 29 May and 3, 5 June 1784. Doane's *Musical Directory* of 1794 listed a Mr Deeble of Fish Street who was an alto singing with the Madrigal Society, and it is likely that this was the same person.

Deeve. *See* DEVOTO.

De Fesch, William *1687–1761, violinist, violoncellist, organist, composer.*

William (Willem) De Fesch was born at Alkmaar in 1687 and baptized on 26 August of that year. After studying under Alphonse d'Ève at Antwerp, De Fesch organized two concerts there between 1718 and 1722 and was made organist of the cathedral. In 1725 he became chapel master, succeeding his teacher. It was while he held this position in 1730 that he composed his *Missa Paschalis* for four voices and orchestra, which is preserved at the cathedral. He also wrote a number of works for the violoncello and six sonatas for violin, German flute, and organ.

In 1731 the hot-tempered De Fesch was dismissed for ill-treating and overworking the choir boys at Antwerp and came to London. His first appearance in England seems to have been on 13 March 1732 at Hickford's music room at a benefit for himself. On the following 10 May at the same place Mrs De Fesch had a shared benefit at which some of William's church music was performed; he played a new piece on the violin and Mrs De Fesch sang several songs in Italian. At Lincoln's Inn Fields on 16 February 1733 De Fesch's oratorio *Judith* was performed, but only after it had been announced for several previous dates, and De Fesch published an apology:

The Composer humbly hopes the Disappointment the Town met with by its being postpon'd, will be in no means imputed to him, it being occasioned by such an Accident as any one might unfortunately fall under, that of the Misconduct and pretended Sickness of Cecilia Young, who had ingaged for the Part of Judith.

What Cecilia Young pretended to be sick of (De Fesch's irascible temper perhaps) is not known. Hogarth celebrated the oratorio with his drawing of "A Chorus of Singers," which shows a rehearsal of *Judith*.

De Fesch had a benefit concert at the Devil Tavern on 30 May 1733, another at York Buildings on 8 April 1734, one at the Haymarket Theatre on 26 March 1735, and one at the Crown and Anchor Tavern on 29 February 1740 (a performance of *Judith*, tickets for which were available from the composer "on the pav'd stones in St. Martin's lane, next door to the Golden Peruke").

Harvard Theatre Collection

WILLIAM DE FESCH
engraving by Le Cave, after Soldi

Little was heard of De Fesch in London for the next few years, but on 21 March 1744 at the Crown and Anchor his new serenata, *Love and Friendship*, was performed, tickets for which were available from Mrs Misaubain at his old address. On 30 January 1745 De Fesch advertised subscriptions to three Wednesday performances at Covent Garden during Lent. *Love and Friendship* and another new piece by him, the oratorio *Joseph*, were presented on 6 and 20 March and 3 April.

De Fesch played in Handel's band when the master's *New Occasional Oratorio* was performed at Covent Garden on 14 February 1746, and on the following 8 April at Drury Lane De Fesch's *Love and Friendship* was revived, tickets from him at this time being available at the Ironmonger's in St Martin's Court, Leicester Fields. Beginning in 1748 De Fesch was the leader of the band at Marylebone Gardens, and during the years that followed he wrote most of his songs. The British Museum *Catalogue of Printed Music* contains three pages of works by the composer, the bulk of the pieces being light songs which such popular singers as Vernon, Miss Falkner, Miss Lenton, and Mrs Chambers sang at this pleasure garden. On 23 March 1754 another new theatre piece by De Fesch, the operetta *The London Prentice*, was given its first performance at Drury Lane. William De Fesch died on 3 January 1761 in London.

An engraved portrait of the musician by F. M. Le Cave after a painting by A. Soldi was published in 1751.

De Fesch, Mrs [William?] [fl. 1732], singer.

Mrs De Fesch, presumably the wife of the violinist and composer William, made her first English appearance singing several songs in Italian at Hickford's music room on 10 May 1732. She shared the benefits with a Mr St Helene, who was making his first public appearance; William De Fesch also appeared on the program.

De Florence, Ferdinand [fl. 1663–1665], musician.

On 19 October 1663 Ferdinand de Florence was appointed a French musician in ordinary in the King's Musick. He may have been the Mr Ferdinando who was in charge of the Chapel Royal choristers in 1664 and 1665. Ferdinand de Florence was possibly dismissed from the King's Musick in 1665.

De Fompré, Mons [fl. 1724–1736], actor, dancer.

Monsieur De Fompré was one of the masters of the troupe of "Italian" comedians who performed at the Haymarket Theatre from 17 December 1724 to 13 May 1725. De Fompré was the harlequin of the company and doubtless appeared in most of the productions, though the bills noted him only once, for his benefit on 8 March 1725. Most bills carried no casts. During their stay in London the foreign players ran themselves into debt, and on 18 April De Fompré had to place a notice in the newspapers that he would not be responsible for any debts contracted by members of the troupe.

De Fompré did not appear in London again until 8 April 1736, when he played Arlequin in *Le Mariage forcé* at Covent Garden, billed as having been received with great applause by the nobility and gentry ten years before. The Madame De Fompré who was active in London in 1734–35 must have been related to our subject, but they seem not to have played in England at the same time.

De Fompré, Mme [fl. 1734–1735], actress, dancer.

Madame De Fompré, surely related to Monsieur De Fompré who performed in London in 1724–25 and 1735–36, was one of the leading actresses in Francisque Moylin's troupe of players who visited London in 1734–35. The company played at the Haymarket Theatre from 26 October 1734 through 2 June 1735. The roles played by Madame De Fompré are most impressive: Marianne in *Le Tartuffe* (her first notice, on 20 November 1734), Alcmena in *Amphitryon*, Angelique in *La Malade imaginaire*, the title role in *Zaire*, Lucille in *Le Bourgeois gentilhomme*, the title role in *Inès de Castro*, Adelaide in *Gustave Vasa*, and Agnès in *L'École des femmes*. At the last performance at the Haymarket Theatre on 2 June and at a repetition of it on 4 June at Goodman's Fields Madame De Fompré joined in the grand ballet which concluded the evening.

De Fourmantelles. *See* FOURMANTEL.

De Franchetti, Rose. *See* ROSE, MISS.

De Frano, Mlle [fl. 1737], dancer.

Mademoiselle De Frano danced at Hallam's Bartholomew Fair booth on 23 August 1737 and at Hallam and Lee's Southwark Fair booth on the following 7 September.

De Frompe. *See* DE FOMPRÉ.

Degamar, Mr ₁*fl. 1760s?*₁, *actor.*

In his *Memoirs* James De Castro stated that "A person named *Degamar*, was a very inferior actor of his day; yet he stood high in the opinion of Mr Garrick, and used frequently to take more liberties with him in the mode of speech than those who ranked higher in the theatre." De Castro tells of Degamar visiting Garrick at his villa at Hampton, which Garrick bought in 1753, so perhaps Degamar was active in the theatre in the 1750s or 1760s. There is no other record of him.

De Gambarini, Elisabetta, later Mrs Chazal *b. 1731?, singer, composer, organist.*

Elisabetta de Gambarini may have been born in 1731, the birth date furnished on the portrait frontispiece to her two volumes of harpsichord lessons published in 1748. But it is likely that she was born somewhat earlier. She may have been singing for Handel as early as 1745, and perhaps she sang in the *Occasional Oratorio* in 1746 and 1747 and in *Joseph* in 1747. Certainly she sang the role of the first Israelite Woman in *Judas Maccabaeus* on 1 April 1747 at Covent Garden.

Though *The London Stage* does not record it, a benefit performance for Miss Gambarini was supposed to have been given at the Haymarket Theatre on 28 March 1748, at which she sang and played "on the Organ, accompanied by the best Masters, a War March and a Victory of her own composing . . ." She was living at this time in Argyll Buildings. She published *English and Italian Songs* about 1750. A song, *Tho' Mars, still Friends to*

France, published about 1759, was sung by her at her concert in Bath. On 15 April 1761 a benefit for her was presented at the concert room in Soho; *The Enchanted Forest* was performed, but no cast was listed. As Mrs Chazal, Elisabetta gave a concert at which she appeared as organist and composer, according to Dean's *Handel's Dramatic Oratorios and Masques.* Gerber, in his *Lexicon,* states that she was also a painter.

De Giardini, Felice. *See* GIARDINI.

De Giovanni, Pasquale ₁*fl. 1796–1820*₁, *singer.*

Pasquale De Giovanni's Italian career is obscure. He made his English debut at the King's Theatre on 2 January 1796, singing Mitrane in *Semiramide.* He appeared that season also as Zopiro in *Piramo e Tisbe* (first on 9 February), Nearco in *Antigona* (24 May), and Mordicone in *Il Tesoro.*

De Giovanni remained a constant singer of secondary roles in London's Italian opera through at least the season of 1819–20, except for the season of 11 January through 12 August 1817, when his name was not found in the bills. From 1815 or earlier he was (when present in the company) deputy stage manager. Besides those roles named above, he added the following (in approximate order chronologically):

Bartologgio in *L'amor fra le vendemmie,* Cecotto in *La modista raggiratrice,* Ufficiale in *Evalina,* Nardone in *Le gelosie villane,* Adrasto in *Ipermestra,* Messala in *Evalina,* Murena in *Cinna,* Riccardo in *Il consiglio imprudente,* Osmondo in *Elfrida,* Nearco in *Antigono,* Talete in *Medonte,* Fernando in *Ines de Castro,* Osmida in *Didone,* Efestioni in *Alessandro e Timoteo,* Farnace in *La morte di Mitridate,* Evandro in *Alceste,* Castiglione in *Zaira,* Marzio in *La clemenza di Scipione,* Demofoonte in *Die Zauberflöte,* Lisargo in *La cosa rara,* Antonio in *Le nozze di Figaro,* Fiorello in *La barbiere di Siviglia,* and one of the slaves in *Il flauto magico* (*Die Zauber-flöte*).

After the turn of the century Smith (*The Italian Opera . . . 1789–1820*) gives De Giovanni unspecified roles in some 33 operas.

Degnum. *See* DIGNUM.

"De Gomez, Madame." *See* HAY-WOOD, ELIZA.

Degon. *See* D'EGVILLE.

Degotti, Mr [*fl. 1797–1798*], *scene painter.*
Mr Degotti worked with Marinari as a scene painter at the King's Theatre in the Haymarket during the 1797–98 season and was noticed in the bill on 28 November 1797 when he and his partner executed new scenes for *Ipermestra.*

De Graeff. *See* GRAF.

De Grange. *See* LA GRANGE.

De Granger, Claude [*fl. 1663*], *musician.*
As of autumn 1663 Claude de Granger was a musician in ordinary in the musical service of Charles II.

De Gremont, Mlle [*fl. 1720*], *performer?*
A member of the French troupe that played at the King's Theatre in the Haymarket in the spring of 1720, Mlle De Gremont shared a benefit with two others on 20 June. She was, presumably, one of the performers in the company.

De Grimbergue, Jean-Baptiste *d. 1722, manager.*
Jean-Baptiste de Grimbergue (or Grimberghs, Grimberque) was the manager of the Grand Theatre in his native Brussels from 1709 to 1714, when he went into bankruptcy. Early in 1720 he brought a troupe of players, described later as belonging to the King of Sweden, to play from 5 March to 21 June 1720 at the King's Theatre in the Haymarket and, for performances on 4 and 5 April, the Lincoln's Inn Fields playhouse. The company was supported by royal commands and had a subscription of £1000 collected by 4 February before they set foot in England. Their fare was chiefly farces and comedies, including *Le Bourgeois gentilhomme* and *Le Malade imaginaire*. De Grimbergue had some troubles with his performers and published an apology in the *Daily Courant* of 2 May:

Monsieur de Grimbergue, Director of the French Comedians hereby gives Notice, that he is extreamly sorry he could not give on Friday last all the Entertainment he had promised in his Publick Bills, by reason that Signora VIOLENTA unluckily fell sick that very day; and Mons DANGEVILLE refused to Dance, being puft up by the Applause he had the good furtune to meet with; fancying he hath a Right to do so whenever he pleases.

But the season was successful enough to encourage the manager to return later in the year.

On 29 December 1720 he opened the new Haymarket Theatre with *La Fille à la mode ou le badeau de Paris*. The company was not as successful this time, and on 21 January 1721 the *London Journal* reported that they were going to return to the Continent. De Grimbergue denied the rumor, and the company stayed in London until 4 May, presenting a total of 51 performances. The repertory was again mostly farces and comedies, augmented with dancing and tumbling. Molière was a favored playwright, and Londoners saw for the first time *L'École des femmes, Le Médecin malgré lui,* and *L'Avare*—among others. The players ran themselves into debt, however, and later foreign troupes met resistance in London because of it. After returning to Brussels, de Grimbergue died on 16 August 1722.

D'Egville, Mons [fl. 1794], violinist.

Doane's *Musical Directory* of 1794 lists a violinist named D'Egville of No 18, Broad Street, Carnaby Market, who performed at Drury Lane Theatre and the King's Theatre. Inasmuch as most dancing masters also played the violin after some fashion, the entry may possibly refer to James Harvey D'Egville, who had danced at both patent houses. The rest of the D'Egvilles, dancers, lived at the Broad Street address in June 1792.

D'Egville, Miss [fl. 1794], singer.

Doane's *Musical Directory* of 1794 lists a soprano singer, Miss D'Egville, who was then living at No 18, Broad Street, Carnaby Market. This was the address of Peter D'Egville, ballet master, and she was doubtless one of his daughters.

D'Egville, Master [fl. 1794], singer.

Doane's *Musical Directory* of 1794 lists a male soprano singer, Master D'Egville, then living at No 18, Broad Street, Carnaby Market, the address of Peter D'Egville the dancing-master, probably the lad's father.

D'Egville, Fanny [fl. 1779–1800], dancer.

Fanny D'Egville was the elder daughter and probably the third child of the dancers Peter D'Egville (Dagueville) and his wife. She was the sister of James Harvey, George, Sophia, and Lewis, all professional dancers in the London theatres.

Fanny made her debut as a juvenile under the wing of her father at Covent Garden Theatre on 8 May 1779, dancing a minuet with Dumay at the end of Act II of *Love in a Village*. She returned to that house in 1779–80, being named first in the bill of 8 January, dancing with her elder brother Master James and Master Holland,

her father's pupil, at the end of Act IV of *The Merchant of Venice*. Her father confined her to anonymous choruses thereafter that season, though she was carried on the account book with a salary of £1 10s. per week. She did not reappear in the bills until 16 May 1780, when she assisted Dumay's benefit night by dancing with him "a new Minuet and Allemande" of her father's composition. She danced a minuet with her brother James for her father's benefit of 18 May.

Fanny D'Egville did not reappear on any London bill for the next eight years. She was almost certainly the Miss D'Egville who danced with her two older brothers and Miss Blanchet and Miss De Camp for her and her brothers' partial benefit) at Drury Lane Theatre on 5 June 1788. She had not been seen in the bills previously that season but in fact probably danced occasionally. It is uncertain whether or not she is to be understood as one of "the young Degvilles" occasionally in the Covent Garden bills for 1788–89, for this was a designation previously reserved for James and George. The boys went to Drury Lane the next season, but "Miss D'Egville" was distinguished in the bills only on 1 June when her brothers took their benefit along with Johnston and Dale. It seems likely that she was occupied in the pleasure gardens, fairs, and circuses during these *lacunae* in the record. At any rate, Fanny was with Sophia and George at Drury Lane from 16 November 1791 through 7 June 1792, like them earning £2 per week for a variety of humbler terpsichorean tasks. She joined George, Sophia, and Lewis in George Colman's Little Theatre in the Haymarket on 25 August 1792 to dance under James's direction in the afterpiece *The Enchanted Wood*; these dances were several times repeated through 7 August.

From 21 November 1792 through 10 June 1793, Fanny was frequently in the specialty and entr'acte dances with the

Drury Lane company at the King's Theatre, where James was now employed as ballet master and choreographer. Her salary was still a constant £2 per week. She returned to the company between 16 and 30 May 1794 at the same salary, then disappeared from all London bills until she rejoined the Drury Lane ballet and most of her family on 27 October 1794, remaining with them through 8 June. On the latter date she danced James's new device, *The Princess of Wales's New Minuet and Gavot*, for his and others' benefit. The town saw her no more, until, on 4 and 7 November 1797, she impersonated one of the Graces in Noverre's ballet *Cupid et Psyche* at Covent Garden.

At Drury Lane on 9 May 1798, Fanny appeared with the Labories, St Pierre, the Hilligsbergs, and others, the bill certifying "The whole Corps de Ballet from the Opera House," and thus, though there is no other record of her service at the King's Theatre, she nevertheless may have been dancing there during the periods when the records are blank. Her last recorded dance was with her brother, Master Lewis, in *The Duchess of York's New Minuet and Waltz*, composed by James D'Egville for Mrs George Mattocks's benefit performance at Covent Garden on 2 May 1800. There is every likelihood that Fanny D'Egville danced often in London until far into the nineteenth century.

D'Egville, George *fl. 1786–1806*, *dancer, dancing master.*

George D'Egville was the second son of Peter D'Egville and his wife, well-known London dancers. His older brother, James Harvey D'Egville, and his brother Lewis and sisters Fanny and Sophia were also dancers, and he bore some relationship to various other theatrical D'Egvilles.

George danced for the first time with his brother James and the twelve-year-old Maria Theresa De Camp at the Haymarket on 6 July 1786: "End of mainpiece a new

dance, *Jamie's Return* (in which a *Scotch Reel*) by the two Master Degvilles and Miss DeCamp." The youngsters were with the company all summer and were featured again in this number several times. On 1 September and several times following, they presented "a new Dance, *The Spanish Serenade; or, The Old Lover Outwitted.*"

The two brothers were brought to Drury Lane during the following fall and danced frequently together, singly, with other children, and with some adults, from 24 October 1786 through 6 June 1787.

George and James returned to the Haymarket during the summer of 1787 and to Drury Lane ("the two young Devilles") from 20 September 1787 through 13 June 1788. As in the previous season, the boys appeared often in dances created for them and Maria Theresa De Camp, such as the "new Dance, *La Soirée Provençalle*" which the trio presented at the end of Act III of *A New Way to Pay Old Debts* on 13 January 1787 and following and the one which they always danced in Act III of *Richard Coeur de Lion* from its first performance on 8 November 1787. They continued as staples of the fare of the house through 1788–89 and 1789–90, when they were paid jointly £7 10s. per week, and although Miss De Camp was now carried as an actress, she continued to appear frequently with them in dances.

In the 1790–91 season the brothers D'Egville were present at Drury Lane only from 27 December through 25 May. Their absence in the early part of the season is mysterious, as is the recession of their joint salary to only £6 per week. In 1792–93 the brothers' long juvenile partnership was severed. James, now grown, turned to choreography for the moment. But George was joined by his sisters Fanny (who had already appeared briefly with her brothers in 1788, 1790, and 1791) and Sophia. All were at the theatre from 16 November 1791 through 7 June 1792 at £2 per week apiece. Fanny and George and their young brother Lewis danced occasionally at the Haymarket in the summer of 1792. George was very probably the "Master D'Aigueville" who appeared several times at Bristol in January of 1792.

He continued at Drury Lane in 1792–93 and was busily employed that season from 21 November through 3 June, presumably at the weekly wage of £2 which was recorded for his siblings Lewis and Fanny. They all performed on 21 November 1792 in their brother James's composition accompanying Cobb and Storace's *The Pirates,* brought out with much fanfare. The piece held the boards for many performances that season and the next. George showed up only once in 1793–94, on 2 July; he was Philip in the first performance

Harvard Theatre Collection

MASTER JAMES HARVEY D'EGVILLE, MASTER GEORGE D'EGVILLE, MARIA THERESA DE CAMP (later MRS CHARLES KEMBLE), in *Jamie's Return*

engraving by Saillier, after Miller

of his brother's spectacle *Alexander the Great* on 12 February 1795.

All the D'Egvilles were absent from the London patent houses in 1795–96 and 1796–97, though they probably found work at the pleasure gardens or circuses, for which bills are far from complete. George was probably the D'Egville who danced a minuet with Miss Goddard at Drury Lane on 10 November 1797. The dancer Mrs Wybrow was advertised as his pupil in 1798.

George went to the King's Theatre to dance under the direction of James in the season of 14 January–4 August 1804. He was still there in 1805–6. The *Authentic History of the Green Room* (1804) placed him with Colman at the Haymarket in 1803–4 and testified that he had "been at the Royalty Theatre with Mr M'Cready, and since played at the Circus, and several parts of the kingdoms." The writer added: "He has lately been married to his second wife, and at present assists his brother in teaching."

An engraving by Saillier, after W. Miller, published in 1787, pictures George and his brother James, when the Masters D'Egville, with Maria Theresa De Camp (later Mrs Charles Kemble) in the dance of *Jamie's Return.*

D'Egville, James Harvey [*fl.* 1782– 1827?], *dancer, choreographer.*

James Harvey D'Egville was the eldest child of Peter D'Egville and his wife, dancers, and the brother of George, Fanny, Sophia, and Lewis, also dancers. He was also related in some fashion to other D'Egvilles (dancers, actors, and musicians) of the late eighteenth and early nineteenth centuries.

James first danced as a juvenile in performances in 1782 (or earlier) at the Royal Circus. His first appearance in a London theatre was with the twelve-year-old Maria Theresa De Camp at the Haymarket on 14 June 1786, dancing a piece

JAMES HARVEY D'EGVILLE
engraving by Freeman

called *The Nosegay.* On 6 July he and his brother George and Miss De Camp danced a "Scotch reel" *Jamie's Return,* which was favorably received and inspired an engraving of the three youngsters by Saillier in 1787. The brothers were professionally inseparable at Drury Lane in the winters and the Haymarket in the summers until the end of the 1792–93 season, in which apparently not only James and (probably) George, but Lewis, Fanny, and Sophia were with the Drury Lane company at the King's Theatre and Haymarket. James perhaps had entered on his majority by 1791 when he began to be referred to in the playbills as "Mr" rather than "Master."

Beginning with the winter of 1791 James danced some principal roles in the ballets accompanying the operas in O'Reilly's converted Pantheon, appearing first in the part of Mentor in a command performance of a new ballet by D'Auberval, *Telemachus in the Island of Calypso.* (In the second

performance, on 22 March, he was designated "D'Egville Jun." to distinguish him from Peter his father, still resident and active in London.) On 24 March he danced, in addition to Mentor, the title role in a dramatic ballet called *The Deserter.*

D'Egville returned to the Pantheon the following winter season, dancing there from 17 December until the disastrous fire of 14 January and with the Pantheon company at the Haymarket from 14 February through 9 June. He appeared as "Satyre" in D'Auberval's "New Pantomimic, Anacreontic Ballet," as a principal in the same choreographer's *La Fête villageoise,* and *Le Volage fixé* and as Pacha in his *La Foire de Smirne; ou, Les Amans réunis.* On 26 April 1792 "James Degueville" married Catherine Berry at St Marylebone. He directed some dance spectacles for Colman at the Haymarket the following summer.

When on 26 January 1793 the King's Theatre in the Haymarket became once again the permanent home of London's opera and ballet, James D'Egville joined the tiny *corps de ballet* as master and remained through the end of the season on 29 June 1793. He was Jupiter in Noverre's "new Heroic Pantomime Ballet *Venus and Adonis,*" Agamemnon in his *Iphiginia in Aulide,* and a principal in his *Le Faune infidèle,* all frequently repeated.

On 1 June 1793 at the end of the opera, D'Egville commenced his career as choreographer by unveiling "a new Pastoral Ballet" called *Le Jaloux puni,* which caused little stir. He was absent from the opera during most of the 1794 season, rejoining the corps of dancers there only on 1 April when he danced an unspecified part in Noverre's *Les Ruses de l'amour,* which he repeated frequently until the season ended on 8 July. He was paid £2 on 2 July for supplying some short dance figures and dancing in them ("by permission of the Proprietor of the King's Theatre") in a benefit performance at Drury Lane for the relicts of the men who had died in Lord

Howe's naval action of 1 June. He evidently lost heavily on his benefit that season for on 7 July 1794 the account book noted a payment from him of £13 1s. 6d. toward making up the discrepancy between his receipts and the charges of the house.

James danced again for the opera's ballet corps during the 1794–95 seasons but only from 6 to 16 December inclusive, appearing six times in Onorati's "Grand Heroic Pantomime Ballet" *Giustino I, imperatore dei Romani* and then leaving the King's Theatre. According to Cecil Price: *"The Times,* 26 Dec 1794, reported that D'Egville had been dismissed rather cavalierly from his post as dancer at the King's Theatre. He began a lawsuit against Taylor, but lost it because 'the contract was not on a stamp' (The *True Briton,* 2 June 1795)." D'Egville joined George, Lewis, Fanny, and Sophia at Drury Lane on 12 February 1795, for which date he contrived the pantomime *Alexander the Great; or, The Conquest of Persia* for the music of Krazinski Miller. The *Biographia Dramatica* reported that John Philip Kemble wrote a description of the action which he "distributed gratis at the theatre."

This ponderous pantomime was generally well received, but despite 54 rehearsals before its performance, some of the curious devices encountered difficulties and consequent stricture. The spectacle required, besides the acting company and dancers, 200 soldiers, each of whose costumes cost £5. Because of the mob of extras the grand procession of Alexander's entry into Babylon could not be properly formed backstage and "was sent on in a very confused manner." Moreover, Alexander's car was not ready for the premier performance. It was, however, completed for the second performance, on 13 February, and entered to applause, being drawn by two elephants, and accompanied by Darius's car, drawn by white horses. James played Alexander himself and involved all his brothers and sisters in minor actions. The preparation of

Alexander was the most arduous enterprise of James's year, which was nevertheless filled with dancing engagements and kept him running from his lodging at No 29, Lichfield Street, Soho, to Drury Lane and the opera house. His salary from Drury Lane was £8 per week.

Neither James nor his relatives are to be found in any London playbills for the 1795–96 or 1796–97 seasons, and during the following season only George and Fanny performed—once apiece. A notation of 13 November 1795 in the Drury Lane account book shows payment of £30 to

Harvard Theatre Collection

JAMES HARVEY D'EGVILLE, as Caractacus

artist unknown

James "for waving [*sic*] his Claim to an Engagement this Season." One D'Egville—probably James—performed a few times at the Royal Circus in 1798, and Willson Disher found James also dancing the clown at Sadler's Wells that year, in Joseph Grimaldi's absence.

On 26 March 1799 James returned to his old association with the King's Theatre as ballet master. On that date he refurbished D'Auberval's ballet *Télémaque*. During this season James's wife was among the female dancers. The D'Egvilles remained at the King's through 1801–2, going to Drury Lane the next season. James's name appeared in a *London Chronicle* account of 4 April 1800 of the trial (at which he was a witness) of the murderers of the dancer Louis Barthelemici. He apparently also produced, on special commission, a few spectacular productions at Covent Garden in 1801–2, although the *Monthly Mirror* was severe upon his work for the regular theatres: "We rather think that his abilities, powerful and scientific as unquestionably they are, are not exactly calculated for an English ballet." Mr and Mrs D'Egville were at Nottingham in May of 1802, and he went on to Birmingham alone in June. This brief surviving glimpse of provincial ramblings probably explains where they were during the gaps in the London chronology.

James, without his wife, returned to the opera for the brilliant season of 14 January–4 August 1804 and there met again his brother George. James was performing in "a new Caledonian Ballet of his own composition" at the Royal Circus on 21 October 1804. George remained in the company in 1805–6 but James was absent, being again employed as ballet master at Drury Lane where on 5 June 1806 he showed his *Mountain Robbers; or, the Terrific Horn*. He was still in the Drury Lane company the following season, and on 16 September 1807 the management gave him a new contract, to run to the end

of the 1809–10 season. He was to be master and principal dancer at a salary of £18 per week with "the Privilege of using his own new Pieces for his Benefit." He was also to be given payments from time to time, as the subsequent accounts show, for his many young pupils. In the Public Record Office is a notice of a license to him for "Juvenile Entertainments of Burlettas, Operettas, Ballets, Pantomimes, Action Songs &c. by his own Pupils under 12 years of Age." Though the custom of introducing one's pupils singly or in reasonable numbers was a time-honored one, evidently D'Egville was responsible for the vogue of introducing what the *Monthly Mirror* called "a numerous troop of infants" into classical and popular ballets. The practice, doubtless a consequence of the sentimental craze for the "Young Roscius" William Henry West Betty and his imitators, like little Miss Mudie, spread at the patent theatres and the opera and was much and justly complained of in the critical press.

The contract notwithstanding, James returned to the King's Theatre in 1808, this time not only as the master and principal dancer but as acting manager of the entire company as well. No doubt the Opera had offered him more money. (James does not appear to have been overscrupulous; when he had gone to Drury Lane on his latter tour, he had lured the Opera's star dancer Parisot with him by dangling a fee of 1000 guineas and devising new ballet spectacles for her, like *Terpsichore* and *Emily, or, Juvenile Indiscretion*.) The season of James's return to the King's was a very difficult one. Counter-claims to the patenteeship of the opera house advanced by Edmund Waters against William Taylor in the autumn of 1807 had not been finally adjudicated by the Lord Chamberlain when the redecorated house opened in January 1808. It was necessary for D'Egville to pacify the temperamental Madame Catalani, who had been engaged by Taylor at the enormous fee of £5250 and who at first refused to sing until the entire sum had been advanced—a manifest impossibility for the harassed D'Egville and his treasurer Schelmerdine. But D'Egville directed a season which was by and large successful, and he grossed £465 19s. at his benefit. His own salary was a handsome £800.

James Harvey D'Egville's full name was signed to a petition circulated after the Drury Lane fire of 24 February 1809. The Lord Chamberlain was asked to lend his influence to efforts at the theatre's resuscitation. All the other signatories—R. W. Elliston, Richard Wroughton, John Bannister, John Braham, John Johnstone, and William Dowton—were functionaries or stellar performers of Drury Lane; some were both. Thus the inference should be that D'Egville was in 1809 ballet master at Drury Lane as well as at the opera.

William Taylor regained effective control of the King's Theatre in the fall of 1808, quarreled with D'Egville, and dismissed him at the end of the 1809 season. The Public Record Office holds a petition of 28 August 1809 from "James Harvey D'Egville late acting Manager and now Ballet Master of the Opera House and his pupils" (A^y Noble, C. Twamly, A. Twamly, C. Davis, B. Green, N. Toose, A. Smith, S. Peto, the sisters B., F., and H. Dennet, C. Bristow, H. Davis, N. Gayton, and one Hodges). D'Egville alleged that for the "greater part" of his life "he has been Constantly employed in directing the Ballet department at the King's Theatre" and that he "by his sole and laborious exertions" had "again established Mr Taylor as Manager of the Opera." The ingrate had, nevertheless, dismissed him and his pupils without warning or reason on 4 July 1809. D'Egville asserted that he had a written contract for five years.

William Taylor's reply also survives: that D'Egville had been employed only pro tem while Taylor waited upon Joseph Rossi's arrival; that D'Egville was a turbulent character, well-known for his offen-sive behavior and physical assaults on some of the players, which had brought him into the law courts; that of the 15 pupils he had named only eight had been employed by Taylor, D'Egville having insisted on bringing in the rest; and that, as to remuneration, "within about 15 months that he was actually engaged in the business of this concern, he received in Salaries and Benefits above £4000—besides the sums paid to his pupils (exceeding £1200) of which it is generally understood that he enjoyed a considerable portion." D'Egville evidently lost the argument.

From 1804 through at least 1810, D'Egville and his pupils were frequently to be seen also in the summer offerings at the Haymarket. Though he was exiled from the King's in 1809–10, he was there again in 1810–11. After these dates his career as a dancer cannot be followed, and his death date is not known to us. Nicoll cites, however, the productions of his ballet *Naissance de Venus* at the King's Theatre in 1826 and his *Le Siège de Cythère* in 1827.

In addition to the ballets and other dance productions noted in passing, a list of D'Egville's works would include the following. Except where noted all were produced at the King's Theatre: *Achille et Deidamie*, Drury Lane, 21 June 1804; *Amintas et Sylvie*, 29 December 1801; *Les Amours de Glauque et Circé*, 6 January 1809; *Barbara and Allen*, 17 February 1801; *La Belle laitière*, 26 January 1805; *Le Bon prince*, 31 May 1794; *Constance et Almazor*, 19 May 1808; *La Coquette villageoise*, 20 March 1802; *Crazy Jane*, 4 April 1805; *Don Quichotte*, 14 February 1809; *La Double épreuve*, 17 June 1808; *L'Enlèvement de Déjanire*, 9 February 1808; *La Fête chinoise*, 20 February 1808; *La Fille sauvage*, 6 June 1805; *Heliska*, 16 June 1801; *Hylas et témire*, 23 April 1799; *Hyppomène et Atalante*, 8 March 1800; *Irza*, 2 February 1802; *Les Jeux floraux*, Haymarket, 20 March 1809; *Le Jugement de Midas*, 20 February 1802; *Le Mariage mexicain*, 25 February 1800; *Le Mariage secret*, 26 March 1808; *Mora's Love*, 15 June 1809; *La Naissance de Flore*, 27 April 1809; *La Naissance de Venus*, Haymarket, 1826; *L'Offrande à l'amour*, 2 March 1805; *L'Offrande à Bacchus*, 2 January 1808; *Ossian*, 23 May 1805; *Paul and Virginia*, Lyceum, 11 May 1810; *Pygmalion*, 3 January 1801; *Des Quatre nations*, 21 April 1801; *Rinaldo and Leonara*, 29 May 1800; *Le Siège de Cythère*, Haymarket 1827; *Telasco and Amgahi*, Drury Lane, 14 May 1800; *Télémaque*, 26 March 1799; *Terpsichore's Return*, Drury Lane, 1 November 1805; *Le Voeu témeraire*, 14 January 1804.

Portraits of James Harvey D'Egville include the following:

1. A portrait engraved by S. W. Reynolds.

2. A portrait engraved by S. Freeman for the *Monthly Mirror*, 1809; the same engraving was also published by W. Smith.

3. As Caractacus; a vignette etching, colored.

4. With Deshayes, in *Achilles and Deidamia*, engraved and printed (in color) by A. Cardon, 1804; D'Egville's figure alone, from this engraving, was also published by Cardon.

5. When Master D'Egville, with his brother George and Maria Theresa De Camp (later Mrs Charles Kemble) in the dance *Jamie's Return*, engraved by Saillier, after W. Miller, 1787.

D'Egville, Mrs James Harvey, Catherine, née Berry ⟨*fl.* *1791–1802*⟩, *dancer.* See **D'EGVILLE, JAMES HARVEY.**

D'Egville, Lewis ⟨*fl.* *1792–1799*⟩, *dancer.*

Lewis D'Egville was apparently a younger son of the dancers Peter D'Egville (Dagueville) and his wife and thus the brother of James Harvey, George, Fanny, and Sophia D'Egville (and perhaps others).

Lewis was first noticed by name dancing as a juvenile at the Haymarket with his brother George and other young people in *The Enchanted Wood* on 25 July 1792, an entertainment which was repeated several times thereafter. The following fall found him at Drury Lane with his brother James (and probably George also) and his sisters Sophia and Fanny. He was earning £2 a week doing chorus dancing and was sometimes featured in afterpieces and entr'acte performances. He danced with some regularity from 13 October through 3 June with Drury Lane's dispossessed company, first at the King's Theatre and then alternately both there and across the street at the Little Theatre in the Haymarket.

He was the "Master D'Egville" who performed with his sisters dances composed by James his brother for Cobb's opera *The Pirates* on 16 May 1794. The D'Egvilles were not noticed earlier that season and appeared only twice more, in that same piece, on 16 and 30 May.

All the D'Egvilles were with the Drury Lane dance company at some point in the 1795–96 season, but Master Lewis was evidently brought in only to dance again in *The Pirates* on 27 October and 17 and 25 November.

Lewis's last known appearance in London (still as "Master") was with one of his sisters in dances at the end of the mainpiece and afterpiece at Covent Garden Theatre on 2 May 1799.

D'Egville, Peter ⟨*fl.* *1768–1794*⟩, *dancer, ballet master, choreographer.*

The dancer Peter D'Egville was evidently an immigrant, though we find no record of a French or other continental career. (The name is spelled variously in the bills. Peter, the head of the family in England, evidently persisted in spelling it, or allowing it to be spelled "Daigueville," but the second generation preferred "D'Egville.")

Peter was first noticed in London dancing

with Mrs King during the intervals of *Artaxerxes* at Drury Lane on 1 November 1768 in "A New Dance call'd *The Piedmontese Mountaineer*," repeated on 3 November 1768 and subsequently. He was "first dancer" and by perhaps 1770 also ballet master at the theatre. He and his wife were paid £200 by Drury Lane in 1772–73. On 19 October 1769 he had also entered into an agreement with Thomas King, "Manager and Director" of Sadler's Wells, "for and in behalf of himself and his five pupils namely John Holland, Richard Scriven, Mary Ross [later Madame Texier], Elizabeth Armstrong and Harriet Medlicot." They were to receive jointly £175 for dancing at the Wells "as often as required" and were to agree to perform nowhere else in London except there and the Theatres Royal.

On 17 March 1772 Peter exploited this dual exposure of his talents by advertising "to the Nobility and Gentry, that he has an elegant dancing room No 38 Cow Lane, Snowhill; where he continues to teach every day the *Dauphin's Minuet* and others." He was willing to teach "abroad . . . when required; and at the request of his scholars he will give a Ball on the 10th instant," admission 10s. 6d. He thus evidently drew to his tutelage many private pupils. His professional scholars included his own five (or more) children, James Harvey, George, Fanny, Sophia, and Lewis (and perhaps C. D. D'Egville).

Peter and his wife were evidently discharged from Drury Lane by Garrick, along with Jean Baptiste Vidini, in the middle of the 1773–74 season. An obscurely worded letter from Joseph Yorke to Garrick dated 22 March 1774 seems to give that implication; and on 24 February 1774 D'Egville had advertised for students from "his house in King-Square Court, Dean St. Soho," as "late Ballet-Master, and First Dancer, at Drury Lane Playhouse." (He offered "the Minuet, Louvre, Cotillons, Allemande, Dauphine, Country Dances &c.") "Daig-

ville's scholars" were dancing after the opera performances at the King's Theatre on 24 and 26 March 1774.

The following season, 1774–75, found D'Egville and his wife dancing at Covent Garden, with Peter serving as principal dancer and ballet master. On 7 October he furnished a "New Grand Ballet call'd *The Village Festival*" for his friend Vidini's first Covent Garden appearance and Helm's English debut. It was repeated several times. On the night of the D'Egvilles' benefit, 12 May 1775, he and "his Scholar" danced in a comic dance of his own contriving called *The Country Macaroni Assembly*; he did a "wooden Shoe Dance," and his wife was featured as the Queen in *Boadicea Queen of Britain*, assisted by "her two daughters."

Madame D'Egville does not seem to have returned to Covent Garden in 1775–76, though Peter was fully employed and for his benefit on 3 May introduced "Mas. Dagueville dancing a Minuet and an Allemande" with a "girl only 5 years old." On 7 May 1776 "Peter Dagville," as he signed himself this time, wrote the following letter to Willoughby Lacy at Drury Lane from "mr jrland upholster bow Street Covent Garden":

Mr Dagville Compliment to Mr Lacy and wille be Glad to know if it is anny Room in your house next Saison for me as a ballet master principal Dancer and to act in the pantomine a principall charactere if is Wanted — at the Sallery of 160 pounds for the Saison an a benefitte in aprile 20 as j huse to have before. Mr Lacy will oblige mr Dagville of an ansWhere j am Sir your most obeidient   Servante

Lacy evidently declined to reinstate him at Drury Lane. D'Egville had presumably displeased the management at Covent Garden, for he appeared there only twice in the next season, both times for benefits and toward the end of the season — on 28 April 1777, for Quick, "End of Mainpiece *The*

Humours of Newmarket, with the Poney Races, by Dagueville (1st appearance this season)," a performance repeated for the benefit of Wild the prompter on 5 May.

It is probable, then, that the "Dagueville" who danced at Bristol in 1776 was Peter D'Egville, but his movements from that point until his return to London and Covent Garden for the 1777–78 season are obscure. Perhaps he busied himself with private teaching in London, as he had done earlier, or in Bristol, as he seems to have done later.

His powers were now declining, and he was no longer top-billed at Covent Garden, nor did he receive the highest salary among the dancers. He was third on the list, at £4 13*s.* per week (behind Sga Tinte at £6 6*s.* and Aldridge at £6), and the sum may have paid also for the occasional services of his son Master (James Harvey) D'Egville. In 1778–79 the two male "Daguevilles" were at Covent Garden from 14 October through 24 May and 10 November through 8 May respectively, and on 14 May they also danced at Drury Lane, in the popular *The Humours of Newmarket.* On 8 May at Covent Garden first appeared "Miss Dagueville," certainly Peter's elder daughter Fanny, dancing a minuet with Dumay at the end of the mainpiece.

The 1779–80 season was Peter D'Egville's last year of service at Covent Garden. He still received £4 13*s.* per week. During most of the season his son was in the *corps de ballet,* and so, through the spring only, was Fanny. "Mme Dagueville" was featured once in out-of-season performances at the Haymarket in the spring of 1784 and once in the following summer's regular Haymarket season.

The elder D'Egvilles were employed as figure dancers for the opera at the King's Theatre in 1782–83 and again in 1785–86. "Mme Dageville" danced the principal part in a dramatic dance called *The Skirmish* at the Haymarket at least twice in the summer of 1785, but Peter does not seem to have

been of that company. Again, the gaps in Peter's chronology may be conjecturally filled by supposing that he taught or that he went to the provinces. He and his wife drop from the records for a long period after 1785–86.

Though the name is not carried in the Drury Lane bills for 1789–90 through 1793–94, Peter evidently did dance sometimes there, for the surviving manuscript pay books of the theatre show payments almost weekly to "Degville Sr" and two "Juniors" or sometimes (early in 1789–90) to "Degville and Sons," later the same season to "Degville" and two "Nephews," but quite evidently refering to James and George. Coupled with them in the accounts is a pupil of Peter's named Blanchett. Peter was receiving salaries for all. After this year the usual designation is "Degvilles," though once "Degville's 2 lads." In 1794 (17 May) "Degville Sen" was "raised 0:6:8 per day" and his sons identified: "G[eorge] Degville [31 May] raised 6*s.* 8*d.*"; and on 7 June James Degville received a payment of £8. At the time of a benefit the "young Degvilles" shared with several others on 7 June 1792, they were living at No 18, Broad Street, and presumably so were their parents. It seems likely that Peter and son James were the "D'Aigueville and Son, Dancing Masters" who set up an academy at No 19, College Street, Bristol, in December 1791; and we believe it almost certain that the Mr, Miss, and Master d'Aigueville who danced at Bristol in January 1792 were Peter, his daughter (probably Fanny), and his son George.

After about 1794 it is sometimes difficult to tell whether notices refer to Peter or to James, and it may be that during the 1794–95 season some of the dances credited to "D'Egville, Sen" are not by him but by his son James. Peter's death date is not known to us. (A Mr C. D. D'Egville who was on the Drury Lane roster as a dancer in 1814–15 was perhaps a son or grandson.)

D'Egville, Mme Peter [fl. 1772–1786], dancer. See D'EGVILLE, PETER.

D'Egville, Sophia [fl. 1791–1795], dancer.

Sophia D'Egville was the younger daughter of the dancer Peter D'Egville and his wife and the sister of James, George, Fanny, and Lewis D'Egville, also dancers.

Sophia's first professional appearances were as a small child in the Drury Lane company playing at the King's Theatre. She earned £2 per week from 16 November 1791 through 7 June 1792. It is not clear from the bills whether Sophia and her brother Lewis and sister Fanny (with whom she invariably appeared) were regulars in the corps or were simply hired for the nine occasions when they were listed as dancing in the afterpiece *Richard Coeur de Lion.* We conclude, however, that inasmuch as they shared a benefit performance with Johnson, Nix, and Dale on 7 June, they belonged to the company. They were said to live at that time at No 18, Broad Street (known to have been Peter D'Egville's address).

Sophia and all her siblings were connected with the Drury Lane company in 1792–93. She danced, again infrequently featured, mostly with her brother Lewis. She still earned £2 per week from 13 October through 10 June doing *gavottes, minuets de la cour,* or an occasional *pas russe* or comic dance, most of them of her brother James's devising.

In the following season the younger D'Egvilles failed to appear anywhere, so far as the bills tell, until 16 May 1794. They then performed their brother's dances for *The Pirate,* repeated again on 30 May. But they were not noted afterward that season.

All the D'Egvilles were together again with the displaced Drury Lane company in 1794–95, and again their principal activity was the dancing in *The Pirates* from 27 October through 8 June. They were, however, involved in the premier performance of their brother James's heroic pantomime spectacle *Alexander the Great* on 12 February 1795. Sophia was one of the 10 "Attendant Females." The pantomime was repeated some half dozen times that season. There is no record of Sophia's career or life after that date.

De Henney, [Mme?] [fl. 1753], dancer.

A Madame, or possibly Mademoiselle, De Henney shared a benefit at Covent Garden on 14 May 1753. She was, according to the *Public Advertiser,* a dancer.

De Hervigni. See D'HERVIGNI.

De Hesse. See DESHAYES and DESSE.

De Hightrehight, Mr [fl. 1718], fire-eater.

Malcolm's *Anecdotes* contains a description of a performance in 1718 by the Swiss fire-eater from the valley of Annivi, Mr De Hightrehight:

This tremendous person ate burning coals, chewed flaming brimstone and *swallowed* it, licked a red-hot poker, placed a red-hot heater on his tongue, kindled coals on his tongue, suffered them to be blown, and broiled meat on them, ate melted pitch, brimstone, beeswax, sealing-wax, and rosin, with a spoon; and to complete the business he performed all these impossibilities five times *per diem* at the Duke of Marlborough's head in Fleet-street, for the trifling receipts of 2*s.* 6*d.* 1*s.* 6*d.* and 1*s.* Master Hightrehight had the honour of exhibiting before Lewis XIV. the Emperor of Germany, the King of Sicily, the Doge of Venice, and an infinite number of princes and nobles—and the Prince of Wales, who had nearly lost his inconceivable pleasure by the envious interposition of the Inquisition at Bologna and in Piedmont, which holy office seemed inclined to try *their mode of burning* on his *body,* leaving to him the care of resisting the flames and rendering them harmless; but he was preserved from the unwelcome ordeal by the interference of the

Duchess Royal Regent of Savoy and the Marquis Bentivoglia.

Deighton. *See* **DIGHTON.**

Deitrich. *See* **DIETRICH.**

De Jardin, Mons ₁*fl. 1750–1751₁, *dancer.*

On 8 January 1750 Monsieur De Jardin presented a *Tambourin* dance in Act III of *Volpone* at the Covent Garden Theatre in his first appearance on the English stage. This became one of his most popular dances, one which he offered as a specialty dance for the rest of the season and revived the following fall. In addition, De Jardin participated in the spring of 1750 in *The Fair,* the masquerade dance in *Romeo and Juliet,* and a Dutch dance. His salary during his engagement was £3 weekly. In 1750–51 he appeared as Mars (Leander) in *Merlin's Cave,* Zephyrus in *Apollo and Daphne,* and in a grand ballet called *The Gondoliers.*

Delaboyde. *See* **DELAHOYDE.**

De La Brun. *See* **LE BRUN.**

De La Chapelle, Mons ₁*fl. 1791–1792₁, *dancer.*

Monsieur De La Chapelle was a French dancer in the King's company in 1791–92. During that season the King's company played at the Pantheon until it burned to the ground on 14 February 1792 and played thereafter at the Haymarket. De La Chapelle made his first appearance dancing in the ballet *La Fête villageoise* on 31 December 1791. On 10 March he danced in the pantomime ballet *Le Volage fixé* and on 14 April he danced the role of Almozadin in *La Foire de Smirne.* After their initial performances, all three pieces were danced regularly during the season, with De La Chapelle making his final appearance, on 9 June 1792, in the latter two.

Perhaps he was related to Jean Baptiste Armand Chapelle (1755–1823), who acted at the Théâtre du Vaudeville in Paris.

De La Cointrie, Mons ₁*fl. 1751–1753₁. *See* **DE LA COINTRIE, MME.**

De La Cointrie, Mme ₁*fl. 1749–1752₁, *dancer.*

Madame De La Cointrie made her first appearance on the English stage on 15 April 1749, when she danced with Villeneuve at Covent Garden. At that time her name was printed on the bill as "Contair"; at other times during her career it appeared as "Contri." On 21 April 1749, now billed as "Madame De La Cointrie," she made her second appearance, dancing again with Villeneuve, and on 21 April her third, dancing this time with Froment in a *Scotch Measure,* a *Highland Reel,* and a minuet. In the following season she moved over to Drury Lane, where she made her debut on 11 October 1749 as an aerial spirit in the dancing chorus of *Comus,* a role she repeated a number of times throughout her brief career in London. On 9 November she performed as one of the peasant dancers in *The Savoyard Travellers* (also repeated throughout the season), on 20 April she danced a minuet with Mathews, and on 28 April she shared a benefit with Master Mattocks.

For the season of 1750–51, Madame De La Cointrie returned to Covent Garden; she danced as an aerial spirit in *Merlin's Cave* on 21 December (repeated throughout the season) and the parts of Daphne and Flora in *Apollo and Daphne* on 26 December; on 4 May 1751, she shared a benefit with other dancers and some house servants, an indication of her minor status in the company. Back at Covent Garden in 1751–52, she danced again in *Merlin's Cave* and probably appeared as a chorus member in other dances. Her name did not appear after that season, but a Mr Cointrie danced Scaramouche in the *Necromancer* on 20

December 1751 and many times throughout this season and the following one. He may also have been the "La Cointe" who danced at Covent Garden in 1755–56.

De la Cour, W. *fl. 1740–1763*, *scene painter.*

The Monsieur de la Cour who painted a new scene for the production of *Busiri* at the Haymarket Theatre on 10 May 1740 was probably the "Lacourt" who was paid £21 for painting scenes for *The Fair* at Covent Garden on 7 February 1750. He was doubtless the W. de la Cour who worked in Scotland from at least 1759 through 1763. Boswell and Gentleman in *A View of the Edinburgh Theatre* remarked on the summer season of 1759:

We cannot conclude this Work without observing, of what infinite Advantage it is to The Edinburgh Theatre, to have the Decorations done by so good a Painter as Mr. De la Cour, who was brought hither during the Administration of Mr. DIGGES. Some of our Number have the Pleasure of being acquainted with this ingenious Artist, who are of the Opinion, that his amiable Character in private Life, is no less to be esteemed, than his beautiful and elegant Landschapes are to be admired. We are happy to find him gaining Patronage of People of Taste in this Country; and, we hope, he shall continue to meet with Encouragement equal to his Merit.

Unfortunately the painter did not continue to meet with that encouragement. On 5 March 1763 he complained in the *Edinburgh Courant*:

Mr De la Cour to the Public.

As the managers of the theatre, in order to prejudice me, do now employ another to paint their decorations for both here and Glasgow, spreading about that I have been too dear, the only remedie I could think of to expose this false report and undeceive the public, was by giving an account of my prices, as also in what manner I have been paid. For the front scenes, such as towns, chambers,

forests, &c., of fifteen feet square each, never above £7, 7s.; for the wings, £1, 1s.; and so in proportion for the rest, though those I did for Newcastle were still cheaper. As I received the payment of above only by benefits, the managers, instead of being losers, must have considerably gained, because they were always on such nights as the charges of the house could not otherwise have been cleared. Last year, for instance, they gave me Monday, February 1st, as this was a fast day of the Church of England. Had it not been for the goodness of my friends, I could not have defrayed expenses, which amounted to £22.

Dibdin, in his *Annals of the Edinburgh Stage*, noted that the house at Edinburgh could hold only £60, so that the house charges noted by De la Cour were as high in proportion as those of any London playhouse at this time. In any case, the painter's plea seems to have done him little good, for the records of the Edinburgh theatre make no mention of him after this.

Del'Acqua, Teresa *fl. 1790*, *singer.*

Signora Teresa Del'Acqua sang in the first act of *La buona figliuola* when that act alone was presented as part of a program at the Haymarket Theatre on 25 March 1790. It was her first public appearance. On 27 May she had a role in *Gli schiava per amore.*

De la Croix, Mlle *fl. 1790–1799*, *dancer.*

Mlle De la Croix was first recorded dancing in London when she took an unspecified "principal part" in "A new comic Dance . . . called *Old Age Metamorphosed*" at Hughes's Royal Circus on 3 July 1790, a performance repeated several other times that summer.

She had perhaps danced earlier that year in the *corps de ballet* of the Italian opera, then in temporary quarters at Covent Garden. Smith lists her as in the company, but no bills are cited. Certainly she was at the King's Theatre with the ballet of the Italian opera by 28 June 1791 when she took the role of Cateau, "mère de Colette," in the ballet *La Fête du seigneur*.

Mlle De la Croix was absent from London's boards until 16 March 1797 when the Covent Garden playbill announced that she was appearing for the first time on that stage, in the leading part of Maugrette in Charles Farley's musical gothic extravaganza *Raymond and Agnes*. The piece was repeated many times during the season. She was advertised as "from the Opera House" when she danced at the theatre in Richmond, Surrey, on 1 September. She signed articles at Covent Garden for £2 2*s*. per night in the 1797–98 season, appearing again as Maugrette on 7 October and many times thereafter and being featured in several specialty dances and ballets.

Evidently the Covent Garden management adopted a lenient attitude to her appearances outside the patent theatre, unless the *Madame* De la Croix who is listed in the cast of *Blackbeard; or, the Captive Princess*, "Performed for the first time at the Royal Circus on Easter Monday, 1798, and repeated upwards of One-hundred Nights in the course of the Season" is some other person. Madame De la Croix figured in a news item in the *Times* of 5 June 1798:

The Managers of the Opera house, it seems, have very politely given permission to those of their dancers to appear on the boards of the R[oyal] C[ircus] tomorrow night, for the benefit of Mad. De la Croix, whose apartments were lately robbed to a very considerable amount. . . . the Managers of the Circus, with their usual liberality, have given her the receipts of to-morrow night.

If Mlle (or Mme) De la Croix was in the regular dance company at Covent Garden in the 1798–99 season the fact was not publicly noted. She played Maugrette twice more, on 20 and 24 April 1799, but her name did not appear again in the bills.

De la Fond, Mr ₁*fl. 1716*₁, *impresario*.

Dudley Ryder recorded in his diary on 25 January 1716:

Went to brother's and then to concert of music at Mr. De la Fond which he has every Wednesday night at 7 o'clock. There was pretty good music and a boy that belongs to St. Paul's of about nine year old that sung several songs to the Harpsichord and viol; he had the strongest and finest [voice] I ever heard in my life from a child.

Delagar, Mr ₁*fl. 1775*₁, *dancer*.

The Drury Lane account books for 25 February 1775 show Mr Delagar (or Delegal) as a dancer receiving a weekly salary of £1 10*s*.

Delagarde, ₁Charles?₁ ₁*fl. 1705–1736*₁, *dancer, choreographer, dancing master*.

There were at least three male dancers named Delagarde (or D'Legard, Legard) performing in London in the first half of the eighteenth century—a father and his two sons. The father may have been named Charles, since that was the Christian name of the son usually called Delagarde Junior. The elder Delagarde was first noticed in contemporary advertisements on 12 December 1705 when he participated in a Grand Dance (repeated on 15 and 17 December) at the Queen's Theatre in the Haymarket. He was mentioned again on 25 April and participated in a dance called *Three Clowns* on 13 June. He danced at Drury Lane in 1706–7 and 1707–8, appearing on 4 November 1707 with his student Miss Morris and on 21 February 1708 in *The Saltarella* with Hester Santlow. The Coke papers at Harvard show him to have been at the Queen's Theatre again in 1708–9 at a salary of 12*s*. 6*d*. daily. In 1708, 1710, and 1711 he wrote down Isaac's dances for the Queen's birthday; on 26 January 1710 at Drury Lane and on 7 April 1711 at the Queen's Theatre he was billed as dancing with Mrs Delagarde—presumably his wife; and on 2 May 1712 he performed at Drury Lane with Miss Santlow for her benefit.

On 1 January 1715, billed for some reason as appearing for the first time in six years, Delagarde danced at the Lincoln's Inn Fields playhouse, and there he continued through 31 October 1716 before his name again disappeared from the bills.

On 3 October 1718 at the Lincoln's Inn Fields Theatre Delagarde appeared in a group dance and, with Mrs Bullock, in the popular *Dutch Skipper*. He danced regularly throughout the season and composed the *Burghermaster and his Frow*, which he and Mrs Bullock performed. On 18 October 1718 his two sons, Charles and J. Delagarde, made their London debuts, after which they often appeared with their father and Mrs Bullock in specialty dances, some of them composed by the elder Delagarde. At the end of the season Delagarde shared a benefit with Hall on 30 April 1719.

Delagarde apparently turned his attention to teaching and choreography for the several seasons that followed. In 1721 John Weaver listed him as one of England's dancing masters, and at the theatres in 1721 and 1724 dances composed by Delagarde were performed. He was, according to *The London Stage*, a member of the Lincoln's Inn Fields company again in 1728–29, though he was rarely cited in the bills. In 1729–30 he was mentioned for the roles of the Gardener in *The Rape of Proserpine*, and a Cyclops in *Perseus and Andromeda*, and was seen in dances with Miss Wherrit and with groups. So he continued through 1732–33 at Lincoln's Inn Fields and, from December 1732, at Covent Garden.

From 1733–34 through 1735–36 he danced regularly in pantomimes and specialty turns. He was seen in a *Scottish Dance, The Nassau, Pygmalion, Swedish Dal Karl* (with Mrs Ogden, born Bullock), *The Medley, The Faithful Shepherd, Two Pierrots, The Grecian Sailors*, and *English Maggot*. His pantomime roles included an Infernal in *Perseus and Andromeda*, a Grecian, Haymaker, and Pierrot in *The Necromancer*, a Zephyr and Bridal Swain in *The Nuptial Masque*, a Bridal Swain in *Apollo and Daphne*, and Pluto (Punch) in *The Royal Chace*. During 1735–36, his last full season, he was on a straight salary of 4s. 2d. daily and was paid £32 10s. for performing on 156 days—an indication that he was far more active than the bills would suggest but not a very important member of the *corps de ballet*.

Delagarde was in a *Scots Dance* on 29 September 1736, but when the dance was repeated, on 4 October and subsequent dates, he had been dropped. He seems not to have stayed with the Covent Garden company for the season, and the following year neither he nor his sons were mentioned in London playbills. It is probable that the elder Delagarde retired or died and that the dancer who appeared at Covent Garden in 1738–39 and subsequent years was his son, J. Delagarde.

Possibly the following entry in the St Paul, Covent Garden, parish registers concerns the dancer: on 3 December 1717 Anne, the daughter of Charles Delagarde, was buried.

Delagarde, Mrs [Charles?] [*fl.* 1710–1711], dancer.

Mrs Delagarde, presumably the wife of the dancer Delagarde who appeared in London beginning in 1705 and whose Christian name was possibly Charles, danced with Delagarde on 26 January 1710 at Drury Lane (a new *Swedish Peasant*) and on 7 April 1711 at the Queen's Theatre in the Haymarket. She seems not to have performed again in London.

Delagarde, Charles [*fl.* 1718–1734], dancer.

Charles Delagarde and his brother J. Delagarde made their debuts at the Lincoln's Inn Fields Theatre on 18 October

1718 performing a dance with *The Double Dealer*. Their father, also a dancer, presumably trained them, and he often appeared in specialty numbers with the two "children." Some of the dances which the boys offered during the 1718–19 and 1719–20 seasons with John Rich's company were the *French Peasant, Harlequin, Scots Dance, Scotch Highlander, Scaramouch, Sultan and Sultaness*, and *The Italian Shadows*. The boys seem not to have appeared separately, and each season they were granted shared benefits. After May 1720 they dropped from sight, though both reappeared as dancers in later years and pursued their separate careers.

Charles came back on the stage in London on 9 October 1728 at Lincoln's Inn Fields, billed as Delagarde Junior to distinguish him from his father, who was a member of the same company. In 1728–29 the younger Charles participated in several untitled entr'acte dances and was a Sicilian and a Countryman in *The Rape of Proserpine* and a Masquerader in *Italian Jealousy*. He stayed with Rich's troupe at Lincoln's Inn Fields and, after November 1732, Covent Garden, dancing regularly, perhaps, but receiving scant mention in the bills. In addition to his old parts he was assigned a Peasant in *Apollo and Daphne* and Ixion in *Harlequin a Sorcerer*. His greatest feat seems to have been getting permission to perform at Goodman's Fields on 15 January 1732 and a few subsequent days, but all this yielded was the information that his Christian name was Charles, for so he was billed. In 1733–34, his last season at Covent Garden, he was mentioned for only one part: the Peasant in *Apollo and Daphne*. His last appearance was on 1 April 1734.

Delagarde, J. [*fl. 1718–1750*], *dancer*.

J. Delagarde and his brother Charles, sons of the Lincoln's Inn Fields dancer and choreographer, made their first appearance on 18 October 1718 at that playhouse. The two "children" danced a heavy schedule through the 1719–20 season, appearing always together and sometimes joined by their father and Mrs Bullock in dances which the elder Delagarde composed. Many of their dances had no names, but some were titled: *French Peasant, Harlequin, Scotch Highlander, The Italian Shadows*, and *Sultan and Sultaness*. The boys shared benefits in 1719 and 1720. They were not mentioned again in London until years later, when each followed his own career.

J. Delagarde was noticed again on 20 December 1732 when he played a Follower in *The Amorous Sportsman* at Goodman's Fields. During this season and subsequent ones he was identified by his initial to distinguish him from his father and brother, both of whom were again active in London. J. Delagarde stayed at Goodman's Fields with Giffard's troupe through 1735–36, after which he moved with the company to Lincoln's Inn Fields for the 1736–37 season. He danced many undescribed specialty numbers, performed in untitled group dances, and played minor roles in pantomimes throughout these years. Among his billed roles were Punch in a dance called *Masquerade*, a Follower in *The Happy Nuptials*, a Waterman, Deity, and Follower in *Britannia*, a Companion in *Diana and Acteon*, a Triton in *Harlequin Shipwrecked*, and a Sylvan in *Hymen's Triumph*. Specialty dances in which he appeared were *Pierrot and Pierrate* (quickly shortened in the bills to *Two Pierrots*) —a popular dance he performed with Vallois, a *Milk Pail Dance, Tambourine Dance*, and *Pyrrhic Dance*. He shared benefits in 1734 and 1735 and received solo benefits on 12 April 1736 and 27 April 1737. Tickets for the last were available from him at his lodgings at Mrs Stafford's in Dean Street, Fetter Lane. His tickets were also accepted at the theatre on 15 June 1737 at the benefit of Miss Oates, his future wife.

The Delagarde who appeared at Covent Garden in 1738–39 and remained until 1750 was apparently J. Delagarde. Once, at a shared benefit on 29 April 1740, he was identified as "I. Delegarde," and, unlike his father and brother, who had performed at Covent Garden earlier in the 1730s, he was given regular benefits, just as he had been at Lincoln's Inn Fields. It is likely that the elder Delagarde left the stage, as did young Charles, while J. Delagarde—often just "Delagarde" in the bills—continued his career. At Covent Garden he was not one of the important dancers; he seems to have started at 3s. 4d. daily and to have moved up to 5s. by the end of November 1740, and perhaps he never earned much more than that. In 1749–50 (his last full season) he was paid £4 11s. 8d. for five days, but this was shared with his wife. He married Miss Oates sometime between 21 and 30 March 1741.

At Covent Garden Delagarde's duties were similar to those he had known before. Titled specialty dances in which he appeared included *The Grecian Sailors*, the popular and quaintly spelled *Je ne scais quoy*, *Two Pierrots*, *English Peasants*, *La Provençale*, *Villagers*, *Les Maquignons*, and *Le Gondalier*. His pantomime roles included an Infernal and a Fawn in *Perseus and Andromeda*, a Huntsman, a Peasant, and a Polonese in *Apollo and Daphne*, a Demon and a Swain in *Orpheus and Eurydice*, Hercules (Brighella) in *The Royal Chace*, and the second Sylvan, Fire, and a Country Lad in *The Rape of Proserpine*. After 1745–46 he danced only in pantomimes. His benefits, usually shared with two others, continued through 1749–50, his last being on 17 April 1750.

J. Delagarde played his old role of an Infernal in *Perseus and Andromeda* on 29 October 1750, but when the work was repeated the next day he was replaced by Gardiner. His stage career ended just as his father's had, abruptly, after a single performance at the beginning of a season.

Delagarde, Mrs J., née Oates ₁*fl.* 1730–1751₁, *actress, dancer.*

Miss Oates was the daughter of James Oates, a performer at Drury Lane and a fair booth operator. Her first notice came on 20 August 1730 at the Bartholomew Fair booth operated by Fielding and her father; she played Maria in *The Generous Free Mason*. The work ran through 7 September, after which it was shown at Southwark Fair through 23 September. Miss Oates then joined her father at Drury Lane for the 1730–31 season, probably playing small parts during much of the season. When spring came she was given some billed roles: Jenny in *Patie and Peggy* on 31 May 1731, one of the Wives in *Don John* on 11 June, Dulceda in *Bayes's Opera* on 23 July, Lucy in *The Devil to Pay* on 6 August, and Selena in *The Triumphs of Love and Honour* on 18 August. She concluded the summer playing Arbella in *The Banished General* at Bartholomew Fair beginning on 26 August at a booth run by Mills, Miller, and her father.

She stayed at Drury Lane for another season, adding to her repertoire such small roles as a Bridesmaid in *Perseus and Andromeda* and Clara in *The Lover's Opera*. The Mrs Oates listed in *The London Stage* on 1 January 1732 as playing a Lady in *The Lottery* was surely Miss Oates. Again she finished the season at Bartholomew Fair, acting Clarinda in *Henry VIII* at the Miller-Mills-Oates booth in August. A Miss Ann Oates, probably her sister, also appeared in this production.

Miss Oates struck out on her own in 1732–33 and joined John Rich's company at Lincoln's Inn Fields just before the troupe moved into their new Covent Garden Theatre. Her first appearance was on 16 November 1732 when she took the title role in *Flora*. After this she appeared as Philoe in *Achilles* and Nell in *The Devil to Pay*, and on 10 May 1733 at Covent Garden she shared a benefit with two others which brought in £146 4s. Miss Oates played the second Phillis in *The Livery Rake* at Drury Lane in May 1733 and then

acted the title role in *Jane Shore* at Bartholomew Fair in August.

When Theophilus Cibber led a contin-
gent of Drury Lane discontents to the Hay-
market Theatre in the fall of 1733, Miss
Oates joined him and busied herself playing
Sylvia in *The Old Bachelor*, Mustacha in
The Opera of Operas, Philadelphia in *The
Amorous Widow*, a Peasant Woman in
The Burgomaster Trick'd, and a Lady in
Chrononhotonthologos. She also appeared
in such specialty dances as *Les Amantes
constants*. When Cibber's group returned to
Drury Lane in the spring of 1734 she
added to her list a Grace in *Love and Glory*
(later retitled *Britannia*) and the title role
in *The School Boy*. On 16 May 1734 she
and Master Oates, doubtless her brother,
paired off in a comic dance at their teacher
Davenport's benefit. Miss Oates shared a
benefit on 23 May, but for some reason it
was given at Lincoln's Inn Fields. At Bartholomew Fair in August she played Arabella in *The Constant Lovers* and danced
with Master Oates and the Davenports.

At Drury Lane in 1734–35 Miss Oates
performed infrequently, but she danced at
York Buildings on 3 June 1735 and spent
the summer months at Lincoln's Inn Fields
playing Estifania in *Rule a Wife and Have
a Wife*, the School Boy, and Nell in *The
Devil to Pay*. In 1736–37 she joined Giffard's troupe at Lincoln's Inn Fields where
she appeared in *King Arthur, The Worms
Doctor*, and a number of specialty dances,
and she was also a Shepherdess in *Harlequin Shipwrecked* and a Follower in both
Britannia and *Hymen's Triumph*.

She rejoined Rich's company at Covent
Garden in 1737–38, and except for a brief
appearance at Drury Lane in April 1742,
she finally settled down there for the rest
of her career. Perhaps she accepted the fact
that she was not destined for much more
than small roles in pantomimes and participation in specialty dances, for typical of
her activity from 1737 to 1751 were such
parts as a Harlequin Woman and the Mill-

er's Wife in *The Necromancer*, an Amazon
in *Perseus and Andromeda*, and a number
of small roles in *The Rape of Proserpine*,
plus dancing in *Je ne scais quoy, Faithful
Lovers, Le Bergères fidelle, La Villageoise,
Les Paisans moisonneurs*, and *Le Gondalier*.
Her salary, at least in the 1740–41 season,
was 6*s*. 8*d*. daily.

Sometime between 21 and 30 March
1741 Miss Oates married the dancer
J. Delagarde, after which she gave up benefits and went on a straight salary. By the
mid-1740s her activity had diminished to
the point where she did little specialty
dancing and appeared in only one or two
pantomimes each season. She had long since
given up dramatic roles. Oddly, the peak in
her career came in the 1748–49 season
when she was Daphne (and Flora, representing an Inconstant) in *Apollo and
Daphne*, but while she played in that pantomime she participated in nothing else,
and the next season she relinquished the
roles to others. The last mention of Mrs
Delagarde was on 4 December 1751 when
she played a Follower in *Apollo and
Daphne*. When the work was repeated the
next day, she was dropped from the bill—a
virtual duplication of the manner in which
the careers of her husband and father-in-
law ended.

Del'Agata or **Delagatha**. *See* **DELL
AGATA**.

De La Grange, Mons ₁*fl. 1738*₁,
dancer.

At the Fielding-Hallam booth at Tottenham Court on 7 August 1738 and Hallam's
booth at Southwark Fair on 5 September
The Mad Lovers (called *The Man's Bewitch'd* on the latter date) was presented.
Monsieur De La Grange played one of
the Bride Men and Mademoiselle De La
Grange, probably his daughter, was one of
the Bride Maids; both participated also in a
comic *Peasant Dance*. At Pinkethman's
Bartholomew Fair booth on 23 August of

this same year a variant work called *The Man's Bewitch'd* was performed, with the two De La Granges playing Friends of Don Furioso and participating in a comic ballet.

De La Grange, Mlle *(fl. 1738)*, dancer. *See* DE LA GRANGE, MONS.

De La Guard. *See* DELAGARDE.

De La Hay, Mons *(fl. 1707)*, dancer.
At Mr Duffield's Old Wells in Hampstead on 1 August 1707 one of the comic dancers was a Monsieur De La Hay.

De La Hay, Mr *(fl. 1736–1738)*, dancer.
At the Haymarket Theatre on 20 February 1736 Messrs De La Hay (or Hayes) and Shawford revived, with alterations, the old Sorin-and-Baxter *Italian Night Scenes*; De La Hay danced Harlequin and Shawford Scaramouch. At the Hallam-Fielding booth at Tottenham Court on 7 August 1738 De La Hay appeared as Captain Atall (Harlequin) in *The Mad Lovers*, a show that was repeated under the title *The Man's Bewitch'd* at Hallam's Southwark Fair booth on the following 5 September.

Delahoy, [Master?] *(fl. 1799)*, dancer.
A dancer named Delahoy, very likely a juvenile, was named by the bills at Covent Garden as a participant in the pantomime *The Magic Oak; or, Harlequin Woodcutter*, at its premier performance on 29 January 1799 and 15 times before the end of February. He then disappeared from public notice.

Delahoyde, Mr *(fl. 1745–1750)*, musician.
Either Oliver or Thomas Delahoyde, both musicians at the Theatre Royal, Dublin, in 1750, played at Drury Lane in the 1745–46 and 1746–47 seasons. On 30 April 1746 "Delaboyde" had his benefit

tickets accepted, and on 12 May 1747 "Delahyde" shared a benefit with three others.

Delahyde. *See* DELAHOYDE.

Delaistre. *See* DE LAÎTRE.

De Laître, Mons *(fl. 1752–1759)*, dancer.
A "Mr and Mrs Delaistre," both dancers, appeared at Strasbourg in 1752–53. Though no more was heard of his wife, Monsieur de Laître was recommended to Garrick by Noverre on 31 January 1755 and brought to London to appear in *The Chinese Festival* on 8 November of that year. Richard Cross the prompter noted in his diary that "Mr. Delaistre is a good dancer," yet when the spectacle was repeated on 15 November the Frenchman was one of many who were omitted from the cast. The performances of *The Chinese Festival* caused a show of patriotism by Londoners which nearly wrecked the production, but by 8 January 1756 when de Laître offered a *Peasant Dance*, Cross jotted down in his diary that there was "no notice taken of the french."

Perhaps the dancer stayed in England the following season, but the bills did not mention him again until 1757–58, when he again appeared at Drury Lane. During the season he was in a *Pastoral Dance*, the Masque in *The Tempest*, the pantomime *Harlequin Ranger* (Cross noted: "The pant: was hiss'd & Dull"), a *Furies Dance* in *Macbeth*, *The Prussian Camp*, *The Market*, a *Masquerade Polish Dance*, and *Amphitryon*. Arthur Murphy in the London *Chronicle* of 26–29 November 1757, after seeing de Laître in *The Market*, said "the Publick . . . spoke with the greatest Applause their approbation of Mr Delater both as a Dancer and as Designer [i.e., choreographer]." The dancer was praised again about January 1758 when Garrick wrote to Noverre's wife that her "Brother

& Mr D'Latre are highly approv'd of, & their Names are in our Bills at large, every time they Dance."

In 1758–59 de Laître was back in London at Covent Garden. On 16 November 1758 he was one of the Tartars in *The Feast of Bacchus*, and later in the season he appeared in a Pastoral Dance in *Florizel and Perdita* and such specialty dances as *Tambourine, The Prussian Rope-Makers*, and a minuet. After the season ended de Laître did not appear in London again.

De La Magre. *See* DELAMAINE.

Delamaine, Henry [*fl. 1733–1755?*], dancer, choreographer.

At the Goodman's Fields Theatre on 10 September 1733 Henry Delamaine made his first appearance on the English stage offering an untitled specialty dance. Perhaps he continued performing at the theatre, but notices of him did not turn up again until 15 September 1735, when he was cast as a Mandarin Gormogon in *Harlequin Grand Volgi* at Drury Lane. He stayed at that playhouse for the full 1735–36 season, dancing in such entr'acte specialties as *Newmarket's Delight, Le Badinage de Provence*, and (with Villeneuve) *Two Pierrots*. Some of his solo dances were *The Whim, Mason's Dance*, and *A Harlequin*. He was also a Turkish Dancer in the pantomime *The Fall of Phaeton*. He shared a benefit with Davenport on 15 May 1736. The printers, as might be expected, had difficulties with his name, once spelling it "de la Magre."

The fall of 1736 found Delamaine at Lincoln's Inn Fields with Giffard's troupe. He appeared there on 9 November 1736 and a few subsequent dates before the end of the year, after which his name dropped from the bills. By 18 September 1737 he was in Dublin, dancing at the Aungier Street Theatre, but he returned to London to appear in *The Dragon of Wantley* at Covent Garden on 26 October. Having made little progress, Delamaine went to the Continent and danced at the St Laurent Fair in 1738 and 1739. The first year he offered a *pantomime anglaise*, apparently of his own devising, which won his troupe an engagement at the Opéra Comique. In 1739 Delamaine's company played at the St Laurent and St Germain fairs with good success, but differences with his French sponsor Pontou (the director of the Opéra Comique) caused Delamaine to disband the company.

On 31 October 1741 the dancer reappeared at Drury Lane, dancing a comic turn in *The Harlot's Progress*. Subsequently he appeared in a solo *Dutch Dance*, was in *Les Jardiniers*, played a Satyr in a dance called *Les Satires puny*, performed a *Miller's Dance* by himself, and was the chief performer in a piece called *Les Maquignons*, from which he excerpted his own part to serve as a solo in later performances. At the end of the season he seems to have gone to Dublin, but he was back in London on 25 October 1743 dancing the *Dutch Skipper* with Anne Auretti. With the Aurettis and Mlle Auguste he appeared several times during the 1742–43 season in such dances as *Les Pasteurs joyeux, Italian Peasants*, and *Les Boufons du cour*. For his benefit with Janneton Auretti on 22 April 1743, Delamaine performed an *Italian Dance* with Mlle Auguste, a minuet with Janneton Auretti, and a solo louvre. John Rich, the Covent Garden manager, seems to have given Delamaine permission to appear on 22 March 1743 at Lincoln's Inn Fields, where he offered a minuet, a louvre, and a *Sailor's Dance* with Mlle Roland, and then raced back to Covent Garden to perform there.

On 2 March 1745 the papers announced that a company of Dutch children under Delamaine's direction would appear at the Haymarket Theatre. The dancer-choreographer had received a license for the performance on 28 February. The group numbered 25, including a number of English, German, and Italian performers. On 5 or 6 March they opened with music, dancing, exercises, and a pantomime called *Arlequino triomphante*, but in order to "get several Things ready" Delamaine had to postpone some scheduled performances and did not play again until 12 and 14 March. Though the Duke of Cumberland and other notables graced the opening night, Delamaine's project seems not to have caught the fancy of the town.

What happened to Henry Delamaine after 14 March 1745 is not known. An interesting note in the Covent Garden accounts on 25 September 1749 indicates that Delamaine, presumably the dancer, paid the balance of his account, £30. Had he rented or purchased some theatrical goods from Covent Garden for his Haymarket venture of 1745? A "Harry Delamain" ran the Shakespeare's Head tavern in Covent Garden in 1755, and perhaps he was the ex-dancer.

Two other Delamaines, probably relatives of Henry, appeared in Dublin but apparently not in London: William was there from 1731 to 1738 and Robert in 1736–37.

Delan, [**B.?**] [*fl. 1797*], *house servant?*

The Drury Lane accounts for 3 December 1797 show a payment of £6 (or possibly 6s.) to a B. (or R.?) Delan, possibly one of the house servants.

"De La Nash, Mme." *See* FIELDING, HENRY.

Delane, Miss. *See* WETHERILT, MRS ROBERT.

Delane, Dennis *d. 1750, actor.*

A native of Ireland, Dennis Delane was educated at Trinity College, Dublin, and was originally intended for the bar. His Dublin debut was at the Smock Alley

Theatre in 1729 where he was, according to Chetwood's *General History*, well received. Before coming to England Delane developed a sizeable repertoire of important roles, mostly tragic, which he displayed during his early seasons in London.

After a benefit in Dublin on 8 March 1731 Delane negotiated for a London engagement at Drury Lane, but the company was "brimful" according to Chetwood, and Delane was hired instead by Giffard at Goodman's Fields. There he made his first appearance on 24 November 1731 as Chamont in *The Orphan*, after which he offered a number of other important roles: Othello on 26 November, Aimwell in *The Stratagem* on 27 November, Torrismond in *The Spanish Fryar* on 3 December, Orestes in *The Distrest Mother* on 7 December, the King in *The Mourning Bride* on 9 December, Oroonoko on 13 December, Essex in *The Unhappy Favorite* on 20 December, Pembroke in *Lady Jane Gray* on 30 December, Hotspur in *1 Henry IV* on 29 January 1732, Manly in *The Provok'd Husband* on 17 February, a role in *The Jealous Husband* on 21 February, the Ghost in *Hamlet* on 26 February, Richard III for his benefit on 20 March, Clerimont Senior in *The Tender Husband* on 27 March, Tamerlane on 28 March, Osmyn in *The Mourning Bride* on 1 April, Roderigo in *The Pilgrim* on 12 April, and Leon in *Rule a Wife and Have a Wife* on 27 April. With his "good person; excellent voice" and rich repertoire, Delane was an immediate success.

But his opening season, remarkable though it was, did not display to London all that Delane had to offer. At Goodman's Fields in 1732–33 and 1733–34 he added Standard in *The Constant Couple*, possibly Castalio in *The Orphan*, Brutus in *Julius Caesar*, Piercy in *Virtue Betray'd*, Bevil in *The Conscious Lovers*, Dumont in *Jane Shore*, Macbeth, Timoleon, Amurat in *Scanderbeg*, King Lear, Worthy in *The Relapse*, Cato, Hardy in *The Funeral*, Polydor in *The Orphan*, Briton in *The Wonder*, Alexander in *The Rival Queens*, Varanes in *Theodosius*, Guyomar in *The Indian Emperor*, Lothario in *The Fair Penitent*, and Carlos in *Love Makes a Man*. Between these two seasons he returned to Ireland to play with the Smock Alley company at Cork in mid-July 1733, and he went back to Ireland for a brief stay in August 1734. While in London he lived in Mansel Street near the playhouse.

Delane was at Goodman's Fields again in 1734–35, but Heartwell in *The Country Lasses* was the only new role he played, and in early March 1735 he was ill. He was again in Dublin on 12 June 1735, and with Henry Giffard and other visiting actors from England, he played with the Aungier Street company at Carlow and Cork during the summer. When he re-

DENNIS DELANE, as Comus(?)

artist unknown

turned to London in the fall, it was to Covent Garden, where he had been recommended by James Quin. This brought him under the management of John Rich, and when Rich formed the Sublime Society of Beefsteaks in 1735, Delane was one of the original 24 members.

His first appearance at Covent Garden was on 25 October 1735 as Alexander in *The Rival Queens*. Following that he acted many of his old parts and also Bajazet in *Tamerlane*, the title role in *The False Friend*, Antony in *All for Love*, Davison in *The Albion Queens*, Hastings in *Jane Shore* (for his benefit on 15 March 1736), Falstaff in *The Merry Wives of Windsor*, and Valentine in *Wit Without Money*. His benefit brought in £121 17s. 6d., and the bill noted that he was living then at the sign of the Dial, Covent Garden. The 1736–37 Covent Garden season saw him in such new parts as Jaffeir in *Venice Preserv'd*, Pyrrhus in *The Distrest Mother*, Volpone, Francisco in *Wit Without Money*, Welford in *The Scornful Lady*, Ursaces in *Cymbeline*, and King John. In the summer of 1737 he was off again to Ireland to play Othello, Brutus, Volpone, and Torrismond at Smock Alley. He also put in an appearance at Waterford.

During the rest of the 1730s at Covent Garden Delane showed London audiences such parts as Richard II, the King in *2 Henry IV*, Henry V, Ziphares in *Mithridates*, Hengist in *The Royal Convert*, Herod in *Herod and Mariamne*, Smith in *The Rehearsal*, Medley in *The Man of Mode*, and Scandal in *Love for Love*. He made summer jaunts to Ireland in 1738 and 1739. In London in the spring of 1739 he was living at the Golden Ball in Exeter Court, near Exeter Exchange in the Strand, but a year later was at No 6, Wild Court, Wild Street. In March 1740 his benefit tickets, in addition to being available from him, could be had of Mrs Delane (his mother?) at the Fig Tree, opposite Salisbury Street in the Strand. By 1740 Delane's salary was £1 10s. daily plus a free benefit from which he often realized at least £100 profit.

The critics started taking notice of the actor in 1740. Perhaps Fielding was the author of the *Apology for the Life of T...... C......* who wrote:

D..l..ne is also esteemed a just Player; and though he has often a more loud Violence of Voice, yet either from an Imitation of Q[ui]n, or his own natural Manner, he has a Sameness of Tone and Expression, and drawls out his Lines to a displeasing Length: But that loud Violence of Voice is useful to him when Anger, Indignation, or such enrag'd Passions are to be expres'd; for the shrill Loudness marks the Passion, which the sweet Cadence of Q[ui]n's natural Voice is unequal to. In such Parts, especially *Alexander*, D..l..ne pleases many; for the Million, as C[olley] C[ibber] says, are apt to be transported when the Drum of the Ear is soundly rattled; [but] D..l..ne is young enough to rise to greater Perfection.

On 10 September 1741 Delane made his first appearance at Drury Lane, as Othello. He acted many of his old parts there during the 1740s, playing more frequently in comedies than before, though tragic roles remained his staple fare. Among his new roles at Drury Lane from 1741–42 through 1747–48 were Comus, Antonio in *The Merchant of Venice*, the King in *All's Well that Ends Well*, Hamlet (for his benefit on 15 March 1742), Morelove in *The Careless Husband*, Heartwell in *The Old Bachelor*, the Elder Woudbe in *The Twin Rivals*, Silvio in *Women Pleased*, the title role in *Mahomet the Imposter*, the Bastard in *King John*, Osmond in *Tancred and Sigismunda*, Ferdinand in *The Tempest*, Macduff in *Macbeth*, De Gard in *The Wild Goose Chase*, and Blenheim in *The Fine Lady's Airs*.

During these years his career was affected by the competition of David Garrick and Spranger Barry, both of whom played

similar lines. At Drury Lane in 1742–43, for instance, Garrick took Delane's usual role of Hastings in *Jane Shore* and Delane played Dumont; in *The Fair Penitent* Garrick acted Lothario and Delane Horatio. In 1746–47 Barry took Macbeth away from Delane, relegating Delane to Macduff (though only temporarily). Both Garrick and Barry were at Drury Lane in 1747–48, which meant that Delane was then reduced to King Henry in *Richard III* (Garrick played Richard), the Archbishop of Canterbury in *Henry V* (Barry played the lead), and Gloster in *Jane Shore* (Garrick was Hastings, and Barry, Dumont). But Delane played less frequently as the years went on, turned more to comedy and the bottle, and had fewer opportunities to play choice leading roles.

Delane's trips to Ireland were less frequent in the 1740s, and again the competition from Garrick may have been the cause. In the summer of 1742 both actors were playing in Dublin, and on 23 June Garrick wrote to his brother Peter that "Delane has play'd against Me, but wanting allies has quitted ye field."

In London Delane's benefits still drew well, though no better than in earlier years. He shifted lodgings as frequently as before. From 1742 to 1744 he was living in Queen's Court, King Street, Covent Garden; then he moved to the Unicorn in New Exchange Row in the Strand. By March 1748 he had moved to Broad Court at the upper end of Bow Street, Covent Garden.

His critics were still commenting on his voice, which Thomas Gray described in a letter to Walpole in October 1746 as "deep-mouth'd" and "like a Passing Bell." *A Letter of Complaint* in 1747 asked someone to "Help Mr Delane to a new manner and judgment to display the best pipe that ever was heard." In his own way, Garrick made his comment on Delane's voice and manner. In *The Rehearsal*, probably in the early 1740s, he had mimicked Delane. According to Murphy, Garrick retired to the upper part of the stage, and drawing his left arm across his breast, rested his right elbow on it, raising a finger to his nose, and then came forward in a stately gait, nodding his head as he advanced, and, in the exact tone of Delane, spoke the following lines:

So boar and sow, when any storm is nigh . . .

Tate Wilkinson said that Garrick's mimicry drove Delane to drink and death, and as late as 1772 David Williams wrote to Garrick, accusing the actor of murdering Delane's reputation, which had "such an affect on the mind of poor Delane (a man many degrees your superior in birth, education, fortune, and character) that it absolutely occasioned his death." Perhaps there was some truth in the accusations, but Garrick's imitation of Delane was surely not the only cause of Delane's deterioration in the late 1740s.

The great falling out between the two actors apparently came after the summer of 1748. Delane acted in Dublin and Edinburgh and at the latter worked with Sparks and Mrs Ward. On his return to London Delane recommended Mrs Ward to John Rich at Covent Garden rather than to Garrick at Drury Lane. Why he chose to do this is not known; he may have had very good reasons. In any case, it is said that Garrick was furious and cut his old friend dead when they met. Delane thereupon left Drury Lane and played at Covent Garden during the remainder of his career. If Delane flew to the bottle "for relief to his hurt mind" and "continued to use it with such excess that he was never himself again," as Wilkinson reported, the conflict with Garrick in 1748 may simply have been the last of many straws. Delane had started bravely in London, success had come quickly before he had matured as an actor, and then he had met competition he could not match.

However adversely affected he may have been by Garrick's snub, his 1748–49 season at Covent Garden showed him playing as vigorously as ever. For the first time in his career he acted with Quin, sharing leading roles with his old mentor. During the season Delane was seen as Hotspur, Hastings, Polydore, Torrismond, Manly, Tamerlane, Oroonoko, Antony in *Julius Caesar*, Young Belvil, Carlos in *The Revenge*, Aimwell, Varanes, Juba in *Cato*, Cinthio in *The Emperor of the Moon*, Galesus in *Coriolanus*, Morelove, Henry IV, Standard, Lothario, Alexander, and Buckingham in *Henry VIII*. He played as heavy a schedule as he had done in his earlier years and even put in a special appearance at Twickenham on 21 September 1749 to play Manly in *The Provok'd Husband*.

By 1749, according to Chetwood, Delane had started to get "bulky," but Chetwood thought this was "a Recommendation to many capital Parts that may sit easy, and give Pleasure, when the Bloom of Youth is gone." Perhaps he was being kind, for Delane did not have long to live, and that fact was apparent to his contemporaries. In the fall of 1749 he went to work again at Covent Garden at a salary of £1 9s. 2d. daily. He acted mostly in his old roles, but he played Banquo in *Macbeth* for the first time. His last appearance was on 17 March 1750 as Piercy in *Virtue Betray'd*, for Ryan's benefit. On 31 March (apparently not 29 March or 1 April as in some sources) Dennis Delane died. *Faulkner's Dublin Journal* on 5 June spoke of the actor as "Dennis Delane Esq. of Killinough in the County of Roscommon, a Gentleman of exceeding good character."

Delane left a wife, the former Margaretta Horsington. They had married at St Paul, Covent Garden, on 9 November 1745, both declaring themselves to be of the parish of St Martin-in-the-Fields. On 11 July 1746 they buried a child Susanna at the church where they were married. Delane was buried there on 6 April 1750. He had written a will, but it was not dated. In it he bequeathed all his estate, including land in the County Roscommon which he had inherited and land in County Galway, to his wife. She proved the will, rather hurriedly, on 3 April 1750.

After Delane's death the critics were ready with opinions on what Delane should have done with his career. Hill's *The Actor* in 1750 said:

We remember Mr. Delane to have charm'd us in Alexander; and in Hotspur to have excell'd every body in that character; but we were not quite so fond of the figure he made in Viscount Aimwell. The man who has a strength of voice and dignity of figure proper for such characters as the former, wou'd certainly play them better if never taken off by things less fit for him; and this gentleman's reputation wou'd unquestionably have been much higher than it was, and the manager of the house he belong'd to wou'd have been a greater gainer by him, if he had play'd only these sort of characters . . .

Thomas Davies, in his *Life of Garrick* and *Dramatic Miscellanies*, noted that Alexander in *The Rival Queens* was Delane's greatest role, that his Richard II missed revealing the tender feelings and despondency because of his loud voice, that his King John failed to display the turbulent and gloomy passions proper to the character, and that his chief merit was not generally understood. Delane, thought Davies, excelled in well-bred gentlemen, such as Bevil in *The Conscious Lovers* and Manly in *The Provok'd Husband*, rather than in the heroic parts that brought him to prominence.

Dennis Delane's real name, according to W. J. Lawrence's report of a copy of his will in the Dublin Public Record Office, was Delany. Francis Gentleman in *The Theatre* rhymed the actor's stage name with "again." An engraving of Delane as Comus is in an extra-illustrated edition of Davies's *Life of Garrick* in the Folger Shakespeare Library, but no engraver is mentioned, and the attribution cannot be substantiated.

Delane, Mrs Dennis. *See* HORSINGTON, MARGARETTA.

Delany. *See* DELANE.

De la Porte, [Gérard?] [*fl.* 1660s?], violinist.

Roger North, commenting on foreign musicians who came to England after the Restoration, mentioned "One Porter, as they called him, [who] had an incomparable aiery manner on the violin." This musician may have been Gérard de la Porte, who published some chamber music in 1689.

De la Roche-Guilhen, Mme [*fl.* 1677], director, playwright.

On 22 May 1677 a warrant from the Lord Chamberlain ordered members of the King's Musick to attend Mme de la Roche-Guilhen at rehearsals of her play, *Rare en tout*, at Whitehall, which she apparently directed with the help of James Paisible the musician.

De la Rovere, Luigi [*fl.* 1790–1791], scene painter.

One Luigi de la Rovere (or Della Rovere) was on the house list at the Pantheon in 1790–91 as a scene painter, working under Hodges.

De La Salle. *See* SALLÉ.

Delascey, Mr [*fl.* 1757], dancer.

Mr Delascey played a Frenchman in a dance entitled *Le Carneval de Venice* at the Haymarket Theatre on 26 December 1757.

"De La Soup Maigre." *See* LOWDER.

Delater. *See* DE LAÎTRE.

De la Tour. *See also* LA TOUR.

De la Tour, Alexander [*fl.* 1689–1700], violinist?

Alexander de la Tour, probably a violinist, was appointed to the King's private music on 27 July 1689, and livery accounts indicate he remained in the royal musical establishment until at least 1700. Except for notices in livery warrants de la Tour (sometimes de Lature or D'Lature) was rarely cited in the Lord Chamberlain's accounts. He was mentioned on 27 February 1692 as one of the 24 musicians serving under Nicholas Staggins (hence the probability of de la Tour having been a violinist), and his salary in 1697 was cited as £40 yearly.

It is quite possible that an entry in the parish registers of St Martin-in-the-Fields concerns the musician: Philadelphia De la Tour, daughter of Alexandr (*sic*) and Hester was born on 11 February 1690 and christened the following 23 February.

Delatre. *See* DE LAITRE.

De Lature. *See* DE LA TOUR.

De La Valle, Mme [*fl. 1790–1796*], *harpist, pianist.*
A Madame De La Valle (sometimes Delaval) seems to have been an accomplished executant on the harp, playing in London near the end of the century.

She was employed by Johann Peter Salomon in his concerts in the Hanover Square Rooms beginning in March 1790, along with musicians of the excellence of Muzio Clementi, Giovanni Battista Viotti, Johann Nepomuk Hummel, Michael Kelly, and Anna Storace.

She appeared on Haydn's list of the musical people he had met in London, and she played at the first Haydn concert of 1792. He remarked that she was a pupil of Krumpholz and that she also played the piano.

Madame De La Valle was employed by the Ashleys in their oratorio season from 12 February through 18 March 1796 at Covent Garden.

De la Volee, Jean [*fl. 1663*], *musician.*
On 19 October 1663 Jean de la Volee was sworn one of the French musicians in ordinary in the King's Musick.

Delawn, Mr [*fl. 1734*], *dancer.*
On 28 August 1734 at York Buildings a Mr Delawn danced between the acts of a production of *The Orphan.*

Del Bene. *See* FERRARESE.

Del Campo, Thomazio Alegro [*fl. 1718*], *acrobat.*
At Angel Court on 24 September 1718, to augment a performance of *The Recruiting Officer*, Thomazio Alegro Del Campo, "lately arrived from Italy," performed a ladder dance and vaulted on a managed horse.

Del Caro, Mlle, later Mme Cesare Bossi [*fl. 1794–1803*], *dancer. See* DEL CARO, MLLE [*fl. 1790–1815*].

Del Caro, Mlle [*fl. 1790–1815*], *dancer.*
The elder Mlle Del Caro (sometimes De'Caro) was invariably called *Madame* in the bills of her first season in the Italian Opera's *corps de ballet.* She danced some dozens of times from the opening of the season with the dispossessed opera company at the Haymarket on 7 January through the close of the season at Covent Garden on 17 July 1790. She was not seen in the opera dances at either the King's Theatre or the Pantheon in the following season, 1790–91, nor in 1791–92. Some part of this time she was in Dublin where, according to W. H. Grattan Flood, "she captivated the citizens by her dancing of the hornpipe, to which she gave her name, and which long continued a favorite."

Still denominated "Madame" Del Caro, she rejoined the opera ballet (now again at the King's Theatre) in the season running from 11 January through 8 July 1794. She was seen in several popular ballets contrived by Jean Georges Noverre, the ballet master, especially *Adelaide; ou, la bergère des alpes*, *L'Union des bergères*, and *Les Ruses de l'amour*, many times repeated. On 2 July 1794 she accompanied the Hilligsbergs and other opera dancers to Drury Lane to participate in the great benefit evening for the relief of the widows and orphans of the men killed in the action of 1 June 1794 under Lord Howe. Some of these appearances perhaps should be credited to her younger sister, whose existence *The London Stage* does not acknowledge but who is said by Smith (*The Italian Opera . . . 1789–1820*) to have come to the *corps* during the season.

From this point on it is not always easy to distinguish one sister from the other. Both were in the company at the King's Theatre from 6 December 1794 through 11 July 1795, and during the year the younger sister (now married to the composer Cesare Bossi) began to be referred to in the bills as Signora, Mlle, or Mme Bossi del Caro (and sometimes still Mlle Del Caro). One of the girls, probably the elder and more experienced one, received a salary of £600 in 1795–96. The *Monthly Mirror* of 29 October 1796 commended "A lively Scotch dance, that does credit to the taste of Gentili [the choreographer], and gives Miss Del Caro, a charming opportunity of displaying her abilities, which approach very near to the excellence of her sister."

Smith notices the younger sister at the King's Theatre occasionally in the 1802–3 season and the elder dancing with the Vestris family there in *La Calife de Bagdad* on 17 January 1815.

Delegal. *See* DELAGAR.

Delemain. *See* DELAMAINE.

De Lepine, Mr [*fl. 1719*], *machinist.*
Malcolm's *Anecdotes* mention a Mr De

Lepine who was a machinist at the King's Theatre in the Haymarket in 1719:

The close of the same year presented the eighth wonder of the world to the Londoners, as Mr. De Lepine, the inventor, had the vanity to call it. This was a machine, moved by springs and wheels, impelling figures to advance on a stage, where they performed a pantomimic opera, aided by the usual changes of scenes, musick, &c, &c.

De l'Épine, Francesca Margherita, later Mrs John Christopher Pepusch
d. 1746, singer.

Margherita de l'Épine, or, as she once signed herself, Françoise Marguerite de l'Épine, was probably of Italian or French-Italian parentage. She very likely came to England late in 1692. She is said to have arrived with her German music teacher Jacob Greber, though his earliest notice in England seems to have been in 1703. The *London Gazette* of 3–5 January 1692/93 reported: "The Italian lady (that is lately come over that is so famous for her singing)" had been falsely rumored to have cancelled her advertised "consort at York-buildings." But, the *Gazette* assured everyone, "next Tuesday, being the 10th instant, she will sing at the Consort in York Buildings, and so continue during this season." The same journal on 23 January said that the Italian lady would sing "every Tuesday in York-Buildings, and Thursdays in Freeman's Yard in Cornhill . . ." E. L. Moor in *Music and Letters* (1947) questions whether the singer spoken of was in fact Signora de l'Épine, since she was not mentioned again in England until 1703, but she cannot be identified as anyone else, and if she was not spoken of again for several years she had doubtless returned to the Continent.

Perhaps Margherita de l'Épine was one of the performers "lately come from Rome and Venice" who gave recitals at York Buildings on 3 November 1702 and subsequent dates, but the prompter Downes reported that his manager Thomas Betterton was instrumental in bringing her to England to sing at Lincoln's Inn Fields. Grove claims that she received "20 gns for one day's singing in ye play call'd the Fickle Shepherdess" in May 1703, but no source is cited for the quotation. The play was presented at Lincoln's Inn Fields in March, and a May repetition would have been likely. Grove also cites an advertisement on 1 June 1703 saying that her performance on that date would be "positively the last time of her singing on the stage during her stay in England," but *The London Stage* does not report a performance for her on that date. In any case, she did not leave England, for she appeared at Lincoln's Inn Fields on 8 June singing, among other pieces, a "Nightingale Song." She sang again at the theatre on 11 June and was billed at Tunbridge Wells on 12 August. She sang weekly at the Wells, but the extent of her stay there is not known.

On 29 January 1704 she made her Drury Lane debut singing Greber's music. When she repeated that recital on 5 February, she met with a violent reception. Her rival Mrs Tofts published a note in the *Daily Courant* on 8 February concerning the matter: "I was very much surpriz'd when I was inform'd that Ann Barwick, who was lately my Servant, had committed a Rudeness last night, by throwing of Oranges, and hissing when Mrs l'Epine, the Italian Gentlewoman Sung. I hope no one can think that it was in the least with my Privity, as I assure you it was not." The lady seemed to protest too much.

Signora de l'Épine continued singing regularly at Drury Lane through 5 July 1704, taking time off for a concert on 7 June at Chelsea College. Her songs were usually by Greber or Purcell. Finally she made good her intention to leave, but she was back at Drury Lane on 30 December 1704, billed as "lately return'd to England." On 16 January 1705 she sang songs

before and after the performance of *Arsinoe*, and she was regularly billed as offering vocal entertainments with plays through March. Her popularity was enormous. One jingle said that those who "hear L'pine Italian squeak. / Subscribe themselves her Bubbles by the Week." The *Diverting Post* of 16 June 1705 printed an epilogue complaining that audiences were being split between the two theatres, and "L'Epine, and Tofts sneak off with all our Gains." In the same paper on 30 June a poet wrote that "L'Epine, and Tofts, the Hearts of all have won."

Greber left England in 1705. After his departure Signora de l'Épine attracted the eye of Daniel Finch, Earl of Nottingham. Rowe commented on the affair in one of his poems:

> Did not base Greber's Peg inflame
> The sober Earle of Nott——g——m,
>   Of sober sire descended?
> That carelesse of his soul & Fame
>   To Play-houses he nightly came
> And left church undefended.

Signora de l'Épine remained in London performing regularly through 1720 at Drury Lane, the Queen's (later the King's) Theatre in the Haymarket, Hickford's Music Room, Coignand's Great Room, Lincoln's Inn Fields, Stationers' Hall, and the Duchess of Shrewsbury's in Kensington. As opera became the rage in London she turned more and more to operatic singing, though she continued appearing at occasional recitals.

Grove states that her first appearance in an opera was on 7 March 1706 at the Queen's Theatre when *The Temple of Love* was given its premiere, but the Signora Margarita who sang in that work was Maria Margarita Gallia, the wife of the opera's composer Saggione. Nicola Haym wrote Vice Chamberlain Coke on 21 April 1706 that Signora Margherita was learning her part in *Camilla*, but again the reference may have been to Maria Gallia. The opera advertisements rarely cited more than "Signora Margherita" (or "Margarita"), and though many such references may have been to Signora de l'Épine, there is no way to be certain. Perhaps she sang the title role in *Thomyris* at Drury Lane on 1 April (but a year later her part in that work was Tigrane). And possibly she was Presento in *Camilla* on 6 December 1707 at the same house. It is certain that she sang Olindo in *Love's Triumph* at the Queen's Theatre on 26 February 1708.

Signora de l'Épine's income in England was enough to make her want to settle there and learn the language. Downes, writing in 1708, said that "since her Arrival in England, by Modest Computation [she] got by the Stage and Gentry, above 10000 Guineas." That was probably an exaggeration, but her salary at the Queen's, stated in March 1708 was £400; only the *castrato* Nicolini earned more (£430). Yet the opera singers had problems: English weather and Christopher Rich. On 31 December 1707 Signora de l'Épine complained to the Vice Chamberlain that the Drury Lane manager owed her £25 5s. from the previous year, and the singers all pleaded that because their opera season was short, the weather a hazard to their voices, and no other employment for them available, they at least should get their pay.

What the operas may have sounded like during these early years is a question. In *Camilla* in 1707 Signora "Margarita" sang in Italian part of the time, "The Baroness" most of the time, and Valentino all of the time. As the years passed, operas were performed in English but the Italians never quite mastered the tongue. Signora de l'Épine made a valiant effort, however, and by 1715 was able to sing in English tolerably well—at least her English was more understandable to most of her audience than Italian would have been. Whether they could follow the language or not, Englishmen were quite taken with the sing-

ers. Lord Halifax wrote a poem entitled "On Orpheus [Nicolini?] and Signora Francesca Margarita:"

> Hail, tuneful pair! say by what won-
>   drous charms,
> One scap'd from Hell, and one from
>   Greber's arms?
> When the soft Thracian touch'd the
>   trembling strings,
> The winds were hush'd, and curl'd their
>   airy wings;
> And when the tawny Tuscan raised her
>   strain,
> Rook furls the sails, and dares it on the
>   main.
> Treaties unfinish'd in the office sleep,
> And Shovell yawns for orders on the
>   deep.
> Thus equal charms and equal conquests
>   claim,
> To him high woods, and bending timber
>   came,
> To her shrub-hedges, and tall Notting-
>   ham.

The 1708–9 opera season was at the Queen's Theatre. On 14 December 1708 Signora de l'Épine ("Signora Margarita") appeared as Mario in *Pirro e Demetrio*. On 12 February, billed as Signora de l'Épine, she took Mrs Toft's place in the title role in *Camilla*; on 2 March she sang the title part in *La Clotilde*; and on 9 April for her benefit *Pirro e Demetrio* was repeated. She remained at the Queen's Theatre until the middle of the 1714–15 season, singing the title role in *Almahide*, Berenice and Dario in *Idaspe*, Janisbe in *Antioco*, Godofredo in *Rinaldo* (her first appearance in a Handel work, on 23 January 1712), Valdemaro in *Ambleto*, Calypso in *Calypso and Telemachus*, Eurillo in *Pastor fido*, Agilea in *Teseo*, Rodoaldo and Edwigge in *Ernelinde*, Nicea in *Dorinda*, Adraspe in *Creso*, and Cilene in *Arminio*. At Drury Lane in the last half of the 1714–15 season and in 1715–16 she appeared as Adonis in *Venus and Adonis*, the title role in *Myrtillo*, Apollo in

Apollo and Daphne, and Dido in Pepusch and Booth's *The Death of Dido*. She also sang in the cantata *The Britannia* and rendered Pepusch's "The Meditation" in *Lady Jane Gray*.

Swift wrote in his *Journal to Stella* on 6 August 1711 of going to an opera rehearsal where he saw "*Margarita* and her sister, and another drab, and a parcel of fiddlers." Signora de l'Épine's sister, according to Burney, was Maria Gallia, though Grove says his statement seems to have no foundation.

In the spring of 1717 Signora de l'Épine began an engagement with John Rich at the Lincoln's Inn Fields Theatre. Her first role there may have been Presento in *Camilla* on 2 January 1717, after which, in 1717 and 1718, she sang Mentor in *Calypso and Telemachus*, Tigranes in *Thomyris*, Adonis in *Venus and Adonis*, and an unnamed role in *Circe*. She apparently did not sing in London during the 1719–20 season.

At some point Signora de l'Épine married the composer John Christopher Pepusch, whose music she had frequently sung. Grove dates their marriage 1718 and says the singer then retired from the stage, but there is no proof of the wedding, and the singer actually continued performing until the middle of 1720. Her absence from the stage in the winter season of 1719–20 might suggest that she and Pepusch were married then. In May 1720 at Drury Lane "a Boy," a scholar of hers, sang an entr'acte number, and in June at the King's Theatre Signora de l'Épine joined Handel and the Royal Academy of Music for their first season of opera offerings. She was Procris in *Narciso* on 18 June, Polissena in *Radamisto* on 22 June, and Rhea Silvia in *Numitore* on 25 June. She appeared no more for 13 years, though her student Isabella Chambers sang in the 1720s.

Hawkins in his *General History* placed the marriage of Pepusch and Signora de l'Épine in 1722 or 1724 but gave evidence

for neither date. Moor suggests 1726 but seems unaware that the Pepusches had a child in 1724. Hawkins decorated his story of the marriage by stating that the couple lived in Boswell Court, Carey Street, and had a parrot in their window who was taught to sing "*Non e si vago e bello*" from *Giulio Cesare*. Hawkins also reported that Signora de l'Épine's mother lived with the couple and that Margherita had a son who died before the age of 13. Burney dated the son's death 1739 (but he had Margherita dying in 1740, whereas she lived until 1746).

It is pleasant to come upon at least one piece of factual information: John Pepusch, son of John Christopher and "Margaretta," was baptized on 9 January 1724 at St Clement Danes. Perhaps this was the son said by Hawkins to have been "a child of very promising parts" who died before he was 13; if so, his death would have been about 1736, not 1739. If Pepusch and his wife were living in Boswell Court, Carey Street, by 1730 they had moved to Fetter Lane, off Fleet Street, according to the Holborn Library records.

Mrs Pepusch made one more recorded appearance as a singer: on 21 May 1733 at Drury Lane she sang at Seedo's benefit. The bill stated that she had not performed "on any theatre these 14 [*recte* 13] years." On 19 July 1746, according to Benjamin Cooke's diary, she became ill, and by 10 August she was dead. Cooke said on 10 August that Mrs Pepusch had been "extremely sick" the day before.

Burney may have been incorrect on some of his dates, but his knowledge of Margherita's musical talent was probably sound. He said she became very proficient on the harpsichord, though she never mastered Bull's *Walsingham Variations*. On her singing and personal appearance he had this to say:

Her execution was of a very different order [from that of English singers] and involved real difficulties [i.e., embellishments]. Indeed, her musical merit must have been very considerable to have kept so long in favour on the English stage, where, till employed at the opera, she sang either in musical entertainments, or between the acts, almost every night. Besides being *out-landish*, she was so swarthy and ill-favoured, that her husband used to call her *Hecate*, a name to which she answered with as much good humour as if he had called her Helen. But with such a total absence of personal charms, our galleries would have made her songs very short, had they not been executed in such a manner as to silence theatrical snakes, and command applause.

John Hughes was one of those who heard her in her prime and testified in verse to her powers:

Music hath learn'd the discords of the state,
And concerts jar whig and tory hate.
Here Somerset and Devonshire attend
The British Tofts, and every note commend,
To native merit just, and pleas'd to see
We've Roman arts, from Roman bondage free.
Then fam'd L'Epine does equal skill employ,
While list'ning peers crowd to th' ecstatic joy:
Bedford, to hear her song, his dice forsakes,
And Nottingham is raptur'd when she shakes:
Lull'd statesmen melt away their drowsy cares
Of England's safety in Italian airs.
Who would not send each year blank passes o'er,
Rather than keep such strangers from our Shore?

Margherita de l'Épine was pictured in a painting by Sebastiano and Marco Ricci called "A Rehearsal at the Opera" at Castle Howard, the seat of the Earl of Carlisle, in Yorkshire. A replica of the painting, according to *The Dictionary of National Biography*, was owned by the piano makers John Broadwood and Sons. Eric Walter White in *Theatre Notebook* XIV and Mollie Sands in Volume XIX of the same journal discuss in detail six related Ricci paintings or copies of them. The painting at Castle Howard shows Margherita in black, standing, and holding a muff. Similar paintings are owned by Sir Watkin Williams-Wynn, bart., and Major Christopher Turnor. A second rehearsal scene may show Signora de l'Épine singing with Mrs Tofts, though it may, on the other hand, depict "The Baroness" and Mrs Tofts. Versions of this painting belonged to Mr A. W. Holliday and the late Mrs Leonard Messel. A third scene shows Signora de l'Épine, again in black, seated, listening to Nicolini sing. Versions of this are owned by Mrs. E. C. Graham and Lady Knutsford.

Deleval. *See* DE LA VALLE.

Delfevre, Mme [*fl.* 1786–1787], *dancer.*

At the King's Theatre in the Haymarket in 1786–87 Mme Delfevre danced in *La Chercheuse d'esprit* on 23 December, *Le Berger inconstant* on 6 January, and *L'Heureux événement* on 20 January and was the Mischievous Fairy in the pantomime ballet *Zemira and Azor* on 23 February.

Delicati, Luigi [*fl.* 1789], *singer.*

Luigi Delicati and his wife Margherita sang second *buffo* and first *buffa* respectively at the King's Theatre in the Haymarket early in the year 1789 for a combined salary of £520 and a clear shared benefit. In *La cosa rara* on 10 January he sang Lisargo and she Lilla; in *Il disertore* on 28 February she was Belinda; in *La villana riconosciuta* on 24 March he sang Gianotto and she Madama Enrichetta; and in *Il barbiere di Siviglia* on 11 June he sang Il Giovinetto and she was assigned an unnamed role. Signor Delicati received no critical appraisal, but his wife was taken to task in the *Morning Post* of 19 February 1789: "though Delicati is not wanting in personal attractions, her figure has more of the maternal *em bon point* [*sic*] in it necessary for the occasion." The *Biographical and Imperial Magazine* of January 1789 was somewhat kinder: Signora Delicati "has a charming voice but wants instruction."

Delicati, Signora Luigi, Margherita [*fl. 1789*], *singer. See* DELICATI, LUIGI.

Deligny, Louise [*fl. 1791*], *dancer.*

Mlle Louise Deligny danced Venus in *Telemachus in the Island of Calypso* on 22 March 1791 at the Pantheon Theatre and a Nymph in *Le Siège de Cythère* on 9 May at the same house.

De Lile. *See* DE LISLE.

De L'Inconu. *See* "L'INCONNUE."

De Lisle, Mons [*fl. 1675*], *dancer.*

Monsieur De Lisle danced in the court masque *Calisto* on 15 February 1675.

Delisle, Mons [*fl. 1734–1735*], *actor, dancer.*

Monsieur Delisle was the scaramouch of the French troupe that Francisque Moylin brought to England to play at the Haymarket Theatre (and twice at Goodman's Fields) from 26 October 1734 through 4 June 1735. He appeared as both an actor and a dancer, unless there were two men of this name in the company; Delisle's benefit on 1 May 1735, shared with Dubuisson, identified him as "Delisle, Dancer." During their stay Delisle played Azael in *Sampson Judge of Israel* (his first appearance, on 2 December 1734), a "Rare-Show Man" in *Arlequin balourd*, Le Pelerin in *Le Festin de Pierre*, Meledor in *Zaire*, Nabal in *Athalie*, and Briareus in *L'Embarras de*

richesses. As a specialty dancer he appeared with Badouin in *Two Pierrots* (also called *Pierrot and Pierraite*) and, at the last two performances the company gave at the Haymarket on 2 June 1735 and Goodman's Fields on 4 June, he participated in a *Grand Ballet*. Delisle was probably related to the Mlle de L'Isle who danced at Covent Garden in 1735–36 and perhaps to the Mlle Delisle who first appeared in London in the spring of 1720.

Delisle, Mlle *c. 1684–c. 1758, actress.*

Born about 1684, Mademoiselle Delisle made her acting debut at the Opéra in Lyon, where she performed until 1715. In 1716 she joined the troupe of Madame Baron in Paris, playing Colombine in a number of comic pieces. From that company she moved to the troupe of Saint-Edme, where she stayed through 1718. She left Paris to perform in the provinces, and early in 1720 she was a member of de Grimbergue's company, which came to London to perform at the King's and Lincoln's Inn Fields theatres from 5 March through 21 June.

Mlle Delisle was first mentioned in the playbills on 22 March, when she acted an unnamed role in *The Amorous Follies*. On 4 April she had principal parts in *The Gamester* and *The School for Lovers*; on 26 April she was in *Arlequin galerien* (the troupe sometimes advertised their titles in English, sometimes in French, but they performed in their own tongue); *Le Bourgeois gentilhomme* was performed for her benefit on 10 May; and she played Colombine in *Les Bains de la porte de St Bernard* on 27 May.

The troupe returned to London in December 1720 to play a total of 51 performances by 4 May 1721 at the new Haymarket Theatre, the first company to act there. Mlle Delisle arrived after the engagement had begun, for on 9 February 1721 when she had a role in *L'Arlequin nouvelliste* she was hailed as "late arriv'd from France."

On 10 February she took a role in *Medecin Malgre Luy*, and on 25 February when *Les Folies Amoureuses* was performed she offered "Jouves par Mademoiselle de Lisle."

She returned to Paris to play at Francisque's theatre, specializing as before in colombine roles. In 1725 she joined the Opéra Comique under Honoré. Mlle Delisle performed there until her retirement in 1740. She died about 1758.

De L'Isle, Mlle ⟨fl. 1735–1736⟩, dancer.

On 22 November 1735 at Covent Garden Mlle de L'Isle made her first appearance on the stage in a new comic dance with Nivelon. She was probably related to the actor-dancer Delisle who had performed with the French company at the Haymarket the previous season. During 1735–36 at Covent Garden (and twice with the same company but at Lincoln's Inn Fields) Mlle de L'Isle offered such solo dances as *Harlequine*, *Tambourine*, and a comic dance in the character of Polonese, and with Nivelon she appeared in a comic ballet and a dance called *Peasant*. She, Nivelon, and Lalauze danced a ballet in which she took the part of Colombine. Mlle de L'Isle did not appear frequently in group dances, but she was an Amazon in the pantomime *Perseus and Andromeda* and a participant in a *Grotesque Pantomime Dance*.

De Lissale, Mr ⟨fl. 1742⟩, house servant?

On 8 February 1742 at Covent Garden, benefit tickets given out by Mr De Lissale, possibly one of the house servants, were accepted at the theatre.

De Liury, Mlle ⟨fl. 1720⟩, performer?

The French troupe which had played at the King's Theatre in the Haymarket in the spring of 1720 granted Mlle De Liury and two others a benefit on 20 June. She was probably one of the performers, but no roles are known for her.

Dell, Mr ⟨fl. 1760–1761⟩, horn player.

Mr Dell was a French horn player at Covent Garden in 1760–61, apparently hired especially for *Thomas and Sally*. The account book for 28 November 1760 noted that though the new piece was popular it cost John Rich 10s. 6d. for Mr Wrexell the clarinetist and 5s. for Dell for each night in the season.

Dell, James d. c. 1774, musician.

James Dell was described as a musician in ordinary to the King when administration of his estate was granted his widow Hannah on 27 July 1774. He must also have been a member of the Royal Society of Musicians, for when his widow died the Society provided £5 for funeral costs on 6 November 1808 and another £5 on the following 4 December.

Dell Agata, Michele ⟨fl. 1758–1763⟩, dancer.

On 9 October 1762 at Drury Lane Signor Dell Agata (or Del'Agata) made his first appearance in England dancing with Signora Fiorentini in two new pantomime ballets, *The Bavarian Shoemakers* and *The Italian Robbers*. On 3 January 1763 he danced in *The Magician of the Mountain*, and on 24 February he participated in *Phoebe*. The dancer was presumably Michele Dell Agata (or Delagatha) who was ballet master to Karl Eugene, Duke of Württemberg, in 1758.

Della Rovere. *See* DE LA ROVERE.

Delli Angioli. *See* ANGELI.

Deloney, the Messrs ⟨fl. 1675⟩, guitar players.

When the court masque *Calisto* was performed on 15 February 1675, two musicians named Deloney, probably a father and son or perhaps brothers, played guitars.

Delorme, Mme [fl. 1730–1737], dancer.

Madame Delorme (or D'Lorme) danced at Drury Lane from 1730 through 1733–34 and at Covent Garden from 1734–35 through 1736–37, seldom rising to assignments of much importance. Frequently dancing the same or similar roles or entr'actes during the same period at the same theatres was Mlle Delorme, doubtless Madame's daughter. Though she may have been active at Drury Lane earlier, Mme Delorme's first notice in the bills seems to have been on 14 April 1730, when she danced *La Pieraite* with Roger and participated in a group dance. On 23 April she was a Follower of Diana in *Diana and Daphne*. During the rest of her stay at Drury Lane Mme Delorme had such assignments as a Syren in *Cephalus and Procris*, an Hour of Sleep, a Punch Woman, and an Attendant in *Perseus and Andromeda*, Betty in *The Beggar's Opera*, a Milkmaid in *The Country Revels*, a Scaramouch Woman in *Harlequin Restored*, a Shepherdess in *The Judgment of Paris* and in *The Harlot's Progress*, and a Nymph in *Cupid and Psyche*. She also appeared in a variety of specialty dances, such as *The Masques, La Badine, The Revellers*, and *La Badinage* (the last at Lincoln's Inn Fields at a special benefit for Lally given by Drury Lane performers). With Le Brun she often joined in a Pierot and Pierette dance.

At Covent Garden, where her salary was 4s. 4d. nightly (she was paid £37 5s. 4d. in 1735–36 for 172 nights), her dancing chores were similarly small: an Amazon in *Perseus and Andromeda*, a Harlequin Woman in *The Necromancer*, a Nymph and sometimes a French or Spanish woman in *Apollo and Daphne*, and participation in such entr'acte pieces as a *Scot's Dance*, *The Faithful Shepherd, Fawns* (*sic*), and a *Grand Comic Dance*.

Delorme, Mlle [fl. 1730–1737], dancer, actress.

Mademoiselle Delorme probably appeared in the dance *Myrtillo* at Drury Lane on 13 April 1730, and by the end of May she had performed *La Pieraite* with Roger (as had Mme Delorme—doubtless her mother), a Shepherdess in *The Fairy Queen*, and a number of untitled dances. On 20 August at the Fielding-Oates Bartholomew Fair booth she danced with St Luce, "particularly *Wooden Shoe, Pierrot and Pierraite*, and *Black Joke*." In the fall of 1730 she was again at Drury Lane offering entr'acte dances and playing a Syren and a Follower of the Deities of Pleasure in *Cephalus and Procris*, but she seems not to have been noticed again during the season. (A citation in *The London Stage* on 8 October 1730 of "Mrs Delorme" seems to be an error for "Miss.")

On 23 August 1733 Mlle Delorme danced at the Fielding-Hippisley booth at Bartholomew Fair, and in the fall she appeared again at Drury Lane, as Flora in *Harlequin Dr Faustus,* a Nymph in *Cupid and Psyche,* and in *Pierrots* with Le Brun. Again, Mme Delorme was in the troupe, often dancing the same numbers or playing the same or similar pantomime roles.

The Delormes moved to Covent Garden in 1734–35, where they remained until 1736–37. There Mlle Delorme was a Sylvan and a Female in *The Rape of Proserpine*, a Grace in *The Royal Chace*, and an Amazon in *Perseus and Andromeda*. She had other small roles. She joined a visiting French group on 8 April 1736 to act Sylvia in *Le Mariage forcé*. Specialty dances in which she participated were *The Princess Ann's Chacone* with Dupré, a *Pastoral Dance* with Mlle Grognet, *Les Bergers champêtre, The Faithful Shepherd*, a *Scot's Dance, Le Depit amoureux* with Desse, a *Ball Dance* with Dupré, and

French Peasant. On 23 August 1736 she danced *Two Pierrots* with Livier at Bartholomew Fair. Her last season at Drury Lane was 1736–37.

De Loutherbourg, Philip James (Philippe Jacques) *1740–1812, painter, scene designer.*

Philippe Jacques De Loutherbourg was born on 31 October 1740 in Strasbourg, according to the baptismal register of the Neue Kirche there. But his father later declared that he had been born on 1 November 1740 in Fulda, Hesse-Nassau, and his monument in the churchyard of St Nicholas, Chiswick, perpetuates that testimony.

The ancestors of the De Loutherbourgs were Poles, whose patents of nobility were said to have been bestowed by King Sigismund in 1564. Philippe's immediate forebears were recusants who had fled to Switzerland to escape persecution from the Roman Church. His father, Philippe, resettled in Strasbourg after appointment as painter to the Court of Darmstadt.

Philippe's mother, Catherine-Barbe Heitz, had wanted him to become a Lutheran cleric; his father had intended him for engineering. Philippe's own inclinations were for painting, but he allowed himself to be sent to the University of Strasbourg where for a time he tried to content both parents, studying mathematics, philosophy, science, and theology. He prevailed on his father finally, however, to give him instruction in drawing and then he studied with J. H. Tischbein the elder.

The De Loutherbourg family moved to Paris in 1755 (where the father was to die in 1768). Young Philippe Jacques then studied with Carle van Loo, a most successful painter and at that time Recteur of the Académie Royale. Van Loo excelled in the portrayal of historic, mythological, and religious subjects. De Loutherbourg also sought instruction in printmaking from Jean-Georges Wille, head of an engraving academy, before entering the studio of

François Joseph Casanova. While in Casanova's studio in 1763 De Loutherbourg prepared for exhibition at the Salon a picture which won the acclaim of Diderot.

It was said that De Loutherbourg, by virtue of his earlier education in chemistry, had developed a new method of preparing and blending colors to make them more durable. In later years his employment of colors was to become one of the most inventive aspects of his scene designing technique. At Paris he achieved acclaim for numerous pictures exhibited at the Salon, and in 1766 he was nominated as a "peintre du roi" in the Académie Royale and was elected a member on 22 August 1767, before he had reached the normally required age of 30. Scandal delayed the actual certification because of reports that his wife, Barbe Burlat, whom he had married on 10 January 1764, was engaged in criminal behavior. Subsequently he sired five children by her, but the marriage, which had taken place against the wishes of his wife's parents, was an unhappy one. In 1768 he was elected to the Académie de Peinture et de Sculpture de Marseille, preceded by a letter of recommendation which described him as "one of those few geniuses that centuries only produce from time to time."

De Loutherbourg was well acquainted with Boucher and Servandoni and perhaps even worked with them on scenery in the Paris theatres. It was, in fact, Jean Monnet, the director of the Opéra-Comique who introduced De Loutherbourg to David Garrick, by letter, as "un de nos plus grand peintres, et garçon fort aimable." In November 1771 the artist journeyed to London, perhaps driven from Paris by his domestic troubles, with the intention of obtaining commissions to support a short stay. He was accompanied by Giovanni Battista Torré, a pyrotechnist who also became a publisher and dealer in prints at London, including the first by De Loutherbourg. (From this time he was commonly known as Philip James De Loutherbourg; his last

Dulwich College Art Gallery

PHILIP JAMES DE LOUTHERBOURG
by Gainsborough

name was spelled in a variety of ways in the theatre account books and other documents, including Lutherberg, Lutherbury, Luthenburg, and Lutherbourg.)

Although he eventually settled in a house at No 45, Titchfield Street, where he was to remain until 1783, during his first several months at London he resided in the house of the riding and fencing master Domenico Angelo in Carlisle Street. There he soon met Garrick. In response to the great actor-manager's request for some ideas about a new piece at Drury Lane, De

Loutherbourg presented (in a letter now in the Harvard Theatre Collection) a most comprehensive proposal for the alteration and improvement of the lighting, scenic, and mechanical systems in the theatre under his coordination and supervision. He offered to provide models and drawings for the workmen, painters, and machinists, and to do some painting of the scenery himself. He also proposed to design the costumes for actors and dancers, in harmony with the composer and ballet master. In effect, he was putting forward a new concept for coordinating all the scenic elements under one artistic master.

Obviously attracted by the proposals, Garrick engaged him. The account books indicate that De Loutherbourg was paid £300 between 20 March and 18 June 1773, the total figure the painter had requested for three months' work. Precisely what productions De Loutherbourg prepared in that season are not known, as his name was not publicly associated with Drury Lane until the next season. One of them may have been *The Pigmy Revels*, a new pantomime with music by Dibdin which was produced on 26 December 1772 with "New Scenes, Habits, and Machines." In view of the new lighting techniques which De Loutherbourg proposed in his let-ter, and which indeed we know were achieved no later than the following season, it seems that Gainsborough's letter to Garrick in late 1772 complaining that Drury Lane's stage had become too bright and glaring might have been a reaction to the changes the designer had already made.

In a subsequent letter, also undated, to Garrick and Lacy, De Loutherbourg requested more sweeping authority and a salary of 600 guineas, for which he would work year 'round, proposing to use the summers to prepare for the spectacles and novelties which he assured would fill the coffers of the Drury Lane treasury. Garrick agreed, but gave him the lesser salary of £500 per year, and made some reduction, according to Charles Dibdin (*Complete*

Harvard Theatre Collection

A scene from *A Christmas Tale*

by DE LOUTHERBOURG

History of the Stage), in the proposals for the scenic department. In the season of 1773–74 De Loutherbourg began in earnest to change the nature of theatrical production in England.

On 9 October 1773, Dr Arne's grand masque *Alfred* was revived for the first time in 16 years, with designs by De Loutherbourg and scenery painted by Carver, John French and Royer, and ship models by Serres. The production had "New Scenes, Machines, Decorations &c. The Characters dress'd in the Habits of the Times." "This Masque is very well got up . . ." wrote the prompter Hopkins in his diary, "particularly a Representation of the Grand Naval Review design'd by Mons De Loutherberg & vastly well Executed had great Applause the piece is very dull." The *St James's Chronicle* (4–9 October 1773) reported that "The two Lines of Men of War are not painted flat upon the Scenes, but are made with all their Rigging, Masts &c." The scene of the grand naval review was introduced again in *The Fair Quaker* on 9 November 1773.

On 27 December 1773 Garrick's extravaganza *A Christmas Tale* was produced. It had been written "in a hurry & on purpose to Shew Some fine Scenes" which were designed by De Loutherbourg, wrote Hopkins, "particularly a Burning Palace &c.

Courtesy of the Victoria and Albert Museum

Scene design, by DE LOUTHERBOURG

which was extremely fine & Novel." The production was not appreciated by the *Westminster Magazine*, but the *London Magazine* for that month claimed that "the alteration of the colour of the trees and flowers in the second act, the rising of the moon, the palace which tumbles into ruin, the grand garden scene at the conclusion, and the sea prospect which bounds it are of a sort rarely seen in this country." Horace Walpole wrote that the production was "adorned with the most beautiful scenes"; and Henry Angelo in his *Reminiscences* (1828–30) described how De Loutherbourg had

astonished the audience, not merely by beautiful colouring and designs, far superior to what they had been accustomed to, but by a sudden transition in a forest scene, where the foliage varies from green to blood colour. This contrivance was entirely new, and the effect was produced by placing different coloured silks in the flies, or side-scenes, which turned on a pivot, and with lights behind, which so illumined the stage, as to give the effect of enchantment.

Sethona, a new tragedy by Alexander Dow, on 19 February 1774 was the next piece for which scenery was designed by De Loutherbourg. The play was well supported by the extraordinary acting of Spranger and Anne Barry, and the scenes, by the testimony of Hopkins, were applauded. "The Dresses, Decorations and Scenery of this Play are much superior to those of any modern Tragedy," wrote the *Public Advertiser* (21 February 1774); "they do ample Justice to the Author, and likewise do Honour to the Taste and Spirit of the Manager, who seems to have spared no Expence to furnish a splendid and rational Entertainment. The Scene of the Temple of Osiris, and the View of the Egyptian Catacombs were particularly admired, and are worthy of the Brush of Mr Loutherbourg."

At the end of his second year of employment at Drury Lane, De Loutherbourg married a Staffordshire beauty, Lucy Paget, at Marylebone Church in May 1774. Having experienced artistic and financial success, and now some tranquillity in his personal life, he evidently decided to settle in England.

In 1774–75, his next season with Garrick, De Loutherbourg received a total of £333 5s. 8d. in eight monthly payments of £41 13s. 4d. each commencing on 14 October 1774 and ending on 26 May 1775. He did designs—painted by French and Royer—for Francklin's *Electra* on 15 October, including a perspective of Argos, the palace of Aegisthus, and the tomb of Agamemnon which the *Westminster Magazine* (October 1774) called "warm and spirited." For the premiere of Burgoyne's *The Maid of the Oaks*, the *Westminster Magazine* (November 1774) asserted that the excellent scenery "preserved the piece from that damnation, which as a dramatic production, it justly deserved," since obviously it had been got up "as a mere vehicle for *splendid spectacle*." The *London Magazine* (November 1774) reported that the scenery for this piece had cost £1500 (a figure the account books do not support), "yet it will not appear extravagant to anybody who sees it." "The most remarkable scenes" described by the latter periodical:

were Mr. Oldworth's mansion, which we are informed is taken from a view of Lord Stanley's house and improvements: the portico is an imitation of the temporary building at the late celebrated Fête Champêtre; the magnificent scene of the saloon is also similar to that nobleman's grand apartment, which changes to one of the most beautiful scenes ever exhibited, representing a celestial garden, terminated by a prospect of the Temple of Love, in which the statue of the Cyprian goddess appears in the attitude of the Venus of the Medicis. The background is illuminated by the rays of the sun, which have a most splendid and astonishing effect.

The 20 crowded houses which the *London Magazine* predicted for *The Maid of the*

Oaks was exceeded by four. For the *Grand Provençale Dance* on 8 December 1774, De Loutherbourg created a sunrise over Marseilles which had, reported the *Public Advertiser* (8 December 1774), "a most natural and pleasing Effect." According to Sybil Rosenfeld's detailed list of De Loutherbourg's work in London, which appeared in *Theatre Notebook* (Spring 1965), and from which many press notices quoted here are gratefully drawn, he designed a tent scene for *Mathilda* on 21 January 1775. Probably De Loutherbourg supplied the new scenes and costumes for the first performance of Jephson's *Braganza* on 17 February 1775 — no expense was denied "for the Cloaths & Scenery both of which was Superb" wrote Hopkins.

De Loutherbourg's inventions, painted by French and Greenwood, in *Queen Mab* on 11 November 1775 — which Hopkins characterized in his diary as "a representation of a Regatta very well executed but is too much like the Naval Review" — brought high praise from the *Morning Post* (13 November 1775). The scene showed Red House, the entrance to Smith's gardens, which changed to the regatta on the Thames going by Ranelagh: "The effect produced by this united scenery and machinery, is wonderful; every barge is rowed to the time of the band of music . . . the sky flat behind is finely designed and executed for the general relief, and the disposition of men and boats near shore, in the foreground, is beautiful and masterly." (The same account was printed in the *Westminster Magazine* for November 1775.) The scenery was used again for *The Genii* on 11 December 1775 and for *The Waterman* on 12 April 1776. His new scenes for *The Runaway* on 15 February 1776 moved the *Morning Chronicle* (17 February 1776) to acclaim De Loutherbourg as "The first artist who showed our theatre directors that by a just disposition of light and shade, and critical preservation of perspective, the eye of the spectator might be so effectually deceived in a play-house as to be induced to take the produce of art for real nature."

The last assignment which De Loutherbourg executed under Garrick's management was for Colman's farce *The Spleen* on 7 March 1776; the scenes, according to *London Magazine* (March 1776) included a view of Spa Fields, the Pantheon, and adjoining buildings. In 1775–76 De Loutherbourg received monthly payments of £31 13s. 4d. for a total of £261 10s. 4d., representing a large reduction in salary from his previous year's figure of £333 5s. 8d.

Recent scholarly speculation has been seen about the possibility that De Loutherbourg may have designed scenery for *Richard III* under Garrick's management. In 1874 some drawings by De Loutherbourg came into Henry Irving's hands from "his old friend," whose initials were C. R. or C. A. On these drawings in the handwriting of 1874 appear the words "the first practical Bridge" and "Sketch for the play 'Richard the 3rd.' — made for David Garrick by de Loutherbourg." Photographs of the drawings were published by W. J. Lawrence in 1895 in the *Magazine of Art*. These photographs were later reproduced by Richard Southern as reconstructions from maquettes — pastiches or collages — and shown by W. Moelwyn Merchant in *Shakespeare and the Artist* (1959). There seems little doubt that the attribution of the original drawings to De Loutherbourg is correct, but as Merchant wondered, "what scene in *Richard III* do they purport to set and what text was used by Garrick in the production?" In *Theatre Notebook* (XIX:110) Rosenfeld and Croft-Murray questioned the suitability of the sketches to a production of *Richard III*, finding the sketch of the rocky chasm spanned by a bridge difficult "to fit in with any scene in the Cibber version." Neither Shakespeare nor Cibber specified the use of a bridge, and a "practical" one at that.

From the time De Loutherbourg came to work for Garrick until the end of 1775–76, *Richard III* was performed at Drury Lane nine times; only in the last two of these performances did Garrick play the role. The part was perhaps his greatest physical challenge. Sturz saw him in 1768 after a performance reclining on a bench "like the dying Germanicus in Poussin's picture, with heaving breast, pale, and covered with perspiration, his hands limp and quivering, speechless." When Garrick was preparing his final round of roles in the spring of 1776 he told Joseph Cradock, "I can play Richard; but I dread the fight and the fall. I am afterwards in agonies." A routine stage fall by an experienced actor standing on the boards themselves, after a violent stage battle, could be responsible for "agonies," of course, but if Garrick had fallen from the bridge, it would not then have been a presumptuous addition of stage business despite the fact that neither version of the play requires it. There is, unfortunately, no surviving account of a "fall" by Garrick in the production, except his own testimony in which he fails to mention a bridge, nor is there any notice in the bills or advertisement of new scenery for revivals of *Richard III* during De Loutherbourg's tenure under Garrick. But built-up stage pieces were in use on the English stage as early as 1716 in Hill's *The Fatal Vision*, and a bridge upon which actors appeared was specified by Hill for his *Henry the Fifth* in 1723. The inscription put on the drawing about 1874 that it was a representation of "the first practical Bridge" is incorrect, but that circumstance does not necessarily negate the possibility that these sketches by De Loutherbourg were, indeed, for *Richard III*.

After Garrick's retirement, De Loutherbourg continued on with the new Drury Lane management under Richard B. Sheridan. The fall of 1776, however, brought a unique and inexplicable event in De Loutherbourg's theatrical career. The name "Loutherbourg"—presumably belonging to the designer—appeared in the bill of 14 October 1776 to perform the role of Harlequin ("for that night only") in a production of the pantomime *The Life and Death of Harlequin* at China Hall Theatre in Rotherhithe.

Under Sheridan, the designer's salary was raised again to £500 per season for 1776–77, 1777–78, and 1778–79. Payments to him as shown in the account books for the subsequent years are erratic, but it seems that De Loutherbourg was still earning £500 in 1779–80. His salary payment in 1780–81, according to Rosenfeld, totalled £247, about half of his customary wages; the figure supports William Pyne's information that the designer finally left Drury Lane because of Sheridan's attempts to reduce his salary.

His fairy palace for *Selima and Azor* on 5 December 1777 was criticised for its similarity to scenery in *The Maid of the Oaks*. He created a palace with hanging gardens for *Semiramis* on 14 December 1777. He provided new scenes for a revival of *Queen Mab* on 1 January 1778—his view of Greenwich Hospital with the Thames and Greenwich Park in the background was "certainly one of the finest perspectives that ever was exhibited." The romantic exterior of a castle in moonlight for *The Battle of Hastings* on 24 January 1778 was also his work.

It was perhaps during this season of 1777–78 that De Loutherbourg had an encounter with the elder Grimaldi. A clipping from an unidentified newspaper reported:

The Painter and the Ballet Master have had a terrible quarrel. Signor de Grimaldi drew his fiddle stick upon Monsieur de Loutherbourg —upon which the last, with a brush of red oaker, gave a diagonal line across Pantaloon's face, which looked as if he had cut his head into two parts—the Frenchman retired and left the Italian with his mouth open, as we have often seen in a pantomime. As they are both sprung from great families, it is not expected this affair will end so comically.

During the summer of 1778 De Loutherbourg made excursions to Coxheath Camp in Kent and to the Peak section of Derby-shire to make sketches in preparation for two productions in 1778–79. He was re-imbursed £35 by the theatre for the trips. One of these productions was Sheridan's musical entertainment *The Camp* which opened at Drury Lane on 15 October 1778. De Loutherbourg created a perspective of Coxheath Camp, a new military encamp-ment near Maidstone, "from which, by a kind of magic peculiar to himself, he makes the different battalions, composed of small figures, march out in excellent order, into the front of their lines." The designs were also used at the Theatre Royal in Bristol on 15 March 1779.

For the two-act pantomime of *The Won-ders of Derbyshire*, also probably contrived by Sheridan, De Loutherbourg created spec-tacularly exotic and romantic designs which were such accurate depictions of the actual locales that they formed a veritable trav-elogue. The picturesque settings, which capitalized on the growing interest in Eng-lish landscapes, included views of Matlock, Dovedale, leadmines and landscape at day-break, the outside and inside of Peak's Hole, and Buxton Wells, among others. A scene of Chatsworth closed the first act. De Loutherbourg's ingenuity was praised in a long review in the *London Packet* (8–11 January 1779).

Last night was performed at Drury-lane Theatre, a new patomime [*sic*], called *The Wonders of Derbyshire*, or *Harlequin in the Peak*, in which all the scenes are designed by Mr. Loutherbourg. This artist ranks so de-servedly high as a man of genius, taste, and brilliant execution, that the warmest eepecta-tions [*sic*] have been entertained of his suc-cess, in a province of painting, where a loose is given to the imagination, and where the wildest flights of fancy may be characteristi-cally employed. The scenes exhibited last night were infinitely superior to every thing that has been seen since those of Servandoni, and with several advantages in the disposition and illumination. . . .

The sublime stile of the paintings seemed to have awed the genius of buffoonery and low humour; a succession of most elegant scenery was displayed, in which few attempts were made to move the muscles of the audience, or to interrupt the admiration ex-cited by the exhibition.

The business is pretty much in the usual stile; Harlequin appears in a most beautiful scene, in which the setting sun is admirably imitated; he is in despair for the loss of Colombine, and attempts to destroy himself, but is prevented by a fairy (Miss Abrams, a child, who sung a pleasing air); a Magician (Mr. Bannister) rises and presents Harlequin with a talisman, with power sufficient for the accomplishment of his wishes, which he is particularly charged not to lose. A French gentleman, who is betrothed to Columbine, then appears, with a train of servants, and undergoes a great variety of insults and morti-fications; by the power of Harlequin, he is tormented with various supernatural and ter-rific appearances in his chamber; he after-wards appears at the Peak, and descends into one of the pits, but leaves his cloaths as usual above; they are carried off by Harlequin, who introduces himself to Columbine and her father, in a grand scene, in which Chatsworth House and Gardens appear in the back ground; he is soon detected, flies off with Columbine, and the pursuit commences through all the wonders of the Peak, of which a succession of beautiful, correct, and mas-terly views are exhibited. Harlequin, in the midst of his adventure, loses his hat, wherein he had fixed his talisman, which is found by his clown, who on handling it, as it is a pretty plaything, is surrounded by demons, the servants of the tallisman [*sic*] by whom he is carried off; Harlequin, deprived of the greater part of his power, is seized, and thrown into a cavern, from which he is borne by a flying dragon, he is afterwards caught and sinks into the earth, but leaves his arms behind him, which becomes animated, plays a variety of gambols, and then sinks; Harle-quin is again pursued and caught in a gloomy cave; but here the magician rises and changes the scene into a magnificent palace and gar-dens, in which a chorus of spirits descend, and the lovers are united.

Considered as a vehicle for elegant scenery, machinery, and music (the only light in which a Pantomime deserves to be considered,) the piece exhibited last night deserves the highest praise, as it is on the whole generally superior to any we have ever seen . . .

Angelo asserted that "never were such romantic and picturesque paintings exhibited in that theatre before." A pamphlet published several weeks after the first performance, written by "A Derbyshire Man," described the actual locales of 12 of the 21 scenes shown in the pantomime and provided a kind of libretto for the production. An account of this pamphlet and its relationship to the pantomime, along with analysis and reviews, was presented by Ralph Allen in "*The Wonders of Derbyshire*: A Spectacular Eighteenth-Century Travelogue," *Theatre Survey* (1961).

Among the many tributes to Garrick after his death in January 1779 was Sheridan's *A Monody On the Death of Garrick* which was presented at Drury Lane on 11 March 1779 with a new scene "invented and designed" by De Loutherbourg. Over the next several years, the designer concentrated his talents on a series of nautical stage adventures. In his scenery of Tilbury Fort and the battle of the Armada in Sheridan's *The Critic* on 29 October 1779, "The deception of the sea was very strong," reported the *General Advertiser* (1 November 1779), "and the perspective of the ships together with the mode of their sailing truly picturesque." Some of these scenes were later used at Bristol on 27 May 1780. Tribute was paid to him by Sheridan within the text of *The Critic*, itself, when the principal character remarks, "As to the scenery, the miraculous powers of Mr. De Loutherbourg's pencil are universally acknowledged."

He provided, on 13 December 1779, new dresses, scenes, and decorations to *Zoraida*. On 1 January 1780 he staged *Harlequin Fortunatus* which contained, among others, a scene of the "Representation of the Storming Fort Omoa in the Bay of Honduras" by land and sea. But technical errors on opening night diminished the effect as "The sceneman blundered egregiously all through the entertainment," according to the *London Chronicle* (4 January 1779). "During the siege of the fort so much gunpowder was fired off that the stage was so filled with smoke that the officers, men, &c. were scarcely discernible from the boxes." In *Artifice* on 14 April 1780, Tower Hill with the launching of a land frigate was depicted, and on 17 May 1780 *The Genii* was revived with a sea fight. After executing scenery for *The Lord of the Manor* on 27 December 1780, De Loutherbourg did elaborate settings for *Robinson Crusoe* on 29 January 1781, again depicting several nautical scenes, as well as transformation effects such as a fat friar changing into a hogshead, a chair into a lanthorn, a room into a dyer's shop, a convent into a windmill, and an *auto da fe* into a garden. "The scene of Crusoe's bower, and several others, are beautiful," reported the *London Magazine* (February 1781), "but the inside of the prison of the Inquisition is greatly beyond any of the rest." A scene of "eastern magnificence" with temples and arcades was provided for *The Fair Circassion* on 11 November 1781.

De Loutherbourg's last designs for Drury Lane were for *The Carnival of Venice* on 13 December 1781, a piece which concluded with "a View of St. Mark's Place, and a grand *Representation of the Carnival*." Evidently he had anticipated the dispute with Sheridan over salary which caused him to leave Drury Lane, for during this last season at that theatre he had also taken up another enterprise. In a house in Lisle Street, near Leicester Square, daily from 26 February 1781, he exhibited his "*Eidophusikon*; or, Various Imitations of Natural Phenomena represented by Moving Pictures," on a miniature stage six feet wide by eight feet deep. The exhibition con-

Mr. DE LOUTHERBOURG intending very ſhortly to finally cloſe his Exhibition, that the Public at large may have an Opportunity of ſeeing the *EIDOPHUSIKON*, he has made a Diviſion of his Room into Front Seats at 5s. each, and the Back Rows at 2s. 6d.—And for the future, the Evenings of Exhibiting will be *MONDAY*'s, *WEDNESDAY*'s, and *FRIDAY*'s, at his Houſe in *Liſle-Street*, *Leiceſter-Square*. The Doors will be opened at *Half paſt Seven*, and the Performance to begin *preciſely at Eight*.

Eidophuſikon:

An intire New Set of

MOVING PICTURES,

Repreſenting the following

Phœnomena of Nature,

Invented and Painted by

Mr. DE LOUTHERBOURG.

The PERFORMANCE divided into TWO ACTS.

1ſt Scene. The SUN RISING in the FOG, an ITALIAN SEA-PORT.

2d. The CATARACT of NIAGARA, in NORTH AMERICA.

3d. And (by particular Deſire) the FAVOURITE SCENE (exhibited 60 Nights laſt Seaſon) of the

STORM and SHIPWRECK.

ACT the SECOND.

1ſt. The SETTING of the SUN after a RAINY DAY; with a View of the CASTLE, TOWN, and CLIFFS of DOVER.

2d. The RISING of the MOON, with a WATER-SPOUT, exhibiting the EFFECTS of THREE different LIGHTS, with a View of a ROCKY SHORE on the COAST of JAPAN.

The concluſive SCENE,

3d. SATAN arraying his TROOPS on the BANKS of the FIERY LAKE, with the RAISING of the PALACE of PANDEMONIUM, from MILTON.

The Muſic for the Scenes compoſed and performed,

By Mr. BURNEY,

Who will Play a Sonata before the laſt Scene, on the Harpſichord.

The Vocal Part by Mrs. BADDELEY.

☞ Ladies and Gentlemen who chuſe to have Places kept, will pleaſe to ſend to the Office, in *Liſle-Street*, where a Perſon attends.

Harvard Theatre Collection

Announcement of the *Eidophusikon*

sisted, as Sybil Rosenfeld has described it, of a "display of scenery for [its] own sake." The audience was treated to five scenes: dawn at Greenwich Park, noon in Tangier, sunset near Naples, a moon rise over the Mediterranean, and a shipwreck at sea. The displays were interspersed with four transparencies and by musical interludes written by Michael Arne and sung "with the truest taste" by Mrs Arne who also sang two songs composed by J. C. Bach. The popular *Eidophusikon* was greatly admired by Gainsborough (who had painted De Loutherbourg's portrait about 1778). When the designer was prosecuted for offering a public exhibition without a musical license, a license was issued at once, without penalty, by the justices who presided.

The *Eidophusikon* ran through May 1781, closed for the summer, and reopened on 10 December 1781, with new music by Burney. On 31 January 1782 five new scenes were shown, which were described in some detail by the *European Magazine* (March 1782). They consisted of a sunrise over an Italian seaport, a view of Niagara Falls, sunset at Dover, a spectacular light and water display on the coast of Japan, and "a view of the Miltonic Hell, cloathed in all its terrors" as the grand climax. A watercolor of the last scene, by Edward Francis Burney, is in the British Museum and has been described in some detail by Rosenfeld in "The *Eidophusikon* Illustrated," *Theatre Notebook* (XXVIII). De Loutherbourg used the show to continue experiments in light-

ing, movement of clouds, and transparencies lit from the rear by Argand lamps. The entire spectacle was accompanied by sound effects of rain, hail, thunder, and roaring seas. A vivid description of the hell scene was given by William Pyne in *Wine and Walnuts* (1823):

Here, in the foreground of a vista, stretching an immeasurable length between mountains, ignited from their bases to their lofty summits, with many-coloured flame, a chaotic mass rose in dark majesty, which gradually assumed form until it stood, the interior of a vast temple of gorgeous architecture, bright as molten brass, seemingly composed of unconsuming and unquenchable fire. In this tremendous scene, the effect of coloured glasses before the lamps was fully displayed; which, being hidden from the audience, threw their whole influence upon the scene, as it

DE LOUTHERBOURG's *Eidophusikon*
by E. F. Burney

rapidly changed, now to a sulphurous blue, then to a lurid red, and then again to a pale vivid light, and ultimately to a mysterious combination of the glasses such as a bright furnace exhibits, in fusing various metals. The sounds which accompanied the wondrous picture struck the astonished ear of the spectator as no less preternatural; for, to add a more awful character to peals of thunder, and the accompaniments of all the hollow machinery that hurled balls and stones with indescribable rumbling and noise, an expert assistant swept his thumb over the surface of the tambourine, which produced a variety of groans, that struck the imagination as issuing from infernal spirits.

De Loutherbourg continued to exhibit the *Eidophusikon* until 31 May 1782. In 1786 it was revived in a room over the Exeter Exchange, formerly the Patagonian Theatre, between 30 January and 12 May, with the storm scene updated to exhibit the wreck of the *Halsewell*. The *Eidophusikon* did much, as Rosenfeld noted, "to foster taste for subtler light effects and naturalistic landscape scenery on stage." De Loutherbourg later sold his stock to [George?] Chapman who exhibited it at Davis's Great Room, No 60, Great George's Street, Dublin, in February 1792, and as the *New Eidophusikon* in Panton Street, Haymarket, London, in April 1799. It was destroyed by a fire in Panton Street and James Street in March 1800.

De Loutherbourg has been credited with designs, executed by A. M. Bigari, for a production of *Harlequin Foundling* at the Smock Alley Theatre, Dublin, in March 1783. Earlier, at Christmas 1781, he had worked on lighting effects for a fête given by William Beckford at Fonthill. His last known work for the theatre was at Covent Garden on 20 December 1785 for the afterpiece *Omai*, with the assistance of Richards, Carver, Hodgins, Turner, the younger Catton, and the Rev Matthew William Peters, a "celebrated artist." Nineteen scenes based on the sketches which

John Webber had made when he accompanied Captain Cook to the South Seas were put on the stage, as indicated in the manuscript of the piece now in the Library of the Society for Theatre Research, London. The author of *Omai*, John O'Keeffe, wrote about the production in his *Recollections* (1826):

At Barnes I composed a grand spectacle for Covent Garden, called *Omai*; the incidents, characters, &c. appropriate to the newly-discovered islands in the southern hemisphere, and closing with the apotheosis of Captain Cook. The effect of this piece was most happy. Shield's melodies were beautifully wild, as suiting his romantic theme; and the dresses and scenery were done from drawings of Mr. Webber, the artist, who had made the voyages with Captain Cook. . . . Loutherbourg planned the scenery. He had previously invented transparent scenery — moonshine, sunshine, fire, volcanoes, &c. as also breaking the scene into several pieces by the laws of perspective, showing miles and miles distance. Before his time, the back was one broad flat, the whole breadth and height of the stage. *Omai* was acted forty nights [actually 49] the first season. Loutherbourg had £100 for his designs, and I another £100 for the composition of the piece, besides the sale of my songs, which brought me about £40.

The spectacle has been reconstructed in detail by Ralph G. Allen in "De Loutherbourg and Captain Cook," *Theatre Research* (1962).

In an article in *Theatre Notebook* (XX), Anthony Oliver and John Saunders argue that De Loutherbourg was the likely designer for the famous production of *Pizarro* at Drury Lane on 24 May 1799 and that a painting, oil on glass, depicting Rolla and Pizarro, now in the possession of Messrs Oliver and Saunders, was done by him.

In 1780 De Loutherbourg was elected an associate of the Royal Academy where he had frequently exhibited since 1772. He was made an academician on 28 November

1781. After a visit to Switzerland in 1783, he moved to a house in Hammersmith Terrace, Chiswick, devoting himself to mysticism under the influence of Cagliostro, Mesmer, and the prophet Richard Brothers. Even earlier, while Garrick was alive, De Loutherbourg had written to Mrs Garrick about his interest in alchemy, an interest which Mrs Garrick and his friend the pyrotechnist Torré shared with him. De Loutherbourg and his wife claimed the powers of prophecy and healing by faith; and in 1789 a fellow believer, Mary Pratt, published *A List of a few Cures performed by Mr. and Mrs. De Loutherbourg of Hammersmith Terrace without Medicine, by a Lover of the Lamb of God.* In *Old and New London,* Walford related a riot caused by one of their unsuccessful attempts at faith healing. A mob attacked their home, breaking windows and threatening their safety. On 13 November 1789 the *Morning Chronicle* reported that "Loutherbourg has entirely given up the practice of working miracles and taken to his pencil again." He turned earnestly now to history painting, religious subjects, and battle scenes.

By the nineteenth century his artistry, business, and influence waned. Although in 1806 he was put up for the presidency of the Royal Academy, the incumbent Benjamin West was re-elected. In 1807 De Loutherbourg was appointed "Historical Painter to HRH the Duke of Gloucester," but no works under that patronage are known.

De Loutherbourg died at Hammersmith Terrace on 11 March 1812 at the age of 72 and was buried in the churchyard of St Nicholas, Chiswick, where also are buried Hogarth and the actor Henry Holland. A large Romanesque monument designed by Sir John Soane contains his remains. The inscription written by Dr C. L. Moody reads, in part:

With Talents Brilliant and Super Eminent / As an Artist / He united the still more en-viable endowments / Of a cultivated, enlarged, and elegant Mind, / Adding to both, those superior qualities of the Heart / Which entitled him / As a man, and as a Christian, / To the cordial respect of the Wise and Good / In him Science was Associated with Faith, / Piety with Liberality, / Virtue with Suavity of Manners, / And the rational use of this World / With the ennobling hope of a world to Come / A deathless Fame will record his professional excellence / But to the hand of Friendship belongs the office / Of strewing on his tomb those moral flowers / Which displayed themselves in his Life, / And which rendered him estimable as a Social Being /

*Here Loutherbourg repose
thy laurell'd head
While art is cherish'd thou canst
ne'er be dead
Salvatore, Pouissin, Claude thy
skill combines
And beauteous Nature lives
in thy designs.*

Also reposing in the sarcophagus are the remains of his widow "Lucy de Loutherbourg / Who closed a life of active benevolence and utility with the resignation, fortitude / and hopes of a Christian / on the 20th of September 1828 / in the 83rd Year of her Age" and William Philip James Lodder, probably a son, "formerly Captain in the 6th Foot / Born the 3rd of July 1779 / Died the 31st of January 1867 / in his 88th Year." A portrait of Lucy De Loutherbourg by her husband, engraved by G. Scorodomoff, is in the Huntington Library. In a painting entitled "Winter Morning," De Loutherbourg included his wife and himself, along with V. M. Picot, John Webber, and Jean Georges Noverre. De Loutherbourg left a collection of ship models and many sketches and stage maquettes, as well as an eclectic and large library of books, many of which are now in the British Museum.

De Loutherbourg is commonly acknowledged to have been the most influential designer in the English theatre since Inigo

Jones by virtue of his advances along the path to both a romantic and more realistic treatment of stage space. He refined the technical use of ramps, levels, set-pieces, and profile wings—all items which had been seen on the English stage before. Although he did not introduce scenic transparencies and colored sidelights to the English stage—Garrick had used them for a production of *Harlequin's Invasion* on 31 December 1759—his experiments with them led to startling effects. The encouragement given to him by Garrick can be realized by a comparison of investments in technical effects over the years. In 1766–67, Drury Lane spent £652 on scenes and machines and £1240 on lighting. By 1775–76, the last year of Garrick's management, expenditures for scenes and machines were £1674 and for lighting £1970.

Probably more important than his use of transparencies, filters of colored silk, and marvels of perspective painting was the fact that his lighting and scenic arrangements allowed the actor to step farther back into the scenic areas without becoming obscured by dark shadows or looking disproportionate to his environment. As a result of the new spirit of freedom in his stage designs many aspects of the rigid system of stage mounting which had persisted for over a century were discarded and the way was readied for the coming of the pictorial art of the next century.

Portraits of De Loutherbourg include:

1. A self-portrait, in oil. Painted between 1805 and 1810. In his wife's possession until her death. Now in the National Portrait Gallery. Engraved by R. Page and published by R. Jones, 1814.

2. A self-portrait in pencil and chalk, done about the age of 40. In the Hessian Landesmuseum, Darmstadt.

3. "Landscape in which the artist has introduced a portrait of himself with his gun and dog." Sold at Foster's, 29 May 1829, present location unknown.

4. In full figure, skating, in his own painting, "Winter Morning," mentioned in the biography above.

5. A miniature by Richard Cosway. As part of the F. N. and O. S. Ashcroft Collection, this portrait was on loan to the Victoria and Albert Museum until 1938. The portrait was reproduced in the *Connoisseur* in 1926. The Ashcroft Collection was sold at Sotheby's in May 1946, and subsequently the portrait was in the possession of Minto Wilson, who lent it to the exhibition, "The First Hundred Years of the Royal Academy," held at Burlington House in 1951–52. The present location is unknown.

6. An oil painting by Gainsborough, exhibited at the Royal Academy in 1778. Bequeathed by Sir Francis Bourgeois in 1811 to Dulwich College, where it still hangs.

7. A miniature by J. Jackson. Engraved by H. Meyer for Cadell's *Contemporary Portraits*, 1813.

8. An anonymous engraving, after a portrait by S. Singleton, published in 1798.

9. De Loutherbourg is pictured with numerous other artists in a painting by H. Singleton which belongs to the Royal Academy. The painting was published in an engraving by C. Bestland in 1803 with the title "The Royal Academicians assembled in their Council Chamber to adjudge the Medals to the successful Students in Painting, Sculpture, Architecture, and Drawing in 1793."

De Loutherbourg's own paintings of theatrical persons include a portrait of Dr Arne, engraved by Bartolozzi; a portrait of the elder George Colman, engraved by Cheesman, published 1807; G. F. Cooke as Macbeth, engraved by Parker, 1803; G. F. Cooke as Shylock, engraved by Skelton, 1803; David Garrick, a pen-and-ink sketch done shortly before the actor's death, engraved by R. Sawyer, 1825; Garrick as Richard III, a portrait originally listed in the *Mathews Collection Catalogue* (#321) but not in the Garrick Club and its present location unknown; Garrick as Don John in *The Chances*, probably exhibited at the Royal Academy, now in the Victoria and Albert Museum; a watercolor sketch of the previous painting, also at the V. & A.; a version of the previous painting, engraved by Hall for the *New English Theatre*, 1777; Garrick as Don John, a pencil sketch (perhaps a tracing from the engraving by C. Phillips) at the British Museum; Charles Kemble as Orlando in *As You Like It*, engraved by C. Warren, 1804; John Philip Kemble as Wolsey in *Henry VIII*, engraved by DeLatre, 1803; Charles Macklin as Shylock and Michael Dyer as Gratiano in *The Merchant of Venice*, engraved by T. B. Simonet; Giovanni Morelli, vocalist at the Haymarket, engraved by the artist, 1790; Alexander Pope as Leontes and Mrs Powell as Paulina in *The Winter's Tale*, engraved by J. Neagle; Thomas Weston as Spy in *The Rival Candidates*, engraved and published by M. Torré, 1775; Richard Wroughton as Bolingbroke and Charles Kemble as Aumerle in *Richard III*, engraved by A. Warren, 1804.

Numerous examples of De Loutherbourg's landscape and marine subjects are found in galleries and private collections in England and on the Continent. Two of his landscapes with cattle are at the Dulwich College Picture Gallery; a canvas called "The Milkmaid" is at the Birmingham Art Gallery; a "View of Cumberland" is in the National Portrait Gallery, London (it was engraved by W. Richardson); a landscape is at the Victoria and Albert Museum; his large canvas of the "Grand Attack on Valenciennes," for which he made studies in 1793 with the Duke of York's expedition, was engraved by W. Bromley; his battle piece of "Earl Howe's Victory on 1 June 1794" is at Greenwich Hospital; his painting "Summer Afternoon with a Methodist Preacher," about 1774, is in the National Gallery of Canada, Ottawa; a painting "Gig Upsetting on Derby Day,"

attributed to De Loutherbourg, was acquired by the Boston Museum of Fine Arts by the bequest of Mary Le Ware in 1937. In the British Museum are drawings and etchings, mostly dating from his earlier period. De Loutherbourg did plates and vignettes for Macklin's *Bible*, Bowyer's *History of England*, and Bell's *British Theatre*. Engravings after his drawings were published in *Picturesque Scenery of Great Britain* in 1801 and 1805. The Victoria and Albert Museum possesses a number of De Loutherbourg's drawings and engravings, including one of Peaks Hole for *The Wonders of Derbyshire* and mountain scenery for the *Eidophusikon*. Sepia sketches for *A Christmas Tale* are in the Musée des Beaux-Arts, Strasbourg, and in the Collection of Colonel Brinsley Ford. His original painting of "Mr Weston in the character of Tycho fighting the evil spirits" in *A Christmas Tale* was exhibited at the Royal Academy in 1774 but is now lost; engravings of the scene by Charles Phillips are in the Harvard Theatre Collection and the British Museum. His oil painting of Macbeth and the Witches is at the American Shakespeare Festival Theatre, Stratford, Connecticut. There have been two doctoral dissertations on De Loutherbourg: Ralph Allen's "The Stage Spectacles of Philip James De Loutherbourg" (Yale University, 1960) and Lillian Preston's "Philippe Jacques De Loutherbourg. 18th Century Romantic Artist and Scene Designer" (Florida State University, 1957). A *Catalogue of Drawings* executed by the artist which was printed for a sale held on 18 June 1812 lists 380 pieces, ranging over the entire spectrum of De Loutherbourg's works. A major exhibition of De Loutherbourg's works was held at Kenwood (the Iveagh Bequest) in Hampstead from 2 June through 13 August 1973. A handsome and detailed catalog of that exhibition, edited by Rüdiger Joppien of Cologne University, was published by the Greater London Council.

Delpine. *See* **DE L'ÉPINE.**

Delpini, Carlo Antonio *1740–1828,*
actor, dancer, choreographer, singer.

Carlo Antonio Delpini was born at
Rome (perhaps in the parish of St
Martin's) in 1740 and was said to have
been trained by Nicolini. His continental
career is not known, but he was a polished
performer nearing the height of his pantomimic powers when he came to London.
It is possible that he was the "Chas Del-
phini" who signed a letter, now in the
Smith manuscript collection at the Garrick
Club, dated 7 January 1767, and whose
address was said then to be No 14, Drury
Lane. But he is not certainly known to have
been engaged in theatrical activity in Britain before his first appearance at Covent
Garden on 26 December 1776 when he
danced as Pierrot in the pantomime *Harlequin's Frolicks.* On this occasion the playbills announced his "first appearance on
the English stage." But halfway through his
exertions in the afterpiece he injured himself seriously in some manner, and on the
next evening, when the *Frolicks* played
again, according to the *Morning Chronicle*:

[Hull] made an apology for the illness of
Delpini, telling the audience that the Signor
had hurt himself so much the preceding
evening in performing . . . that he could
not come out of his room; the managers
therefore hoped that the audience would accept of [Ralph] Wewitzer in the character . . .

Not until 9 January was Delpini able to
resume the role. He danced it half a dozen
times more through 27 January but after
that date seems not to have been employed
in another piece until 23 April when, for
Lee Lewes's benefit night, he danced as
Pierrot in *The Royal Chace; or, Harlequin
Skelton.* Nor was he used in either the
corps de ballet or in specialty dances. He
was, however, probably already assisting in
arranging the spectacle and business for

the harlequinades. For his performances,
whatever they were, he received £1 10s.
per week.

Delpini danced and acted a few times
in October 1777 in *The Royal Chace* and
was seen on 1 October in a booth at Cambridge, performing as Pierrot for a benefit
for Lee Lewes, but his emphasis shifted
now to the behind-the-scenes activity of
writing and staging his first original pantomime. On 25 November he brought out in
collaboration with the machinist James
Messink the elaborate afterpiece called *The
Norwood Gypsies,* with music composed by
John Abraham Fisher, in which Lee Lewes
starred as Harlequin and Delpini was the
Clown. The piece was enormously expensive but also was greatly popular, being
played 44 times before the end of the
1777–78 season. Delpini's salary was raised
to £2 10s. in that season.

He was back at Covent Garden from 14
October 1778 through 24 May 1779, dancing and miming in Messink's *The Medley;
or, Harlequin At-All,* which was played
some two dozen times. As Scaramouch, he
was a prime reason for the great success of
Dibdin's *The Touchstone; or, Harlequin
Traveller,* which was played some 45 times
that season.

Delpini was in the Drury Lane company
in 1779–80, but he also danced and acted
several times at Covent Garden, when *The
Touchstone* and his own *Norwood Gypsies*
were performed. He came on for the first
time at Drury Lane that season at the end
of the mainpiece (*The Stratagem*) on 10
December in a "New Comic Pantomimic
Dance" of his own composition, *The Sports-
men Deceiv'd,* under the rubric "first appearance as a dancer in England." Certainly this advice was incorrect, inasmuch as
interpretations of Pierrot and Scaramouch
involve some dancing. It was, however, the
first featured specialty dancing he had done.
He appeared in the bills that season very
infrequently and was no doubt busily
assisting in the preparation of the panto-

Harvard Theatre Collection

CARLO ANTONIO DELPINI, "Shooting at
the Spaniards"

artist unknown

mimes which had the inestimable advantage over those of Covent Garden of being
set by the scenic genius De Loutherbourg.

In May 1780 Delpini was living at No
1, Haymarket. On 30 May he made his
debut in the summer theatre at the Haymarket, playing the Clown in *The Genius
of Nonsense*. From this period until the
end of the century he was in and out of
the London theatres. He was at the Haymarket from 19 July to 26 August 1784,
was absent from the winter theatres in
1784–85 except for a few specially licensed
performances at the Haymarket, was re-
hired by Covent Garden from 26 December through 5 June 1785–86, and disappeared from the London bills again in
1786–87. He was hired by Palmer for the
ill-fated Royalty Theatre, and his pantomimes *Don Juan* and *The Deserter of Naples* were given there on 12 August 1787
and 1 January 1788, respectively. (M.

Willson Disher, in an entry in the *Enciclopedia dello spettacolo*, dates his service
to the Royalty as 1782, long before the
theatre was built.)

Delpini sang and his wife made her London debut for Goodwin's benefit at the
Haymarket on 29 May 1788. He was paid
£8 per week by Covent Garden in 1788–
89 and acted often from 26 December
through 18 June. He thrust his wife into
a part at his benefit, on 28 May 1789, and
the pair gleaned £224 11*s*., before house
charges. *The Dictionary of National Biography's* short entry on Delpini states that
"On 17 February 1789 Delpini was severely hurt at the Haymarket, acting in the
'Death of Captain Cook,' a serious ballet
from the French." The date may be accurate, but the ballet was being given only
at Covent Garden that season, so far as
The London Stage shows, and the playbill
for 17 February does not announce it.
However, the Covent Garden bill of 26
March notes: "Delpini being entirely recovered from his late Accident will perform his original Character this Evening
in the new Serious Pantomime." He was
living in the spring of 1790 at No 17,
Tavistock Street, Covent Garden. He
earned £6 per week at Covent Garden
from 16 September 1789 through 14 June
1790. His benefit on 26 May 1790 brought
£285 2*s*. before charges.

Delpini was again absent from the winter patent theatres from the fall of 1790
through the fall of 1793. He was engaged
in the winter season at the Haymarket
from 10 October through 17 February
1793–94, was absent from the winter theatres again in 1794–95 and 1795–96, and
was re-engaged by Covent Garden from 5
November through 9 June in the season of
1796–97, at £5 per week. The Delpinis
lived at least part of that season at No 27,
Maiden Lane, Southampton Street.

No winter bills carried his name in
1797–98 and 1798–99, but he returned to
Covent Garden on 21 October 1799, re-

maining through 6 June 1800 at the much reduced salary of £3, which he was paid at least through 1802–3. He was apparently on the wane, and evidence for his activities in the London theatres after about 1804 is lacking.

The gaps in Delpini's London record during the latter years of the eighteenth century can be filled conjecturally and partially with the help of the few hints we have. He busied himself at the London amphitheatres, for one of the surviving vagrant bills for Hughes's Royal Circus (23 August 1788) mentions him prominently as "Acting Manager," as the composer and director of "A new comic Divertissement called *A Dutch Tea-Garden*" and one of the same called *The Impress'd Recruits; or, the Siege of Belgrade*, plus "Mr Delpini's last new grand, Pantomime Entertainment, called, *What You Please.*" A review (from an unidentified clipping) praises the presentation of his "long-expected pantomime of *What You Please,*" which displayed "such a combination of fine scenery, excellent business, and numerous changes, as to keep the eye and ear fully engaged from beginning to end: the whole closes with a procession, representing the four quarters of the world . . . " (This last was one of Delpini's favorite devices and frequently involved representative animals of various localities —"cavalli, tigri, leopardi e altre bestie," according to the *Enciclopedia.*) "Mr Delpini, who invented the business, has given another proof that his fancy is inexhaustible. —The managers have likewise done him justice, in sparing no expence in the execution of such excellent ideas."

Delpini is reported by several sources to have been engaged at the King's Theatre, and he may have served there before coming to the patent theatres, for a satirical print by his sometime ally in spectacle P. J. De Loutherbourg, published in 1776 and described by Angelo as the caricature of "a Signor, a celebrated performer at the

Italian Opera House," is thought by M. Dorothy George to be of Delpini. When he took a special benefit at the Haymarket on 30 April 1784 "The Band from the Opera House" played as he introduced "a specimen of singing in French, Italian and English" in his "new pantomimical, operatical, farcical interlude, *The Peasant Metamorphos'd; or, Delpini's Voyage from Dublin in an Air Balloon.*" He and the dancer Blake were performing "by permission of the managers of the Opera-house." And in 1789 the journals described his support of "Sir John" Gallini during a riot at the Opera.

Delpini was blasted critically by the *Monthly Mirror* in August 1798 for an unspecified September production at Astley's Amphitheatre. He had stolen bits and pieces of pantomimes from other houses, "and this is called the *invention* of Mr

By permission of the Trustees of the British Museum

CARLO ANTONIO DELPINI
"Delpini a la Rossi"

by Sayres

Delpini. . . . Mr Delpini, we know very well, *can* invent if he please . . ."

Finally, he may have toured professionally in the provinces oftener than we know. The *Monthly Mirror* placed him with Macready at Birmingham during at least some part of 1797–98.

Delpini was in demand to direct and oversee amateur productions. In 1790 he produced his *Don Juan; or, the Libertine Destroy'd. A Tragic Pantomimical Entertainment* (first produced at Covent Garden on 28 May 1789) at the Wargrave theatricals. At a royal *fête* at Frogmore where Mr and Mrs Delpini and the younger John Follett were playing in pantomime, "in firing a pistol, Follet wounded Delpini in the right eye, but not so dangerously as was at first imagined. The Stadtholder and Prince of Wales were particularly attentive to Delpini, whose accident dampened the remainder of the Day's Entertainment."

At some time early in the nineteenth century he gave at the Pantheon a grand masquerade in honor of George IV when that monarch was Prince Regent, called *La fiera di Venezia*, tickets for which sold for three guineas each. Later, he arranged elaborate entertainments in the Pavilion at Brighton for George IV.

At least two songs "as sung by" Delpini were published separately: *Oh What a Misfortune befel me today* from *Hobson's Choice* (1790), and *See that pretty creature there* from *Don Juan* (1787). He was also mentioned in *The Favorite Airs . . . in the Critic*. "Sung . . . by Miss Field, Miss Abrahams and Sigʳ Delpini," (1781).

In addition to the productions mentioned above and *The Life and Death of Pantaloon,* produced at the Haymarket 11 March 1806 (and attributed to him by Nicoll), Delpini must have had a creative hand, not now distinguishable, in scores of other works, especially many at the amphitheatres.

An unattributed clipping in the Beard collection at the Victoria and Albert Museum offers the following testimony about the close of Delpini's life:

Such were the volatility and eccentricity of Delpini's character, that he never once thought of the future, either by providing for his old age, or even subscribing to the Theatrical Fund, or any such provident institution; so that he was laid on a bed of sickness for some years, and afflicted with a complication of disorders . . .

Delpini had no relief except the kindness of his friends until his old patron, "the Prince—his present Majesty," granted him £200.

The decline of poor Delpini's life was solaced by the unremitting attentions of his widow, who attended his bed of sickness, misery, and suffering, with the most praiseworthy affection and care, wholly disregarding her own privations and fatigues, and who is now left in a state of entire and frightful destitution. Delpini had a very strong and singular presentiment, that he should not die till the year "Eight," as he often declared to the writer of this, which was exactly realized, for he died in the year 1828, at the age of 88.

Delpini expired on 20 January 1828 in his lodgings in Lancaster Court, St Martin's Churchyard.

Portraits of Carlo Antonio Delpini include:

1. Engraving, holding glass, toasting "Here's a health to all good lasses!" Drawn and engraved by J. N[ixon], 1788. Published E. Harding, 1789.

2. As Pierrot in *Aladdin*. Drawn and engraved by W. Hincks.

3. Caricature engraving of Delpini in woman's attire, captioned "Delpini a la Rossi." Engraved by Sayres, 1785.

4. Engraving by B. Rebecca, 1798.

5. In the pantomime *Robinson Crusoe*. Anonymous. 1782.

6. Delpini "Shooting at the Spaniards." Anonymous engraving.

Delpini, Signora Carlo Antonio [fl. 1784–1828], actress, singer.

Carlo Antonio Delpini, the notable Pierrot and impresario of harlequinades at Covent Garden, Drury Lane, and the London circuses, was married in 1784, according to the 1805 edition of the *Thespian Dictionary*, to an actress who had "performed at several provincial theatres with applause." Her first and family names are unknown.

Presumably Mrs Delpini accompanied her husband to London for the 1785–86 season, but her name did not then appear on the Covent Garden roster or anywhere else. The Delpinis were absent from the record again in 1786–87. He was with Palmer at the Royalty in 1787–88 and it is possible that Mrs Delpini was too, for the records of that ill-starred adventure are by no means complete.

The first documented appearance of Mrs Delpini on any London stage, then, was on 29 May 1788 in a specially licensed benefit performance for the actor Goodwin. She played Tag in the afterpiece *Miss in Her Teens*, and Carlo sang a comic entr'acte song. Evidently her effort attracted no managerial eye, for she was in no regular company the following season, though she may have performed at the circuses or pleasure gardens. Another opportunity to display her talents came with Delpini's benefit at Covent Garden on 28 May 1789, when she played Mary the Buxom in Pilon's farce *Barataria*. Again she was ignored, and she was not seen again at Covent Garden until Delpini's next yearly benefit, on 26 May 1790. This time she played in the mainpiece, as Kitty Pry in *The Lying Valet*.

After these dates she appeared only one more time in a London patent theatre, so far as is known. This was, once again, on the occasion of a benefit for her husband, at Covent Garden on 9 June 1797. She was then again Mary the Buxom in what the bills pointed out was her "first appearance these 8 years." She had played with

Delpini in a pantomime at the royal *fête* at Frogmore on 23 May 1797, when Delpini was accidentally wounded in the eye by the clown Follet. And she appears to have superintended the singing for her husband when he directed the Wargrave theatricals for the Earl of Barrymore.

She was still alive at her husband's death in 1828 and is said to have nursed him devotedly through his last illness.

Del Pò. *See* STRADA DEL PO.

Demaimbray, [Stephen Triboudet?] [fl. 1735?–1744], machinist.

A Mr Demaimbray, machinist, received benefits at Drury Lane in May 1742, 1743, and 1744. Probably he was the Stephen Triboudette Demaimbray whose daughter Elizabeth-Maria, by Mary his wife, was christened at St Paul, Covent Garden, on 29 April 1735. A son, Stephen-Charles, was also christened there on 22 April 1736. A century later, on 28 October 1836, administration of the estate (valued at £200) of Louisa Maria Triboudet Demaimbray, late of Richmond, Surrey, and spinster, was granted to her sister Sara Lydia Triboudet Demaimbray, spinster.

De Majo, Signor [fl. 1766], singer?

In a program of singing at the King's Theatre on 13 March 1766, a new *Duetto* and *Cananetto* were given, "accompanied by Recitations by Sg De Majo."

Demar, Mons [fl. 1736], dancer.

On 20 February 1736 at the Haymarket Theatre Monsieur Demar, billed as newly arrived from Paris, performed a *Flag Dance*.

Demaria, Mr [fl. 1773–1775], dancer?

Mr Demaria, Signora Crespi, and Signor Como were paid a total of £4 3s. 3d. by Drury Lane Theatre on 2 October 1773 for "3 days not on list," and on 15 November 1775 "Mr Damaria" was paid £8 8s. by

order of David Garrick. Demaria was probably a dancer, as were Signora Crespi and
Signor Como.

Demaria, J. ₍fl. 1793?–1814₎, *scene
painter.*

J. Demaria, the painter, was paid £6 16s.
6d. by Covent Garden on 23 December
1793 for 12½ days' work; a week later on
30 December he was paid another £2 12s.
6d. for five days. In August 1794 that
theatre paid him a total of £20 6s., at the
rate of 14s. per day, presumably for preparing scenes for the coming season. Demaria
was employed as a painter at the new
Drury Lane when it opened in March 1794,
at a rate of £2 2s. per week. He assisted
Malton with scenes for *Lodoiska* on 9 June
1794. The Drury Lane account books show
he was regularly employed through 1796–
97 at a salary of £3 3s. per week. He was
at Drury Lane again in 1798–99, at a
salary of a guinea a day, and was among
the several painters employed for the production of *Pizarro* (24 May 1799).

Demaria was back at Covent Garden by
September 1799, where he received £30
on 7 September, £7 on 7 October for eight
days, £10 on 22 October for two weeks,
£65 10s. 6d. for a bill on 23 October, and
£4 7s. 6d. on 5 February 1800 for five
days. He also seems to have painted for the
King's Theatre, for when he was working
at the Birmingham Theatre in the summer
of 1800 he was described as from the
Opera House.

There is no further notice of Demaria
until he offered his services to James Winston at the Haymarket by a letter sent from
No 58, Berwick Street, Soho, on 13 February 1811 in which he stated that salary was
not a principal consideration but that "honourable employ" was. He offered to repair
the old scenes and to paint new ones before
the summer season opened. For the Haymarket he worked on *Royal Oak* and
Quadruped of Quedlinburgh in 1811 and
Look at Home in 1812. In the latter year

at the new Drury Lane he was one of a
team which painted scenes for *Hamlet, As
You Like It, All in the Wrong, Up All
Night, The Wonder, The Merry Wives of
Windsor, Lionel and Clarissa,* and *She
Wou'd and She Wou'd Not.* In a letter
to Winston in 1814 he said he was retiring
and would not work again at the Haymarket though he had received "polite attention and friendly intercourse" in the
seasons he had been connected with that
theatre. (Letters in possession of Miss Sybil
Rosenfeld.)

Demby. *See* DANBY.

Demembray. *See* DEMAIMBRAY.

Demera, Signora ₍fl. 1771₎, *singer.*
A Signora Demera sang the role of Tan-
cia in *La contadina in corte* at the King's
Theatre on 14 March 1771.

De Micheli, Mr ₍fl. 1783–1785₎,
boxkeeper.

A Mr De Micheli, Junior, was a boxkeeper at the King's Theatre in 1783–85.
No doubt he was a son of Leopoldo De
Micheli (fl. 1761–1791) the basso at the
same theatre. De Micheli, Junior, perhaps
was the John Holland De Micheli whose
son, John George, was baptized at St Paul,
Covent Garden, on 28 March 1799.

De Micheli, Leopoldo ₍fl. 1761–
1791₎, *singer, music copyist.*

In a letter written to the Lord Chamberlain on 26 November 1785, Leopoldo De
Micheli claimed to have been "in the service of the King's Theatre" for 24 years, or
since 1761. No doubt in his earlier years
with the Opera, De Micheli served as a
minor member of the chorus, but the record
of his long career in London, which lasted
at least until 1790–91, is spasmodic and incomplete. The first notice of his name in
the bills was as a basso at the King's Theatre in 1764–65, when he sang Aquilio in

Adriano in Syria on 26 January and six other times through 23 February. Possibly in that season he also appeared in several other operas for which no casts are known. Several years later the *Public Advertiser* announced on 9 September 1767 that De Micheli had been engaged for the serious operas for the ensuing season. Unfortunately, opera casts are not known for 1767–68, but no doubt De Micheli sang in such pieces as *Sifare, Ifigenia in Aulide, La buona figliuola,* and *La moglie fedele.* Six years later, he was again at the King's Theatre; although not mentioned in the management's announcement of appointments on 23 October 1773, he sang Flavio in *Lucio vero* on 20 November 1773, Mengorto in *La buona figliuola* on 17 March 1774, and unspecified roles in *Il puntiglio amoroso* on 7 December, *Antigono* on 8 March, and *L'Olimpiade* on 3 June.

After an apparent hiatus of two years De Micheli was once more engaged at the King's Theatre and remained a very busy singer there for six consecutive seasons, 1776–77 through 1781–82. Among the roles he regularly performed during this period (with date of first performance) were: Pagnotta in *La fraschetana* (5 November 1776), Lisimaco in *Germondo* (21 January 1777), Clearco in *Antigono* (1 March 1777), Silvano in *L'ali d'amore* (13 March 1777), Oracolo in *Orione* (24 May 1777), Sibari in *Creso* (8 November 1777), Roberto in *Vittorina* (16 December 1777), Masino in *La vera costanza* (10 February 1778), Pasquino in *L'amore soldato* (5 May 1778), Adrasto in *Demofoonte* (28 November 1778), Timagene in *Alessandro nell' Indie* (27 November 1779), Marco Fabio in *Quinto Fabio* (22 January 1780), Clotarco in *Rinaldo* (22 April 1780), Malgoverno in *L'arcifanfano* (25 November 1780), Don Grillo in *Le serve rivali* (19 December 1780), Varo in *Ezio* (17 November 1781), Pasquino in *I viaggiatori felici* (11 December 1781), and Procolo in *Giunio Bruto* (12 Jan-

uary 1782). He also sang principal roles in *Il geloso in cimento, Telemaco, La schiava, I capricci del sesso, L'amore artigiano, Il marchese villano, L'omaggio, Euriso,* and *Il duca d'Atene.*

De Micheli seems to have given his last performance in London on 3 June 1783 in *La buona figliuola;* it was also his only performance during that season. No longer singing, De Micheli took up the position of music copyist for the King's Theatre. Accounts in the Public Record Office show De Micheli to have filled this position by 1783; in 1785 he was paid the handsome sum of £414 for copying music. The last notice of him was as a music copyist at the Pantheon in 1790–91.

During the mid-1780s, De Micheli was also involved in the squabbles and litigation concerning the management of the Opera. He was one of six persons to whom Taylor, a manager for a brief time, assigned interest as trustees of the King's Theatre in a deed of trust on 17 July 1783. The trustees were empowered to collect and distribute funds to keep up the house, pay salaries and bills, and to pay off Taylor's creditors. How significant a role De Micheli actually had in this trusteeship is not clear, and by 1784, he and John Siscotti resigned from it, expressing a dislike for the conduct of the other four trustees—George Grant, Simon Slingsby, Michael Novosielski, and James Sutton. In his letter to the Lord Chamberlain on 26 November 1785, De Micheli claimed that Taylor and the trustees owed him a sum of £926. He complained that the new manager, Gallini, would not re-employ him (employment was De Micheli's right, as a creditor) and had denied him the right of printing the music.

In his complaint to the Lord Chamberlain, De Micheli stated that he was the father of a large family. His wife, Mary Ann De Micheli, was no doubt the "Sga Michelli" who sang roles in *La contessina* and *Nitteti* at the King's Theatre in the spring of 1778. A De Micheli, Junior, was a boxkeeper at the King's Theatre from 1783–84 through 1784–85. Another son, Henry Joseph De Micheli, was born on 6 September 1775 and baptized at St James, Westminster, on 5 October 1775. Henry Joseph married Susannah Manning at St George, Hanover Square, on 13 July 1797. When recommended to the Royal Society of Musicians on 1 August 1802 (elected 5 December 1802), Henry Joseph De Micheli was described as married, with one child. He was said to have had teaching engagements at the Bryan House School and to have offered private teaching on the pianoforte. He died shortly before 5 October 1828, on which date his widow Susannah was granted a full widow's allowance of 30 guineas per year by the Royal Society of Musicians. She was still alive in July 1837. One John Holland De Micheli was probably another son of Leopoldo De Micheli. Perhaps he was the De Micheli, Junior, who was the boxkeeper at the King's Theatre, 1783–85. A child, John George, born on 19 February 1799 to John Holland De Micheli and his wife Catherine, was baptized at St Paul, Covent Garden, on 28 March 1799.

De Micheli, Signora Leopoldo, Mary Ann [fl. 1775–1778], singer.

Mary Ann De Micheli sang unspecified roles at the King's Theatre in *La contessino* on 11 and 17 January 1778 and in *Nitteti* on 19, 23, 26, and 30 April 1778. She had married the basso, Leopoldo De Micheli (fl. 1761–1791) by 1775, and she became the mother of a large family; see her husband's entry for details.

De Mira, Signora [fl. 1793–1800], singer.

Signora De Mira first sang in the King's Theatre, London, on 26 February 1793 as Livietta in *Le nozze de Dorina*. She repeated the role on 12 March, 9 and 30 April, and 7 May. Her other part that season was

Cecca in *I zingari in fiera*, on 14, 17, 21, and 28 May, and 1 June. In the following season, she sang Sondrina in *Le contadine bizzare* on 1 February 1794, repeating it 13 times, Dorinda in *Il capriccio drammatico* on 1 March and seven times more, Donna Xemena in *Don Giovanni* also on 1 March and on 8 March, and a role in *La frascatana* on 5 June. She did not return to the King's Theatre until 18 February 1800, when she sang Dorinda, repeating the role nine times that season.

De Mirail. *See* DUMIRAIL.

Demodore, Mr [fl. 1715], flutist.

On 5 August, 2 September, and 17 November 1715 Dudley Ryder noted in his diary that he had heard Mr Demodore play on the flute. On the second date Demodore was playing at the London Coffee House with Smith, and on the last he was at some unidentified tavern.

Demourier, Mr [fl. 1774–1775?], dancer.

Mr Demourier was a dancer at Drury Lane about 1774–75, but no specific mention of him was ever made in the bills.

Denande. *See* VANDENAND.

Denby. *See also* DANBY.

Denby, Mr [fl. 1784], violinist.

Mr Denby (or possibly Derby) was one of the first violins at the Handel memorial concerts at Westminster Abbey and the Pantheon on 26, 27, 29 May and 3, 5 June 1784.

Denett. *See* DENNETT.

Denham, Miss. *See* DURHAM, MISS.

Denham, Robert c. 1723–1782, singer.

Born about 1723, Robert Denham was

probably the Master Denham who sang one of the Israelites in the oratorio *Esther* at the Crown and Anchor Tavern, the Strand, at a private performance given on 23 February 1732. It is likely that he was one of the children of the Chapel Royal under Bernard Gates. In 1755 he sang at the Three Choirs Meeting in Worcester, and at some point he was made a Gentleman in the Chapel Royal and a member of the Abbey choir. On 5 November 1774 he made his will, leaving his freehold house in Church Lane, Chelsea, to his wife Katherine, along with all his other personal property. He described himself as of St Luke's, Chelsea. Robert Denham died at the age of 59 on 7 December 1782 and was buried at Westminster Abbey on 13 December. His widow proved his will on 17 December.

Denis. *See* **DENNETT** and **DENNIS.**

Denison. *See* **DENNISON.**

Denman, Edmund   *c. 1754–1827, instrumentalist.*

Edmund Denman the bassoonist may have been the son of, or otherwise related to "Edmund Denman of the Parish of St Dunstan in the West . . . and Elizabeth Voutron of St Mary le Bone" who were married at St Paul, Covent Garden, on 21 May 1736.

Our Edmund the musician and his wife Margaret were the parents of Henry (1774–1816) and James Denman (b. 14 September 1791), both musicians, and of a twin of James, whose name is not known and who died young. Henry is noticed separately in this dictionary; James's career was entirely in the nineteenth century. There was at least one more child, born c. 1776, about whom nothing is known.

When, on 1 February 1784, Miles Coyle proposed Edmund Denman for membership in the Royal Society of Musicians the deposition said of him that he had "prac-

tic'd music upwards of seven years, is in the first troop of Grenadier Guards, plays the Bassoon, Clarinett & French Horn, is a married man, has two children, one 10 and the other 8 years old, [and he is] about 30 years of age."

Edmund was doubtless the Denman, bassoonist, who appears on Burney's list of instrumentalists for the first Handel Memorial Concerts in May and June of 1784, at Westminster Abbey and the Pantheon. He assisted with his bassoon at the annual May charity concerts at St Paul's Cathedral in 1790 and in every year from 1792 through 1798. He suffered a long illness in the spring of 1800 and two members of the Society advanced him 10 guineas. An order from the Society dated 6 April 1800 directed that they be reimbursed from the general funds.

A petition for assistance was received from him on 4 January 1807 and the Governors of the Society granted him £5 5s. per month. He was granted a further 10 guineas for medical assistance upon his application on 3 April 1808, for which he thanked the Society on 5 June. He proposed his son James for membership in the Society on 7 September 1817. On 1 September 1822 he was granted a pension "commencing from August last." On 2 December 1827 the Society paid a bill for £6 2s. covering his funeral expenses.

Denman, Henry   *1774–1816, singer, actor, instrumentalist.*

The musician and actor Henry Denman was born the son of Edmund and Margaret Denman on 30 April 1774 and baptized at St Marylebone church on 29 May following. Henry's father was a prominent bassoonist. Henry also had a younger brother, James, who played the bassoon professionally (but probably not until the beginning of the nineteenth century) and still another brother, James's twin, whose name is not known.

When Henry was proposed by his father

for membership in the Royal Society of Musicians on 3 May 1795 (elected unanimously on 2 August), he was said to be engaged at that time as a chorus singer at Drury Lane Theatre (the bills show a Denman in the chorus there for the first time on 23 May 1792, singing in the production of *Dido, Queen of Carthage*) and employed also "at Miss Olivers school on Bloomsbury Square as performer on the violin (which latter place he has attended several years)." He had "served an apprenticeship to music" and performed "on the Piano Forte, Violin and Tenor [viola]." (Doane's *Musical Directory* of 1794, however, gives opposite his name: "Organ. Bass. Bassoon. Composer.")

After his first night singing in *Dido* and in two subsequent performances of the same work in 1792, Henry Denman was evidently occupied with the other strings to his bow until the theatrical season of 1794–95 which found him back at Drury Lane. He was one of a large "chorus of Goatherds and Villagers" singing Dr Arnold's music in *The Mountaineers* on 31 October 1794, a popular presentation that season. He served thus humbly in choruses to *The Roman Father*, *The Cherokee*, and perhaps other productions. This was his task at Drury Lane for the rest of his association with musical drama. But he also acted small parts in nonmusical productions on occasion and contributed his voice (his range was bass through baritone) to concert choruses and to oratorios, earning in 1799 a constant £2 per week. He was picked out for praise by the reviewer for the *Monthly Mirror* who had enjoyed the presentation of the oratorio *Ruth* in the concert room of the King's Theatre on 22 April 1799. Denman had "displayed great merit" in an unspecified part.

By 2 April 1800 he had become prominent enough to be included among the "principal singers" on the bill for the first production in London of Haydn's new oratorio *The Creation of the World*. For

that production he was traveling in excellent musical company indeed. John Ashley was the leader, Samuel Wesley was organist, and the other principal singers were Mme Mara, Mme Dussek, Small, Page, and Bartleman.

Henry Denman was occasionally active in provincial theatrical and musical affairs, particularly in summers, and is traceable in 1792 and 1794 to Rochester and Canterbury, in 1799 to Hull, and in 1802 to Hull and to Nottingham.

Fragmentary news of Denman's activities survives in the records of the Royal Society of Musicians. He was chosen to play violin in the May charity concerts of the Society from 1796 through 1800 and in 1803, 1804, and 1806 and was then nominated to be one of the Society's Governors. But at the meeting of 4 September 1803 "it was made apparent that his affairs would prevent his attendance as Governor," and Mr Sale, seconded by Mr Oliver, moved that Arthur Betts should replace him in the office.

The Minute Books of the Society contain a certificate of baptism for "Rose Charlotte Denman, daughter of Henry and Jane" born 1 December 1802 and baptized 9 February 1803 at St James, Westminster. An entry of 5 July 1812 records the granting of five guineas ("to be spent at the direction of Mr Oliver & Simcock") for the relief of the family of Henry Denman, so he may have been at that time out of employment. He himself, on 1 August 1813, "made request for relief, but being neither aged nor infirmed, it was rejected." On 4 February 1815 he was "ill & needed medical aid" and was granted 10 guineas to be used at the "discretion of Mr Howes." The Minute Book entry of 3 August 1816 reported that Denman was to be removed to hospital and that the Society was pledged to "afford him whatever necessaries he may require," and on 1 September he was placed in St Bartholomew's Hospital and £14 for support of Denman and "his daughters" was paid by the Society. By 6 October 1816 Denman was dead, and the Society had contributed £8 for his funeral.

Henry Denman's widow Jane (née Burgess) was granted an allowance of a guinea a month on 3 November 1816, after furnishing, on 6 October, a certificate from William Mead, curate of St Marylebone, attesting to her marriage to Henry on 28 February 1794. Jane was illiterate, for she made her mark when witnessing an affidavit dated 3 November which declared that "Rose Charlotte Denman, the only child" of her "late Husband Henry" was then living, was under 14 years of age, and desired the Society's care and assistance.

Other entries in the Society's Books concerned the increase in Jane's pension to £2 12s. 6d. (on 1 February 1824), her application to succeed Mrs Rost as Housekeeper to the Society (1 May 1825), and a declaration that her weakened eyes made her unfit for needlework (6 August 1826). The entry of 7 January 1827 said simply that Mrs Jane Denman had "died last Tuesday."

Henry Denman published a good many popular works, and the ones following survive in the collection of the British Museum: *Three Sonatas for the Piano Forte or Harpsichord with an Accompanyment for a Violin . . . Opera Primo.* (1780?); *When Lovely Sue I left behind. A Favorite Sea Song . . .* (London, 1790?); *Six Glees for Three & Four Voices.* (London? 1790?); *Three Sonatas for the Piano Forte. Opera 2ᵈ.*; *Three Sonatas for the Piano Forte. Opera IV.* (London, 1794?); *Two Grand Marches. 1st, The Westminster March. 2nd, General Washington's March, for the Piano-Forte or Harpsichord.* (London, 1795?); *A Favorite Sonata for the Piano Forte or Harpsichord.* (London, 1795?); *Morpeth Rant, adapted as a Rondo for the Piano Forte, with an Accompaniment for the Lute, Flute or Violin.* (London, 1800?).

A number of songs, most of them by James Hook, were published "as sung by" Denman at Vauxhall from 1796 to 1800: *It was one Eve in Summer Weather, Along the Flow'r Invested Shore, The Albion, the Pride of the Sea, Elfin Away, The Birth of the Rose, Near a Neat Little Cot, Unfurl'd Were the Sails,* and (with Charles Dignum) *When We Dwell on the Lips of the Lass we adore* are typical.

Denman, William 1766–1806, *actor, singer.*

The actor William Denman, born in 1766, was reported by the *Authentic Memoirs of the Green Room* (1804) to have been the son of "an Officer in the Royal Navy, and we find also two of his brothers in the list of Lieutenants." He, too, was destined for the sea service, but his mother, wishing to have at least one of her men near home, apprenticed him to "an eminent Bookseller in the city of Rochester." He came to London, the account continues, to pursue the bookselling trade but instead went on the stage with a provincial company in the South.

Denman first appeared in Kingston, Surrey, in 1790 and at Canterbury a little later. A Denman (probably William but conceivably Henry) was present also in the Tunbridge Wells summer company in 1794, 1795, 1796, and 1797. William Denman, by his later testimony, seems also to have acted at Swansea or elsewhere in Wales with Henry Masterman, and since Masterman died in 1803, very likely Denman acted with him before coming to London.

Denman was in country companies for nearly a decade if he underwent the normal seven-year apprenticeship beginning at age 14, and if he went on the stage immediately after completing it, as the *Authentic Memoirs* author suggests that he did. For he did not come to London until the fall of 1796, at which time John Grubb hired him at Drury Lane to replace John Moody in Irish characters. He was advertised as from the Margate Theatre when he came onto the Drury Lane stage for the first time, as Foigard in *The Beaux' Stratagem*, on 27 October. He was paid £2 per week during the season for acting such parts as O'Whiskey in *The Charity Boy*, the Earl of Oxford in *Richard III*, Kilmallock in *The Mountaineers*, Father Paul in *Robinson Crusoe*, Antonio in *The Enchanted Island*, the Priest in *Love Makes a Man*, Seacoal in *Much Ado about Nothing*, and Caius Lucius in *Cymbeline* (though some of these roles may have belonged to Henry Denman).

The *Authentic Memoirs* thought that he was summoned back for a second season but resigned because he regarded both his salary and his scope for performance as too small. But the only criticisms surviving suggest that he may have gone to Ireland for further seasoning. The *Monthly Mirror's* comment on his Foigard was that "he has some brogue, but very little humour," and John Williams, in *A Pin Basket to the Children of Thespis* (1797), agreed:

> Manly DENMAN came o'er, to fill up
> MOODY'S place,
> And assume the Stage Shamrock, *but not
> with much grace,*
> Thus Critics have urg'd, when this
> claimant's address'd,
> He is kind to the brogue, *but he murders
> the jest.*

Denman left London for Edinburgh in the fall of 1797 and remained there for a season. Criticism was again severe. When he shifted to a sober part, that of Old Norval in *Douglas*, the local theatrical pundit "Timothy Plain" observed "In the hands even of a decent performer, this part must always be interesting, and of much consequence in the piece—On Saturday, it passed over almost as much unnoticed as the officer who announces that the banquet waits."

Denman joined Tate Wilkinson on the York circuit in 1799, where his brief Drury

Courtesy of the Garrick Club

WILLIAM DENMAN
by Wellings

Lane connection was exploited in the bills. The *Monthly Mirror* observed that he was likely to prove "an useful actor, but not in the cast for which the manager engaged him (*old men*)." He remained with Wilkinson through the summer of 1803 in a fairly humble station and was not extremely popular, judging from a comparison of his benefit receipts with those of the rest of the company.

He was critically respectable in rustic and Irish characters, however. W. Burton, in *A Pasquinade Upon the Performers at York* (1801), was complimentary:

*Respect shall attend him wherever he
    goes.
And all will allow, a bright Hawthorn ∗
    he blows;
Could I wish to say more to make him
    the vogue,
I then should add much to the praise of
    his brogue:
When around the huge oak he stands
    forward to sing,
With attention I listen, and feel my heart
    ring.
∗Mr. D. is exactly calculated for that
    character in "Love in a Village."*

George Colman, visiting York, was somehow impressed with his work and made
him a "liberal offer" (if the *Authentic
Memoirs* may be credited) to come to the
summer company at the Haymarket. There
he was delayed for the first five weeks by a
cold and hoarseness but finally settled into
John Johnstone's lines of characters—Irishmen and old men and sympathetic fatherly
and avuncular figures. He also sang musical characters with such success that Colman gave him an important part in his
new musical play *Love Laughs at Lock-
smiths*, produced on 25 August 1803.

The Manchester *Townsman* of 15 February 1804, in process of scolding the Manchester managers Bellamy and Ward for
their parsimony and consequently inferior
company, cited "Mr. Denman, the successful Irishman of the Haymarket-theatre,
[who] is now performing in an *insignificant country* company" and asked why
"such persons" were not engaged.

That country company may have been a
strolling troupe on the Isle of Wight, for
by one account Denman is said to have died
at Newport either on 19 June or in October 1806, aged 40.

Denman had married, in 1800, a lady
whose surname was Close. He does not
appear to have been related to Edmund and
Henry Denman.

In the Garrick Club are two watercolor
drawings of Denman: one as the Quaker,

drawn by W. Wellings; the other a portrait by W. Carroll.

Denner, Mr [*fl. 1758*], *violinist.*
Mr Denner played the violin in the performance of the *Messiah* at the Chapel of
the Foundling Hospital on 27 April 1758
and was paid 10s.

Dennet, Mr [*fl. 1753*], *actor.*
A Mr Dennet was a member of the company playing at Richmond in the summer
of 1753. He played Seyton in *Macbeth* on
28 July.

Dennett, Miss B. [*fl. 1799?–1820?*],
dancer, actress? See **DENNETT, ELIZA.**

**Dennett, Eliza, later Mrs Robert
O'Neill** [*fl. 1799?–1820?*], *dancer,
actress?*
Miss Eliza Dennett was "the youngest of
the Miss Dennetts, [and] the tallest of the
three" according to William Hazlitt; and
there were only three dancing when he
wrote, in 1820. There were also only three
active in the closing years of the eighteenth
century. But in between, in the early years
of the nineteenth century, there were others,
according to manuscript account books and
letters. There is no way of telling whether
or not Eliza was one who came on before
the end of the century.

Eliza is the only one of the sisters whose
first name we have; two others are identified in the bills of the eighteenth century
only by the initials E. and B. when, indeed,
any distinction at all is made. Later, there
were perhaps a Miss C., a Miss F., and a
Miss H. Dennett. For these reasons, as well
as the fact that much of the time several
sisters danced together, it is virtually impossible to place them exactly. An additional difficulty is offered by the bill com-
positors who spelled their surname variously: "Denis," "Denny," "Dennys,"
"Denys" as well as (properly) "Dennett."

A Miss "Denys" came with eight other

dancers from the opera *corps de ballet* at the King's Theatre to dance in a "Grand Anacreontic Ballet, *Bacchus et Ariadne*" for Kelly's benefit at Drury Lane on 9 May 1798. One Miss Dennys was listed on some bills of the Birmingham Theatre in the summer of 1798. When Thomas John Dibdin and Charles Farley's new pantomime *The Magic Oak* opened at Covent Garden on 29 January 1799, a dancer called Miss "Denny" was listed with many others and assisted in the piece through 28 February. At Drury Lane on 14 May 1800 "Mlle Denis and B. Denis" were shepherdesses in an elaborate ballet, *Atalanta and Hypponemus*, by D'Egville. On 2 June that theatre's bill (of a performance for the benefit of the celebrated dancer Madame Bossi del Caro) advertised among the "Principal Performers" in the evening's ballet, *The Lucky Escape*, "Miss B. Denis . . . Miss E. Denis." Certainly concealed in the catch-all phrase "and the whole Corps de Ballet" was a third Miss Dennett, for the *Monthly Mirror*, in reviewing the performance, thought that "the Miss Denis (three young ladies of uncommon merit) from Sadler's Wells, displayed a degree of grace and activity, which met with universal applause." The comment furnishes the first hard evidence of any of the Dennett sisters at Sadler's Wells.

As Hazlitt was to remark about some of them later, the Dennetts were essentially minor-house performers, despite their excellence and despite the evidence of their popularity; and their style was suited to pantomime and country dance—what Hazlitt called "nature"—rather than formal French ballet. So it is not surprising to find them at work assisting the hippodrama of William Davis at the New Royal Circus in St George's Fields on 17 August 1801 (and doubtless they were there long before). On the date cited, at least two of the sisters were dancing in the pantomime *The Eclipse; or, Harlequin in China*, "Miss Denny" (i.e., the eldest) as Mirth, "Miss

E. Denny" as Joy. There was also "a new Hornpipe by Miss Denny." A clipping of 1801 (otherwise undated) praises the work (again of two) of the Dennetts in "The New Grand Spectacle of RINALDINI," saying "Miss Denny's Aurelia is supported most ably, and strongly touches the heart. . . . Miss E. Denny's *Pas Seul* is in the highest style of perfection." One, two, or three (or more) of the Dennetts (always as "Denny") are in scattered remaining bills for the New Royal Circus in 1804, 1805, and 1806. They occasionally lent their talents, which included acting and (for the eldest, at least) singing, to the patent theatres.

At Drury Lane on 20 April 1801 Cecilia

By permission of the Trustees of the British Museum

MISS F. DENNETT, as Columbine
engraving by "W. B."

in the "Musical Farce of the Son in Law" was taken "By a YOUNG LADY," anonymous. But a playbill for the evening in the Enthoven collection is annotated "Miss Dennett" in a contemporary hand. Is this the youngest of all the Misses Dennett making her first dramatic appearance in a patent house?

Drury Lane, in fact, occasionally employed some of the Dennetts through at least 1814–15. The Folger pay books always lump them together as "the Dennetts." But manuscript accounts in the British Museum are sometimes more explicit: In 1800–1801 there were two Dennetts sharing £10 per week with eight other dancers. From 1805–6 through 1808–9 there were Dennetts on the list. In September 1806 a Miss C. Dennett, a "child dancer," was paid £1 per six-day week, as was another (also described as a child), Miss E. Dennett. Their pay under these designations was constant at £1 per week each through 1808–9. In the 1807–8 season Miss F. signed the paybook for both of these children.

The (elder?) sisters served the opera at the King's Theatre for some time before 4 July 1809, for the ballet master James Harvey D'Egville, discharged on that date, named Misses H., F., and B. "Dennet" as among his pupils who were discharged and who had fled to the New English Opera. Two Dennett girls were on the Drury Lane

By permission of the Trustees of the British Museum

THE THREE MISSES DENNETT
engraving by "W. B."

accounts in 1812–13, 1813–14, and 1814–15. According to yet another manuscript in the British Museum "3 Misses Dennett" were at Covent Garden in 1816–17. The American manager Edmund Simpson saw them dance there in June 1818.

William Hazlitt was the most ardent partisan of the Dennett girls—at least of the three who were current in his time. But he names only one of these, Eliza. One of the others he calls "Miss F." In the *Examiner* of 29 December 1816 Hazlitt reports on a Grimaldi pantomime in which

Miss F. Dennett was the Columbine, and played very prettily as the daughter of the Blind Beggar. But who shall describe the *pas de trois* by the three Miss Dennetts, 'ever charming, ever new,' and yet just the same. . . . If they were at all different from what they are, or from each other, it would be for the worse. The charm is in seeing the same grace, the same looks, the same motions in three persons. They are a lovely reflection of each other. The colours in the rainbow are not more harmonious . . .

In the *Examiner* of 2 February 1817 "the three Miss Dennetts" are like " 'the Sirens three.' "

Hazlitt reported for the *London Magazine* of 1820 a performance at the Adelphi, where he had gone to "snatch a grace beyond the reach of art from the Miss Dennetts." He defends their style against "the dancing-school critics," saying of "our three English graces" that "Theirs is the only performance on the stage . . . that gives the uninitiated spectator an idea that dancing can be an emanation of instinctive gaiety, or express the language of sentiment."

Our last news from Hazlitt about these ladies was in the *London Magazine* for May 1820, and it concerns Eliza, who "resumes the part of Cinderella at Covent Garden,—restored, like Psyche, to her late-lost home, and transformed by the little hump-backed fairy, from a poor house-maid to a bright

princess, drinking pleasure and treading air." Eliza "combines a little cluster of graces in her own person, and 'in herself seems all delight.' She has learnt to add precision to ease, and firmness of movement to the utmost harmony of form."

"The Three Misses Dennetts of Covent Garden Theatre" were shown dancing together in a vignette engraving by "W. B." now at the British Museum. An engraving by "W. B.," published by H. Gray, depicts Miss F. Dennett as Columbine in *The Blind Beggar of Bethnal Green*.

Dennett, Miss F. [*fl.* 1799?–1820?], *dancer, actress?* See **DENNETT, ELIZA.**

Dennis. *See also* **DENNETT.**

Dennis, Mr [*fl.* 1725–1731], *performer?*
A Mr Dennis received benefits at the Lincoln's Inn Fields Theatre on 4 January 1725 and 4 January 1731. Possibly he was connected with the troupe, though his name is not otherwise known in theatre annals of that time. Perhaps he was John Dennis the critic, though help for him from the theatres did not come until shortly before he died in 1734.

Dennis, Mr [*fl.* 1752–1780?], *singer, dancer.*
Mr and Mrs Dennis sang and danced at the Great Tiled Booth on the Bowling Green at Southwark on 29 September 1752 and sang at Widow Yeates's booth at Bartholomew Fair on 3 September 1755. *To the Wood Robin Red Breast is flown*, published about 1760, and *Young Strephon woo'd me long before*, published about 1770, were sung by Mrs Dennis at Sadler's Wells. Mr Dennis was at Sadler's Wells in 1769, and *Good Mother if you please you may*, published about 1780, was sung by him there at some point.

Dennis, Mr [*fl.* 1779], *actor.*

Mr Dennis played Ratcliff in *Jane Shore* at the Haymarket Theatre on 20 December 1779.

Dennis, Mrs ₍*fl. 1720*₎, *singer.*

"Mrs Dennis, who never yet perform'd in Publick," sang at a benefit concert for herself at York Buildings on 15 February 1720. When the opera *Numitore* opened at the King's Theatre in the Haymarket on 2 April she sang Dorilla.

Dennis, Mrs ₍*fl. 1752–1770?*₎, *singer, dancer. See* **DENNIS, MR** ₍*fl. 1752–1780?*₎.

Dennison, Mr *d. 1756, dancer.*

A scholar of Lalauze, Mr Dennison made his first appearance on the stage dancing with his master on 18 April 1750 at Covent Garden. A year later, on 1 May 1751, Settree, another Lalauze student, joined with Dennison at the same house to make their second appearance "on that stage" — which suggests unrecorded dancing elsewhere in the interim. In 1751–52 Dennison was a regular member of the Covent Garden troupe and appeared as an Infernal in *Perseus and Andromeda* on 30 September 1751, a Pierrot Woman in *The Necromancer* on 11 November, and a Spirit in *Merlin's Cave* on 16 January 1752. At Lalauze's benefit on 15 April Dennison and Settree danced *Two Pierrots* and Dennison was in a dance called *Le je ne scay quois.* A Mr and Mrs Dennison sang and danced at Phillips's Southwark Fair booth on 21 September, but this may have been an error for Mr and Mrs Dennis, who did precisely the same thing at Southwark on 29 September.

Dennison appeared again at Covent Garden in 1752–53 but was rarely mentioned in the bills, which may explain his move to Drury Lane in the following season. There he was given better encouragement. His first notice there was on 17 October 1753, when he was in *Queen Mab.* After this he

appeared in *The Genii* and *Fortunatus* and danced in a number of entr'acte specialties, such as *L'Entree de Flore, The Savoyard Travellers,* and *The Pierrots* (with Granier). He also joined with Mlle Auguste in a pastoral dance in *The Shepherd's Lottery,* and on 4 May 1754, when his benefit tickets were accepted, he offered a solo *Punch Dance.*

Dennison remained at Drury Lane for the next two seasons, appearing in a few pantomimes, dancing in occasional plays (as in the masquerade in *Romeo and Juliet*), and offering specialty numbers. With Mrs Addison he performed a minuet and louvre at his shared benefit with three others on 29 April 1755 (which brought in £104). The *Daily Advertiser* of 31 March 1756 reported that "Dennison one of the Dancers at Drury Lane" had died on 29 March.

Dennison, Mrs ₍*fl. 1752*₎, *singer, dancer.*

Unless an error was made in the bill, Mrs Dennison and her husband sang and danced on 21 September 1752 at Phillips's Southwark Fair booth. Though Mr Dennison was active at the theatres from 1750 to 1755, his wife was cited only this once. Since a Mr and Mrs Dennis sang and danced at Southwark on 29 September 1752, perhaps the billing of Mr and Mrs Dennison should have read Dennis.

Denny. *See also* **DENNETT.**

Denny, Mr ₍*fl. 1757–1768*₎, *doorkeeper.*

Mr Denny (or once, apparently in error, Danny) was a doorkeeper at Drury Lane earning, as of 9 February 1765, 1s. 6d. daily or 9s. weekly. His benefit tickets were taken throughout the years, from the 1757–58 season through the 1767–68 season.

Denny, Mr ₍*fl. 1784*₎, *violoncellist.*

Mr Denny played the violoncello at the

Handel Memorial Concerts at Westminster Abbey and the Pantheon on 26, 27, 29 May and 3, 5 June 1784.

Denny, Mrs [*fl.* 1783–1785], *dresser.*

Mrs Denny was a dresser at the King's Theatre in the Haymarket from 1783 to 1785 – and possibly before and after these years.

Denny, Henry [*fl.* 1783–1791], *carpenter.*

Henry Denny was a journeyman carpenter at the King's Theatre in the Haymarket from 1783 to 1785 (and possibly before and after these dates), and he served in a similar capacity at the Pantheon in 1790–91.

Denoyer, [**G.? Philip?**] *d.* 1788, *dancer, choreographer.*

Mystery surrounds the dancer Denoyer's name. The spelling most commonly found is used here, but it appeared as Desnoyer, Denoye, Dunoyer, and Desnoye as well. He signed himself in a letter to a newspaper in 1739 "G. Desnoyer" but was identified at his death as Philip Denoyer.

Perhaps this dancer's father was the "Desnoyers" who arranged ballets for the opera *La festa del Himineo* in 1701 at Lietzenburg (now Charlottenburg) where Queen Sophia-Charlotte, the wife of Frederick I of Prussia, had a summer palace. The first notice of Denoyer in London was on 11 January 1721 when he danced at Drury Lane, billed as lately arrived in England. His dances during the rest of the season were rarely titled, but on 16 May he, Boval, and Miss Smith participated in a new comic dance. Two days later Denoyer received a solo benefit. He was with Drury Lane again in 1721–22 dancing, principally, unnamed entr'acte numbers, though on 10 March 1722 the bill announced that he and Mrs Younger would offer a dance called *Myrtillo*. After the season was over he accepted an offer to teach Prince Frederick at Hanover for a rumored salary of £500 annually.

Not until 1731–32 did Denoyer return to Drury Lane. On 22 December 1731 a *Grand Ballet d'amour* of his composing was performed by Denoyer, Mrs Booth, and others. The bill noted that Denoyer was dancing master to the Prince of Wales and that he was making his first appearance since his arrival in England. During the rest of the season he offered specialty dances and played Adonis in *Cephalus and Procris*. At the end of the 1731–32 season he went to Poland, according to Reed, returning to Drury Lane to appear as Paris in *The Judgment of Paris* on 8 February 1733. The *Grub Street Journal* on 17 October 1734 reported that Denoyer had been to Poland again, this time sent by George II to report on the merits of Mlle Sallé. His report was evidently favorable, for she appeared at Covent Garden on 26 December 1734.

In 1734–35 Denoyer was busy in London. In addition to the services he rendered to the royal family, he danced frequently at Drury Lane, sometimes in solo pieces, sometimes in group dances, and occasionally in pantomimes. He danced the *Russian Sailor* by himself; he often paired off with Mrs Walter or Mlle Roland in a *pas de deux*; he was in such group dances as *La Coquette* and *Les Jaloux*; he composed and danced in *The Shepherd's Mount*; and he played Pluto in *Merlin*. When benefit time came in the spring of 1735, the managers of the two patent houses graciously allowed Denoyer and Mlle Sallé to appear at one another's benefits.

Denoyer stayed at Drury Lane through 1739–40. Two of his new pantomime roles were Adonis in *The Fall of Phaeton* and Mars in *Mars and Venus*, but he seemed to prefer such entr'acte entertainments as *Le Chasseur royal*, the *Venetian Gondalier and Courtezan, Biscaien, La Folie amoreuse*, a *Hungarian Dance* ("in the manner of the country"), and *A Voyage to the Island of*

Cytheria. He also appeared in what were called grand ballets. His partners varied from season to season, but his favorites seem to have been Mlle Roland, Mrs Walter, and Mlle Chateauneuf. He brought some of his scholars before the public in 1732, 1735, 1735–36, and 1736–37, but they were always left nameless, so it is impossible to tell how many he introduced. In 1736 he served as an emissary for Fleetwood to engage Mlle Sallé for the following winter. Denoyer's lodgings were in St James's Street, over against Park Place in March 1737, but by April 1739 he had moved to the corner of St James's Square in Pall Mall.

The dancer's stay at Drury Lane had a disastrous ending. First he had a quarrel with Mlle Roland, and then he and Mlle Chateauneuf unwittingly started a riot. The first incident occurred in January 1739. A letter from "G Desnoyer" appeared in the *Daily Post* on 24 January answering an earlier one published by "Mad^m" Roland. Denoyer denied to one and all that he had called her a bitch, and he complained that she had required him to attend rehearsals at her lodgings rather than at the theatre. Why a Frenchman should object to that he did not explain, but when he refused to go to her house she had her revenge by affronting him on stage on 13 January. The Drury Lane managers supported Denoyer, and Mlle Roland moved to Covent Garden the following season.

A year later, on 23 January 1740, Denoyer and his new partner Mlle Chateauneuf were supposed to dance. Unfortunately, she was ill shortly before that but advised the managers that she thought she would be able to appear on 23 January. Her name was placed on the bill, as was Denoyer's, but without confirmation from the dancers that they would in fact perform. She did not appear, nor did Denoyer —who probably could not have danced without her. The results of the misunderstanding and the incorrect billing were reported in the *Daily Advertiser* on 25 January:

> On Wednesday night last a Disturbance happen'd at Drury-Lane Playhouse, occasion'd by one of the principal Dancers not being there to dance at the end of the Entertainment, and after most of the People in the Pit and Galleries were gone, several Gentlemen in the Boxes pull'd up the Seats and Flooring of the same, tore down the Hangings, broke down the Partitions, all the Glasses and Sconces, the King's Arms over the middle front Box was pull'd down and broke to Pieces; they also destroy'd the Harpsichord, Bass Viol, and other Instruments of the Orchestra; the Curtain they cut to pieces with their Swords, forc'd their way into the lesser Green-Room, where they broke the Glasses, &c. and after destroying every thing they could well get asunder, to the amount of about three to four hundred Pounds Damage, left the House in a very ruinous Condition.

One gentleman concerned in the affair sent the manager £100 for his share in the damage.

Perhaps Denoyer thought audiences at Covent Garden would be less violent. He danced there in 1740–41 and 1741–42 at a daily salary of £1 10*s.* plus a free benefit which, on 7 March 1741, brought in £222 12*s.* 6*d.* His frequent partner was Barbarina Campanini, with whom he danced in *Mars and Venus, Les Amants heureux, The Italian Peasants*, chaconnes, louvres, minuets, and a *Tambourine.* As in previous years he also appeared in group dances (*Fawns and Nymphs, Tyrolean Dance, Pan and Syrinx*), and he was Chasseur in a dance titled *Rural Assembly* in the production of *The Winter's Tale.* His benefit on 1 April 1742 was his last on record. Tickets from him were available at his lodgings in Gloucester Court, St James's Street.

Denoyer abandoned theatrical dancing after that, though he remained active as a teacher. Three generations of the royal family came under his tutelage, and Denoyer resided near the royal palace at Kew when the future George IV lived there with his parents. In 1769 Denoyer created a little masque done by the royal children to celebrate Prince Edward's birthday, and in the 1770s Denoyer was much involved with the court circle and their intrigues, serving, in 1773, as a confidant of Princess Caroline. It is likely that after his retirement from the theatre Denoyer also had other pupils, and we know that the actor Spranger Barry learned deportment from him. Denoyer died in 1788.

The only picture of Denoyer seems to be a cartoon by Hogarth called "The Charmers of the Age." Denoyer and Signora Campanini are shown in mid-air. Hogarth repeated the view in miniature in a picture on the wall in his views called "Taste in High Life" and "The Analysis."

Dens. *See* **DENTS.**

Dent, Richard ₁*fl. c. 1714–1728*₁, *barber.*

Richard Dent was the Drury Lane barber about 1714–15, and a bill has survived for 2*s.* 6*d.* which he charged for a wig he had made for Dupré at the order of Robert Wilks, one of the company managers. By 1726–27 he was working at Lincoln's Inn Fields, one of the payments to him there being 6*s.* for "curling hair" on 5 June 1727. He was cited on the theatre's free list in 1727–28 as Mr Dent the "Hair cutter."

Denton, Mrs ₁*fl. 1749–1767?*₁, *actress.*

On 26 May 1749 at the Haymarket Theatre Mrs Denton's benefit tickets were accepted. She was perhaps the Mrs Denton who acted Julia in *Theodosius* on 8 July and Mrs Motherly in *The Provok'd Husband* on 22 July 1767 at the same house.

Denton, "Thomas" ₁actually John₁ *d. 1789, artificer, exhibitor.*

Born in the North Riding of Yorkshire, John, called Thomas, Denton started life as a tinman. He then became a bookseller in York, after which he came to London about 1780 and made a speaking figure which he exhibited. Public interest encouraged him to create next a writing figure. He was, in addition to an artificer and exhibitor, an amateur chemist, the translator of a French book on conjuring, a silver plater, and a coiner. For the last-named activity he was convicted and hanged at Newgate on 1 July 1789.

Dents, ₁Master?₁ ₁*fl. 1723*₁, *dancer.* *See* **DENTS, DE LONG.**

Dents, ₁Miss?₁ ₁*fl. 1723*₁, *dancer. See* **DENTS, DE LONG.**

Dents, De Long ₁*fl. 1723*₁, *dancer.*

At Pinkethman and Norris's booth at Bartholomew Fair on 22 August 1723 Monsieur De Long Dents (or Dens) and his two children danced the popular *Dutch Skipper*. They danced again on 2 September at Pinkethman's theatre in Richmond, offering both comic and grotesque dances. The bills did not specify the sex of either of the children.

Denys. *See* **DENNETT** and **DENNIS.**

Deodore, Peter ₁*fl. 1674*₁, *performer?*

A Lord Chamberlain's warrant dated 9 November 1674 lists Peter Deodore as a member of the King's Company but does not name his specialty.

D'Éon De Beaumont, Charles Geneviève Louis Auguste André Timothée *1728–1810, swordsman, impresario, diplomatist.*

Nearly every circumstance and action of the Chevalier Charles D'Éon De Beaumont's life was either sensational or equivocal, or both. Many matters of fact are still in dispute. Information both veritable and speculative is extensive. It includes his own

Harvard Theatre Collection

CHEVALIER D'EON
by Condé

testimony in *Lettres, mémoires et négocia-
tions particulières* (1764) and in many of
his later books and pamphlets and a large
mass of manuscripts in his hand now in the
British Museum. Most of the accounts
printed since his death have emphasized the
sensational aspects of the unquestionably
eccentric and bizarre activities of a man
who was nevertheless an important minor
figure in diplomatic history. Every account
has either scanted or omitted the theatrical
fencing which entitles him to a place in
this dictionary. A still dependable short account of D'Éon's military and diplomatic
career is J. K. Laughton's sketch in *The
Dictionary of National Biography*. A more
recent narrative is that which is worked
into J. D. Aylward's *The House of Angelo*.
The summary account which follows has
derived information from these, as well as
from early sources.

D'Éon was born on 5 October and baptized on 7 October 1728 at Clermont-
Tonnerre in Burgundy. His family belonged to the minor nobility. He studied
law, and when the death of his father left
him in reduced circumstances he called
upon powerful family friends for assistance.
The Prince de Conti procured him a coro-
netcy in the dragoons and, in 1755, sent
him to St Petersburg as a secret agent. It
was rumored that D'Éon was received as a
woman by the Russian Empress Elizabeth.
At any rate, his diplomacy at St Petersburg
played a part in bringing Russia into alliance with France and Austria.

D'Éon returned to France in June 1756
and was sent immediately back to St Petersburg, on each journey carrying important
messages between the sovereigns of France
and Russia. In April 1757 he was sent from
St Petersburg to Vienna with letters from
the Empress Elizabeth to Maria Theresa.
He was dispatched to Versailles with news
of the battle of Prague. His coach overturned, and his leg was broken, but he still
reached the French court 36 hours ahead of
the Austrians' special courier. Louis xv
awarded him the Military Cross of St Louis
and a gold snuffbox.

D'Éon was again at St Petersburg till August 1760. He was promoted captain and
joined the staff of Marshal de Broglie, distinguishing himself during the campaign of
1761. In 1762 he accompanied the French
Ambassador, the Duc De Nivernois, to
London. When De Nivernois was recalled
in 1763, D'Éon remained at the embassy,
first as chargé d'affaires and then as minister plenipotentiary. He had been instructed
to correspond secretly with the King,
through the Comte De Broglie and without
the knowledge of Nivernois, on the progress of a French scheme to invade England.
Thus he had been, in fact, not only an
agent for espionage against Britain, but
against one faction in his own foreign office. At the conclusion of the peace he was
left in possession of documents which com-
promised the King. When the Comte De
Guerchy, designated successor to Nivernois,
arrived in London, D'Éon, most likely at
the command of Louis xv, refused to sur-

render either his papers or his person; he was threatened by De Guerchy. D'Éon obtained from a certain De Vergy an affidavit that De Vergy had been bribed to murder him. De Guerchy was indicted, but the indictment was dropped. Somehow D'Éon had become a popular figure. The mob threatened De Guerchy in his turn and smashed the windows of his residence.

During his school days in Paris, D'Éon had begun studying fencing, at which he was to become in time professionally adept, in the *salle* of the famous master Teillagory. A fellow pupil had been Domenico Angelo. They had resumed their friendship in London and D'Éon had sought refuge from De Guerchy's menaces at Carlisle House, where Angelo was conducting his fencing academy. D'Éon had remained in residence after the threat subsided, repaying Angelo's hospitality by helping with the pupils. The friendship would again become important toward the end of the century.

D'Éon's supposed exploit in women's clothes at the Russian court in time became notorious, and wagers as to his sex were being feverishly laid by the sporting British. Some of the bets—or "policies," as they were called—involved enormous sums. D'Éon's insertion of an advertisement in the *Morning Post*, expressing his displeasure at the wagering, had no effect. In 1777, because of a dispute over settlement of one such wager, Samuel Hays, a surgeon, brought an action against a broker named Jaques. Lord Mansfield heard the case. Le Goux, a surgeon, swore that he had attended the Chevalier, who was, indeed, a woman. A Mons De Moraude, an editor, swore that he had known "Madame" D'Éon intimately. Mansfield charged the jury to the effect that such wagering was legal, and the jury returned the decision that D'Éon had been proved a woman. George Colman altered Taverner's comedy *The Artful Husband* to *The Female Chevalier* to capitalize on the Chevalier's notoriety, but the play

lasted only seven performances in the summer of 1778.

After the death of Louis XV on 10 May 1774 the existence of the secret correspondence which D'Éon still had in his possession began to trouble Louis XVI. Beaumarchais had been sent to London to retrieve the correspondence. D'Éon seems to have extracted a promise of £5,000 (which it appears he never got) and a pension of £500 a year. Among the conditions attached was one that on his return to France he should wear women's attire, a stipulation which remains mysterious. It was, nevertheless, enforced when he appeared at Versailles in August 1777 in the uniform of a captain of dragoons. Marie Antoinette herself ordered a complete outfit of women's clothing for D'Éon, who was ordered not to leave the precincts of the Court for two years. During this entire period D'Éon remained in skirts, though the King gave "her" permission to wear the star of the Order of St Louis on "her" corsage. When war with England was again declared in 1778 D'Éon petitioned that he be allowed to don a uniform and serve in the fleet, but the request was refused. He retired to his mother's house at Clermont-Tonnerre, where he apparently remained for over six years in increasing debt. Deprived of his pension by political change, he sold his valuable library and other effects at auction.

In 1785 D'Éon returned to England, still in feminine attire. He was aided in his return by the Angelos, who had perhaps suggested that he might recoup his fortunes through his swordsmanship. The Prince of Wales invited D'Éon and Harry Angelo to preside over bouts of fencing demonstrated before the Prince at Carlisle House in 1787, when all the leading masters were invited to meet the famous Chevalier St George. D'Éon was said to have distinguished "herself" in dexterity, despite the encumbrance of the female clothing of the period.

Through Harry Angelo's influence D'Éon

Harvard Theatre Collection

CHEVALIER D'EON

artist unknown

was given a benefit at Vauxhall in 1791, where he was presented with a specially struck medal which represented him in the character of the "Gallic Minerva." In 1792 D'Éon took as a fencing pupil a Mrs Bateman, a young woman who was probably already an actress. From January 1793 in a house in Carlisle Street, Soho, she and D'Éon gave a series of subscription breakfasts. A newspaper clipping of 18 January reported that D'Éon, "yesterday morning, gave a public dejeune at Mrs. Bateman's, Carlisle-street, to upwards of two hundred Nobility and Gentry. At one, breakfast being finished, Mademoiselle [D'Éon] assumed her former character, and sustained two assaults; the first with Captain Ross, an Irish Gentleman, the second with Mr. Scott. It was allowed by all the company, that a greater display of science and dexterity was scarcely ever seen."

The bills recording displays and performances by D'Éon, in London and elsewhere are scattered and perhaps some appearances are now unknown. Mrs Bateman apparently attempted to secure permanent theatrical employment in London by acting at the Haymarket in the spring and summer of 1793, but she was badly reviewed. On her benefit night, 30 May, she brought the Chevalier D'Éon onto the stage. D'Éon fenced with Mrs Bateman and then with a member of the audience. Two clippings in the Winston collection describe the occasions, though somewhat differently:

Le Chevaliere D'Eon fenced, on Thursday night, upon the Haymarket stage, with her pretty friend, Mrs Bateman. . . . The officer, who was expected, did not appear, but another Gentleman, a volunteer, came on in a [fencing] mask, and had, at first, the strange success of hitting his able antagonist, who did not coolly nor long bear the disadvantage. In some succeeding onsets, of astonishing vigour and skill, she, twice, or three times, wrenched his sword from his hand and threw it into the air. It was pleasant to observe, that the audience received Madame D'Eon, not only with the applause, always excited by superior skill, but with the respect, due to the talents, conduct, and serious exertions of a person, who will long be considered as the wonder of the eighteenth century.

The second writer discerned no such respect:

[She] greatly pleased the audience by her inimitable science with the foil, but her dress excited the merriment of the company to such a degree, that several minutes elapsed before the bursts of laughter subsided. Her dress, (or rather un-dress) was a petticoat that reached a few inches below her knees; a short brown jacket, which she pulled off on the stage, and then appeared in her shift sleeves. This was too much for the serious John Bull, who therefore indulged himself in the laugh at the poor Chevalier's expense—

On June 19, again according to an un-attributed clipping and at some place un-named, D'Éon fenced for public mirth and appreciation. Very likely the location was Ranelagh Gardens, in the Rotunda, where Warwick Wroth (in *London Pleasure Gardens of the Eighteenth Century*, citing a bill we have not seen) says D'Éon fenced "with M. Sainville, and received the congratula-tions of the Prince of Wales and Mrs. Fitzherbert [the royal mistress]" on 27 June. In the 19 June appearance, also op-posite Sainville, she displayed "a vigour and firmness incredible to her age . . ." Sain-ville was commended for "his tranquillity in fighting unmasked . . . and the exceed-ing advantage which he has had in his two assaults upon that intrepid adversary . . ."

Mrs Bateman and D'Éon were engaged for several nights at the Richmond Theatre in July and August 1793, their bill of 23 August announcing "The celebrated Cheva-lier d'Eon will fence with a nobleman." An anonymous writer, in a clipping found in the Richmond Library, reviewed the event as "a disgusting sight," a fine display of fencing by the Chevalier but "in a dress that was scarcely decent." In July the pair also appeared at Brighton and in October they were at Margate. In between engage-ments they apparently still offered their fencing breakfasts in the Carlisle Street residence of Mrs Bateman. An announce-ment of July 1794 promised "cold iron is always a standing dish to regale the loung-ers."

On 16 September 1794 a newspaper re-ported "Madame D'Eon and Mrs Bateman set out for Cork, where they were engaged to perform six nights in the Theatre Royal; from thence they proceed to Dublin, where they have a similar engagement." Clark in *The Irish Stage in the County Towns*, re-ports that they were on bills at Cork on 15 August and 14 October, but they were doubtless there between those dates as well. They played, briefly it seems, in Dublin and returned to England in February 1795. The

Chevalier's journey toward London was in-terrupted by illness at Liverpool. Aylward states that the pair fenced again at Ranelagh and at the Opera House in 1795 and that later in 1795 they toured in Gloucestershire, where D'Éon appeared sometimes in female attire, sometimes in uniform. In the bills for these performances D'Éon stated that "she" no longer had the pension granted "her" by Louis XVI and, "having been frustrated in the receipt of £5,000 deposited for her in the hands of an English noble, she was obliged to cut her bread with her sword."

On 26 August 1796 D'Éon received a deep wound in the armpit through the ac-cidental use of a foil from which the pro-tective button had broken. He never fully recovered from the effects of the accident, and having been forced to give up exhibi-tions and lessons, he fell back on the sale of his few remaining mementos and the good offices of a diminishing circle of friends. He lived some years in the house of a Mrs Cole in Millman Street, near the Foundling Hospital, where he died on 21 May 1810. Mrs Cole, in laying out the body for burial, discovered to her astonish-ment that her long-time companion was a man. An autopsy was conducted by the Père Elysée, surgeon to the French Embassy, Mr Copeland, a surgeon of Golden Square, Mr Watson, a professor of anatomy, Sir Sidney Smith, and the Hon Mr Lyttleton. A certificate was issued by this committee stating that they "found the male organs in every respect perfectly formed." Yet, they continued, there was "an unusual roundness in the formation of the limbs. The throat was by no means masculine; breast remark-ably full; arms, hands, and fingers those of a stout female; legs and feet corresponding with the arms." Horace Walpole reported that "Lord Mount-Edgecumbe said excel-lently, 'Mademoiselle D'Éon is her own widow.'"

D'Éon was buried in the churchyard of St Pancras. In 1868, during the construction of St Pancras station, the marker on his grave disappeared.

An estate valued at £300 was granted in August 1811 to Thomas Williams, attorney "of Lewis Augustus O'Gorman the Nephew and one of the next of kin," who was "residing at the City of Cadiz."

D'Éon's notoriety was of course a magnet for portraitists and satirists. The following engravings survive:

1. Portrait by J. B. Bradel, engraved after his own drawing. Published at Paris, undated.

2. As Minerva. By J. Condé after his own drawing. Published 1791.

3. In female attire. By T. Chambers after R. Cosway. Published 1787.

4. J. Condé after J. Condé. A copy of or similar to the preceding. Plate to the *European Magazine*, 1791.

5. Copy of preceding, engraved by R. Cooper; published by J. Bell, 1810.

6. Engraving by W. Daniell of a drawing by G. Dance, 1793. Published 1810.

7. In female attire. By L. J. Cathelin after J. Ducreux.

8. In uniform. By T. Burke after J. G. Huquier.

9. At age 24; in female attire. Engraved by F. Haward after a picture by A. Kauffmann, after a picture by Latour.

10. Fencing with M. de St George in the presence of the Prince of Wales and others. By V. M. Picot after Robineau, 1789.

11. Copy from D'Éon's figure in the preceding. Anonymous engraver. Plate to Kirby's *Wonderful Museum*, 1813.

12. In uniform. By Vispré after his own drawing.

13. In female attire; oval frame with ornaments. Engraved by A. Stoettrup, 1779.

14. Profile vignette from death mask. Engraved by C. Turner, 1810.

15. In uniform; oval in rectangular frame of masonry. Anonymous engraver.

16. Copy of preceding, with different ornaments. Anonymous engraver, 1807.

17. Half in male, half in female attire. Anonymous engraver. Plate to *London Magazine*, 1777.

18. As Minerva, standing before a tent; account of D'Éon engraved on separate plate. Anonymous engraver. Published by S. Hooper, 1773.

19. A satirical print, "The Trial of M. D'Éon by a Jury of Matrons." Anonymous etching from the *Town and Country Magazine*, June 1771. The Chevalier, wearing a military hat, the order of St Louis on a ribband around his neck and a drapery around his middle, stands on a pedestal before a jury of 12 ladies who are to decide on his sex: Lady Har[ringto]n, L[ad]y R[ochfor]d[?], L[ad]y T[own]sh[en]d, L[ad]y G[rosveno]r, L[ad]y Sarah B[unbur]y, L[ad]y Lig[onie]r, L[ad]y R[odne]y, The D[uchess] of N[orthumberland?]. One reaches behind the drapery and wears a look of surprise on her face.

20. *The Rape of Miss Deon from France to England.* July 1771. This political cartoon is one of a set of at least three, including 21, 22, and perhaps 23 below. They have been attributed to Bartolozzi.

21. *A Deputation from Jonathan's and the Free-Masons.* July 1771.

22. *The Nuptials of Miss Epicene D'Éon.* July 1771.

23. *Don Quixote's Procession to the Installation.* July 1771. The four cartoons immediately preceding comment on the suspicion that D'Éon and the politician John Wilkes were in collusion and somehow profiting from the trafficking in "policies" on D'Éon's sex.

24. *Chevalier D-E-N Return'd or the Stock-Brokers Outwitted.* 1771. Anonymous satire on the "policies."

25. Untitled frontispiece from *An Epistle from Mademoiselle D'Éon to the Right Honourable L[or]d M[ansfield] . . . on his Determination in Regard to her Sex,* 1778. Anonymous satirical print. A manwoman figure.

26. D'Éon is represented as one of sev-

eral figures in the political cartoon *Evidence Against Certain Persons* by an anonymous engraver in 1769.

De Paoli, Gaetano ₍*fl.* 1795₎, *singer.*
Gaetano De Paoli sang Conte di Belfiore in *Le nozze di Dorina* at the King's Theatre in the Haymarket on 16 and 23 June 1795.

"De Paris, Mlle à la mode" ₍*fl.* 1731₎, *dancer.*
A dancer masquerading under the name of Mlle à la mode de Paris performed *The Sailor's Mistress* at Lincoln's Inn Fields on 15 March 1731.

De Parr. *See* DIEUPART.

De Po. *See* STRADA DEL PO.

Deport, Mr ₍*fl.* 1749₎, *wigmaker.*
It is not clear whether Mr Deport was on the staff of the Drury Lane Theatre or was in business for himself, but the accounts show a payment of £1 11s. 6d. to him on 3 October 1749 for a wig for Eumenes in *Tamerlane*.

Derby. *See also* DARBY.

Derby, Mr ₍*fl.* 1757–1762₎, *office keeper.*
As the second gallery office keeper at Covent Garden, Mr Derby (or Darby) shared benefits from 1757–58 through 1761–62. The accounts show that he received half value for his tickets on 19 May 1760 so that he collected only £19 6s.; even this was an overcharge, and he had to give 6s. 6d. back. His salary, at least in 1760–61, was 2s. daily. A Mr Darby was mentioned in the Covent Garden accounts on 13 October 1802, but there is no certainty that he was the same person.

Derby, Countess of. *See* FARREN, ELIZABETH.

Derham, Miss. *See* DURHAM, MISS.

Derle. *See* DEARLE.

Deroissi, Miss ₍*fl.* 1763₎, *dancer.*
At Covent Garden Theatre on 7 May 1763 Miss Deroissi, a student of Duquesney, made her first appearance on any stage in a solo dance.

De Rossenaw, Ninetta ₍*fl.* 1754–1755₎, *actress.*
The London Stage lists Ninetta de Rossenaw as one of the actresses in the Covent Garden company in 1754–55.

De Roy, Mr. *See* ROYER.

De Ruell. *See* DU RUEL.

Desabaye, Mr ₍*fl.* 1687–1711₎, *bass viol player, violoncellist.*
Mr Desabaye on 5 July 1687 was a member of the King's Musick at a yearly salary of £50. In the summers of 1687 and 1688 he attended the King at Windsor, but the Lord Chamberlain's accounts scarcely mention him otherwise. On 1 December 1707 he and other court musicians were given leave to play for the operas at the new Queen's Theatre in the Haymarket. The records are not too clear, but it seems that Desabaye may have been refused at the Queen's when he first offered to play for £1 nightly, but he was soon hired, apparently as a bass viol player only, at 10s. nightly. He remained at the Queen's Theatre until 1711, once (in November–December 1710) being noted as a violoncellist. As one of the gentlemen in "the Musick room" at the theatre he never rose above his starting salary.

Desaguliers, ₍Dr?₎ ₍*fl.* 1740₎, *pyrotechnist.*
A Dr Desaguliers (or possibly Mr De Desaguliers) provided fireworks on 1 Au-

gust 1740 in the gardens of Cliveden when the birth of Princess Augusta and commemoration of the accession of George I were celebrated. Other entertainment included performances of the masques *Alfred* and *The Judgment of Paris*.

De St Leu, Mr *fl. 1794*, *flutist*.

Doane's *Musical Directory* of 1794 identified Mr De St Leu of Spittal Square as a flutist who performed with the Cecilian Society.

De St Luce. *See* ST LUCE.

Desbarques, Mons *fl. 1705–1708*, *dancer*.

John Weaver in his *Essay Towards a History of Dancing* (1712) said "The best Performer of [serious] *Dancing* that ever was in *England*, I take to be Monsieur Desbargues, who had a certain *Address* and Artfulness in his *Gestures* . . ." Desbarques (for that seems to be the most common spelling) was billed as newly arrived from Paris when he danced at the Queen's Theatre in the Haymarket on 6 November 1705. The confusing changes in management at the Queen's and at Drury Lane brought Desbarques to Drury Lane for the first time on 3 December 1706, where he danced until he returned to the Queen's in January 1708. Unfortunately, the bills during the early years of the eighteenth century rarely described or titled dances, but we know that at his benefit on 13 June 1706 Desbarques, Fairbank, and de la Garde danced *Three Clowns* and on 20 February 1707 he participated in *Three French Peasants*.

Accompanying Desbarques, perhaps throughout his stay but certainly from 1707 on, was either Madame Desbarques or Mademoiselle Desbarques or both. A petition of 1707 to the Vice Chamberlain, asking restitution for various losses suffered by the opera performers, names the dancers Cherrier, Desbarques, and Mlle Desbarques as

having lost money because of the shifts in the Drury Lane and Queen's Theatre management; a note dated 31 December 1707 specified that Mlle Desbarques was owed £12. Though not mentioned in the bills, she must have been dancing during the season. *The London Stage* lists a Mrs Desbarques as dancing at the Queen's on 7 February 1708, and documents in the Coke papers at Harvard dating about this time list a Mrs Desbarques at a daily salary of £1 3s. 4d. and Desbarques at £2 10s. No mention is made of Mlle Desbarques. The evidence seems to suggest a husband, wife, and daughter, however, and not a confusion between the two latter. After 1708 the family apparently returned to the Continent.

Desbarques, Mme *fl. 1708*, *dancer*. *See* DESBARQUES, MONS.

Desbarques, Mlle *fl. 1707*, *dancer*. *See* DESBARQUES, MONS.

Deschalliez, Louise, later Louise Deschalliez de Vaurenville *fl. 1720–1722*, *dancer*.

The Louise Deschalliez de Vaurenville who was active in Holland in 1722 was probably the Mlle Deschalliez who danced in London in 1720–21. A member of de Grimbergue's French troupe that played at the King's Theatre in the Haymarket and at Lincoln's Inn Fields from 5 March to 21 June 1720, Mlle Deschalliez danced with the pierrot of the company, Roger, in most of her appearances. On 17 June at the King's Theatre she was granted a benefit. *The London Stage* seems to be in error in calling her "Mrs Deschalliez" on 3 May 1720, for there is no evidence that a second female dancer of this name was in the group.

The company returned to London to perform at the new Haymarket Theatre from 29 December 1720 to 4 May 1721. On

21 and 27 February and 4 March Mlle Deschalliez danced with Roger. The bill for 6 March (as recorded in *The London Stage*) names Roger, Mlle Deschalliez, "and" (*recte* alias?) Mlle "Vaurentille" as the dancers. On 20 April "Mlle de Vaurinville" received a benefit, and on 27 April at Lincoln's Inn Fields there was dancing by "Monsieur Pierrot and Mademoiselle Vaurinville, formerly call'd Mademoiselle de Chalier from the French House." This statement seems explicit enough to point to an error in the bill of 6 March.

Descoate, John *(fl. 1695)*, *trumpeter.*

A warrant dated 4 April 1695 in the Lord Chamberlain's accounts names John Descoate as one of four musicians in the King's Musick to receive new trumpets.

Desdechina, Signora *(fl. 1749)*, *dancer.*

Signora Desdechina (or Dedeschina) made her first appearance on the English stage dancing with Monsieur Billioni at Covent Garden on 11 January 1749.

Dese. *See* DESSE.

De Shade, Mons *(fl. 1743)*, *dancer.*

A British Museum manuscript lists Monsieur De Shade as one of the dancers at Drury Lane in 1743.

Deshaln, Mr *(fl. 1737)*, *house servant?*

A Mr Deshaln (or Deshalu, De Chanlue), possibly a house servant at Lincoln's Inn Fields, had his benefit tickets accepted on 10 and 18 May 1737.

Des Hayes, André J. J. *(fl. 1797?–1811)*, *dancer, choreographer.*

William Smith's *The Italian Opera in London* lists the dancer Des Hayes as a member of the opera company at the King's Theatre in the Haymarket during the 1797–98 season, but on 11 January 1800 Des Hayes was billed as making his first appearance in England. He danced in a new divertissement on that date, and during the rest of the season appeared in *Témire* (later titled *Hylas et Témire*), *Le Mariage mexicain*, the male lead in *Hyppomène et Atalante*, "*A New Bacchanalian Divertissement Ballet*," a *Divertissement Bayadaire*, and *Laura et Lenza*. On 14 May he and the rest of the *corps de ballet* from the opera danced at Drury Lane in *Telasco and Amgahi* and *Hyppomène et Atalante*.

André J. J. Des Hayes (for that appears to have been his signature) returned to the Continent after the 1799–1800 season, possibly to the opera in Madrid from whence he had come. In 1803 he was in Milan, and from 1804 through 1811 he was back at the King's Theatre in London with his wife, earning, in 1808 at least, £2100 plus £300 for their costumes annually. Monsieur Des Hayes was billed as the composer of the ballet *Figaro*, a work in which he also danced on 16 May 1811. The *Examiner* on 9 June reported that "The two great rivals in public favour, Messrs. Deshayes and Vestris, have each tried their skill in the composition of new ballets, which have been brought out on their respective benefit nights, and proved to be as unequal in merit as the performers who have produced them." Des Hayes was praised for creating "one of the most entertaining ballets that have been produced for many seasons." He gave to Vestris and Angiolini the more vigorous dances and reserved "to himself and Madame MONROY such as require the more gentle and elegant movements of the figure." Des Hayes seems not to have stayed in London after the spring of 1811.

An engraving by A. Cardon shows J. H. D'Egville and a Monsieur Des Hayes in the ballet pantomime *Achilles and Deidamia*. It is probable that the Des Hayes pictured is our subject.

ANDRÉ J. J. DES HAYES, with J. H. D'EGVILLE, in *Achilles and Deidamia*
engraving by Cardon

Deshayes, ₁Jean Baptiste François
*1705–1779?*₁, *actor, choreographer?*

A Monsieur Deshayes (or De Shayes) was a member of Francisque Moylin's troupe at the Haymarket, Lincoln's Inn Fields, and Goodman's Fields theatres during the 1734–35 season. He was first mentioned in the bills on 16 April 1735 when he acted Abner in *Athalie* at the Haymarket. On 9 May there he played Clitendra in *Georges Dandin*, and on 23 May at Good-

man's Fields he was Pamphile in *L'Embarras de richesses.* He may have performed other parts for the troupe, but the bills made no other mention of him. There is a possibility that he joined the company part way through the season. Moylin began on 26 October 1734, almost six months before Deshayes's name was cited in the bills; but on 24 February 1735 an unnamed actor, hailed as recently arrived from Paris, played the title role in *Le François à Londres.*

If Deshayes did, in fact, arrive in London in February 1735, he may have been Jean Baptiste François Dehesse (also called Deshayes), a Hollander of French parentage who became a sharer in the Comédie Italienne in 1734 and made his debut on 2 December of that year at Fontainebleau as the Valet in *Le Petit maître amoureux*. What is known of the Dutchman's continental career would fit with the brief stay in London of Monsieur Deshayes.

Dehesse was born at the Hague in September 1705. He acted juvenile roles in the French provinces, especially at Valenciennes. At that town in 1730 he met Marie Madeleine Hamon, to whom he gave dancing lessons. He asked for her hand in marriage, but her father refused, so the young performer abducted her and fled to Paris. The couple passed as man and wife for a few years, but in 1737 Dehesse met the actress Catherine Antoinette Viscentini. He married her on 30 July 1742. Dehesse began composing ballets in 1748, was placed in charge of the ballets at the Comédie Italienne in 1760, and retired in 1769. His wife died on 5 August 1774 and Dehesse died on 22 May 1779. Information concerning Dehesse in Campardon's *Les Comédiens italiens* provides no clue to link the continental performer with the Deshayes who appeared in London, but the dates and types of roles make it quite possible that the two were one and the same.

De Sisley, Mme ₁*fl. 1794*₁, *singer.*

Doane's *Musical Directory* of 1794 identified Madame De Sisley as a soprano living at No 4, Hanover Street, Longacre.

Desmoulins, John ₁*fl. 1778*₁, *house servant?*

John Desmoulins was receiving £1 5*s.* weekly at Drury Lane in October 1778, apparently as one of the house servants.

Desmoulins, Mrs ₁John?₁ ₁*fl. 1778*₁, *house servant?*

The Drury Lane account books cited Mrs Desmoulins on 14 November 1778 as receiving a salary of £1 5*s.* weekly. It is probable that she was the wife of John Desmoulins and that she was a house servant.

Desnoyer. *See* DENOYER.

Desormes, Mons ₁*fl. 1749*₁, *actor.*

Monsieur Desormes was an actor in Monnet's troupe of French comedians at the Haymarket Theatre from 14 November through December 1749, though he was mentioned only once in the bills: on 14 November he was in the cast of *Les Amans réunis*. The company did not have a successful season, and Monnet lost £1306 12*s.* 8*d.* Desormes volunteered the opinion that the manager had not chosen a sufficient number of Molière works to satisfy English audiences, but the engagement had been plagued from the start with disturbances at the theatre occasioned by anti-Gallic sentiment and English political differences. Desormes, one of the most highly paid players in the troupe, contracted with Monnet for £227 7*s.* 6*d.* but received only £197 2*s.* 9*d.* in money and notes.

Despréaux. *See* GUIMARD.

Desse. *See also* DESHAYES.

Desse, Mons ₁*fl. 1735–1761*₁, *dancer.*

In his *Shakespeare in the Theatre* Charles Beecher Hogan identifies the Monsieur Desse who danced in London from 1735 to 1761 as Jean Baptiste De Hesse (1705–1769) (*recte* Jean Baptiste François Dehesse [1705–1779]), the Dutch actor-choreographer of French parentage. That identification seems most unlikely, for Dehesse was active in France during the years Desse danced in England, and the continental performer seems to have been a far more successful person than the one who appeared in London. The Dutchman may, on the other hand, have been the actor Deshayes who played in London in 1735.

In 1735–36 Desse (for so he was designated in the London bills for many years) danced 172 nights with the Covent Garden company at 5s. nightly, his first notice being on 26 September 1735 when he was a Harlequin Man in *The Necromancer*. Subsequently that season he appeared as a Frenchman in *Apollo and Daphne*, a Demon and Earth in *The Rape of Proserpine*, a Zephyr in *The Royal Chace*, and an Infernal in *Perseus and Andromeda*. In addition to his roles in pantomimes he danced in such entr'acte turns as *Faithful Shepherd*, *Scot's Dane*, *Dance of Sailors* (from *Orestes*), *French Peasants*, and *Le Depit amoureux* (with Mlle Delorme). On 28 April 1736 he had a solo benefit which brought in only £44 10s., not enough to cover house charges. His address on his bill was given as Bagnio Lane, Newgate Street.

Desse remained at Covent Garden through 1739–40, appearing in a few new roles: Water and Fire in *The Rape of Proserpine*, a Fury in *The Necromancer*, Cupid and Hercules (Brighella) in *The Royal Chace*, a Huntsman in *Apollo and Daphne*, and a Swain and Country Lad in *Orpheus and Eurydice*. New specialty dances in which he participated were a *Grand Comic Dance*, *Faithful Lovers*, and *Two Pierrots* (with Lalauze). The last proved very popular, as did an untitled ballet which Desse danced with Miss Oates. He took no benefit in 1737; in 1738 his benefit tickets were accepted; and in 1739 and 1740 he shared benefits with two other performers.

The records would suggest that he was making little progress at Covent Garden, and from 1740–41 through 1745–46 he tried his luck at Drury Lane. There he was at first advertised more frequently. His debut was on 13 October 1740 in a *Peasant Dance*. Other dances he appeared in during his stay were *Shepherd and Shepherdesses*, *Les Masons* and *Les Sabotiers*,

Diane à la chasse, *Les Jardiniers suèdois*, *The Peasants' Triumph*, *Le Généreux corsaire*, *A Voyage to the Island of Cytherea*, a *Tyrolean Dance*, *Les Amants volages*, an *Italian Masquerade*, and *a Grand Turkish Dance*. Occasionally he did a solo chaconne or danced a minuet or louvre with Miss Hilliard. He took small roles in pantomimes less frequently than in earlier years, some of his parts being a Sea God in *Harlequin Shipwrecked*, a Fantastic "Spright" in *The Amorous Goddess*, and an unnamed role in *Harlequin Incendiary*. He also danced within such works as *Comus*, *Robin Goodfellow*, and *The Tempest*. At benefit time he normally shared receipts with one or two others, though in 1744 he split the profits with five. In the spring of 1742 his tickets were available at Mr Gresham's the shoemaker in York Street, Covent Garden, but by 1747 he had moved to Brownly Street, Longacre.

In 1746–47 Desse returned to Covent Garden for the rest of his long career. His dancing was sharply reduced, and perhaps he was earning part of his £2 weekly salary as a choreographer. Over the years his appearances in new roles included Mars (Leander) in *The Royal Chace*, Scaramouch and a Spaniard in *Apollo and Daphne*, Pan (Scaramouch) and an Aerial Spirit in *Merlin's Cave*, and a Demon (Pierrot) in *The Necromancer*. Specialty dances in which he performed included *The Gondaliers*, *The Threshers*, *The Feast of Bacchus*, and *The Hungarian Gambols*. He also danced in *Macbeth*, *The Muses Looking-Glass*, *The Prophetess*, and *The Fair*. His yearly benefits were always shared with one or more persons, and sometimes, as in 1760, though he sold more tickets than his colleagues, he had to turn back money to help cover a deficit.

Part way through his stay at Covent Garden, from 1753–54 through 1756–57, his name disappeared from the bills, though he still received his benefits. But he was cited in bills once again in 1757–58 and appeared occasionally in subsequent seasons. By 1761–62, his last season on record, he must have been well along in years. In September 1761 he danced Water and a Demon in *The Rape of Proserpine* and was a Croat in *The Hungarian Gambols*. The latter work was not repeated, and Desse was replaced in both of his roles in *Proserpine* by the end of the month. After that he apparently retired.

Desse had a son, advertised as "Desse Junior," who danced in 1761 and who presented one of his own scholars to the public the same year.

Desse, Mr ₁*fl. 1761₁, dancer.*

On 9 March 1761 Desse "Jr" appeared in the comic ballet *The Hungarian Gambols* at Covent Garden, where the elder Desse, presumably his father, had performed for many years. On the following 8 May a minuet was performed by a young gentleman and a young lady five years old, a scholar of Desse Jr.

D'Esser, Mr ₁*fl. 1748₁, dancer.*

A Mr D'Esser (possibly the popular dancer Desse) participated in a *Grand Dance of Furies* at Phillips's Southwark Fair booth on 7 September 1748.

Dessessars, Mons ₁*fl. 1734–1735₁, actor.*

The pantaloon of Francisque Moylin's company, which played at the Haymarket and Goodman's Fields theatres from 26 October 1734 to 4 June 1735, Monsieur Dessessars appeared in leading roles in most of the troupe's mainpieces. His first appearance in London was on 20 November 1734, when he acted Orgon in *Le Tartuffe*. During the rest of the busy season he played Emanuel in *Sampson Judge of Israel* (presumably in French, despite the English title), Roast Beef in *Le François à Londres*, Hector in *Le Joueur*, Sosia in *Amphitryon*, Argante in *Le Malade imaginaire*, the Doc-

tor in *Arlequin Balourd*, the Embassador in *Ines de Castro*, Tortillon in *La Fille capitaine*, Chatillon in *Zaire*, Jourdain in *Le Bourgeois Gentilhomme*, Clotalde in *La Vie est un songe*, Casimir in *Gustave Vasa*, Le Marquis Mascarille in *Les Précieuses ridicules* (for his benefit on 10 March 1735), the Prudent Governour in *La Fausse coquette*, Mathan in *Athalie*, Dandin in *Georges Dandin*, and Chrisanthe in *L'Embarras de richesses*.

Of his individual performances the critics seem to have said nothing, though the play *Le François à Londres* raised considerable comment because the character he played, Roast Beef, was a satire on the English. The Earl of Egmont, however, found the piece "very diverting and well acted."

Dessessars, Mme ₁*fl. 1734–1735₁, actress.*

The wife of the pantaloon in Francisque Moylin's troupe of French players, Madame Dessessars acted several roles at the Haymarket Theatre during the company's 1734–35 visit. On 20 November 1734 she played Mme Pernelle in *Le Tartuffe*, and she followed that with Mme La Ressource in *Le Joueur*, Belina in *Le Malade imaginaire*, and Mme Jourdain in *Le Bourgeois gentilhomme*. She and her husband shared a benefit on 10 March 1735.

"Des Singes, Le Chevalier" ₁*fl. 1767–1768₁, performing monkey.*

At Sadler's Wells in 1767–68 Signor Spinacuti displayed a trained monkey named "Le Chevalier des Singes." An engraving shows some of the animal's tricks, mostly on a tight rope, juggling candelabra and pushing a wheelbarrow.

Dessuslefour, Françoise-Marie. *See* DURANCY, MME.

Destrade, ₁Francis?₁ *d. 1754, dancer, actor.*

Monsieur Destrade was a member of the Covent Garden company from 1740–41 through 1746–47. His first notice in the bills was on 10 October 1740 when he danced a Swain in *Orpheus and Eurydice.* Other roles he played in pantomimes over the years were similarly small: an Infernal, the Petit Maître and a Country Lad in *Perseus and Andromeda*, the fifth Fury in *The Necromancer*, a Gardener and Earth in *The Rape of Proserpine*, a Follower in *The Loves of Mars and Venus*, and Pan (Scaramouch) and an Aerial Spirit in *The Royal Chace.* He also appeared in such entr'acte dances as *La Provençale, Les Maquignons, La Villageoise*, and *Le Gondalier.*

Occasionally at benefit time Destrade had an opportunity to appear alone (as in *Peasant de Bordeaux*) or in a *pas de deux* (as in *Two Pierrots* with Richardson or a minuet with Mlle Auguste). On 19 April 1744 he played the French Soldier in *Henry V* ("being the first time of his attempting to speak on the stage"). At first his benefits were shared with one other performer, but in 1745 he had to share with three, and in 1747 he received no benefit at all. On 22 March 1754 the *Public Advertiser* reported that Monsieur Destrade the dancing-master, formerly of Covent Garden, had died on 20 March. Very likely he was the Francis Destrade of the parish of St George, Hanover Square, whose widow Mary was granted administration of his estate in 1755.

De Surlis, Jean ₁*fl. 1663–1707*₁, *actor, manager.*
Jean de Surlis (or de Sureis) was active in February and March 1663 with Dennis Lavoy at the Théâtre à Gand in Brussels. In the summer of 1688 he was either the manager or leading player of a troupe of French comedians who were brought to England to perform for the King at Windsor. The playhouse there was ordered prepared on 25 July, and the company of foreigners arrived on 11 August. They were housed by the Groom Porter at Windsor in

his own house from 13 August to 22 September. The troupe's goods were exported on 29 September and de Surlis was paid £200 in October for the services he and the 11 other members of the company rendered. The irony is that there seems to be no record of how often they performed or what they played.

In 1697 de Surlis was a principal actor in *"la troupe de Sa Majesté Britannique"* at the Hague, and in February 1707 he and his wife acted at Mons.

Dettey, Miss ₁*fl. 1794*₁, *singer.*
According to Doane's *Musical Directory* of 1794 Miss Dettey was a soprano who sang about this time at the Foundling Hospital.

De Vallois. *See* **VALLOIS.**

Devan. *See* **DAVANT.**

Devant. *See also* **DAVANT.**

Devant, Anthony ₁*fl. 1669*₁, *musician?*
On 18 June 1669 Anthony Devant was one of several men to be apprehended for "keeping playhouses and sounding trumpets, drums and fifes at dumb shows and modells" without paying the necessary fee to the sergeant trumpeter.

De Vaul. *See* **DUVAL.**

De Vaurenville or **De Vaurinville.** *See* **DESCHALLIEZ.**

D'Evelyn, Miss ₁*fl. 1797–1798*₁, *actress, singer.*
Miss D'Evelyn (or Devlen, Devilyn) made her first appearance on any stage, billed as "A Young Lady," playing Margaretta in *No Song No Supper* at Drury Lane on 19 January 1797. The *Monthly Mirror* said she was well received: "Her

figure is petite, but agreeable, and she displayed considerable taste in the 'plaintive ditty,' but her voice wants power, at present, for this immense theatre. Miss D'Evelyn has repeated her performance two or three times with success."

In the spring of 1797, at a weekly salary of £2, Miss D'Evelyn also played Amphitrite in the masque *Neptune and Amphitrite* in *The Tempest* on 22 February, Angelica Goto in *The Shipwreck* on 27 February, Mary in *Cape St Vincent* on 17 April, Charlotte in *My Grandmother* on 3 May, Katharina in *Don John* on 19 May, and Norah in *The Poor Soldier* on 7 June. In 1797–98 she moved to Covent Garden, but her only notice in the bills there was on 12 February when (for £2 the account book noted) she was one of the choristers in *Joan of Arc*. She was replaced by Mrs Blurton the following night and not heard from again.

Devenish, Mrs. *See* PLUNKETT, ELIZABETH.

De Verneuil, ₁Louis François Joseph?₁ ₁*fl. 1718–1735*₁, *actor*.
The Monsieur de Verneuil who appeared with his wife in London in 1734–35 was probably Louis François Joseph de Verneuil. He and his wife, the former Marie-Louise Chabot, were active in Holland as early as 1718 and played at the Théâtre Français at the Hague in 1729. With Francisque Moylin's troupe they acted at the Haymarket and Goodman's Fields theatres in London from 26 October 1734 to 4 June 1735. With them was Mlle Mimi de Verneuil, probably their daughter, who had apparently appeared at Drury Lane during the 1733–34 season. The trio shared a benefit on 24 March 1735.

Monsieur de Verneuil's roles were Cléanthe in *Le Tartuffe*, Phanor in *Sampson Judge of Israel*, Lord Cross in *Le François à Londres*, Dorante in *La Joueur*, Mercury in *Amphitryon*, Beralt in *Le Malade imag-*inaire, Geronte in *Arlequin balourd*, Alphonsus in *Inès de Castro*, the Ghost of Don Pedro in *Le Festin de Pierre*, Lusignan in *Zaire*, Covielle in *Le Bourgeois gentilhomme*, King Basil in *La Vie est un songe*, Christierne in *Gustave Vasa*, Joad in *Athalie*, De Sotenville in *Georges Dandin*, and Plutus in *L'Embarras de richesses*.

Madame de Verneuil played Dorine in *Le Tartuffe*, Tinette in *Le François à Londres*, La Comtesse in *Le Joueur*, the Queen in *Inès de Castro*, Leonor in *Gustave Vasa*, and the title role in *Athalie*.

Mademoiselle de Verneuil seems to have been a dancer only, unless she was the "Miss Mimie" who acted Angeline in *Le Joueur* on 13 December 1734. There was a Madame Mimi Fourçade in the troupe, and the casting may be an error for her. Mlle de Verneuil danced *Pierrot and Pierraite* with Le Sage Junior and *The Wedding* with Mlle Grognet.

De Verneuil, ₁Mme Louis François Joseph, Marie-Louise, née Chabot?₁ ₁*fl. 1718–1735*₁, *actress*. *See* DE VERNEUIL, ₁LOUIS FRANCOIS JOSEPH?₁.

De Verneuil, Mimi ₁*fl. 1733–1735*₁, *dancer, actress?* *See* DE VERNEUIL, ₁LOUIS FRANCOIS JOSEPH?₁.

Devesse. *See* DÉVISSE.

Devienne, Mr ₁*fl. 1797–1798*₁, *flutist*.
Mr Devienne played the flute in the band of the King's Theatre during the 1797–98 season.

"Devil, the Great." *See* LAWRENCE, JOSEPH and NEVIT, MR.

"Devil, the Little." *See* REDIGÉ, PAULO.

De Villiers. *See* VILLIERS.

Devilyn. *See* D'EVELYN.

Dévisse, Mons [*fl.* 1750–1754],
dancer.

Monsieur Dévisse, a leading dancer at
the Paris Opéra, made his first appearance
in England on 2 November 1750 at Drury
Lane dancing a new comic dance and
Pigmalion with Mlle Auretti. The *General
Advertiser* the next day reported that Dévisse was "received with general Applause."
During the rest of the season the Frenchman appeared many times with Mme Auretti in a dance called *Peasants*, danced in
the masque *Alfred*, and with Mme Auretti
at benefit time performed a *New Dance*,
Provincial Dance, louvre, and minuet.
Tickets for his benefit on 16 April 1751
were available at the Distillers at the corner
of the Little Piazza, Covent Garden.

Dévisse then returned to Paris as an
agent for Garrick and immediately got
himself into trouble with the authorities.
Oman's *Garrick* contains a translation of a
letter Louis Basile de Bernage, Provost of
the merchants of Paris, wrote to Mons
Berryer, Commissioner of Police, in June
1751:

On what you were good enough to acquaint
me with, Monsieur, as to the design which
brought to this place Messieurs Garrick and
Levié, I have had them sought for but have
not succeeded in discovering them. You had
given me hopes of sending me information
should anything come to your knowledge on
this subject, so I am led to believe that you
have heard no more on the matter. But *I
know without any doubt that one of our
dancers, named Dévisse, who left furtively
in the month of August last year, and passed
into England,* is at present in Paris. One of
our actors assures me that he saw him and
spoke to him in this town only a few days
ago, and I have reason to believe that the
object of his voyage, about which he addressed certain entreaties to me, alleging
business affairs, is to help forward by his
special knowledge, the steps that Messieurs

Garrick and Levié may take to entice some of
our actors and actresses and to carry them off
with them; perhaps he has already taken
measures to succeed in that.

I hope, Monsieur, that independently of
these reasons, his infringement of the Regulations and orders of the King will decide you
*to give orders to have him arrested and car-
ried to Fort L'Evêque.* Monsieur le Duc de
Gesvres, to whom I have reported this, is of
my opinion; and Monsieur d'Argenson will
approve your action. The example is absolutely necessary, first to keep our actors and
actresses within bounds and to assure that the
public service be properly carried out, and
secondly to forestall M. Dévisse's evil inten-
tions, and the manoeuvres of these foreigners.

This apparently stirred the police to action,
but they did not arrest Dévisse until September 1751, and he apparently continued
his recruiting in spite of it.

A year later, on 25 August 1752, David
Garrick wrote to his brother George that
he hoped Dévisse would not bring the
dancer "Pitro" with him from Paris, since
the Drury Lane company was already over-
loaded. As the following season bills reveal,
Dévisse did bring "Pitro." They arrived in
September, and before the season started
"Devesse" put in an appearance in 22 September at Southwark Fair dancing Pantaloon in *Harlequin Triumphant.* He
reported to Drury Lane for his new engagement on 17 October, dancing in *Les Bû-
cherons* and *Les Tonneliers de Strasburgh.*
He was kept busy the rest of the 1752–53
season and again in 1753–54 dancing in
*Macbeth, The Genii, Bayes in Petticoats,
Fortunatus, The Man of Mode, Romeo and
Juliet,* and other productions. He also appeared in such specialties as *Italian Gardeners, Country Amusements, La Chacone
des caractères* (in which he was Punch),
*The Englishman in Paris, The Savoyard
Travellers,* and a *Dutch Dance.* He often
danced with Mlle Auretti or Mlle Auguste
in a louvre or a minuet. Tickets for his 26
March 1753 benefit were available at Mrs

Jones's, the hoop-petticoat maker in Bow Street, Covent Garden. In the spring of 1754 he seems to have been granted no benefit, though the prompter Cross wrote in his diary on 6 April 1754 that "Mr Devisse has Tickets." After this season Dévisse disappeared from London.

Devlen. *See* D'EVELYN.

Devoes. *See* DEVOTO.

"De Voltore, Mons" ⟨*fl.* 1734⟩, *acrobat.*
At the Hippisley-Bullock-Hallam booth at Bartholomew Fair on 24 August 1734 feats of tumbling were presented by "Monsieur De Voltore" (a pseudonym?) and others.

Devonshire, Mr ⟨*fl.* 1795⟩, *exhibitor.*
A Mr Devonshire exhibited transparencies at Bartholomew Fair in 1795.

"Devonshire Girl." *See* MOSSE, MRS

Devoto, Mr ⟨*fl.* 1778–1784⟩, *house servant?*
On 23 May 1778 a Mr Devoto, possibly a house servant, shared a benefit with four others at Drury Lane. Every May thereafter (except in 1782) through 1784 Devoto's benefit tickets were accepted. Possibly Devoto was descended from the scene painter John Devoto of earlier in the century. A John Devoto of the second generation is said to have set up in 1775 as a teacher of painting. He may possibly have done some work at Drury Lane, but our subject's lowly position, as revealed at benefit time each year, suggests theatre work more menial than painting.

Devoto, Miss ⟨*fl.* 1746⟩, *actress.*
On 29 January 1746 at Goodman's Fields *Love Makes a Man* and *The Stage Coach* were performed for the scene painter John Devoto's benefit. He had announced

The Orphan, with his daughter making her debut on stage as Monimia, but for some reason a change had to be made. It is not known whether or not Miss Devoto acted in one of the pieces given at her father's benefit. Since she was referred to only as Devoto's daughter, she may have acted under some other name. A Jane Devoto of St Martin-in-the-Fields married a John Tempest on 3 April 1742 at St George's Chapel, Mayfair, and this may have been the painter's daughter.

Devoto, Anthony ⟨*fl. c.* 1662–1677⟩, *puppeteer.*
Perhaps as early as 1662 Anthony Devoto (or Deeve, Devoes, Devotti, di Voto) was showing his puppets at a booth in Charing Cross. He was certainly active there in 1667, 1668, 1669, and 1672, and

Public Record Office

playbill for ANTHONY DEVOTO's Charing Cross booth, 11 November 1672

from 1672 to 1677; in addition to his Charing Cross venture he worked at Bartholomew Fair. In 1669 Gervase Price, the Sergeant Trumpeter to Charles II, demanded the usual 12*s*. daily fee which players were supposed to pay him. Devoto refused to pay and took his case to the Master of the Revels, Sir Henry Herbert, pleading that he made "shewe of puppettes only." Herbert supported his plea and on 15 July wrote his recommendation to the Lord Chamberlain that Devoto be released from the arrest under which Price had placed him.

On 11 November 1672 a warrant directed to "Antonio Divoto punchenello" permitted Devoto to "Exercise & Play all Drolls and Interludes, He not receiuing into his Company any person belonging to his Ma^tes or Royal Highnesse Theatres Nor Act any Play usually acted at any of ye said Theatres." Armed with this permission and winking at some of its provisions, Devoto advertised for the same day:

At the Booth at Charing-Cross, every day in the Week will be presented variety of Farces Drolls, and Comical Entertainments by Mr Anthony Devo, His Majesties Servant. And this present Monday being the Eleventh of November, will be presented the Dutch cruelties at Amboyna [cribbed from Dryden's play], with the humours of the Valiant Welch-Man. Acted by Men and Women. Beginning exactly at Two of the Clock in the Afternoon, and at Four. Vivat Rex.

Devoto, John ₁*fl. 1672–1676*₁, *property man, manager.*

The John Devoto who hired a booth at Bartholomew Fair in 1672, 1674, 1675, and 1676 was possibly the Mr Devoto (Deeve, Devoes, Divoe, Divoto are variants) who prepared the properties for the court masque *Calisto,* which was performed in February 1675.

Devoto, John ₁*fl. 1708–1752*₁, *scene painter.*

JOHN DEVOTO
engraving by J. Faber, Jr, after Damini

John Devoto was referred to in his time as French, though his parents were probably Italian and possibly from Genoa. In 1708 he was an assistant to Gerard Lanscroon, doing paintings in the Earl of Nottingham's house in Rutland; unfortunately, fire destroyed the paintings there in 1913 and no photographs of them have survived. By 1718 Devoto was established as a decorative painter in the parish of St Clement Danes and had sufficient business to need an assistant. Three drawings dating about 1719 show Devoto's decorative painting style, and it is similar enough to that of Sir James Thornhill to suggest that the two may have worked together at some time.

The earliest example of Devoto's scene designs dates from the same year; it is typically Baroque and reminiscent of the work of the Bibienas. All known Devoto designs for scenery are at the British Museum. In 1719–20 he was making copies (perhaps for practice) of the designs of his contemporaries Juvarra and Righini. Possibly by this time he had painted some scenes for London productions, but the earliest mention of him in theatrical advertisements came on 24 September 1723 at Drury Lane when *Julius Caesar* was performed "With an intire new Sett of Scenes representing Anciant Rome, painted by Monsieur Devoto." When the pantomime *Harlequin Shepherd* was presented at Drury Lane on 28 November 1724 there was in it "A New Night Scene. The Scenes being all painted from the real Place of Action." By December 1724 Devoto's work was well enough known that Hogarth, when he drew "A Just View of the British Stage," satirically ascribed the "Scene Newgate, by M D—V——to."

Devoto provided the scenes for Thurmond's *The Miser*, which opened at Drury Lane on 30 December 1726, and for *Perseus and Andromeda*, which had its premiere on 15 November 1728. For the production of *Othello* on 15 November 1731 he painted "a new set of Scenes being a prospect of the Ponte Rialto at Venice . . ." In 1732 the painter apparently planned to publish a collection of his designs, but he did only a drawing for a subscriber's receipt and the project came to nothing. Theophilus Cibber's *The Harlot's Progress* at Drury Lane on 31 March 1733 apparently used Devoto designs. Henry Angelo claimed that the artist worked for John Rich at Lincoln's Inn Fields after 1732–33, but this seems unlikely. Rich moved to Covent Garden in 1732 and no bills for that house name Devoto.

The painter did leave Drury Lane, however. In 1734–35 he was at the Goodman's Fields playhouse, his designs for *Jupiter and Io* being seen there for the first time on 24 January 1735. A year later, on 27 January 1736, the London *Daily Post and General Advertiser* said, "We hear the Designs of

By permission of the Trustees of the British Museum

Scene design by JOHN DEVOTO

Merlin's Cave [in *King Arthur*], that were presented last week to her Majesty by Mr Giffard, have been so well approv'd of, by many Persons of Quality, that Mr Devoto, who made the Draughts, has had several Copies bespoke by the Nobility."

In January 1739 Devoto painted some scenes for the White Swan playhouse in Norwich. He may have gone there to supervise their use, but he painted them in London and shipped them to Norwich with the paint still wet, causing a delay in the opening of the theatre. His scenery was used at the New Wells, Clerkenwell, in June 1740 for an entertainment called *A Hint to the Theatres; Or, Merlin in Labour.* Depicted

was Merlin's Cave, and it is probable that Devoto arranged with his manager Giffard to rent to the New Wells the scenery he had painted for *King Arthur* four years before. He was still in Giffard's troupe, for on 3 March 1741 at Goodman's Fields he supplied scenes and machines for *Harlequin Student*, especially a scene "of Shakespeare's Monument As lately erected in Westminster Abbey." The *Daily Post* on 3 July 1742 advertised a show of scenes by Devoto at the New Wells featuring "A Grand Representation of Water Works, as in the Doge's Gardens at Venice."

Devoto worked for Garrick when the actor supervised private theatricals for the

Scene design by JOHN DEVOTO

Duke of Bedford in 1744. On 11 September a payment of £10 10s. was requested for Devoto for "one Flat Scene and 4 Wings." The painter was given a benefit at Goodman's Fields on 29 January 1746 and presumably painted scenery for the theatre that season. The benefit was planned for his daughter, who was to play Monimia in *The Orphan* for her maiden effort on stage. The play was changed, however, and it is not clear whether or not Miss Devoto ever appeared subsequently.

Perhaps the painter gave up theatre work after this, for later records of his activity make no mention of scenery. In the 1750s he drew a frontispiece for *Twelve English Songs* by Barnabas Gunn, and in 1752 he designed admission tickets for the Handel oratorios *The Choice of Hercules* and *Samson* at Covent Garden. After that, no more was heard of Devoto, though a second generation John Devoto, possibly his son, opened a school in Longacre to teach drawing in December 1775 and exhibited some of his work the following year. He lived at Mrs Goadsby's, Bedford Street, Covent Garden.

John Devoto the scene painter was drawn by Vincenzo Damini in 1738; an engraving after Damini was made by J. Faber, Jr. Though no full study has been made of Devoto, in 1952 Edward Croft-Murray published a pamphlet on him for the Society for Theatre Research, from which much of the material in this entry was drawn.

Dewell, Nicholas   [fl. 1689–1699], *trumpeter.*

If Nicholas Dewell's name was an anglicizing of Duvall, perhaps he was a descendant of the court singer of pre-Restoration days, Nicholas Duvall. Dewell was sworn a trumpeter in the King's Musick on 12 September 1689, was given a new trumpet on 4 April 1695 (his name then being spelled "Dewitt"), was listed as receiving an annual salary of £91 5s. in 1697, and

was last mentioned in the Lord Chamberlain's accounts in a warrant dated 1699.

Dewitt. *See* **DEWELL.**

Dexter, John   1726–1764, *actor.*

John Dexter was born in Ireland in 1726 and, according to the *Alumni Dublinenses*, matriculated at Trinity College in 1743, at age 17. Francis Gentleman called Dexter "Schoolfellow" with himself, Mossop, and Derrick. He found Dexter still at Trinity as Gentleman mustered out of the Army after "the Rebellion" (i.e., in 1746).

According to Davies's recollection in his *Life of Garrick*, the great actor-manager encouraged three young performers from the Dublin theatres to come to him in the fall of 1751—Mossop, Ross, and Dexter. But there is no record of Dexter's having appeared in Ireland or anywhere else before his coming on at Drury Lane on 22 October 1751 in the title role of *Oroonoko*. And the prompter Cross entered in his diary: "One Mr Dexter did Oroonoko, a gent of Ireland—who never appear'd upon a Stage before—he had yᵉ Greatest applause ever heard & indeed deservedly a Sweet Voice, great feeling &c.—his name was not in yᵉ Bills—only by a Gent &c."

Perhaps the fact that the old piece had not been acted in five years helped precipitate the praise which showered down on Dexter. The "Inspector" No 201 in the *Daily Advertiser and Literary Gazette* thought that "Mr Dexter has given us in the character of Oroonoko the greatest first essay that perhaps any stage has produced. He has great feeling, and equal expression; a fine figure, a vast deal of grace in his deportment, and uncommon tenderness in his manner, and a voice formed by nature for expressing it." Dexter played the part again on 25 November and when on 28 November he played Hippolitus in *Phaedra and Hippolitus*, with his friend Mossop as Theseus, Cross noted: "Went off well."

His next essay was on 6 February 1752

in the revival, after seven years, of *Lady Jane Gray*, playing Pembroke. Cross's comment: "Very Dull Play & No Garrick." But the tragedy was repeated the next night. On 17 February Dexter stepped into a secondary part, Clerval in Francis's translation from the French, *Eugenia*, and Garrick took the lead, Mercour. It "went off with great Applause" but only after a small riot, occasioned by the audience's disapproval of the music, was quelled.

Dexter finished the 1751–52 season with his benefit on 17 March when he played Castalio in *The Orphan* and tickets could be had of him at "his lodgings at Mr Gibson's in James Street, Covent Garden." Receipts were £120, out of which house charges of about £60 were taken.

Dexter repeated his Oroonoko on 5 October 1752, his first appearance of the new season, but evidently some of his lustre had worn off, as there was a very thin house, with receipts of only £80. The managers allowed him to lie fallow until 8 November when, with a complete change of pace, they sent him forth to try Carlos in *Love Makes a Man*. The receipts on this occasion of Dexter's first venture into comedy increased a little, to £90, not too poor for a Wednesday night, but not good. He was next tried in a masque, *Comus*, playing one of the brothers while his friend Mossop took the title part. The bill drew £70 on Tuesday, 28 November. On 2 December Dexter went back to tragedy and began to descend a little, playing Cranmer in *Henry VIII*, and on 7 December came somewhat to the fore again as the title character in *Don Sebastian, King of Portugal*. He was Orsino in *Twelfth Night* on 8 January 1753, played the Colonel, a secondary character in *The Non-Juror*, on 6 February for the special benefit of Theophilus Cibber, who was in the King's Bench prison. On 22 February Dexter played Dudley in *Lady Jane Gray*. For his benefit on 3 April, he essayed Young Mirabel in *The Inconstant*. He still invited

ticket seekers to James Street, and his total receipts, before charges, amounted to a very respectable £170.

But Garrick and his assistants had given Dexter a fair trial in a variety of leading and supporting roles and had found him in need of further grooming. His contract was not renewed. It was a disappointment for all concerned. Davies, who was of the company at the time, recalled that on the night of his debut a half hour before curtain time the confident and insouciant Dexter was still engaged in conversation with friends in the pit and had to be reminded of the passing time. And after that triumphant first night Garrick had written to friends in the strongest terms about his wonderful expectations for Dexter's career.

The Present State of the Stage (1753) summed up Dexter's London attempts by observing that "Mr. Dexter's first performance of Oroonoko, we all remember, was amazing" but that he had not equalled it in subsequent efforts. Yet he was a "man of good sense" and his voice, though weak, was melodious. *A General View of the Stage* echoed and expanded these sentiments: "Mr Dexter has a genteel figure, agreeable voice, an easy carriage, and good sense. He has acquitted himself with applause in several parts of genteel Comedy; and some of those he has attempted in Tragedy have been equally deserving of it."

But Dexter could now honestly be said to be "from the Theatre-Royal, Drury Lane," and he made straightway to Dublin to exploit his newspaper notices. At Dublin he remained until his death, playing with considerable success and often pleasing audiences though never achieving the eminence he had once promised himself. John Lee, however, in a letter of 1757 to Thomas Sheridan called Dexter "the principal Performer next to" Sheridan and King in Dublin. He was at Cork in the summers of 1756, 1758, 1760, 1761, and 1762. He played also at Edinburgh, and *A View of the Edinburgh Theatre During the Sum-*

mer Season 1759, very likely the joint production of James Boswell and Dexter's old friend Francis Gentleman, furnishes some criticism of his mature style.

On 20 June 1759 the authors first warned him that the extravagant puffing he had enjoyed in Dublin was a danger to his success in Edinburgh. He was mildly commended, and thought to be better as a hero than as a lover, being "deficient in Point of Tenderness." He had evidently overcome the vocal weakness of his salad days for "His being accustomed to play in a large House renders his Voice . . . too strong for this"; yet its shrillness made him unfit for Hamlet. On 25 June he was excellent as Archer in *The Beaux' Stratagem* and was congratulated "on having followed our Advice, in reducing his Voice to a lower, and consequently less disagreeable Pitch" and on 27 July "not amiss" in Lord Townly in *The Provok'd Husband* and seen to be "daily improving" under critical tutelage. Romeo, on 30 June, was too youthful for him: "We could not, indeed, but smile, when we heard his Mistress talking of cutting him up into little Stars, in order to enlighten the Heavens. We will, however, candidly acknowledge [he] was very great in the dying scene." On 2 July he was not perfect in his part of Sir Charles Easy in *The Careless Husband*, though good in the "gentle raillery." On 11 July his Captain Plume, in *The Recruiting Officer*

had but very little of the Briskness and Fire of a sprightly young Officer, newly come Home from serving a Campaign. He rather gave us the Conception of some good-natured Man of Fortune, who, to oblige his Friends and Acquaintances, had condescended to put on a Suit of Regimentals, and shuffle through the Character, in order to pass away an Evening Agreeably. This Gentleman's Manner of playing in Comedy (by Reason of his being overstudious to avoid Affectation) is simple, even to a Fault. These Graces in Acting, which commonly go under the Denomination of Bye-play, or Stage Tricks, are not only great Embellishments, but are essentially necessary to a Performer; without which, he can never be reckoned compleat. We are sorry that Mr. Dexter has not payed enough Regard to these, as it were *minutiae* of his Employment; for which Reason, although he seldom offends, yet he never can charm an Audience.

On 21 July his Orestes in *The Distrest Mother* was "greatly too languid."

A Person who had not read the Play, would never have thought, from Mr. Dexter's Manner of *managing* the two first Acts, to have seen him go distracted. — Actors, in general, have a Way of what they call *saving themselves*, than which, nothing can be more dangerous to make free with. It is very allowable, that a Performer should reserve the utmost Strength of his Abilities, for any Scene that is distinguishably grand; But, then, he must observe some Kind of Proportion, and not shew a Person in the End of a Play, directly opposite to what he was in the Beginning. Mr. *Dexter's* raving Scene was incredibly well performed. His Attitudes were bold and striking; the Expression of his Countenance just and forcible. Our Terror increased at every Line, till he gradually rose to all the Wildness and Fury of a heroic Madman. Altho' this justly claims as it's Due, the greatest Commendation, yet he went through the former Scenes with such a negligent Inattention, and tame Composure, as rendered them flat and spiritless; by which Means, the Richness of Colouring, and Glow of Imagery, which the Author has in several Places displayed, was entirely lost to us.

The close criticism of Dexter's technique and our record of his acting virtually end with the Edinburgh critics' comment about *Love for Love* on 23 July: "We were very well pleased with Mr Dexters Valentine." Years later, Francis Gentleman, again anonymously, in *The Dramatic Censor* (1770) recalled his Mark Antony, which "was pretty and inoffensive, but very faint and lukewarm."

Dexter's wife, a Dublin actress, died 10 June 1764. He himself died on 8 August following, "much esteemed," says Davies, "for his regular conduct and genteel behaviour."

Deyman, Mrs ₍fl. 1714₎, *actress.*

Mrs Deyman was a member of a troupe called the Duke of Southampton and Cleaveland's Servants playing at Richmond in the summer of 1714. They presented *Injured Virtue*, in which Mrs Deyman acted Artimia and spoke the epilogue when it was given on 1 November 1714 at the King's Arms in Southwark, so her role in the summer at Richmond was probably the same.

D'Ferrou Ville, Mons ₍fl. 1732₎, *dancer.*

Monsieur D'Ferrou Ville (if the name is transcribed correctly) danced at the Fielding-Hippisley booth at Bartholomew Fair on 22 August 1732, billed as lately arrived from Paris.

D'Fesch. *See* DE FESCH.

D'Herbage, Mons ₍fl. 1736₎, *actor.*
Monsieur D'Herbage played one of the Countrymen in *Tumble Down Dick* at the Haymarket Theatre on 29 April 1736.

D'Hervigni, Mlle ₍fl. 1735–1736₎, *dancer.*

On 31 December 1735 at Covent Garden Mlle D'Hervigni made her first appearance on the English stage dancing in a *Serious Ballet* and a comic piece called *Les Puisans*. She was billed as from Paris. During the rest of the 1735–36 season she appeared as a Nymph in *The Royal Chace* and participated, often with Lalauze as her partner, in such specialty dances as *French Peasant*. On 8 April 1736 she played Colombine in *Le Mariage forcé* with a visiting troupe of French players, and at her shared benefit

with Mrs Kilby on 26 April she danced a solo louvre and *Rigadoon.*

Diamond. *See also* DIMOND.

Diamond, Mr ₍fl. 1660₎, *acrobat.*
Mr Diamond (or Dymond) performed acrobatic feats in the pageant given for the Lord Mayor on 29 October 1660.

Diamond, Mr ₍fl. 1784–1790₎, *actor.*
On several widely spaced occasions from 1784 through 1790 one Mr Diamond (or several) acted in specially licensed performances at the Haymarket Theatre. Because of certain conflicts in dating it is very unlikely that the references are to the well-known William Wyatt Dimond of the Bath-Bristol company.

On 16 November 1784 Diamond played Captain Savage in *The School for Wives* and on 31 January Fairfax in *King Charles I*. On 6 March 1786 a Diamond was Axalla in *Tamerlane the Great.* On 29 September 1790 he or another Diamond took the part of Captain Sightly in *The Romp.*

"Diana." *See* COSTANTINI, SIGNORA GIOVANNI BATTISTA.

"Diana, Signora" ₍fl. 1726–1727₎, *actress.*
"Signora Diana"—which is probably a Christian name, not a surname—was a member of the Italian troupe that arrived in London on 21 September 1726 and opened their season at the King's Theatre in the Haymarket two days later. She was given a benefit on 9 February 1727 and was cited in the 8 April bill for *La Dama demonio* as playing Mistress Demon, presumably the title role.

Di Aspino, Diego ₍fl. 1744–1745₎, *singer.*
Don Diego di Aspino sang the Spaniard in *The Queen of Spain* at the Haymarket

Theatre on 19 January 1744 and again on 14 February 1745.

"Diavolino, Signor" *[fl. 1754], musician.*

Mrs Midnight's New Carnival Concert at the Haymarket Theatre on 13 September 1754 was "Set for a Smoking Pipe, a Tankard, a Bassoon, a Pair of Tongs, two Wooden Spoons, a Salt Box, and a Pair of Slippers"—to be played by "the best Italian masters," including "Signor Diavolino." "Mrs Midnight" was Christopher Smart's pseudonym, but who "Diavolino" was is not known.

Dibble, Robert *[fl. 1793–1817], singer.*

Robert Dibble was a minor singer in choruses at the Haymarket and Drury Lane from 1793 through at least 1816–17. His name first appeared on a Haymarket bill for 3 August 1793 when he sang in *The Mountaineers.* In that summer he also sang in *Caernarvon Castle.* On 19 November 1793 he sang in the chorus for *The Tempest* at the Haymarket and in the following summer at the same theatre he sang in *The Surrender of Calais, The Battle of Hexham, The Mountaineers,* and *Comus.* Again at the Haymarket in 1794 he was in *The Surrender of Calais* and *Zorinski.* In that year Doane listed him in the *Musical Directory* as a tenor, a member of the New Musical Fund, the Portland Chapel Society, and the Haymarket Theatre. In the listing his full name was provided, as well as his address, No 3, Mitre Court, Milk Street, Cheapside.

For 1795–96, Dibble was engaged as an extra chorus tenor by Drury Lane, where in that season he appeared in such musical extravaganzas as *The Pirates, The Cherokee, The Iron Chest,* and *The Surrender of Calais.* He remained at Drury Lane in a similarly obscure capacity until 1816–17, the season his name is last noted by us in the pay accounts. In that last season he was earning the modest sum of £1 5s. per week, a salary constant since at least 1808–9. His chorus role as one of "The Horde" in *Lodoiska* (for which he was first billed on 1 January 1800) is typical of his function at the theatre. Dibble also continued during summers to sing at the Haymarket, at least through 1801. Possibly he was related to Thomas Dibble Davis (d. 1795), who acted in London from 1758 to 1788.

Dibble, Thomas. *See* DAVIS, THOMAS DIBBLE.

Dibdin, Miss *[fl. 1799–1804], dancer.*

A Miss Dibdin danced at Covent Garden for the first time on 29 January 1799, in an unspecified role in a pantomime, *The Magic Oak; or, Harlequin Woodcutter.* She was a Female Domestick in *Oscar and Malvina; or, The Hall of Fingal* on 2 March, repeated in *The Magic Oak* on 25 March, and was a Domestick again, this time in *Raymond and Agnes; or, The Castle of Lindenbergh,* on 13 April.

Her activities were even less frequent in 1799–1800. On 1 January 1800 she was named to replace Miss Coombs in one of the unnamed pantomime characters of *The Volcano,* danced in *Paul and Virginia* on 1 May, and executed (with 17 others) a "New Dance" at the end of the mainpiece on 17 May. She was on the Haymarket bill of 2 July 1800 as a Dancing Negress in *Obi; or, Three-Finger'd Jack.*

Miss Dibdin continued dancing at Covent Garden in the winters and occasionally at the Haymarket in the summers through the summer of 1804. To which of the Dibdin families she belonged is not known.

Dibdin, Charles *1745–1814, actor, singer, dramatist, composer, pianist, manager.*

Charles Dibdin "Son of Thomas Dibdin, Clerk of this Parish," was "baptized in private March 4" 1745, according to the entry in the register of Holyrood Church, Southampton.

Charles was probably the twelfth of fourteen children of his father, whom he called "a silversmith, a man of considerable credit." Nothing is known of Charles's mother. (The tradition, adopted from the *Penny Cyclopoedia* by Husk in *Grove's Dictionary*, that Charles's grandfather "had founded the village near Southampton which bears his name" was disproved by H. W. S. Taylor in *Notes and Queries* Nov. 1860, who cites its Domesday mention, "Depe-dene [from its] situation in a thickly wooded dell," and says that "no traditions with a family of the name exist in the village." Where the family originated is not known.)

In his *Professional Life* Dibdin casually details many circumstances of his life up to 1803. But this account must be heavily supplemented by other sources. Foregoing

formal education, even in music, he "not only cut a great figure at the college and the cathedral, at Winchester, where" he "sung anthems," but "at the concert rooms, at the races and the assizes [which] echoed with my vocal fame." A weekly subscription concert, patronized by Archdeacon Eden, Dr John Hoadley, Colonel Caesar (the lover of Mrs Woffington), and others, was established. The performers were local clergymen, and young Dibdin was the vocal star soloist. He was "put up for an organist's place at Waltham, in Hampshire," but was rejected "on account of my youth."

At the age of 12 (according to his memoir, but more likely at 14 or 15) he went to London on the invitation of his brother Thomas, 29 years his senior.

To town I came; visited all the churches; fell in love with extempore playing; soon learned to handle *Moll Peatley, Bobbin Joan,* and *Lilaballero* [*sic*], in a voluntary; and, little as such a circumstance may be suspected of me, by favour of a deputy-organist, I often played the congregation out of church, at St. Bride's, before I was sixteen years old.

His brother Thomas sailed in the *Hope* ("This was at the time of Byng's war, as it was called"). The ship was captured by a French vessel, and young Charles was on his own, in the employment that Thomas had provided for him—apprenticed to "old Johnson who . . . kept a capital music-shop in Cheapside." But there he "saw no chance for advancement to the organ-loft," for he was kept tuning harpsichords all day, and Johnson rejected the "songs and sonatas" which he was already bringing for sale. "I am ready to allow," Dibdin later said, "they were puerile, imperfect, and crude," for except for a few lessons from Peter Fussel, later organist at Winchester Cathedral, he had had literally no instruction.

Soon, however, Charles persuaded "the notorious [Thomas] Kear, of stentorian

Harvard Theatre Collection

CHARLES DIBDIN

engraving, after Dighton

memory," a popular bass singer, to sing six of his ballads at Finch's Grotto Gardens, and the Thompsons, publishers in St Paul's Churchyard, generously gave him three guineas for their copyright.

Casting about for a permanent situation, Dibdin was befriended by one Berenger, a "*bon vivant*, and intimate with Garrick, Beard, Bonnel Thornton, and all the first-rate literary and theatrical geniuses of that day." Berenger advised him to think of the stage, and he soon entered "a new world." Charles had never even seen a play or opera, but "in less than a month, through the influence of my friend, I had break-fasted with Johnny Beard; dined with Rich; and joined Tommy Warren and Lord Sandwich, at the St Alban's-street tavern, in a new prize-glee, composed by . . . Mr Arne."

He set about learning for the first time the rudiments of harmony by dissecting Correlli's concertos, and found that, after close attention at the theatre, he could go home and write from memory the whole score.

The Covent Garden account book for 5 December 1760 carried the notation "Paid Dibdin for singing 5 nights in *Thomas and Sally* and 1 night in *Romeo* £1 10s." On 11 December he was named in the Chorus for *Comus*, and on 18 April 1761 he shared a benefit with other minor players.

The eccentric Covent Garden patentee John Rich took a liking to his new chorus singer and conceived that he should in time "have exactly the same kind of deep bass voice that Leveridge had." Rich's ancient prompter John Stede, a veteran 80 years of age, and a marvellous repository of theatrical lore and wisdom, also took the lad under instruction. At Rich's levees Charles met all the people of theatrical importance; and though the manager's death in 1761 destroyed the hopes of immediate stardom erected on Rich's extravagant promises, John Beard, Rich's son-in-law and partial

heir to the patent, continued to encourage him. He gained wider acting experience with Burton and Bransby, the managers, and Weston, Shuter, and Jane Pope, performers, at the "Histrionic Academy" at Richmond in the summer of 1762.

Dibdin's theatrical career was fairly launched when Beard accepted his first full-length work, the pastoral operetta *The Shepherd's Artifice*, for which Dibdin had written both words and music. This trifle was produced as the afterpiece of a performance for Dibdin's benefit, shared with the minor players Holton, Buck, and Miss Sledge on 22 May 1764, when Charles performed the character of Strephon. It was twice staged the next season, on 12 April 1765 and for the benefit of Dibdin and Perry on 13 May, and on those occasions the bills advertised that "Books of the Entertainment" were to be sold at the theatre.

Meanwhile Dibdin had continued to be employed in the choruses to harlequinades and musical comedies, for a salary of 5s. per night. He later boasted: "I was perfectly a bell-weather [*sic*] to the chorus-singers, who have always a knack of going astray, as bad as Handel's sheep in the *Messiah*, and it was my constant employ to keep them together." Charles was again picked out for a "named part" in the bills when on 2 November 1762 he was a Harvest Man in *Harlequin Sorcerer, with the Loves of Pluto and Proserpine*. In the summer of 1763 he joined Younger's company at Birmingham, sang his own popular songs at the local Vauxhall, and made excursions to act at Hagley, Leasowes, Meridon, and other towns. When he came back to London he began work with Michael Arne on music for Garrick's alteration of *A Midsummer Night's Dream* called *A Fairy Tale*. In the season of 1763–64 also he three times stood forth from the ruck of chorus singers: as the witch in the same pantomime on 3 October 1763, as the Magician in *Perseus and Andromeda* on

Harvard Theatre Collection
CHARLES DIBDIN
engraving by B. Smith, after J. Kearsley

14 January 1764, and as Strephon, afore-mentioned. He apparently returned to play at Birmingham in the summer of 1764.

Charles Dibdin's great opportunity, so far as performance was concerned, came on 31 January 1765. He had been suddenly thrust into rehearsal by Beard as Ralph in Isaac Bickerstaffe's *The Maid of the Mill*, in place of the aging Dunstall, and had feigned an indifference he did not feel while spiteful and envious attacks rained on him from older aspirants. He had re-hearsed casually, and his undeserved ene-mies anticipated his abject failure. Instead, he enjoyed one of the most brilliant suc-cesses of the decade, being encored in every song, and even setting a sartorial fashion: the "Ralph-hankerchiefs" he introduced be-gan to be worn by young bucks. On each of three successive Saturdays Charles's salary was raised by 10 shillings; *The Maid of the Mill* ran for more than 50 nights, and it was not long until Beard proposed that articles "be prepared for three years, at a salary of three, four, and five pounds a week . . ." An additional, though informal, stipulation was that Dibdin should never be required to perform in any but musical pieces, a device Charles thought might prevent the envy and bad feeling from fellow actors which, he says, very nearly drove him from the stage.

In the summer of 1765 Dibdin was engaged by Love for the first season of his new theatre at Richmond, and in the fall he rejoined the chorus at Covent Garden, singing also specialty songs and performing parts like Damaetas in *Midas* and the Shepherd in *The Royal Chace*. For the next two years he alternated between Covent Garden in the winters and Richmond in the summers, where, he says, Garrick paid him much attention and taught him how to play Lord Ogleby in *The Clandestine Marriage*.

In the season of 1766–67 Dibdin was named in bills 15 times and was kept busy learning new parts and writing songs. He had a huge success on 21 February 1767 as the original Watty Cockney in *Love in the City* (afterward altered to *The Romp*), for which he composed the first chorus, the finales of the first and second acts, and three songs. He was saved from a plot to oust him hatched by Simpson the oboe player and others of the band by the personal intercession of Dr Thomas Augustine Arne. During the season he was also Robin in *The Accomplish'd Maid*, Sir Trusty in *Rosamond*, a Sailor in *Thomas and Sally*, Mercury in *Perseus and Andromeda*, and Palaemon in *The Chaplet*. At season's end he shared a benefit with Davis (for which the door receipts were small—£4 5s. 6d. for each—but the sharers also retained an undisclosed income from tickets they sold). In addition to all this the young man introduced the pianoforte to the English theatre on 16 May 1767 when, playing upon one, he accompanied Miss Brickler in "a favourite song from *Judith*." His *The Village Wedding* was produced at Richmond on 18 July 1767. In 1767–68 he acted and sang at least 16 times. On 25 February 1768 Bickerstaffe's *Lionel and Clarissa*, for which

he wrote two-thirds of the music, came on the boards. The opera was very popular, but Dibdin received only £48 for his contributions to it.

By this time most of Charles Dibdin's varied theatrical talents had been displayed and his principal direction laid out. He sang (solo and in chorus), very likely danced a little, acted, and played both piano and harpsichord. But the production of his musical pieces—operettas, burlettas, pantomimes, songs—which were to bring him the greatest fame, now began to occupy most of his attention.

John Beard sold the patent of Covent Garden in July 1767, and George Colman assumed the management. Colman and Dibdin did not jibe, and Dibdin wore out the last year of his Covent Garden articles chafing under all sorts of petty tyrannies. Fate added a final blow when his benefit, announced for 13 May 1768, was postponed because of the death of Princess Louisa Anne, the King's sister. The rearranged benefit brought him only £22 13s. after charges. But he was becoming a recognized member of an inner circle of male professional singers. The *bon vivant* William Hickey, taken to the Globe Tavern in Craven Street for an evening's entertainment by a "lodge" called The Euphrates, in 1768, found Dibdin one of the members, along with Hook, Champness, Charles Bannister, and Dodd.

Dibdin joined the Drury Lane company in the fall of 1768 precisely in time to profit from the acquisition by Garrick of Covent Garden's star author and librettist Bickerstaffe. *The Padlock*, originally planned for production at the Haymarket in the summer of 1768 but deferred because of Samuel Foote's "indolence," according to Dibdin, brought both Bickerstaffe, the author of the story, and Dibdin, the composer, great acclaim at Drury Lane. But Bickerstaffe also cleared, in time, over £1700 by it, whereas Dibdin says he received only £45. Dibdin later charged both

CHARLES DIBDIN, as Mungo

artist unknown

Bickerstaffe and Garrick with deviousness and rapacity, "for the first wanted, of course, to get my music as cheap as possible, and the latter my theatrical exertions." The part of Mungo, at first rehearsed and then abandoned by John Moody, went to Dibdin, and the public praised him deliriously. He wrote both words and music for *Damon and Phillida*, which took the boards on 21 December 1768. Said Hopkins's diary, "went off very dull, and some hisses—the musick not vastly liked . . ."

Dibdin's older brother Thomas was that year confined for debt, and before he was released to take up an appointment in India, his misfortune had caused Charles to run up a money obligation to Garrick which he deplored as a "mental slavery" which caused "a perpetual conflict between

my duty and my inclination." Under the spur of this financial exigency Dibdin secured an agreement with the proprietors of Ranelagh to compose music for two summers at £100 per season. On 12 May 1769 at Ranelagh House the Bickerstaffe-Dibdin *Ephesian Matron* was shown. On 21 June 1769 Bickerstaffe's *The Captive*, with Dibdin's music, appeared at the Haymarket.

The Stratford Jubilee in the fall of 1769 employed much music by Dibdin and involved him in a bitter contention with Garrick which threatened to disrupt the festival. Garrick was finally mollified by Dibdin's composition of "Let beauty with the sun arise," which he had threatened to withhold: "I . . . got down to Stratford the evening before the *Jubilee*, made the musicians sit up all night, and as soon as it was daylight we sallied forth as a band of masqueraders, and to the astonishment of Garrick serenaded him with the thing he had set his heart upon, but which he had given up as lost."

On 30 August 1769 was published *Shakespear's Garland or the Warwickshire Jubilee Being a Collection of Ballads as Perform'd at the Theatre Royal Drury Lane Composed by Mr Dibdin*. On 31 August at the Haymarket he sang a part in *The Ephesian Matron*, advertised as his first appearance at that theatre. He also sang ballads that summer at Ranelagh.

At Drury Lane in the season of 1769–70 Dibdin continued to perform: Mungo, a Female Ballad Singer in the representation of *The Jubilee*, and for his first time, Ogleby in *The Clandestine Marriage*. In the summer of 1770 he furnished music for Bickerstaffe's *The Maid the Mistress* and *The Recruiting Sergeant* (the fruits of his £100 compact with Ranelagh) and contributed songs to *The Madmen*, "A new Burletta," at Marylebone Gardens on 28 August and *Cupid's Frolick* at Sadler's Wells on 25 July. At some time during the year he collaborated with David Garrick on *Cupid and Damon* and with Bicker-staffe on *Dr Ballardo*, neither of which was performed. In 1770–71 his appearances at Drury Lane were few, though he attracted attention in "the character of an Old Lady" in *He Would if he Could*, a burletta adapted by Bickerstaffe from Pergolesi's *La serva padrona* for which Dibdin had furnished the music when it had been called *The Maid the Mistress* at Ranelagh. At the Haymarket on 5 June 1771 he played Bully in *The Provok'd Wife*, again advertised as being for the first time on that stage.

In 1771–72 Dibdin was doubtless engaged in chorus singing, and he set Garrick's masque, *The Institution of the Garter*, and composed several glees and catches for entr'acte performance, some of which he sang for his benefit on 1 May, when he garnered £65 12s. profit. He is credited by Grove (but not by *The London Stage*) with music for Cumberland's after-piece *Amelia* (14 December 1771), which the *Theatrical Review* called a failure. He seems to have borrowed heavily from the theatre during the season. In the spring and summer he composed the interludes *The Brickdust Man* (with Bickerstaffe), *The Monster of the Woods* (with Hook and Fisher), and *The Palace of Mirth* for his friend Tom King, who had just become proprietor of Sadler's Wells. At that time he had a house in Peter Street, Bloomsbury.

Notwithstanding his hearty dislike of Garrick, Dibdin came publicly to his defense in 1772 when, after Bickerstaffe fled to France under the accusation of sodomy, Kenrick launched his infamous *Roscius's Lamentation for the loss of His Nyky*. In 1772–73 Dibdin continued to perform at Drury Lane—Buckskin in *The Rose*, Pandolpho in *The Wedding Ring*, a Countryman in *The Recruiting Sergeant*, and minor vocal parts in several musical entertainments. He furnished music for Messink's pantomime *Harlequin Foundling* on 26 December, and the *Westminster Maga-*

Harvard Theatre Collection

CHARLES DIBDIN, as Ralph

artist unknown

zine praised his contribution. His successful comic opera *The Wedding Ring*, purloined from Goldoni, was produced anonymously on 1 February, but the Drury Lane audience, suspecting it to be Bickerstaffe's, turned riotous until Dibdin owned his authorship. In the summer he ingratiated himself with fellow professionals by singing in Barthélemon's benefit presentation of *La zingara* at Marylebone Gardens and assuming his excellent part of Ralph in *The Maid of the Mill* at the Haymarket for the benefit of Aiken and Mrs Fearon. For his friend Tom King he wrote *The Ladle* (12 April), *The Mischance* and *The Whim-Wham* (26 July), *Vineyard Revels* (3 May), *The Grenadier* (10 August), and *The Pilgrim* (23 August). He also favored his friend the deputy manager of the Haymarket, George Alexander Stevens, by setting verses for Stevens's sketch *A Trip to Portsmouth*, "a poor rickety thing," which on 11 August perished despite Bannister's charming rendition of the songs.

Dibdin was now 28. He was earning £6 per week, plus extras for his services at Drury Lane—about the middle of the salary range for principals there—and no doubt picking up extra emoluments for published songs and evenings singing at public gardens. The high tide of his fortune carried on into the season of 1773–74 when his interlude *The Deserter*, an adaptation from Sedaine, came out on 2 November, and he contributed the music, while De Loutherbourg devised the scintillating scenery, for Garrick's extravaganza *A Christmas Tale*. But both his personal life and his relations with Garrick were worsening.

On 4 April 1774 he was again at Sadler's Wells with his *Bower of Flora* and *The Cave of Enchantment*. His *Harlequin Restor'd* was presented on 27 June and his *Cross Purposes* daily in August.

David Garrick, whose lack of an ear for music Dibdin derides in his memoir, had rejected *The Waterman* with contempt. Foote put it on at the Haymarket in the summer of 1774; it ran for 15 performances, and Garrick at once sent his brother George to charge Dibdin with disloyalty in giving it to Foote. Garrick, according to Dibdin, next commissioned from him a ballad farce, *The Cobler*, based on *La Savetier* of Sedaine, and then threw all sorts of obstacles in the way of its production. It was a success for nine nights but "on the tenth night was damned by a party." The strange feud continued: "After *The Cobler* came out, matters went on worse than ever. The more I studied to please, the less I succeeded; yet I buckled to all manner of druggery [*sic*]. If Grimaldi wanted a dance of furies, or Messink a pantomime tune, I was required to furnish it at a moment's warning."

At the beginning of the 1774–75 season

Garrick's treasurer had found Dibdin to be indebted to the theatre for some £200. Dibdin claimed that, had justice been done him in payments for his music, he would have been not only solvent but affluent. He was nevertheless "required to leave the whole of my salary in the office, at the rate of seven pounds a week, till the two hundred pounds should be liquidated." *The Quaker* was sold to Brereton for his benefit for £10, and Brereton's profits were only £36 15*s*. 6*d*. on his night, according to the account books. Garrick bought the work from Brereton for £100 and suppressed it. It did not again come out until 1777, when Garrick had left Drury Lane. Dibdin charges that Garrick stole the outline for the entertainment *May-Day; or, The Little Gipsey*.

The transcription by James Winston of the record book of the Drury Lane actors' fund shows Dibdin's premium of a guinea as having been paid in 1775. He "neg. pay." in 1776, for Garrick had discharged him from the company. Whether the open break came, as some have suggested, because of Garrick's abhorrence of Dibdin's treatment of his mistress Harriet Pitt or (as undated letters of the fall of 1775 between Dibdin and Garrick hint) because Dibdin had neglected rehearsals and had grown undependable (he defended himself against this charge in another extant letter) or because of Garrick's jealousy and caprice (as Dibdin everywhere charges) cannot now be known. It was a mutually profitable relationship and could earlier have been made much more so. In any case, Garrick now contemplated retirement. Dibdin carried the disagreement to its final stages with a spleenful pamphlet, *David Little* (which he issued then suppressed), and a puppet-play, *The Comic Mirror; or, The World as It Wags* at the Grand Saloon at Exeter Change (24 June 1775) in which Garrick was among others satirized. On the first night of the little entertainment, the toy boats stuck in the river during the spectacular view of the Ranelagh Regatta, and some of the quite large puppets—two feet, six inches high—refused to work, but being "admirably constructed" they were eventually mastered and the *Comic Mirror* ran from June to September, three times a week. The bill of fare was offered again in February and then, a few weeks later, was transferred to Marylebone Gardens.

Harried now by creditors and with no steady employment, Dibdin extracted a promise from Arnold to "superintend" any pieces he should send and with several of his illegitimate children flew to France, where he remained for two years. During his stormy 13-hours' outward passage to Calais, Dibdin wrote the popular sea song "Blow High, Blow Low," which was a prominent feature of his next comic opera, *The Seraglio*, produced (though much altered) by Thomas Harris at Covent Garden on 14 November 1776. He remained five months at Calais, avoiding the English locals, whom he describes as a set of absconding financiers, duellists, smugglers, bankrupts, "and Morgan, the highwayman." The theatrical innkeeper Desien sponsored him socially and helped liberate his piano from the customs. He then took his brood to the provincial city of Nancy. He had left behind at Drury Lane the music for Henry Bate's (later Sir Henry Bate Dudley) *The Blackamoor Wash'd White*, and it was produced on 1 February 1776 to violent ructions. The Hopkins diary notes: "Much hissing and Crying out no more no more . . . as soon as the Blackamoor was given out for the next Night they kept a great Noise and call'd for another Farce to be given out—." The disturbance recurred on the second and third nights.

Dibdin contributed his usual trio to Sadler's Wells for the spring and summer: *The Sister Witches; or, Mirth and Magic* on 8 April, *The Impostors; or, All is Not Gold that Glitters* on 13 May, and *The Mountebank* on 29 July. As was becoming customary in his work at the minor houses, Dibdin wrote both words and music for

these. His *Metamorphosis*, based on Molière's *Le Sicilien* and *Georges Dandin*, were offered at the Haymarket on 26, 27, 29, and 30 September 1776. Still *in absentia*, he sent his *The Razor Grinder* (21 April 1777) to Tom King at Sadler's Wells and gave him also *Yo Yeah; or, The Friendly Tars* (18 August). His burletta, *Poor Vulcan*, suffering the weakening alterations of Thomas Hull and enjoying musical interpolations by Arne and Arnold, came out at Covent Garden on 4 February 1778 and earned him a much-needed £200. He seems also to have furnished John Ellis of the Patagonian puppet theatre with a sketch called *Macaroni* in March 1778. Moreover, he sent two more offerings to Sadler's Wells—*She Is Mad for a Husband* (20 April) and *The Old Woman of Eighty* (1 June).

In June 1778, evicted from France because of impending hostilities, Dibdin returned to England, engaging at once with Harris to write three afterpieces or the equivalent for £300 during the season of 1778–79. He next wrote the libretto for the comic opera *The Gipsies*, based on *La Bohémienne* by Charles Simon Favart. Arnold set it to music and it was produced at the Haymarket on 3 August 1778. For 18 September he wrote both words and music of the comic opera *Rose and Colin*, based on *Rose et Colas* by Michel Jean Sedaine, and also *The Wives Revenged*, based on *Les Femmes Vengées* by Favart, and on 2 October, *Annette and Lubin*, based on a French work of the same title by Favart and de Santerre. Despite the "rooted dislike" and "ineffable pity and sovereign contempt" which Dibdin openly professed for the French, he evidently had put to practical use his stay in their country and his acquisition of their language. He had, he says, completed six operas and farces—little more than thefts to which he added music—before landing at Dover, his aim being, in time, "an epitome of the comic-opera in France."

In the seasons 1778–79 through 1781–

82 he was carried on the roster of Covent Garden as composer to the theatre at £10 per week. On 14 October 1778 *The Medley; or, Harlequin At-All,* by Messink, carried new music by Dibdin. On 4 January 1779 he contributed *The Touchstone; or Harlequin Traveller,* a pantomime; on 6 May *The Chelsea Pensioner,* a comic opera. Early that season Dibdin had become more and more disenchanted with Harris but had become reconciled with Garrick, "with infinite pleasure." Garrick had attended some rehearsals of *The Touchstone,* including "an evening-repetition a night or two before its appearance. It was the last time he ever was on a stage . . ." Dibdin wrote the music for Edward Neville's musical farce *Plymouth in an Uproar* for 20 October 1779, the pantomime *The Mirror; or, Harlequin Everywhere* for 30 November, and the comic opera *The Shepherdess of the Alps* (based on J. F. Marmontel's *La bergère des Alps*) for 18 January 1780.

Uneasy in his relationship with Covent Garden, Dibdin resolved to act upon the invitation of his brother, now "master-attendant at Nagore" and a wealthy man, to join him in India. But at this juncture, he says:

I was informed by Sir Thomas Rumbold [his brother's patron], that my brother had been struck with lightning; in consequence of which he had lost the use of one side; and that, having gathered his fortune together, which he assured me was very considerable, he had embarked for England, with his wife, and his infant son, but could hold out no further than the Cape of Good Hope, where he died.

For that moment then, and for some time afterward, Dibdin was forced to remain with Harris, though he rebelled to the extent of trying an independent venture at the Haymarket (usually dark at that time of the year) on 1 March 1780. He fell in with a suggestion—"an absurd scheme"—

to revive his puppet show *The Comic Mirror,* so

with puppets, Chinese Shadows, and other vehicles, a performance was got up, called *Pasquin's Budget* . . . which could not but fail at the Haymarket; for, though both the Bannisters performed . . . it was impossible to hear a single syllable; and, to make all sure, a celebrated equestrian instructed one of his people, an Italian, to apply for an engagement to conduct the *ombres chinois,* not forgetting to give him previous orders to spoil everything he undertook.

The audience, most of whom had mistaken the bills to mean that all the actors would be human, rioted and nearly destroyed the interior of Colman's theatre. He disclaimed any responsibility for the production, and Dibdin was forced onstage to make an apology.

Dibdin staged *The Surprise* as his only offering at Sadler's Wells that spring, on 17 April 1780. He went back to Covent Garden in the fall and there presented a series of his pieces: *The Islanders* (25 November 1780, a comic opera abridged the next year as *The Marriage Act*); *Harlequin Freemason* (a pantomime, "the tricks" devised by the machinist Messink, the songs by Dibdin, 29 December 1780); and the burletta *Jupiter and Alcmena* (based on John Dryden's *Amphitryon,* the music by Dibdin and Shield), by which Dibdin ultimately realized £285, 27 October 1781. *Jupiter and Alcmena* was an abject financial failure for Harris and his theatre, and the thin fabric of mutual tolerance between Dibdin and Harris parted.

Dibdin turned next to the equestrian theatre, the popularity of which Astley had now successfully demonstrated to the "legitimate" managers. Moving to the Surrey side of Blackfriar's Bridge, where the jurisdiction of the Lord Chamberlain over theatrical affairs did not extend, he entered into a partnership with Col West, the son of Vice Admiral Temple West, and some other inexperienced amateurs, to erect an amphitheatre on ground controlled by West. Though the Surrey magistrates had granted no license, Dibdin set about finding a company, his idea being "to have a stage on which might be represented spectacles, each to terminate with a just [*sic*] or tilting-match, or some other grand object, so managed as to form a novel, and striking *coup-de-theatre . . .* that the business of the stage and ring might be united."

The Royal Circus and Philharmonic Academy opened in November 1782. But Charles Hughes, who was supposed to manage only the equestrian business, and Grimaldi, whose province was only the pantomimes, according to Dibdin had sinister designs on the whole amphitheatre: "While the leech Hughes, was sucking the blood of the proprietors, and fastening on the concern, the serpent Grimaldi, was coiled up till a proper opportunity should arrive to seize the management." Dibdin attributes to their machinations the fact that, after the sudden death of his ally West, "after most unexampled industry . . . I was accused, and found guilty of flagrant neglect, and voted out of that concern which had derived all its consequence from me, and which, but for me, would never have had existence."

But Dibdin seems to have been adept both at making enemies and at self-justification, and it is hard to avoid the conclusion that the wreck of the Royal Circus was in large measure the fault of his grandiose plan. He had assembled, in addition to equestrians, musicians, and adult performers of all kinds, "A number of children, not less, I believe, than sixty," presided over by a schoolmaster and a schoolmistress. "Thus," he says, "had I formed a seminary to mature actors and actresses for the theatre." But the cost of this "nursery for the stage, like the schools of Oudinet, and Nicholet, at Paris," along with the scenery and costumes of the "grand ballets," may have caused the proprietors to "cut up the scheme" and exclude him despite a season of five months in which, Dibdin asserted,

£9500 came into the house. During that season and the next, he said, the following pieces by him were put on: *The Barrier of Parnassus, The Saloon, The Milkmaid, The Refusal of Harlequin, The Land of Simplicity, The Passions, The Statue, The Benevolent Tar, The Regions of Accomplishment, Pandora, Tom Thumb* (none of which are listed by Nicoll), *The Lancashire Witches, The Cestus, The Long Odds,* and *Clump and Cudden. Harlequin the Phantom of a Day* was also produced at the Royal Circus in 1783. In addition, he says, "two or three pantomimes; four or five other *intermezzos* of a more trifling kind; and, at least, fifteen ballets, each taking twelve or fourteen airs; and an overture; and a variety of things more inconsiderable, make up what I did for that strange, and to me very unfortunate place." Grove lists at the Royal Circus in 1783 and 1784 in addition to those above, given by Dibdin in his *Life* and found by us in other sources, the following: (1783) *The Temple of Confusius, Rus in Urbe or Jack in the Green, The Passions, The Quakers, The Talisman, Robin Hood, La Melange Universal, The Sicilian Peasants, The Graces, Sappho,* and *A Breaking Up;* (1784) *The Olive Branch,* and *The Magic of Orasmantes.*

After the Surrey magistrates abruptly closed the theatre Hughes obtained a license for himself. Dibdin went to law for his share of the moveables, but evidently unsuccessfully. (He seems to have been imprisoned briefly for debt in 1783.) He composed, nevertheless, for the Royal Circus from time to time for years.

Linley was well entrenched as principal composer at Drury Lane. Nevertheless Dibdin contrived to have his own comic opera *Liberty Hall* produced as an afterpiece at the house on 8 February 1785, and it played ten times that spring. But despite assiduous efforts his *A Game at Commerce, or, The Rooks Pigeoned* was rejected everywhere he sent it.

By now Dibdin's affairs must have been

fairly desperate, for except for the *Liberty Hall* success and perhaps a few sales of songs he was during the 1784–85 season "completely turned . . . out of the theatres" and thus was "ripe for any feasible adventure that might offer." The Clerkenwell architect, brick-maker, and trading justice Jacob Leroux at this juncture brought him a proposal to build a theatre "not far from Pancras . . . where has since been created Pentonville, and Somer's-Town." Ever optimistic, Dibdin "planted poplars, and went on with a good deal of spirit."

I staked out my ground; planned my building; and took advantage of a very fine piece of water, on which I placed my best dependance, having intended to produce the effect of my grandest spectacles through the medium of hydraulics. . . . My entertainments were all to have been classical, and, therefore, I named the place *Helicon*.

Despite many promises, a license was refused. At that time also Dibdin's mother died and while he was in Southampton for her funeral, "A letter from town . . . informed me that a gale of wind, on the very night that the mail-coach conveyed me to Southampton, had annihilated Helicon." By the time he returned to London Leroux had removed and sold all the fallen timbers. Dibdin was out some £290.

Soon after those disasters he was incautious enough to provide to Daly, the despicable Dublin manager, musical works to the value of £600. Daly bilked him of £460 in the transaction, paying only £140 and returning none of the music. Perhaps some of it was employed in Joseph Atkinson's *A Match for a Widow*, at Smock Alley Theatre on 17 April 1786.

Dibdin repaired to the country, began a novel, wrote some songs, saw his *The Fortune Hunters* come out at Sadler's Wells on 17 July, junketed through the countryside, and began to publish "a hebdomadal work, called *The Devil*," of which 4,000 copies were sold in a day. He found it impossible

to carry on without a "confederacy," and (of course) the confederacy "betrayed me; they connived at a counter publication," and after 21 numbers Dibdin gave over. In 1786 he achieved the distinction of being imitated by G. S. Carey in the latter's *Lecture on Mimicry*. His *Harlequin Conjuror* was featured at the Royal Circus on 9 April; his spectacular *England Against Italy* was featured at Sadler's Wells on 30 April. *Harvest Home* was produced on 16 May 1787 at the Haymarket on the eve of his departure on a 14-month campaign offering solo musical entertainment to Worcester, Leeds, Liverpool, Litchfield, Huntington, Nottingham, Oxford, Ipswich, Colchester, Cambridge, Hereford, Hull, York, Durham, Grantham, Bury, Yarmouth, Norwich, and Lincoln. His purpose was, he said, "to bid adieu to a generous public, who have afforded me a long and liberal patronage"—for he had decided once more to go to India. In May 1787 *The Deception* and *The Maid's Disaster* and in June 1788 his musical farce *Lovely Nancy, or, The Miller's Grist* were presented at the Royal Circus.

An account of his *Musical Tour* seen through the press in the summer of 1788, a final quarrel with Thomas Harris over a manuscript now behind him, and the bailiffs once more on his heels, he sold a few songs for what he could get and set sail for India. But he never got closer than Dunkirk. Heavy weather forced his bark (he quarrelled with the captain) into Torbay, and he made his way back to London to face threatening creditors.

In 1789, taking lodgings near the Old Bailey, he set up in Hutchins's Auction Room, King Street, Covent Garden, a series of "table entertainments," one-man shows of narration, singing, and playing, under the general title *The Whim of the Moment*. On his opening evening only 16 people came in. He could not get his excellent song "Poor Jack" published and so sold it with 11 other songs for £60. "Scarcely had I parted with it a fortnight," he laments typically, "when it began to spread itself over the kingdom. . . . it may be safely averred, that it has cleared the purchaser five hundred pounds." This statement is in direct contradiction to the following testimony by E. Beresford Chancellor in his *The Annals of Covent Garden*:

Charles Dibdin began his entertainment called *London Amusements*. One of the items was the famous song *Poor Jack*, and so popular was this that it was not only regularly and vociferously encored when given, but copies could hardly be printed quickly enough to meet the demand for them. This being so, Dibdin—I may as well give J. T. Smith's actual words—"Dibdin actually hired a stall, which then stood close to the Piazza in Russell Street . . . being large enough for Wood, his man, to stand in to deliver out the songs. The crowd and scramble to get them, even wet from the press, was such, that I have seen persons fight for their turn."

Dibdin then moved to the Lyceum and began to bring out his *Oddities*, which were very successful. He contrived to furnish farces as well for the Royal Circus: *The What Is It?*, altered from Gay's *What D'Ye Call It* for 4 May and *The Spirit of Fancy; or, I Don't Know What* for 20 May. During this period he again tried periodical journalism, with his *The Bystander; or, Universal Weekly Expositor* (22 numbers from 15 August 1789 to 6 February 1790) but gave that up because he "grew most intolerably sick of a traffic with music-shops."

But from about 1790 Dibdin's life seems to have settled into a more even tempo. His was one of the principal hands in the Wargrave Theatricals of 1790–91. He revised his *Oddities* and the show ran for 79 nights. His *Wags* was performed for 109 nights. He brought out *The Fortune Hunters* at Sadler's Wells on 13 April 1789, *Private Theatricals*, *Tippoo Saib* (with Hook), and *The Quizzes* in 1791, *The Recruiting Manager* (at Sadler's Wells) and *Coalition* in

Harvard Theatre Collection

CHARLES DIBDIN, at the Sans Souci

artist unknown

1792, *Castles in the Air* in 1793, and *Will of the Wisp* in 1794. Also to 1794, apparently, belong *Nature in Nubibus* and *Great News*, at the Royal Circus, and *A Loyal Effusion*, at Covent Garden; in 1795 *Quaverina and Crotchetini* was at Sadler's Wells.

In 1791 he had left the Lyceum for a room at No 411, opposite Beaufort Buildings, in the Strand, which he called the Sans Souci. He was there into 1795. In the winter of 1795 Dibdin published his three-volume novel *Hannah Hewit; or, the Female Crusoe*, reputed to contain the life of his brother Thomas as "Captain Higgins," and *The Younger Brother*, three volumes, and produced his interlude *Christmas Gambols*. In 1796 he erected a house to shelter his second Sans Souci Theatre. Since this little house is rarely even mentioned by theatre historians, it may be well to quote extensively from "a daily paper" as it was quoted by the *How Do You Do*, No 7, of 22 October 1796, particularly as it introduces us to still another facet of Dibdin's talents, his sketching, and also since we know the *How Do You Do* (eight numbers, 30 July–5 November 1796) to have been written by Dibdin and the actor F. G. Waldron:

On Saturday evening that enterprising genius, Mr. DIBDIN, opened his entertainment for the season, under the title of *The General Election*, in a building erected for the purpose in Leicester-Place, Leicester-Fields; and when we recollect that not one brick of the new building was laid till after the month of June last had commenced, the mere side walls standing at the time, it is a matter of admiration that a dwelling-house, on rather a large scale, and the *New Sans Souci* behind it, should have been got up in the time; the latter is completely finished, and fitted up in a stile of peculiar neatness and elegance. The shell of the dwelling house is meant to stand all the winter before the inside-work is gone on with. The situation of *Sans Souci* is certainly changed considerably for the better, as the wide expanse of Leicester-Fields is much better adapted for the commodious disposition of the carriages of the Nobility and Gentry, than the confined limits of the narrowest part of the Strand. The passages to the boxes, area, and gallery, are convenient and comfortable, and they will be still more so when the covered colonade, which we understand is to range along the whole front of the building is put up. The interior of *Sans Souci* presents, literally speaking, a most picturesque appearance, being decorated with a number of paintings from the pencil of Mr. DIBDIN, who unites in his own person the character of a votary to the Sister Arts, and equally divides his time in the exercise and composition of Painting, Poetry, and Music. His pictures are chiefly landscape of character, and prove him to be no mean artist. His subjects are well selected, and his manner of disposing and finishing

them evinces a considerable share of fancy, taste, and skill. In the two largest pieces are figures from the masterly hand of STODDART. When the curtain draws up, the stage presents the interior of an elegant tent, with the front and back parts of it open, so that Mr. DIBDIN appears to stand within it, while the back view presents a perspective of a garden scene, enriched with a temple and a sheet of water.

The critic of the *Monthly Mirror* was contemptuous:

The decorations of the new room are tawdry and effeminate. The *paintings*, all from the pencil of Mr. Dibdin, except two or three figures by an *artist*, form quite a *picture gallery*: there is *spring*, and *summer*, and *autumn*, and *winter*, and *morning*, and *evening*, and various other landscapes, which Pether and Freebairn, Farringdon and Sir George Beaumont, we hope, will inspect the first opportunity, for they may rely upon it there never was seen *any thing like them* before. 'Ut pictura poesis.' Mr. Dibdin is assuredly as good a *poet* as he is a *painter*.

Dibdin remained at the second Sans Souci for 10 years, producing there and elsewhere such entertainments as *Datchet Mead* (1796), *The Sphinx* and *The Goose and the Gridiron* (1797); a dramatization of his novel (at Drury Lane) *Hannah Hewitt* (1799); *King and Queen, The Vanguard; or, British Tars Regaling after a Battle* (Covent Garden) and *Tom Wilkins* (1799); *The Cake House* and (at Covent Garden) *The Siege of Acre* (1800); *A Frisk* (1801); *Most Votes* (1802); *Britons Strike Home* (1803); *Valentine's Day, The Election, The Frolic*, and *A Trip to the Coast* (1804); and *Heads and Tails* and *Cecilia* (1805). As insubstantial and hastily contrived as most of these offerings were, each contributed a fresh augmentation to his by now enormous stock of songs, for the "entertainments" were really little more than a series of ditties, sung by Dibdin himself and strung together by a thread of jocularity and anecdote told in his winsome and graceful style.

The Public Record Office has records of licenses granted Dibdin yearly from 1792 through 1808 "for Recitative Singing & Music by himself only" three times a week, except on Christmas Eve and Day, 30 January, Ash Wednesday, and Passion Week. He usually accompanied himself on the piano, but he also evolved what the Edinburgh *Courant* described (when Dibdin took the Sans Souci bill north in 1799) as "an organised instrument, which has the properties of a band" and which he could operate alone. But his amazing fecundity and quick facility at turning out songs was the driving force of whatever success he had. He was not uniformly successful in the eyes of all critics, however, and by 1797 the strain of constant performance was beginning to exact its toll, both on his delivery and his inventiveness. The *Monthly Mirror* was especially harsh to some of his performances, though the journal praised others. The issue of October 1797 condemned his *Sphinx* (7 October 1797 at the Sans Souci) as dull and insipid, employing music Dibdin had used before. Moreover:

His voice and articulation are considerably worse this year than we have observed them heretofore. These however may have been injured by the ravages of time, and therefore may be mentioned without reprobation, but the manner in which he blunders and flounders through the whole of his amusement deserves, nightly, the execration and the hisses of the audience.

Throughout those Sans Souci years Dibdin pushed many projects, setting about writing *A Complete History of the English Stage* (5 vols., 1800); overseeing, as his own publisher, the distribution of his songs and the books of the play frequently hawked at the theatres; composing an epitaph for his friend the actor William Parsons (1795); acting at Tunbridge

Wells in 1797; becoming a shareholder at Sadler's Wells in 1802. In 1798 he took a second tour, a circuit of Kent and Sussex, and to exploit it devised *A Tour To Land's End*. In 1799 he showed his theatrical wares at Bath and Bristol. In 1800 he made still another trip of above 1800 miles "during which time I visited forty-three places, including Edinburgh and Glasgow, my route being through Northamptonshire, Leicestershire, Derbyshire, Lancashire, Westmoreland, and Cumberland into Scotland; and, on my return, through Northumberland, Durham, Yorkshire, Lincolnshire, Norfolk, Suffolk, and Essex." On the way he gestated his next winter's entertainment *Tom Wilkins* and sketched many natural scenes.

In 1801 he was on the road again and covered most of lowland and highland Scotland and northern England. The results were his next entertainment, *The Cakehouse*, and also *Observations of a Tour Through . . . Scotland and England* (2 vols, 1801–2) containing his own and his daughter's pencil sketches and dedicated, rather presumptuously, to the renowned classical cameo sculptor and draughtsman John Flaxman. Dibdin boasted in false-modest terms that "Sir Joshua Reynolds saw a strange daubing by me, in which he however discovered something he liked, and, at the instance of Goldsmith, he lent me several capital landscapes to copy." Eight pictures which Dibdin painted on the latter tour were exhibited at Somerset House in 1801. The following summer he took one last tour, to visit his friend Sheldon "on the river Ex," and to Plymouth, Portsmouth, and the Isle of Wight, determining on the way to prepare one last entertainment, *The Frisk*, and then retire. But he could find no suitable offers for his premises or his theatrical stock, and so, a general election being then fought, he satirized it in *Most Votes* in 1802. At that point also Dibdin put the finishing touches on the strange combination apology for his life and collection of the words of 600 of his songs, published in 1803 as *The Professional Life of Mr Dibdin*.

In June 1803 the government had granted this "Tyrtaeus of the British Navy" a pension of £200 *per annum* for his nearly 100 sea songs which, it was said, did more to bring in recruits than did all the press gangs together. In 1805 he sold his stock and copyright to Bland and Weller, the Oxford Street music sellers, for £1800, left his theatre in Leicester Place, and retired to Cranford. On 8 February 1806 he produced his last piece at Drury Lane, *Broken Gold*.

But Dibdin's pension was withdrawn by the Grenville ministry in 1806 and, though failing in strength and voice, he was forced back to the Lyceum. In 1807 he published a novel, *Henry Hooka*. At the Lyceum in 1808 he produced the entertainments *Professional Volunteers*, *The Rent Day*, *A Thanksgiving*, and *Commodore Pennant*. He also opened a music shop opposite the theatre, but it quickly failed. The accounts of the Public Record Office show that he was in 1808 granted a license "for Song Recitation and Music" at the Sans Pareil Theatre for an unstated period and at "a Music Room in his house in the Strand" for the period 14 December to 14 June 1809. These were his last attempts at minstrelsy.

In 1810 a public subscription dinner promoted by the Earl of Dartmouth and supported by numbers of London musicians raised £653, of which he received £80 at once, the rest being invested in annuities for him and his family. He was then, and until his death, resident in Arlington Street, Camden Town.

In 1811 he wrote the music for *The Round Robin*, for which his son furnished the libretto. They put in on the stage of the Haymarket on 21 June and it failed abysmally.

Dibdin was stricken with paralysis in 1813. He died at the age of 69, on 25 July 1814, and was buried in the ground owned by St Martin-in-the-Fields in Pratt Street, Camden Town. A slab over his grave, placed by his wife, bore the lines from his great song "Tom Bowling" (which were said to have been intended to describe his brother Thomas):

His form was of the manliest beauty;
His heart was kind and Soft,
Faithful below he did his duty,
And now he's gone aloft.

A will he signed on 24 November 1798 at Leicester Place, Leicester Square, and in which he defined himself "music seller," left all his estate and effects unspecified to his wife and executrix Ann. An amendment of 16 June 1808 specified his daughter Ann as residuary legatee. The will was proved by Ann Dibdin, widow, on 25 October 1814.

Details of Dibdin's domestic life, which he carefully avoided in his voluminous biographical writings, are obscure and disputed. In 1768 William Hickey witnessed and later recorded in his memoirs a savage fight between two women of the town in a drinking den called Wetherby's. One, named Miss Burgess (who on another occasion he says "sang admirable songs"), "lived for several years afterwards with Dibdin, the actor, who had just at the above period commenced his theatrical career in the character of Hodge in the comic opera of *The Maid of the Mill*." But Dibdin's triumph as Ralph had begun early in 1765. In any case Dibdin's extended affair with the dancer Harriet Pitt (d. 1814) produced Charles Isaac Mungo Pitt in 1768. In 1771 Thomas John Dibdin was born to the couple. There may have been other children as well. By 1775 Garrick is said to have become sufficiently indignant at Dibdin's treatment of his family to discharge the singer from the Drury Lane company. Harriet Pitt later acted under the name of Davenett. A manuscript note in the hand of James Winston, in the Folger Library, reads:

Extract of a Letter from Mrs Davenett to
Const [?]

Dibdin was ever a thoughtless man, a false
and [illeg.] pride—always lived beyond his
means—which obliged him when distressed to
raise money on his own prop^y. Mr. David
Garrick offered to take the affairs in hand
(The public papers having spoke of his ill
treatment to me) & make him do me justice.
I refused, thinking time would convince him
of his impropriety towards me & his child—
Ap 30, 1790—

John Woodfall Ebsworth states in *The
Dictionary of National Biography* that by
the time of that discharge Charles Dibdin
had "transferred himself and his truant
affections to a Miss Anne Maria Wylde, of
Portsea, probably a relation of James Wild,
the prompter, but was unable to marry her
until long afterwards, when his first wife
died." In a short "Early Life" chapter
supplied to the *Memoirs of Charles Dibdin
the Younger*, the editor of that work,
George Speaight, says that "When he was
only twenty two [1767?], Charles Dibdin
abandoned his wife and formed a liaison
with Harriet Pitt." But we know of no evidence for a marriage before the liaison with
Harriet Pitt. Moreover, the relationship of
Dibdin and Harriet Pitt has always been
considered irregular and was doubtless so,
although there seem to have been genteel
efforts in later generations to rewrite that
history. Thus, Harriet can scarcely have
been an impediment to a marriage with
Miss Wyld.

Harriet Pitt earlier had lived with
George Mattocks the actor and by him had
produced at least two other children. There
was Cecil Pitt, who played in the band at
Sadler's Wells in 1803 during the management of his half-brother Charles Dibdin
the younger, and Cecil's sister Harriet the
dancer, whom Arundell describes as fat and
who usually came on as the last of the
figurantes and in the crowd scenes. Pinks
in his *History of Clerkenwell* says that during this time "the mother and sister" of
Charles the younger and Thomas Dibdin

lived in an old building called the Goose
Farm, next door to the Angel Inn in St
John Street, Clerkenwell. He also reports
that the sister (presumably Harriet: "a
short squat figure") died in Clerkenwell
Poor House. Their mother had by 1793
taken the stage name "Mrs Davenett."

Charles Dibdin's wife Ann Wyld Dibdin
(1757–1835) gave him at least one child,
who, according to John Britton's *Autobiography*, was still living in 1850, was
then Mrs Dacre, and was "preparing for
publication" a memoir of her father, which
does not seem to have been finished. There
was perhaps also a second daughter by Ann
Wyld Dibdin, for Mrs Dibdin signed a will
on 7 July 1834 leaving her property, unspecified, to her daughter (Mrs.) Anne
Jane, widow, "with whom I am now residing." The residuary legatee was "Cecilia
Ann Frances Jane who now lives with her
mother." She was the granddaughter of
Mrs Dibdin. Did Mrs Jane, still "widow"
when she proved the will on 30 April
1836, later become Mrs Dacre?

Charles Dibdin the elder was the very
epitome of the popular showman, scram-
bling always for subsistence, often caught
between more powerful and conflicting theatrical interests, the toast of the taverns,
perpetually flying before creditors. In the
Folger Library is an undated letter from
Bickerstaffe to Mrs Garrick asking her to
intercede with her husband for Dibdin,
"this poor, unthinking young man . . ." If
she should do so "I am almost positive they
[the managers?] would not have any more
trouble from the same quarter; his wants
really now arising from the sole unfortunate circumstance of his Benefit, & his
having furnished a house on the strength of
his hopes from it. An hundred pound will
entirely set him free . . ." He never was
set entirely free from this anxiety, and
though he made a great deal of money for
himself, in John Britton's words, he was
"ill-versed in the science of domestic economy, or the art of saving money."

Dibdin's defensive autobiographical writings make him seem tense, quarrelsome, mock-modest, and self-justifying, even when allowances are made for his misfortunes. But onstage Dibdin had a broad and proletarian appeal, hearty, sentimental, and friendly. John O'Keeffe remembered that

Dibdin's manner of coming on the stage was in happy style; he ran on sprightly, and with nearly a laughing face, like a friend who enters hastily to impart to you some good news. . . . A few lines of speaking happily introduced his admirable songs, full of wit and character, and his peculiar mode of singing them surpassed all I had ever heard.

W. B. Wood recollected that "without other assistance" he "was enabled to furnish an evening's entertainment, scarcely excelled in after days by Mathew's [sic] wonderful dramatic feats."

Not all critics endorsed him. In *The Dramatic Censor* (1770) Francis Gentleman voiced a minority opinion on Dibdin's portrayal of Ralph in *Maid of the Mill*: "Whatever merit Mr Didbin may have in composition, he certainly has not the shadow of any in acting; wherefore, we are hardy enough to say, the young miller could scarce have fallen into worse hands." And Gentleman later jingled in *The Theatres* (1772)

Dibdin, alas! we nearly had forgot,
Perhaps oblivion were the kindest lot:
How he composes, 'tis not fit, we say,
But grant kind stars that he may never
      play
Nor, to enlarge our wish, may ever sing;
Mungo in this, in that, in ev'ry thing.

However, that opinion came well before the height of Dibdin's popularity either as a singer or a composer-librettist. Such critical dissidents were soon whelmed under by the deluge of Dibdin's songs, dramatic and musical stage productions, and his thousands of personal appearances before delighted audiences.

The bibliography of Charles Dibdin the elder can scarcely ever be considered complete. To the attributions of major stage offerings furnished by Dibdin himself, Allardyce Nicoll's "Handlists," *The London Stage*, Alfred Loewenberg in *Grove's Dictionary*, and the British Museum's *Catalogue of Printed Music*, we have added, above, a few from other sources. But his torrent of "entertainments," as well as his comic operas, pantomimes, farces, spectacles, reviews, and burlettas produced at least 900 songs which he claimed as his own. No attempt has been made here to list them. Dibdin privately published a great many of his songs himself. In addition, he brought out, or other publishers brought out for him, many collections of the words and music of his ballads. He also left behind in manuscript form a number of librettos.

Dibdin continued to paint, and Redgrave says that there were "some pleasing views of Lake scenery, which were engraved in aqua tint by John Hill." He is said also to have assisted in scene painting. There is in the Harvard Theatre Collection his original drawing of the interior of the Sans Souci Theatre.

In addition, the indefatigable Dibdin was a teacher of singing (Mrs Mountain was one of his pupils) and a pedagogical author. Grove credits him with *A Letter on Musical Education* (1791); *Music Epitomized*; *The Musical Mentor, or St. Cecilia at School* (1808); and *The English Pythagoras, or Every Man His own Music Master* (1808). He published also several volumes of "poetry" and some ephemeral pamphlets.

The following likenesses of the elder Charles Dibdin are known:

1. Portrait, oil on canvas, by S. J. Arnold. In the Garrick Club.

2. By W. Beechey, oil, location not now known. (British Museum *Catalogue of Engraved British Portraits* cites a photogravure from this painting, plate to a pamphlet by W. Roberts, 1922.)

3. Engraving by B. Smith, after J. Kearsley.

4. By John Opie, oil. Exhibited at Grosvenor Gallery, 1888, and sold at Christie's 29 May 1897 (Sir John Pender's sale); "bought by Tooth."

5. Engraved portrait, B. Smith after T. Kearsley; frontispiece to *The Professional Life of Mr. Dibdin*, 1803. The same picture was engraved by J. Heath and published by Longman, Hurst, Rees & Orme, 1809; an anonymous copy was published without date, and a reversed copy was engraved by C. Phillips.

6. Engraved portrait, by W. Ridley after S. De Wilde; published by T. Bellamy, 1794.

7. Portrait by an anonymous engraver after Dighton; printed for Bowles & Carver, 1794.

8. Portrait by an anonymous engraver after S. Drummond. Plate to the *European Magazine*, 1809.

9. Portrait engraved by B. Smith after J. Kearsley, published by B. Smith and J. P. Thompson, 1801. An anonymous engraver reversed the plate for *The Thespian Dictionary*, 1805.

10. Portrait engraved by J. Young, after T. Phillips, 1799. Same picture, vignetted, engraved by W. Greatbach as a plate to Hogarth's *Memoirs of the Musical Drama*, 1838. Same picture, vignette, engraved by A. Dick. Same, engraved by G. Stodart.

11. "Performing at the Sans Souci," Dibdin seated at the piano. Anonymous. Undated.

12. As Mungo in *The Padlock*, engraved by B. Clowes. Printed for Carington Bowles.

13. As Mungo. Plate to *Dramatic Characters . . . in the Days of Garrick*. Published by R. Sayer.

14. As Mungo. Plate to the *Political Register*.

15. As Ralph in *Maid of the Mill*. Published by J. Bew, 1779.

16. "A Lyceum Oddity or Stop Him Who Can!" "C. W. *fecit* / Dublin, Publish'd Octr 1. 1788," caricatures Dibdin.

17. "Attic Miscellany. A Musico-Oratorical Portrait," engraved by "Annabal Scratch," published by Bentley & Co., March 1791, caricatures Dibdin.

18. There is an engraving of a picture of Charles Dibdin's tomb in the Harvard Theatre Collection.

Dibdin, Mrs Charles. *See* PITT, HARRIET.

Dibdin, Charles Isaac Mungo *1768–1833, actor, singer, manager, playwright.*

Charles Isaac Mungo Dibdin was born on 27 October 1768 in Russell Court, the elder of two illegitimate sons of Charles Dibdin by his connection with the actress Harriet Pitt (d. 1814). The curious name derived from his father's friendship with Isaac Bickerstaffe the playwright and fame in the character of Mungo in Bickerstaffe's farce *The Padlock*. The names of Charles and a younger brother, Thomas John (1771–1841) have sometimes been oddly conflated to produce a "Charles John Dibdin," as on some late portraits, but the reference is always to Charles I. M. Dibdin, or "Charles the younger," as he was usually called in his day. Charles also had a half-brother Cecil and a half-sister Harriet, illegitimate children of their mother by the actor George Mattocks. They took their mother's surname Pitt. Particulars of Dibdin's life from his birth to within three years of his death are set forth in a lengthy memoir which was discovered only recently and edited by George Speaight for the Society of Theatre Research in 1956.

The elder Charles was discharged by Garrick from the Drury Lane company at the end of the 1774–75 season at least in part because of his desertion of Harriet Pitt and her sons (both of whom had already been onstage, walking in the procession in the 1775 revival of the Shakespeare *Jubilee*). But the youngsters were soon snatched from their theatrical environment by a disapproving great-uncle, Cecil Pitt, a wealthy City goods broker, and kept away from the theatre and from both parents for many years.

Charles was treated as an adopted son and, under the name Pitt, was sent to school, first at Hackney, and then near Durham, where he imbibed rudimentary classics and contracted an enthusiasm for modern literature. At 14 he was bound apprentice to a kindly pawnbroker, a Mr Cordy of Snow Hill, and served the normal apprenticeship of seven years plus seven more as Cordy's shopman. Dibdin began to write for minor literary magazines, and in 1792 he published by subscription his first book, *Poetical Attempts: by a Young Man.* Other works followed: *Investigation, a Poem,* 1792; *The Age: a Satire,* 1793; and *The Royal Cradle,* 1796, to celebrate the birth of Princess Charlotte. In 1796 he was involved for a few months as joint proprietor of *The Cabinet Magazine.* C. I. Pitt was the name under which he published up to that time.

Charles was nearly 29 when he succumbed simultaneously to his aversion to pawnbroking and to the attraction of the theatre. His master Cordy generously gave him his blessing and a year's wages. His brother Tom was already stage manager at Sadler's Wells, having given up his own preparation for trade at the age of eighteen.

For his first foray into the profession, Charles wrote, "I proposed to myself to start in London with an entertainment, in the nature of those with which my father had so long entertained the Town . . ." Unlike his father, who had composed most of the music, as well as the words, to his songs, Charles "compiled" the tunes from various composers but principally from James Sanderson. He called his first entertainment *Sans Six Sous,* a play on *Sans Souci,* his father's theatre, and an allusion to his own poverty. Sanderson rented the Royalty Theatre and engaged Dibdin to present his entertainment for three guineas a week on a trial basis.

Dibdin came on, fortified by claret and the presence in the house of his old master with a claque of pawnbrokers. He was tongue-tied with apprehension but managed to deliver a disarming address. His "alternation of monologue and song" proved too long for his impatient audience, but he reduced it by two-thirds and on the last five nights of his week "came off with flying colours."

On 14 June 1797, he wrote, he was "united, at St. George's Hanover Square, to Miss Mary Bates, with whom, the previous summer I had met behind the scenes of Sadler's Wells Theatre . . ." The marriage register of the church, however, shows the marriage between "Charles Isaac Pitt & Mary Bates" to have been celebrated on 13 June.

Charles was now married, in debt for £200 "to Publishers, Printers and others," and without employment. He devised a pantomime ("my heroes Don Quixote and Sancho Panca, whom I transformed to Harlequin and Clown. It consisted of 24 Scenes. I invented all the mechanical changes and pantomime tricks; made models of them in pasteboard and coloured them"). Then he set off to the Amphitheatre of the Arts to try to sell his invention to the Astleys. They gave him five guineas, a discouraging reward for the six weeks the work had taken. But the contact led to auditions and three-year engagements for both Charles and Mary. The sharp-dealing Astley, recognizing desperation, offered only three guineas a week for both performers.

I was, moreover, bound to produce annually *Twelve Burlettas; Twelve Serious Pantomimes!! Twelve Harlequinades!!!* exclusive of such comic songs as might be wanted . . . write Puffs, etc. etc. etc. . . . neither to be paid but for such nights on which the Theatre was open; to pay all our travelling expenses to [Astley's] Theatres in Dublin, Liverpool, Manchester, or wheresoever he might take his Company to, in the Winter; and back again to Westminster Bridge; with the exception of Water Carriage to and from Dublin.

The Dibdins took lodgings in 1797 at a house back of the Amphitheatre and Dibdin wrote the burletta *The Comet* for his wife's first appearance, George Broad, Astley's composer, furnishing the music. Next stop for the young couple was the Astleys' Peter Street Amphitheatre in Dublin, where they revelled innocently in the rate of currency exchange, a blessing to the starveling English performers, ruinous to the Irish economy though it was.

The Astleys' season in Ireland was that year a failure for the first time since the company first crossed St George's Channel because of the older showman's bullheaded insistence on flaunting his Englishness and his adherence to the ministry of Pitt. Ireland was in 1797 on the verge of serious uprising, and Astley's indiscretions provoked several riots in the theatre. In the midst of these perturbations Dibdin was obliged to advertise "A New comic Melange of recitation and singing, called *The Universal Panacea, or Smith's Recipe*, written and to be spoken and sung by Mr. C. Dibdin. Junr, his first appearance in Dublin." But he carried it off with tact "combining with the general subject, local notices of Dublin and the Irish Character; and concluding with an appropriate compliment to the Shamrock, Shalaly and Harp . . ." It was a success all six nights of performance.

During that season of 1797–98 Dibdin wrote and saw produced—exclusive of addresses, prologues, epilogues, songs for Johannot, and other trifles—*The Blank, or The Tar and the Ticket* and *The Stratagem*, musical pieces of one act; *Irish Courtship, or the Lasses of Leixlip*, a farce with Songs; and *Duncan's Victory*, an "occasional spectacle, commemorating that brave Admiral's celebrated Victory over the Dutch at Camp-

Harvard Theatre Collection

CHARLES ISAAC MUNGO DIBDIN
engraving by Thomson, after Satchwell

erdown." The list is significant, both as an illustration of how closely he was adhering to the types of light drama created by Charles his father but also as representative of most of the kinds of ephemerae he was to continue to produce in great profusion. Some 210 comic operas, operatic farces, burlettas, pantomimes and extravaganzas are in Nicoll's "Hand-List."

On 13 March 1798 Mrs Dibdin gave birth to the first of their 11 children, John Bates Dibdin, at her parents' Hotel at Holyhead. Charles remained in Liverpool, where the Astleys' company habitually rented the Theatre Royal from Francis Aickin "to fill up the spare time between the closing of the Peter Street Theatre, to the opening of the Amphitheatre Royal, Westminster Bridge on Easter Monday." At Liverpool Dibdin performed *The Panacea* on opening night and it was received with contempt. So he "left the Stage very unceremoniously and indignantly declaring to Mr Astley that I never would perform for him again; and I kept my word."

Just why his dudgeon should have been directed at Astley rather than at the unappreciative Liverpudlians is unclear, but at any rate, he was not sufficiently exercised to resign from all association with Astley. He continued to write for the Amphitheatre, contributing for the London spring season of 1798 *Ways and Means, The Astronomer, The Triumph of Peace, Harlequin in Malabar, A Trip to the Nore, The Fool's Cap,* and *The Turk,* as well as songs for Delpini's *More Beards and More Ghosts.*

But presently his wife offended the dictatorial Astley "by employing her Needle, on the Stage, while waiting at rehearsal; and not 'putting away her work' when he *commanded* her . . ." She received a month's notice, and that left Dibdin as the only wage earner in the family.

In the fall of 1798 Dibdin accompanied the younger Astley back to Dublin as assistant manager of the enterprise at Peter Street, but their chief singer Johannot had defected to Crow Street, and their season was again unsuccessful. In February 1799 the Dibdins sailed on the packet *Venus* to Holyhead, nearly perishing in a violent storm en route. After the following summer season at Liverpool they severed their connection with Astley's "amphitheatricals." The Dibdin's second child Mary Ann, later a professional harpist, was born in the spring of 1799.

Dibdin was now, in the fall of 1799, engaged by the peripatetic equestrian company jointly conducted by William Parker, William Davis, Robert Handy, George Smith, John Crossman, and Richard Johannot. The emolument was "Two Guineas and an half per week, the year round, and a Guinea per week for my Wife, whenever they could employ her . . ." He joined the company at Liverpool in a temporary circus, "in which a Box, not unlike the perpendicular parallelogramatical Theatre, in which Punch is exhibited in London Streets, only higher and wider, was constructed . . ." Here in the "singing box" he and Johannot caroled out the songs Dibdin wrote. One, "Abraham Newland," became so famous that the publisher Hine gave him four guineas for it.

With the company going to Bristol next, Dibdin advertised his benefit with a long bill in rhyme and sang comic duets with Johannot in a small stage projecting over the horse circle. He was disappointed of the large benefit he had hoped for because a few nights previously part of the makeshift gallery had collapsed, injuring several, one woman being so badly bruised that she later died. In July they went to Manchester. Though the summer was the happiest of Dibdin's career, the company lost much money. At Manchester, Dibdin produced *The Mouth of the Texel,* (a "Ballad Pantomime"), *Harlequin and Uncate,* and *Harlequin Phoenix.* Attempting to sing a song which he had composed only two hours before, and with his prompter unable to read his scrawl, he suffered another embarrassment—"somebody in the Gallery cried 'There's the Poet can't sing his own Song!' this was followed by a general Horselaugh." He ran off the stage determined never to perform anywhere again.

The playbill advertising the first performance of *The Volcano,* invented by Thomas Dibdin, with Moorehead's music, produced by Farley at Covent Garden Theatre on 23 December 1799, mentions "Machinery by Cresswell, Sloper, Goostree, C. Dibdin Jun."

Receiving an indication from Mrs Dibdin's grandmother, then wardrobe keeper at Sadler's Wells, of the imminent resignation there of the manager Mark Lonsdale, Dibdin applied in 1800 to Richard Hughes the proprietor, proposing terms of two guineas per week for his wife, three for himself, the salary for him to begin three weeks before opening. He impulsively resigned his job and he and his wife set off for London. A drunken coachman overturned their vehicle and broke Dibdin's collarbone.

Though his salary and "bits of Benefits" had brought him £9 per week on tour and the Sadler's Wells position would at first bring no more than £3, he was nevertheless relieved to be convalescing at home in London near his and his wife's families. He and his wife and children took lodgings ("at an easy rent") with his wife's grandmother Mrs Holmes in a house she rented in the vernal precincts of Tunbridge Spa Gardens, his "Islington Paradise," where he could wander, "studying and meditating" his productions.

The Wells proprietors—William Siddons, Richard Hughes, Thomas Arnold, Richard Wroughton, and John Coates—hired Dibdin but beat his price down to two guineas per week. He went quickly to work and engaged a troupe, some of whom were already veterans of performance there. Among them were the not-yet-famous Joe Grimaldi; the clown Dubois "and all his pupils"; Richer the great ropedancer; Mrs Tetherington (née Collet), a celebrated Columbine; Mons and Mme St Pierre and Mons Gouriet, dancers; "Jew" Davis the comedian; the harlequins Banks and Simpson; the singer Phillips; and the actresses Mrs Pyne and the 14-year-old Miss Minton. John Moorhead and William Russell were the composers, the clever Robert Andrews the scene painter, and Alexander Johnston the machinist.

With this talent, on Easter Monday 1800 Dibdin opened the Wells, offering his burletta *Old Fools; or, Love's Stratagem*, his "serious Pantomime" called *Boadicea, or the British Amazon*, and another pantomime, *Peter Wilkins, or the Flying World*, by Dibdin and Andrews. The night and the season were successful, and Dibdin was re-engaged by the proprietors.

In 1802 Charles and Thomas John Dibdin his brother bought William Siddons's share of the Wells for £1400, and a new group of proprietors was formed, consisting, with the Dibdins, of Richard Hughes, William Reeve the composer, R. C. Andrews the scene designer, W. Yarnold, and a grocer of Clare Market named Barfoot.

Charles Dibdin went on managing Sadler's Wells productions year after year until 1819 with the exception of his disastrous managerial venture to Dublin in 1805–6 (when he and Tom signed for the Peter Street Amphitheatre, during the rebuilding of Crow Street, at a rental of £450, and lost £2,000). After 19 years and six months, he relinquished management of Sadler's Wells.

Dibdin's *Memoirs* detail vividly the vicissitudes and triumphs of management, the accidents and innovations—pony races, the Aquatic Theatre (with realistic naval battles and Newfoundland dogs rescuing drowning children), pugilism and melodrama, the ghastly tragedy of 15 October 1807 when 18 people were killed when someone shouted "Fire!" In 1820, at a time when he was confined for debt within the rules of the King's Bench, he sold his share in the Wells to some of the other partners. At this low point in his life, Dibdin was (while still confined) hired by Elliston to write some pantomimes. In 1822–23 he became stage director for his old friend William Davis of the Royal Amphitheatre, Westminster Bridge. From March 1825 to Michaelmas 1826 he managed the Surrey Theatre and after that left off management altogether. In 1825 his admirers founded the Melodists' Club.

Even after severing ties with management, Dibdin continued to be a compulsive writer of pantomimes, farces, and entertainments. His last effort, the farce *Nothing Superfluous*, was produced at Hull on 5 August 1829. He died 13 January 1833.

Charles I. M. Dibdin was an agreeable man, seemingly without his father's fondness for quarreling and blame-placing but with only a modest share of his father's talents in singing, painting, set devising, and acting, and none at all in composing and playing keyboard instruments. Like the elder Charles he essayed ambitious nondramatic works: *Mirth and Metre: consisting of Poems, Serious, Humorous, and Satirical* (1807); *Young Arthur, or the Child of Mystery. A Metrical Romance* (1819); and *Comic Tales and Lyrical Fancies; including the Chessiad, a Mock Heroic, in Five Cantos, and the Wreath of Love, in Four Cantos* (1825).

Dibdin's wife Mary, who died in 1816, bore him at least 11 children: John Bates Dibdin (13 March 1798–10 May 1828), Charles Lamb's friend; Mary Ann Dibdin, (1799–1886), an excellent harpist, who became Mrs Tonna; Charles Richard Dibdin (20 December 1800–5 December 1820), the scene painter; Susan Harriet Dibdin (1802–1859); Frances Holmes Dibdin (27 January 1804–25 February 1805); Robert William Dibdin (1805–1887), a clergyman; Sophia Amelia Dibdin (1807–1882); Thomas Charteris Dibdin (16 August 1809–3 November 1813); Ann Augusta Dibdin (1810–1872), a pianist; Edward Henry Dibdin (8–20 September 1813) and his surviving twin Henry Edward Dibdin (d. 6 May 1866), an organist and composer.

C. I. M. Dibdin's portrait, engraved by J. Thomson after R. W. Satchwell, as a plate for the *European Magazine*, was published by J. Asperne, 1819.

Dibdin, Mrs Charles Isaac Mungo, Mary, née Bates *1782–1816, actress, singer.*

Mary Bates was said by Charles Isaac Mungo Dibdin to have been 14 years of age and an actress at Sadler's Wells when he met her there in 1796. Her parents kept a hotel at Holyhead. They were married at St George, Hanover Square, on 13 June 1797 (not 14 June, as he states in his *Memoirs*), while he was still employing his mother's surname Pitt.

I may here remark that she had been at Sadler's Wells from 8 years of age, and at the time / "When I went wooing," / sustained principal singing and comic Characters; but at the end of the season previous to our marriage, owing to a dispute between her Grandmother (. . . Mrs. Holmes, then Wardrobe Keeper and Mantua Maker of the Wells, who had brought her up from 2 years of age) and the Proprietors of the Wells, concerning her Salary, which she wanted raised from 15/- to a Guinea and a half a week; and which they declined doing, Miss Bates was withdrawn from the Wells: . . . she was, therefore, when we married unemployed.

So, too, was Dibdin. But he soon talked his, and her, way onto the Astleys' payroll at the Royal Amphitheatre, he as "Author to the Theatre," and "she to play all the principal singing and comic acting Business."

From that point onward Mrs Dibdin followed the peregrinations of her husband,

Harvard Theatre Collection

MARY DIBDIN

artist unknown

from London to the Peter Street Amphitheatre, Dublin, in 1797, back to London and again to Dublin in 1798, and once again to London, via Liverpool in 1799, then to the touring equestrian company of Parkes, Davis, Handy, South, Crossman, and Johannot, which crisscrossed the British Isles playing in disused theatres and temporary circuses.

In 1800, Mrs Dibdin's grandmother was influential in securing for Charles the post of manager of Sadler's Wells vacated by Mark Lonsdale. There he remained for nearly two decades (as proprietor from 1802), pouring out of his seemingly inexhaustible imagination a flood of popular farces and musical pieces, while his wife sang and acted to supplement the income needed to sustain their growing family. She eventually gave birth to at least 11 children. (See her husband's entry for names and dates.)

Mrs Dibdin had been subject to epileptic fits since suffering an attack of typhus fever at the age of eight. She was forced to retire from the stage at the close of the 1814–15 season. On 16 August 1816 she died at the age of 35. Charles called her as an actress and singer "much admired, as a mother exemplary, and as a wife inestimable – the effects of her being a christian." Her brother-in-law Thomas Dibdin wrote that she had been "one of the best of wives and mothers."

Mrs Dibdin was a niece of Mrs Thomas Kennedy, the actress.

A stipple portrait engraving of Mrs Dibdin, unattributed and undated, is in the Harvard Theatre Collection.

Dibdin, Thomas John 1771–1841, actor, playwright, singer, manager.

Thomas John Dibdin was the second of two illegitimate children of the elder Charles Dibdin and the actress Harriet Pitt. He was born in Peter Street, London, on 21 March 1771. His godfathers were David Garrick and Francis Aickin. His younger full brother was Charles Isaac Mungo Dibdin, and he had also two half-siblings, Cecil and Harriet, illegitimate children of Harriet Pitt by the actor George Mattocks, both of whom took their mother's surname.

A rambling, florid, but often valuable and entertaining two-volume memoir, *The Reminiscences of Thomas Dibdin*, gives many of the circumstances of his life from birth until near the date of its publication in 1827. It also judiciously omits some key occurrences.

Thomas and his brother were virtually abandoned, along with their mother, by their father Charles about 1775. Garrick, incensed by the desertion, discharged the father and assisted Miss Pitt. The two boys were allowed to march in the procession of characters in the revised Shakespeare Jubilee at Drury Lane. Thomas, "an extraordinarily beautiful boy," according to his own *Reminiscences*, was selected as Cupid to walk hand-in-hand with Mrs Siddons, who played Venus. One of his wings dropped off and Mrs Siddons borrowed a pin from Mrs Garrick's servant to reattach it. "At the nightly conclusion of the Jubilee, tarts, cheesecakes, and other pastry were very liberally distributed to the juvenile corps, who personated fairies, &c . . . and Mr. Garrick himself, on those nights, stayed, for the pleasure he felt in witnessing a due distribution of said bonbons."

But, delightful as the theatrical life seemed to the four-year-old, it was not yet his to be enjoyed. Miss Pitt could not afford to keep her family together, and her uncle Cecil Pitt, a City upholsterer of wealth and respectability, packed the boys off to school. Charles was his favorite, was virtually adopted by his uncle, and called himself Charles Pitt until he was a grown man. It does not appear, however, that Thomas used the surname.

When he was about eight years old, Thomas was, "for the sake of musical tuition, and in the hope of making me as clever a man as my dad," placed in the juvenile choir of St Paul's Cathedral under the tenor singer, organist, and composer Robert Hudson (1732–1815), who was almoner and master of the children. He next studied for a "twelvemonth, under Mr. Tempest, of Half-farthing-lane Academy, Wandsworth," and finally was removed to the tuition of a classical scholar, a Mr Galland at Durham, where he remained for three years.

At about 14 he was brought back to London and apprenticed to his uncle Cecil, who then turned his articles over to William Rawlins, afterwards Sir William and Sheriff of London, an eccentric man who doted on the drama but did not think it meet for apprentices. After several thrashings over the issue and after his model theatres were destroyed by his master, Dibdin, his rage for theatre further inflamed by attendance in the sixpenny gallery of the Royalty, decamped.

Cockran Joseph Booth, "second prompter and a respectable actor at Covent Garden," was also a joint proprietor of the new Theatre Royal, Margate. After Dibdin auditioned for him in the part of Marcus in *Cato*, Booth, a kindly man, gave him a letter to Robson and Mate, his fellow proprietors, and Dibdin fled London in "the cabin of a Margate hoy," entertaining deck passengers on the way.

Dibdin says he selected Margate because his half-brother, the musician Cecil Pitt, was in the band. But there was no room for Tom at Margate, and Mate sent him to Mr Richland, manager of a sharing company on the Dover circuit. That company being then on the road, he had to walk 70 miles to catch up. He made his first stage appearance in a barn at Eastbourne, under the assumed name of S. Merchant, as Valentine in O'Keeffe's *The Farmer*, singing his father's new and popular song "Poor Jack," which he repeated nearly every night of the season. In this company he "wrote the first of nearly two thousand ditties which I have been since guilty of," a hunting song set by

"our leader of three fiddles," named Benfield. Here also he embarked on a parallel career of scene painting, like his brother Charles, and, like his father Charles, composed a burletta of dialogue and songs called *Something New*.

Dibdin soon stepped up from the joint-stock world of starveling sharing companies, joining a salaried company under James Gardner, Mrs Baker's acting manager on the Kent circuit of Canterbury, Rochester, Tunbridge Wells, Maidstone, Feversham, and Deal. Mrs Baker, herself an eccentric, ruled a rural dramatic empire populated largely by eccentrics. But she was a managerial genius and a humane and generous person, and the alert young Dibdin learned much under her direction. Acting at Beverley, he met Ann Hilliar, his future wife. At Beverley and Harrowgate he boarded with Jones, later first violin in the band of the Adelphi Theatre, who began teaching him to play that instrument.

In 1791 he accepted an offer from Ward and Banks to play at Liverpool, arriving there on the eve of the opening by those managers of the new theatre at Manchester. Because a London player, W. Bates, failed to show up, Dibdin was allowed to star on the opening night as Mungo in *The Padlock*, the most famous part of his father. In this good provincial company Dibdin (still as "Merchant") sang, acted, and painted scenery. At the end of the Manchester Theatre's season he was reintroduced to Francis Aickin, the Liverpool summer manager, also his godfather, who had not seen him since his christening. Aickin hired him.

The Liverpool summer enterprise, under the joint proprietorship of Aickin and J. P. Kemble, represented the greatest professional advance yet for Dibdin, not only because of its famous managers but also because the rotating company was populated from time to time by the most experienced London actors—both Aickins, Quick, Holman, King, Mrs Mattocks, Mrs Ward, and Mrs Mountain, among others. Dibdin also was brought for the first time into the management side of show business, becoming assistant to William Powell, prompter and treasurer. When Mrs Ward, of Drury Lane and wife of his Manchester manager, took her benefit at Liverpool he wrote "a *petite pièce* on the subject of 'Botany Bay,' . . . a new and interesting colony, and painted some scenery for it from designs in Cook's Voyage." Dibdin says that afterward he "sold the manuscript, music, and sketches of the scenes, to an agent of Mr. Wignell, proprietor of the Philadelphia theatre, for—not much . . ."

Dibdin rejoined Ward and Banks at Chester and Manchester at the end of the summer, used his influence to obtain the leadership of the band for his half-brother Cecil Pitt, painted scenery, and produced *Sunshine after Rain*.

In 1792 he traveled for the first time to Scotland, sight-seeing at Edinburgh, painting scenes, being entertained in the countryside by the Earl of Finlator's mother, the commander of Fort George, Frazer of Lovat, and other notables, and playing for a week at Banff and another at Inverness.

Back to Manchester went this "young man, who could" now, as he boasted, "sing 'Poor Jack,' paint scenes, play the fiddle, write a farce, get up a pantomime, attempt Sir Francis, Gripe, Apollo in 'Midas,' Mungo in the 'Padlock,' Darby in the 'Poor Soldier,' Captain Valentine in the 'Farmer,' and Polonius in 'Hamlet;' not to mention all dialects, as the Irishman in 'Rosina' . . . with French and German characters . . ." At Manchester he again met Ann Hilliar, and on 23 May 1793 he married her in the old collegiate church there. At Manchester also in 1792 he acted and assisted in scene painting at the elegant new Ardwick Green Circus.

There followed in quick succession engagements for the newlyweds with Stanton at Bury, Huddersfield, and Rochdale and with Henry Masterman at Swansea, Carmarthen, and Haverford-West. At the place

Harvard Theatre Collection

THOMAS JOHN DIBDIN

engraving by Freeman, after Owen

last-named his wife gave birth to their first child, a daughter Maria, and he was delivered of the burletta which was to be his first London production, *The Rival Loyalists, or Shelah's Choice*. It came out at Sadler's Wells and brought him five guineas.

The little family moved to London in 1794, reunited with Charles and the Dibdins' mother, renewed intimacy with many actor friends, and secured steady work at Sadler's Wells. But the happy time was darkened by the loss of their little girl Maria, "as we have since lost several others, who rest in the cemeteries of Lambeth, Rochester, Richmond, and Covent Garden." Up to that point Tom was still "S. Merchant" but he now made peace with his quondam master Sir William Rawlins, who declined to prosecute him for breach of apprentice articles, and so he resumed the Dibdin name, over the objection of his father.

There followed a period of some years

of intense activity for Tom Dibdin. In 1794, 1795, and 1796 he brought out at Sadler's Wells at least sixteen productions, with music by Lavesque, John Davy, John Moorehead, and Reeve. He also went to work to produce pantomimes for the other minor theatres, on one occasion selling Philip Astley four pieces in one day "for FOURTEEN GUINEAS the lot." He enacted the role of Firelock in his own *Love's Trial* at Handy's New Circus at the Lyceum on 10 December 1794. He began to write songs for publication by Longman and Company. During the winter holidays he traveled to Canterbury to paint scenery and produce spectacles for Mrs Baker, and the result was another engagement with the manageress "constituting me comic actor of all work, with profits of scene-painting, two salaries, and two benefits in each town . . ."

This portion of Dibdin's account, of around 1796 and 1797, when, he says, he was happier than ever before or after, is sprinkled generously with the names of gentle and noble patrons—the Earl and Countess of Mount Edgecumbe, Sir John Mackintosh, Lord Cremorne. At Maidstone Tom took Masonic instruction and contrived his farces of *The British Raft*, ridiculing the French invasion scare, and *The Jew and the Doctor* (produced for his benefit). There also he wrote his famous song "The Snug Little Island," which procured him the favor of "his Grace the Duke of Leeds, whose warm, friendly, and condescending patronage continued during his life." The "new theatre in High-Street, opposite the Conduit" in Maidstone, Kent, was opened on 12 April 1798 with several of Dibdin's pieces. He sang and acted there and on 12 July brought on for the first time his subsequently enormously popular farce *The Jew and the Doctor* under the title *The Jew Guardian*, with the comic genius Dowton as Abednego and the author as Old Bromley.

Nelson's victory at the Nile in June

1798 being rumored about London before it was officially gazetted, Richard Cumberland advised Dibdin to steal a march on his competitors and write a musical celebration. The Covent Garden manager Harris asked for the piece *The Mouth of the Nile* on a Friday, and Dibdin delivered it on the following Monday. Attwood wrote the music, it was quickly put into rehearsal, and when official confirmation came of the victory it was put on and ran for 32 nights during the 1798–99 season, with Dibdin in the character of Pat.

Dibdin was engaged for £5 per week at Covent Garden in that season and he remained there for eight years; his first-named character on that stage was Mr Pickle in *The Spoiled Child*, which he assumed when Powell became ill. He twice that first season played Abednego in *The Jew and the Doctor* when Fawcett, the actor for whom the character had been written, was indisposed. The farce was a favorite with George III, who often commanded it.

But T. J. Dibdin's facile quill was far more important to management than anything he could contribute from the stage, and his tours of duty as actor-singer came less and less frequently. Out of the easy imagination of this most productive of the Dibdins tumbled burlettas and burlesques and ballets, musical dramas and farces, operettas and spectacles and songs. Between 1795 and 1837 he wrote certainly more than 250 dramatic and musical vehicles (he says "twelve dozen and three-score plays" in his comic epitaph; but he was able to recall the titles of only 196 in his autobiography), countless prologues and epilogues, and more than 2000 songs. (Lists of many of his dramatic pieces may be found in the third and fourth volumes of Allardyce Nicoll's *A History of English Drama 1660–1900*.) Many of his mainpieces and afterpieces were founded on some feature of another's work—as in the case, for instance, of his comedy *The Birth-*

Day, which was taken from Kotzebue's *Reconciliation* — but he set his own unmistakable seal on the dialogue and business of each. He was neither a literary nor a dramatic genius, but he was very vigilant of and immediately responsive to the changing tastes of a public more and more avid for spectacle and blatant sentimentality. The only difference he ever had with the turbulent and demanding audiences was the series of near riots in December 1802 by Jewish auditors over a song sung by Fawcett in *The Cabinet* which they misapprehended to be anti-Semitic.

Dibdin made large sums by some of his productions — in 1803-4, for instance, clearing £1515. But unfortunate business ventures, like the speculation with his brother Charles in a Dublin circus enterprise which failed in 1806 and lost them £2,000, sometimes brought him near bankruptcy. In 1802 Thomas John and his brother Charles had bought William Siddons's share of Sadler's Wells for £1400, and a new partnership was formed with Richard Hughes, William Reeve, R. C. Andrews, W. Yarnold, and a Mr Barfoot. Charles continued as stage manager there through 1819, but Thomas John was not very active in the direction of affairs. In 1807 he was saddened and shocked by the trampling to death at the Wells of 18 people after someone shouted "Fire!" In September 1808 he witnessed the destruction by fire of Covent Garden theatre, for which he was also writing. (The first novelty after the Covent Garden company entered temporary quarters at the Opera House was his *Princess and No Princess.*) He and his wife were dancing at a ball given by the proprietors of the Golden Lane Brewery hard by Drury Lane Theatre when, on the night of 24 February 1809, that theatre burned to the ground.

Dibdin and his wife usually spent their summers acting at Richmond, until her retirement and move to Cheltenham after the 1808-9 season, and one or both of them occasionally acted outside the London area, usually for friends' benefits. In 1811-12 he managed the old Royal Circus, then called the Surrey Theatre, for Elliston at £15 a week and then, when the new Drury Lane Theatre was built, signed on there as prompter and writer of pantomimes for a season's salary of £520. After the death of Samuel Whitbread in 1815 Dibdin became joint manager of Drury Lane with Alexander Roe. In July 1816 he again took command of the Surrey. But in 1816 also Elliston discharged him from the Drury Lane management, giving as his reason that Dibdin could not at one time manage two theatres successfully, though Dibdin had the friendship and support of most of the Committee of noblemen and gentlemen then ostensibly in charge of Drury Lane. Lord Byron, one of their number, gave him a handsome sum at his parting benefit and presented him "with about two hundred beautiful drawings of Turkish costume, exhibiting the correct habits of all classes in the Ottoman Empire, executed under his lordship's immediate inspection When he was first in the Levant . . ." Dibdin found them "invaluable" for his "Eastern spectacles" at the Surrey.

But despite his enormous diligence in management and his writing "upwards of eighty pieces" there, the Surrey effort was foredoomed. Before it had opened he had expended over £4,000 in tearing out the horse ring of the old Circus, erecting a stage, and redecorating. His costumes were sumptuous, his scenery elaborate, and his company first-rate. But the patent theatres were raising legal objections and his house would not hold enough people to justify his expenditures. On 19 March 1822 he closed the theatre and turned the remainder of his lease over to Watkyns Burroughs.

Dibdin went next to the Haymarket for three seasons, where D. E. Morris had offered him the post of stage manager and principal author and Mrs Dibdin the superintendency of the wardrobe. But quarrels with Elliston and Morris, a brace of lawsuits, and a brief sojourn in debtor's prison marred and finally ended his tenure there.

Dibdin spent his declining years in comfort, a little bitter that so much bad luck had prevented his spending them in luxury. He died on 16 September 1841 and was buried on 21 September near the grave of his grandmother Ann Pitt and his old friend the clown Grimaldi in the burial ground of St James, Pentonville.

In addition to his voluminous theatrical writing and his autobiography, Dibdin produced *A Metrical History of England* (2 vols, 1813); *Bunyan's Pilgrim's Progress Metrically Condensed* (1834); and a periodical, *Tom Dibdin's Penny Trumpet*, which died after four numbers. He edited, in 26 volumes, *The London Theatre, a Collection of the most Celebrated Dramatic Pieces* (1815–18).

T. J. Dibdin lacked the spirit and some of the talents of his father Charles and he inherited few of his faults of character. Tom seems to have been a kindly man, fond of the merry meetings with his companions of the Covent Garden Beef Steak Club, the Ad Libitum, and the Literary Fund Club, convivial but not bibulous. He was a little boastful of his wide acquaintance among the socially elect, yet friendly, direct, and democratic. He was a faithful husband, a good father and brother, and a dutiful son, caring for both his mother Harriet Pitt and the aged actress his grandmother Anne Pitt until their deaths. He wrote his own epitaph in the Ad Libitum Club:

> *Longing while living for laurel and bays,*
> *Under this willow a poor poet "lays,"*
> *With little to censure, and less to praise,*
> *He wrote twelve dozen and three score*
>   *plays:*
> *He finished his "Life," and he went his*
>   *ways.*

Thomas John Dibdin and Nancy his wife were (according to a genealogy published in *Who's Who in the Theatre*) parents of George Dibdin Pitt (1799–1855)

the dramatist; Eliza Pitt (1801–1885), an actress who married an actor named Stoker; Charles Dibdin Pitt (1818–1866), an actor who married the actress Ellen Coveney and from whom a large collection of stage people of the nineteenth and twentieth centuries are descended; and Cecil Pitt, an actor. These people evidently reverted to the surname Pitt as adults, for one finds additional children of Tom and Nancy recorded in the baptismal records of the "actors' church," St Paul, Covent Garden: 28 June 1811 "Thomas Robert Coleman, Son of Thomas and Ann Dibden [*sic*] Born Octo^r 22^d 1810," "May Ann Daughter of Thomas & Ann Dibden: Southampton Street: Gentleman: Born 12 April 1813," (doubtless the "Ann Dibdin, Russell S^t., . . . Aged 1" buried at St Paul's on 4 April 1814), and "Charles Alexander Son of Thomas & Ann Dibden: Russell St.: Gent^n: Born 6 Mar 1815." Speaking of his circumstances in 1821 Dibdin rather bafflingly says in his autobiography that he by then had had "some seven daughters and two sons to support, bury, and otherwise provide for," and we recall the death of the first-born, Maria, in 1794 (probably the child he mentioned as buried at Lambeth) and the other children he says were interred at Rochester and Richmond. Probably the Sophia Dibdon (*sic*) buried at St Paul, Covent Garden, on 4 September 1795 was another of the children of Tom and Ann.

The following engraved portraits of Thomas John Dibdin are known:

1. Plate to *The Monthly Mirror*, engraved by W. Ridley after C. Allingham and published by Vernor & Hood, 1802.

2. Plate to the *European Magazine*, by H. Meyer after S. Drummond, published by J. Asperne, 1817.

3. An etching, vignette, with a facsimile autograph, by "A. Crowquill" (A. H. Forrester).

4. By H. Meyer after T. Wageman, published by H. Colburn, 1827.

5. By J. Young after W. Owen, 1807. The same picture was engraved by S. Free-

man as a plate to Mrs Inchbald's collection of farces. It was published also by Longman, Hurst, Rees & Orme, 1809.

Thomas John Dibdin said that he had been painted once by Allingham and once by Dighton. Neither original portrait is now known to exist, though very likely the Ridley engraving enumerated first above was taken from Allingham's oil.

Dibdin, Mrs Thomas John, Ann, née Hilliar d. 1828, actress, singer.

When the young singer Thomas John Dibdin arrived from Hull at Beverley in 1790 to take up his new duties in the company managed by Wright he met, among others, a Miss Ann Hilliar. She was a sister to the manager's wife and had formerly acted at Edinburgh and Newcastle. Dibdin went on to the company of Ward and Banks at Liverpool early in 1791. While he was acting and prompting at Manchester in the spring of 1793, another of Ann Hilliar's sisters, passing through town with her husband, was surprised by the premature birth of a daughter, and Ann was summoned to Manchester. Ann and Tom renewed acquaintance when she visited the theatre, were joint baptismal sponsors for her little niece at the old Collegiate Church, and a few weeks later, on 23 May 1793, were married at the same church.

Ann accompanied her husband in his peripatetic wanderings of 1793 and 1794 acting and singing in Stanton's company at Bury, Huddersfield, and Rochdale, then with Masterman at Swansea, Carmarthen, and Haverford-West, where she gave birth to their first child, Maria. The couple had assumed the name "Merchant." When Tom Dibdin was called to Sadler's Wells in 1794 to begin his long London career of singing, writing, painting, and managing, Ann joined the company in minor singing roles. Both played in Mrs Baker's company at Tunbridge Wells in September 1797, where, according to the *Monthly Mirror*, she was "a great favourite. She played Cap-

tain Macheath for her benefit with great spirit and vivacity," now under her husband's real name, Dibdin.

On 18 September 1799 Mrs Dibdin made her first London patent-house appearance, at Covent Garden, as Aura in the afterpiece *The Farmhouse*. She was then said to be from the Rochester theatre, but that fact need not indicate that she had acted there immediately before her Covent Garden appearance. She was carried on the roster at £3 weekly through the end of the season, in June, sustaining Patty in *Inkle and Yarico*, Damaris in *Barnaby Brittle*, Beatrice in *True Friends*, the Widow Volatile in *Fashionable Levities*, Mrs Tempest in *The School for Wives*, a Lass in *The Deserter of Naples*, and (rather oddly) Goneril in *King Lear* and the Queen in *Cymbeline*. She was also the original Lady

Harvard Theatre Collection

ANN DIBDIN, as Queen Caroline
engraving by Picart, after De Wilde

Handy in Thomas Morton's popular *Speed the Plough*, which was introduced on 8 February 1800 and had a run of 37 performances that season. Thomas Dutton in his *Dramatic Censor* of April, 1800, thought little either of Lady Handy or of Mrs Dibdin; it was a bad part which "suffers additional degradation from Mrs Dibdin's manner of performance." She was important enough, however, to share her benefit with John Emery and Mrs Johnson on 28 May and share gross receipts of £326 12s. Of her acting that night, as Lady Mary Raffle in *Wives as They Were, and Maids as They Are*, Dutton remarked only: "Mrs. Dibdin follows in Mrs. Mattocks's walk, but 'haud passibus aequis.'"

In fact, more or less in Mrs Mattocks's walk, she continued until Mrs Mattocks's fate—age and corpulency—began to overtake her. The "breeches figure" she had revealed so pleasingly to Tunbridge Wells audiences in 1797 was fading by 1801 when the *Authentic History of the Green Room* judged: "With respect to person, she is tall, and of figure not unpleasing, but favouring rather too much of the Cheshire breed, to delight upon the stage."

Ann Dibdin remained at Covent Garden until 1808 and sang also at Sadler's Wells off and on. In most summers she accompanied her husband to the theatre at Richmond, Surrey. But her rigorous performance schedule was often interrupted by pregnancy and her life repeatedly saddened by the deaths of children. (For a discussion of the children of Thomas and Ann Dibdin see his entry.) She was a good trouper, a popular performer, and a faithful theatrical wife, supporting her husband through his triumphs and disasters. After the failure of his Surrey Theatre venture, in 1822, she accompanied him to the Haymarket, signing on "as superintendant of the ladies' wardrobe, though," Dibdin adds, "at a very trifling salary."

Ann Hilliar Dibdin died on 29 August 1828. Her portrait was engraved by Picart,

after De Wilde, in the character of Queen Caroline in *The Heart of Midlothian*, as a plate to *The Theatrical Inquisitor*, 1819.

There were numerous Hilliars, Hilliards, and Hillyards on the provincial and London stages from the beginning of the eighteenth century. Possibly all were related. Richard Ryan in his *Dramatic Table Talk* (1825) cited a bill of a provincial theatre in June 1797 where a family of at least seven Hillyards sustained all the parts of mainpiece and afterpiece.

Dick, Mr *fl. 1790–1805*, *tailor*.

Mr Dick was the chief tailor at Covent Garden from at least the 1790–91 season through 1804–5 and was often mentioned in the bills when new spectacle productions were presented. Usually the bills simply stated that the "dresses" were by Dick and Mrs Egan or by Lupino, Dick, and Mrs Egan, so it is not possible to tell how much of a hand in the design of the costumes Dick may have had. The bill for *Hercules and Omphale* on 17 November 1794 stated specifically that the dresses were chiefly designed by Lupino and executed under Dick's direction, but from 1795–96 on, Lupino's name was no longer mentioned in connection with costumes, and perhaps Dick assumed the role of designer as well as tailor.

On 16 March 1797 when *Raymond and Agnes* was first performed, Dick, Goostree, and Mrs Egan were credited with the dresses and decorations. When *Joanna* was done on 16 January 1800, the *Universal Magazine* complimented Dick and Mrs Egan: "the richness of the dresses [has] been rarely equalled." Dick's salary is not known, though he was paid £80 in 1794–95, according to the theatre's account book, and perhaps that was his annual stipend. A Mr Dick was at the Theatre Royal, Edinburgh, in 1818–19, but it is unclear whether or not that person was the tailor.

Dick, Mrs *fl. 1797*, *house servant?*

On 18 May 1797 at Covent Garden a

Mrs Dick's benefit tickets were accepted. Since this is the only reference to her, perhaps the bill contained a typographical error; if so, the reference may have been to Mr Dick, the Covent Garden tailor.

Dickens. *See* DICKINS *and* DICKONS.

Dickenson, Mrs [*fl.* 1746–1765], *boxkeeper.*

Mrs Dickenson was the keeper of the center middle gallery box at Drury Lane known since the 1720s as "Burton's Box" —in memory of the earlier keeper of it. Mrs Dickenson received a shared benefit with three others on 29 April 1747, so she had presumably worked at the theatre the full 1746–47 season. On 9 February 1765 she was still there, earning 2*s.* daily or 12*s.* weekly, the only woman in the group of boxkeepers but paid at the same rate as her colleagues. Perhaps she was the wife of the Drury Lane first gallery office keeper, John Dickinson, though her name seems clearly and invariably to have been spelled Dickenson.

Dickenson, [Samuel?] [*fl.* 1784–1810], *oboist.*

Mr Dickenson played second oboe at the Handel Memorial concerts at Westminster Abbey and the Pantheon on 26, 27, 29 May and 3, 5 June 1784 and participated in the St Paul's concerts in May 1791, 1792, and 1793. Doane's *Musical Directory* of 1794 listed the oboist as a member of the Academy of Ancient Music living in Bentinck Street, Soho. Dickenson played in the *Messiah* performance at the Haymarket Theatre on 15 January 1798 and on the following 27 February was paid £9 by Drury Lane as an extra member of the band.

Probably the oboist was Samuel Dickenson, a member of the Court of Assistants of the Royal Society of Musicians in August 1799 and later. He seems to have played at Drury Lane in the spring of 1800

and at the Haymarket in the summers of 1804 through 1810. The Royal Society granted him £3 13*s.* 6*d.* on 4 January 1807, but the nature of Dickenson's need was not specified. Possibly he found himself employed only during the summers and required financial assistance during the winters.

Dickerson, Mr [*fl.* 1794], *violinist.*

Doane's *Musical Directory* of 1794 listed Mr Dickerson of Lincoln as a violinist who played at the performances commemorating Handel at Westminster Abbey. The *Dictionary* did not specify which of the several performances he played in, that of 1784 or those of other years.

Dickins, Mr [*fl.* 1705–1706], *actor.*

Mr Dickins acted Count Cogdie in *The Gamester* on 22 February 1705 at Lincoln's Inn Fields. At the Queen's Theatre in the Haymarket he was Cleon in *Ulysses* on 23 November 1705 and the Ensign in *The Faithful General* on 3 January 1706.

Dickinson, John [*fl.* 1745–1779], *gallery office keeper.*

John Dickinson served as the gallery office keeper and then the first gallery office keeper at Drury Lane from 1745 through 1779, the only season unaccounted for being 1749–50. He was recorded for benefits throughout the years, first with two to three others, then, beginning in 1757 and continuing through 1778, alone. Once, in 1765, he was billed in error as a doorkeeper. His salary, at least as of 9 February 1765, was 3*s.* 4*d.* daily or £1 weekly; his address, from 1775 on, was No 5, Wild Court, Wild Street, Lincoln's Inn Fields. His luck at benefit time was not always recorded, but we know that in 1767 he suffered a deficit of £54 14*s.* and in 1776 of £55 6*s.* Usually, however, he made a very substantial profit, one of his greatest being £203 2*s.* in 1774. The records indicate that at most benefits he could expect to make at least £170 after the house charges were paid.

Dickinson was named in two theatrical wills. The patentee James Lacy asked him to be his trustee in his will dated 20 May 1768 and proved on 17 February 1774, and the machinist Alexander Johnston asked Dickinson and Thomas Hewett to administer his estate for his wife in his will dated 2 July 1775 and proved on the following 19 October.

Dickons, Mrs Peter. *See* POOLE, MARTHA FRANCES CAROLINE.

Dickson. *See* DIXON.

"Dick Whittington." *See* COLMAN, GEORGE *1732–1794.*

"Dicky, Jubilee." *See* NORRIS, HENRY.

Diddear, Harriet Elizabeth, later Mrs John Saville Faucit and then the second Mrs William Farren the younger, *1789–1857, actress.*

Harriet Elizabeth Diddear was born, according to the account in the *Authentic Memoirs of the Green Room* (1814), at Penzance, Cornwall, on 31 July 1789. Her father was the merchant-turned-manager who acted and managed in theatrical companies all over Kent and Surrey, and elsewhere. She assisted him by acting juvenile characters in several of his locations, including once or twice at Richmond before the end of the eighteenth century.

The *Memoirs* state that, when she was 15, because of "misfortunes [which] deprived her father of his management" she was "compelled to accept an engagement in the Dover company" to help her parents and her siblings "of which she was the eldest member."

At Dover she met the young actor John Saville Faucit. In the summer of 1805, while both were engaged at Richmond,

they were married at St George, Southwark. Shortly after the ceremony the young couple went back to Richmond where she played Bertha in *The Point of Honour,* for his benefit.

In 1806 the pair went to the Norwich Theatre, where Harriet became a great favorite, and (except for the winter of 1810, spent in the North with Macready) at Norwich they remained until 1813. An eminent barrister traveling the Norfolk circuit came back to London full of enthusiasm for her Lady Macbeth and reported his find to Harris at Covent Garden. Harris sent Fawcett his acting manager (no relation to her husband) to engage her. She appeared for the first time at Covent Garden on 7 October 1813 as a successful Desdemona and then played an equally successful Juliet.

Her career continued to flourish for some time, both in London and on the Kent Circuit, which her actor-author husband managed for thirty years. But her principal claim to remembrance may be the five among her six children by Faucit whom she gave to the nineteenth-century stage: John F. Saville (1807–1855); Edmund F. Saville (1811–1857); Alfred Saville; Harriet (d. 1847), who married the actor W. H. Bland; and the famous Helena, Lady Martin (Helen Faucit, 1817–1898).

John Saville Faucit died at No 31, Primrose Street, Bishopsgate, on 1 November 1853, aged 70. Harriet Elizabeth Diddear Faucit married the notable actor William Farren the younger in 1856. She died on 16 June 1857, aged 67.

Diddear, [John? Charles?] *1761–1841, actor, manager.*

"Mr. Diddear, a nephew of the late celebrated Major La Valeire," according to a notice of his daughter, in *Authentic Memoirs of the Green Room* (1814), "was in early life a merchant in the East Indies, but owing to several losses in the Island of Antigua, he came to England, and having purchased his freedom of the City of London, commenced business as a silk-mercer in Fleet-Street. Being, however, still unfortunate [,] to prevent a failure, he sold off his effects . . ."—and went on the stage. None of these misfortunes are dated and they may be fictitious. But Diddear certainly seems to have begun his stage service at Bath around 1783. "For the winter of 1784–85 he joined the Exeter company, in which circuit he remained nine years, when, by a fall, he unfortunately broke one of his legs. Soon after his recovery he commenced manager, and as such speculated at Brighton, Dover, Deal, Richmond, &c."

Actually, his Brighton managership lasted from the summer of 1796, when he succeeded John Bernard, through that of 1798, when he was succeeded by Blogg and Archer. At Brighton he assembled or retained a company in which Holland was scenic artist and Field stage manager and in which Alexander Archer, John Emery, Kelp, Mote, Walcot, Wheeler, Morton, Fulham, the Misses Fulham, and Miss Diddear were the principals. In the following season, along with some of these, he employed the female Wilmots, Adcock, John Quick, Gurton, William Wallack, Joe Munden, and Pritchard, with Incledon occasionally singing. But Diddear seems also to have been occupied elsewhere. Robert Copeland wrote James Winston on 13 December 1803 from Sandwich, referring him to Diddear "who has managed this circuit for many years."

In the summer of 1800 Diddear took the management and proprietorship at Richmond, Surrey, in partnership with Copeland, "groom to the late Mr. Fector, banker, and principal proprietor of the Dover theatre, and formerly of superior excellence as a private actor," according to Thomas Gilliland, who added that in 1803 a "kind of coalition took place, by admitting Messrs. Powell and Russell." Diddear remained in the management there until 1805, when Cherry of Drury Lane assumed

control. Charles Mate's letter to James Winston dated 14 January 1804 speaks vaguely of Diddear being "jockeyed out of the concern."

Diddear attracted good summer talent from the patent theatres—Quick, Dora Jordan, the Dormers, the Beverlys, Lewis, Powell, and the Dibdins. The *Monthly Mirror* of 1801 showered compliment upon him for taking "this convenient, but hitherto unprofitable, little theatre" to afford a proof "that good management will not be lost upon the inhabitants of Richmond." In fact, "The management of Mr. Diddear affords the most general satisfaction."

Porter, in his history of the Brighton theatre, called Diddear "Charles." But a license (in the Lord Chamberlain's records) to perform at Richmond between "20 30 Sept" 1800 was granted to "Messrs. John Diddear and Robert Copland and Co." The same names were given in 1801–2.

Diddear managed and acted at Dover, Deal, and other places for a good many more years. He died, according to the *Gentleman's Magazine* for April 1841, on 19 February 1841, aged 80. His daughter Harriet Elizabeth became Mrs John Saville Faucit and then the second Mrs William Farren, Jr. Diddear had several other children of whom nothing seems to be recorded.

Didelot, Charles-Louis *1767–1837,* *dancer, choreographer.*

Charles-Louis Didelot, the son of the dancer Charles Didelot and his wife Magdalaine, née Maréchal, was born in Stockholm in 1767. The King of Sweden took notice of Charles-Louis in a court divertissement, and the young dancer was sent to Paris to study under D'Auberval, Vestris, and Deshayes. In Paris Didelot danced at Audinot's theatre; then, in 1786, he returned to Sweden and there composed his first ballet, *Frigga (Freya)*.

On 8 December 1787 Didelot made his first appearance in England, dancing in *Les Offrondes à l'amour* at the King's Theatre. At an annual salary of £400 he appeared during the rest of the 1787–88 season in *The Military Dance*, a *pas de deux* with Mlle Coulon, *Adèle de Ponthieu*, his own *La Bonté du Seigneur*, *Richard Coeur de Lion* (also his work), *The Deserter*, several untitled dances, and three ballets by Noverre: *L'Amour et Psiché* (in which he danced Adonis), *Les Fêtes du temps*, and *Euthyme et Eucharis* (in which he danced Mars). As of 22 May 1788, when he was granted a benefit, Didelot was issuing tickets at No 37, Silver Street, Golden Square.

Didelot returned to the King's Theatre in 1788–89 at a salary of £600 plus a benefit free of house charges. He danced in such works as *L'Embarquement pour Cythère* (which *The London Stage* calls his composition—possibly an incorrect attribution), *Les Fêtes provençales*, *La Nymphe et le chasseur*, *Les Jalousies du sérail*, *Admète*, *Le Tuteur trompé*, and *Les Folies d'Espagne*. Except for a brief period in mid-February 1789 when he was unable to dance because of an injured leg, Didelot was busy all season.

During the 1789–90 season he danced at Bordeaux, but he returned to England in early 1791 to perform at the Pantheon from 17 February through June in such pieces as *Amphion et Thalie*, in which he was Amphion, and *Telemachus in the Is-*

The Metropolitan Museum of Art, Elisha Whittelsey Fund, 1959

CHARLES-LOUIS DIDELOT and MME THÉODORE D'AUBERVAL in *Amphion et Thalie*

by Rowlandson

land of Calypso, in which he danced the title role. With him at the Pantheon was his wife Marie-Rose. Didelot returned to Paris to appear at the Opéra and was not seen in London again until the spring of 1796 when he performed at the King's Theatre from February through July for a fee of £1000. On 20 February, when he danced with his wife a *pas de deux* of his own composition, Didelot was advertised as making his first appearance at the new opera house and his wife was incorrectly noted as making her first appearance in England. During the season Didelot served as choreographer and leading dancer, appearing in such works as *Les Trois sultanes, Le Bouquet, Little Peggy's Love, L'Amant statue, The Caravan at Rest*, and *L'Heureux naufrage*.

The *Monthly Mirror* in February 1796 called Didelot and his wife "indisputably two of the best performers in Europe." At Mme Didelot's benefit on 2 June 1796 a new dance by Didelot was presented, and a critic in the *Morning Chronicle* was enchanted:

The most bewitching dance ever witnessed, for novelty of idea, charm of fancy, and delicacy of passion was performed last night. Not content with the common praise, the audience called forward the author, Didelot, and paid him the tribute due to original and inventive talents. The ballet was entitled L'AMOUR VANGÉ. The invention, which was perfectly new, was that of bands of Cupids floating in air – suspended on their own wings, without the intervention of any grosser medium.

The Didelots were living at that time at No 9, Haymarket, but they moved next door to No 8 the following year and by June 1800 were residing at No 13, Panton Street.

Didelot remained at the King's Theatre through 1801, making occasional appearances (for £16 nightly) at Covent Garden and Drury Lane. As before, he regularly offered new pieces of his own composition

and normally danced in them. Some of these were *Sapho et Phaon, Acis et Galathée*, and *Laura et Lenza*. He was more frequently seen as the leading dancer in works by others, especially pieces by the theatre's ballet master Gallet, such as *Pizarre, L'Heureux retour, L'Offrande à Terpsichore, Ariadne et Bacchus*, and *La Vengeance de l'amour*. Once, on 31 March 1798, it was reported that Didelot was unable to dance as scheduled because of a "severe contusion he received in consequence of a fall, on Tuesday [27 March]."

Fuchs in his *Lexique* reports that Didelot appeared at Paris, Bordeaux, and Lyon during the late 1790s and in Russia in 1801; it is evident that between his London seasons he regularly returned to the Continent. The Didelots had a son, Karl, who was probably born in 1800 (Russian sources date his birth 2 May 1801, but the *Morning Chronicle* stated that Mme Didelot danced that day). At the King's Theatre in 1800–1801 Didelot, his wife, and another son were still appearing, after which time the elder Didelot and his wife went to Russia. Mme Didelot died there in 1803.

In either 1805 or 1806 Didelot married Marie-Rose Colinette, who had danced in Russia in 1799. After their marriage the second Mme Didelot became famous as a teacher of ballroom dancing to the royal family in St Petersburg. Didelot choreographed the dances she taught. After an unsuccessful season in Paris in 1811 the Didelots came to England in 1812. Charles-Louis served as dancing master at the King's Theatre, where both Didelots danced, through 1814, after which the couple returned to the Continent. Didelot was in Paris in 1815 and then went again to Russia in 1816 to serve as ballet master there until his retirement in 1829. He died in Kiev on 7 November 1837.

Mary Grace Swift of Loyola University, New Orleans, has written a study of Charles-Louis Didelot, *A Loftier Flight*, which will now be the definitive biography.

Collection of Harry R. Beard, Victoria and Albert Museum

CHARLES-LOUIS DIDELOT, MARIE-ROSE DIDELOT, and MME PARISOT in *Alonzo e Caro*

artist unknown

She very graciously offered helpful suggestions for this entry and clarified the careers of the two Mmes Didelot.

A portrait said to be of Didelot, in the Chaffee Collection at the Harvard Theatre Collection, is not considered authentic by Mary Grace Swift or by Ivor Guest. Three satirical prints depict Didelot. One by Rowlandson shows Didelot and Mme Théodore (D'Auberval) in *Amphion et Thalie* at the Pantheon in 1791. An anonymous print of 1796 satirizing the costumes of the dancers was published by H. Humphrey; it shows Didelot with his wife and Mme Parisot. Mme Didelot is shown in a transparent gown and Mme Parisot bare-breasted. An engraving by W. H. Brooke in volume XII of the *Satirist* shows Didelot and his second wife in the midst of a riot at the King's Theatre on 1 May 1813.

Didelot, Mme Charles-Louis, Marie-Rose, née Paul *d. 1803, dancer.*

Marie-Rose Paul (or Pole) became the first wife of the dancer Charles-Louis Didelot sometime before her first notice in England on 17 February 1791, when she danced the Muse of Tragedy in *Amphion et Thalie* at the Pantheon. She appeared in performances of the ballet through 15 March. Smith, in *The Italian Opera*, lists Mme Didelot as dancing also at the King's Theatre in 1791 and at the Pantheon and the Haymarket during the 1791–92 season, but *The London Stage* contains no such evidence. The Didelots went to Paris after their London engagement and did not return until 1796.

On 20 February 1796 at the new King's Theatre the Didelots danced a *pas de deux* composed by Charles-Louis; he was advertised as making his first appearance at that theatre (he had danced at the old King's Theatre in the late 1780s), and Mme Didelot was incorrectly hailed as making her first appearance in England. The couple also appeared in *Les Trois sultanes* at the end of the evening. "Mme Rose," as she was frequently cited in the bills, danced during the months that followed in *Alonso e Cora*, *Little Peggy's Love* (at Drury Lane), *The Caravan at Rest* (in which she was a Malabar Woman), *L'Amour vangé*, *Flore et Zéphire* (she danced Flore), *L'Heureux naufrage*, and several untitled pieces. For her season's work from February through July 1796 she received £1000, as did her husband.

From 1796–97 through 1800–1801 the Didelots appeared at the King's Theatre and, occasionally, at the patent houses. Among the many dances in which Mme Didelot was seen over the years were *L'Amour et Psiché*, *Les Délassements militaires*, *Pizarre*, *Sapho et Phaon* (in which she danced Sapho), *Acis et Galathée*, *L'Offrande à Terpsichore*, *Constante et Alcidonis*, *Enée et Didon*, *Les Deux jumelles* ("The pas de deux of Didelot and Rose was particularly admired," said the *Morning Chronicle* of 30 January 1799), *Télémaque* (in which she danced Calypso), *Tarare et Irza*, *Hyppomène et Atalante*, *Laura et Lenza*, and *The Four Quarters of the World* (*Des Quatre nations*).

Mme Didelot was much praised in London. On 28 November 1796, for example, the *Morning Chronicle* commented on the performance of *Zémire et Azor* two nights before at the King's: "never . . . did the English stage see such a female dancer as Madame Rose shewed herself to be. Having recovered the full vigour of health, she displayed talents that drew forth the most vehement bursts of applause; and Didelot, enchanted with the music of this praise, emulated the exertion of his wife."

The Didelots went to Russia after 1801, and there Marie-Rose died in the spring of 1803.

Three satirical prints show Mme Didelot. The first, published by H. Humphrey in 1796, is titled *Modern Grace,—Or—the Operatical Finale to the Ballet of Alonzo*

MARIE-ROSE DIDELOT, as Calipso
engraving by Condé, after Henard

E Caro. Mme Didelot is pictured in transparent dress, and Mme Parisot is shown bare-breasted; also in the picture is Mons Didelot. In 1796 Gillray published the print, *No Flower That Blows Is Like This Rose*, showing Mme Didelot dancing, with a garland of roses. Another Gillray engraving of 1798 shows Mme Didelot and two other opera dancers in scanty costumes. Beneath the picture is a verse from the *Morning Herald*:

'Tis hard for such new fangled orthodox rules,
That our Opera-Troop should be blam'd,
Since like our first parents, they only, poor fools,
Danc'd Naked, & were not asham'd.

Henard pictured Mme Didelot as Calipso in *Télémaque*.

Didier, Abraham J.   *1739–1823, actor.*

The entry for "Mr Didier" in *Theatrical Biography* (1772) presented him as the eldest son of a gentleman who was "in an office of considerable trust at Harwich" and who gave him a fine education. According to that account, the boy was placed as a midshipman in the Navy but rejected a permanent commission to join a "small straggling party of irregulars who were nightly murdering blank verse" before audiences at Dover. He is supposed to have strolled with them from town to town, developing his theatrical ability. But (the account continues) when he was left a legacy of £700 he spent it all in a year of wild debauchery.

At Dublin's Smock Alley Theatre (at some date undetermined but certainly before 1770, when the first mention of her as Mrs Didier occurs) he met the actress Margaret Du Bellamy, who curbed his bibulous behavior and then married him. Whether the Dublin visit was before or after his first London appearance in 1764 is not known.

Abraham Didier was first on the company lists at Drury Lane on 2 October 1764 as Cleremont in *The Old Maid*. He played Don Luis in *She Wou'd and She Wou'd Not* on 22 October and Fabian in *The Capricious Lovers* on 2 November. He earned 5*s.* per acting day during the season and then slipped back to the country.

In 1766 and 1767 he was at Edinburgh. On 12 January 1767 he was one of a group of actors issuing a handbill protesting the method (a suborned riot) which the actor Stayley had employed for forcing his way back into the Edinburgh company, which had rejected him. On this occasion "A. J. Didier" appeared among the signers. A Mr and Mrs "Dedier" were seen several times at Bath in 1767–68. Records of Edinburgh's theatrical affairs are scarce for 1768–69 and 1769–70, but perhaps Didier was again playing in the Scottish capital,

for he occurs in bills of 1770–71, filling such parts as Sharper in *The Old Bachelor,* and that season Mrs Didier was in the company too.

Samuel Foote had just taken a three-year lease of the Edinburgh house, and when he came south to open his usual summer season at London's Haymarket Theatre, he brought the Didiers along. On 17 May 1771 Abraham played Young Knowell in *Every Man in His Humour* and followed with Young Cope in *The Lame Lover,* Young Loveit in *The Commissary,* Biondello in *Catharine and Petruchio,* Philip in *The Brothers,* Jersey in *The Maid of Bath,* Loveit in *Miss in Her Teens,* Prattle in *The Deuce is in Him,* Charles Dudley in *The West Indian,* and Sharper in *The Old Bachelor.*

Almost upon his first appearance the *Town and Country Magazine* decided: "Mr. Didier is genteel and easy, and appears to have a just conception of his author" and mildly praised Mrs Didier as well. But no London winter managers were interested in acquiring the Didiers, and their sponsor Foote had quickly tired of his Edinburgh enterprise and had passed the lease on to West Digges. The Didiers drifted back to the provinces.

Probably at some time in 1772 both Abraham and Margaret Didier signed on with Palmer at Bath, and there both played steadily until Abraham retired from that company about 1785 (she continued there until well into the nineteenth century). They appeared also at Bristol in 1776, in the spring and summer of 1779, in 1779–80, and in 1780–81 (she continued much longer). Didier also played at Richmond in the summer of 1778.

So far as records show Abraham Didier was seen only one more time on a stage after he left the Bath-Bristol troupe. On 13 December 1786 he turned up inexplicably at Covent Garden to act Dashwou'd in *Know Your Own Mind.*

He continued residence in Bristol and

died there on 26 October 1823, aged 84 according to Genest. The will of Abraham Didier of Bristol, "gent.", signed 3 May 1817 and witnessed by William Tanner and John I. Williams, left in trust to John Araman and Philip Jones, merchants of Bristol, for the benefit of his wife Margaret all his "Close or parcel of land situate at Mangotsfield" in the County of Gloucester. The residuary legatees were Ann Gibbons, wife of William Gibbons of Abbot Leigh, Somerset, and her children. Household goods and several government annuities also went to Abraham's widow. The will was proved by the oath of Margaret Didier on 6 December 1823. She survived him by six years.

Didier, Mrs Abraham J., Margaret, née Evans 1741–1829, actress, singer.

Margaret Dubellamy was the sister of the well-known actor and singer Charles Clementine Dubellamy. They had forsaken their more prosaic surname, Evans, when they had begun to appear on the stage, and "Charles Clementine" was really plain "John."

The date of Margaret's first appearance is not known to us. Very likely it was at Dublin where she was said by *Theatrical Biography* (1772) to have met her future husband Abraham Didier when both were engaged by the Smock Alley company. He was called drunken and dissolute by that account and she was said to have reformed his manners and made him apply himself to his profession. The date of their marriage is not known, but she appeared as "Mrs Didier" on the bills of 1767–68 and on the Edinburgh bills of 1770–71, playing such roles as Patch in *The Busybody* and singing Lucy in *The Beggar's Opera*.

Samuel Foote brought both the Didiers from Edinburgh to London's Haymarket in the summer of 1771. Margaret's debut at the Haymarket was on 15 May 1771 but the bill for the mainpiece, Foote's old standby *The Devil Upon Two Sticks*, listed only actors, no parts. She was Bridget in *Every Man in His Humour* on 17 May and Lucy in *The Minor* on 20 May. Thereafter that season she was steadily employed, as Miranda in *The Busy Body*, Mrs Cadwallader in *The Author*, Ann Lovely in *A Bold Stroke for a Wife*, Lucy in *The Virgin Unmask'd*, Lady Fanciful in *The Provok'd Wife*, Ursula in *The Padlock*, Juliet in *The Patron*, Sophia in *The Brothers*, Miss Grantham in *The Lyar*, Charlotte in *The Apprentice*, Nell in *The Devil to Pay*, Dorcas in *The Mock Doctor*, Mlle Florival in *The Deuce is in Him*, Arethusa in *The Contrivances*, Miss Rantipole in *The Tobacconist*, the title part in *Dido*, Elvira in *Love Makes a Man*, Charlotte in *The West Indian*, Silvia in *The Old Bachelor*, Rosetta in *Love in a Village*, and Frill in *The Coxcombs*—a solid line of leads and secondary parts in comedy and farce.

A London newspaper critic had found both the Didiers valuable acquisitions to Foote's theatre, "the lady in particular." She had a pleasing figure, good voice, and a "just conception of an author and an agreeable delivery, with peculiar vivacity and spirit." Yet none of London's winter managers seized upon this treasure or her husband, and when summer returned the Didiers were absent from the Haymarket. Foote had repented his Edinburgh bargain, and the Didiers perhaps did not appeal to his successor, West Digges (or more likely Digges did not appeal to them). The couple went instead about that time to Bath, where both played fairly steadily until Abraham's retirement in 1781.

Margaret continued to play at Bath and at Bristol every season between 1772–73 and 1806–7, first in her usual soubrettes and young comic eccentrics and later as character women of an elderly cast. (She was also at Richmond, Surrey, in the summer of 1778.) Garrick wrote Colman from "the Bath" on 20 April 1775 that he had written a prologue for Mrs Didier's benefit and that it had been given a good reception.

She often sang songs in her comedy roles (though apparently she had no sustained singing parts in opera or ballad opera) and her "Old Maid's Song" became a desideratum of great value to her colleagues when they had a benefit night. After some 34 years on the Bath stage, and now 66, she retired at the end of the season of 1806–7. She gave her famous Mrs Hardcastle in *She Stoops to Conquer* for her last benefit on 17 February, "after which," Genest reports the bill as predicting, "Mrs Didier will deliver a new poetic address, and take an oblique retrospect of her stage-life, stating many reasons for her intended retirement." The "many reasons" were her 66 years, and the idea had been borrowed from the farewell address of Mrs Siddons, with whom in earlier years at Bath she had been in rivalry for parts.

Mrs Didier's husband Abraham had died in 1823. She died at Bristol in 1829, aged 88. Abraham had left her substantial real properties and annuities. When she made her own will on 20 January 1825 she passed along the property to Ann (Mrs William) Gibbons and her children of Leigh in Somerset, as provided for already in Abraham's will. (The relationship is not understood. Mrs Gibbons could hardly have been a daughter of the Didiers, inasmuch as *Miss* Elizabeth Every "Mrs Gibbons's sister" was left £10.) Mary Hobbs, servant, received £5, as did William Gibbons. Mrs Burton and Miss Harriet Burton "of Stokes Croft Bristol" received £10 each.

Didsbury, Robert   ₁fl. 1787–1794₁, singer.

Robert Didsbury was paid £2 15s. (weekly? per performance?) as a basso by the Academy of Ancient Music for the 1787–88 season. Doane's *Musical Directory* of 1794 listed him as living at No 8, Gwyn's Buildings, Islington, and a participant in the oratorio performances at Drury Lane.

Diesey, Mr   ₁fl. 1767₁, dancer.

All that is known of Mr Diesey is that he was a dancer at Drury Lane in 1767.

Dietrich, Christian   d. 1760, bass player.

On 28 August 1739 Christian Dietrich, a double bass player, became one of the original subscribers to the Royal Society of Musicians. He participated in performances of the *Messiah* at the Chapel of the Foundling Hospital in May 1754 and on 27 April 1758 and in each case was paid 15s. After his death on 5 April 1760 the *Gentleman's Magazine* called him an "excellent performer on the double bass."

Dieupart, Charles   d. c. 1740, violinist, harpsichordist, composer, impresario.

The French musician Charles Dieupart (variously spelled by baffled English printers De Parr, Diopar, Dioupast, Dupar) settled in England about 1700. His *Pièces de clavecin* were perhaps written about this time, though they were not published until about 1735. Dieupart's earliest appearances were probably as a harpsichordist. At Drury Lane on 11 February 1703 and at Richmond Wells on 12 August he accompanied Gasperini, and on 18 May 1704 at York Buildings he played for Giuseppe Olzi. He continued playing at concerts but found time for composing as well. On 22 February 1704 his music for the interlude *Britain's Happiness* was first heard.

By 28 January 1706 he had become an agent for the celebrated singer Mrs Tofts, proposing terms for her to Christopher Rich, the manager of Drury Lane. He continued in that capacity for at least another year and similarly served the singer Littleton Ramondon in dealings with the opera impresario Heidegger in 1707 and 1708. This contact with managers may have gone to his head, for when he petitioned for a position in the opera band at the Queen's Theatre in the Haymarket in 1707, he asked an outrageous £3 nightly while his colleagues asked no more than £1 10s. He was not at first hired. This would not have upset him perhaps, had his post in the band at Drury Lane been secure, but when Christopher Rich heard that some of his musicians were negotiating to play at the Queen's Theatre, he turned them out. The musicians appealed to the Lord Chamberlain, asking restitution for six days' lost time. Most of them asked for £1 10s. or £2; Dieupart asked for £4. What Dieupart settled for is not known.

By 1 December 1707 matters had been straightenend out and Dieupart was hired at the Queen's for £1 5s. daily, the highest fee paid any of the musicians. His annual income at the theatre seems to have been £70. The Coke papers at Harvard, which provide us with much of this information, also make it clear that Dieupart, in addition to being an agent, accompanist, composer, and member of the Drury Lane and then the Queen's Theatre bands, was probably a court musician. His demands for high pay were probably justified, for he was apparently proficient on the violin as well as the harpsichord.

Dieupart's association with the Queen's Theatre brought him another opportunity to compose. On 26 February 1708 Motteux' *Love's Triumph* was performed, the music being partly composed by Dieupart and partly adapted by him from works by Scarlatti and others. Since the opera was in English, Dieupart's task was to fit the music to the English text, and the librettist was pleased with the results: "it will owe not a little to Mr. Dieupart," he wrote in his Preface, "for his share in the contrivance of the entertainments and his supplying what recitative and other music was necessary."

Dieupart's association with the Queen's Theatre may have ended about 1711. In 1711–12 he joined with Nicola Haym and Thomas Clayton in an interesting attempt to promote English opera by presenting concerts at York Buildings at which poems were recited to a musical background.

Clayton was the chief composer, though Dieupart may also have written some music for these events. The trio sought the aid of Sir Richard Steele through letters to *The Spectator* in December 1711 and January 1712, but their venture was not very successful.

In the years following 1710 some of Dieupart's music was published. His *Select Lessons for the Harpsichord or Spinnett*, a reprint of part of *Six Suittes de clavessin* (Amsterdam, n.d.), came out about 1710. A song called *The Lovely Caelia* was printed about 1715, as was *As Amoret wth Phillis sat* from *The Man of Mode. If Tears wou'd once restore my Rest*, from *Oroonoko*, was published about 1720, and *The Wheedler* reached print about 1735.

Much of Dieupart's music was performed but not published. On 14 March 1722 at Drury Lane was heard his concerto for two oboes and two flutes; the following May Baston played a Dieupart concerto for the little flute; and on 15 May 1723 a concerto by Dieupart was performed after ACT I of *The Plain Dealer*. In May 1724 his music was ridiculed in the *Session of Musicians*. The scene is a court held by Apollo to determine who is the best composer in England:

> D——p——rt, *well powder'd, gave himself an Air,*
> *As if he could not fail of Fortune there,*
> *Who always prov'd successful with the Fair.*
> *The God his Passion hardly could contain,*
> *For spoiling Opera-Songs in* Drury Lane:
> *But hop'd his Skill he'd in it's Sphere confine,*
> *His Fire betwixt the Acts would brilliant shine.*

Composing incidental music as entr'acte entertainment at plays was probably Dieupart's métier. He was at this time playing in the Drury Lane band again and well situated to have his pieces performed. One of his last works was a trumpet concerto played there on 4 May 1726.

The following 9 September Dieupart's salary at Drury Lane was reduced to 6s. 8d. nightly. What it had been before is not known, but it is clear that he was no longer in much demand. It is said that he wasted away the rest of his life performing in taverns, growing more indolent as the years passed, yet reports were that his playing of Corelli on the violin remained neat and elegant. His last known appearance was on 11 September 1734 at Hampstead; he was billed as "Capt Dupar," scholar to the late Corelli and late music master to his present highness the Prince of Orange. But his past glories seem not to have interested music lovers of the 1730s. Dieupart died about 1740, far advanced in years and, according to Hawkins, in "very necessitated circumstances."

Dieupree. *See* **Dupré.**

Digby, Mr *fl. 1781], actor, singer.*

At the Haymarket Theatre on 22 January 1781 Mr Digby sang "Stand to your Guns" and acted Sneaksby in *A Wife to be Let.*

Digges. *See also* **Diggs.**

Digges, West Dudley *1720?–1786, actor, singer, manager.*

The father of West Dudley Digges the actor was probably Thomas Digges, Esq, of an ancient Kentish family. His mother was Elizabeth, daughter of John West, sixth Baron De La Warr and sister of John West, first Earl De La Warr. These connections, affirmed in Digges's obituary in Flynn's *Hibernian Chronicle* of 12 November 1786 and confirmed by Collins's *Peerage* (1812), were obscured in Digges's lifetime—perhaps deliberately—because of the reluctance of his relations to own either his profession or his reputation for profligacy. Colman in his *Random Records*

WEST DUDLEY DIGGES
artist unknown

(1830) and Peake in *Memoirs of the Colman Family* (1841) hinted falsely that Digges was the illegitimate son of the Earl De La Warr. Other sources—certainly equally erroneous—made him the son of a Colonel Digges of the Guards who had lost a fortune when the South Sea bubble burst. That he may have been the illegitimate son (by Thomas Digges or another) of the Lady Elizabeth West has also been suggested. If the birth year of 1720 given by Joseph Knight in Digges's short entry in *The Dictionary of National Biography* is correct, then that conclusion is inescapable, for according to the *Peerage* the Honorable Miss West and Thomas Digges were married in August 1724.

Perhaps West Digges spent his youth at the Digges estate, Chilham Castle in Kent. But none of the circumstances of his early life or of his education (which seems to have been classical and extensive) are known. Knight (following an uncited source) states that "A commission was obtained for him, and he was sent to Scotland, where he encumbered himself with a burden of debt of which he was never able to get rid." That is another statement about Digges which must be received with both caution and respect. He did not come to the stage until 1749—when he was 29 (or 25?). Military service seems a reasonable explanation of his late start in the theatre and is rendered the more probable because the Lords De La Warr were eminent generals.

On 29 November 1749 at Smock Alley Theatre, Dublin, West Digges appeared as Jaffeir in *Venice Preserv'd*, billed only as "a Gentleman lately arrived from England, who never yet appeared on any Stage." Hitchcock says that Digges had been introduced to Sheridan's management by Theophilus Cibber. The young man was an instant success with Dubliners and succeeded well even in some leading tragedy roles despite the fact that Sheridan himself laid claim to them much of the time and another young star, Henry Mossop, was also at that time in the ascendant. Digges soon took over Hamlet, was seen as Lear, and, acting the role of Antony, aided Sheridan as Brutus and Mossop as Cassius to present one of the century's finest stagings of *Julius Caesar*. He did as well in several lines of comedy, which he inaugurated on 12 March 1750 with his first performance of Plume in *The Recruiting Officer*. His season was in fact so successful that Garrick heard about it and wrote to Draper while on a visit to the Duke of Devonshire at Chatsworth on 2 June 1750:

I have made some enquiry after *Digges*, from a Mr. Ponsonby, son-in-law to the Duke, who is just come from Ireland; he says the young man has great wants, but was liked very well. I wish I had him at a moderate, or even almost any price—not exceeding *five hundred* pounds and no clear benefit.

The £500 was a jest—it was what Garrick himself took for a season—but the desire to hire Digges probably was not. However, Smock Alley and its excellent company and the gentlemanly and enlightened management of Sheridan held Digges in Dublin for six seasons, through 1753–54.

Among the parts he played there were the following: both Jaques and Orlando in *As You Like It*, Macheath in *The Beggar's Opera*, Juba in *Cato*, First Spirit in *Comus*, Myrtle in *The Conscious Lovers*, Aufidius in *Coriolanus*, Pyrrhus in *The Distrest Mother*, the title role in *Don Sebastian*, Careless in *The Double Dealer*, Southampton in *The Earl of Essex*, both Lothario and Sciolto in *The Fair Penitent*, Lord Hardy in *The Funeral*, the Ghost in *Hamlet*, both Dumont and Hastings in *Jane Shore*, Buckingham in *Henry VIII*, the title role in *King John*, Lord Guilford Dudley in *Lady Jane Grey*, Barnwell in *The London Merchant*, Scandal in *Love for Love*, Macduff in *Macbeth*, Alcanor in *Mahomet*, Charles in *The Non-Juror*, Tiresias in *Oedipus*, Bellmour in *The Old Bachelor*, Castalio in *The Orphan*, Hippolitus in *Phaedra and Hippolitus*, Lord Townly in *The Provok'd Husband*, Sir John Brute in *The Provok'd Wife*, Loveless in *The Relapse*, Publius in *The Roman Father*, Romeo in *Romeo and Juliet*, Eumenes in *The Siege of Damascus*, Torrismond in *The Spanish Fryar*, Frankly in *The Suspicious Husband*, Clerimont in *The Tender Husband*, Elder Wou'dbe in *The Twin Rivals*, Mirabel in *The Way of the World*, and Nerestan in *Zara*.

The list shows a nice balance between comedy and tragedy and it also shows the breadth of Digges's abilities at this stage of his life, abilities which to a considerable extent remained with him to the end of his career. He was described in *The Present State of the Stage* (1753) as one

whose Mien is noble, his Person very engaging; he is not quite so tall as Mr. Barry, but extremely genteel; his Eye is brisk and spirited; all his Features happily disposed for the Stage, and capable of marking strongly the Variety of Passions natural to the human Frame. This he manifests in Lear and Jaffier . . . [but] fails too often, by endeavoring to imitate Mr. Garrick, in Things, to execute which requires the Judgment, as well as the Powers of a Garrick.

But Digges was displaying his formidable talent for making trouble for himself. He had run up many debts in Dublin and had contracted what his century called an "irregular connection" with Sarah Ward (née Achurch), estranged wife of Henry Ward the provincial actor and playwright. The relationship probably had begun when Digges and James Love in the summer of 1752 joined a company of strollers which Lee headed. The troupe had erected a wooden booth against a wall of the Bishop's Palace in Castle Yard, Glasgow, which had constituted the first Glasgow Theatre but which had been immediately torn down by George Whitefield the Methodist and his fanatical followers.

An intimate but interrupted and incomplete record of their common-law marriage is furnished by a series of letters which passed between West Digges and Sarah Ward from 1752 through their final separation in 1758. From Glasgow the pair sailed to Ireland by way of Liverpool and played at Cork until September, when she joined and he rejoined the Smock Alley company for the 1752–53 season.

By the end of that season Digges's creditors became so clamorous that, leaving Sarah behind to try to reach some agreement with them, he fled Dublin for England. Somehow he raised enough money by September to dispatch his friend the actor John Sowdon to appease his Dublin duns, which expedient allowed him to return uneasily to the Smock Alley stage that fall.

The 1753–54 season was marred by a political riot in the theatre. Adherents of one of the warring factions demanded that Digges repeat an inflammatory passage in *Mahomet* which had been applauded in a previous performance and which Sheridan had forbidden Digges to utter again. When Digges informed the audience of this prohibition the result was a demand that Sheridan come forward and apologize. He refused to do so and went home. The audience sent messengers after him, and when he remained adamant they demolished the interior of the theatre in a riot which lasted from eight o'clock in the evening until two in the morning. Sheridan, in disgust, left Ireland for two years.

Digges also left the country, being again harassed for debt. He crossed to London and went to ground in the sanctuary of St James ("in the verge of the Court so I shall escape arrests") along with the actor George Bland. He wrote Sarah to "Direct to Charles West, Esq. to be left at the coffee house in Buckingham Court, near the Admiralty, Spring Gardens, London." On 8 June 1754 his alias and address were "Richard Templeton, Esq. at the post-house at Wakefield."

Meanwhile, Sarah Ward resumed her professional travels. In May 1754 she was acting at Chester. Late in June she was "going to York or Doncaster secretly." In October she was again in Dublin. She was at Waltham Abbey, Essex, in April and May 1755, then at Birmingham, then Glasgow, and finally Edinburgh, where she remained until Digges joined her, probably by March 1756.

James Dibdin was undoubtedly correct in considering that the "gentleman from the Theatre Royal in Dublin" who was advertised on the Canongate bill for 6 March as making "his second appearance on this stage" in the role of Lord Townly was West Digges. The same "gentleman" played another of Digges's best roles—Cardinal Wolsey in *Henry VIII*—on 29 March 1756. On 28 September Digges and Sarah were reunited on the stage as Romeo and Juliet.

On 1 October 1756 he sang Macheath in *The Beggar's Opera*.

By that October Digges had also supplanted the weak James Callender as manager of the Canongate, by appointment of the theatre's proprietors. In that season he precipitated a celebrated crisis in the Scottish kirk when on 14 December 1756 he produced the premiere of the Reverend John Home's tragedy *Douglas*, in which he played Douglas and Sarah Ward was Lady Randolph. It played for perhaps seven consecutive nights (a long run for Edinburgh) and caused a sensation and a schism in Scottish society, the disciplining of several clerics who dared to visit the Canongate to see and praise it, and the eventual resignation from the kirk of the Reverend Mr Home.

Digges went energetically to work the next season trying to improve the company and the dramatic offerings at the Canongate and at the same time expanded his own repertoire to include Othello, Captain Bobadil in *Every Man in His Humour*, Dr Caius in *The Merry Wives of Windsor*, and Kastril in *The Alchemist*. A ludicrous squabble with the musicians in the band, which spilled over into "Declarations" and "Defenses" distributed about the streets on broadsides, occupied much of his time until April 1758, and so did a growing pile of debts. Moreover, David Beatt, the Newcastle manager, and the deposed James Callender conspired successfully to wrest the management from him, although the astute Sarah Ward (acting in Liverpool that summer) had advised him by letter to sue the proprietors for a third share of the concern.

Sarah moved on from Liverpool to Newcastle, where she assumed for the first time the name "Mrs Digges" in the bills and entered into an agreement on Digges's behalf. Digges arrived, but after they had acted for a few nights Sarah abruptly left for London and Covent Garden. Miss George Anne Bellamy (soon to replace

Sarah in West Digges's affections and then acting at Covent Garden) later in her *Apology* described Sarah's arrival spitefully:

This lady had one of the most beautiful faces I ever beheld. But her figure was vulgar to a degree. By the stoop and magnitude of her shoulders it might be imagined that she had formerly carried milk pails. Her beauty would have been much more conspicuous in that line . . . than in the character of a queen or young princess. Yet . . . being pregnant into the bargain, it was determined that she should appear as Cordelia . . .

And, much more significantly: "She was accompanied by a frightful being, to whom she gave the title of husband." Had the glorious prospects of London success and Covent Garden money brought the long-lost Henry Ward rushing loyally to his wife's side? Probably. Certainly the eight-year association of Sarah Ward and West Digges was at an end.

The letters appear to offer ample evidence that the infidelities and, before the end, the coldness and indifference of West Digges were principally at fault for the end of the affair between "Westy" and his "Dear Sally," his "Dearest Life." He is revealed as a proud, vain, extravagant, rather childish and irritable lover, uxorious and jealous even during his own infidelities. And though she, on her side, was jealous and a complainer, self-pitying and self-justifying, and not above exaggerating their children's illnesses in order to keep him from deserting, she evidently had much to bear. Extracts from only one of the letters will suffice to show that. She has detected one of his intrigues. He has brought a "Mrs Betty" into the house "and left me not werewithal (and at a time too when my condition required it) even to purchase a bottle of ale." Did he not know that "You was killing *poor forsaken Mrs Ward* by inches, a person whose whole sould was wrapt up in Mr Digges . . ." and

Did you not tell her at Mrs Waterson's where your idol lodg'd, that you were not marred, and that you *hated* both *me* and the *children*, but that you was obliged to keep up *appearances*? . . . Was this well done? Have I *deserved* this from you? 'Tis true I am *not* your wife by *law*, but if the most *sincear* love that ever *woman* had can be binding, Mr Digges had that from me. . . .

—and much more. The last letter (undated) among the surviving ones might have been taken from a sentimental novel:

I hear give you up your vows: give them and your person where you have bestowed your affection; you shall never hear that I make the least complaint of you; tis not yours but nature's fault that deprives me of you. Of what then can I blame you? My sorrows shall be silent, and to myself alone. You know I have not a wish beyond you; and that though I am now writeing to you for the last time, and to take my leve of you for ever, I can't help tell you that all my happeness is gone with you; and find, form what resolution I will, I am doom'd to be wretched without you. Judg then what I must suffer; but everything to affoard ease is deny'd me; the friendly release of tears, which should sometimes come to my ade, is now refused me. The love I bear Mr Digges will I cherish in my breast, and give it to his child, if it shall please God to let it see the light. Excuse me for mentioning what perhaps you do not choose to remember; I could not help it. That you may be ever happy, is the wish of her who is your sincear friend and humble servant.

The plea seems the more pitiable for its shop-worn rhetoric and even for its transparency. It did not work.

There is no way of numbering the children, living, dead, and embryonic, who had kept them together. There were at least six. In July 1753 Digges had commiserated "I am much concerned at the loss of poor little Charlotte, since I know how much you felt on so tender an occasion," an expression perhaps too cool even for Digges if Charlotte was his own child and not Henry Ward's. In June 1754 Digges speaks of an expected birth. Evidently the eldest, Poppy, accompanied Sarah when she toured and the rest were left in Edinburgh with West. In June (1757?) Sarah mentions a young "Westy." She is delighted that he "can walk again, and that my sweet Peggy is well. . . . Pray has my Tommy got his cloaths. . . . Poppey . . . begs her duty to you and love to her brothers and sisters." In another letter a little later she asks: "Pray what has gone with my son Bob? Has he left Scotland?" This reference also must be to a child fathered by Henry Ward.

Digges was now free to make his own arrangements, theatrical as well as domestic, but he was startled when Beatt discharged him from the company in the later summer of 1758, seizing the excuse that he had hired a man-and-wife team and that one of them had now broken the contract by departing. Dibdin thought that "Beat had other reasons for getting rid of Digges. The actor's popularity was great, and his known wish [again] to become manager, if not proprietor, made it dangerous to have him on the premises."

Digges took himself off to Ireland for a season and a summer and forgot chill Caledonia in the warmth of George Anne Bellamy's smiles. But he was not forgotten in Edinburgh, and the anonymous pamphlet (almost certainly by James Boswell and Francis Gentleman) called *A View of the Edinborough Theatre During the Summer Season, 1759* was dedicated to him. In the preface the putative single author praised Digges's acting in general terms adding

As to your *private* Character, into whatever scenes of Folly and Impudence the World may imagine you have been hurried, through a too great Gaiety and Easiness of Disposition; yet, Sir, allow me to say, without Flattery, that if they knew your many amiable Qualifications as well as I do, they would look upon your Imperfections with the most favorable Eye; they would pardon, excuse and forget them.

In Dublin he and Miss Bellamy soon formed a furtive liaison and also very soon found themselves dangerously in debt. Digges once more fled Dublin.

On 8 November 1759 he was back in the Scottish capital puffing his own abilities by inserting anonymous paragraphs in the *Courant* (for which, that paper's accounts show, he paid 3s. 6d.):

> The excellent performance of this *actor* gives the most pleasing expectations to all lovers of dramatic entertainments, that we shall once more see theatrical representations worth our attention. *Ribaldry* and *trash* will give place to *taste* and *truth*, and the works of a Shakespeare will be exhibited by a Gentleman who has established his merit as an actor; as well by a judicious taste in the conception of character, as by equal abilities in the public performance of it.

By this means Digges hoped to put pressure on Beatt to rehire him by drumming up a demand by the public, which vastly admired him still. A paper war ensued, there was indeed a public outcry in Digges's behalf, the theatre opened in November—and Digges was snugly in the company. He appeared as Hamlet on 15 December 1759 and the critic of the *Chronicle* said that "Nature has happily adapted his figure to the dignity and gracefullness of the part; and his knowledge of the author is conspicuous in every line he utters."

In 1760–61 Digges was drawn back to Dublin again where awaited him a good array of his favorite characters and George Anne Bellamy—her liaison with John Calcraft her "keeper" now severed. She and Digges began openly to live together. But she had been attacked by Edward Thompson in *The Meretriciad*, which placed her on a level with the prostitutes there celebrated, she was anxious to leave Calcraft's

vicinity, and she had a lucrative offer from Covent Garden for 1761–62. So she and Digges were separated for a season.

But on 5 May 1762, long before the Covent Garden season was over, George Anne was in Edinburgh to play, as the *Courant* announced, "for the first time on the stage of this kingdom." She states in her *Apology* that she had come to Scotland firmly resolved not to act, had, indeed, fled London because of insistent creditors. But Digges had placed advertisements in the Edinburgh papers proclaiming that she was, in a limited engagement, to appear in *Tancred and Sigismunda*, *Rule a Wife and Have a Wife*, *Jane Shore*, and *The Provok'd Husband*. Digges had also announced that he had written, and would speak, an "Occasional prologue." So, despite the fact that she had even gone the length, in her angry impulsive way, of taking "a pair of scissors" and cutting "my hair off quite close to my head, to prevent my being solicited to appear in public," Digges, with his silver tongue, worked his will. Appear she did, not in four plays but in eight, with Digges her co-star in six of them. Digges pressed for more but she threw one of her famous tantrums. She shortly afterward left to play an engagement in Glasgow—only to find that a mob had burned the stage of the new theatre and with it the costumes she had sent ahead.

On 4 September the *Courant* published a cryptic and curious item of news: "For family reasons, a gentleman of the theatre has been obliged to alter his name in the public bills." On the same date the bills of the theatre carried both a Mrs and a *Mr* Bellamy. No satisfactory reason has ever been advanced for this strange occurrence.

Digges and George Anne Bellamy bought a cottage at nearby Bonnington where they quarrelled energetically and entertained extravagantly, once more running up debts with local tradesmen. ("He indulged me with every pleasure he could procure for me," George Anne wrote later.

"But my temper was so much soured by the continual demands for the debts he had contracted before my union with him, that I could not relish any enjoyment, or behave towards him with that complacency I could have wished.") The cottage was sold off by the creditors; the lovers took leave of Edinburgh (separately, for George Anne took a side trip to act in Glasgow) and departed for London. Digges had already been to London once that summer of 1764 to treat with his brother Captain Dudley Digges "upon some family concerns," as George Anne remembered it. On his return West brought her a present—"a large silver repeater, to be placed at the head of my bed, as I had often wished for a machine of that kind, to know the hours when I was to take the medicines my indifferent state of health rendered necessary."

It is hardly easier to determine the chronology of events in George Anne Bellamy's *Apology* than it is to validate them. But apparently it was at about the time that she and Digges prepared to leave Edinburgh, she to take up her engagement at Covent Garden, that his mother "the honourable Mrs Digges" died, "which made it necessary for her son to go to England. She left eight thousand pounds between her two sons, upon condition that the elder should quit the stage, and take her maiden name of West." Digges preceded George Anne to London, traveling on money that she had obtained by pawning the repeating watch.

At this juncture, George Anne's memoirs provide two more pieces of these dubious data:

Having one day received a letter from Mr. Digges, now West, with a demand for a larger sum than I could spare, I could not help being much affected whilst I read it. Upon which a gentleman, who happened to be present [!], told me, he was well assured the union that had taken place between Mr. Digges and me could not be valid, as to his knowledge a former wife was still living. Being alarmed at this information, and doubt-

ing the truth of it, the gentleman promised to send me well-authenticated proofs of it as soon as he got to London. . . .

Accordingly I received, soon after, an affidavit, confirming the truth of this assertion, by which I was again set at liberty; and found, as I had done more than once, an union I thought to be *indissoluble*, suddenly dissolved. The gentleman at the same time informed me, that he had seen Mrs. Digges, who told him that she had announced her death in the public papers, in order to deceive her husband, by whom she was apprehensive of being molested.

We can find no record of any marriage ceremony in which West Digges was involved as one of the principals, even though in the passage quoted above and at other places in her *Apology* George Anne seems to point to some sort of marriage ceremony performed to unite her and West. Lee Lewes, who knew them both well, flatly denied a marriage, though he says George Anne, like Mrs Ward, much desired one. When George Anne brought the matter up, says Lewes, Digges's reply was always, "Madame, I give you leave to treat me like a foot-pad, rob me and let me go, but don't tie me neck and heels."

Digges apparently was faithful to the terms of his mother's bequest for several years. But he was acting in Ireland again by 1767, for he was in the Limerick bills that summer. After that there is another large gap in our knowledge of his activities. He was off and on at Dublin, it seems certain. An unidentified newspaper clipping of August 1771 announced that "Mr. Foote has sold the remaining Term in the Lease of the Theatre at Edinburgh, to Mr Digges, a capital Performer from Dublin."

He reappeared in glory before his old votaries the Edinburghers as Macbeth on 23 November 1771. "On Mr Digges appearance," reported the *Courant*, "the applause was the most universal that ever was heard; it was several minutes before he was permitted to speak, and the audience welcomed him not only with thundering claps but with loud and repeated huzzas."

In the summer of 1772 Digges took John Bland as partner in the Edinburgh enterprise. Traveling to London to look for recruits before the season opened, Digges fell into the hands of bailiffs, who arrested him for an old debt, but by a series of legal maneuvers involving the Scottish statute of limitations he freed himself both from durance and from payment.

Digges evidently worked hard at his managing but his inveterate extravagance never let him get far enough ahead financially to make the Canongate a rival in excellence to Smock Alley, or even Bath-Bristol, let alone the London houses. John Topham, an astute London visitor, put his finger on another difficulty in a letter of 1775 quoted by Dibdin:

[Digges] is now at the head of a company who seem intended as foils to himself, and though they change every year, I am informed they never change for the better. The small-ness of the salaries accounts for this. There is only one or two whose pay exceeds a guinea a week, nor can the receipts of the house afford more, while the rent is so high.

Thus, though he augmented his resident company (the likes of Inchbald, Wood, Webb, Fleetwood, Miss Glassington, Mrs Welton, Beynon, the Charterises, Simpson, Hallion, Granger) with many larger names who drifted through Edinburgh (Ann Cat-ley, Ned Shuter, Tate Wilkinson, Mrs Yates, et al.), as "Auld Reekie" became more sophisticated Digges's offerings and company were seen as less than satisfactory.

His personal popularity seems never to have dwindled, except among that grow-ing number of people to whom he owed money. He exploited his popularity to the full, not only at Edinburgh but elsewhere. He was at both Cork and Limerick in Sep-tember 1774. As early as 1775 he played a run of five nights of his principal characters for Tate Wilkinson at York. He went to

WEST DUDLEY DIGGES, as Cato

by Roberts

Liverpool to play five nights from 30 Oc-tober 1776 (Cato, Dr Faustus, Henry VIII, Macheath) and pocketed £43 14s. 3d., after expenses, and had a similarly successful five nights there in October 1777. But such extra emoluments were quickly sucked into the quicksand of his financial swamp, larger and deeper year by year. Eventually he found it impossible to continue; indeed he found himself in the Canongate Prison, from which only a process of bankruptcy and the friendly assistance of Tate Wilkin-son extracted him.

Considering Garrick's early interest, Digges's wide acquaintance with London actors and managers, and his reputation as a fine actor and great "draw," it is astonishing that only after he had virtually exhausted his resources at both Dublin and Edinburgh did he ever set foot on a London stage. His debut in London was at the Haymarket on 14 August 1777 in the title part of Addison's *Cato*, a play, it was claimed by the bills, never performed at the Haymarket before that date. It certainly appears that Digges had something larger in mind than a casual summer performance, and it seems probable that he was determined to make an impression on the London managers. For he approached the performance in an antiquary spirit. Not that he went back to the time of Cato Uticensis in dressing the part, but he did go back to the time of Addison. Peake recalled:

Digges 'discharged the character' in the same costume as it is to be supposed was adopted by Booth, when the play was originally acted [in 1713], that is, in a shape, as it is technically termed [i.e., a costume] of the stiffest order, decorated with gilt leather upon a black ground, with black stockings, black gloves, and a powdered periwig.

On 29 August he did his famous Wolsey in *Henry VIII* in his rather agreeably pompous manner, winning the approval of the *London Chronicle* at least, which said that Digges eschewed "the too familiar manner of speaking blank verse." On 10 September he presented his equally famous Sir John Brute in the *The Provok'd Wife*, which he had brought forth first at Edinburgh in 1757. On 19 September he was Lord Townly in *The Provok'd Husband*, a part which he probably played first at Edinburgh on 6 March 1756. On 6 October 1777 he sang Macheath in *The Beggar's Opera*.

The question of where Digges spent the winter is mysterious. He does not appear to have been in London. We do know that at the insistence of his old friend Wilkinson he was four nights at York in February, where he played Sir John Brute, Falstaff, and Sir John Restless in *All in the Wrong*. But by June of 1778 he was back at the Haymarket and played 26 times in a typical offering of his characters—Wolsey, Macheath, Townly, Brute. And on 30 July and a dozen other times he played the leading role of Caratach in a revival (after 150 years, the bill claimed) of Beaumont and Fletcher's *Bonduca*. The play had been heavily altered by George Colman.

In the fall of the year 1778, when he was at least 53 and perhaps as advanced as 58 years of age, Digges finally attained a place on the regular pay list of a London patent theatre, being added to the list at Covent Garden. He remained in the company for one season only, however, playing for the most part his gruffer, blunter, rougher, or older roles: Ventidius in *All for Love*, Caractacus, Lear, Sir John Brute, Cato, Wolsey, and Horatio in *The Roman Father*. His salary is not known and no benefit is recorded. He played substantially the same roles at the Haymarket in the summers of 1779 and 1780 and then left London. He had been living at Mr Addinall's, painter, in Whitehall. J. Keith Angus claimed in his *A Scotch Playhouse* (1878) that "in 1779 there is a fragmentary record of a theatre being run in Shoe Lane [Aberdeen], by West Digges," and he had a few well-puffed performances at Edinburgh in February 1781. Seemingly they were his last in that city.

Digges returned to the Haymarket again in the summer of 1781, was at Cork in September and October of 1781 and in August and October of 1782, and in September of that year was playing at Limerick. He was again at Cork in September of 1783. These conclusions are from scattered bills furnished by Clark, *The Irish Stage in the County Towns,* and may represent either isolated performances or all that remain of full seasons but, perhaps significantly, no winter dates survive.

Digges seems to have been in Daly's company at Dublin in 1782–83 and 1783–84. On 2 July 1784, while rehearsing with Mrs Siddons, who was bestowing on Ireland one of her whirlwind series of guest appearances, he suffered a paralytic stroke. According to the tradition, his part was Jaffeir in *Venice Preserv'd*. Some newspapers reported him as dead, but he survived, though he was incapacitated for acting. Mrs Siddons played a benefit performance for him, and Daly, in one of his few decent gestures on record, retained him as deputy manager (or "confidential assistant," according to one of the O. Smith memoranda in the British Museum).

West Dudley Digges died, according to Flyn's *Hibernian Chronicle* of Cork, on 11 November (all other sources say 10 November) 1786, "at his lodgings on the Coal Quay." He was buried on 12 November in the cathedral of St Fin Barre in Cork. "He was," the obituary notice continues, "a gentleman [in] whom a perfect acquaintance with good breeding, and elegant qualifications for social converse" had combined with "a most pleasing person" to make a distinguished performer. These were the most frequent notes struck in criticisms of Digges—his "breeding" and "gentility" and the beauty (or, later, grandeur) of his person.

John Topham in a letter of 1775 observed, probably truly, that "Digges having had no opportunity of forming his style on the London models, has evolved a style of his own." Having come to the profession late and having been held away from the London stages during his development as an actor and having been himself a dominating influence in the provinces, Digges was very little influenced by changes that took place in the acting techniques practised at the great London patent houses and by their overwhelming personalities, even though he employed those people from time to time. For these reasons he had excited and disturbed London critics and audiences when, a middle-aged and striking figure of whom many had heard much, ("the Magnus Apollo of . . . Edinburgh," as one paper called him), he had come to

"Mr Colman's theatre" to make his London debut in the summer of 1777.

The *Chronicle* of 14 August 1777 had approached him gingerly after he came out in Cato. "As a veteran of the old school, it would be unfair to try him by the rigid and more refined laws of the modern drama." He had "A good person, striking figure, a fine voice" but "his action and declamation wage continual war with one another, and so it is painful to be spectator and auditor at the same time." Yet he had "a number of beauties . . . lost in a chaos of wild and unnatural ranting." As Cato, his "singularity of manner . . . the extreme difference between the stile of the old school . . . and the modern" upset the *Chronicle's* critic. "In the early parts of the play, Mr. Digges, who is evidently formed on Quin and Sheridan, affected us rather ludicrously" but "before the end . . . he awed us into esteem and admiration. His deportment was generally majestic, but often affected; his delivery pompous, but sometimes harsh and grating." The *Gazeteer* was of like mind but found more of the orator than the actor and recalled that "both Cicero and Quintilian agree, that a graceful and commanding figure are very essential requisites in a public declaimer . . ." Condemned was "his broad pronunciation of the Irish accent, than which nothing is more intolerable on the stage." Again and again the *Chronicle's* writers emphasized his "dignity of manner," and the contribution for 25 August by one who was a "theatrical antiquarian" commended Digges's ponderous manner.

I do not remember an instant in which any performer more perfectly . . . looked the part. The publick have been too long accustomed to see the heroes and demi-gods of antiquity personated by men whose appearance and deportment form the most disagreeable contrast with the noble personages whose characters they assume.

Most of the penetrating criticism of Digges is from that late London period when he was past his prime and when, also, he had reluctantly banished from his repertoire some of the youthful characters—Romeo, for instance—which had set the fair auditors of Dublin and Edinburgh afire in the 1750s and 1760s. But he was always a man who attracted publicity and curiosity. Robert Jephson, writing to Garrick in 1773, testified: "Diggs, when I saw him, was one of the most spiritless, inarticulate mummers I ever beheld. Time, that makes a calf an ox, perhaps may have made him a good performer." As late as 1833 Charles Kirkpatrick Sharpe was collecting memories for Maidment, who published the Digges-Ward letters. He contributed the following tidbits from Dibdin:

He acted Hamlet in a sort of military uniform, and Macbeth in a Highland dress. His face was extremely handsome, and he was perfectly well shaped: he possessed the air noble (all the Delawares I ever saw had it) so as to be remarkable, even on the streets. My mother describes him as about the common height; with a high nose, and very fine teeth; dark brown hair and a very powerful voice. His singing in the *Beggar's Opera* was admired by Lord Kellie and all the best judges of music.

Digges put his learning to no literary use except for an English adaptation (1759) of Ramsay's *The Gentle Shepherd*.

Sharpe says he

never saw a print of Digges, but I remember well a picture (by Runciman) of him in the character of King Lear, which hung in Martin's sale-room many years ago. . . . It gave one no notion of the actor's face, if I remember right, as the mouth and chin were muffled in an immense white beard, which, mingled with a copious white periwig, 'rode on the Whirlwind' over the unlucky canvas. It was a shocking daub . . .

A drawing in sepia of Digges by an anonymous artist is in the Harvard Theatre Collection (but is not listed in the Hall *Catalogue*). A colored drawing by J. Roberts of Digges as Cato is in the British Museum. An engraving of him by an unknown artist as John Brute in *The Provok'd Wife* was published as a plate to an edition of the play in 1788 by Harrison.

Diggs. *See also* **DIGGES.**

Diggs, Richard *d. 1727, actor.*
The 1718 edition of *Richard III* listed Richard Diggs as Catesby, and perhaps he played the role at Drury Lane on 6 December 1715, but it is more likely he acted it at some unrecorded performance in 1717, during which year we have other records of his activity. On 30 May 1717 he shared a benefit with Jones at Drury Lane, and on 9 September at the Pack-Pinkethman booth at Southwark Fair he appeared as Lord Worthy in *Twice Married*.

Diggs joined the Lincoln's Inn Fields troupe in 1718–19 and acted a full season that is fairly completely recorded: Worthy in *The Recruiting Officer* (his debut there, on 29 September 1718), Sir Charles in *The Fair Quaker of Deal*, Hephestion in *The Rival Queens*, Alonzo in *The Traitor*, Marcus in *Cato*, a role in *Platonic Love*, and Octavius Caesar in *Julius Caesar*. He shared a benefit with Ogden on 29 May 1719. In 1719–20 he added such parts as Richmore in *The Twin Rivals*, Rosny in Beckingham's *Henry IV*, Seberto in *The Pilgrim*, Ross in *Richard II*, Lucius in *Cymbeline*, Truelove in *Hob's Wedding*, Jack Stanmore in *Oroonoko*, and Narbal in *The Imperial Captives*. His benefit on 28 April 1720 was shared with Mrs Robertson. At Bartholomew Fair he played the King in *Love's Triumph* on 23 August to complete his season's activity.

Diggs remained at Lincoln's Inn Fields for the rest of his career, occasionally taking parts of some importance, but usually appearing in middling roles. Over the years between 1720 and his death in 1727 he expanded his repertoire to include such characters as Agamemnon in *Troilus and Cressida*, Escalus in *Measure for Measure*, Albany in *King Lear*, Dervise in *Tamerlane*, Lorenzo in *The Merchant of Venice*, Page in *The Merry Wives of Windsor*, Sir Charles in *The Stratagem*, Blandford in *Oroonoko*, the Duke in *Venice Preserv'd*, Story in *The Committee*, Bertran in *The Spanish Fryar*, Haemon in *Oedipus*, Truman in *The Squire of Alsatia*, Cardenio in *Don Quixote*, Hemskirk in *The Royal Merchant*, Lodovico in *Othello*, Demetrius in *Titus Andronicus*, Horatio in *Hamlet*, Stanley in *Richard III*, Dorilant in *The Country Wife*, and Sharper in *The Old Bachelor*.

Occasionally the bills and accounts for Lincoln's Inn Fields gave some indication of the actor's financial state. His daily salary in 1724–25 was 16s. 8d., but by 1726–27 he was receiving £1 10s. His individual benefits in 1724, 1725, and 1726 all brought in over £115, his best showing being in 1724 when the income was £145 1s. The house charges during these years would have been about £40.

Diggs played Banquo in *Macbeth* for the ailing Boheme on 3 April 1727. Perhaps Diggs himself was not well at the time, for he died the following 12 April. The papers called him "a noted Actor at the New Play-House," and the record of his roles would suggest that he was a young player of promise. His widow was granted a benefit on 28 April which made a profit for her of £74 17s. Richard Diggs seems to have been one of those solid, hard-working actors, good in secondary roles, whose contributions seldom attracted critical attention but were essential to the life of the theatre.

Dighton, Mr *[fl. 1733–1748]*, actor.

On 20 February 1733 at the Haymarket Theatre Mr Dighton played Moneses in *Tamerlane*. Perhaps he toured the provinces after this, for his name did not appear in London bills again until 30 December 1741, when he acted Buckram in *Love for*

Love with Giffard's troupe at the Goodman's Fields Theatre. He remained there to play Scale in *The Recruiting Officer*, Pedro in *The Spanish Fryar*, Vainlove in *The Old Bachelor*, Frederick in *The Wonder*, Blunt in *George Barnwell*, Cornwall and Albany in *King Lear*, and Ratcliff in *Richard III*. On 24 April 1742 he shared a benefit with four other performers.

He followed Giffard to Lincoln's Inn Fields in 1742–43 and added there such new parts as Catch in *The Committee*, Pallas in *The Rehearsal*, Friendly in *The Recruiting Officer*, Catesby in both *Richard III* and *Jane Shore*, and Ben in *The Beggar's Opera*. After a strong beginning, Giffard's troupe ran into financial difficulties and disbanded in the spring of 1743. Dighton left London, for in 1748 he was acting for 5s. nightly at the Jacob's Wells Theatre in Bristol.

Dighton, Robert *c. 1752–1814, actor, singer, dramatist, scene painter, portrait painter.*

Robert Dighton's entry in *The Dictionary of National Biography* is concerned entirely with his career as a portraitist, art-shop keeper, and purloiner of original works from the British Museum. It makes no mention of his parallel career as a theatrical performer. But there is no doubt that the clever caricaturist and the lively actor-singer were one and the same person.

Dighton was born about 1752. He first gained notice as an artist when he contributed some small portraits in chalk to the exhibit of the Free Society of Artists in 1769, and he exhibited such portraits at the Society through 1773.

In 1775 he was living and painting at "Mr Glanville's, opposite St. Clement's Church," and from that address he sent his first pictures, "a frame of stained drawings" (according to Redgrave), to the Royal Academy's exhibit. In 1777 he sent to the Academy "A Conversation," "A Drawing of a Gentleman from Memory," and some

By permission of the Trustees of the British Museum

ROBERT DIGHTON

artist unknown

small whole-length figures. He was then resident at No 266, High Holborn.

The *Morning Post* for 27 August 1776 identified him as the "Gentleman" who had acted an unspecified part at the Haymarket the night before. In 1777, we find the first probable reference to him by name as a theatrical performer, when a "Deighton" was in the company of Joseph Fox in his first season as lessee of the Brighton Theatre, beginning 1 July. But "Deighton's" roles are unknown.

There is no record of Dighton's theatrical activities from 1777 until 26 March 1781, when he bobbed up again in a nonce company assembled by special permission of the Lord Chamberlain to act for their joint benefits at the Haymarket, usually dark at that season. Several of the actors were appearing for the first time, and Dighton acted Mungo in *The Padlock* "for that night only." He must have been successful in the comic part for he repeated it

with the regular company at Covent Garden on 5 May 1781. The bill for the evening perhaps stretched truth a little when he was advertised for his "second appearance on any stage."

But Dighton did not, then or ever, gain a permanent billet in a London patent theatre. Indeed, not until 28 April 1784 was he seen again on a London stage, this time when he sang the popular rustic part of Hawthorne in *Love in a Village* "(for that night only)" for the benefit of Johnstone. It was his sole performance that season. On 13 December 1784 he organized his own benefit at the Haymarket, obtained from the Lord Chamberlain special permission to play, and persuaded some friends —Popplewell, Decastro, Ingall, Mrs Henley, Mrs Barnard, Mrs Woodman, and others—to support his Captain Macheath in *The Beggar's Opera*. On 12 February 1785 some of these and other players gave for their joint benefit, again at the Haymarket, *A Trip to Elysium* and *The Quaker*. In the afterpiece Dighton appeared for the first time in the character of the Quaker. Dighton repeated his Macheath for Mrs Pinto's benefit night at the Haymarket on 15 March. He lived in 1785 in Henrietta Street. On 9 April 1788 he obliged Mrs Greville on her benefit night at the Haymarket (another specially licensed performance) by playing Centinel in the afterpiece *The Ephesian Matron*.

Meanwhile, Dighton had probably been singing at several pleasure gardens in London, and by 9 April 1792, at latest, he was an occasional performer at Sadler's Wells. On that date he participated (according to a Folger manuscript transcript of a bill) in "A Comic Piece in Song and Recitative call'd the Coquette," with Dubois and Mrs Baker, and also in "An entirely new Comic Extravaganza, consisting of Song, Recit[ative] and Spectacle call'd Queen Dido, or the Trojan Ramblers," with Wordsworth from Bath and Perry from Exeter, assisted also by Mrs Dighton.

How often Dighton sang at Sadler's Wells is impossible to know, given the scattered state of the bills. He was Jack Marlinspike in *England's Glory* at the Wells on 31 August 1795. He was on the payroll there in 1797. And there are published songs in the British Museum's collection which reflect his activities there: *Guardian Frigate. We be three poor Fishermen. The Fisherman's Glee. Sung by Messrs. Dighton, Lowe and Gray in The Guardian Frigate . . . at Sadler's Wells. Written by Mr. Lonsdale . . .* Longman and Broderip: (London, 1790?); Reeve's *The Picture Shop* [as sung by Dighton at Sadler's Wells] . . . 1794; Reeve's *The Loyal Cobbler* [as sung by Dighton at Sadler's Wells] (1795?), and *You may sing of your Waggoners, Ploughboys and Watchmen* [as sung by Dighton at Sadler's Wells] (1795?). Doane's *Musical Directory* (1794) called him "Prin[cipal] Tenor" at the Wells and gave his address as No 12, Charing Cross.

On 28 May 1800 a forgetful (or deceptive) management at Covent Garden called his appearance singing T. Dibdin's *The Muffin Man* "the first on this stage." On 13 June he sang "The Laughing Song" on the occasion of that theatre's benefit for the General Lying-In Hospital. In the season of 1800–1801 he earned a guinea a night singing in several pantomimes at Covent Garden and was still appearing there, but only occasionally, in 1805–6. Redgrave credited him also with "some scenery" but did not specify the scenes.

But Dighton had been earning his living principally as a drawing master and painter and as proprietor of a printshop near Charing Cross. His wide acquaintance among theatrical people and other celebrities led him early into portraiture and caricature, and his satirical etchings of barristers, military officers, and performers, each tinted by hand, were much sought after. In 1795 he etched *A Book of Heads*, published by Bowles and Carver of No 69, St Paul's Churchyard, as well as his own portrait in left profile, a crayon holder in his right hand and under his left arm a portfolio inscribed "A Book of Heads by Robert Dighton Portrait Painter and Drawing Master." His theatrical subjects included James and Frances Aickin, all the Kembles, Ann Catley, John Braham, David Garrick, Signora Catalani, and J. S. Munden.

Dighton was involved in a scandal when, in 1806, his theft of a number of etchings and prints from the British Museum was discovered. He had sold to Samuel Woodburn, the art dealer, Rembrandt's "Coach Landscape" for 12 guineas, and Woodburn had taken it innocently to the British Museum to compare it with the impression he knew was there. The episode led to the dismissal of an official of the Museum,

Harvard Theatre Collection

ROBERT DIGHTON, as Dennis O'Neal
artist unknown

though apparently most of the prints were recovered and Dighton escaped punishment. Dighton died at No 4, Spring Gardens, in 1814. He had married the singer Miss Bertles in 1791 and they had had at least two children.

There is in the British Museum a rather pathetic manuscript letter sent from Dighton, at No 4, Spring Gardens, Charing Cross, and dated 22 October 1812, to the manager of Sadler's Wells asking for consideration for Dighton's daughter. (She has "strong powers and sings well," age has impaired his abilities as an artist, he has a large family, and the hardness of the times press on him heavily.) The letter is endorsed on the back: "To be answered the company entirely full."

Robert Dighton had also a son, Denis Dighton, born in London in 1792 and admitted early as a student to the Royal Academy. He was a painter of battles and military scenes and was also a caricaturist. He was a close friend of the Prince of Wales and was appointed his military draughtsman in 1815. He died on 8 August 1827.

In addition to the graphic work already mentioned, Robert Dighton drew and engraved a portrait of himself: "Mr Dighton in the Character of the Muffin Man at Sadler's Wells," published 9 May 1797.

The British Museum owns a set of Dighton's etchings, his lithograph of a boy at an easel, and the following watercolors: "Glee Singers executing a Catch," "The Reward of Virtue," "Comme ce Corse nous mène," "There is gallantry for you!" and "Men of War Bound for the Port of Pleasure."

An engraving of him as Dennis O'Neal, by an unknown artist, is in the Harvard Theatre Collection.

Dighton, Mrs Robert, née Bertles
ιfl. 1787–1794ι, *singer.*

Miss Bertles was mentioned as a featured singer at Vauxhall Gardens in two collec-

MRS ROBERT DIGHTON
by Dighton

tions of James Hook's songs published in 1787. In 1788 she was apparently still, or again, singing at Vauxhall when Hook's *Hark, hark the dreadful Din of War* was published, "as sung by" her. She sang in a concert under the direction of Hindmarsh on 16 February 1790 at the Paul's Head Tavern, Cateaton Street.

An unattributed clipping in the British Museum, dated 3 August 1791 announces one of her appearances at Sadler's Wells as "Mrs Dighton late Miss Bertles," so it cannot then have been very long since her marriage to the singer and caricaturist Robert-Dighton. She was singing at the Wells in 1792, and Doane's *Musical Directory* of 1794 gave her professional address as Sadler's Wells Theatre and her home address as No 12, Charing Cross. She was a soprano.

She was the mother of at least two children by Robert Dighton—a daughter, who appears to have been a singer, and a son, Denis, the battle painter (1792–1827).

An engraved portrait of Mrs Dighton, by her husband, is in the British Museum.

Dignam, Mr *(fl. 1743)*, *house servant?*

Mr Dignam shared a benefit with four others at Lincoln's Inn Fields on 6 April 1743. He was, perhaps, one of the house servants.

Dignum, Charles *c. 1765–1827, singer, actor, composer.*

Charles Dignum was born about 1765 in Rotherhithe, the son of an impoverished Irish Catholic master tailor. After the removal of his father's residence and business to Wild Street, Lincoln's Inn Fields, Charles was placed as a chorister in the chapel of the Sardinian ambassador in Duke Street, where very shortly he was noticed by Samuel Webbe, the organist and vocal teacher, who took him as a pupil.

Harvard Theatre Collection

CHARLES DIGNUM

engraving by Heath, after Callcott

Charles's own early preference was for the Church, and he obtained consent to go to Douai to be instructed and to take orders, but he was disappointed in this aim by his father's inability to pay for the journey. He was then articled to a carver and gilder named Egglesoe, but the engagement was broken mutually after nine months of quarrelsome association, and Dignum fetched up finally apprenticed to Thomas Linley, the composer and singing master.

Linley seems to have proved the ideal mentor who, unlike some masters of young singers or dancers, refused to exploit his pupil's growing powers and forbade him any public performance until his voice had completely matured. Linley judged that moment had arrived in the spring of 1784, for a "Degnum" was listed by Burney as among the tenor singers in the Handel Memorial celebrations at Westminster Abbey and the Pantheon in May and June.

On 14 October 1784 Dignum made his patent-theatre debut at Drury Lane, singing in the role of Young Meadows in *Love in a Village,* billed only as "A Young Gentleman." He "was received by a very crowded House, with the most unbounded Applause," according to a newsclipping dated 15 October. His "second appearance on any stage" was a repetition of the part on 21 October. On 26 November he performed the title role in Michael Arne's *Cymon,* on 18 December was Damon in Boyce's *The Chaplet,* and on 27 December repeated Young Meadows, being then for the first time named in the bill. He sang in a chorus in *Macbeth* on 2 February 1785, was William in *Rosina* on 28 March, played Lord Aimworth in *The Maid of the Mill* on 8 April, was one of the Voters in *St Giles's Scrutiny* on 11 April, bore a "principal Vocal Part" in *The Sons of Anacreon* for John Bannister's benefit on 18 April, assisted Bannister, Chapman, Suett, Barrymore and others in Danby's prize glee "Awake, Æolean Lyre" for the benefit of Barrymore and Miss Field on 22 April, and

CHARLES DIGNUM, as Tom Tug
engraving by Bond, after De Wilde

acted Captain Greville in *The Flitch of Bacon*, and sang three songs at his own benefit, shared with Mrs Wilson and bringing them £193 4s. 6d. On 3 May, he sang three songs ("Bright Phoebus has mounted the chariot of day," "Jack, thou art a toper," and "Toby's brown jug") for Spencer and Mrs Hedges's benefit on 11 May, repeated "Bright Phoebus" for the benefit of Phillimore, Chaplin, and Nix on 13 May, and on 26 May wound up his crowded and successful first season warbling "Bright Phoebus" once again for the benefit of Wood, Percey, and Cameron.

That first season, 1784–85, was almost a paradigm of seasons to come: Dignum played primary and secondary characters in ballad opera, pantomime, and musical romance, did journeyman background work

in choruses, and (especially) gave enthusiastic renditions of patriotic songs, sea songs, military songs, ballads, and sentimental favorites in the tenor tradition of John Beard. Among the innumerable parts he was to add in the nearly thirty years during which he trod the Drury Lane boards were the following, occurring oftenest in afterpieces and almost always farcical, sentimental, or eccentric: Octavio in *The Strangers at Home*, Mercury in *Harlequin Invasion*, Osmyn in *The Sultan; or, A Peep into the Seraglio*, Lubin in *The Quaker*, Tom in *The Mistake of a Minute*, Macheath in *The Beggar's Opera*, Hawthorne in *Love in a Village*, a Bacchanal in *Comus*, the title role in *Artaxerxes*, the Magician in *Hurly-Burly*, the Magician in *Harlequin Junior*, Giles in *The Maid of the Mill*, Stanmore in *Love in the East*, Tugg in *The Waterman*, Captain Sightly in *The Romp*, Lord Heartwell in *The Double Disguise*, Sir Owen in *Richard Coeur de Lion*, Sir John Loverule in *The Devil to Pay*, Rashly in *The Lord of the Manor*, Belville in *Rosina*, Leander in *The Padlock*, Harman in *A School for Fathers*, Carlos in *The Doctor and the Apothecary*, Colin in *Belphegor*, Campley in *Inkle and Yarico*, Robert in *The Haunted Tower*, Crop in *No Song No Supper*, Careful in *True Blue*, a Noble Buck in *The Buck's Lodge*, Peter in *The Siege of Belgrade*, Quaver in *The Virgin Unmask'd*, Corin in *The Cave of Trophonius*, Apollo in *Poor Old Drury!!!*, a Muleteer in *The Mountaineers*, Lord Alford in *The Children in the Wood*, the title role in *Harlequin Peasant*, the Squire in *Thomas and Sally*, a Tartar in *Lodoiska*, and Selim in *Bluebeard*.

Rather surprisingly, he was called upon for a variety of minor Shakespearian roles, not alone Amiens in *As You Like It* and Balthazar "(with songs)" in *Much Ado About Nothing*, which to a singer were natural enough, but also Bedford and Gower in *Henry V*, Burgundy and the Esquire in *King Lear*, a Gentleman in

Measure for Measure, Norfolk and Ratcliff in *Richard III*, Pembroke in *King John*, Marcellus in *Hamlet*, Sir Thomas Lovell in *Henry VIII*, and Lorenzo in *The Merchant of Venice*.

Dignum seems to have left Drury Lane in the winters only once—the first part of the season of 1793–94, when he went over to the Haymarket. But he was at Liverpool's Theatre Royal in the summer of 1786, where, the theatre's account books show, he earned a benefit of £122 2*s*., with charges of £35. He seems to have returned in 1792 and other years.

At Drury Lane he gradually ascended to £4 per week from before 1796 until 1804–5, when he dropped to £2 for part-time effort, but this modest salary was handsomely supplemented by substantial payments to him as one of the perennial leading singers in the March oratorios at Drury Lane (£37 16*s*. in 1794) and by sometimes enormous takings on his benefit nights. On 8 June 1798 he cleared £422 8*s*. 10*d*. On 4 June 1800 his receipts were £628 6*d*., with charges of £70 7*s*. 11*d*. He sang, moreover, at Vauxhall in the summers until at least 1810, at the Anacreontic Society's songfests, at Freemasons' Hall, at Willis's Rooms, and in the taverns. He retired with a small fortune of his own, in addition to his wife's property.

He was living in 1785–86 in Little Wild Street, Drury Lane; in 1787–88 he was living in "Red Lion Square, the corner of Leigh-street," and in 1790–91 he was at No 23, New North Street, Red Lion Square, where he remained until some time well after 1800. In 1814 he was in Gloucester Street, Queen Square. In 1816 he gave his address on a letter as "22 Knightsbridge, near the Foot Barracks, facing Hyde Park on the left hand side of the way," but evidently he soon moved back to Queen Square.

Dignum was indeed physically unprepossessing, especially in his later years, when his corpulency became unwieldy on the stage. *The Secret History of the Green Room* suggested that, once he achieved a degree of affluence, he ate compulsively, remembering his early poverty and hunger. "His voice," according to that critic's opinion, "is a soft agreeable tenor, but rendered somewhat unpleasant by being formed too much in his throat."

Dignum had an uphill struggle to achieve popularity, but his open goodwill toward fellow performers, his real and apparent moral worth and rectitude, and (most of all) his insensitivity to the jibes leveled at him from the pit and gallery on account of his gross appearance and his origins finally won him a rough partisanship among his auditors. "Anthony Pasquin" was one of the more talented of his insulters in print:

> The wight has each requisite fitting a
> clown,
> Save bashfulness, that is a sense he's
> ne'er known:
> Did the varlet affect but to blush, he
> would cheat us,
> For Nature imbronz'd him when scarcely
> a foetus:

Dignum's popularity slipped a little after the arrival on the scene of Kelly, but only comparatively. He was a favorite of audiences until the very end of his career. And, according to the *Authentic Memoirs of the Green Room*, he was "generally resorted to on occasions of public festivity, and convivial meetings, to enhance the charm of good fellowship and good cheer, by the attraction of a good song."

There was also a difference of opinion as to the quality of his voice. F. G. Waldron, a fellow performer writing anonymously in *Candid and Impartial Strictures on the Performers Belonging to the . . . Theatres* (1795), was unmerciful but may have had personal motives:

This gentleman's voice has very little resemblance of those notes which generally come from an English singer. His tones are mostly like those of a cracked reed, but possess occasionally a *fatness* of sound if we may so express ourselves, that are certainly in unison with the *doughy* bulk and flabby appearance of his person, but are not very pleasing to the ear of a British audience. As far as these defects admit, in tender plaintive airs he is heard with some pleasure.

But Thomas Bellamy in *The London Theatres* (1795) exclaimed:

> DIGNUM, *thou jolly child of pleasing song,*
> I never yet have thought [*thy*] *air too long*

The judicious Thomas Gilliland agreed in his *Dramatic Synopsis* (1804), saying:

Mr. Dignum as a singer, deserves all the admiration his vocal powers have obtained him, there is a sweetness of voice which renders his warblings particularly gratifying to the ear. As an actor he can only be rated with the rest of our vocal performers, who seldom blend the study of action with the contemplation of music. Mr. D. has however played *Sir Richard Vernon* in "Henry the Fourth," and several other parts with more than common ability, the beauties of this gentleman's voice are said to be more effective in a room than on the Stage; in either, we must consider him a delightful singer.

Dignum's mannerisms were occasionally objected to: a newspaper correspondent of 21 December 1786 thought "If Mr. Dignum could get rid of the dimpled smile of *self-approval*, in the stanzas of 'Behold this Fair Goblet!' [in the *Jubilee*] which do not require the decoration of a *broad grin*, it would be well." On 24 November 1789 he was advised: "If Mr DIGNUM would not run towards the pitt—with *head-long* zeal, whenever he has a good thing to repeat, it would be as well," and on 26 November the advice was more insistent:

By the bye Dignum should never conceive himself to be the go-between the Poet and the Pit. . . . His manner of running forward and announcing the approaching character, was like exercising the office of a Chorus, and give the audience the idea that it was his duty to insinuate the plot, or rather plunge it into the Pit . . .

In 1786 Dignum had married a Miss Rennett, an attorney's daughter. They had several children only one of whom, a daughter, survived. The *Monthly Mirror* of November 1796 reported that "Mrs. Dignum, wife of the singer, had lately a narrow escape of being consumed: a spark from the fire caught her dress, which was of muslin, and burnt it; her neck and arms were much hurt." She died at No 23, New North Street, Red Lion Square, in 1799. Dignum's mother also died that year, in July, aged 74.

Charles Dignum died of "inflammation of the lungs" at his house in Gloucester Street on 29 March 1827. He is reported to have been worth over £30,000 at the time of his death. His will left all his own real property, unspecified, to his daughter Sarah Elizabeth, Mrs Joseph Horsley, except for an income of £13 per year left to his brother Peter Dignum, £20 to Charles Butler, Esq, and his collection of the works of Handel to Mrs Linley of Southampton Street, Covent Garden. In addition, the Westmoon Estate, which had been the property of his wife and had been held in trust for Mrs Horsley, went to her with the provision that at her death half of its value would be at the disposal of her husband Joseph and the other half would be divided equally between Charles's two brothers Peter and Thomas Dignum, his wife's nephew Charles Rennett, and her niece Anna Maria Nicholls. Mourning rings were left for his brothers, his wife's niece Charlotte Fennell, and Thomas Wright, Esq (perhaps the organist, composer and inventor, 1763–1829), of Henrietta Street, Covent Garden.

By a codicil of 3 July 1816, Dignum provided that Thomas Wright (who, with Charles Butler, was his executor) should hold in trust for Sarah Elizabeth Horsley £1000 in four-percent stock, rents of his four houses in Grafton Court, Paradise Street, Marylebone, and five one-hundred-pound shares of the Theatre Royal, Drury Lane. On 4 January 1820 he wrote "In consequence of the death of Mrs Linley I give my works of Handel to her two sons Ozias and Wm Linley." But on 2 February 1827 the Linley brothers were given £5 each in lieu of the Handel works.

Charles Dignum composed a good number of songs and some were published and survive in the British Museum's collection: *Caroline of Dartmouth, a celebrated Song . . . The Words by Mr. Upton.* (1790?); *The Disabled Seaman. A . . . Ballad. The Words by M. G. Lewis, etc.* (1798); *Fair Rosalie, a favorite Song, Sung by Mrs. Crouch . . . The Melody by Mr. Dignum.* (1795?); *On that lone bank where Lubin died, . . .* [Melody by C. Dignum.] (1794?); *The Fight off Camperdown. A celebrated Song, the Melody . . . by Mr. Dignum* (1798?); *The Horse Guards Penelope, a Celebrated Song . . . the Words by M. G. Lewis, . . .* (1800?); *The Maid of the Rock. A celebrated Song, sung . . . by Master Welsh . . . The Melody . . . by Mr. Dignum, the Accompaniments by Mr. Florio Junr., the Words by G. S. Carey.* (1795?); *The Neglected Tar, a Celebrated Song, adapted . . . by Mr. Dignum, etc.* (1790?); *The Poor Recruit, a Celebrated Song . . . The Words by S. Carey. The Accompaniments by Mr. Florio Jun. The Melody . . . by Mr. Dignum.* (1795?); *The Soldier and his Dog. A Much admired Song, the Melody . . . by Mr. Dignum . . . The Words by Capt. C. James.* (1795?); *The Soldier encamp'd on the Coast. A celebrated Ballad. Sung by Master Welsh . . . The Words by Capt. C. James. The Melody . . . by Mr. Dignum.* (1795?); *The Soldier's Consolation,* *a much admired Song. The Melody . . . by Mr. Dignum . . . The Words by Capt. C. James.* (1795?); *Sweet Jane, I always thought on you. A much admired Song. The Melody . . . by Mr. Dignum . . . The Words by Mr. Upton.* (1795?), and *William of Allerton Green. A celebrated Ballad. Sung by Master Welsh . . . The Words by G. S. Carey. The Melody . . . by Mr. Dignum.* (1795?).

In addition, an enormous number of songs (principally of James Hook's composition) "as sung by" Dignum at Vauxhall, Ranelagh, the taverns, and the theatres were published. A few representative ones were: *Bright Phoebus Has Mounted the Chariot of Day* (1790) by Hook, as sung with King at Ranelagh; *The Bonny Collier's Daughter* (1795) by Hook, as sung at Vauxhall Gardens; *The Cottage in the Grove* (1796) by Hook, Vauxhall; *The Maid of the Green, Pretty Sally* (1797) by Hook, Vauxhall; *O Fine London Town* (1800) by Hook, Vauxhall; *The Unfortunate Sailor* (1800) by Hook, Vauxhall. There were many more by Hook, a few by Kelly, some by a Captain Morris. At least one was by Haydn: *Outrageous Storms Now Dreadful Rose* (1800), sung by Dignum with Mrs Second, Incledon, and Sale.

A watercolor drawing by De Wilde of Dignum as Tom Tug in *The Waterman* is in the Garrick Club; it was engraved by W. Bond for Cawthorn's *Minor British Theatre*, 1806. An original pencil sketch of him by Samuel De Wilde is in the Harvard Theatre Collection. Other portraits of Charles Dignum include: an engraving by J. Heath, after A. Callcott; an engraving by K. Mackenzie, after Dighton, published by West & Hughes, 1800; an engraving by W. Ridley, after S. Drummond, published in the *European Magazine*, 1799; and an engraving by Ridley, after Smith, published in Parson's *Minor Theatre*, 1793.

Dike, Mr [fl. 1799–1800], *performer.*

Mr Dike was a performer at Covent Garden earning £1 10s. weekly in 1799–1800, but his specialty is not known.

Dil, Mr [fl. 1796], *house servant?*
The Drury Lane accounts at the British Museum contain an entry dated 3 December 1796 citing a 5s. (or £5?) payment to a Mr Dil – if the name has been deciphered correctly. He may have been a house servant.

Diller, Mons [fl. 1788], *pyrotechnist.*
At the Royalty Theatre on 29 September 1788 Monsieur Diller, who described himself as "Professor of Natural Philosophy from Holland," provided an entertainment of "Philosophical Fireworks" for the first time in England. He also exhibited at the Lyceum and was imitated at Astley's Amphitheatre by Monsieur Henry. Diller's fireworks were created "from Inflammable Air without smell, smoke or Detonation." His machinery apparently consisted of jets arranged in patterns and designs, some revolving and some stationary. Air was forced from a bladder through a sponge saturated with ether. Movement and variation were produced by turning on and off the gas from separate sets of holes.

Dillon, Baron [fl. 1784], *singer.*
Charles Burney's *An Account of the Musical Performances in Westminster Abbey, and the Pantheon* (1784) listed a Baron Dillon as one of the countertenors who sang in the Handel Memorial Concerts in May and June of that year. Perhaps the name is an error; there was a singer named Baron who was in the chorus of *Joanna* at Covent Garden on 16 January 1800.

Dimirail. *See* DUMIRAIL.

Dimknell, Mr [fl. 1799], *house servant.*
Mr Dimknell – if the spelling is correct – was listed as a bill deliverer and pit checktaker at the Richmond Theatre in 1799 in the manuscript accounts at the Richmond Reference Library.

Dimmock, Mr [fl. 1758–1762], *doorkeeper, billsticker.*
Mr Dimmock (or Dymuck) served the Covent Garden Theatre as lobby doorkeeper and billsticker from 1758 to 1762. He was granted benefit tickets each spring. He sold them to augment his salary which was, as of 22 September 1760, 2s. daily.

Dimmock, Master [fl. 1739], *actor.*
"Young Dimmock" played Pompey in *The Harlot's Progress* at Drury Lane on 15 October 1739 and subsequent performances through 29 December.

Dimond. *See also* DIAMOND.

Dimond, William Wyatt d. 1812, *actor, manager.*
"Mr. Dimond was bred to the business of a chaser" (an engraver on silver or other fine metals), James Winston recalled in his *Theatric Tourist* (1805). That is the sole bit of information surviving about the early life of the actor William Wyatt Dimond.
Dimond essayed Romeo to Miss Mansell's Juliet at Drury Lane on 1 October 1772 under the rubric "young Gentleman, first appearance on any stage." Hopkins noted that night in his prompter's diary "Mr. Diamond [*sic*] made his first appearance upon the Stage in the Part of Romeo he is very younge a Smart Figure good Voice & made a very tolerable first appearance he met with great Applause." He was again anonymous, identified only as "A Young Gentleman who performed Romeo" when he was cast as Dorilas in *Merope* on 13 January 1773. He and Miss Mansell shared a benefit profit of £79 18s. on 14 May when he played Moneses in *Tamerlane.* During the season the treasurer's book

Harvard Theatre Collection

WILLIAM WYATT DIMOND, as Philaster
by De Wilde

had recorded four payments to him of 10 guineas each and one of 10 shillings. Looking back at that season several years later, William Hawkins in *Miscellanies in Prose and Verse* (1775) found that he had "very conspicuous merit in some scenes of Romeo; in others, he was totally insufficient, in judgment, voice, and expression, particularly in the frantic scenes; but on the whole, he supported that character (considering his age, which was then but nineteen,) with tolerable ease and propriety . . ."

According to W. W. Penley, Dimond assisted Hurst in managing the "Theatre over the butter market" at Canterbury during the summer of 1772. But a letter now in the Birmingham Public Library from the country manager Charles Mate to James Winston in 1804 mentions (certainly cor-

rectly) that Dimond "opend Canterbury Theatre—in 1773."

Dimond's newspaper notices and his impression on audiences had been sufficient to ensure his return to the Drury Lane company for the winter season of 1773–74. He added a number of secondary characters to his small repertoire—Rovewell in *The Fair Quaker*, Radel in *A Christmas Tale*, the Dauphin in *King John*, Lorenzo in *The Heroine of the Cave*, and an unnamed part in *The Pantheonites*. For his joint benefit with F. G. Waldron on 7 May 1774 he acted both George in *The Maid of Kent* and Florizel in *Florizel and Perdita*, dividing £123 6d., after house charges, with Waldron. Ticket seekers were directed to apply at his lodging at "No 3, in Hyde-Street, Bloomsbury."

Dimond was playing in Birmingham on 17 August 1774, the date of the only bill available for that summer season. He came to the Haymarket for the first time on 7 July 1775 to play some unspecified part in a new play by John Jackson called *Eldred*, and at various other times that summer and the next he acted for the company at Richmond, Surrey. He was then said to be "from the Theatre Royal, Bath."

The *Morning Chronicle* of 15 September 1778 had the "pleasure to inform the public that Mr. Dimond of the Theatre Royal, Bath, has kindly consented . . . to perform the part of Edgar" for West Digges's benefit on 17 September at Drury Lane. When he took the role of Charles in *The Jealous Wife* at the Haymarket on 18 June 1779, the *Gazetteer* reported that it was his first time at that theatre and that "since his first appearance in London [he] has been the hero of the Bath company." On 16 July following, he was Lord Falbridge in *The English Merchant*. On 31 July he played Edward in the first performance of Hannah Cowley's tragedy *Albina, Countess Raimond*, and the *Gazetteer* thought his presentation "so striking as to cause a very general enquiry why the London theatres have been so long deprived of his assistance (of which they stand much in need)." He repeated Charles in *The Jealous Wife* for his benefit on 10 August (ticket seekers were directed to his residence at No 3, Upper James Street, Golden Square). He perhaps played Aimwell in *The Stratagem* (one source gives the part to Aickin) on 17 August, was Constant in *The Provok'd Wife* on 18 August, and was the first representative of Lord Newbery in the elder George Colman's new comedy *The Separate Maintenance* on 31 August and 11 other times until near the end of the summer season.

At what date Dimond's long association with Bath's excellent theatre began is not known. But he remained there (and after the "union" of the two theatres in 1779, also at Bristol) from about 1774–75 until his death in 1812. The Bath proprietor John Palmer became so involved with the business of the national Post Office by 1785 that he relinquished the actual management to William Keasberry, and by 1786 Dimond had joined Keasberry in the direction of the business and the productions. Dimond continued to act the juvenile leads, often opposite the young Sarah Siddons, then in the company at £3 per week. He was an efficient manager, an encourager of the younger players, and a much-admired actor of sentimental comedy whose one flaw seems to have been an amiable weakness for gaudy costume. As Sir George Airy in *The Busy Body* he wore "a pea-green silk with silver and foil embroidery" and as Lothario in *The Fair Penitent* he wore spangles. As for tragedy he was particularly admired in the title parts of *The Stranger* and *Hamlet*, and as George Barnwell in *The London Merchant*. After R. W. Elliston rejoined the Bath-Bristol company from York in 1793, Dimond began to share some roles with him and relinquish others. He and Elliston continued competition but remained friends. He witnessed Elliston's marriage to Elizabeth Randall at Bath Abbey on 1 June 1796.

Harvard Theatre Collection

WILLIAM WYATT DIMOND, as Don Felix

engraving by Audinet, after De Wilde

Felix Farley's Bristol Journal analyzed Dimond's acting method and commended the soundness of his ear and judgment and found that "in genteel Comedy he has scarcely his equal,—certainly not a superior." Genest testified that "tho' a very sober man, he was happy in acting a drunken scene." Sheridan is supposed to have said that Dimond was the best Joseph Surface that he had ever seen.

After Keasberry retired in 1795 (he died in 1797) Charles Charlton, who had come into the company in 1791, was appointed assistant to Dimond in the management. At that time Dimond acquired shares in the theatre. In 1799 the other proprietors agreed to Dimond's proposals for a long new lease of the Bristol theatre—eighteen years. On 1 July 1801 he retired from acting, playing Edgar in *King Lear* for his last appearance. He retained a share in the management, however, and on 12 October 1805 he took over the direction of the magnificent new Theatre Royal in Beaufort Square, Bath. He had participated in the planning before the decoration was executed by Dance and Hayes. He had even attended the sale of the celebrated William Beckford's gaudy collection of effects at Fonthill Abbey in 1801 and had there purchased among other objects the pictures by Cassali which he caused to be set in the sectioned ceiling of the Beaufort Square theatre. (At the same sale he acquired for his own use Beckford's "State Bed," made of crimson velvet, and matching chairs, curtains, and sofas, all embroidered in gold. King George III had once slept in the bed when it had belonged to Lord Melcombe and it had cost £1500 to build.)

Dimond died on 2 January 1812, at his house in Norfolk Crescent, Bath, of the effects of a stroke he had suffered on the previous Christmas Eve. He was buried in Bath Abbey on 10 January. He was said by the Bath *Herald* to have been 62 years of age at his death, which estimate conflicts with Hawkins's statement that he was 19 in 1773. He had married Matilda Martha Baker on 2 December 1779. Winston called her "a woman of property." They had at least three children. A son, William, succeeded to the Bath-Bristol management and was the author of a number of melodramatic theatrical pieces and a volume of verse. There were also a daughter, Matilda, who died on 23 November 1801, and another son, Charles Palmer Dimond, who died on 12 January 1853, aged 63.

William Wyatt Dimond's will, dated from Albion Place, Bath ("in perfect health") on 17 June 1809 and witnessed by the actors Charles Charlton, Abraham Taylor, and John Quick, was proved at London on 19 September 1812 by Dimond's widow Matilda Martha. It left all his household goods to her and the "Real

Estate and the rest and residue of my personal Estate and Effects (independent of the property settled on my Marriage)" in trust to the widow and her two brothers Thomas Baker and John Richard Baker. One third of the property was to be for the immediate use of Dimond's widow and two thirds to be divided equally among his children when they should attain their majorities. He mentioned his "interest and property in the Bath and Bristol theatres" but made no further specification of property.

Portraits of Dimond include:

1. As Don Felix in *The Wonder*, oil painting by Samuel De Wilde now in the Garrick Club. Engraved by P. Audinet for Bell's *British Library*, 1792. Same picture, with ornaments, published as plate to *British Drama*, 1817.

2. As Philaster; watercolor drawing by De Wilde, now in the Harvard Theatre Collection. Engraved by P. Audinet, plate to Bell's *British Library*, 1791.

3. Nine silhouettes on paper, of "Mr Dimond." In Garrick Club.

4. Bust, engraved by Freeman after Bennett, 1808.

5. Half-length, by S. Freeman after J. Reynolds; plate to *Monthly Mirror*, 1808.

6. With Miss Wells. Engraved by F. Bartolozzi after C. Shirreff.

7. As Lord Edward in *Albina, Countess Raimond*, drawn and engraved by T. Bonnor, 1779.

8. As Lord Edward; with Mrs Massey as Albina. Plate to *The Lady's Magazine*. Anonymous.

Dine. *See* DYNE.

"Dingdong" [*fl. 1774*], *musician*.

On 15 March 1774 at the Haymarket Theatre for Dr Arne's benefit was presented a *"Comic Ode"* in which "Clatterbane" played the Saltbox, "Shadrach Twanglyre" and his assistants played the Jew's Harp, "Bladderbridge" held forth on the Hurdy-

Gurdy, and "Dingdong" and his assistants made music on the Marrow Bones and Cleavers. The identity of the performers who hid behind these pseudonyms is not known, and the names sound suspiciously like those concocted by the zany poet and manager Christopher Smart.

Ding——, Mr *(fl. 1661–1662)*, *actor*.

A manuscript cast in a Folger Shakespeare Library copy of *The Royall King* includes an actor's name, unfortunately cropped; all that is left of it is "Ding"—possibly to be read as Dingle or Dinger. Other cropped names seem to be missing two letters. The play was presented by the King's Company at the Vere Street Theatre about 1661–62.

Dingley, Joseph *(fl. 1766)*, *proprietor*.

In 1766 appeared the following advertisement:

Mr. Price will exhibit Horsemanship, this and every afternoon, if the Weather permits, in a field adjoining to The Three Hats, at Islington: Where Gentlemen and Ladies may be accommodated with Coffee and Tea, Hot Loaves, and Sullybubs [*sic*], the Loaves to be ready at Half an Hour after Four O'Clock every afternoon, by your humble servant, Joseph Dingley.

Perhaps Dingley was merely the owner of the tavern, though the advertisement hints at his having been a proprietor of the equestrian show in the field nearby.

Diopar, Diopart, or **Dioupast.** *See* DIEUPART.

Disabaye. *See* DESABAYE.

Disney, Thomas *(fl. 1671–1698)*, *actor*.

Thomas Disney acted Antipholus of Syracuse in *The Comedy of Errors*, probably about 1671–72 either at the Nursery for young players in Hatton Garden or on tour with John Coysh's company of strollers. He also appeared about this same time in *The Wise Woman of Hogsdon*. On 28 September 1677 he and other younger members of the King's Company in London signed an agreement with Charles Killigrew and the building sharers to form a reconstituted troupe, and in late February 1678 he acted Contentious Surly in *The Rambling Justice* at Drury Lane under the new articles of agreement that had been drawn up. In the spring of 1679 Disney was possibly on tour again with Coysh in a troupe styled the Duke of Monmouth's Company, and perhaps he played in Edinburgh. By the spring of 1681 he was back in London and is known to have acted Sir Walter Raleigh in *The Unhappy Favorite* at Drury Lane in May. His last known role with the King's Company was Ishmael in *The Heir of Morocco* on 11 March 1682.

Disney was not active in London again until mid-April 1695 when he played Garrucca in *The Indian Queen* with Christopher Rich's company at the Dorset Garden Theatre. He remained with Rich through March 1698, performing at Dorset Garden occasionally but mostly at the troupe's primary playhouse, Drury Lane. His roles included Lord Goodland in *The Mock Marriage*, Vilarezo in *The Rival Sisters*, Memnon in *Neglected Virtue*, Azema in Pix's *Ibrahim*, Sorano in *The Unhappy Kindness*, Fidelio in *The Triumphs of Virtue*, Old Stanmore in *The World in the Moon*, and Philo in *Caligula*.

There was a Thomas Disney who lived in the parish of St Clement Danes, where several other actors lived during the Restoration period. This Disney had a wife Mary, and they baptized a son Thomas on 24 March 1679, a son Charles on 18 June 1682, and a son Carey on 18 July 1683. One of the actor Thomas Disney's fellow players in the King's Company was Carey Perin.

Diswell, Mr *(fl. 1794–1795)*, *puppeteer.*

Mr Diswell exhibited puppets at Bartholomew Fair in 1794 and 1795.

Ditcher, Mr *(fl. 1797–1813)*, *doorkeeper.*

The Drury Lane accounts first cited Mr Ditcher in 1797 and last mentioned him in 1812–13. He was a doorkeeper earning, by 1812, 18*s.* weekly. There seem to have been two other men named Ditcher working at Drury Lane, both of them after the turn of the century: one was an upper gallery check taker earning 9*s.* weekly and the other was a sweeper, who by 1815 was earning 12*s.* per week. The Mr Ditcher who was a doorkeeper may have been the one advanced to free list checker at £1 10*s.* weekly in 1813–14.

"Divito." *See* RICH, CHRISTOPHER.

Divoe or **Di Voto.** *See* DEVOTO.

Dixon, Mr *(fl. 1762–1771)*, *doorkeeper.*

A Mr Dixon was a pit doorkeeper at Covent Garden theatre from at least 1762–63 through 1770–71. His salary in 1767–68 was 2*s.* per day.

Dixon, Clara Ann, later Mrs Smith, then Mrs Sterling *(fl. 1795–1822)*, *singer, actress.*

According to a brief and dubious memoir in the 1814 edition of the *Authentic Memoirs of the Green Room*, Clara Ann Dixon was the daughter of an army officer and the granddaughter of Major-General Dixon; she was the niece of Admiral Dixon and had two brothers who were military officers. She is known to have performed as a young lady in private theatricals given by the Society of Kentish Bowmen in its lodge at Dartford Heath in 1795. A sketch by John Nixon, artist and amateur actor, in his *Dramatic Annals* (in the Garrick Club), shows her in a Green Room scene with other actors. At the age of sixteen, she was articled as a singing pupil to Maria Anna Crouch and Michael Kelly, but it is not clear whether the arrangement occurred before or after her appearance at the Bowmen's lodge.

Announced as "A Young Lady" making her first appearance on any stage, she played Beda in *Blue Beard* at Drury Lane on 15 April 1799, for the benefit of her tutor Mrs Crouch. The *European Magazine* (April 1799) identified her as Miss Dixon. During the following winter she was engaged at the King's Theatre. Using the name of Signora Clara, she made her debut on 11 January 1800 in the comic opera *I zingari in fiera.* "There is much sweetness and delicacy in her voice," reported the *Monthly Visitor* (January 1800), "and perhaps it may be owing to her evident timidity that it did not seem to possess strength and compass in proportion." The piece was played a total of 15 times during that season. On 8 February she sang Azema in the serious opera *Semiramide.* On 6 June 1800 she came from the King's Theatre to play Ghita in *The Siege of Belgrade* at Drury Lane for Mrs Crouch's benefit, billed as Miss Clara Dixon.

Miss Dixon was engaged subsequently by Harris, the manager of Covent Garden, where she made her debut as Polly in *The Beggar's Opera* on 24 September 1800 and "met with a most flattering reception." After her second appearance at Covent Garden, on 6 October, in *Selima and Azor*, it was reported in the *Monthly Mirror* (November 1800) that the musical tale had been revived "chiefly for the purpose of exhibiting Miss Dixon in Selima, a character in which Mrs Crouch has so often appeared to the greatest advantage at Drury-Lane. Miss Dixon was very happy in the songs, particularly in the celebrated air of 'No flower that blows is like the Rose,' which produced an *encore*." She played

Courtesy of the Garrick Club

CLARA ANN DIXON
by J. Nixon

Louisa in *The Duenna* for the first time on 22 October, Jessica in *The Merchant of Venice* on 10 November, Harriet in *The Reprisal* on 23 April, and Olivia in *Twelfth Night* for her benefit on 9 June 1801. For her services during this first season at Covent Garden she was paid a salary of £167 10s. In the summer of 1801 she acted at Liverpool, where her benefit brought £110. After spending the winter season of 1801–2 at Covent Garden, she joined the Plymouth and Exeter company for the summer of 1802. She soon married the deputy manager, Smith. At her benefit at the end of her third season at Covent Garden, on 15 June 1803, her name was printed in the bills as "Mrs Smith (late Miss Dixon)."

The new Mrs Smith gave up the stage temporarily but she and her husband proved incompatible, and the couple separated. In order to sustain herself and three of Smith's children, she returned to the boards and played during the first decade of the nineteenth century at Bath, Bristol, Manchester, Liverpool, Hull, and York. In 1812–13 she was back at Covent Garden, but now with her name changed, for some reason, to Mrs Sterling. Her engagement at Covent Garden was for three seasons, at successive salaries of six, seven, and eight guineas per week. As Mrs Sterling she also sang at Vauxhall Gardens in the summers of 1812 (at £10 10s. per week) and 1814. In the 1821–22 season Mrs Sterling was on the Drury Lane list at £4 per week.

Dixon, Cornelius [*fl.* 1770–1821], *scene painter, architect.*

The architect Cornelius Dixon, about whose earlier life nothing is known, was residing in Pimlico, London, in 1770. In 1783–84 and 1784–85 he served as scene-painting assistant to Novosielski at the King's Theatre; the listing of his name in a deed of trust relating to that theatre, dated 7 July 1783, indicates that he was probably working at the King's in earlier seasons. According to Redgrave, Dixon was the architect of the Royalty Theatre, which John Palmer opened in Wellclose Square on 21 June 1787 with *As You Like It* and *Miss in Her Teens.* Dixon was also engaged by Palmer as scene painter and machinist. Productions at the Royalty in 1787 for which he provided scenes included *Hobson's Choice, Don Juan, Harlequin Mungo, The Deserter of Naples* (with Vesuvius in eruption), and *Hero and Leander.* The author of the last piece, Jackman, wrote rather extravagantly in the dedication of the published text that "This Artist has burst upon the Public with such astonishing powers that he distances every competitor. . . . His knowledge of stage effects, the best judges positively declare, surpasses even the genius of our favourite Loutherbourg."

In 1788 at the Royalty, Dixon painted scenes for Bates's pantomime *Gil Blas.* The

Mrs Dixon who danced in the pastoral *The Birthday* at the Royalty on 31 October 1787 probably was his wife. In May of that year he painted the royal box at the Duke of Richmond's private theatre in Privy Gardens and also provided an extra scene when *The Way to Keep Him* was offered to the royal visitors.

From 17 February to 19 July 1791, Dixon was an assistant to Hodges during the engagement at the Pantheon of the King's company. He painted new scenes for *The Surrender of Calais* at the Haymarket on 10 September 1792. In 1795, with Greenwood and others, he painted three sets of wings and back scenes for the opening of the new Theatre Royal in Birmingham on 18 June.

We have no record of Cornelius Dixon's work at a patent theatre before the new Drury Lane Theatre opened in 1812. In the first season of that new and vast theatre, he (or another C. Dixon, possibly a son) painted scenery with Capon, Greenwood, Marinari, and others for *Hamlet, As You Like It, All in the Wrong, Up All Night, The Wonder, The Merry Wives of Windsor, Lionel and Clarissa,* and *She Wou'd and She Wou'd Not.* In that year he also provided scenes at Covent Garden for *Love, Law and Physick.*

In 1813–14 a C. Dixon was employed at Covent Garden as painter and on 2 November 1813 he was paid £100 on account for the season. Indeed, there seem to have been two Dixons at Covent Garden, for on 2 April 1814 a sum of £40 was paid on account to "Messrs Dixon."

In 1819 Dixon designed new decorations in *basso relievo* for the Drury Lane house. He also did scenery for Kean's performances at Drury Lane of *Coriolanus* and *King Lear* in 1820. His last known work was for a coronation spectacle at Drury Lane in 1821. He should not be mistaken for William Dixon, who was a scene painter and decorator at the Ipswich theatre, 1796–1803.

Dixon, Mrs [Cornelius?] [*fl. 1787*], *dancer.*

A Mrs Dixon danced with Miss Bithmere in a musical pastoral called *The Birthday* at the Royalty Theatre on 31 October 1787. She was probably the wife of Cornelius Dixon, a scene painter at the Royalty in that season.

Dixon, Elinor. *See* LEIGH, MRS ANTHONY.

Dixon, James [*fl. 1660–1662*], *actor.*

James Dixon was a member of John Rhodes's troupe playing at the Cockpit in Drury Lane by 24 March 1660, and by the end of the year he had joined the Duke's Company under Sir William Davenant. His only recorded role was Rosencrantz in *Hamlet,* performed at Lincoln's Inn Fields on 24 August 1661, though Dixon was still a member of the troupe in 1661–62. On 4 July 1662 when Sir Henry Herbert, Master of the Revels, sent a messenger with a warrant to the playhouse, Dixon was one of 12 Duke's Company players who beat up the messenger and held him prisoner for two hours. At the trial on 18 July all the actors identified themselves as from the parish of St Clement Danes, admitted their guilt, and were fined 3s. 4d. each. After this, James Dixon was heard from no more. There is a good possibility that he was related to Elinor Dixon, the actress who married Anthony Leigh.

Dixon, Thomas [*fl. 1794*], *violinist.*
In Doane's *Musical Directory* (1794), Thomas Dixon was listed as a violinist, a member of the Choral Fund, with an address at No 6, Francis Court, Lambeth Walk.

Dixon, William [*fl. 1792–1796?*], *singer, music engraver and copyist.*
In Doane's *Musical Directory,* 1794, William Dixon was listed as an alto (countertenor), a music engraver and copyist, a

member of the Choral Fund, and a singer in the Handel festival at Westminster Abbey and the oratorios at Drury Lane. His address was No 6, Borough Road, St George's Fields. He was probably the Mr Dixon whose name is found in the bills as a minor chorus person at Covent Garden in 1791–92 and at Drury Lane from 1793–94 through 1795–96. On 28 February 1792 at Covent Garden he sang in *Orpheus and Eurydice*. Productions in which he sang at Drury Lane included: (1793–94) *The Pirates* and *Lodoiska*; (1794–95) *The Roman Father* and *The Cherokee*; and (1795–96) *The Cherokee, The Pirates,* and *The Surrender of Calais*. A Mr Dixon was a member of the Drury Lane chorus in 1812–13 and 1813–14 at £1 5s. per week.

D'Lapine. *See* DE L'ÉPINE.

D'Latre. *See* DE LAÎTRE.

D'Lature. *See* DE LA TOUR.

D'Legard. *See* DELAGARDE.

D'Lorme. *See* DELORME.

D'Muraile. *See* DUMIRAIL.

Doane, Joseph [fl. 1793–1794], *singer.*

Joseph Doane was probably the J. Doane whose *Musical Directory* of 1794 provides us with a fund of useful information about musicians of the late eighteenth century who were rarely recorded elsewhere. Joseph Doane was a basso, living at No 45, Orchard Street, Westminster. He was a member of the Oxford Meeting in 1793, and in 1794 he participated as a singer in performances by the Choral Fund, the Cecilian Society, and the Surrey Chapel Society. He also sang in the Handel memorial concerts at Westminster Abbey and in the oratorios given at Drury Lane.

Doberval. *See* D'AUBERVAL.

Dobney, Ann *c. 1670–1760, proprietor.*

Upon the death of her husband, Mrs Ann Dobney (sometimes Dabney, D'Aubney, or D'Aubigney) kept the Bowling Green House, at the back of Panton Street, Islington, for many years. She died on 15 March 1760, at about the age of 90, and was succeeded at her establishment by Thomas Johnson. About 1767 the equestrian Price performed there.

Dobson, Mr [fl. 1728–1734], *violoncellist.*

Mr Dobson was one of the musicians who helped sustain the Academy of Ancient Music after Maurice Greene left it about 1728. The diary of the Earl of Egmont notes a concert, apparently at the Crown Tavern, on 8 March 1734 in which Dobson played the violoncello. Perhaps the references to "Mr Dobson's Son. Renter" in the Lincoln's Inn Fields Theatre free lists in 1726–27 and 1727–28 are to the musician.

Dobson, Mr [fl. 1792], *actor.*

Mr Dobson played Gradus in *Who's the Dupe?* on 15 October 1792 at the Haymarket Theatre—his first and last notice in the eighteenth century. Possibly he was the Dobson who received £1 5s. in 1815 at the same house, but that Dobson appears to have been a house servant.

Dobson, Benjamin [fl. 1664–1669], *fencing master, manager?*

On 30 May 1664 a student of the fencing master Benjamin Dobson fought a trial at eight weapons at the old Red Bull playhouse with a student of William Wright's. The weapons were back sword, single rapier, sword and dagger, rapier and dagger, sword and buckler, half pike, sword and gauntlet, and single falchion. On 18 June 1669 a warrant was issued by the Lord

Chamberlain to apprehend Dobson and others "for keeping playhouses and sounding trumpets, drums and fifes at dumb shows and modells" without paying the usual 12*d*. fee to the sergeant trumpeter.

Doctor, Joseph [*fl.* 1787–1800], *clown, equilibrist, tumbler, actor.*

In 1787 Joseph Doctor (sometimes "Dortor") headed a troupe of acrobats, said to be Spaniards, who performed various physical evolutions at Sadler's Wells. For seven years, off and on, Doctor's name appeared as a clown in the pantomime bills at the Wells. He was frequently referred to as "Senor."

For 12 February 1794 "Surprizing Feats of Activity, by the celebrated Signor Doctor, from Sadler's Wells" were advertised at the theatre in Charleston, South Carolina, that "being his first appearance in America." He remained in Thomas Wade West and John Bignall's Charleston company through the season of 1794–95, sometimes billed as "the celebrated Spaniard," clowning in pantomimes, tumbling, and acting minor roles. (His wife also acted small parts; so far as is known she had not performed in London. During her stay in Charleston and later at Philadelphia her invariable lot was the insignificant minor roles in comedy and melodrama.)

Thomas Wignell and Alexander Reinagle brought the Doctors to Philadelphia's Chestnut Street Theatre for the season of 1795–96 to compete with John Bill Ricketts's equestrians and his pantomimists—Reano, the Sullys, and the Spinacutas—in the circus at the Pantheon. Doctor made his first appearance at Chestnut Street in "A Grand Exhibition of Scenery, Action, Spectacle, Dance, and Feats of Activity, called T'Other Side of the Gutter," billed as "Signior Doctor from Sadler's Wells." He remained at Philadelphia through the winter of 1799–1800. Charles Durang wrote in his memoirs that on 18 February 1799, during the course of James Byrne's pantomime *Diana and Actaeon*, Doctor "threw a somerset from the second tier of boxes to the stage."

On 9 April 1800 the bills at New York's Park Street Theatre announced: "Signior Joseph Doctor, from Sadler's Wells (late from Philadelphia)" would do both "Ground" and "Lofty" tumbling, as well as "Postures" and equilibriums. He would "go through a Hoop with a Pyramid of Thirteen Glasses of Wine on his Forehead." The bill was "to conclude with the Italian Serpentine, on a Ladder 20 Feet High. Signior Doctor is only engaged for two nights, after which he is under the necessity of embarking for the Havannah." After 14 April, when he again astonished the New York spectators, he was heard from no more.

Dodd, James Solas 1721–1805, *actor, lecturer.*

Among the papers left by the eleventh Earl of Buchan was a memorandum written by the surgeon, actor, adventurer, and lecturer James Solas Dodd, giving in considerable detail his lineage and the circumstances of his life down to 1782. The account sounds romantic in the extreme but at least in its principal facts is quite true.

Dodd's grandfather John "(who had been Master in the Navy during Queen Anne's Wars)" commanded the *St Quinten*, a merchantman trading to Barcelona. He there grew friendly with a young officer, one Don Jago Mendozo Vasconcellos de Solis "Knight of the Order of Calatrava and a younger brother of Don Antonio de Solis, author of the History of Mexico." Captain Dodd saved the young man from the consequences of a fatal duel with the son of the Governor of Barcelona by spiriting him to England. There Don Jago met and married Captain Dodd's daughter Rebecca and "took the name of Dodd in order to perpetuate to his issue a small estate near Newcastle-upon-Tyne." The "sole issue" of the union "was a Son" in 1721, "who to continue his father's Name, was baptized

James Solis, but by error of the Parish clerk was entered on the parish Register James Solas, which mode of spelling he hath ever since continued."

In 1727 Don Jago died without receiving his father Don Gaspard's forgiveness for marrying a heretic. In 1728 the old man entered a monastery and left his properties to the Church after the refusal of James's mother to surrender her child to him.

James Solas Dodd "received a Classical education and was at first designed for the [Anglican] Church" but was apprenticed "to Mr John Hills Surgeon & Man Midwife in the Minories London." In 1745, at the end of his apprenticeship, Dodd "went into the Royal Navy as Surgeon's Mate of the Blenheim Hospital Ship" and then served successively "till the end of the then war" in the *Devonshire* and the *St Albans*. In 1751 he quit the Navy, "took up his diploma as a member of the Corporation of Surgeons at London, and followed his business in Gough Square Fleet Street & Suffock Street Haymarket." In 1752 he published *An Essay towards a Natural History of the Herring* and in 1753 a pamphlet in the controversy over Elizabeth Canning the perjurer. In January 1754 "on account of some deaths in his family" he "went abroad and travelled over most of Europe till May . . ." In 1759 he went again into the Navy, serving in the *Sheerness* and the *Prince Admiral*. In 1762 he "was again examined at Surgeon's Hall and Qualified as Master Surgeon of any Ship of the first Rate . . ." But by 1763 he had "settled in London chiefly in the Literary Line."

His "Literary Line" included the writing and public dramatic delivery in 1766 in the Great Room at Exeter 'Change and later the same year at Plaisterers' Hall of an entertainment published as *A Satyrical Lecture on Hearts, to which is Added a Critical Dissertation on Noses* (1767).

In 1767 also, his house near the Saracen's Head Inn on Snow Hill collapsed. His wife

and children were "dug out of the ruins alive" but the family lost all its belongings. Two other persons were killed. "His Wife's head being affected by this fatal accident, he quitted business and went to Bath and Bristol for her recovery, and from thence to Ireland, where he followed his Business & Literary Employments in Dublin."

While in Ireland Dodd published (at Cork in 1770) his *Essays and Poems*, which purported to contain "A Collection of all the Airs, Catches, Glees, Contatas, and Roundelays . . . performed at Stratford upon Avon, on occasion of the Jubilee . . . in Honour of Shakespeare" in 1769. The implications are ambiguous, but evidently the musical collection was an anthology and not Dodd's work. More important were the last 98 pages of the book, which Christian Deelman, a modern chronicler of the celebration, calls "one of the fullest and least-known first-hand accounts of the Jubilee." And on 9 October 1769 Dodd was engaged by William Parsons, the manager of the Birmingham Theatre, to re-read Garrick's "Jubilee Ode to Shakespeare," backed up by "several eminent singers, and an elegant and numerous band of music," for the edification of Birmingham's burghers. When Dodd returned to London in 1779 he bore with him a play he called *Gallic Gratitude*, which had first been acted at Smock Alley Theatre, Dublin, in 1772 as *The Funeral Pile*. It was not much more than a translation of Joseph de Lafont's *Le Naufrage*. It was performed twice only in London, at Covent Garden on 30 April and 19 May 1779.

In 1781 Dodd was induced by an adventurer, a Major John Savage who styled himself "Baron Weildmeister," to embark with his entire family on a voyage to Russia. There, said Savage, he had a plan of secret alliance to propose to the Empress from a foreign power, which would earn them "the order of St. Catherine & . . . £1,000 a year pension." By the time they reached Riga the deluded Dodd had been disenchanted. He and his family took ship for Scotland, landing destitute at Leith in September 1781.

In 1782 Dodd acted at the Edinburgh Theatre and delivered his lectures at various places around town. After that year all record of his movements and activities is absent, except for a license taken out in 1786 to marry one Ann Hurley Mason, which is now in the office of the Keeper of the Public Records in Dublin.

Dodd died in Mecklenburgh Street, Dublin, sometime early in 1805, aged 84. O'Keeffe, in his *Recollections*, said that "His learning and general knowledge were great; and though he had but small wit himself, [he] delighted to find it in another. He turned actor but was indifferent at that trade. He was a lively, smart little man, with a cheerful laughing face." A newspaper obituary called him "a gentleman of amiable and entertaining manners, whose converse with the literary world and fund of anecdote rendered his company extremely agreeable."

Dodd, James William   *1740?–1796, actor, singer, manager.*

James William Dodd was born the son of a hairdresser in London, probably in 1740, and was educated at a grammar school in Holborn, according to *Theatrical Biography* (1772). He is also said by that source to have decided to become an actor after playing with success in a school presentation of Terence's *Andria*. Certainly many of the titles in the catalogue printed for the sale of his library in 1797 strongly suggest that he had classical training.

Dodd is supposed to have been in a country company playing Roderigo in *Othello* on the Sheffield circuit when he was 16 years old. But certainly he was seen by Tate Wilkinson acting at the excellent theatre in Norwich in 1763. There he became a "servant of all work" until John Arthur, manager of the Bath company, saw him and hired him. At Bath he began to

develop the expertise which made him by common agreement the finest actor of fops and coxcombs since the death of Colley Cibber.

By 1764 rumors of his excellence had already reached the ears of those omnivorous talent seekers, the London managers. Garrick had written to the actor James Love from Paris on 27 January 1765 imploring "Give me an Acc^t I beseech You (an impartial one) of Youngsters of Either Sex, who promise something" and again on 3 March: "Your account of Dodd pleases Me. I dread a Stroler, they contract such insufferable Affectation that they disgust me . . . Pray Enquire, & let me know more about that *Dodd*—We want a Second [William] Obrien most dreadfully . . ." James's wife Martha was not mentioned in this letter, but evidently Garrick was interested in her acting abilities, too. (The Dodds must have married young. Their

Harvard Theatre Collection

JAMES WILLIAM DODD

engraving by Laurie, after Dighton

son, James William, was born in 1760.)

On 4 May 1765 Garrick wrote to Dr John Hoadly, who was sojourning at "the Bath," and thanked him for information he had already sent relative to the Dodds. On 23 May, Hoadly wrote a scrupulous letter about Dodd:

My own opinion of him is, that his *person* is good enough, but his motion is too much under restraint and form; more the stalk and *menage* of a dancing master, than the ease of a gentleman. I speak of his legs; his action seems easy enough and unstudied. He has a white *calf-like* stupid face, that disgusted me much till I heard him speak and throw some sensibility into it. His voice is good and well heard everywhere; and he seems sensible, alive, and attentive to what is going on, and properly so. I fear there must be a dash of the *coxcomb* in every part in which you would see him in perfection; and in that cast he will be an excellent successor to O'Brien. . . . He sings agreeably well, and with more *feeling* than he acts with. . . . In singing, his voice seemed to me remarkably low, but that might only be by comparing it with his *speaking* voice, which is very distinct. One excellence I observed in him, that he is not in a hurry, and his *pauses* are sensible, and filled with proper action and looks . . .

Hoadly, a playwright himself, was, like Love, a careful observer and Garrick knew it. He decided to engage both Dodd and his wife Martha, whom Hoadly also warmly approved.

So in the fall of 1765 James and Martha Dodd went into rehearsal with the glittering company at Drury Lane Theatre. Dodd made his London debut on 3 October in the comic part of Faddle in *The Foundling*, singing in the part a "new song." During the rest of the season he added Lord Trinket in *The Jealous Wife*, Jack Maggot in *The Suspicious Husband*, Quaver in *The Virgin Unmask'd*, Plausible in *The Plain Dealer*, the Squire in *Thomas and Sally*, Osric in *Hamlet*, the Fine Gentleman in *Lethe*, Slender in *The Merry Wives of Windsor*,

Sir Harry Wildair in *The Constant Couple*, Roderigo in *Othello*, Alexas in *All for Love*, Mercury in *Harlequin's Invasion*, Sparkish in *The Country Wife*, Sir Novelty Fashion in *Love's Last Shift* (for his benefit), Marplot in *The Busy Body*, Master Stephen in *Every Man in His Humour*, and several unspecified parts in harlequinades. He had firmly established the related lines he was to follow for the next 31 years— fops, coxcombs, beaux, occasional country boobies, and silly fellows generally. His real métier quickly became comedy of manners and sentimental comedy, though he occasionally descended to low buffoonery or flew up to tragedy, at which he always failed. (He too often chose a tragic character for his benefits—on one lamentable occasion Richard III, on another Hamlet, and on yet another Mark Antony.) For these labors he was already, by 1766–67, rewarded with £5 per week. Kelly found, in his *Thespis* of 1766, that Dodd was framed for a coxcomb at birth and would always excel at playing the nice, prim, epitome of a man who blends the worthless and the vain—the fopling. The judgment stood up. There were some critics who thought of Dodd as striving to dethrone Thomas King as chief comic actor at Drury Lane. The *Rational Rosciad* (1767) railed:

The height of folly, self conceit and
    pride,
In strutting Dod are visibly descry'd;
As well could Ackman touch Othello's
    woe;
Or Hamlet's meeting grief from Moody
    flow;
As well hoarse Vincent like soft Pinto
    sing,
As Dod take off inimitable King;
The want of native strength his effort
    mocks;
A frog can never swell into an ox.

But King and Dodd—though both played fops—were utterly unlike in personality and presentation, and though both had enormous repertoires, King's effective range was perhaps wider. Dodd, too, was a swift and accurate study and he never wanted for parts on which to exert his peculiar talents. A selection of his roles follows: the original Sir Benjamin Backbite in *The School for Scandal*, Scribble in *Polly Honeycombe*, Trinket in *The Jealous Wife*, Novel in *The Plain Dealer*, Sparkish in *The Country Girl*, Dapper in *The Alchemist*, Coupée in *The Virgin Unmask'd*, Tom in *The Conscious Lovers*, Mask in *The Musical Lady*, Young Clackit in *The Guardian*, Rovewell in *The Contrivances*, Lord Foppington in *The Careless Husband*, Count Basset in *The Provok'd Husband*, both Sir Macaroni Virtue and Old Shepherd in *A Peep Behind the Curtain*, Dr Mineral in *The Widow'd Wife*, Damon in *The Chaplet*, Sir Brilliant in *The Way to Keep Him*, Modely in *The School for Lovers*, Apollo in *Midas*, Razor in *The Provok'd Wife*, Damon in *Damon and Phillida*, Willis in *The School for Rakes*, Fribble in *A Miss in Her Teens*, Young Philpot in *The Citizen*, Tattle in *Love for Love*, Jessamy in *Lionel and Clarissa*, Humphrey Gubbin in *The Tender Husband*, Campley in *The Funeral*, Oliver in *The Ladies' Frolick*, Jessamy in *The School for Fathers*, Crispin in *The Anatomist*, Lord Aberville in *The Fashionable Lover*, Sharp in *The Lying Valet*, Kecksy in *The Irish Widow*, the Old Woman in *Harlequin's Invasion*, the Nephew in *The Gamester*, Daffodil in *The Male Coquette*, Brisk in *The Double Dealer*, Jack Rattle in *The Rose*, Petruchio in *Catharine and Petruchio*, Captain Mizen in *The Humours of the Navy*, Sapling in *The Note of Hand*, Sir Benjamin Dove in *The Brothers*, Ralph in *The Maid of the Mill*, Dupely in *The Maid of the Oaks*, Sir Harry Muff in *The Rival Candidates*, Lord Minikin in *Bon Ton*, Young Meadows in *Love in a Village*, Sharp in *The Contrast*, Scrub in *The Stratagem*, Tycho in *A Christmas Tale*, Robin in *The Waterman*, Tinsel in *The Drummer*, Ali in *Selima and Azor*, Quicksilver in *Old City Manners*, Bob Acres in *The Rivals*, Sir Brilliant Fashion in *The Way to Keep Him*, Charles Marlove in *The Milesian*, Stephen in *Every Man in His Humour*, Beau in *Æsop*, Linco in *Cymon*, Sir Harry Flutter in *The Discovery*, Cadwallader in *The Author*, Jerry Sneak in *The Mayor of Garrett*, Sir Harry Bouquet in *The Camp*, Captain Duretete in *The Inconstant*, Young Philpot in *The Citizen*, Dangle in *The Critic*, George Oldgrove in *The Generous Impostor*, Le Nippe in *The Lord of the Manor*, Bauldy in *The Gentle Shepherd*, Charles in *The Carnival of Venice*, Faddle in *The Foundling*, Abel Drugger in *The Alchemist*, Lord Frolic in *The School for Vanity*, Lord Beauboot in *The Best Bidder*, Sir Harry's Servant in *High Life Below Stairs*, Ben in *Love for Love*, Toupee in *The*

JAMES WILLIAM DODD, as Campley
engraving by Godfrey, after Roberts

FRANCIS WALDRON as Fabian, ELIZABETH YOUNGE as Viola, JAMES WILLIAM DODD as Sir Andrew, and JAMES LOVE as Sir Toby

by Wheatley

Metamorphosis, Jerry Blackacre in *The Plain Dealer*, Lord Hectic in *The Reparation*, Tinsel in *The Double Disguise*, Shatterbrain in *The Absent Man*, King Arthur in *Tom Thumb*, Sturmwald in *The Doctor and the Apothecary*, Master Johnny in *The School Boy*, Don Manuel in *She Wou'd and She Wou'd Not*, and Watty Cockney in *The Romp*.

Dodd had few Shakespearean parts and their execution was uneven. He made a rather strange Balthazar in *Much Ado About Nothing* and must have cut an odd figure as Mercutio in *Romeo and Juliet* and also as Lorenzo and later Gratiano in *The Merchant of Venice*. He was, however, an amusing Launce in *Two Gentlemen of Verona*, a frolicsome Autolycus in *The Winter's Tale*, and one of the best of the century's Osrics in *Hamlet*. He tried Polonius late (in fact on 29 April 1796, just before his retirement) and with mixed results. His best large attempt in Shakespeare was, by such accounts as remain, Sir Andrew Aguecheek in *Twelfth Night*, and he played the role at every opportunity. His fellow performer Thomas Bellamy thought (in *The London Theatres*, 1795) that one might "In Ague Cheek, the pure comedian view" when Dodd presented the character.

"What an Aguecheek the stage lost in him!" remembered Charles Lamb:

In expressing slowness of apprehension this actor surpassed all others. You could see the first dawn of an idea stealing slowly over his countenance, climbing up by little and little with a painful process, till it cleared up at last to the fulness of a twilight conception, its highest meridian. He seemed to keep back his intellect as some have power to retard their pulsation.

He must have been accepted as Cloten in *Cymbeline*, because it was his part from 21 October 1766 until the end of his life. He was, moreover, with Moody and Suett, a part of the eighteenth century's most notable trio of witches in *Macbeth*. But as Roderigo in *Othello* he was lamentable. The *Thespian Magazine* of June 1793 deplored his attempt: "We were sorry to see such an actor as Dodd descend into Buffoonery; in the dying scene of Roderigo he reminded us of the death of the Clown in Harlequin Skeleton."

As late as the year of his death the *Monthly Mirror* was reporting (28 May) "Poor Dodd tottered through 'the young Mercutio,' as well as his age and corpulency would permit him." His benefit-night Hamlets were disastrous. The leisurely pauses and lack of haste which Garrick and others rightly thought in his earlier years betokened a youngster in command of himself had lengthened out until, Winston recalled in the *Theatric Tourist* (1805), "Mr Kemble is reckoned to be twenty minutes longer in his performance of Hamlet than most of his contemporaries; but Mr Dodd, when he played that part . . . was twenty minutes longer than Mr Kemble;—so much for speaking looks, and dignity of pauses!"

The "high red-heeled stage dandy of the old school of comedy" as Mrs Charles Mathews recalled him in *Tea Table Talk* had, according to his colleague Charles Dibdin, "a perfect knowledge of his profession." Mrs Mathews remembered that his rotund person was ably supported upon two short though well-formed legs, always elegantly covered with silk stockings, and his feet with Spanish leather shoes, secured by costly buckles. His hair *bien poudré, the* queue of which was folded curiously into a sort of knocker, which fell below the collar of . . . a scarlet coat. The little man, in short was a decided fop of his day, both off and on the stage.

Despite a certain amount of critical sniping, often invited by his pomposity of manner off the stage, critics were in substantial agreement as to his talents. William Hawkins, in *Miscellanies in Prose and Verse*, singled him out in 1775 for praise as "the genteel affected coxcomb . . . certainly an original" but attributed Dodd's success to some extent to the fact that "he is no less so by nature in his private deportment." *The Garrickiad* (1780?) thought the "little comic dog [was] equalled not in ten." James Henry Leigh in *The New Rosciad* (1786) wrote sourly

What petit-maître, trifling, pert and vain,
By tinsel frippery hopes to raise his
      name?
Tis DODD! . . .
. . . .
A hopping, skipping, prattling, little
      thing;
. . . .
A fop in miniature, with studied ease,
A gaudy insect fluttering at a breeze
. . . .
Or how could'st thou presume the stage
      to tread,
With all these imperfections on thy
      head?

But "Anthony Pasquin" [John Williams] in *The Children of Thespis* the same year rhymed

Behold sprightly Dodd *amble light o'er*
      the stage,
And mimic young fops in despite of his
      age!

He poses his cane 'twixt his finger and
  thum,
And trips to the fair, with a jut of the
  bum;
His figure on Gallantry's sons is a satire;
So frothy his manners, so stinted by
  Nature

. . . .

We may swear from his mien, that his
  humour was cast
In the light mould of Fashion, full thirty
  years past;
For thro' the gay drama, if I am no
  fibber,
He steers in midway between Lewis and
  Cibber;
Partaking of both, as all authors agree,
The crocodile steals from the land and
  the sea;
And varies in nought from our grand-
  mother's beaus,
But the curls on his pate, and the cut
  of his cloathes.

James Boaden, in his *Memoirs of the
Life of John Philip Kemble* (1825), in-
serted the following delightful character of
Dodd:

Dodd was one of the most perfect actors
that I have ever seen. He was the fopling of
the *drama* rather than the age. I mean by this,
that his own times rarely shewed us anything
so highly charged with the vanity of personal
exhibition. He was, to be sure, the prince of
pink heels, and the soul of empty eminence.
As he tottered rather than walked down the
stage, in all the protuberance of endless muslin and lace in his cravats and frills, he reminded you of the jutting motion of the
pigeon. He took his snuff, or his bergamot,
with a delight so beyond all grosser enjoy-
ments that he left you no doubt whatever of
the superior happiness of a coxcomb.

Dodd was no mean singer, and though
he did not emphasize this talent beyond an
occasional appearance in ballad opera, he
sometimes burst into song in straight comedy parts, and some of the songs he sang
were published as identified with him: William Boyce's *Thrice Happy the Nations*

that *Shakespeare has charm'd. Sung by
Mr Dodd in Harlequin's Invation* . . .
(1770?); *The Sluggish Moon as yet un-
drest* (1770?); and the drinking song *O
Doctor, O Doctor* (1780?). He sang at the
Anacreontic Society's soirées, and when the
young rake William Hickey was taken "to
the Globe Tavern in Craven Street" in
1768, he "spent a night of infinite gratifica-
tion" listening to "the best singing I ever
heard. . . . There I first had the pleasure
to hear Dodd, the player, sing his famous
song of 'Cease rude Boreas,' and a charming performance he made it. He was followed by Hook, Champness, Banister [*sic*],
Dibdin, and many other celebrated voices,
who were all members of the Lodge, which
was distinguished by the name of 'The
Euphrates.' "

Dodd's salary at Drury Lane ascended
little by little until, in the season of 1792–
93, it reached the very respectable figure of
£12 per week. It declined to £11 in his last
season when he was plagued by illness. His
benefits invariably came out well after
house charges were paid: in 1773, about
£166; 1774, over £102; 1775, £216; 1784,
£101; 1785, £184; 1786, £128; 1787,
£163; 1788, £153; 1789, £190; and 1796,
£183. He worked sustainedly at his parts
and was regularly at Drury Lane in the
winters until his death (except for the
season of 1793–94, when he did not play
anywhere in London until 21 April, and
that of 1788–89, when an illness forced
him out of action from mid-November until April). His residences in London were:
at No 2, Chancery Lane, at the time of his
benefit in 1775, in New Ormond Street
from about 1777 until 1786, when he had
removed to Gray's Inn, where he lived until sometime in 1791–92, after which his
residence was No 8, Southampton Row,
Bloomsbury.

As early as 1767 Dodd had begun to go
to Bristol and Bath to act in the summers,
at first as a backup to the comedian John
Arthur and then as a favorite with his own

large constituency in the audiences of both cities. In 1769 he lost much of that favor because he began an *amour* with the beautiful and talented actress Mary Bulkley, wife of George Bulkley, leader of the Bristol Theatre's band.

Dodd and Martha his wife had not got on well together for some time, and in July the London newspapers had been agog over their latest rather operatic quarrel. According to the accounts, Dodd had first insisted on a separation and gone off to Bristol while his wife had engaged at Richmond, Surrey. Dodd then changed his mind and "wrote in very peremptory terms to Mr Love, the manager . . . to discharge her, threatening, in case of refusal, to take her away by force." She swore out a warrant against him. He came to Richmond and, pistol in hand, stopped a post chaise in which he mistakenly thought she was hiding, discovered his error, and attempted to escape. He was captured, taken before a magistrate, and committed to Kingston jail for two nights. He had then to find two friends who would provide security for his good behavior.

All public sympathy in the Bulkley affair was on the side of Martha Dodd, and when she died at Bury St Edmunds in October following the altercation at Richmond, Dodd found it necessary to absent himself from some of his London haunts. A London news clipping in the Burney collection dated 28 October 1769 states that he "now lies at the point of death near Drury Lane Theatre." (He was not shown in the Drury Lane bills from 14 October until 19 December 1769. Feeling was so strong at Bristol that he did not play again there for two years.)

Dodd revived though, and so did his interest in acting, in managing, and in Mary Anne Bulkley. In 1772 he bought Thomas King's share of the Bristol Theatre, Matthew Clarke and Samuel Reddish being the other partners. His resumption of the liaison with Mrs Bulkley caused a fresh up-

roar. The *Bath Chronicle* of 20 August 1772 reported that "A celebrated actress at Bristol has been detected in bed with the sing-song insignificant Mr. D——," and the allegation was denied in several letters to the paper. There were other headaches for the Bristol managers in that year and the next. First, Kennedy and Booth attempted to set up a rival house. Then Dodd and his colleagues, attempting to finesse the interlopers by seeking a royal patent as a theatrical monopoly, met with evasions by the Bishop of Bristol and the local Members of Parliament. At the end of the summer of 1773 Dodd gave up; and he sold his share to Reddish in January 1774.

In the summer of 1774 Dodd and Mrs Bulkley eloped to Ireland, but the Dublin audiences were as censorious as those of Bristol and London, and the lovers were not accepted. On 8 September Garrick wrote to the actor John Moody, "Dodd has been much worse for his voyage (as I suppose he is not ye better for his intrigue) he is money bound in Dublin and I shall release him. . . . Mrs Bakley [*sic*] is returned safe to her husband." But, though Dodd struggled back to Drury Lane in the fall, Mrs Bulkley was not "safe" for long. Tate Wilkinson engaged the lovers together for four nights at York, for race week, in August 1777. The affair continued for some two or three additional years, with intermissions, but Mrs Bulkley's ardour had cooled by 1780 at latest, when she seems to have been the mistress of the harlequin John ("Big") Banks.

Besides the Sheffield, Norwich, Bath, Bristol, and Dublin record, Dodd seems to have acted very few times outside London. He was said to have been at Edinburgh during some part of 1782–83.

James William Dodd died at his house in Southampton Row on 17 September 1796 as he prepared for another theatrical campaign. Administration of his property, which was of unspecified worth, was granted to his son Rev James William

Dodd (1760–1818), Second Usher of Westminster School from 1784. The younger Dodd was a cleric of some distinction, a graduate and fellow of Trinity College, Cambridge. He compiled *Ballads of Archery*, published with music in 1818. He became Vicar of Swineshead, Lincolnshire, in 1800 and Rector of North Runcton, Norfolk, in 1812. He married Ann Whitaker of St Pancras parish, Middlesex, on 16 May 1811 and she bore him six children: Edmund James, Charles William, Ann Sally, Susan, Frances, and Martha Ann. The Rev Mr Dodd is buried in the East Cloister of Westminster Abbey.

A Catalogue of the very curious and Valuable Library of the late Mr James William Dodd of the Theatre-Royal, Drury Lane . . . was published by Leigh and Sotheby for the auction sale held on 19 January 1797 and eight subsequent days. The 2,435 lots listed contain about 2600 titles of astonishing diversity, displaying Dodd's morbid fascination with violence and death. There were volumes of trials for murder, manuals for poisoners, histories of rogues like Rob Roy, Holwell's *Account of the Deaths of the Gentlemen in the Black Hole of Calcutta*, Tyburn confessions, with scandals and erotica (*The History of Pudica, a Lady of Norfolk and Her Five Lovers* [1754]; Mills's *Night Search, or the Cunning Courtizan Discovered* [1652]; *Onania, or the Heinous Sin of Self-Pollution* [1752]), but also with sixteenth-century Latin treatises, freemasonry, magic and demonology, travel, boxing, medicine, fishing, British antiquities, music—a bewildering variety of subjects, from Coryat's *Crudities* (1611) to first editions of Udall's *Terence*. There were many joke books, complete runs of magazines, folios of prints, and over 1,000 separate plays, as well as many collected editions. Early editions of Heywood, Lodge, Massinger, Peele, Middleton, Jonson, Marston and Chapman were listed. Among all the rest were 41 early quartos—from 1599 through 1621—

of Shakespeare's plays, a 1623 folio (which sold for £7 7s.), a 1684 folio (17s.), and a 1685 (10s.). Dodd also collected weapons of North American Indians.

"Duodecimo" Dodd, as Francis Gentleman called him in *The Theatres* (1772), "A pretty, pert, significant pantine," was a popular subject for artists. Portraits of him include:

1. Oil, probably by Robert Dighton, now in the Garrick Club. Engraved by R. Laurie, 1779.

2. As Sir Andrew Aguecheek in *Twelfth Night*. With Elizabeth Younge as Viola, James Love as Sir Toby Belch, and Francis Waldron as Fabian. Oil by Francis Wheatley, now at the City Art Gallery, Manchester, England. Engraved by J. R. Smith, 1774.

3. As Dr Cantwell in Bickerstaffe's *The Hypocrite*. Watercolor by De Wilde, in the Burney Collection, British Museum.

4. As Abel Drugger in *The Alchymist*. Watercolor by Samuel De Wilde, now at the Garrick Club. Engraved by Thornthwaite for Bell's *British Library*, 1791.

5. As Lord Foppington in *A Trip to Scarborough*. Watercolor by Robert Dighton, now at the Garrick Club.

6. As Sparkish in *The Country Girl*. Watercolor by Robert Dighton, now at the Garrick Club.

7. As Tinsel in *The Drummer*. Colored drawing on vellum by J. Roberts, 1777.

8. As Campley in *The Funeral*, engraved by Godfrey after Roberts. Plate to Bell's *British Theatre*, 1794. There is a woodcut of the same picture.

9. As Clodio in *Love Makes a Man*, by J. Collyer after J. J. Barrolet. Plate to *New English Theatre*, 1777.

10. As Faddle in *The Foundling*. Engraved by Terry, 1780.

11. As Lord Foppington in *The Careless Husband*. By Thornthwaite after J. Roberts. Plate to Bell's *British Theatre*, 1776.

12. As Linco in *Cymon*. Anonymous. 1778.

13. As Mercutio in *Romeo and Juliet*. By C. Grignion after T. Parkinson. Plate to Bell's edition of Shakespeare, 1775.

Dodd, Mrs James William, Martha
d. 1769, actress, singer.

The circumstances of Martha Dodd's early life are unknown. She must have been very young when she married the country actor James William Dodd, for he himself can have been no more than 19 at the time. (Their son the younger James William Dodd was born in 1760 and his father in 1740.)

James Dodd was acting at Sheffield at 16 and at Bath a little later. It is not known whether or not Martha was a native of one of these towns, or whether or not she was already established as an actress. James Love saw the Dodds in Bath and spoke to Garrick about them, and Garrick commissioned Dr John Hoadly to see them and report on their worth. Hoadly turned in a meticulous critique recommending Dodd as a replacement for O'Brien at Drury Lane. He also commended Martha Dodd as "a very genteel, sensible woman, fit to fill any part of high life, especially if written with any sensibility and tenderness. . . . She is tall and made no bad figure in breeches . . ."

Martha accompanied her husband to London in the fall of 1765. Dodd made his Drury Lane debut on 3 October acting and singing as Faddle in *The Foundling*, and was thrust at once into many of the foppish parts which were to make him famous. But Mrs Dodd did not appear in a featured role until 29 January 1766, when the season was half over, at which time she was Lady Lurewell in *The Constant Couple*, on the night when her husband first essayed Sir Harry Wildair in that play. She played Amanda in *Love's Last Shift* on 25 April for her second and last appearance at Drury Lane.

In the summers of 1766, 1767, and 1768 Martha accompanied her husband to the Bath and Bristol theatres and played such roles as Roxana in *The Rival Queens* and Daphne in *Midas*. But the marriage had begun to deteriorate because of Dodd's philandering, and there was a temporary separation after a quarrel in the spring of 1769. That summer Dodd went off to Bristol and she signed with James Love's troupe at Richmond, Surrey. Dodd demanded that Love discharge her and when Love refused to do so Dodd descended on Richmond with a pistol, threatening his wife. The result was two nights in Kingston jail for Dodd and the temporary cessation of hostilities. Dodd then began (or continued) an affair with the actress Mary Ann Bulkley, wife of George Bulkley, leader of the band at the Bristol Theatre.

In the fall of the year 1769 Mrs Dodd left her husband and signed on with the Norwich company. Both she and Dodd fell gravely ill in November, and on the twenty-eighth of that month she died at Bury St Edmunds "of an inflammation of the lungs, which she bore with true Christian resignation," according to a newspaper obituary. She was survived by a son, the Rev James William Dodd, Second Usher of Westminster School.

Dodd, John   ₁fl. 1784?–1794₁,   *singer.*
A bass singer, John Dodd sang for the Long Acre Society concerts, was among the vocalists in some of the Handelian celebrations at Westminster Abbey, and subscribed to the Choral Fund—all according to Doane's *Musical Directory* (1794).

Dodimear, Mr   ₁fl. 1793₁,   *dancer.*
On 11 March 1793 and periodically through 23 April Mr Dodimear danced one of the Natives of the Island in *The Governor*.

Dodson, Mr   ₁fl. 1731–1734₁,   *singer, actor.*
Mr Dodson sang "New Mad Tom" at Goodman's Fields on 14 May 1731 and

played Razor, the French barber, in *The Gardener's Wedding* at Mile End Green on 30 September 1734.

Dodson, Mrs ₁*fl. 1740–1749*₁, *actress, singer.*

On 18 November 1740 at Covent Garden Mrs Dodson made her first appearance on any stage as Dorcas in *The Mock Doctor.* She may have stayed with the company for the rest of the season, but she was not mentioned further in the bills, and her next appearance was on 23 August 1743 at the Hippisley and Chapman booth at Bartholomew Fair when she played Angelica in *The French Doctor Outwitted.* In March and June (and perhaps other months) 1748 Mrs Dodson sang at Sadler's Wells, and on 10 and 15 May 1749 she sang at the New Wells, Shepherd's Market, during May Fair. She was presumably related to the Miss Dodson who appeared at Covent Garden from 1740 to 1742.

Dodson, Miss ₁*fl. 1740–1742*₁, *actress, dancer.*

Miss Dodson performed at Covent Garden in 1740–41 for 10*s.* weekly. Her first notice in the bills was on 7 February 1741 when she was Betty in *The Gamester.* During the rest of the season she played an Amazon in *Perseus and Andromeda,* Kate in *The King and the Miller of Mansfield,* and Tippet in *The Provok'd Wife.* She appeared at the Hippisley and Chapman booth at Bartholomew Fair on 22 August 1741 at Flametta in *The Devil of a Duke.*

Miss Dodson returned to Covent Garden for the 1741–42 and 1742–43 seasons, but her activity was rarely mentioned in the bills. In the former season she was a Villager in *Orpheus and Eurydice,* and in the latter she played a Country Lass in *The Rape of Proserpine.* She was replaced in *Proserpine* on 29 December 1742 and may not have finished the season. She was probably related to the Mrs Dodson who ap-

peared at Covent Garden in 1740, acted at the fairs, and sang at Sadler's Wells.

Doe, Miss ₁*fl. 1772*₁, *actress.*

Miss Doe played the Child in *Isabella* at Covent Garden on 30 March 1772. She was doubtless related to Doe the house servant, probably his daughter.

Doe, John ₁*fl. 1766–1804*₁, *house servant, actor.*

A British Museum manuscript lists a Mr Doe as the second gallery office keeper at Covent Garden in 1766. He was probably the Doe, variously styled Mr or John, who was a billsticker, actor, and doorman at Covent Garden through 1804. Doe's salary on 14 September 1767 was 2*s.* daily—exactly what he was earning at the end of his long career. But he there augmented his pittance by serving the playhouse in other capacities. On 26 March 1768 and on many dates thereafter, John Doe was paid for sticking the "Black Bills," a task still assigned him in 1802. On 13 November 1771 and several other dates throughout the 1771–72 and 1772–73 seasons, he received extra pay for performing "in the Ass" in Mother Shipton. His stipend for this ignominious duty seems to have been 2*s. 6d.* each performance. At the end of each season Doe's benefit tickets were accepted, but many times he received only half value and settled for less than £5 profit. Perhaps Doe picked up extra change playing in other productions, but the accounts made no further mention of such activity after 1772–73. In 1794–95 he was cited as a doorkeeper, a duty he may have performed in other seasons. Miss Doe who appeared as a child in 1772 was doubtless related to John, perhaps was his daughter.

"Doge of Drury, The." *See* STEELE, RICHARD.

Dogget, Mr ₁*fl. 1748*₁, *actor.*
At Yates's booth at Bartholomew Fair

on 24 August 1748 Mr Dogget played Taylor in the droll *The Consequences of Industry and Idleness*.

Dogget, James [*fl.* 1794], *singer.*

Doane's *Musical Directory* of 1794 listed James Dogget of No 40, the Strand, as a tenor who had been in the choir at St Paul's Cathedral and who had sung in the oratorios at Westminster Abbey and Drury Lane.

Doggett, Mr [*fl.* 1791], *actor, dancer.*

A Mr Doggett played Lord Rake "(with *Hippisley's Drunken Man*)" in *The Humours of Sir John Brute* at the Haymarket Theatre on 26 December 1791—his only known appearance in London.

Doggett, Thomas *c.* 1670?–1721, *actor, singer, manager.*

Though most sources place Thomas Doggett's birth date about 1670, T. A. Cook in his biography of the actor argues for a date closer to 1650, largely on the basis of Doggett's having married a Mary Owen by 1682. But another Thomas Doggett may have married Mary Owen, for the name was remarkably common, and what we know of the actor's early roles argues for the later date. Doggett was born in Castle Street, Dublin, and, according to Clark's *The Early Irish Stage*, acted in Ireland from 1684 to 1688 before coming to England. A manuscript cast for *The Night Walker*, performed at Smock Alley in 1684–85, lists "[D]oggy" as the Boy.

After his Dublin years Doggett became a strolling player and perhaps appeared at the London fairs before being engaged by Christopher Rich at 10*s.* weekly to act at Drury Lane. He is known to have played Deputy Nincompoop there in *Love for Money* in January 1691, but he was not noticed by the critics until he acted Solon in *The Marriage-Hater Match'd* in January 1692. On 26 February the *London Mercury* asked "Whether in Justice [D'Urfey, the author] is not obliged to present Mr Dog-

get (who acted Solon to so much Advantage) with half the Profit of his Third Day, since in the Opinions of most Persons, the good Success of his Comedy was half owing to that admirable Actor?" Indeed, "Solon" quickly became Doggett's nickname. He also acted the title role in *Sauny the Scot* about 1692, and Anthony Aston later wrote that Doggett "was the best Face-player and Gesticulator, and a thorough Master of the several Dialects, except the *Scots* (for he never was in *Scotland*)." Yet he made an admirable Sauny.

In 1692–93 Doggett played a full schedule at Drury Lane. Perhaps he had acted there regularly since 1690—the records are too sparse to be sure—but the fullness of his 1692–93 season suggests that perhaps he had made only sporadic London appearances previously and spent much of his time elsewhere. In 1692–93 he played Bertrand in *Henry II*, Colonel Hackwell Senior in *The Volunteers*, Lord Malepert in *The Maid's Last Prayer*, Fondlewife in *The Old Bachelor*, Quickwit (and the prologue) in *The Richmond Heiress*, and Wittless (and the prologue) in *The Female Vertuosos*. His Fondlewife was especially noteworthy, and Colley Cibber paid Doggett the compliment of imitating as exactly as possible his makeup and manner in the role. The season also brought Doggett new articles of agreement with Rich and a salary of £2 weekly.

In addition to his comic talent, Doggett was also a respectable singer. Dryden wrote to Walsh in April 1693 after seeing *The Richmond Heiress*, praising Anne Bracegirdle and Doggett especially: "the Singing was wonderfully good, And the two whom I nam'd sung better than Redding and Mrs Ayloff, whose trade it was . . ." On the following 9 May Dryden wrote again to Walsh that "This morning I had [the United Company's] chief Comedian whom they call Solon, with me; to consult with him concerning his own Character [of Sancho in *Love Triumphant*]: & truly I

Part of Articles of Agreement, 3 April 1696, between THOMAS DOGGETT and Skipwith

thinke he has the best Understanding of any man in the Playhouse."

Doggett's new parts in 1693–94, in addition to Sancho, were Coridon in *The Rape of Europa*, Sir Paul Plyant in *The Double Dealer*, Ferdinando in *The Fatal Marriage,* Thorneback (and the epilogue) in *The Married Beau*, and Sancho Panza (and the epilogue) in 1 *Don Quixote*. He also sang and acted in *The Lancashire Witches*. Sometime during the season Doggett and William Bowen bolted the company and tried to negotiate new terms as a pair. Betterton, the leading actor, refused them readmission until they treated sepa-

rately, and Doggett ended with a raise in his weekly salary to £2 10s. But the United Company was torn by dissension, and in the fall of 1694 Betterton and a group of dissatisfied older players charged the Drury Lane proprietors Rich and Skipwith with unfair treatment and rebelled. Dash in *The Canterbury Guests* in late September was Doggett's last recorded role with the United Company.

When Betterton received a license to form a new troupe, Doggett joined him. At the reconverted Lincoln's Inn Fields tennis court theatre the new company opened on 30 April 1695 with *Love for*

Love with Doggett as Ben. Cibber later wrote that "*Congreve* was a great Admirer of [Doggett], and found his Account in the Characters he expresly wrote for him. In those of *Fondlewife*, and his *Old Bachelor*, and *Ben*, in *Love for Love*, no Author and Actor could be more obliged to their mutual masterly Performances." In preparation for the role of Ben, Doggett, according to *An Essay on Acting* (1744) "took Lodgings in *Wapping*, and *gather'd thence a Nosegay* for the whole Town." The care with which Doggett worked up his roles particularly impressed Cibber. Colley said Doggett was

the strictest Observer of Nature, of all his Contemporaries. He borrow'd from none of them: His Manner was his own: He was a Pattern to others, whose greatest Merit was that they had sometimes tolerably imitated him. In dressing a Character to the greatest Exactness he was remarkably skilful; the least Article of whatever Habit he wore seem'd in some degree to speak and mark the different Humour he presented. . . . He could be extremely ridiculous without stepping into the least Impropriety to make him so. His greatest Success was in Characters of lower Life, which he improv'd from the Delight he took in his Observations of that Kind in the real World.

With Betterton's troupe in 1695–96 Doggett played Squire Wouldbe (and spoke the epilogue) in *She Ventures and He Wins*, Sapless in *Lover's Luck*, Vaunter in *The She-Gallants*, and Young Hob in his own play *The Country Wake* (published in 1696 and performed in April of that year). In *A Comparison Between the Two Stages* the character Ramble says of *The Country Wake*: "Oh, that's Dogget's: The Players have all got the itching Leprosie of Scribling as Ben. Johnson calls it; 'twill in time descend to the Scene-keepers and Candle-snuffers: Come, what came on't?" To which Sullen replies, "Not then directly Damn'd, because he had a part in't

himself, but it's now [1702] dead and buried." But not so dead as Sullen thought. In 1715 *Hob: or The Country Wake* was published, and though some authorities have assigned the work to Colley Cibber, Hughes and Scouten in *Ten English Farces* make a good case for its being Doggett's revision of his earlier play. Variations on *The Country Wake* were performed well into the eighteenth century.

Before the 1695–96 season was over Doggett negotiated with Skipwith and Rich to return to Drury Lane. He drove a hard bargain. Two different agreements dated 3 April 1696 spelled out the details of his new engagement. He was to receive at once £50. Another £50 was to be paid him the following 12 October, two days after his new engagement at Drury Lane was scheduled to begin. If Doggett could arrange to leave Betterton's troupe by 20 July, he would get an additional £10 and spend the summer learning five new roles and improving himself by travel. If he could leave Betterton within three weeks (that is, before the end of April), still another £10 would be paid him, for which he would make "Observaçons for yᵉ benefitt of this Company" during his travels. His salary at Drury Lane was to be £4 for every six acting days or a share equal to that being received by George Powell or John Verbruggen (who were paid £4 out of every £20 profit). Doggett was to have his benefit during Lent, and as long as he did not choose an opera or a recently revived play, Drury Lane would bear all but 10s. of the house charges. Doggett and Skipwith both posted bonds of £500 each.

Doggett probably toured during the summer of 1696; Anthony Aston later said Doggett, Booker, Mins, and others strolled with him about this time. Perhaps Doggett carried out his agreement to make observations for Drury Lane and was able to bring back recommendations for the recruitment of actors. He does not appear to have fulfilled his agreement to start playing at

Drury Lane on 10 October 1696, however, and he may well have begun the fall season with Betterton's troupe. The part of Gallus in *The Loves of Mars and Venus* was designed for Doggett at Lincoln's Inn Fields that fall, but Lee took over the role. On 26 October 1696 the Lord Chamberlain, who usually tried to prevent actors from switching companies, gave Doggett special permission to act at either Lincoln's Inn Fields or Drury Lane. This allowed him to make the transfer he had planned the previous April. On 21 November he played Lory in *The Relapse*, his first recorded appearance at Drury Lane under his new contract. After that he spoke the epilogue to *Cinthia and Endimion* and played Learchus in both parts of *Aesop*, Mass Johnny in *Woman's Wit*, Massetto in *The Triumphs of Virtue*, and Bull Senior in *A Plot and No Plot*.

The role of Lory in *The Relapse* was unsuited to Doggett, and he quickly relinquished it to Pinkethman. His Mass Johnny in *Woman's Wit*, on the other hand, was tailor-made for him by Cibber. Colley had originally planned the play for Betterton's players, with whom he worked briefly the previous season, but he reshaped the characters for the Drury Lane comedians and was pleased with the result. In his Preface he wrote that

not to miss the advantage of Mr. *Dogget's* excellent action, I prepar'd a low character, which (though I dare not recommend it to the reader) I knew from him cou'd not fail of diverting. I have seen him play with more success I own, but never saw any man bear a truer face of nature; and indeed the two last acts were much better perform'd than I could have propos'd in that other house . . .

After the 1696–97 season Doggett left Drury Lane, apparently without permission. Cibber later said that Doggett, because of the "Exactness of his Nature" was often restless in any given theatre. In this instance, "having some Reason to think the

Patentee had not dealt fairly with him, he quitted the Stage and would act no more, rather chusing to lose his whatever unsatisfy'd Demands than go through the chargeable and tedious Course of the Law to recover it." The exact nature of his dissatisfaction in 1696–97 is not known but may be guessed at. Rich was a tyrannical and scheming manager and Doggett "a prudent, honest Man"; a conflict between the two would have been almost inevitable.

On 13 October 1697 Doggett received permission from the Duke of Norfolk to act at Norwich with a company previously managed by the strolling player John Coysh. Back in London the Drury Lane managers complained to the Lord Chamberlain about Doggett's desertion, and a warrant was issued for his apprehension. Cibber related what happened after that:

A Messenger was immediately dispatch'd to *Norwich*, where *Dogget* then was, to bring him up in Custody: But doughty *Dogget*, who had Money in his Pocket and the Cause of Liberty at his Heart, was not in the least intimidated by the formidable Summons. He was observ'd to obey it with a particular Chearfulness, entertaining his Fellow-traveller, the Messenger, all the way in the Coach (for he had protested against Riding) with as much Humour as a Man of his Business might be capable of tasting. And as he found his Charges were to be defray'd, he, at every Inn, call'd for the best Dainties the Country could afford or a pretended weak Appetite could digest. At this rate they jollily roll'd on, more with the Air of a Jaunt than a Journey, or a Party of Pleasure than of a poor Devil in Durance. Upon his Arrival in Town he immediately apply'd to the Lord Chief Justice *Holt* for his *Habeas Corpus*. As his Case was something particular, that eminent and learned Minister of the Law took a particular Notice of it: For *Dogget* was not only discharg'd, but the Process of his Confinement (according to common Fame) had a Censure pass'd upon it in Court . . .

Drury Lane did not get Doggett back, and the records show that he succeeded in obtaining an extension of his permit in Norwich on 12 January 1698 and that he returned there to act in the fall of that year. On 24 September he was given permission to perform at St Andrew's Hall, and by 27 January 1699 he was acting at the Angel Inn. Unfortunately, his engagement at the latter place of entertainment was marred when the gallery broke down at one performance, killing a young woman and injuring another.

Doggett came back to London to act Ralph in *Friar Bacon* at a Bartholomew Fair booth he and Parker operated on 23 August 1699 and subsequent days. Ned Ward saw the production in September and left a description of it:

Having heard much of a comedian's [Doggett's] fame, who had manfully run the hazard of losing that reputation in the Fair which he had got in the playhouse, and having never seen him in his proper element, we thought the time might not be very illspent if we took a sight of another best show in the Fair (for so they all styled themselves) that we might judge of his performances.

. . . Then entered the miller and his son Ralph. The father seemed to be the same thing he imitated and as for his hopeful progeny, he was the only person we were desirous of seeing. I think he kept up so true a behaviour of an idiot, that it was enough to persuade the audience that he really was by Nature what he only artfully represented. I could not but conclude the part was particularly adapted to his genius, or he could never have expressed the humour with such agreeable simplicity. But, I fancy, if he was to play the part of a wise man, it would be quite out of his way. There was nothing in the part itself but what was purely owing to his own gesture, for it was the comedian only, and not the poet, that rendered the character diverting. To be plain, they both acted and became their characters extremely well, for I cannot but acknowledge that I never saw anybody look more like a fool than the son, nor any miller look more like a cozening knave than the father.

Doggett returned to Norwich in the fall of 1699 but encountered resistance. On 29 December Humphrey Prideaux wrote from Norwich to John Ellis: "The D[uke] of N[orfolk] hath been here; and some will have it that his only businesse was to fix Dogget and his players here, who have now their stage up at ye Dukes place, and are helping all they can to undoe this place, w^ch, on ye decay of their weaveing trade, now sinks apace."

By 18 December 1699 Doggett was back in London, acting Barnaby Brittle in *The Amorous Widow* with Betterton's troupe at Lincoln's Inn Fields. Vanbrugh wrote in a letter on 25 December that Doggett had been acting at Norwich but was in town "last week" and acted six times for £30, filling the house every time. He was in Norwich again on 17 January 1700 offering the town *Dioclesian*, billed as the first opera ever attempted outside London. He received another permit to act in October, but by November he was again in London, working with Betterton for £3 weekly and a clear benefit. The players were harassed by the authorities for using blasphemous language on stage, but in general Doggett had a successful season. During 1700–1701 he played Sir Testy in *The Ladies Visiting Day*, Shylock in *The Jew of Venice*, probably Fernando in *The Fatal Marriage*, perhaps Shallow in *Henry IV*, and a singing part in *The Mad Lover*. He and Wilks shared the profit of the galleries at Dorset Garden on 11 April and 6 May 1701 when *The Judgment of Paris* was performed.

In the summer of 1701 the actor strolled again. On 1 July he entered into a £500 bond not to act during the time of the Stourbridge Fair or in the liberties of Cambridge, but he performed anyway, could not fulfill the bond, and was jailed by the Vice Chancellor of Cambridge, Richard Bentley. Doggett was not heard from again until 9 September 1702 when the *Secret Mercury* noted that he had appeared at Bartholomew Fair, dressed in an old woman's petticoat and a red waistcoat, presumably in *The Distressed Virgin*, at his own booth. The play was a version of *The Fair Maid of the West*, tricked out with "the Comical Travels of Poor Trusty in Search of his Master's Daughter, and his Encounter with Three Witches."

Doggett entered into a three-year contract with Betterton in the fall of 1702 which, due to unforeseen circumstances, neither side was able to keep. He did, however, play at Lincoln's Inn Fields in 1702–3 and 1703–4. Among his new parts these seasons were Savil in *The Scornful Lady*, Sir Abel Single in *As You Find It*, Nicodemus Somebody in *The Stage Coach*, Sir Arthur Addle in *Sir Salomon*, the title role in *Squire Trelooby*, Sir Oliver in *She Wou'd If She Cou'd*, and Sir Hugh in *The Merry Wives of Windsor*. As before, he often spoke prologues and epilogues and sang. His contract permitted him to leave the company during the summers, and in 1703 he journeyed to Bath. At the request of Betterton's troupe, he joined the company to act at Oxford for £20 or a share of the profits, but on his arrival Betterton offered Doggett different terms. Doggett refused, his parts were given to others, and in a fit of pique he asked for his discharge. The matter was apparently settled amicably, since he rejoined Betterton the following fall after putting in an appearance at Bartholomew Fair in *Bateman*.

The theatrical situation in London changed considerably in 1704–5, and Doggett's contract with Betterton could not be completed. Vanbrugh's new Queen's Theatre in the Haymarket opened during the season, and Betterton, now weary and old, stepped down from the management of his troupe and accepted Vanbrugh's offer to play at the Queen's Theatre. Doggett seems to have been inactive in the fall of 1704, but he played at Drury Lane in the spring of 1705, taking such roles as Sir Nicholas Cully in *The Comical Revenge* and Polonius in *Hamlet*. He moved to the Queen's

Theatre for the 1705–6 season to act Moneytrap in *The Confederacy* and Sancho in *The Mistake* and to sing a comic dialogue with Cook. As Moneytrap, according to Wilkes's *General View of the Stage* of 1759, Doggett

wore an old thread-bare black coat, to which he had put new cuffs, pocket-lids, and buttons, on purpose to make its rustiness more conspicuous. The neck was stuffed so as to make him appear round-shouldered and give his head the greater prominency; his square-toed shoes were large enough to buckle over those he wore in common, which made his legs appear much smaller than usual.

During the 1706–7 season Doggett led the Duke of Norfolk's company in the provinces, but he was replaced by Thomas Ager about 1707, probably at the conclusion of the season.

In March 1708 he contracted to play six times at Drury Lane, and he chose only his favorite old roles: Ben, Sir Oliver, Solon, Fondlewife, and Savil. After that he did not play in London again until the special benefit for Betterton on 7 April 1709 when *Love for Love* was presented. But he was much concerned in London theatrical affairs and joined with other actors to bring about the downfall of the wily Christopher Rich on 6 June 1709. With Wilks and Cibber (and Anne Oldfield for a short period), Doggett treated with Owen Swiney, the holder of Vanbrugh's lease on the Queen's Theatre, and thus became involved in London theatrical management. The trio of actors agreed to pay Swiney £300 and accept £200 each as actor-managers. After these payments were made, any profit or loss would be split between Swiney and the triumvirate.

At the Queen's in 1709–10 Doggett acted, in addition to his old parts, Marplot in *The Busy Body*, the Mad Welshman in *The Pilgrim*, Roger in *Acis and Galatea*, Tom Thimble in *The Rehearsal*, Nykin in *The Old Bachelor*, Num in *The Man's Be-*

witch'd, Tipkin in *The Tender Husband*, Floro in *Almahide*, Dapper in *The Alchemist*, Eitherside in *Edward III*, Floro in *Floro and Beesa*, the title role in *Roger's Wedding*, and the first Gravedigger in *Hamlet*. As usual, he sang, and now he also had chores as a manager.

In 1710–11 the companies shifted. After opening the season at the Queen's Theatre, the actors gave up the new playhouse to the opera singers and moved to Drury Lane. During the season Doggett added to his repertoire a Witch in *Macbeth*, Don Perriera in *Marplot*, Postscript in *The Generous Husband*, and Young Scrape in *Injur'd Love*. He also spoke a comic dialogue with Pinkethman after *Injur'd Love*, dressed as a woman. The trio continued managing Drury Lane the ensuing season, during which Doggett tried Toby in *Madam Fickle* and Sir Tristram Cash in *The Wife's Relief* in addition to such old parts as Ben, Barnaby Brittle, Sir Oliver, and Hob. Hob was a special favorite of Sir Richard Steele, who wrote in *Spectator* No 502 that "There is something so miraculously pleasant in Doggett's acting the awkward triumph and comic sorrow of Hob in different circumstances, that I shall not be able to stay away whenever it is acted."

By the end of 1711–12 the three actor-managers had brought Drury Lane to a flourishing state. Wilks, Cibber, and Doggett earned from their shares at Drury Lane no less than £1000 annually up to the end of Queen Anne's reign in 1714. Though Doggett was eventually replaced by Booth, Drury Lane enjoyed 20 years of effective management by men to whom theatre was life, not just business. Wilks's extravagance was balanced by Doggett's caution, for Doggett, as Cibber said, was "one of those close Oeconimists whom Prodigals call a Miser." Cibber, on the other hand, was the perfect mediator and had a gift for handling his two difficult partners.

On many important matters all three men were in agreement: they discharged all debts every Monday before taking any profits for themselves; they kept strict payrolls, open for public inspection; and they gained the trust of their company members so that no written contracts were needed. All three were also fine actors who had the favor of the town and the respect of their fellows.

Yet the triumvirate wrangled on occasion, often over petty matters such as Wilks's wanting to give a benefit to two visiting Irish actors, at which, according to Cibber, Doggett "bounc'd and grew almost as untractable as Wilks . . ." The one serious matter over which they disagreed concerned the actor Barton Booth, who was ambitious to become a sharer. Booth had friends at court and, on 14 April 1713, won the favor of the town as Cato. Booth petitioned to become a sharer in the management at the beginning of the 1713–14 season, and the trio spent much of the fall arguing the matter. They knew that with his court connections Booth could work his way into the management if he wished, but the company's stock of costumes, scenery, and other valuables were in the names of Wilks, Cibber, and Doggett, and no one could force them to share the stock if they did not want to. Cibber was willing to accept any terms Wilks and Doggett would agree upon. Wilks proposed setting an outrageously high price on the stock to make up for allowing Booth to share in it. But Doggett flatly refused to part with any of the stock or place a value on it.

Cibber tried to get his partners to reach an agreement, for he favored letting Booth fully into the management, since Booth was in favor with town and Court and could help the company. Doggett refused to compromise and walked out, "After which," wrote Cibber, "he never came among us more, either as an Actor or Menager." Doggett's share of the stock fell to Cibber and Wilks, but they could not dispose of any part of it without Doggett's permission, which he refused to give. Further, he insisted on receiving his full share of the company profits whether he worked or not. Booth was admitted to the managership, and the new trio tried to lure Doggett back to the fold, offering him half a share as a sinecure if he no longer wished to perform. Again he refused. Matters were at a standstill: Doggett complained to the Lord Chamberlain that he would not consider any further discussion with the managers until they gave him his share of the profits, and the managers refused to pay him as long as he refused to work. An exchange of remonstrances went on into the winter of 1714–15, when another problem aggravated the situation.

At the death of Queen Anne a new patent had to be issued to Drury Lane. Sir Richard Steele engineered the matter for the managers, and the patent was issued on 18 October 1714 naming Wilks, Cibber, Booth, Doggett, and Steele. Steele informed Doggett of this on 19 January 1715, and the ex-actor was furious because it had been negotiated without his consent. Finally, Doggett went to Chancery in a bill against Wilks, Cibber, and Booth, and the matter was tied up in court for two years before a settlement was reached on 6 March 1716. Doggett was left with £600 for his share in the Drury Lane stock plus 15 percent interest from the date of the last license (presumably the one issued on 11 November 1713 which had added Booth's name to the list of managers). After paying his legal fees Doggett received less than he would have done had he accepted an earlier offer from Drury Lane of £500 and a sinecure for life.

Though the parsimonious Doggett was a man of considerable wealth, the lengthy litigation forced him to dig into his savings and borrow money. In February 1715 he took out a loan for £500 which he did not repay until 30 April 1717, and in March 1715 (1715/16?) he wrote to a Mr Grigsby "to pay to James Jemblin on Order my divid: due att Christmas Last of Five Thousand Pounds Southsea Stock . . ."

Once the vexatious matter of the Drury Lane managership was settled, Doggett got back on amicable terms with Cibber and confessed that it had been Wilks, not Booth, who had irked him so. After the 16 March 1716 settlement Doggett was also able to turn his attention to other things. Long a staunch Whig and supporter of the Hanoverian succession, he placed an advertisement in the papers on 1 August 1716:

This being the day of his majesty's happy accession to the throne, there will be given by Mr. Doggett an orange colour livery with a badge representing liberty, to be rowed for by six watermen that are out of their time within the year past [that is, having undergone their apprenticeships]. They are to row from London Bridge to Chelsea. It will be continued annually on the same day for ever.

What made the prize so attractive was that guineas were sewn into each of the many pockets of the coat.

Doggett also made a brief return to the stage. At Drury Lane he played Barnaby Brittle in *The Amorous Widow* for Mrs Porter's benefit and Ben in *Love for Love* for Hester Santlow's benefit in the spring of 1717. On 1 April 1717 he made his last appearance, playing Hob in his own *The Country Wake*. Then he turned his attention to matrimony. Perhaps, as Cook states, he married Mary Owen about 1682; if so, she was out of his life by 1718, for the *Original Weekly Journal* on 23–30 August of that year reported that Doggett the player was "lately married to a gentlewoman of 20,000 l. fortune."

On 10 September 1721 Thomas Doggett made his will, describing himself as from the parish of St Paul, Covent Garden. He asked his executors, Sir George Markham and Thomas Reynolds, to choose 20 poor shopkeepers who were never worth more than £50 and give them £50 each. To his kinsman Captain Jacob Hallister of Bristol he left his gold watch and £200. To Mrs Mary Peck of Eltham, Kent, widow, he bequeathed £100, and to his niece Mary Young in Ireland, if still alive, he left £200. He provided his servant Ann Gibbons with £20 for mourning, all his household movables, and a £30 annuity, and he gave her sister Catherine £10. To Mrs Thomas Reynolds he left his best diamond ring. His executors were made residuary legatees of what must have been a considerable estate accumulated by Doggett and contributed to by the woman he had married in 1718 and who was, by 1721, dead.

The will also contained detailed instructions concerning the watermen's race Doggett had instituted. He asked his executors to purchase freehold lands to the value of £10 per year, to be conveyed to Edward Burt of the Admiralty office, his heirs and assigns. From this income the race was to be supported. Doggett carefully specified that £5 yearly was to be spent on the 12-ounce silver badge, 18s. for cloth, £1 1s. for making up the prize coat, and 30s. for the clerk of Watermen's Hall for handling the race arrangements.

Doggett requested that he be "decently buried in like manner as my late Wife was, both as to privacy and Expence." The *Weekly Journal or Saturday's Post* of 23 September 1721 reported that "Last Wednesday [20 September] died the Celebrated Comedian, Mr Tho Doggett, formerly one of the Masters of the Play-House in Drury Lane." Doggett was buried at Eltham, Kent, on 25 September, and his will was proved on 2 October.

Anthony Aston, who toured with Doggett, described him as a little, lively man, modest and cheerful in his behavior, a good singer and dancer, a man of sense, a neat and fine dresser, but somewhat illiterate. He found Doggett an honest actor, especially fine in comedy, but hopeless in tragedy, which he seldom essayed. "On the Stage," Aston said, "he's very Aspectbund wearing a Farce in his Face; his Thoughts deliberately framing his Utterance Congruous to his Looks: He is the only Comick

Original now [1708] Extant . . ." His skill at makeup, according to Wilkes's *General View of the Stage* (1759), was so great that

he could with the greatest exactness, paint his face so as to represent the age of seventy, eighty, and ninety distinctly; which occasioned Sir Godfery Kneller to tell him one day, at Buttons' Coffee-house, that he excelled him in Painting, for, that he could only copy nature from the originals before him, but [Doggert] could vary them at pleasure, and yet keep a close likeness.

A description of the actor was preserved at Watermen's Hall, but it surely must have been of Doggett in some character:

He wore an enormous wig with long lappets of hair hanging over his shoulders which enveloped his head, and on the top of it was stuck a small cocked hat which it would have been a great effort of balancing to retain in its place without the aid of pins. His coat, very broad on the tails, reaches below his knees, his waistcoat, with flap pockets of large size, extends half way down his thighs. His small-clothes are light and buckled at the knees, where they are met by coloured stockings which rise out of square-toed, red-heeled, silver-buckled shoes. Under his left arm he carries a clouded or amber-coloured cane, while his right hand is continually titillating his olfactory nerve with snuff from out of a box set with precious stones, and the indispensible rapier hangs at his side.

The description smacks of the care with which Doggett attended to details when creating a character. Offstage, according to Dibdin, Doggett was well-bred, and he never chose to be the actor anywhere but in performance.

The Garrick Club has a portrait called "Thomas Doggett," but its authenticity has been questioned. It shows the fat, strong, good-humored face of a man close to developing a double chin. It was once thought that Doggett was pictured dancing the Cheshire Round, but that drawing too, has been found spurious. An engraving by G. Van der Gucht showing the characters Miss Prue, Ben, Mrs Foresight, and Mrs Frail in a scene from *Love for Love* was taken by an anonymous annotator of the copy in the Harvard Theatre Collection to represent Mrs Ayliff, Doggett, Mrs Boman, and Mrs Barry, but though those players did act the roles in 1695, the engraver (who was not born until the following year) was probably not trying to depict the performers named but only his conception of the characters. It is unfortunate that no verifiably authentic portrait of Thomas Doggett has survived, for he seems to have been one of those rare birds in the theatre, an actor's actor.

Doile. *See also* **DOYLE.**

Doile, Ann ₁*fl.* 1797₁, *house servant?*
The account books for Drury Lane contain an entry of 21 October 1797 concerning a payment of 13*s.* 4*d.* to Miss Ann Doile. She may have been one of the house servants.

Doile, Margaret ₁*fl.* 1797–1800₁, *house servant?*
The Drury Lane accounts from 1797 through 1800 contain several references to Margaret Doile. "Peggy," as she was frequently called in the accounts, was paid 13*s.* 4*d.* on 21 October 1797, the earliest notice of her, and the same amount on 4 March 1800, the last time she was mentioned. She was perhaps one of the house servants, but the books do not make clear what her duties were or whether the sums she received were her daily or her weekly wages.

"Doll Common." *See* **COREY, MRS JOHN.**

Dominic, Mr ₁*fl.* 1726₁, *scene painter.*

Mr Dominic, along with Devoto, Tillemans, and Eberlin, painted the scenes for John Thurmond's *The Miser,* performed at Drury Lane on 30 December 1726.

"Dominichino." *See* **ANNIBALI, DOMENICO.**

Dominique, Mons ₁*fl.* 1742–1751₁, *actor, acrobat, manager.*
Monsieur Dominique belonged to the Grande Troupe Étrangère in 1742, serving under Restier and the widow Lavigne. For them on 15 February at the Saint-Germain fair he played a countryman friend of Harlequin in *Le Diable boiteux.*

In June and July 1742 Dominique appeared as a tumbler with Hendrick Kerman's troupe at Sadler's Wells; in July 1743 he was at Stoke's Croft, Bristol; and in August 1744, at the New Wells, Clerkenwell, he flung himself over 24 men with drawn swords, "a thing never done before in England," according to the bill. Dominique had his own company at Stoke's Croft in November 1745, advertised as from Sadler's Wells in London. It was reported in Bristol that Dominique "suffered greatly in the opinion of the Town . . . by being supposed to be the Master of a French Company," but he said in his defense that he was from Berne, Switzerland, and other members of his troupe were from Amsterdam, Milan, and Great Britain. With Dominique in Bristol was Miss Polly Dominique, age four, who was doubtless his daughter. Dominique was still active in 1751 when, on 30 September in Glasgow, he entertained the Scots by flying over a double fountain.

Dominique, Mme ₁*fl.* 1748₁, *singer, dancer.*
On 24 August 1748 at Hussey's booth at Bartholomew Fair, Madame Dominique (the wife of the acrobat-manager, perhaps) participated in the singing and dancing between the acts of *The Constant Quaker.*

With Master Harrison she presented *Foote's Vagaries.*

Dominique, Polly *b. 1741, performer.*

Miss Polly Dominique, age four, was a member of Dominique's troupe of acrobats and rope dancers who performed at Stoke's Croft Theatre in Bristol in November 1745. The company was hailed as having come from Sadler's Wells. Polly was probably Dominique's daughter and presumably a performer, but her specialty is not known.

Domitilla, Miriamne, née Campanini *[fl. 1741–1748], dancer.*

Signora Miriamne Domitilla was one of two sisters of the celebrated dancer Barbarina Campanini (1721–1799). She made her debut, billed as Signora Domitilla, at Covent Garden on 30 October 1741, when she danced a *New Tambourine* with Barbarina, Mrs LeBrun, Mrs Wright, and Mrs Villeneuve. On 7 November she performed as "a nymph" in *Orpheus and Eurydice* and on 21 January appeared in a new ballet called *The Rural Assembly,* which was introduced into a performance of *The Winter's Tale.* The ballet was subsequently inserted into performances of *As You Like It* on 22 January 1742 and *The Way of the World* on 25 January. For a command performance before the Prince of Wales on 5 April, she shared a benefit with Picq for which she performed a *Hussar* dance with Denoyer. Her salary for the season, which she concluded on 1 May in *Les Savoyards* with Villeneuve, was £5 per week.

At Covent Garden again in 1742–43, Signora Domitilla danced before the Prince of Wales once more on 9 December in a *Musette.* Her other performances that season included *Les Savoyards* and a Sylvan character in *The Rape of Proserpine.* When she performed in *Les Savoyards* on 18 December 1742, a young man in the gallery named William Wright expressed his disapproval of her dancing and "was without any provocation, beat kicked & abused in so violent & terrible a manner" that his life was "despaired of." A reward of five guineas was offered for the "discovery of the offender."

Signora Domitilla continued at Covent Garden for another season as a regular featured dancer, making her final appearance in *The Royal Chace* on 25 May 1744. She then returned to the Continent. She is known to have danced at Paris and in 1747 at Berlin with her sister. On 25 July 1748 the *General Advertiser* reported that "On Wednesday last arrived here from Berlin, the Celebrated Signiora Barbarini, with her Sister Signiora Domitilla," but there is no record of any performances given by either of them at London at that time.

Donadieu, Miss *[fl. 1775], singer.*

Miss Donadieu appeared as Clarinda in Arne's burletta *The Sot* on 1 May 1775 at the Haymarket Theatre. Tickets delivered by her for the previous 27 April were accepted.

Donaldson, Mr *[fl. 1772], actor.*

Mr Donaldson played Madge in *The Gentle Shepherd* at the Haymarket Theatre on 21 December 1772 with a group of Scotsmen in town for the occasion.

Donaldson, Alexander *d. 1794, printer, bookseller, treasurer.*

Alexander Donaldson was a printer and bookseller in Edinburgh from 1750 to 1763 and in London from 1763 to about 1788. His specialty was selling books at great discounts, often by publishing without recognition of copyright; this practice involved him in legal frays with his fellow printers and brought upon him an injunction from Chancery not to print certain English books. The House of Commons finally reversed the decision in 1774. Donaldson was Boswell's early printer and friend, and Boswell was able to defend him to Dr Johnson, who called him a "Robin Hood."

In 1771 Donaldson was made one of the treasurers of Drury Lane by Garrick. Donaldson bought property near Edinburgh in 1786, left London about 1788, and died in Scotland on 11 March 1794.

Donaldson, Mrs William. *See* FALKNER, ANNA MARIA.

Donallan, Mr *fl. 1798–1819*, *sweeper, watchman.*

A Mr Donallan (or Donnelly) was a sweeper and watchman at Drury Lane earning 12s. weekly from at least 1 December 1798 to the end of the 1818–19 season.

Dondell, Sprackling *fl. 1712*, *musician?*

The Coke papers at Harvard contain a receipt for payment made on 24 June 1712, signed by Sprackling Dondell and W. Armstrong. Armstrong was a violist in the band at the Queen's Theatre, and it is probable that Dondell was also a member.

"Don Jumpedo." *See* **"JUMPEDO, DON."**

Donman, Mr *fl. 1785–1789*, *bassoonist.*

Mr Donman played the bassoon at the St Paul's concerts on 10 and 12 May 1785 and 12 and 14 May 1789.

Donnelly. *See* DONALLAN.

Donovan, Master *fl. 1739–1741*, *actor.*

On 10 October 1739, 14 October 1740, and 26 December 1741 Master Donovan was cited in the Drury Lane bill as Moth in *Robin Goodfellow.*

"Don Piaffo." *See* **"PIAFFO, DON."**

"Don Saltero." *See* SALTER, JAMES.

Donwalt, Mr *fl. 1767*, *musician.*

Mr Donwalt was a member of the Covent Garden band, earning, as of 14 September 1767, 5s. nightly.

Doorescourt, John *fl. 1689–1699*, *trumpeter.*

John Doorescourt (or Dorescourt) was sworn a trumpeter in the King's Musick on 12 September 1689 at an annual wage of £91 5s. He was still in the royal service in 1699.

Doorsming, Mr *fl. 1748*, *singer.*

Mr Doorsming made his first, and perhaps his last, public appearance at the Haymarket Theatre on 5 September 1748 singing a cantata.

Dorcase, Mr *fl. 1675*, *singer.*

Mr Dorcase sang in the court masque *Calisto* on 15 February 1675.

Dore, Mrs *fl. 1785*, *actress.*

A Mrs Dore played Mrs Riot in *Lethe* at the Haymarket Theatre on 25 April 1785 for that night only.

Dorell, Miss *fl. 1797*, *actress.*

Billed as "A Young Lady," Miss Dorell made her first appearance at Drury Lane on 2 June 1797 as Lady Ruby in *First Love.* Where she had performed before coming to Drury Lane is not known. She was not noticed in the bills again.

Dorelli, Signor *fl. 1791–1795*, *singer.*

According to Smith's *Italian Opera* a singer named Dorelli was in the opera company which was playing at the King's Theatre in the Haymarket from 26 March to 6 June 1791. Haydn in his *First London Notebook* in 1792 mentioned Dorelli, and in his fourth book he told a story of a Signora "Donellis' " narrowly escaping the claws of a tiger at the Tower of London when the trap door in the beast's cage was left open by the careless keeper. *The Lon-*

don Stage does not list Dorelli, though both it and Smith cite the basso Giovanni Morelli who sang at the Pantheon from 14 May to 18 July 1791 and was popular in London before and after this season. Perhaps the two names were confused.

Dorescourt. *See* **DOORESCOURT.**

Dorien, Mr *fl. 1773*, *actor.*

On 3 September 1773 Mr Dorien played one of the Arval Brothers in *Ambarvalia* at Marylebone Gardens.

Dorion, Mr *fl. 1784–1795*, *singer.*

Fierman Joseph Dorion's son, as "Master Dorion," sang treble in the Handel Memorial Concerts at Westminster Abbey and the Pantheon in May and June 1784. As "Dorion Junior" he sang in the chorus of the Drury Lane company from 1791 through 1794 at the King's Theatre, the Haymarket, and the new Drury Lane. In 1791–92 he was in *The Cave of Trophonius, Dido Queen of Carthage,* and *The Surrender of Calais*; in 1792–93 he sang in *The Prisoner, The Pirates, Ozmyn and Daraxa, The Mountaineers, Caernarvon Castle,* and *Comus*; in 1793–94 he was in *Royal Clemency, The Tempest, Lodoiska,* and *The Battle of Hexham*; and in 1794–95 he was in *The Roman Father* and *The Cherokee.* No references to a Dorion "Junior" appeared after 1795.

Dorion, Fierman Joseph *fl. 1781–1804*, *singer, music copyist.*

Fierman Joseph Dorion sang the role of Violon in *A Preludio* at the Haymarket Theatre on 8 August 1781; he returned there the following summer, singing the same role on 3 June 1782 and playing an Anchor Smith in *Harlequin Teague* on 17 August. In May and June 1784 Dorion was one of the tenors who sang at the Handel Memorial Concerts at Westminster Abbey and the Pantheon, and by 1 November 1787 he was working at Drury Lane

as a music copyist and singer. He continued there at least through the 1794–95 season and also appeared as a singer in the summers at the Haymarket.

Dorion's characters were seldom named in the playbills, but he was in *The Battle of Hexham, The Island of St Marguerite, New Spain, The Surrender of Calais, The Cave of Trophonius, Richard Coeur de Lion, Dido Queen of Carthage, The Pirates, Ozmyn and Daraxa, The Mountaineers, Caernarvon Castle, Comus, Royal Clemency, The Tempest, Thomas and Sally, Lodoiska, The Roman Father, The Cherokee,* and *Zorinski.* Singing with him in many of these productions was his son, whose career began in 1784.

Doane's *Musical Directory* of 1794 listed the elder Dorion as a singer in performances sponsored by the New Musical Fund and the Academy of Ancient Music as well as in the oratorios and other productions at Drury Lane. Dorion's address in 1794 was No 126, Drury Lane. From 23 February to 30 March 1798 he sang in the oratorios at Covent Garden. In 1803 a "Mons Dorion" sang at Sadler's Wells, and in April 1804 one "Dorian" appeared there. Perhaps these references are to Fierman Joseph Dorian, for Dorian Junior was not mentioned in contemporary documents after 1795.

Dorival, Anne Marguerite *d. 1788, dancer.*

Mademoiselle (sometimes, apparently in error, Madame) Anne Marguerite Dorival was dancing in Paris as early as 1773 and was one of the solo dancers at the Opéra in 1776. She came to the King's Theatre in London for the 1784–85 season at a salary of £350, her first notice being on 18 December 1784 when she danced in a new divertissement choreographed by Lepicq. Thereafter she appeared in such dances as *Le Tuteur trompé, The Deserter, Il convito degli dei, Le Jugement de Paris, Il convitato di pietra, Macbeth* (a ballet based on the play), and *À la plus sage.* She also danced in the opera *Orfeo* and participated in untitled specialty dances. At the time of her solo benefit on 7 April 1785 she was living at No 127, Pall Mall. According to Campardon, Anne Marguerite Dorival died in Marseilles in 1788.

Dorival à Corifet, stage name of Marie Catherine Brida   *b. c. 1754, dancer.*

Born about 1754, Marie Catherine Brida, called Mademoiselle Dorival à Corifet, was living in Paris by 1777 and dancing at the Opéra by 1786. William C. Smith in *The Italian Opera* places her in London at the King's Theatre in the spring of 1789, though *The London Stage* notes her for the first time on 7 January 1790 in *La bergère des Alpes* at the Haymarket Theatre (where the opera company was performing). In the early months of 1790 Mlle Dorival was seen in such other dances as *Les Mariages flammands, Les Caprices, La Jalousie sans raison,* and *The Generous Slave*. When she was granted a solo benefit on 20 May she advertised that tickets would be available from her at No 36, St Martin's Street.

In the spring and summer of 1791 she danced at the new King's Theatre in *Orpheus and Eurydice, La Mort d'Hercule, and his Apothéosis, Ninette à la cour, Les Folies d'Espagne,* and *La Fête du seigneur*. Perhaps her most important night was on 6 June 1791 when she danced a *minuet de la cour* with Vestris. They repeated that dance on 9 July, the last performance of the season and Mlle Dorival's last notice in England.

Dorman, Mr   [*fl.* 1740–1741], *house servant?*

A Mr Dorman worked at the Covent Garden Theatre in 1740–41 at an unspecified salary and task. Perhaps he was one of the house servants, though there is a chance that he was Ridley Dorman, the violinist of later decades.

Dorman, Ridley   [*fl.* 1752–1773?], *violinist.*

On 15 August 1752 Ridley Dorman the violinist was given a benefit concert at the Long Room in Hampstead. The following 9 October he married the singer Elizabeth Young at her parish church, St Paul, Covent Garden. The register shows that Dorman was from the parish of St George the Martyr and was a bachelor; the witnesses were J. and Isabella Scott and Cecilia Arne.

Both Mr and Mrs Dorman were active in the Drury Lane Theatre in 1767, she as a singer and he, apparently, as an instrumentalist. *The London Stage* cites a singer Dorman that year at Drury Lane at a salary of £1 10*s.* weekly, but the reference is surely to Elizabeth, not Ridley. On 1 June 1767 Ridley was paid £10 10*s.* for attending rehearsals – probably as an accompanist or member of the band.

After 1767 Ridley Dorman's career is difficult to trace. A Mr Dorman was paid by Drury Lane for coal: £45 10*s.* on 28 October 1771 and £46 5*s.* on 19 October 1773. The coal dealer may have been a different Dorman, but Ridley may have given up his undistinguished musical career for a trade. In 1815–16 and 1816–17 a Mr Dorman was earning £3 weekly as a member of the Drury Lane band; he may have been one of Ridley's descendants.

Dorman, Mrs Ridley, Elizabeth, née Young   *d. 1773, singer, actress.*

Elizabeth Young, the niece of Cecilia Young Arne, is said by Grove to have accompanied her aunt to Ireland in 1755 and perhaps to have made her debut in Dublin on 20 March 1756. Grove may have confused Elizabeth Young and Elizabeth Younge (later Mrs Alexander Pope), for the latter was certainly in Dublin in 1755 and after.

Indeed, on 22 June 1758 "Miss E. Young" made what was billed as her first appearance on any stage, singing Lucy in *The Beggar's Opera* at Drury Lane. The singer in question was Elizabeth, substituting for Kitty Clive, who had refused to perform. The work was then given only one performance, a special post-season benefit for some distressed actors.

In the fall of 1759 Elizabeth joined the Drury Lane company on a permanent basis. In 1759–60, 1760–61, and 1761–62 she sang in *Romeo and Juliet*, the *Epithalamium* in *Isabella*, the interlude *Hearts of Oak*, and *The Reprisal*, but she also appeared in named roles: Dorcas in *The Mock Doctor* on 15 November 1759 (replacing Mrs Abington), a Nymph in *Comus* on 24 November, Pastora in *The Chaplet* on 18 April 1761 (replacing Mrs Clive), and her debut role of Lucy (again replacing Mrs Clive) on 25 May 1762.

On 9 October 1762 at her parish church, St Paul, Covent Garden, Miss Young married the violinist Ridley Dorman. Witnesses were J. Scott, Isabella Young Scott (probably Elizabeth's sister), and Cecilia Arne. For the ten years that followed, Mrs Dorman sang and acted at Drury Lane, and on occasion she made appearances elsewhere.

At Drury Lane she essayed such roles as Mrs Peachum in *The Beggar's Opera*, Tippet in *Phoebe*, Agenor in *The Royal Shepherd* (replacing the ailing Mr Norris on 24 February 1764; "much applauded," wrote the prompter Cross in his diary), Dorcas in *Thomas and Sally*, Gilades in *Pharnaces*, Grideline in *Rosamond*, Dol Tearsheet in *Falstaff's Wedding*, Mrs Day in *The Committee*, Ariel in *The Tempest* (in place of Miss Young on 30 April 1766), a Shepherdess in *Cymon*, Ceres in *The Tempest*, Ursula in *The Padlock* ("Mrs Dorman was hissed at first," wrote Cross on 3 October 1768), Rheum in the entertainment *The Old Women Weatherwise*, Traplass in *The Country Madcap in London*, and the Mother in *The Chances*. As of 9 February 1765 Mrs Dorman was earning 5s. daily, a lowly wage considering her obvious willingness to substitute on a short notice for others.

In addition to her Drury Lane appearances she sang at Finch's Grotto Gardens in August 1765 and the summer of 1771; she made an appearance at the Haymarket Theatre on 7 October 1768 as Dorcas in *Thomas and Sally*; at Signora Frasi's benefit at the King's Theatre on 1 June 1769 she sang the title role in *Artaxerxes*; and she was in *The Noble Pedlar* at Marylebone Gardens on 21 August 1770.

Elizabeth Young Dorman died on 12 April 1773 and was buried at St Paul, Covent Garden, on 19 April. The parish register scribe noted her as Mrs "Darman" from St Anne, Westminster.

Dormond. *See* **DORMAN.**

Dorney, Richard *1620–1681, violinist.*

On 3 November 1641 Richard Dorney's mother, a widow with six small children, petitioned the Lord Chamberlain for a place in the King's Musick for Richard. She stated that her late husband Richard had been a violinist in ordinary to Charles I, had served for seven months with his Majesty in Spain, and had left no maintenance for his wife and children upon his death. The elder Dorney, however, had, during his long last illness, procured a promise from Charles I, as earlier from James I, that his son Richard would be admitted to the King's Musick in his father's place. On 8 November 1641 the Lord Chamberlain signed a certificate assuring Richard Dorney Jr of a place as soon as he became fit, "he being at present in his minority, and not capable of taking the necessary oath. In the meantime his place to be filled by some able man." On 11 November a payment was made to Dorney of 1s. 8d. daily wages and £16 2s. 6d. annual livery allowance as a violinist in ordinary in place of his deceased father. All this suggests that Dorney's twenty-first birthday must have fallen between 8 and 11

November 1641 and that he was born in 1620.

Richard Dorney (sometimes Darney) was reappointed at the Restoration and served until his death in 1681. The accounts mention Dorney occasionally, usually in connection with his livery payments (which were often in arrears) or his annual salary. Other notices include those on 15 March 1662 when he was paid £7 for a tenor violin, 30 August 1662 when he received 5s. daily for attending the King at Hampton Court, 13 August 1669 when he assigned £10 7s. 9d. to Sir William Boreman of Whitehall (probably a loan or payment of a debt), 19 April 1673 when he assigned over five years of his arrears in pay to Roger Sizer of St Martin-in-the-Fields (presumably in return for a loan), 4 July 1674 when he practiced under Monsieur Cambert at the theatre in Whitehall, and 15 February 1675 when he played in the court masque *Calisto*. His salary was £46 10s. 10d. yearly, though in the summer of 1662 it would seem he was getting only £20.

Though Charles II was slow in paying his employees, replacements moved with lightning speed into positions made vacant by death. It is likely, then, that Richard Dorney died shortly before 2 August 1681 when John Lenton was appointed to his place in the violins.

Dorsion, Mlle   [fl. 1792], dancer.

Fuchs's *Lexique* lists the dancer Mademoiselle Dorsion as appearing in the pantomime ballet *La Foire de Smirne* on 16 April 1792. She is not listed in *The London Stage*, but the ballet was performed at the Haymarket Theatre on 14 April and Mlle Dorsion may well have been one of the minor dancers.

D'Orta, Rachele, later Signora Giorgi   [fl. 1784–1785], singer.

Signora Rachele D'Orta's first appearance in England was on 6 January 1784 at the King's Theatre when she sang Dorina in *I rivali delusi*. She went on to sing Arminda in *La schiava* on 24 February, Giannina in *Le gelosie villane* on 15 April, and Livietta in *Li due gemelle* on 12 June. When she took her benefit on 10 June she advertised that tickets would be available from her at No 72, the west side of the Haymarket.

At a season salary of £500 she returned to the King's Theatre in 1784–85 to sing Clorinda in *Il curioso indiscreto*, a role in *Demetrio*, Cintia in *Il pittor parigino*, a vocal part in the ballet version of *Macbeth*, and roles in *La finta principessa* and *La buona figliuola*. On 25 January 1785 (but not regularly thereafter) she was billed as Signora Rachele D'Orta Giorgi. For her benefit with Tasca on 28 April 1785 she advertised that she was living at No 234, Piccadilly. From that address, probably during the 1784–85 season, she wrote a letter beseeching the aid of the Lord Chamberlain in a dispute over the salaries at the opera house, and she described herself as "first comic woman" at the King's Theatre.

The Signor Giorgi whose name Rachele D'Orta took is difficult to identify. He may have been Giorgi the dancer, whose first wife's name disappeared from the records after 1772, or he may have been Joseph Giorgi, a harpsichordist at the King's about 1785. A third possibility is James Georgi (or Giorgi), a musician who committed suicide in Ireland in April or May 1798 and whose widow, after receiving financial aid from the Irish Musical Fund, died in July or August 1800.

D'Orta, Rosina   [fl. 1784], singer.

Signora Rosina D'Orta sang Rosalba in *La schiava* on 24 February and Sandrina in *Le gelosie villane* on 15 April 1784 at the King's Theatre in the Haymarket.

Dortor. *See* DOCTOR.

Dosel, [William?]   [fl. 1788–1796], doorkeeper.

Mr Dosel was a doorkeeper at Covent Garden from 1788–89 to 1795–96 at 12*s.* weekly. Possibly he was the William Dosell who married Charlotte Thornton at St George, Hanover Square, on 10 August 1794.

Doser, Mr [*fl.* 1789], *house servant?*

A Mr Doser's benefit tickets were accepted at Covent Garden on 13 June 1789. He appears to have been one of the house servants and a different person from Mr Dosel the doorkeeper.

Dothwait, Mr [*fl.* 1794], *flutist.*

Doane's *Musical Directory* of 1794 listed Mr Dothwait of the New River Company Office, Islington, as a flutist who played in concerts presented by the Handelian Society.

Dotti, Anna [*fl.* 1724–1727], *singer.*

When Anna Dotti sang Irene in Handel's *Tamerlano* at the King's Theatre in the Haymarket on 31 October 1724, Lady Bristol wrote that "the woman is so great a joke that there was more laughing at her than at a farce, but her opinion of herself gets the better of that . . ." Nevertheless, Signora Dotti went on to sing Agamira in *Artaserse* on 1 December, Cornelia in *Giulio Cesare* on 2 January 1725, Eduige in *Rodelinda* on 13 February, and Mandane in *Dario* on 10 April. She returned in 1726 to sing Emilia in *Elisa* on 15 January and Cleone in *Alessandro* on 5 May. Her last season was in 1727 when she sang Amiceto in *Lucio Vero* on 7 January, Orindo in *Admeto* on 31 January, and Pilades in *Astianatte* on 6 May.

Doubourg. *See* DUBOURG.

Doughty, Jane. *See* WILKINSON, MRS TATE.

Douglas, Mr [*fl.* 1770], *actor.*

A Mr Douglas played Glumdalca in *Tom Thumb the Great* at the Haymarket Theatre on 19 December 1770.

Douglas, Mr [*fl.* 1776–1817], *house servant.*

Perhaps there were two or even three men named Douglas who worked at Drury Lane in the late eighteenth century, but the citations to a male Douglas in the bills and accounts from 1776 through 1817 will be treated here as referring to one person only. At a salary of 9*s.* weekly Douglas worked as a lobby keeper in 1776–77 and 1777–78. In June of 1787, 1797, and 1800 a Douglas was listed with many others whose benefit tickets were accepted at the theatre. In 1800 Douglas was cited in the accounts as one of the men's dressers at 9*s.* weekly, a post he still held at the same salary in 1816–17.

Douglas, Miss [*fl.* 1777], *actress.*

A Miss Douglas made her first, and apparently last, appearance on the London stage on 22 April 1777 when she played Peggy in *The Gentle Shepherd* at the Haymarket Theatre.

Douglas, Alexander [*fl.* 1672–1673], *actor?*

The Lord Chamberlain's accounts listed Alexander Douglas apparently as a new member of the King's Company on 2 March 1672 and *The London Stage* includes him in the company roster for 1672–73. Perhaps he was an actor, though no roles are known for him.

Douglas, William [*fl.* 1720–1745], *trumpeter.*

William Douglas, commonly called "the Black Prince," was given a benefit concert at Hickford's music room on 23 February 1720. Similar benefits were held for him on 15 March 1721, 16 February 1722, 6 March 1723, and 26 February 1724. None of the bills gave any indication of Douglas's participation in the concerts. On 28

August 1739 he was one of the original subscribers ("being musicians") to the Royal Society of Musicians. He shared a benefit with Valentine Snow on 20 February 1745 at the Haymarket Theatre, and the bill helpfully stated that several pieces on the trumpet would be played by Mr Snow and Mr Douglas. Tickets for the concert were made available at Douglas's lodgings in Little Castle Street, Oxford Market.

Douglass, Mrs David. *See* HALLAM, MRS LEWIS.

Doumorier. *See* DUMORIER.

Dove, Henry *(fl. 1674–1678?)*, *violinist.*

On 27 August 1674 Henry Dove was appointed a violinist in the King's Musick, replacing Philip Beckett; his wages were £46 12s. 8d. yearly. In January 1676 he was paid £12 for a new violin, but on the following 12 August he was replaced by Giles Stevens. Perhaps two entries in the parish registers of St Bride, Fleet Street, concern the musician: Henry and Thomasine Dove christened a daughter Elizabeth on 25 April 1675 and a son Henry on 11 April 1678.

Dove, Michael *d. 1747, actor, dancer.*
Michael Dove's first theatrical notice came on 11 February 1729 when he played the Duke in *Venice Preserv'd* and shared a benefit with two others at the Haymarket Theatre. He remained at the Haymarket through July, playing the Third Countryman in *The Humours of Harlequin* on 25 February, Colonel Countermine in *Hurlothrumbo* on 29 March, Bluet in *The Smugglers* on 7 May, the Miller's Man in *The Humours of Harlequin* on 26 May, and Gage in *The Beggar's Wedding* on 29 May. On 26 June he shared a second benefit, this time with only one colleague.

In August 1729 Dove acted Aegon in *Damon and Phillida* at Drury Lane, after which he joined Reynolds's troupe at Bartholomew and Southwark fairs to play in *The Beggar's Wedding* and act Shallow in *Southwark Fair.*

His 1729–30 season was similar. In the winter at the Haymarket Theatre he played Shameless in *Love and Revenge*, Diego in *Fatal Love*, Sukey in *The Beggar's Opera*, Dr Fillgrave in *Tom Thumb*, and Lomporhomock in *Hurlothrumbo*, and in the summer he appeared at Tottenham Court and Bartholomew and Southwark fairs. His 1730–31 season at the Haymarket saw him as Sullen and Gibbet in *The Stratagem*, Pedro in *The Spanish Fryar*, the Miller in *The Cobler of Preston*, and in other roles, and he returned to Tottenham Court in August 1731 to play the Laughing Brother in *Damon and Phillida*. He repeated the pattern again in 1731–32, though he seems to have been inactive in the first half of the season. At the Haymarket he played Shift in *The Cheats of Scapin*, both Bullock and the Chaplain in *The Recruiting Officer*, Dominic in *The Spanish Fryar*, and Mopsus in *Damon and Phillida*, and in August 1732 he went again to Tottenham Court to play Gregory in *The Mock Doctor* and Bumkin in *The Metamorphosis of Harlequin.*

From January through May 1733 – if not for the whole 1732–33 season – Dove worked at Goodman's Fields with Giffard's troupe. His first role there was the Landlord in *The Tavern Bilkers* on 13 January, after which he played Harry in *The Beggar's Opera*, the Corporal in *The Mad Captain*, and Forrest in *Richard III*. On 16 May he shared a benefit with three others. Mrs Dove joined him at Goodman's Fields for the 1733–34 season, and the pair remained with Giffard's company through 1736–37, the last season being at Lincoln's Inn Fields. Dove played several of his old roles plus a Waterman, Priest of Hymen, and a Guinea Dropper in *Britannia*, Mortar in *The Chymical Counterfeits* and in *Jupiter and Io*, Kate in *The Funeral*, Sly in *Love's Last*

Shift, Poundage in *The Provok'd Husband*, Errand in *The Constant Couple*, Bernardo in *Hamlet*, Curtis in *Sauny the Scot*, Alphonso in *The Spanish Fryar*, Pantaloon in *Harlequin Shipwrecked*, Decoy in *The Miser*, Blunder in *The Honest Yorkshireman*, Jacques in *Love Makes a Man*, Bardolph in *1 Henry IV*, and other minor roles, almost all comic or involving dance. During these years he also appeared at the Haymarket Theatre in the summer of 1735 as the lead in *The Mock Doctor*, Dreary in *The Beggar's Opera*, Fairbank in *The Twin Rivals*, Hounslow in *The Stratagem*, and Antonio in *Love Makes a Man*.

After Giffard's venture collapsed in the spring of 1737 the Doves were without a theatrical home, and Michael acted here, there, and everywhere. In August and September of 1738 he appeared at Tottenham Court, Southwark Fair, and (on 22 August) at Covent Garden. His 1738–39 season was spent at Covent Garden, followed by an appearance at Bartholomew Fair. He apparently did not act in London in 1739–40, but he was at the fair again in August 1740. At Goodman's Fields in 1740–41 he was mentioned for one role, and he returned again to Bartholomew Fair in the summer of 1742. In 1742–43 he played a full season at Lincoln's Inn Fields, acted at and shared the operation of a Bartholomew Fair booth in August, and danced regularly at the New Wells, Clerkenwell. He appeared in one role at Drury Lane in the early part of the 1743–44 season but was otherwise inactive in London.

During these peripatetic years Dove acted such new parts as Clodpole in *The Amorous Widow*, Bardolph in *The Merry Wives of Windsor*, Bumpkin in both *The Funeral* and *Harlequin Turned Philosopher*, Bullcalf in *The Rambling Lovers*, John Trott in *Harlequin Student*, the Bookseller in *The Committee*, Seringe in *The Relapse*, Tyrell in *Richard III*, Moody in *The Provok'd Husband*, and Trapland in *Love for Love*. He played Tim Guzzle in *The Glorious*

Queen of Hungary and Clodpole in *Harlequin Dissected* at his booth with Turbutt in 1743. He received benefits off and on, and his bill for 22 April 1741 noted that he (and presumably his wife) were living at The Sun in Hooper's Square.

In 1744–45 he settled down at Goodman's Fields for the rest of his career. He revived a number of his earlier parts at first and played infrequently, but as his career neared its end he acted Sycorax in *The Tempest*, Tradelove in *A Bold Stroke for a Wife*, Jobson in *The Devil to Pay*, the First Murderer in *Macbeth*, the Second Gravedigger in *Hamlet*, Decius in *Cato*, Antonio in *The Tempest*, Stratocles in *Tamerlane*, a Carrier in *1 Henry IV*, Elliot in *Venice Preserv'd*, the Duke in *Othello*, and Ernesto in *The Orphan*. Virtually all of these parts he played in 1746–47, and it would appear that Dove's life in the theatre had taken a new turn; gone were his roles in pantomimes and farces, though for his benefit with his wife on 9 April 1747 he chose two old favorites of his, Jobson in *The Devil to Pay* and Vandunck in *The Royal Merchant*. But just as his career seemed to be accelerating again, his life ended. He died sometime before 16 November 1747, on which date Covent Garden gave a special benefit to his widow.

Dove, Mrs Michael, Elizabeth [*fl.* 1731–1747], *actress, dancer.*

The 1731 edition of *The Tragedy of Tragedies* named Elizabeth Dove, wife of the actor Michael, in the role of Glumdalca; the work was performed at the Haymarket Theatre on 24 March of that year. A year later Mrs Dove returned to the Haymarket to play La Robauld in *The Wanton Justice* on 17 March 1732, after which she again dropped from sight until 1733–34. She joined her husband as a member of Henry Giffard's company at the Goodman's Fields Theatre, her first part there being Molly in *The Beggar's Opera* on 17 October 1733. The bills for the season also show her dancing in a *Rural Dance* and a *Milk Pail Song and Dance* and playing an Attendant in *Britannia* and Ricorta in *Don Quixote*. She remained at Goodman's Fields through 1735–36, adding such credits as a Haymaker in *The Necromancer*, the Maid in *The Chymical Counterfeits*, the Queen of Spades in *A Dance of Court Cards* in *The Emperor of the Moon*, and Colombine in *Harlequin Shipwrecked*.

The Doves moved with Giffard to Lincoln's Inn Fields in 1736–37 where Mrs Dove was the Maid in *The Worm Doctor* and Jenny Diver in *The Beggar's Pantomime*, but her activity for the several seasons which followed was restricted to the fairs. In August and September 1738 she played Lady Graygoose (Colombine) in a piece variously titled *The Mad Lovers* and *The Man's Bewitch'd* at Tottenham Court and at Bartholomew and Southwark fairs. She returned to Bartholomew Fair on 23 August 1739 to play Colombine in *Harlequin Turned Philosopher* and on 23 August 1740 to take the same role in *The Rambling Lovers*. On 14 September 1741 she played Colombine in *Harlequin the Man in the Moon* at Southwark Fair, and on 25 August 1742 she acted the same character in *The Miser Bit* and danced, with Phillips, *La Mason* and *Les Sabotiers* at Bartholomew Fair. The latter entertainments were repeated at Southwark Fair on 8 September. On the following 27 September at the same fair she was Colombine in *Harlequin Reveller* and again danced with Phillips. Her husband joined with Turbutt to operate a Bartholomew Fair booth on 23 August 1743 and the days following, and Mrs Dove's Colombine was seen in *Harlequin Dissected*.

In 1744–45 she and Dove were back at Goodman's Fields, but except for her appearance as Colombine in *The Amorous Sportsman* she was not noticed in the bills until her benefit with Dove on 11 March 1745. In 1745–46, however, she performed regularly at Goodman's Fields and, for a

change, did not appear as Colombine in anything. She was Myrtillo in *The Provok'd Husband*, Betty in *The Twin Rivals* and in *The Old Bachelor*, Lady Welldon in *Oroonoko*, Advocate in *The Fair Quaker of Deal*, Mrs Chat in *The Committee*, probably Rose in *The Recruiting Officer*, and Amphytrite in *The Tempest*. The following season she added the Nurse in *Love for Love*, Miss Jenny in *The Provok'd Husband*, Dolly in *The Stage Coach*, Betty in *The School Boy*, Mrs Slammekin in *The Beggar's Opera*, Lettice in *The Devil to Pay*, and Aranthe in *King Lear*. After those two busy seasons, she left the stage. Her husband died in 1747, and Mrs Dove was given a benefit at Covent Garden on 16 November of that year.

Dovey, Mr ₍fl. 1724–1727₎, *house servant.*

The Lincoln's Inn Fields Theatre accounts include several items relating to Mr Dovey, who appears to have been a house servant in charge of the supernumeraries and of wardrobe supplies. The earliest mention of him was on 23 September 1724 when he was paid £1 11s. 4d. for the supernumeraries, and the last was on 25 May 1727 when he was cited on the theatre's free list.

Dowdell, Mr ₍fl. c. 1710₎, *bass player.*

The Coke papers at Harvard include a document dating from about 1710 which names a Mr Dowdell, a double-bass player, as a member of the band which played at a concert at the Duchess of Shrewsbury's mansion in Kensington. The musicians involved were all, apparently, members of the band at the Queen's Theatre in the Haymarket.

Dowden. *See* **DOWTON.**

Dowding, Mr ₍fl. 1784₎, *singer.*

A countertenor, Mr Dowding sang in the Handel Memorial Concerts at Westminster

Abbey and the Pantheon on 26, 27, and 29 May and 3 and 5 June 1784.

Dowler, Mrs ₁*fl. 1794–1795*₁, *dresser.*
During the 1794–95 season at Covent Garden Mrs Dowler worked as a dresser for 12*s.* 6*d.* weekly.

Down, Mr ₁*fl. 1731*₁, *house servant?*
On 14 May 1731 Mr Down shared a benefit at Goodman's Fields Theatre with Beeson; probably both were house servants.

Downes, Mr ₁*fl. 1729*₁, *actor.*
A Mr Downes, possibly a descendant of the Restoration prompter, acted a few roles in the spring and summer of 1729. At the Haymarket Theatre he played Temo in *Hurlothrumbo* on 22 April, the Prince of Tanais in *Tamerlane* for his shared benefit with Hulett on 2 May, and Alspike in *The Smugglers* on 7 May. At the Hall-Oates Bartholomew Fair booth on 26 August he acted the Boatswain in *Maudlin.*

Downes, John ₁*fl. 1661–1719*₁, *prompter, actor.*
John Downes was the prompter for the Duke's, United, and Betterton companies from 1661 to 1706. At the end of his career he set down, as best he could, a history of the Restoration theatre which he called *Roscius Anglicanus* (1708). He stated in the Preface that he, "Being long Conversant with the Plays and Actors of the Original Company, under the Patent of Sir William Davenant, at his Theatre in Lincoln's-Inn-Fields, Open'd there 1662 [*recte* 1661]. And as Book keeper and Prompter, continu'd so, till October 1706. He Writing out all the Parts in each Play; and Attending every Morning the Actors Rehearsals, and their Performances in Afternoons . . ."
At the beginning of his career he had tried acting, with unhappy results: "I must not forget my self, being Listed for an Actor. . . . The very first Day of opening the House there, with the Siege of Rhodes [on

28 June 1661], being to act Haly; (The King, Duke of York, and all the Nobility in the House, and the first time the King was in a Publick Theatre). The sight of that August presence, spoil'd me for an Actor too." Because his task at the theatre was behind the scenes, little was ever said about Downes, but the Lord Chamberlain's accounts occasionally mentioned him: on 3 April 1665 James Gowslaw sued Downes, perhaps for a debt; Rich Skayfe also sued him, on 26 June 1667; and on 15 October

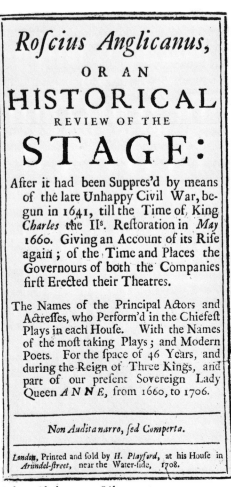

Title page of JOHN DOWNES's *Roscius Anglicanus* (1708)

1689 a hearing was called on a complaint of the actor Joe Haines against Mountfort and other United Company members, including the "Bookkeeper"—presumably Downes, though perhaps the reference was to an office worker. Despite his initial failure as an actor, Downes may have appeared on stage again in later years. Two plays staged in the spring of 1698 at Lincoln's Inn Fields under Betterton's management have prologues in which the "prompter" appears—though whether or not Downes played himself is not known.

Downes retired in October 1706 but lost none of his interest in the theatre. He may have been the father of a young musician about whom the opera manager Owen Swiney wrote the Lord Chamberlain on 27 January 1707. Swiney explained that he had not hired young Downes at the Queen's Theatre in the Haymarket (where Downes the prompter had finished his career) because the lad was utterly unqualified. Swiney said he was prepared to give young Downes's father whatever pension the Lord Chamberlain thought fit.

Purportedly, John Downes wrote to Sir Richard Steele on 1 July 1710 the following letter, but the style is so unlike the Downes of *Roscius Anglicanus* that very likely Steele wrote it himself:

Honoured Sir,—Finding by divers of your late papers that you are a friend to the profession of which I was many years an unworthy member, I the rather make bold to crave your advice touching a proposal that has been lately made me of coming again into business and the sub-administration of stage affairs. I have from my youth been bred up behind the curtain, and been a prompter from the time of the Restoration. I have seen many changes, as well of scenes as of actors, and have known men within my remembrance arrive to the highest dignities of the theatre, who made their entrance in the quality of mutes, joint-stools, flower-pots, and tapestry hangings. It cannot be unknown to the nobility and gentry that a gentleman [Christopher Rich, undoubtedly] of the Inns of Court, and a deep intriguer, had some time since worked himself into the sole management and direction of the theatre. Nor is it less notorious that his restless ambition and subtle machinations did manifestly tend to the extirpation of the good old British actors, and the introduction of foreign pretenders—such as harlequins, French Dancers, and Roman singers—which, though they impoverished the proprietors and imposed on the audience, were for some time tolerated, by reason of his dexterous insinuations, which prevailed upon a few deluded women, especially the vizard masks, to believe that the stage was in danger. But his schemes were soon exposed, and the great ones that supported him withdrawing their favour, he made his exit, and remained for a season in obscurity. During this retreat the Machiavelian was not idle, but secretly fomented divisions and wrought over to his side some of the inferior actors, reserving a trap-door to himself, to which only he had a key. This entrance secured, this cunning person, to complete his company, bethought himself of calling in the most eminent strollers from all parts of the kingdom. I have seen them all ranged together behind the scenes; but they are many of them persons that never trod the stage before, and so very awkward and ungainly, that it is impossible to believe the audience will bear them. He was looking over his catalogue of plays, and indeed picked up a good tolerable set of grave faces for counsellors to appear in the famous scene of "Venice Preserved," when the danger is over; but they being but mere outsides, and the actors having a great mind to play "The Tempest," there is not a man of them, when he is to perform anything above dumb show, is capable of acting with a good grace so much as the part of Trinculo. However, the master persists in his design, and is fitting up the old "Storm;" but I am afraid he will not be able to procure able sailors or experienced officers for love or money. Besides all this when he comes to cast the parts, there is so great a confusion amongst them for want of proper actors, that for my part I am wholly discouraged. The play with which they design to open is "The Duke and no Duke," and they are so put to it that the master himself is to play the Conjuror, and they have no one for the General but honest George Powel.

Now, sir, they being so much at a loss for the *dramatis personae*, viz. the persons to enact, and the whole frame of the house being designed to be altered, I desire your opinion whether you think it advisable for me to undertake to prompt them? For though I can clash swords when they represent a battle, and have yet lungs enough left to huzza their victories, I question, if I should prompt them right, whether they would act accordingly.

I am, your Honour's most humble Servant,
JOHN DOWNES

There is no evidence to show that Downes ever returned to theatre work.

The Postman Robbed of his Mail (1719) referred to Downes as one still alive, but by then he must have been a very old man. He left behind his invaluable *Roscius Anglicanus*, a work sometimes inaccurate and frustratingly incomplete, yet one of the small handful of primary sources to which we can turn for information about the Restoration theatre.

Downing, George *d. 1780, actor, playwright.*

According to his own testimony in an autobiographical sketch published with *The Temple of Taste* in 1763, George Downing's father was a tradesman with an independent fortune. George married in secret at the age of 19 the daughter of Captain Edward Randolph, a merchant, and the parents on both sides "discarded" the newlyweds. By 1761 Downing and his wife had a family of three children, one boy and two girls.

Downing's theatrical career started in 1758 at Norwich, and he wrote the prologue spoken at the opening of the new theatre there in 1759. He joined Herbert's provincial strollers, probably in 1760, but after a quarrel with Herbert in September

1761, Downing left the company at Spalding and headed for London, his first visit there in 12 years. He said he frequented the theatres, hoping for a job, but all he could find was a position with Warner at his booth in Islington at Borough Fair. Warner hired him for a guinea a day on the recommendation of George Stevens, whom Downing had earlier befriended. The actor's first and only known London role was a King in Stevens's *St George for England*.

Through another friend Downing was recommended to, and read for, George (and probably David) Garrick, and he was assured a place in the company the following season. John Rich of Covent Garden sought him out, said Downing, and hired him for the planned production of *The Coronation* in November 1761. Rich died on 26 November, and the new manager, John Beard, replaced Downing before George had a chance to appear in public at Covent Garden. (*The Coronation* opened on 13 November, before Rich died; Downing was not in the cast. George may have exaggerated his story about Rich's promise of a part.)

Downing acted at Norwich again from 1764 to 1766, but by then he was enfeebled by age and his "person and declining powr's" made him suited only for such roles as Adam in *As You Like It*, Sciolto in *The Orphan*, and Sealand in *The Conscious Lovers*, according to a contemporary report. He acted at Worcester and York, but, said the *Thespian Dictionary* (1805), he tired of the stage, became a schoolmaster in Birmingham, and died there late in 1780.

George Downing wrote a number of plays: *The Tricks of Harlequin* (1739), *The Temple of Taste* (1763), *Newmarket* (1763, according to the *Thespian Dictionary*, but published in 1774 according to most sources; it was played at Drury Lane in 1772), *The Parthian Exile* (1774), and *The Volunteers* (1780, performed that year at Covent Garden).

Mrs George Downing did not act in London, though she performed with her husband at Spalding in 1761 and Worcester in 1772. A Miss Downing, probably their daughter, acted at Norwich from 1765 to 1767 but never appeared in London.

Downman, Mr ₁*fl. 1788₁, *scene painter.*

A newspaper clipping dated 14 April 1788, preserved at the Richmond Library, advertises portraits of noble persons "as they were drawn by Mr Downman for the Scenery at Richmond House Theatre."

Dowse, Mr *d. 1783, singer.*

The newspapers reported about January 1783 that Mr Dowse, formerly a singer at Vauxhall Gardens and Sadler's Wells, had been found dead on a dunghill near an inn in Holborn. Possibly related was Elizabeth Dowse, daughter of a Thomas Dowse, who was buried at St Paul, Covent Garden, on 26 July 1783.

Dowsing, John ₁*fl. 1678₁, *singer.*

John Dowsing was sworn a Gentleman of the Chapel Royal on 4 December 1678, but there is no further record of his participation in that group.

Dowson, Mr ₁*fl. 1777₁, *actor.*

A Mr Dowson had principal but unnamed roles in *The Coquette* and *The True-Born Irishman* on 9 October 1777 at the Haymarket Theatre.

Dowson, Ann ₁*fl. c. 1765–1779₁, *singer.*

Miss Ann Dowson sang at Finch's Grotto Gardens about 1765, and she was there again in the summer of 1771, when she was in *The Gamester* and sang such entr'acte tunes as "Soldier Tir'd." She shared a benefit with the composer Smith on 30 August 1771. Miss Dowson sang at Sadler's Wells from 1772 to 1775 and was

there again on 5 April 1779, the last notice of her in the bills.

Dowson, John ₁*fl. 1680₁, *dancing master.*

John Dowson, dancing master of the King's Company, was discharged on 10 December 1680.

Dowton, William *1764–1851, actor, manager.*

William Dowton was born in Exeter on 25 April 1764, the son of an innkeeper and grocer. He was given a liberal education, and he was apprenticed to an architect in 1780. William engaged in amateur theatricals in Exeter, became stage-struck, and in 1781 left his master to join some strolling actors at Ashburton, Devonshire. His first appearance as a professional was as Carlos in *The Revenge*, which the troupe performed in a barn. Dowton then acted with Hughes at Weymouth and next returned to Exeter and played Macbeth and Romeo. He may have acted briefly at Bath. In September 1791, he joined Sarah Baker's company in Kent. He married Mrs Baker's daughter Sarah (1768–1817) in 1793 or 1794. Dowton played at Rochester and Canterbury from 1792 to 1796, mostly in comic roles.

His first appearance in London was as Sheva in *The Jew* at Drury Lane on 10 October 1796, billed as from the theatre at Tunbridge Wells, where he had played the role. On 22 October *How Do You Do?* observed that the part actually required little more of a player than "a plain, clear, and unaffected delivery, with a tolerable imitation of the *Jewish* pronunciation of the English tongue." The critic found Dowton effective in his delivery and accent, and in some scenes "he also evinced a degree of sensibility and feeling, the judicious management of which shot like the electric shock into the bosoms of the audience, and drew forth such loud plaudits as could not but be highly gratifying to him." The

Monthly Mirror was cooler in its response and preferred the Sheva of the younger Bannister or of Elliston. Gilliland in 1806 recalled Dowton's London debut as a triumph: "we never recollect a first appearance greeted with greater approbation . . . In pourtraying the Israelite he never betrayed the imitator, but evinced the real passions of the man . . ." It was, Gilliland thought, "an unique piece of playing."

After his initial role at Drury Lane, Dowton earned his £4 or £5 weekly salary in 1796–97 playing Scrub in *The Stratagem* on 27 October 1796, the First Gravedigger in *Hamlet* on 21 November, Sir Francis Wronghead in *The Provok'd Husband* on 22 November, Michael Goto in *The Shipwreck* on 10 December, Cacafogo in *Rule a Wife and Have a Wife* on 1 Feb-

WILLIAM DOWTON, as Colonel Oldboy engraving by Thomson, after De Wilde

ruary 1797, Commodore Broadside in *Cape St Vincent* on 9 March, Sir Solomon Cynic in *The Will* on 24 April, Sir John Manfred in *The Last of the Family* on 8 May, Sir Fretful Plagiary in *The Critic* on 12 May, Feste in *Twelfth Night* on 17 May, Hugo in *The Haunted Tower* on 22 May, a role in *The Hovel* on 23 May, Polonius in *Hamlet* on 25 May, Fitzherbert in *The Haunted Tower* on 6 June, and Antonio in *Love Makes a Man* on 12 June.

John Williams commented on Dowton's first London season in *A Pin Basket to the Children of Thespis* (1797):

> His Grave-digger *proves him adroit at low wit,*
> And his Scrub *shews his faculties pliant and fit*
>
> . . . .
>
> *Though he's been overpuff'd, overstrain'd, and run hard,*
> *He's a natural claimant on Laughter's reward*
>
> . . . .
>
> *It is urg'd he's too dry and too costive—Admitted;*
> *Yet this failing shall make him in future more fitted;*
> *To underdo aught in an early attempt,*
> *Speaks a modest advance which suspends my contempt.*

After his successful London season, Dowton spent the summer of 1797 performing at Margate, Richmond, Tunbridge Wells, and, apparently, Canterbury.

He was running hard indeed the following fall. He played Frank Oakland in *A Cure for the Heart-Ache* at Tunbridge Wells on 2 October 1797 and was on the boards at Drury Lane the next night to act Sterling in *The Clandestine Marriage*. During 1797–98 he appeared in some of his old roles and a great many new ones: Walter in *The Children in the Wood*, Whittle in *The Irish Widow*, Farmer Cole in *Cheap Living*, a Witch in *Macbeth*, Barnardine in *Measure for Measure*, a Carrier in *1 Henry IV*, Hassan in *The Castle*

Spectre, Ibrahim in *Blue-Beard*, Malvolio in *Twelfth Night* ("Mr Dowton may be considered as chaste a painter of the love-sick steward as ever trod the Stage," wrote Gilliland), Governor Tempest in *The Wheel of Fortune*, Appesley in *She's Eloped!*, Verges in *Much Ado About Nothing*, Shin in *The Ugly Cub*, Lingo in *A Nosegay of Weeds*, and Jobson in *The Devil to Pay*. His salary for this considerable expenditure of energy was only £5 weekly, and at his benefit on 6 June 1798 he had to share the £204 1s. 9d. profits with two others. He was living at the time at No 5, Strand Lane, Surrey Street, the Strand.

The 1798–99 season saw him in such new roles as Sir Anthony Absolute in *The Rivals*, Clod in *The Young Quaker* (in which part Gilliland found him superior to the late John Edwin), Peachum in *The Beggar's Opera*, Moody in *The Country Girl*, Latitat in *The Twins*, Orozembo in *Pizarro*, and Sir Tunbelly Clumsey in *A Trip to Scarborough*. During the season he went over to the Haymarket Theatre to play Lovel in *High Life Below Stairs* (on 17 December 1798) for Lacy's benefit. Dowton's 1799–1800 season brought him out as Jerome in *De Montfort*, Old Mirabel in *The Inconstant*, Hardcastle in *She Stoops to Conquer*, and some of his earlier characters.

At the beginning of the 1800–1801 season Dowton was criticized in two roles. In the Enthoven Collection is a clipping concerning his Polonius on 16 September 1800: he acted the part "in a stile that would have suited Foresight, or any silly old man on the stage." Polonius, the anonymous critic thought, should be "foolish, pretending, ceremonious, but not vulgar, coarse, and farcical." And on 20 September when Dowton acted the Baron in *The Haunted Tower* for the first time, a critic said "his conception of the part was good, but he was more than once at a loss for his *speech*!" Other new parts Dowton tried

Harvard Theatre Collection

WILLIAM DOWTON, as Falstaff
engraving by Dean, after Wageman

that season were Tobias in *The Stranger*, Sir Sampson in *Love for Love*, Sir David Dunder in *Ways and Means*, and Adam Winterton in *The Iron Chest*.

Dowton may have been absent from Drury Lane in 1801–2, but he acted with the company from 1802–3 through 1819–20, making a number of appearances elsewhere and expanding his interests as a provincial manager. One of his excursions away from Drury Lane was in the summer of 1805. On 15 August he revived Foote's *The Tailors* at the Haymarket Theatre. The tailors of London rose up in anger and 700 of the guild descended on Dowton's house at No 7, Charing Cross and rioted, notwithstanding an offer from the management to withdraw the play and Dowton as well. A detachment of Horse Guards helped magistrates and constables restore order.

Among his other activities away from Drury Lane were: a brief acting visit to Manchester in 1806, a plan with other players in 1810 to set up a third patent company in London, an engagement at the New Theatre, Worthing in September 1812, a visit to Canterbury in January 1814 (he became snowbound), managerial duties at the Haymarket in 1815 and 1816, and his involvement in the management of the theatres at Maidstone and Canterbury until 1815. His provincial interests did not prosper. The obituary cited above makes it plain that "his want of success in the provinces became at length proverbial among managers." At Faversham, for example, he once acted to an audience of one in the pit, and at Rochester on one occasion he played to a seven-shilling house.

Dowton continued to act at Drury Lane until 1820. His salary increased over the years from £7 in 1800 to £20 in 1814, but there it remained. He continued playing a variety of roles. In addition to those already mentioned, he acted Obadiah Prim in *A Bold Stroke for a Wife*, Foresight in *Love for Love*, Dogberry in *Much Ado About Nothing*, Sir Hugh Evans in *The Merry Wives of Windsor*, Sir Oliver in *The School for Scandal*, and, at the request of Lord Byron, an unsuccessful Shylock in *The Merchant of Venice*. The list could go on. Because Dowton's provincial acting is not fully documented, it is impossible to say how many roles he attempted during his career.

In 1836 Dowton went to America, but he was not very successful. His debut there was on 21 June at the Park Theatre in New York as Falstaff in *Henry IV*. He appeared the following September in Philadelphia and took a farewell benefit on 23 November before returning to England. On 8 June 1840 he was given a farewell charity benefit at the opera house in London.

In private life Dowton is said to have been cheerful, gentlemanly, and unobtrusive, but he could fly into a passion at a

Harvard Theatre Collection

WILLIAM DOWTON, as Dr Cantwell engraving by Cooper, after De Wilde

trifle and as quickly fly out of it. Much of that mercurial quality he brought to the characters he played. Leigh Hunt in his *Critical Essays* asked,

Who is so impressive, so striking, so thrilling as this actor in scenes of angry perturbation or of anger subdued by the patience or pleasantry of its object? . . . Dowton preserves the great features of rage, impatience, he twists about his fingers, changes his attitude and his gesture, mutters hastily with his lips, turns away at intervals from the speaker with a mouth of contempt, or seems unable to wait for his conclusion. . . . But

Courtesy of the Garrick Club

S. T. RUSSELL as Jerry Sneak, MRS HARLOWE as Mrs Sneak, and WILLIAM DOWTON as Major Sturgeon

by De Wilde

then, who at the same time can drop with such a fall of nature from the height of passion to the most soft emotions and the most social pleasantry? His expression of satisfaction with another, his grateful shake of the hands, and his hurried thanks breaking through the intervals of overpowering joy, exhibit the perfection of social enjoyment.

William Dowton wrote his will on 10 October 1849 at his house, No 27, Brighton Terrace, Brixton, Surrey. To his (apparently) only surviving son, William Patten Dowton, he left his entire estate. One of his witnesses was George William Dowton, presumably a relative. William Dowton died on 19 April 1851, and his son proved his will on the following 2 July.

On 16 October 1817 Dowton's wife had died at Rochester. She had acted in Tunbridge Wells, Maidstone, Canterbury, and elsewhere in the provinces but had not appeared in London. Dowton's son Henry died on 9 June 1818 after a brief acting career. Dowton's son William took over his father's interest in the Kent circuit in 1815 and appeared at Drury Lane in 1832; he died in 1883 at close to 90 years of age.

Portraits of William Dowton include:

1. A watercolor portrait by Samuel De Wilde in the Harvard Theatre Collection.

2. As Falstaff. Oil by R. W. Buss. Now in the Garrick Club.

3. As Falstaff in *1 Henry IV*, with George Smith as Bardolph. Oil by George Clint. In the Raymond Mander and Joe Mitchenson Theatre Collection.

4. As Governor Heartall in *The Soldier's Daughter*, with Thomas Collins as Timothy Quaint. Oil by Samuel De Wilde. In the Garrick Club.

5. As Colonel Oldboy in *Lionel and Clarissa*. Oil by De Wilde. Engraved by Thomson as a plate to Oxberry's *New English Drama.*

6. As Peachum in *The Beggar's Opera*, with Munden as Lockit. Oil by Smirke, 1815. In 1960 in the possession of J. O. Flatter.

7. As Major Sturgeon in *The Mayor of Garratt*, with S. T. Russell as Jerry Sneak, and Mrs Harlowe as Mrs Sneak. Oil by Samuel De Wilde. In the Garrick Club.

8. As Dr Cantwell in *The Hypocrite*. Watercolor by Samuel De Wilde, 1812. Now in the British Museum.

9. As Cantwell. Watercolor by Samuel De Wilde. Now in the Harvard Theatre Collection. Engraved by Cooper.

10. As Sir Oliver Cypress in *Grieving's a Folly*. Watercolor by De Wilde.

11. As Drugget in *Three Weeks after Marriage*. Watercolor by De Wilde. At Harvard.

12. As Falstaff. Watercolor by Thomas Charles Wageman; engraved by Dean. In the Folger Library.

13. As Justice Woodcock in *Love in a Village*. Watercolor by De Wilde. At Harvard.

14. As Restive in *Time Out*. Watercolor by De Wilde. At Harvard.

15. In Elizabethan costume. Watercolor by De Wilde. Dated 2 December 1819. At Harvard.

16. Portrait engraving. Anonymous. Full face. In Harvard Theatre Collection.

17. Bust. Engraved by T. Cheesman after S. De Wilde, 1807.

18. Bust. T. Blood after S. Drummond. Plate to *European Magazine*, 1813.

19. Bust. Engraved by W. Ridley. Plate to *Monthly Mirror*, 1804.

20. As Sir Anthony Absolute. By S. Scriven after S. De Wilde, 1808.

21. As Sir Anthony Absolute. Drawn and engraved by R. Page, 1824.

22. As Sir Anthony Absolute. By J. Rogers after R. Page. Plate to Oxberry's *Dramatic Biography*, 1826.

23. As Balthazar in *The Fisherman's Hut*. By I. R. Cruikshank. Colored plate to *British Stage*.

24. As Sir Robert Bramble in *The Poor Gentleman* "On his Farewell Benefit at Her Majesty's Theatre, June 8th, 1840." Engraved by W. Clerk. A copy of No 25, below.

25. As Sir Robert Bramble. Drawn and engraved by F. E. George, 1840.

26. As Drugget in *Three Weeks after Marriage*. By R. Cooper after De Wilde.

27. As Sir Francis in *The Provok'd Husband*. Anonymous.

28. As "Francisco." Engraved by Alais.

29. As Sir Oliver Surface in *The School for Scandal*. By J. Rogers after J. W. Gear. Plate to *Dramatic Magazine*.

Doyle. *See also* **DOILE.**

Doyle, Mr [*fl.* 1800–1809], *house servant?*

On 13 June 1800 at Drury Lane a Mr Doyle's benefit tickets were accepted. The account books show a Mr Doyle as recipient of 11s. in 1803–4 and £5 19s. 3d. in 1804–5. Doyle was a member of the Drury Lane company working at the Lyceum Theatre in the summer of 1809. Perhaps he was one of the house servants.

Doyle, Mrs [*fl.* 1789–1801], *house servant?*

On 6 June 1789 at Covent Garden Mrs Doyle's benefit tickets were accepted. She was cited in the Drury Lane account books on 21 October 1797 for a payment of 13s. 4d.—perhaps her daily salary. Mrs Doyle was mentioned in the accounts in 1799, 1800, and 1801, her weekly salary (apparently) being £1. Perhaps Mrs Doyle was one of the house servants.

Doyle, James *[fl. 1794], singer?*

Doane's *Musical Directory* of 1794 listed a James Doyle of Saffron Hill, Hatton Garden, as a bass (singer, presumably) who performed for the Handelian Society and in the oratorios at Covent Garden and Westminster Abbey. The well-known singer and actor John Doyle was listed by Doane as living at the same address, but their relationship is not understood. Probably they were brothers. John was the brother of Margaret Doyle the singer, who became Mrs Kennedy.

Doyle, John *d. 1794, singer, actor.*

John Doyle's first known role was Clodden in *The Lady of the Manor* on 23 November 1778 at Covent Garden. The following 8 February 1779 he replaced Wilson as Keel in *The Touchstone*, and on 13 February he played Hodge in *Love in a Village*. He continued at Covent Garden through 1785–86, was gone in 1786–87, returned in 1787–88, and apparently left after the 1788–89 season. He was paid £1 10s. weekly throughout his Covent Garden career.

While at Covent Garden he sang regularly in performances of *Macbeth, A Fête* (in which he offered a hunting song), *Romeo and Juliet, Alexander the Great, The Magic Picture, Robin Hood,* and *The Roman Father.* He was also assigned such parts as Astorath in *The Mirror,* Filch and Crookfingered Jack in *The Beggar's Opera,* Damaetas and Pan in *Midas,* Hatter in *Lord Mayor's Day,* Tanner in *The Magic Cavern,* Drill in *The Campaign,* and Mercury in *Poor Vulcan!*

Occasionally Doyle sang elsewhere: in the summer of 1779 he was at Birmingham; in May 1783 he was at Sadler's Wells; he played Harry in *Who's Who* at the Royal Circus in the spring of 1786; and he appeared at the Circus again in October 1786 and in 1787. Doane's *Musical Directory* of 1794 listed John and James Doyle as living in Saffron Hill, Hatton Garden;

John, according to Doane, sang tenor in the oratorios at Covent Garden and Westminster Abbey.

A note in the O. Smith collection at the British Museum tells us that John Doyle "Died at his House Little Queen Street, Lincoln's Inn Fields," in 1794. He was "well known as a vocalist. The immediate cause of his death was the rupture of a blood vessel, occasioned by too great an exertion in singing." John was the brother of the singer Margaret Doyle who, as Mrs Kennedy, sang at Covent Garden during the years John appeared there.

Doyle, Margaret *d. 1793.* See KENNEDY, MRS MORGAN HUGH.

Doyle, Mrs Michael. *See* GLANVILLE, MISS.

Draghi, Giovanni Battista *b. c. 1640, organist, harpsichordist, composer, librettist.*

It is possible that Giovanni Battista Draghi was the brother of the composer Antonio Draghi and that he was born in Rimini. His birth is said by Grove to have been about 1640. Draghi came to England at or immediately after the Restoration and soon established himself as a musician of distinction. On 12 February 1667 Pepys reported enthusiastically on hearing him at Lord Brouncker's house:

[T]he Italian Signor Baptista . . . hath composed a play in Italian for the Opera, which T. Killigrew do intend to have up; and here he did sing one of the acts. He himself is the poet as well as the musician; which is very much, and did sing the whole from the words, without any musique prickt, and played all along on a harpsicon most admirable, and the composition most excellent. The words I did not understand, and so know not how they are fitted, but believe very well, and all in the recitativo very fine. . . . But the whole composition is certainly most excellent; and the poetry, T. Killigrew and Sir

R. Murray, who understood the words, did say was excellent. I confess I was mightily pleased with the musique. He pretends not to voice, though it be good, but not excellent. . . . My great wonder is, how that man do keep in memory so perfectly the musique of the whole act, both for the voice and the instrument too. I confess I do admire it: but in recitativo the sense much helps him, for there is but one proper way of discoursing and giving the accents.

Following the entertainment the group went to Mrs Knepp's lodgings where Draghi taught the actress to sing her role in the work, "and there she did sing an Italian song or two very fine, while he played the base upon a harpsicon . . ." It is disappointing to find, after such enthusiasm, that the opera seems never to have been performed.

Draghi was sought after by dramatists, patronized by Queen Catherine, and made Master of the King's Italian music. His music for the dances in the Shadwell version of *The Tempest* was heard at the end of April 1674 (but is now lost), and for the same author's *Psyche* at the Dorset Garden Theatre in February 1675 Draghi wrote "All the Instrumental Musick (which is not mingled with the Vocal)." The *Psyche* music was published in 1675. On the death of Matthew Locke in 1677 Draghi became organist to Queen Catherine in the Catholic Chapel at Somerset House, where he had lived since 1671. His salary at court in 1677–78 was £150 yearly, and the King favored him on occasion (as in 1684) with bounties of £50 from the Secret Service funds. His position was secure enough that the Popish Plot in 1678 did not affect him seriously, though he and other musicians complained of their fear of being driven away from their adopted country. Draghi retained his organist's position, however, and later taught the princesses Anne and Mary.

On 28 January 1685 John Evelyn referred to Draghi as "that excellent & stupendous Artist" who was exceeded on the harpsichord by few if any in Europe. Evelyn may not have appreciated, as so many playgoers did, Draghi's talents as a songwriter. Among his songs, which appeared in Playford's *Theater of Music* in 1685, 1686, and 1687, were "Tell me no more I am deceiv'd," "To high, oh Cupid!," "The Pleasures that I now possess," and "Who can resist my Celia's Charms," from *A Duke and No Duke*; "There never was Swain so unhappy" and "Awake, oh Constantine" (from *Constantine*), and "Dialogue between Damon and Phillis," "How Pow'rful is the God of Love," "Where art thou, God of Dreams!," "Must I ever sigh in vain?" and "When I see my Strephon Languish." In 1687 Draghi set Dryden's St Cecilia Ode, scored for a five part chorus and orchestra. He is also said to have composed songs for *Romulus and Hersilia* and *The City Heiress* in 1682, *The Injured Lovers* in 1688, and *The City Bride* in 1696.

On 15 July 1696 Draghi witnessed articles of agreement between the actor-manager Betterton and the dancer Sorin. His presence on that occasion suggests his continuing association with the theatre. But he also composed for concerts. At York Buildings on 24 February 1697 was heard his new song composed for the Princess's birthday, and on 30 March 1698 at the same music room works by "Seignior Baptist" were performed. At some point he left England, probably to follow Catherine of Braganza. Works by him continued to be published. *Six Select Suites or Lessons for the harpsichord* appeared about 1700, and when *Wit and Mirth* came out in 1719 it contained several Draghi pieces.

"Dragon" [fl. 1775], *performing dog.*
When *The Rival Candidates* was presented at Drury Lane on 1 February 1775, Weston spoke a humorous Epilogue

accompanied by a large dog named **DRAGON** which had a good effect, but as it was poor

DRAGON's first time of appearing on the stage, he, like all young performers of true feeling, seemed a good deal frightened . . . but having conquered his fears, and recovered himself a little, he performed his part very *chastely*, and to the entire satisfaction of all present.

He seems, however, not to have pursued his stage career further.

Dragonetti, Domenico *1763–1846, double-bass player, composer.*

Born on 7 April 1763 at Venice, Domenico Dragonetti manifested a talent for music at a very early age, taught himself the violin and guitar, and studied the double bass under Berini. By the time he was 13 he was playing in the band at the Teatro San Bernadetto, and at 18, at Berini's request, Dragonetti succeeded his master at St Mark's. In addition to his astonishing skill on the awkward instrument he had chosen, he composed for it sonatas, concertos, and capriccios.

The Imperial Opera in St Petersburg offered Dragonetti a contract which he declined. Then, in 1794, at the invitation of Banti and Pachierotti, he came to London to play at the King's Theatre. His first English appearance was on 20 December 1794 at a performance of Anfossi's *Zenobia.* He won immediate acclaim for his skill and soon received invitations to play in all the major provincial concerts. At the King's Theatre in 1795–96 his annual salary was £250, and he was allowed a benefit.

Though Dragonetti made occasional trips to the Continent (to Italy and Vienna in 1798, Vienna in 1808 and 1809, Bonn in 1845), he chose England as his home and developed many close friendships there. Robert Lindley, the cellist with whom he shared a desk at the opera house for 52 years, became one of Dragonetti's constant companions. Haydn, when he visited London in 1794 and 1795, became good friends with Dragonetti, and Dragonetti visited Haydn in Vienna in later years. Domenico

knew well most of the professional musicians and serious musical enthusiasts in London, as his remarkable will attests, and he was on intimate terms with many members of the nobility and gentry.

His continental trips brought him into contact with important musicians there. On a visit to Vienna in 1809 he met Sechter and Beethoven. Many years later (in August 1845) he honored his friend by leading the double basses at the Beethoven Festival at Bonn, and that brought him another admirer, Berlioz.

Dragonetti's execution must have been remarkable indeed. It is said that he could play on the double bass the cello parts in string quartets, and the *Times* on January 1818 called him "one of the most extraordinary performers on the double bass that perhaps has ever existed." He was content with his place in the orchestra, but on 24 April 1837 his close friends Vincent and Clara Novello persuaded him "to depart from his resolution of not playing Solos in

Harvard Theatre Collection

DOMENICO DRAGONETTI
by Bartolozzi

public, and FOR THIS TIME ONLY he will accompany [Clara Novello] in a New Song, with Contra Basso obligato, composed expressly for this Concert, by Vincent Novello."

The double-bass player was as celebrated for his eccentricities as for his musical talent. His double bass was his "wife"; he adored snuff and had a sizeable collection of snuff boxes; he collected and played with dolls, to the delight of little girls who would visit him; he had a dog named Carlo who regularly sat with him in his place in the orchestra; and he spoke a delightful patois made up of Italian, bad French, and worse English.

A shrewd investor, Dragonetti amassed a fortune of considerable size, houses at No 4 and No 6, Leicester Square, and a remarkable collection of music, musical instruments, and pictures. He drew up his will in Italian on 6 April 1846, ten days before his death. A notarized translation was made for purposes of probate after the musician's death. Dragonetti listed 59 bequests, many of them to friends who were figures in the theatrical and musical world of London in the first half of the nineteenth century. Among these were George Piggott the violin teacher (to whom Dragonetti left some of the instrumental music he had collected), Teresa Milanollo the violinist (a Stradivarius once used by Paganini), Camillo Sivori (an Amati violin), Anfossi the composer and double-bass player (one of Dragonetti's several double basses), Monsieur Deloffre the violin teacher (a violin), Mr Rosselot the cello teacher (a cello), Mr Calcott the horn player at the Haymarket Theatre (a French horn), Mr Beaumann (two bassoons), Robert Lindley (a cello), Vincent and Clara Novello (some vocal music from Dragonetti's sizeable collection and two bonds of old Portuguese stock valued at £10 per annum), Eliza Fontaine of Paris, a harpist (a £5 bond and a harp), and Cipriani Potter (two £10 bonds with the

proviso that Potter should transcribe for piano six of Dragonetti's double-bass compositions "without adding a note of his own").

Dragonetti's collection of musical instruments must have been vast, for, in addition to the above bequests, he left violins and viols to most (if not all) of the members of the string section at the "Theatre Royal of the Italian Opera"—his fellow players for so many years. To the British Museum went the bulk of his music collection, including 182 volumes of scores of classical operas. To friends among the nobility Dragonetti left many of his paintings (the Duke of Leinster was given most of the collection of art work). His favorite double bass, made by Gasparo di Salò, had originally come from the convent of San Pietro in Vicenza; Dragonetti bequeathed it to St Mark's in Venice, to be played at services there by their most skilled specialist on the instrument.

Domenico Dragonetti died at his house in Leicester Square (No 4) on 16 April 1846. His will was proved on 14 May by his executors, Vincent Novello, John Benjamin Heath, and Count Carlo Pepoli.

The musician was pictured in crayons by Salabert, and Bartolozzi painted and engraved Dragonetti, seated, with his treasured double bass nearby. An engraving by F. Hellemacher shows Dragonetti when young, and one by M. Gauci shows him when old. Luigi Scotti pictured Dragonetti with many other musicians, about 1805.

Drake, Mr [fl. 1799–1802], dancer.

Though the Drury Lane accounts for 1799–1802 did not distinguish carefully between Mr, Mrs, and Miss Drake, all three seem to have been dancers, and probably all three were of the same family. Mr and Mrs Drake were not named in the bills, though the account books indicate that he was earning £1 10d. and that he worked from at least the fall of 1799 to the fall of 1802. Mrs Drake's salary was not cited, but she seems to have been a member of the *corps de ballet* at least in October, November, and December 1799.

Miss Drake danced at Drury Lane for £1 5*s.* weekly in 1798–99, 1799–1800, and 1800–1801. Her assignments included the small parts of a Female Slave in *Blue-Beard* and a Vassal in *Feudal Times* and singing as a member of the chorus in *The Egyptian Festival.* She occupied her summers of 1800 and 1801 at the Haymarket Theatre taking minor singing and dancing parts such as a Dancing Negress in *Obi.* Most bills gave her no mention, and she was probably among those designated as "etc." A Miss Drake was in Philadelphia in 1821, but there seems little likelihood that she was the dancer-singer of two decades before.

Drake, Mrs ₁*fl. 1799*₁, *dancer. See* **DRAKE, MR.**

Drake, Miss ₁*fl. 1798–1801*₁, *dancer, singer. See* **DRAKE, MR.**

Draper, Mr ₁*fl. 1776*₁, *singer.*
Mr Draper sang in a performance of the *Messiah* given on 2 April 1776 at the Chapel of the Foundling Hospital.

Draper, Miss ₁*fl. 1776–1782*₁, *singer.*
Miss Draper was a principal singer in the oratorios at Drury Lane every spring from 1776 through 1782. Her first notice was on 1 March 1776 and her last on 15 February 1782. Once, on 12 March 1779, she was mentioned as singing Sacchini's "*Tergi il pianto.*"

Drench, Master ₁*fl. 1795*₁, *actor.*
On 22 August 1795 at Astley's Amphitheatre Master Drench played one of the Cupids in *Harlequin Invincible.*

Dressler, John ₁*fl. 1777–1808*₁, *double-bass player, trombonist, composer.*
John Dressler, the German musician of

the late eighteenth century, was said to have been the first person to introduce the trombone to English orchestras, though that seems unlikely in view of the instrument's use by Handel in *Saul* in 1739 and the popularity of the sackbut in England in the seventeenth century. Dressler seems not to have made a specialty of the trombone until late in his stay in England.

On 6 April 1777 John Dressler, described as a single man and a professional musician, was recommended for membership in the Royal Society of Musicians, but he withdrew his name and did not join the Society until some time later. He played the double bass in the Handel Memorial Concerts at Westminster Abbey and the Pantheon in May and June 1784, and by 6 March 1785 he had, indeed, become a member of the Society. He played double bass at the Society's charity concerts at St Paul's Cathedral in May 1785 and again from 1789 through 1796, with the possible exception of 1795.

As early as 24 February 1792 Dressler played at the King's Theatre. On that date he performed in *The Redemption,* but what instrument he played was not noted in the records. On the following 7 March he played in *Acis and Galatea.* On 15 February 1793 he was a trombonist at the oratorio concert at the King's—the first mention of his performance on that instrument. At the opening of the new Drury Lane Theatre on 12 March 1794 Dressler was a member of the band. Doane's *Musical Directory* of that year listed him as both a double-bass player and a trombonist, living in King Street, Soho. Doane said he had played at the Handel concerts at Westminster Abbey.

Dressler performed at Covent Garden in *Alexander's Feast* on 12 February 1796, in the *Messiah* there on 3 March 1797, in the *Messiah* at the Haymarket Theatre on 15 January 1798, at Covent Garden on the following 23 February, and in the Handel concerts at Covent Garden on 8

February 1799 and 28 February 1800. During that period, however, his regular post was in the band at Drury Lane. The account books for that playhouse mention him frequently as a trombonist from 27 October 1798 through January 1808. His salary by 1803–4 was £3 weekly and it seems not to have changed over the years.

John Dressler published some concertos and quartets for wind instruments. He had a daughter who married Samuel Thomas Lyon, and perhaps Raphael Dressler was John's son. Raphael was proposed for membership in the Royal Society of Musicians in 1829, but his name was withdrawn by a Mr Lyon (his brother-in-law?) on 6 December of that year.

Dreussart, Mr (fl. 1707), *proprietor?*
Littleton Ramondon's contract at the Queen's Theatre in the Haymarket on 2 December 1707 named John James Heidegger and a Mr Dreussart as representatives of the opera house. Perhaps Dreussart was one of the proprietors, or possibly the treasurer.

Drew, Mr (fl. 1722–1723), *actor.*
At the Haymarket Theatre Mr Drew played Spitfire in *The Wife's Relief* on 17 December 1722, Corporal Macer in *Bonduca* on 31 January 1723, Antonio in *Venice Preserv'd* on 13 February, Scrub in *The Stratagem* on 14 March, Bullock in *The Recruiting Officer* on 15 April, and Crispin in *The Anatomist* on 22 April. The following 22 July he was Foresight in *Love for Love* at Hampstead Wells.

Dridge, Mr (fl. 1740), *dancer?*
Mr Dridge, probably a dancer, was one of the Followers in *The Rural Sports*, a pantomime given at Drury Lane on 27 October 1740.

Driscoll, Mr (fl. 1745–1756), *house servant.*
Mr Driscoll shared benefits at Covent Garden from 1745–46 through 1755–56, but his specific function in the theatre was never mentioned. The account books describe him only as a house servant and mention once his salary: on 29 September 1749 he was paid 4s. for two days. Perhaps he was, or was related to, Driscol the peruke maker in Broad Court, Bow Street, who handled benefit tickets for Miss Young in April 1755.

"Droghierina, La." *See* CHIMENTI, MARGHERITA.

"Drollelo, Mynheer" (fl. 1746), *dancer.*
At the Lee and Yeates Southwark Fair booth on 8 September 1746 Signor and Signora "Capuchino" and "Mynheer Drollelo," children from Holland said to be making their first appearance "on any stage," danced. Their names were pseudonyms, very likely.

Dromat, [Marianne?] (fl. 1792–1795), *dancer.*
Fuchs's *Lexique* lists Mlle Dromat (or Droma) as one of the minor dancers in *La Foire de Smyrne* at the Haymarket Theatre on 14 April 1792, though the bill for that date did not mention her. On 26 February 1793 she was a Grace in the dance *Venus and Adonis* at the King's Theatre in the Haymarket, and on 6 April 1795 she made her first appearance at Covent Garden as Discord in the Grand Masque in *Windsor Castle*. Possibly she was the Marianne Dromat who married David Dimblebe on 24 March 1810 at St George, Hanover Square.

Drouville, Mons (fl. 1771–1773), *dancer.*
On 28 May 1771 a "New Dance" was performed at the King's Theatre in the Haymarket by an unnamed dancer lately arrived from France. This was doubtless Monsieur Drouville, who appeared in a

"New Comic Dance" of his own composition on 1 June. The following 4 November Drouville made his first appearance at Covent Garden in *Jovial Gardeners*, but he seems not to have stayed with the company for the season.

At Norwich on 24 August 1772 the manager wished to "engage Mr Drouville if he will come and bring a proper lady with him to Dance. If not Mr Griffith may engage two others but not to let the Salaries of both exceed £2 12s. 6d." Drouville may have been engaged, but the records fail to show it. His next and last mention in England was on 16 June 1773 when he was in a new *Pantomimical Pastoral Dance* at the Haymarket Theatre.

Droz, Henri Louis Jaquet *1752–1791, exhibitor, mechanician.*

In *Les Spectacles de la foire* Campardon states that the Swiss mechanician and exhibitor Henri Louis Jaquet Droz was born in Chaux-de-Fond on 13 October 1752. Droz was in Paris in 1774, by which time he already had a reputation for building automatons. In 1775 he exhibited there a mechanical two-year-old child who took dictation.

Droz was in London in the late 1770s. Oxberry's *Dramatic Biography* cited "Jacques" Droz as an "ingenious mechanist" active about 1778, and Charles Dibdin in his *Professional Life* mentioned giving a show at "an auction-room in King-Street, Covent-Garden. I believe the very place once celebrated by the chess-playing automaton of Jacky Droz."

Droz was back in Paris in 1782 presenting an elaborate mechanical show lasting half an hour. He died in Naples on 18 November 1791.

Drummond, Mr *[fl. 1738–1769], proprietor.*

The Mr Drummond, banker, who worked with Heidegger on the plans for the 1738–39 opera season was probably the same Mr Drummond who by 1766–67 was one of the "proprietors and Managers of the Opera" at the King's Theatre in the Haymarket. Heidegger made reference to Drummond in advertisements on 23 and 24 May and 26 July 1738 when he was trying in vain to find subscribers for the ensuing opera season; he named Drummond as the banker to whom subscribers should send their 20 guineas, and it was ultimately Drummond who repaid subscribers when insufficient funds were raised. On 6 August 1766 Drummond and his partners (Vincent and Gordon) announced the procurement of "the best Company that can be got in Italy" for the 1766–67 season at the King's Theatre. The triumvirate lost money on their venture, according to Dr Burney, and gave up the management of the King's Theatre in 1769.

Drummond, Mr *[fl. 1756], actor.*

A Mr Drummond acted Lopez in *The Intriguing Captains* on 20 September 1756 at Bence's booth at Southwark Fair.

Drury, Robert *[fl. 1732–1741], playwright, actor.*

Robert Drury wrote the ballad opera *The Devil of a Duke*, performed at Drury Lane in August 1732 and published the same year. On 17 August it was announced that "further performances would be deferred in order that the piece might be shortened." Drury's next work was another ballad opera, *The Mad Captain*, performed at Goodman's Fields in March 1733 and published that year. The following August at Covent Garden *The Fancy'd Queen*, his third ballad opera, came out. It, too, was published in 1733.

Drury, partly in order to further his own pieces and partly to initiate his career as an actor, played Othello on 19 and 29 November 1734 at York Buildings for his benefit. *The Mad Captain* was given as an afterpiece. His next piece, *The Rival Milliners*, he described as "A Tragi-Comi-

Operatic-Pastoral Farce." It was presented at the Haymarket Theatre in January 1736, and when it was repeated on 2 February, Drury played Bellmour in the mainpiece, *The Fatal Extravagance*. Again, his stage appearance was for his benefit.

For reasons unknown, he apparently "maliciously spread a report about the Town" that Mrs Thomas Reading would not appear on 16 February at her own benefit at the Haymarket in *The Careless Husband*. She published a denial of the rumor but failed to explain why Drury had tried to ruin her benefit. Possibly she had interfered in some way with his own benefit earlier in the month.

Drury abandoned playwriting after this, and he seems not to have acted in London again. He appeared at Norwich for the first time on 6 February 1739 and performed there until 1741.

Du Barques. *See* DESBARQUES.

Dubellamy, Charles Clementine, stage name of John Evans   *d. 1793, actor, singer.*

"Charles Clementine Dubellamy" was the name the singer John Evans affected when he came on the stage. (His sister Margaret [1741–1829] also used the name Dubellamy in the provinces, before she married the actor Abraham J. Didier and came to perform in London.) Evans was said by R. B. Peake in his *Memoirs of the Colman Family* to have followed his father's trade of shoemaking before his debut as a provincial player.

He appeared first upon the stage of the Norwich theatre but in what year is not known. Pinn in his *Roscius* (1767) states that Dubellamy was at Norwich "last season," by which Pinn must have meant 1765–1766. Pinn damned him in tragedy but praised him highly in comedy.

Dubellamy possessed a handsome appearance and a voice of considerable, if not operatic, quality. He first exercised it in

Harvard Theatre Collection

CHARLES DUBELLAMY as Young Meadows, and ANN CARGILL as Rosetta

engraving by Collyer, after Dodd

London, so far as the bills reveal, when "a Gentleman [,] first appearance" (at the King's Theatre) sang a song in Act II of *The Conscious Lovers* on 9 September 1766. "The Gentleman who sang in the *Conscious Lovers*" was billed as Amiens in *As You Like It* on 13 September, again with Barry's company at the King's, and was identified by a letter in the *Public Advertiser* of 20 September:

Being at the Opera House last week to see the *Conscious Lovers* and *As You Like It*, not to mention the various and allowed excellencies of each performer, I was most agreeably surprised at the songs, in the bills said to be sung by a Gentleman, which indeed his genteel figure and polite address, at first sight well authenticated; but for the songs, viz If Love's a Sweet Passion, — Blow, Blow Thou Winter's Winds, — with some others I must confess I never heard the like; his voice was finely masculine, strong, sweet, clear and articulate; his manner not servilely confined to the pedantic stiffness of some, or the affectation of others; in a word he sung like a Gentleman; and the sound, as Milton elegantly expresses it, "Floated on the Wings of Silence." This is not intended (by doing justice to Mr D. B——y) to depreciate any [one else]. . . . I am told he has applied to Mr Beard, with what success I know not . . .

John Beard, the great tenor singer and then manager and joint patentee at Covent Garden, was a superb judge of voices, and he agreed with the letter writer. He hired Dubellamy, and his wife Frances Maria as well, for the 1766–67 season.

On 12 November 1766 Dubellamy made his first appearance in a regular London patent theatre, as Young Meadows in *Love in a Village* (his wife having preceded him as Lavinia in *The Fair Penitent* on 7 November). He had an unspecified part in *Harlequin Dr Faustus* on 18 November and sang, with many others, "a Solemn Hymn, set by Purcel" which was "Introduced" in *The Royal Convert* on 21 November. On 3 December he was Sir John Lofty in *The Accomplish'd Maid* a "New Comic Opera never perform'd before," an adaptation from Goldini's *La buona figliuola* by Edward Toms, the music by Niccolo Piccini, in opposition to the original, then playing at the opera house. He was the Third Spirit in *Comus* on 14 February 1767 and sang the part of Sightly on the first night (and subsequent nights) of Isaac Bickerstaffe's pastiche comic opera *Love in the City* on 21 February. He played Hilliard in *The Jovial Crew* on 3 March, substituted for Beard in the "vocal parts" of *Romeo and Juliet* on 17 March (and was retained in this spot even after Beard returned on 20

April), and played Gower in *Henry V* before the royal family on 23 April. Dubellamy chose to play for his benefit shared with Mrs Pitt on 5 May the farcical part of Moor of Moor Hall in *The Dragon of Wantley* and to sing "by Particular Desire" the *"Cantata* of *Cymon and Iphegenia."* He played and sang a sailor in *Thomas and Sally,* the afterpiece on 20 May, and finished his season with gravity as Salisbury in *King John,* on 28 May. Dubellamy sang once as an adjunct to the program at the Haymarket on 14 August 1767.

The Dubellamys returned to Covent Garden in the season of 1767–68, he with a salary of £3 for a six-day week. To his repertoire he added that season the following roles, most of them singing parts: Palaemon in *The Chaplet*, Mervin in *The Maid of the Mill*, Lorenzo in *The Merchant of Venice*, Mercury in *Lethe*, Chasseur Royal in *The Royal Chace*, Lord Aimworth in *The Maid of the Mill*, Apollo in *Midas* (substituting for Mattocks), a Bacchanal in *Comus*, a vocal part in *Lycidas*, Rook in George Colman's new comedy *The Oxonian in Town*, Charles Freeman in *The Stratagem*, a vocal part in an episode of *The Roman Father* called "The Triumphal Entry of Publius," a vocal part in the background music to *Macbeth*, Titus in *Coriolanus*, Quaver in *The Virgin Unmask'd*, and, for his benefit jointly with his wife, Octavio in *She Wou'd and She Wou'd Not*. (They realized only £33 16s. after house charges were subtracted from the receipts.)

During the trial-at-law which capped the three years of quarreling over mistresses and precedents between the Harris and Colman factions at Covent Garden, Dubellamy testified that in June 1768 Colman had offered him and his wife articles for three years at £3 10s. and £2 10s. respectively, binding the proprietors for £1000 against default. The Dubellamys returned to Colman's company in each winter season through 1772–73 and lived near the theatre in Wild Court, Great Wild Street. She is said to have died on 15 August 1773.

In the winter of 1775–76 Charles Dubellamy returned alone to Covent Garden. The *Public Advertiser* for 10 May 1776 reported that, on 8 May at St George, Bloomsbury, he had married a widow, Mrs Buttar, an American and a daughter of the late General Bradstreet. John Bradstreet (c. 1711–1774) was a Colonial officer. He had left two daughters by his wife Mary and evidently he left also a considerable fortune.

Dubellamy had joined Samuel Foote's band of comedians at the Haymarket for the summer campaigns of 1769, 1770, and 1773. He had sung at Marylebone Gardens in the summer of 1774 and he played and sang at Liverpool (for £2 each four-day week) in the summer of 1776. Throughout 1776–77 he was probably trouping in Ireland. Clark's *The Irish Stage in the County Towns* places him at the Crow Street Theatre, Dublin, sometime in 1777.

The records are as dim concerning Dubellamy's activities in the seasons of 1777–78 through 1779–80, but he was certainly at Bath and Bristol during some parts of 1779 and 1780. He returned to the Haymarket on 30 May 1780 to play Apollo in *Midas*, and the bills then stated that he was playing in London for the first time "these three years." His benefit bill of 27 July shows that he lodged that summer in Bow Street "next door to the Theatre Coffee-House."

Dubellamy's debut at Drury Lane Theatre came late in his career. On 26 September 1780 he came onstage there as Young Meadows in *Love in a Village*, the part he had used for his initial London appearance in 1766. One critic thought that "Mr Dubellamy's singing made ample amends for the few deficiencies which appeared in his delivery of the dialogue." He added a few new parts to his repertoire during the season, notably the Huntsman in the first performances of General "Gentleman Johnny" Burgoyne and William

Jackson's comic opera *The Lord of the Manor*. He continued in his constant line of lyrical roles again in 1781–82, but he also "created" Melvie in Richard Tickell's *Carnival of Venice* and Summers in Frederick Pilon's comic opera *The Fair American* and was borrowed by his old friend Miss Younge to play Moor of Moor Hall in *The Dragon of Wantley* for her benefit.

After the season of 1781–82 Dubellamy disappeared from London's (and from Britain's) boards and bills. He was reported by Dunlap to be in New York by 1789 where he had perhaps reassumed his real name of Evans. "He was now past his meridian," said Dunlap, but was "still a handsome man" and "full of the courtesy of the old school." Dubellamy, Dunlap says vaguely, was "a medium of communication between the play-writer and the managers," and perhaps his function was that of what we would today call a literary agent. He is said to have introduced Dunlap's first play, *The Modest Soldier*, to the Hallam-Henry management. He died at New York on 6 August 1793, and the *European Magazine* declared in a brief notice of his death that he had been in America for nine years.

Not many critics were as blunt as Francis Gentleman in *The Dramatic Censor*, (1770) who declared that Dubellamy had "much merit as a singer, not one grain as a speaker," but there was common agreement that his value lay principally in his singing, not his acting, because of what Gentleman called his "faintness of expression." R. B. Peake thought him very awkward in deportment and "remarkable, while singing and speaking for the cocking up of his thumbs."

Among the roles, not given above, which Dubellamy played were: Cawawkee in *Polly*, Hastings in *She Stoops to Conquer*, Major Belford in *The Deuce is in Him*, Count Folatre in *April Day*, Frederick in *Fire and Water*, Lionel in *Lionel and Clarissa*, Roger in *The Gentle Shepherd*, Captain Greville in *The Flitch of Bacon*,

Macheath in *The Beggar's Opera*, Worthy in *The Recruiting Officer*, Eustace in *Love in a Village*, Antonio in *The Duenna*, Leander in *The Padlock*, Rimines in *Artaxerxes*, William in *The Camp*, and Honour in *King Arthur*. Like most of his other parts these were lyrical, comic, or romantic (or all three). He was thus more often seen in afterpieces than were most stars of his secondary magnitude. His Shakespearean parts were rather extensive, however, and often went beyond the expected singing roles like Amiens in *As You Like It*. They were Autolycus in *The Winter's Tale*, Balthazar in *Much Ado about Nothing*, Camperus and Capucius in *Henry VIII*, the Duke in *All's Well that Ends Well*, the Duke in *Othello*, Florizel in *The Sheep Shearing* (Colman's alteration of *The Winter's Tale*), France in *King Lear*, Gower in *Henry V*, Guiderius in *Cymbeline*, Horatio in *Hamlet*, Lorenzo in *The Merchant of Venice*, Octavius in *Julius Caesar*, Salisbury in *King John*, Stanley in (Cibber's) *Richard III*, and Titus in (Sheridan's) *Coriolanus*.

The popularity of several of the songs presented by Dubellamy at the theatres and Marylebone Gardens carried them to publication "as sung by" him: *For Sally I Sigh, Lovely Nymph Asswage my Anguish* (from *Midas*), *Sweet are the Banks when Spring Perfumes, For Polly I Sigh*. Also published was *Seek ye the Lord*, which he sang (in 1775?) at the Bedford Chapel of Lincoln Cathedral.

Dubellamy was pictured by D. Dodd as Young Meadows in *Love in a Village*, with Mrs Cargill as Rosetta, in a plate engraved by J. Collyer for the *New English Theatre* in 1784. A Dodd-Angus print of c. 1781 shows him, Palmer, and Mrs Cargill in a scene from *The Carnival of Venice*.

Dubellamy, Mrs Charles Clementine the first, Frances Maria   *d. 1773, actress, singer.*

Mrs Charles Clementine Dubellamy may have appeared on the stage for the first time

at Norwich, whence she and her husband came in the summer of 1766 to act at Foote's Haymarket. Her first and middle names were Frances Maria, but her family name is, like her early life, unknown. Charles Dubellamy enjoyed a critical success with his first vocal performances at the Haymarket and consequently John Beard hired both husband and wife for Covent Garden at the beginning of the 1766–67 winter season.

Mrs Dubellamy preceded her husband to the Covent Garden stage, being given the supporting role of Lavinia in *The Fair Penitent* on 7 November. It was a night for experiments, apparently, inasmuch as the play was being revived after nine years. Ross was playing Horatio for the first time, Miss Barowby, as Lucilla, was making her "first attempt as an actress," and Miss Elliot, as Calista, was making her "first attempt in tragedy."

Charles Dubellamy gained the favor of audiences and consequently of management almost immediately, and he was employed in a variety of ways. But after two more performances of *The Fair Penitent*, Frances Maria Dubellamy went back to rehearsal until she was ready to be thrust into the not very taxing role of the Countess of Rousillon in *All's Well that Ends Well* on 23 January 1767. Three days later she played Gertrude, with Ross as Hamlet, but the combination must have failed for it was never tried afterward. Mrs Dubellamy was seen in nothing more during that season; but in June, after the house was shut and most of its actors had departed, it was reopened for Shuter's benefit and she acted Isabinda in *The Busy Body*.

Mrs Dubellamy was utilized far more frequently to earn her nightly 3s. 4d. during her second season at Covent Garden. On the opening night, 14 September 1767, she had an unspecified part in *The Rehearsal*, revived after 12 years, according to the bills. On 23 September she was the Lady Blanch in *King John*, on 19 October Serina in *The Orphan*, on 22 October

Lucilla in *The Fair Penitent* (she had given up Lavinia and the management was trying Mrs Lessingham in the part "for the first time"), and on 30 October she assumed one of the Bacchants in *Comus*. She was in both the mainpiece and the afterpiece on 20 November: *The Fair Penitent* was repeated and she came on again in the farce *The Upholsterer*. On 1 January 1768 she assumed the Lady in *Love à-la-Mode*. She moved into heavy tragedy as Regan in Colman's alteration of *King Lear* on 20 February, and on 13 April she returned to her accustomed lighter vein with Alithea in *The Country Wife*. She played Selima in *Zara* on 10 May, and the next night, for the Dubellamys' joint benefit, she was Hypolita in *She Wou'd and She Wou'd Not*.

Mrs Dubellamy played, but with diminishing frequency, at Covent Garden in the winters and at the Haymarket in the summers through the season of 1771–72. Probably she was in ill health, for she was not seen at all at Covent Garden in 1772–73 and appeared only once more, on 26 May, at the very beginning of the Haymarket's summer season of 1773. The *Morning Chronicle* reported the death, on 15 August, of Frances Maria Dubellamy, the *Theatrical Monitor* of the following 5 November identified that decedent as Charles's wife, and the Fawcett notebooks in the Folger Library also record her death under 1773.

In addition to the characters named, Mrs Dubellamy added the following to her repertoire during her short London career: Harriet in *The Upholsterer*, Eleanor in *The Countess of Salisbury*, Louisa in *Love Makes a Man*, Charlotte in *Catharine and Petruchio*, an unspecified vocal part in John Hoole's new tragedy *Timanthes* (which first played on 24 February 1770), Lucy in *The Brothers*, Mrs Mecklin in *The Commissary*, Queen Elizabeth in *Richard III*, Lucy Waters in *The Brothers*, Milwood in *The London Merchant*, Mrs Midnight in *The Country Madcap*, Tappet in *The Miser*, Mrs Subtle in *The Englishman in Paris* (probably), and Mrs Sneak in *The Mayor of Garratt*.

Dubellamy, Margaret. *See* DIDIER, MRS ABRAHAM J.

Duberval. *See* D'AUBERVAL.

Dubia. *See* DUBOIS.

Dubisson. *See* DUBOISON and DUBUIS-SON.

"Dublin Roscius, The." *See* RYDER, THOMAS.

Duboia. *See* DUBOIS.

Du Bois, [Mons?] [*fl.* 1730], *dancer?*
The performance of 24 April 1730 at Lincoln's Inn Fields Theatre was for the benefit Du Pre and Du Bois. Du Pre was a well-known dancer, thus very likely so was Du Bois. Receipts of the night totalled £87 18*s.*

Dubois, Charles [*fl.* 1792–1807], *dancer.*
Master Charles Dubois, the son of Jean Baptiste Dubois the celebrated clown, was a dancer. He performed in *Meadea's* [*sic*] *Kettle* at Sadler's Wells on 9 April 1792 and was there again in 1800 as Harlequin Junior in *Harlequin Benedick*. Billed as one of his father's scholars, he reappeared at the Wells in 1801 and, with his father, toured to Plymouth and (probably) Exeter, Salisbury, Portsmouth, and Gosport. By 13 April 1807, when he danced a *pas de deux* at the Royal Circus, he was billed as C. Dubois or Dubois Junior. There, in the spring and summer of 1807, he was a principal dancer in *Rudolph and Rosa* and played Sir Topaz in *Edwin of the Green*, Caius Lucias in *Imogen*, and Caled in *Almoran and Hamet*. The last notice we

have found of Charles Dubois was on 22 September 1807 when he danced in *Rodolph and Rosa* and repeated his role of Sir Topaz also at the Royal Circus.

Dubois, Frank [fl. 1696], actor.

Prompt copy traces in the 1696 edition of *She Ventures and He Wins* reveal the Drawer to be Frank Dubois—the name of the actor, apparently, not the character. He is otherwise unknown, and *The London Stage* does not list him.

Dubois, Jean Baptiste 1762–1817, clown, acrobat, dancer, actor, singer.

Born in 1762, the French performer Jean Baptiste Dubois may have come to England in the 1770s. In the Manchester Theatre bill for 27 December 1776 was a "Sig Dubia" who rope danced and a Mr "Duboia" who was a tumbler; the performing troupe was headed by (Philip) Astley of London. Both references may well be to Dubois, who was both a rope dancer and a tumbler and who worked with Astley in later years. Dubois was certainly in England by 1780, according to Findlater, and in the summer of 1782 "Mr Baptiste" was a clown to the horsemanship and "Duboa" was a tumbler at Astley's Amphitheatre. The clown, with Griffin, Jones, and Miss Hutton, formed a pyramid on three galloping horses. Again, Dubois was probably both the clown and tumbler referred to. He was probably the acrobat "Dupuis" at Bristol in October 1783, Sadler's Wells in May, and Astley's from August to October 1784.

In 1787 Dubois worked briefly as clown to the horsemanship at Jones's Equestrian Amphitheatre in Whitehall (and, as "Dupuis," performed on the trampoline at the Royal Circus). The following year he served as clown to horsemanship at Sadler's Wells. He appeared at Drury Lane in 1789–90, making his debut there as the Clown in *Harlequin's Frolick* on 26 December 1789. His salary was £3 weekly,

but he was not mentioned in the bills as performing in any other productions during the season.

The 1790–91 season at Drury Lane brought him out as Scaramouch "(with a song)" in *Don John* on 26 October 1790, Signor Pasticio Ritornello in *The Critic* on 27 October, a Soldier in *The Siege of Belgrade* on 1 January 1791, and the Clown in *The Fairy Favour* on 7 February. The account book on 5 March 1791 shows a payment to Dubois of 7s. for "Macaronis" —probably medley entertainments of some sort.

Dubois made no known appearances at Drury Lane in 1791–92, but according to a Folger Library manuscript he was in *Meadea's Kettle* at Sadler's Wells on 9 April 1792 and some time that year "revived" his egg dance—a traditional turn in which a dancer did an intricate dance blindfolded among eggs placed at intervals on the stage floor. Dubois did a hornpipe in wooden clogs and broke no eggs.

The Drury Lane accounts mention the name Dubois frequently in 1792–93. Several entries show payments to a Dubois who kept horses for the theatre, and he may well have been the enterprising and multifaceted clown-equestrian Jean Baptiste. The pay for looking after the horses was £6 6s. weekly. Dubois, with one Jacobs, sold horses to the theatre as well and collected sizeable sums for taking care of them. A (second?) Dubois was paid for timber that season. Jean Baptiste played a Pirate in *The Pirates* and a Knight in a *Tournament* which he directed for *Cymon*; these were presented by the Drury Lane troupe at the King's Theatre. For the season Dubois was paid £4 weekly as a performer.

Dubois was not at Drury Lane in 1793–94, but he appeared at Sadler's Wells as a dancer in October 1793, received regular payments from Drury Lane for keeping horses, played the Wild Man in *Valentine and Orson* at Sadler's Wells, entertained there on the cymbals, and was manifestly skilled at archery (in May 1794 at the Wells he shot an apple from a child's head). Dubois was listed in Doane's *Musical Directory* in 1794 as a tenor singer living at No 53, Taylor's Buildings, Islington Road, and an employee of the Sadler's Wells Theatre.

In 1794–95 Dubois was back on the boards at Drury Lane playing an Indian Warrior in *The Cherokee* and Clytus in *Alexander the Great,* but he still handled the horses and seems to have been empowered to rent horses to other playhouses. In August 1795 he was back at Sadler's Wells, acting Lord Percy in *Chevy Chase.*

His salary at Drury Lane rose to £6 weekly in the fall of 1795, though he was not assigned many roles: he played Aglogan in *The Cherokee* and the Clown in *Harlequin Captive,* but from 26 January 1796 onward his name was dropped from the bills. Dubois left the troupe and visited America, making his first appearance in March 1796 at the John Street Theatre in New York. He was back at Drury Lane by October, however, and in 1796–97 played such parts as the Seneschal in *Richard Coeur de Lion,* Glaude in a dance called *The Scotch Ghost,* and his old role of the Clown in *Harlequin Captive.* The spring of 1797 saw him at Sadler's Wells again where, according to the *Monthly Mirror* in April, Dubois was "the life and spirit of this place," giving "energy and effect to every character he undertakes." Dubois could perform as any type of clown, do trick riding on horseback, dance, sing, tumble, juggle, and act.

On 27 March 1798 a Mr Dubois, probably Jean Baptiste, appeared with Lailson's Circus in Philadelphia, serving as one of the dancers. On 18 May he acted Tipperary in *The Sufferings of the Maddison Family* for the troupe. By the winter of 1798 Dubois was again in London. The *Authentic Memoirs of the Green Room* (1799) stated that he was often harassed by creditors and was planning to set up a theatrical academy for ladies and gentlemen.

Dubois was back at Drury Lane on 6 December 1798 acting Jamie in *The Scotch Ghost* dance for £3 weekly, but he was not mentioned in the bills for any other activity. In 1799 he was "clown to the rope" at Sadler's Wells; there in 1800 he played Gobble, the eating clown, in *Peter Wilkins; or, Harlequin in the Flying World* and sang, to Joe Grimaldi's salt box accompaniment, a mock Italian air. Grimaldi and Dubois performed together for many years; Findlater states that Dubois had a great influence on Grimaldi, who watched him for 12 years, though Grimaldi denied ever having been Jean Baptiste's student.

In 1801 Dubois "and his pupils from Sadler's Wells" (including his son Charles, Masters I. and C. Bland, and Miss Bland) performed for six weeks at the Plymouth and Dock theatres, entertaining the sailors with dancing and pantomimes. Dubois also toured to Exeter, Salisbury, Portsmouth, and Gosport, but he was back at Sadler's Wells in May 1801 to perform with Grimaldi a satire on duelling in *The Philosopher's Stone.* At the end of the summer Dubois left the Wells, apparently because he did not receive a requested raise in salary. In 1803–4 he was at Covent Garden earning about £5 weekly for doing entr'acte turns such as his egg hornpipe. He returned to the Wells in time, for Gilliland in 1805–6 said that "Dubois is entitled to a great eulogium for his masterly acting; it is a great pity that the energies of this Performer's frame and mind, should have been so long suffered to waste at Sadler's Well's—he certainly is the best buffoon on the Stage."

From March to September 1807 Dubois performed at the Royal Circus for the first time. He was clown to the rope, played Mahomed Shah in *Solima,* Wolsberg in *Rodolph and Rosa,* Cymbeline and Leonatus Posthumus in *Imogen,* and Almoran in *Almoran and Hamet*, and danced his egg hornpipe. He was probably the Monsieur Dubois who danced in the summer of 1809 at the Haymarket Theatre, but by that time Grimaldi had succeeded Dubois as the leading clown in London.

Little is known of the personal life of Dubois. On 2 January 1796 the *Morning Herald* reported that his wife had died recently. She and Jean Baptiste had had two sons: Charles, who was trained by his father as a dancer and who performed with him in the late 1790s and early 1800s, and Joseph, who died in 1812.

Jean Baptiste Dubois died in 1817. A portrait of him by Van Assen was engraved by Dumee and published in the *Thespian Magazine* on 1 March 1794. A print in the Finsbury Public Library showing the interior of Sadler's Wells in 1795 depicts the ropedancer Richer with Dubois.

Duboison. *See also* DUBUISSON.

Duboison, Mr (fl. 1795), *performer?*
The Drury Lane account books contain an entry dated 24 October 1795 which reads, "acct of saly. he [Duboison] says to begin 13th 5.0.0." The size of the salary would suggest a performer rather than a house servant.

Dubourg, Isaac. *See* ISAAC.

Dubourg, Matthew *1703–1767, violinist, composer.*
Matthew Dubourg was born in London in 1703, the natural son of the dancer Isaac. He made his first appearance at one of Thomas Britton's concerts about 1712, playing a Corelli sonata, standing on a stool. When Geminiani came to England in 1714, Dubourg became his pupil. Billed as "the famous Matthew Dubourg" on 7 April 1715, he played a solo at the Lincoln's Inn Fields Theatre, and perhaps he had been displaying his talent all season under the billing of the "Boy." On 19

April 1716 at Hickford's Music Room he was given a benefit concert. He was granted another one there on 22 March 1717, and he performed at Hickford's again on 3 April and 3 May. On 10 May he played at Stationers' Hall and on 22 May at Drury Lane. And so it went for the rest of the decade: regular appearances at Hickford's, Stationers' Hall, York Buildings, Drury Lane, Lincoln's Inn Fields, and the Haymarket Theatre.

Dubourg went to Dublin in 1724 but was back in London by 1 June 1727 for a concert at York Buildings. On 17 June at Stanmore he married Frances, the daughter of the musician Bernard Gates. The violinist played in the St Cecilia Day concert at the Crown and Anchor on 22 November 1727 and stayed in London, at least through 15 May 1728 when he performed at Hickford's.

He returned to Dublin in 1728 to succeed Cousser (or Kusser) as leader of the Viceroy's band, and in that position until 1764 Dubourg wrote many birthday odes for the Lord Lieutenant. In 1735 he was appointed chamber musician to the Prince of Wales. The violinist was in Dublin for the concerts which Handel gave there in November 1741 and played in the first performance of the *Messiah* on 13 April 1742. Van der Straeten reports that in Dublin Dubourg played a cadenza at a Handel performance and wandered so far afield that, when the violinist finally finished, Handel said, "Welcome home, Monsieur Dubourg," —to the delight of the audience.

In March 1743 Dubourg returned to London for a short time to play violin solos in the Covent Garden performances of Handel's *Samson, L'Allegro ed il Penseroso*, and the *Messiah*. By October he was back in Dublin working on a subscription series of Handel oratorios with Arne. He also taught violin while in Dublin, one of his students being Miss Plunkett, who made her first appearance at the Haymarket Theatre in London on 27 January 1744.

Dubourg returned to London (while still keeping his official post in Dublin) to organize a concert at Hickford's on 21 April 1749. For a number of years he appeared at the annual concerts for the benefit of decayed musicians and their families at the King's Theatre in the Haymarket (1750, 1751, 1754, 1755, 1756, 1758, 1759, and 1761), and he occasionally wrote overtures for these events.

On 25 January 1752 Dubourg was performing in Ireland, but on the following 2 December he was being considered for the sinecure appointment as Sergeant Trumpeter in London, a post to which Valentine Snow finally succeeded. The violinist did, however, receive an appointment in London as leader of the King's Band, even though he still held his Dublin post. In 1761 he was made Master of Her Majesty's Band of Musick at a fee of £200 yearly. Though he kept a London residence in Sherrard Street, Golden Square, he seems not to have returned permanently until 1765, after he had relinquished his Dublin position.

On 3 July 1767 Matthew Dubourg made a brief will, leaving 60 guineas to Bridget Byrn and 50 guineas each to Benjamin and George Johnson. The rest of his estate he bequeathed to his wife Frances. He made no mention of his daughter Elizabeth, who had married the oboist Redmond Simpson on 22 September 1753, so perhaps she had died or had been otherwise provided for. According to Grove, Dubourg died on the day he made his will, though the description on a memorial tablet at Paddington Church states that he died on 5 July. The inscription reads:

Here lyeth the body of Matthew Dubourg, chief composer and master of music in the kingdom of Ireland, servant to four generations of the illustrious House of Hanover, George I. and II., his Royal Highness the late Prince of Wales, and His present Majesty; as also instructor in Music to their Royal Highnesses the Duke of Cumberland and the late Prince Frederick. He died July 5, 1767, aged 64.

> Tho' sweet as Orpheus thou coulds't bring
> Soft pleadings from the trembling string,
> Unmov'd the King of Terror stands,
> Nor owns the magic of thy hands.

Dubourg was buried at Paddington on 7 July, and his widow proved his will on 13 July.

Some of Dubourg's music appeared in such collections as the *Delightful Pocket Companion for the German Flute, Musica belicosa, or Warlike Musick*, and *Serenading Trumpet Tunes*. But his chief importance was not as a composer but as a violin virtuoso, and his contribution to the progress of violin playing in England and Ireland was considerable. Philip Hussey painted Dubourg; the portrait was owned by Joseph Cooper Walker of Dublin.

Du Breil, Mons [fl. 1711], *dancer.*
Monsieur Du Breil (or Du Brill) from the Brussels opera, danced with Mlle le Fèvre at the Queen's Theatre in the Haymarket from 20 March through 21 April 1711, after which Du Breil announced he would be leaving England. The following summer at Pinkethman's playhouse in Greenwich the younger Thurmond danced "that excellent and much admired *Scaramouch*, as it was performed by the famous Monsieur du Brill from the Opera at Brussels."

Dubreuil, Mons [fl. 1721–1722], *actor? dancer?*
Monsieur and Madame Dubreuil were members of a French troupe that played at the Haymarket Theatre from 4 December 1721 to 10 April 1722. The Dubreuils shared a benefit with two others on 26 February 1722. Perhaps Dubreuil should be identified as the dancer Du Breil who performed in London in 1711.

Dubreuil, Mme [*fl. 1721–1722*], *actress? dancer? See* **DUBREUIL, MONS.**

Du Brill. *See* **DU BREIL.**

Du Brocq. *See* **DEBROC.**

Dubuisson, Mons [*fl. 1734–1742*], *dancer, actor.*

Monsieur Dubuisson was a member of Francisque Moylin's French troupe at the Haymarket and Goodman's Fields theatres from 26 October 1734 to 4 June 1735. His first billing came on 2 December 1734 when he played Zamec in *Sampson Judge of Israel*. Following this he appeared as Geronte in *Le Joueur*, Diaphoirus in *La Malade imaginaire*, the News Cryer in *Arlequin Balourd*, Don Henriquez in *Inès de Castro*, L'Arc and Ciel in *La Fille capitain et Arlequin son sergeant*, Don Alvarez in *Le Festin de Pierre*, Corasmir in *Zaire*, the Singing Master in *Le Bourgeois gentilhomme*, Ulric in *La Vie est un songe*, Rodolphe in *Gustave Vasa*, Ismael in *Athalie*, and Midas in *L'Embarras de richesses*. He shared a benefit with Delisle on 1 May 1735.

On 11 November 1741 Dubuisson returned from Paris to London, this time accompanied by his dancing partner Mlle Bonneval, to dance at Covent Garden. Their specialty dances were rarely described in the bills, but when they shared a benefit on 21 April 1742 the pair danced *Quarrelling Lovers Reconciled* and *Les Matelots*. Tickets for the benefit were made available at Dubuisson's house in St Martin's Street, near Leicester Fields.

Dubus or **Du Bus.** *See* **CHAMPVILLE.**

Duchemin, [**Mlle?**] [*fl. 1789*], *dancer.*

Smith's *Italian Opera* lists a female dancer named Duchemin as a member of the opera company playing at the King's Theatre in the Haymarket and, after the fire, at Covent Garden in 1789. She is not listed in *The London Stage*.

Duchesne, Mons [*fl. 1791–1792*], *dancer.*

Monsieur and Madame Duchesne danced in *Amphion et Thalie* at the Pantheon on 17 February 1791, though both were omitted from the dance on 26 February. Fuchs in his *Lexique* indicates that Mons Duchesne danced in *La Foire de Smyrne* at the Haymarket Theatre on 14 April 1792, though *The London Stage* does not include him in the cast.

Duchesne, Mme [*fl. 1791*], *dancer. See* **DUCHESNE, MONS.**

Duck, Mr [*fl. 1735–1744*], *doorkeeper.*

Mr Duck was the first gallery doorkeeper at Covent Garden, the first mention of him in the accounts occurring in 1735–36 when he was "Allowed 162 Nights attendance at 20^d £13.10.– and is charged with Tickets taken in his name £15.3.–." He shared yearly benefits through the 1743–44 season, his last coming on 14 May 1744; he was not, however, listed for benefits in the 1738–39 and 1739–40 seasons, so he may have worked elsewhere for a period.

Duckworth, Mr [*fl. 1792–1793*], *manager.*

Mr Duckworth led the company which played at Parsons Green, Fulham, in 1792 and 1793. The theatre he used had been opened in 1789 in a barn adjoining the White Horse Inn, at the corner of Parsons Green and Ackmar Road.

Duckworth, Mr [*fl. 1794*], *violinist.*

Doane's *Musical Directory* of 1794 listed Mr Duckworth of Oakley Street, Lambeth, as a violinist who played at Westminster Abbey, Astley's Amphitheatre, and the Apollo Gardens.

Ducrast, Mme *(fl. 1794), singer.*

Doane's *Musical Directory* of 1794 listed Madame Ducrast, a soprano, as a participant in concerts presented by the Society of Ancient Music and Johann Peter Salomon.

Ducros. *See* DUCROW, ANDREW.

Ducrow, Andrew *1793–1842, equestrian, ropedancer, equilibrist, manager.*

Andrew Ducrow was born at the Nag's Head, No 102, High Street, Southwark, on 10 October 1793 only a few days after his father Peter, the "Flemish Hercules," had brought his family from Paris to London to perform at Astley's Amphitheatre.

Andrew was strong but slight of build, not fitted by physique to succeed in Peter's rugged line of performance, though he had been set to train for it at the age of three. Being found insufficient, he was sent instead to the accomplished harlequin and dancer Richer, who taught him the arts of harlequinade, vaulting, tumbling, and fencing, but also the fundamentals of funambulism. He varied his studies with lessons from the equestrian Collet at Astley's.

He performed in his father's troupe both at Astley's and elsewhere in London before his fourth birthday. He was with a company his father led to a temporary amphitheatre at the bottom of Greve Street, near Bathwick Fields, Bath, at some time in the 1790s. A circumstantial and persistent story was told, supposedly illustrative of the father Peter's iron discipline. During a performance the boy fell from his horse to the tanbark and broke his leg. His father rushed to him and carried him from the arena. Presently, cries of pain were heard issuing from the dressing tent, and one of the audience, investigating, found Peter Ducrow horsewhipping his son for his clumsiness.

Andrew accompanied his father to the provinces and even toured on the Continent. *The Memoirs of J. De Castro, Comedian* (1824) reproduces a bill of 1797

From the Collection of Marian Hannah Winter

ANDREW DUCROW, in *The Gladiators*
self-portrait

for the San Carlo Theatre at Lisbon, in which appear "Principiarao Mr. Du Crow, e Mr. Smith, e o Infante Hercules," who was certainly Andrew.

The rigor of his father's training did not abate, and the youth inherited Peter's courage and ability, though not his strength. In 1800 he attracted the fascinated attention of George III and the nobility assembled at a fête given at Frogmore. By 1808 or earlier Andrew was a principal equestrian and ropedancer at Astley's at £10 per week. He rejoined his father when Peter assumed direction of the Royal Circus in St George's Fields, Blackfriar's Road, and added pantomime to his repertoire during the few months before Peter went into bankruptcy, and then he rejoined Astley.

Peter Ducrow died in 1814. Andrew performed during the winter of 1817–18 at the Olympic Circus at Liverpool and there he was married to Margaret Griffith, an equestrienne from that city. The responsibility of his wife, mother, brothers, and sisters had fallen upon Andrew. Taking them all and his trick horse Jack he joined Blondell's Cirque Olympique at Brussels. His success brought him to the notice of the great manager Franconi at the Cirque Olympique in Paris. After protracted negotiation Franconi bound him contractually in 1818 by offering him all the profits exceeding three hundred francs a performance. After his debut at the Cirque on 16 December 1818 Ducrow startled the French with a number of imaginative innovations, including the kind of equestrian pageant which he called an *entrée*. Ducrow recruited for personnel in London in the spring of 1819. Together with his younger sisters Margaret, Louisa (later Mrs Wood), and Emily (later Mrs William Irwin Broadfoot) and his brother John (d. 23 May 1834) who was clown to the ring, he returned to France and toured through 1822.

For the rest of his career Andrew confined his professional activities to the British Isles. On 5 November 1823 he and his horses appeared in Planché's mildly successful drama *Cortez, or the Conquest of Mexico*, at Covent Garden, and among his other presentations at the patent theatres was *The Enchanted Courser, or the Sultan of Kurdistan* at Drury Lane on 28 October 1824. But the arena was his natural habitat, and his association with Astley's Amphitheatre (of which he was by now manager and of which, about 1825, he became joint proprietor with William West) is that for which he is principally remembered. He brought Astley's to a peak of prosperity not achieved in the days of its founder. He employed over 150 persons and seldom took in less than £500 per week.

In 1831 Ducrow's spectacular melodrama *The Days of Athens* was seen at Drury Lane. In 1832 William IV fitted up an arena in his pavilion at Brighton so that Ducrow might perform there. In 1832 Ducrow produced for Alfred Bunn at

Harvard Theatre Collection

ANDREW DUCROW, as the Spanish Bull Fighter

engraving by Rogers, after Wageman

Drury Lane the spectacle of *St George and the Dragon*. This success was followed by *King Arthur and the Knights of the Round Table*, for which Queen Adelaide rewarded Ducrow with a gift of £100.

Ducrow toured the British Isles extensively in the summers and played to overflowing arenas at Dublin, Norwich, Leeds, Hull, Edinburgh, Liverpool, Manchester, Bath, York, and Glasgow. As James Winston wrote, he "had no fixed season" at any location but remained "as long as the receipts justified his expectations."

A newspaper clipping of 12 October 1833 speaks of "a splendid national arena" he had "lately" constructed at Norwich. "It is fitted up in great style, and contains a circle as large as Astley's." Another clipping of 30 November 1835 describes his "Olympic Arena" at Hull, "a new building, and embellished with taste," where Ducrow and his horse Pegasus attracted great crowds. In July 1837 his spectacle *Crichton* was lavishly produced at the Royal Amphitheatre in London.

On 8 June 1841 Astley's Amphitheatre was totally destroyed by fire. The pecuniary loss was partially recovered by subscriptions and a benefit in Ducrow's favor; but an old female servant, long with Ducrow's family, had been burned to death in the fire, and the tragedy obsessed him so that his mind gave way. He was brought back to partial health by a Dr Wray and a Dr Sutherland but died after a paralytic stroke at his house, No 19, York Road, Lambeth, on 27 January 1842. His funeral on 5 February was attended by hordes of curiosity seekers as well as his mourning family and devoted employees. The *Gentleman's Magazine* (April 1842) described the order of procession to the elaborate mausoleum, which had been designed for him in 1837, in Kensal Green Cemetery:

A body of police to clear the way; Mr. Gawler, the undertaker, mounted on horseback; four mounted porters; plume of feathers with two pages; two mounted porters; the deceased's three favourite horses, led by two grooms to each; the horses were Vienna, Beauty, and Pegasus, each caparisoned in deep mourning. Beauty was the last horse Mr. Ducrow ever entered the ring with. (John Lump, his old and favourite horse, was to have been the fourth, but, as if prescient of his master's decease, he expired with old age a few days before, after a servitude . . . of 17 years. . . . Hearse, with six horses, richly caparisoned. Four postilions and ten pages . . .

Ducrow, styled variously as "King of Mimics," "Colossus of Equestrians," "Kean of the Arena," "Emperor of Horseflesh," and, in France, "Vestris à Cheval," was famous for many additions to the list of equestrian spectacles, pantomimes, and melodramas (including at least one melodramatic equestrian pantomime, *The Magic Tomb*), *poses plastiques, tableaux vivants,* and impersonations of antique statues introduced into his "scene" of "Raphael's Dream," to the accompaniment of William Callcott's music. To the end, he was devoted to extravagant and romantic spectacles and his last, *Charlemagne* (Drury Lane, 1841), was one of his most lavish. Most of the present-day acts of horsemanship which survive in the ring are descended from Ducrow. Fair-complexioned and handsome, only some five feet eight inches in height, he was slight, elegant, and shapely of figure, but he could contort his limbs as astonishingly as any posturemaker.

Ducrow was a complex and perhaps neurotic personality (which should not be wondered at, given the circumstances of his youth). James Winston remembered him as "a dutiful son, a kind brother, a tender husband, and a doting father," and also a favorite of children. But he was "passionate to excess" and rough of language, and his rages were terrifying. Many anecdotes of his courage survive, such as the occasion when he arose from his sickbed to chain a rampaging elephant. He was a clever draftsman and frequently suggested his ideas for scenery to his painters by sketching them on the boards of the stage.

Ducrow's annual dinners for his actors and friends, given in his theatre at Westminster Bridge at the height of his winter season, were celebrated for their jollity. He would always make a speech, interlaced with the rough talk from the horse ring which he affected, and ending invariably, according to James Winston, with the avowal "that of all the fine dishes that were put on Table give me a baked shoulder of mutton and taters."

Ducrow's first wife died on 15 June 1837 at Newcastle-on-Tyne. Winston's notes contain the following observation:

The first Mrs. Ducrow died 100 miles from Town but notwithstanding they were not the most affectionate couple he wanted [to]

MR DUCROW AS THE WINDSOR POST BOY.

Pub. by M & M. SKELT, 11, Swan S.t Minories, London.

Harvard Theatre Collection

ANDREW DUCROW, as the Windsor Post Boy
engraving by Lloyd, after Cocking

bring her body for interment to the Kensal Green Cemetery at no small expense and at the funeral exhibited some excentric conduct which can not be written down to the great annoyance of the officiating clergyman & the delay of the interment—and as Ducrow does nothing in the common way he has since expended upwards of £800 on a monument on which he has placed emblems of his Ladies—and very conspicuous engraved The Family Vault of Andrew Ducros Esq.

He married his second wife, Louisa Woolforth, another equestrienne, in June 1838. She survived him, along with (according to Winston's notations) his mother and his children—Peter, Andrew, Louisa,

and his adopted son "Master Chafe, commonly called *Le Petit Ducrow*." Which of those children, if any, were by his second wife is not known. But Mrs Ducrow was pregnant at the time of her husband's death.

Andrew Ducrow's will, which he signed on 10 November 1841, was proved at London on 17 February 1843. The will furnishes the second wife's first name, speaks of John, another son, and gives other details employed above. The *Gentleman's Magazine* estimated the worth of Andrew's properties to be over £60,000 at his death. The will speaks only of monies and securities and real and personal estate, worth unspecified, to be left in trust for his widow and children after certain bequests: £200 each to his widow Louisa, his sisters Margaret Ducrow and Mrs Louisa Wood, and to his sister Emily, Mrs W. D. Broadfoot, £150. To Joseph Hillier £300; interest on £100 for the maintenance of his apprentice Susan Beechdale until age 21, with the principal sum then to be given her; interest on £200 to maintain his apprentice Andrew Chaffe (the "Master Chafe" of Winston's note), with £100 of the principal to go to him at his majority; £200 to Andrew Byrne (son of the celebrated dancer Oscar Byrne); £150 to William David Broadfoot; and £25 to one Tissey Avery, perhaps a servant. His wife Louisa, George Searle "the elder of Stangate Lambeth boat builder," James Auberton "of the West of England Fire Office Number 20, New Bridge Street, Blackfriars," and Oscar Byrne "of Burton Crescent Mddx," are named as executors.

The will gives specific directions for the obsequies described above, down to the request that his favorite horses should attend. Ducrow sets aside £500 for funeral expenses and £800 (presumably the sum Winston alluded to) to enlarge the family's monument. His wife Louisa, as one of the executors, is rather insensitively directed to erect "two marble truncated or broken obelisks or columns to be placed by the side of the said monument," the one to the right to "be dedicated to" Andrew and that on the left to "his dear departed wife Margaret."

Andrew Ducrow was a favorite study for engravers of theatrical prints, particularly of the "penny plain and tuppence coloured" variety. All of the graphic representations of him listed below are of that series unless otherwise indicated:

1. An anonymous woodcut, arm over the back of a chair, holding a whip.

2. Playing violin for a dancing horse. Anonymous.

3. As the Brigand, standing on a horse, holding a gun. Pub. W. West, 1830.

4. As the Brigand, standing on a horse, sword and pistol. Anonymous.

5. As the Dying Brigand, standing beside horse, gun in r. hand. Pub. W. West, 1830.

6. As Charles II. Oval surrounded by views of equestrian feats. Engraved by C. Clutterbuck.

7. As the Chinese Enchanter standing on three prancing horses, torch in hand. R. Lloyd after W. Cocking.

8. As the Courier of Petersburgh. Engraved by R. Lloyd after W. Cocking.

9. As the Dying Moor, balanced on r. knee on a horse, holding a banner. R. Lloyd after W. Cocking.

10. As Fame, standing on one foot on a prancing horse, blowing a trumpet. R. Lloyd after W. Cocking.

11. As St George, standing, l. arm raised, a battleaxe in r. hand. A. Park. No. 67. Anonymous.

12. As the God of Fame, standing on a horse, blowing a trumpet. Pub. O. Hodgson. No. 63. New Series.

13. As the Greek Brother, seated on a prancing horse, sword upraised. Pub. W. West, 1829.

14. As Jack Junk, standing on a running horse, a gun in r. hand, a flag in l. Pub. M. & M. Skelt. No. 22.

15. Jack Junk, Brigand, Adonis, and Troubadour Page; four characters by Ducrow on one plate. Pub. Skelt.

16. As Omrah, standing beside a horse, elbow on the horse's neck. Pub. W. West, 1828.

17. Patrick Greek, Paul Pry, St George and the Dragon, and Rob Roy Macgregor; four characters by Ducrow on one plate. Pub. O. Hodgson, 1831. No 11.

18. Dancing a Persia Minuet with his favorite horse in *Charlemagne*, playing a stringed instrument. 1839.

19. As Rob Roy, standing on horseback holding sword and shield. 1828.

20. In his "Roman Defense"; in four different attitudes of Gladiators. From

drawings made for Napoleon Bonaparte. 1817.

21. As Sanbalat in *Timour the Tartar.* Engraved by Marks.

22. As Sanbalat, seated on a horse, scimitar in r. hand. Pub. M. Skelt. No 11.

23. As the Spanish Bull Fighter, hand at his throat, wearing a large hat. J. Rogers after T. Wageman. Plate to Oxberry's *Dramatic Biography,* 1827.

24. In *Vicissitudes of a Tar,* standing on a prancing horse, bundle on a stick. R. Lloyd after W. Cocking. No 6.

25. As the Wild Indian Hunter, standing, driving two horses in tandem. Drawn and engraved by T. Lane.

26. As the Wild Indian Hunter, standing, driving two horses in tandem. E. Lloyd after W. Cocking. No 12.

27. As the Wild Indian Hunter, standing on two horses driven in tandem, a spear upraised in r. hand, an arrow in l. Anonymous.

28. As the Windsor Post Boy, standing on two prancing horses, whip in hand. R. Lloyd after W. Cocking.

29. "Rôle de Zamba dans le Cheval du Diable." Standing, l. hand on hip. Artist A. Lacauchie, engraver unknown. Plate to *Galerie Dramatique,* pub. Martinet.

30. As Zelicos in *The Fall of Athens,* in armor and helmet. Anonymous.

31. As Zephyr, standing on one foot, holding up a child. Pub. R. Lloyd, 1830.

MR J. DUCROW,
THE CELEBRATED CLOWN TO THE CIRCLE
IN THE GROTESQUE SCENE, THE TEA AND SUPPER PARTY.
London, Pub. June 1.st 1831 by R.LLOYD, Dramatic Repository 40 Gibson S.t near the Coburg Theatre.

Harvard Theatre Collection

JOHN DUCROW, in "The Tea and Supper Party"
engraving by Lloyd

Same picture published by M. & M. Skelt.

32. In character, standing on a horse, holding Cupid on r. shoulder. *Villain* after Reverchon.

33. View of six feats of horsemanship at Astley's. Pub. J. Fairburn. Pl. 12.

34. View of six feats of horsemanship at Astley's. Pub. J. Fairburn. Pl. 13.

35. View of six feats of horsemanship at Astley's. Pub. J. Fairburn. Pl. 14.

36. A bust, sculptured by J. Howe, was exhibited at the Royal Academy in 1842.

37. With Miss Woolford (later his wife); as Flora and Zephyr on the double ropes. Pub. R. Lloyd, Lambeth.

Ducrow drew a self-portrait which was engraved by Badoureau for a print published in Paris about 1819. It was captioned "Foremost Equestrian of London" and depicts him in armor, brandishing sword and shield, standing on a galloping horse in his act *The Gladiators* which he produced at Franconi's Cirque Olympique.

Ducrow, John   *d. 1834, equestrian, clown.*

The exploits of John Ducrow, a great clown to the ring in his day in the British circus, have been overshadowed in history by the exploits of his famous brother, Andrew. Both were sons of the patriarchal strong man, acrobat, and manager Peter Ducrow (or Von Ducrow) whom Astley brought to England in 1793 and who fathered a numerous family.

The details of John Ducrow's life are unknown, but he was probably Andrew's elder brother and was, therefore, born in Belgium, perhaps around 1790. The scattered bills of the London circuses in the last decade of the century mention several Ducrows who cannot now be identified. By 11 May 1795 or earlier there was at Davis's Royal Circus in St George's Fields a "Dacrow" doing "GROUND and LOFTY TUMBLING" and a "Ducrow" in an "Equestrian Exercise" on the same bill. It is likely that the "Dacrow" was John; it cannot have been the two-year-old Andrew.

John assisted both his father in the ill-fated venture of the Royal Circus in 1813, and afterwards his brother Andrew at Astley's. John Ducrow died in 1834. He seems early to have performed ahorse, but later he won fame as a clown.

A "penny plain" print was published by R. Lloyd in 1831, in which Ducrow is shown in a grotesque scene, "The Tea and Supper Party," holding a cup and saucer in his hand. He dips his toe into the cup. A donkey and pony are seated at table, eating.

Ducrow, Peter   *d. 1814, strong man, acrobat, manager.*

Peter Ducrow (or Von Ducrow), the "Flemish Hercules," was born in Bruges, Belgium. He performed extensively on the Continent as a strong man before being hired by Philip Astley, who had established his *Cirque* in Paris in 1783. Jottings in James Winston's "Manager's Notebook," taken from one of Astley's letters dated 4 December 1786, establish Ducrow's presence in the company: "the Strong Man is gone to Brussells for his children I don't know when he will arrive" and "Mr Hercule is not arrived from Brussels . . ."

Ducrow came to London with his wife and several small children early in October 1793 and took lodgings at the Nag's Head, No 102, High Street, Southwark. Within a week of their arrival, on the tenth of October, Andrew, the most prominent of the performing Ducrows, was born. There is no foundation whatever for the assertions by William Rendle and Philip Norman in *The Inns of Old Southwark* (1888) that Andrew was born on 12 May 1796, his family "having arrived from Germany on the same day," and there seems none for the claims that "His father was a German clown and acrobat, patronized by Queen Charlotte, being a native of the small state of Mecklenburg-Strelitz, to which she belonged. His mother had been a ladies'-maid at Buckingham House."

Peter's métier was always demonstration of his phenomenal strength and agility of limb, and his milieu was invariably the world of fair booth and circus which supplemented and increasingly competed with "legitimate" theatre. Some bills of Philip Astley's amphitheatre describe his feats of strength, such as lifting from the ground and holding between his teeth a table with four of his children on it, or, lying on his back, supporting a platform with 18 fully equipped grenadiers.

According to the sketchy chronology of Willson Disher in *Greatest Show on Earth*, the elder Ducrow about 1798 or 1799 took a company to a "crazy amphitheatre in Bathwick Fields" in Bath and remained for some time. Exhibitions and evolutions, or "Herculean Equilibriums" there and elsewhere were performed by Peter Ducrow and his troupe, which probably included his sons Andrew and John and perhaps others of his children.

By (at latest) 11 May 1795 there was at Davis's Royal Circus in St George's Fields a "Dacrow" doing "GROUND and LOFTY TUMBLING" and a "Ducrow" in an "Equestrian Exercise" on the same bill. The "Dacrow" may have been Peter, but the equestrian was probably one of his sons, likely John, but certainly not the two-year-old Andrew.

In 1813 Peter Ducrow took a lease of the Royal Circus, ran the hippodrama there for a few months and then went into bankruptcy. He died in 1814. There was a Miss Ducrow performing as an equestrienne early in the nineteenth century. An anonymous "penny plain" engraving of her as "the Spanish Girl," standing on a racing horse, was published by Dyer in Bath (c. 1830?). She was very likely a granddaughter of Peter Ducrow.

Duddy, John ₍*fl. 1794*₎, *singer.*

Doane's *Musical Directory* of 1794 listed John Duddy, of Lower Street, Islington, as a basso who sang in performances given by the Choral Fund.

Duddy, Thomas ₍*fl. 1794*₎, *instrumentalist.*

Doane's *Musical Directory* of 1794 listed Thomas Duddy of Lower Street, Islington, as a bassoonist, violoncellist, and clarinettist who participated in performances given by the Choral Fund.

Dudley, Mr ₍*fl. 1794*₎, *singer.*

Doane's *Musical Directory* of 1794 listed Mr Dudley, a tenor; J. Dudley, a bass; and S. Dudley, an alto, all from Derby. They participated at some date unspecified in the Handel performances at Westminster Abbey.

Dudley, Mr ₍*fl. 1800–1812*₎, *house servant.*

Mr Dudley was a doorkeeper or ticket taker — the account books are unclear — at Drury Lane from as early as 14 June 1800 when his benefit tickets were accepted. He was with the company in 1811–12 when it played at the Lyceum Theatre, and it is probable that he also served during the intervening years.

Dudley, Miss ₍*fl. 1778–1783*₎, *actress, dancer.*

Miss Dudley made her first appearance on any stage on 28 December 1778 at the Haymarket Theatre playing an unnamed part in *The Macaroni Adventurers* and Kissinda in *The Covent Garden Tragedy*. On 15 March 1779 she reappeared at the same house as Kitty in *The Humours of Oxford* and Columbine in an entertainment called *Pantomimical Scenes*. On 18 October 1779 she was in *The Touchstone of Invention* and played Isabinda in *The Busy Body*; on 3 January 1780 she acted Ruelle in *The Modish Wife* and Myra in *Wit's Last Stake*; and on 28 March 1780 she was Victoria in *The Humours of Oxford* and Lady Bab in *High Life Below Stairs*. A Haymarket bill for 17 September 1783 indicated that Miss Dudley acted principal characters in *Cheapside* and *A New Way to Keep a Wife at Home*, but the roles were not named, and despite all these efforts to make her mark in London, Miss Dudley was not heard from again.

Dudley, J. (*fl. 1794*), *singer. See* **DUDLEY, MR** (*fl. 1794*).

Dudley, S. (*fl. 1794*), *singer. See* **DUDLEY, MR** (*fl. 1794*).

Duel, Mr (*fl. 1724–1727*), *house servant.*

Mr Duel worked in the office at Lincoln's Inn Fields at £1 1s. weekly from at least September 1724 through the 1726–27 season, according to the playhouse account books.

Dufainanas, Miss (*fl. 1799*), *house servant?*

A Miss Dufainanas—if the transcription of her name is correct—was twice noted in the Drury Lane account books in 1799: on 7 and again on 23 January she was put down for 10s. What her function was in the playhouse was not noted; she may have been one of the house servants.

Duffel. *See* **DUFFIELD.**

Duffey, Peter (*fl. 1768–1805*), *singer, actor.*

The Secret History of the Green Rooms (1790) claimed that Peter Duffey had been a hatter in Dublin and that he had been talked into pursuing a stage career by friends who heard his fine singing voice. He performed at Kilkenny as early as 1 February 1768, played at Belfast and Kilkenny in 1770, and on 9 October 1771 is known to have acted Polybius in *Love and Despair* in Waterford. In 1778 Duffey acted at Kilkenny once more, and the following year he joined the opera company at the Capel Street Theatre in Dublin, then managed by Giordani and Leoni, making his first appearance in *The Enchanted Island.* He made his Smock Alley debut on 24 October 1785 and in 1786 and 1787 was seen at Waterford and Cork. He played at Cork again in 1788 and performed at the Crow Street Theatre in Dublin in 1788–

89. On 8 March 1789 he was expelled from the Irish Musical Fund, having been a member since 1 April 1787.

On 23 September 1789 Duffey played Alphonso in *The Castle of Andalusia* at Covent Garden. The *European Magazine* found his voice harmonious, various, and powerful but thought that as an actor he lacked ease and clarity in his speech. His figure and features, the critic said, were neither very excellent nor exceptionable. Despite this lukewarm reception, Duffey went on during the 1789–90 season at Covent Garden (at £4 weekly) to play Dermot in *The Poor Soldier*, Saib in *Love and War*, Allen o'Dale in *Robin Hood*, Antonio in *The Duenna*, Sir Charles Manly in *The Lady of the Moon*, Mervin in *The Maid of the Mill*, a Witch in *Harlequin's Chaplet*, and Young Meadows in *Love in a Village*. He also sang in *Macbeth, Romeo and Juliet, The Way of the World, The Soldier's Festival, The Widow of Malabar,* and *All for Love*. On 3 June 1790 he shared a benefit with Cox which grossed £315 10s. 6d. His address was given in the benefit bill as No 115, St Martin's Lane. Duffey was discharged from Covent Garden at the end of the 1789–90 season to make room for Incledon.

Duffey made his first appearance at Hull on 25 January 1791 playing Lionel in *Lionel and Clarissa*, and during 1791 he also appeared at Hull, at York, and at Vauxhall Gardens in London. By 1792 he was back in Dublin. Duffey acted at Carrick-on-Suir in October 1795. He is said to have left the stage and to have returned to a trade different from his original one, and in 1805 he was reported recently married.

Duffield, Caesar (*fl. 1669–1707*), *violinist.*

Caesar Duffield the City wait was probably the same person as the violinist active at court in the 1670s. His name was variously spelled Duffil and Duffel. On 28 June 1669 he was one of five musicians ordered arrested for "teaching, practising and executing music in companies or otherwise" without a license from the Marshall and Corporation of Music. He was in another scrape with the authorities on 15 April 1673 when he and other musicians playing at the "Nursery" for young actors operated by the patent theatres were ordered apprehended for some misdemeanor, but on the following 19 April he was discharged from custody. By 9 November 1674 he was playing in the King's Musick, for on that date he and others were to be paid for attending Charles II at Newmarket from 22 September to 12 October of that year. He was one of the added violins in the band when the court masque *Calisto* was played on 15 February 1675. He was still active after the turn of the century, for on 7 February Duffield and Walter Cole were paid £5 for music by the Middle Temple, and on 1 August 1707 at the Old Wells in Hampstead he held a musical concert.

Duffield, John [*fl.* 1720–1722], dancer.

Possibly John Duffield the dancer in the early 1720s was the son Walter and Margaret Duffield baptized at St Bride, Fleet Street, on 19 August 1686, but the name is not unusual enough to be certain. Duffield was Scaramouch in *The Cheats* (*The Tavern Bilkers*) on 23 January 1720 at Lincoln's Inn Fields and danced with *The Double Dealer* on 11 May. The following season at the same house he reappeared in his Scaramouch role, danced entr'acte turns occasionally, and added Scaramouch in *The Jealous Doctor* to his limited line. A British Museum manuscript dated 1722 provides us with his Christian name.

Duffour, Mr [*fl.* 1777–1797], property man?

There are two entries, 20 years apart, concerning Mr Duffour, in the Drury Lane account books. On 19 June 1777 he was paid £6 4s. 6d. for carving heads; this would suggest that he was a property man, though he may well have been a tradesman contracted for the work. On 28 October 1797 his name appeared in the accounts again: "7 days not on pay list 7/0/0." The implication here is that he was, or had been, a salaried employee.

Duffy. *See* DUFFEY.

Dufour, Mr [*fl.* 1760–1763], dancer.

On 22 September 1760 Mr Dufour was receiving 5s. daily at Covent Garden as a minor dancer. His name was infrequently cited in the bills in 1760–61, 1761–62, and 1762–63, but we know that he danced a Pandour in the comic ballet *The Hungarian Gambols* on 9 March 1761, *The Pierrots* with Hussey on 13 May 1762, and a Daemon in *The Rape of Proserpine* on 26 January 1763.

Dufour, Camilla, later Mrs Jacob Henry Sarratt [*fl.* 1796–1809], singer, actress.

The *Oracle* of 11 February 1796 tells us that Camilla Dufour's first appearance in public had been in a recent concert at the King's Theatre. She sang in music rooms and in Salomon's concerts and studied under Mrs Crouch and Michael Kelly prior to her appearance on 19 October 1797 at Drury Lane in her first speaking part, Adela in *The Haunted Tower*. The *Monthly Mirror* gave her a fearful drubbing:

Miss Dufour, who has obtained considerable credit at the concert rooms &c. made her appearance in Adela, Storace's introductory character. This lady has no talents for the stage. As a singer she has taste and science, but that is not enough for a first opera woman, in such a theatre as Drury Lane. It has unfortunately been too much admitted, that a singer need not be an actress; and hence it is we have had so many insipid females conveyed from the orchestra to the stage, who never learnt to read any thing beyond the ti-tum-ti of a Vauxhall ballad; and, as far as regards action, know only that the right hand must be carried to the left breast, and the chest tortured so as to imitate the throbbings and heavings of some admired soparano. Miss Dufour is one of the ladies thus accomplished. Her figure is short and thick—"so was Storace's" her friends will say; but they can carry the comparison no further. She has ten pounds a week, however, according to report, and if her engagement is for any long period, she may congratulate herself on her good fortune, notwithstanding we thus set her down as a *vox et praeterea nihil*.

Camilla's salary seems not to have been the extravagant £10 rumored, but rather £6, part of which went to her teachers, if they had the courage to accept it.

Miss Dufour was not given many more important assignments at Drury Lane, though she stayed there for the rest of the 1797–98 season and returned the following season. On 9 December 1797 she was Amphitrite in the masque *Neptune and Amphitrite* in Act I of *The Tempest*; on 23 February 1798 she sang in the *Messiah*; in March she was in the oratorio concerts; and the following season, on 24 May 1799, she appeared in *Pizarro*.

In the early years of the nineteenth century she seems to have appeared at the Haymarket Theatre, and she is reported to have published a novel, *Aurora* in 1803 — though the new *Cambridge Bibliography of English Literature* does not list it. By that year she had married Jacob Henry Sarratt (who died on 6 November 1819). As Mrs Sarratt she sang Polly Peachum to Elliston's Macheath in *The Beggar's Opera* at the Royal Circus on 17 July 1809. The last notice of her was in the same role there on the following 18 September.

Dugay, Mons ₁*fl.* 1741–1748₁, *dancer, slackrope dancer.*

Monsieur Dugay (or Duge—probably an error for Dugé) offered a new comic dance at Goodman's Fields on 7 October 1741 for his first appearance at that house. His previous activity is not known; at Goodman's Fields he danced in a *Grand Ballet* on 9 October but was not involved in any other new dances receiving mention in the bills. *The London Stage* lists Dugay as a member of both Goodman's Fields and Covent Garden this season, but the Covent Garden calendar reveals no activity for him there. On 15 and 16 April 1745 Dugay turned up at Goodman's Fields again, this time offering "several new exercises of Rope Dancing and Tumbling" with Vangable and others. His last notice on record was in 1748 when he appeared at the New Wells, Goodman's Fields, playing the Doctor in *Harlequin Collector* and giving "several new performances on the Slack Rope" with Granier and his troupe.

Dugdale, Mr ₁*fl.* 1779₁, *actor.*

Mr Dugdale was in the cast of *The Touchstone of Invention* and acted Whisper in *The Busy Body* on 18 October 1779 at the Haymarket Theatre.

Duge. *See* DUGAY.

Dugermay. *See* DUQUESNEY.

Dugrande, ₁Mons₁ ₁*fl.* 1743₁, *dancer.*

A dancer named Dugrande appeared as the Petit Maître in *Perseus and Andromeda* at Covent Garden on 8 January 1743.

Duill, Mrs John Lewis, Catherine Mary, née Satchell, later Mrs John Taylor the first *d.* 1789, *actress.*

On 13 May 1786 at Covent Garden Mrs John Lewis Duill, billed as "A Young Lady," made her first and last appearance on stage as Evandra in *Timon of Athens*. She had been born Catherine Mary Satchell. On 4 January 1780 she had married John Lewis Duill of the Inner Temple at St George, Hanover Square. She was a minor at the time and married with the consent of her father, John Satchell. On 27 March 1788 at St James, Piccadilly, she was married a second time, to the poet John Taylor. Taylor wrote in his *Records of My Life* (1832), "I married one of [Mrs Stephen Kemble's] sisters. . . . I had the misery of losing her, about nine months after our union." She died in January 1789.

Dujoncel, Mons ιfl. 1749–1762?ι, *dancer.*

Monsieur Dujoncel was a dancer in Monnet's troupe of French comedians who played at the Haymarket Theatre in the fall of 1749. Dujoncel was in *Les Amans réunis* at the opening performance on 14 November, but no further notice of him was taken in the bills. The troupe had much difficulty. Anti-Gallic sentiment plus local political battles upset the opening performance, and the rest of the troupe's engagement was marred from time to time. Monnet lost money on the venture, and though some of the actors were not given their full pay, Dujoncel received all of the £36 15s. he had contracted for.

Perhaps the dancer was the Monsieur du Poncel who contracted with Noverre's company at Stuttgart on 5 May 1762 to dance for three years at a salary of 800 florins plus 120 florins for shoes.

"Duke." *See* WATSON, MARMADUKE.

Duke, Mr. *See* DYKE, MR ιfl. c. 1661–1662ι.

Dukes, N. ιfl. 1730–1755ι, *dancer.*

Mr Dukes (or Duke) was first mentioned in playbills on 28 April 1730 when at Goodman's Fields he danced the title role in *Harlequin Turn'd Dancing-Master.* On 28 May he was Pantalon in *The Fashionable Lady*, and on 27 July he took the role of Harlequin in that work. He reverted to Pantalon on 11 November 1730. He appeared again on 25 October 1731 as a dancer at Goodman's Fields and then was

not heard of again until the 1733–34 season, when he danced with the Covent Garden company. There he played an Infernal in *Perseus and Andromeda*, a Fawn in *The Necromancer*, a Zephyr in *The Nuptial Masque*, and a Bridal Swain in *Apollo and Daphne.* He also participated in such entr'acte dances as *Pygmalion*, and, with Miss Baston for his shared benefit on 8 May 1734, *Les Amants constants* in the characters of a highlander and his lass. He stayed at Covent Garden for the following season, again playing small parts in pantomimes and joining other dancers in such specialty turns as *Grecian Sailors* or *The Faithful Shepherd.* He and Delagarde performed a popular *Pierrots* dance a number of times, and he joined with Mrs Ogden in *The Flanderkins* in May 1735 with great success.

For the 1735–36 and 1736–37 seasons Dukes danced at Drury Lane, his first notice there being on 22 October 1735 when he danced in *Le Badinage de Provence.* He took small parts in pantomimes on occasion, such as a Peasant Man in *The Harlot's Progress*, Colin in *Harlequin Restored*, a Moor in *The Fall of Phaeton*, and a Bridesman in *Poor Pierrot Married.* He also danced a Dutchman in an entr'acte called *The Rover*, performed a minuet and *The Medley of Jokes* with Mrs Bullock (at a special benefit allowed him at Goodman's Fields), participated in a *Grand Polonese Ballet*, and danced in *The Tempest.*

Not until 20 April 1742 did Dukes's name appear again in London bills; on that date he received a solo benefit at Goodman's Fields, tickets for which could be had of him at his lodgings near The Three Tuns, Spital Fields. He is not known to have performed during the season. On 3 March 1743 at Lincoln's Inn Fields he shared a benefit with Mrs Freeman and danced a minuet and louvre with her, and at May Fair on 3 May 1744 he played Gonzales in the droll *The Captive Prince* at Hallam's booth. At the Haymarket on the following 10 May he received an individual benefit, but he seems not to have performed. It is likely that during these years he was spending much of his time teaching rather than performing.

At some point Dukes opened an academy "for the purpose of teaching grown Gentlemen to dance." This was ridiculed about 1754–55 in *The Connoisseur* as "Geometry made easy, and adapted to the meanest Capacity, By N. Dukes, Dancing-Master to Grown Gentlemen."

Dulane. *See* DELANE.

Dulin, [Mons] [*fl.* 1767], *dancer.*

A dancer named Dulin was in Samuel Foote's company that played 58 times at the Haymarket Theatre during the summer of 1767.

Dulisse, Mme [*fl.* 1757–1758], *dancer.*

On 2 September 1757 Madame Dulisse danced with Joly in a *Medley Concert* produced by Theophilus Cibber and (judging by the personnel in the program) Christopher Smart. Among other performers were "Mynheer von Poop-Poop Broomstickado," a bassoonist hiding under one of the pseudonyms affected by Smart's company, but Madame Dulisse was presumably our dancer's real name. A Mlle Dulisse, presumably her daughter, also danced in some of these late summer entertainments. Madame Dulisse appeared with Froment in a minuet on 8 September and a new *Scots Dance* on 14 September. She was in *Le Carneval de Venice* on 26 December and danced again with Froment on 27 January 1758.

She was at Covent Garden for at least the first few months of the 1758–59 season and she danced in *The Threshers* on 14 October 1758 and played a Bacchant in the pantomime ballet *The Feast of Bacchus* on 16 November.

Dulisse, Mlle [*fl.* 1757–1759], *dancer.*

As part of Theophilus Cibber's *Medley Concert*, Mlle Dulisse (or Dulies) danced *Bohemian Peasants* with Joly at the Haymarket Theatre on 1 July 1757. At her benefit on 22 August, shared with her dancing partner, she played Colombine in *Harlequin Maggot*. She joined with Joly again on 31 August in *Italian Peasants*.

In 1757–58 she performed occasionally at the Haymarket, sometimes paired off with Joly and Settree in such dances as *The Drunken Peasant* and *The Irish Landlord and Landlady*. On 25 January 1758 she was the Statue in *Pigmalion* at Froment's benefit, and at her own benefit on 18 May she danced with Joly and offered a solo *Fingalian Dance*.

On 16 May 1759 she was granted a shared benefit with two others at Covent Garden, though there are no records of her having performed there; she may have been a minor member of the group of dancers at the theatre who never received notice in the bills. Mlle Dulisse was presumably the daughter of the Mme Dulisse active in London about the same time.

Dulondel, Mons [*fl.* 1720], *actor.*

Monsieur Dulondel played young lovers in De Grimberque's troupe when it appeared at the King's Theatre in the Haymarket from 5 March to 21 June 1720. He shared a benefit with two others on 20 June.

Dumai, D. [*fl.* 1756–1783], *dancer.*

The first mention of D. Dumai (or Dumay) in the bills was on 11 May 1756 when he performed a new *Harlequin* dance at Covent Garden. His only other citation that year was on 18 May when he was in *Les Savoyards*. Perhaps he was in the company in 1756–57, though the bills made no mention of him. He was there from 1757–58 through 1782–83, however, each season receiving occasional citations in the bills and each spring selling benefit tickets. His salary was 5s. daily in 1767–68, and he was still paid the same amount at the end of his long period of service. His earnings at benefit time usually were between £50 and £75, but in the 1760s he often had to give a portion back to the management to help cover an overall deficit.

Dumai's dancing must not have been distinguished, for only occasionally was he singled out. He performed in *Macbeth, The Threshers* (a dance), *The Prophetess, The Fair, Comus, Harlequin Doctor Faustus, Rural Love* (a dance), and *The Festival of the Black Prince* (a ballet). He also appeared in cotillions, gavottes, and untitled group dances. From time to time he was assigned characters, such as a Satyr in *The Feast of Bacchus*, a Daemon in *The Rape of Proserpine*, a Hussar in *The Hungarian Gambols*, an Infernal in *Perseus and Andromeda*, Hercules (Brighella) in *The Royal Chace*, and a Farmer in *Harlequin's Jubilee*. Beginning in 1763–64 he was periodically seen in minuets, his partners being Miss Macklin, Miss Twist, Mrs Heard, or his own unidentified scholars. Dumai's last named part was Hercules in *The Royal Chace* in April and May 1783. After the 1782–83 season he seems to have retired.

Dumeney, Mrs ₁*fl. 1709–1717?*₁, *actress.*

Mrs Dumeney played Flora in Anthony Aston's *The Coy Shepherdess* in Dublin about 1709 and continued active there until about 1716. Though proof is lacking, she may have been part of Aston's troupe performing in London in 1717.

Dumfie. *See* **DUMPHEY.**

Dumirail, Mons ₁*fl. 1674–1716*₁, *dancer.*

A "Mr D'muraile" was one of a group of French dancers who appeared in the production of *Ariadne* at Drury Lane on 30 March 1674. They apparently stayed on at the playhouse for the rest of the season, but there was a dispute over their wages. The

actor John Lacy had agreed with the court musician Louis Grabu that the dancers would be paid 10s. daily, but Thomas Killigrew, Charles Hart, and Lacy made an agreement with them on 2 May 1674 for 5s. daily even when they did not dance. The Lord Chamberlain settled the matter on 6 May by ordering the dancers to attend Killigrew at the theatre and observe his commands per agreement. The following 15 February 1675 saw the dancers participating in the court masque *Calisto*.

It was perhaps D'muraile who was the Monsieur Dumirail who appeared with his son at Hickford's music room on 12 April 1716. A ball and masquerade were presented, plus "several entertainments of dancing performed by Mr. Dumirail and his son, who is lately come from Paris, and others. This being the last time of their appearing in Publick before their return to Paris." During his stay Dumirail took on as one of his scholars Glover, who was to become popular in later years.

The dancer Dumirail was possibly related to the actor of that name who made his debut in Paris in 1712, left the stage in 1717, reappeared as Mitridate on 21 March 1724, and retired on 11 January 1730. That Dumirail was a *pensionnaire* of the Comédie Française in January 1752, receiving 1000 livres.

Dumirail fils ₁*fl. 1716*₁, *dancer. See* **DUMIRAIL, MONS.**

Dumont, Mons ₁*fl. 1734–1735*₁, *scenekeeper.*

Monsieur Dumont was one of the scenekeepers in the company of French comedians managed by Francisque Moylin. They played at the Haymarket and Goodman's Fields theatres from 26 October 1734 to 4 June 1735.

Dumont, Mons ₁*fl. 1737–1750*₁, *dancer.*

Monsieur Dumont, billed as lately arrived from Paris, performed *Dancing Punch* at the Smock Alley Theatre in Dublin on 17 May 1737. Possibly his wife came over with him from France, but she was not mentioned in the bills until a year later when the couple danced at Smock Alley on 8 May 1738. On 4 December 1740 they danced at the Aungier Street Theatre in Dublin. The bills give no indication that the pair returned to France between the performances we know of; they may well have performed regularly in Dublin over the years. In 1741–42 Monsieur Dumont was in London, dancing at Drury Lane such entr'acte turns as a *Sailor's Dance* with Mrs Walter, *Le Jardiniers suédois*, and *Les Masons* and *Les Saboties*. He appeared also in *Comus*, was a Triton in *Harlequin Shipwrecked*, and danced a Pilgrim in *A Voyage to the Island of Citherea*. He danced with Hendrick Kernan's troupe at Sadler's Wells on 3 July 1742 and returned to Covent Garden in 1742–43 to appear in such specialty dances as *La Villageoise*, *Les Bourgeoise*, and *The Peasants* and to dance a Demon, Gardener, and Fire in *The Rape of Proserpine*, an Infernal in *Perseus and Andromeda*, and Pluto (Punch) in *The Royal Chace*.

Madame Dumont seems not to have appeared in London during these seasons. She was with Thomas Este's troupe at Taylor's Hall in Edinburgh sometime between December 1741 and February 1745, but Monsieur Dumont was apparently not with her. She was in the Covent Garden company in 1746–47, though no roles are known for her; again her husband seems not to have been with her. In 1747–48 she was billed as dancing a Follower in *Apollo and Daphne* and dancing a minuet and louvre with Froment at Covent Garden, while Monsieur Dumont performed again at Smock Alley. Madame Dumont repeated her pantomime role at Covent Garden in late October 1748, after which time her name disappeared from the bills. A year later it was her husband's turn at Covent

Garden; he played an Infernal in *Perseus and Andromeda* in late November 1749 and repeated in late October 1750, after which his name also dropped from sight.

It seems unlikely that this couple could have been part of the "Dumont and family" who danced at the Mill Gate Theatre in Belfast about October 1771, but perhaps they were.

Dumont, Mme (*fl.* 1724–1725), *actress*.

Madame Dumont was the colombine in the Italian troupe which played in London from 17 December 1724 to 13 May 1725 at the Haymarket Theatre. On 29 March 1725 she split a benefit with Monsieur Phillipe, the scaramouch.

Dumont, Mme (*fl.* 1738–1748), *dancer*. See DUMONT, MONS (*fl.* 1737–1750).

Dumont, Mrs (*fl.* 1799–1800), *singer*.

Mrs Dumont was a minor singer at Bristol in 1799 and apparently appeared at Drury Lane in London sometime in 1799–1800. She made her first appearance at the Birmingham theatre on 4 June 1800, billed as from Drury Lane.

Dumont, Mlle (*fl.* 1748), *dancer*.

On 28 April 1748 at Covent Garden Mademoiselle Dumont was the Statue in the pantomime dance *Pigmalion*.

Dumont, Mlle (*fl.* 1781), *dancer*.

Mademoiselle Dumont was in a pastoral dance and *Les Amans réunis* on 17 November 1781 at the King's Theatre in the Haymarket.

Dumorier, Mr (*fl.* 1792–1793), *scene painter?*

The Covent Garden account books for 1792–93 show several payments to Mr Dumorier (or Doumorier) spaced out over the season. On the fifth night he was paid £10, on the fifty-eighth £12 6s., on the eighty-fifth £10 4s., and on the one hundred thirty-fifth £7 7s. The payments presumably covered painting he had done at the theatre.

Du Moulins. *See* DESMOULINS.

Du Mouriez. *See* DU PÉRIER.

Dumphey, Mrs *d. 1782, actress.*
The Drury Lane account books show that Mrs Dumphey (or Dumfie, Dumfy) was an actress at that theatre in 1774–75 and 1776–77 at a salary of £1 weekly. She subscribed 10s. 6d. to the retirement fund at the theatre in 1775. Winston noted that she died in September 1782.

Dunant, Mr (*fl. 1799*), *actor.*
Mr Dunant acted an Officer in *Douglas* and Fitzroy in *The Poor Soldier* at the Old Crown Inn, Highgate, on 15 May 1799. He probably performed on other dates at the Inn, but the bills have been lost.

Dunbar, Mr *d. c. 1762, boxkeeper.*
Mr Dunbar was a boxkeeper at Drury Lane from 1743–44 through 1760–61. Every spring he received shared benefits with two or three other employees (occasionally more), the average total income being about £175 before house charges. Dunbar died about 1762. His last benefit was on 14 May 1761; on 21 May 1762 his widow shared a benefit with three others.

Dunbridge. *See* DURBRIDGE.

Duncalfe, Henry (*fl. 1732–1739*), *musician.*
Henry Duncalfe held a benefit concert at the George and Vulture Tavern, Cornhill, on 10 February 1732 and became one of the original subscribers to the Royal Society of Musicians on 28 August 1739.

Duncan, Timothy *d. 1801, actor.*
Timothy Duncan's earliest theatrical notice was in 1766 when he acted at the Smock Alley Theatre in Dublin. He performed in Limerick in 1768 and appeared at the Capel Street Theatre in Dublin, perhaps about 1770–71. He left Ireland on 25 March 1771 and about 1772 was in Whitely's company at Newcastle. He was in Austin's troupe at Chester in the fall of 1778 and on 3 October married an actress in the company, Miss Legg (his second wife?), at the Chester Cathedral. The marriage was reported in the *Morning Post*, but there is no record of it in the Cathedral books, nor at St John's or Holy Trinity.

Duncan was acting in Chester again from July to October 1779, and both he and his wife appeared there in October and November 1780. Their daughter Maria Rebecca was born at Liverpool about 1780. From March through July 1784 the Duncans performed at Belfast. On 3 March when Timothy played Major O'Flaherty in *The West Indian* at the Rosemary Lane Theatre he elicited a note of praise from the *Belfast Mercury*: "It is usual to represent the Major as a vulgar brogueineering Irishman; but Duncan with true propriety, tho' he still retained the Irish characteristics in his terminations, showed O'Flaherty the man of travel, of Mars, of the world." For his wife's benefit on 23 June 1784 Timothy wrote a song, "The Gift of the Gods; or, Establishment of Irish Freedom."

The Duncans were at Edinburgh in 1784–85, and on 17 September 1788 they made their first London appearances, hailed as from Chester, he in his proven part of the Major and she as Charlotte Rusport in *The West Indian*. The *European Magazine* found them both "well acquainted with the business of the theatre" but felt that neither exhibited proofs of great excellence. *The West Indian* was not repeated and the pair left London.

On 5 November 1788 the Duncans made their first appearances at the Crow

Street Theatre, billed as from Covent Garden. Dublin became Timothy's home base for the ensuing nine years, but he also appeared at Cork in September and Waterford in October 1789, at Drogheda in the autumn of 1791, at Derry in December 1795, and at Belfast in the first half of 1796. Mrs Duncan seems to have confined herself to appearances in Dublin. The Duncans appeared at York early in 1797, billed as from Dublin, and with their daughter acted at Leeds in June of that year.

Perhaps the Mr Duncan who acted one of the two Mutineers in *Cato* at the Haymarket Theatre in London, for one performance only (on 5 December 1797) was Timothy; in the cast was Bellamy from York, and Timothy was at York when the season began there in January 1798. The Duncans played at York in 1798 and 1799, and Timothy was there again in 1800. Possibly Timothy was the dancer named Duncan who was at Covent Garden in 1800–1801, but that seems unlikely. Timothy Duncan died in Edinburgh in February 1801.

Duncan, Mrs Timothy, née Legg [fl. 1778–1801], *actress.*

The Miss Legg who married Timothy Duncan on 3 October 1778 at Chester Cathedral may have been the daughter of Jonathan and Mary Legg. Jonathan had acted in London from 1755 until his death in 1778. Miss Legg played at Chester from August to November 1778. Duncan was one of the actors in the troupe. The Duncans were at Chester again in October and November 1780, at Belfast from March through July 1784, and at Edinburgh in 1784–85. Their daughter Maria Rebecca, born about 1780 in Liverpool, made her debut in Newcastle as the Child in *Isabella* on 13 March 1786.

On 17 September 1788 at Covent Garden Mrs Duncan made her first London appearance playing Charlotte Rusport in *The West Indian*, but the play was not repeated and Mrs Duncan seems not to have performed in London again. She made her Crow Street, Dublin, debut on 5 November 1788 and acted in Dublin again in 1791–92 and 1794–95. With her husband she acted at Leeds in June 1797 and at York from 1797 through 1799. In 1801 she was in Liverpool and Edinburgh, but after her husband died in Edinburgh in February 1801 Mrs Duncan seems to have left the stage.

The Duncans' daughter, Maria Rebecca, after some performing in the provinces, made her London debut in 1804, married James Davison in 1812, had a considerable acting career as Mrs Davison, and died in 1858.

Duncomb, Mr [fl. 1784–1794], *singer.*

Mr Duncomb, a basso, sang in the Handel Memorial Concerts at Westminster Abbey and the Pantheon on 26, 27, and 29 May and 3 and 5 June 1784; and in 1794, according to Doane's *Musical Directory*, he had recently sung in some Handelian performances at the Abbey. He may well have been, or been related to, the Duncomb who was at that period organist of St Dunstan's Church, Kensington, according also to Doane.

Duncombe, John [fl. 1710–1716], *singer.*

The *Calendar of Treasury Books* shows a payment of £40 to John Duncombe and Thomas Gethyn, former children of the Chapel Royal whose voices had changed. They were paid for the period 25 December 1715 to 25 December 1716, so their service as boy singers probably ran from about 1710 to 1715.

Dunembray. *See* DEMAIMBRAY.

Dunn, [John? fl. 1745–1762?], *violinist, composer?*

A Mr Dunn was paid 10s. for playing violin in a performance of the *Messiah* given at the Foundling Hospital in May 1754. A number of songs published between 1745 and 1762 by a John Dunn are listed in the British Museum *Catalogue of Printed Music*, but there is no indication that he was the violinist.

Dunn, William Nathaniel 1782–1855, *treasurer*.

Born in 1782, William Nathaniel Dunn became a clerk at the Drury Lane Theatre at least as early as 13 January 1798 when the accounts there first cited him. His starting salary was apparently £1 5s. weekly, but by the 1799–1800 season he was raised to £1 10s. and by the fall of 1800 he was being paid £2. In 1807–8 he was up to £5 weekly and was called the chief clerk, and by 1812–13 he was serving as deputy treasurer at £6. He was still working at the theatre in 1816–17. On 15 March 1852 Dunn, describing himself as of Norwood, Surrey, but formerly of Charlotte Street, Bedford Square, London, made his will, leaving everything to his wife Rosa. He died at Norwood on 3 March 1855 at the age of 73, and his widow proved his will on 25 April.

The Garrick Club has a painting of Dunn by an anonymous artist.

Dunning. *See also* DOWNING.

Dunning, Mr [fl. 1747–1748], *actor*.

Mr Dunning played Bajazet in *Tamerlane* at the Cole Hole in Red Lion Street on 27 January 1747 with a group of other gentlemen performing "for their Diversion." On 29 February 1748 he made his debut as a professional at the Haymarket Theatre playing Chamont in *The Orphan* for his shared benefit with Mrs Rowley. He does not seem to have remained in the profession.

Dunnraile. *See* DUMIRAIL.

Dunoyer. *See* DENOYER.

Dunstall, Henrietta. *See* HUNT, MRS WILLIAM.

Dunstall, John 1717–1778, *actor, singer*.

John Dunstall was born on 30 January 1717. His first London season on record was 1740–41 when he played at Goodman's Fields, but his schedule was so heavy that he must have been working professionally for some time. His first notice was on 20 October 1740 when he played Driver in *Oroonoko*.

Since his roles during the 1740–41 season were typical of those he essayed during the rest of his life, and include many which he acted year after year, a full listing of them may be useful. The starred roles Dunstall was still performing in the 1770s: *Driver in *Oroonoko*, Bluff in *The Old Bachelor*, *Bullock in *The Recruiting Officer*, the Duke in *Othello*, *Tradelove in *A Bold Stroke for a Wife*, Polidorus in *Aesop*, *Dominic in *The Spanish Fryar*, Sir Sampson in *Love for Love*, Butler in *The Drummer*, *Moody in *The Provok'd Husband*, Mirvan in *Tamerlane*, the Doctor in *The Chymical Counterfeits*, the Host in *The Merry Wives of Windsor*, *Antonio in *Love Makes a Man*, Old Mirabel in *The Inconstant*, Blister in *The Virgin Unmask'd*, Obadiah in *The Committee*, Bardolph in *1 Henry IV*, Old Wilful in *The Double Gallant*, the second Gravedigger in *Hamlet*, Woodcock in *Tunbridge Walks*, *Jobson in *The Devil to Pay*, Sir Tunbelly in *The Relapse*, the second Witch in *Macbeth*, Club in *Love and a Bottle*, the Keeper in *The Imprisonment of Harlequin*, the Clown in *The Winter's Tale*, *Boniface in *The Stratagem*, Mat in *The Beggar's Opera*, Pedro in *The Wonder*, the Lord Mayor in *Richard III*, Simon in *The Anatomist*, Albanact in *King Arthur*, a Watchman and a Countryman in *Harlequin Student*, the Steward in *All's Well that Ends Well*, James in *The Miser*, Phaeax in *Timon of Athens*, and Charon and Aesop in *Lethe*.

Despite Dunstall's busy schedule in 1740–41, the Goodman's Fields management was apparently not paying him much, and at benefit time he was merely one of several whose benefit tickets were accepted. After the season was over, Dunstall played at Ipswich, and on 22 August 1741 he acted Corporal Bounce in *Thamas Kouli Kan* at Bartholomew Fair. With him throughout the season was his wife Mary, who played an equally heavy schedule and whose career paralleled Dunstall's until her death in 1758.

The actor stayed with Giffard's troupe at Goodman's Fields in 1741–42, adding such new parts as Cacafogo in *Rule a Wife and Have a Wife*, Sir Wilful in *The Way of the World*, Thunder and Lightning in *The Rehearsal*, and the Physician in *King Lear*. He had moved up in the company, for, instead of sharing tickets, on 6 April 1742 he shared a benefit with Peterson. Dunstall followed Giffard to Lincoln's Inn Fields in 1742–43, repeating many of his old parts but adding some others which were to be favorites of his throughout the years that followed, especially Sir Jealous Traffic in *The Busy Body* and Rakish in *The School Boy*. The Giffard venture foundered in the spring of 1743, and Dunstall put in appearances at Southwark and the Haymarket Theatre to fill out his season.

In 1743–44 Dunstall played the first half of the season at Covent Garden and the last at Drury Lane, adding to his repertoire three more roles with which he remained identified for many years: the title part in *The Mock Doctor*, Stocks in *The Lottery*, and Lockit in *The Beggar's Opera*. While at Covent Garden in the fall of 1743 John and his wife introduced their daughter Henrietta to the stage; she eventually became Mrs William Hunt, under which name she did most of her performing.

Dunstall was at Covent Garden in 1744–45 and there remained for the rest of his career. By this time his line was well

Harvard Theatre Collection

JOHN DUNSTALL, as Dominic
after Dodd

established, and though he added new roles to his repertoire almost every season, he tended to concentrate on the parts to which he had already laid claim. Seldom over the years did he try his hand at tragedy; he confined himself to the more rough-hewn comic types or parts that required singing. Between 1744–45 and his death in 1778 the most significant new roles he played were Sir William Bedford in *The Squire of Alsatia*, the Duke in *Venice Preserv'd*, Antonio in *Love Makes a Man*, Puff in *Miss in Her Teens*, Prigg in *The Royal Merchant*, Mopsus in *Damon and Phillida*, Hob in *Flora*, Mustapha in *Don Sebastian*, Tyrrel in *Richard III*, Jamy in *Henry V*, Hob in *Hob in the Well*, Robin in *The Contrivances*, Puzzle in *The Funeral*, Corin in *As You Like It*, Falstaff in *The Merry Wives* of *Windsor* and *1 Henry IV* (though he did not stay with these), Sullen in *The Stratagem* (though not regularly), a Plebeian in *Julius Caesar*, the Drunken Man in *Lethe*, Waitwell in *The Way of the World*, Launcelot in *The Merchant of Venice* (but he played it infrequently), Soto in *She Wou'd and She Wou'd Not*, Hodge in *Love in a Village*, Brainworm in *Every Man in His Humour*, Jarvis in *The Good Natured Man*, Sterling in *The Clandestine Marriage*, a Ballad Singer in *Harlequin Skeleton* (and in several other works), Sir Toby in *Twelfth Night*, and Caliban in *The Tempest* (but only for a short time). He also advanced from the second to the first Witch in *Macbeth*.

Over the years he acted during the summers, though only a portion of his work is known. In 1746, 1748, and 1749, for instance, he appeared at Richmond and Twickenham in some of his standard parts: Lockit, Moody, Bullock, and Jobson. In September 1758 he joined with Vaughan and Warner to operate a booth at Bartholomew Fair. He was probably the Dunstall who appeared in Birmingham in the summers of 1762, 1775, and 1776. In the summer of 1765 he was at the Jacob's Wells Theatre in Bristol, and the 1760s also saw him at Liverpool. During the winters he confined himself to Covent Garden except for occasional appearances at Drury Lane, usually to help some fellow actor's benefit.

Dunstall's dogged determination gradually raised him to the second salary grade at Covent Garden. In 1746–47 his pay was 12s. 6d. weekly, and in mid-May he shared with one other person a benefit which brought in £107 11s. 6d. before house charges. In the 1750s some of his benefits showed deficits, but he usually sold enough tickets to cover the loss and to end up with a few pounds in his pocket. By 1758 (after his wife's death) Dunstall must have been doing better, for though his benefit on 28 April that year, shared with Miss Ferguson, showed a loss at the door of £25 19s.,

Harvard Theatre Collection

CHARLES MACKLIN as Sir Francis Wronghead, and JOHN DUNSTALL as John Moody

engraving by Reading, after Dodd

Dunstall sold £140 5s. worth of tickets and gallantly absorbed the whole deficit. In 1759 for the first time he had a solo benefit, an honor he kept to the end of his career. By 1761 his weekly salary was up to £4, and his benefit brought him a profit of £153 18s. 6d. He was earning £1 daily (normally £6 weekly) by 1767, and by the 1770s he could count on his April benefits bringing him a profit of at least £160, and sometimes the figure was close to £190. But Dunstall worked hard for his modest success. In 1776–77, when he was almost sixty, he was still acting 176 days per season, and his repertoire had not appreciably narrowed over the years.

The actor and his wife lived in Hunt's

Court, Castle Street, Leicester Fields, in 1747; by 1777 Dunstall was living, apparently by himself, in Little Queen Street, Lincoln's Inn Fields.

In the fall of 1778 Dunstall went to work at Covent Garden as he had done year after year. Many of his old parts were still in his repertoire: Captain Jamy, Moody, Sir Jealous, Tradelove, the First Gravedigger, Bullock, and Lockit. He played all of these, plus several others, between September and December. On 23 December he took an unnamed role in a new play, *The Spendthrift.* A week later he was dead. He died on 31 December 1778, just a month short of his sixty-first birthday. Dunstall was buried at St Paul, Covent Garden, on 8 January 1779, attended by many of the actors with whom he had worked.

On 29 June 1774 Dunstall had made his will. He was apparently not in good health at the time, and he failed rapidly during the last three or four years of his life. He asked in his will that his body be kept unburied as long as possible after his death, for he had a fear, not uncommon at the time, of burial alive. He proposed that his funeral should not cost more than 10 guineas. He asked his executors to sell the property he owned in the Borough of Huntington and elsewhere and invest the proceeds for the benefit of his daughter Henrietta Hunt. He also provided for any children Henrietta might bear. The rest of his estate he left to his kinsman Jonathan Dunstall of Bermondsey, Surrey, and to the Theatrical Fund at Covent Garden, an association for which the actor had served as an accountant for some years. Dunstall's will was proved on 2 January 1779, six days before his delayed burial.

John Dunstall's talent was described by his contemporaries in guarded terms. *The Rational Rosciad* of 1767, for instance, said:

> Dunstall, designed by nature for a
>   clown,

> Pleases (*in country characters*) the
>   Town;
> Should he attempt in elegance to rise,
> Smiles of contempt would be his only
>   prize.

Kelly's *Thespis* the same year said Dunstall "blends the jarring compounds of a part" and is correctly warm, vehemently true, best in the rough yet cultivated mold, and has the stern strong face of nature. "*D* was for Dunstall, abounding in merit," a poet wrote in the January 1772 *Gentleman's Magazine.* But Francis Gentleman in *Theatres* that year said

> Old dog-trot Dunstall keeps the beaten
>   way,
> And very seldom mends, or mars a
>   play . . .

In 1775 William Hawkins in *Miscellanies in Prose and Verse* wrote that Dunstall was a good low comedian but was "too much of a mouther: notwithstanding, his Hodge, and Sir Jealous Traffick, are inimitable, such characters being happily suited to his manner." The same year in the poem *Drama,* Downman said

> In the harsh parent, or the rustic boor,
> Dunstall and Parsons shew great comic
>   pow'r.

Writing in 1784 after the actor's death, Thomas Davies in his *Dramatic Miscellanies* remembered Dunstall as a popular singer, a man of honesty and good nature, and a member of several respectable societies. Dunstall had the bad habit, however, of acknowledging his friends in the audience during performances. Davies credited Dunstall with the role of Ben in *Love for Love,* a part *The London Stage* does not record for him.

John Williams in *A Pin Basket to the Children of Thespis* in 1797 commented that Dunstall "was remarkable for his affectation of grecisms, and words of many syllables—insomuch, that when he was missing at a Rehearsal, NED SHUTER told the elder COLMAN, who was acting Manager, that DUNSTALL had found out another hard word, and was gone to Whitechapel with it."

Portraits of Dunstall include:

1. As Dominic in *The Spanish Fryar*. A photograph in the Harvard Theatre Collection of a painting, probably after Dodd. The portrait was engraved by Walker for the *New England Theatre*, 1776.

2. As Dominic. Drawing by unknown artist. In the British Museum.

3. As Dromio in *The Comedy of Errors*. Drawing by Parkinson. In the British Museum. Engraved by Grignion for Bell's *British Theatre*, 1776.

4. As Hodge in *Love in a Village*, with Shuter as Justice Woodcock and Beard as Hawthorn. Painting by Zoffany, in the possession of the National Theatre. Engraved by Finlayson, published by Zoffany, Finlayson, and Parker. An anonymous engraving of the figure of Hodge was published by Sayer and Smith, 1769.

5. As Dominic. Anonymous engraving published by Wenman, 1777.

6. As Jobson in *The Devil to Pay*. Anonymous engraving.

7. As John Moody in *The Provok'd Husband*, with Macklin as Sir Francis. Engraving by Reading, after Dodd, for *New English Theatre*, 1776.

Dunstall, Mrs John, Mary *d. 1758, actress, singer.*

Mrs John Dunstall joined the Goodman's Fields company with her husband in 1740 and played many different characters during the 1740–41 season. She must therefore have had considerable provincial acting experience behind her. Her first role was Melinda in *The Recruiting Officer* on 22 October 1740, after which she acted Euphronia in *Aesop*, Elvira in *The Spanish Fryar*, Mrs Foresight in *Love for Love*, Lady Grace in *The Provok'd Husband*, Mrs Ford in *The Merry Wives of Windsor*, Serina in

The Orphan, Mrs Frail in *Love for Love*, Arbella in *The Committee*, Cephisa in *The Distrest Mother*, Lucy in *The Recruiting Officer*, Sylvia in *The Double Gallant*, Belinda in *Tunbridge Walks*, Hillaria in *Love's Last Shift*, Nell in *The Devil to Pay*, Pindress in *Love and a Bottle*, Colombine in *The Imprisonment of Harlequin*, Mopsa in *The Winter's Tale*, Gipsey in *The Stratagem*, Jenny Diver in *The Beggar's Opera*, Isabella in *The Wonder*, Teraminta in *The Wife's Relief*, Prince Edward in *Richard III*, a Waiting Woman in *The Anatomist*, Philide in *King Arthur*, Ganymede in *Harlequin Student*, Mariana in *All's Well that Ends Well*, Wheedle in *The Miser*, Phryne in *Timon of Athens*, and the First Lady in *Lethe*. She concluded her season playing Mercury in *Lethe* at Ipswich in July 1741 and appearing as Karanza in *Thamas Kouli Kan* at Bartholomew Fair on 22 August.

Mrs Dunstall and her husband stayed with Giffard's troupe at Goodman's Fields in 1741–42 and at Lincoln's Inn Fields in 1742–43, during which seasons she added to her repertoire such parts as Myrtilla in *The Provok'd Husband*, Scentwell, Patch, and Isabinda in *The Busy Body*, Priscilla (and, at James Street) Kitty Pry in *The Lying Valet*, Altea in *Rule a Wife and Have a Wife*, Araminta in *The Old Bachelor*, Elvira in *Love Makes a Man*, Foible in *The Way of the World*, Hoyden and Amanda in *The Relapse*, Mrs Peachum in *The Beggar's Opera*, Dorcas in *The Mock Doctor*, and the title role in *Flora*. When Giffard's venture collapsed, Mrs Dunstall finished the season acting and singing at Southwark and the Haymarket Theatre.

She was inactive in 1742–43, though perhaps she was grooming her daughter Henrietta (later Mrs William Hunt) for her debut in 1743. From 1743–44 on, Mrs Dunstall played at Covent Garden. Though her career in London had started vigorously, over the years she acted less and less. Still, she added to her list of roles before her death in 1758 such characters as Jane in *The London Cuckolds*, Lucy in *The Country Wife*, Miss Prue in *Love for Love*, Doll Tearsheet in 2 *Henry IV*, Colombine in *The Royal Chace*, the title role in *Phebe*, Mrs Day in *The Committee*, Arabella in *The Fair Quaker of Deal*, Phillida in *Damon and Phillida*, Parley in *The Constant Couple*, the Nurse in *Romeo and Juliet*, and Colombine in *Harlequin Skeleton*.

Mrs Dunstall was earning 12s. 6d. weekly in 1746–47, and though she was occasionally granted benefits, she appears to have been on a straight salary during most of her career. She acted at Richmond in the summers of 1746 and 1749, but in most years she contented herself with her winter schedule at Covent Garden. By 1750 she had reduced her appearances considerably; by 1755–56 she played only a handfull of parts and appeared infrequently; and in 1757–58 she acted only two roles: Mrs Fardingale in *The Funeral* and Mrs Peachum in *The Beggar's Opera*. She played Mrs Peachum on 30 March 1758, her last recorded appearance. She was buried at St Paul, Covent Garden, on 28 May 1758. The critics of the time apparently took no notice of her talent.

Dunstone, Mrs ₁*fl. 1735*₁, *actress.*
Mrs Dunstone, otherwise unknown, appeared as Monimia in *The Orphan* at the Haymarket Theatre, for her benefit on 4 August 1735.

"Duodecimo." *See* DODD, JAMES WILLIAM.

Du Pain, ₁Mlle?₁ ₁*fl. 1789*₁, *dancer.*
Smith's *The Italian Opera* lists a female Du Pain as one of the principal dancers in the opera company at the King's Theatre in the Haymarket and, after the fire there, at Covent Garden in 1789. She is not listed in *The London Stage.*

Dupar. *See* DIEUPART.

Duparc. *See* "FRANCESINA, LA."

Du Park, Miss ₁*fl. 1800*₁, *harpist.*
Miss Du Park performed on the harp at Mrs Franklin's concert in Willis's Rooms on 27 March 1800.

Duparr or **Dupart.** *See* DIEUPART and DUPORT.

Dupee, William ₁*fl. 1794*₁, *music porter.*
Doane's *Musical Directory* of 1794 listed William Dupee of No 23, Gravel Lane, Southwark, as a music porter at the Drury Lane Theatre.

Du Périer, François du Mouriez *c. 1650–1723, manager, actor.*
François du Mouriez Du Périer was born at Aix about 1650 and served Molière as a *valet de chambre* until the playwright's death in 1673. He acted in the provinces, married Madeleine Jannequin, and in 1681 succeeded the Sieur de Brécourt (his wife's uncle) as manager of the Prince of Orange's Company of comedians. He was active at the Hague in 1681, and it was from Holland that he and his troupe came when they visited England in 1684.

The company's properties were admitted duty-free on 26 May 1684, and the troupe arrived early in June for a four-month stay. Their first performance was supposed to have been at court on 10 June. The company traveled with the King to Windsor and Winchester, and on 29 October money from the Secret Services was used to pay Du Périer £49 "for the charge and expences of yᵉ French players." The troupe left England in December. After a career that brought him honor and wealth, Du Périer died on 21 June 1723.

Dupin, Mons ₁*fl. 1661–1663*₁, *actor.*
As a member of the Lavoy and Alcidor troupe, Monsieur Dupin performed in Belgium and Holland in 1661, 1662, and 1663. He was probably in the troupe when it received permission to come to London

on 25 August 1663. From 1662 the company traveled under the name of the *Comédiens du Roy d'Angleterre*, though they were sometimes also called the *Comédiens du Séré nissime Prince de Liège*.

Duplaisir. *See* DUPLESSIS.

Duplessis, Lewis [*fl.* 1724–1776?], *dancer.*

Lewis Duplessis (or Duplaisir, Duplessey, Duplissy) danced at Lincoln's Inn Fields in 1724–25 and was three times cited in the account books as receiving £1; whether this was for the day or the week is not clear, though one would assume it was his daily salary. He is known to have taken a role in *Mars and Venus* on 17 April 1725 and to have played Sysiphus in *Harlequin a Sorcerer* on 26 May. On 13 September 1725 the manager John Rich notified the Drury Lane managers that Duplessis was discharged, upon which the dancer contracted to work at the rival house.

From 1725–26 through 1727–28 he appeared at Drury Lane though not often in roles of importance or in specialty dances which were given titles. He was a Shepherd in the masque at the end of *Apollo and Daphne* on 11 February 1726 and Punch in *Harlequin Doctor Faustus* on 3 June; he played Countrymen in *Apollo and Daphne, The Miser,* and *Harlequin's Triumph* in 1726–27; and in his last season at Drury Lane he was not noticed except for his benefit shared with two others on 17 May 1727.

A concert at the Devil Tavern was given for Lewis Duplessis on 28 January 1736, but after that date his performing activity seems to have ended in London.

The will of Michael Festing the musician left £10 to Festing's sister "Elizabeth Duplaisey now at Dublin." She may well have been the dancer's wife. On 12 October 1776 an L. Duplessy and an E. Duplessy witnessed the marriage at St George, Hanover Square, of Louis Bartholomew Pasquier and Ann Hornby. The initials fit, so perhaps the witnesses were Duplessis and his wife.

Du Poncel. *See* DUJONCEL.

Duport, Miss [*fl.* 1770], *singer.*
Miss Duport (or Dupart) sang in the chorus at the end of *La Passione* at the King's Theatre on 8 March 1770.

Duport, Jean Pierre 1741–1818, *violoncellist, composer.*
Jean Pierre Duport was born in Paris on 27 November 1741, the son of a dancing master at the Opéra. He became a student of Berthaut and, in time, the teacher of his brilliant younger brother Jean Louis Duport. Jean Pierre played at the Concert Spirituel in Paris in 1761 and was a member of the orchestra of the Prince de Conti until he came to England in 1769.

On 1 March 1770 at the King's Theatre he played a violoncello solo, billed as "the celebrated M. Dupart." Thereafter he made frequent appearances: on 8 March at the King's, on 14, 16, and 21 March at Drury Lane, on 22 March at the King's, on 28 March at Drury Lane, on 29 March at the King's, on 6 April at Drury Lane, and on 3 and 4 May at the Haymarket. In January, February, and April 1771 he played again at the same three theatres, after which he made a trip to Spain.

Duport was back in London in February, March, and April 1772 to play at the King's, Haymarket, and Covent Garden. On 27 April he had a benefit concert at the Haymarket at which he played a duet with the violinist Vachon and a solo. The *Theatrical Review* on 11 March commented that Duport's "execution is truly masterly, his tone very brilliant, and his taste pleasingly delicate and chaste. What he performs on this instrument is wonderful, when the genius of it is considered."

By 1773 Duport was in Berlin, playing first chair cello in the royal orchestra of

Frederick the Great. He taught the future monarch, Frederick William II, and wrote a few compositions for the cello. His brother Jean Louis, though he came to England for six months in 1782, seems not to have performed in public in London. Jean Pierre Duport died in Berlin on 31 December 1818.

Dupré. *See also* **BRAY** and **DUPUIS.**

Dupré, Mons [*fl.* 1679–1705], *lutenist.*

John Evelyn heard the lutenist Monsieur Dupré (or Du Prue, Dupree) at Mr Slingsby's on 20 November 1679. The London *Gazette* of 10 June 1703 announced that "Mr Dupre, Lute Master, has set up a School at the White Periwig in King Street by Guildhall . . . where he teaches to play upon the Lute, and the Theorbo in Consort, at reasonable Rates." On 8 November 1704 and again on 21 March 1705 Dupré was given benefit concerts at York Buildings.

Dupré, Mons [*fl.* 1715–1717], *dancer.*

The dancer who appeared in London from 1715 to 1717 billed as Dupré Junior may have been one of the Duprés active in the following decade, but certain identification is impossible. On 14 October 1715 at Drury Lane Dupré Junior and Dupré (presumably his father) were noticed as dancers. On 24 October *Harlequin and Two Punchanellos*, a dance composed by the elder Dupré, was performed by the two Duprés and Boval. Dupré Junior continued dancing at Drury Lane in 1715–16 and returned in 1716–17, after which his notices stopped.

Dupré, Mons *d. c. 1735, dancer, choreographer.*

Monsieur Dupré was first mentioned in London bills on 22 December 1714 when he danced at Lincoln's Inn Fields. He con-

tinued appearing in entr'acte turns during the rest of the season and received a benefit on 7 April 1715. In 1715–16 he moved to Drury Lane and there brought out Dupré Junior, presumably his son. The pair joined Boval in *Harlequin and Two Punchanellos*, a dance composed by the elder Dupré, on 24 October 1715, and on 10 April 1716 Dupré was given a solo benefit. He continued at Drury Lane in 1716–17, one of his roles being Mars in *The Loves of Mars and Venus.*

He reappeared at Lincoln's Inn Fields on 9 January 1719 in the title role in *Amadis*, a part he repeated frequently in the years that followed. During what was left of the 1718–19 season he also appeared in dances with Mrs Bullock, and on 10 March he was granted a benefit. He did not dance again until 18 November 1720 at Lincoln's Inn Fields, after which he danced entr'actes and played Amadis repeatedly for the rest of the 1720–21 season. His name then dropped from the bills once more, this time for two years, and the pattern of his London appearances certainly suggests a French dancer (for there were many Duprés in the profession there) who came over from the Continent periodically for special engagements. On 27 April 1723 he danced Mars in *Mars and Venus* at Lincoln's Inn Fields, and the following fall he joined the company full time as dancer and choreographer, an association which continued until his death about 1735.

During his first regular season at Lincoln's Inn Fields he danced in specialty numbers (often undescribed) and played Leander (Mars) in *Jupiter and Europa*, a Harlequin Man in *The Necromancer*, the Mad Soldier in *The Humours of Bedlam*, and his old role of Amadis. For his benefit on 8 April 1724 he danced *Myrtillo* and attracted a crowd that brought £120 4s. 6d. to the box office.

Dupré's daily salary for the four seasons which followed was £1, and for that salary he both danced and choreographed. He revived his early roles and added a Fury in *Harlequin Sorcerer*, Mars (Harlequin) in *Mars and Venus*, and a Spaniard in *Apollo and Daphne*, and in addition he appeared regularly in specialty dances, some of his own composing. In the fall of 1725 a Dupré Junior appeared at Lincoln's Inn Fields; he may have been the Dupré Junior of ten years before, but it is more likely he was another and younger son, James, for he continued dancing until 1751. Identification is made more complicated by the fact that some sources report that the French dancer Jean-Denis Dupré and / or Louis ("Le Grand") Dupré danced at Lincoln's Inn Fields about this time. The London bills, however, show the continued appearances of the Dupré we have been following here, the appearance in 1725 of James Dupré, and no indication of a brief engagement by any other dancers of that name. Indeed, it is unlikely that so famous a performer as Louis Dupré would have appeared in London without fanfare, and the Dupré Junior who began his appearances in 1725 took only minor assignments.

From the fall of 1725 onward the bills at Lincoln's Inn Fields contained two Duprés. The elder one appeared regularly in his old roles of a Harlequin Man, the Spaniard, and the Fury, and added to his list such new pantomime parts as a God of the Woods, a Demon, a Countryman, and Earth in *The Rape of Proserpine* and a Masquerader in *Italian Jealousy*. He danced through November 1729, as did Dupré Junior, and then both names dropped from the bills until September 1730, suggesting a possible tour to the Continent or the British provinces. Some sources state that "Le Grand" Dupré danced at Lincoln's Inn Fields in 1730, but again the records show only the return of our subject, still dancing the parts with which he had been identified earlier.

From 1730 to his death about 1735 our Monsieur Dupré decreased his performing activity and added few new roles or dances

to his repertory. One new part was an Infernal in *Perseus and Andromeda*. He participated also in a number called *The Masqueraders* in *The Provok'd Husband*. He expended most of his energy on such specialty dances as *Moors, Spanish Entry, The Matelot,* and *La Mariee*. His scholars— Miss La Tour and Young Weeks—came on during the early 1730s. On 8 May 1734 Dupré shared a benefit with two others but apparently he did not dance. Sometime between early May and 1 December 1735 Monsieur Dupré died. On that date a benefit was held for Dupré (i.e. Dupré Junior); the next night Widow Dupré's tickets from the night before were accepted; and thereafter the elder Dupré's roles were taken by others. His son James continued dancing until 1751, and the Widow Dupré received benefits through 1753.

Dupré, Mr ₁fl. 1754₁, *singer.*

A Mr Dupré sang in the *Messiah* at the Chapel of the Foundling Hospital on 15 May 1754 at a fee of 10s. 6d.

Dupré, Mme ₁fl. 1735–1755₁, *dancer?*

The Widow Dupré who was a beneficiary of various benefit performances at Covent Garden from 1735 to 1753 seems clearly to have been the wife of the Monsieur Dupré who danced fairly regularly in London from 1714 to his death about 1735, and the mother of the dancer James Dupré who danced from 1725 to 1751. If the identification is correct, the Dupré Junior who danced from 1715 to 1717 in London was another son (unless he should be identified as James Dupré when young).

On 1 December 1735 "Dupré" was given a benefit at Covent Garden; on 2 December, according to Latreille, "Tickets delivered out for the benefit of Monsʳ Dupre's Widow & others that could not be admitted last night will be taken this night." It would appear that the elder Dupré had died, the theatre gave a benefit for the family under the umbrella "Dupré," and then the widow and her son continued their own careers. Widow Dupré received shared benefits or had her benefit tickets accepted at Covent Garden almost every spring from 1735 through 1753. Had she received benefits for only a year or two after her husband's death we might assume a charity on the part of manager John Rich. But the continued benefits suggest that she was a member of the company and, in view of the specialties of her husband and son, a dancer. Probable confirmation of this is the billing of a Mrs Dupré on 8 October 1755; she danced in *Romeo and Juliet*. She may have been an unheralded member of the Covent Garden *corps de ballet* through the years. No further mention of her seems to have survived.

Dupré, Éléonore [Caroline?] [fl. 1776–1787], dancer.

The libretto of *Il trionfo di Clelia* (Turin, 1787) gave Mademoiselle Dupré's first name as Éléonore, but that for *Medonte* (Alexandria, 1783) had called her Caroline. Éléonore would seem, however, to have been the correct name of the dancer who made her first appearance in England on 7 November 1776 at Drury Lane in two ballets—*The Double Festival* and *The Triumph of Love*. Her season salary in 1776–77 is not known, though the account books show that in May 1777 she and Gallet received £100 in lieu of a benefit and that she was paid £39 10s. 8d. for the period 9 June to 19 July 1777. In 1777–78 she was paid £400.

In the course of her two seasons at Drury Lane she was seldom mentioned in the bills, though she is known to have appeared in a "Dance of Spirits" in *The Tempest* and in the dance "Rural Grace" in *Love in a Village*. The critics said little of her dancing, though Hopkins noted in his diary that at her debut on 7 November 1776 "Mlle Dupré fell down, and a little after Gallet fell down, but [they] did not hurt

themselves, and the Dance went on—and even with all these Disadvantages was much applauded." The evening had been plagued with problems, for the costumes were not at the theatre on time, the schedule had to be altered, and the music was imperfect.

Dupré, James [fl. 1725–1751], dancer.

James Dupré, who danced regularly in London from 1725 to 1751 may have been one of the two Duprés who appeared earlier in the century, but the evidence is too confusing to allow a positive identification. Further, there were numerous Duprés dancing in France in the first half of the eighteenth century; many of them have not been identified by Christian name, and some of them probably appeared in England. James may have been one of them. When he was first noticed in London on 13 November 1725 as Sysiphus in *Harlequin Sorcerer* at Lincoln's Inn Fields, he was billed as Dupré Junior to distinguish him from an elder Dupré (his father?) who danced at the same theatre. The designation "Junior" was attached to James until the elder Dupré died about 1735, after which James was billed usually as "Dupré." His Christian name was not mentioned in the press until 1741.

Dupré Junior (or James, if we have identified him correctly) danced in Rich's company at Lincoln's Inn Fields and, beginning in 1732, Covent Garden. His pantomime roles included a Bacchanal and a Peasant in *Apollo and Daphne*, the Doctor (Neptune) in *Jupiter and Europa*, a Sicilian in *The Rape of Proserpine*, a Masquerader in *Italian Jealousy*, a Cyclops in *Perseus and Andromeda*, and a Scaramouch Man in *The Necromancer*. His entr'acte turns included a *Scaramouch* dance and, with Miss Baston, a minuet. Rich seems to have paid Dupré between 6s. 8d. 10s. weekly.

After the 1733–34 season at Covent Garden the elder Dupré's activity ended, and his widow was a beneficiary of the performance on 2 December 1735. James then dropped the "Junior" after his name in the bills, continued dancing such old parts of his as a Peasant in *Apollo and Daphne* and a Scaramouch Man in *The Necromancer* and added a number of new parts to his repertoire, such as a Gardener and a Countryman in *The Rape of Proserpine*, Neptune (Pantaloon) in *The Royal Chace*, and one role the elder Dupré had danced, an Infernal in *Perseus and Andromeda*. He continued appearing in specialty dances, some of them being *The Faithful Shepherd, Grecian Sailors, French Peasants*, and, with Mlle Delorme, *The Princess Ann's Chacone* and a *Ball Dance*. This increase in activity in 1734–35 and 1735–36 would seem to be directly related to the elder Dupré's retirement and death. On 1 December 1735 a benefit was given for "Dupré" which brought in a total of £148 5s. 6d.; tickets given out by Widow Dupré for that date were accepted again the following day. It seems clear that the benefit was designed for the bereaved family and that the elder Dupré was James's father. James received his own benefit (shared with others) the following 8 May 1736, and the Widow Dupré, presumably his mother, was granted benefits for many years in her own right.

In 1735–36 James Dupré performed 172 times at a salary of 3s. 4d. per day for a total of £28 13s. 4d. His benefit in May 1736, unfortunately, suffered a loss, and he was charged with a £30 deficiency.

In the years which followed, Dupré continued in many of his old minor roles in pantomimes and added such new ones as a Zephyr and an Aerial Spirit in *The Royal Chace*, a Swain and a Country Lad in *Orpheus and Eurydice*, and a Follower in *The Loves of Mars and Venus*. Some of his new specialty turns from 1736 to 1751 were a *Scotch Dance* with Mrs Pelling, minuets with Mlle Ozanne and Miss Norman, and *La Provençale*. He also danced in *The Rural Assembly* in *The Winter's*

Tale, a ballet called *Mars and Venus*, and *Comus*. Like the elder Dupré, James had scholars, one of whom (unnamed) appeared with him on 29 April 1742 in a louvre and minuet at his shared benefit with Bencraft. By the 1746–47 season Dupré was performing only one billed role per season, and his benefits in the 1740s did not bring him much profit. In 1750–51 he danced only an Infernal in *Perseus and Andromeda*, and on 9 May 1751, the last mention of him, he was one of several whose benefit tickets were accepted.

Dupree, Miss [fl. 1797], *harpist*.

Miss Dupree made her first, and apparently her last, appearance in public playing a concerto on the harp at the end of the first part of the *Messiah* at Covent Garden on 10 March 1797.

Dupres, Mr [fl. 1761], *dancer*.

A Mr Dupres (possibly an error for Dupré) was listed on the Covent Garden payroll on 26 November 1761 as a dancer receiving a salary of £20 per year. He seems not to have been the same person as the dancer Duprez at Drury Lane in the 1770s whose salary was much higher.

Dupret, Mr [fl. 1800], *choreographer*.

On 2 June 1800 at Drury Lane was presented a new ballet *The Lucky Escape*, composed by one Dupret, with music by Bossi, the leader of the band at the King's Theatre. Dupret may have been a ballet master.

Duprez, Mr [fl. 1776–1782], *dancer*.

Mr Duprez (or Dupres) was on the payroll at Drury Lane in 1776 at an unspecified salary and in 1777–78 at £400 annually. The bills seldom mentioned him, but on 17 May 1780 his benefit tickets were accepted; on 5 May 1781 he danced a minuet and shared in proceeds from benefit tickets, and in 1782 he performed in *Lun's Ghost* on 4 January, danced in *The*

Devonshire Minuet on 27 April (when his benefit tickets were accepted), and played Don Pedro in *Don Juan* on 10 May. The account books show that by the spring of 1781 his salary was up to £500 per season.

Du Prue. *See* DUPRÉ.

Dupuis. *See also* DUBOIS, JEAN BAPTISTE.

Dupuis, Mons [*fl.* 1757–1759], *dancer.*

Monsieur Dupuis danced in a specialty number titled *Le Carneval de Venice* on 26 December 1757 at the Haymarket Theatre, after which he became a member of the Drury Lane company. On 2 November 1758 he was in a number called *The Swiss* and the next day danced in *Comus.* But on 3 February 1759 he "ran away" from the company and was not heard from again.

Dupuis, Mr [*fl.* 1797–1800], *watchman.*

The Drury Lane accounts at the end of the eighteenth century show payments of 12*s.* weekly to a Mr Dupuis (or Dupuy, Dupree), the watchman. The first mention of him was on 23 September 1797 and the last on 10 May 1800; by 8 January 1800 he was referred to as the "late watchman" and was being paid arrears in his salary.

Dupuis, Charles [*fl.* 1794–1804], *organist, singer?*

Though Doane's *Musical Directory* of 1794 refers to Charles Dupuis as "Junior," he was not named after his father, the organist and composer Thomas Sanders Dupuis. Charles was an organist and a bass (singer, apparently) who performed for the Academy of Ancient Music. In 1794 he was living at No 4, Park Lane. He was doubtless the Mr Dupuis who was refused financial aid by the Royal Society of Musicians on 2 December 1804 because of restrictions in the Society's laws. In 1796

Charles Dupuis had been the residuary legatee of his father's estate; by 1796 Charles's brother, the Rev Thomas-Skelton Dupuis, had died.

Dupuis, Thomas Sanders 1733–1796, *organist, composer.*

Thomas Sanders Dupuis was the third son and fourth child of John and Susannah Dupuis, natives of France who had migrated to England. Thomas was born in London on 5 November 1733. His father had a position at court which may have helped him place young Thomas in the Chapel Royal under Bernard Gates. Dupuis also studied under the organist John Travers. On 3 December 1758 Thomas was elected to the Royal Society of Musicians.

As early as 21 January 1761 Dupuis gave public performances on the organ; on that date he appeared in concert at the Great Room in Dean Street, Soho. On 26 and 31 March 1762 he played a concerto on the organ at a performance of the *Messiah* at Drury Lane, and he may have played other public recitals about which no information has survived. *Mortimer's London Directory* of 1763 listed him as a harpsichord teacher living in King's Row, Grosvenor Square. On 16 July 1765 he married Martha Skelton of Fulham at St George, Hanover Square.

By 1773 Dupuis was organist of the Charlotte Street Chapel. In that year his mentor Bernard Gates died, making Dupuis one of his residuary legatees. Dupuis erected a tablet to his teacher's memory in the church at North Aston. When William Boyce died in 1779, Dupuis succeeded him as organist of the Chapel Royal, and he seems also to have served as composer to the Chapel and master of the children. In 1784 he was the assistant director of the Handel Memorial Concerts, and on 26 June 1790 he received a Doctor of Music degree from Oxford. When Haydn visited London in 1792 he heard Dupuis play at St James's Chapel and, to the astonishment of Du-

By permission of the Trustees of the British Museum

THOMAS SANDERS DUPUIS

engraving by Turner, after Russell

puis's pupil George Smart, expressed his admiration by falling on the organist's neck and kissing him.

By 1794 Dr Dupuis was living at No 4, Park Lane, and was still active in the affairs of the Royal Society of Musicians and at court concerts. On 8 April 1795, for example, he and Dr Arnold conducted the choir and Dupuis played the organ at the wedding of the Prince of Wales. On 17 July 1796 Thomas Sanders Dupuis died at his house in King's Row, Park Lane, of an overdose of opium. The day before, he had written his will, requesting burial at Fulham on the coffin of his wife, a wish which was not carried out. He was buried in the West Cloister of Westminster Abbey on 24 July. He left £50 to Letitia Dupuis, the widow of his late son Rev Thomas Skelton Dupuis, small legacies to several friends, £100 to the Royal Society of Musicians, and

the rest of his estate to his son Charles. Dr Samuel Arnold was a residuary legatee.

Dupuis wrote a number of works for piano, organ, and voice, many of which are listed in the British Museum *Catalogue of Printed Music*. John Spencer, one of Dupuis's students, edited a selection of his master's cathedral music and provided as a frontispiece a portrait of Dupuis by J. Russell. Probably that engraving is after the painting of Dupuis by J. Russell which is in the Conway collection at Turville; one engraving of it was made by C. Turner.

Du Qua, Mrs [*fl. 1697*], *actress.*

At the Lincoln's Inn Fields Theatre under Betterton's management in late June 1697 Mrs Du Qua played Dresswell in *The Innocent Mistress.*

Duquesney, Mons [*fl. 1784–1786*], *dancer.*

Monsieur Duquesney the younger, presumably the son of the dancer Jacques Alexandre Duquesney, appeared in the comic pantomime *The Country Squabble* on 30 April 1784 at the Haymarket Theatre. With Mlle Constance on 10 May he danced a *Pastoral pas de deux.* He performed at Astley's Amphitheatre on 27 September 1785 and was a member of the opera company at the King's Theatre in the first half of 1786. At the King's he appeared in a *Divertissement sérieux* and a *Divertissement villageoise* on 24 January, the dance *Acis and Galatea* on 18 February, a dance in *Perseo* on 21 March, *Le Premier Navigateur* on 23 March (as a "Lover of Melody"), *L'Amour jardinier* on 1 April, a *pas de trois* from the opera *L'Épreuve villageoise* on 27 April, and *Les Deux solitaires* on 23 May. The season ended on 11 July, after which Duquesney Junior is not known to have danced again in London, though there is a possibility that some of the references to a dancer named Duquesney in later years could be to the younger man rather than to Jacques Alexandre, to whom they have been assigned here.

Duquesney, Jacques Alexandre ⟨*fl.* *1756?–1791*⟩, *dancer.*

The Duquesney who danced at Toulouse in 1756 may have been Jacques Alexandre Duquesney, who made his first appearance in England on 23 October 1762 dancing *The Jealous Woodcutter* at Covent Garden. With Miss Wilford on 1 Janaury 1763 he performed *The Dutch Skipper*; he may have been a Demon in *The Rape of Proserpine* on 26 January; he was in a comic dance called *The Catalonian Marriage* on 8 March and in *The Jovial Gardeners* on 12 March; he and Miss Twist entertained with a minuet on 26 March; and at his shared benefit on 7 May he introduced his student Miss Deroissi to the public.

In 1763–64 and 1764–65 at Covent Garden he was seen in such new dances as *The Amorous Knife Grinders, The Cudgell'd Husband, Hymen's Triumph, The Tricks of Pierrot, The Tyrolese Peasants, Les Caprices de Galatée*, and a minuet in *Romeo and Juliet*. He also danced Thyrsus in *Perseus and Andromeda*, appeared in a number of untitled comic dances, and participated in pantomimes.

Duquesney did not dance in London in 1765–66, but he reappeared on 11 November 1766, this time at Drury Lane, in a comic dance entitled *The Jealous Peasant*. His salary at Drury Lane was apparently £3 weekly, and he stayed there for two seasons. He performed in a *Dance of Slaves* in *Oroonoko*, in the dances in *Cymon*, in a pantomime dance called *The Millers and the Colliers*, in a number entitled *The Nosegay, The Gallant Shepherd* (for his solo benefit on 18 May 1767), in a *Masquerade Dance* in *Romeo and Juliet*, in a *Dance of Furies* in *Macbeth*, in a cotillion in *The National Prejudice*, and in other pieces. His second Drury Lane benefit, on 30 April 1768, was shared with John Palmer.

On 30 May 1768 Duquesney danced between the acts at the Haymarket Theatre, and there he continued working through September as a member of Foote's company. He then left London, and perhaps it

should be questioned whether the Duquesney who appeared in London 15 years later was Jacques Alexandre or his son.

In 1783, according to the Lord Chamberlain's accounts, a Duquesney was second dancer at the King's Theatre, though the bills made no mention of him. In 1784–85 he danced at the Haymarket, playing unnamed parts in *The Deserter* on 14 February 1785 and *Medea and Jason* on 10 March and occasionally offering an entr'acte turn. He danced in a new divertissement at the King's on 18 June and replaced Lepicq in the dances in *Orfeo* on 25 June. On 1 August, billed as Duquesney "Sr." (which suggests that the dancer we have followed *was* Jacques Alexander), he danced at Astley's Amphitheatre, after which he again left London.

At a season salary of £250 plus a free benefit, Duquesney danced at the King's Theatre in the first half of 1789, his first appearance of the season being on 10 January when he was in a divertissement and *L'Embarquement pour Cythère*. He later appeared in *Les Fêtes provençales, La Nymphe et le chasseur, Les Jalousies du Sérail, Admète, Les Caprices de Galatée*, and *Les Folies d'Espagne*. In 1789–90 the opera company performed at the Haymarket Theatre, and Duquesney once again appeared in group dances, among them *La Bergère des Alpes, Les Mariages Flamands, Les Caprices, La Jalousie sans raison*, and *The Generous Slave*.

In 1790–91 Duquesney danced at the Pantheon, appearing as a Shepherd in the pantomime ballet *Amphion et Thalie* on 17 February and subsequent dates. He probably danced until the last performance of the season on 19 July, but after that date his name no longer appeared in the London bills.

Durac. *See* DUTAC.

Duranci, Mr *d. 1793, actor, swordsman?*

Perhaps the actor Duranci who appeared

at Drury Lane in 1791 was the Monsieur "Durenci" who gave exhibitions with the broadsword, small sword, and battle axe at Sadler's Wells in 1788. Those exhibitions were interspersed with an entertainment called *The Four Valiant Brothers* in which Durenci acted Renaux, and one critic was so impressed that he advised "our English Tragedians to take a lesson."

On 17 December 1791 a Mr "Durancey" was entered on the Drury Lane company books; his salary was £4 weekly. On 31 December, according to the playbill, "Duranci" (the correct spelling, apparently) made his first appearance as a Knight in *Cymon* at the King's Theatre, where the company was then performing. On 19 March he was in the cast of *The American Heroine*. The actor's career was cut short by his death on 3 January 1793, at which time he was still a member of the Drury Lane troupe, though no roles are known for him after March 1792.

Durancy, Mons, stage name of Jean-François Fienzal ₍fl. 1746–1766₎, actor.

Jean-François Fienzal, called Durancy, and his wife, the former Françoise-Marie Dessuslefour, called Mlle Darimate, were performers at Brussels with Favart in 1746. In the fall of 1749 they joined Monnet's troupe for an engagement at the Haymarket Theatre in London which they hoped would last until Lent. The opening night, 14 November, was marred by disturbances caused by local political differences and anti-Gallic sentiment, and the season in general was a failure. Durancy and his wife had contracted to act for £361 17s. 1d. but were lucky to receive £357 7s.; some players in the troupe received much less than they had bargained for. The bills during their London stay rarely provided casts, but Durancy and his wife were mentioned as being in *Les Amans réunis*, the opening production on 14 November.

Durancy made his debut at the Comédie Française on 18 January 1762 but did not stay with the company long; he returned to Brussels where he was better appreciated and continued performing until 1766. After her London engagement Madame Durancy appeared again at Brussels in 1753, was at Versailles in 1760, and made her debut at the Comédie Française in 1762. The couple had a daughter, Magdelaine-Celeste Fienzal de Frossac, called Durancy, born on 21 May 1746, who acted as a child in the 1750s.

Durancy, Mme, stage name of Mme Jean-François Fienzal, Françoise-Marie, née Dessuslefour ₍fl. 1746–1762₎, actress. See DURANCY, MONS.

Durand, Mlle ₍fl. 1791₎, dancer.

Mademoiselle Durand was a Nymph in the ballet *Amphion et Thalie* at the Pantheon on 17 February 1791 and subsequent dates. On 22 March she was assigned to dance a Nymph again, in *Telemachus in the Island of Calypso*.

Durastanti, Margherita ₍Signora Casimiro Avelloni₎ b. c. 1685, singer.

Margherita Durastanti was born about 1685 in Italy. Her first recorded theatrical appearance was at the Teatro San Giovanni Crisostomo in Venice in 1709. She sang the title role in Handel's *Agrippina* there on 26 December 1709, by which time she must already have had considerable performing experience. She was the leading singer at the theatre until 1712, after which she sang at Naples during the 1715–16 season.

The date of Durastanti's marriage to Casimiro Avelloni is not known, but she employed her maiden name in her professional affairs throughout her career. By April 1719 she was in Dresden, where Handel engaged her at £1600 for 18 months to sing with Senesino and others in London for the newly-formed Royal Academy of Music. When Rolli heard the news, he sent a despairing note to his friend Riva in August 1719: "Durastanti will be coming for the Operas: Oh! What a bad choice for England! . . . she really is an Elephant!"

Signora Durastanti made her first appearance in London at the King's Theatre in the Haymarket on 2 April 1720 singing Romolo in *Numitore*. On 27 April she took the title role in *Radamisto*, and on 30 May she sang the leading part in *Narciso*. Then she threw the Academy into a fit. Rolli wrote Riva on 29 August 1720:

Mrs. Margherita is pregnant and the Directors are very much annoyed about it. Some of them complained with me of it, especially now that she was expected to be the leading lady in the Opera. Honest Avelloni is distressed about it, and she flew into a rage, and you will see the result: she will return to Italy, regardless of her salary here of a thousand pounds and more per year. The half of this if saved means a lot of money in Italy, especially for someone like her who germinates yearly.

But the elephantine soprano did not let her germination interfere with her career. She sang Elisa in *Astarto* in November 1720, Zenobia in *Radamisto* in December, and Statira in *Arsace* in February. Burney reported that she sang Zenobia on 25 February 1721, so she certainly performed right up to the last possible minute.

On 7 March 1721 the *Evening Post* announced that on 2 March "his Majesty was pleased to stand Godfather, and the Princess and Lady Bruce, Godmothers, to a Daughter of Mrs Darastanti, chief Singer in the Opera-house. The Marquis Visconti [appeared] for the King, and the Lady Litchfield for the Princess." By 28 March the singer was back on stage warbling in a Scarlatti *Serenata* at a King's Theatre concert. She finished the opera season singing Clelia in *Mutius Scaevola* on 15 April, Tomiri in *Ciro* on 20 May, and participating in concerts on 14 June and (for her benefit) 5 July.

Sir John Vanbrugh wrote to Lord

Carlisle on 16 November 1721, "We are a little Cripled in our Opera, by a Letter from Durastanta; that She is not well, and can't be here this Winter, they go on however and two New Operas are preparing. . . ." Margherita returned in the fall of 1722, and though casts were not listed in the opera bills, she doubtless sang in *Crispo, Mutius Scaevola, Ciro*, and *Floridante*. On 12 January 1723 she sang Gismonda in *Ottone* and on 19 February she was Veturia in *Coriolano*. She sang the title role in *Erminia* on 30 March and Vitige in *Flavio* on 14 May. She was probably one of the five singers invited to go to Paris for the summer of 1723.

During the 1723–24 season in London, Signora Durastanti sang Clitarco in *Farnace*, Domiziano in *Vespasiano*, Sesto Pompeo in *Giulio Cesare*, Giulia in *Calfurnia*, and Lincestes in *Aquilio*. Her benefit on 17 March 1724 drew the following comment on 31 March from Lecoq (in a letter to Manteuffel translated in Deutsch's *Handel*):

Durastante, whom you know, retired the day of her benefit with a cantata in praise of the English nation. She said that she was making way for younger enchantresses. That one day brought her more than a thousand pounds sterling. Her benefit last year brought in nearly as much, not to mention her salary of 1200 guineas a year. Have you ever heard, Monseigneur, of prodigality and favour to equal this towards a woman [already] old, whose voice is both mediocre and worn out? That is what the English are like.

The information on the singer's retirement was not quite correct. "Black Peggy," as she was called in the *Session of Musicians* (1724), finished the season before leaving the stage to the far greater Signora Cuzzoni.

On 30 October 1733 Signora Durastanti, her voice mellowed to mezzo, returned to the King's Theatre to sing the title role in *Semiramis*. Lady Bristol heard her on 3

November and wrote her husband that most of the singers "are all scrubbs except for old Durastante, that sings as well as ever she did." During the rest of the 1733–34 season Signora Durastanti sang Gismonda in *Ottone*, Byrcema in *Cajo Fabricio*, Tauride in *Arianna in Creta*, Calliope in *Il Parnasso in festa*, a role in *Arbace*, the Israelite Woman in the oratorio *Deborah*, Haliate in *Sosarme*, and probably Eurilla in *Pastor fido*. After that season, Margherita Durastanti was not heard from again.

Durbridge, Mr (fl. *1783–1785*), *box and lobby keeper.*

The Lord Chamberlain's accounts show a Mr Durbridge (or Dunbridge) to have been a box and lobby keeper at the King's Theatre in the Haymarket from 1783 to 1785.

D'Urfey, Thomas *c. 1653–1723, orator, author, singer, composer, actor?*

Born about 1653 in Devonshire, Thomas D'Urfey was the son of Severinus D'Urfey and his wife Frances. Young D'Urfey may have been trained for the law, though most sources indicate that he was a scrivener's apprentice. He turned to playwriting, producing his first work, *The Siege of Memphis*, in September 1676. There followed over the years an astounding outpouring of dramatic work: at least 29 comedies, tragedies, and dramatic operas which were performed, plus three unacted pieces.

In addition to writing plays by the dozens, D'Urfey turned out song lyrics by the hundreds. These he occasionally set to music himself, and he frequently sang them in his rich bass voice for his friends' (and perhaps the public's) pleasure. Most of his songs were collected in 1719 in his *Wit and Mirth*. D'Urfey also wrote a poem on archery in collaboration with the actor Shatterell, and numerous poems, pamphlets, and tales.

Despite a bad stutter, which he lost

Harvard Theatre Collection

THOMAS D'URFEY

engraving by Pye, after Thurston's copy of Van der Gucht's portrait

when he swore or sang, and a grotesque countenance, about which he could do nothing, D'Urfey became a favorite of Charles II. Addison wrote that he recalled the King "leaning on *Tom d'Urfey's* Shoulder more than once, and humming over a Song with him." D'Urfey's songs were performed by himself and others at Whitehall, Winchester, Newmarket, Windsor, and other places visited by the King. The second Duke of Albemarle, the Earl of Carlisle, the Earl of Berkeley, the Duchess of Grafton, Lord Morpeth, and other highly placed people befriended D'Urfey during the reign of Charles.

On 8 May 1676 a Thomas Durfey was sworn a "Comoedian" in the King's Company under the manager Thomas Killigrew. Perhaps he was another person of the same name, but it is significant that the playwright's first stage work was produced by the King's Company at Drury Lane in September of that year. The term "Comoedian" was indifferently used in the Lord Chamberlain's accounts for all members of the troupe, actors, scenekeepers, and orange-women alike, so there is no assurance that the Thomas Durfey so described performed. He may have served the company in any capacity, and if he was the playwright, perhaps he sang, acted, or served as a house playwright.

James II did not find D'Urfey as amusing as Charles II had found him, though the author had written satires in the early 1680s against the Whigs who had tried to prevent the Duke of York from succeeding to the throne. The Revolution of 1688 lost D'Urfey the courtly connections he had developed, so that he had to turn to other means of support. He taught singing to the girls at Josias Priest's school in Chelsea and wrote the epilogue to *Dido and Aeneas* when it was presented there in 1689–90. He turned out a newspaper called *Momus Ridens* in 1690 and 1691 and published anonymously a number of political poems and pamphlets. When William III came to the throne, D'Urfey switched his political affections to the Whigs and wrote several songs for the new King which again brought him royal patronage. Though he could not afford it, D'Ufrey tried to live the life of a man of fashion. He added the apostrophe to his name after 1683; he hired a liveried page to follow him around; he fought a duel with the musician Bell; he took the waters at Epsom and Tunbridge Wells; and he developed friendships with the third Earl of Leicester, Charles Montague, Sir Charles Sedley, and others.

His pretensions to fashion (and indeed even to the laureateship) only amused his friends, for D'Urfey was, at best, a good hack writer of bawdy songs and lively popular plays. The 1690s saw the birth of most of his best dramatic work, especially the first two parts of *Don Quixote*, for which Purcell wrote the music. With the accession of Queen Anne, D'Urfey's star began to

Harvard Theatre Collection

THOMAS D'URFEY
engraving by Grignion, after Gouge

decline, though he continued writing and though he pleased the Queen with his songs. Upon her death in 1714, however, he was left with a monarch who was deaf to D'Urfey's kind of light entertainment. In desperation, perhaps, D'Urfey turned to the writing and speaking of flattering "orations," (prologues, actually) at the theatre, hoping to attract the favor of King George. On 3 June 1714 at Drury Lane he delivered an oration to the King, Prince, and Princess, and on 7 June he delivered another to the "ladies." On 29 May 1716 for his benefit at Drury Lane he spoke a "New Oration on several famous Heads" addressed to the Prince of Wales, and at the same house on 27 May 1717, again for his benefit, he spoke a similar oration.

D'Urfey's greatest patron during his last years was the Duke of Dorset, who frequently entertained him at Knole, where D'Urfey's portrait by J. Thurston hangs today. When D'Urfey died, he was buried at Dorset's expense at St James, Westminster (now Piccadilly), on 26 February 1723. Administration of his estate was granted on 15 March to his chief creditor, John Bates. D'Urfey was described in the letters of administration as a bachelor from the parish of St Martin-in-the-Fields.

C. Pye engraved Thurston's copy of Van der Gucht's portrait of D'Urfey, and W. Walker published it in 1821. E. Gouge's portrait of him was engraved by G. Vertue to serve as a frontispiece to *Wit and Mirth* in 1719. C. Grignion engraved Gouge's portrait for Hawkins's *History of Musick* in 1776, and an anonymous engraver copied it for Caulfield's *Remarkable Persons* in 1819.

Durham, Mr ₁fl. 1714₁, *actor.*

Mr Durham played Dioclesian in *Injured Virtue* when it was performed by the Duke of Southampton and Cleaveland's Servants at Richmond in the summer of 1714 and at the King's Arms Tavern in Southwark on 1 November 1714.

Durham, Miss ₁fl. 1757–1758₁, *dancer.*

It is probable that the references in the Haymarket Theatre bills in the summers of 1757 and 1758 to Miss Denham, Miss Derham, and Miss Durham are all to the same young dancer. What her name actually was cannot be determined, and the choice here of Durham is arbitrary. As part of Theophilus Cibber's troupe Miss Durham participated in a number of "Medley Concerts." She was sometimes paired off with Morris in a hornpipe, and for her benefit on 27 August 1757 she danced with Joly. On 1 June 1758 she had a second benefit when *The Old Woman's Oratory*, a Christopher Smart production, was presented, but after that she seems to have dropped from the notices.

Durivall. *See* DORIVAL.

Durley. *See* DARLEY.

Durravan, Malachy ₁fl. 1772–1783₁, *actor.*

On 30 April 1772 Malachy Durravan made his Irish debut at the Crow Street Theatre in Dublin. He performed in Dublin through 1774. Durravan appeared once in London: at the Haymarket Theatre on 22 February 1779 he acted Jonathan in *The Prejudice of Fashion* and Sir Roger Belmont in *The Foundling*. In 1783 he was performing with his son at Wolverhampton.

Du Ruel, Mons ₁fl. 1703–1706₁, *dancer.*

On 2 January 1703 at Drury Lane Monsieur Du Ruel made his first recorded appearance in England. He was billed as a scholar of Pettour and lately a dancer at the Opéra in Paris. He danced regularly through July, but rarely did the bills give much indication of the kind of specialties he performed. Once, however, on 18 May 1703, the bill stated that there would be "several Entertainments of Dancing by the Famous Monsieur Du Ruel, particularly an Extraordinary Comical Country Mans Dance never perform'd before." He performed at Drury Lane again in 1703–4, two of his popular dances being the *Dutch Skipper* and *Scaramouch*. During the season he was allowed to appear at least twice at special concerts at Lincoln's Inn Fields, on 21 December 1703 and 1 February 1704. On 20 April his wife joined him on stage at Drury Lane, and from that time forward they frequently appeared together, one of their specialties being the *Country Frenchman and his Wife*. Du Ruel alone often danced to Gasperini's playing of *The Echo*.

Du Ruel danced at Drury Lane with his wife during the 1704–5 season, and she was with him again in the fall of 1705. On 2 November of that year Christopher Rich of Drury Lane discovered that Du Ruel and his wife had entered into articles to perform at the Queen's Theatre in the Haymarket. The pair had been in France the previous summer, during which time they had apparently negotiated for a change of theatres. On 24 November, however, they made their first appearance of the season at Drury Lane, and on 29 November Rich was notified that they had been officially discharged from the Queen's Theatre. The pair danced at Drury Lane, but less frequently than before, during the 1705–6 season, after which Madame Du Ruel seems to have given up performing in London. Du Ruel, however, appeared at Drury Lane on 18 December 1706.

Du Ruel, Mme [fl. 1704–1706], dancer.

On 20 April 1704 Madame Du Ruel joined her husband to dance at Drury Lane. She appeared regularly through July, dancing the *Country Frenchman and his Wife*, the *Dutch Skipper*, and other turns which were left undescribed in the bills. On 1 July she danced a solo chaconne. The pair danced again at Drury Lane in the 1704–5 season. On 24 February 1705 Madame Du Ruel composed and danced a piece called *The Heroine*, and on 1 March she received a benefit.

She and her husband returned to France for the summer and upon their return were engaged to dance at the Queen's Theatre in the Haymarket. The Drury Lane manager, Christopher Rich, seems to have prevented this, however, and on 24 November 1705 the pair were at Drury Lane, making their first appearance since their return. They danced there for the rest of the season, but not as frequently as before. After the spring of 1706 Madame Du Ruel disappeared from the London stage.

Her seasons in England brought her enough fame to warrant a poem by Samuel Phillips, published in the *Diverting Post* on 17 March 1705:

> *Gods, how she steps! see how the blushing Fair,*
> *With nimble Feet, divides the yielding Air,*
> *As tho' she'd throw the common Method by,*
> *And teach us not to Walk, but how to Fly!*
> *Look with what Art the Nymph displays her Charms;*
> *Observe the curling Motions of her Arms!*
> *See in what Folds her flowing Garments stream;*
> *At once they cool and kindle up a Flame*
> *In e'ery Breast, but her's!—she's still the same.*
> *She, like chast Cynthia, does on all Men shine,*
> *But to Endymion she is only kind:*
> *Ill-sorted Fate! that only One must be*
> *Repriev'd from Death, enjoy Felicity,*
> *While Thousands daily do dispair, and die.*

Whether "Endymion" was Monsieur Du Ruel or some other lover we may never know.

Duser, Mons [fl. 1775?–1790?], clown, tumbler.

On 24 July 1786 at Astley's Amphitheatre "Duser (the celebrated clown)" participated in a new dance called *The Country Wake* which involved tumbling. On 4 September Duser was the clown in the pantomime *At the Village Sports*, and on 9 October he performed a tumbling act.

References to a clown at Astley's date from as early as August 1775 to 28 June 1790, but none can be assigned to Duser with any certainty. Perhaps, however, he was the "clown to the horses," puffed on 24 October 1782 as "one of the most eminent Performers in Europe, lately arrived from France, a pupil of Mr Astley's." Or he may have been the clown on 26 May 1785 when "the Clown's Great Grandmother will carry him in an Italian basket, on the Rope." The performer's "feats are so uncommon," wrote a critic, "that the audience seems to vie with each other who shall applaud most."

Dusharroll. *See* SHAROLE.

Dussek, Jan Ladislav *1760–1812, pianist, organist, composer.*

Born in Čáslav, Bohemia, on 12 February 1760, Jan Ladislav Dussek was the son of the organist and music teacher Johan Joseph Dussek. At the age of five Jan began studying piano and at nine the organ. In his youth he was also a singer at the Minorite church in Jihlava, where he received his formal education and further musical training at the College of Jesuits. He went to Prague to take a bachelor's degree in theology and then to Mechlin, where he performed on 16 December 1779.

Dussek accepted a post as organist at Bergen-op-Zoom in Holland and about 1782 went to Amsterdam and then to the Hague. He was a great success as a pianist, and he also taught piano and composed. In 1783 he journeyed to Hamburg to study further under Carl Philipp Emanuel Bach, then on to Berlin in 1784 where he performed not only on the piano but also the armonica. Dussek spent a year at the estate of Prince Radziwill in St Petersburg and then, in late 1786, went to Paris, thence to Milan, and back to Paris in 1788. Everywhere he played he was highly acclaimed.

In early 1790 Dussek came to London, and his first public appearance was on 2 March at one of Johann Peter Salomon's concerts at Hanover Square. The next night he appeared at Drury Lane playing a piano concerto at the Handel oratorio concert. When Haydn visited London in 1792 he wrote a flattering letter about Dussek to the pianist's father in Bohemia, saying that the younger Dussek was "a most honourable and polished man who is a distinguished musician." This same year, on 4 September at St Ann (Soho, presumably), Dussek married the singer Sophia Corri, the daughter of the musician and music publisher Domenico Corri. The union led to the formation of Corri, Dussek & Co at No 67, Dean Street, Soho (where Jan and

Sophia lived in 1794), a location at which Domenico Corri had already set up a music shop. The firm prospered at first and added new quarters at No 28, Haymarket. They brought out some works by Haydn, Pleyel, and, of course, Dussek.

The music business, however, was not Dussek's chief concern during the 1790s in London. He taught, composed a great deal, and concertized regularly. At the King's Theatre on 15 and 22 February 1793, for example, he played a piano concerto, and until the end of the century Dussek kept appearing as a soloist at oratorio concerts at the King's Theatre and Covent Garden. He also put in at least one appearance, on 1 June 1798, at Ranelagh Gardens.

At his shop, in addition to publishing and selling music, Dussek and his partner vended tickets to special events, as, for instance, the masquerade ball and supper for Princess Charlotte's birthday on 7 April 1796. The firm also built pianos—probably

Harvard Theatre Collection

JAN LADISLAV DUSSEK
engraving by Condé, after Cosway

the instrument patented in 1799 by Joseph Smith—and on 21 March 1800 at Covent Garden Dussek's wife played a "military concerto" (probably by her husband) "on the new Patent Grand Piano Forte by Corri and Dussek, with tambourine and triangle."

Dussek turned out many musical compositions while he was in London, including music written in collaboration with Michael Kelly for *The Captive of Spilburg*, which was performed at Drury Lane on 14 November 1798. Dussek's other theatrical music consisted of an overture for *Feudal Times*, played at Drury Lane on 19 January 1799, and instrumental music for *Pizarro*, given at the same playhouse on 24 May. The *Times* on 15 November 1798 wrote of Dussek's composing:

> Mr. Dussek, in the music which is entirely new, has displayed a complete knowledge of the principles of the art. Composition is chiefly of the melancholy cast, and so far it is appropriate to the subject [of *The Captive of Spilberg*]. . . . The melody is natural and the choruses are, without exception, as perfect specimens of scientific taste as we can find in the works of the theatrical composers of the present day. The overture is entitled to encomium for the delicacy, sweetness and just combination of its movements, and was received with repeated plaudits.

Though his stay in England was a musical success, Dussek's home and business life was unfortunate. His wife Sophia was 14 years younger than he and not very faithful. She had a daughter, Olivia, born on 29 September 1801, over a year after Dussek left England. Olivia in time became Mrs George Buckley, had a career as a musician, and died in 1847. When it became apparent in 1800 that the Corri-Dussek firm was going bankrupt, Dussek left England in secrecy to avoid his creditors. On 16 May 1800 he wrote from Hamburg to Longman, Clementi & Co in London asking the firm to ship him two grand pianos, care of Messrs Lubert and Dumas.

Dussek performed in Hamburg in 1800 and 1801 and at Prague in 1802 before returning to his home to spend a few months with his father. He was in Magdeburg in 1803 and found a new patron in Prince Louis Ferdinand of Prussia. After the Prince died in 1806 Dussek was patronized by the Prince von Ysenburg, in whose court he served as a chamber musician.

Dussek and his wife apparently never saw one another after his departure from England, but they anticipated a reconciliation, for on 22 April 1806 when Dussek was in Berlin he wrote his wife a letter (preserved at the Bibliothèque du Conservatoire):

My Dear,

I receive Your lettre this moment, and as the post goes of in a few hours, I only have time to say that in such a case as You, & Your Father mention I cannot help retourning to London, for although I might live very happy anny where out of England, I could not bear the Idea of being outlawed in anny Country what ever. —Therefore press Your Father to send me that paper from the Chancelor, and a passport, for I would be glad this Business might terminate before the end of Mid Summer, that I might have time to resume my Journey to Bohemia. . . .

As soon as the Chancellor's Paper, and the Passeport will be send to me, take for me a little lodging in the Country, no matter whereabout, if it is but out of town, for after spending the Spring in this beautifull place where I am know, it would be impossible for me to stay two months in London. —Let a Forte Piano be brought there and I shall compose You some new Music.—

Adieu my dear You cannot conceive how happy I am at the Idea of seeing You so soon, although it deranges me in my projects. I shall write more the next post.

God bless you.

　　　　　　　　　Yours
　　　　　　　　　Dussek.

Perhaps, since the letter has been preserved, it was never sent. In any case, Dussek seems not to have returned to England.

In 1807 he was befriended by the Prince de Bénévente (Talleyrand), with whom he lived near Paris for several years. Dussek died at St-Germaine-en-Laye on 20 March 1812. His widow married John Alvis (or Alois) Moralt soon after her husband's death. *Grove's Dictionary* contains as complete a list of Dussek's compositions as can be found, along with an evaluation of his abilities as a composer and pianist.

Dussek's friend John Godefroi made an engraving of the musician which was published by Lesauvage. An engraving by P. Condé after R. Cosway was published by Cianchettini and Sperati in 1808. In the Nationalbibliothek in Vienna are engravings of Dussek by Arndt, Lemoine, and Maurin—all after unknown artists—and an engraving by Queneday after a painting by Callamorel.

Dussek, Mrs Jan Ladislav, Sophia Giustina, née Corri, later Mrs John Alvis Moralt   *1775–c. 1830, singer, harpist, pianist, composer.*

Sophia, the daughter of Domenico Corri the musician and music publisher, was born in Edinburgh on 1 May 1775. She had an elder brother Giovanni and younger brothers Montague, Haydn, and Philip Anthony, all of whom in one way or another became involved in London musical life. Sophia studied under her father and made her first public appearance as a pianist at the age of four in Edinburgh. The family moved to London in the late 1780s, and Sophia began appearing at the music rooms in London with considerable success. She sang soprano at the Hanover Square Rooms, perhaps as early as March 1790, though the London *Gazette* of 15 April 1791 reported her first public appearance as in those rooms in early 1791.

Miss Corri married the eminent pianist and composer Jan Ladislav Dussek on 4 September 1792 at St Anne's (St Anne, Soho, presumably). Though their marriage was not very successful, Sophia had the ad-

vantage of her husband's teaching and became expert on the piano and harp. She sang at Salomon's concerts, toured the three kingdoms (Cambridge, Oxford, Liverpool, Manchester, Edinburgh, and Dublin), and was in demand at the London theatres in oratorios. Among her London appearances were the Handel concert at Covent Garden on 8 March 1793 when she sang "I know that my redeemer liveth" from the *Messiah* and "Let the bright seraphim" from *Samson*, the concert at the King's Theatre on 27 February 1795 when she provided a harp accompaniment for Madame Banti, the Covent Garden concert on 7 March 1800 when she played a duet with Cimador —she on the harp and he on the piano—and the Covent Garden concert on 21 March 1800 when she played a "Military Concerto" (doubtless of her husband's composition) on a new patented grand piano built by the firm of Corri and Dussek.

She was apparently not faithful to Dussek, who was 14 years her senior, and it is said that she once ran away from him but was brought back. The couple lived for a while at her father's house and place of business, No 67, Dean Street, Soho, but they moved some time in the 1790s to Hammersmith. When the music business run by her husband and father became insolvent, Dussek fled to the Continent, leaving Sophia behind. A daughter, Olivia, was born to Mrs Dussek in 1801, over a year after the departure of her husband. Though there was talk of a reconciliation in 1806, the Dusseks seem not to have met again after 1800. When Dussek died in 1812, Sophia married the musician John Alvis (or Alois?) Moralt.

Sophia continued her musical career in the early nineteenth century, composing, playing the harp at the Oxford Music Room and elsewhere, singing in concerts, and teaching her daughter. In 1808 she was engaged "to perform in serious opera and to take the part of principal buffa, in case Mme Catalani is ill and unable to perform" at the King's Theatre for a season salary of £500. The *Examiner* on 1 May wrote of her performance in *La festa d'Iside*: "Madame Dussek appeared to more advantage, as a singer, in this opera than in any other; but from her strange dress, closely wrapped round her face, she appeared to be labouring under the agonies of an inveterate tooth-ache."

After her marriage to Moralt she lived at No 8, Winchester Row, Paddington, where she established a successful academy of music for teaching piano. Her daughter Olivia became Mrs George Buckley. She died in 1847. Sophia Dussek Moralt died about 1830.

Dutac, Mons [fl. 1724–1725], *actor.*
Monsieur Dutac (or Durac) was the *pantalone* in the Italian troupe which played at the Haymarket Theatre from 17 December 1724 to 13 May 1725. On 19 April 1725 he and Soulart shared a benefit.

"Dutch Woman, The." *See* SAFTRY, MRS.

Dutton, Mr [fl. 1730], *actor.*
Mr Dutton acted Stitch in *Scipio's Triumph* at Reynolds's booth at Bartholomew Fair on 22 August 1730, and Mrs Dutton, presumably his wife, played Zara in *Amurath the Great* and a Woman Peasant in *Harlequin's Contrivance* on 9 September 1730 at Pinkethman's Southwark Fair booth. In the latter performance Dutton played one of the Foresters.

Dutton, Mrs [fl. 1730], *actress. See* DUTTON, MR [fl. 1730].

Dutton, Frederick [fl. 1768–1785], *actor.*
Mr and Mrs Frederick Dutton acted at Norwich as early as 1768–69 and remained there through 1771. Frederick's salary in 1770 was £2 weekly, as was his wife's, but the Committee Books at Norwich show that

on 25 May 1771 it was agreed that Dutton's pay for the ensuing season should be 10s. 6d. weekly and that of his wife £1 11s. 6d. Dutton's wife Elizabeth did not complete the 1771–72 season; she died at Bury on 27 December 1771 and was buried on 31 December. From 1774 to 1777 Dutton acted low comedy parts at Edinburgh, two of his roles being Scrub in *The Stratagem* and Mungo in *The Padlock*. In 1777 he performed at Bristol.

The summer of 1781 found Frederick at Richmond, and on 12 November of that year he appeared at the Haymarket Theatre in London, acting, for that night only, a principal character in *The Spendthrift* and delivering a monologue called *Shuter's Post Haste Observations on his Journey to Paris*. On 21 September 1782 he made his first appearance at Bath, and he was with the Bristol troupe for the 1782–83 season, doubtless performing at both towns. On 22 March 1784 he was back at the Haymarket, playing Sharp in *The Lying Valet* and delivering his monologue again, and he returned there for the last time on 15 March 1785 as Filch in *The Beggar's Opera*, Diggory in *All the World's a Stage*, and speaker of the *Shuter* monologue.

Duval, Mr [fl. 1742], *dancer.*
On 29 September 1742 at Covent Garden, billed as making his first appearance on that stage, Mr Duval danced the *Drunken Peasant*. He danced again on 9 October, but he seems not to have stayed with the company the full season.

Duval, Mr [fl. 1764–1767], *dancer.*
On 10 March 1764 at the King's Theatre in the Haymarket Mr Duval (or Duvall) joined Berardi and Miss Tetley in a *Terzetto*. The following 20 March he danced with them in *The Turkish Coffee House*, and on 31 March he was Harlequin in *Le Masquerade*. At some time during 1764 he danced at Sadler's Wells, and he was there again in 1767. On 13 May 1767 he was

one of the dancers in the production of *Merlin*.

Duval, Mme ₁*fl.* 1741–1745₁, *dancer.*

On 28 September 1741 Mme Duval (or Duvall) and Froment danced *Les Bergiers* at Goodman's Fields; she was billed as making her first appearance on that stage. This might suggest that she was the Mlle Duval who danced at Drury Lane the previous season, though billings in later seasons make it clear that there were two dancers of the name in London.

Mme Duval did not receive further notices at Goodman's Fields in 1741–42, but she appeared occasionally at Covent Garden in 1744–45. She danced in *Le Gondalier* on 27 November 1744, was a Follower and Earth in *The Rape of Proserpine*, a Country Lass in *Orpheus and Eurydice*, danced in *Comus* and *Pyramus and Thisbe*, and performed a minuet with Destrade. On 23 November 1745 she repeated her small part in *Orpheus and Eurydice*, but on 25 November she was replaced, never to be noticed again.

Duval, Mlle ₁*fl.* 1740–1744₁, *dancer.*

Mlle Duval (or Duvall) danced *French Peasants* with Nivelon at Drury Lane on 26 December 1740 and on several subsequent dates and appeared in *Les Masons*, *Les Sabotiers*, and *Diane à la chasse*. On 22 August 1741 she danced Britannia in *The Triumph of Britannia* at Hallam's Bartholomew Fair booth. She and Mme Duval performed at Goodman's Fields in the fall of 1741, Mlle Duval appearing in a ballet introduced into *The Imprisonment, Release, Stratagems, and Marriage of Harlequin* on 9 October. She danced again on 19 October but was dropped from the bill on 23 October. On 10 October 1744 she put in an appearance at Covent Garden, dancing in *La Provençale*, a number which was dropped by the end of the month.

DuVal, John ₁*fl.* 1730₁, *dancer.*

Dickson's Dublin Intelligence of 12 May 1730 advertised a benefit at Smock Alley in Dublin for John DuVal, a dancer who had arrived "lately from London." There appears to be no record of DuVal's London activity, but the Dublin bill would suggest that he performed there shortly before his arrival.

D'Vallois. *See* **VALLOIS.**

Dworshak, Mr ₁*fl.* 1791₁, *clarinettist, basset-horn player.*

With his colleagues David and Springer, Mr Dworshak played at a number of concerts at Vauxhall Gardens in 1791. He was proficient on both the clarinet and basset horn.

Dyamond. *See* **DIAMOND** and **DIMOND.**

Dyan, Ursula. *See* **VAN BECK, MRS MICHAEL.**

Dyble, Richard ₁*fl.* 1672₁, *musician.*

Along with three others, Richard Dyble was ordered arrested on 29 February 1672 for playing music without a license.

Dyell, Mr ₁*fl.* 1776₁, *actor.*

Mr Dyell acted Lawyer in *The Miser* at the Haymarket Theatre on 18 September 1776.

Dyer, Mr ₁*fl.* 1716?–1720?₁, *singer.*

The British Museum *Catalogue of Printed Music* lists a song, *Here's a Health to the King*, published about 1716, that was sung by a Mr Dyer at Bullock's booth at Southwark Fair. The same song, with additional stanzas by Dyer, he sang at Lincoln's Inn Fields, and it was printed about 1720. *The London Stage* seems to contain no reference either to performances or to Dyer. Perhaps Dyer should be identified with the musician William Dyer.

Dyer, Mr (fl. 1732–1734), actor.

Mr Dyer played Sir Jealous in *The Busy Body* on 14 November 1732 at Lincoln's Inn Fields for his first appearance on that stage. During the rest of the season there he acted Woodcock in *Tunbridge Walks*, Kite in *The Recruiting Officer*, Cleon in *Timon of Athens*, Antonio in *Love Makes a Man* (on 7 May 1733 for his benefit, split with Haughton), and Obadiah in *The Committee*. On 27 September 1733 at Covent Garden he acted Sir Jealous again; on 29 September he was Shallow in *The Merry Wives of Windsor*; and on 11 October he played the third Witch in *Macbeth*. On 7 December at Drury Lane his wife made her debut on that stage in *Oroonoko*, for Dyer's benefit—an odd arrangement, since he had previously been with the rival troupe. He seems not to have acted another role until 7 October 1734 at the Haymarket Theatre, when he played Sir Sampson in *Love for Love*, and he was last noted in the bills on the following 4 November when he acted Bajazet in *Tamerlane* with a mixed group of professionals from the patent houses at the Great Room at the Ship Tavern.

Dyer, Mrs (fl. 1692–1693), singer.

As a member of the United Company Mrs Dyer sang in *The Fairy Queen* at Dorset Garden on 2 May 1692, and then, at Drury Lane during the winter, she sang in *Henry II* on 8 November 1692 and in *The Maid's Last Prayer* at the end of February 1693. Her songs in all three productions were by Henry Purcell, one of them being "I come to lock all fast" in *The Fairy Queen*. The *Thesaurus Musicus* of 1693 assigned her "Tho you make no return to my passion" in *The Maid's Last Prayer*, but this song was given to Mrs Hodgson in the printed edition of the play.

Dyer, Mrs (fl. 1733–1734), actress.

Mrs Dyer acted Widow Lackit in *Oroonoko* at Drury Lane on 7 December 1733 for her first appearance on that stage, and on 27 May 1734 at the Haymarket Theatre she played the Hostess in *1 Henry IV*. She must have been the wife of the actor who worked in London about this time; the *Oroonoko* performance was for his benefit.

Dyer, [Benjamin? John?] (fl. 1675), dancer.

On 15 February 1675 a Mr Dyer danced in the court masque *Calisto*. There were two Dyers who were dancing masters about this time, and perhaps one of them was the participant cited. Benjamin Dyer, whose wife was named Mary, lived in Shoe Lane next to the Wheat Sheaf and "against" the church of St Andrew, Holborn. The registers for that parish contain several references to Dyer's children: Mary Magdalen was baptized on 6 August 1671; Bridget was buried on 28 January 1673; Harman was buried on 22 July 1673; Mary was baptized on 26 December 1673; Elizabeth was baptized on 24 May 1674; Lucey was baptized on 6 June 1678; Ellinor was baptized on 10 November 1679; Martha was baptized on 15 July 1681; and a second Elizabeth, the first apparently having died, was baptized on 2 December 1682. On most of the entries Dyer was described as a dancing master, and on three of them he was styled "Gentleman."

Very likely related to Benjamin was John Dyer of the same parish, also described in the registers as a dancing master and gentleman, who lived with his wife Elizabeth at what the registers describe variously at Holborn Bridge, Shoe Lane, at the King's Head, against "ye Gloab," and near or next Dr Nurse's. The registers contain several mentions of their family: "Coocke" was born on 12 and baptized on 22 July 1660; Sarah was born on 29 June, baptized on 6 July, and buried on 17 August 1662; Anne was born on 29 August and baptized on 6 September 1663; John was born on 21 September, baptized on 4

October 1664, and buried on 2 March 1669; Matthew was baptized on 19 January 1666; John Dyer the elder "an antient man from John Dyer's his sonne's house" was buried on 10 October 1669; and Elizabeth was baptized on 13 November 1671 and buried on 1 January 1674.

Dyer, Edward *[fl. 1672–1686],* *violinist, composer.*

Edward Dyer was appointed a musician in ordinary in the King's Musick on 10 September 1672 and appointed to replace Locke as composer at a lifetime stipend of £40 annually starting 29 September 1677. As a violinist his salary, in addition to his composer's stipend, was £46 12s. 3d. yearly, in addition to which he received, but not usually on time, an annual livery allowance of £16 2s. 6d. The last mention of him in the Lord Chamberlain's accounts was on 21 September 1686 when he was to receive arrears of £112 17s. 6d. He may have been the Edward Dyer who was cited several times in the St Margaret, Westminster, parish registers. Edward and his wife Mary Magdalin christened the following children over the years: Dorothyah on 30 January 1668, Mary on 26 July 1670, Younge on 11 June 1671, Martha on 27 May 1672, "Yonne" on 13 January 1674, and Mary Magdalin on 27 January 1675.

Dyer, Harriet. *See* CHAMBERS, HARRIET.

Dyer, James *[fl. 1770],* *dancer.*

On 6 January 1770 James Dyer was paid £1 17s. 6d. by Covent Garden for nine nights as an extra dancer – possibly in *The Rape of Proserpine,* which had been running recently. At the ballet master Fishar's benefit on 20 April 1770 Dyer (presumably James), described as one of Fishar's scholars, danced a hornpipe in *Thomas and Sally.*

Dyer, Michael *d. 1774, actor, singer.*

Michael Dyer is said by a Burney notation in the British Museum to have made his stage debut as Tattle in *Love for Love* in Dublin in 1742, though Clark in *The Irish Stage in the County Towns* places the actor at the Smock Alley Theatre in Dublin as early as 1739. Clark may be in error, for he also has Dyer at Covent Garden in 1733, many years before he came to England. Dyer led a company of players at Cork in 1741–42, was erroneously reported on 15 May 1742 by the *Dublin Mercury* as "barbarously murdered," but was playing at the Aungier Street Theatre in Dublin in November 1743. On 26 December 1744 Dyer, identified as of Smock Alley, married Harriet Bullock of the same playhouse. She was the daughter of Christopher and Jane Bullock and had acted and danced at Smock Alley as early as 1737–38. The Dyers performed in Dublin for several years and then toured the English provinces before coming to London in 1749.

On 27 October 1749, billed as from Dublin, Michael Dyer made his first appearance at Covent Garden playing Tom in *The Conscious Lovers,* a role that allowed him to display his singing talent as well as his acting and which was one of his favorite vehicles for many years. Chetwood, writing in his *General History* in 1749, called Dyer a useful and pleasing actor, a fine singer, and a splendid mimic; "he can *take off* (as the Theatrical Term expresses it) not only every Actor, Male and Female, he has seen and heard . . . but also Singers and Dancers, foreign and domestic." During the 1749–50 season Dyer was also seen as Brazen in *The Recruiting Officer,* Atall in *The Double Gallant,* Beau Clincher in *The Constant Couple,* Marplot in *The Busy Body,* Clodio in *Love Makes a Man* (another of his favorite parts), Tinsel in *The Drummer,* Pistol in *Henry V,* Trim in *The Funeral,* Mercutio in *Romeo and Juliet* (one of his best characters), and Macheath in *The Beggar's Opera.* He was granted a benefit by himself on 20 April 1750 which was apparently clear of house charges.

MICHAEL DYER as Gratiano, with CHARLES MACKLIN as Shylock
engraving by Simonet, after De Loutherbourg

He could hardly bring out all his roles during his first season, but by the end of 1750–51 London had seen Dyer in most of the parts with which he was identified for the following 24 years. That season he appeared as Roderigo in *Othello*, Ramilie in *The Miser*, Gratiano in *The Merchant of Venice*, Brisk in *The Double Dealer*, Fribble in *Miss in Her Teens*, Basset in *The Provok'd Husband* (another of his favor-

ites), Mortimer in *1 Henry IV*, Setter in *The Old Bachelor*, Alexas in *All for Love* (which he played for many years), Chatillon in *King John*, Nerestan in *Zara*, Joe in *The King and the Miller*, Dick in *The City Wives Confederacy*, Jack Stocks in *The Lottery*, Witwoud in *The Way of the World*, Ranger in *The Suspicious Husband*, and others.

Until his death in 1774 Dyer played at

Covent Garden. From 1753 on he received benefits regularly, and though his salary is not known for every year, he was earning £7 weekly in 1759, £1 1s. 3d. daily in 1767, and £1 3s. daily in 1768. His benefits brought him profits that averaged £150. Over the years he attempted many roles in new plays but also added to his repertoire new parts in revived works. Among them might be mentioned Chamont in *The Orphan*, Lovemore in *The Amorous Widow*, Dudley in *Lady Jane Gray*, Sparkish in *The Country Wife*, Laertes in *Hamlet* (though he declined to Osric in later years), Young Fashion in *The Relapse*, Richmond in *Richard III*, Archer in *The Stratagem*, Marcus in *Cato*, Garcia in *The Mourning Bride*, Romeo (for his benefit on 11 April 1755; he did not keep the role), Hephestion in *The Rival Queens*, Macduff in *Macbeth* (again for a benefit), Altamont and Lothario in *The Fair Penitent*, the title roles in both *Sir Courtly Nice* and *The Minor* (which he did not play often), Razor in *The Provok'd Wife*, Knowell in *Every Man In His Humour*, Eustace in *Love in a Village*, Jeremy in *Love for Love*, Young Bellair in *The Man of Mode*, Brush in *The Clandestine Marriage*, and Feste with the epilogue song in *Twelfth Night* (late in his career and seldom performed).

By 1753 Dyer had attracted the attention of the critics, and he may have had mixed feelings about what they said. *The Present State of the Stage* that year found in Dyer a "Lightness in his Deportment, which does not suit well with Characters of Gravity; yet I have seen him perform some Things in Tragedy extremely well." In 1757 *The Theatrical Examiner* was more detailed:

Mr. D——r is a little smart figure; his hair is light and features small,——therefore express always one thing.——His manner tolerably free, rather with a sort of sameness; he plays Mercutio much better than any

person I have seen, from not playing the fool in it. Atall he is much at a loss in; the town too often see Mr. G——k in Ranger, to give [Dyer] any great share of applause in the part.—Tom in the Conscious Lovers he plays very agreeable.

The *Theatrical Review* of 1757–58 liked Dyer's Modely in *The Country Lasses*, "where his ease, his prodigious flow of spirits, and his figure, struck and pleased me; but on a second, third, and fourth visit, I fancied I discovered too much resemblance between his Count Basset, his Modely, his Clodio, and even his Tom in the Conscious Lovers." The author went on to analyze the problem and offer Dyer advice:

I will not pronounce this sameness want of genius; for he has variety; but one would imagine that he exhausts and displays his whole stock of gestures and action in each part, so as to be forced in the next to borrow from the former, to fill up the performance; in a word, what variety he is master of, he employs entirely in adorning each particular part, not in distinguishing the parts from each other. I therefore would advise him, as the only means of procuring further success, to make it henceforth his study to find out the characteristick differences between this and that character, so that he may vary his exhibition of them accordingly. He pleases already, thereby he will please more; but it would be very imprudent in him to roam out of that set of lively characters which he now acts in comedy, as they are the only parts where he can make any advantage of the uneven smartness of his own voice. Those dancing and airy notes would but ill-become more sedate characters; they have something ludicrous, which, tho' genteel, debar him from all hopes of ever making a figure in the buskin; where, to be useful, he may from time to time supply a vacancy, but never fill a character.

In 1762 *The Rosciad of C——v——nt G——rd—n* had similar views but expressed them more lightly:

NEXT D——R came on, by nature's hand design'd,

To please each hearer, and to charm
  each mind;
So just, so true, the servant's part he
  plays,
That all must own he well deserves our
  praise.—
. . . Nor can we less applaud his mimic
  rage,
When loud he swaggers round the
  trembling stage;
And whilst his words the blust'ring hero
  speak,
Tamely submits to eat FLUELLIN's leek.
But when from Common-Sense he goes
  astray,
To follow where his fancy leads the way,
Begins the scene, where most he shines,
  to quit
And imitates the sprightly coxcomb's
  wit:
We must those parts, so ill employ'd
  deplore,
Whose native lustre charm'd so oft
  before.

The Battle of the Players of 1762 was probably right in categorizing Dyer as a general in John Rich's "Light-Infantry" at Covent Garden. When Dyer went off to Bristol in the summer of 1766, on the other hand, "he took a higher flight," as Jenkins wrote in his *Memoirs* in 1826, "and I have seen him play Zaphna in 'Mahomet,' with great and deserved applause."

But Dyer chose to be tested against London standards, so he had to suffer such slings and arrows as those in *The Rational Rosciad* of 1767:

True to the poets meaning, dapper Dyer,
Neither replete nor destitute of fire,
Plays all his various characters with skill,
Not absolutely great, but far from ill.

Or Francis Gentleman's sharper thrusts in *The Theatres* (1771–72):

Dyer was never any thing to boast,
A sufferable coxcomb at the most;

Now sinking fast into the vale of years,
The remnant of a remnant he appears.

Theatrical Biography in 1772 summed up matters and also offered some anecdotes about Dyer's life. The author noted that over a period of 27 years Dyer's appearance, manner, and style of acting had scarcely changed—a somewhat left-handed compliment. Dyer was a prudent actor and saved his money (over £2000, the author said), but he was fleeced of his savings by a friend who represented himself as a man of fortune, took Dyer's money to invest, and absconded with it. After this sad affair (undated by the author), Dyer acted with Spranger Barry at the Crow Street Theatre in Dublin and at Cork (activity for which there is no other record). The writer concluded that Dyer's "*forte*, we think, lies in footmen; there is a pertness in his face and manner, that answers to this cast of parts, which does not suit well with those of gentlemen."

The 1772–73 season was Dyer's last full one. He was still playing Tom, Tressel, Jeremy, Hephestion, and others of his accustomed parts, and he also appeared in a role in a new comedy, Robin in *Cross Purposes* and participated in an *Occasional Prelude*. His earning power was still considerable: on 13 April 1773 his benefit brought him a profit of £182 16s. 6d. In 1773–74 he essayed two new roles, an unnamed one in *Achilles in Petticoats* and Handy in *The Man of Business*. For his benefit on 5 April 1774 he acted Jeremy in *Love for Love* and collected a profit of £152 11s. 6d., but that was his last appearance, and he did not complete the season. On 9 April 1774 Michael Dyer died. The next day one T. M. wrote a blank-verse "Impromptu on the Death of Mr Dyer, of Covent Garden Theatre, who died Last Night at Nine o'Clock:"

He's gone; the solemn, slow, funeral Toll
Minutely echoing from yon sacred Dome

*Confirms th'expected news, and gives the
    World
One Instance more of Death's insatiate
    Pow'r.
Oh Dyer! born to feel the keenest Strokes
Affliction's Hand could give, who liv'dst
    unpaid
The social Duties thou didest well de-
    serve;
How shall I sing thy much-lamented
    Death!
How shall I sing thy Worth—thou
    injur'd Man!
But needless all the afflicted Muse can
    say,
And him whom Angels hymn lacks not
    her Praise.
The Trial's o'er, he soars to meet the
    Crown,
The bright Reward of all his Suff'rings
    past;
And Envy's Self must own he liv'd a
    Man,
"More sinn'd against than sinning."*

Was Dyer's eulogist thinking of the actor's loss of £2000 and his deception by a friend? Or was he referring to the report (undocumented) that Mrs Dyer made a false step for which the actor never forgave her? Or did the comedian suffer some other calamity of which existing records say nothing?

Of Dyer's married life a few facts have suvived, though there is confusion about his spouse. His marriage to Harriet Bullock in 1744 bore fruit, as the parish registers of St Paul, Covent Garden, testify. They had a son John, baptized on 13 December 1750 and buried the next day; a daughter Barbarina, baptized on 2 May 1752; and a son William, baptized on 25 August 1754 and buried on the following 19 October. Possibly the provincial actor Joseph Dyer was a son of Michael and Harriet, for he named a daughter (or granddaughter) Harriot in 1818.

But Michael Dyer's will, dated 15 June 1772 and proved on 18 April 1774 (the day after the actor's burial at St Paul, Cov-

ent Garden), contains references which conflict with the baptismal records. The will refers to Dyer's wife as Henrietta and cites a daughter Harriet Taplin. A scribal error which Dyer may have overlooked might account for the Harriet-Henrietta confusion, or, as Hogan suggests in *Shakespeare in the Theatre*, Dyer may have married a second time to a woman named Henrietta. The daughter Harriet Dyer Taplin, judging by her Christian name, was surely a child of Michael and Harriet, and either her baptismal record has not been found or the daughter Barbarina was actually Barbarina Harriet. (Harriet Dyer married William Taplin about 1770 but by 1784 went under the name of Mrs Chambers.)

In any case, Michael Dyer's will specified that his three-percent consolidated annuities and his goods, valuables, and clothes were to be sold and invested at three percent for the benefit of his daughter Mrs Harriet Taplin "without the controul of her husband" and for the benefit of her children if she should have any. If she should die without issue, £100 was to be given to the Theatrical Fund for "decayed actors" at Covent Garden and the overplus of £100 was to go to Dyer's wife "Henrietta" for her life and then to Edward Tighe of the Middle Temple.

Michael Dyer was shown as Gratiano in *The Merchant of Venice*, with Macklin as Shylock, in an engraving by T. B. Simonet after De Loutherbourg. An anonymous engraver showed Dyer as Young Wilding in *The Citizen*, with Shuter as Old Philpot and Woodward as the Citizen.

Dyer, Mrs Michael, Harriet, · née Bullock *b. 1721?, actress, dancer.*

Harriet (or Harriot) Bullock may have been the child who was born to Christopher Bullock and his wife Jane in February or March 1721, though there is no proof. Harriet was doubtless the granddaughter of William Bullock referred to in the Lincoln's Inn Fields free list on 29 October 1728, and perhaps she was the Miss Bullock who played Maria in *The London Merchant* at the elder Bullock's Bartholomew Fair booth on 26 August 1731. In that production were Henrietta Maria Bullock Ogden, Ann Russell Bullock, and William Bullock the elder.

Harriet's father died in 1722, but his widow continued acting in London until 1737, after which she took Harriet with her to Dublin. At the Smock Alley Theatre on 8 May 1738 "Bullock's daughter" acted, and on 23 November she made her first public attempt at dancing. Her mother died in 1739, and Harriet apparently stayed on in Ireland, perhaps performing occasionally. She was with the Smock Alley company when she married a young actor in the troupe, Michael Dyer, on 26 December 1744. She was described by the papers as "a young actress of very good character."

Mrs Dyer and her husband played at Smock Alley for several seasons, and on one occasion she was the unwilling object of a lustful attack by a drunken playgoer. On 19 January 1747 at a performance of *Aesop* a tipsy young gentleman found his way to the green room where he accosted Mrs Dyer, trod on her foot, abused her with obscene language, and started to attack her. George Anne Bellamy came to the rescue and whisked Mrs Dyer to the safety of a dressing room, while the playhouse guards controlled the ardor of the impulsive inebriate.

In October 1749 the Dyers came to London to play at Covent Garden, the theatre with which both were chiefly associated for the rest of their lives. Mrs Dyer played Imoinda in *Oroonoko* for her debut on 3 November, but she seems not to have been an active member of the troupe the rest of the season. For several years she made only occasional appearances. On 15 April 1751 she acted Octavia in *All for Love* to swell her husband's benefit receipts, but that was the only billing she

received that season. She played at the Jacob's Wells Theatre in Bristol in the summer of 1751, and upon her return to Covent Garden in 1751–52 she appeared only as Clarissa in *The City Wives Confederacy*, Flora in *The Country Lasses*, and Mrs Brittle in *The Amorous Widow*. The author of *The Present State of the Stage* in 1753 complained that he could not understand why Mrs Dyer was seen so seldom, since she was a pleasant and just performer.

During the rest of the 1750s Mrs Dyer added the following new parts to her small repertoire: Angelina in *Love Makes a Man*, Lady Dainty in *The Double Gallant*, Aurelia in *The Twin Rivals*, Celia in *Volpone*, Catherine in *Henry V*, the Duchess of York in *Richard III*, Rose in *The Recruiting Officer*, Angelica in *The Constant Couple*, Lucinda in *The English Woman in Paris*, Lady Percy in *Henry IV*, Violante in *The Wonder*, Araminta and Arabella in *The Committee*, Jaqueline in *The Royal Merchant*, and Colombine in a number of pantomimes: *The Jealous Farmer Deceived, Harlequin Skeleton, The Jealous Farmer, Harlequin Statue, Colombine Courtezan, Merlin's Cave, The Fair, The Rape of Proserpine,* and *The Siege of Quebec*. In Colombine she had clearly found a line which pleased her and the public; *The Theatrical Examiner* in 1757 said she was "at present the best Columbine we have." By 1759 the Covent Garden management allowed her to share a benefit with three others, whereas she had been on a straight salary before. And in the summer of 1759 she was invited back to the theatre at Bristol.

The 1760s saw little change in the pattern Mrs Dyer had set for herself. She was content to work a relatively light schedule each season, concentrate on colombine parts, and occasionally play new roles in comedies. For this she received 7s. 8d. daily or £70 yearly and usually enjoyed a shared benefit each spring. As Colombine she appeared in the 1760s in *Harlequin Sorcerer*,

Perseus and Andromeda, The Royal Chace, Orpheus and Eurydice, Apollo and Daphne, and *The Farmer Outwitted,* and she played another popular pantomime role, Lady Relish in *Harlequin Doctor Faustus.* Other parts she tried during the decade included Harriet in *The Jealous Wife,* Melinda in *The Recruiting Officer,* Hillaria in *Love's Last Shift,* the Lady in *Love à la Mode,* Isabinda in *The Busy Body,* Dorinda in *The Stratagem,* and Lady Grace in *The Provok'd Husband.* Her salary dropped to 6s. 8d. daily in 1767, but she received a small windfall that year when Thomas Phillips left her £10 10s. in his will. In 1765 she broke her routine by playing at Lynn; there she spoke a special epilogue at a performance of *Love for Love,* but the rest of her activity has not been discovered.

Mr and Mrs Dyer had started a family, perhaps as early as the late 1740s. Their daughter Harriet, who later became Mrs William Taplin, may have been born before 1750, but her baptismal record has not been found. The Dyers had a son John who died in infancy in 1750, a daughter Barbarina (or Barbarina Harriet?) who was born in 1752, and a son William who died in infancy in 1754. Possibly the Joseph Dyer who acted in the provinces later in the century was also a son of Michael and Harriet, but no birth record for him has been located.

In 1768–69 at Covent Garden Mrs Dyer played some of her old parts and added Lady Constant in *The Way to Keep Him,* Araminta in *The Confederacy,* Lamorce in *The Inconstant,* and Harriet in *The Miser.* At the Haymarket Theatre in the summer of 1769 she was Sukey in *The Beggar's Opera,* Dolly in *The Commissary,* Kitty in *The Liar,* Araminta in *The Old Bachelor,* Portia in *Julius Caesar,* Lucy in *The Minor,* and an unnamed character in *The Doctor Last in His Chariot.* Perhaps this sudden increase in her activity and expansion of her repertoire occurred because her children were old enough to need less atten-

tion. Hogan in *Shakespeare on the Stage* suggests that Michael Dyer married a second time (Dyer's will calls his wife Henrietta, not Harriet), but the busy Mrs Dyer of 1768–69 was clearly the same performer of earlier years, for she played a number of parts that had been her property for some time: Colombine in *Orpheus and Eurydice, The Royal Chace,* and *Harlequin Skeleton,* Lady Relish in *Harlequin Doctor Faustus,* and a number of others.

In 1769–70 Mrs Dyer passed a season at Covent Garden much like the 1768–69 season, and she acted again at the Haymarket in the summer, but she added little to her repertoire beyond the role of Eleanor in *King John.* On 1 October 1770, unless the bills were in error, she played the Farmer's Wife in *Harlequin's Jubilee* at Covent Garden and Desdemona in *Othello* at the Haymarket—a feat difficult but not impossible.

By 1771–72 she was no longer the attraction she had once been. One critic described her as "Dyer, who seldom can please." She acted infrequently, and the 1772–73 season was her last at Covent Garden. She played Colombine in *The Royal Chace,* Dolly in *The Commissary,* Mrs Foresight in *Love for Love,* and, for her shared benefit with two others on 18 May 1773, Bridget in *Every Man in His Humour.* The accounts show that each beneficiary had to contribute £7 16s. 8d. to cover a deficit. This Mrs Dyer was able to do with part of the receipts from the £37 8s. worth of tickets she had sold, but that was a rather sad ending to her long career. She acted only once more in London: on 16 September 1773 at the Haymarket Theatre she had an unnamed role in Samuel Foote's production of *The Macaroni.*

Tate Wilkinson testified in his *Wandering Patentee* (1795) that Mrs Dyer "had made a false step, which her husband . . . never forgave, and by which she rushed precipitately into vice and sudden distraction, and died in great distress . . ."

Wilkinson elaborated little: "Her person was neat and genteel; she was a good Colombine: But her ill fate gave her up from the comforts of Covent Garden Theatre, to the miseries of a little country company, where she ended her days in remorse, and an accumulation of woe and calamity." How true the story is cannot now be determined. When Michael Dyer died on 9 April 1774, perhaps Mrs Dyer was no longer with him; the press was silent on the matter. Dyer's will, written in 1772, named Mrs Dyer a secondary legatee but called her (possibly in error) "Henrietta." Harriet Taplin, the daughter of Michael Dyer, was to receive the benefit of income from the sale of Dyer's possessions; if she died childless, £100 was to be given to the Covent Garden fund and the overplus to "Henrietta" Dyer, Michael's wife. The name Henrietta was used again in reference to Dyer's widow on 9 August 1814 when the estate was administered following the death of Harriet Taplin in 1804. Perhaps Michael Dyer married twice, but the career of the Mrs Dyer we have been following here seems all of a piece and should be assigned to Harriet Bullock Dyer; if there was a Henrietta Dyer, she was apparently not an actress.

Dyer, William   *fl.* 1727?–1739], musician.

William Dyer was one of the original subscribers to the Royal Society of Musicians on 28 August 1739. He may have been the William Dyer mentioned on 19 October 1727 when administration of the estate of John Hart of Northington, Southampton, was granted to Susanne Dyer alias Hart, wife of William Dyer and relict of John Hart.

Dyke, Mr   [*fl. c. 1661–1662*], actor.

An actor named Dyke, or possibly Duke, played a role in *The Royall King* at the Vere Street Theatre about 1661–62, according to a manuscript cast in a Folger Shakespeare Library copy of the play. Perhaps this performer should be identified as Marmaduke Watson, who was sometimes called "Duke."

Dyke, Mr   [*fl. 1754*], bassoonist.

Mr Dyke played the bassoon for a fee of 8s. in the May 1754 performance of the *Messiah* given at the Foundling Hospital.

Dyke, John   [*fl. 1789?–1814?*], actor, singer, dancer.

The name Dyke (or Dykes) appears in a number of theatrical documents in and out of London in the late eighteenth century, and perhaps all the references are to the performer John Dyke. A Mr Dyke was a principal character in *The What Is It?* at the Royal Circus on 12 May 1789; a Dykes was playing at the theatre in Salisbury in 1792; at Sadler's Wells on 4 August 1795 a Mr Dyke was a Hunter in *Chevy Chase* and on 31 August a Sailor in *England's Glory*; and a Mr Dyke played in the summer of 1797 at Birmingham, hailed as from the Royalty Theatre in London.

On 26 May 1797 and for a fortnight thereafter a Dyke danced in *Harlequin and Oberon* at Covent Garden. He returned for the 1797–98 and 1798–99 seasons at £1 10s. weekly to appear as a messenger in *1 Henry IV*, the Count of Lindenbergh in *Raymond and Agnes*, Paris in *The Jealous Wife*, Don Quixote in both *Barataria* and *Harlequin and Quixote*, a Danish Soldier in *The Round Tower*, the second Irishman in *Voluntary Contributions*, a Witch in *The Witches' Revels*, the Woodcutter in *Harlequin's Chaplet*, and a number of unspecified but principal characters in other pantomimes. In addition, he sang in the choruses in *Hamlet, Macbeth,* and *Romeo and Juliet*. Between seasons, in the summer of 1798, a Mr Dyke performed again at Birmingham.

Dyke began the 1799–1800 season at Covent Garden, but after appearing as the

Jailor in *The Beggar's Opera*, singing in *Macbeth* and *Romeo and Juliet*, and playing a Countryman in *Lovers' Vows*, and an Islander in *The Death of Captain Cook*, he seems to have left the company. His last appearance at Covent Garden was on 28 October 1799. In 1800 John Dyke and Mary Smith were granted a license to produce an entertainment at the Haymarket Theatre, and perhaps this venture caused him to desert Covent Garden. Nothing is known of the Haymarket production Dyke planned. A Mr Dyke, perhaps the same person, was at Drury Lane in 1813–14 at a salary of £1 1s. weekly; also on the roster was a Miss Dyke at £2 10s.

Dykes, Mr ₁fl. 1710–1725₁, *boxkeeper.*

On 8 May 1710 Mr Dykes and two other boxkeepers at the Queen's Theatre in the Haymarket received a benefit. Though Dykes's name did not appear again in theatrical documents until 15 December 1716, one supposes that he was regularly employed at the Queen's Theatre (renamed the King's after the death of Queen Anne). His position in 1716 was front boxkeeper at the King's. In the 1720s he received benefits on 14 March 1723 and 16 April 1725 at the Haymarket Theatre, though he was in both instances described as boxkeeper at the King's Theatre.

Dymond. *See* **DIAMOND** and **DIMOND.**

Dymuch or **Dymuck.** *See* **DIMMOCK.**

Dyne, John *d. 1788, singer, composer.*

John Dyne, a countertenor, wrote a number of glees, one of which, "Fill the bowl," won a prize from the Catch Club in 1768. He became a Gentleman of the Chapel Royal in 1772, sang in *Samson* at Drury Lane on 22 March 1776, and sang in the *Messiah* at the Chapel of the Foundling Hospital on 2 April 1776. He was a member of the Academy of Antient Music from its inception in 1776 and became a lay vicar of Westminster Abbey in 1779. He was one of the singers in the Handel Memorial concerts at the Abbey and the Pantheon in May and June 1784. He died by his own hand on 30 October 1788 and was buried the following 3 November at St Paul's Cathedral.

The Royal Society of Musicians in 1789, 1792, and 1795 helped arrange for the children of John Dyne to be apprenticed: George Muscat Dyne was placed with a surgeon, the eldest daughter (unnamed) was apprenticed to a mantua maker, and Julia and Wilhelmina Dyne were placed with Wilhelmina Muscat and Wilhelmina Dyne of Grantham. On 5 December 1795 the Society ordered the widow Dyne's allowance stopped and requested from her proof that she had a further claim on the Society's funds. Action was postponed, her allowance was continued, and not until 1 March 1812 was she informed finally that funds would be stopped. A Mrs Dyne, presumably the widow of John, started sending letters of thanks to the Society for benefactions in 1821, however, so there must have been a change of heart or circumstances. A Mr Dyne, probably John's son George, thanked the Society on 6 December 1835 for the donations they had given his mother during the years he was abroad.

Dyne, Richard ₁fl. c. 1760–1776₁, *singer.*

In the 1760s or possibly later Richard Dyne (or Dine) petitioned the Lord Chamberlain for allowances of clothing for Children of the Chapel Royal. Normally, such a request would have come from the master of the young choristers, though Dyne may have been an assistant. On 22 March 1776 at Drury Lane Dyne was one of the chorus of Israelites in the oratorio *Samson.*

Dynion. *See* **BENION.**

Illustrations

THEATRE PLANS AND SITES

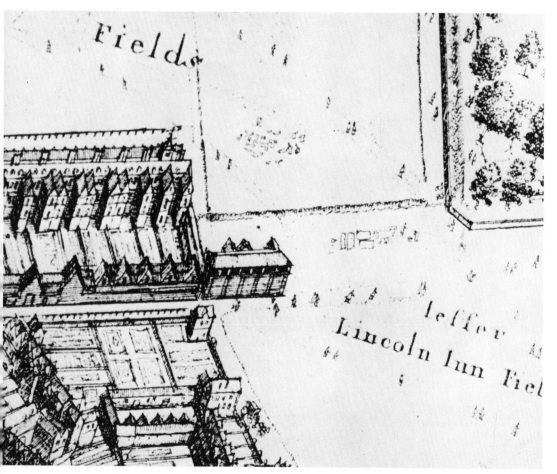

Lisle's Tennis Court, later the Lincoln's Inn Fields Theatre
from Hollar's map of London, c. 1657

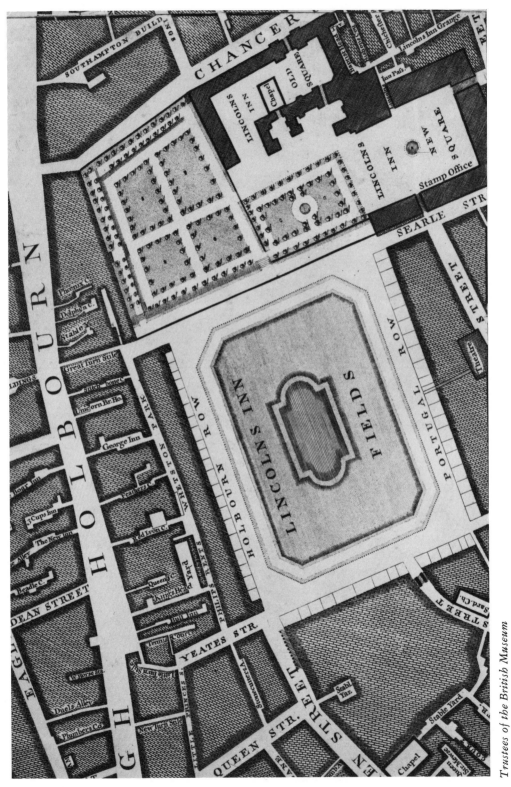

Trustees of the British Museum
Lincoln's Inn Fields and the site of the theatre
from Roque's map of London, 1746

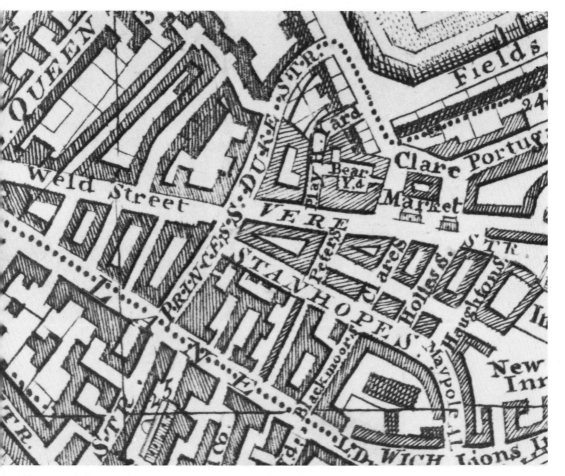

Sites of the Vere Street Theatre (in "Play H. Yard" west of Clare Market) and
the Bridges Street Theatre (shown in profile at lower left and numbered 25)
from Foster's map of London, 1738, though the sites are of theatres of the 1660s

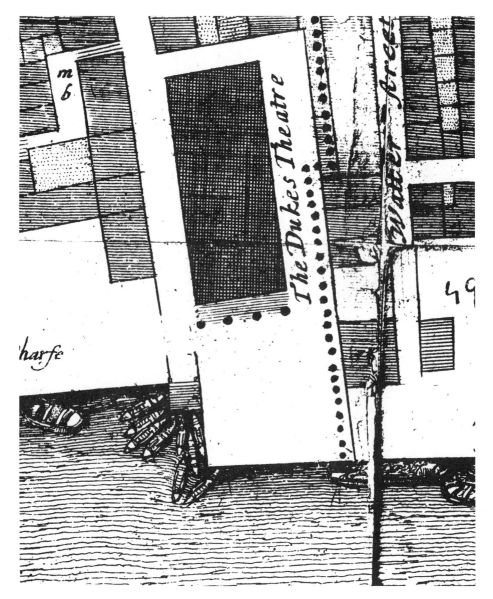

Site of the Dorset Garden Theatre
from Ogilby and Morgan's map of London, 1677

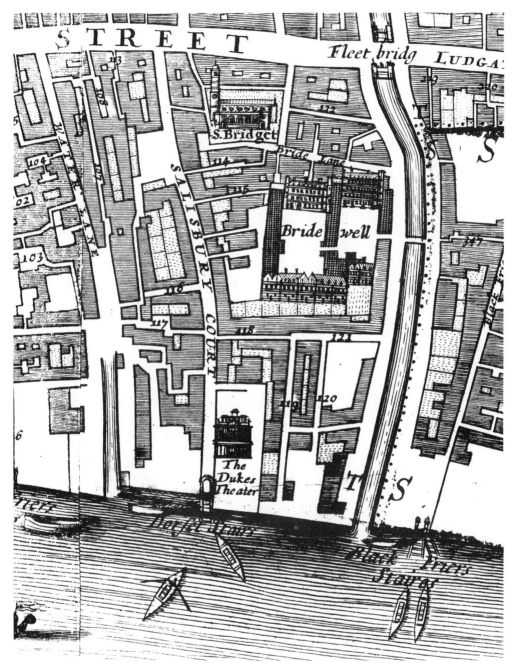

Site and façade view of the Dorset Garden Theatre ("The Dukes Theater")
from Ogilby and Morgan's map of London, 1681–82

548

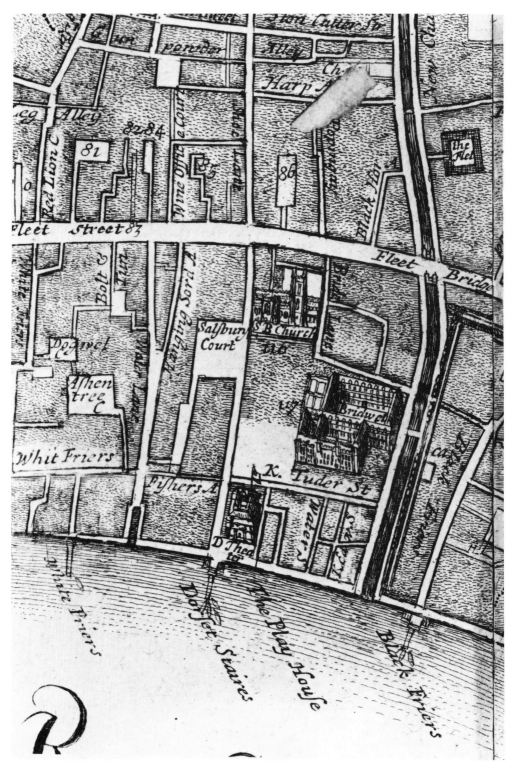

Trustees of the British Museum

Site of the Dorset Garden Theatre—but the bird's-eye view of the building may
picture the older Salisbury Court playhouse, which was not on the same site but nearby
from Lea and Glynne's map of London, 1706

549

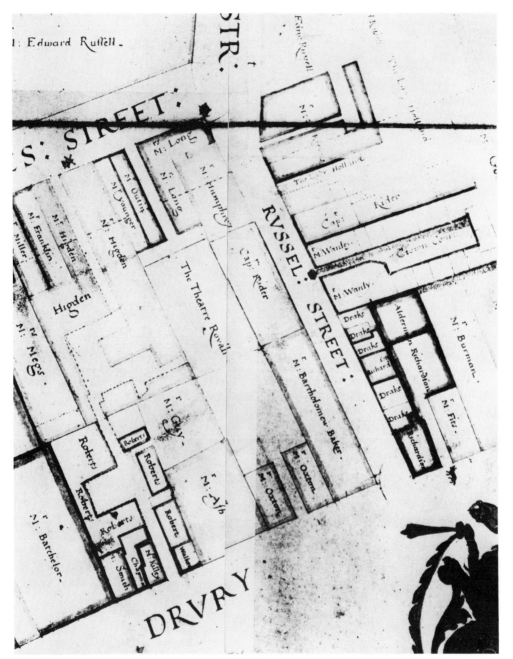

Site of the Bridges Street (and later, Drury Lane) Theatre ("The Theatre Royall")
from Lacy's map of the parish of St Paul, Covent Garden, 1673

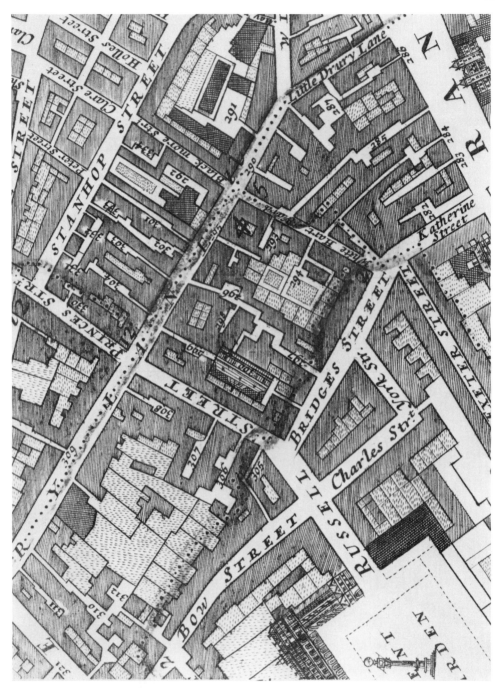

Site and profile view of the Bridges Street Theatre
(numbered 300 in the center of the picture)
from Morgan and Ogilby's map of London, 1681–82, showing a playhouse which had
burned down 10 years before

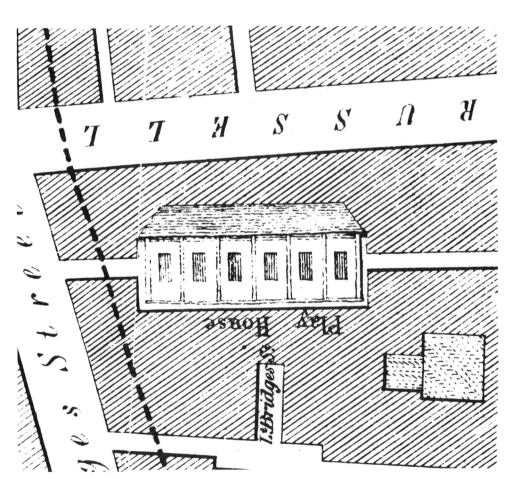

Site and profile view of the Drury Lane Theatre
from Lyborn's map of Covent Garden, 1686

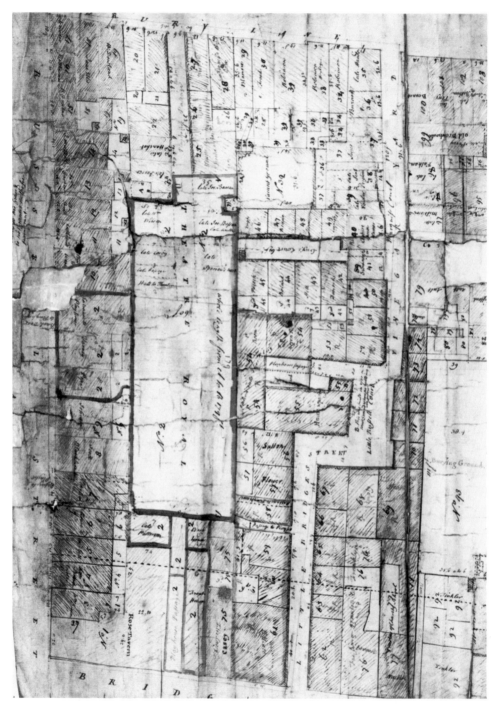

Trustees of the Bedford Settled Estates and of the Greater London Record Office
Site of the Drury Lane Theater, c. 1748, from a Bedford Estate map

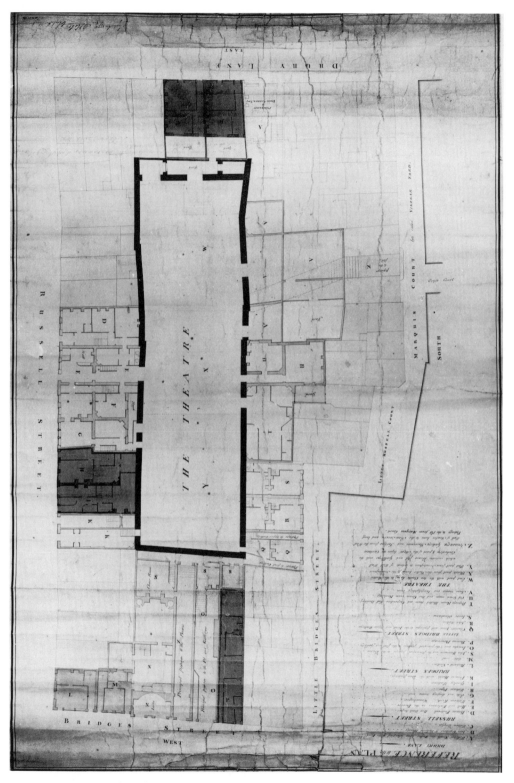

Trustees of the Bedford Settled Estates and of the Greater London Record Office
Site of the Drury Lane Theatre, by J. Hele, 1778

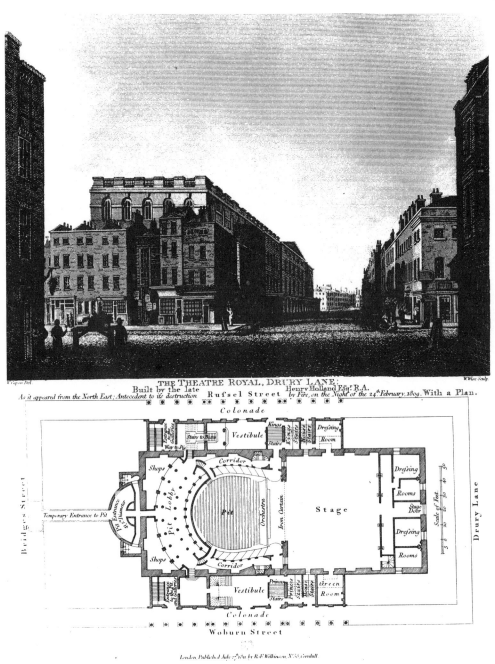

Exterior view from the northeast (Russell Street front) and interior plan of the Drury Lane Theatre before the fire of 1809 drawing by the scene designer William Capon from Wilkinson's *Londina Illustrata*, 1819–25

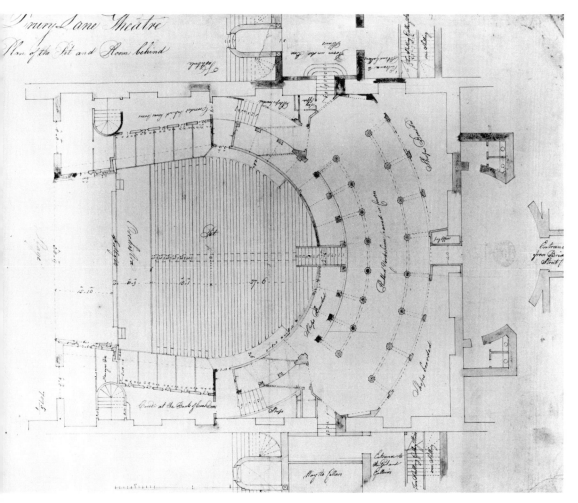

Enthoven Collection, Theatre Museum
Henry Holland's first design for the auditorium of the Drury Lane Theatre, 1792.

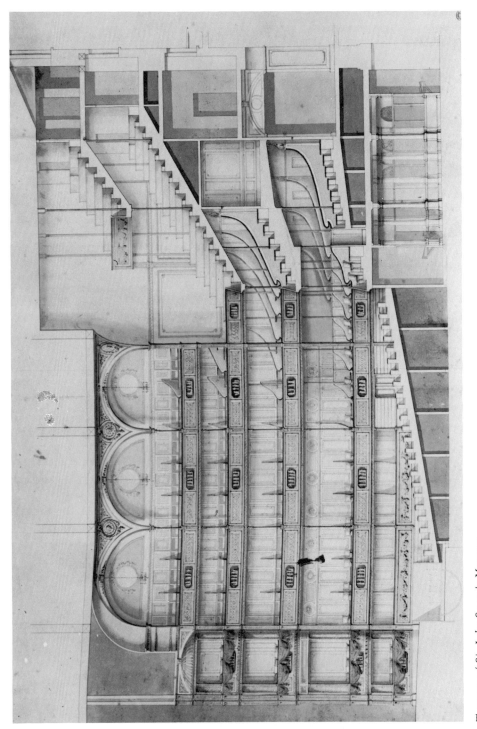

Henry Holland's section view of the Drury Lane auditorium, 1793

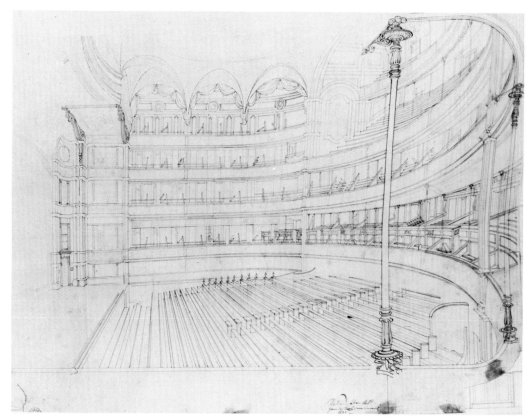

Drawing of the Drury Lane auditorium by the scene designer William Capon, 1805

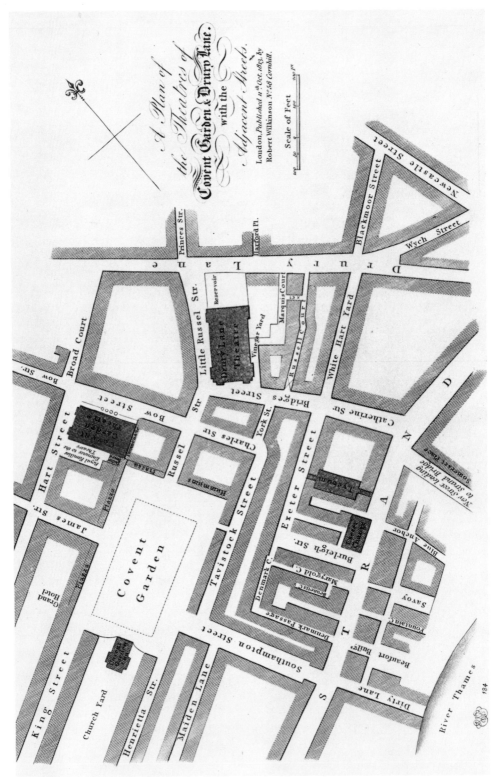

Sites of the Covent Garden and Drury Lane theatres, 1813
from Wilkinson's *Londina Illustrata*, 1819–25

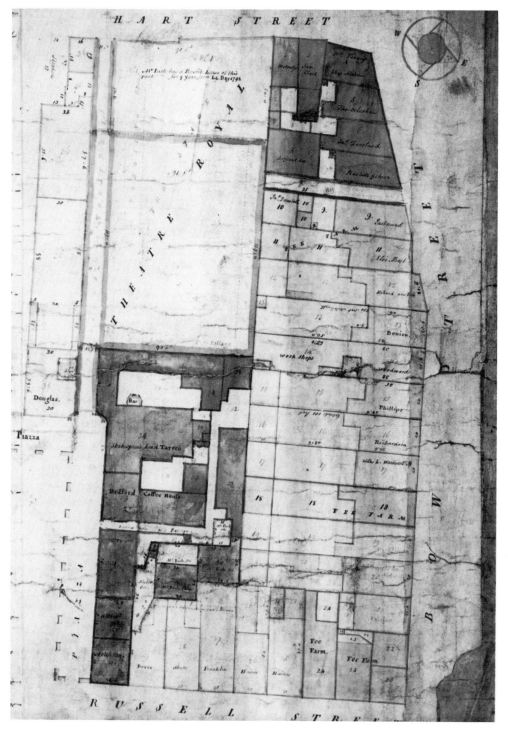

Trustees of the Bedford Settled Estates and of the Greater London Record Office
Site of the Covent Garden Theatre, c. 1760

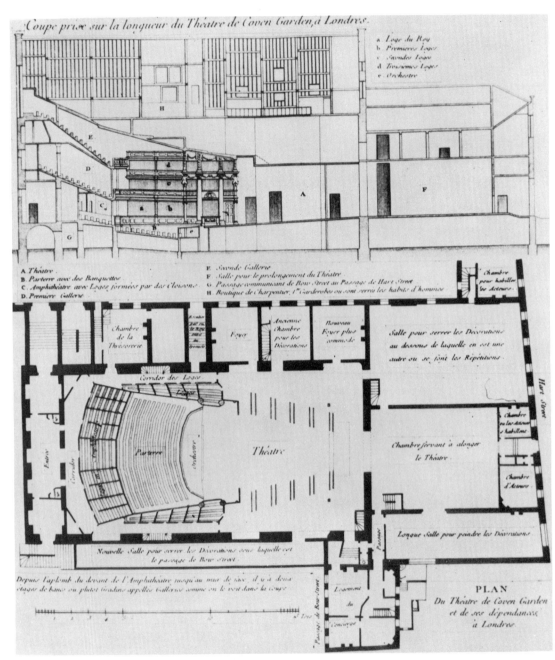

Section and plan of the Covent Garden Theatre of 1731–32, engraved about 1774
from Dumont's *Parallele de Plans des Plus Belles Salles de Spectacles d'Italie et de France*

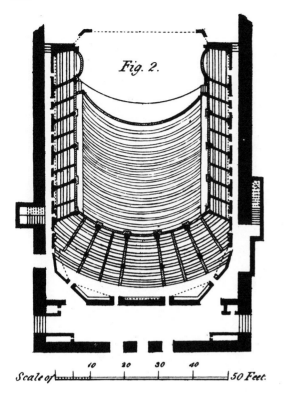

Fig. 2.

Scale of   10   20   30   40   50 Feet.

Covent Garden Theatre.

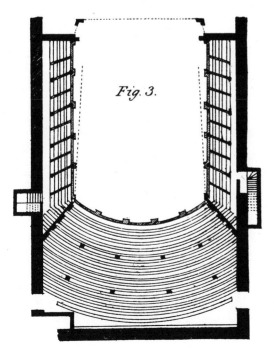

Fig. 3.

Plans of the Covent Garden Theatre after the
1782 remodelling by Richards
from Saunders's *A Treatise on Theatres,* 1790

Folger Shakespeare Library
Site of the King's Theatre in the Haymarket ("Opera House" in upper right corner). Nearby were the Haymarket Theatre, the tennis court theatre in James Street, and the concert rooms in Panton and Dean streets
from Roque's map of London, 1746

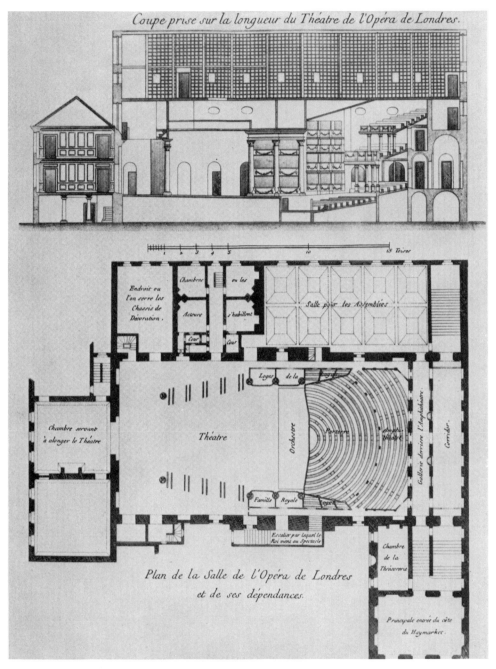

Coupe prise sur la longueur du Théâtre de l'Opéra de Londres.

Plan de la Salle de L'Opéra de Londres
et de ses dépendances.

Section and plan of the King's Theatre in the Haymarket, 1764
from Dumont's *Parallele de Plans des Plus Belles Salles de Spectacles d'Italie et de France*

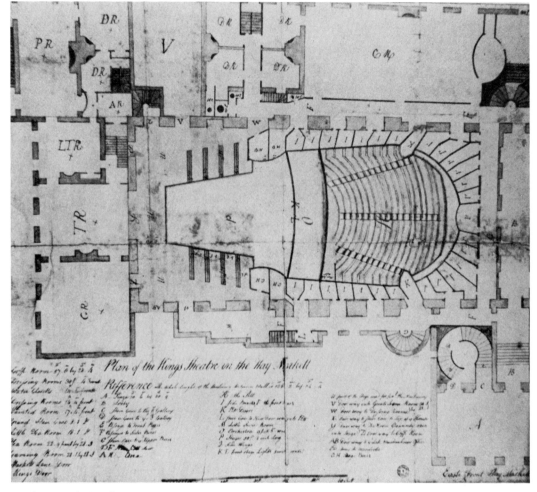

Plan of the King's Theatre in the Haymarket, probably drawn by Novosielski for the 1782 alterations

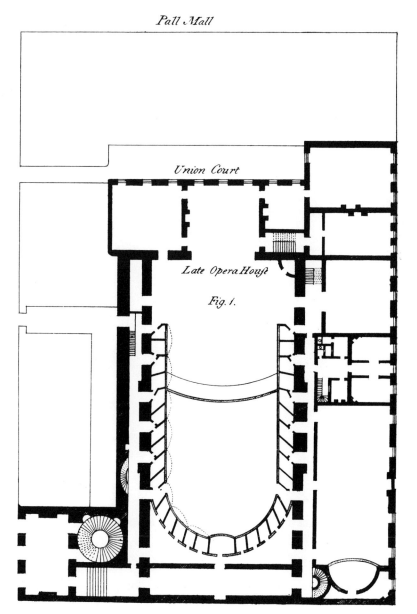

Pall Mall

Union Court

Late Opera Houſe

Fig. 1.

Plan of the King's Theatre in the Haymarket, c. 1782
from Saunders's *A Treatise on Theatres*, 1790

Harvard Theatre Collection
Sketch by Dibdin of the auditorium of his second Sans Souci Theatre, 1796

567

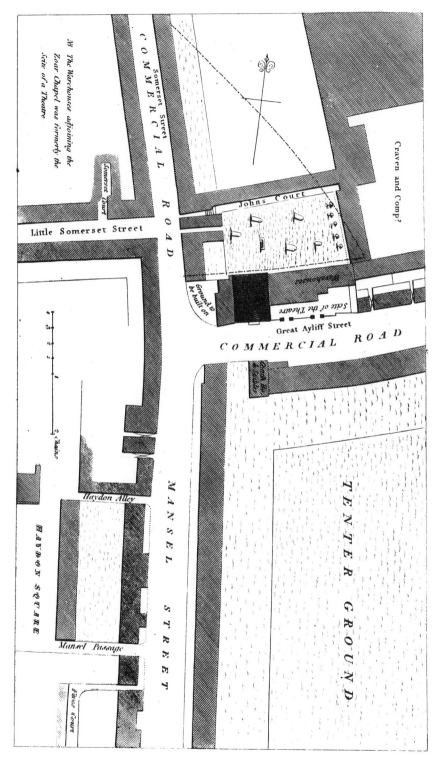

Folger Shakespeare Library
Site of the Goodman's Fields Theatre
print by Robert Wilkinson, 1813

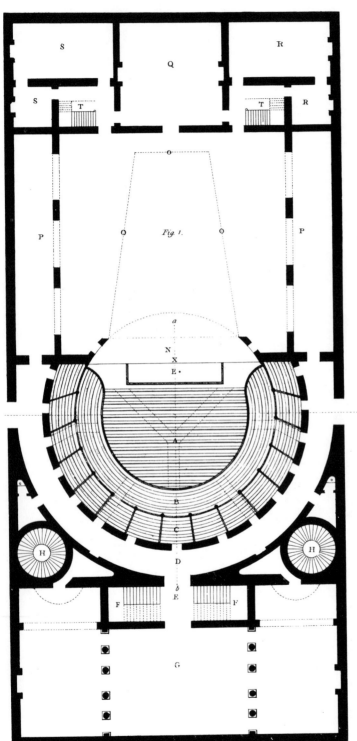

Theatre.

A. *Pit*
B. *Balcony*
C. *Boxes*
D. *Coviadore*
E. *Lobby*
F F. *Principal Stair Cases*
G. *Coffee Room*
H H. *Gallery Stair Cases*
I. *Entrance under Coffee Room*
K. *Waiting Room*
L. *Receivers Room*
M. *Servants Hall open to the Street*
E.* *Orchestre*

Plan for an ideal theatre by George Saunders
from Saunders's *A Treatise on Theatres*, 1790